Cast spelter Art Nouveau figural clock, 24 1/2" h., $1,000; Porcelain stein with dragon handle, pine cone decoration, $85; Cigarette card with cowboy scene, $12-20; Diamond Dye store cabinet, $1,320; 1907 Marlin Rifles poster, $2,145.

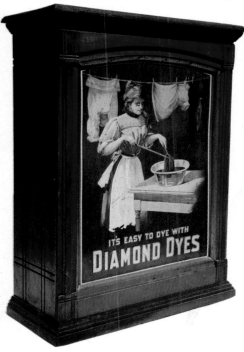

Clockwise, top left to right: 1966 Cub Scout book, $15; Blue Holanda Budweiser decanter set, CS35, $1,224; Northwestern "Zacherl" beer tray, $6,050; four beer tap knobs, E&B Ale, $42, Frederick's Extra Pale, $178, Piel's Light Beer, $33 and Trommer's White Label, $33; early paper-covered box with painted landscape, early 19th c., $9,350.

*Clockwise, top left to right: Jackie Robinson dime bank, 1950s, $679; Bust of girl lipstick holder by Josef Originals, $75; ceramic windmill juice reamer, $125-175; ceramic juice reamer with clown head, $65-85; brass hand bell with Jacobean head finial, 4" h., $95.*

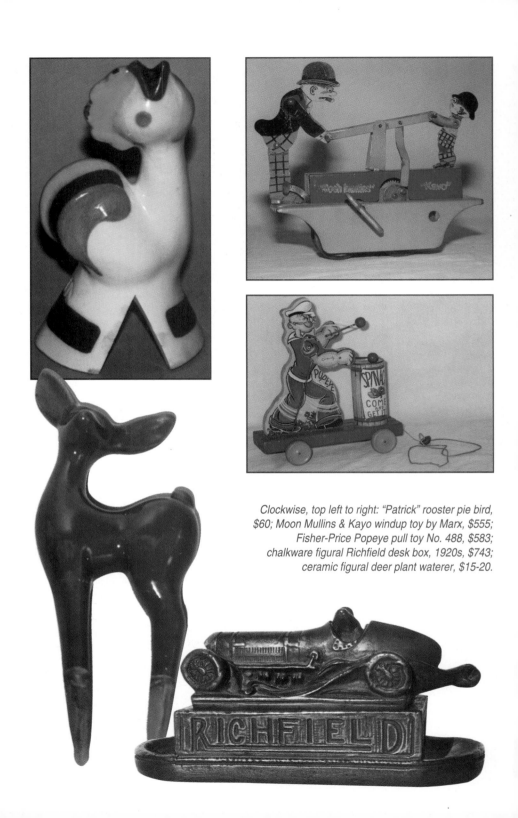

*Clockwise, top left to right: "Patrick" rooster pie bird, $60; Moon Mullins & Kayo windup toy by Marx, $555; Fisher-Price Popeye pull toy No. 488, $583; chalkware figural Richfield desk box, 1920s, $743; ceramic figural deer plant waterer, $15-20.*

*Clockwise, top left to right: Amphora pottery figural dragon vase, 22" h., $4,000-5,000; Blue & White pottery Stag pattern pitcher, 9" h., $650-850; Shawnee Pottery figural Scottie Head wall pocket, $65-95; Florence Ceramics "Georgette" Godey Woman figurine, $325-400; Chintz China rose bowl with frog insert, Florida pattern, $2,600.*

*Clockwise, top left to right: Watt Pottery Dutch Tulip mixing bowls, Nos. 63, 64 and 65, each $125; Josef Original ceramic cat figure, $65; Czechoslovakian glass 'spiderweb' type vase, 8" h., $150; Campbell Kid girl doll by Horsman, 1930s, $193; National Cash Register Model No. 2, $1,800.*

*Clockwise, top left to right: Fun-E-Flex jointed wood Mickey Mouse toy by Borgfedlt, 7" h., $2,860; Colonial Woman ribbon doll, $50-60; Simon & Halbig No. 1249 25" h. girl doll, $1,200; Mickey's Mousekemovers moving van by Marx, $250; early Pinocchio jointed wood doll, 6" h., $95.*

Clockwise, top left to right: complete Sonja Henie trousseau in box by Madame Alexander, $3,100; early Federal style jelly cupboard with grain painting, $7,150; Ward Brothers drake and hen Pintail decoys, pr. $12,100; Belter three-piece parlor suite in Rosalie without Grapes pattern, $7,000; Wooton Patent "Standard Grade" secretary, ca. 1880, $12,000.

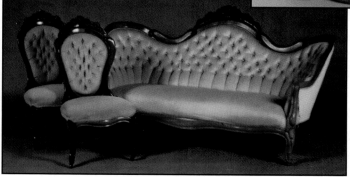

*Clockwise, top left to right: ornate turn-of-the-century mahogany veneer tall chest of drawers, $1,750; Victorian Eastlake style tall chest of drawers, $975; Louis XV-Style bureau plat, late 19th c., $6,000; early 20th century child's wicker rocker, $110; tall oak Arts & Crafts stacking bookcase, $2,800.*

Clockwise, top left to right: Victorian Rococo substyle rosewood full-tester bed, ca. 1850, $13,500; Carnival glass Orange Tree 10" bowl in marigold, $175; country Victorian walnut wall cupboard, $770; Duncan & Miller Canterbury pattern Jasmine rose bowl, $90-110; Amberina vase with applied decoration 8 1/2" h. $175.

*Clockwise, top left to right: cobalt blue Chevron pattern creamer, $12-15; Mary Gregory sapphire blue glass decanter, 8 1/2" h., $195; unsigned Wave Crest cracker jar, 8 1/4" h., $295; Wurlitzer Model 61 juke box, $1,750; hand-painted porcelain belt buckle brooch, 1 3/4 x 2 1/8", $100.*

Clockwise, top left to right: Handel reverse-painted table lamp with parrots, $20,000; late Victorian blue satin glass hanging parlor kerosene lamp, $4,480; Steuben brown Aurene gas shade, 5 1/2" h., $1,000; Heintz Art Metal Shop bowl No. 1852, $450; Tiffany "Acorn" pattern table lamp, 22 3/4" h., $15,000.

Clockwise, top left to right: Solid core tri-level latticinio swirl cane-clipped marble, 2 1/16" d., $250-275; Cane-dipped latticinio swirl marble, 2 3/8" d., $175-200; Mira floor model disc music box, 41 1/2" h. $6,600; English sterling silver coffee urn, ca. 1804-05, $3,025; cast-iron Civil War mortar, $45,932.

Clockwise, top left to right: Pyrex "Bluebelle" refrigerator jar, $40-45; World War I poster by Howard Chandler Christy, 19 x 29", $275; Czechoslovakian jeweled glass perfume bottle, 5 1/2" h., $2,200; Victorian cranberry glass enameled perfume bottle with hinged cap, $225; English cameo lay-down perfume bottle, 8 1/2" l., $2,016.

Clockwise, top left to right: General Electric floor model radio, 1939, $175; Victor Talking Machine Model 143 table top radio, 1930s, $150; 1964 Lily Munster mint-in-box doll, $2,090 and Grandpa Munster doll, $1,760; Star Wars Chewbacca bank by Sigma, $95; Fred Flintstone on Dino battery-operated toy by Marx, 1960s, $743.

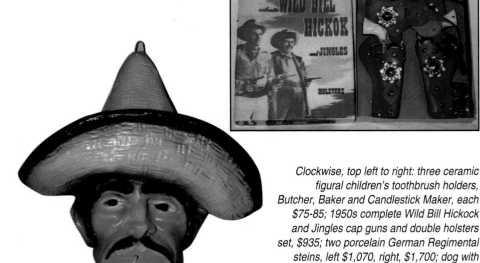

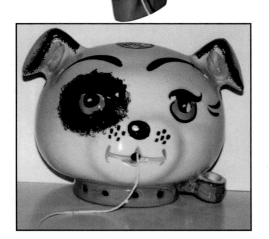

Clockwise, top left to right: three ceramic figural children's toothbrush holders, Butcher, Baker and Candlestick Maker, each $75-85; 1950s complete Wild Bill Hickock and Jingles cap guns and double holsters set, $935; two porcelain German Regimental steins, left $1,070, right, $1,700; dog with black eye ceramic string holder, $95; Pancho Villa chalkware string holder, $275.

# *Antique Trader*®
# ANTIQUES &
# COLLECTIBLES

**EDITED BY KYLE HUSFLOEN**

Published by
Antique Trader Books, A Division of

# krause
# publications

700 E. State Street • Iola, WI 54990-0001
Telephone: 715/445-2214
Web: www.krause.com

Please, call or write us for our free catalog of antiques and collectibles publications.
To place an order or receive our free catalog, call 800-258-0929.
For editorial comment and further information,
use our regular business telephone at (715) 445-2214.

ISBN: 0-87341-890-5

Printed in the United States of America

# Cover photo credits:

**Front cover:** clockwise from top left: Marklin windup tin racer missing driver, $1,650, courtesy of Jackson's Auctioneers, Cedar Falls, Iowa; European 19th century ornate cabinet with mirror, $1,760, courtesy of Garth's Auctions, Delaware, Ohio; row of "Big Hit" brand spice canisters with paper labels, Jeannette Glass Co., each $28-35, courtesy of Kate Trabue, Eureka, California; Italian carved walnut grotto chair, ca. 1880, $1,500, courtesy of DuMouchelles, Detroit, Michigan; Limoges porcelain hand-painted punch bowl and base, 14" d., $990, courtesy of Jackson's Auctioneers, Cedar Falls, Iowa.

**Back cover:** upper left: Crown Ducal Chintz China juice reamer, $350-400, courtesy of Bobbie Zucker Bryson, Tuckahoe, New York; lower right: Van Briggle Pottery "Three-Headed Indian" vase, 11" h., ca. 1920s, $275-375, courtesy of Scott H. Nelson.

# A WORD TO THE READER

It has been over thirty years since The Antique Trader first began publishing detailed and authoritative pricing guides to the world of antiques and collectibles, a tradition we are proud to carry into the new century and millennium. Now that the 20th century is behind us we are all wondering what the future trends in collecting will be. In the last years of the past century many things became very collectible which did not officially meet the 100 year old standard for a "true" antique. This trend is likely to continue as more and more collectors, baby boomers and Generation Xers in particular, take up serious collecting.

Traditional categories of antiques such as furniture, glassware and ceramics certainly will continue to have a strong following, however, as you'll see in the listings in this new volume, many new and unusual items are also catching the fancy of collectors.

The core of our price guide remains the three major fields of collecting as noted above: Furniture, Ceramics and Glass, but over the years the subcategories of pieces listed in these fields has grown tremendously and we have always done our very best to keep abreast of these trends. For instance, fine chinawares of the 19th and early 20th century are still much sought after, but added to these is the current widespread appeal of mid-20th century dinnerwares such as Blue Ridge China and Russel Wright Designs as well as novelty and figural items from a variety of companies such as Lefton China, Florence Ceramics, Kay Finch and many more. This great broadening of the collecting realm is also seen among furniture lovers and those who enjoy the sparkling appeal of all types of glassware. Today nearly everyone agrees that there is a collectible to appeal to almost every interest, taste and pocketbook. In recent years such diverse items as Costume Jewelry, Kitchenwares, Czechoslovakian Collectibles and Sports Memorabilia have all come to be accepted as vital segments of the collecting marketplace. We include these and many other specialty collectibles in this issue and have introduced a number which are of interest to even newer niches in the collecting world including: Cow Creamers, Mustache Cups, Lipstick Holder Ladies, Plant Waters and more.

The editors and staff of our price guide always take great care to offer the most accurate and up-to-date information with careful descriptions and thorough indexing and cross-referencing. Our list of Special Contributors continues to grow and we're pleased to make use of their insights and expertise to ensure that our readers have the most in-depth and authoritative data available. I want to offer special thanks to all these fine people and organizations for their efforts and you'll find a complete listing of them on the following pages.

Good photos of pieces listed are always a great asset to any pricing guide and we're pleased to once again be able to offer hundreds of black and white photos which highlight the dozens and dozens of categories we cover. In addition, we're proud to include a new 16 page full-color supplement to further add to the value and visual appeal of our 2001 Antiques & Collectibles Price Guide. A great many of our categories also include a brief introduction as well as often including some background on markings found on pieces and notes on reference books which will be of additional value to collectors. Especially in our Ceramics and Glass sections you find the sketches of factory or artists' marks a valuable aid.

It is important for readers to remember that, although our listings are thorough and authoritative, this book should be used only as a guide to pricing. A number of factors can influence what a particular item may sell for at a particular time and in a particular location. Regional differences in pricing aren't as noticeable, perhaps, as in years past, but they do occur in pricing and, of course, rarity and condition always play a major part in what a piece may bring on the open market. In general the prices we list will be for "retail replacement" value of a piece, but the law of supply and demand is almost always at work so working within a retail value range is generally the best method to establish a realistic price.

Antique Trader's Antiques & Collectibles Price Guide follows a basically alphabetical format for most categories. However, we have arranged the larger categories of Ceramics, Furniture and Glass into their own sections where each specific type or maker will be listed alphabetically within that section. If you have a question about where a specific category is to be found please refer to the detailed INDEX we provide at the back of this book. We have cross-referenced as many of the categories as possible to make your research easier.

Please remember that although our descriptions, prices and illustrations have been double-checked and every effort has been made to ensure accuracy, neither the editor nor publisher can assume responsibility for any losses that might be incurred as a result of consulting this guide, or of typographical or other errors.

Photographers who have contributed to this issue include: E. A. Babka, East Dubuque, Illinois; Stanley L. Baker, Minneapolis, Minnesota; Dorothy Beckwith, Platteville, Wisconsin; Johanna S. Billings, Danielsville, Pennsylvannia; Donna Bruun, Galena, Illinois; Herman C. Carter, Tulsa, Oklahoma; Susan N. Cox, El Cajon, California; J. D. Dalessandro, Cincinnati, Ohio; Ruth Eaves, Marmora, New Jersey; Susan Eberman, Bedford, Indianna; Scott Green, Manchester, New Hampshire; Jeff Grunewald, Chicago, Illinois; Vance Hall, Wichita, Kansas; Charles Hippler, Monticello, Illinois; Robert G. Jason-Ickes, Olympia, Washington; Dorothy Kamm, Port St. Lucie, Florida; Marlyn Margulis, Cherry Hill, New Jersey; Robert T. Matthews, West Friendship, Maryland; Louise Paradis, Sparta, Wisconsin; David H. Surgan, Brooklyn, New York; Ann Sutton, Lakeland, Florida; and Tom Wallace, Chicago, Illinois.

For other photographs, artwork, data or permission to photograph in their shops, we sincerely express appreciation to the following auctioneers, galleries, museums, individuals and shops: Albrecht Auction Service, Vassar, Michigan; Alderfers, Hatfield, Pennsylvannia; American Eagle Auction Company, Circleville, Ohio; American Social History and Social Movements, Pittsburgh, Pennsylvannia; Brown Auction & Real Estate, Greensburg, Kansas; The Burmese Cruet, Montgomeryville, Pennsylvannia; Charles Casad, Monticello, Illinois; The Cedars - Antiques, Aurelia, Iowa; I.M. Chait Gallery, Beverly Hills, California; Frank Chiarenza, Newington, Connecticut; Christie's, New York, New York; Cincinnati Art Galleries, Cincinnati, Ohio; Collector's Auction Service, Oil City, Pennsylvannia; Collector's Sales & Services, Pomfret Center, Conneticut; Copake Country Auction, Copake, New York; Craftsman Auctions, Pittsfield, Massachusetts; S. Davis, Williamsburg, Ohio; DeFina Auctions, Austenburg, Ohio; William Doyle Galleries, New York, New York; DuMouchelles, Detroit, Michigan; Early American History

Auctions, Inc., La Jolla, California; T. Ermert, Cincinnati, Ohio; Garth's Auctions, Inc., Delaware, Ohio; Glass-Works Auctions, East Greenville, Pennsylvannia; Glick's Antiques, Galena, Illinois; Green Valley Auctions, Mt. Crawford, Virginia; Grunewald Antiques, Hillsborough, North Carolina; and Guyette and Schmidt, West Farmington, Maine.

Also to Vicki Harmon, San Marcos, California; the Gene Harris Antique Auction Center, Marshalltown, Iowa; the late William Heacock, Marietta, Ohio; International Toy Collectors Association, Athens, Illinois; Michael Ivankovich Antiques & Auctions, Doylestown, Pennsylvannia; Jackson's Auctions, Cedar Falls, Iowa; James Julia, Fairfield, Maine; Peter Kroll, Sun Prairie, Wisconsin; Bev Kubesheski, Dubuque, Iowa; Lang's Sporting Collectibles, Raymond, Maine; Leland's Auctions, New York, New York; Jim Ludescher, Dubuque, Iowa; Joy Luke Gallery, Bloomington, Illinois; J. Martin, Mt. Orab, Ohio; Mastro & Steinbeck Fine Sports Auctions, Oakbrook, Illinois; Randall McKee, Kenosha, Wisconsin; McMasters Doll Auctions, Cambridge, Ohio; Dr. James Measell, Marietta, Ohio; Gary Metz's Muddy River Trading Company, Salem, Virginia; Pacific Glass Auctions, Sacramento, California; Parker-Braden Auctions, Carlsbad, New Mexico; Past Tyme Treasures, Los Altos, California; Dave Rago Arts & Crafts, Lambertville, New Jersey; Jane Rosenow, Galva, Illinois; Tammy Roth, East Dubuque, Illinois; Running Rabit Productions, Waverly, Tennessee; L.H. Selman, Ltd., Santa Cruz, California; Skinner, Inc., Bolton, Massachusetts; Slawinski Auction Company, Felton, California; Sotheby's, New York, New York; Stanton's Auctioneers, Vermontville, Michigan; Michael Strawser, Wolcottville, Indiana; Temples Antiques, Eden Prairie, Minnesota; Tin Pan Alley Antiques, Galena, Illinois; Town Crier Auction Service, Burlington, Wisconsin; Tradewinds Antiques, Manchester-by-the-Sea, Massachusetts; Treadway Gallery, Cincinnati, Ohio; Lee Vines, Hewlett, New York; Doris Virtue, Galena, Illinois; Woody Auctions, Douglass, Kansas; and Yesterday's Treasures, Galena, Illinois.

We hope that everyone who consults our Antiques & Collectibles Price Guide will find it the most thorough, accurate and informative guide to the ever-changing world of collecting.

The staff of Antique Trader's Antiques & Collectibles Price Guide welcomes all letters from readers, especially those of constructive critique, and we make every effort to respond personally.

- Kyle Husfloen, Editor

# SPECIAL CATEGORY CONTRIBUTORS

## GENERAL CATEGORIES

### Advertising Items
Mr. Peanut Collectibles
Richard Reddoc
914 Isle Court
N. Bellmore, NY 11710
(516) 826-2247
e-mail: NB887929@nassau-net.org

### Boy Scout Memorabilia
Jim Trautman
R.R. 1
Ontario, Canada, L0N 1N0
(519) 855-6077

### Books
Civil War-Related
Bill Butts
Main Street Fine Books &
Manuscripts
206 N. Main
Galena, IL 61036

### Bottles
Milk
John Tutton
1967 Ridgeway Road
Front Royal, VA 22630
(540) 635-7058
e.mail:jtutton@rma.edu
Publications: *Udderly Delightful*, three editions and *Udderly Beautiful*

### Buttons
Millicent Safro
Tender Buttons
143 E. 62nd St.
New York, NY 10021
(212) 758-7004
fax: (212) 319-8474
Author of Buttons

### Cans & Containers
Spice Tins
Joan M. Rhoden, edited by
Connie Rhoden
8693 N. 1950 East Road
Georgetown, IL 61846-6264
(217) 662-8046
fax: (217) 662-8223
e-mail: rhoden@soltec.net
Publications: Co-author
*Those Wonderful Yard-Long Prints and More, More Wonderful Yard-Long Prints and Yard-Long Prints*

### Cat Collectibles
Marilyn Dipboye
33161 Wendy Dr.
Sterling Heights, MI 48310

### Children's Toothbrush Holders
Debbie Gillham
Gaithersburg, MD 20878
e-mail:dgillham@erols.com

## Clothing
Neckties
Michael J. Goldbert
823 SE 25th Ave.
Portland, OR 97214
e-mail: emjaygee@ine-tarena.com

### Coffee Memorabilia
B. J. Summers
233 Darnell Road
Benton, KY 42025
(270) 898-3097
fax: 401-683-1644
e-mail: bsummers@apex.net
Publications: *B.J. Summers Guide to Coco-Cola I & II, Value Guide to Advertising Memorabilia I & II, Value Guide to Gas Station Memorabilia* and *B.J. Summers Pocket Guide to Coca-Cola I & II*

### Country Store Collectibles
Rich Penn
Box 1355
Waterloo, IA 50704-1355
(319) 291-6688
fax: 319-291-7136
e-mail: PNYFLDS@aol.com
Author of *Mom and Pop Stores: A Country Store Compendium of Merchandising Tools for Display and Value Guide*

### Czechoslovakian Collectibles
Ruth A. Forsythe
Galena, OH

### Dollhouse Furniture & Accessories
Patty Cooper
e-mail: Gardenmont@aol.com

### Goldilocks and the Three Bears Collectibles
Kerra Davis
1779 Mershon Road
Mershon, GA 31551
(912) 647-1886
Publications: *Contemporary Doll, Georgia Magazine, American Country Collectibles, Collectible Flea Market Finds, Victorian Decorating Ideas, Antique Trader Weekly*

### Hardware
H. Weber Wilson
P.O. Box 506
Portsmouth, RI 02871
(800) 508-0022
e.mail: hww@webwilson.com
Publications: *Antique Hardware Price Guide*

### Hatpins and Hatpin Holders
Audrae Heath
P.O. Box 1009
Bonners Ferry, Idaho 83805

## Heintz Art Metal Shop Wares
David Surgan
328 Flatbush Ave.
Suite 123, Brooklyn, NY 11238
(718) 638-3768

### Indian Artifacts
Gary L. Fogelman
Rd. 1, Box 240
Turbotville, PA 17772-9599
(470) 437-3698
fax: 570-437-3411
e-mail: iam@csrlink.com
Author of *A Projectile Point Topology* for Pennsylvania & the Northeast, An Identification & Price Guide for Indian Artifacts of the Northeast & The Pennsylvania Artifact Series
Editor & publisher of *Indian Artifact Magazine*

### Jewelry (Costume)
Marion Cohen
P.O. Box 39
Albertson, NY 11507

### Jigsaw Puzzles
Chris McCann
Collectors Press, Inc.
P.O. Box 230986
Portland, OR 97281
(503) 684-3030
fax: 503-684-3777
e-mail: rperry@collectorspress.com

### Kitchenwares
General
Carol Bohn, KOOKS
501 Mark St.
Mifflinburg, PA 17844
(717) 966-1198

Egg Timers, Pie Birds & String Holders
Ellen Bercovici
5118 Hampden La.
Bethesda, MD 20814
(301) 652-1140

Figural Teapots
Eve Hill
e-mail: teapoteve@yahoo.com
Publications: *Maine Antique Digest, TEA-Magazine, Tea-Time Gazette, Antique Trader Weekly, Auction Guide & Collector*

Juice Reamers, Napkin Dolls
Bobbie Zucker Bryson
1 St. Eleanoras La.
Tuckahoe, NY 10707
e-mail: Napkindoll@aol.com
(914) 779-1405

Toasters
Carl Roles
P.O. Box 529
Temecula, CA 92593
(909) 699-8556 or (909) 699-5139

**Laundry Room Items**
Irons
David Irons
223 Covered Bridge Rd.
Northampton, PA 18607
Fax: (610) 262-3853,
Author, *Irons by Irons, More Irons by Irons and Pressing Iron Patents*

Jimmy & Carol Walker
Iron Talk
P.O Box 68
Waelder, TX 78959-0068

**Melmac Dinnerware**
Michael J. Goldberg
823 S.E. 25th Ave.
Portland, OR 97214
e-mail: emjaygee@netarena.com
Author of several books & articles on
antiques and collectibles including *"I Remember Melmac"*

**Nutcrackers**
Claudia Davis
2350 Finch Road
Hayden Lane, ID 83835
phone & fax: (208) 772-6801
e-mail: cjdavis@icehouse.net

**Office Equipment**
Typewriters
Darryl Rehr
P.O. Box 641824
Los Angeles, CA 90064
(310) 477-5229
fax: 310-268-8420
e-mail: dcrehr@earthlink.net
http://home.earthlink.net/~dcrehr

Frank Briola
P.O. Box 44022
Pittsburgh, PA 15205
(800) 372-6509
fax: 412-937-8787
e-mail: americana@mail.com

**Phonographs**
Mike Ellingson
1412 2nd Ave., S.
Fargo, ND
(701) 280-1413
e-mail: MikEllingson@webtv.net

**Photographic Items**
Cameras
Chicago Photographic
Collectors Society
Chicago, IL

**Plant Waterers**
Bobbie Zucker Bryson
1 St. Eleanoras La.
Tuckahoe, NY 10707
e-mail: Napkindoll@aol.com
(914) 779-1405

**Playing Cards**
Rhonda Hawes
Secretary/Treasurer, 52 Plus
Joker
204 Gorham Ave.
Hamden, CT 06514
web: www52plusjoker.org

**Radios**
Harry Poster
P.O. Box 1883
S. Hackensack, NJ 07606
(201) 794-9606
Fax: (201) 794-9553
e-mail: hposter@world-net.att.net

Jim Trautman
R.R. 1
Orton Ontario, Canada,
L0N 1N0
(519) 855-6077

Hammond Museum of Radio
Guelph Ontario

**Recipe Booklets**
Michael J. Goldberg
823 SE 25th Ave.
Portland, OR 97214

**Ribbon Dolls**
Bobbie Zucker Bryson
1 St. Eleanoras La.
Tuckahoe, NY 10707
e-mail: Napkindoll@aol.com
(914) 779-1405

**Scottish Tartanware**
Ellen Bercovici
5118 Hampden La.
Bethesda, MD 20814
(301) 652-1140

**Sewing Adjuncts**
Beth Pulsipher
Praire Home Antiques
240 N. Grand
Schoolcraft, MI 49087
(616) 679-20962

**Thimbles**
Cal Holden
P.O. Box 264
Doylestown, OH 44230
(330) 658-2793

**Sheet Music**
Lois Cordrey
Editor & publisher of
*Remember That Song* newsletter
5623 N. 64th Avenue
Glendale, AZ 85301
e-mail:rtsnews@doitnow.com

**Textiles**
Linens & Needlework
Elizabeth Kurella
Box 222
Plainwell, MI 49080
e-mail: ekurella@accn.org
Publications: *The Complete Guide to Lace & Linens, Guide to Lace and Linens, Pocket Guide to Valuable Old Lace and Lacy Linens, The Lace Merchant, Secrets of Real Lace & the Lace Merchant*

Quilts
Craig Ambrose
3717 6th Ave., Apt.
244, Des Moines, IA 50313
(515) 288-4595
e-mail:
Camb485361@aol.com
Author of self-published book,
*A Picture Book and Price Guide to Antique Quilts*

**Tools**
Martin & Kathy Donnelly
Donnelly Antique Tools
31 Rumsey St., P.O. Box 281
Bath, NY 14810

**Toothpick Holders**
Judy Knauer
P.O. Box 452
Devault, PA 19433-0452
(610) 431-3477
e-mail: winkjk@netaxs.com
Founder of the National Toothpick Holder Collectors Society 1973 & publisher of *The Toothpick Bulletin, 1973-1997*

**Toys**
Lionel Trains
Jim Trautman
R.R. 1
Orton Ontario, Canada
L0N 1N0
e-mail: emjaygee@inetarena.com
Author of several books & articles including "I Remember Melmac" American Country Collectibles
(519) 855-6077

Train Cars
Todd Waagner
P.O. Box 516
New Middletown, OH 44442-0516
(330) 757-3119
e-mail: papertrw@aol.com

Wooden Toys
Richard Friz
P.O. Box 472
Peterborough, NH 03458
(603) 563-8155
e-mail: joshdickmad@monad-net.com
Publications: *Maine Antique Digest,*
Antique Toy World, Antique and the Arts Weekly, Antiques Reveiw

**Trump Indicators**
Ellen Bercovici
5118 Hampden La.
Bethesda, MD 20814
(301) 652-1140

**Wall Pockets**
Joy & Marvin Gibson
P.O. Box 217
Ozark, MO 65721
(417) 581-6931
e-mail: ozarkhoot!aol.com
Authors of Collectors *Guide to Wall Pockets: Book I & Book II*

## Watches
Pocket Watches &
Wristwatches
Cooksey Shugart
P.O. Box 3147
Cleveland, TN 37320
(423) 479-4813
Publication: *Complete Price Guide to Watches*

## Western Americana
Dick & Terry Engel
P.O. Box 1429
Ennis MT 59729
(406) 682-4499

## Whistle Cups
Deborah Gillham
47 Midline Ct.
Gaithersburg, MD 20878-1996
(301) 977-5727
e-mail: reamers@erols.com

## Whistles
Harry D. Barry
2785 Windswept Drive
North East, PA 16428
(814) 725-8150

## Windmill Weights
Richard C. Tucker
Argyle Antiques
406 Country Club Road
Argyle, TX 76226

## World's Fair Collectibles
Richard Friz
P.O. Box 472
Peterborough, NH 03458
(603) 563-8155
e-mail: jmd-friz@top.monad.net
Publications: *Yankee, Maine Antique Digest, Antique Toy World and Antique & Arts Weekly*

## Writing Accessories
Letter Openers
Ray & Bevy Jaegers
P.O. Box 29396
St. Louis, MO 63126
e-mail: upsisquad@aol.com
Publications:*The Write Stuff*

# CERAMICS

## Abingdon
Elaine Westover
210 Knox Hwy. 5
Abingdon, IL 61410-9332
(309) 462-3267

## American Painted Porcelain
Dorothy Kamm
P. O. Box 7460
Port St. Lucia, FL 34985-7460
(561) 465-4008
e-mail: dorothy.kamm@usa.net

## Bauer, Catalina Island, Vernon Kilns
Steven R. Soukup
P. O. Box 7662
15459 Wyandotte St.
Van Nuys, CA 91406
e-mail: soukup@dfhaia.com

## Blue & White Pottery
Steven E. Stone
18102 East Oxford Dr.
Aurora, CO 80013
fax: (303) 969-2737

## Ceramic Arts Studio of Madison
James Petzold
P. O. Box 46
Madison, WI 53701-8770
(608) 241-9138
fax: (608) 241-8770
e-mail: ceramics@execpc.com

## Chintz
Jane Fehrenbocher
600 Columbia St.
Pasadena, CA 91105
e-mail: Chintz4u@aol.com

## Clarice Cliff
Carole A. Berk
4918 Fairmont Ave.
Bethesda, MD 20814
(800) 382-2413 or (301) 656-0355
fax: (301) 652-5859
e-mail: cab@caroleberk.com
web: http://www.carole-berk.com

## Coors
Jo Ellen Winther
(800) 872-2345 days
(303) 421-2371 home
fax: (303) 431-5350
e-mail: Repofam@aol.com

## Cowan Pottery
Tim & Jamie Saloff
e-mail: tgsaloff@erie.net
web:
http://www.erie.net/~jlsaloff

## Fiesta
Matthew Whalen
734 S. 26th St.
Arlington, VA 22202
e-mail: fiesta@medi-umgreen.com
web: http://www.medi-umgreen.com

## Florence Ceramics
Rita Bee, Editor
Florence Collector Club
Newsletter
(909) 683-1485
e-mail: AR2Bee@aol.com

## Franciscan
Alan Phair
P. O. Box 30373
Long Beach, CA 90853-0373
e-mail: ALAN-PHAIR@aol.com

## Geisha Girl Porcelain
E. Litts
P. O. Box 394
Morris Plains, NJ 07950-0394
(973) 361-4087
e-mail: happy-memories@worldnet.att.net
web:
http://home.att.net/~happy-memories

## Gonder Pottery
Jim & Carol Boshears
917 Hurl Dr.
Pittsburgh, PA 15236-3636
(412) 655-1380
e-mail: gondernut@aol.com

## Hall China
Steve Cagle & Dave Periord
e-mail: slcagle@aol.com

## Harker Pottery
Don & Neva Colbert
69565 Crescent Rd.
St. Clairsville, OH 43950-9350
(740) 695-2355
e-mail: colbert@1st.net
web: http://users.1st.net/col-bert/harker/harker/htm

## Haviland
Nora Travis
P. O. Box 6008
Cerritos, CA 90701
(714) 521-9283

## Homer Laughlin China
Matthew Whalen
e-mail: president@hlcca.org
Homer Laughlin Collectors Association
Magazine: *Dish, The*
P. O. Box 26021
Arlington, VA 22215-6201
(500) 674-5222
e-mail: hlcoa-info@medi-umgreen.com
web: http://www.medi-umgreen.com/hlcca/

## Hull Pottery
Joan Gray Hull
1376 Nevada S. W.
Huron, SD 57350-3135
(605) 352-1685

## Hummel Figurines
Dean A. Genth
Miller's Hallmark & Gift Gallery
Northedge Mall
1322 North Barron St.
Eaton, OH 45320
(513) 456-4151

## Ironstone
General, all-white
Dieringer's Arts & Antiques
P. O. Box 536
Redding Ridge, CT 06876
fax: (203) 938-8378
e-mail: Dieringer1@aol.com

## Lefton
Loretta DeLozier
P. O. Box 50201
Knoxville, TN 37950-0201
(865) 539-2140
e-mail: LeftonLady@aol.com
Author: *Collector's Encyclopedia of Lefton China (Books I & II)*

## LuRay
Joe Zacharias
P. O. Box 99516
Raleigh, NC 27624-9516
(919) 848-6966
e-mail:
IBUYLURAY2@aol.com

## Majolica

Michael G. Strawser
Strawsers Auctions
P. O. Box 332
Wolcottville, IN 46795-0332
(219) 854-2859 or (219) 854-2235
fax: (219) 854-3979
web: http://www.majolicaauctions.com/

## McCoy

Craig Nissen
P. O. Box 223
Grafton, WI 53024-0223
(414) 377-7932
e-mail: McCoyCN@aol.com

## Moorcroft

Robert G. Jason-Ickes
Olympia, WA
e-mail: antiqueappraisers@hom.com

## Morton Potteries

Burdell Hall
210 W. Sassafras Dr.
Morton, IL 61550-1254
(309) 263-2988
e-mail: bnbhall@mtco.com

## Nippon

John Crisman
Jackson's Auctioneers &
Appraisers
2229 Lincoln St.
Cedar Falls, IA 50613
(319) 277-2256

## Noritake

Tim Trapani
145 Andover Place
West Hempstead, NY 11552-1603
(516) 292-8355 or (718) 464-9009
fax: (718) 464-8448
e-mail: ttrapani@aol.com
President: Noritake Collectors' Society

## Old Ivory

Alma Hillman
362 East Maine St.
Searsport, ME 04974
(207) 548-6658
e-mail: oldivory@acadia.net

## Owens Pottery

Frank Hahn
P. O. Box 934
Lima, OH 45802-0934
(419) 225-3816 or (419) 222-3816
fax: (419) 227-3816
e-mail: ggb@wcoil.com

## Red Wing

Charles W. Casad
Monticello, IL

## Royal Bayreuth

Howard & Sarah Wade
P. O. Box 325
Orrville, OH 44667-0325
(330) 682-8551
fax: (330) 682-3655
e-mail: ukdolls@aol.com
Club: Royal Bayreuth International Collector's Society
Newsletter: RBICS Newsletter

## Royal Bayreuth & R. S. Prussia

Mary J. McCaslin
6887 Black Oak Ct. E.
Avon, IN 46123
(317) 272-7776
fax: (317) 272-7776
e-mail: maryjack@iquest.net

## Royal Copley

Dan Benton
1639 North Catalina St.
Burbank, CA 91505-1605
e-mail: copleydbi@aol.com

## Russel Wright

Ann M. Kerr
P. O. Box 437
Sidney, OH 45365-0437
(937) 472-6369

## Shawnee

Ellen Supnick
2771 Oakbrook Manor
Weston, FL 33332
(954) 578-8787

Linda A. Guffey
2004 Fiat Ct.
El Cajon, CA. 92019
e-mail: Gufantique@aol.com

## Shelley

Mannie Banner
6412 Silverbrook W.
W. Bloomfield, MI 48322

## Teplitz-Amphora

Les & Irene Cohen
P. O. Box 17001
Pittsburgh, PA 15325-0001
(412) 793-0222 or (412) 795-3030
fax: (412) 793-0222
e-mail: www.am4ah@hotbot.com

## Torquay

J. Wucherer
Transitions of Wales, Ltd.
P. O. Box 1441
Brookfield, WI 53008

## Uhl Pottery

Lloyd Martin
1582 Gregory Lane
Jasper, IN 47546

## Warwick

Donald C. Huffmann
1291 N. Elmwood Dr.
Aurora, IL 60506
(630) 859-3435

## Watt Pottery

Dennis Thompson
6715 Stearns Rd.
No. Olmsted, OH 44070
e-mail: dthomp@stratos.net

## Willow Wares

Jeff Siptak
P. O. Box 41312
Nashville, TN 37204
(615) 383-7855
fax: (615) 269-7123
e-mail: WillowWare@aol.com

# GLASS

## Carnival Glass

Bruce Dooley
2571 7th Ave.
Sweetwater, NJ 08037,
(609) 965-2535

## Cut Glass

Vance Hall A Touch of Glass,
Ltd., 9107 Autumn Chase
Wichita, KS 67206
(316) 634-2220

## Imperial 'Candlewick'

Mary M. Wetzel-Tomalka
P.O. Box 594
Notre Dame, IN 46556
(219) 254-9817
Author: *Candlewick—The Jewel of Imperial*

## Milk Glass

Frank Chiarenza National Milk
Glass Collectors Society 80
Crestvew Newington, CT
06111-2405 (860) 666-5576

## Pattern

Iris Cottage Interiors
Andrea & Alan Koppel
Rt. 295 & County Rt. 5
P.O. Box 254, Canaan, NY
12029
(518) 781-4379

Tim Timmerman
11655 S.W. Allen Blvd., #31
Beaverton, OR 97005
(U.S. Coin pattern)

## Rose Bowls and Jack-in-the-Pulpit Vases

Johanna S. Billings
P.O. Box 244
Danielsville, PA 18038-0244,
e-mail: bankie@concentric.net Author: *Collectible Glass Rose Bowls*

## Tiffany & Tiffany Lamps

Carl Heck
Box 8416
Aspen, Co. 81612
Phone & Fax: (970) 925-8011

# ADVERTISING ITEMS

*Thousands of objects made in various materials, some intended as gifts with purchases, others used for display or given away for publicity are now being collected. Also see various other categories.*

*Alarm Clock*

**Alarm clock,** "Planters Peanuts," round yellow face, red clock body, Mr. Peanut, clock hands & numbers in black, Mr. Peanut's arms serve as the hour & minute hands, ca. 1960s (ILLUS.).............. **$250**

**Ashtray,** "Valencia Cafe & Bar, Cheyenne, Wyo." pottery, model of cowboy hat, cobalt blue w/white trim, ca. 1940-50s, 2 x 4 3/4" ..................................................... 143

**Bag rack,** "Whistle," tin w/silk screen detail w/elves different from the norm, 16 1/2 x 37" (some rust & wear)................... 625

*Ball Point Pen*

**Ball point pen,** "Planters Peanuts," advertising type, by Cross, blue & yellow, ca. 1970s (ILLUS.).............................................. 18

**Bank,** "Planters Peanuts," figural molded plastic, Mr. Peanut found in various col-

*Plastic Mr. Peanut Bank*

ors, coin slot in top of removable hat, pale blue, green, red & peanut tan, 7" h., each (ILLUS.) ...................................... 15

**Bill hook,** "Arlington Brand," celluloid w/lithograph by Parisan Novelty Company, Chicago, Illinois, white, red & yellow & "Arlington Pickles - Vinegar - Sauerkraut," 3 1/2" d. ................................. 99

**Bill hook,** "Butter-Nut Coffee," celluloid, blue w/can shown in shades of brown & marked "Ask For Butter-Nut - Coffee Delicious," button 2 x 2 3/4", overall 7" l. ..... 176

**Blotter,** "Dr. Pepper," rectangular, green, shows three tilted bottles wrapped w/ribbon banner reading "Ten - Two - Four" (light mildew & wear).................................... 110

**Bottle carrier,** "7-Up," aluminum, marked "Fresh Up," six-pack size .............................. 50

**Bottle carrier,** "Pepsi Cola," wood, six-pack size, original finish .............................. 140

**Bottle opener,** metal, folding-type w/cork-screw, marked "Gooderham & Worts Limited, Distillers of Fine Whiskey Since 1832" ........................................................... 125

**Cake box,** Schepps tin, embossed on front & top w/artwork by Kaulbach on sides & front, front opening, 13" sq., 14" h. (paint chips, scratches & soiling, minor rust at bottom) .......................................................... 182

**Calendar,** 1898 "Hood's Coupon Calendar," circle in center w/bust of infant w/curly blonde hair, border w/floral decoration, unused, full pad & coupons, 4 1/2 x 7" .......................................................... 77

**Calendar,** 1910, "Osborne Harvesting," paper lithograph showing woman standing by grazing horse, framed under glass, image 15 1/2" h. (minor creases)....... 400

**Calendar,** 1913, "Deering," paper lithograph of boys playing baseball, matted & framed, 19" h. (minor creases & stains) .... **2,300**

**Calendar,** 1913, "Selby Loads," colorful scene w/California quail by Edward Wilson Currier, Olsen Litho Co., S.F., December page only, complete bands top & bottom w/minor cracks from rolling, 21 x 27 1/2" (ILLUS. next page) ................ **4,455**

**Calendar,** 1916, "Winchester Guns and Cartridges," rectangular, colorful scene of two men w/a dog climbing a rocky hillside trail (ILLUS. next page)...................... **1,925**

**Calendar,** 1918, "DeLaval Cream Separator," paper lithograph shows woman standing w/horse, full pad, framed under glass, 17 1/2" h. (minor stains & tears) ........ 550

**Calendar,** 1920, "Sharples Separator," mother standing on porch step, young girl & boy in foreground, she is holding a pan while the boy drinks from it, top band, complete calendar pad, small tears & creases upper right, 12 x 22" ......... **237**

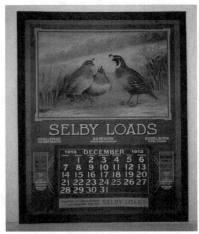

*1913 Selby Calendar*

*Winchester 1916 Calendar*

**Chair,** "Fairbank's Gold Dust Washing Powders," tin insets, slat seat ...................... **300**

**Clock,** "Calumet Baking Powder," reverse painting on glass front panels, 31-day face, 34 1/4" h. (minor flaking) .................... **650**

**Clock,** "Dr. Pepper," octagonal, neon, black numbers w/red 2, 4 & 10, late 1930s, soiling, (stains & wear w/light rusting on interior of case) .......................................... **688**

**Clock,** "International Harvester," square, electric wall-mount, metal body w/tin face & glass cover, neon light tube around edge, 15 1/2" (scuffs to body) ........ **715**

**Clock,** "Liberty Coal," electric, glass dome w/metal case, by Gillco Mfg., 19 1/2" d. ....... **450**

**Coin,** "Planters Peanuts," limited edition Mr. Peanut 75th anniversary, silver, 1 oz. ...................................................... **175-200**

**Counter display,** "Planters Peanuts" four-sided red pyramid display for bags of peanuts, several white Mr. Peanut figures on sides & top w/"Planters Salted Nuts" in white letters at top, ca. 1950s, 15" h. (light soiling, bew bends) ............... **1,760**

**Counter display,** "Smith Brothers'," pressed steel & black enamel marked "Smith Brothers' S.B. Cough Drops" on top above graphic of product box & "5¢," 3 3/4 x 4 1/4 x 9 3/4" ................................ **413**

*Counter Display Box*

**Counter display box,** "Planters Defend America Peanuts," 24 count cardboard box, w/"For a Victorious America, Buy U.S. War Bonds and Stamps" on top in white lettering, depending on condition & die-cut (ILLUS.) ..................................... **150-900**

*Counter Display Box*

**Counter display box,** "Planters Salted Peanuts," 24-count cardboard box, w/"For a Victorious America, Buy U.S. War Bonds and Stamps" across the top in white lettering, Mr. Peanut & unshelled peanuts in blue ink, depending on condition & die-cut (ILLUS.) ....... **150-900**

**Counter display cabinet,** "Diamond Dyes," wood w/lithograph of woman standing at a table dying article of clothing, other clothes hanging on line behind her, marked "It's Easy to Dye With Diamond Dyes," includes some products & three-page color card & distributor label from Sacramento, California, 10 x 22 x 29 3/4" (ILLUS. next page) ........ **1,320**

**Counter display cabinet,** "Diamond Dyes," wooden front opening w/embossed tin lithograph front showing children playing w/balloon, tin lithographed rear door, 24 1/2" h. (minor repair) ...................................................... **1,200**

*Diamond Dyes Cabinet*

*Counter Display Jar*

*Counter Display Jar*

**Counter display cabinet,** "Dr. Daniel's Veterinary," wood, front-opening w/embossed tin lithographed front panel, 26 3/4" h. (some rust & stains) .................. **1,700**

**Counter display cabinet,** "Elgin Watches," wooden front opening w/reverse painting on glass front, small drawers on inside (several missing), image of Father Time, 37 3/4" h. (some scratches) ........................ **900**

**Counter display cabinet,** "Humphrey's Veterinary," wood, front-opening w/heavily embossed molded profile of a horse, 27 1/2" h. (some cracks) .............. **3,100**

**Counter display cabinet,** "James Needles," wood w/reverse painting on glass labels, two dovetailed drawers, 15 1/2" h. (cracks & flaking) ........................ **450**

**Counter display cabinet,** "Magic Dyes," wood, rear opening w/tin lithograph front, 36 3/4" h. (stains & scratches) ......... **2,400**

**Counter display cabinet,** "Ward's Bread," oak w/acid etched lettering, sliding back doors, 32" h. ................................................... **500**

**Counter display case,** "E & W Collar," glass & wood, contains 14 collars, 25" h. (minor scratch to decal) ............................... **550**

**Counter display case,** "Primley's Gum," wood frame & base, curved glass front & glass sides, gold leaf lettering on front, 12 x 18" (some wear to wood) ...................... **550**

**Counter display jar,** cov., "Fish Globe Planters Peanuts," clear glass fish bowl jar w/tin lid, fish-shaped white label on front (ILLUS. top next column) .................... **375**

**Counter display jar,** cov., "Planters Brand Peanuts," clear glass fish bowl jar w/clear glass lid w/peanut handle, yellow rectangular label w/black & red lettering ...... **450**

**Counter display jar,** cov., "Planters Peanuts," clear glass barrel jar w/clear glass lid w/peanut handle ..................................... **550**

**Counter display jar,** cov., "Planters Peanuts," clear glass four-sided jar, sides are blown glass peanuts & clear glass lid w/peanut handle .......................................... **525**

**Counter display jar,** cov., "Planters Peanuts," clear glass hexagonal jar and clear glass lid w/peanut handle, yellow lettering reads "Planters," yellow Mr. Peanut figure (ILLUS.) ................................. **155**

**Counter display jar,** cov., "Planters Peanuts," clear glass square jar & clear glass lid w/peanut handle ............................ **110**

**Counter display jar,** cov., "Planters Peanuts," w/"Please Keep Jar Always Covered," clear glass slant jar w/tin lid, lid embossed w/Mr. Peanut & black, gold & white lettering ................................................. **175**

**Counter display jar,** cov., "Planters Salted Peanuts," clear glass lid w/peanut base & clear glass lid w/peanut handle, imprint of a football .................................... **425**

**Counter display jar,** cov., "Zatek Chocolate Billets," embossed clear glass, 16 1/2" h. (rim chips to lid) .......................... **300**

**Counter display sign,** "Alaska Refrigerator," cardboard die-cut standup, lithograph of seal & Eskimo child in furry white suit w/hood, holding green sign w/snow on top, marked "Alaska Refrigerator," child's hood marked "Alaska" & "The Seal of Perfection" on side of brown seal, litho by Edwards & Deutsch, Chicago, Illinois, minor scrapes & creases w/tape, small tack hole, 12 1/2 x 16 1/4 (ILLUS. next page) ............. **187**

**Counter spool cabinet,** "Brainard Armstong," walnut, incised side plaques, slanted front, 24 glass front drawers, four lower wood drawers w/incised wood, 36" l., 32" h. ..................................... **950**

*Alaska Refrigerator Counter Display*

**Counter spool cabinet,** "Brooks," ornate oak front, paneled sides, solid panel back, 25" h. (slight checking) ..................... **725**

**Counter spool cabinet,** "Clark's - O.N.T. - Geo. A. Clark, Sole Agt.," walnut, thin rectangular top wmolded edges above a low case w/a stack of three narrow long drawers each w/an oval recessed panel enclosing a ruby glass pane etched w/clear lettering, a pair of small brass & black knobs on each drawer, narrow molded base, old finish, late 19th c., 16 1/2 x 22 3/4", 9 1/2" h. (drawer bottoms replaced w/masonite) .......................... **330**

**Counter spool cabinet,** "Merricks," round, revolving, w/two curved glass panels w/lettering, 12 1/2" h................................. **1,100**

**Crock,** cov., "Heinz Apple Jelly," stoneware w/bail handle, 7 3/4" h. ............................... **950**

**Crock,** cov., "Heinz Grape Jelly," stoneware w/bail handle, 9 1/2" h. (tears to label) ..................................................... **1,050**

**Crumb catchers,** "Eagle Lye," lithograph by Chas. Shonk, Chicago, Illinois, semicircular form, one w/product container shown in center &"Use Eagle Lye - Purest & Best" & the other is marked "Send for Our Book of Valuable Information - Eagly Lye Works - Milwaukee Wis." 1/2 x 6 1/2 x 9 1/4 & 3/8 x 3 x 7", the pr. ..................................................... **193**

**Deck chairs,** "Piedmont Cigarettes," folding-type, wood w/double sided porcelain sign back, 31" h., pr..................................... **475**

**Dispenser,** "Zeno Gum," oak w/tin lithographed embossed front panel, 16 1/4" h. (some flaking & scratches)........ **1,100**

**Display bottle,** "Heinz Cider Vinegar," on base, frosted & clear embossed glass w/"Heinz" etched in pickle cork stopper, spigot at bottom, 14 1/2" h. (edge wear to labels, rim chips, hairline on base)........... **450**

**Display bottle,** "Heinz Pickles," clear glass w/ground stopper, 11" h. (rim chips & soiling to label) ........................................... **300**

**Display box,** "Campbell's Soup," featuring Tomato Soup can on two sides & the Campbell Kids on each end, red & white, front reads "Campbell's Soups - Tomato Juice - Pork and Beans - Franco American Spaghetti," ca. 1920s-30s, 17 x 27 x 27" (light insect damage & minor wear & soiling)..................................... **253**

*Peters Popular Cartridge Box*

**Display box,** "Peters Cartridge Co." pointer-type hunting dog on front flanked by "25 Load - 10 Ga. 230" w/"Popular Cartridge" above & "The Peters Cartridge Co." below (ILLUS.) ........................ **2,173**

**Display case,** "Colgan's Gum," wood frame, base & top w/glass sides & shelves, acid etching highlighting six different flavors, 8 x 9 x 18" (new shelves, pin supports, finish & hinges ....................... **660**

**Display rack,** "National Biscuit," oak w/stylized decal, curved kickplate, 68" h.............. **525**

**Door push,** "Butternut Bread," die-cut heavy tin, 8 3/4 x 19 3/4"............................. **300**

**Door push,** "King Cole Tea-Coffee," 3 x 31 1/2"............................................... **200**

**Door push,** "Sunbeam Bread," leaf-shaped, red, white & blue, depicts Miss Sunbeam w/"Sunbeam - Batter Whipped," 9 x 19"....................................... **413**

**Door push,** "Vick's," porcelain, palm press type w/"For Colds," 3 3/4 x 7 3/4"................. **400**

*Draw-string Pants*

**Drawstring pants,** "Planters Peanuts," Mr. Peanut pattern on blue background, lightweight denim, adult sizes, ca. 1960s (ILLUS.)......................................................... **50**

**Fan,** "Dr. Pepper," two-sided cardboard w/wooden handle, pretty girl in yellow dress by Earl Moran, reverse w/bottle & "Drink a Bite to Eat - at 10 2 and 4 o'clock," ca. 1930s-40s (light wear on front, back w/soiling on left side & paper tears) .......................................................... **358**

**Fan pull,** two-sided, cardboard figural scarecrow bust w/jack-o-lantern head, white shirt & blue jacket, straw hands, holding bottle, w/"Drink a Bite to Eat at 10 - 2 - 4" across shirt, 7-8" l. (ILLUS. left) ............................................................ **1,760**

*Dr. Pepper Fan Pulls*

**Fan pull,** two-sided, cardboard w/scene of bathing beauty holding ship's wheel w/clock hands at 10 - 2 - 4, marked "Drink Dr. Pepper - Good For Life - or When You're Hungry, Thirsty or Tired," 7-8" l. (ILLUS. right).................................. **2,200**

**Glassine bag,** "Planters Pennant, The Nickel Lunch," five cent bag, ca. 1940s ........ **10**

*1908 Ithaca Gun Poster*

**Guns,** "Ithaca," 1908, rectangular, "Wild Gobbler" above snowy outdoor scene w/large turkey in foreground w/"Ithaco Guns - Guaranteed" below (ILLUS.) ....... **1,540**

**Hat badge,** "National Trailways Bus System," die-cut, from Carolina Scenic Trailways, 2 1/2 x 2 5/8" ..................................... **425**

**Key chain,** "Planters Peanuts," limited edition Mr. Peanut 75th anniversary coin, silver, rare, 1 oz..................................... **375-400**

**Key chain,** "Planters Peanuts," limited edition Mr. Peanut 75th anniversary coin, brass ................................................. **100-125**

**Key chain,** "Planters Peanuts," limited edition Mr. Peanut 75th anniversary coin, brass, prototype ................................... **100-125**

**Light globe,** "Kentucky Fried Chicken," milk glass w/likeness of Colonel Sanders in black & white logo on rectangular red panels, 1960s, 10" h. (light wear & soiling) ................................................................ **110**

*Light Pulls*

**Light pulls,** "Planters Peanuts," figural Mr. Peanut, molded plastic, various colors, ca. 1960s, each (ILLUS.)................... **15**

**Match holder,** "Dr. Pepper," wall-mount type, light green, 3 1/8 x 3 1/4 x 6"................ **80**

*DeLaval Souvenir Matchsafe*

**Matchsafe,** "DeLaval," souvenir, bright plating & colors on tin litho by American Art Sign, New York, 1908, w/original 1 1/4 x 4 x 6 3/4" cardboard box (ILLUS.)......................................................... **418**

**Mechanical pencil,** "Planters Peanuts," figural molded plastic Mr. Peanut on top, yellow & blue ................................................. **18**

**Megaphone,** "Dr. Pepper," heavy paper w/metal ring at top, ca. 1950s, unused (light wear & soiling) ..................................... **358**

**Mirror,** "Angelus Marshmallows," pocket-type, oval, depicts angel holding a box & standing on a square base marked "Angelus Marshmallows" .......................... **143**

**Mirror,** "Cherry Brand," ornate gold handle & rim, celluloid advertising "Fine Chocolates & Bon Bons - Cherry Brand - Cy Gousset 137-141 Prince St. New York," minor soiling & scratches, wear to gold, 2" w., 4" h. (ILLUS. top next page)................ **99**

**Mirror,** "Gillette," pocket-type, round, marked "Shave Yourself - Gillette Safety Razor - No Stropping - No Honing" .............. **110**

**Mirror,** "Horlick's Malted Milk," depicts woman holding can standing next to cow marked "Ask for Horlick's at All Druggists," border marked "The Diet for Infants, Invalids and Nursing Mothers - Ask for Horlick's - Avoid Substitutions," Bastian Bros., 2" d. (surface scratches, mirror streaked) ........................................... **121**

*Cherry Brand Mirror*

**Mirror,** "Thompson's Ice Cream," pocket type, round, depicts colorful bust of Andy Gump w/"Thompson's Unexcelled Ice Cream" around edge & "Andy Gump - for President" flanking the figure ..................... **231**

*Planters Novola Peanut Oil Tin*

**Oil tin,** "Planters Peanuts," Novola peanut oil, blue label w/red border, 5 gal. (ILLUS.)...................................................... **225**
**Oil tin,** "Planters Peanuts," Novola peanut oil, blue label w/red border, colorful printed carton, 5 gal. ................................... **425**
**Order flag,** "Borden Dairy," circular die-cut cardboard insert to place in empty milk bottle to order various dairy products, center shows delivery person in white holding two bottles of milk w/"Borden's Dairy Delivery Company" around border & colored flags attached showing the

*Borden Dairy Order Flag*

various products, tab at bottom w/ "For Extra Orders Turn Up Flag and Put in Top of Bottle," 1932, 5 3/4 x 7 3/4" (ILLUS.) ..................................................... **231**
**Pail,** "Planters Peanuts," Mr. Peanut circus peanut butter pail w/lid, 1 lb. ................. **775-800**

*Telephone Co. Paperweight*

**Paperweight,** "Bell System," blue glass, bell-shaped w/white lettering "Bell System - New York Telephone Company" on one side & "Local and Long Distance Telephone" on reverse, 3 1/4" w., 3" h. (ILLUS.) ..................................................... **209**
**Paperweight,** "Planters Peanuts," figural pot metal Mr. Peanut............................ **775-800**
**Paperweight,** "State Milling & Elevator Co., Cache Junction, Utah," rectangular, depicts image of three different flour sacks on milk glass back, 7/8 x 2 3/4 x 4 1/4" ...................... **149**
**Parade costume,** "Planters Peanuts," Mr. Peanut, w/cane, adult sized, fiberglass w/foam padded shoulders (ILLUS. next page)........................................................ **600**
**Peanut dispenser,** "Planters Peanuts," toy-type, molded plastic, upright style w/molded figure of Mr. Peanut, made once, used as store display, Tarco, 1978 ....... **45**
**Pen & pencil set,** "Planters Peanuts," w/"Mr. Peanut's 75th Birthday," by Cross, gold-filled, Mr. Peanut engraved on clip, rare ................................................. **200**
**Pencil,** "Planters Peanuts," advertising type, green w/eraser tip, unsharpened .......... **18**

*Parade Costume*

*Dr. Pepper Pin Trays*

black boy wearing yellow hat, eating watermelon, blue background w/"Drink Dr. Pepper At All Soda Fountains 5¢" in red letters around edge, light rusting at border near face, pit marks on outer border, 3 1/4" l. (ILLUS. top right) ................ **2,530**

**Playing cards,** "Dr. Pepper," black w/logo & pretty girl in red dress holding bottle, complete deck w/calendar card & bridge card, ca. 1946, original box ......................... **385**

**Poster,** "Daisy Air Rifles," titled "Two Daisies" by Calvert Litho Co., Detroit, Michigan, shows boy walking arm in arm w/girl & holding rifle on his shoulder, other children at play in background, top & bottom bands w/hanger, reverse pictures No. 1, No. 2, No. 3, No. 30 & the "Little Daisey" w/full descriptions, 15 1/2 x 22 3/4" ........................................ **4,620**

*Marlin Rifle Poster*

**Poster,** "Marlin," 1907, rectangular, outdoor scene w/one man in canoe & a second man pushing the canoe away from the river bank , a campsite in the wooded background, w/"Marlin Repeating Rifles and Shotguns - 'The Gun For the Man Who Knows'" (ILLUS.)............................. **2,145**

*Morton's Salt Poster*

**Poster,** "Morton Salt," rectangular, depicts product in center w/potatoes on left & a split baked potato & salt shaker on right, "What's a potato without Morton's?," ca. 1940s-50s, framed under glass, wrinkles, light edge wear, minor marks & stains, 18 x 36" (ILLUS.) .............................. **187**

**Pin tray,** "Dr. Pepper," metal, round, center w/scene of two kittens drinking milk from a bowl, one w/pink ribbon, the other blue, light green background, tan border w/scalloped edge w/"Drink Dr. Pepper At All Soda Fountains 5¢" in red letters, light crazing & edge wear, 2 1/2" d. (ILLUS. top left) ...................................... **1,210**

**Pin tray,** "Dr. Pepper," metal, round, center w/scene of two puppies, light blue background, pink border w/scalloped edge w/"Drink Dr. Pepper At All Soda Fountains 5¢" in red letters, few shallow dents & marks, border wear,2 1/2" d. (ILLUS. bottom right) ............................................. **1,430**

**Pin tray,** "Dr. Pepper," metal, oval, center w/black & white dog against yellow ground, white & light blue border w/scalloped edge w/"Drink Dr. Pepper At All Soda Fountains 5¢" in red letters, light soiling, minor marks, light edge wear, 3 1/4" l. (ILLUS. bottom left) ..................... **1,650**

**Pin tray,** "Dr. Pepper," metal, oval w/white & green scalloped edge, center scene of

*Display Punchboard*

**Punchboard display,** "Planters Peanuts," rectangular, layered cardboard, orange, blue, yellow & black lettering, across the top reads "Planters Cocktail Peanuts," 1940s-50s (ILLUS.) .............................. **100-300**

**Radio,** "Dr. Pepper," transistor-type, plastic, ca. 1960s, 3 x 7" ............................ **297**

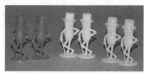

*Plastic Mr. Peanut Salt and Pepper Shakers*

**Salt & pepper shakers,** "Planters Peanuts," figural Mr. Peanut, molded plastic, various colors, each set (ILLUS.) .................. **20**

**Scale,** "Planters Peanuts," molded figural Mr. Peanut, plastic, coin slot in top hat, originals have brass tag w/item number on back of hat, ca. 1940s, hat circumference 8 1/2" (only 8" on reproductions), 3' 8" h. ...................................................... **16,000**

**Sidewalk scale,** "Planters Peanuts," figural Mr. Peanut, restored, 20 x 22" .............. **20,700**

**Sign,** "DeLaval Cream Separator," paper lithograph shows five different images of farm women w/machines, framed under glass .......................................................... **1,050**

**Sign,** "Grape-Nuts," embossed tin lithograph of girl walking to school w/St. Bernard dog, 30" h (light damage) .................. **1,150**

**Sign,** "Heinz's Pickles," embossed cardboard logo on side & "Established 1869 - Heinz's Preserved Sweet Mixed Pickles - Keystone Brand," 4 x 11" .......................... **187**

**Sign,** "Planters Peanuts," 3-D hand carved wood Mr. Peanut, green & yellow, approximately 24 x 33" ......................... **500-525**

**Sign,** "Shirley President Suspenders," lithographed cardboqrd w/scenes of six women engaged in various sports, under glass in wood frame, 52 1/2" l. (tearing).... **1,900**

**Sign,** "Sweet-Orr," porcelain, depicts six men in a tug-of-war w/pair of overalls w/"Sweet-Orr - Union Made - Overalls" in white letters on blue, fading & scratches to graphic, chips to "w" & edges, cracking, 14 x 20" (ILLUS. top next column) ....... **413**

**Sign,** "Witter's Laundry," embossed die-cut of a cute baby seated in a cloth sling tied at the top w/blue ribbon, decorated w/blue flowers at top & around baby who holds a card which reads "My Clothes

are at Witter's Laundry - Are Yours?," image 4 3/4 x 11 3/4 in 13 x 17" period frame (ILLUS. below) ..................... **583**

*Sweet-Orr Overalls Sign*

*Witter's Laundry Sign*

*Woolrich Outdoorwear Sign*

**Sign,** "Woolrich Rugged Outdoorwear," genuine birchbark canoe w/hanger, 2 1/2 x 4 1/2 x 18" (ILLUS.) ......................... **605**

**Sign,** Moxie, diecut cardboard, jockey on horse & horse-form Moxiemobile, Moxie written on each side, ca. 1918, excellent condition, 9" l., ........................................ **1,650**

**Store bin,** "Capital Coffee," pine w/original red stain & black stenciled labels on the sides & front panel, late 19th - early 20th c., 16 1/2 x 21", 32 1/2" h. ........................... **550**

**Store bin,** "Jersey Coffee," painted salmon w/stenciled decoration on top front, 32" h. .......................................................... **850**

**Store bin,** "Luxury Coffee," painted yellow, stenciled top & front w/shipping stencils on ends, 32" h. ..................................... 1,050

**Store bin,** "Wilbur's Seed Meal," four-sided, painted & stenciled yellow, 36" h. ...... 850

**String holder,** "Red Goose Shoes," tin lithograph, 14" h. ..................................... 1,300

**Thermometer,** "Burress Implement Co.," rectangular w/rounded top, aluminum w/red tractor & "McCormick Deering Farm Machinery - International Trucks - Booneville, Miss.," 3 3/4 x 13 1/4" ............... 176

**Thermometer,** "Carter White Lead Paint," porcelain, white, red & black, "Carter White Lead - The All Weather Paint" at the top, paint bucket at bottom marked "Carter Soft Paste White Lead," by Beach Coshocton, Ohio, 3/4 x 7 x 27" (chips top & bottom edges ........................... 259

**Thermometer,** "Dr. Pepper," circular dial w/"Hot or cold," 18" d.................................... 110

**Thermometer,** "Dr. Pepper," die-cut figural classic bottle cap, 11" d................................ 100

*Dr. Pepper Thermometer*

**Thermometer,** "Dr. Pepper," tin & glass, white & red w/aqua highlights, bottle shown opposite thermometer w/clock at top marked "Drink A Bite To Eat At 10 2 4" & "Dr. Pepper - Good For Life - 5¢" at the bottom, soiling, small edge bend lower right, few marks & light scuffs, ca. 1930s, 4 1/2 x 13" (ILLUS.) ................... 2,310

**Thermometer,** "Ex Lax," porcelain w/horizontal bulb, 1 1/4 x 8 x 36" .......................... 325

**Thermometer,** "Frostie Root Beer," tin, 8 x 36" (some rust & damage) .................... 145

**Thermometer,** "Keen Kutter," metal on wood w/hanger, by Simmons Hardware Co., 1/2 x 1 3/4 x 7 1/4 ................................. 176

**Thermometer,** "Pepsi-Cola," metal w/glass lens, "Drink Pepsi-Cola Ice-Cold," red, white & blue, ca. 1951, 12" d..................... 1,100

**Thermometer,** "Planters Peanuts," Mr. Peanut, tin, 1978, 6 x 7" ............................ 65-80

**Thermometer,** "Red Goose Shoes," porcelain, 27" h. (minor screw hole & edge chip) ............................................................. 650

**Thermometer,** "Royal Crown Cola," tin w/detailed deep embossing.......................... 185

**Thermometer,** "Sunbeam Bread," metal & glass, "Reach for Sunbeam Bread - Let's Be Friends" above Miss Sunbeam Trademark, copyright Quality Bakers of American Cooperative, Inc., 1957, 12" d. (soiling & surface stain & marks).................. 413

**Thermometer,** "Tums," aluminum w/glass tube, rectangular w/"Tums for the Tummy" at the top & "Tums Quick Relief for Acid Indigestion - Heartburn" at the bottom, 4 x 9" .................................................. 55

*Log Cabin Express Wagon*

**Toy,** "Log Cabin," tin wagon pull toy for small size syrup can, red, side marked "Log Cabin Express," & stamped "798" on bottom, 1 1/2 x 4 x 5 1/4" (ILLUS.) .......... 259

*Wood-jointed Mr. Peanut*

**Toy,** "Planters Peanuts," figure of Mr. Peanut, wood jointed, painted yellow, black & white w/blue top hat, ca. 1930s (ILLUS.)....................................................... 225

**Toy,** "Planters Peanuts," Mr. Peanut black & tan wind-up, rare................................. 400-425

**Toy,** "Planters Peanuts" Mr. Peanut, plastic windup walking figure, green, 8 1/2" h. (very light wear)......................................... 413

*Toy Train Car*

Toy train car, "Planters Peanuts," coal car, printed on side w/Planters advertising in red, white & yellow, Tyco, 1977, mint in original box (ILLUS.) ...................................... 50

*Clear Glass Tumblers*

Tumblers, "Planters Peanuts," clear glass w/Mr. Peanut decal, each (ILLUS.) ................ 25
Tumblers, "Planters Peanuts," Mr. Peanut 75th anniversary six-piece set.............. 250-275
Uniform badge, "Signal Trucking," cloisonne on brass, 2" w................................... 450
Whistle, "Planters Peanuts," figural Mr. Peanut, various colors, 2 1/2" ................... 10-15

# ARCHITECTURAL ITEMS

*In recent years the growing interest in and support for historic preservation has spawned a greater appreciation of the fine architectural elements which were an integral part of early building, both public and private. Where, in decades past, structures might be razed and doors, fireplace mantels, windows, etc., hauled to the dump, today all interior and exterior details from unrestorable buildings are salvaged to be offered to home restorers, museums and even builders who want to include a bit of history in a new construction project.*

*Fine Victorian Building Finial*

Building finial, copper, a conical wide floriform base supporting a ribbed balusterform w/ball on top, 19th c., minor dents, 48" h. (ILLUS.)........................................ $1,955
Building mounts, patinated copper, each relief-molded in the form of a massive scroll volute, possibly American, late 19th c., 10 1/2 x 60", 20" h., pr. .................... 920

Building ornament, carved & painted wood fan, demi-lune form centering a carved fan & rayed louvers in a molded frame, old green paint, New England, ca. 1800, 53" l., 21 1/4" h. ............ 748
Building ornament, cast lead model of an eagle & shield mounted on a threaded rod, America, 11 1/2 x 12" (some corrosion) ......................................................... 403
Building ornaments, eagles' heads, cast iron, a large feathered head w/beak open, from 19th c. courthouse, 12 x 13", 16" h., pr. (losses, rust) ............................ 2,415

*Art Deco Elevator Doors*

Elevator doors, Art Deco style, pale brass, each tall door w/two panels incised w/geometric & stylized flora & fauna, small dents, ca. 1930s, each panel 20 1/2" w., 84 3/4" h., pr. (ILLUS.)............. 2,587

*Fine Cast Iron Victorian Gate*

Fireplace surround, cast iron, Arts & Crafts style, the two-part surround comprised of a frame w/raised flower & leaf borders, the screen w/central profile bust of an Egyptian pharaoh w/raised flower & wood grain borders, early 20th c., 30 1/2 x 30 1/2" (discoloration, rust)............ **230**

**Gate,** cast iron, square frame w/arched vined cresting centering a banner readings "Edward R. Dolan," above a scrolling arch over a scene w/a large weeping willow tree w/two doves in the branches above a pair of recumbent lambs on a grassy mound, old black, green & white paint, ca. 1860, 29" w., 41" h. (ILLUS. previous page) ......................................... **1,380**

# ART DECO

*Interest in Art Deco, a name given an art movement stemming from the Paris International Exhibition of 1925, continues to grow today. This style flowered in the 1930s and actually continued into the 1940s. A mood of flippancy is found in its varied characteristics - zigzag lines resembling the lightning bolt, sometimes steps, often the use of sharply contrasting colors such as black and white and others. Look for prices for the best examples of Art Deco design to continue to rise. Also see JEWELRY, MODERN.*

**Andirons,** cast iron, figural, designed as an owl w/angled geometric features, a "P" at lower center, ca. 1930, 15 7/8" h., pr. .... **$115**

*Rare Art Deco Steel Book Ends*

**Book ends,** hammered steel, figural, modeled as upright open-mouthed cobra w/the coiled tail on a rectangular low platform, by Edgar Brandt, impressed mark, ca. 1925, 7 3/4" h., pr. (ILLUS.)....... **7,475**

**Candlesticks,** white metal w/brass patina, hexagonal paneled standard & base w/geometric grid decorative band, impressed Pairpoint mark & "B6119" on base, 8" h., pr. (patina wear) ........................ **288**

**Chandelier,** five-light, five press-molded frosted amber glass shades w/floral decoration suspended from a gilt & enameled metal mount w/linear & floral decoration, impressed & raised marks include "Halcolite Co P750 Pat Pend" on ceiling mount, America, ca. 1930, shaded 17 1/2" w., 21" l. (gilt wear, minor glass chips) ........................................ **518**

**Cigarette dispenser,** metal, a covered square patinated metal & enameled chrome box-form dispenser w/a cast-metal mechanical monkey w/arm outstretched to grab a cigarette, on a shaped rectangular base, impressed mark on base "Ronson - PIK - A - CiG - Art Metal Works, Inc., Newark, New Jersey," ca. 1935, 5 x 8 1/2", 5 1/4" h. (missing attachment, patination loss) ........... **518**

**Clock,** table model, enameled metal, the flat square top w/enameled tile-like surround depicting a parrot & cockatoo in red, green, blue, white & black on a green & orange speckled cream ground & centered by a small square dial w/Roman numerals, raised on a four-footed patinated metal frame & forked leg stand, impressed "C.H. Deposé" in an oval & "347-1 - 16 - France," ca. 1920s, 7 1/4" h. (patination loss) ............... **1,093**

*Art Deco Decanter Set*

**Decanter set:** three glass decanters in a chrome-plated framework; a flat rectangular platform base w/tiny ball feet & incurved end uprights joined by a hinged top crossbar w/arched black Bakelite handle, fitted w/three bottle-form glass decanters in green, blue & amber each w/a looped chrome base frame & chrome ball stoppers, impressed mark of Krome Kraft by Farber Bros., New York on the base, ca. 1925, some metal corrosion, 3 1/2 x 12", 10 1/2" h. (ILLUS.)......... **230**

**Floor lamp,** cast metal, a geometric finial above a three-socket candlestick w/chain pulls, standard w/hammered & geometric decoration raised on a flared stepped base w/stylized floral decoration, ca. 1938, 53 1/2" h. ................... **173**

**Floor lamp,** wrought & patinated iron, a tall slender standard topped w/a crimped fanned finial over a down-curved socket arm w/a crimped & fanned bracket, the lower half of the standard tapering to a small round platform on a triangular foot, by John Sartori, striated bronze finish, fitted w/a later cylindrical frosted & clear green glass shade w/a geometric design, overall 69 1/4" h.............................. **805**

**Lamp,** table model, a conical glass shade & spherical base in frosted dark amber glass, decorated w/acid-etched & enameled geometric diamond & triangle patterns in orange & green, silver stamp "Bulova - Czechoslovakia" on base, ca. 1930, shade 13 1/4" d. overall 14 1/2" h. .. **2,645**

**Lamp,** table model, figural, a model of an airplane w/a frosted colorless glass body accented w/silver paint, nickel-plated wings, propellers, tail & looped strap support above the flat rectangular base w/rolled-under ends, American, ca. 1935, 11 1/4" l., 7 5/8" h. (corrosion, paint loss)..................................................... **374**

**Wall scones,** bronze, each w/a shaped rectangular back plate supporting a single curved socket arm, polished, in the manner of Emile-Jacques Ruhlmann, unsigned, France, ca. 1925, 18" h, pr. ...... **3,335**

# ART NOUVEAU

*Art Nouveau's primary thrust was between 1890 and 1905, but commercial Art Nouveau productions continued until about World War I. This style was a rebellion against historic tradition in art. Using natural forms as inspiration, it is primarily characterized by undulating or wave-like lines and whiplashes. Many objects were made in materials ranging from glass to metals. Figural pieces with seductive maidens with long, flowing hair are especially popular in this style. Interest in Art Nouveau remains high, with the best pieces by well known designers bringing strong prices. Also see JEWELRY, ANTIQUE.*

**Bowl,** sterling silver, the domed foot repoussé & chased w/scrolls & animal heads, the deep rounded bowl decorated w/lilies & leaves, three cast & applied hollow looped handles chased w/leaves & scrolls, cast & applied rim, gilded interior, mark & date symbol for the Gorham Mfg. Co., Providence, Rhode Island, 1903, body 10 1/2" d....... **$3,680**

**Candlestick,** bronze, figural, modeled as a kneeling nude female w/long flowing hair incorporated into a petal-form candle-socket above, impressed "E.B. Parsons - Roman Bronze Works - New York" on base, dark brown patina, early 20th c., 7 1/2" h. ...................................................... **863**

**Candlesticks,** figural, gilt-metal, figures of partially clad maidens carrying vessels on their heads, impressed "MP," "D.P. Muller" around the base, Europe, early 20th c., 10 1/2" h., pr. (patina & gilt loss) ..... **374**

**Clock,** figural, silvered spelter, the top w/a tall figure of a standing Art Nouveau maiden w/one hand to her mouth, wearing a diaphanous gown, on an upright squared base cast w/swirling vines & flowers flaring at the base & forming loop feet, round central clock dial, time-and-strike movement, ca. 1910, 12" w., 24 1/2" h. (ILLUS. top next column) .......... **1,000**

**Lamp,** table model, figural, a domical copper shade w/round glass jewels in florette mounts around the top & plain jewels around the drop rim, raised on a cast-metal figural base in the form of a Daphne-style Art Nouveau maiden

w/leaf-form arms, squared & twisted standard w/leaf-cast base, painted green & tan, Europe, ca. 1900, light wear, 20 1/2" h. (ILLUS. below) ......................... **1,380**

*Figural Art Nouveau Clock*

**Lamp,** table model, patinated cast metal, figural, a standing Art Nouveau maiden wearing a long flowing gown, her arms held out w/a leaf-cast electric socket suspended from each hand, each socket fitted w/a gold Aurene ribbed & bell-shaped marked Steuben shade, dark brown & green patina, spotting to patina, early 20th c., 29" h. (ILLUS. top next page) ............................................................**1,093**

*Figural Art Nouveau Lamp*

**Mirror,** dressing table-type, silver-mounted, the arched irregular outline w/a border composed of scrolls & flowers, a female figure in the upper left-hand corner, the back of mahogany w/a pierced hinged strut, marked "RP," probably for Robert Pringle & Sons, Birmingham, England, 1902, 13 1/2" w., 17 1/2" h. (ILLUS. below)...................................................... **2,300**

*Art Nouveau Lamp & Steuben Shades*

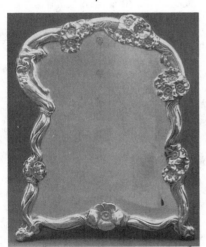

*English Art Nouveau Silver Mirror*

**Vase,** bronze-mounted glass, an iridescent cylindrical glass vase mounted in a naturalistic conforming iris bronze mount w/a large gilt-bronze blossom, Austria, early 20th c., 10 1/4" h. ...................................... **518**

**Vase,** metal-mounted glass, a slender tapering cylindrical pale amber glass vase mounted within a dark metal openwork mount of stylized flowers & leaves, Bohemia, ca. 1900, 9 3/4" h. (nick to rim)..... **173**

**Vase,** mold-blown bulbed cylinder of cornflower blue glass w/iridescent lustre, enamel-decorated w/stylized dahlias in lavender & white on green stems rising from grass base, signed in enamel, possibly by Fritz Heckert, ca. 1900, minor

enamel neck at rim, 9 1/2" h. (ILLUS. below)...................................................... **1,150**

*Art Nouveau Enameled Glass Vase*

# AUTOGRAPHS

*This section highlights 100 desirable autographs out of the panorama of interesting historical figures who populate every field of human endeavor.*

*Autograph values continue strong, although collectors should be aware of vast numbers of non-authentic contemporary sports & celebrity items entering the market via popular internet auction sites & other venues, often offered by part-time dealers or other novices not qualified to guarantee authenticity & acquired by collectors trusting the expertise of the seller. There are also a small number of unscrupulous types who have saturated this market with their phony wares. The best advice is to avoid or be extremely circumspect in purchasing from anyone the autographs of living persons. After all, why do that then, with a little persistence, imagination & a dash of luck it remains possible to obtain authentic specimens of your heroes John Hancock either by mail or occasionally in person? Secretarial, printed & Autopen signatures are recurring dilemma, of course, but getting around that is simply part of the challenge & fun.*

*Full-time professional autograph dealers who guarantee the authenticity of all material without time limit remain the collector's most reliable source of genuine autographs. Look for membership in professional associations such as the Antiquarian Booksellers Association of America. (The Manuscript Society & Universal Autograph Collectors Club are outstanding organizations, but membership is open to all.) Never be fooled by ornate "COAs" (Certificates of Authenticity), which are often crutches used by inexperienced dealers to lend credibility to their material. Remember, anyone can print up & issue such certificates, which sometimes aren't worth the paper they are printed on.*

*"Go for the best content & the best condition you can afford" may sound hackneyed, yet it remains*

the soundest advice—& the most often neglected! "If it looks too good to be true, it probably is" follows a close second. Work only with serious dealers whose expertise & integrity you trust, & back up this trust by becoming a signature sleuth yourself, reading & studying all you can get hold of about autographs.

The following are all items that sold recently at reputable auction houses, & are chosen for their variety & for values that are typical. Standard autograph descriptions have been greatly shortened. Abbreviations (which apply to most but not all items described below):

ALS = Autograph Letter Signed

LS = Letter Signed

DS = Document Signed

PS = Photograph Signed

**Arbuckle, Roscoe "Fatty" (1887-1933),** silent film comedian, original pen & ink portrait by unknown artist, inscribed & signed & dated August 24, 1927, framed together w/photograph ............................... $325

**Armstrong, Neil (born 1930),** astronaut & first to set foot on moon, PS, undated.......... 300

**Auden, W. H. (1907-1973),** Pulitzer-prize winning poet, ALS, agrees to meet poet Edgar Lee Masters, framed w/portrait, 1 page ........................................................... 325

**Austin, Stephen F. (1793-1836),** Texas colonizer & city namesake, DS,"Texas Loan" Certificate, dated January 11, 1836, 1 page, 9 x 11" ................................ 1,500

**Baker, Josephine (1906-1975),** American jazz singer who became Parisian legend, signed concert program, elaborate leatherbound illustrated "Folies Bergere" 1937 program, 4 pages........................ 325

**Barnum, Phineas T. ("P.T.") (1810-91),** showman & circus owner, unsigned Autograph Quotation, reading: "All the world's a stage & all the men & women merely players," 1 page ............................. 700

**Basie, William "Count" (1904-1984),** jazz pianist & Big Band leader, PS, inscribed promotional portrait ..................................... 275

**Beauvoir, Simone de (1908-1986),** French author long affiliated w/Jean-Paul Sartre, ALS, declines to attend meeting, undated, 1 page ......................................... 300

**Bernhardt, Sarah (1844-1923),** great French dramatic actress known as "The Divine Sarah," postcard size PS, undated (mounting traces on verso) ........... 300

**Boone, Daniel (1734-1820),** famed frontiersman, rare DS, certifying that a horse was used for public service in an expedition, framed w/engraving, dated November 23, 1782, 1 page ...............................6,000

**Burger, Warren (1907-1995),** Supreme Court chief justice, ALS, to former justice Arthur Goldberg regretting absence at Goldberg's "Medal of Freedom" award ceremony, 1 page ...................................... 250

**Byrd, Richard E. (1888-1957),** American explorer of the Antarctic, small PS, dated April 24, 1957 .............................................. 275

**Cain, James M. (1892-1977),** American novelist of "The Postman Always Rings Twice" fame, LS, to an editor w/interesting writing content, dated April 2, 1946, 1 page ............................................................. 475

**Capote, Truman (1924-84),** Southern novelist acclaimed for "In Cold Blood," ALS, discusses Sicily, dated June 24, 1952, 2 pages ............................................................ 175

**Carver, George Washington (1864-1943),** agricultural chemist & educator who discovered numerous industrial uses for peanuts, soybeans & sweet potatoes, rare PS, undated, some damage ............. 2,200

**Charles (born 1948) & Diana (1961-97),** Prince & Princess of Wales, color PS, within 1983 Christmas card, inscribed & signed by both, in original envelope .......... 3,750

**Coleridge, Samuel Taylor (1772-1834),** English critic & poet remembered for "The Rime of the Ancient Mariner," rare ALS, third-person text regarding the borrowing of books, dated December 27, 1818, 1 page ........................................... 650

**Coolidge, Calvin (1872-1933),** 30th U. S. President nicknamed "Silent Cal," ALS, recommends a friend for a bank loan, dated October 12, 1911, 1 page ................ 500

**Coolidge, Grace (1879-1957),** First Lady, small signed card w/engraved White House vignette, undated ............................ 100

**Dalton, Emmett (1871-1937),** Old West outlaw turned screenwriter, LS, to silent film cowboy star Ken Maynard, dated September 5, 1934, 1 page....................... 1,300

**Darrow, Clarence (1857-1938),** defense attorney of Leopold-Loeb murder trial & Scopes monkey trial fame, PS, inscribed undated portrait ........................................ 700

**Darwin, Charles (1809-82),** British naturalist & originator of evolution theory, ALS, about botanical matters, dated December 21, 1880, 1 page ................................ 2,600

**Davis, Sammy, Jr. (1925-1990),** versatile singer, dancer, actor & "Rat Pack" member, small PS, undated.................................. 85

**Dietrich, Marlene (1901-1992),** sultry German film actress best known for "The Blue Angel," unusual PS, oversize portrait inscribed to Ethel Merman, undated (slight damage at corners) .......................... 750

**Eliot, T. S. (1888-1965),** influential American poet & critic, ALS, thanks a hostess for a lunch, dated May 22, 1955, 2 pages..... 375

**Farrell, James T. (1904-1979),** American novelist famed for 1930s "Studs Lonigan" trilogy, ALS, to a newspaper editor about his review of an H. L. Mencken book, dated November 11, 1961, 12 pages ............................................................ 500

**Field, Eugene (1850-1895),** Chicago poet of "Little Boy Blue" fame, ALS, discusses his book & autograph collection, dated February 4, 1890, 4 pages ......................... 550

**Fields, W.C. (1880-1946),** film & vaudeville comedian famed for his love of liquor & dislike of children, PS, undated ................. 1,000

**Flynn, Errol (1909-1959),** film heartthrob, LS, to Warner Brothers about posing for publicity stills, dated April 28, 1948, 1 page ........ 450

**Gacy, John Wayne (1942-1994),** mass murderer, LS, to actor Brian Dennehy about his portrayal of Gacy in a made-for-TV film, dated June 2, 1991, 1 page ....... 150

**Garfield, James A. (1831-81),** 20th U.S. president, assassinated by Charles J. Guiteau, PS, undated (some surface damage) ..................... 1,300

**Garrison, William Lloyd (1805-1879),** abolitionists & newspaper founder, unsigned Autograph Manuscript, text of poem "Sonnet to Liberty," dated October 9, 1863, 1 page ...................... 1,300

**Gould, Chester (1900-1985),** "Dick Tracy" cartoonist, small original ink sketch, undated ..................... 160

**Grant, Julia Dent (1826-1902),** First Lady, ALS, regards purchasing bonds, dated December 27, 1897, 4 pages ...................... 950

**Handy, W. C. (1873-1958),** "Father of the Blues" who composed "St. Louis Blues," PS, dated June 1, 1956 (some damage) ..... 350

**Harrison, William H. (1773-1841),** 9th U. S. President & first to die in office, ALS, concerns military provisions, dated October 6, 1797, 2 pages ...................... 950

**Hoover, J. Edgar (1895-1972),** long-time FBI chief, LS, concerns his appointment as director of investigations at Justice Department, dated August 8, 1933, 1 page ..................... 80

**Hughes, Langston (1902-67),** "Harlem Renaissance" movement poet & writer, rare PS, undated ......................... 425

**Irving, Washington (1783-1859),** author remembered for "The Legend of Sleepy Hollow" and "Rip Van Winkle" ," Autograph Note Signed, concerns a dinner invitation, undated, 1 page (shows restoration work) ..................... 300

**Jackson, Andrew (1767-1845),** War of 1812 hero & 7th U.S. president, DS, presidential pardon, dated June 3, 1831, 1 page ..................... 1,800

**Jackson, Thomas "Stonewall" (1824-63),** revered Confederate general, ALS, dated January 1, 1846, to his sister concerning leaving West Point, 2 pages ......... 7,000

**James, Henry (1843-1916),** American novelist whose many works include "The Turn of the Screw," ALS, routine content, undated, 3 pages ...................... 280

**Jung, Carl (1875-1961),** "Father of Analytical Psychology," signed typescript, essay "Psychoanalysis & the Cure of Souls," undated, 11 pages ......................... 850

**Kai-shek, Chiang (1887-1975),** Chinese officer & statesman exiled by Communists to Taiwan, PS, framed portrait inscribed on mount ..................... 200

**Kennedy, Robert F. (1925-1968),** attorney general & assassinated presidential candidate, ALS, congratulates Arthur Goldberg on appointment as U.N. ambassador, dated 1965, 1 page ............. 1,600

**L'Amour, Louis (1908-1988),** prolific & bestselling Western novelist, LS, discusses his mail & his stories, dated April 27, 1980, 1 page ......................... 425

**Leigh, Vivien (1913-1967),** "Gone With the Wind" actress, ALS, discusses a trip to Brazil & an upcoming role, dated September 20, 1962, 2 pages ......................... 450

**Longstreet, James (1821-1904),** controversial Confederate general, rare war-date ALS, concerns a possible offensive in northern Virginia, dated September 27, 1861, 2 pages ......................... 5,500

**Lugosi, Bela (1882-1956),** actor typecast as "Dracula," signature on small slip, framed w/portrait, undated (stained) ........... 260

**Mack, Connie (1862-1956),** Hall of Fame baseball team manager & owner, ALS, discusses a major league team in Baltimore, dated October 28, 1953, 2 pages ...... 550

**Malcolm X (1925-1965),** radical assassinated civil rights leader, rare ALS, choice content to a colleague on his prison time & its effect on his faith & plans, dated February 15, 1950, 2 pages.. 6,500

**Marconi, Guglielmo (1874-1937),** inventor of the wireless telegraph, PS, dated April 4, 1934, inscribed circular portrait also signed by photographer; accompanied by PS of his wife ..................... 600

**Matisse, Henri (1869-1954),** French artist, ALS, mentions his illustrations for James Joyce's "Ulysses" among other things, dated March 16, 1934, 2 pages (worn & damaged but repaired) ..................... 2,100

**Miller, Henry (1891-1980),** author of long-banned "Tropic of Cancer" & other racy novels, pair of ALSs, regarding an exhibit of his paintings, dated 1960, 2 pages ......................... 425

**Mussolini, Benito (1883-1945),** Italian fascist party leader & later prime minister who allied his country w/Hitler, DS, military appointment co-signed by King Vittorio Emmanuel III, dated November 2, 1938, 1 page ......................... 250

**Nelson, Horatio (1758-1805),** English naval officer who defeated the French at Trafalgar, ALS, to Emma Hamilton discussing an upcoming battle, dated March 23, 1801, 1 page ......................... 3,000

**Nimitz, Chester W. (1885-1966),** American commander of the Pacific fleet during World War II, PS, famed shot of the Allied powers gathered to sign the Japanese surrender aboard the U.S.S. Missouri, undated ......................... 1,600

**O'Keeffe, Georgia (1887-1986),** American artist known for her large paintings of brilliant flowers & bleached animal skulls, ALS, arranging a meeting, dated January 28, 1934, , 1 page ................... 750

**O'Neill, Eugene (1888-1953),** Nobel Prize- & Pulitzer Prize-winning American playwright, PS, undated, inscribed newspaper portrait, framed ......................... 350

**Osler, Sir William (1849-1919),** Canadian physician who developed modern medical practices, ALS, arranging a meeting & other matters, undated, 1 page .............. **1,000**

**Paine, Thomas (1737-1809),** colonial patriot remembered for "Common Sense," rare ALS, discussing finances, undated, 2 pages ....................... **7,500**

**Parrish, Maxfield (1870-1966),** American artist known for book illustrations, ALS, discussing an exhibition, dated November 18, 1904, 1 page (rather worn) ............. **550**

**Penn, William (1644-1718),** English colonizer & founder of Pennsylvania, DS, dated April 4, 1695, selling 600 acres of land, framed w/period engraving, 1 page.. **3,200**

**Pickford, Mary (1893-1979),** silent film star known as "America's Sweetheart," LS, discussing Hollywood & Charlie Chaplin, dated April 28, 1925, 3 pages ..................... **500**

**Poe, Edgar Allan (1809-49),** American writer known for dark themes in short stories & poems such as "The Raven," rare ALS, regarding a female poet, dated February 18, 1844 ............................... **16,000**

**Puccini, Giacomo (1858-1924),** Italian composer of "Madame Butterfly" fame, ALS, discussing problems with a symphony he is composing, undated, 1 page.. **1,000**

**Rand, Ayn (1905-1982),** American novelist ("Atlas Shrugged") whose "objectivist" philosophy is reflected in her writings, rare PS, portrait w/choice inscription, dated March 15, 1952 ............................... **2,750**

**Reeves, George (1914-1959),** "Superman" actor, signature & inscription on 5 1/4" x 3 1/2" slip, framed with "Superman" portrait, undated................................... **375**

**Remington, Frederic (1861-1909),** Western artist, ALS, discusses health & other matters & sketches an artist at work w/alligator observing at top of page, undated, 1 page ........................................ **2,600**

**Ripley, Robert L. (1893-1949),** cartoonist & "Believe It or Not" creator, PS, undated (slightly creased portrait)................ **120**

**Rubinstein, Anton (1829-1894),** Russian pianist & composer, ALS, concerning his opera "Nero," 2 pages .................................. **350**

**Rush, Benjamin (1745-1813),** influential physician & signer of the Declaration of Independence, DS, a medical diploma on vellum from the College of Philadelphia, signed by Rush & other professors, dated 1790, 1 page (some damage) ......... **1,100**

**Sartre, Jean-Paul (1905-1980),** French existentialist philosopher & writer, ALS, discussing the publishing of his plays in the Soviet Union, dated November 2, 1965, 2 pages ............................................. **500**

**Schulz, Charles (1922-2000),** "Peanuts" cartoonist, original marker sketch of "Snoopy," undated, 1 page........................... **425**

**Sennett, Mack (1880-1960),** silent film director & "Keystone Kops" creator, DS, promissory note for $10,000, framed w/portrait, dated October 11, 1916, 1 page (some damage) .................................. **270**

**Seuss, Dr. (1904-1991),** author of many children's classics such as "Green Eggs & Ham," small color PS, photo of front cover of "The Cat in the Hat," undated......... **180**

**Shaw, George Bernard (1856-1950),** Nobel Prize-winning British dramatist, ALS, scathing response to a request for an unedited version of one of his plays, dated April 29, 1927, 1 page ...................... **475**

**Sinatra, Frank (1915-1998),** crooner & actor, rare PS, early portrait from his Tommy Dorsey Orchestra days, undated..... **500**

**Speer, Albert (1905-1981),** Hitler confidante & official Third Reich architect, unusual LS, denying idea that Holocaust ever occurred, dated October 4, 1980, 1 page ................................................................. **1,500**

**Stewart, Jimmy (1908-1997),** beloved "It's a Wonderful Life" actor, original signed ink sketch of "Harvey," framed w/portrait, undated ................................................................. **325**

**Stuart, J.E.B. (1833-1864),** revered Confederate cavalry officer, rare ALS, congratulates cousin on marriage & discusses politics & his army career, dated February 23, 1859, 4 pages ............ **8,500**

**Swanson, Gloria (1899-1983),** silent film star, large PS, undated ............................... **110**

**Thomas, Dylan (1914-1953),** colorful Welch poet, ALS, agrees to read at a poetry event, dated July 26, 1948, 1 page (some damage) ................................ **1,100**

**Thurston, Howard (1869-1936),** renowned magician, rare PS, dated 1935............... **750**

**Trollope, Anthony (1815-1882),** prolific British novelist, ALS, discusses a journey, dated September 1, 1868, 2 pages ...... **800**

**Truman, Harry S (1884-1972),** 33rd U.S. president, LS, thanks comedian Jack Benny for attending his birthday party, framed w/photo of Benny & Truman at the gathering, dated December 18, 1961, 1 page ................................................ **500**

**Utrillo, Maurice (1883-1955),** French artist, ALS, sends New Year's greetings, dated January 1, 1934, 1 page (slight damage)..... **350**

**Van Buren, Martin (1782-1862),** 8th U.S. president, ALS, offers financial advice, dated September 15, 1832, 1 page............. **550**

**Verdi, Giuseppe (1813-1901),** prolific Italian opera composer, ALS, concerns an article, undated, 1 page............................ **1,400**

**Verne, Jules (1828-1905),** French author known as "the founder of science fiction," small ALS, responds to an autograph request, framed w/portrait, dated November 2, 1897, 1 page .......................... **950**

**Warhol, Andy (1928-1987),** leading pop artist known for Campbell soup can paintings, DS, typescript of a brief essay, undated, 1 page ......................................... **230**

**Washington, Booker T. (1856-1915),** prominent black educator who founded the famous Tuskegee Institute in Alabama in 1881, DS, graduation certficate from the Calhoun Colored School, signed by Washington as trustee, dated May 20, 1913, 1 page .................................. **325**

**Welles, Orson (1915-1985),** multi-talented film actor, director, writer & producer, DS, check for $22.40, dated August 14, 1957, 1 page .................................... **190**
**Wells, H. G. (1866-1946),** prolific British novelist, ALS, discussing some books, undated, 1 page ................................ **325**
**West, Mae (1892-1980),** film comedian in suggestive, sexy roles, PS, large portrait inscribed to Ethel Merman ................ **325**
**Whistler, James Abbott McNeil (1834-1903),** American artist best known for "Arrangement in Gray & Black No. 1" (better known as "Whistler's Mother"!), ALS, regarding transporting his work to an exhibition, undated, 3 pages ............... **1,600**
**York, Alvin C. (1887-1964),** World War One hero portrayed by Gary Cooper in film "Sgt. York," LS, sends thanks for seed packets, dated March 24, 1928, 1 page ............................................. **300**
**Zapata, Emiliano (1877-1919),** assassinated Mexican revolutionary leader, DS, details on a civil case, dated March 10, 1916, 1 page .................................... **1,600**
**Zola, Emile (1840-1902),** French author famed as the defender of Dreyfus, ALS, discusses an invitation & his wife's illness, dated June 12, 1875, 1 page ............. **400**

# AUTOMOTIVE COLLECTIBLES
*Also see ADVERTISING ITEMS and CANS & CONTAINERS*

*Arno Air Meter*

**Air Meter,** "Arno" white stepped base w/tapering cylindrical body, rectangular red meter at top, air hose & two air gauges, by Romort Mfg. Co., Oakfield, Wis., cracked glass face, older restoration, 9 x 12", 62" h. (ILLUS.) ................ **$1,210**
**Bank,** "Fire Chief" metal figural gas pump w/trap & paper label, 5 3/4" h. (minor paint chips) ................................ **303**

**Banner,** "Ford," cloth w/gold fringe at bottom, white lettering, "1942" on blue at top, "Ford SIX 90 Horsepower" on red center & "America's Most Modern SIX" on blue at bottom, 40" w., 60" h. ............. **187**

*Sunoco Banner w/Donald Duck*

**Banner,** "Sunoco," cloth w/cloth backing, colorful scene depicting Donald Duck driving red hot rod near road sign reading "Change Now to summer type Oil and Grease Sunoco" & "Unexcelled Lubrication" & "Form A700 15.5m 3-39 Litho in U.S.A. Copyright 1939 Walt Disney Productions" at bottom, soiling & fading, touch-up in spots, 56" w., 35 1/2" h. (ILLUS.)................................ **770**
**Banner,** "Texaco," white cloth showing two Scottie dogs w/heads to one side & "Drain—Fill—then LISTEN" in black & red letters, The Texas Company Sweeney Litho Co. Inc. Belleville, NJ, 80" w., 36" h. (soiling, creases) ................... **209**
**Bottle rack,** "Mobil Oil," w/porcelain sign & six completge bottles .................... **325**
**Calendar,** 1929 "Socony Gasoline," partial pad, 13 1/4 x 26 1/2" (cleaned & repaired) ....................................... **425**
**Calendar,** 1952 "Texaco," die-cut paper & cardboard, circular top w/logo, top of calendar w/"Texaco Asphalt Roofing Products," full pad, 15" w., 26 1/2" h. creases & some soiling)............................ **358**
**Chauffeur's badge,** 1948 Illinois ...................... **35**
**Cigarette lighter,** "Cities Service," plastic, model of 8-ball, top lifts to expose lighter, logo at base, w/original packet of flints & box, N.O.S., 3 1/2" d.......................... **77**

*Richfield Oil Co. Cigarette/Cigar Box*

**Cigarette/cigar box,** "Richfield Oil Co.," copper flashed over chalkware, model of racing car on cover, "Richfield" on side, ca. 1920s-30s, 4 x 4 3/4 x 10" (ILLUS.) ....................................... **743**

*Dunlop Tire Clock*

**Clock,** "Dunlop Tires," black metal tire frame w/"Dunlop" in yellow plastic letters, tin face, iron bracket to side for mounting, minor scratches, soiling & paint chips,48" w., 36" h. (ILLUS.) .............. **770**

**Clock,** "Mobil Pegasus," electric, wall-type, glass dome w/aluminum case by American Time Corp. (new movement/motor & matching hand set)...................................... **625**

**Flag,** "Texaco," sewn wool, 48 x 75", rare ....... **500**

**Gas pump globe,** "Elreco Gill," one premium & one regular lens ............................ **600**

**Gas pump globe,** "Kyso" (Standard Oil Kentucky), three-piece, wide body glass, rare ................................................................ **800**

**Gas pump globe,** "Mobil Premium" w/original Capcolite body, 13 1/2" d. .................... **250**

**Gas pump globe,** "Red Indian," high profile black metal body w/two milk glass lenses, profile of Native American w/full headdress, red, white & black, black lettering, 13 1/2" d. (newer body) ..................... **605**

**Gas pump globe,** "Shamrock," plastic body w/two milk glass lenses, green shamrock, white lettering, 13 1/2" d. (melting at base of body, chips to mounting areas on lenses).................................... **231**

*Socony Motor Gasoline Globe*

**Gas pump globe,** "Socony Motor Gasoline," low profile metal body w/one embossed milk glass lens, shield form also marked "Reg. U.S. Pat. Off. - Standard Oil Co. of New York," flanked by "N - Y" w/"SO" white letters on blue, minor yellowing & scratches to lens, paint chips to body base, 16 1/2" d. (ILLUS.) .... **1,980**

**Gas pump globe,** "Standard Oil Gold Crown," one piece globe w/original mount ring/base, all original ........................ **450**

*Texaco One-piece Globe*

**Gas pump globe,** "Texaco," one-piece milk glass w/raised letters & copper base w/"Pat. No. 1604773," 16" d. (ILLUS.)....... **1,238**

**Gas pump globe,** "Tydol," double-sided glass inserts in glass frame, 17" h. .............. **550**

*Union Gasoline Globe*

**Gas pump globe,** "Union Gasoline" high profile metal body w/one milk glass lens w/shield-form design, blue top & red & white striped bottom, "Property of Union Oil" bottom of globe, newer metal body, cracking to paint around edge, minor scratches, 15" d. (ILLUS.) ........................ **1,870**

**Gas pump globe,** "Zephyr" two milk glass lenses w/red ripple frame, red lettering 13 1/2" d. (soiling on body & lenses, paint chips on metal rims) ........................ **1,320**

**Gas pump globe lens,** "Gulf Coast" (New Orleans Tenneco Affliate), 15" d. ................ **200**

**Gas pump globe lens,** "Kyso" (Standard Oil Kentucky, 16 1/2" d. ............................... **375**

**Gas pump globe lens,** "Red Indian," 13 1/2" d. ....................................................... **890**

**Gasoline pump,** American Oil Visible Pump Standard No. 70730, cylindrical red base w/black trim, side slides open to expose interior, round glass top, w/Flying A reproduction globe, restored w/original parts, 18" d., 102" h. (BB hole in glass cylinder) ...................................... **1,540**

*Eco Meter Gasoline Pump*

**Gasoline pump,** "Eco," red roof-shaped top over round glass clock dial-style gallon register w/white dial, dial No. R2, tapering red body w/black trim, no identifing numbers, restored w/one original & one replaced new glass face, 19 x 20", 84" h. (ILLUS.) ........................................... **6,160**

**Gasoline pump sign,** "Texaco Fire-Chief Gasoline," rounded porcelain w/logo & fire hat & marked "Made in USA 9-20," 10" w., 18" h. (waterstain, chips & cracking) ........................................................... **176**

*Texaco Gas Pump Gumball Machine*

**Gumball Machine,** "Texaco" gas pump form w/battery-operated plastic light-up sign at top, side handle dispenses gum ball stored in glass top, Olde Tyme Reproductions, Inc., Serial No. 90-012183, 21" h. (ILLUS.)................................. **121**

**Hat badge,** "Mobilgas/Mobiloil," cloisonné w/original hat ................................................. **300**

**Hat badge,** "Tydol/Flying A Gasoline" cloisonné over nickel, 1 3/4" ............................. **500**

**Lantern,** Dietz "Nightdriver's Friend," large clear lens w/small red lens on other side ..... **100**

*"Florida" License Plate Alligator*

**License plate decoration,** figural cast metal alligator w/open jaws, glass eye, marked "Florida" in red script, by Erskine, Tampa, Florida, original paint, 14" l., 4 1/2" h. (ILLUS.)........................................... **171**

*Shell Oil License Plate Reflector*

**License plate reflector,** "Shell Oil Co." tin lithograph, shell-shaped w/three flags in the center, 1 x 3 1/4 x 5" (ILLUS.) ............... **121**

**Map,** 1928, "Fyre Drop Gasoline," motor trails, 4 x 9"................................................... **210**

**Motor oil,** "Phillips Trop-Artic" 1 qt. tin, lithograph shows artic scene w/igloo in upper half & tropical scene w/palm trees below, "Phillips Petroleum Company" at bottom, w/contents, 5 1/2" h. (minor denting & scratches) .................................. **715**

**Name badge,** "Sunoco," die-cut brass w/cloisonné detail, by Galfour, 1 3/4 x 3" ..... **200**

*Handy Oil Bottles*

**Oil,** "Esso Handy Oil," plastic yellow 5 1/2" h. handy man image w/contents, original die-cut display box, set of 20 w/10 x 15" display (ILLUS.) ........................... **385**

**Paper clip,** "Packard," brass, bell-shaped, embossed w/Packard radiator logo, floral decoration at sides, 2 1/2" w., 3 1/4" h. (some tarnish) .............................. **363**

**Paperweight,** "Chevrolet," metal w/embossed bow tie logo, 1 1/2 x 3 1/2", 2" h. .................................................................. **88**

**Pump sign,** "Douglas Blend Gasoline" embossed aluminum, 10 x 14" ................... **450**

**Pump sign,** "Shell Gasoline" die-cut porcelain, 12 x 12 1/4" ......................................... **925**

**Pump sign,** "Sunray D-S Petroleum Products," porcelain, 9" sq. .............................. **1,000**

**Salt & pepper shakers,** "Mobilgas" plastic, figural gas pump, "Central Oil Co., Plainview, Nebraska," 2 3/4" h., pr. .................. **200**

**Salt & pepper shakers,** "Richfield Ethyl" plastic, figural gas pump, stamped "Boise, Idaho," 2 3/4" h., pr. ........................ **425**

**Service pin/necktie bar,** "Texaco Oil Co." rectangular bar marked "14k" on back, octagonal center wnameled pin w/star logo & "20 Years Service," 1/2 x 2" ............. **77**

**Sign,** "Esso Elephant Kerosene," one-sided porcelain, elephant depicted in center, 12" w., 24" h. (minor edge chips) ................. **688**

**Sign,** "Fisk Tire," one-sided tin w/attached hanger, model of clock, logo in center, w/movable hands to show when attendant will return, H.D. Beach Co., Coshocton, Ohio, 6 1/8" d. (minor scratches, denting & soiling) ...................... **330**

*Fisk Tires Sign*

**Sign,** "Fisk Tires," two-sided wood sign & frame, logo of small child w/tire & candle in center & "Tires - Tubes - Service Station" at bottom, image sanded, cracking of wood, soiling & fading of graphic on both sides, 30 1/2" w., 41 1/2" h. (ILLUS.) ..................................................... **825**

**Sign,** "Goodyear Tires," one-sided, die-cut porcelain model of hot air blimp w/"Good Year #1 in Tires," few edge chips & scratches, manufacturers defect to color

blue, probably a proto-type, 40" w., 18 1/2" h. (ILLUS. below) ......................... **3,300**

*Goodyear Tires Sign*

**Sign,** "Shell Gasoline," two-sided die-cut painted orange shell-shaped metal, flange-type, 21 1/2" w., 17 1/2" h. (minor scratches to both sides) ........................... **1,595**

**Sign,** "Sunoco" two-sided porcelain w/iron hanger, "Rest Room," 22" w., 14" h. (few chips to both sides & edges, wear to hanger) ................................................................. **825**

**Signs,** "Fina" porcelain "Rest Room," 4 x 9", pr. ........................................................ **450**

**Thermometer,** "Dominion Tires," porcelain, rectangular w/rounded top, marked "Drive Safely - Ride On Dominion Royals," intact tube positioned over tire graphic in center, 10" w., 30" h. (chips on edges & edge of tube) ........................... **825**

**Thermometer,** "Shell Gasoline - Shell Motor Oil," porcelain, rectangular w/rounded top & bottom, "Pt. Mar. 16, 1915" at bottom, tube intact, 7" w., 27" h. (chips to mounting holes & by 90 degree mark) ......................................................... **1,100**

**Thermometer,** "Signal Products" plastic pole-shaped, 2 1/2 x 7", rare ...................... **530**

**Thermometer,** "Texaco," die-cut embossed tin, pole-type, in original box, 2 5/8 x 6 1/4" ................................................ **355**

**Uniform badge,** "Chevron Station Manager," 1 1/4 x 1 1/2" ..................................... **230**

**Uniform badge,** "Shell" die-struck brass w/cloisonné detail, 2 1/2 x 2 5/8" ................. **450**

# BANKS

*Original early mechanical and cast-iron still banks are in great demand with collectors. Their scarcity has caused numerous reproductions of both types and the novice collector is urged to exercise caution. The early mechanical banks are especially scarce and some versions are seldom offered for sale but, rather, are traded with fellow collectors attempting to upgrade an existing collection. Numbers before mechanical banks refer to those in John Meyer's Handbook of Old Mechanical Banks. However, another book Penny Lane---A History of Antique Mechanical Toy Banks, by Al Davidson, provides updated information and the number from this new volume is indicated in parenthesis at the end of each mechanical bank listing.*

*In past years, our standard reference for cast-iron still banks was Hubert B. Whiting's book Old Iron Still Banks, but because this work is out of print and a beautiful new book, The Penny Lane Bank Book---Collecting Still Banks by Andy and Susan Moore pictures and describes numerous additional*

banks, we will use the Moore numbers as a reference preceding each listing and indicate the Whiting reference in parenthesis at the end. The still
banks listed are old and in good original condition
with good paint and no repair unless otherwise
noted. An asterisk (*) indicates this bank has been
reproduced at some time.

# MECHANICAL

*Frog On Round Lattice Base Bank*

**102 Frog on Round Lattice Base,** w/foot
operated opening mouth & eyes, yellow
lattice work on base, 4 1/4" d., PL 204
(ILLUS.)...................................................... **$489**

*Indian Shooting Bear Mechanical Bank*

**129 Indian Shooting Bear,** Indian kneeling
w/rifle shooting coin into bear, ca. 1883,
10 1/2" l., PL 257 (ILLUS.) ........................ **2,722**
**132 "Jolly Nigger,"** w/red shirt, moving
arm, tongue & rolling eyes, patented on
March 14, 1882, 6 1/2" h. (PL 275) .............. **374**
**138 Jonah & the Whale,** Jonah in boat
w/whale in water, pat. July 15, 1890 (PL
282) ........................................................ **1,725**
**156 Mason Bank,** Irish hod carrier working
w/Italian bricklayer, patented in 1887 (PL
321) ........................................................ **4,140**
**169 Mule Entering Barn,** marked "Pat'd.
Aug. 30, 1880," replaced trap, polychrome has wear & light rust, 8 1/2" l
(PL 342) ...................................................... **900**
**176 Novelty Bank,** in light brown w/open-
ing door to reveal teller, inoperative lock-
ing trap (PL 361) .......................................... **173**
**177 - Organ Bank (Cat & Dog),** by Kyser &
Rex, w/colored moving figures of monkey, cat, & dog on top of organ, bell
mechanism, 5 1/2" (lacking trap), PL 369
(ILLUS. top next column) ............................. **460**

*Organ Bank w/Cat & Dog*

*Organ Bank w/Boy & Girl*

**178 Organ Bank (Boy & Girl),** by Kyser &
Rex, cast in the form of a portable barrel
organ, w/hand-turned mechanism causing the monkey to drop a coin into the
top, and tip his cap, the boy & girl to
dance, & the bell to ring, (slight chipping
to figures), 7 3/4" h., PL 368 (ILLUS.) ....... **2,300**

*Organ Bank (Miniature)*

**179 Organ Bank (miniature),** by Kyser &
Rex, in the form of a barrel organ,
w/hand-turned mechanism causing turning monkey in red jacket to deposit coin,
tip his hat, & bell to ring, , 6 1/2" h. (lack-
ing bell) PL 371 (ILLUS.)............................. **748**

**185 Paddy & His Pig,** Irish figure holding pig in his lap, brown coat, some wear (PL 376) .................................................... **2,433**

*Pig In Highchair Mechanical Bank*

**194 - Pig in Highchair,** nickel plated, cast w/floral & foliate motifs, the pig lifts tray, swallows the coin & moves his tongue, pat. Aug. 24, 1897, 6" h., PL 390 (ILLUS.)...................................................... **690**

*Trick Pony Bank*

**196 Pony - Trick Bank,** cast iron, the pony lowers its head to deposit the coin in the trough trap door which opens & closes to receive the coin , 7 in. w. PL 484 (ILLUS.) ..................................................... **1,208**

**231 Uncle Sam w/Satchel & Umbrella,** coin is dropped into opening satchel, w/moving hand & mouth, 11" h., 4 3/4" w., PL 493 (ILLUS. top next column)......................................................... **1,821**

**244 World's Fair Bank,** the Indian chief appears after lever is pushed, then hands Columbus a peace pipe as Columbus salutes, w/"Columbus" cast into base, "World's Fair Bank" cast on front (finish worn on tree trunk), 8 1/4" w., (PL 573 ).......................................... **863**

**33 Cabin,** cabin w/man standing in doorway, w/yellow walls, pivoting man kicks coin through roof, 4 1/4" deep (PL 93) ......... **580**

**37 U.S. and Spain,** cast iron, grey cannon pointed at a ship's mast, PL 500 (ILLUS. middle next column) ................................. **3,080**

*"Uncle Sam" Mechanical Bank*

*U. S. & Spain Mechanical Bank*

*"I Always Did 'Spise A Mule" Bank*

**4 (I) Always Did 'Spise a Mule,** boy on bench facing mule, w/tan base, by J. E. Stevens Co., 10" w., PL 250 (ILLUS.)...... **1,150**

**49 Clown on Globe,** w/turning & flipping mechanism, red & orange outfit, blue sphere & tan base, (lacking trap), unextended 9" h. PL 127 ................................. **3,105**

**5 - "(I)Always Did 'Spise a Mule,"** (Jockey Over), by John Harper & Co., England, w/kicking mule & pivoting rider, 10" w. (PL 252) ...................................................... **475**

**53 "Creedmoor Bank,"** by J & E Stevens Co., w/gray trousers (PL 137) ...................... **446**

**53 Creedmore Bank,** soldier aims rifle at target in tree trunk (PL 137) ......................... **633**

**69 Speaking Dog Bank,** seated girl w/large dog, rectangular coin trap & maroon base variation, , 7" h. (PL 447)........ **748**

*Eagle & Eaglets Bank*

**75 Eagle & Eaglets,** w/bending mother & rising young, w/bellows that simulate birds chirping, 6 3/4" w. (one eaglet's wing broken) PL 165 (ILLUS.)..................... **604**

*Elephant Pull Tail Bank*

**80 Elephant Howdah - "Pull Tail,"** modern, w/white body, PL 174 (ILLUS.) ............. **431**

## POTTERY

**Building,** circular tower form w/thick base band & domed roof, good detail, mottled brown Rockingham glaze, Ohio, 19th c., 5 1/4" h. ...................................................... **468**

*Fine Decorated Stoneware Bank*

**Cylindrical,** stoneware cylindrical body w/base band & angled shoulder to a thick ring at the base of the cylindrical neck, greyish tan glaze w/dark brown Albany slip w/flowers, New Geneva,

19th c., wear, glaze chips around coin slot, 6 1/2" h. (ILLUS.) ............................... **1,870**
**Model of a house,** rectangular two-story brick w/end chimneys, overall mottled dark brown Rockingham glaze, 4 3/4" h. (chips) ...................................................... **165**

## STILL

**1053 Building - U.S. Treasury Bank,** cast iron w/sheet metal base, white & red, replica of Sub-Treasury Building in New York, Grey Iron Casting Co., 1925-28, minor wear, 3 1/4 x 3 3/4 x 3 1/4" h. (W. 379) ................................................................. **55**

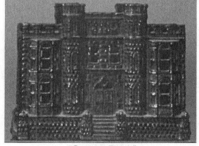

*"Columbian Magic Savings Bank"*

**1065 "Columbian Magic Savings Bank,"** by Magic, w/pivoting slide & combination lock (ILLUS.) ............................................... **230**
**107 Man in Top Hat - "Transvaal Money Box,"** cast iron w/bronze finish, inscribed "By permission of the proprietors of the Westminster Gazette, Made in England," John Harper Ltd., England, ca. 1885, 4 1/4" l., 6 3/16" h. ......... **550**
**1079 Building - State Bank,** cast iron, roof w/arched dormers & cupola, arched door & windows, Kenton Grey Iron Casting Co., ca. 1899-1900, 4 1/4 x 5 1/2 x 6 3/4" h. ...................................................... **575**
**1083 Building - State Bank,** cast iron, Arcade Mfg. Co. 1913-25 & Grey Iron Casting Co. 1889, 2 3/8 x 3 1/16 x 4 1/8" h. ................................................... **121**

*"County Bank"*

**1110 Building - County Bank,** cast iron, w/battlement roof & 1891 registration number, John Harper Ltd., England, ca. 1892, 2 3/4 x 5 1/4 x 4 1/4" h. (ILLUS.) ........ **345**
**1111 Building - City Bank, with Director's Room on Top,** cast iron, John Harper Ltd., Chamberlain & Hill, England, ca.

1902, 1 1/2 x 3 1/2 x 4 1/8" h., W. 380 (ILLUS. below) ............................................ **259**

*City Bank w/Director's Room on Top*

**1160 Building - "Flat Iron Building Bank,"** cast iron, small trap, Kenton Mfg. Co., 1904-26, triangular, silver finish w/gold roof, 4 1/2 x 4 3/4 x 5 3/4" h. ............ **211**

*New Bank Building*

**1229 Building - New Bank,** by J. & E. Stevens, 1872, finished in red, green, blue & cream w/brass-plated figure & left-front lever, 6" h. (ILLUS.) ................. **10,063**
**1240 Building - Skyscraper,** cast iron, by A.C. Williams Co., 1900-31, w/four corner towers & gilt finish, 2 1/2" sq., 5 1/2" h. (W. 412) ...................................... **86**
**1290 "Uncle Sam's Register Bank,"** cold rolled sheet steel w/black & gold, Durable Toy & Novelty Corp, 1912-present, 4 1/2 x 5 1/4 x 6 1/4" h. ....................... **39**
**1373 - "The North Pole Bank,"** nickeled cast iron, Grey Iron Casting Co., US 1922-1928, 4 1/4" h., 2 5/8" d. .................... **220**

*"Graf Zeppelin" Cast Iron Bank*

**1428 Zeppelin - "Graf Zeppelin,"** cast iron, A.C. Williams Co., 1920-34, 6 5/8" h., 1 3/4" h., W. 171 (ILLUS.) ............ **141**
**1437 Tank - "U.S. Tank Bank 1918,"** cast iron, model of a WWI tank, gold, A.C. Williams Co., 1920s, 4 1/4" l., 2 3/8" h. (W. 162) ...................................... **193**
**150 Pershing - Gen. "Pershing,"** bronze electroplated cast iron, bust of the general, Grey Iron Casting Co., patented 1918, 7 3/4" h. (W. 312) ................................ **55**

*"A Money Saver" Still Bank*

**1544 Clock - "A Money Saver,"** cast iron & steel, clock-form embossed face, Arcade Mfg. Co., 1909-20s, 3 1/2" h., W. 224 (ILLUS.) ...................................... **58**
**163 - "Campbell Kids,"** cast iron, A.C. Williams Co., 1910-21, gold repaint has minor wear, 3 1/4" h. .................................... **193**
**\* 168 Black Woman - Aunt Jemima (Mammy with Spoon),** cast iron, A.C. Williams Co., 1905-30, worn polychrome, good color, screw replaced, 5 7/8" h., (W. 17) ......................................... **220**
**177 - Mulligan (Policeman),** cast iron, A.C. Williams Co. 1905-32 & Hubley Mfg. Co. 1914, good color w/minor wear, 5 3/4" h. (W. 8) ......................................... **220**

*Clown w/Crooked Hat Still Bank*

**210 Clown with Crooked Hat,** cast iron, American-made, worn gold repaint, glued feet, 2 1/4" w., 6 3/4" h., W. 28 (ILLUS.)...................................................... 358

**211 Clown,** cast iron, standing figure w/pointed hat, A.C. Williams Co., 1908, worn old blue paint w/red & gold, 6 3/16" h. (W. 29) ...................................... 248

**228 Indian - Indian with Tomahawk,** cast iron, Hubley Mfg. Co., 1915-30s, pristine, 5 7/8" h. (W. 39) ................................. 269

**270 Rabbit - Bugs Bunny at Barrel,** white metal, by Metal Moss Mfg. Co., American-made, late 1930s, 5 3/4" w., 5 1/2" h........................................................ 148

**28 - Sailor (medium),** cast iron, Hubley?, US, worn silver, light rust, 5 1/2" h. ............... 72

**357 Dog - Boxer (Bulldog),** cast iron, seated, A.C. Williams Co. 1912-28 & Hubley Mfg. Co., worn gold & red, 3 7/8" l., 4 1/2" h. (W. 105) ........................... 39

**366 Cat - Seated Cat with Soft Hair,** cast iron, Arcade Mfg. Co., ca. 1910-29, 2 7/8" l., 4 1/4" h. (W. 248) ........................... 76

**367 Cat - Seated Cat with Fine Lines,** cast iron, American-made, ca. 1912, traces of black, 3" l., 4" h............................. 165

*Seated Bulldog Still Bank*

**396 Dog - Bulldog, Seated** cast iron, Hubley Mfg. Co., ca. 1928, 3 7/8" h., W. 102 (ILLUS.)...................................................... 173

**416 Dog - Puppo,** cast iron, w/bee on side, Hubley Mfg. Co., 1920s-30s, polychrome has wear but good color, 4 7/8" h. (W. 338) ...................................... 72

*Fido on Pillow Bank*

**443 Dog - Fido on Pillow,** cast iron, white & brown dog w/pillow, Hubley Mfg.

Co., ca. 1920s, very good, 7 3/8" base, 5 3/4" h., W. 336 (ILLUS.) ........................... 182

**446 Elephant - Elephant on Wheels,** cast iron, A.C. Williams Co., 1920s, 4 1/8" h., 4 3/8" l., pristine (W-75)................................ 319

**450 Elephant - Art Deco Elephant ("G.O.P."),** cast iron, trunk uplifted, American-made, red & gold, minor wear, 5 1/2" l., 4 3/8" h. (W. 72) ........................... 275

**48 Doughboy (Soldier),** cast iron, World War I soldier, Grey Iron Casting Co., 1919, 7" h. (W. 40) ...................................... 413

*Donkey Still Bank*

**500 Donkey (large),** cast iron, grey overall w/brown saddle, A.C. Williams Co., ca. 1920s, pristine, 6 1/4" l., 6 13/16" h., W. 197 (ILLUS.)................................................ 241

**520 Horse - Prancing Horse,** cast iron, large, rectangular base, Arcade Mfg. Co. 1910 & A.C. Williams Co., worn paint, 1910-34, 7 3/16" h. (W. 78) ........................... 94

**54 General Butler,** cast iron, man in the form of a frog reads "Bonds & Yachts for Me - For the Masses This is $1,000,000," J. & E. Stevens Co., 1884, 6 1/2" h. (W. 294) .................................. 2,495

**553 Cow,** cast iron, standing animal, A.C. Williams Co., ca. 1920, 5 1/4" l., 3 3/8" h. (W. 200) ...................................... 69

**566 Rabbit - Begging Rabbit,** cast iron, gold & red, A.C. Williams Co., 1908-20s, minor wear, 5 1/8" h. (W. 98) ...................... 160

**574 Rabbit - Rabbit Standing,** cast iron, A.C. Williams Co., 1908 to mid 1920s, 5 5/8" l., 6 1/4" h., traces of red & gold (W. 99)................................................ 220

*Bear w/Honey Pot Still Bank*

* **717 Bear - Bear with Honey Pot,** cast iron, Hubley Mfg. Co., 1936, 6 1/2" h., minor wear, W. 327 (ILLUS.)......................... **87**

*"Billiken" on Throne Still Bank*

**73 - "Billiken" on Throne,** cast iron, A.C. Williams Co., gold & red, 1909, minor wear, 3 1/8" w., 6 1/2" h. (ILLUS.).................. **55**

**732 Sea Lion (Seal on Rock),** cast iron, black overall, Arcade Mfg. Co., 1910-13, minor wear, 3 1/2" h., 4 1/4" l. (W. 199) ...... **385**

**746 Lion - Lion on Tub,** cast iron, decorated, A.C. Williams Co., 1920s-34, wear but good color, tub 2 1/2" d., 5 1/2" h. (W. 57) ......................................................... **152**

*Lion on Wheels Still Bank*

**760 Lion - Lion on Wheels,** cast iron, A.C. Williams Co., 1920s, 4 5/8" l., 4 1/2" h., W. 95 (ILLUS.) ............................................ **115**

**762 Lion - Large Lion, Tail Right,** cast iron, American-made, 6 1/4" l., 5 1/2" h. ........ **83**

**782 Liberty Bell - Liberty Bell ("1926"),** cast iron, also called "Sesquicentennial, Liberty," Grey Iron Casting Co., 1928, traces of old finish, 3 7/8" d., 3 3/4" h............. **39**

**789 Globe - Globe on Arc,** cast iron, red & gold, Grey Iron Casting Co., 1900-03, 5 1/4" h. (ILLUS. top next column) ............... **104**

**80 "Billiken,"** cast iron, gold & red, on base, embossed "Billiken Shoes Bring Luck" across chest, A.C. Williams Co., 1909 (some wear, screw replaced) 4 1/4 x 2 1/2" ................................................. **72**

**807 Liberty Bell - "Bailey's Centennial Money Bank,"** cast iron on square wooden base, embossed "Proclaim 1776 Liberty - Centennial Money 1876 Bank," J.S. Semon, 1875, worn gold & black, overall 4 1/2" h. (W. 280) .................... **55**

*Globe On Arc Still Bank*

**821 Radio - "Radio Bank,"** painted cast iron, blue & gold, two dials, Hubley Mfg. Co., ca. 1928, minor wear, 2 5/16" l., 3 5/16" h. (W. 136) ........................................ **138**

**84 Black Boy - Two-Faced Black Boy (Negro Toy Bank),** cast iron, black, gold & silver, A.C. Williams Co., 1901-19, 3 1/8" h. (W. 44) ......................................... **248**

*Floral Safe*

**885 Safe - Floral Safe,** cast iron, key-locked trap, embossed w/colored floral decorations on gold ground, J. & E. Stevens Co., 1898, 4 5/8" h., W. 347 (ILLUS.)........................................................ **345**

**948 - Savings Chest,** cast iron, w/key, Van Elyen-Henstep, Detroit, US 1892, wear & some rust, 6 1/4 x 4 5/16 x 3 11/16 ......... **248**

**951 Bean Pot,** cast iron, "Nickel Register" w/pail handle, American-made, worn nickel plate & red paint, 3 7/16" d., 3" h. ........ **55**

*Egyptian Safe Bank*

**Building - Egyptian Safe Bank,** w/gilt motifs on black ground, 4 1/2" h. (ILLUS.)........................................... **518**

*People's Savings Bank*

**Buildng - People's Savings Bank** w/brown gabled roof, cream walls & caption "Property of People's Savings Bank, Grand Rapids, Mich.," 10 3/4" h. (ILLUS.).................................................. **1,093**

*"Columbian Recording Bank"*

**"Columbian Recording Bank,"** by Magic, w/indicator dial, marked "Columbian Exposition" on base of bank, 1892 (ILLUS).......................................................... **201**

# BARBERIANA

*A wide variety of antiques related to the tonsorial arts have been highly collectible for many years, especially 19th and early 20th century shaving mugs and barber bottles and, more recently, razors. We are now combining these closely related categories under one heading for easier reference. A selection of other varied pieces relating to barbering will also be found below.*

## BARBER BOTTLES

**Amber,** Optic Rib patt. w/orange, white & yellow enamel decoration, pontil scarred base, rolled lip, about perfect, ca. 1885 - 1925, 8 1/4" h. .......................................... **$105**
**Amber,** w/multicolored label under glass floral decoration & words "Hair Oil," smooth base, tooled lip, 7 1/8" h. ................. **176**
**Black amethyst,** w/white enamel decoration of a sailing vessel on rough water,

detailed, rare, pontil scarred base, rolled lip, perfect, 6 1/2" h. .................................... **468**
**Clear,** copper wheel-cut floral decoration, tooled lip, decorations on polished base, original sterling silver stopper w/matching engraved decoration, perfect, ca. 1885-1925, 7 1/2" h...................................... **132**
**Clear,** pink & white, alternating Swirl patt., pontil scarred base, rolled lip, ca. 1885-1925, 5 3/4" h. ............................................... **358**
**Clear,** slight silver coating, two-tone brown soft enamel floral decoration, smooth base, ABM lip, perfect, 8" h........................ **132**
**Clear,** square shape w/"T. NOONAN & SONS - CO. - BARBERS SUPPLIES - BOSTON, MASS." written in circle on front, smooth base, ABM lip w/original stopper embossed "T. Noonan & Sons, Boston," perfect, 4 3/8" h............................... **66**

*Clear w/Light Purple Satin Finish Bottle*

**Clear,** w/light purple satin finish & silver overlay of geometric & swirl decoration, smooth base, tooled lip, original hinged sterling silver cap, bottle perfect, but silvering is worn, 7 7/8" h. (ILLUS.) ................. **176**

*Bottle with "Persian" Style Decoration*

**Cobalt blue,** Optic Rib patt. w/silver & yellow enamel "Persian" style decoration, pontil scarred base, sheared lip, perfect, 6 3/4" h. (ILLUS.)........................................ **143**
**Cranberry opalescent,** Hobnail patt., 8 1/4" h. ......................................................... **193**

**Deep cobalt blue,** corset waist w/red & white enamel design, pontil scarred base, sheared lip, perfect, somewhat unique decoration, 7 3/4" h., .......................... **94**

**Deep cobalt blue,** Optic Rib patt. w/gold & heavy silver "Persian" style enamel decoration, pontil scarred base, sheared lip, perfect, ca. 1885 - 1925, 6 3/4" h. .................. **94**

**Deep cobalt blue,** w/orange & white enamel decoration, pontil scarred base, rolled lip, perfect, ca. 1885 - 1925, 6 5/8" h. .......................................................... **88**

**Deep grass green,** Optic Rib patt. w/white enamel decoration, smooth base, sheared lip, perfect, ca. 1885 - 1925, 6 3/4" h. ................................................................ **99**

**Deep purple amethyst,** Hobnail patt., smooth base, rolled lip, perfect, ca. 1885-1925, 7 1/4" h. .................................... **253**

**Deep purple amethyst,** Optic Rib patt. w/small repeating red & white leaf enamel decoration, pontil scarred base, rolled lip, perfect, 7 1/2" h............................. **83**

**Deep purple amethyst,** Optic Rib patt., white enameled Mary Gregory girl w/basket decoration, pontil scarred base, rolled lip, ca. 1885-1925, 7 7/8" h. ....... **303**

**Deep turquoise blue,** Optic Rib patt., smooth oval shape in middle, smooth base, flared lip, original stopper, perfect, 8" h. ................................................................ **110**

**Frosted deep green,** silver overlay berry & leaf decoration, pontil scarred base, rolled lip, excellent condition, ca. 1885-1925, 7 3/4" h. ......................................... **1,540**

**Frosted grass green,** white & gold Art Nouveau leaf & flower-style decoration, pontil scarred base, sheared lip, ca. 1885 - 1925, 8" h. (some gold missing near base) ..................................... **358**

**Frosted purple amethyst,** Optic Rib patt. w/silver overlay floral decoration, pontil scarred base, rolled lip, perfect, ca. 1885 - 1925, 7 1/2" h. ..................................... **1,265**

*Frosted Purple Amethyst Barber Bottle*

**Frosted purple amethyst,** Optic Rib patt. w/white & gilt, Art Nouveau style, large floral decoration, all gold intact, pontil scarred base, rolled lip, ca. 1885-1925, 7 7/8" h. (ILLUS.)......................................... **330**

**Grass green,** Optic Rib patt. w/white & brown enameled decoration of a stag within an oval frame, pontil scarred base, sheared lip, 8" h. (bottle perfect, but some of painted stag missing) .............. **110**

**Iridescent,** orange w/pink & light blue tones, smooth base, polished lip, ca. 1885-1925, 7 7/8" h........................ **194**

**Iridescent,** ruby red w/gold, blue, pink, & green highlights, overall "alligatored" design, smooth base, polished lip, 7 7/8" h. ..................................................... **908**

**Opalescent canary yellow,** Optic Rib body w/Daisy & Fern patt., smooth base, rolled lip, perfect, ca. 1885-1925, 7 1/4" h. ................................................... **132**

**Opalescent clear,** white Seaweed patt., polished pontil, rolled lip, ca. 1885-1925, 8 1/4" h. ................................................. **253**

*Opalescent Cranberry Barber Bottle*

**Opalescent cranberry,** Coin Spot patt., polished pontil, rolled lip, perfect, ca. 1885-1925, 7" h. (ILLUS.) ........................... **495**

**Opalescent cranberry,** melon-ribbed sides w/Coin Spot patt., smooth base, rolled lip, ca. 1885-1925, 8 1/2" h. ........................ **210**

**Opalescent cranberry,** Stripe patt., melon-lobed shape, smooth base, rolled lip, perfect, ca. 1885-1925, 7 3/8" h. ................. **132**

**Opalescent turquoise blue,** Stars & Stripes patt., unique & attractive, polished pontil, rolled lip, ca. 1885-1925, 7 1/4" h. ....................................................... **550**

**Pale apple green,** Coin Spot patt., w/yellow, orange & white enamel design, pontil scarred base, rolled lip, 8 1/4" h. ............ **121**

**Red cut to clear,** flashed ruby red cut to clear & frosted, Bohemian-style decoration, smooth base, rolled lip, ca. 1885-1925, 7 7/8" h. ............................................... **358**

**Spatter,** clear w/white & dark red alternating spatter design, smooth base, flared lip, perfect, 7 7/8" h. ..................................... **385**

**Turquoise blue,** Optic Rib patt. w/red & white enamel decoration, pontil scarred base, sheared lip, perfect, ca. 1885-1925, 7 1/2" h. ............................................. **121**

**Turquoise blue,** Optic Rib patt. w/red, yellow & white enamel floral decoration,

pontil scarred base, rolled lip, perfect,
7 3/4" h. ....................................................... **176**

**Turquoise blue,** Optic Rib patt. w/yellow,
red & white enamel design, pontil
scarred base, sheared lip, 7 5/8" h. (1/8"
flake on edge of lip)................................... **77**

**Yellow,** Hobnail patt., smooth base, rolled
lip, ca. 1885 - 1925, 7 1/8" h. ...................... **121**

**Yellowish green,** Optic Rib patt. w/multi-
colored enamel floral decoration, pontil
scarred base, sheared lip, perfect, ca.
1885-1925, 6 1/8" h.................................... **187**

# MUGS

## FRATERNAL

**Brotherhood of Railroad Trainmen,**
shows their emblem, owner's name
above, base marked "Limoges W.G. &
Co. France" & "E. Berninghaus Cincin-
nati. O.," 3 1/2" h. .......................................... **99**

**Fraternal Order Eagles,** No. 293, shows
emblem, owner's name below, base
marked in gold "P. Germany" & "P. Eis-
mann 4. 11.," 3 3/4" h................................. **209**

*Fraternal Order of Eagles Mug*

**Fraternal Order of Eagles,** shows
emblem, owner's name below, base
marked "T & V Limoges France,"
3 5/8" h. (ILLUS.) ......................................... **143**

**Fraternal Order of Eagles and Shriners,**
shows emblem w/owner's name below,
perfect, 3 5/8" h.......................................... **110**

**Knights of Maltese Cross,** shows emblem
w/owner's name above, perfect,
3 3/4" h...................................................... **242**

**Knights of Tented Maccobees,** shows
emblem w/owner's name below, base
marked "V x D Austria," 3 3/4" h.................. **198**

**Knights of the Golden Eagle,** shows
emblem w/owner's name above, base
marked "T & V Limoges France" &
"Natl.," 3 5/8" h. .......................................... **209**

**Loyal Order of Moose,** shows emblem,
"William Harrison Lodge No. 27
L.O.O.M. No. 2 Mt. Pleasant PA" written
below, base stamped "Felda China Ger-
many," 3 5/8" h............................................ **468**

**Odd Fellows,** shows the All Seeing Eye
above their emblem & a Bible, owner's
name in ribbon around design, base
marked "C.A Smith Barber Supplies
Philadelphia," perfect (ILLUS. next col-
umn) ......................................................... **231**

**Order of Redmen,** shows emblem,
owner's name below, base marked "T &
V Limoges France," 3 1/2" h......................... **121**

*Odd Fellows All Seeing Eye Mug*

## OCCUPATIONAL

**Bartender,** scene of bartender behind bar
waiting on male customer, "Otto
Johnson" written above, 3 7/8" h. ................. **187**

**Boating,** scene of man driving a motorboat,
waves, scene expands around 2/3 of
mug, "Albert R. Russ" written above,
base marked "Royal China International"
& "G.B.S.," semi-vitrious, 3 5/8" h.
(repair to left of handle but does not
affect decoration) ...................................... **1,100**

**Boiler operator,** scene of large double
door boiler, "Albert Goldner" written
above, 3 1/2" h. .......................................... **358**

**Buggy driver,** scene shows a man driving
a horse-drawn buggy, "W.F. Danner"
written below scene, base stamped w/"T
& V Limoges France," perfect ...................... **330**

**Butcher,** shows steer's head w/crossed
butcher's tools on either side & surrounded by laurel wreath, made for
"W.S. Snover," 3 1/2" h. .............................. **154**

**Captain,** detailed scene of captain in front
of stern-wheel paddleboat w/two
women, "The Captain" written in gold
below scene, full pink wrap, perfect, ca.
1953, 3 7/8" h. ............................................ **105**

**Carpenter,** highly detailed scene shows a
carpenter or cabinetmaker planing a
piece of wood at his bench, "Chas. F.
Burton" written above, base marked
"M.M.F." & "T & V Limoges France,"
3 5/8" h...................................................... **468**

**Cigar maker,** shows a banded roll of cigars
w/a band of holly decoration around
entire top of mug, "John Bruner" written
below, base marked "Leonard Vienna" &
"R.H. Hegener Minneapolis," 4" h. .............. **303**

**Engineer,** shows large, detailed stationary
engine, "Albert Horstbrink" written
above, base marked "Decorated by
Koken & Boppert St. Louis Telephone
Razors Oriental Shaving Soap & Cos-
metic," 3 7/8" h. .......................................... **358**

**Engineer,** shows locomotive & tender, "H.
Werth" written below, base marked
"Leonard Stenka," 3 7/8" h. ......................... **132**

**Express Co.,** scene of winged safe or
strong box inside a horseshoe w/"United
States Express Co. 1854" written on
horseshoe, owner's name below, "T & V
Limoges France" marked on base, rare
subject matter, 3 5/8" h. .............................. **1,760**

**Farmer,** scene of farmer plowing his field
w/two horses, house in background,
"Wm. Orth" written below, detailed, looks
unused, 3 1/2" h. ........................................ **358**

**Horse track,** colorful, detailed race scene w/two horses in a horseshoe in lower right hand corner, owner's name in banner, "Limoges W.G. & Co. France" & "The World Our Field Koken St. Louis Trade Mark" on base, perfect....................... **908**

![Shaving Mug with Hunting Scene]

*Shaving Mug with Hunting Scene*

**Hunter,** scene of hunter & his dog in a boat w/hunter's gun discharging at three ducks, owner's name below, nice color & detail, mug has full black wrap, base marked "T & V Limoges France," 3 1/2" h. (ILLUS.)......................................... **495**
**Mason,** shows a mason's trough & board, "Thomas Boyd" written above, perfect, 3 5/8" h....................................................... **121**
**Military,** shows crossed cannons, w/owner's name above & "69 Artillery Corps" below, base marked "T & V Limoges France," 3 5/8" h. (crack in area of handle extends from top of rim downward) ......................................................... **578**
**Milk delivery man,** large scene of man driving a horse-drawn "Milk" wagon, owner's name above, perfect, 3 7/8" h......... **523**
**Musician,** scene of man playing oboe in front of music stand, "Wm. H. Gerhart" written above, decoration at sides, "Alpha" in gilt on base, 3 5/8" h. (repair exists on top rim above name "Wm.") .......... **330**
**Musician,** shows a detailed coronet, vine design on sides, "J.P. McGhinny" written above, base stamped "D. & Co. France," 3 5/8" h. (professional repair on top of base rim near handle) ................................. **121**

*Detailed Pharmacist Shaving Mug*

**Pharmacist,** shows a well-detailed mortar & pestle, owner's name below, base marked "V x D Austria," perfect (ILLUS.) ..... **220**
**Pharmacist,** well-detailed scene of pharmacy w/male clerk waiting on a woman, sign for "Omega Oil" hanging on front of counter, mug w/full pink wrap, owner's name above, 3 3/4" h. (small area of

shallow chipping exists in rim above decoration) ...................................................... **578**
**Plasterer,** scene of man plastering an interior wall, "J.A.G. Broome" written above, base marked "T & V France," 3 5/8" h......... **908**

![Printer Shaving Mug]

*Printer Shaving Mug*

**Printer,** scene of printer setting type at a type set desk, "Herman Roethig" written below scene, sprigs of flowers decorate sides, "V x D Austria" mark on base, 3 5/8" h. (ILLUS.)........................................ **458**
**Railroad worker,** shows red caboose w/letters "I.C.R.R." (Illinois Central) on side, "W. Mosby" written above, base impressed "Germany," 3 3/4" h. .................. **275**
**Shoemaker,** shows a woman's high shoe w/"Chas Boon" written above, full black wrap, base marked "T & V France" & "Aug. Kern Barber Supply Co. St. Louis Trade Mark Always Upright," 3 5/8" h. ........ **358**

*Occupational Electric Trolley Mug*

**Trolley driver,** shows a brown & yellow electric trolley w/people inside, "William Smith" written above, 3 5/8" h. (ILLUS.) ...... **413**

## PATRIOTIC

![Crossed American & Swiss Flags]

*Crossed American & Swiss Flags*

**American flags,** scuttle-type, "Williams Shaving Soap Healing Antiseptic" on one side w/crossed American flags on other, base marked "Rd. No. 376,419" & "Made in Germany," 4 1/8" h. ....................... **231**
**American & Italian flags,** shows eagle w/shield & crossed flags, owner's name

above, full green wrap, base stamped "Homer Laughlin Made in U.S.A.," 3 5/8" h. ...................................... **176**

**American & Swiss flags,** large decoration of crossed Swiss & American flags above a large pipe wrench, owner's name above, ca. 1890-1925, professional repair to rim edge above last name, 3 5/8" h. (ILLUS. previous page) ....... **187**

## MUSTACHE CUPS

*Inside of a mustache cup showing a typical, decorated mustache guard w/the one semicurcular opening against the side of the cup.*

*Inside of a Mustache Cup*

**Cup,** ceramic, copper lustre w/raised design, four-footed, applied mustache guard, unmarked, country unknown, ca. 1845-1855 ............................................ **170-190**

*Royal Bavarian Mustache Cup*

**Cup,** china, figural, hand-painted & transfer design, marked "PM/B Royal Bavarian China, Germany," ca. 1891-1910 (ILLUS.)................................................ **130-140**

**Cup,** china, hand-painted, applied mustache guard, marked "Haviland, Limoges," France, ca. 1881-1885 ................. **145-155**

**Cup,** china, hand-painted, applied mustache guard, unmarked, country unknown, ca. 1880-1890 ......................... **95-110**

**Cup,** china, hand-painted, bamboo handle, applied mustache guard, unmarked, country unknown, ca. 1880-1890 .......... **100-125**

**Cup,** china, hand-painted & decal, applied mustache guard, unmarked, country unknown, ca. 1880-1890 ............................ **70-90**

**Cup,** china, hand-painted & decal, half-scissors handle, applied mustache guard, unmarked, country unknown, ca. 1870-1880 ................................................. **60-75**

**Cup,** china, hand-painted & decal, lustre, applied mustache guard, marked "Kahla, Germany," ca. 1890 ............................. **110-120**

**Cup,** china, hand-painted, matte finish, rare fan handle, repair to cup, applied mustache guard, unmarked, country unknown, ca. 1865-1875 ...................... **165-175**

**Cup,** china, hand-painted, modified moriage decoration, applied mustache guard, unmarked, Oriental, country unknown, ca. 1875-1885 ...................... **110-120**

**Cup,** china hand-painted on molded design, applied mustache guard, unmarked, country unknown, ca. 1870-1880 ...................................................... **115-125**

**Cup,** china, hand-painted outside & inside, applied mustache guard, marked "Haviland, France," overglaze-green, "Haviland & Co., Limoges," underglaze-red, ca. 1889-1905 ................................ **135-150**

**Cup,** china, hand-painted over swirl mold, applied mustache guard, unmarked, country unknown, ca. 1880-1890 ......... **120-140**

**Cup,** china, hand-painted, raised gold, applied mustache guard, marked "Made In Germany" (oversize mark), overglaze-black, ca. 1920s .................................... **100-125**

**Cup,** china, hand-painted, rare raised & molded mustache guard, unmarked, country unknown, ca. 1870-1880 ......... **160-180**

**Cup,** china, hand-painted, unusual boxcar handle, signed, applied mustache guard, unmarked, country unknown, ca. 1886 ................................................. **175-200**

*Kettle-form Mustache Cup*

**Cup,** china, kettle-form, hand-painted, applied floral design, four-footed, modified bamboo handle, applied mustache guard, unmarked, country unknown, ca. 1880-1890 (ILLUS.)............................... **135-155**

**Cup,** china, kettle-form, hand-painted, four-footed, applied mustache guard, unmarked, country unknown, ca. 1880-1890 ...................................................... **135-155**

**Cup,** china, kettle-form, hand-painted, lustre, blown-out & applied gold design, four-footed, applied mustache guard, unmarked, country unknown, ca. 1870-1880 ...................................................... **155-165**

**Cup,** china, Oriental design, applied mustache guard, blue mark unknown, country unknown, ca. pre-1891 ..................... **135-145**

**Cup,** china, rare left-handed, hand-painted & rare horse decal, applied mustache guard, unmarked, country unknown, ca.

1865-1875, some wear (ILLUS. below)................................................. **300-325**

**Cup,** china, rare seashell shape, hand-painted, wishbone handle, four-footed, applied mustache guard, unmarked, country unknown, ca. 1880-1890 ......... **145-175**

*Rare Left-handed Mustache Cup*

**Cup,** majolica, rare hand-painted, flakes, applied mustache guard, unmarked, USA/England, ca. 1870--1880 .............. **325-350**

**Cup & saucer,** ceramic, left-handed, copper lustre & transfer, applied mustache guard, unmarked, country unknown, ca. 1880-1890 ............................................ **550-600**

**Cup & saucer,** china, decals, applied mustache guard, marked "KPM" (Kranichfeld Porcelain Manufactory), "Germany," underglaze-green, ca. 1903-193 .......... **180-200**

**Cup & saucer,** china, decals, twisted handle, applied mustache guard, marked "USA, Royal Crown, RG," underglaze-blue, USA, circa 1949+ ............................ **65-70**

**Cup & saucer,** china, hand-painted, applied design, applied mustache guard, unmarked, country unknown, ca. 1880-1890 .................................................. **150-160**

**Cup & saucer,** china, hand-painted, applied design, deep saucer, applied mustache guard, marked "Germany" in tiny circle, underglaze, ca. 1892-1900 .. **175-195**

**Cup & saucer,** china, hand-painted applied gold design, applied mustache guard, unmarked, country unknown, ca. 1870-1880 .................................................. **175-200**

**Cup & saucer,** china, hand-painted, applied mustache guard, Lefton China, ca. 1950-60s ................................. **60-65**

**Cup & saucer,** china, hand-painted, applied mustache guard, marked crossed arrows & "Blue Onion" in script, country unknown, ca. 1892+ ................. **170-180**

**Cup & saucer,** china, hand-painted, applied mustache guard, marked "Hand Painted, Nippon" w/rising sun, overglaze-bluish green, Japan, ca. 1890-1921 ...................................................... **225-250**

**Cup & saucer,** china, hand-painted, applied mustache guard, marked "KPM" (Kranichfeld Porcelain Manufactory), "Germany," underglaze-green, ca. 1903-1913 ........................................... **175-200**

**Cup & saucer,** ironstone china, farmer size, transfer design, applied mustache guard, marked "Ironstone Staffordshire, England," ca. 1968+ ............................... **75-100**

**Cup & saucer,** majolica, hand-painted, floral handle, applied purple mustache guard, marked w/English registry mark (partly indistinct), England, ca. 1868-1883 ..................................................... **800-900**

**Cup & saucer,** majolica, rare hand-painted w/lavender inside cup & center of saucer, applied mustache guard, unmarked, England or USA, ca. 1870-1880 ........... **450-500**

**Cup & saucer,** silver plate, applied rope design, thumbprint, raised mustache guard, marked "Wilcox Silverplate Co., Meriden, Conn., Quadruple Plate," symbol of crossed hammers in a circle, USA, ca. 1870-1880 ............................. **375-400**

**Cup & saucer,** silver plate, chased design, applied mustache guard, marked "Meriden Silverplate Co.," quadruple plate, symbol of lion holding a goblet, USA, ca. 1869-1874 ..................................................... **400-425**

**Cup & saucer,** silver plate, chased design, applied mustache guard, marked "Pairpoint Mfg. Co., New Bedford, Mass., Quadruple Plate," symbol of "P" in diamond in circle, USA, ca. 1875-1885 ...... **350-400**

**Cup & saucer,** silver plate, engraved design, applied mustache guard, marked "Rogers & Bro., Patented Sept. 6, 1887, Triple Plate," USA, ca. 1885-1890 ........ **400-425**

**Cup & saucer,** silver plate, engraved design, pedestaled bases, scalloped mustache guard, marked "Woodman Cook Co., Quadruple Plate," USA, ca. 1880-1890 ..................................................... **300-325**

**Cup & saucer,** silver plate, engraved design, unmatched saucer, applied mustache guard, marked "Derby Silver Co., Derby, Conn., Quadruple Plate," symbol of anchor, over a crown in a circle, USA, ca. 1870-1875 ............................. **225-275**

**Cup & saucer,** silver plate, engraved, French horn handle, pedestaled bases, applied mustache guard, marked "Pairpoint Mfg. Co.," quadruple plate, symbol of "P" in a diamond shape, USA, ca. 1870-1880 ........................................... **400-425**

*Silver-plated Mustache Cup & Saucer*

**Cup & saucer,** silver plate, quadruple plate, etched lighthouse design, pedestaled bases, applied French horn handle, applied mustache guard, USA, ca. 1870-1880 (ILLUS.).............................. **400-425**

**Cup & saucer,** silver plate, raised design, monogram on applied mustache guard, marked "Derby Silver Co., Derby, Conn., Quadruple Plate," symbol of anchor over a crown in a circle, USA, ca. 1870-1885 .......................................................... **400-425**

**Cup & saucer,** silver plate, satin engraved design, pedestaled saucer, applied mustache guard, unmarked, country unknown, ca. 1870-1880 ...................... **275-300**

**Cup & saucer,** silver plate, satin engraved overall design, monogram, gold-lined, applied mustache guard, marked "Meriden B., Co., Quadruple Plate," symbol of scales of justice in a circle, USA, ca. 1870-1880 ............................................. **450-475**

**Cup & saucer,** silver plate, satin engraved, unmatched saucer, applied mustache guard, mark illegible, USA, ca. 1870-1880 .................................................... **175-200**

*His & Hers Mustache Cup Set*

**Cup & saucer set,** china, rare, two his and one hers, elaborate gold applied design, applied mustache guards, unmarked, country unknown, ca. 1870-1880, set (ILLUS.)................................................ **850-890**

**Demitasse cup,** china, hand-painted, applied mustache guard, marked "R S Germany" (green wreath mark), Germany, ca. 1915-1925 ..................... **150-175**

*Hand-painted Demitasse Cup*

**Demitasse cup,** china, hand-painted floral design, elaborate applied gold handle, applied mustache guard, early Royal Bayreuth mark, Germany ca. 1887-1902 (ILLUS.)................................................ **135-145**

**Demitasse cup,** china, hand-painted, unusual shape, unusual latch design handle, applied mustache guard, unmarked, country unknown, ca. 1850-1860 ...................................................... **125-145**

**Demitasse cup & saucer,** china, hand-painted, applied mustache guard, unmarked, country unknown, ca. 1875-1880 ..................................................... **200-250**

**Demitasse cup & saucer,** china, hand-painted unusual colors, applied mustache guard, marked, "T" (Tettau), "Germany, Sontag & Sons" (Royal Bayreuth), underglaze-green, ca. 1887-1902 ......... **225-250**

**Demitasse cup & saucer,** china, hand-painted, unusual design, rare molded & raised mustache guard, unmarked, country unknown, ca. 1875-1885 ......... **300-325**

**Demitasse cup & saucer,** china, square, ribbon handled, four footed, applied mustache guard, unmarked, country unknown, ca. 1860-1870...................... **350-375**

**Mug,** china, hand-painted raised design, four-footed, applied mustache guard, unmarked, country unknown, ca. 1865-1875 ....................................................... **125-145**

**Mug,** china, presentation-type, hand-painted, applied mustache guard, marked "Made In Germany" underglaze-red, ca. 1920s, much wear....... **65-115**

**Mug,** china, presentation-type, hand-painted cobalt & raised gold, rare cherub handle, applied mustache guard, unmarked, country unknown, ca. 1885-1890 ...................................................... **250-300**

**Mug,** china, presentation-type, hand-painted raised design, applied mustache guard, unmarked, country unknown, ca. 1885-1890 .............................................. **120-130**

**Mug,** china, presentation-type, hand-painted, rare cherub handle, applied mustache guard, unmarked, country unknown, ca. 1880-1890, much wear ... **100-190**

# RAZOR BLADE BANKS

*Occupied Japan Razor Blade Bank*

**Barber,** holding pole, Occupied Japan, 4" h. (ILLUS.)........................................... **50-60**

*"Looie" Razor Bank*

**Barber,** "Looie" found in right handed & left handed versions, 7" h. (ILLUS.) .............. **85-100**

**Barber,** "Tony," Ceramic Arts Studio, 4 3/4" h. (ILLUS. top next page)............. **90-100**

**Barber,** "Tony," standing wearing blue coat & stroking chin, 5 3/4" h. (ILLUS. next page) ........................................................ **60-80**

*"Tony" Razor Blade Bank*

*Barber Stroking Chin Razor Blade Bank*

*Wooden Barber Razor Blade Bank*

**Barber,** wooden, "The Old Blade," bottom
unscrews, Woodcroft,1950, 6" h.
(ILLUS.) ..................................................... **65-75**
**Barber,** wooden, w/key & metal holders for
razor & brush, 9" h. ................................... **85-95**
**Barber chair,** small, 4 3/4" h. .................... **100-125**

*Barber Chair Razor Blade Bank*

**Barber chair,** large, 5 3/4" h. (ILLUS.) ...... **125-150**

*Cleminson Barber Head Blade Bank*

**Barber head,** Cleminson, different colors
on collar, 4" h. (ILLUS.) ............................. **30-35**
**Barber pole,** ceramic, half-round hanging-
type, "Razor Blades," by Kreiss, 5" h.
(ILLUS. top next column) ......................... **40-60**

*Hanging Barber Pole Razor Blade Bank*

*Barber Pole Razor Blade Bank*

**Barber poles,** red & white (various
designs), 6" h. (ILLUS.) ............................. **25-35**

*Barbershop Quartet Razor Blade Bank*

**Barbershop quartet,** "The Gay Blades,"
5 1/4 x 4 1/4" (ILLUS.) ............................. **75-100**

*Bell-Shaped Cleminson Blade Bank*

**Bell-shaped,** man shaving, Cleminson,
3 1/4" h. (ILLUS.) ...................................... **25-35**

*Wooden Razor Blade Bank*

**Box,** wooden, souvenir, "Old Razor Blades
- For Gay Old Blades By Cracky," w/hill-
billy, side w/names of city & state,
5 1/2" h. (ILLUS.) ...................................... **35-45**

*Donkey Razor Blade Bank*

**Donkey,** ceramic, Listerine, 2 1/4" h.
(ILLUS.)..................................................... **20-30**

*Elephant Razor Blade Bank*

**Elephant,** ceramic, Listerine, 2 1/2" h.
(ILLUS.)..................................................... **25-35**

*Plastic Dandy Dan Razor Blade Bank*

**Figure of Dandy Dan,** plastic, 6 3/4" h.
(ILLUS.)..................................................... **25-35**

*Frog Razor Blade Bank*

**Frog,** ceramic, Listerine, 3" h. (ILLUS) .......... **15-25**

*Green & Yellow Frog Razor Blade Bank*

**Frog,** "For Used Blades," found in green &
yellow, 3" h. (ILLUS.)................................. **60-70**
**Metal box,** policeman holding up one hand,
reads "Old Razor Blades," 4" h. .............. **75-100**

*Safe Razor Blade Bank*

**Safe,** green, says "Blade Safe" on the front,
2 1/2" h. (ILLUS.)....................................... **45-55**

*Shaving Brush Razor Blade Bank*

**Shaving Brush,** ceramic, wide at top
w/decal, 4 1/2" h. (ILLUS.) ...................... **50-60**
**Shaving cup,** half-round hanging-type,
"Gay Old Blade," w/quartet, 4" h. .............. **65-75**

*Villain Razor Blade Bank*

**Villain,** or Matador, "Gay Blade" 6" h.
(ILLUS.)..................................................... **55-65**

# MISCELLANEOUS

*Electric Barber Pole*

**Barber pole,** carved wood, carved at the top w/the head of a man w/a large dark beard on a red block above the columnar red, white & blue central section above the blue block base, 8" w., 55" h. (head loose,some soiling, cracking & paint chips)................................................. **1,045**

**Barber pole,** electric light-up type, milk glass cylinder w/a red stripe, mounted in a light green porcelainized metal frame w/domed top, now painted white, some chips, galvanized metal at base added, some fading, 11" w., 26" h. (ILLUS. previous page)....................................................... **468**

**Barber pole,** electric, porcelainized metal, a milk glass globe above a top light fixture on a white & green metal cap above two red & white twisted stripe metal pole sections divided by a center waisted band, another band at the bottom resting on a tall square green base, early 20th c., 13" d., 82" h. (water stain, some chips)......................................................... **1,100**

**Barber pole,** turned & painted wood, a white ball finial above a turned top over the long red & white striped pole above another turned ball on the shorter striped lower section, added flat square foot base, late 19th - early 20th c., overall 79" h. (some paint touch up) ........................ **420**

**Book,** "The Barber's Manual," by A.B. Moler, copright 1910, illustrated, hard cover, 210 pp., 6 x 9" (some fading, edge wear & tears, binding splitting) .............. **17**

*Rare Barber Shop Globe Sign*

**Globe sign,** milk glass, large squared form w/peaked top & round base flange, fired-on lettering & narrow border of stripes in black, reads "Barber Shop," early 20th c., some water stain & overall wear, 9 1/2" w., 12" h. (ILLUS.).............................. **825**

**Hot water heater,** electric, "The Superior," milk glass globe above the metal columnar body w/spigot above the wide round base, metal tag w/"National Stamping and Electric Works - Chicago, Ill. - Pat. Aug. 30, 1910," 110 volts, soiling, wear, 8" w., 17 1/2" h. (ILLUS. next column) ........ **253**

**Poster,** "Wildroot Hair Oil," elegantly dressed man & woman on blue background w/"Wildroot with Oil for the Hair - 3 action  - 1 Grooms the Hair - 2 Relieves Dryness - 3 Removes Loose Dandruff," Union Made, Cleveland, ca. 1940s, 25 x 36" ..................................... **116**

*Early Barber Shop Water Heater*

**Razor kit,** "Curvfit Woman's Razor," metal & cardboard, gold-plated razor w/two packages of razors, unopened, Curvfit Sales Corp., Stamford, Connecticut, early 20th c. (box wedge wear & surface loss)........................................................... **17**

**Razor kit,** man's, Everready, three-inch chrome-plated safety razor & chrome blade box w/two razors, metal kit box w/felt lining, , 3 1/8" w., 3/4" deep, the set (minor wear, stain & fading on box).......... **22**

**Razor kit,** man's safety-type, Army-issue, metal razor blade holder & sharpening stone, metal razor, engraved "Property of US Army," in canvas kit holder, kit 2 1/4 x 4 1/2" (canvas worn, snap missing) ....................................................... **22**

**Razor kit,** man's safety-type, "Heljestrand Shaving Kit," a 16" l. leather strap razor marked "Heljestrand Sweden," & eleven single-edge blades, w/original printed paper directions in English & Swedish, leather-covered fitted case, 20th c., case 2 1/4 x 4 1/2", the set (case worn, clasp not working)..................................... **22**

**Razor storage box,** oak, square upright form w/hinged flat lid opening to small compartments for storing upright straight razors, contains seventeen early razors w/various makers' names, some w/ivory handles, others w/plastic, usual soiling & scratches, early 20th c., box 6 1/4" w., 9" h., the group............................................. **198**

**Sign,** flange-type, porcelain, square w/dark green ground printed w/white lettering & a large safety razor, a man's head in brown in the upper left, reads "The Clemak Face - 5/ - The Clemak Safety Razor," foreign, 12" sq. (chips to edges, scratches)...................................................... **880**

**Sign,** pole-type, one-side porcelain, long curved rectangular form w/advertising at the top reading "Read! - The Milwaukee Sentinel - First News of the Day - A.C. Backus - Publisher," long lower section in curved red, white & blue stripes, 10 x 48" (some fading, chipping & scratches)................................................... **248**

Sterilizer cabinet, wood & glass, upright wood cabinet w/a top drawer above a middle glazed door printed w/"Antiseptic Sterilizer" & opening to a glass shelf, another glazed door below, flat base, early 20th c., 11 x 11 1/2", 24" h. (overall wear) .......................................................... 209

# BASEBALL MEMORABILIA

*Baseball was named by Abner Doubleday as he laid out a diamond-shaped field with four bases at Cooperstown, New York. A popular game from its inception, by 1869 it was able to support its first all-professional team, the Cincinnati Red Stockings. The National League was organized in 1876 and though the American League was first formed in 1900, it was not officially recognized until 1903. Today, the "national pastime" has millions of fans and collecting baseball memorabilia has become a major hobby with enthusiastic collectors seeking out items associated with players such as Babe Ruth, Lou Gehrig, and others who became legends in their own lifetimes. Though baseball cards, issued as advertising premiums for bubble gum and other products, seem to dominate the field there are numerous other items available.*

Base, original canvas sack w/leather ties on one side, stamped "Brooklyn Dodgers National Association," game-used, 1930s ....................................................... $1,190

Baseball, black-skinned 'figure-eight' style, Civil War era, completely solid & round .... 1,019

*Babe Ruth-signed 1938 Baseball*

Baseball, Brooklyn Dodgers team-signed, 1938, signed by Babe Ruth as team coach as well as team members, heavy shellac w/cracking & chipping (ILLUS.)..... 1,235

Baseball, from Mark McGwire's home run record-breaking series, signed by McGwire's hitting coach Dave Parker & inscribed "9 - 8 - 98 - Game Used Ball - Big Mac HR #62...," also signed by McGwire & mounted above a game ticket stub, w/an 8 x 10" color photo of the actual hit ............................................................... 4,047

Baseball, Mickey Mantle-signed, home run model, Official Harridge ball, late 1950s ball hit in Briggs Stadium, signed in the 1970s ......................................................... 766

Baseball, red lemon peel-type, original blood red color, 1850s................................. 894

Baseball, signed by Casey Stengel, inscribed "To Johnny Krell...Glad we could win for you, Casey Stengel, NY Yankees, 1956" ....................................... 1,852

Baseball, signed by Ty Cobb & Honus Wagner in the 1940s, aged to an even brown, Cobb dated his signature "8/6/46" ................................................... 1,149

Baseball, team-signed, 1937 New York Yankees, twenty-two team signatures including Gehrig, Ruffing, DiMaggio, Mazzeri, Gomez & others, evenly browned w/age........................................... 1,808

Baseball, team-signed, 1946 Brooklyn Dodgers, w/twenty-five player signatures including Durocher, Reese, Medwick, etc., excellent condition........................... 1,083

Baseball, team-signed, 1947 New York Yankees, signed by twenty-two team members including DiMaggio, Reynolds, Page, Henrich & Brown............................. 575

Baseball, team-signed, 1951 New York Yankees, signed by twenty-six members of the World Series champs including Mize, Martin, Berra, Mantle, Stengel & others, signed by DiMaggio in the 1980s, bright white color ..................................... 1,643

Baseball, team-signed, 1954 Brooklyn Dodgers, Official National League ball by Giles, twenty-seven mostly blue ink signatures including Robinson, Hodges, Campanella & Roe .................................... 1,480

Baseball bat, personal model autographed by Luis Aparicio, Adirondack Bat #302 ........ 184

Baseball bat, wooden, Massachusetts-style, two flattened sided w/narrow rounded top & bottom, 1850s, 32" l. (chip missing on barrel)................................ 766

Baseball cap, Montreal Royals, navy blue w/large "M" in white on front, white button on top, size 7 1/8, game-worn, late 1940s ....................................................... 1,035

Baseball card, 1933 Lou Gehrig Goudy Gum Co. #160, well-centered .................. 1,110

Baseball card, Babe Ruth 1933 Sport Kings, nice centering, color on face, verso very lightly bled-through ................. 1,793

Baseball card, Christy Mathewson 1909-11 T206, w/dark cap, sharp edges & corners, near mint ......................................... 1,084

Baseball card, Eddie Mathews 1952 Topps, rookie card .................................... 2,644

Baseball card, Henry Aaron 1954 Topps, No. 128, rookie card, fine color & contrast ............................................................... 3,149

Baseball card, Mickey Mantle 1951 Bowman, No. 253, his first baseball card, nice color, edges & corners...................... 7,717

Baseball card, Mickey Mantle 1965 Topps, No. 350, nice color, full gloss ................... 2,803

Baseball card, Roberto Clemente 1955 Topps, No. 164, fine color & contrast........ 1,121

Baseball card, Ted Williams 1948 Leaf No. 76, orange background, strong corners & edges ......................................................... 814

**Baseball card,** Topps 1969 complete set, near mint ................................................... **2,300**

**Baseball card,** Willie Mays 1951 Rookie card, Bowman No. 305, fine color & contrast ..................................................... **1,961**

*Jackie Robinson Dime Register Bank*

**Dime bank,** lithographed tin, "Save and Win with Jackie Robinson - Daily Dime Register Bank," square w/cut corners, yellow ground w/figure of Robinson on the left, lettering in red & black, very minimal edge scratching, 1950s, 2 1/2" sq. (ILLUS.) ....................................................... **679**

**Employee badge,** silver-colored metal w/impressed wording around rim in black, raised number in center on green ground, reads "Ebbets Field Employee" & "151," 1940s, 2" d. (some wear to green) ............................................................... **2,130**

**Gum display box,** cardboard, "Indian Gum," Goudey, bright yellow ground w/large color Indian chief bust profile, 1933, excellent condition, 6 x 9 3/4" .......... **1,439**

**Jersey,** white cloth, game-worn by Ken Griffey, Jr., printed "Mariners" across the chest in blue & "Griffey - 24" on the back, circular team patch on left sleeve, tagging at bottom reads "Russell Athletic...Diamond Collection ...1993...2," extra length, 1993 ..................................... **1,297**

**Letter,** handwritten by Adrian "Cap" Anson, major star of 19th century baseball, letter to his daughter dated September 4, 1906, two signatures at the end, framed 12 x 14 1/2" ............................................... **1,682**

**Letter,** Kenesaw Mountain Landis handwritten letter in two columns, on his Judge's Chambers, United States Courts letterhead, dated 1921 ..................... **417**

**Letter,** type-written copy signed by Roy Campanella, notes receipt of his salary while w/the Montreal Royal farm team, dated January 24, 1947 ............................ **1,112**

**Magazine,** "Life," June 8, 1953, Roy Campanella on cover ............................................ **25**

**Magazine,** "Life," September 27, 1948, Doak Walker on cover .................................... **15**

**Magazine,** "Now," January 1954, color cover shot of Joe DiMaggio & Marilyn Monroe seated in a restaurant, near mint (ILLUS. top next column) ............................ **421**

*DiMaggio & Monroe on "Now" Cover*

*1870 Baseball Manuel*

**Manual,** "Chadwick's Convention Base Ball Manuel For 1870," hard cover red binding w/early engraving of baseball pitcher under the title, rebound, original pages yellowed, a couple missing (ILLUS.) ............ **843**

**Pennant,** Brooklyn Dodgers souvenir-type, red felt w/white lettering & colored ball park scene, reads "National League Champions - Brooklyn Dodgers," 1949, 26" l. (only slight dark staining) ................... **560**

*Fine Babe Ruth-signed Photograph*

**Photograph,** Babe Ruth-signed, sepia tone full-length shot of Ruth posing in a batting stance, inscribed "To Wm. E. Mack - From "Babe" Ruth - April 24, 1927," some toning & edge wear, 7 x 9" (ILLUS.) ...................................................... **7,928**

**Photograph,** black & white posed shot of Babe Ruth playfully borrowing a newsman's camera & shooting a picture of Lou Gehrig for the benefit of a UPI photographer, dated April 12, 1932, original wire service photo printed in the 1940s, 8 x 10" .......................................................... 509

**Photograph,** Lou Gehrig wire photo, black & white three-quarters standing portrait of Gehrig leaning on a bat & smiling, AP credit & photographer's pencil marks on back, 1936, 8 x 10" (some corner creases) ....................................................... 996

**Photograph,** movie still in black & white, from "Babe Comes Home," shows Babe Ruth offering flowers to his girl, co-star Anna Q. Nilsson, original caption describes the scene & film, 1927, glossy 8 x 10" .......................................................... 285

**Photograph,** team shot of Moxie Baseball team, each player w/"Moxie" on his uniform, w/two managers, original mount, ca. 1905, 13 1/2 x 17" (slight mount staining, tack holes near corners) ..... 421

**Photograph,** Ty Cobb-signed, sepia tone full-length shot of Cobb standing in batting pose in uniform, signed "To W.E. Mack - From His Friend - Ty Cobb. 4/14/27," 7 x 9" .................................... 4,365

**Photograph,** Babe Ruth w/seven friends, inscribed & dated "1940," 8 x 10", mint ... 2,650

**Photographic negative,** original negative of Ted Williams in a posed batting stance, this pose often used later w/the background blotted out, w/two prints made from the negative, negative 4 x 5", the group ...................................................... 919

**Pinback button,** printed round metal, white ground w/black & white bust portrait of Jackie Robinson w/black & red wording reading "Brooklyn 1947 Dodgers - Congratulations - 'Jackie,'" commemorates his first year in the major leagues & being the 1947 Rookie of the Year, 1 1/4" d. ...................................................... 222

*Brooklyn Dodgers Pocket Knife*

**Pocket knife,** single folding blade in yellow plastic ivory colored handle printed in red "Official Souvenir - Brooklyn Dodgers," ring for keys at end, 1940s, near mint (ILLUS.) .............................................. 463

**Press pin,** 1940 Detroit Tigers World Series model, brass, oval w/incurved ends, relief-cast w/a snarling tiger head & crossed bats w/"Tigers - 1940 Press - World Series," near mint, 1" l. (ILLUS. top next column) .......................................... 316

**Press pin,** N.Y. Yankees, 1955 ....................... 125

**Program,** 1939 game w/Athletics vs the Red Sox, notes Ted Williams first career home run, pencil-marked, white & red cover w/black & white photos of six players ...................................................... 1,441

**Program,** 1955 Red Sox program & scorecard .................................................................. 35

*1940 Detroit Tigers Press Pin*

**Program,** Brooklyn "Official Score Card," cover w/printed image of old-time batsman, shows of the publisher, Pittsburgh Fire Arms Co. on back, used, 19th c., 4 x 6" (tear along fold, stains on back) ......... 380

**Ring,** 1950 New York Yankees World Series Championship model, Regal Balfour salesman's sample in 14k gold, size 9 1/2 .......................................................... 3,057

**Soap bar,** "Mickey Mantle's Holiday Inn," Ivory soap in original sealed green & white wrapped w/sketch of Mantle swinging bat & Holiday Inn sign on the left side, from Joplin, Missouri, 2 x 3" ........... 348

**Stock certificate,** Brooklyn Dodgers, ten shares, team seal pressed into the bottom right, issued in 1948, near mint .......... 2,406

*1939 Brooklyn Dodgers Game Ticket*

**Ticket,** opening day, 1939 Brooklyn Dodgers, baseball-shaped w/stub torn-away to show home schedule across the sweet spot, yellow w/red & black printing (ILLUS.) ....................................................... 903

**Ticket,** "Union B.B. Grounds - Brooklyn" printed in black on a lavender ground, red printed facsimile signature of "Wm. N. Cammeyer," builder of the first enclosed baseball field, Civil War era, 2 x 3 1/2" ............................................... 4,233

*1939 All-Star Game Ticket Stub*

**Ticket stub,** 1939 All-Star game, played July 11, 1939 at Yankee Stadium (ILLUS.)................................................ **746**

**Trophy,** silver plate, chalice-form w/deep oval bowl engraved w/a wide band of scrolls at the top above the engraved inscription "Presented to Edwin B. Swadkins from the members of the Criterion Baseball Club 1867," 7" h................ **1,725**

# BASKETS

*The American Indians were the first basket weavers on this continent and, of necessity, the early Colonial settlers and their descendants pursued this artistic handicraft to provide essential containers for berries, eggs and endless other items to be carried or stored. Rye straw, split willow and reeds are but a few of the wide variety of materials used. The Nantucket baskets, plainly and sturdily constructed, along with those made by specialized groups, would seem to draw the greatest attention to this area of collecting.*

**Bushel basket,** woven splint, oval w/nailed rim & handle, stamped "Genoa Apple Basket," old patina, 12 1/2 x 20 1/2", 8" h. ........................................................... **$165**

**Bushel basket,** splint stave construction, deep rounded sides joined at the top by a bentwood band, small bentwood handles, old dark red, 19" d., 11" h. ................... **385**

**"Buttocks" basket,** woven splint, 24-rib construction w/diamond design at bentwood handle, sun-bleached finish w/faded green stripes, 7 x 8 1/2", 3 1/2" h. ..................................................... **127**

**"Buttocks" basket,** woven splint, 38-rib construction, bentwood handle, 6 x 6 1/4", 2 3/4" h. (wear, stain & some damage)..................................................... **165**

*Small "Buttocks" Basket*

**"Buttocks" basket,** woven splint, 24-rib construction, minor damage, 5 1/2 x 6 1/2", 3" h. plus handle (ILLUS.) ................ **248**

**"Buttocks" basket,** woven splint, 22-rib construction, deep sides w/wrapped rim & slender bentwood handle, good old patina, 7 1/4 x 7 1/2", 4" h. plus handle (minor damage) ......................................... **215**

**"Buttocks" basket,** 37-rib construction, woven splint w/bentwood handle, marked "Ohio State Fair 1938," old patina, 8 1/2 x 9 1/2", 4 3/4" h. ..................... **303**

**"Buttocks" basket,** woven splint, 22-rib construction, deep sides w/wrapped rim & slender bentwood handle, good patina

w/dark brown color, 11 x 12 1/2", 6" h. plus handle.................................................. **220**

*Large "Buttocks" Basket*

**"Buttocks" basket,** woven splint, 26-rib construction, old varnish, 11 x 11", 6 1/4" h. plus bentwood handle (ILLUS.)...... **171**

**"Buttocks" basket,** woven splint, 16-rib construction w/wrapped rim & center bentwood twig handle w/Eye of God design, 12 x 14", 6 1/2" h. plus handle......... **105**

**"Buttocks" basket,** woven splint, 36-rib construction, good old patina, 10 3/4 x 9 1/2", 7" h. plus bentwood handle (some damage) ..................................... **495**

**"Buttocks" basket,** tightly woven splint, 40-rib construction, boat-shaped w/incurved ends, twisted twig center handle, old finish, 10 1/2 x 17", 8" h. plus handle (minor damage) ............................... **325**

*Cheese & Pitcher Baskets*

**Cheese basket,** woven splint, round w/wide honeycomb woven design & wrapped bentwood rim w/six bentwood rim handles, minor breaks, 19th c., 17 3/4" d., 6 1/2" h. (ILLUS. right) ............... **805**

**Cheese basket,** woven splint, shallow round form w/honeycomb design, old patina, 21" d. (some damage, string-wrapped rim repairs) ..................................... **105**

**Gathering basket,** woven splint, flat-bottomed shallow round form w/wrapped rim & small bentwood rim handles, some breaks near center, 10" d. (ILLUS. top next page) ............................................... **165**

**Half basket,** woven splint, 17-rib construction, pocket-form w/flat back & rounded front, bentwood fixed handle, 5 1/2" w., 4 1/2" h. plus handle.................................... **138**

*Round Shallow Gathering Basket*

*Rare Early Key Basket*

**Key basket,** plantation-type, black leather w/tooled leaves, vines & floral designs & heart cut-out at the base of the strap handle, possibly Virginia, overall wear, replaced lining, replaced end tabs below heart cut-outs & stitching added around rim, w/five old keys, 8 3/4" l., 4 1/2" h. plus handle (ILLUS.) ................................ **4,400**

*Two Woven Wicker Baskets*

**Laundry basket,** woven wicker, deep round slightly flaring sides w/wrapped rim & wrapped loop end rim handles, attributed to Zoar, Ohio, 22" d. (ILLUS. bottom) .......................................... **165**

**Laundry basket,** woven wicker, oblong w/wrapped rim & rim handles, attributed to Zoar, Ohio, 26 1/2 x 32" (some damage) ............................................ **220**

**Market basket,** woven splint, rectangular w/oblong sides & oval wrapped rim, central bentwood handle, 9 x 12", 5 1/2" h. plus handle ...................................... **88**

**Market basket,** woven splint, rectangular w/upright sides, fanned ribbing, wrapped rim, center bentwood handle, natural patina, 11 1/2 x 17"', 6 1/2" h. plus handle (some damage) ...................... **110**

**Market basket,** woven splint, deep rectangular sides w/radiating ribs & rounded bottom ends, wrapped rim, bentwood center handle, old patina, 9 1/2 x 14", 7" h. ........................................... **149**

**Market basket,** woven splint, deep rectangular sides w/rounded corners & wrapped rim, high bentwood central handle, 13 1/2 x 14", 8" h. plus handle ......... **110**

*Large Painted Market Basket*

**Market basket,** woven splint, wrapped bottom ring below the deep round sides w/bentwood wrapped rim & shaped bentwood fixed handle, painted blue, minor paint wear, breaks, 19th c., 13" d., 13 1/4" h. (ILLUS.) .................................... **1,380**

**"Melon" basket,** woven splint, 11-rib construction, end-to-end bentwood handle w/diamond design at each end, good patina, 10 1/2" d., 6" h. plus handle (some damage) ............................. **176**

**Nantucket basket,** splint ribs & cane weaving w/whip-wrapped rim & swivel bentwood handle w/brass attachment, turned wooden base, faded ink inscription on bottom, old patina, 7 x 7 1/2", 3 1/4" h. plus handle ............................................. **1,045**

**Nantucket basket-purse,** finely woven splint, oval w/flat wooden lid decorated w/a carved ivory whale, ivory pin closure & handle fasteners, 20th c., 7 x 9 1/2", 6" h. ...................................................... **690**

**Pitcher basket,** woven splint, bulbous ovoid pitcher-form w/wrapped bentwood rim & bentwood ash handle, minor breaks, 19th c., 4 1/2" d., 7 3/4" h. (ILLUS. left) .................................... **863**

**Storage basket,** cov., woven wicker, a deep bulbous oval body w/a deep fitted top & two large wrapped swing handles, natural finish, ca. 1920, 17" l. ...................... **86**

**Storage basket,** cov., woven splint, shaped cylindrical form w/a fancy porcupine & plain weaving w/two ring-shaped handles at the sides & two looped handles on the cover, 19th c., 28" h. ................... **460**

Utility basket, woven splint, oval, woven in wide & narrow splint, painted dark red & red w/alternating yellow & red flowers, 19th c., 4 1/2 x 8 x 13" (minor losses) .......... 354

Utility basket, woven splint, flat-bottomed round form w/wrapped rim & swivel bentwood handle, old patina, 5 1/2" d., 2 3/4" h. ....... 385

Utility basket, woven splint, 64-rib construction, flat bottom w/rounded sides & wrapped rim w/small bentwood end handles, good patina, 15 " d., 5 3/4" h. (some wear & damage) ................ 193

Utility basket, woven splint, deep cylindrical sides w/narrow wrapped rim, slender bentwood swivel handle, worn red exterior paint, 9 1/2" d., 6 3/4" h. .......... 330

Utility basket, woven splint, rectangular w/flat sides & wrapped rim, bentwood end-to-end handle, good age & color, 5 3/4 x 7", 3 3/8" h. plus handle ......... 193

Utility basket, woven splint, deep round tapering sides w/small wrapped bottom band & wide round wrapped top band, high bentwood handle, good patina, 10 1/4 x 11 1/2", 7" h. plus handle ......... 110

Utility basket, woven splint, slightly tapering deep round sides w/wrapped rim & slender bentwood swing handle, overall worn blue paint, 11" d., 7 1/4" h. (some damage) ....... 402

Utility basket, woven splint, cylindrical sides w/33-rib construction, overhead bentwood handle, good color, 12" d., 7 1/2" h. plus handle ....... 220

Utility basket, woven splint, cylindrical sides w/wrapped rim & swivel bentwood handles, good old dark patina, 12 x 13", 7 1/2" h. (damage in bottom) ...... 220

Utility basket, woven splint, cylindrical sides w/33-rib construction & narrow wrapped rim, high angular overhead bentwood handle, good color, 13" d., 7 3/4" h. plus handle ......... 138

Utility basket, woven splint, round cylindrical sides w/a heavy wrapped rim & bentwood handle, grey scrubbed patina, 15" d., 8" h. plus handle ......... 193

Utility basket, woven wicker, round w/low gently flaring sides, wrapped rim & wrapped rim handles, attributed to Zoar, Ohio, 17" d. (ILLUS. top with laundry basket) ....... 275

*Large Utility Basket*

Utility basket, woven splint & cane, deep slightly tapering round sides w/vertical

wood straps & a heavy bentwood rim w/hand hole handles, rim stenciled "Harker Pottery Co.," 12 1/2" h., 27" d. (ILLUS.) ....... 193

Wall basket, woven splint, oval, stamped red & blue geometric flowers & dots, 19th c., 4 x 6 1/4 x 12 1/2" (minor losses to bottom) ....... 431

# BELLS

*Figural Jacobean Head Bell*

Figural bell, brass, a Jacobean head handle above the sides cast w/various figures, embossed inscription around the rim, 3 1/4" d., 4" h. (ILLUS.) ....... $95

Glass, high body w/flaring rim in shaded yellow to peach, applied tall tapering clear hollow handle w/tapering ring top, clear clapper w/custard-colored tip, late 19th c., 11 3/4" h. ....... 413

Glass, wide body w/flaring rim in cranberry Swirl patt., replastered waisted white opaque glass hollow handle swelled at the top w/a pointed finial, replaced interior wire w/glass bead clapper, late 19th c., 9 3/4" h. ....... 275

Railroad engine bell, nickel-plated, suspended in a heavy arched yoke w/U-form support on pedestal base, on modern mahogany foot, 25" h. ....... 2,145

School bell, hand-type, brass bell w/a turned hardwood handle, late 19th c. ...... 66

# BICYCLES

Alenax, 1985 mountain bike, Model TRB 5000 ....... $330

Apex, pneumatic tire safety model, probably a track racer, Taylor adjustable handlebars, rat trap pedals, wheels & tires excellent, unrestored, ca. 1903 ....... 743

Bone shaker, primitive type w/wooden-spoked wheels, front 39" d., rear 24" d., 19th c., restored ....... 2,640

Columbia, All Bright 54" ordinary model, correct brake hardware, fine restoration, ca. 1885 ....... 413

Columbia, Model 81 man's pneumatic chainless model, rare original decal, restored, 1902 ....... 1,375

**Credenda,** Convertible model, by A.C. Spalding Co., correct brake hardware, restored, ca. 1889 .................................... **1,650**

**Dayton,** 1940 Champion Single Flex, dual headlights in tank & horn, springer front fork & chrome tubular rack w/tail light, name transfer on tank, very good original, very scarce ...................................... **4,620**

**Elgin** 1934 Black Hawk model, original headlight, correct Lobdell 26" wood steel overlay rims, restored................................ **2,200**

**Elgin,** 1937 girl's model, good original paint, Allstate whitewall tires, very complete .................................................................... **715**

**Elgin,** 1938 Deluxe girl's, Allstate whitewall tires, very original, good condition............... **468**

**Elgin,** 1939 Four Star boy's, deluxe chainguard & Blue Bird stem, repainted w/housepaint, restorable ........................... **1,210**

**Elgin,** 1939 Miss America model, all correct parts, repainted w/house paint, restorable ......................................................... **1,320**

*Rare Elliot Hickory Youth Bicycle*

**Elliott Hickory,** wood & metal, youth's, hard tire safety, wooden-spoked wheels, coil spring suspension on seat, fine unrestored condition, 19th c., front wheel 20" d., rear wheel 26" d. (ILLUS.) ............. **8,800**

**Greyhound,** lady's balloon-tire model, maroon & white paint, includes tires, Emblem Mfg. Co., Angola, NY, ca. 1920s .......................................................... **165**

**Hartford,** Cushion Tire Safety man's model w/cross frame, correct brake hardware, coaster pegs, tires & seat leather replaced, first model used by the U.S. Army, ca. 1889 ......................................... **2,090**

*English Kangaroo Highwheel Saftety*

**Herbert, Hillman & Cooper,** Kangaroo highwell safety model, 36" d. wheel w/geared chain drive, brake hardware,

recovered seat, new rubber tires, made in England, ca. 1889 (ILLUS.) .................. **9,350**

**Ingersoll Co.,** 1936 Ingo-bike, correct foot rubber, restored, red frame ......................... **798**

**Iver Johnson,** 1938 boy's Roadster, very good original condition ................................ **495**

**Monarch,** 1937 Silver King boy's Wing Bar model, semi-restored, new old-stock tires ......................................................... **2,970**

**Monarch,** 1937 Silver King Deluxe boy's model, open lug frame, stainless fenders, rare rear carrier & two-position handlebars ..................................................... **1,320**

**Otto,** 42" d. ordinary-type w/X-boxed open head w/brake hardware, woodenspoked wheels, original logo in cast-iron seat, ca. 1890, restored ........................... **2,090**

**Roadmaster,** 1937 Super Deluxe Zep lady's model, Lobdell seat, front brake, twin Silver Ray lights, fair original red paint, rare................................................... **1,320**

**Safety model,** hard tire type w/front brake hardware, unknown maker but similar to The National Safety, 19th c., restorable (needs seat leather) ................................. **1,595**

**Schwinn,** 1964 Corvette, rare coppertone color, 100% complete w/correct pedals, grips & tires ................................................. **193**

**Schwinn,** Sting-Ray girl's 'Slik-Chik' model, green w/white accents, ca. 1965 ............. **165**

**Schwinn,** Sting-Ray 'Pea Picker,' 1968, first year of production, very original ........... **578**

**Shelby,** 1938 Air Flow lady's model, Western Flyer badge, aluminum rack & chainguard, teardrop pedals, Davis Deluxe white wall tires, proper tail light, very good original red & black paint ................ **2,530**

**Silver King,** 1948 Hex Tube boy's model, fine original piece w/rare aluminum pedestal light, complete, very correct, Davis Deluxe whitewall tires........................... **1,705**

**Stoddard Mfg. Co.,** Tiger man's pneumatic safety model, rare eclipse bicycle brake, adjustable handlebars, excellent tires, restored, 1898 ............................................. **908**

**Tricycle,** child's, wooden frame w/angled bar supporting seat, wooden spokedtires, late 19th c.......................................... **633**

**Union Cycle Co.,** hard tire safety model, unusual front & rear suspension, lever & hairspring suspension, restored, 1892 .... **11,550**

**Victor,** man's tall-frame pneumatic safety model, rare original 'slick tire' (holding air), unrestored, good, ca. 1890 .................. **440**

**Victor,** Model C man's hard tire safety model, complete w/brake hardware, tire rubber & seat leather replaced, frame unrestored, ca. 1889 ............................... **7,700**

**Victor** Victoria lady's hard tire safety model, w/optional tip-down seat, correct brake hardware & coaster pegs, restored, ca. 1892 ..................................... **1,650**

**Waverly,** Scorcher man's pneumatic tire safety, by Indiana Cycle Co., early style handlebars, cork grips, Jameson tires, excellent unrestored condition, ca. 1894... **1,760**

**White Cycle Co.,** Bronco safety model w/unusual cross frame pneumatic tire type w/gear-driven rear axle crank, wooden handlebars, apparently original tires marked "Departure Road Tire - the Fish Rubber Co., Chicopee Falls, Mass.," nickel-plate frame w/wear............. **5,500**

*Rare White Flyer Bicycle*

**White Flyer,** hard tire safety model, unique drive system incorporating chains & pulleys hooked to rear axle, White Cycle Co., Westboro, Massachusetts, ca. 1890s (ILLUS.) ...................................... **33,000**

*Whizzer Model H Roadmaster*

**Whizzer,** Model H on Roadmaster model motor bike, heavy duty frame loaded w/accessories including Cadet speedometer, generator set, front brake & Goodyear double eagle white wall tires, original unrestored condition, Vermont 1948 license plate, original manual (ILLUS.)................................................... **2,210**

**Wooden,** lady's safety model w/wooden-spoked wheels w/new tires, ca. 1894........ **2,420**

# BLACK AMERICANA

*Over the past decade or so, this field of collecting has rapidly grown and today almost anything that relates to Black culture or illustrates Black Americana is considered a desirable collectible. Although many representations of African-Americans, especially on 19th and early 20th century advertising pieces and housewares, were cruel stereotypes, even these are collected as poignant reminders of how far American society has come since the dawning of the Civil Rights movement, and how far we still have to go. Other pieces related to this category will be found from time to time in such categories as Advertising Items, Banks, Character Collectibles, Kitchenwares, Cookie Jars, Signs and Signboards, Toys and several others. For a complete overview of this subject see Antique Trader Books' Black Americana Price Guide with a special introduction by Julian Bond.*

*Ambrotype of African-American Lady*

**Ambrotype,** cased half-length portrait of an African-American lady seated wearing a print dress w/white collar & brooch, on her lap is a wide-brimmed hat w/striped cloth around the crown, leather case w/separation at the hinge, some lines in the emulsion, mid-19th c., 2 x 2 1/2" (ILLUS.)...................................................... **$193**

*Rare Black Minstrel Automaton*

**Automaton group,** carved gesso & polychrome, a large black minstrel ground w/sixteen animated figures & a dog, late 19th - early 20th c. (ILLUS.) ................... **29,325**

**Baby rattle,** celluloid, figural, a standing well-dressed black man in top hat & tails holding a bouquet of flowers, white & red w/black face & hands, made in Japan, 8" h. (some fading & soiling) ............................. **44**

**Badge,** rectangular light card stock w/black letters on brown ground, for a marcher w/Martin Luther King & others on the GOP Convention in July 1960, "Marching for Equal Rights Now! To Be Free By 1963 - 'Emancipation' 100 Years," 3 1/2 x 7 1/2" .......................................... **204**

**Banner,** black printing on white poly-cotton, reads "Martin Luther King Jr. - 1929 - 1968 (flanking bust sketch of King) - Make His Dream a Reality," about the time of his assassination, grommets in corners, slightly browned, minor soil & stains, 40 x 46" (ILLUS. top next page)........ **439**

**Baseball cap,** white cloth w/grey pinstripes & well worn black visor, for Kansas City Black Royals Negro League team, large black "KC" stitched on front, ca. 1920s ........ **927**

*Martin Luther King Jr. Banner*

**Book,** "Negroes and Negro Slavery -The First an Inferior Race - The Latter Its Normal Condition," by J.H. Van Evrie, noted slavery apologist, published in New York City, 1861, 340 pp. (blank end pages missing, general wear, soiling, browning) ..................... **231**

**Book,** "The Black Phalanx," by Joseph T. Wilson, 1889, American Publishing Company, Hartford, first edition, early history of black soldiers in the American Revolutionary War, War of 1812 & Civil War, hard leather covers, 528 pp. (spine crudely reglued) ........................ **165**

**Book,** "The Work of Colored Women - YWCA - 1919," from the War Work Council of the YWCA, many photos, end chart, paperback, 136 pp. (worn, small spine tear) .................................... **424**

**Booklet,** "Equality, Land and Freendom - a Program For Negro Liberation," a Communist Party publication from the League of Struggle for Negro Rights, fine cover graphics, New York, 1933, 48 pp., 4 1/2 x 6" ................................ **73**

**Booklet,** "Songs, Sketch of the Life, Blind Tom - the Negro Boy Pianist," brief biography & sample songs & rave reviews about this young black prodigy, ca. 1868, sketched bust portrait on cover, 30 pp., 5 1/2 x 8 3/4" (soil, worn, tears, pieces missing on back cover) .................... **121**

**Booklet,** "The Black Star Line Passenger List - S.S. Olympus," lists 62 passengers aboard this cruise ship, Black Star Line founded by Marcus Garvey, ca. 1920, 2 pp., 5 x 8" (spine slightly worn) ................... **660**

**Broadside,** baseball, full-length photo of player Satchel Paige, white ground w/red & black lettering reading "Coming - Look for Date - Satchel Paige - at Holden, Mo. - Thurs. June 22 8:30 P.M. - Holden Chiefs vs Hilton Smith's Eagles...," 1939, 5 1/2 x 14" (some toning, slight corner wear, some pencil writing on back).............................. **2,628**

**Carte-de-visite,** "Baptist Church, Colored, Petersburg, Va.," exterior view w/men & women sitting on front fence, Lazell & McMullin, Petersburg, photographers, 1866, pencil inscription "Church of Petersburg Negroes burned by rebels.

Given by Lottie, Feb. 9th, 1868" (soil, wear, slight crimp) ........................ **342**

**Carte-de-visite,** Frederick Douglass, half-length portrait seated w/one arm resting on a table, erased pencil marks on top border, ca. 1860 ............................. **550**

**Carte-de-visite,** Sojourner Truth, three-quarters view seated beside table & holding knitting, printed across the bottom "I Sell the Shadow to Support the Substance," 1864 (corners clipped, foxing, light browning) ......................... **660**

**Carte-de-visite,** titled "Runaway Slave - 60 Mile Marcher," seated black man barefoot & ragged, photographed by McPherson & Oliver, Baton Rouge, Louisiana, an escaped slave who took refuge behind Union lines, back noted "Contraband that marched 60 mi. to get to our lines," probably 1862 ..................... **1,029**

**Chapbook,** "The Slave's Friend - Vol. III, No. V," cover engraving of "Old Lilly and Little Mary," children's anti-slavery publication, homemade wallpaper cover, late 1830s, 16 pp. (slight foxing) ........................ **103**

*Rare Ronson Figural Lighter*

**Cigarette dispenser & lighter,** figural metal, a cast-metal African-American bartender mixing a a cocktail behind a fully stocked bar, flanking side compartments opening to hold cigarettes, center panel fitted w/a lighter, striated woodgrain brown & black enameled bar raised on a black-painted base, marked, Ronson Touch-Tip, Art Metal Works, Incentury, Newark, New Jersey, ca. 1936, one shaker replaced, 3 x 6", 6 3/4" h. (ILLUS.)...................................... **1,472**

**Doll,** stuffed cloth, Mammy figure w/hand-embroidered features, simple stitch-trimmed red dress & blue & white dust cap, 18" h. (wear, damage)......................... **220**

**Doll,** topsy-turvy-type, handmade reversible type w/painted faces & cotton, calico & chintz clothing, hand-stitched borders, ca. 1860s, some soil & wear on white doll, black doll clean & bright, 27 1/2" h. ..................................... **1,313**

**Doll family,** stuffed cloth, Aunt Jemima, Uncle Mose, Diana & Wade, color-printed cloth, cut-out & sewn, possibly by Grinnell Lithographic Co., New York, New York, ca. 1924, 12" to 15 1/2" h., the set (slight wear) .................... **403**

**Game,** dart board, lithographed tin, crude caricature of a black boy grinning & wearing a straw hat marked "Sambo," standing behind a round target w/blocks w/numbers around him, Wyandotte Toys, for suction darts, 14 x 23" (slight wear, scratches) ............................................. 97

**Handbill,** "Save Our Lives -" w/photos of the heads of Clarence Norris & Hayward Patterson, the Scottsboro Boys, also reads "They Must Not Burn Dec. 7 - Join The Fight To Free Them!," probably 1934, 5 1/2 x 8 1/2" (fold in center, slightly soiled) ............................................. 244

**Homecoming program,** black college Thanksgiving homecoming program w/advertisements & photos of the teams & cheerleaders, Swift College vs Knoxville College, ca. 1930s, 8 pp. ........................ 28

**Incense burner,** cast iron, figural, a standing black Mammy wearing a green dress & yellow shawl balancing a wide shallow yellow basket-shaped holder on her head, 5" h. (paint chips) ................................. 94

**Letter,** hand-written stampless cover, writer apologizes to recipient concerning a proposed sale of married slaves; he owned the wife & the other party the husband & wished to purchase the wife but her mistress would not sell her, written in Paris, Tennessee, October 27, 1833, 7 3/4 x 9 3/4" (soil on exterior, slightly smudged) ...................................................... 200

**Magazine,** "Labor Defender," June 1931, dramatic cover photo of young black man w/his head in a noose, cover story title "Dreiser on Scottsboro," 16 pp. (separation at bottom spine, creases at bottom, slight wear) ......................................... 145

**Medallion,** black basalt pottery, oval, slavery theme, embossed image of a kneeling black slave man surrounded by the phrase "Am I Not a Man and a Brother?," England, late 18th - early 19th c., unmarked, 1 1/8 x 1 1/4" .......................... 978

**Mirror,** pocket-type, oval cellulioid, top w/photo of W.T. Brown, Jr., owner of a black funeral home in Chicago, ca. 1920s or '30s, 1 3/4 x 2 3/4" ..................... 124

**Movie poster,** "The Flaming Crisis," fine multicolored poster of black man in jail cell w/ghost of another man pointing at him, noted at bottom "with a Notable Cast of Colored Artists," a Monarch Production, ca. 1920s, corner chips, archival backing, 28 x 42" (ILLUS. top next column)` ............................................. 825

**Pamphlet,** "Vote Against Jim Crow!," published by the Socialist Workers Party in 1940 attacking the civil rights record of both the Democrats & Republications, graphic cover, 8 pp., 4 x 5 1/4" (soiled, worn) .............................................................. 42

**Photograph,** cabinet card-size, full-length portrait of a black woman wearing ragged blouse & skirt drawn up around waist, perhaps a farm worker, marked in lower right "Aunt Nancy," photographer Haweris, Jacksonville, Florida (ILLUS. next column) ................................................ 212

*Rare Monarch Productions Poster*

*Cabinet Photo of "Aunt Nancy"*

**Photograph,** group team photo of the all-girl black basketball team the Cardinals, written inscription "YWCA 27-28," 8 x 10" (corner creases, some wear) .......... 342

**Pinback button,** celluloid, "National Association of Colored Women's Clubs, Inc., - Organized 1896," center w/bust photo of older lady above "Dr. Mary Church Terrell - Founding President - Educator - Emancipator, yellow & red, 2 1/2" d. (foxing along bottom) ................................. 275

**Pinback button,** celluloid, "Save the Scottsboro Boys - ILD," sketch of arms pulling on jail bars in red & white, Eagle Regalia Co., 7/8" d. ..................................... 182

**Pinback button,** celluloid, "SNCC" w/black & white hand shaking, 1" d. (light wear) ......... 35

**Pinback button,** lithographed tin, "Abolish Poll Tax - 100% Democracy," black & white, 3/4" d. (some light blue marks) ............ 47

*Postcard of Catholic School Class*

**Postcard,** real photo-type, black Catholic girl's school group, titled "Senior Pupils. Holy Providence, Cornwells, PA," inscribed & dated on the back 1908, minor wear & soil (ILLUS.) ........................... **193**

*Black Big Band Battle Poster*

**Poster,** Big Band era, "War! War! War! - Curry vs Lunceford...," with illustrated panels advertising the black female band leaders Edith Curry & Joan Lunceford, rare theme, 1940s, red & blue, 28 x 42" (ILLUS.)........................................ **484**

**Poster,** cardboard, "Somebody paid the price for your right - Register/Vote," photo of Martin Luther King Jr. in background left, portion of large U.S. flag in the right foreground, published by the A. Philip Randolph Ed. Fund, ca. 1968, black & white, 17 x 24" ................................ **154**

**Poster,** World War II, "Twice A Patriot!," brown-toned photograph of ex-Private Obie Bartlett who lost an arm at Pearl Harbor, shown working as a welder at a West Coast shipyard, government publication, 1943, 28 x 40" (folds, slight separations at edges) ........................................ **908**

**Sign,** enameled tin, rectangular, yellow ground w/black & red scene of a black shoeshine boy & a man's legs in the upper right, wording in black & red reads

"Yes sah! - 'Star Brand Shoes are better' - Sold at Best Stores," 18 x 23" (few dents & scratches, small paint chips) .......... **550**

**Slave tax badge,** copper, flat diamond shape, stamped "Charleston 2083 Servant 1835," Charleston, South Carolina, early 19th c., 2 x 2" (wear, cleaned, lacquered)...... **1,840**

**Slave tax badge,** copper, flat rectangular form stamped "Charleston 1828 Porter No 254" on the front & "La Far" on the reverse, Charleston, South Carolina, early 19th c., 2 x 2 1/8" (wear, cleaned, lacquered) ................................................ **3,220**

**Stereo view card,** rectangular cardboard, "Colored Troops Taking Train Rest," World War I black Doughboys in formation at a train stop en route to Europe, Keystone, 1918 ............................................. **109**

**Stereo view card,** rectangular cardboard w/view of the interior of an elegant restaurant w/black waiters standing at attention, unidentified but possibly a Florida series, ca. 1900.................................. **42**

**Tintype,** policeman, shown seated wearing a police bowler & badge w/night stick, rare occupational, from Ohio-Pennsylvania area album, 2 1/4 x 3 3/8" (lightly rubbed, few tiny nicks) ................................. **224**

*Tintype of Black Girl with Doll*

**Tintype,** sixth plate, an attractive young black girl seated holding a small white doll on her lap, full case, emulsion not evenly applied, bright image (ILLUS.) .......... **363**

**Token,** bronze, American Colonization Society 1¢ Contribution token, Liberia on obverse w/a ship nearing shore, man & tree of liberty on reverse, 1833, 1 1/8" d. (some wear) ................................................ **333**

**Toy,** embossed lithographed tin, round head of a black native woman w/large eyes & yellow ring earrings, pull string at the bottom makes the eyes move, 2" d. (soiling, minor paint chips) ............................ **49**

**Toy,** windup tin, "Walking Porter," black porter carries suitcases, Louis Marx, original box, 8 1/2" h. (minor wear) ............. **440**

# BOOK ENDS

**Brass,** Arts & Crafts style, rectangular form w/etched & embossed flower stalks outlined in green, impressed "Carence Craft" mark, Chicago, early 20th c., 4 x 7", 4 3/4" h., pr. (some discoloration) ... **$288**

**Brass,** cast, figural masted sailing ship, ca. 1920, 4 1/2" h., pr. .......................................... **28**

**Brass,** model of a cat in a whimsical geometric design, possibly by Chase, 4" w., 7 1/2" h., pr. .................................................. **173**

**Bronze,** figural "End of the Trail," Native American on horseback, Pompeian mark, pr. .................................................... **185**

**Bronze,** Zodiac patt., decorated w/the signs of the zodiac in relief, dark patina, impressed "Tiffany Studios New York 1091," early 20th c., 4 5/8 x 5 1/4", 6" h., pr. ...................................................................... **690**

*Bronze Lion Book End*

**Bronze,** figural, lion & lioness, modeled after Antoine-Louis Barye, greenish black patina, each w/mahogany base, Barbedienne Fondeur, retailed by Tiffany & Co., 20th c., 11" l, pr. (ILLUS. of lion) ...................................................... **2,649**

**Cast metal,** a full-figure elf sitting atop a giant book & reading, late 19th c., 3 1/2" h., pr.................................................... **80**

**Cast metal,** Cottage in Woods, No. 292, near mint, Hubley, 5 1/2" h., pr..................... **308**

**Cast metal,** Cottage in Woods, painted sky w/white moon, pristine, Albany Foundry, 6 1/2" h., pr..................................................... **468**

**Cast metal,** Edgar Allen Poe House, original paper label on bottom of each, Bradley & Hubbard, mint, 4 x 4 5/8", pr. ............. **770**

**Cast metal,** Lady in Garden scene w/fence, pristine, 4 3/8" h., pr. ................................... **352**

**Cast metal,** Mansion Door, near mint, Bradley & Hubbard, 4 x 5 1/2", pr................... **308**

**Cast metal,** Old Doorway, shrubbery & railed fence, attributed to Sarah Simonds, 4 1/4" h., pr. ......................................... **605**

**Cast metal,** Peacocks on Fence, near mint, Bradley & Hubbard, 6 3/16" h.pr. ............... **352**

**Cast metal,** Puppies in Basket, original paper label on back, pristine, 5 1/8" h., pr................................................................... **352**

**Cast metal,** scenic, House & Waterwheel, different scenes, mint, Bradley & Hubbard, 3 3/4 x 5", pr........................................ **528**

**Cast metal,** scenic, Seascape & Village, different scenes, mint, Bradley & Hubbard, pr.............................................................. **550**

**Chromed metal,** figural, Art Deco style, female head turned upward w/one shoulder raised, black wood base, 4 1/2 x 6 1/4, 6 1/4" h., pr. (ILLUS. top of next column)................................................. **403**

**Copper,** hand-hammered Arts & Crafts style, flat egg-form uprights w/small side flanges at the base, impressed mark of Dirk van Erp, 5 1/2" h., pr. (cleaned patina) .......................................................... **330**

*Figural Art Deco Book Ends*

**Leather,** Arts & Crafts design, hand-tooled w/a daffodil design, square, early 20th c., 6" sq., pr. .................................................. **485**

# BOOKS

## CIVIL WAR-RELATED

*Although one hundred titles barely scratches the surface of this enormous field, what follows are a representative sampling of acknowledged Civil War classics --biographies, memoirs and letters, general references, regimental and battle histories, fiction and more.*

*Values given represent the average retail price for first editions in the original binding in fine condition. Note that some of the earlier titles were issued in both cloth and leather editions; the leather editions command higher prices. For post-1930 titles, the dust jacket is assumed to be present. Remember that age is no excuse for poor condition. Serious collectors have little interest in ex-library copies or copies with torn or damaged bindings, broken hinges, detached or absent covers or spines or other unsightly defects. Beware: Reprints and facsimile editions of these popular titles abound and may cause confusion, especially with the older titles. These other editions can certainly be of interest and have value, but a knowledgeable antiquarian book dealer will be able to separate the true firsts from other editions.*

**Adams, George W.,** "Doctors in Blue: The Medical History of the Union Army in the Civil War," New York, 1952 ......................... **$75**

**Alexander, Edward P.,** "Military Memoirs of a Confederate," New York, 1907............. **300**

**Benet, Stephen Vincent,** "John Brown's Body," Garden City, 1928............................... **40**

**Boatner, Mark M.,** "The Civil War Dictionary," New York, 1959 ..................................... **40**

**Butler, Benjamin F.,** "Butler's Book: Autobiography and Personal Reminiscences," Boston, 1892 ................................. **75**

**Catton, Bruce,** "The Army of the Potomac," New York, 1962, three volume set ................. **50**

**Catton, Bruce,** "The Centennial History of the Civil War," Garden City, 1961-65, three volume set.......................................... **50**

**Chamberlain Joshua L.,** "The Passing of the Armies," New York, 1915 ..................... **300**

Chesnut, Mary Boykin, "A Diary from Dixie," New York, 1905 ............... 150

Cleaves, Freeman, "Rock of Chikamauga: The Life of General George H. Thomas," Norman, 1948 ............ 75

Crane, Stephen, "The Red Badge of Courage," New York, 1895 ............... 500

Curry, William Leontes, "Four Years in the Saddle," Columbus, 1898 ............ 300

Custer, Elizabeth B., "Boots and Saddles" or "Life in Dakota with General Custer," New York, 1885............ 75

Dabney, R.L., "Life and Campaigns of Lieut. Gen. Thomas J. Jackson," London, 1864-66, two volume set ..................... 400

Davis, Jefferson, "The Rise and Fall of the Confederate Government," New York, 1881, two volume set ................................. 250

Dawson, Sarah Morgan, "A Confederate Girl's Diary," Boston, 1913 ............... 175

De Forest, John William, "Miss Ravenal's Conversion from Secession to Loyalty," N.p., 1867............ 200

Dornbusch, Charles, E., "Military Bibliography of the Civil War," New York, 1971-88, four volume set...................... 100

Douglas, Henry Kyd, "I Rode with Stonewall," Chapel Hill, 1940 ............... 65

Duke, Basil W., "A History of Morgan's Cavalry," Cincinnati, 1867 ............ 300

Early, Jubal A., "A Memoir of the Last Year of the War for Independence in the Confederate States of America," Toronto, 1866 ............ 250

Eggleston, George Gary, "A Rebel's Recollections," New York, 1875 ......... 200

Evans, Robley D., "A Sailor's Log: Recollections of Forty Years of Naval Life," New York, 1901............ 75

Fletcher, William Andrew, "Rebel Private Front and Rear," Beaumont, TX, 1908...... 2,500

Foote, Shelby, "The Civil War: A Narrative," New York, 1958-74, three volume set." ............ 200

Forbes, Edwin, "An Artist's Story of the Great War," New York, 1890, 20 parts......... 600

Freeman, Douglas Southall, "Lee's Lieutenants," New York, 1942-44, three volume set ............ 325

Freeman, Douglas Southall, "R.E. Lee," New York, 1934-35, four volume set........... 250

Fremantle, Arthur James Lyon, "Three Months in the Southern States," New York, 1863............ 300

Gardner, Alexander, "Photographic Sketchbook of the Civil War," Washington, D.C., 1865-66, two volume set......... 25,000

Giles, Leonidas B., "Terry's Texas Rangers," Austin, 1911 ............... 1,500

Gordon, John B., "Reminiscences of the Civil War," New York, 1903 ............ 200

Grant, Ulysses S., "Personal Memoirs of U.S. Grant," New York, 1885-86, two volume set............ 125

Greeley, Horace, "The American Conflict: A History of the Great Rebellion," Hartford, 1864, two volume set............ 60

Hamilton, Charles, and Ostendorf, Lloyd, "Lincoln in Photographs," Norman, 1963 ............ 100

"Harper's Pictorial History of the Great Rebellion," New York, 1866, two volume set ............ 250

Harwell, Richard B., "The Battle of Gettysburg," N.p., 1908 ............ 100

Hattaway, Herman, and Jones, Archer, "How the North Won: A Military History of the Civil War," Champaign, 1983 ............... 50

Heartsill, William W., "Fourteen Hundred and 91 Days in the Confederate Army," Marshall, TX, 1876 ............ 20,000

Henderson, G.F.R., "Stonewall Jackson and the American Civil War," London, 1898, two volume set ............ 400

Henry, Robert Selph, "'First with the Most,' Forrest," Indianapolis, 1944 ............... 75

Hood, John Bell, "Advance and Retreat: Personal Experiences in the United States and Confederate States Armies," New Orleans, 1880 ............ 300

Horn, Stanley F., "The Army of Tennessee," Indianapolis, 1941 ............ 150

Jackson, Mary Anna, "Life and Letters of General Thomas J. Jackson," New York, 1892 ............ 200

Johnson, Robert U., and Buel, Clarence C., "Battles and Leaders of the Civil War," New York, 1884-88 ............ 350

Johnston, Joseph E., "Narrative of Military Operations," New York, 1874...................... 250

Jones, John Beauchamp, "A Rebel War Clerk's Diary at the Confederate States Capital," Philadelphia, 1866, two volume set ............ 450

Jones, Virgil Carrington, "The Civil War at Sea," New York, 1960-62, three volume set ............ 150

Kantor, MacKinlay, "Andersonville," New York, 1955............ 50

Lee, Robert F., recollections & letters of General Robert E. Lee, New York, 1904........ 75

Leslie, Frank, "Frank Leslie's Illustrated Newspaper 1861-65," New York, five bound volume set...................... 2,500

Lewis, Lloyd, "Sherman, Fighting Prophet," New York, 1932............... 60

Lincoln, Abraham, "Complete Works of Abraham Lincoln," Nicolay & Hay ed., New York, 1905, twelve volume set ............ 300

Livermore, Mary A., "My Story of the War: A Woman's Narrative of Four Years Personal Experience," Hartford, 1888 ............ 50

Long, E.B., "The Civil War Day by Day: An Almanac 1861-1865," Garden City, 1971....... 40

Longstreet, James, "From Manassas to Appomattox," Philadelphia, 1896 ................. 350

Malone, Bartlett Yancey, "Whipt 'em Everytime," N.p., 1919 ............... 100

McCarthy, Carlton, "Detailed Minutiae of Soldier Life in the Army of Northern Virginia 1861-1865," Richmond, 1882............. 200

McClellan, George B., "McClellan's Own Story," New York, 1887 ............... 100

McClellan, Henry B., "The Life and Campaigns of Major General J.E.B. Stuart," Boston, 1885............ 250

**Meade, George,** "The Life and Letters of George Gordon Meade," New York, 1913, two volume set .................................... 250

**Miller, Francis T.,** "The Photographic History of the Civil War," New York, 1911-12, ten volume set........................... 500

**Mitchell, Margaret,** "Gone with the Wind," New York, May 1936............................. 2,750

**Mosby, John S.,** "Mosby's War Reminiscences," Boston, 1887 ................................. 225

**Mosgrove, George Dallas,** "Kentucky Cavaliers in Dixie," Louisville, 1895 ............. 600

**Naisawald, L. Van Loan,** "Grape and Canister," New York, 1960.............................. 75

**Nevins, Allan, et. al.,** "Civil War Books: A Critical Bibliography," Baton Rouge, 1967, two volume set .................................. 100

**Nolan, Alan T.,** "The Iron Brigade," New York, 1961....................................................... 50

**Oates, Stephen B.,** "With Malice Toward None: The Life of Abraham Lincoln," New York, 1977............................................. 40

**Official Records,** of the Union and Confederate Armies, Washington, DC, 1880-1901, 128 volume set................................ 750

**Olmsted, Frederick Law,** "The Cotton Kingdom," London, 1861 ............................ 450

**Paris, Comte de,** "The Battle of Gettysburg," Philadelphia, 1886 ............................ 100

**Pember, Phoebe Yates,** "A Southern Woman's Story," New York, 1897 ................ 650

**Porter, David D.,** "The Naval History of the Civil War," New York, 1886 ......................... 200

**Porter, Horace,** "Campaigning with Grant," New York, 1897.......................................... 100

**Pullen, John J.,** "The Twentieth Maine," Philadelphia, 1957....................................... 75

**Ransom, John L.,** "Andersonville Diary," Auburn, NY, 1881...................................... 175

**Rhodes, James Ford,** "History of the Civil War 1861-1865," New York, 1917................. 65

**Russell, William Howard,** "My Diary North and South," New York, 1863, two volume set ...................................................... 300

**Sandburg, Carl,** "Abraham Lincoln: The Prairie Years and the War Years," New York: 1926-39, six volume set..................... 150

**Semmes, Raphael,** "The Cruise of the Alabama and the Sumter," London, 1864, two volume set ........................................... 450

**Shaara, Michael,** "Killer Angels," New York, 1974.................................................. 400

**Sheridan, Philip H.,** "Personal Memoirs of Philip Henry Sheridan," New York, 1888, two volume set ........................................... 175

**Sherman, William T.,** "Memoirs of General William T. Sherman," New York, 1875, two volume set ........................................... 125

**Simpson, Harold B.,** "Hood's Texas Brigade: Lee's Grenadier Guard," Waco, 1970 .................................................................... 200

**Sorrel, G. Moxley,** "Recollections of a Confederate Staff Officer," New York, 1905 ....... 400

**Starr, Stephen Z.,** "The Union Cavalry in the Civil War," Baton Rouge, 1979-85 ......... 125

**Stern, Philip Van Doren,** "Secret Missions of the Civil War," Chicago, 1959 ............... 35

**Stevenson, William G.,** "Thirteen Months in the Rebel Army," New York, 1862............. 75

**Stowe, Harriet Beecher,** "Uncle Tom's Cabin," Boston, 1852, two volume set ...... 2,500

**Strode, Hudson,** "Jefferson Davis," New York, 1955-66, four volume set................... 200

**Taylor, Richard,** "Deconstruction and Reconstruction: Personal Experiences of the Late War," New York, 1879............... 200

**Thomas, Benjamin P.,** "Abraham Lincoln," New York, 1952.................................... 30

**Tucker, Glenn,** "Hancock the Superb," Indianapolis, 1960...................................... 75

**Van Horne, Thomas B.,** "History of the Army of the Cumberland," Cincinnati, 1875, three volume set................................ 500

**Vandiver, Frank E.,** "Mighty Stonewall," New York, 1957......................................... 50

**Watson, Sam R.,** "'Co. Aytch' Maury Grays First Tennessee Regiment," Nashville, 1882 ................................................... 1,500

**Wiley, Bell,** "The Life of Billy Yank," Indianapolis, 1952.......................................... 50

**Wiley, Bell,** "The Life of Johnny Reb," Indianapolis, 1943.......................................... 50

# BOTTLE OPENERS

*Before the turn of the century, the crown cap for bottled drinks was invented and immediately there was a need for a bottle cap remover or bottle opener.*

*There are many variations of openers, some in combination with other tools, others are utilitarian with fancy handles. Perhaps the most important type of bottle opener today is the figural bottle opener. There are 22 classifications or types of figural bottle openers, with Type 1 being the most important and sought after by collectors. Figures for openers include people, animals, birds, pretzels, keys, etc. Wall-mount openers are mostly faces of people or animals with the opener located in or near the mouth.*

*The important early producers (ca. 1940-50) of iron and pot-metal (zinc) figural openers were Wilton Products, John Wright Inc., Gadzik Sales and L & L Favors. Figural openers were made primarily as souvenirs from vacation spots around the country.*

*Today, new original figural openers are produced in limited numbered editions and sold to collectors. Manufacturers such as Reynolds Toys have produced over 40 different figural bottle opener editions since 1988.*

*There are two clubs for bottle opener collectors: Figural Bottle Opener Collectors (F.B.O.C.) and Just For Openers (J.F.O.). J.F.O. is a club primarily for beer opener collectors, but includes collectors of figural openers, corkscrews and can openers.*

*The numbers used at the end of the entries refer to Figural Bottle Openers Identification Guide, a new book printed by F.B.O.C.*

*Bottle Openers By TypeType 1—Figural bottle openers, free-standing or in natural position or wall-mounted, the opener an integral part of the figure.Type 2—Figural openers with corkscrew, lighter or nutcracker, etc.Type 3—Figural openers, three-*

dimensional on both sides but do not stand. Type 4—Figural openers with loop openers an integral part of design. Type 5—Figural openers with a loop inserted in the casting process. The loop or opener is not part of the casting process. Type 6—Same as Type 5 with an added can punch. Type 7—Same as Type 5 with an added corkscrew or lighter. Type 8—Flat, back not three-dimensional, loop part of casting. Type 9—Same as Type 8, loop inserted in the casting process. Type 10—Same as Type 8 with a corkscrew. Type 11—Openers are coin or medallion shape, one- or two-sided, with an insert or cast integral loop opener. (These are very common.) Type 12—Figural stamped openers, formed by the stamping process (steel, aluminum, or brass). Type 13—Extruded metal openers. Type 14—Johnny guitars or figural holders. Johnny Guitars are figures made of wood, shells, string, etc.; they have a magnet that holds a stamped steel (Type 12) opener; figural holders or display holders are cast holders that have a clip that holds one or two cast figural openers. Type 15—Church keys with a figure riveted or cast on the opener. Some do not have a punch key. Type 16—Figural church-key openers with corkscrew. Type 17—Decorated church-key openers (church-key loop or wire loop openers with names and jewels attached). Type 18—Base opener (opener molded in bottom as integral part). Type 19—Base opener added (opener added to bottom by brazing or soldering). Type 20—Baseplate opener (opener screwed in base of figure). Type 21—Wooden openers/Syroco openers (metal insert, cast stamped or wire type). Type 22—Knives, hatchets, scissors, etc., with openers.

Rarity A—Most Common B—Difficult C—Very difficult D—Very hard to find E—Rare to Very Rare (few known)

## TYPE 21
**Man in tuxedo,** Syroco, wearing top hat, metal opener attached to head inside body ............................................................. **90**

# FIGURAL (FULL DIMENSIONAL)

## TYPE 1
**Alligator w/boy,** cast iron, figural group of black boy being bitten in the behind by an alligator, rarity B, 3" h., F-133 .......... **$75-150**

*Aviator Bottle Opener*

**Aviator,** aluminum, figure of pilot dressed in brown flight suit & goggles w/his right hand raised, rarity B, 3 3/4", N-591 (ILLUS.) ...................................................... **45-90**

**Bar wolf,** cast iron, rarity C, 9 1/2", F-149 ..................................................... **150-250**
**Bear,** mama, aluminum, model of mama bear wearing a yellow & green dress, rarity C, 4" h., N-561 ................................. **45-90**
**Bear,** papa, aluminum, model of papa bear wearing a blue jacket, red vest & grey pants, rarity C, 4 5/8" h., N-560 ......... **45-90**
**Bear at fence,** aluminum, model of a bear standing at a fence marked "FIGURAL - BOTTLE - OPENERS," rarity B, 4 5/8" h., N-582 ...................................... **75-150**
**Bicycle FBOC 1990,** aluminum, model of a gold bike on a base marked "FBOC," 2 5/8" h., N-572 ...................................... **45-90**
**Bird's Birch Beer,** aluminum, model of a grey bird perched atop a branch, the bird marked "Blrd's," the branch marked "Birch Beer," 3" h., N-574 ......................... **45-90**
**Black horse,** aluminum, model of a rearing horse, rarity A, 3 3/4" h., N-584 ............... **50-75**

*Cathy Coed Bottle Opener*

**Cathy Coed,** cast iron, figure of a young woman wearing a yellow hat, blue V-neck blouse, short flared yellow skirt & black Mary Jane-type shoes, standing on a base marked "Women's Weekend," rarity E, 4 5/16" h., F-39 (ILLUS.) ............ **1,200+**
**Chili pepper '93,** cast iron, model of a red chili pepper, rarity B, 5 7/8" h., N-658 .... **75-150**
**Dodo bird,** cast iron, model of a bird w/black body, colorful markings on wings, head & an orange beak, rarity E, 2 13/16", F-122 ...................................... **450-650**
**Dolphin,** aluminum, model of stylized goldfish green dolphin w/tail curled over its head, 4" h., N-616 ................................. **75-150**
**Donkey,** aluminum, w/3" ears, rarity D, 3 3/8" h., F-59 ...................................... **350-550**
**Donkey,** brass, base marked "Norwood," rare, 4 1/8" h. .............................................. **550+**
**Dragon,** cast iron, model of dragon w/open mouth, arched back & curled tail, rarity E, 5" h. ............................................... **550+**
**Dumbbell,** cast iron, rare, 4 5/8", F-220 ......... **550+**
**Elephant,** cast iron, rarity E, 3 1/4", F-47 .. **450-650**
**Father Time,** aluminum, figure of Father Time dressed in grey robe, holding a sickle & an hour glass, rarity B, 4 3/4" h., N-599 ................................................. **75-150**
**Freddie Frosh,** cast iron, model of young man w/his hands in his pockets wearing a beanie-style cap, sweater w/Greek letter across the front, standing on a green

base, rarity D, 4" h., F-37 (ILLUS.
below).................................................... **450-650**

*Freddie Frosh Bottle Opener*

**Good luck,** aluminum, model of a hand in the form of a fist w/forefinger overlapping thumb, wrist marked "Good Luck," rarity A, 3 3/4" h., N-624 .................................... **50-75**

**Grass skirt Greek,** cast iron, figure of a black boy wearing a grass skirt, clutching a sign that reads "Phi Gamma Delta - Fiji Island Party - '53," rarity D, 5" h., F-43 ............................................................... **650+**

**Heart in hand,** cast iron, model of an upturned hand w/a cut-out heart in the palm, rarity E, 4 1/4" h., F-203 ............. **350-550**

**Hunting dogs,** aluminum, model of two dogs, one chocolate brown & one light brown, 2" h., N-587 .................................... **50-75**

**Iroquois Indian,** cast iron, figural, aluminum, rarity A, 4 3/4" h., F-197 ...................... **50-75**

**Lady in the wind,** aluminum, figure of woman wearing royal blue dress & hat, she is leaning into the wind clutching her hat, 4" h., N-598 ...................................... **50-75**

**Lion hoop,** cast iron, model of a lion jumping through hoop, 3 5/8" l., N-576 ........ **250-350**

**Mademoiselle lamp/sign,** cast iron, rarity A, 4 1/2", F-10 .................................... **50-75**

**Male nude w/garment,** brass, rarity E, 2 7/8" h., F-24 ...................................... **200-300**

*Miner Bottle Opener*

**Miner,** FBOC '95, cast iron, figure of miner wearing blue pants, yellow shirt & brown hat holding pan & pick on base marked "FBOC 1995," rarity A, 4 1/8", N-670 (ILLUS.).................................................... **50-75**

**Missouri mule,** bronze, model of stylized kicking mule, rarity A, 2 7/8" h., N-551 ..... **50-75**

**New Year baby,** aluminum, figure of baby New Year holding a parrot & wearing a black top hat, diaper & sash marked "1989," 4 5/8" h., N-567 ......................... **75-100**

**Nude w/wreath,** chrome, female nude w/raised arms & spread wings, rarity B, 5 3/16", F-173 ........................................ **75-150**

*Oriental Clown Bottle Opener*

**Oriental clown,** aluminum, figure of Oriental man w/hands in pockets dressed in brown, black & red clown suit, rarity C, 4 3/8" h., N-559 (ILLUS.)......................... **90-110**

**Palm tree,** cast iron, rarity B, 4 9/16", F-21........................................................ **90-200**

**Parrot,** FBOC, 1987, cast iron, model of a colorful parrot on black perch, rarity A, 5 1/2" h., F-108c .................................... **50-75**

**Parrot,** large, cast iron, rarity A, 5 1/2" h., F-108............................................................. **50-75**

**Pelican,** cast iron, model of a pelican w/upturned orange beak, 4" h., F-130 .... **75-150**

**Pelican w/flat head,** cast iron, model of pelican w/black head, colorful body & yellow beak, rare, 3 7/16" h., like F-129 .... **550+**

**Polar bear,** aluminum, model of polar bear standing on its hind legs holding a brown stick, rarity C, 3 3/4" h., N-557 .............. **90-125**

**Pretzel,** cast iron or aluminum, rarity A, 3 3/8" w., F-230 ...................................... **50-75**

**Pumpkin head,** aluminum, figure of a person w/pumpkin head wearing black robe, rarity B, 4 1/4" h., N-565 ............... **75-150**

**Rooster,** cast iron, 4" h., F-100 ................ **75-100**

**Rooster,** cast iron, rarity A, 3 1/8" h., F-97 .. **50-75**

**Rooster (large),** cast iron, tail down, rarity B, 3 3/4" h., F-98 ...................................... **75-150**

**Rooster (tail down),** cast iron, rarity B, 3 3/4" h., F-99 .......................................... **550+**

**Sailor,** aluminum, cast iron, painted, rarity D, 5 7/8", F-18........................................ **350-700**

**Sea horse,** cast iron, 4" h., F-140 .............. **75-150**

**Shoe,** aluminum, rarity C, 3 3/4" h., F-209.................................................... **150-250**

**Skeleton,** aluminum, rarity B, 4 7/8" h., N-566 ................................................... **75-150**

**Skunk,** cast iron, 2" h., F-92c ................... **150-250**

**Steering wheel,** brass, rarity A, 2 7/8", F-225 ........................................................ **50-75**

**Straw hat/sign,** FBOC 15th, cast iron, figural group of man clutching sign post that reads "F.B.O.C. 15th Conv.," rarity A, 3 7/8" h., N-618 ................................. **50-75**

**Swimmer,** aluminum, rare, 3 1/4", F-195 ....... **850+**

**Teen girl,** cast iron, figure of a teen-aged girl lying on her stomach w/her chin in her hands & her feet in the air, wearing black pants, white shirt & a red ribbon in her blond hair, 2" l, N-577 ................... **250-350**

**Top hatter,** bronze, model of stylized bird wearing a top hat, rarity A, 2 1/2" h., N-606 ................................................................ **50-75**

**Totem pole,** aluminum, rarity B, 3 3/4" h., N-573 ................................................................ **45-90**

## WALL MOUNT

**Beer drinker,** cast iron, model of older man wearing cap, white shirt & orange vest holding a mug of beer, surrounded by cast-iron frame w/banner at the bottom marked "Spencer Brewing Co. - Lancaster, Pa.," rarity E, 6 3/8" h., F-406 ................................................................ **550-850**

**Black face,** cast iron, black face w/red mouth & hole in the ears, marked "Crowley," 4" h., F-404 ...................................... **550+**

**Bronze pirate,** pirate head wearing a red scarf on his head, an eye patch & holding a knife between his teeth, 5" h., N-512 ................................................................ **75-150**

**Bulldog,** cast iron, rarity B, 4" h., F-425 ..... **75-150**

**Four-eyed man,** cast iron, four-eyed man w/mustache, rarity B, 3 15/16" h., F-413 ................................................................ **75-150**

*Wall Mount Hanging Drunk Opener*

**Hanging drunk,** cast iron, figure of a man dressed in a black tuxedo & top hat, holding bottle in left hand w/right hand outstretched, rarity B, 5" h., F-415 (ILLUS.) .......................................................... **75-150**

**Sun,** aluminum, orangish red-painted smiling sun w/black eyebrows, rarity B, 4" h, N-663 ................................................................ **75-150**

## TYPE 21

**Figure,** wooden, figure of bird, Danish ......... **10-30**

**Figure,** wooden, figure of golfer w/wooden golf club serving as opener, Danish ......... **10-30**

# BOTTLES

## BITTERS

*(Numbers with some listings below refer to those used in Carlyn Ring's For Bitters Only.)*

*Rare American Life Cabin-form Bottle*

**American Life Bitters - P.E. Iler, Manufacturer, Tiffin, Ohio - American Life Bitters,** cabin-shaped w/rounded shoulder & pointed lower doors & windows, applied sloping collar mouth, smooth base, ca. 1865-75, medium amber, 9" h. (ILLUS.) .................................................. **$9,625**

**Baker's - Orange Grove - Bitters,** square w/ropetwist corners, applied sloping collar mouth, ca. 1865-75, cherry puce, 9 3/8" h. ....................................................... **1,265**

**Bell's (Dr.) - Golden Tonic - Bitters,** figural bell w/tall neck & applied mouth, red iron pontil, ca. 1870-75, medium amber, 10" h. ........................................................ **12,650**

*Berkshire Bitters Pig Bottle*

**Berkshire Bitters - Amann. Co. Cincinnati. O.,** figural pig, applied mouth, ca. 1865-76, amber, 10" l. (ILLUS.) ................ **1,540**

**Big Bill Best Bitters,** tapering square, golden amber, ca. 1870-90, 12 1/8" h. ........ **154**

**Birmingham's (Dr.) Anti Bilious Blood Purifying Bitters - This Bottle No Sold,** cylindrical w/narrow panels up the sides, applied sloping collar mouth, smooth base, ca. 1855-65, some overall inside stain, medium blue green, 8 7/8" h. (ILLUS. top next page) ................ **4,180**

**Brown (F.) Boston - Sarsaparilla - & Tomato - Bitters,** cylindrical w/applied sloping double collar mouth, pontiled base, ca. 1845-55, aqua, 9 1/4" h. ............... **303**

**Brown's Celebrated Indian Herb Bitters - Patented 1867,** figural Indian Queen, rolled lip, light yellow, 12 1/8" h. .............. **3,300**

*Rare Dr. Birmingham's Bitters Bottle*

**Brown's Celebrated Indian Herb Bitters -
Patented 1868,** figural Indian Queen,
golden amber, rolled lip, 12 1/8" h. (area
of lip unrolled w/minor roughness) .............. **578**
**Brown's Celebrated Indian Herb Bitters -
Patented Feb. 11 1868,** figural Indian
Queen, rolled lip, medium to deep amber
w/some red, 12 1/8" h. ................................ **715**
**Bryant's Stomach - Bitters,** octagonal
w/lady's leg neck w/applied sloping double collar mouth, ca. 1860-70, deep olive
green, 12" h. ............................................... **7,975**

*Very Rare Cassin,s Bitters Bottle*

**Cassin,s Grape Brandy Bitters,** nearly
square w/violin-shaped sides, applied
lip, ca. 1871-75, medium golden amber,
tiny flakes on lip, very rare, 10" h.
(ILLUS.) ................................................... **44,000**
**Clarke's Sherry Wine Bitters,** rectangular,
most original label & tax stamp, aqua,
8" h. ............................................................ **88**

**Cock's Celebrated Stomach Bitters
(label only),** square, tooled top, medium
to light amber ................................................. **66**
**Corwitz - Stomach Bitters,** rectangular
w/paneled sides, tooled mouth, ca.
1880-90, deep bluish aqua, 7 5/8" h. .......... **264**

*H.M. Crooke's Stomach Bitters Bottle*

**Crooke's (H.M.) Stomach Bitters,** cylindrical w/bulbed lady's leg neck, applied
sloping collar mouth, smooth base, ca.
1850-60, olive amber, 10 3/8" h.
(ILLUS.) ..................................................... **1,595**
**Curtis - Cordial - Calisaya - The Great -
Stomach - Bitters - 1 - 8 - 6 - 6 -C - C -
C -1- 9 - 0 - 0,** cylindrical w/tall tapering
paneled shoulder, cylindrical short neck
w/applied mouth, ca. 1866-75, deep root
beer amber, dug, 11 1/2" h. (some minor
scratches) .................................................... **1,018**
**Davis's Kidney and - Liver Bitters - Best
Invigorator - and Cathartic,** square
w/paneled sides, tooled mouth, ca.
1880-90, medium golden amber, 10" h. ...... **143**
**Doyle's - Hop - Bitters - 1872,** around
sides of sloping shoulder, square w/pan-
eled sides w/raised clusters of hop berries & leaves, applied sloping double
collar mouth, partial paper labels, ca.
1872-80, amber, 9 7/8" h. ............................. **66**
**Doyle's - Hop - Bitters - 1872,** around
sides of sloping shoulder, square w/pan-
eled sides w/raised clusters of hop berries & leaves, applied sloping double
collar mouth, ca. 1872-80, yellowish
green, 9 7/8" h. (very shallow flake at
one base corner) ......................................... **413**
**Drake's (S T) - 1860 - Plantation - X - Bit-
ters - Patented - 1862,** cabin-shaped,
four-log, applied sloping collar mouth,
95% original paper labels, ca. 1862-70,
amber, 10" h. (D-110)................................... **264**
**Drake's (S T) - 1860 - Plantation - X - Bit-
ters - Patented - 1862,** cabin-shaped,
four-log, applied sloping collar
mouth, ca. 1862-70, amber, 10" h. (D-
110) ............................................................... **88**

Drake's (S T) - 1860 - Plantation - X - Bitters - Patented - 1862, cabin-shaped,
four-log, applied sloping collar
mouth, ca. 1862-70, yellowish amber,
10 1/8" h. (D-110)...................................... **264**

Drake's (S T) - 1860 - Plantation - X - Bitters - Patented - 1862, cabin-shaped,
six-log, ca. 1862-70, deep cherry puce,
10" h. (D-105)........................................... **220**

Drake's (S T) - 1860 - Plantation - X - Bitters - Patented - 1862, cabin-shaped,
six-log, ca.1862-70, medium grape
puce, 9 7/8" h. (D-106)........................... **1,650**

*Drakes Plantation Bitters Bottle*

Drakes (arabesque) - Plantation (arabesque) - Bitters - Patented 1862,
cabin-shaped, six-log, three-tier roof,
square, applied sloping collar mouth,
smooth base, ca. 1865-75, medium apri-
cot puce, 9 7/8" h., D-102 (ILLUS.) ............. **743**

Electric Bitters (on front & back labels),
square, light amber, pt. .................................. **44**

Fenner's (Dr. M.M.) - Capitol Bitters -
Fredonia, N.Y., rectangular, applied top,
original paper label & tax stamp, aqua,
10 1/2" h. ...................................................... **66**

Gates (C.) & Cos - Life of Man - Bitters,
rectangular w/short neck & tooled
mouth, 95% of paper label, Canada, ca.
1890-1900, pale green, 8" h. ......................... **55**

Globe (The) Tonic Bitters, square w/pan-
eled sides, applied sloping collar mouth,
smooth base, 98% original paper
label, ca. 1865-75, thin cooling check in
shoulder, yellow amber, 9 7/8" h.
(ILLUS. top next column) ............................. **660**

Great Tonic (The) - Caldwell's - Herb Bitters, triangular w/tall neck & applied
sloping collar mouth, iron pontil, ca.
1870-80, medium golden amber,
12 3/4" h. ...................................................... **209**

Hall's Bitters - E.E. Hall New Haven -
Established 1842, barrel-shaped,
applied square collar top, smooth base,
light yellow olive, 9 1/8" h. ........................... **825**

*The Globe Tonic Bitters*

Hartwig - Kantorowicz - (Star of David) -
Posen - Berlin - Hamburg, tall lobed
form w/tall slender neck & applied
mouth, Germany, ca. 1880-95, bright
grass green, 13" h. .................................... **3,960**

Henley's (Dr.) California IXL Bitters,
cylindrical w/applied lip ring, open
pontil, ca. 1870s, light sapphire blue,
12" h. (some interior stain, tiny ding on
inside lip) ..................................................... **275**

Henley's (Dr.) Wild Grape Root IXL Bitters, cylindrical w/applied rim, dark
aqua, 12" h. (some scratching, tiny pot-
stone) ........................................................... **523**

Henley's (Dr.) Wild Grape Root IXL Bitters, cylindrical w/applied rim, light
green, 12" h. (some minor interior haze)...... **413**

Holtzermann's - Patent - Stomach - Bitters, cabin-shaped, four-roof, tooled
mouth, ca. 1880-1895, medium amber,
9 3/4" h. ...................................................... **209**

Holtzermann's - Patent - Stomach - Bitters, cabin-shaped, four-roof, tooled
mouth, ca. 1880-1895, reddish amber,
9 3/4" h. ...................................................... **253**

Hopkins (Dr. A.S.) - Union Stomach Bitters - F.S. Amidon, Sole Prop. - Hartford, Conn U.S.A., rectangular
w/paneled sides, tooled mouth, ca.
1880-1900, medium golden amber,
9 1/2" h. ........................................................ **71**

Hostetter's (Dr. J.) - Stomach Bitters,
square w/beveled corners, short neck
w/applied sloping collar mouth, ca.
1860-70, deep olive green w/amber
tone, 9 1/4" h. .............................................. **231**

Keystone Bitters, barrel-shaped w/ribs,
applied sloping collar mouth, smooth
base, ca. 1870-80, golden amber,
9 3/4" h. (ILLUS. top next page).................. **743**

Kuyper's (D) Orange Bitters, short cylindrical body w/rounded shoulder to tall
neck, ABM, complete original labels,
1920s, dark green .......................................... **44**

*Keystone Bitters Barrel-shaped Bottle*

*Rare Lacour's Bitters Bottle*

**Lacour's Bitters Sarsapariphere,** cylindrical w/sunken side panels & ringed rim & base, applied mouth, ca. 1866-79, deep green, 9 3/8" h. (ILLUS.) ........................ **11,000**

**Langley's (Dr.) - Root & Herb - Bitters - 99 Union St. - Boston,** cylindrical w/short neck & flattened applied mouth, ca. 1855-65, yellowish amber, 7" h. ............................................................ **330**

**Morning (design of star) Bitters - Inceptum 5869 - Patented - 5869,** triangular slender form w/slanted ridges on neck, applied sloping collar mouth, iron pontil, ca. 1870-80, medium amber, 12 1/2" h. .................................................... **198**

**National Bitters,** figural ear of corn, medium yellowish amber, "Patent 1867" on base, applied mouth, 12 1/2" h. ............. **550**

**National Bitters - Patent 1867,** figural ear of corn, "Patent 1867" on base, applied mouth, medium amber w/hint of puce, 95% of original paper label, 12 5/8" h. ........ **770**

**Old - Homestead - Wild Cherry - Bitters - Patent,** cabin-shaped, scalloped shingles on four-sided roof, applied sloping collar mouth, ca. 1865-80, golden yellow amber, 9 3/8" h. (partially open bubble on inside of lip) ............................................. **385**

**Old Sachem - Bitters - and - Wigwam Tonic,** barrel-shaped, ten-rib, applied mouth, ca. 1855-70, deep strawberry puce, 9 1/2" h. (shallow flake on side of lip) ................................................................. **633**

*Old Sachem Bitters Bottle*

**Old Sachem - Bitters - and - Wigwam Tonic,** barrel-shaped, ten-rib, applied mouth, smooth base, ca. 1855-70, peach puce, 9 1/4" h. (ILLUS.) ..................... **770**

*Rare Original Pocahontas Bitters*

**Original Pocahontas Bitters - Y. Ferguson,** barrel-shaped w/ten horizontal ribs above & below embossing, applied mouth, smooth base, ca. 1855-65, deep bluish aqua, 9 1/4" h. (ILLUS.) .................. **5,500**

**Owen (Garry.) Strengthening Bitters - Ball & Lyons New Orleans, LA Sole Proprietors,** square, applied top, amber, 9" h. ..................................................... **132**

**Oxygenated - For Dyspepsia - Asthma & - General Debility - Bitters,** rectangular w/paneled sides, applied sloping collar mouth, pontiled base, ca. 1845-55, aqua, 7 1/2" h. ............................................ **132**

**P.D. H. & Co. (monogram on shoulder) - Sazerac Aromatic Bitters,** cylindrical w/tall lady's leg neck & applied mouth, ca. 1865-75, milk glass, 12 1/8" h. ..................................................... **303**

**Petzold's (Dr.) Genuine German Bitters Incept. 1862,** oval w/twenty side ribs, tooled top, amber, 10 5/8" h. (potstone w/ding on base) ........................................... **110**

**Pineapple figural,** embossed diamond-shaped panel, applied top, amber, 8 7/8" h. .................................................. **187**

**Rising Sun Bitters - John C. Hurst, Philada.,** square, applied top, amber, 9 3/8" h. .................................................. **143**

**Roback's (Dr. C.W.) - Stomach Bitters - Cincinnati, O.,** barrel-shaped, applied sloping collar mouth, iron pontil, ca. 1855-65, medium amber, 9 7/8" h. .............. **495**

**Roback's (Dr. C.W.) - Stomach Bitters - Cincinnati, O.,** barrel-shaped, applied sloping collar mouth, smooth base, ca. 1860-70, golden yellow w/olive tone, 9 1/4" h. ..................................................... **1,100**

*Dr. A.H. Smith Old Style Bitters*

**Smith (Dr. A.H.) Celebrated Old Style Bitters - O.S. 2781 The Standard Tonic and Blood Purifier,** square w/beveled corners, applied sloping collar mouth, ca. 1875-85, deep chocolate amber, 8 7/8" h. (ILLUS.) ............................ **143**

**Soule (Dr.) - Hop - Bitters - 1872 (on shoulders),** square w/embossed hop flowers & leaves design on one side, crocked neck, amber, 9 1/4" h. ..................... **176**

**Southern Aromatic - Cock Tail - Bitters - J. Grossman - New Orleans - Sole Manufacturer,** cylindrical w/tall lady's leg neck & tooled mouth, ca. 1880-90, yellow w/amber tone, 12 5/8" h. (some spotty inside stain) ................................... **1,430**

**Sun Kidney and Liver Bitters - Vegetable Laxative, Bowel Regulator and Blood Purifier (one front & back paper labels),** square, amber, 95% of labels, 9 1/2" h. ................................................ **66**

**Toneco Stomach Bitters - Appetizer & Tonic (one front & back labels),** square, clear, 9" h. ...................................... **66**

*Rare Old Dr. Townsend's Bitters Flask*

**Townsend's - (Old Dr.) - Celebrated - Stomach - Bitters,** chestnut flask-shaped w/applied mouth & applied handle, open pontilca. 1860-70, golden yellow amber, 8 3/4" h. (ILLUS.) ...... **12,000-14,300**

**Traudt's Alterative Bitters (label only),** over embossed Dr. J. Hostetter's Stomach Bitters, square, amber, 10 1/2" h. .......... **143**

**Von Hopf's (Dr. E.R.) Curacoa Bitters - Chamberlain & Co. Des Moines Iowa,** rectangular, w/100% original paper label, amber, 7 1/2" h. .................................... **99**

**Von Koster - Stomach - Bitters - Fairfield - Conn.,** rectangular w/beveled corners, short neck w/tooled mouth, ca. 1880-1900, amber, 9" h. ............................................ **99**

**Wahoo - & - Calisaya - Bitters - Jacob Pinkerton - Y!! - O.K. - I.M. - Y!!!,** semi-cabin w/paneled sides, applied sloping collar mouth, ca. 1865-75, amber, 10 3/8" h. (ILLUS. top next page) ................. **660**

**Wallace's Tonic Stomach Bitters,** square, applied top, full front & rear labels w/a peacock, amber, 9 1/4" h. .......................... **440**

**Warner's (Dr. C.D.) German Hop Bitters - 1880 - Reading, Mich.,** square, tooled top, amber, 9 1/2" h. ................................. **143**

*Wahoo & Calisaya Bitters Semi-Cabin*

**Wilder's (Edw) - Stomach Bitters - (design of a building) - Edw. Wilder's - Wholesale Druggists - Louisville, KY.,** square semi-cabin w/paneled sides & beaded corners, tooled mouth, ca. 1885-95, clear, 9 3/4" h. ........................................ **148**

**Wood's (Dr.) - Sarsaparilla - & - Wild Cherry - Bitters,** rectangular w/beveled edges, applied sloping collar mouth, ca. 1845-55, aqua, 8 3/4" h. (lightly cleaned)..... **308**

**Zingari Bitters - F. Rahter,** round, lady's leg neck, amber, 12" h. ............................... **468**

# FIGURALS

*Figural Kummel Bear Bottle*

**Bear,** "Kummel," seated on haunches w/shaped base, applied mouth, black olive amber, ca. 1880-95, 11 1/8" h. (ILLUS.) ......................................................... **$39**

*Belgian Bear Bottle*

**Bear,** seated w/shield in front, embossed on back "Distrie 'Mercator' SA - Anvers Belgique - Deposé," tooled mouth, smooth base, ca. 1890-1910, Belgium, clear, 9 7/8" h. (ILLUS.)................................ **181**

*Clam Flask with Metal Cap*

**Clam,** ground lip, smooth base, original metal screw cap, ca. 1885-95, medium amber, 5 1/4" h. (ILLUS.) ............................ **121**

**Coachman,** three-quarters length bust w/top hat & holding pipe & glass, ground lip, smooth base, milk glass, ca. 1880-95, 10 1/4" h. (slight chip on side of lip) .... **1,650**

**Harrison Monument,** frosted clear bust of Benjamin Harrison atop tall reeded black glass column, ground lip, smooth base, ca. 1888, 11 1/4" h. ......................... **1,073**

**Man standing leaning on stump,** wearing 18th c. costume, flared lip, pontil, ca. 1870-90, Europe, cobalt blue, 7 1/8" h. ....... **578**

*French Orange-shaped Bottle*

**Orange or tangerine,** "P. Bardinet Bordeaux," oblong w/ground lip & smooth base, center band w/wording, ca. 1900-20, straw yellow w/orange tone, probably French, 4 1/8" h. (ILLUS.) .......................... **44**

*Fine Figural of Standing Woman*

**Woman standing wearing peasant dress,** rolled lip, pontil, base of back embossed "Deposé," ca. 1890-1910, France, medium green, 13 1/8" h. (ILLUS.) .................................................. **1,265**

# FLASKS

*Flasks are listed according to the numbers provided in American Bottles & Flasks and Their Ancestry by Helen McKearin and Kenneth M. Wilson.*

**Chestnut,** eighteen ribs swirled to the right, short flared neck, cobalt blue, 6" h. ............. **715**

**Chestnut,** fifteen vertical ribs, attributed to Mantua, Ohio, early 19th c., citron, 1/2 pt., 5 1/8" h. ............................................... **605**

**Chestnut,** mold-blown, twenty-four vertical ribs, Zanesville, Ohio, golden amber, 5 1/4" h. (wear, scratches) ........................... **275**

*Early Chestnut Flask*

**Chestnut,** twenty ribs swirled to the right, tooled & flared lip, open pontil, deep cobalt blue, 3 3/4" h. (ILLUS.) ..................... **633**

**Chestnut,** twenty-four vertical ribs, grandfather-size, sheered top, open pontil,

medium to light amber, Zanesville, Ohio (interior haze) .............................................. **440**

**Chestnut,** twenty-four vertical ribs, sheared lip, open pontil, medium to deep amber, Zanesville, Ohio (some scratches) .............. **187**

*Jenny Lind - Kossuth Calabash Flask*

**GI-100 -** "Jenny Lind" above bust of Jenny Lind within wreath - "Kossuth" above bust of Kossuth, calabash, applied ringed mouth, open pontil, aqua, qt. (ILLUS.) ...................................................... **176**

**GI-103 -** "Jeny. Lind (sic)" above bust within wreath - View of Glasshouse, no wording, vertically ribbed sides, calabash, aqua, qt. .................................. **80**

**GI-111 -** Kossuth bust facing right w/heavy beard, "Bridgeton." at right & "New Jersey" at left - Sloop sailing left w/flying pennant, sheared lip, open pontil, aqua, pt. ................................................................ **242**

*Kossuth & Frigate Flask*

GI-112 - "Louis Kossuth" above full-faced bust of Kossuth in uniform above crossed flags - Frigate sailing left flying flags above "U.S. Steam Frigate Mississippi S. Huffsey," "Ph. Doflein Mould Maker Nth.5t St 84" on base, calabash, applied sloping collar, iron pontil, bluish aqua, qt. (ILLUS.) ............................... 275

GI-114 - Classical bust obverse & reverse, sheared lip, open pontil, olive green, 1/2 pt. ...................................................... 303

GI-2 - Washington bust below "General Washington" - American Eagle w/shield w/seven bars on breast, head turned to right, edges w/horizontal beading w/vertical medial rib, sheared lip, open pontil, pale greenish aqua, pt. ......................... 187

GI-20 - Washington bust facing left w/"Fells" above & "Point" below - Monument without statue above "Balto.," vertical medial rib, light to medium pink amethyst, pt. ................................. 1,760

GI-28 - Washington bust below "Albany Glass Works," "Albany NY" below bust - full-rigged ship sailing to right, applied tapering top, open pontil, vertically ribbed edges, aqua, pt. ................ 253

*Washington - Taylor Flask*

GI-42 - Washington bust below "The Father of His Country" - Taylor bust below "A Little More Grape Captain Bragg, Dyottville Glass Works, Philad.a," smooth edges, sheared lip, open pontil, light teal blue, qt. (ILLUS.) ...................... 413

GI-47 - Washington bust below "The Father of His Country" - plain reverse, applied collar mouth, iron pontil, medium bluish green, qt. ................................. 330

GI-54 - Washington bust without queue - Taylor bust in uniform, open pontil, applied sloping double collar mouth, deep yellowish olive green, qt. .................. 605

GI-79 - Grant bust in medallion - American Eagle on shield & carrying ribbon in beak all above oval framed w/"Union," smooth edges, applied mouth, smooth base, deep aqua, pt. (tiny flake on edge of lip) .......................................... 231

GI-95 - Franklin bust below "Benjamin Franklin" - Dyott bust below "T.W. Dyott,

M.D.," three vertical ribs w/heavy medial rib, sheared lip, open pontil, aqua, pt. .......... 358

GI-99 - "Jenny Lind" above bust - View of Glasshouse w/"Glass Works" above & "Huffsey" below, calabash, smooth sides, broad sloping shoulder, pale bluish green, qt. .................................... 77

GII-10 - American Eagle w/"W. Ihmsen's" above "Glass" below - Sheaf of Rye w/"Agriculture" above & farm implements below, vertically ribbed edges, sheared lip, open pontil, aqua, pt. .......................... 440

GII-106 - American Eagle above oval obverse & reverse, w/"Pittsburgh, PA" in oval on obverse, narrow vertical rib on edges, deep green, pt. (small lip ding) ......... 176

GII-11 - American Eagle facing left w/eleven stars above, standing on plain oval - Cornucopia with Produce vertically ribbed edges, plain lip, pontil, yellowish amber, 1/2 pt. ................................. 88

GII-11 - American Eagle facing left w/eleven stars above, standing on plain oval - Cornucopia with Produce vertically ribbed edges, plain lip, pontil, aqua, 1/2 pt. (small lip flake) ...................... 231

GII-13 - American Eagle w/head turned to left & w/large beak & no shield above an oval frame cut-off at the bottom & enclosing ten large pearls, a semicircle of eighteen stars above eagle - Cornucopia inverted & coiled to left filled w/produce, horizontally beaded border w/medial rib, light to medium yellowish green, 1/2 pt. (lightly cleaned) .................. 5,500

GII-15 - American Eagle with head to the right & surrounded by sunrays, shield on breast, on oval beaded panel w/"F.L." - Cornucopia filled w/produce, sheared lip, open pontil, aqua, 1/2 pt. ............................. 330

*Eagle - Lyre Flask*

GII-22 - American Eagle w/head turned to left holding a banner reading "Union" w/two rows of stars above & an oval frame enclosing an eight-point star below - Lyre below two rows of fourteen stars, corrugated edges, sheared lip, open pontil, deep aqua, pt. (ILLUS.of back & front) .............................. 1,100

GII-26 - American Eagle above stellar motif obverse & reverse, horizontally corrugated edges, plain lip, smooth base, aqua, 1/2 pt. .................................................... **55**

**GII-26 -** American Eagle above stellar motif obverse & reverse, horizontally corrugated edges, plain lip, open pontil, medium to deep bluish green, 1/2 pt. ........ **2,145**

**GII-45 -** American Eagle facing right w/wings spread, shield on breast, within an oval border & standing on a plain oval - Cornucopia filled with produce, sheared lip, open pontil, aqua, 1/2 pt. ......... **198**

*Rare Eagle & Furled Flag Flask*

**GII-54 -** American Eagle facing left on large shield, sunrays around head - U.S. flag furled on standard above "For Our Country," sheared lip, open pontil, chocolate tobacco amber, pt. (ILLUS.) ...................... **5,280**

**GII-56 -** American Eagle facing left within oval panels, larger shield on breast, thirteen small stars above - Large cluster of grapes, sheared lip, open pontil, aqua, 1/2 pt. .................................................. **209**

**GII-60 -** American Eagle in oval beaded medallion - "Liberty" in scroll above beaded medallion around leafy tree, sheared lip, open pontil, aqua, 1/2 pt. .......... **413**

**GII-72 -** American Eagle w/head turned right & standing on rocks - Cornucopia w/produce, vertically ribbed edges, sheared neck, open pontil, yellowish olive amber, pt............................................ **165**

**GII-73 -** American Eagle w/head turned right & standing on rocks - Cornucopia w/produce & X to the left, vertically ribbed edges, sheared neck, open pontil, yellow amber, pt. (ILLUS. top next column) ............................................................ **176**

**GIII-4 -** Cornucopia with Produce - Urn with Produce, vertically ribbed edges, plain lip, pontil, dark olive green, pt. ...................... **77**

**GIII-4 -** Cornucopia with Produce - Urn with Produce, vertically ribbed edges, plain lip, pontil, dark amber, pt............................... **88**

**GIII-4 -** Cornucopia with Produce - Urn with Produce, vertically ribbed edges, tooled lip, pontil, olive green, pt. (ILLUS. center next column)................................................. **104**

**GIII-4 -** Cornucopia with Produce - Urn with Produce, vertically ribbed edges, plain lip, pontil, dark emerald green, pt. ................ **468**

*Eagle - Cornucopia Flask*

*Cornucopia - Urn Flask*

**GIII-8 -** Cornucopia with Produce & large pearl at left - Urn with Produce, vertically ribbed sides, sheared lip, pontil, amber, 1/2 pt. (slight interior stain)................ **88**

**GIV-1 -** Masonic Emblems - American Eagle w/ribbon reading "E Pluribus Unum" above & "P" (old-fashioned J) below in oval frame, sheared lip, open pontil, aqua, pt............................................. **413**

**GIV-18 -** Masonic Arch w/pillars & payment & six stars around quarter moon - American Eagle over plain oval frame w/"KCCNC," light yellow amber, pt.............. **220**

**GIV-19 -** Masonic Arch w/pillars & pavement - American Eagle above oval frame w/"KCCNC," sheared lip, open pontil, dark olive green, pt. (minor interior stain)..... **176**

**GIV-2 -** Masonic Emblems - American Eagle w/ribbon reading "E Pluribus Unum" above & "HS" below in oval frame, rolled lip, open pontil, light bluish green, pt. ....................................................... **385**

**GIV-3 -** Masonic Emblems - American Eagle w/heavily crimped ribbon above &

"J.K. - B." below in oval frame, thick rolled lip, open pontil, yellowish topaz shading to yellowish green, pt. .................. **4,510**

GIX-48 - "M'Carty & Torreyson" arched above a star w/"Manufacturers, Wellsburg, Va." below - Large sunbrust w/twenty-four rays in circular frame, fiddle-shaped w/sheared & tooled lip, open pontil, deep aqua, pt. ................................. **1,073**

GV-1 - "Success to the Railroad" around embossed locomotive - similar reverse, sheared lip, open pontil, yellow-amber, pt. ........................................................ **3,740**

GV-10 - "Railroad" above horse-drawn cart on rail & "Lowell" below - American Eagle lengthwise & 13 five-point stars, vertically ribbed edges, plain lip, pontil, olive green, half pint ................................. **237**

GV-3 - "Success to the Railroad" around embossed horse pulling cart - similar reverse, sheared lip, open pontil, olive green, pt. ....................................................... **209**

GV-3 - "Success to the Railroad" around embossed horse pulling cart - similar reverse, sheared lip, open pontil, yellow amber, pt. .................................................... **303**

*Horse Pulling Cart Flask*

GV-7 - Horse pulling loaded cart obverse & reverse, no inscription, applied mouth, open pontil, deep olive green, pt. (ILLUS.) ...................................................... **880**

GVI-4 - "Baltimore" below monument - "Corn For The World" in semicircle above ear of corn, smooth edges, applied lip band, open pontil, copper puce, qt. .................................................. **1,320**

GVI-4 - "Baltimore" below monument - "Corn For The World" in semicircle above ear of corn, smooth edges, applied lip band, open pontil, golden yellow amber, qt. (ILLUS. top next column)... **1,375**

GVI-6 - "Baltimore" below monument - "Corn For The World" in semicircle above ear of corn, sheared & tooled lip, open pontil, bright yellow green, pt. .......... **6,875**

GVIII-16 - Sunburst w/twenty-one triangular sectioned rays obverse & reverse, sheared & tooled lip, open pontil, olive amber, 1/2 pt. ............................................... **385**

*Corn For The World Flask*

*Moss Green Sunburst Flask*

GVIII-16 - Sunburst w/twenty-one triangular sectioned rays obverse & reverse, sheared & tooled lip, open pontil, moss green, 1/2 pt. (ILLUS.)................................. **935**

GVIII-20 - Sunburst w/thirty-six slender rays forming a scalloped ellipse w/five small oval ornaments in center - similar but variations in size of center oval ornaments, sheared lip, open pontil, aqua, pt...... **220**

GVIII-27 - Sunburst w/sixteen rays obverse & reverse, rays converging to a definite point at center & covering entire side of flask horizontally, ribbed edges, sheared lip, open pontil, light blue, 1/2 pt. .................. **358**

GVIII-8 - Sunburst w/twenty-eight triangular sectioned rays, obverse & reverse, center raised oval w/"KEEN" on obverse & w/"P & W" on reverse, olive amber, pt. ..... **523**

GX-18 - Spring Tree (leaves & buds) - Summer Tree, smooth edges, smoky ice blue, qt. ...................................................... **413**

GXI-27 - "For Pike's Peak" above prospector w/knapsack on shoulder & walking w/a cane above an oval - American Eagle w/shield & banner above oval, aqua, pt. ................................................... **88**

GXI-34 - "For Pike's Peak" above prospector w/tools & cane standing on oblong frame - American Eagle w/pennant above frame "Ceredo," crude square band lip, aqua, qt............................................ **88**

**GXII-30 -** Clasped hands above oval, all inside large shield w/"Union" above - American Eagle w/shield w/bars above oval frame, amber, 1/2 pt. ......................... **176**

**GXII-43 -** Clasped hands above square & compass above oval w/"Union" all inside shield - American Eagle, calabash, amber, qt. ..................................................... **385**

**GXII-17 -** Horseman wearing cap & short tight coat on a racing horse w/flying tail - Hound walking to the right, aqua, pt............. **105**

**GXIII-23 -** Flora Temple obverse, plain reverse, smooth edges w/beads at lower neck & shoulder, blue green, pt. .................. **105**

**GXIII-35 -** Sheaf of Grain w/rake & pitchfork crossed behind sheaf - "Westford Glass Co., Westford Conn," smooth edges, olive green, pint................................ **121**

*Sheaf of Grain - Westford Glass Flask*

**GXIII-37 -** Sheaf of grain on crossed rack & pitchfork - "Westford Glass Co., Westford, Conn.," applied double collar mouth, smooth base, tobacco amber, 1/2 pt. (ILLUS.)................................. **132**

**GXIII-4 -** Hunter facing left wearing flat-top stovepipe hat, short coat & full trousers, game bag hanging at left side, firing gun at two birds flying upward at left, large puff of smoke from muzzle, two dogs running to left toward section of rail fence - Fisherman standing on shore near large rock, wearing round-top stovepipe hat, V-neck jacket, full trousers, fishing rod held in left hand w/end resting on ground, right hand holding large fish, creel below left arm, mill w/bushes & tree in left background, calabash, edged w/wide flutes, open pontil, aqua, qt. ..................................... **88**

**GXIII-41 -** Sheaf of grain on rake & pitchfork below arched laurel branches - eight-petal ornament below "Sheets & Duffy," calabash, ribbed edges, tapering lip, open pontil, deep bluish aqua, qt............ **165**

**GXIII-42** Sheaf of grain in front of rake & pitchfork, two laurel branches above - eight-petal ornament w/no inscription, calabash, tapered lip, open pontil, aqua, qt. ................................................................. **77**

**GXIII-46 -** Sheaf of Grain above crossed rake & pitchfork - Tree & foliage, calabash, vertically ribbed, applied mouth, open pontil, dark claret, qt............................ **825**

**GXV-19 -** "Geo. W. Robinson" in an arc & "Main St. W. V.A" in a reverse arc on obverse, plain reverse, strapside flask, smooth base, applied mouth, deep bluish aqua, pt................................................... **198**

**Pitkin** sixteen broken ribs swirled to the right, Midwestern, light green, 5 1/4" h. (exterior worn) ............................................... **413**

**Pumpkinseed,** picnic-type, tooled lip, amber, 1/2 pt. (some interior stain) .............. **121**

# INKS

**Cone-shaped,** amber, bubbly ............................ **55**

**Cone-shaped,** "Carters" on the base, cobalt blue......................................................... **66**

**Cone-shaped,** light blue...................................... **66**

**Cone-shaped,** light green, some bubbles.......... **66**

**Cone-shaped,** marked "Sanford's" on base, deep purple ........................................... **55**

**Cylindrical,** light to medium green w/olive tone, thin flared lip, open pontil, embossed "Hover - Phila," ca. 1845-55, 2 5/8" h. (several tiny flakes off lip) .............. **165**

*Hover Master Ink Bottle with Spout*

**Cylindrical,** master-size, medium emerald green, applied sloping double-collar mouth w/crimped pour spout, open pontil, embossed around shoulder "Hover - Phila," ca. 1845-55, 7 1/2" h. (ILLUS.) ......... **358**

**Cylindrical,** medium green, rolled lip, open pontil, embossed "S. Fine Blk. Ink," ca. 1845-55, 3" h. (some faint scratches) .......... **176**

**Eight-sided w/central neck,** light to medium bluish green, rolled lip, pontil, embossed "Harrison' Columbian Ink," ca. 1845-55, 1 7/8" h. (ILLUS. top next page) ..................................................... **633**

**Eight-sided w/central neck,** master-size, medium bluish green, applied mouth, open pontil, embossed "Estes - N.Y. - Ink," ca. 1845-55, 6 1/4" h. .......................... **715**

*Scarce Harrison' Columbian Ink*

**Eight-sided w/central neck,** medium apple green, rolled lip, pontil, embossed "Harrison' Columbian Ink," ca. 1845-55, 2" h. .......................................................... **990**

*Very Rare Farley's Ink*

**Eight-sided w/central neck,** yellowish amber, thin flared lip, open pontil, embossed "Farley's Ink," ca. 1845-55, very faint content haze, 3 3/4" h. (ILLUS.)...................................................... **1,760**

*Rare Train Engine Inkwell*

**Figural,** model of an early train engine, aqua glass, marked "Trademark Pat. Oct. 1874," 2 1/8" l. (ILLUS.) .................... **1,320**

**Rectangular,** flared lip, open pontil, "J Kidd Improved Indelible Ink," clear ...................... **143**

**Teakettle-type fountain inkwell w/neck extending up at angle from base,** black amethyst glass, sheared lip, smooth base, ribbed & slightly domed tapering sides, probably Europe, ca. 1880-1900, 2 1/8" h. (tiny chip on lid & flake on edge of top) .................................. **440**

**Teakettle-type fountain inkwell w/neck extending up at angle from base,** cut overlay glass, cobalt blue cut to clear w/a bold cross & punty design, polished lip, cut base, ca. 1880-95, 2 1/4" h. .............. **688**

**Teakettle-type fountain inkwell w/neck extending up at angle from base,** cut overlay glass, cobalt cut to clear w/clear polished ribs, lip w/original brass press-on cap, polished pontil, ca. 1880-95, 1 1/2" h. ....................................................... **633**

**Teakettle-type fountain inkwell w/neck extending up at angle from base,** cut overlay glass, jade green cut to clear in a tiered scallop design, cut starburst on base, ground lip w/original brass neck ring, ca. 1880-95, 2 1/8" h. (missing hinged lid)...................................... **743**

**Teakettle-type fountain inkwell w/neck extending up at angle from base,** deep cobalt blue glass, eight-sided, sheared lip, smooth base, ca. 1880-90, 2" h. (needs cleaning)......................................... **165**

**Teakettle-type fountain inkwell w/neck extending up at angle from base,** deep cobalt blue glass, four-sided w/beveled corner panels, sheared & ground lip, smooth base, ca. 1870-90, 1 5/8" h. ............ **358**

*Blue English Teakettle Ink*

**Teakettle-type fountain inkwell w/neck extending up at angle from base,** deep cobalt blue glass, polished pontil & original silver hinged lid, applied top brass medal reading "G. Riddle London," England, ca. 1870-90, 2" h. (ILLUS.) .......... **523**

**Teakettle-type fountain inkwell w/neck extending up at angle from base,** deep emerald green glass, eight-sides, ground lip, smooth base, ca. 1875-95, 2" h. (small chip along one panel edge) ....... **143**

**Teakettle-type fountain inkwell w/neck extending up at angle from base,** milk glass w/embossed flowers & leaves, rounded tapering form, original sterling silver neck ring, smooth base, ca. 1875-95, 2 1/2" h. ................................................. **303**

*Fine Decorated Teakettle Ink*

**Teakettle-type fountain inkwell w/neck extending up at angle from base,** opalescent milk glass, eight-sided, ground lip w/original brass neck ring & hinged lid, smooth base, original gold & yellow paint on the embossed floral decoration, ca. 1875-95, 3" h. (ILLUS.) ............... **578**

**Teakettle-type fountain inkwell w/neck extending up at angle from base,** stoneware pottery, unglazed greyish brown, five-sided, impressed on base "Boss Brothers Middlebury," ca. 1875-90, 1 5/8" h. ............... **121**

*Small Hover - Phila. Umbrella Ink*

**Umbrella-type (12-panel cone shape),** medium bluish green, rolled lip, open pontil, embossed "Hover - Phila," ca. 1845-55, light overall stain, 2" h. (ILLUS.) ............... **220**

**Umbrella-type (6-panel cone shape),** aqua, rounded sides w/rolled lip & open pontil, embossed "Waters - Ink - Troy N.Y.," ca. 1845-55, 2 7/8" h. (overall stain, some minor ground wear) ............... **660**

**Umbrella-type (6-panel cone shape),** pale apple green, waisted base & rounded shoulders to rolled lip, open pontil, embossed "Boss - Patent," ca. 1845-55, 2 3/4" h. (lightly cleaned) ............... **358**

**Umbrella-type (8-panel cone shape),** aqua, rolled lip, open pontil, embossed "S.O. Dunbar - Taunton," ca. 1845-55, 2 1/2" h. (overall stain) ............... **105**

**Umbrella-type (8-panel cone shape),** bluish aqua, rolled lip, pontil, ca. 1845-55, 3 1/8" h. ............... **121**

**Umbrella-type (8-panel cone shape),** deep cobalt blue, tooled lip, "N.Y." on smooth base, ca. 1870-80, 2 5/8" h. (lightly cleaned) ............... **495**

*Rare Purple Umbrella Ink*

**Umbrella-type (8-panel cone shape),** deep purple, rolled lip, open pontil, ca. 1845-55, shallow chip off flat base, 2 5/8" h. (ILLUS.) ............... **358**

**Umbrella-type (8-panel cone shape),** medium orangey puce glass, rolled lip, open pontil, some roughness on lip, late 19th c. (ILLUS top next column) ............... **605**

**Umbrella-type (8-panel cone shape),** medium yellowish olive amber, rolled lip, pontil, ca. 1845-55, crude, 2 3/8" h. ............ **187**

*Rare Umbrella Ink*

# MEDICINES

**Arnold's (Dr. S.) Balsam,** eight-sided, flared lip, open pontil, ca. 1845-55, pale aqua, 2 3/8" h. ............... **176**

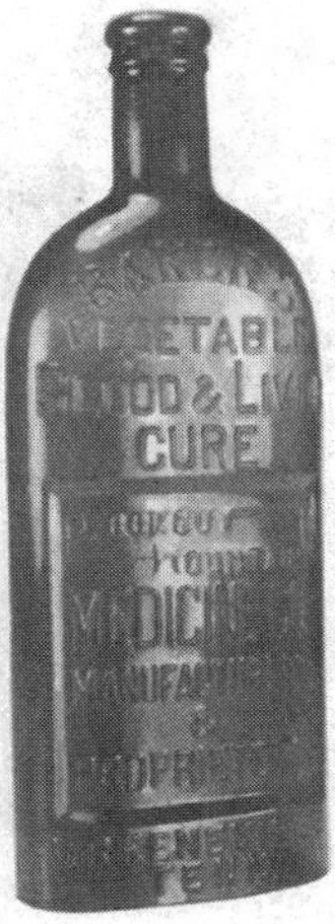

*Baker's Vegetable Blood & Liver Cure*

**Baker's Vegetable Blood & Liver Cure, Lookout Mountain Medicine Co. Manufacturers & Proprietors, Greenville, Tenn.,** oval w/tooled mouth & smooth base, ca. 1880-90, reddish amber, minor content stain, 9 7/8" h. (ILLUS.) ............... **385**

**Budwell's Emulsion of Cod Liver Oil No. 2 with Guaiacol and Creosote Carbonate - budwell Pharmacal Co., Lynchburg, Va.,** oval w/tooled mouth & "W.T. & Co. U.S.A. Pat Jan 18 1898" on smooth base, ca. 1890-1900, deep cobalt blue, 8" h. (dug) ............... **187**

**Cook's Balm of Life,** oval w/strap sides, tooled mouth smooth base, ca. 1880-90, light cobalt blue, 8 1/4" h. ............... **176**

**Cure (The) for Fits - Dr. Chas. T. Price - 67 William St. New York,** oval w/tooled mouth & smooth base, ca. 1880-95, clear, 8 1/2" h. (lightly cleaned) ............... **330**

**Davis's (Dr.) - Depurative - Phila.,** square w/beveled corners, applied sloping collar mouth, iron pontil, ca. 1845-55, medium bluish green, 9 3/4" h. ............... **2,970**

Duffy's Tower Mint (below) - Est. (castle moftif) 184 Trade Mark, tall tapering three-story building-shaped, applied mouth, smooth base, ca. 1875-85, medium amber, 9" h. ...................................... **578**

*Duffy's Tower Mint Cure*

Duffy's Tower Mint Cure (below) - Est. (castle moftif) 184 Trade Mark, tall tapering three-story building-shaped, applied mouth, smooth base, ca. 1875-85, yellowish amber, partially polished small chip on lid, cleaned, 9" h. (ILLUS.) .. **1,073**

Fenner's (Dr. M.M.) Peoples Remedies - Fredonia N.Y. U.S.A. - Kidney & Backache Cure 1872-1898, oval w/tooled mouth & smooth base, ca. 1890-1900, 98% original label, contents, tax stamp & box, medium amber, 10" h. ..................... **385**

Foster's (Dr.) Anti-Catarrh, eight-sided bullet-shape, tooled mouth, smooth base, ca. 1890-1900, deep teal green, 3 3/4" l. ...................................................... **149**

Gargling Oil, Lockport, N.Y., rectangular w/ABM lip & smooth base, 99% of original paper label, ca. 1910-15, cobalt blue, 5 1/8" h. .................................................. **143**

Gleet Seven-Days Gonorrhea, rectangular w/tooled mouth & "M.B.W. Millville" on smooth base, ca. 1890-1910, some inside & outside milky stain, deep cobalt blue, 5" h. (ILLUS. top next column) ............ **798**

Gogings Wild Cherry Tonic, square w/beveled corners, tooled mouth, smooth base, ca. 1890-1900, medium amber, 8 3/4" h. .................................... **66**

Graefenberg & Co. - Dysentery Syrup - New York, rectangular w/beveled corners & paneled sides, applied sloping collar mouth, open pontil, ca. 1845-55, aqua, 6" h. ............................................... **77**

Ham's (Dr.) Aromatic Invigorating Spirit, N.Y., cylindrical w/applied mouth & smooth base, ca. 1875-85, orangish amber, 8 1/2" h. ..................................... **61**

*Rare Gleet Gonorrhea Bottle*

Heimstreet (C.) & Co. - Troy, N.Y., tall octagonal shape w/applied double collar mouth & open pontil, ca. 1845-55, medium sapphire blue, 7 1/8" h. ................... **303**

Houcks Vegetable Pancea - Goodletsville Tenn., rectangular w/beveled corners, applied double collar mouth, smooth base, ca. 1855-60, deep bluish aqua, 7 1/8" h. ........................................... **688**

*Rare Western Medicine Bottle*

Indian Tla-Quillaugh's Balsam - Dr. R. Parker, S.F., cylindrical w/applied mouth & smooth base, ca. 1864-67, copper shading light to dark from shoulder, rare, 8 1/2" h. (ILLUS.)..................................... **11,650**

Mother Putnam's Blackberry Cordial - Rheinstrom Bros. Proprietors, rectangular w/paneled sides, applied mouth on tall ringed neck, smooth base, ca. 1880-90, medium amber, 10 7/8" h. (tiny chip off lip) ............................................................ **220**

**N.Y. Medical - University,** rectangular w/tooled mouth & smooth base, 100% original paper label w/"Compound Fluid Extract of Cancer-Plant," ca. 1885-95, deep cobalt blue, 7 3/8" h............................ **798**

**Orcutt's Sure Rheumatic Cure,** rectangular w/paneled sides, tooled lip, smooth base, ca. 1885-95, deep cobalt blue, 6 1/8" h. ....................................................... **633**

**Pearl's White Glycerine,** rectangular w/sunken panel, tooled mouth, smooth base, ca. 1880-90, deep cobalt blue, 6 3/8" h........................................................ **143**

**Sanford's Extract of Hamamelis or Witch Hazel,** round w/sunken panel, tooled mouth, smooth base, ca. 1885-95, deep cobalt blue, 10 1/4" h.................................. **330**

**Sanford's Radical Cure,** rectangular w/tooled mouth & smooth base, 95% of original paper label w/"Sandford's Radical Cure for Catarrh," ca. 1870-80, deep cobalt blue, 7 5/8" h.................................... **165**

**Shaker (The) Family Pills - Dose 2 to 4 - A.J. White,** rectangular w/paneled sides, sheared lip, smooth base, ca. 1890-1900, medium amber, 2 1/4" h. ............ **94**

**Sparks Perfect Health (below Trade Mark) - bust of man - for Kidney & Liver Diseases,** rectangular w/beveled corners, tooled mouth, smooth base, ca. 1880-95, medium amber, 9 1/2" h. .............. **275**

*Rare Stone's Liquid Cathartic Bottle*

**Stone's (G.W.) Liquid Cathartic & Family Physic, Lowell Mass.,** rectangular w/beveled corners & three indented panels, applied double collar mouth, smooth base, ca. 1850-60, tobacco or root beer amber, 8 7/8" h. (ILLUS.) ........................ **9,625**

**Swaim's Panacea - Genuine - Philadelphia,** rectangular w/applied sloping collar mouth & open pontil, ca. 1840-50, aqua, 7 3/4" h. ............................................. **853**

**Swaim's - Panacea - Philada,** paneled cylinder, applied sloping double collar, open pontil, ca. 1840-50, medium yellowish olive, 7 3/4" h. (ILLUS.) ..................... **853**

*Fine Swaim's Panacea Bottle*

**Swift's Syphilitic Specific,** strap-side flask form, applied mouth, smooth base, ca. 1870-80, deep cobalt blue, 9 1/8" h. (spot of roughness on one strap edge) ........ **633**

**U.S.A.- Hosp. Dept. (in oval),** cylindrical w/applied mouth & smooth base, ca. 1860-75, deep cobalt blue, rare size, 6 1/4" h. ...................................................... **6,160**

**(Warner's) Log Cabin Extract - Rochester, N.Y.,** three indented panels on front, flat back, smooth base, tooled mouth, ca. 1880-90, w/original box & directions, medium amber, 6 3/8" h. ............ **264**

*Warner's Safe Cure - Frankfort*

**Warner's Safe Cure (motif of safe) Frankfut A/M,** oval w/applied mouth & smooth base, ca. 1890-1900, deep olive green, 9" h. (ILLUS.) .................................... **358**

**Warner's Safe Cure (motif of safe) Melbourne, Aus - London, Eng - Toronto, Can - Rochester, N.Y. U.S.A.,** oval w/applied blob top & smooth base, late 19th c., medium copper, 9 5/8" h. (shallow open bubble) .......................................... **176**

**Warner's Safe Cure (motif of safe) Melbourne, Aus - London, Eng - Toronto, Can - Rochester, N.Y. U.S.A.,** oval w/applied double collar mouth & smooth base, late 19th c., reddish amber, 9 5/8" h. ......................................................... **99**

*Dr. Weaver's Canker Syrup Bottle*

**Weaver's (Dr. S.A.) Canker & Salt Rheum Syrup,** oval w/applied mouth & iron pontil, ca. 1845-55, aqua, 9 3/8" h. (ILLUS.) ........................................................ **66**

**Wilder's (Edward) Compound Extract of Wild Cherry (motif of five-story building) - Edward Wilder & Co. Wholesale Druggists Louisville, KY.,** semi-cabin shaped w/paneled sides, tooled mouth, smooth base, ca. 1885-95, clear, 7 1/2" h. ...................................................... **121**

**Wishart's (L.Q.C.) - Pine Tree Tar Cordial, Phila. - Patent (design of pine tree) 1859,** square w/beveled corners, applied sloping collar, smooth base, ca. 1859-70, medium emerald green, 9 1/2" h. ...................................................... **220**

**Wistar's (Dr.) Balsam of Wild Cherry - Sanford & Park - Cincinnati, O.,** eight-sided w/applied sloping collar mouth & iron pontil, ca. 1845-55, deep ice blue, 6 3/8" h. (some light haze) .......................... **159**

**Wood's (Dr. J.S.) Elixir, Albany , N.Y.,** rectangular w/deeply cut corners & tombstone shoulders, applied sloping collar mouth, iron pontil, ca. 1845-55, deep bluish green, 8 3/4" h. (tiny flake on front panel) ......................................... **4,400**

**Wynkoop's Katharismic Sarsaparilla - New York,** rectangular w/sunken panels, applied sloping collar mouth, iron pontil, ca. 1845-55, medium cobalt blue, 10" h. (ILLUS. top next column) ................ **7,975**

*Rare Wynkoop's Medicine Bottle*

# MILK

*The milk bottles in this listing are all glass with dairy names. Milk bottles were patented in 1886 and handmade until the introduction of the Owens semi-automatic bottle machine. The turn-of-the-century saw a large increase in the use of milk bottles by small dairies in most every town in America. These lowly utilitarian glass bottles have become a prized collectable because of the pride of the farmer who produced the milk and the way he promoted the sale of milk through these bottles. Also nearly all folks have ties to a family farm, some close, some far, which causes us to want part of the past. Our listing will note size, square or round, embossed (raised glass lettering) or pyro (painted label). All pricing is for milk bottles in good plus condition, meaning free from cracks, chips, stain or paint wear or fading.*

*Aldrich Dairy Milk Bottle*

**Aldrich Dairy - Norwich, NY,** quart, round, pyro (ILLUS.) ................................................. **35**

**Baxter's Dairy - Watkins Glen, NY,** quart, square, pyro ...................................................... **8**

**Birch Lawn Dairy J.M. Leighty - Tarrs, Pa.,** quart, round, pyro, farm scene ................ **55**

**Branglebrink Farm - St. James, N.Y.,**
　half-pint, round, embossed.............................. 6
**Brookefield Dairy - Hellerstown, Pa.,**
　half-pint, round, embossed, baby top............. 35
**C.N. Baker - Charlotte, N.C.,** pint, round,
　embossed......................................................... 16
**Chapman's Dairy - Greenville, S.C.,**
　quart, round, pyro.......................................... 40
**Chestnut Farm Chevy Chase Dairy -
　Washington, DC,** quart, round,
　embossed, carton............................................ 30

*Churchill's Dairy Quart Milk Bottle*

**Churchill's Dairy - Bethlehem, NH,** quart,
　round, pyro (ILLUS.)....................................... 35
**Clay County Farms - Middleburg, Fl.,** jer-
　sey cow ........................................................... 50

*Coop Golden Crust Bread Milk Bottle*

**Coop Golden Crust Bread,** quart, round,
　pyro (ILLUS.).................................................. 50
**Cream Valley Dairy - Woodstown, N.J.,**
　quart, square, pyro.......................................... 10
**Dairy Gold,** quart, round, pyro, 2 color
　(ILLUS. top next column) ............................... 60
**Dairylea,** quart, round, pyro, 2 color, eagle,
　girl/hoop, family.............................................. 30
**Damascus Cream Top Milk - Portland,
　Ore.,** quart, round, pyro, cream top............... 35
**David Fiske Warehouse - Point, Conn.,**
　quart, round, embossed ................................. 18
**Dellinger Dairy - Jeffersonville, IN,** quart,
　round, pyro, 2 color, gold medal herd ........... 55
**Dykes Dairy - Warren/Youngstown, Pa.,**
　quart, round, pyro, 2 color, "United
　States is a Sound Investment Buy War
　Bonds & Stamps," Statue of Liberty .............. 75

**Earl Lapan's Dairy - South Burlington,
　Vt.,** half-pint, round, pyro............................... 12
**Eveleth Creamery - Eveleth, Minn.,** quart,
　round, pyro, cream top ................................... 45

*Franz Dairy Knox Clarion Milk Bottle*

**Franz Dairy Knox Clarion - Emlenton,
　PA,** quart, round, pyro (ILLUS.) ..................... 45
**Frink Serving Denver Make America
　Strong,** quart, round, pyro, eagle,
　girl/hoop ......................................................... 60
**Fryes Dairy - Leominster, Mass.,** quart,
　square, pyro, baby top ................................... 75
**Furman Bros. - Ithaca, N.Y.,** quart, round,
　pyro, cop the cream ..................................... 200

*Harris Dairy Quart Milk Bottle*

**Harris Dairy - St. Joseph, Mo,** quart,
　round, pyro squat (ILLUS.)............................. 30

G.C. Kaufman - Kingston, N.Y., half-pint,
round, embossed, tin top............................... 50
Gayoso Farms - Horn Lake, Miss., quart,
round, pyro..................................................... 55
George Godin - Richfort, Vt., quart,
round, pyro..................................................... 60
Greenhill Dairy - Wilmington, Del., quart,
round, embossed ........................................... 35
H.E. Larrimore's Dairy - Seaford, Del.,
quart, round, pyro.......................................... 50
H & L Hometown Dairy - Keokuk, Ia.,
quart, round, pyro.. 45Harris Dairy - St.
Joseph, MO, quart, round, pyro squat
(ILLUS. bottom previous page) ...................... 30

*Homecroft Dairy Quart Milk Bottle*

Homecroft Dairy - Bessember, PA, quart,
round, pyro (ILLUS.)....................................... 40
Independent Riviera Dairy - Santa Bar-
bara, Calif., quart, round, pyro ...................... 35
Julius Heretick Dairy - Hopewell, Va.,
pint, round, embossed.................................... 10
Kilfasset Farms - Passumpsic, Vt., quart,
square, pyro ................................................... 10

*Lackrone Dairy Milk Bottle*

Lackrone Dairy - Salem, IL, quart, round,
pyro (ILLUS.).................................................. 45
Leadbelt Dairy - Bonne Terre, Mo., quart,
round, pyro..................................................... 45
Leake Bros. Dairy Fountain Inn, half-pint,
round, pyro, stork .......................................... 18
M.H. Williams Ayrshire Dairy, quart,
round, pyro, four Ayrshire cows ..................... 45
Maple Farm - Boston, Mass., quart,
round, embossed, store bottle........................ 25
Meadowsweet Dairies - Tacoma, Wash.,
quart, round, embossed ................................. 22

Midland Creamery - Colorado Springs,
Colo., pint, round, pyro, two-color................. 40

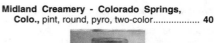

*Midwest Dairy Bottle*

Midwest Dairy - St. Louis, MO, quart,
round, pyro, war slogan (ILLUS.) .................. 65
Mohawk Farms - Staten Island, N.Y.,
quart, round, embossed, Indian .................... 50
Newton Farm Dairy - Ellicott City, Md.,
quart, round, embossed ................................ 35
Oak Grove Dairy - Windsor, N.C., quart,
round, embossed ........................................... 30
Peapack Gladstone Dairy, quart, round,
embossed....................................................... 15
Pet Milk Company, quart, round, pyro.............. 30
Quality Coughlin Dairy - Pierre, S.D.,
quart, round, pyro.......................................... 60
Quality Dairy W. Fudge - El Dorado, Ark.,
quart, round, embossed ................................ 30
Redford Farm D. Cardillo - Stockbridge,
Mass., quart, round, pyro.............................. 35
Rices Dairy Benzie County - Benzonia,
Mich., quart, round, pyro............................... 45
Riverview Farms - Frankfort, Ky., pint,
round, pyro..................................................... 18
Sanitary Dairy - Fort Dodge, Ia., quart,
round, pyro, cream top .................................. 35
Sawyer Farms - Gilford, N.H., quart,
round, pyro, baby top .................................. 125
Silver Leaf Dairy Guernsey - Ironwood,
Mich., pint, round, pyro .................................
Southern Dairy Farm - Tuscaloosa, Ala.,
quart, round, pyro.......................................... 70
Southside Dairy - Oneonta, N.Y., quart,
round, pyro, large tree................................... 40
Sunny Brook Farm - Alhambra, Calif.,
half-pint, round, pyro ..................................... 15

*Walthours Dairy Milk Bottle*

**Sweet's Dairy - Fredonia, N.Y.,** quart, round, pyro, cop the cream .......................... 200
**The Dell Newtown Bucks Co. - PA,** quart, round, pyro ................................................ 125
**Tyoga Farms Dairy,** quart, square, pyro, bulk milk truck .................................... 15
**Walthours Dairy - Greensburg, PA,** quart, round, pyro, 2 color (ILLUS. bottom previous page)...................................................... 75
**Winchester Creamery - Winchester, Va.,** half-pint, round, pyro ..................................... 40

*Winona Quart Milk Bottle*

**Winona - Winona Lake, IN,** quart, round, pyro (ILLUS.).................................................. 95

# MINERAL WATERS, SODAS & SARSAPARILLAS

**Adirondack Spring - Westport, N.Y.,** cylindrical w/applied sloping double collar mouth, ca. 1865-80, deep emerald green, qt. ..................................................... 242
**Andrae (C.) Port Huron, Michigan,** Hutchinson stopper w/applied top, cobalt blue (some wear & scratches, needs cleaning) ............................................................. 550
**B.B.W. San Rafael,** Hutchinson stopper w/tooled top, California, late 19th c., light aqua (some wear) ......................................... 33
**Blaffer (J.A.) & Co. - New Orleans,** cylindrical w/tall neck & applied double collar mouth, ca. 1865-75, deep golden amber, 6 3/8" h. (some scratching) .......................... 242

*Rare Ten Pin-Shaped Mineral Water*

**Borcman (H.) Mineral Water Manufacturer - Cumberland, MD.,** ten pinshaped, applied mouth, iron pontil, ca. 1845-55, pinhead flake on lip, deep cobalt blue, 8 1/4" h. (ILLUS.) ................... 3,850
**C & K Eagle Works Sac. City,** applied top, smooth base, California, 1858-66, light cobalt blue (polished) ........................... 66

*Owen Casey Soda Water Bottle*

**Casey (Owen) Eagle Soda Works - Sac City,** cylindrical w/applied mouth & smooth base, ca. 1860-70, medium cobalt blue, 7 1/8" h. (ILLUS.) ...................... 143
**Champion Spouting Spring - Saratoga Mineral - Spring - (superimposed over) C.S.S. Co. (monogram) - Limited - Saratoga N.Y. - Champion - Water,** cylindrical w/applied sloping collar mouth, bluish aqua, ca. 1865-80, pt. ......... 72
**Clark (Charles) - Charleston - SC - Soda - Water,** cylindrical w/applied sloping collar mouth, iron pontil, ca. 1845-55, medium green, 7 7/8" h. (some overall stain & ground lines) .................................... 143

*Clarke & Co. Mineral Water Bottle*

**Clarke & Co. - New-York,** cylindrical w/applied ringed mouth & smooth base, ca. 1855-65, black olive amber, 7 5/8" h. (ILLUS.)......................................... 440

Clarke (John) - New York (around shoulder), cylindrical w/applied sloping double collar mouth, pontiled base, ca. 1855-60, medium yellowish olive amber, qt. .............. 176

Clarke & White - New York, cylindrical w/applied sloping double collar mouth, ca. 1860-75, deep forest green, pt. .............. 55

Clarke & White - New York, cylindrical w/applied sloping double collar mouth, ca. 1860-75, deep emerald or forest green, qt. ....................... 66

Clarke & White - New York, cylindrical w/applied sloping double collar mouth, ca. 1860-75, deep emerald green, pt. ........... 77

Classen & Co. - design of crossed anchors - Sparkling, cylindrical w/applied mouth, sapphire blue, dug, 7 5/8" h. ....................................... 330

*Early Coca-Cola Bottle*

Coca-Cola Bottling Co., Inc. Binghamton, cylindrical machine-made w/crown top, ca. 1900-10, yellow olive, 7 3/4" h. (ILLUS.)....................... 105

Congress & Empire - Spring (C in frame) - Saratoga. N.Y. - Congress - Water, cylindrical w/applied sloping double collar mouth, deep emerald green, ca. 1865-75, dug, pt. ......................... 853

Congress & Empire Spring - C - Saratoga, N.Y. - Congress - Water, cylindrical w/applied sloping double collar mouth, deep emerald green, crude, ca. 1860-75, pt. .............. 143

Congress & Empire Spring Co. - Hotchkiss' Sons - C - New-York - Saratoga, N.Y., cylindrical w/applied sloping double collar mouth, ca. 1865-75, deep emerald green, qt. ....................... 116

Cooper's Well Water - Miss. - B.B. Co., cylindrical w/applied straight double collar mouth, heavy overall ground stain, ca. 1875-85, amber, qt. ...................... 121

D.S. & Co. San Francisco, applied top, smooth base, 1861-64, dark cobalt blue (lightly cleaned) ............................................. 231

Deep Rock Spring - Trade - Deep Rock - Mark - Oswego N.Y. - DRS (monogram), cylindrical w/applied sloping double collar, aqua, 1870-80, pt. ...................... 231

Dewer (James). Elko, Nevada, Hutchinson stopper, 1892-95, clear ..................... 1,870

Eagle (W.) - New-York - Union Glass Works Phila. - Superior - Mineral Water, cylindrical w/paneled base & applied sloping collar mouth, iron pontil, ca. 1845-55, medium sapphire blue, 7 1/2" h. (lightly cleaned, faint bruise on lip)................. 385

Empire Soda Works - Vallejo (design of eagle), cylindrical w/applied mouth, ca. 1860-70, bluish green, 7 3/8" h. .................. 110

Eureka - California Soda Water Co. S.F., w/eagle design, Hutchinson stopper w/tooled mouth, aqua (minor case wear) ....... 88

Excelsior Spring, Saratoga, N.Y., cylindrical w/applied sloping double collar, ca. 1870-80, deep yellowish olive amber, pt., 7 3/4" h. (minor inside stain).................. 121

Excelsior Spring - Saratoga, N.Y., cylindrical w/applied sloping double collar, ca. 1870-80, deep bluish green, qt. (minor scratches) ................. 121

Fehr (John) - Reading, wide cylindrical form w/applied sloping double collar mouth, iron pontil, ca. 1845-55, medium bluish green, 7" h. (lightly cleaned) ............. 198

Fields - Superior - Soda Water - Charleston - S. C., octagonal w/applied sloping collar mouth, iron pontil, ca. 1845-55, deep cobalt blue, 7 5/8" h. (two tiny under collar flakes, interior & exterior stain) ................. 358

Gardner (John H.) & Son - Sharon Springs - N.Y., cylindrical w/rounded shoulder & applied sloping double collar mouth, medium teal blue, ca. 1865-75, pt. ................. 303

Gettysburg Katalysine Water, cylindrical w/tall neck & applied sloping double collar, ca. 1865-80, lots of bubbles, emerald green, qt., 9 5/8" h. ........................ 88

Gettysburg Katalysine Water, cylindrical w/tall neck & applied sloping double collar, ca. 1865-80, olive green, qt., 9 5/8" h. ................. 132

Guilford Mineral - GMWS (inside circle) - Guilford - VT - Spring Water, cylindrical w/tall tapering neck & applied sloping double collar mouth, deep bluish green, ca. 1870-80, qt. ................. 159

Guilford Mineral - GMWS (inside circle) - Guilford - VT - Spring Water, cylindrical w/tall tapering neck & applied sloping double collar mouth, 99% original paper labels, deep teal green, ca. 1870-80, qt. (potstone w/small stress crack) .................. 209

Haas Bros - Natural - Mineral Water - Napa - Soda, cylindrical w/applied mouth, ca. 1860-70, deep sapphire blue, lightly cleaned, 7 3/8" h. ......................... 121

Harris (J.W.) Soda New Haven, Conn., applied top, iron pontil, ca. 1845-55, clear ....... 440

Harris Lithia Water - Harris Springs - S.C., cylindrical w/short neck & tooled mouth, ca. 1890-1910, greenish aqua, 1/2 gal. ................................................ 66

**Highrock Congress Spring- 1767- (design of a rock), C. & W. Saratoga N.Y.,** cylindrical w/applied sloping double collar mouth, deep chocolate amber, ca. 1865-75, qt. ............................... 242

**Highrock Congress Spring (design of a rock), C. & W. Saratoga N.Y.,** cylindrical w/applied sloping double collar, ca. 1865-75, medium root beer amber, pt. ........ 198

**Highrock Congress Spring (variant design of a rock), C. & W. Saratoga N.Y.,** cylindrical w/applied sloping double collar, ca. 1865-75, medium root beer amber, pt. ............................................ 358

**Jackson's Napa Soda,** applied top, 1873-85, cobalt blue (minor interior stain) ............. 605

**Kensington - Glassworks,** wide cylindrical form w/applied sloping double collar mouth, iron pontil, ca. 1845-55, medium emerald green, 7 1/4" h. (inside stain) ........ 187

**Kissingen Water - Patterson & Brazeau,** cylindrical w/applied sloping collar mouth, yellowish lime green, ca. 1870-85, pt. ...................................................... 143

**Knowlton (D.A.) - Saratoga - N.Y.,** cylindrical w/applied sloping double collar mouth, deep olive green, ca. 1855-70, dug, pt. ...................................................... 154

**L. & Cochcrane - Selzer (on shoulder),** bulbous cylindrical w/slender neck & applied blob top, ca. 1865-75, English, medium pinkish puce w/wisps of darker color, 7" h. (lightly cleaned, illegible words on back) ........................................... 187

*Lappeus Soda Water Bottle*

**Lappeus (Wm. W.) Premium Soda & Mineral Water - Albany,** ten-sided w/applied blob top & iron pontil, ca. 1845-55, cobalt blue, 7" h. (ILLUS.) .......... **1,073**

**Ledic (A.) - Utica - Bottling Establishment - Superior - Water - Mineral,** cylindrical 24-sided 'teepee' form w/applied mouth, iron pontil, ca. 1845-55, deep cobalt blue, 7 5/8" h ................... **1,165**

**Massena Spring - (monogram in frame above bird) - Water,** cylindrical w/applied sloping double collar mouth, ca. 1870-80, medium amber, qt. ...... 132

**Massena Spring - (monogram in frame above bird) - Water,** cylindrical w/applied sloping double collar mouth, ca. 1870-80, medium teal blue, qt. ..................................................................... 165

**McIntire (E.) - Mineral - Patent,** cylindrical w/applied sloping collar mouth, iron pontil, ca. 1835-45, medium green, 6 3/4" h. (minor case wear) ......................... 495

**Missisquoi - A - Springs,** cylindrical w/applied sloping double collar mouth, ca. 1865-80, deep emerald amber, qt. (in-making chip from under applied collar) ...................................... 99

**Naturliches - Miner Wasser - Doppelkohlens. - Fullung - Des - Apollinaris - Brunnen,** cylindrical w/tall neck & applied mouth, ca. 1865-75, Germany, olive green, crude, dug, 10" h. ................... 121

**Nevada City Soda Works - L. Seibert,** applied top, smooth base, 1880s, aqua ......... 66

**New Liberty - Soda W. Co. - Trade (design of Liberty head) Mark - S.F.,** cylindrical w/short neck & tooled mouth, Hutchinson closure-type, ca. 1890-1900, aqua, 6 3/4" h. (very minor ground pecks) ...................................................... 66

**Oak Orchard - Acid Springs - Alabama - Genesee Co. N.Y. (around shoulder),** cylindrical w/applied sloping double collar mouth, ca. 1865-80, deep bluish green, qt. ...................................................... 200

**Oak Orchard - Acid Springs - H.W. Bostwick - Agt. No. 574 - Broadway, New York,** cylindrical w/applied sloping double collar mouth, embossed on smooth base "Glass From F. Hitchins Factory - Lockport, N.Y.," deep root beer amber, qt. ...................................................... 154

*Rare Townsend's Sarsaparilla Bottle*

**Old Dr. Townsend's Sarsaparilla - New York,** square w/beveled corners, applied sloping collar mouth, open pontil, ca. 1845-55, tiny flake on lip, deep tobacco amber, 9 1/2" h. (ILLUS.) ........................... **2,530**

*Ormsby Soda Water Bottle*

**Ormsby (D.L.) New York Union Glass Works - Phila.,** cylindrical w/applied blob top & iron pontil, ca. 1845-55, deep vivid cobalt blue, 7 3/8" h. (ILLUS.) .............. **605**
**Pavilion & United States Spring Co. - Saratoga, N.Y. - Pavilion Water - Aperient,** cylindrical w/rounded shoulder & applied sloping double collar mouth, deep Lockport green, ca. 1865-80, pt. ......... **242**
**Pavilion & United States Spring Co. - Saratoga, N.Y. - Pavilion Water - Aperient,** cylindrical w/rounded shoulder & applied sloping double collar mouth, yellowish olive amber, ca. 1865-80, pt. .............. **330**

*Scarce Clear Poland Water Bottle*

**Poland - Water - Poland Mineral Spring Water (around monogram) - H. Ricker & Sons Proprietors,** figural, seated

Moses Poland, applied sloping collar mouth, unusual pontil-scarred base, lightly cleaned, ca. 1880-90, clear, 11 1/2" h. (ILLUS.) ....................................... **303**

*Rare Florida Mineral Water Bottle*

**Ponce de Leon Spring (monogram) Water - St. Augustine, Fl.,** cylindrical w/applied ringed mouth, smooth base, very minor imperfections, ca. 1870-80, yellowish olive green, pt., 7 1/2" h. (ILLUS.) .................................................... **4,070**
**Post (E.A.) Portland, Ogn.,** w/eagle motif, applied top, smooth base, 1881-83, clear ............................................................. **560**

*Cobalt Blue Ginger Ale Bottle*

**Ray (James) Savannah, Geo. - Ginger Ale,** Hutchinson stopper, cylindrical w/tooled mouth & smooth base, ca. 1870-80, lightly cleaned, deep cobalt blue, 8" h. (ILLUS.) ..................................... **468**
**Saint Leon - Spring Water (inside diamond enclosing) - Earl W. Johnson -**

27 - Congress St. - Boston - Mass., cylindrical w/applied sloping double collar mouth, medium emerald green, ca. 1870-80, pt. (faint bruise inside lip) .............. 148

Saratoga (design of star) Spring (backwards S), cylindrical w/applied sloping double collar mouth, deep yellowish olive green, ca. 1865-80, qt ......................... 121

Seedorff (J.) - Charleston - S.C., cylindrical w/applied blob top, ca. 1855-70, medium bluish green, 7" h. (light scratching) ..................................................... 330

Seedorff (John) - Charleston, S.C. (in slug plate), cylindrical w/applied blob top, iron pontil, ca. 1845-55, deep sapphire blue, 7 1/8" h. ............................... 253

Seedorff (John) - Charleston, S.C. (in slug plate), cylindrical w/applied mouth, iron pontil, ca. 1845-55, medium sapphire blue, 6 7/8" h. (tiny open shoulder bubble, minor stain & wear) ........................ 154

Smith (A.P.) - Charleston, S.C. (arched embossing variant), cylindrical w/applied sloping collar & iron pontil, deep cobalt blue, ca. 1845-55, 7 5/8" h. ...... 413

Smith (A.P.) - Charleston (slug plate variant), cylindrical w/applied sloping collar mouth, iron pontil, ca. 1845-55, deep cobalt blue, 7 3/8" h. (lightly cleaned) ..................................................... 242

Smith & - Fotheringham - Soda Water - St. Louis - This Bottle - Is Never Sold, ten-sided w/applied sloping collar mouth, iron pontil, ca. 1845-55, deep sapphire blue, 7 1/2" h. (light stain, some case wear) ........................................................... 605

*Southwick & Tupper Soda Bottle*

Southwick & G.O. Tupper - New York - Adna - H, ten-sided w/applied sloping collar mouth, iron pontil, ca. 1845-55, cobalt blue, 7 3/8" h. (ILLUS.) ..................... 550

Southwick & Tupper New York, applied top, iron pontil, early, dark cobalt blue (some resin repair in top) ............................ 132

*Unlisted Mineral Water Bottle*

St. Louis Artesian Mineral Water by W.H. Stevens & Co., cylindrical w/ringed applied mouth, smooth base, ca. 1865-75, unlisted, tiny cooling crack & lip flake, deep bluish aqua, 9 1/2" h. (ILLUS.) ..................................... **2,640**

St. Regis - Water - Massena Springs, cylindrical w/tall tapering neck & applied sloping double collar mouth, ca. 1870-80, medium teal blue, qt. ............................. 176

Star Spring Co. (design of star) Saratoga, N.Y., cylindrical w/applied sloping double collar, ca. 1865-80, deep reddish amber, pt., 7 5/8" h. (faint bruise inside lip) ......................................................... 61

Stenson (James) Chicago, Ills., wide cylindrical body w/rounded shoulder tapering to applied ringed top, amber ......... 121

Thomas (C.) - Truckee, Hutchinson stopper four-piece tooled top, California, ca. 1890s, aqua ................................................. 330

Townsend's (Dr.) - Sarsaparilla - Albany, N.Y., square w/beveled corners & applied sloping collar, ca. 1845-55, deep forest green, 9 1/2" h. ................................... 385

Townsend's (Dr.) - Sarsaparilla - Albany, N.Y., square w/beveled corners & applied sloping collar, iron pontil, ca. 1845-55, sapphire blue, 9 1/2" h. (repair in base) ......................................................... 523

Tweddale's - Mineral Waters, cylindrical w/applied sloping collar mouth, open pontil, ca. 1840-50, medium emerald green, 6 1/8" h. (chip off side of lip) .............. 303

Tweddale's Celebrated Soda or Mineral Water - Courtland Street - 38 New York, cylindrical w/applied blob top & iron pontil, very minor ground imperfections, ca. 1845-55, cobalt blue, 7 1/4" h. (ILLUS. top next page) .................. 209

V - Vincent & Hathaway - Boston - H - A.B.C. Co. - New Haven Ct - Pat. Jan. 5th 1864, cylindrical w/applied mouth & smooth base, ca. 1864-70, cobalt blue, 6 1/2" h. (ILLUS. center next page) .............. 275

*Tweddle's Soda Water Bottle*

*Vincent & Hathaway Soda Bottle*

**Vermont Spring - Saxe & Co. - Sheldon Vt.,** cylindrical w/a tall tapering neck & applied sloping double collar mouth, olive green, ca. 1870-80, qt. .......................... 99

**Vermont Spring - Saxe & Co. - Sheldon Vt.,** cylindrical w/a tall tapering neck & applied sloping double collar mouth, peach puce, ca. 1870-80, qt. (faint bruise on shoulder) ...................................... 330

**Voelker and Bro. Cleveland, O,** w/"V&B" on base, applied top, smooth base, light cobalt blue (needs cleaning) .......................... 77

**Washington Spring - Saratoga - N.Y.,** cylindrical w/rounded shoulder, applied sloping double collar mouth, medium emerald green, ca. 1865-80, pt. ................... 198

**Washington Spring - Saratoga - N.Y.,** cylindrical w/rounded shoulder, applied sloping double collar mouth, deep emerald green, ca. 1865-80, pt. .......................... 231

**Winkle (Henry) Sac. City,** applied top, iron pontil, California, 1852-54, greenish aqua (minor haze) ....................................... 209

**Wise (J.) - Allentown - PA - This Bottle - Belongs To - James Wise,** cylindrical w/long neck & applied sloping double collar, ca. 1855-65, deep cobalt blue, 7" h. ............................................................. 121

# PEPPERSAUCES

**Aqua,** cylindrical lobed sides below angled shoulder & tall ringed neck w/double rolled collar, open pontil, crude, 9 1/2" h. (cleaned) ......................................................... 88

**Aqua,** cylindrical lobed sides below angled shoulder & tall ringed neck w/double rolled collar, ground pontil, shoulder embossed "Wells Miller Provost Pepper Sauce," 9 1/2" h. (cleaned)............................ 99

**Aqua,** cylindrical lobed sides w/angled shoulder & tall ringed neck w/applied collar, open pontil, embossed "W.A. Lewis & Co." on shoulder, ca. 1850s, 8 1/4" h. ......................................................... 99

*Early Decorative Peppersauce Bottle*

**Deep bluish aqua,** four-sided square tapering shape w/ropetwist corners, applied double collar mouth, iron pontil, band of embossed stars up three sides, ca. 1855-65, 9" h. (ILLUS.) ............... 203

# PICKLE BOTTLES & JARS

**Aqua,** four-sided cathedral pickle, double-ring tooled mouth, smooth base, "S.J.G." on one panel, ca. 1855-65, 7 1/4" h. ........... 209

**Aqua,** four-sided cathedral shape, rolled lip, double neck ring, graphite pontil, 8 1/4" h. (lightly cleaned)............................. 358

**Deep bluish aqua,** four-sided cathedral shape, diamond lattice design in windows, double-ringed molded mouth, smooth base, 7 3/8" h. ................................. 193

**Deep greenish aqua,** four-sided cathedral shape, double-ringed tooled neck, smooth base, crude, 11 1/2" h. .................... **220**

**Deep purple,** four-sided w/rounded panels, double-ringed tooled neck, 7" h...................... **77**

*Golden Amber Early Pickle Bottle*

**Golden amber,** four-sided w/rounded panels, double-ringed tooled neck, 8" h. (ILLUS.)........................................................ **121**

*Early Sanborn Boston Pickle Bottle*

**Golden yellow amber,** tapering cylindrical form w/molded ground lip & smooth base, embossed on the side w/"G.P. Sanborn & Son - Union (inside shield & star) - Boston Pickle," ground lip, smooth base, 5 1/8" h. (ILLUS.)............................... **143**

**Green aqua,** four-sided cathedral shape w/star & diamond design in windows & molded shoulders, double-ringed molded mouth, smooth base, ca. 1860-70, 11 1/2" h. ............................................... **242**

**Medium blue green,** four-sided cathedral shape, double-ringed molded mouth, iron pontil, ca. 1855-65, small bruise inside lip, some minor grinding, 11 3/8" h. (ILLUS. top next column) ............. **468**

**Medium green,** cylindrical w/top & base rings & paneled rounded shoulder, applied mouth, iron pontil, ca. 1855-65, some milky inside stain, 12 1/4" h. (ILLUS. center next column) ..................... **1,705**

*Four-sided Cathedral Pickle*

*Rare Cylindrical Pickle Bottle*

**Pale blue aqua,** six-sided cathedral shape, double-ring tooled neck, embossed "I.C. CO." on base, one gal., 13" h. (some scratches).................................................... **165**

*Early Reddish Amber Pickle Bottle*

**Red amber,** four-sided w/recessed ribbing & outset columnar corners, applied top, smooth base, ca. 1860-75, lightly cleaned, 8 1/4" h. (ILLUS.) .......................... **358**

# POISONS

**Amber,** cylindrical embossed "Poison - Wyeth," 100% of original front & back paper labels, ABM lip, smooth base, ca. 1890-1910, 2 1/4" h. ..... **220**

**Clear,** cylindrical w/tooled top & some exterior striations, embossed "Strychinia Poison," 2 1/2" h. ................................. **44**

**Clear,** flask-shaped w/overall mold-blown Hobnail patt., sheared lip, pontil, ca. 1845-55, 4 3/8" h. ........................................ **110**

*Large Diamond Lattice Poison Bottle*

**Cobalt blue,** cylindrical w/overall embossed diamond lattice design, tooled lip, smooth base, ca. 1890-1910, 11 1/4" h. (ILLUS.) ...................................... **413**

**Cobalt blue,** rectangular w/beveled ribbed corners, "Poison" down the side, 4 1/4" h. ...................................................... **44**

**Cobalt blue,** square w/beveled corners w/"Poison," embossed stars & skull & crossbones on sides, w/original paper label, ABM, probably ca. 1915, small ........... **143**

**Cobalt blue,** three-sided w/embossed "Poison" on one side, design of owl & mortar & pestle on second & "The Owl Drug Co." on third, tooled lip, smooth base, ca. 1900-1910, 4 7/8" h. ...................... **88**

**Green,** rectangular w/ribbed beveled corners w/"Poison" & "The Sun Drug Company" on the front, 4" h. .............................. **231**

**Medium moss green,** three-sided embossed w/skull & crossbones & "De-Dro Gift Flasche Der Deutscher Drogisten Verbandes," ABM lip, smooth base, ca. 1910-20, Germany, 4 3/8" h. ........ **605**

**Olive green,** six-sided w/embossed skull & crossbones panels alternating w/"Poison - Gift" on panels, ABM lip, smooth base, Germany, ca. 1910-20, 9 3/4" h. (ILLUS.) ..... **358**

*German Green Poison Bottle*

**Turquoise blue overlay,** three-sided w/diamond lattice design & "Poison - Poison," tooled mouth, smooth base, w/original coffin-shaped pills each marked "Poison," ca. 1890-1910, slight wear, 5 1/4" h. ........................................... **132**

# WHISKEY & OTHER SPIRITS

**Beer,** "Capitol Bottling Works Petaluma, Cal." w/monogram, "P.C.G.W." on base, cylindrical w/tall neck, amber, qt. (minor stain) ................................................................ **44**

**Beer,** "Fredericksburg Bottling Co. S.F." in ring w/shield & monogram, cylindrical w/tall neck & wire & porcelain stopper, green, qt. ...................................................... **44**

*Unique Beer Bottle with Seal*

**Beer,** "Phoenix Bott'g Phila This Bottle Not To Be Sold" on applied shoulder seal, cylindrical w/applied mouth & smooth base, original lightning-type closure, ca. 1885-95, olive green, chip on lower edge of seal, 9 3/8" h. (ILLUS.) .............................. **413**

**Beer,** "Richmond Bottling Works," cylindrical w/tall neck & wire & porcelain stopper, amber, qt. (some interior haze) .............. **77**

**Beer,** "The Phoenix Brewery Co. Victoria B.C." w/embossed phoenix, cylindrical w/pontiled base & applied top, dark olive green, qt. (cleaned, some scratches) .......... **154**

**Beer,** "Tivoli Brewing Co. Registered Detroit Mich." in seal on shoulder, cylindrical w/tall neck, dark amber, qt. (few scratches) ...................................................... **33**

**Beer,** "Wreden's Lager Oakland Cal.," cylindrical w/tall neck, amber, qt. ................. **44**

**Case gin,** free-blown square tapering shape w/small crude applied top, open pontil, 1770-1830, light olive green ............. **143**

**Case gin,** free-blown tall slender square tapering shape w/applied flared lip, large open pontil, possibly 17th c., medium olive green, 9 1/2" h. .................................... **66**

**Gin,** "Cosmopoliet J.J. Melchers W.Z. Schiedam," tall square tapering form, dark green, 1850-70, 11" h. ........................ **121**

**Gin,** "London - Jockey - Club House - Gin" w/design of jockey on horse, square w/rounded shoulder & short neck w/applied sloping collar, iron pontil, ca. 1855-70, amber, 9 5/8" h. (tiny collar flake) ......................................................... **523**

**Schnapps,** "Burke's (E. & J.) Schiedam Schnapps," square w/beveled corners, applied sloping collar mouth, smooth base, ca. 1880-1900, deep olive amber, 8" h. ........................................................... **77**

**Schnapps,** "Gayen (J.T.) Schiedam Schnapps," square w/beveled corners, applied mouth, smooth base, ca. 1880-90, medium yellow olive green, 7 5/8" h. ........ **54**

**Schnapps,** "Nolet (A.C.A.) Schiedam Aromatic Schnapps," square w/beveled corners, applied sloping collar mouth, smooth base, ca. 1875-90, bright yellow olive, 9 3/8" h. ..................................... **94**

**Schnapps,** "Royal Club - Schnapps - Schiedam," square w/beveled corners, applied sloping collar mouth, smooth base, ca. 1880-1900, yellowish olive green, 7 3/4" h. ..................................... **54**

**Schnapps,** "Schade & Buysing's - Schiedam - Aromatic Schnapps," square w/beveled corners, applied sloping collar mouth, smooth base, 80% paper label w/"Sparrow Schiedam," ca. 1885-1900, medium olive green, 9" h. (ILLUS. top next column) ..................................... **88**

**Schnapps,** "Schiedam Schnapps - Aromatico," square w/beveled corners, applied sloping collar, smooth base, ca. 1855-65, deep olive amber, 9 1/4" h. ..................... **55**

**Schnapps,** "Silver Stream Schnapps - W & A Gilbey," tall square form w/beveled corners, applied sloping collar mouth, smooth base, ca. 1880-90, olive green w/amber tone, 8 3/8" h. (ILLUS. center next column) ..................................... **77**

**Schnapps,** "Udolpho Wolfe's Aromatic Schnapps, Schiedam," rectangular w/beveled corners, applied sloping collar mouth, dark green w/yellow tone, 9 3/8" h. ......................................................... **55**

*Schade & Buysing's Schnapps Bottle*

*Silver Stream Schnapps Bottle*

**Schnapps,** "Udolpho Wolfe's Aromatic Schnapps, Schiedam," rectangular w/beveled corners, applied sloping collar mouth, ca. 1880-90, medium olive green, 3 1/2" h. ............................................. **198**

**Schnapps,** "Udolpho Wolfe's Aromatic Schnapps, Schiedam," rectangular w/beveled corners, applied sloping collar mouth, smooth base, ca. 1860-70, medium apricot puce, 8 1/4" h. (ILLUS. top next page) ............................................. **220**

**Schnapps,** "Udolpho Wolfe's Aromatic Schnapps, Schiedam," rectangular w/beveled corners, applied sloping collar mouth, smooth base, ca. 1885-90, medium blue green, 9" h. ............................ **275**

*Udolpho Wolfe's Schnapps Bottle*

**Schnapps,** "Voldner's Aromatic Schnapps Schiedam," applied top, smooth base, bright medium lime green (minor scratches)....................................................... **88**

**Schnapps,** "Vollmar Schnapps," square w/beveled corners, tooled mouth, smooth base, ca. 1890-1900, bluish aqua, 8" h. ................................................. **39**

**Schnapps,** "Wolfe's (Hudson G.) - large embossed bell - Bell Schnapps," square w/beveled corners, applied mouth, smooth base, ca. 1870-80, medium amber, 9 7/8" h. (cleaned)............................. **99**

**Spirits,** club-shaped, twenty-four swirled ribs, aqua, early 19th c., 7 3/8" h. (minor wear) ............................................................. **94**

**Spirits,** free-blown, globular, amber, 11 3/4" h. (broken surface blisters, light stain) ........................................................... **303**

**Spirits,** globular, mold-blown, twenty-four swirled ribs, good impression, aqua, 7 1/2" h. (stain, lip chips) ............................. **154**

*Rare Early English Seal Bottle*

**Spirits,** "Greive (B) - 1727" seal bottle, bulbous cylindrical body tapering to a tall neck w/applied string lip & applied seal, open pontil, England, ca.1727, medium olive green, 4 1/2" d. base, 6 1/4" h. (ILLUS.)....................................................... **5,720**

**Spirits,** mold-blown, globular, twenty-four swirled ribs, Zanesville, Ohio, amber, 7 1/2" h. (stain, wear) .................................. **220**

**Spirits,** mold-blown, globular, twenty-four swirled ribs, Zanesville, Ohio, amber, 7 1/2" h. (stain)............................................ **385**

**Spirits,** squat bulbous form w/tall tapering neck w/applied ring, free-blown open pontil, deep emerald green-black, ca. 1650, 7 1/4" h. (chipping on lip in making) ..................................................................... **1,210**

**Spirits,** squatty onion-form, free-blown, tall tapering neck w/applied ring, open pontil, Holland, 1720-35, emerald green ........... **198**

*Early Dated Onion-shaped Bottle*

**Spirits,** "Watt (Nath) - 1718" seal bottle, squatty bulbous onion shape, tall tapering neck w/silver mouth band & applied seal, open pontil, minor content stain, England, ca. 1718, 5 3/4" d. base, 6 7/8" h. (ILLUS.)....................................... **3,630**

*Ambrosial Sealed Chestnut Flask*

Whiskey, "Ambrosial - B.M. & E.A.W. & Co." on seal, chestnut flask-shaped w/applied mouth, handle & seal, open pontil, ca. 1860-70, yellowish amber, 9 1/2" h. (ILLUS.) .......................................... **413**

*Rare Bininger Cannon Bottle*

Whiskey, "Bininger (A.M.) & Co. - 19 Broad St. - N.Y.," cannon-shaped, sheared lip, smooth base, 60% original paper label w/"Great Gun Bourbon," ca. 1855-70, medium amber, 12 1/2" h. (ILLUS. front & back) ........................................................ **585**

*Bininger Barrel-shaped Bottle*

Whiskey, "Bininger (A.M.) & Co. 19 Broad St. N.Y. - Distilled in 1848 - Old Kentucky - Bourbon - 1849 Reserve" w/embossed clock face, ringed barrel shape w/applied double collar mouth, open pontil, ca. 1855-65, medium amber, 8 1/8" h. (ILLUS.) ............................ **253**

Whiskey, "Bininger (A.M.) & Co 338 Broadway N.Y. - Distilled in 1848 - Old Kentucky - 1849 Reserve Bourbon," ringed barrel shape w/applied double collar mouth, open pontil, ca. 1855-65, medium amber, 8" h. .................................... **204**

Whiskey, "Bininger (A.M.) & Co. New York," square w/beveled corners, applied sloping collar mouth, smooth base, ca. 1855-70, medium amber, 9 3/4" h. ........................................................ **94**

Whiskey, "Bininger's (clock face) Regulator 19 Broad St. New York," round flat shape w/faint clock face, applied double collar mouth, open pontil, ca. 1855-65, yellow amber, 6" h. ........................................ **495**

Whiskey, "Bininger's Night Cap No. 19 Broad St. N.Y.," flattened rectangular form w/short neck & applied mouth w/internal screw threads, smooth base, ca. 1855-70, medium amber, 8 1/4" h. (stopper missing) ........................... **209**

Whiskey, "Brent. Warder & Co. - Louisville, KY," ringed barrel-shape w/applied mouth, smooth base, ca. 1865-75, medium copper puce, 6 7/8" h. (light content stain) ............................................. **2,255**

Whiskey, "Buffalo Old Bourbon (design of buffalo) Geo. E. Dierssen & Co. Sacramento, Cal.," cylindrical w/tall neck & tooled mouth, smooth base, ca. 1890-1910, clear, 11 7/8" h. ............................ **605**

Whiskey, "Carhart & Brother N.Y." on applied seal, handled chestnut flask-shape, applied mouth & handle, iron pontil, ca.1855-70, deep puce, 9" h. .......... **1,705**

*Rare Carhart Chestnut Flask Whiskey*

Whiskey, "Carhart & Brother N.Y." on applied seal, handled chestnut flask-shape, applied mouth & handle, iron pontil, ca.1855-70, medium smoky topaz puce, 8 3/4" h. (ILLUS.) .............................. **2,035**

Whiskey, "Caspers Whiskey - Made by Honest - North - Carolina People," cylindrical w/long lappets w/dots around the shoulder & a reeded neck w/a tooled mouth, smooth base, ca. 1880-90, deep cobalt blue, 12 3/8" h. .................................... **523**

*Rare Caspers Whiskey Clear Bottle*

**Whiskey,** "Caspers Whiskey - Made by Honest - North - Carolina People," cylindrical w/long lappets w/dots around the shoulder & a reeded neck w/a tooled mouth, smooth base, ca. 1880-90, clear w/amethystine tint, 12" h. (ILLUS.) .............. **578**

**Whiskey,** "Ce Tooraen Bayou Sara, La." embossed around shoulder, cylindrical w/tall neck & applied collar, stepped base, dark olive green, early rare Louisiana bottle, 11 1/2" h. ................................ **3,520**

**Whiskey,** "Chestnut Grove Whiskey, C.W." on applied seal, chestnut flask-shaped w/applied mouth w/spout & applied handle, open pontil, medium root beer amber, 8 1/2" h. ................................ **209**

**Whiskey,** "Chestnut Grove Whiskey, C.W." on applied seal, chestnut flask-shaped w/applied mouth w/spout & applied handle, open pontil, ca. 1860-70, yellow olive, 8 5/8" h. ............................................ **2,090**

**Whiskey,** "Crown Distilleries Company," cylindrical w/tall neck w/tooled lip & inside screw threads, amber, pt. (half-open bubble on shoulder) ............................ **55**

**Whiskey,** "Cutter (R.B.) Pure Bourbon," ovoid body w/applied mouth & handle, iron pontil, ca. 1855-65, two small stress cracks at handle, strawberry puce, 8 3/4" h. (ILLUS. top next column) ............. **303**

**Whiskey,** "Duffy' Formula" embossed on one side, original intact paper label on other side, tall slender cylindrical shape w/applied mouth & smooth base, ca. 1880-90, medium amber, 9 7/8" h. ............... **242**

**Whiskey,** "Duffy's Malt Whiskey Company - D.M.W. Co. (monogram) - Rochester, N.Y. U.S.A.," on base "Patd. Aug. 24 - 1886," cylindrical w/tooled mouth & smooth base, 85% original front & back paper labels, ca. 1890-1910, amber, 8 1/4" h. ......................................................... **44**

*R.B. Cutter Pure Bourbon Bottle*

*Forest Lawn Whiskey Bottle*

**Whiskey,** "Forest Lawn - J.V.H.," spherical body w/tall neck & applied mouth, iron pontil, ca. 1855-65, deep olive green, 7 1/2" h. (ILLUS.) ......................................... **440**

**Whiskey,** "G.D. & M. Baltimore" on applied shoulder seal, wide cylindrical body w/rounded shoulder & tall neck w/applied sloping double collar mouth, ca. 1870-85, medium amber, 9 1/2" h. ............................................................ **303**

**Whiskey,** "Good Old Bourbon - In A Hogs" w/arrow, pig-shaped, ca. 1885-1900, clear, 6 7/8" l. ................................................. **99**

**Whiskey,** "Graves (Jno.H.) Old Kentucky Whiskey San Jose Cal.," w/full paper label 90% intact, cylindrical w/tall neck & tooled top, amber, 1910-15, fifth .................... **88**

**Whiskey,** "Griffith Hyatt & Co. - Baltimore," bulbous ovoid shape tapering to neck w/applied mouth & applied handle, open

pontil, ca. 1860-70, medium tobacco
amber, 7 1/8" h. .......................................... **523**
Whiskey, "Lilienthal and Co. Distillers"
w/embossed crown in circular slug plate,
coffin flask-form, amber, 1885-90, pt. ...... **2,090**
Whiskey, "McFarlane & Co. Honolulu"
w/monogram, cylindrical w/tall tapering
neck & applied collar, amber, fifth ................. **99**
Whiskey, "Miller's Extra Trade Mark - E.
Martin & Co. Old Bourbon," flask-shape
w/applied mouth & smooth base, small
letter variant, ca. 1875-80, rich yellow
olive, 7 1/2" h. (small stress crack in
neck) ........................................................ **1,540**

*Rare Moore Western Whiskey Flask*

Whiskey, "Moore (Jesse) and Co. Louisville KY. Trademark Moore Hunt and
Co.," flask-shaped w/double applied collar mouth, w/monogram & deer antlers,
deep olive amber, minor imperfections,
cleaned (ILLUS.) ...................................... **6,050**
Whiskey, "Patent" on shoulder, "Wm.
McCully & Co. Pittsburgh" (on base),
cylindrical w/lady's leg neck, applied
double collar mouth, smooth base, ca.
1860-70, yellowish beer amber,
11 1/2" h. .................................................... **121**
Whiskey, "R. & S. (monogram) - Roehling
& Schutz, Inc. - Chicago," four-roof
cabin-shape, smooth base, tooled
mouth, ca. 1880-1890, amber, 9 3/4" h.
(small flake on edge of one roof panel) ........ **242**
Whiskey, "Rothenberg (D.) Co. Old Judge
Kentucky Whiskey," w/picture of the
judge drinking, cylindrical w/tall tapering
neck w/applied collar, amber, fifth ................. **33**
Whiskey, "Sacken Belcher & Co. 26 Pearl
St. N.Y." on applied seal, chestnut flask-
shape w/applied mouth & handle, open
pontil, ca. 1860-70, amber, 9" h. ............... **1,650**
Whiskey, "Simmond's Nabob Pure KY
Bourbon Whiskey," cylindrical
w/embossed scene of nabob, tooled
neck, small annealing check in neck,
open bubble on top, cleaned, clear
(ILLUS. top next column) ............................ **523**

*Scarce Clear Nabob Whiskey Bottle*

*Rare Semi-Cabin Whiskey Bottle*

Whiskey, "Smith (S.S.) & Co. - Cincinnati,"
semi-cabin shape, applied sloping collar
mouth, smooth base, ca. 1860-70,
medium cobalt blue, 9 5/8" h. (ILLUS.) ..... **3,190**
Whiskey, "Star Whiskey New York W.B.
Growell Jr." in oval, conical body
w/applied mouth w/spout & applied handle w/tip of finial missing, large open
pontil, ca. 1865-75, medium yellowish
amber, 8" h. (ILLUS. top next page) ............. **242**
Whiskey, "Taylor (G.O.)" on base, paper
label w/"G.O. Taylor Pure Rye," cylindri-
cal w/tall neck & tooled top, amber, fifth ......... **44**
Whiskey, "Teakettle Old Bourbon Shea,
Bocqueraz & McKee Agents San Francisco" w/embossed teakettle, cylindrical
w/tall neck & applied collar, bright
amber, fifth (pressure ding on lip, open
bubble on front) .........................................., **385**

*Star Whiskey Handled Bottle*

**Whiskey,** "Warranted Flask From The Culpepper Liquor Co Culpeper, VA," flattened strap-sided flask, smooth base, tooled mouth, ca. 1890-1900, clear ............. **413**

**Whiskey,** "Wertz (S.A.) Phila Superior Old Rye Whiskey" on appled shoulder seal, wide cylindrical body w/rounded shoulder & neck w/applied sloping double collar mouth, smooth base, ca. 1870-80, yellow amber, 9 1/2" h. (tiny potstone on back) ................................................................ **94**

**Whiskey,** "Wolters Bros. & Co. 115 & 117 Front Street SF," cylindrical w/tall neck & applied collar, brownish amber, fifth (minor dirt inside) ......................................... **285**

**Wine,** "Heller (A.) & Bro." under crest on applied neck seal, tall slender tapering cylindrical body w/applied mouth, smooth base, ca. 1880-90, reddish amber, 14" h. ................................................. **121**

**Wine,** "Kohler & Van Bergen San Francisco" w/monogram & "1883," cylindrical w/slender neck & ringed mouth, seal on shoulder, dark green, qt. ............................ **143**

**Wine,** "Napa Valley Wine Co. SF 1890" in seal on shoulder, cylindrical w/slender neck & ringed mouth, very dark green, qt. ......................................................................... **55**

**Wine,** "Paul O. Burns Wine Co. Proprietors Yerba Buena San Jose Cal. U.S." on shoulder seal, cylindrical w/lady's leg neck, applied collar, medium to deep olive green, ca. 1890s, qt. ........................... **143**

# BOXES

**Band box,** cov., wallpaper-covered cardboard, deep oval cylindrical base w/flat fitted cover, paper w/a simple design of stripes & panels in blue & white w/pink, green, blue & white in unfaded area inside rim, lined w/"Columbian Centinel" newspaper, Boston, 1820, 20 1/2" l. (wear, stains, some damage) ..................... **$440**

*Three Early Band Boxes*

**Band box,** cov., wallpaper-covered pasteboard, deep oval sides w/fitted flat cover, the "Clayton's Ascent" wallpaper depicting hot air balloons in flight in various colors, labled on underside of cover "From J.M. Hurlbert's paste board band box manufactory no. 25 Court Street, Boston," early 19th c., imperfections, 12 1/2 x 17 3/4", 12 1/4" h. (ILLUS. left) ....... **978**

**Band box,** deep oval sides w/fitted flat cover, the sides w/paper depicting a scene of a stagecoach amid hunters, imperfections, early 19th c., 17 3/4" l., 11" h. (ILLUS. right) .................................... **144**

**Band box,** wallpaper-covered pasteboard, deep oval sides w/fitted flat cover, decorated w/paper showing large birds perched among large flowering ground & w/an architectural view, 19th c., imperfections, 16 3/4" l., 10 3/8" h. (ILLUS. top center) ......................................................... **489**

**Band box,** wallpaper-covered cardboard, round cylindrical form w/a flat fitted cover, the wallpaper w/a bold design of birds among flowering branches in green, yellow, white & faded red on a blue & white ground, first half 19th c., 17 1/2" d., 11 1/4" h. (wear, edge damage) ............................................................. **440**

**Bentwood box,** cylindrical w/lapped seams w/wrought-iron nails, fitted flat cover w/lapped edge band, old worn grey paint, interior w/light colored wash w/some residue, 15" d., 8 1/4" h. (edge damage to base) ......................................... **550**

**Bentwood box,** painted, oval w/deep base w/wide single finger lappet, the fitted flat cover w/single lappet, old grey paint, 17 1/2" l. ......................................................... **633**

*Finely Carved Bride's Box*

**Bride's box,** chip-carved maple & pine, ovoid bentwood, the slightly domed fitted cover decorated w/carved hearts, hex signs & pinwheels, opening to a well w/a mid-molding & molded base, probably Europe, 19th c., 9 x 15 1/2", 7" h. (ILLUS.)...................................................... **3,737**

**Bride's box,** painted pine, oval bentwood w/stitched seams, original blue paint decorated around the sides of the top & bottom w/bands of bold stylized flowers & fruit vines, the top decorated w/a bowl of flowers, Europe, 19th c., 18 1/2" l. (wear, some edge damage, glued lid split)........................................................ **880**

**Bride's box,** pine bentwood, oval w/fitted cover, deep sides decorated w/original floral decoration in red, yellow, orange, green, black & white, the flat cover w/the figure of an angel, interior w/old paper patches, Europe, 19th c., 17" l. (lacing on base missing, wear, edge damage) ..... **1,430**

*Ornately Decorated Glass Box*

**Glass box w/hinged cover,** round squatty bulbous base w/brass fittings, cobalt blue ornately decorated on the top & around the sides w/gold bands w/geometric designs in pink, white, yellow, rust & red, including pendent hearts, late 19th c., 4" d., 2 1/2" h. (ILLUS.)................... **135**

*Floral-decorated Glass Box*

**Glass box w/hinged cover,** squatty round form w/brass fittings, cobalt blue enameled around the cover & base w/bold white & gold-dotted swags divided by large white & pink blossoms & tiny blossoms clusters, the cover w/an inner band of lily-of-the-valley blossoms, Europe, late 19th - early 20th c., 4 3/4" d. (ILLUS.)......................................... **225**

*Porcelain Figural Money Box*

**Money box,** porcelain, figural, modeled as a tan basketweave basket w/a little girl peeking out the top, she wearing a blue dress & w/black hair & painted facial features, money slot in the top, late 19th - early 20th c., 2 x 2 3/4", 2 1/2" h. (ILLUS.)........................................................ **75**

**Paint box,** painted pine, rectangular w/tin latch & interior of various carved compartments including four lined w/tin & two lined w/blue & white floral transfer-decorated ceramic, a lidded compart-

*Walnut & Pine Candle Box*

**Candle box,** hanging-type, walnut & pine, the rectangular raised-panel retractable lid w/shaped handles within a conforming box frame & a matching background pierced for hanging, patch to lower right corner of lid, repair to top of background, batch to base & lacks side moldings, American, early 19th c., 4 1/2 x 9 1/4", 18 3/4" h. (ILLUS.)........................................ **460**

**Candle box,** inlaid cherry, rectangular case w/bevel-edged sliding lid w/a central inlaid ebony diamond & a narrow band around the base, 19th c., 11" l. (age crack in bottom, edge damage & wear) ....... **248**

**Candle box,** painted pine, rectangular w/dovetailed sliding flat lid, worn original red painted ground w/black & yellow striping & gold-stenciled deer, horses & compote of fruit & leaves, first half 19th c., 8 x 12", 9 1/2" h. (lid replacement w/dark weathered finish) ............................. **303**

**Candlebox,** pine, rectangular w/inset sliding flat lid, old red finish, 19th c., 6" l. ............ **440**

ment contains two ceramic & one glass imbibing reservoir, some orange & blue pigments remain, American 19th c., 2 3/4 x 6 1/2", 7/8" h. (lacking three lids for interior compartments, wear, crazing on exterior) ................................................. 316

**Pantry box,** painted wood, stave construction fastened w/two woven lap hoops, carved initials on flat cover "R.P.F.," painted green, mid-19th c., 14 1/2" d., 6 1/2" h. (minor paint loss) .......................... 863

**Patch box,** ivory, steel & jasper ware, narrow oval flat-topped ivory box w/an inlaid oval blue Wedgwood jasper ware medallion w/a white relief classical figure flanked by two smaller jasper ware medallions each within a cut-steel oval frame, no visible marks, England, early 19th c., 3 3/4" l. (slight line in ivory).............. 805

*Stained Poplar Pipe Box*

**Pipe box,** hanging-type, stained poplar, tall upright square form w/scalloped top sides flanking the arched backboard w/hanging hole, a small thumb-molded bottom drawer w/brass knob, molded base, nailed construction, mahogany stain, early 19th c., minor wear, 4 3/4 x 5", 22" h. (ILLUS.) ........................ **2,615**

*Dutch Silver Box*

**Silver box,** round w/hinged cover, the sides chased & embossed w/classical style scrolls & husk swags, the cover

w/fluting & central engraved roundel w/heraldic design & inscription, .934 fine, Holland, late 19th c., 4 3/4" d., 3 1/8" h. (ILLUS.)............................................. **978**

**Storage box,** carved & painted wood, rectangular top w/yellow pinstriped simulated stringing on a conforming box w/horizontal reeding, old red paint, New England, early 19th c., 4 1/2 x 8 3/4", 3 3/4" h. ...................................................... **920**

**Storage box,** curly maple, rectangular w/hinged lid on the dovetailed base, putty inlaid star on cover, soft rubbed-down finish, 19th c., 7 3/8" l. ......................... **715**

**Storage box,** painted & decorated curly maple, rectangular, academy-decorated overall w/h.p. pink & green floral vines & seashells, signed "Maria" in a banner on the back, raised on tiny bun feet, mid-19th c., 6 1/2 x 9 3/4", 3 1/2" h. (surface wear, minor damage at hinge area) .......... **4,025**

*Early Painted Storage Box*

**Storage box,** painted & decorated pine, deep rectangular form w/sliding lid, decorated around the sides w/a continuous primitive landscape w/colorful houses & trees on a white ground, wear & minor repair, 19th c., 8 3/4" l. (ILLUS.)............... **1,100**

**Storage box,** painted & decorated pine, rectangular low domed cover above the flat sides, original orangish red ground w/yellow striping & large stylized flowers in red, white, green & mahogany, wire & tin hinges & tin hasp, attributed to Heinrich Bucher, first half 19th c., 9 3/8" l. (some edge damage) ............................... **7,700**

**Storage box,** painted & decorated pine, rectangular top w/a central rectangular landscape scene w/mountains, a lake & buildings, additional polychrome floral decoration, original dark painted ground w/grey & red red striping, matching decoration on lid interior also inscribed "To Jennie," 19th c., 9 7/8" l. (lock removed)...... **974**

**Storage box,** painted & decorated poplar, rectangular top decorated w/a sailing ship w/the American flag, the dovetailed base decorated w/gold, red & black striping & foliage decoration on the original blue ground w/worn yellowed varnish, w/lock & key, attributed to Baltimore, early 19th c., 7 1/2" l................................. **3,300**

**Storage box,** painted pine, rectangular w/dovetailed construction, interior w/a sliding panel opening to a compartment & a drawer below, painted green, New England, early 19th c., 17 3/4 x 34", 18" h. ....................................................... **460**

*Box with Painted Paper Decoration*

**Storage box,** paper-covered wood, rectangular w/a deep hinged lid, the sides hand-painted w/a village landscape w/a church & large houses among trees, a swag & tassel decoration around the cover, in green, red, brown & yellow on darkened white, early 19th c. (ILLUS.)...... **9,350**

**Tine box,** painted bentwood, oval w/tacked seam, upright end posts spring-fastened to hold the flat oval cover w/central loop handle, green textured repaint, Scandinavian, 19th c., 10 1/2" l. ................... **330**

*Fine Carved Walnut Wall Box*

**Wall box,** carved & painted walnut, the arched cornice molding flanking a carved central leaf crest above tasseled corner pendants & curving sides continuing to a box w/carved vines & leaves flanked by cross-hatching, the leaf & vine designs continue throughout the box, an arched mirror in the center top, dark reddish brown stain w/old black paint, Pennsylvania or Connecticut, ca. 1830-40, minor imperfections, 12" w., 20 1/4" h. (ILLUS.).................................... **1,955**

**Wall box,** grain-painted & stenciled wood, nailed & dovetailed box w/lower drawer & shaped backboard pierced for hanging, grained in red & black & stenciled in bronze, 19th c., 7 x 12 3/4", 10" h.

(repaired crack in backboard, bottom board, surface wear) ................................. **1,840**

# BREWERIANA

*Beer is still popular in this country but the number of breweries has greatly diminished. More than 1,900 breweries were in operation in the 1870s but we find fewer than 40 major breweries supply the demands of the country a century later, although micro-breweries have recently sprung up across the country.*

*Advertising items used to promote various breweries, especially those issued prior to prohibition, now attract an ever growing number of collectors. The breweriana items listed are a sampling of the many items available.*

*Budweiser Girl Advertisement*

**Advertisement,** cardboard w/outdoor scene of lady wearing long red dress holding bottle of Budweiser beer, newer wood frame, water stain, scratches & soiling, top corners missing, nail holes to edges, edge tears to one side, 20 1/2" w., 35" h. (ILLUS.).......................... **$660**

*White Rock Beer Advertisement*

**Advertisement,** tin lithograph in wood frame, scene of girl holding sheath of wheat w/countryside in background, bottle of White Rock to side w/"The Akron Brewing Co., Akron, Ohio" & "White Rock Bottled Beer" on mountain in background, scratches & small paint chips , frame w/overall wear, 24 3/4 x 33" (ILLUS.) ......... **616**

*Cone Top Beer Cans*

**Beer can,** "Cold Spring Lager Beer," metal, cone top w/original cap, greyish green, black, white & red, Cold Spring, Minnesota (ILLUS. left) ......... **125**

**Beer can,** "Fauerbach C B Centennial Brew,"Cold Spring Lager Beer," metal, cone top, white & red w/gold trim, Madison, Wisconsin (ILLUS. center) ......... **128**

**Beer can,** "Royal Bohemian Style Beer," metal, cone top w/original cap, white w/dark blue & red & gold trim, "Duluth Brewing & Malting Co., Duluth, Minn." at bottom (ILLUS. right) ......... **128**

*Pilsner Beer Glasses*

**Beer glass,** "Hamm's" red enameled letters w/"Born in the land of sky blue water" in black enameled letters, St. Paul, Minnesota (ILLUS. far left) ......... **57**

*Enameled Beer Glasses*

**Beer glass,** "Knapstein's Beer," New London, Wisconsin, red enameled lettering (ILLUS. far left) ......... **120**

**Beer glass,** "Manhattan Premium," & logo in red & black enameled letters, Chicago, Illinois (ILLUS. second from left) ......... **95**

**Beer glass,** "Nectar Beer," red enameled lettering & logo w/"Ambrosia Brewing Co. - Chicago, ILL." (ILLUS. second from left) ......... **16**

**Beer glass,** "Pabst Blue Ribbon - Crown Inn," red enameled lettering (ILLUS. second from right) ......... **33**

**Beer glass,** "Royal Select," black enameled lettering, Spokane, Washington (ILLUS. second from right) ......... **151**

**Beer glass,** "Van Merritt Beer," black enameled logo w/Dutch girl & "The World's Most Honored Beer," Burlington, Wisconsin (ILLUS. far right) ......... **52**

**Beer glass,** "Zoller's Beer" black enameled lettering & figure of pirate w/sword, Davenport, Iowa (ILLUS. far right) ......... **83**

**Brochure,** Pabst Brewing Company, titled "A Little Talk Over the Wires" showing a man & a woman talking to each other on old wall phones, ca. 1900s, unfolded, mint condition, 6 1/2 x 7 1/2" ......... **60**

**Clock,** Fort Pitt Beer, electric wall-type, tin clock face, glass cover & reverse painted glass advertising at top w/"Fort Pitt Special Beer," metal housing, 25" w., 16" h. (face paint cracked, scratches & dents) ......... **110**

**Clock,** Schaefer Beer, electric wall model, plastic, barrel-shaped w/lighted advertising, clock on one end, Schaefer logo on other, 9" d., 12" h. ......... **55**

*Budweiser Decanter Set*

**Decanter set:** pottery, tall cylindrical decanter w/tapering shoulder, short cylindrical neck w/original rounded blue top & six cylindrical tumblers; Budweiser CS35, Blue Holanda patt. on white ground, the set (ILLUS.) ......... **1,224**

**Door push,** rectangular, tin, lithograph shows can & bottle w/"We Serve Stegmai's Gold Medal Beer" shield form at top & "Take Home a Supply" at bottom,

3 1/2 x 8" (minor surface dirt & hole scratched) ...................... **94**

**Light globe,** "Record's Ale" high profile metal body w/two round glass lenses, four-leaf clover design w/waterfall scene in center, lenses taped in, 15 1/2" d. (minor scratches & soiling)...................... **1,100**

*Rumph Mugs*

**Mug,** pottery, Rumph, cylindrical w/incurved side near scrolled handle, opposite side slightly rounded, "Drunk Man, Morning After," relief-molded caricature of man's head w/hot water bottle, mottled brown (ILLUS. left) ........................... **40**

**Mug,** pottery, Rumph, tree trunk-form w/branch handle, relief molded long-billed bird perched on top, mottled brown (ILLUS. right)................................... **35**

**Mug,** pottery, Rumph, waisted cylindrical w/C-form handle, relief molded Republican elephant head opposite & stars & "USA" on side, mottled brown (ILLUS. center)........................ **147**

**Sign,** "Bull's Eye Beer," porcelain, square, target in red, white & blue w/"Bull's Eye Beer - Golden West Brewing Co's. Oakland, California," 18" (waterstain & edgewear) ...................... **352**

**Sign,** reverse painted glass, "Gilt Edge Best Ruhstaller Beer Lager," metal enclosure w/two wall brackets, Achrach & Co., San Francisco, California, 18" d........ **550**

*Buffalo Lager Sign*

**Sign,** reverse painted wrap-around corner type, crackle glass lettering against a view of the brewery w/"Buffalo Lager - Buffalo Brewing Co., Sacramento, Cal.," 9 1/4 x 16 x 25 1/2" (ILLUS.)...................... **6,050**

**Sign,** round, electric light-up type, metal & reverse painted glass, "Betz Beer - Ale - Porter," 17" d. (soiling, flaking paint, metal back pitted & rust) .............................. **165**

**Sign,** round, reverse painted glass, red w/gold lettering "We feature Budweiser Bottled Beer," logo at top, 10 1/2" d. ............ **149**

**Sign,** tin lithographed over cardboard, colorful scene of fisherman standing in stream, two other men sitting on bank near woods, oval at sign reads "Champagne Velvet Beer" bottom marked "The Beer With The Million Dollar Flavor" & signed "Hg. Hintermeister," Terre Haute Brewing Co., Inc. Terre Haute, Indiana, 14 1/2 x 19 1/2" (scratches & soiling).......... **176**

*Ceramarte Steins*

**Stein,** Ceramarte, pottery, scalloped foot below rounded base w/bulbous body & rounded rim, white ground w/colorful center scene of man & milkmaid carrying buckets on shoulder yoke flanked by scrolling floral decoration, Brazil (ILLUS. right)......................................................... **294**

**Stein,** Ceramarte, pottery, tapering cylindrical form w/scene of dancing couples, Brazil (ILLUS. left)......................................... **101**

**Stein,** Ceramarte, pottery, tapering cylindrical form w/scene of two men sitting & holding mugs, w/woman standing between them holding a bottle & filling a mug, Brazil (ILLUS. center)......................... **140**

*Delft-like Budweiser Steins*

**Stein,** pottery, Budweiser, CS11, blue Delft-like design, Diamond patt. (ILLUS. far left) .......................................................... **295**

**Stein,** pottery, Budweiser, CS11, blue Delft-like design, Heart patt. (ILLUS. far right) ................................................................ **358**

**Stein,** pottery, Budweiser, CS11, blue Delft-like design, Spade patt. (ILLUS. second from left) .......................................... **358**

**Stein,** pottery, Budweiser, CS11, blue Delft-like design, Staple patt. (ILLUS. second from right) ........................................ **350**

**Stein,** pottery, Budweiser, tall tapering cylindrical body, German Cities series, CS16, Berlin (ILLUS. left top next page) ...... **310**

**Stein,** pottery, Budweiser, tall tapering cylindrical body, German Cities series, CS16, Heidelberg (ILLUS. center next page) ............................................................. **335**

*Budweiser German Cities Steins*

**Stein,** pottery, Budweiser, tall tapering cylindrical body, German Cities series, CS16, Munchen (ILLUS. right) .................... **400**

**Tap knob,** "E&B Ale," E&B Brewing Co., Detroit, Michiagn ivory, blue round disc & red rectangle w/white lettering .................. **42**

**Tap knob,** "Frederick's Extra Pale," red oval disc on silvered metal, Chicago, Illinois ............................................................... **178**

**Tap knob,** "Piel's Light Beer," black w/yellow round disc w/red & black lettering, Brooklyn, New York ....................................... **33**

**Tap knob,** "Trommer's White Label," ivory w/blue round disc, center star & wreath decoration in gold, white lettering ................. **33**

**Tray,** Budweiser Beer, tin lithographed, entitled "St. Louis Levee in Early Seventies" w/"Copyright 1914 Anheuser Busch, Inc.St. Louis - King of Bottled Beer" at the bottom, 12 3/4 x 17 1/2" (soiling & scratches) ...................................... **99**

**Tray,** lithographed metal, round, center scene of factory w/"Ruhstaller Gilt Edge Lager & Steam" in gold lettering at top, by American Art Works, Coshocton, Ohio, 13" d. (minor scrapes & edge dings) ............................................................... **440**

*Budweiser Wine Decanter Set*

**Wine decanter set:** pottery, footed bulbous body tapering to tall wide cylindrical neck w/pinched spout & six footed bulbous cups; Budweiser CS32, white ground decorated w/purple grape clusters & green scrolling leaves & vines, beaded trim at base & around neck of decanter w/scene of three monks in center, the set (ILLUS.) ................................................. **526**

**Yard long print,** double-sided paper lithograph showing young woman in purple dress, framed under glass, Pabst Brewery, 33 3/4" l. .................................................. **350**

# BUSTER BROWN COLLECTIBLES

*Buster Brown was a comic strip created by Richard Outcault in the New York Herald in 1902. It was subsequently syndicated and numerous objects depicting Buster (and often his dog, Tige) were produced.*

**Book,** "Buster Brown Blue Ribbon Book of Jokes & Jingles, No. 2," 1905 ................... **$950**

**Camera,** box-type ................................................ **40**

**Catalog,** 1937, brown leather-like cover, 100 pp. ........................................................... **125**

**Game,** linen-type, "Pin the Tail" game, w/original cardboard folder .......................... **225**

*Early Buster Brown Target Game*

**Game,** target-type, lithographed paper on wood, rectangular form w/the heads of the characters circled as the targets, a landscape background, Bliss, early 20th c., some fading & staining, 10 x 24" (ILLUS.) .............................................................. **575**

**Gun punch-out sheet,** ca. 1940s ...................... **60**

**Mug,** child's, porcelain, color transfer-printed scene of Buster w/a teapot & his dog, Tige ............................................................ **48**

**Playing cards,** complete deck in original box, ca. 1906 ............................................... **118**

**Tea set:** pitcher, creamer & cov. sugar bowl; child's, porcelain, color scenes of Buster & his friends, 3 pcs. .......................... **210**

**Tie slide,** ca. 1940s ............................................. **85**

*Rare Buster Brown Bell Toy*

**Toy,** cast-iron bell-type, four-wheeled w/Buster Brown steering & Tige riding above the bell, early 20th c., 7" l. (ILLUS.) ...................................................... **3,850**

# BUTTONS

*Buttons have reflected the world around us for more than two centuries. They have and continue to give us insights to both social and political movements throughout history.*

Millicent Safro, author of Buttons notes buttons with pictorial designs have been made in many periods, but those known by collectors as "picture buttons" came into vogue during the Victorian era in the second half of the 19th century. Usually metal with stamped designs, their varied array of subjects included animals, children, buildings, scenery, insects, fruit, flowers, birds, people, mythology, theater and opera. Many of the images are derived from contemporary illustrations, trade cards and a wide range of literary works including children's stories and fairy tales.

The following photographs and listings include not only buttons of the Victorian era, but a wide range of other 18th and 19th century buttons.

**Brass,** stamped, round, depicts arrival of Lohengrin in a swan boat, swirled border, Victorian, ca. 1880-90, 1 7/16" d...... **$15-20**

**Brass,** stamped, round, dove holding a branch in beak, mounted over black velvet background surrounded by leafy border, Victorian, ca. 1880-90, 1 1/2" d........ **20-25**

*Brass & Pearl Button*

**Brass,** stamped, round, faceted steel center, applied to pearl background & set in crimped steel border, ca. 1890-1900, 1 7/16" d. (ILLUS.)...................... **25-40**

**Brass,** stamped, round, figure of woman w/a parasol & picking an apple behind a fence, applied to pink tinted background & mounted in a decorative gated border, Victorian, ca. 1880-90, 1 7/16" d.............. **15-20**

*Whippet Brass Button*

**Brass,** stamped, round, large whippet head holding a whip in mouth, petal border decorated w/faceted steels, Victorian, ca. 1870-80, 1 3/8" d. (ILLUS.)........ **35-125**

**Brass,** stamped, round, moon & falling star, applied to wood background, France, ca. 1880-90, 1 3/16" d. ................... **40-45**

**Brass,** stamped, round, oak tree w/a decorative leafy border, applied to white metal background of buildings & a windmill, Victorian, ca. 1880-90, 1 5/8" d......... **20-25**

**Brass,** stamped, round, pierced, swallow with square-cut steels around the border, Victorian, ca. 1880-90, 1 5/8 d. ......... **35-45**

**Brass,** stamped, round, red tint, two kittens in a woven basket, mirrored background on border, Victorian, ca. 1880-90, 1 7/16" d. ...................... **75**

**Brass,** stamped, round, shows popular 19th c. French caricature "French Fop" on balcony holding a crook, Victorian, ca. 1880, 1 3/16" d. ........................... **30-45**

*Glazed Ceramic Button*

**Ceramic,** round, glazed w/transfer printed mythological head touched w/gold & mounted in darkened brass border, France, mid-19th c., 1 1/4" d. (ILLUS.).... **75-125**

*Boar Sporting Button*

**Copper & silver,** round, sporting button of silvered boar within a belt marked "Vautrait De Villeneuve," applied to gilded copper back, mid to late 19th c., 1 1/8" d. (ILLUS.) ...................................................... **30-35**

*Helmet Shell Cameo Button*

**Helmet shell,** round, finely carved Art Nouveau iris cameo, set in silver metal prongs, ca. 1898-1900, 1 1/4" d. (ILLUS.)................................................ **150-175**

**Ivory,** made of Alaskan walrus ivory, etched w/black pigmented decoration, ca. 1880-90, top 1", center 1 1/8", bottom 1 1/2" l., each (ILLUS. top next page) ........................................................ **45-50**

**Ivory under glass,** round, h.p. bust portrait of 18th c. young lady wearing large feathered hat, copper mounting, France, ca. 1770, 1 3/4" d. ................... **600-650**

*Alaskan Walrus Ivory Buttons*

**Painting under glass,** round, miniature portrait of aristocratic woman wearing a flamboyant hat, powdered hair & white lace shawl fastened w/flowers, painted in style of Thomas Gainsborough, set under glass w/a paste border, mid-19th c., 1" d. .......................................................... **200**

*Hand Painted Porcelain Button*

**Porcelain,** round, h.p. in style of 19th c. Dresden china, polychrome floral center surrounded by a French blue border encrusted w/gold, late 19th c., 1 1/4" d. (ILLUS.)...................................................... **30-35**
**Porcelain,** round, transfer-printed design of two children ice skating w/tree, house & two other skaters in background, gold sky & trim, set of 4 representing four seasons, mid-19th c., 1 5/8" d. ........... **150-200**

*Porcelain Button with Robin*

**Porcelain,** round, white glaze h.p. porcelain depicting a red-breasted robin perched on tree branch, naturalistic colors, England, early 19th c., 1" d. (ILLUS.)...................................................... **75**
**Silver plate,** round, pierced metal of cat & lizard on a stone wall, faceted steels decorating top inner border, Victorian, ca. 1880-90, 1 1/4" d. ................ **40-45**

*Turquoise & Garnet Gilded Button*

**Turquoise & garnet,** ball-shaped, ornate gilded design w/stone settings, Austria-Hungary, late 17th to early 18th c., 1 1/8" d. (ILLUS.).................................... **65-100**

# CANDLESTICKS & CANDLEHOLDERS

*Also see METALS, ROYCROFT ITEMS and SANDWICH under Glass.*

*French Second Empire Candelabra*

**Candelabra,** gilt-bronze & cut crystal, four-light, a slender reeded central top shaft supporting a cupped socket surrounded by three scroll leaf-trimmed upturned candlearms w/sockets all connected to a scroll-cast mount above the tall facet-cut crystal shaft fitted into an acanthus leaf-case socket raised on three animal legs resting on a tripartite flat base, Second Empire era, France, mid-19th c., 16" h., pr. (ILLUS.)............................................. **$2,000**
**Candelabra,** brass & crystal, six-light, a pyramid prism finial supporting a crystal beadwork stem, decorated w/scrolling arms, prism garlands & beads, brass base supporting six scrolling arms ending w/candleholders, 19th c., 13" d., 29" h., pr. (some decoration missing).......... **728**
**Candlestand,** cast iron & brass, floor model, a two-armed stand w/two brass candle cups & drip pans fitted to a horizontal sliding carrier & ending w/a tripod base, brass finial & standard decoration, 18th c., 48 1/4" h. (wear) .......................... **3,105**
**Candlestick,** brass, capstan-form, a wide flared cylindrical base supporting a wide flat disk centered by the turned & shaped cylindrical socket w/pick hole at

the side, probably 18th c., 5 1/4" h. (repair to top flange).................................... **495**

**Candlestick,** brass, Queen Anne style, scalloped domed foot below the knob-turned slender shaft below a tapering flange & the tall cylindrical socket w/scalloped socket rim, England, 18th c., 7 7/8" h. (minor casting flaws)...................... **660**

**Candlestick,** brass, round flat-topped domed foot centered by a rod- and ring-turned shaft w/a ring-turned tall cylindrical socket, shaft screws into base, early, 7 1/2" h....................................................... **440**

**Candlestick,** brass, wide round shallow dished base centered by a shaft w/an urn-form section below a spiraled section below the ringed cylindrical candle socket, standard screws into the base, early, 6 3/4" h. .............................................. **303**

**Candlestick,** bronze, figural, two-light, cast in full-relief at the top w/the form of a female bearing a child on her shoulders w/outstretched arms supporting baskets, cast by Gorham, by Willard Paddock, inscribed "1912 by W.D. Paddock," 29 1/2" h..................................................... **1,610**

**Candlestick,** pressed flint glass, a paneled tulip-form socket on a tapering octagonal shaft w/faceted rings on a narrow octagonal base, New England Glass Co., fiery opalescent, first half 19th c., 9 3/8" h. (small chips) ................................................ **743**

*Early Pricket Candlestick*

**Candlesticks,** brass, pricket-type, a dished top centered by a tall tapering candle spike above a baluster-, ring- and knob-turned stem above a lower disk on a flaring cylindrical base raised on ball feet, ecclesiastical markings, early, 15" h., pr. (ILLUS. of one)......................................... **3,300**

**Candlesticks,** pressed flint glass, a wide flaring hexagonal tulip-form socket w/scalloped rim on a ringed tapering hexagonal shaft on a round foot, pewter socket inserts, opaque blue, Pittsburgh, mid-19th c., 9 3/4" h., pr. (small flakes)........ **495**

**Candlesticks,** silver, on shaped square base w/scrolling stylized dolphins to corners, stem w/flat leaf motifs, bell-shaped flat leaf sockets, Russian, 13 3/4" h., pr. (ILLUS. top next column) ............................ **805**

*Russian Silver Candlesticks*

**Candlesticks,** sterling silver, Rococo style w/a slightly domed, stepped & scalloped round foot below the tall slender shaft w/a ringed knob below a slender urn-form section connected to the tall ringed cylindrical candle socket w/wide flattened & scalloped rim, each engraved on side of base "The Gift of Eliz. Sauvaire to her grandson Thos. De Jersey 1759," William Cafe, London, England, 1758-59, 8 1/2" h., pr................................ **5,940**

**Candlesticks,** brass, square bobeche over baluster-shaped stem & square base, ca. 1800, 9 1/2" h., pr. ....................... **280**

**Candlesticks,** brass w/push-ups, baluster-shaped stem resting on chamfered base, early 19th c., 10 1/2" h., pr. ................ **308**

# CANDY CONTAINERS

*\*Indicates the container might not have held candy originally.*

*+Indicates this container might also be found as a reproduction.*

*‡Indicates this container was also made as a bank.*

*All containers are clear glass unless otherwise indicated. Any candy container that retains the original paint is very desirable; readers should follow descriptions carefully realizing that an identical candy container that lacks the original paint will be less valuable.*

**Airplane - "Liberty Motor,"** clear glass, all original tin (no hole in tin for flag) ........... **$2,200**

**Bird on Mound,** glass, traces of paint, original pewter whistle & closure ........................ **660**

**Bus "Victory Glass Co."** 90% yellow paint, tiny base chip, original closure .... **685-850**

**Carpet Sweeper "Dolly Sweeper,"** all original, original closure ........................ **440-525**

**Cash Register,** 85% paint, original closure...... **660**

**Coal Car "Overland Limited,"** minor wheel well wear, original wheels, original closure.................................................. **400-440**

**Fat Boy on Drum,** 95% paint, original closure .......................................................... **660**

**Hat, Irish,** clear glass, marked "Its A Long Way to Tipperary" in semi-circular arc

above three-leaf shamrock in hat band, ca. 1920s, 2 3/4" h. (two interior cracks on both sides above brim, small dings on base of threads, no closure) ....... **1,128**
**Lamp, Library,** metal base w/glass dome top, original fringe & closure......................... **825**

*Monkey Lamp Candy Container*

**Lamp - Monkey,** original closure & candy, paper label (ILLUS.) .................................... **523**
**"Lawn Swing,"** all original tin & closure .......... **963**
**Mackintosh's Toffee Shop,** 3 1/4" h. x 4" w., surface wear...................................... **385**
**Man on Motorcycle with Side Car,** 50% paint, original closure & candy ..................... **975**
**Milk "Toy Town Dairy,"** cardboard lithograph, one side scouts, one side children gardening, two original creamers w/original candy (slight tear) .................... **1,155**
**Phonograph with Glass Horn,** original glass horn & metal sleeve, original closure & candy (small chip top edge)............. **550**
**"Pumpkin Head Policeman,"** 95% paint, original bail & closure ............................... **2,970**
**R. S. McColl Sweet Shop,** tin, 4 7/8" h. (minor paint flake) ........................................ **220**
**Rabbit on Dome,** good paint, tiny ear chip, original closure ............................................ **633**

*Rabbit w/Wheelbarrow*

**"Rabbit w/Wheelbarrow,"** 50% original paint, original closure (ILLUS.)..................... **330**
**Red Cross Confectionery Lifeboat,** probably used as store display, 15 1/4" l., very good ................................................. **550**

**Rocking Horse,** small chip under front, original closure ...................................... **150-275**
**Rocking Horse w/Clown Rider,** 95% paint, original closure .................................... **578**
**Rolling Pin,** clear glass, red tin caps w/red stained wood handles, original closure ........ **275**
**"Safety First,"** good paint, original closure.................................................... **320-440**
**Soldier with Sword.** 85% original paint, original closure ......................................... **1,238**
**Statue of Liberty,** hole in torch hand, original closure (slight repair to upper corner of left rear monument) .............................. **1,540**
**Telephone, Redlich's Cork Top #2,** cardboard disk reads "Compliments of The Season," original closure (no metal bell)...... **308**
**Uncle Sam by Barrel,** 95% original paint, original closure .......................................... **1,045**
**Village "Bank,"** w/glass insert, replaced clip.................................................................. **209**
**Village "Log Cabin,"** with insert (replaced clip)............................................................ **360-385**
**Wagon - Tin,** all roiginal tin (small corner chip) ............................................................. **558**
**Watch,** complete, original closure & candy (tin face not very legible) ............................. **440**
**Watch, Eagle,** w/original strap & fob inside glass, original closure (dirty) ........................ **385**
**Windmill - Candy Guaranteed,** original top & closure (one fin missing on fan).......... **715**

# CANES & WALKING STICKS

**Carved ivory figural "sword" cane,** the L-form handle in walrus ivory in two pieces, the shaft portrion carved in high-relief w/a bust of "Lady Liberty" wearing a liberty cap, carved ivory collar, a button in the collar releases the metal sword blade inside the shaft, silver collar & malacca shaft w/black horn tip, ca. 1880s, 36" l. ............................................. **$1,980**
**Carved ivory & mahogany walking stick,** the elephant ivory handle carved as a realistic chow dog head w/inlaid glass eyes, turned burl collar on the shaft w/a horn ferrule, probably Europe, ca. 1890, 36 1/4" l. .................................................. **610**
**Carved ivory & oak "relic" walking stick,** the knob handle in ivory w/a small blossom carved in the top & two rows of leaves & chain at the base, fitted in a double-ring collar inscribed "Hoc est Siguum Amicitiac - To Dr. John H. Boardman - Piece of the original wood of the U.S. Frigate Constitution," the shaft in oak w/splotches of dark aging, ca. 1850, 34" l. ..................................................... **1,650**
**Carved ivory, silver overlay & hardwood walking stick,** the figural ivory handle carved as a boy wearing a cap decorated w/sterling silver overlay trim, further scrolling silver overlay down the sides of the handle, mahoganized hardwood shaft w/horn ferrule, ca. 1890, 36" l. ..................................................... **1,210**
**Carved ivory, solid gold & hardwood cane,** a "tau" shaped handle w/elephant

ivory sections framed by 14k gold tip & central section w/inscriptions dated 1907, brown hardwood shaft, white metal & iron ferrule antique replacement, American, 32" l. ........................................... **385**

*Ivory & Sterling Silver Cane*

**Carved ivory & sterling silver cane,** a "tau" form handle composed of carved elephant ivory sections silver bands of silver overlay in a twisted angled design, a large "S" on one end & marked "Sterling," heavy rosewood shaft ending in replaced brass tip, ca. 1880, 35" l. (ILLUS.)........................................................ **578**

**Carved rosewood walking stick,** the head carved as two plump cats in a basket, on the back a small oval inset piece of mother-of-pearl w/signature of Japanese carver, oval ivory collar on a black oval ebonized wood shaft w/horn ferrule, probably fashioned in England w/an imported handle, ca. 1900, 36" l. ................. **220**

**Carved whale ivory & exotic wood walking stick,** the handle carved in the form of lady's leg above four ivory & six baleen spacers & a pewter ferrule continuing to a round tapering shaft, 19th c., 33 3/4" l. (handle loose, small crack) ........... **460**

*Gold-filled Presentation Cane*

**Gold-filled & ebony walking stick,** the round gold-filled knob handle w/presentation inscription, finely chased w/flower blossoms & ribbon bands alternating w/plain panels, fine ebony shaft ends in a white metal & iron ferrule, ca. 1880, 37" l. (ILLUS.)............................................. **222**

**Hickory "relic" cane,** a crook handle & plain wood shaft w/bark removed, mounted w/a 5" l. silver medallion inscribed "This cane was cut from The Hornet's Nest Shiloh Battlefield - Sept. 9th, 1894 by J.O. Mason, Mt. Pulaski, Ill.," brass ferrule made from a real thimble, 38" l. .................................................... **1,210**

**Ivory cane,** the T-form ivory handle above the ivory shaft composed of matched segments, 37 1/4" l. (some age cracks & edge damage) .............................................. **468**

**Ivory & wood cane,** angled ivory handle w/scrimshawed design of a whale, a gold-colored ferrule to the greyish shaft streaked w/black & w/an ivory tip, 32 3/4" l. (age cracks in handle).................. **220**

*William J. Bryant Political Souvenir*

**Pewter & hardwood walking stick,** the pewter handle molded in the shape of the head of William Jennings Bryan, "Free Coinage - 16 to 1" embossed along the base of the handle, mounted on an ebonized hardwood shaft, political item from the 1896 presidential campaign, small crack at base of handle, overall 35 1/2" l. (ILLUS.) ............................ **495**

**Plated brass & hardwood "harmonica" cane,** the plated brass angled handle w/a built-in harmonica w/square mouth holes on one side & two rows of round air holes on the other, marked "patented," movable grip at end of handle, w/white metal & iron ferrule, ca. 1880, 35 1/2" l. .................................................... **1,100**

**Porcelain & ebonized wood walking stick,** a round porcelain knob handle elaborately h.p. w/a bouquet of flowers in pink, purple, yellow & blue among green leaves, on a thin decorated gold collar above a long porcelain shaft section similarly painted & joined by a gilt-metal ferrule to the ebonized hardwood shaft, probably England, ca. 1890, 36" l....... **523**

**Rose quartz & mahogany walking stick,** the rose quartz handle w/a low domed top above gently tapering sides to the sterling silver collar on the mahogany shaft w/a replaced brass tip, ca. 1890, overall 34 1/4" l...................................... **495**

**Silver & ebonized wood cane,** the curved & scrolled silver Art Nouveau handle embossed w/a long fox holding a large pheasant in its jaws, ebonized wood shaft w/horn ferrule, Continental hallmarks, ca, 1900, 36" l.................................... **770**

**Silver & oak "relic" walking stick,** the silver knob handle engraved around the sides w/C-scrolls, ferns, leaves & blossoms, the top inscribed "Charter Oak - Oct. 31st, 1687, the Charter of Connecticut was hid in the trunk of this tree - It was restored May 9th, 1689. Blown over 12:50 O'clock A.M. - Aug. 20th 1856," thick, heavy oak shaft w/pierced round silver eyelets, burnished metal ferrule, 35 1/2" l. ..................................................... **1,155**

**Wooden walking stick,** carved & painted w/a spiraling design of large raised leaves, a lizard & a snake in green, rust & yellow against a black ground, American, 19th c., 36 3/4" l. (wear) ....................... **920**

# CANS & CONTAINERS

*The collecting of tin containers has become quite popular within the past several years. Air-tight tins were first produced by hand to keep food fresh and, after the invention of the tin-printing machine in the 1870s, containers were manufactured in a wide variety of shapes and sizes with colorful designs. Also see: ADVERTISING, AUTOMOTIVE COLLECTIBLES, COCA-COLA COLLECTIBLES and TOBACCIANA.*

**Airplane oil,** Texaco, 1 qt. can...................... **$775**

**Baking powder,** Rough Rider tin w/paper label showing man on horse, 2 1/4 x 4 1/2" (minor scrapes & dings) ........... **88**

**Baking Powder,** Vision tin, paper lithographed label depicting angels playing w/fire, 3 x 7" (minor scuffs)............................ **77**

**Biscuit,** Huntley & Palmers tin, stack of books tied w/strap, bright red w/gold, black & tan trim, 6 1/4" l. .............................. **330**

*Debray French Biscuit Tin*

**Biscuits,** Debray French Biscuit two-piece tin, lithographed hunting scene w/hunters on horseback, dogs & stag, 1 3/8 x 3 1/2 x 7 1/2" (ILLUS.) ...................... **110**

**Candy,** Sanders tin pail, cov., w/bail handle, 2 1/2 lbs., colorful figures of children around sides, lithograph by Canco, light surface rust on top rim & top, minor scratches, 5 1/2 x 5 1/2" (ILLUS. top next column)................................................... **330**

**Cleanser,** Gold Dust Scouring Cleanser, Lever Bros, unopened, 3 x 4 1/2".................. **55**

**Cocoa,** Ghiaradelli Cocoa 1 lb. tin w/paper lithograph label, unopened, 3 1/4 x 6 1/2".............................................................. **77**

**Coffee,** Araban Coffee Co. tin, Boston, Massachusetts, Arabian man drinking coffee, lithograph by American Can Co., dated 1929, 4 1/4 x 6" (scrapes & dings) ..... **330**

*Sanders Candy Tin Pail*

**Coffee,** Country Club 1 lb. tin, scene of large country club building on both sides, 4 x 6" (minor scrapes) ................................... **193**

**Coffee,** Fort Pitt tin, red w/gold band at top & bottom, scene of fort, lithograph by Republic Metalware Co., Buffalo, New York, 4 1/4 x 5 1/2" (faded gold).................. **468**

**Coffee,** Matchless 1 lb. tin w/screwtop, green w/gold trim, lithograph w/coffee beans on branch, Continental Can Co., 4 x 6" (minor dings & scrapes) .................... **242**

**Coffee,** Strong Heart tin, Charles Hewill, Des Moines, Iowa, lithograph w/image of Native American by American Can Co. on both sides, 4 1/4 x 5 3/4" (minor scrapes & dings) ......................................... **264**

**Condoms,** Shadows tin, marked "Shadows (letters reflected as shadow image) As Thin as a Shadow - As Strong as an Ox!," Youngs Rubber Co., 1 5/8 x 2 1/8" ....... **66**

**Gasoline,** Powerized Gasoline (Sunburst Refining) emergency 1 qt. can, rare............. **200**

**Honey,** Bradshaws 3 Bears 5 lb. tin w/graphs of bears, dated 1949, 5 x 5 3/4" ............................................................. **55**

**Lubricant,** Shell Hypoid Gear Lubricant 1 gal. can, 11" h. .............................................. **250**

**Lubricant,** Texaco Home Lubricant, 4 oz. can, 5 1/8" h. .............................................. **350**

**Marine Motor Oil,** Texaco, 1 gal. can, 10 1/4" h.................................................. **400**

**Motor oil,** Ben Hur 1 qt. can, red w/white & black lettering, Ben Hur Oil Co., Los Angeles - New Orleans, 4" d., 5 1/2" h. (minor scratches & staining)........................ **165**

**Motor oil,** Mona 1/2 gal. can, 6" h. .................. **235**

**Motor oil,** Pequot Chief Motor Oil, 1/2 gal. can, 6 1/4" h. ...................................... **220**

**Motor oil,** Shell Company of California, 1 gal. can, 11" h. ............................................ **400**

**Motor oil,** Shell/Roxana Petroleum Corp, 1 gal. can, 11" h., rare.................................. **600**

**Motor oil,** Signal Motor Oil/Penn, 1 qt. can (top lid missing) ........................................ **210**

**Motor oil,** Sinclair Opaline 1/2 gal. can w/"Enterprise Stamping Co. Pittsburgh, PA" at bottom edges & "Sinclair Refining Company Chicago" on side (paint chips & scratches) ......................................... **550**

**Motor oil,** Texaco "Medium" handi-grip 1/2 gal. can, 6 1/2" h. ...................................... **220**

*Trop-Artic Auto Oil*

**Motor oil,** Tro-Actic Auto Oil, 1/2 gal. can, lithograph of scene of tropical island w/car parked near palm tree, Manhattan Oil Co., minor denting & scratches, 3 x 8", 6" h. (ILLUS.) .................................. **1,210**

**Motor oil,** Veedol 5 gal. can in wooden box, can w/early touring car on one side, box marked "Veedol Motor Oil - Tidewater Oil Co. New York," 8 1/2" h. can, box 11 1/2 x 15" (minor scratches on can, fading to lettering on box)............................. **314**

**Oysters,** Liberty Brand, 1 gal tin can, both sides w/image of Statue of Liberty w/"Liberty brand - Fresh Oysters - packed by Ivens and Hudson, Rock Hall, MD," 6 1/2 x 7 1/2" ........................................ **215**

**Peanut butter,** FI-NA-ST Peanut Butter tin pail, cov., bail handle. 1 lb., image of a man wearing a white coat on both sides by First National Stores, Somerville, Massachusetts, 3 3/8 x 3 3/4" ..................... **143**

**Peas,** Roundup Grocery Company tin, Spokane, Washington, colorful embossed paper label w/white bowl filled w/peas on one side, scene of cowboy on a bronco on other, marked "Sweet Early June Peas," 2 5/8 x 4" (top cut open)................... **303**

**Shoe polish,** Whittemores "New Era" tin, unused, 1 x 3 1/2" ......................................... **44**

*Tip Top Soda Can*

**Soft drink,** "Tip Top Soda," metal, cone top, shows clown, red, white & blue, Madison, Wisconsin (ILLUS.) ............. **350**

**Spice,** Blue Jewel, 1 1/2 ozs., Jewel Food Stores, Inc., white w/two blue stripes & blue jewel, tin top & bottom, cardboard body, wrap around paper label.................. **30-65**

**Spice,** Country Club, The Kroger Grocery & Baking Co., light green, country club building flying the American flag ............. **75-125**

**Spice,** Durkee's, 1 1/4 ozs., Durkee Famous Foods, white & green w/baked turkey on platter, tin litho ......................... **20-45**

**Spice,** Early Dinner, 2 1/2 ozs., Peyton-Palmer Co., dark blue & white, two couples at dinner table w/waiter serving them, dress is early 1900 ...................... **100-200**

**Spice,** Farmers Pride, 1 1/2 ozs., Hulman & Co., red, white haired man seated in chair wearing straw hat w/arm around shoulders of young girl standing beside him holding a doll, tin top & bottom, cardboard body, wrap around paper label ....... **50-90**

**Spice,** French's, 2 ozs., The R.T. French Co., round, tin litho, tan w/French's red flag flying from black staff......................... **25-55**

**Spice,** Gold Bond, 2 ozs., Jewett & Sherman Co., tin top & bottom, cardboard body, wrap around paper label, red, gold, w/Gold Bond in white circle ............. **20-45**

**Spice,** Happy Hour, 1 3/4 ozs., Campbell Holton & Co., tin wrap around paper label, yellow, pink, blue w/"Happy Hour," written in white ........................................... **10-35**

**Spice,** Jack Sprat, 1 1/2 ozs., Western Grocer Mills, tin top & bottom, cardboard body, wrap around paper label, light yellow w/Jack Sprat in green outfit, red bows at knees, light blue knee socks, tan moccasins, black & green hat, carrying plate & silverware in one hand & glass in other............................................. **35-75**

**Spice,** Little Elf, 1 1/4 ozs., stick cinnamon, Bursley & Co., Inc., cardboard, yellow & dark blue, elf in red holding tray w/spice tin on it...................................................... **10-40**

**Spice,** Monday's, 4 ozs., The P.C. Monday Tea Co., tin litho, white, black, light blue & pink, lettering in black w/white & light blue background........................................ **25-55**

**Spice,** Our Family, 2 ozs., Nash-Finch Co., white & dark blue, silhouette of lady's head in dark blue on white background, "Our Family" in white on dark blue background, other lettering in red, tin top & bottom, cardboard body, wrap around paper label ................................................. **30-65**

**Spice,** Quaker, 1 1/2 ozs., Lee & Cady, red band between white & dark blue bands, Quaker lady in dark dress & hat trimmed in white holding tin in right hand w/left hand on hip, tin litho .................................. **15-35**

**Spice,** Safe Owl, 1 1/4 ozs., Safe Owl Products, Inc., white w/red lettering, head of brown owl at bottom of tin, blue center w/celery seed letters in white, tin litho............................................................. **15-35**

**Spice,** Slade's, 3/4 oz., D. & L. Slade Co., tin litho, light blue w/three camels & palm trees in black at bottom of tin, also man dressed in white leading brown pack camel........................................................... **35-60**

**Spice,** Tea Table, 1 1/2 ozs., Peyton Palmer Co., tin litho, table w/two chairs on veranda set for tea, including teapot, cups & saucers, sugar bowl, bouquet of red flowers, sea in background, striped awning overhead................................... **100-150**

**Spice,** Three Crow, 3 ozs., The Atlantic Spice Co., yellow w/red & black lettering, three black crows sitting on wooden fence in circle at center of tin, tin litho ....... **35-65**

**Spice,** Wish Bone, 3 ozs., J.F. Humphreys and Co., cardboard, unopened, red & steel blue, steel blue lettering on red background w/broken wish bone through the 'o' in bone, other lettering is dark blue on steel blue background .................. **45-80**

**Talcum powder,** Cadette tin, colorfully painted as a cadet figure, Cadette Products Corp., Rutherford, New Jersey, 1 1/4 x 2 1/4 x 7 1/4" .................................... **154**

*Jess Talcum Powder Tin*

**Talcum powder,** Jess embossed tin, depicting young woman, flowers at border, by Wm. Brown & Bros., Baltimore, 1 1/2 x 2 1/2 x 4 1/2" (ILLUS.) ...................... **358**

**Talcum powder,** Winchester After Shave Talc tin w/hunting scene of man & his dog, front & back, by Jolind Dist. Co., New York, 1 x 3 x 4 3/4"............................... **330**

**Tobacco,** Buckingham Bright Cut Plug tin, trial size, 3/4 x 2 1/4 x 3" (few scrapes)........ **176**

**Tobacco,** Hi-Plane vertical pocket tin, flying airplane shown on front w/"Hi-Plane Smooth Cut Tobacco for Pipe and Cigarettes," red w/white letterint, 1 x 3 x 4 1/2" (minor fading).................................... **176**

*Kim-Bo Vertical Pocket tin*

**Tobacco,** Kim-Bo Cut Plug pocket tin, cardboard w/tin top & bottom, young girl pictured on front, Lovell & Buffington Tobacco Co., Covington, Kentucky, complete w/contents, 1910 Revenue Stamp & Union Stamp, 1 x 2 1/4 x 4 1/2" (ILLUS.).......................................................... **385**

**Tobacco,** Sam's Own Mixture tin, rectangular w/dog depicted on front, England, 1 x 3 x 4 1/4" ................................................ **44**

**Tobacco,** Stag Tobacco pocket tin, vertical w/stag depicted on both sides, 3/4 x 2 5/8 x 3 1/2" ............................ **121**

**Tomatoes,** League Brand, paper lithographed label on opened tin can, image of tomato on one side, baseball scene on other, California Packing Co., San Francisco, California, 4 x 4 5/8" (minor dings & scrapes) ......................................... **440**

# CAROUSEL FIGURES

*The ever popular amusement park merry-go-round or carousel has ancient antecedents but evolved into its most colorful and complex form in the decades from 1880 to 1930. In America a number of pioneering firms, begun by men such as Gustav Dentzel, Charles Looff and Allan Herschell, produced these wonderful rides with beautifully hand-carved animals, the horse being the most popular. Some of the noted carvers included M. C. Illusions, Charles Carmel, Solomon Stein and Harry Goldstein.*

*Today many of the grand old carousels are gone and remaining ones are often broken up and the animals sold separately as collectors search for choice examples. A fine reference to this field is Painted Ponies, American Carousel Art, by William Mannas, Peggy Shank and Marianne Stevens (Zon International Publishing Company, Millwood, New York, 1986).*

*Herschell Spillman Carousel Dog*

**Dog,** carved & painted wood, good detail w/brown figure of a Setter w/black, red & yellow studded collar & a carved saddle, old paint, attributed to Herschell Spillman Co., Tonowanda, New York, late 19th to early 20th c., needs reassembling & some additional restoration, 58" l., 18" h. (ILLUS.)............................... **$8,625**

**Fish,** carved & painted as a large, deep-bodied cod-like fish w/wide tail, in green, greenish grey & turquoise blue, glass eyes & carpeted seat, late 19th c., 48" l., 16" h. (paint loss) ....................................... **1,725**

*Carousel Giraffe*

**Giraffe,** carved & painted wood, shades of brown w/green saddle pad, maker unknown, ca. 1900 (ILLUS.).................... **16,000**

*Prancing Carousel Horse*

**Horse,** prancing position, carved wood w/full-bodied white-painted body w/articulated head, ears, eyes, mouth & a black-painted buckled bridle above an articulated mane over a black-painted saddle above red, black & gold details, on articulated legs w/blue & gold-painted hoofs & horse hair tail, American, 20th c., 65" l., 43" h. (ILLUS.)............................ **6,325**

**Horse,** prancing position, carved & painted wood, tan horse w/black mane, rust colored bridle, glass eyes, brown saddle w/floral cantle, flat green blanket w/yellow & tan border, yellow, red & green breast collar, original paint, attributed to Armitage Herschell Company, late 19th c., 41" h., 48" l. (ILLUS. top next column)............................................. **12,650**

**Horse,** running position, carved wood, raised legs & head, good detail w/bridle & carved animal saddle pad, attributed to C.W. Parker Co., Abilene, Kansas, late 19th to early 20th c., old natural finish, imperfections, 16 x 70", 53" h. (ILLUS. center next column) ..................... **3,738**

*Herschell Carousel Horse*

*Parker Carousel Horse*

**Horse,** prancing position, carved & painted wood, grey horse w/blue bridle, eagle carved cantle, yellow, red & orange blanket & red & orange breast collar, late 19th - early 20th c., attributed to Charles Loof, 55" h., 55" l. (restored) .................... **3,450**

*Running Pig Carousel Figure*

**Pig,** running position, carved & painted wood, painted white pig w/protruding tongue, glass eyes, yellow bridle, carved red & blue saddle & blanket, late 19th - early 20th c., paint loss, 16" h., 44" l. (ILLUS.)..................................................... **2,300**

# CARVED BOTTLE STOPPERS

*The world's most renowned woodcarvings are produced by ANRI, a family owned business located in the Groden Mountains of Northern Italy, established in 1912.*

Bottle stoppers were the first item produced for sale and export by the Master Carvers of ANRI in the early 1920s, but the production of stoppers and other bar-related items ended in 1976. Single stoppers, corkscrews, bottle openers, and combinations of all three as bar sets and bar scenes were sold all over the world.

To be considered Mint, an ANRI stopper must have no cracks or chips in the wood or paint, must have the original cork without chips or breaks, and in most cases, have the original paper sticker. Many stoppers were sold without stickers, however, so a sticker increases the value, whereas the lack of one does not reduce the value. Mechanical stoppers must be in perfect working order. Plastic heads and poorly carved stoppers are much less valuable or desirable.

# MECHANICAL

ANRI originally made toys, so as their bottle stoppers evolved, mechanics for movement were incorporated. Manipulating a string-pull, or pressing a lever on the back of a stopper can bring them to life in fascinating ways. Twist pegs are another way of producing movement.

**Accordion player or violinist,** pulling string lifts right arm of accordion player out away from body making it appear his squeeze box is expanding, while violinist draws metal bow back & forth across violin, heads may tilt from side-to-side, hard to find ........................................... **$85-100**

**"Amor Sport,"** full-figured man & woman, w/two pegs when turned moves his head as though he is trying to kiss her & she half-heartedly resisting, can be coerced to kiss w/practice, ANRI patented model, original box.............................. **90-110**

**Arm raiser,** pressing down on head causes both arms to lift upward, rare to find in working order, ca. early 1920s-mid 30s ... **75-85**

**Bacchus & his friends,** carved to resemble sprites & imps w/pointy ears, detailed eyelashes, tiny teeth & facial expressions, wearing wreaths of grapes & grape leaves around their heads, set of six produced & offered for a very short period of time, very rare, each ............. **150-200**

**Ballerina,** delicately carved dancer on point w/upraised arms, wearing umbrella-shaped skirt, sweet & simple face, various dress colors & decorations, turning peg moves figure back & forth bowing or side-to-side ............................ **75-100**

**Barrel sitter,** detailed carving & painting, children as opposed to adults, round heads, tiny pinholes in eyes, girls or boys straddling barrel or keg w/some holding musical instruments or flowers, heads mounted on beads allowing movement ................................................. **25-30**

**Caught at the door,** woman standing w/left hand on doorknob facing a half-opened door, w/upraised right arm holding a shoe, through doorway is a man about to cross threshold, turning peg causes her to lower the shoe aiming for his head

w/his face disappearing as he ducks the assault, her mouth is open probably in a curse of some sort & his expression is a drunken smirk, very rare ............................ **200**

**Cowboy,** riding black & white horse, rifle over shoulder & reins in each hand, turning peg causes horse to rear up on hind legs................................................................. **150+**

**Deadeye,** bandanna tied over one side of face w/only one eye visible ....................... **50-75**

**Deadeye,** Head-in-head type, bandanna tied over one side of face w/only one eye visible, pushing lever down causes hat on head to rise & out pops another smaller head ........................................... **75-85**

*Dickens Character Bottle Stoppers*

**Dickens characters,** character-type including Mr. Pickwick, Dolly Varden, Mr. Pecksniff, Capt. Cuttle, Mrs. Gamp, Artful Dodger, Joe "The Fat Boy," Sam Weller, Job. Trotter, Mr. Dick, & David Copperfield, labeled w/names painted on front or back of wooden collar around top of cork, most valuable & sought after ANRI stoppers ever produced, any Dickens stopper each (ILLUS.) ........................ **150+**

*Donkey or Elephant*

**Donkey or Elephant,** carved ears & tail attached to body by thin metal pins, head is down in sleepy resting position, raising tail moves head up & ears move forward, each (ILLUS.) ............................ **40-60**

**Double hat tipper,** two hat tippers side-by-side, pull string & both tip their hats, rare left-handed tipper ..................................... **65-75**

**Drinker,** model varies, clothing, hat (or no hat) & facial features are endless, usually holds bottle in hand, pushing lever down raises mug to mouth while head tips back as he drinks................................. **20-25**

*Face To Face Kissers*

**Face to face kissers,** kissing couple facing each other, pressing lever causes them to come together in a kiss (ILLUS.) ........... **75-85**

*Man Tipping Hat*

**Hat tipper,** wearing various hats & clothing, faces, expressions & detail vary, pull string in back & he bows his head & doffs his hat, each (ILLUS.) ...................... **20-25**

**Head in Head,** common-type, man wearing hat, some fully carved & others are simple round beads w/painted faces, depressing lever causes hat to rise & out pops another smaller head which varies... **40-45**

**Head in Head,** unusual-type (Gnomes, Santa Claus, Deadeyes), figure wearing hat, some fully-carved & others are simple round beads w/painted faces, depressing lever causes hat to rise & out pops another smaller head which varies........................................................ **75-100**

**Hobo,** w/ruddy cheeks & exaggerated red lips making him look like a black caricature, comprised of hollow beads strung together, holding a knotted handkerchief in his left hand & a metal walking cane in the other, exquisitely detailed clothing including derby hat, extremely rare, pictured in earliest ANRI catalog ...... **200+**

**Kissing couple,** man & woman usually from waist up, standing side-by-side, w/exaggerated carvings to lips, pushing lever down raises heads slightly & turn towards each other bringing lips together in a kiss, releasing lever returns to original position ................................................ **30**

**Kissing couple,** man & woman usually from waist up, standing side-by-side, w/exaggerated carvings to lips, pushing lever down raises heads slightly & turning towards each other bring lips together in a kiss, releasing lever returns to original position, older model w/soft paint, detailed clothing & realistic facial features ....................................................... **40-45**

**Man,** man standing w/right hand resting on barrel w/spigot, mug in left hand & bottle sticking out of pocket, turning peg at back of his heels makes him sway, very rare ......................................................... **150+**

**Man,** pushing lever down makes eyes roll back & tongue stick out, another variation has eyes changing color when they roll back & cigar in mouth going from side-to-side.......................................... **50-65**

**Man or woman,** carved head to toe & perched atop a cork stopper, detailed carving & paint, pulling lever opens & closes mouth, older, 3" ...................... **50-65**

**Man or woman,** carved head to toe & perched atop a cork stopper, pulling lever opens & closes mouth, newer, 5" ..... **30-35**

**Monkey hat tipper,** usually dressed in suit w/short pants & hat w/varying colors, may have mug, glass, or stein in left hand, pressing down on tail causes monkey to tip hat ........................................ **65-70**

**Push puppet,** combination of popular child's toy & bottle cork, carved & jointed people or animals can be found, pulling down on stopper base while holding wooden collar around cork releases tension on strings holding figure upright resulting in it's collapsing into a heap, releasing lever returns to original position ................................................................ **40-50**

**Shootist,** rough-looking "outlaw" type cowboy standing w/pistols in both hands, turning peg causes him to raise one arm then the other & 'shoot' while head tilts from side-to-side, rare ................................. **150+**

**Show me the way home,** English model, man hanging onto signpost w/one hand & dangling bottle of wine in other, turning peg causes him to dip & sway in drunken manner, sign says "Show Me The Way Home" which is printed in several languages for export including German, French, Italian & Spanish ......................... **75-90**

**Sitting man,** carved head & shoulders resting in stand carved in shape of chair, legs of man attached to or part of chair, stopper & stand combination, very rare, ca. 1920-30s ................................... **80-100**

**Switchman,** man sitting w/both hands grasping a pole, sides of perch painted w/distance notation such as "7km" or "2km," turning peg moves figure back & forth ...................................................... **70-85**

**Tip & kiss,** kissing couple sitting side-by-side, he holds hat in left hand w/right arm around her shoulder, pressing lever moves him to tip his hat & kiss his lady, rare ......................................................... **75-85**

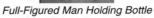

*Full-Figured Man Holding Bottle*

**Tipple tipple,** full-figured man holding bottle in left hand & red umbrella under right arm, wearing yellow top hat & dress coat w/tails, turning peg causes him to dip & sway in a drunken manner, original box (ILLUS.) .................................................... **90-110**

**Toothache,** bandanna tied around head & knotted on top, an old-fashioned way of treating a toothache .................................. **50-75**

*Two Faced Bottle Stopper*

**Two faced,** carved face topped w/oversized hat attached to head w/thin metal pin allowing it to flip forward & backward revealing second face on other side, various faces including happy/sad, old/young, boy/girl, white/black (ILLUS.)................................................. **80-100**

**Yakkities,** clothing, hats & details of paint vary, pulling lever opens & closes mouth, older models have eyes w/4- or 5-step eye painting process, well-carved features, eyeglasses, teeth or other extras ....................................................... **30-35**

## NON-MECHANICAL

*These are basic, non-mobile ANRI stoppers. But, don't misjudge their value. It is within this category that you will find some of the most realistic and artistically done facial carvings. For a strong collection, you should have a fair number of these that were made in the early years.*

**Bear,** w/musical instrument, accordion, or sitting atop beer keg, detail in carving of fur w/red paint in mouth, may be confused w/"Black Forest" carvings of same style................................................................. **40-45**

**Indian chief,** wearing headdress w/metallic gold painted detail, rare ........................... **75-100**

**Man,** wearing top hat, delicate coloring, eyes w/4- or 5-step painting process, mounted on bead allowing movement, original fabric scarf or collar, very rare & early stopper, hat & clothing style varies....................................................... **85-100**

**Man or woman,** caricature-type, full figure carved in detail from head to shoes, jolly faces, detailed painting of clothing w/tiny patterns .................................................. **30-35**

**Man or woman,** closed mouth, wearing typical Tyrolean garb, woman has large-brimmed hat w/large red fruit or flowers around crown, well carved & detailed ....... **25-30**

**Man or woman,** open mouth w/carved & painted teeth, smiling, metal eyeglasses, delicate coloring & detailed carving ......... **25-35**

**Man or woman,** realistic face, detailed carving & painting of clothing & features, eyes w/4- or 5-step painting process, marked "Italy"........................................... **20-30**

**Scottish terrier,** full-figured sitting dog, black w/detailed carving of fur & face, red tongue ................................................. **45-50**

**Squirrel,** European-type, w/large ears, standing on hind legs, painted gray or reddish, front paws together..................... **20-25**

**Woman,** closed mouth, wearing peasant-type clothing including dress w/tiny painted pattern & head scarf, hair in bun at back of neck ......................................... **20-25**

## POURERS

*Another group within the ANRI stopper collection is the dual purpose model that corks a bottle but allows the beverage to pour through a tube running through the stopper into the bottle neck. To differentiate these from simple stoppers, these are called "pourers." Some of the most interesting ANRI stoppers are pourers, so you'll want to watch for these and add them to your collection.*

**Acrobat,** man sitting atop beer keg, legs dangling over edge w/feet covering pouring tube, metal pin anchors hands to each side of barrel, tip forward to pour & he swings clear of keg to expose pouring tube, coming back to rest when returned to upright position, rare ........................... **85-100**

**Crested bird or rooster,** delicate coloring & detailed feathers, rare, heads 2 1/2" to 3" h. excluding cork & tube...................... **85-110**

**Ma Kettle,** character-type, hair in bun under scarf, mouth opens to pour, variety of models including one w/crafty & devious look w/one eye closed in wink or squint & another w/surprised look on face w/eyes looking sharply to side .......... **70-85**

**Man,** figure of man w/bottle between knees, grasping cork w/both hands, pressing down on coat tail causes him to 'uncork' bottle, exposing pouring tube, rare.......... **85-100**

**Man,** full-figured man leaning face down over barrel, right hand covering beer spigot, tip forward to pour & arm swings clear to expose pouring tube, musical playing "How Dry I Am," "Beer Barrel Polka" or variety of German bar tunes, music stops when returned to upright position, rare ...................................... **100-125+**

**Man or woman,** in typical Tyrolean garb, head & shoulders, head must be removed to expose pouring tube, many varieties available in both realistic & caricature-style carving, may have chrome or colored plastic ring around top of cork .. **40-60**

*Mortimer Snerd Type
Character Bottle Stopper*

**Mortimer Snerd,** character-type, modeled after Edgar Bergen's dummy, wearing porkpie hat, w/bulbous nose & wide smile, mouth opens to reveal pouring

**Models No. 129 or 130,** Bohemian case
(cast iron), each (ILLUS. left w/Model 0)... **2,000**
**Models No. 210 or 211,** each ...................... **1,600**
**Models No. 215 or 216,** each ...................... **1,500**
**Models No. 224 or 225,** each ........................ **900**
**Model No. 310** ..................................... **1,000**
**Model No. 311** ...................................... **900**

*NCR Model 313*

**Models No. 312 or 313,** each (ILLUS of
Model 313) ................................................ **900**
**Models No. 316 or 317,** each ......................... **900**
**Models No. 322, 323, 326 or 327,**
(extended base), each .............................. **1,600**
**Models No. 324 or 325,** each ......................... **900**
**Models No. 332, 333, 334, 336, 342, 343,
346, 347, 348, 349, 356, or 359,** each ......... **700**
**Models No. 410, 415, 416, or 420,** each ......... **800**

*NCR Model 442*

**Models No. 441, 442, or 451,** each (ILLUS.
of Model 442) ............................................. **800**
**Models No. 500 through 599,** counter top-
style, multi-drawer, each .......................... **1,600**
**Models No. 500 through 599,** single
drawer, each ............................................. **1,200**
**Models No. 711 or 717,** each ......................... **200**
**Models No. 1054 or 1064,** each ...................... **600**

# NATIONAL FLOOR MODELS

*NCR Floor Model 572*

**Models No. 500 through 599,** floor model,
brass case atop set of wood drawers,
each (ILLUS. of Model 572) ..................... **3,500**

# OTHER MANUFACTURERS:

*American Cash Register Model 50*

**American cash registers** (ILLUS. of
Model 50) ........................................ **1,000-3,000**
**Chicago cash registers** ............................. **RARE**
**Dial cash registers** ................................... **RARE**
**Hallwood cash registers** ......................... **1,000+**
**Ideal cash registers** ................................. **RARE**
**Michigan cash registers** ........................ **200-700**
**St. Louis cash registers** ......................... **200-700**
**Union cash registers** .............................. **3,000+**
**Weller cash registers** ............................. **300-800**

# CAT COLLECTIBLES
## AVON ITEMS

**Backbrush,** plastic, model of the character
Garfield, w/original box (ILLUS. top next
page) ............................................................ **$25**
**Bottle,** ceramic, "Blue Eyes," model of a
white cat w/blue rhinestone eyes, 1975 ......... **10**

**Candle,** fragrance-type, "Snug 'N Cozy," w/glass sleeping cat holder, 1981 .................. **16**
**Cologne bottle,** spray-type, "Tabatha," model of a black cat, 1975 ............................. **12**

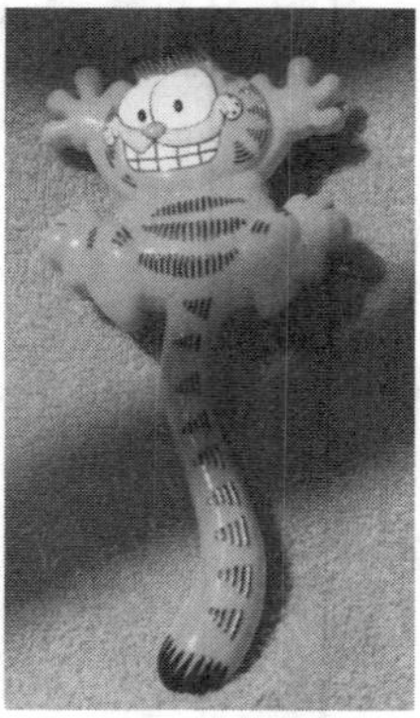

*Garfield Plastic Backbrush*

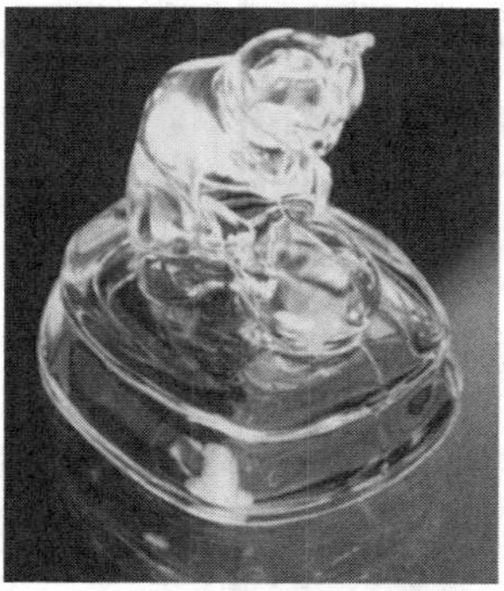

*Avon Clear Glass Cat Figure*

**Model of a cat,** clear glass, seated cat on oblong pillow base, first in a series of three, w/original box, 1994, 3" h. (ILLUS.) ......................................................... **15**

*Avon Cat Pomander*

**Pomander,** ceramic, model of a white kitten curled up on a blue sweater in a brown basket, 1983 (ILLUS.) ......................... **28**

## BANKS

**Cast iron,** mechanical, "Cat & Mouse," late 19th c. ................................................... **51,000**

*Pottery Cat Bank*

**Pottery,** model of a seated "Cubist" looking cat in aqua & gold w/a turquoise bow, Japan, 5 3/4" h. (ILLUS.) ............................... **14**

## BOOKS

**"Book of Cats (A): Being Twenty Drawings by Foujita,"** limited edition of 500, w/extra set of loose plates & signed by the artist in colophon & on one of the extra plates ............................................. **14,950**
**"Drawing A Cat,"** by Clare Turlay Newberry, the Studio Publications, w/dust jacket, 1943, near mint ................................... **50**
**"Hiram and Other Cats,"** by Laurence Dwight Smith, drawings by Gladys Emerson Cook, Grosset & Dunlop, 1941, near mint .............................................. **45**
**"Old Possum's Book of Practical Cats,"** by T.S. Eliot, illustrated by Nicolas Bentley, Faber and Faber, Ltd., 1957, near mint .............................................................. **55**
**"Robber Kitten (The),"** Altemus' Wee Book series, 1904, near mint ......................... **30**

## FIGURALS

*Japanese Tabby Cat Figure*

**Ceramic,** model of a golden tabby w/black stripes, one paw raised, Japan, 4 1/4" h. (ILLUS.) ......................................................... **15**
**Ceramic,** seated grey tabby wearing a white bib & licking its chops, paper labels w/"Joseph Originals" & "Japan," 7 1/2" h. (ILLUS. top next page) ..................... **65**

China, model of a Siamese cat lying down, face looking up, stamped "Goldscheider USA," 1940, 6 1/2" l........................................ 90

*Joseph Originals Grey Tabby*

China, models of a four-piece cat band, designed by Arthur Gredington, Beswick, 1945-73, 2" h., the set ................. 400

Porcelain, "Cats of Character," various colors & poses, Danbury Mint, 1986, from a set of 25, each................................................ 17

*Watcombe Pottery Cat Figure*

Pottery, model of a green cat in top hat, playing a banjo, marked "Watcombe Pottery, Torquay, England," ca. 1890s, 7" h. (ILLUS.) ............................................. 195

Pottery, white Persians w/grey specks, from a line called "Sparklers," incised "Roselane USA," ca. 1950, 3 1/2" h., pr. ........ 75

Redware pottery, figural teapot, black cat w/yellow eyes, gold eyebrows & whiskers, red neck bow, unmarked, attributed to Wales, 8 1/2" h. (some paint flaking)............................................................ 85

## PLATES

China, a series w/cat faces including Siamese, Abyssinian, grey striped tabby & Norwegian forest cat, marked on back "Kaiser Porcelain," 4" d., set of 4.................. 100

China, "My Very Own," a little girl holds a Siamese kitten & looks up at her father, second in a four-plate series titled "Signs of Love," 1984 ................................... 25

# STUFFED TOYS

Kitten, grey w/big furry tail curled around the body, tagged "Applause 1986," near mint, 5 1/2" h. ....................................... 8

Lion cub, gold & white, taggled "Applause 1981," near mint ............................................. 10

Persian long-hair, grey, w/"Dakin 1983" tag & Dakin plastic green disk, near mint, 10" h. ...................................... 15

White cat, fluffy w/pink neck ribbon, tagged "Applause 1985," near mint, overall 15" l........ 20

White cat, w/black & pink ears, tagged "Chubby Cat," near mint, 7" h.......................... 4

# MISCELLANEOUS

*Ceramic Carnation Creamer Holder*

Bowl, ceramic, model of an orange & yellow rounded cat w/the tail forming the handle, Cheshire face grin, stamped "Nestlé Carnation Coffee-Mate Nondairy Creamer - China," for holding creamer packets, 6" l. (ILLUS.) ...................... 30

Candy dish, brass, w/two attached kittens, Victorian, late 19th c.................................... 225

Mug, ceramic, Kliban cat face, marked "Sigma"........................................................... 30

*Fine Barlow-Doulton Pitcher*

Pitcher, tankard-type, stoneware pottery, incised central band of curled up cats, molded upper & lower bands w/brown, blue, white & green trim, designed by Hannah Barlow for Doulton, Lambeth, late 19th c. (ILLUS.) ................................. 2,600

**Salt & pepper shakers,** ceramics, figural, Gingham Dog & Calico Cat, Ceramic Arts Studio of Madison, pr. ........................... 100

**Spoon,** metal, "Cats Kill Mountains," marked "Rebus" .............................................. 65

**Teapot,** cov., stoneware pottery, decorated w/scenes of cats around the sides, decorated by Hannah Barlow for Doulton, Lambeth, late 19th c. ................................... 4,000

**Wall plaque,** papier-maché, round w/a molded figure of a seated cat looking straight at the viewer, cover in brown velvet w/glass eyes, 8 3/4" d. (some wear) ............................................................ 440

# CERAMICS

*ALSO SEE: Antique Trader Books Pottery and Porcelain Ceramics Price Guide, 3rd Edition.*

## ABINGDON

From about 1934 until 1950, Abingdon Pottery Company, Abingdon, Illinois, manufactured decorative pottery, mainly cookie jars, flowerpots and vases. Decorated with various glazes, these items are becoming popular with collectors who are especially attracted to Abingdon's novelty cookie jars.

*Abingdon Mark*

**Book ends,** model of Scottie dog, No. 650, 7 1/2" h., pr. ................................................ $200

**Candleholder,** double, No. 479, Scroll patt., 4 1/2" h. ............................................... 15

*Bamboo Pattern Candleholders & Plate*

**Candleholders,** Bamboo patt., No. 716, pr. (ILLUS.) .......................................................... 30

**Console bowl,** No. 532, Scroll patt., 14 1/2" l. .......................................................... 20

**Console plate,** Bamboo patt., No. 715, 10 1/2" d. (ILLUS. w/candleholders) ............ 125

**Cookie jar,** Baby, No. 561, 11" h. .......... 750-1,000

**Cookie jar,** Clock, No. 563, 9" h. ..................... 100

**Cookie jar,** Daisy, No. 677, 8" h. ....................... 50

*Fat Boy Cookie Jar*

**Cookie jar,** Fat Boy, No. 495, 8 1/4" h. (ILLUS.) ....................................................... 650

**Cookie jar,** Floral/Plaid, No. 697, 8 1/2" h. .......................................................... 350-550

**Cookie jar,** Hippo, No. 549, plain & decorated, 8" h. .............................................. 350-550

**Cookie jar,** Humpty Dumpty, No. 663, 10 1/2" h. ..................................................... 208

**Cookie jar,** Little Girl, No. 693, 9 1/2" h. ......... 225

*Little Ol' Lady Cookie Jars*

**Cookie jar,** Little Ol' Lady, No. 471, 9" h., various decorations, each (ILLUS.) ....... 200-300

**Cookie jar,** Windmill, No. 678, 10 1/2" h. ......... 500

**Cookie jar,** Witch, No. 692, 11 1/2" h. ............ 1,000

**Display sign,** marked "Abingdon" (ILLUS. with candleholders) ................................................. 300

*Scarf Dancer Figure*

**Figure,** Scarf Dancer, No. 3902, 13" h. (ILLUS.) ................................................... 800 up

*Various Flowerpots*

**Flowerpots,** Nos. 149 to 152, floral decoration, 3 to 6" h., each (ILLUS. of three)....... **15-30**

*Abingdon Lamp Base*

**Lamp base,** No. 254, draped shaft, 13" h.
(ILLUS.)...................................................... **200**
**Model of a swan,** No. 661, 3 3/4" h. ............... **150**

*Grecian Pitcher & Vase*

**Pitcher,** 15" h., Grecian patt., No. 613
(ILLUS. right)............................................... **150**
**Planter,** model of a Dutch shoe, No. 655,
5" l. ............................................................. **100**
**Planter,** model of a puppy, No. 652D,
6 3/4" l. ...................................................... **50**
**String holder,** Chinese head, No. 702,
5 1/2" h. ...................................................... **500**
**Vase,** 3 1/2" h., No. A1, what-not type.............. **100**
**Vase,** 4 1/2" h., No. C1, what-not type ............. **100**
**Vase,** 5" h., No. B1, what-not type.................... **100**
**Vase,** 5 1/2" h., No. 142, Classic line ................ **40**
**Vase,** 7" h., No. 171, Classic line ...................... **40**

*Figural Blackamoor Vase*

**Vase,** 7 1/2" h. figure of Blackamoor, No.
497D (ILLUS.) .............................................. **150**
**Vase,** 8" h., No. 132, Classic line ....................... **40**

*Fern Leaf Pattern Vase*

**Vase,** 8 1/2" h., No. 424, Fern Leaf patt.,
medium size (ILLUS.)..................................... **100**

*Swirl Pattern Vase*

**Vase,** 9" h., No. 513, Swirl patt., medium
(ILLUS.)......................................................... **20**

*Boyne Pattern Vase*

**Vase,** 9" h., No. 534, Boyne patt. (ILLUS.) ......... **35**
**Vase,** 10" h., No. 114, Classic line ..................... **25**

*Lung Pattern Vase*

**Vase,** 11" h., Lung patt., No. 302 (ILLUS.) ....... **225**
**Vase,** 15" h., floor-type, Grecian patt., No.
603 (ILLUS. left) ......................................... **150**
**Wall pocket,** figural butterfly, No. 601,
8 1/2" h. ...................................................... **150**
**Wall pocket,** figural Dutch boy, No. 489,
10" h. .......................................................... **150**
**Wall pocket,** figural Dutch girl, No. 490,
10" h. .......................................................... **150**

*Various Size Window Boxes*

**Window boxes,** No. 477, 13 1/2" l., No.
476, 10 1/2" l., No. 475, 7" l., each
(ILLUS.) ..................................................... **25-35**

# AMERICAN PAINTED PORCELAIN

*During the late Victorian era American artisans produced thousands of hand-painted porcelain items, including tableware, dresser sets, desk sets, and bric-a-brac. These pieces of porcelain were imported and usually bear the marks of foreign factories and countries. To learn more about identification, evaluation, history, and appraisal, the following books and newsletter by Dorothy Kamm are recommended:* American Painted Porcelain: Collector's Identification & Value Guide, Comprehensive Guide to American Painted Porcelain, *and* Dorothy Kamm's Porcelain Collector's Companion.

**Berry set:** 8 1/8" d. master bowl & eight
5 1/8" d. sauces; decorated w/various
fruits on polychrome grounds, burnished gold rims, various marks, ca.
1904-33, the set ......................................... **$240**

*Floral-decorated Bonbon Dish*

**Bonbon dish,** round w/one pierced handle,
decorated w/a central medallion of multi-colored flowers in a burnished gold basket, surrounded by a burnished gold frame, ivory ground, pale blue rim, burnished gold handle, border & rim, signed
"MRI," ca. 1925-30, 6 1/4" d. (ILLUS.)............ **35**
**Bonbon dish,** round w/two pierced handles, decorated w/a central medallion &
border design of pink roses, opal lustre interior ground, burnished gold handles
& lip, marked "MZ - Altrohlau - CM-R -
Czechoslovakia," 1918-39, 6 1/2" d.,
1 3/4" h. (ILLUS. top next page)..................... **65**
**Bone dish,** crescent-shaped, decorated
w/seaweed behind a conch shell, burnished gold rim accents, ca. 1888-1896,
6" w. ............................................................. **25**
**Bouillon cup & saucer,** double-handled,
decorated w/a border design of pink roses on a pale green band, burnished
gold scrolls, border bands, rims & handles, marked "T & V - Limoges -
France," ca. 1892-1907, 2 pcs. ...................... **40**

*Two-handled Bonbon with Roses*

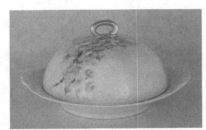

*Butter Dish with Pink Roses*

**Butter dish,** cov., decorated w/branches of pink wild roses on a pale multi-colored ground, yellow enameled flower centers & burnished gold handle, marked "Haviland - France," ca. 1894-1931, 7 1/2" d. (ILLUS.)............ 60

**Butter dish,** cov., individual, decorated w/forget-me-nots, pale blue border, burnished gold rim, signed "E. Keller," marked "H & Co. - France," ca. 1876-1879, 2 5/8" sq. ............ 15

*Calling Card or Manicure Tray*

**Calling card or manicure tray,** rectangular w/rounded corners & dished edges, decorated w/a conventional geometric border design in yellowish browns & burnished gold, pale yellowish brown ground, marked "GDA - France," ca. 1900-25. 5 5/16 x 8 1/4" (ILLUS.)................ 40

**Candlestick,** decorated at the base w/pink & ruby roses, ivory ground, burnished gold rims, marked "France," ca. 1891-1914, 5 1/2" h. ............ 55

**Card holder,** decorated w/pine cones on a multi-colored ground, burnished gold border & rim, signed "S.A.P.," marked "Favorite - Bavaria," ca. 1908-1918, 1 5/16 x 3 1/4", 2 3/4" h. ............ 22

**Celery dish,** pierced handles, decorated w/white roses on a pale green band, ivory ground, burnished gold rim & handles, signed "Julia Hummel," marked "Hutschenreuther - Josephine - Bavaria," ca. 1887, 5 1/2 x 12" ............ 55

**Coffeepot,** cov., decorated w/a conventional-style dragonfly & plant form, opal lustre & ivory ground, burnished gold border bands, rims, handle & knob, signed "Lucille Long," marked w/a crown & shield & "P.A. - Arzberg - Bavaria," ca. 1927, 8 3/8" h. ............ 140

**Collar box,** cov., round, decorated w/a conventional-style floral border on a light grey ground, dull red details, burnished gold knob, marked "Germany," ca. 1892-1914, 2 1/2" d., 1 1/4" h. ............ 20

**Condiment set:** pair of salt & pepper shakers, toothpick holder & 4 1/2 x 7 3/8" tray; decorated w/a border design of red poppies, burnished gold rims & tops, marked "Germany," ca. 1891-1914, the set ............ 50

**Creamer,** decorated w/red poppies, ivory ground, burnished gold rim & handle, marked "KPM - Germany," ca. 1904-1927, 3" h. ............ 20

**Cruet w/stopper,** decorated w/mayflowers on a pale green band, ivory ground, burnished gold rim, handle & stopper, signed "R.A.S.," marked "Oepiag - Czechoslovakia," ca. 1920-1935 ............ 80

**Cup & saucer,** after-dinner size, decorated w/violets on an ivory ground, burnished gold handle, signed "Attai M. Smith," marked w/a circle & "HR - Bavaria," ca. 1887 ............ 30

**Cup & saucer,** decorated w/naturalistic lilacs on a pale ivory ground, pale green border demarcated w/swirling Art Nouveau-style tendrils, burnished gold rims & handle, marked "Haviland - Limoges - France," ca. 1894-1916 ............ 35

**Egg cup,** single, footed, decorated w/yellow roses, burnished gold rim & border band, marked "T & V - Limoges - France," ca. 1892-1907, 3" h. ............ 30

**Ewer,** footring supporting a wide base & tapering cylindrical sides w/an arched rim spout & long arched scroll handle, decorated w/Art Nouveau-style pink & yellowish red tulips on an ivory & burnished gold ground, floral elements outlined in gold, handle, lip & base in burnished gold, signed w/two signatures, one illegible, the other "BEMENT," ca. 1900-15, 11 13/16" h. (ILLUS. top next page) ............ 175

**Game plates,** round, one decorated w/a stylized pheasant, the other a quail, each in landscapes, burnished gold rims, illegible signature, marked "Bavaria," ca. 1903-1917, 8" d. & 9 7/16" d., pr. ............ 65

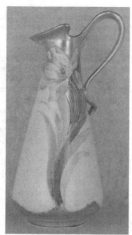

*Ornate Art Nouveau-style Ewer*

**Gravy boat w/attached underplate,** decorated w/pink roses on a light blue & yellow ground, burnished gold rims, marked "T & V - Limoges - France," ca. 1892-1917, 6 x 9 1/2", 3 1/2" h. .............................. **65**

**Nut bowl,** boat-shaped, decorated w/gooseberries on a pastel polychrome ground, burnished gold rim, signed "STONER," marked "Favorite - Bavaria," ca. 1908-1918, 4 1/2 x 5 1/2", 2 5/8" h. .......................................... **40**

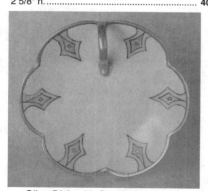

*Olive Dish with Simple Decoration*

**Olive dish,** scalloped rim w/upright ring handle, decorated w/a conventional geometric border design in pink, blue & burnished gold, pale green ground, burnished gold rim & handle, signed "E.J. Fachmann," marked "Z. S. & Co. - Bavaria," ca. 1900-1920, 5 1/2" d. (ILLUS.) ...................................... **20**

**Pickle dish,** leaf-shaped, decorated w/border clusters of maidenhair fern on a pale green ground, burnished gold rim, signed "Ida Lyston Paine," marked "T & V - Limoges - France," ca. 1892-1907, 11 1/4" l. ...................................... **45**

**Pin tray,** rectangular w/pointed ends w/pierced handles, a border design of clusters of conventional blue & yellow flowers, connected by a burnished gold border, burnished gold rim, signed "G G Williamson," marked w/a crowned double-headed eagle & "MZ Austria," 1884-1909, 3 3/4 x 6 3/4" ...................................... **45**

**Pitcher,** 5 3/4" h., lemonade, bulbous body, decorated w/currants on a polychrome ground, ca. 1900-1920 ................... **225**

**Plate,** bread & butter, decorated w/a border design of conventional pink wild roses, burnished gold details & rim, signed "Yeazel" & marked "Imperial - PSL - Empire I" w/a crown in an oval, 1914-18 ....... **20**

*Plate with Wild Rose Decoration*

**Plate,** 7 1/2" d., decorated w/a border design of pink wild roses, ivory ground, pale blue border, burnished gold rim, stamped "Lingquist Art Shop," marked w/the Thomas shield, 1915 (ILLUS.) .............. **40**

*Plate with Oranges & Blossoms*

**Plate,** 8 3/8" d., decorated w/a conventional border design of clusters of oranges & orange blossoms on an ivory ground, pale green rim border, signed "A.E.B.," marked "KPM," 1904-1927 (ILLUS.) ...................................... **45**

**Platter,** 11 1/2 x 17 5/8" oval, meat-type, decorated w/pink carnations on a pale blue & yellow ground, burnished gold rim, marked "H & Co. - Limoges - France," ca. 1891 ........................................ **250**

**Powder box,** cov., round, decorated w/a border design of daisies, ivory ground, burnished gold rim borders & handle, bright gold interior, signed "M. O.," marked w/a Thomas shield, 1908+, 3 3/4" h. ...................................................... **75**

**Ramekin & underplate,** round, ruffled rim, decorated w/dainty border design of ruby roses & forget-me-nots, bands of burnished gold scrolls & rims, pale green ground, signed "Walters," marked w/a bird & "CT," ca. 1899-1918, dish 4 3/8" d., underplate 5 3/16" d., 2 pcs. ........... **45**

**Relish/olive dish,** pierced handles, decorated w/a conventional border design of flowers & scrolls in burnished gold & blackish green, burnished gold rim & handle openings, signed "ERH," marked "Germany," ca. 1900-1914, 4 x 9" ................ **20**

**Salt dip,** decorated w/various flowers & colored panels, burnished gold rim & scrolls, signed "L.J.G.," ca. 1890-1910, 3" d. ...................................................... **30**

**Sandwich tray,** pierced handlse, decorated w/various nuts on a brown & ivory ground, burnished gold rim & handles, signed "WANDS," marked w/a crown, crossed scepters & "Rosenthal - Bavaria," 1910-1916, 5 1/8 x 14 1/2"............. **60**

**Sardine box,** cov., decorated w/fish & seaweeds, white enamel highlights, burnished gold rim & scrolls, marked "T & V - Limoges - France," ca. 1892-1907, 4 3/16 x 5 1/4", 1 5/8" h. (missing underplate) ............................................................. **65**

**Sherbet & underplate,** decorated w/red poppies on a pastel polychrome ground, burnished gold rims & foot rim, signed "S.M.E.," marked w/Thomas shield & "Bavaria" (sherbet) & "J & C - Bavaria" (underplate), ca. 1908-1918, plate 6" d., sherbet 3" h., 2 pcs. ...................................... **35**

*Rose-decorated Spoon Tray*

**Spoon tray,** slender oblong form w/incurved sides & pierced end handles, decorated w/clusters of pink roses, pale blue rim, pale yellow base, mother-of-pearl lustre interior, burnished gold rim & handles, signed "Wheelock Hand Painted" & marked w/a Limoges star & "France," ca. 1891-1914, 3 1/2 x 10 1/4" (ILLUS.)......................................................... **50**

**Stein,** dragon-handled, swelled cylindrical body w/flared base rim, decorated w/a central band of pine cones on a cream ground flanked by wide tan upper & lower bands, signed "Lloyd," ca. 1920-30, 5 3/4" h. (ILLUS. top next column) ........... **85**

*Dragon-handled Stein*

**Sugar bowl,** cov., handled, decorated w/an etched border landscape in burnished gold, ivory ground, burnished gold handles, lip, rim of cover & knob, signed "CE. PULLIS," marked "T & V - Limoges - France," 1917.............................................. **20**

**Talcum powder shaker,** decorated w/pink & ruby roses & greenery on an ivory ground, burnished gold top & base, signed "M. Perl," marked "Favorite - Bavaria," ca. 1908-1920, 2" d., 5" h. .............. **95**

**Tea set:** cov. teapot, cov. sugar bowl & creamer; each decorated w/burnished gold chrysanthemum medallions & panels of squiggled lines, burnished gold rims, handles & spout, signed "MSF," marked "Willets Belleek," ca. mid-1880s to 1909, the set ........................................... **325**

**Teapot stand,** round, decorated w/a Japanese-style painting of a stork on a flowering branch, ivory ground, burnished gold rim, signed "Charlotte Stephens, 4.25," marked "Japan," 6 7/8" d...................... **40**

**Tobacco jar,** cov., decorated w/a geometric design in browns, pale blue & pale yellow w/burnished gold knob, signed "Convent, Key West, Fla.," marked "T & V - Limoges - France," ca. 1892-1907, 5" d., 7 1/2" h.............................................. **295**

# BELLEEK

*Belleek china has been made in Ireland's County Fermanagh for many years. It is exceedingly thin porcelain. Several marks were used, including a hound and harp (1865-1880), and a hound, harp and castle (1863-1891). A printed hound, harp and castle with the words "Co. Fermanagh Ireland" constitutes the mark from 1891. Belleek-type china also was made in the United States last century by several firms, including Ceramic Art Company, Columbian Art Pottery, Lenox Inc., Ott & Brewer and Willets Manufacturing Co. Also see LENOX.*

## AMERICAN BELLEEK

### BASKETS AND BOWLS

**Lenox (palette mark),** bowl, h.p. Art Deco cameos of tulips accented w/heavy gold, artist-signed "Clara May," dated "22," 10 1/2" d., 3" h. .......................................... **$160**

**Ott and Brewer (crown & sword mark),** basket, applied floral & leaf decoration, 6 x 8", 3" h. .................................................. **325**

**Ott and Brewer (crown & sword mark),** bowl, h.p. flowers on a cream ground w/gilded thistle handles .............................. **325**

**Ott and Brewer (crown, sword & O.B. mark),** tazza, hand-decorated w/twig feet & gilt paste ferns, 8" d. ......................... **900**

**Willets (serpent mark),** bowl, handled, h.p. apple blossoms, leaves & twigs accented w/heavy gold, artist-signed "ES James," 6 1/4" d., 5" h. ............. **600**

**Willets (serpent mark),** bowl, handled, h.p. delicate floral sprays, ruffled top trimmed w/gold, gilt shaped handles.............................................................. **350**

## CANDLESTICKS & LAMPS

**Lenox (palette mark),** candlestick lamps, hexagonal inverted tulip shaped shades, h.p. roses joined by green swags & gilding, artist-signed "Trezisc," shades 6" d., overall 18" h., pr. .................... **560**

**Lenox (palette mark),** candlesticks, black w/Art Deco-style enameled flowers accented w/raised gold, 8 1/4" h., pr. ........... **225**

## CUPS AND SAUCERS

*Ceramic Art Company Cabinet Cup*

**Ceramic Art Company (CAC palette mark),** cabinet cup, no saucer, delicately enameled fretwork on footed base, 3 3/4" h. (ILLUS.)............................................ **75**

*CAC Tridacna Shape Cup and Saucer*

**Ceramic Art Company (CAC palette mark),** cup & saucer, "Tridacna" body shape, cream-colored exterior, blue lustre interior w/gold handle & rim, saucer 5 1/4" d. (ILLUS.)........................................ **350**

**Ceramic Art Company (CAC palette mark),** demitasse cup & saucer, decorated w/scenes of elves & pixies inspired by illustrator Palmer Cox, saucer 4" d. ......... **700**

**Coxon Belleek,** cup & saucer, h.p. "Boulevard" patt. gold around the rim of the cup & saucer, saucer 5" d. ............................. **175**

**Lenox (palette mark),** bouillon cup & saucer, cream-colored body w/gold banding around top of cup & saucer, saucer 6" d. ....... **95**

**Lenox (palette mark),** demitasse cup & saucer, filigree sterling silver overlay on two sides of the cup & around the rim of the cup & saucer, saucer 1 1/2" d. ............... **125**

**Lenox (palette mark),** demitasse cup & saucer, sterling silver overlay in an Art Deco design w/orange & green enameling, silver overlay around rim of cup & saucer, saucer 4 1/2" d. ............................. **140**

**Morgan (urn mark),** cup & saucer, h.p. in the "Orient" patt., saucer 5 1/4" d. .............. **250**

**Ott and Brewer (crown & sword mark),** cup & saucer, "Tridacna" body shape, cream-colored exterior, blue lustre interior w/gold handle & rim, saucer 5 1/4" d...... **300**

**Willets (serpent mark),** bouillon cup & saucer, h.p. flowers w/gold trim, saucer 5 1/2" d........................................................ **350**

**Willets (serpent mark),** bouillon cup & saucer, "Tridacna" shape, pearlized cream exterior & yellow interior, saucer 6 1/2" d........................................................ **225**

**Willets (serpent mark),** cup & saucer, coffee-size, cream-colored fluted body w/gold handle & trim, saucer 5 1/2" d. .......... **175**

**Willets (serpent mark),** cup & saucer, "Tridacna" shape, cream-colored exterior, pink lustre interior w/gold handle & trim, saucer 5 1/4" d. .......................................... **250**

**Willets (serpent mark),** demitasse cup & saucer, fluted white body w/purple monogram "W," outlined in gold w/gold-flecked purple dragon-shaped handle, saucer 4" d. ..................................................... **95**

## MUGS

**Ceramic Art Company (CAC palette mark),** mug, Art Deco design w/heavy gold accents, 7" h........................................ **295**

**Ceramic Art Company (CAC palette mark),** mug, h.p. chrysanthemums & leaves, artist-signed in gold "A.B. Wood," 5 1/2" h. ..................................... **125**

**Ceramic Art Company (CAC palette mark),** mug, h.p. design of grapes of various colors & grapevines, accented w/heavy gold on a pink pastel body, artist-signed "KR" & dated 1904, 6" h. .............. **350**

**Ceramic Art Company (CAC palette mark),** mug, h.p. peasant women in the Delft style of monochromatic blue on white, 5 1/2" h............................................. **275**

**Ceramic Art Company (CAC palette mark),** mug, h.p. portrait of a Native American Chief, 6" h. ............................... **1,100**

**Ceramic Art Company (CAC palette mark),** mug, portrait-type, h.p. "Colonial

Drinkers," artist-signed by Fred Little,
5" h. .................................................................. 325
**Ceramic Art Company (CAC palette mark),** mug, portrait-type, h.p. portrait of an old man w/a stein seated at a table, artist-signed "E.D. Westphal," 5 3/4" h. ........ 300
**Lenox (palette mark),** mug, h.p. bird decoration, 4 1/4" h. .............................................. 85
**Lenox (palette mark),** mug, h.p. heavy enameled flowers in the Art Deco style, artist-signed "HRM," 7" h. ............................. 140
**Lenox (palette mark),** mug, h.p. off-white & multicolored poppies on a soft cream matte ground accented w/gold & a gold curved handle, 7" h. ..................................... 200
**Lenox (palette mark),** mug, h.p. w/intense green leaves on a rust & brown ground of berries, 5" h. .............................................. 112

*Lenox Belleek Mug w/Roosters*

**Lenox (palette mark),** cylindrical w/incurved rim & C-form handle, decorated w/a frieze of parading roosters on pink & black mirrored ground, artist-signed, Lenox - Belleek stamp, ca. 1909, 5 1/2" d., 7" h. (ILLUS.) ............................... 165
**Willets (serpent mark),** goblet, toasting-type, "Aforetone," hand-painted, artist-signed "E.S. Wright," dated "1903," 5" d., 11" h. ....................................................... 350
**Willets (serpent mark),** mug, h.p. blackberries & foliage on a pastel ground, 4 1/2" h. .......................................................... 85

*Willets Belleek Mug with Monk*

**Willets (serpent mark),** mug, h.p. scene of a monk w/a wine cask, deep maroon base & handle, 6" h. (ILLUS.)........................ 275
**Willets (serpent mark),** cylindrical w/incurved rim & C-form handle, overglaze decoration of desert scene w/men wearing a fez & red uniform & holding onto a rope attached to a frantic camel which is racing around pyramids, handle, shoulder & base chased w/fired-on gold, marked w/Willets Belleek transfer logo, 5 3/8" h. ............................................. 165

## PITCHERS AND JUGS

**Ceramic Art Company (CAC palette mark),** cider pitcher, h.p. w/large red apples & leaves, accented w/gold w/a gold beaded handle, 5 3/4" w., 9" h............. 450
**Ceramic Art Company (CAC palette mark),** creamer, footed swan-form, gold highlights, artist-signed "ES," dated "1903," 3 1/2" h............................................. 225
**Lenox (palette mark),** cider set: pitcher & six cups; h.p. red apples, leaves & stems in an overall design, cups 5" h., pitcher 6" h., the set .................................................. 950
**Lenox (palette mark),** creamer, cream-colored body w/silver overlay, 4" h. ................... 100
**Lenox (palette mark),** creamer, cream-colored body w/swags of silver overlay, 5 1/4" h. .......................................................... 110
**Lenox (palette mark),** jug, handled, h.p. w/an overall floral design, trimmed in gold, 9" h. ........................................................ 560
**Lenox (palette mark),** lemonade pitcher, undecorated cream body, beaded handle, 6" h. ........................................................ 350
**Ott and Brewer (crown & sword mark),** creamer, cream-colored, hand-decorated w/gold paste foliage & an applied gilded thistle handle, 3 1/2" h. ...................... 450
**Ott and Brewer (crown & sword mark),** ewer, shaped form w/raised gold paste stylized leaf decoration on a matte ground, cactus-shaped handle, 7 1/2" d., 8" h. ........................................................... 1,500

*Willets Jug with Cavalier*

**Willets (serpent mark),** jug, handle, wide ovoid form w/short neck, h.p. scene of a bearded cavalier seated at a table w/a wine jug & goblet, 8" h. (ILLUS.) .................. 420

**Willets (serpent mark),** pitcher, jug-shaped, h.p. large poppies w/soft gold-accented foliage & handle, artist-signed "A.B. Julia," dated "1910," 7" h. .................... **750**

## PLATES

**Lenox (palette mark),** plate, cream-colored w/sterling silver overlay of festoons of ribbons, silver around outer rim, 7 1/2" d. .......................................................... **36**

**Lenox (palette mark),** plate, h.p. medallions surrounded & connected by heavy silver overlay by the Rockwell Silver Company, 7 1/2" d. ........................................ **55**

**Lenox (palette mark),** plate, h.p. w/a few flowers, 8" d. ..................................... **50**

**Lenox (palette mark),** platter, Art Deco design w/h.p. border & solid handles w/gold trim, 16 1/2" l. ................................. **125**

**Ott and Brewer (crown & sword mark),** plate, scalloped rim w/h.p. ferns in pink, dark green, mauve & light green, 8 1/2" d. ............................................................ **120**

## SALT DIPS

**Ceramic Art Pottery (CAC palette mark),** salt, h.p. violets & leaves, scalloped gold rim, 1 1/2" d. ............................................. **96**

**Lenox (palette mark),** salt & pepper shakers, h.p. w/small sprays of flowers, 2 1/2" h., pr. ................................................ **120**

*Artist-signed Lenox Salt Dip*

**Lenox (palette mark),** salt, h.p. w/a stylized band & blossom design, signed by E. Sweeny, 1 1/2" d. (ILLUS.) ...................... **55**

*Footed Lenox Salt Dip*

**Lenox (palette mark),** salt, three-footed, lustre body, gold-trimmed feet & scalloped rim, 1 1/4" d. (ILLUS.) .......................... **56**

*Floral-decorated Lenox Salt Dip*

**Lenox (palette mark),** salt dips, h.p. w/a soft pink ground & small purple blossoms & green leaves w/gold trim, 1 1/4" d., set of 12 (ILLUS. of one) .............. **500**

**Willets (serpent mark),** salt, pink lustre exterior, cream-colored interior, 2" d. (ILLUS. top next column) ...................... **56**

*Willets Salt with Lustre Exterior*

*Footed Willets Salt Dip*

**Willets (serpent mark),** salt, three-footed, lustre exterior w/gold rim & feet, 3" d. (ILLUS.) .......................................... **60**

## SETS

**Lenox (palette mark),** coffee set: pedestal-based cov. coffeepot, cov. sugar & creamer; h.p. flowers in gold shields w/heavy gold accents, artist-signed "Kaufman," the set ..................................... **1,450**

*Lenox Creamer & Sugar Bowl*

**Lenox (palette mark),** creamer & cov. sugar bowl, pedestal base, urn-form bodies, cream ground w/hand-decorated Art Deco design of enameled beading & gold paste, 7" h., pr. (ILLUS.) ...................... **600**

*Lenox Rose-decorated Tea Set*

**Lenox (palette mark),** tea set: cov. teapot, cov. sugar bowl & creamer; each w/a pedestal base & square foot, boat-shaped body w/angled handle, h.p. w/pink roses & blue blossoms w/green leaves, gold handles & finial, teapot 11" l., the set (ILLUS.) .................................. **900**

**Lenox (palette mark),** teapot, cov., pedestal base on square foot, boat-shaped body w/angled handle, h.p. sprays of pink & white roses w/green leaves, gold band trim, 10" l., 8" h. (ILLUS. top next page) .......................................................... **450**

*Lenox Teapot with Roses Decoration*

## VASES

*Ceramic Art Company Vase*

**Ceramic Art Company (CAC palette mark),** compressed bulbous body w/wide shoulder centered by a tiny trumpet-form neck, decorated w/orange & white nasturtiums on a gold & black ground, 4 1/2 x 7" (ILLUS.)............................ **110**

**Ceramic Art Company (CAC palette mark),** vase, ovoid body w/short neck & flared rim, h.p. chrysanthemums on a light green matte ground w/gold trim & gold on neck & neck rim, artist-signed "DeLan," 7 1/2" h. .......................................... **725**

**Ceramic Art Company (CAC palette mark),** vase, ovoid body tapering to a small neck w/fluted & flared rim, h.p. w/large open roses on a pale pink ground, some gold trim, 8 1/2" h. ................. **635**

**Ceramic Art Company (CAC palette mark),** vase, portrait-type, cylindrical, h.p. Art Nouveau style standing lady w/flowing hair, 7" d., 16" h. ........................ **1,400**

**Knowles, Taylor and Knowles Lotus Ware,** vase, front h.p. w/a scene of a Victorian lady standing by a beehive looking up at two flying cherubs, the back w/a bouquet of flowers, applied "fishnet" work on body, 5" d., 8" h. ............ **1,400**

**Lenox (early wreath mark),** vase, urn-shaped on a flaring pedestal & square foot, swan's-neck handles, white ground h.p. w/a central floral medallion on the front & back, 8" h. (ILLUS. top next column)................................................. **265**

**Lenox (palette mark),** vase, bud-type, h.p. & artist-signed, 2" d., 6" h. (mild crazing) ....... **86**

**Lenox (palette mark),** vase, h.p. flowers w/fine gilding, signed "Valborg, 1905," fluted top w/attached handle to side of tilted bowl, 3" d., 8" h.................................... **650**

*Early Lenox Urn-shaped Vase*

**Lenox (palette mark),** vase, bulbous body, h.p. floral decoration in mint condition, 5" d., 8" h. ............................................. **500**

**Lenox (palette mark),** vase, cylindrical, h.p. bird on branch w/flowers, 3" d., 9 1/2" h. ...................................................... **250**

*Lenox Vase with Blossom Seeds*

**Lenox (palette mark),** vase, tapering cylindrical body w/a short wide flared neck, h.p. w/open seed pods w/white & brown seeds & green leaves, shaded brown to cream ground, 10 1/4" h. (ILLUS.)...................................................... **550**

**Lenox (palette mark),** vase, cylindrical, decorated w/a stylized bird highlighted in gold, artist-signed "E.R. Martin," 3" d., 10 1/4" h. ................................................... **300**

**Lenox (palette mark),** vase, painted overall w/a floral design accented w/soft gold, 5" d., 10 1/4" h. .................................... **800**

**Lenox (palette mark),** vase, impressionistic h.p. decoration w/gold trim, 5 1/2" d., 11 1/2" h. ...................................... **475**

**Lenox (palette mark),** vase, ovoid body tapering to a short flared neck, h.p. w/large chrysanthemums w/soft gold highlights, 12 1/2" h. ..................................... **895**

*Lenox Vase with Landscape Band*

**Lenox (palette mark),** vase, cylindrical w/slightly incurved rim, a wide rim band h.p. w/a stylized country landscape & gold border, the lower body w/a pale ground h.p. overall w/diamond devices, 13" h. (ILLUS.)...................................................... 350

**Lenox (palette mark),** vase, cylindrical, h.p. Oriental women, trees & foliage, 15 1/2" h. ....................................................... 350

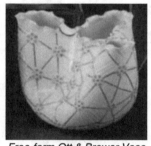

*Free-form Ott & Brewer Vase*

**Ott & Brewer (sword & crown mark),** bulbous base w/sides folded to form three openings w/slightly ruffled rim, decorated w/embossed blue & red forget-me-nots, a few shallow flakes to ruffled rim, 4 x 5 3/4" (ILLUS.)...................................... 825

**Willets (serpent mark),** vase, h.p. chrysanthemums accented w/gold on a white ground, 8" h.............................................. 625

**Willets (serpent mark),** vase, baluster-form w/flared foot & rim, dark green ground decorated w/a h.p. tiger on one side, 4" d., 9" h. (ILLUS. top next column)........................................................ 600

**Willets (serpent mark),** vase, cylindrical, h.p. design of three Japanese women in kimonos on a pale green ground, 3" d., 10" h. ........................ 450

**Willets (serpent mark),** vase, bulbous body w/a short pinched neck & fluted rim, h.p. overall w/large pastel roses & foliage, 8" d., 10" h. ................................ 500

**Willets (serpent mark),** vase, h.p. Pickard decoration of a full-length Art Nouveau lady w/flowing hair & gown on a pink lustre ground, 6" d., 10 1/2" h. ...................... **1,600**

*Willets Vase with a Tiger*

**Willets (serpent mark),** vase, bulbous shape w/a short, small neck w/fluted rim, h.p. w/flowers & heavy gold paste accents, 6 1/2" d., 11" h. ........................... 900

**Willets (serpent mark),** vase, cylindrical, h.p. w/large roses of different shades of pink w/green leaves & gold trim, 11 1/2" h. ....................................................... 625

**Willets (serpent mark),** vase, tapering from a small top to a flared bottom, h.p. clusters of roses, artist-signed "M.A. Minor -1902," 12" h................................ **1,400**

**Willets (serpent mark),** vase, bulbous form w/a short flared neck, h.p. overall w/pink, red & white roses w/soft gold highlights, 6" d., 13" h............................... **1,800**

**Willets (serpent mark),** vase, bulbous shape w/a short pinched neck w/fluted rim, h.p. overall w/pink, red & white roses, 9" d., 13" h. ............................... **1,850**

**Willets (serpent mark),** vase, undecorated, urn-shaped w/curved applied handles, 8" d., 13 3/4" h. ............................. 125

**Willets (serpent mark),** vase, waisted cylindrical form, h.p. overall w/hyacinths w/gold accents, artist-signed "E. Miler," 15 1/2" h. ...................................................... **1,050**

**Willets (serpent mark),** vase, h.p. large flowers, artist-signed "J. Brauer," 3" d., 15 1/2" h. ...................................................... **1,200**

**Willets (serpent mark),** vase, cylindrical w/flared bottom & flared scalloped top, h.p. completely w/pink & red roses on a soft pastel pink ground, 4" d., 15 1/2" h. ...................................................... **1,200**

## IRISH BELLEEK

**Creamer & open sugar bowl,** Lily patt., 3rd black mark, pr. ....................................... 145

**Creamer & open sugar bowl,** Ribbon patt., pr. ............................................................. 150

**Cup & saucer,** Neptune patt., 2nd black mark ........................................................... 225

**Cup & saucer,** Shamrock-Basketweave patt., brown twig-shaped handle .................. 105

**Vase,** 6" h., Shamrock patt., tree trunk-form..... 145

# BRAYTON LAGUNA POTTERY

*Durlin Brayton was ahead of other California upstart companies of the 1940s when he began Brayton Laguna Pottery in Laguna Beach, California in 1927. Collectors need to familiarize themselves with the various lines created by Brayton during their more than forty years in business. Hand-turned pieces were the first to be made but there were many other lines: Children, the mark usually including the name of the child; White Crackle; White Crackle with a small amount of brown stain; Brown Stain with some White Crackle which is not as popular among today's collectors as is the overall White Crackle or the White Crackle with some brown stain; Calasia, an Art Deco line, mostly vases and planters; Gay Nineties; Circus, Provincial, which was a brown stain with gloss glazes in an assortment of colors; African-American; Animals; Walt Disney sanctioned items which are much sought after and treasured; Webton Ware, popular today as it represents a country theme; and there are others.*

*Just as Brayton had numerous lines, the company also had various marks, no less than a dozen. Stickers were also used, sometimes in combination with a mark. Designers incised their initials on some regular sized items and many times their initials were the only mark on a piece that was too small for Brayton's other marks.*

*IForeign imports were instrumental in the failure of many United States companies and Brayton was no exception. Production ceased in 1968.*

## Brayton Leguna Marks

**Bowl,** 10" d., 2" h., Calasia line, feather design in bottom, scalloped rim w/raised circles on inner rim, pale green .................... $75
**Bust of woman's head & shoulders,** White Crackle glaze, 12" h. .......................... 450
**Candleholder,** figural, three choirboys ........... 145
**Candleholders,** figural Blackamoor, pr. ........... 215
**Cookie jar,** cov., light brown matte body w/overall honeycomb texture, dark brown straight tree branches w/five partridges around body in pale blue, yellow & orange, glossy white interior, pale blue lid, Model No. V-12, Mark 2, 7 1/4" h. (ILLUS. top next column) ............................ 185

*Honeycomb Texture Cookie Jar*

**Cookie jar,** figural Mammy, burgundy base & turquoise bandanna, rare early version.. **1,300**
**Cookie jar,** figural Provincial Lady, textured woodtone stain w/high gloss white apron & scarf tied around head, red, green & yellow flowers & hearts motif on clothing, being reproduced so must be marked, "Brayton Laguna Calif. K-27," 13" h. ........... 455
**Cookie jar,** figure of Swedish Maid (Christina), produced 1941, incised mark, 11" h. ........................................................... 600
**Creamer,** figural cat........................................... 45

*Provincial Line Cup with Tea Bag Holder*

**Cup w/tea bag holder,** Provincial line, brown bisque stain w/white & yellow flowers & green leaves outside, gloss yellow inside, marked "Brayton Laguna Calif. K-31," 1 3/4" h. (ILLUS.)........................ 16
**Figure,** African-American baby w/diaper, seated, green eyes, 3 3/4" h. ...................... 115
**Figure,** Blackamoor, kneeling & holding open cornucopia, heavily jeweled w/gold trim, 10" h. .................................................. 215
**Figure,** Blackamoor, kneeling, jeweled trim, 15" h. .............................................................. 275
**Figure,** Blackamoor, walking & carrying a bowl in his hands, glossy gold earrings, white bowl & shoes burgundy scarf, shirt & pantaloons, 8 1/4" h. ................................. 195
**Figure,** boy, Alice in Wonderland, not Walt Disney, marked "R" designer Frances Robinson, 3 3/4" h. ...................................... 300
**Figure,** boy wearing swimming trunks, Hillbilly Shotgun Wedding series, marked, produced 1938, designed by Andy Anderson, 4 1/4" h......................................... 165

**Figure,** Gay Nineties woman holding parasol in right hand, "Brayton Laguna Pottery," and copyright mark, 9 1/2" h. .............. **175**

**Figure,** peasant woman w/basket at her side in front & basket at her left in back, blue dress, yellow vest, incised mark "Brayton Laguna Pottery," 7 1/2" h. ............... **90**

**Figure,** woman w/two wolfhounds, one on each side, woman w/red hair & wearing a long yellow dress, 9 1/2" h. ...................... **145**

*African-American Boy & Girl*

**Figure group,** African-American boy & girl, boy holding basket of flowers in each hand, black shoes, yellow socks, barefoot girl, created by L. A. Dowd, early 1940s, paper label, 4 1/4" base, boy 7" h., girl 5 1/2" h. (ILLUS.) ......................... **375**

**Figure group,** Bride & Groom, the bride standing on the left w/white dress & pink flowers w/green leaves & pink hat, bouquet in left hand, her right hand on the groom's shoulder, man seated wearing striped trousers, black jacket, brown shoes & brown hat in left hand, black hair & mustache, stamp mark, 4 3/4" l., 8 1/2" h. ...................................... **165**

**Figure group,** man & cat blended together in an abstract design on a base, marked in-mold, hard-to-find, mid-1950s, 21" h. ....... **550**

**Figure group,** "One Year Later," Mother seated on left w/green dress holding baby in white dress, man standing w/striped trousers, black hair, mustache, jacket & shoes, stamp mark, 4" l., 8 1/4" h. ...................................... **160**

**Flower holder,** figural, "Francis," girl standing & holding small planter in front, White Crackle glossy glaze dress, yellow pot, brown hair w/blue ribbon, brown-stained face & arms, bluebird on right arm, 6 1/2" h. ................................. **35**

**Model of Carousel horse,** rearing position, 16" h. ...................................... **145**

**Model of cat,** "Kiki," seated on oval base, tail wraps around to hide back legs and paws, socks on front paws, hat perched on head & tied at front, eyes closed, colorful sweater, assorted colors of pink, blue, black & white, marked on unglazed bottom, "Brayton Laguna" above a line & "Kiki" below the line, 6" l. base, 9 1/4" h. ....... **125**

*Brayton-Laguna Cat*

**Model of cat,** lying down, head up, yellow body w/brown accents, green eyes, stamp mark, "Copyright 1941 by Brayton Laguna Pottery," 6 1/2" l., 4 1/4" h. (ILLUS.) ............................................ **55**

**Model of cat,** seated on oval base, socks on front paws w/left paw over right paw, head turned to left looking back, blue eyes open, hat perched on head between ears, bluebird on front of hat, colorful colors of blue, pink, white & black, unglazed, bottom w/no marks, 6 1/4" l. base, 9" h. .................................... **115**

**Model of dog,** sniffing, "Pluto," Walt Disney, 6" l., 3 1/4" h. ..................................... **165**

**Model of duck,** standing w/head down, Provincial line, brown overall stain w/glossy yellow bill, 6 1/2" h. .......................... **50**

**Model of fawn,** standing, ears up, brown & white spots, unmarked, 6 1/2" h. .................... **75**

**Model of fox,** seated, No. H-57....................... **110**

**Model of owl,** brown & white, 7" h. .................... **55**

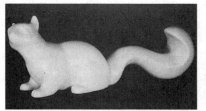

*Brayton-Laguna Quail*

**Model of quail standing on base,** turquoise, black & grey, underglaze mark "Brayton's Laguna Beach, Calif.," 10 3/4" h. (ILLUS.)..................................... **125**

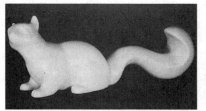

*Brayton-Laguna White Squirrel*

**Model of squirrel,** crouched w/tail behind & curving slightly upward on end, head &

ears up, nondescript face, White Crackle glaze, incised mark, "Brayton's Laguna Calif. T-15," 12 3/4" l, 6" h. (ILLUS.) ............. **125**

**Model of squirrel,** sitting on back feet w/tail up behind body & curved slightly on end, eating a nut, White Crackle glaze, incised mark, "Brayton's Laguna Calif. T-14," 7 1/4" h. ................................... **125**

**Model of St. Bernard dog,** standing, late 1930s, designed by Andy Anderson, brown & white w/partially black ears, 5" h. ...................................................... **250**

**Models of fawns,** woodtone w/white speckles, 5" h. & 7" h., pr. ............................. **95**

*Brayton-Laguna Monkeys*

**Models of monkeys,** male & female, White Crackle w/brown stain faces, unmarked, 13" h., pr. (ILLUS.) ...................................... **370**

**Pitcher,** cream-size, model of a Calico kitten, high glaze white body w/pink, light blue & mauve flowers & brown stitching, pale blue ribbon around neck, black nose & eyes, stamp mark "Copyright 1942 by Brayton Laguna Pottery," 6 1/2" h. ......................................................... **55**

**Salt & pepper shakers,** figural Mammy & Chef, 5 1/2" h., pr. ......................................... **85**

**Tile,** chartreuse & yellow bird, turquoise, yellow & white flowers, black background incised mark, "Laguna Pottery," 7 x 7" ............................................................... **125**

**Vase,** 7 1/4" h., 7" w., 7" l., pillow-shape w/feather design on each side & raised circles on recessed short base, fern green ................................................................ **85**

*Sea Horse Vase*

**Vase,** 8 1/2" h., model of a sea horse, white body w/pink, yellow & turquoise accents, stamp mark underglaze "Brayton Calif. U.S.A.," (ILLUS.) ......................................... **155**

*Russian Lady Wall Plaque*

**Wall plaque,** figure of woman, arms above head, Russian dress, Webton Ware mark, hard-to-find, 13 1/2" h. (ILLUS.) ......... **200**

*Webton Ware Wall Pocket Bowl*

**Wall pocket,** model of a bowl w/shaped rim, two holes for hanging, Webton Ware mark on unglazed back, 2 3/4" w., 4 1/4" h. (ILLUS.)............................................. **65**

# BUFFALO POTTERY

*Buffalo Pottery was established in 1902 in Buffalo, New York, to supply pottery for the Larkin Company. Most desirable today in Deldare Ware, introduced in 1908 in two patterns, "The Fallowfield Hunt" and "Ye Olden Days," which featured central English scenes and a continuous border. Emerald Deldare, introduced in 1911, was banded with stylized flowers and geometric designs and had varied central scenes, the most popular being from "The Tours of Dr. Syntax." Reorganized in 1940, the company now specializes in hotel china.*

*Buffalo Pottery Mark*

## EMERALD DELDARE

**Chamberstick,** Art Nouveau geometric banded & paneled design w/white & celadon green flowers on an olive brown ground, ink stamp mark, 6" d., 7" h. (very small edge chip) ............................................. **990**

*Emerald Deldare Chocolate Pot*

**Coffee/chocolate pot,** cov., tall tapering hexagonal form w/pinched spout & angled D-form handle, inset lid w/blossom finial, stylized symmetrical designs highlighted w/white flowers on body & lid, band just under spout w/stylized moths & large butterfly, decorated by L. Newman, ca. 1911, artist's name in green slip, ink stamp logo & "7," 10 1/2" h. (ILLUS.)..................................... **1,980**

*Dr. Syntax Emerald Deldare Plate*

**Plate,** 7 1/4" d., h.p. floral border & center scene, "Dr. Syntax Soliloquizing," by E. Missel, marked w/Emerald Deldare logo, "1911" & "4," pinhead size glaze nick off edge of rim (ILLUS.) .................................... **303**

## MISCELLANEOUS

**Pitcher,** jug-type, 5 3/4" h., "Holland," decorated w/three colorful h.p. scenes of Dutch children on the body w/band near the rim decorated w/a rural landscape, ca. 1906, marked w/Buffalo transfer logo & date, "Holland" & "9," overall consistent staining (ILLUS.).............. **468**

*"Holland" Pitcher*

*"Cinderella" Pitcher*

**Pitcher,** 6" h., jug-type, "Cinderella," ca. 1907, marked w/Buffalo transfer logo & date, "Cinderella" & "1328" (ILLUS.) ........... **440**

*"Gloriana" Pitcher*

**Pitcher,** 9" h., "Gloriana," blue on white, ca. 1908 (ILLUS.).............................. **550**

## CANTON

*This ware has been decorated for nearly two centuries in factories near Canton, China. Intended for export sale, much of it was originally inexpensive blue-and-white hand-decorated ware. Late 18th and early 19th century pieces are superior to later ones and fetch higher prices.*

**Bowl,** 9 1/2" d., footed deep rounded sides below the squared cut-corner rim, 19th c. (minor interior glaze imperfections) ........ **$920**

**Bowl,** 10" d., 2 3/4" h., round w/scalloped edge, orange peel glaze (minor chips)......... **495**

**Bowl,** 10 1/4" d., 3" h., round w/scalloped rim, orange peel glaze (small chips & spider crack)................................................. **385**

**Cider pitcher,** cov., jug-form, wide ovoid body w/an applied entwined strap handle, mismatched low domed cover w/foo dog figural finial, 19th c., 8" h. .................. **1,265**

**Fruit basket & undertray,** oval upright reticulated sides w/a flared rim, on a conforming reticulated undertray w/a Chinese landscape in the center, orange peel glaze, 19th c., 9 1/8" l., 2 pcs. .......... **1,540**

**Platter,** 14 3/4" l., oblong w/angled corners, orange peel glaze, 19th c. ............................ **385**

**Platter,** 18 3/4" l., large wide oblong shape w/angled corners, large landscape scene in center, 19th c. ............................. **1,430**

*Canton Tea Caddy*

**Tea caddy,** cov., octagonal, 19th c., 5 1/2" h. (ILLUS.)...................................... **2,645**

**Teapot,** cov., oval cylindrical form w/angled spout & entwined strap handle, inset cover w/fruit finial, worn gilt trim, 19th c., 5 1/2" h. ............................................... **770**

**Vegetable dish,** cov., almond-shaped w/flanged rim, low domed cover w/pine cone finial, 19th c., 10 1/2" l. ....................... **220**

**Water bottle,** wide short cylindrical base below the tall waisted neck w/small rim spout, 19th c., 9 7/8" h. (chips).................... **275**

## CATALINA ISLAND POTTERY

*The Clay Products Division of the Santa Catalina Island Co. produced a variety of wares during their brief ten-year operation. The brainchild of chewing-gum magnate, William Wrigley, Jr., owner of Catalina Island at the time, and his business associate D. M. Retton, the plant was established at Pebbly Beach, near Avalon in 1927. Its two-fold goal was to provide year-round work for the island's residents and building material for Wrigley's ongoing development of a major tourist attraction at Avalon. Early production consisted of bricks and roof and patio tiles. Later, art pottery, including vases, flower bowls, lamps and home accessories were made from a local brown-based clay and, about 1930, tablewares were introduced. These early wares carried vivid glazes but had a tendency to chip readily and a white-bodied, more chip-resistant clay, imported from the mainland, was used after 1932. The costs associated with importing clay eventually caused the Catalina pottery to be sold to a California mainland competitor in 1937. These wares were molded and are not hand-thrown but some pieces have hand-painted decoration.*

$\begin{array}{c}\mathcal{C}^{ATALIN\!\!\mathcal{A}} \\ \text{MADE IN} \\ \text{U. S. A.} \\ \mathcal{P}^{OTTERY} \end{array}$

*Catalina Island Pottery Mark*

**Ashtray,** Model No. 657, green glaze .............. **$95**

**Ashtray,** model of a cowboy hat, Descanso green or blue glaze, each............................ **195**

**Ashtray,** figural fish, decorated, Model No. 550, Toyon red glaze, 4 1/2" l. ..................... **150**

**Book ends,** figural monk, pearly white glaze, 4 x 5", pr. ......................................... **1,200**

**Bowl,** fruit, 13" d., footed, blue glaze................ **175**

**Bowl,** 9 1/2 x 14", flared sides, white glaze...... **150**

**Bowl,** 17 1/2" l., oval, flared, pearly white glaze................................................................ **200**

**Candelabra,** No. 382, Descanso green glaze, pr. ......................................................... **950**

**Candleholders,** Descanso green, pr. ............... **150**

**Candleholders,** No. 380, sea foam glaze, pr. ..................................................................... **200**

**Carafe,** cov., handled, Toyon red glaze .......... **125**

**Carafe,** cov., handled, turquoise glaze.............. **95**

*Charger with Marlin*

**Charger,** relief-molded marlin, Monterey brown glaze, 14" d. (ILLUS.) ..................... **1,500**

**Charger,** rolled edge, Toyon red glaze, 14 1/2" d. .......................................................... **225**

**Compote,** footed, w/glass liner, Toyon red glaze.............................................................. **225**

**Flask,** model of a cactus, Descanso green, 6 1/4" h. ......................................................... **600**

**Flowerpot,** Toyon red, 4 1/2" h. ......................... **65**

**Lamp base,** basketweave design, Descanso green glaze .......................................... **1,200**

**Oil jar,** No. 351, Toyon red glaze, 18" h. ........ **1,200**

**Pipe holder/ashtray,** figural napping peon, Descanso green or blue glaze, each ................................................................. **450**

**Pitcher,** 7 1/2" h., Toyon red glaze................... **350**

**Plate,** chop, 11" d., Descanso green glaze ........ **65**

**Plate,** chop, 12 1/2" d., Toyon red glaze ........... **70**

**Relish tray,** handled, clover-shaped, sea foam glaze (ILLUS. top next page) .............. **650**

**Salt & pepper shakers,** figural Senorita & Peon, Toyon red & yellow glaze, pr. ............ **150**

**Salt & pepper shakers,** model of cactus,
tall, pr. ........................................................ **65**

*Clover-shaped Relish Tray*

**Salt & pepper shakers,** model of tulip,
blue glaze, pr.................................................. **85**

*Tile Plaque with Macaw*

**Tile plaque,** depicting green macaw,
12 x 18" (ILLUS.)...................................... **2,000**

*Tortilla Warmer*

**Tortilla warmer,** cov., Monterey brown
glaze (ILLUS.) ........................................... **1,500**
**Tumbler,** blue glaze .......................................... **35**
**Vase,** 5" h., handled, Model No. 612, Man-
darin yellow glaze........................................ **125**
**Vase,** 5" h., stepped form, blue glaze............... **275**
**Vase,** 5" h., stepped, handled, turquoise
glaze............................................................. **350**
**Vase,** bud, 5" h., Model No. 300, Descanso
green glaze ................................................. **100**
**Vase,** 5 1/2" h., Model No. 503, tan glaze ........ **100**
**Vase,** 5 1/2" h., Model No. 600, tan glaze ........ **135**
**Vase,** 6" h., ribbed body, blue glaze .................. **65**
**Vase,** 7" h., Model No. 636, turquoise glaze..... **145**

**Vase,** 7 1/4" h., sawtooth edge on each
side, Model No. 601, turquoise glaze........... **200**
**Vase,** 7 1/2" h., trophy-form, handled,
Toyon red glaze .......................................... **350**
**Vase,** 7 1/2" h., trophy-form, orange glaze ....... **325**
**Vase,** 7 3/4" h., Model No. 627, blue glaze ...... **135**

# CERAMIC ARTS
# STUDIO OF MADISON

*Founded in Madison, Wisconsin in 1941 by two young men, Lawrence Rabbitt and Reuben Sand, this company began as a "studio" pottery. In early 1942 they met an amateur clay sculptor, Betty Harrington and, recognizing her talent for modeling in clay, they eventually hired her as their chief designer. Over the next few years Betty designed over 460 different pieces for their production. Charming figurines of children and animals were a main focus of their output in addition to models of adults in varied costumes and poses, wall plaques, vases and figural salt and pepper shakers.*

*Business boomed during the years of World War II when foreign imports were cut off and, at its peak, the company employed some 100 people to produce the carefully hand-decorated pieces.*

*After World War II many poor-quality copies of Ceramic Arts Studio figurines appeared and when, in the early 1950s, foreign imported figurines began flooding the market, the company found they could no longer compete. They finally closed their doors in 1955*

*Since not all Ceramic Arts Studio pieces are marked, it takes careful study to determine which items are from their production.*

*Ceramic Arts Studio Marks*

*Madonna with Child*

**Ewer,** Ballerina, 4 1/4" h. .................................. **$75**
**Figure group,** Madonna with Child,
6 1/2" h., 1 pc. (ILLUS.) .............................. **120**

*Love Trio: Lover Boy,
Bashful Girl & Willing Girl*

**Figurine,** Bashful Girl, dark hair, 4 1/2" h.
(ILLUS. center) .............................................. **75**
**Figurine,** Burmese Chinthe, 4" h. ..................... **225**
**Figurine,** Daisy, Ballet Group, standing,
5 1/2" h. ...................................................... **175**

*Indian Group: Birch Bark Canoe, Bunny,
Chipmunk, Fawn, Hiawatha, Indian Boy,
Indian Girl, Minnehaha & Sea Gull*

**Figurine,** Hiawatha, Indian group, 3 1/2" h.
(ILLUS. second from right) .......................... **150**
**Figurine,** Indian Boy, Indian group, 3" h.
(ILLUS. center front, left) ............................. **30**
**Figurine,** Indian Girl, Indian group,
3 1/4" h. (ILLUS. center front, right) .............. **30**
**Figurine,** Lady Rowena on charger,
8 1/2" h. ...................................................... **190**
**Figurine,** Lover Boy, 4 1/2" h. (ILLUS. left) ........ **75**
**Figurine,** Minnehaha, Indian group,
6 1/2" h. (ILLUS. back left) .......................... **275**
**Figurine,** Pansy, Ballet Group, standing,
6" h. ............................................................ **375**
**Figurine,** Pied Piper, Nursery Rhyme
Group, 6 1/4" h. ........................................... **225**
**Figurine,** Praying Girl, Nursery Rhyme
Group, 3" h. ................................................. **50**
**Figurine,** Rose, part of Ballet Group, stoop-
ing, 5" h. ...................................................... **200**
**Figurine,** Running Boy, Nursery Rhyme
Group, 3 1/2" h. ........................................... **65**
**Figurine,** Running Girl, Nursery Rhyme
Group, 3 1/4" h. ........................................... **50**
**Figurine,** Saint George on charger,
8 1/2" h. ...................................................... **190**
**Figurine,** Violet, Ballet Group, sitting, 3" h. ....... **150**

**Figurine,** Willing Girl, blonde, 4 1/2" h.
(ILLUS. right) ............................................... **120**
**Figurine,** Winter Willie, 4" h. ....................... **50-70**
**Figurines,** Alice & March Hare, 4 7/8" h. &
6" h., pr. ...................................................... **450**
**Figurines,** Balinese Dancers, Man &
Woman, 9 1/2" h., pr. ................................... **200**

*Bride & Groom Figurines*

**Figurines,** Bride & Groom, 4 3/4" h. &
4 7/8" h., pr. (ILLUS.) ................................... **150**
**Figurines,** Burmese Man & Woman,
4 1/2" h., pr. ................................................ **300**

*Chinese Boy & Girl Figurines*

**Figurines,** Chinese Boy & Girl, 4 1/4" h. &
4" h., pr. (ILLUS. far right & far left) .............. **30**
**Figurines,** Colonial Boy & Girl, 5 1/2" &
5" h., pr. ...................................................... **105**
**Figurines,** Colonial Man & Woman,
6 1/2" h., pr. ................................................ **120**
**Figurines,** Gay Ninety Couple, Harry &
Lillibeth, 6 1/2" h. & 6" h., pr. ....................... **90**

*Gay Ninety Man & Woman*

**Figurines,** Gay Ninety Man & Woman, 6 3/4" h. & 6 1/2" h., pr. (ILLUS.)................. **125**

*Gypsy Man & Woman*

**Figurines,** Gypsy Man & Woman, 6 1/2" h. & 7" h., pr. (ILLUS.)...................................... **120**

*Rare Kabuki Man & Woman*

**Figurines,** Kabuki Dancers, Man & Woman, 8 1/2" h. & 6" h., pr., rare (ILLUS.)...................................................... **2,000**
**Figurines,** Wee Chinese Boy & Girl, 3" h., pr. (ILLUS. center).......................................... **20**
**Figurines,** Wee Dutch Boy & Girl, 3" h., pr. ....... **30**
**Figurines,** Zulu Man & Woman, 5 1/2" h. & 7" h., pr.......................................................... **650**
**Figurines,** shelf-sitters, Colonial Boy & Girl, 5 1/2" h. & 5" h., pr. ............................... **150**

*Farmer Boy & Girl Shelf-sitters*

**Figurines,** shelf-sitters, Farmer Boy & Girl, 4 3/4" h., 4 1/2" h., pr. (ILLUS.) ..................... **90**
**Head vase,** Barbie, 7" h. ................................... **195**
**Head vases,** Lotus & Manchu, 7 3/4" h., pr...... **250**
**Model of birch bark canoe,** Indian group, 8" l. (ILLUS. in background) ......................... **150**
**Model of bunny,** Indian group, 1 3/4" h. (ILLUS. front left)........................................... **50**
**Model of chipmunk,** Indian group, 2" h. (ILLUS. far right)............................................. **60**
**Model of fawn,** Indian group, 4 1/4" h. (ILLUS. far left, front)...................................... **90**
**Model of horse,** Modern colt, 7 1/2" h. ............ **250**
**Model of modern panther,** 6 1/2" h. ............... **200**
**Model of sea gull,** Indian group, (hooks onto side of canoe), 3 3/4" w. wing span (ILLUS. center back on canoe) ................. **1,000**
**Model of tortoise with cane,** 3 1/4" h. ............ **150**
**Mug,** figural Mr. Toby, seated, holding mug, 2 3/4" h........................................................ **125**
**Salt & pepper shakers,** figural Mother & Baby Donkey, 3 1/4" h. & 3" h., pr............... **350**
**Salt & pepper shakers,** figural Mother & Baby Spaniel dog, 2 1/4" h. & 2" h., pr......... **175**

*Running Mother & Baby Bunny*

**Salt & pepper shakers,** figural Running Mother & Baby Bunny, 4 1/2" & 3 1/2" h., pr. (ILLUS.)................................................... **250**
**Salt & pepper shakers,** figural Santa Claus & evergreen tree, 2 1/4" h. & 2 1/2" h., pr. ............................................... **400**
**Salt & pepper shakers,** figural Wee Pig Boy & Girl, 3 1/4" h., & 3 1/2" h., pr. ............... **50**
**Vase,** 4 1/4" h., Comedy & Tragedy, snuggle for Encore man or lady (double sided), 1 pc.................................................... **150**

# CHINTZ CHINA

*There are over fifty flower patterns and myriad colors from which Chintz collectors can choose. That is not surprising considering companies in England began producing these showy, yet sometimes muted, patterns in the early part of this century. Public reception was so great that this production trend continued until the 1960s.*

*Somerset Pattern Salad Bowl*

**Bonbon dish,** Clevedon patt., Royal Winton .............................................................. **225**

**Bowl,** octagonal, Festival patt., Crown Ducal............................................................. **325**

**Bowl,** octagonal, Ivory Chintz patt., Crown Ducal............................................................. **350**

**Bowl,** salad, chrome rim, Somerset patt., Rheims shape, Royal Winton (ILLUS.) ........ **550**

**Bowl,** Sweet Pea patt., Crown shape, Royal Winton ................................................... **750**

*Majestic Pattern Breakfast Set*

**Breakfast set:** cov. teapot, cup, creamer, open sugar bowl, toast rack & oblong paneled tray w/end handles; Majestic patt., Countess shape, Royal Winton, the set (ILLUS.) ........................................ **1,750**

**Breakfast set,** Fireglow Black patt., Royal Winton, the set ............................................ **850**

**Butter dish,** cov., Cranstone patt., Royal Winton....................................................... **375**

**Butter pat,** Anemone patt., Royal Winton .......... **35**

**Butter pat,** Sunshine patt., Royal Winton ....... **135**

*Exotic Bird Cake Plate*

**Cake plate,** Exotic Bird patt., Saville shape, Royal Winton (ILLUS.) ................................. **135**

**Cake plate,** Lichfield patt., James Kent, Ltd. ............................................................... **135**

**Cake plate,** open handles, Carnation patt., Royal Winton.............................................. **125**

**Cake plate,** open handles, Shrewsbury patt., Royal Winton....................................... **295**

**Cake plate,** pedestal base, Cotswold patt., Royal Winton............................................... **275**

**Cake plate,** Royalty patt., Ascot shape, Royal Winton (ILLUS. top next column) ....... **350**

**Cake stand,** three-tier, Skylark patt., Lord Nelson Ware ............................................... **155**

**Cake stand,** two-tier, Clyde patt., Royal Winton ............................................................. **75**

**Candy dish,** cov., low round shape, pointed finial on low domed cover, Stratford patt., Royal Winton (ILLUS. center next column)................................................ **950**

**Candy dish,** Mayfair patt., Royal Winton ......... **135**

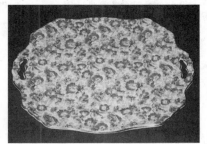

*Royalty Pattern Cake Plate*

*Rare Stratford Pattern Candy Dish*

*Blue Chintz Pattern Cheese Dish*

**Cheese dish,** cov., slanted cover, Blue Chintz patt., Crown Ducal (ILLUS.) ............. **750**

**Cheese dish,** cov., Summertime patt., Dane shape, Royal Winton ........................ **350**

**Coaster,** Paisley patt., Royal Winton............... **135**

**Coffeepot,** cov., Dorset patt., Royal Winton..... **750**

**Coffeepot,** cov., Pink Chintz patt., Crown Ducal ........................................................ **1,595**

*Primula Pattern Coffeepot*

**Coffeepot,** cov., Primula patt., Granville shape, James Kent Ltd. (ILLUS.) .............. **1,400**
**Compote,** open, Blue Tulip patt., Royal Winton ............................................................. **75**

*Welbeck Pattern Compote*

**Compote,** open, low scalloped bowl on a short scalloped pedestal base, Welbeck patt., Royal Winton (ILLUS.) ........................ **595**
**Compote,** open, oblong shallow shaped bowl on a flaring rectangular pedestal base, Queen Anne patt., Royal Winton ....... **225**
**Condiment set on tray,** Delphinium Chintz patt., Royal Winton, the set ......................... **250**

*Marion Pattern Cracker Jar*

**Cracker jar,** cov., Marion patt., Rheims shape, Royal Winton (ILLUS.) .................. **1,500**

*Summertime Pattern Cracker Jar*

**Cracker jar,** cov., Summertime patt., Ninevah shape, Royal Winton (ILLUS.) ............ **1,100**

*Chintz Floral Creamer*

**Creamer,** creamy yellow background w/bunches of pink & blue flowers, green leaves, light green trim, like Unknown 5 patt. by Barker Brothers, Ltd., Sampson Smith, 3 1/4" d., 4" h. (ILLUS.) ..................... **110**
**Creamer & cov. sugar bowl,** Chintz patt., Old Cottage shape, Royal Winton, pr. ......... **250**
**Creamer & cov. sugar bowl,** Primula patt., Crown Ducal, pr. ......................................... **145**
**Creamer & cov. sugar bowl,** Rosalynde patt., James Kent, Ltd., pr. .......................... **150**

*Sweet Pea Creamer & Sugar Bowl*

**Creamer & open sugar bowl,** Sweet Pea patt., Ascot shape, Royal Winton, pr. (ILLUS.) ...................................................... **195**
**Cup & saucer,** Briar Rose patt., Lord Nelson Ware, the set .......................................... **85**
**Cup & saucer,** Cheadle patt., Royal Winton, pr. .......................................................... **125**
**Cup & saucer,** Merton patt., Royal Winton, the set .................................................... **95**
**Demitasse cup & saucer,** Pelham patt., Royal Winton .................................................. **85**
**Dish,** canoe-shaped, Pekin patt., Royal Winton .................................................... **145**
**Egg cup,** Kinver patt., Royal Winton ................ **235**
**Gravy boat & undertray,** Sunshine patt., Royal Winton, 2 pcs. .................................. **295**
**Hot water pitcher,** cov., English Rose patt., Royal Winton ...................................... **750**
**Hot water pot,** cov., Fireglow patt., Sexta shape, Royal Winton (ILLUS. top next page) .......................................................... **700**
**Jam jar,** cov., Peony patt., Crown Ducal .......... **275**
**Jam jar,** cov., Rapture patt., James Kent, Ltd. ................................................................. **125**
**Jam jar, cover & underplate,** Beeston patt., Rheims shape, Royal Winton, the set ................................................................. **395**

*Fireglow Hot Water Pot*

*Sweet Pea Pattern Jam Jar*

**Jam jar, cover & underplate,** Sweet Pea
patt., Ascot shape, Royal Winton, the set
(ILLUS.) ...................................................... **325**
**Juice reamer,** Spring Blossom patt.,
Crown Ducal................................................ **450**
**Lily bowl,** Ascot patt., Crown Ducal................ **145**
**Mustard jar,** cov., footed barrel shape, Tri-
umph patt., Royal Winton ........................... **155**

*DuBarry Pattern Nut Dish*

**Nut dish,** individual, DuBarry patt., James
Kent, Ltd. (ILLUS.) ........................................ **95**
**Nut dish,** individual, Eleanor patt., Royal
Winton ............................................................ **85**
**Pin tray,** June Festival patt., Royal Winton ...... **145**
**Pitcher,** jug-form, Balmoral patt., Royal
Winton .......................................................... **475**
**Pitcher,** jug-form, Mauve Chintz patt.,
Crown Ducal................................................ **175**
**Pitcher,** straight-sided, Green Tulip patt.,
Lord Nelson Ware ....................................... **550**

**Pitcher,** 3" h., jug-form, miniature milk-
type, Chelsea patt., Globe shape, Royal
Winton .......................................................... **110**

*Summertime Milk Pitcher*

**Pitcher,** 5" h., jug-form, milk, Summertime
patt., Albans shape, Royal Winton
(ILLUS.)........................................................ **550**

*Sweet Pea Milk Pitcher*

**Pitcher,** 5" h., jug-form, milk, Sweet Pea
patt., Duval shape, Royal Winton
(ILLUS.)........................................................ **650**
**Plate,** 9" d., dinner, Purple Chintz patt.,
Crown Ducal................................................ **165**
**Plate,** bread & butter, Richmond patt.,
Royal Winton................................................ **195**
**Plate,** chop, Apple Blossom patt., James
Kent, Ltd....................................................... **235**
**Plate,** octagonal, Ivory Fruit patt., Crown
Ducal .............................................................. **65**
**Plate,** salad, Bedale patt., Royal Winton ............ **95**
**Plate,** small, Pansy patt., Lord Nelson
Ware................................................................ **65**
**Plate,** 9" d., dinner, Evesham patt., Royal
Winton .......................................................... **265**

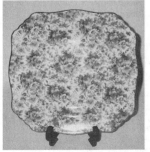

*Summertime Pattern Dinner Plate*

**Plate,** 9" sq., dinner, Summertime patt., Ascot shape, Royal Winton (ILLUS.)............ **225**

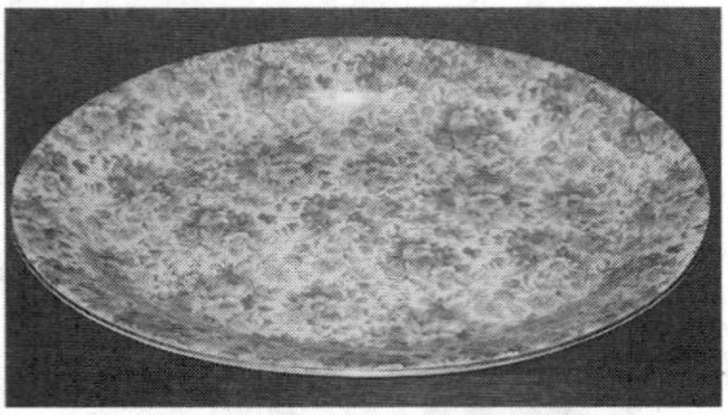

*Summertime Oval Platter*

**Platter,** 12" l., oval, Summertime patt., Royal Winton (ILLUS.) .................................. **325**
**Relish dish,** Hydrangea patt., James Kent, Ltd. .............................................................. **150**

*Primrose Pattern Rose Bowl*

**Rose bowl w/flower frog insert,** Primrose patt., rectangular stepped foot supporting rectangular rounded bowl, Royal Winton (ILLUS.)........................................... **450**

*Florida Rose Bowl with Flower Frog*

**Rose bowl w/frog insert top,** wide rounded urn-form bowl w/large loop shoulder handles & low domed insert flower frog top, raised on a round pedestal base, Florida patt., Crown Ducal (ILLUS.)..................................................... **2,600**
**Salt & pepper shakers on tray,** June Roses patt., Royal Winton, the set............... **295**
**Sandwich tray,** Floral Feast patt., Royal Winton, 7 x 12"...................................... **150**
**Server,** chrome center-handle w/red top, overall floral pattern in pink, blue & yellow w/green leaves, like Anemone patt. by Elijah Cotton Ltd. (Lord Nelson), Parrot & Co., 9" d. (ILLUS. top next column)..... **135**

**Soup plate,** flanged rim, Tapestry patt., James Kent, Ltd. ......................................... **125**

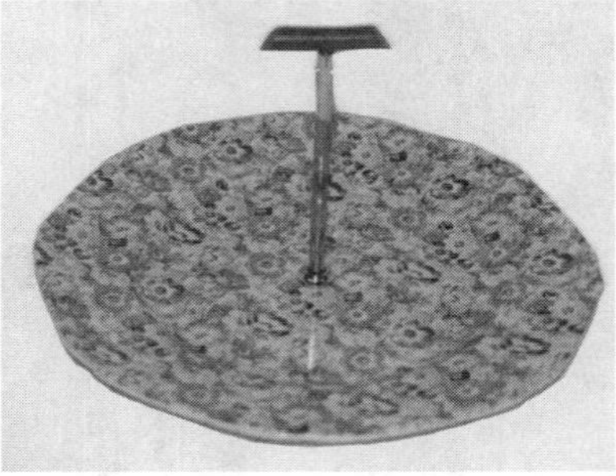

*Chintz Floral Pattern Server*

**Sugar shaker,** Brama patt., Midwinter............. **450**
**Sugar w/metal cover,** squared tapering sides on four small tab feet, Lorna Doone patt., Midwinter, Ltd. ......................... **375**
**Tea set:** stacking-type, cov. creamer, sugar & teapot; Florence patt., Delamere shape, Royal Winton, the set .................... **1,750**
**Tea set:** stacking-type, teapot, sugar & cov. creamer; Black Beauty patt., Lord Nelson Ware, the set........................................ **950**
**Teapot,** cov., DuBarry patt., Diamond shape, James Kent, Ltd. .............................. **950**
**Teapot,** cov., for breakfast set, Chelsea patt., Royal Winton....................................... **450**
**Teapot,** cov., Joyce-Lynn patt., Ascot shape, Royal Winton ................................. **1,295**
**Teapot,** cov., Julia patt., Royal Winton, two-cup...................................................... **800**
**Teapot,** cov., Royal Brocade patt., Lord Nelson Ware ........................................... **800**
**Teapot,** cov., Spring Flower patt., Myott, Son & Co...................................................... **695**
**Teapot,** cov., Summertime patt., Ajax shape, Royal Winton ................................... **950**

*Sweet Pea Pattern Tennis Set*

**Tennis set:** cup & oblong underplate; Sweet Pea patt., Royal Winton, 2 pcs. (ILLUS.)................................................... **165**
**Tennis set,** Marina patt., Lord Nelson Ware, the set............................................. **100**
**Toast rack,** Cromer patt., Royal Winton, small................................................... **165**
**Toast rack,** Orient patt., Royal Winton............. **235**
**Trivet,** round, Silverdale patt., Royal Winton ................................................................ **95**
**Vase,** bud-type, Kew patt., Royal Winton ......... **250**

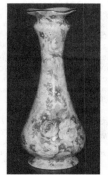

*Rosetime Pattern Bud Vase*

**Vase,** bud-type, Rosetime patt., Lord Nelson Ware (ILLUS.) ...................................... 225
**Vase,** trumpet-shaped, Marigold patt., Crown Ducal................................................. 225

*Summertime Vegetable Dish*

**Vegetable dish,** oblong w/scalloped edges, Summertime patt., Royal Winton (ILLUS.)........................................................ 265
**Vegetable dish,** open, oval, Spring patt., Royal Winton.............................................. 225

# CLARICE CLIFF DESIGNS

*Clarice Cliff Marks*

*Clarice Cliff was a designer for A. J. Wilkinson, Ltd., Royal Staffordshire Pottery, Burslem, England when they acquired the adjoining Newport Pottery Company whose warehouses were filled with undecorated bowls and vases. About 1925 her flair with the Art Deco style was incorporated into designs appropriately named "Bizarre" and "Fantasque" and the warehouse stockpile was decorated in vivid colors. These hand-painted earthenwares, all bearing the printed signature of designer Clarice Cliff, were produced until World War II and are now finding enormous favor with collectors.*

*Note: Reproductions of the Clarice Cliff "Bizarre" marking have been appearing on the market recently.*

**Bone dish,** Tonquin patt., black ...................... $30
**Bowl,** 5" d., Tonquin patt. ................................... 5
**Bowl,** 6 1/4" d., octagonal flanged rim on the rounded body, Woodland patt., stylized landscape w/trees in orange, green, black, blue, purple & yellow, marked........... 550
**Bowl,** 6 1/2" d., 3" h., "Bizarre" ware, footed deep slightly flaring sides, Crocus patt., the sides divided into two horizontal bands of color w/a band of small crocus blossoms along the upper half, in orange, blue, purple & green, stamped mark ............................................................. 550

*Caprice Pattern Bowl & Vase*

**Bowl,** 8" d., "Bizarre" ware, Caprice patt., stylized landscape w/hills, arch & tall trees in lavender, blue, yellow, green & brown (ILLUS. left) .................................. 2,800
**Bowl,** 8" d., 3 3/4" h., "Bizarre" ware, deep gently rounded sides tapering to a footring, Original Bizarre patt., a wide band of blocks & triangles around the upper half in blue, orange, ivory & purple, purple band around the bottom section, marked ....................................................... 650
**Bowl,** 8" d., 4 1/4" h., "Bizarre" ware, octagonal, h.p. w/Original Bizarre patt., large crudely painted bands of maroon, dark orange & dark blue diamonds above an ochre base band, ink mark ........ 1,100
**Bowl,** 9" d., deep rounded sides, the upper half w/a wide band in polychrome featuring large stylized cottages w/pointed orange roofs beneath arching trees, lime green banding, marked .............................. 800
**Bowl,** 9 1/2" d., 4 1/2" h., orange, green & blue h.p. poppies......................................... 600
**Butter dish,** cov., "Bizarre" ware, Crocus patt., a wide shallow base w/low, upright sides fitted w/a shallow, flat-sided cover w/a slightly domed top & flat button finial, the top decorated w/purple, blue & orange blossoms on an ivory ground, marked, 4" d., 2 3/4" h. ................................. 550
**Butter dish,** cov., "Bizarre" ware, short wide cylindrical body w/an inset cover w/large button finial, Secrets patt., decorated w/a stylized landscape in shades of green, yellow & brown w/red-roofed houses on a cream ground, marked, 4" d., 2 5/8" h. (ILLUS. left, top next page) ......................................................... 550

*A Variety of Clarice Cliff Patterns*

*Delecia Citrus Cracker Jar & Vases*

**Cracker jar,** cov., "Bizarre" ware, bulbous barrel shape w/large side knobs to support the arched woven wicker bail handle, wide flat mouth w/a slightly domed cover centered by a large ball finial, Gayday patt., decorated w/a wide band of large stylized flowers in orange, rust, amethyst, blue & green above a lower band in orange on a cream ground, the cover w/an orange finial & yellow band, 5 7/8" d., 6 1/4" h. (ILLUS. right w/butter dish) .......... **975**

**Cracker jar,** cov., "Bizarre" ware, squatty kettle-form w/side knobs supporting the swing bail handle, Delecia Citrus patt. (ILLUS. right) ............ **1,400**

**Cracker jar,** cov., "Bizarre" ware, Blue Chintz patt., stylized blue, green & pink blossom forms w/blue border band (ILLUS. center next page) .......... **1,800**

*"Bizarre" Demitasse Set*

**Demitasse set:** cov. coffeepot, six demitasse cups & saucers, creamer & open sugar bowl; "Bizarre" ware, Fantasque patt., decorated w/a stylized tree on one side, the other w/stylized hollyhocks,

small chips to one saucer, 15 pcs. (ILLUS. of part).......... **3,200**

**Demitasse set:** cov. cylindrical coffeepot, creamer, open sugar bowl & six cylindrical demitasse cups & saucers; Honeyglaze, each body in deep orange, the angled handles in black & dark green, all marked, coffeepot 6" d., 6 1/4" h., the set (chip inside pot cover, minor flake on sugar bowl).......... **3,400**

**Figures** "Bizarre" ware, flat cut-outs, comprising two groups of musicians & two groups of dancing couples, all highly stylized & glazed in reddish orange, yellow, lime green, cream & black, printed factory marks, ca. 1925, 5 5/8 to 7" h., 4 pcs.......... **29,000**

**Gravy boat & underplate,** Tonquin patt., black, 2 pcs. .......... **40**

**Jam jar,** cov., cylindrical body, Melon patt., decorated w/a band of overlapping fruit, predominantly orange w/yellow, blue & green w/brown outline, ca. 1930, restoration to rim & side, marked, 4" h. (ILLUS. top right w/candleholders).......... **690**

**Jam pot,** cov., Blue Firs patt., flat-sided round form on small log feet, domed cover w/flat round knob, stylized landscape w/trees, marked, 4 1/4" h..........**900**

*Canterberry Bells Pattern Jar*

**Jar,** cov., "Bizarre" ware, a sharply tapering conical base supported on four squared buttress feet & w/a sharply inward tapering shoulder supporting the conical cover w/four small buttress tabs at the top, Canterberry Bells patt., decorated in mottled brown rim & shoulder over a stylized floral band in orange, shades of green, blue, amethyst & mottled yellow on a cream ground, 6" d., 8 1/8" h. (ILLUS.).......... **1,300**

**Jardiniere,** "Fantasque" line, Melon patt., Dover shape, deep cylindrical sides on three small tab feet, decorated w/Cubist-style fruits in orange, yellow, blue, green & amber against a cream ground, orange base & rim bands, marked, 6 1/4" d., 6 1/4" h. (minor inside paint wear) .......... **1,900**

**Lemonade set:** 8" h. tankard pitcher & four cylindrical tumblers; each decorated in an abstract geometric pattern in orange, blue, purple, green & yellow, marked, the set .................................................. **1,100**

**Pitcher,** 5 1/8" h., "Fantasque" line, squared base w/flattened spherical sides, Autumn (Balloon Trees) patt. in blue, yellow, green orange, black & purple, stamped on base "Registration Applied For Fantasque Hand Painted Bizarre by Clarice Cliff Newport Pottery England," ca. 1931, minor glaze bubbles & nicks (ILLUS. center right w/candleholders) .................................................. **920**

**Pitcher,** 5 3/4" h., "Fantasque" line, Melon patt., wide conical body w/solid triangular handle, orange & thin black bands flanking a wide central band of stylized melons in yellow, blue, green & orange, marked, ca. 1930 (tiny glaze nicks at rim & base, faint scratch in lower orange band) .................................................. **875**

**Pitcher,** 6 3/8" h., "Fantasque" line, footed ovoid octagonal form w/large D-form handle, Alpine patt., decorated w/trees & house in shades of orange & black w/wide border bands, marked on the base, ca. 1930 (minor glaze flakes) .......... **1,725**

**Pitcher,** 6 7/8" h., "Bizarre" ware, flaring cylindrical body w/a wide rim & wide arched spout opposite an angled handle, Secrets patt., decorated w/a stylized landscape in shades of green, yellow & brown w/a red-roofed house on a cream ground, stamped mark ................................ **900**

**Pitcher,** 7" h., 6" d., jug-type, "Bizarre" ware, Lotus shape, Coral Firs patt., wide ovoid body w/a wide flat rim, heavy applied loop handle, decorated w/a wide landscape band in brown, orange, yellow, brown & grey on an ivory ground, marked ...................................................... **1,200**

**Pitcher,** 7" h., 7" d., "Bizarre" ware, tapering cylindrical body w/flat rim & wide pointed spout, flattened angled handle from rim to base, Sliced Fruit patt., wide band of abstract fruit in yellow, orange & red, stamped mark .................................... **1,800**

**Pitcher,** 7 1/2" h., 7 1/4" d., "Bizarre" ware, My Garden patt., bulbous base below a wide cylindrical body flaring slightly at the rim, an arched bumpy branch handle in mottled purple w/long sprigs of molded green leaves at the base on the all-black matte-glazed body, ink mark (small repaired chip on handle) ................... **413**

**Pitcher,** 9 3/4" h., 7 3/4" d., jug-type, "Bizarre" ware, Isis shape, Summerhouse patt., decorated w/trees & gazebos in yellow, green, purple, red & blue against an ivory ground, marked ............. **3,900**

**Pitcher,** 10" h., 7 1/2" d., "Bizarre" ware, ringed ovoid body tapering to a flat, round mouth, rounded C-form loop handle, Secrets patt., stylized landscape scene in yellow, green & blue, stamped mark ...................................................... **1,400**

**Pitcher,** 10" h., 7 1/2" d., "Bizarre" ware, Viscaria patt., ringed ovoid body tapering to a flat rim w/pinched spout, heavy

rounded C-form handle, large stylized blossoms in blue, yellow & brown, stamped mark ...................................... **900**

**Pitcher,** 11 1/2" h., 8 3/4" d., "Bizarre" ware, wide ringed ovoid body tapering to a wide flat round mouth, rounded C-form handle, Area patt., wide central band of stylized florals in blue, red, yellow, purple, green & black, stamped mark ............. **1,050**

*Lotus Pitcher in Delecia Citrus Pattern*

**Pitcher,** 12" h., "Bizarre" ware, Lotus shape, ringed ovoid body tapering to a wide cylindrical neck, heavy loop handle, Delecia Citrus patt., large stylized red, yellow & orange fruits around the top w/green leaves & streaky green on a cream ground (ILLUS.).............................. **2,200**

**Pitcher,** 12" h., jug-form w/ovoid body w/overall fine molded banding, Lotus shape, Sunrise patt., decorated in bright yellow & orange, marked.......................... **1,200**

*Lotus Pitcher with Sunrise Pattern*

**Pitcher,** 12" h., jug-form w/ovoid body w/overall fine molded banding, Lotus shape, Sunrise patt., decorated in bright yellow & orange, marked (ILLUS.) ............ **2,800**

*Blue Chintz Pattern Pieces*

**Plate,** 8" d., "Bizarre" ware, Blue Chintz patt., stylized blue, green & pink blossom forms w/blue border band (ILLUS. left) .................................................. **600**

**Plate,** 8 3/4" d., "Bizarre" ware, Secrets patt., stylized central landscape scene w/banded borders in greens, yellow & orange, stamped mark (minor paint wear) ................................................... **600**

**Plate,** 9" d., "Bizarre" ware, Blue Chintz patt., decorated w/stylized flowers in green, blue & pink against an ivory ground, marked .................................... **650**

**Plate,** 9" d., "Fantasque" line, h.p. Melon patt., a wide band of stylized fruit in yellow, orange, red, blue & green w/an orange center circle & a narrow orange rim band, ink mark (minor wear) .................. **775**

**Plate,** 9 3/4" d., "Bizarre" ware, Forest Glen patt., decorated in the center w/a landscape w/cottage in green, pale blue, orange, brown & black under a marbleized streaky sky in shades of red, brown & grey on a cream ground, impressed "10/35" (ILLUS. in center w/butter dish) ....... **600**

**Plate,** 9 3/4" d., Forest Glen patt., a stylized cottage in a woodland scene in orange, ivory & green, die-stamped "Clarice Cliff - Newport Pottery - England" .................. **950**

**Plate,** 10" d., "Bizarre" ware, Pansies Delicia patt., decorated w/vivid blue, yellow & rose pansies w/yellow, rose & purple centers on pale & dark green leaves against a blue, green, cocoa, brown & yellow opaque drip glaze background, marked "Pansies - Bizarre by Clarice Cliff - Hand painted - England" & impressed "83" (minor wear) ...................... **121**

**Plate,** 10" d., "Fantasque" line, Autumn (Balloon Trees) patt. w/blue, yellow, green & purple trees & orange striped border bands, base stamped "Fantasque Hand Painted Bizarre by Clarice Cliff Newport Pottery England" (ILLUS. center left w/candleholders) ........................ **1,725**

**Plate,** 10 3/4" d., rounded w/four double-lobe protrusions around the sides, Sunrise patt., colorful center stylized sunrise design banded in orange & green, marked ......................................................... **900**

**Plate,** dinner, Tonquin patt., lavender ............... **28**

**Sauceboat & undertray,** Tonquin patt., green, 2 pcs. ................................................... **29**

**Shaker,** "Bizarre" ware, sharply pointed conical form, Trees and House (Alpine) patt., decorated w/orange & black borders & trees, green rooftop & grass, factory stamp on base, ca. 1930, 5 3/4" h. (minor glaze nicks, hairline in base) .......... **1,380**

**Sugar shaker,** Autumn patt., sharply pointed conical form w/rows of small holes pierced around the top, decorated in pastel autumn colors, marked, 5 1/2" h. .................................................. **1,200**

**Sugar shaker,** "Bizarre" ware, Bonjour shape, a flattened upright oval w/tiny feet across the base, Nasturium patt., stylized orange, red & yellow blossoms & pale green leaves, white at top & burnt orange at the bottom, ink mark, 1 3/4" w., 5" h. ............................................. **550**

**Sugar shaker,** "Bizarre" ware, flattened egg-shaped body set on two tiny log-form feet, Crocus patt., banded body w/a central row of stylized crocus blossoms, in yellow, blue, orange & purple, stamped mark, 2 1/2" w., 5" h. ...................... **750**

**Sugar shaker,** "Bizarre" ware, small footring under slender tapering ovoid body w/rounded top, Viscaria patt., stylized blossom decoration in yellow, green & brown, stamped mark, 2 3/4" d., 4 3/4" h. ........................................................ **850**

*Banded Pattern Bonjour Shape Set*

**Tea for two set:** cov. small teapot, creamer, open sugar, two cups & saucers & two small plates; Banded patt., Bonjour shape, brown & green bands bordering the cream body, the set (ILLUS.) ............................................... **1,800**

**Teapot,** cov., "Bizarre" ware, inverted conical form w/angled handle & spout, glazed in shades of orange, yellow & black, stamped mark on base, ca. 1932, 4 1/4" h. (minor glaze flakes, small spout chip) ............................................................. **2,185**

**Tumbler,** Sunray patt., conical form, polychrome decoration of a stylized sun, orange banding, marked, 3" h. ..................... **600**

**Vase,** 5 1/4" h., "Bizarre" ware, Shape No. 341, squatty bulbous chalice-form, Delecia Citrus patt., bright fruits on a creamy ground (ILLUS. left w/cracker jar) ............... **900**

**Vase,** 6 1/4" h., 3 1/4" d., "Fantasque" line, Shape No. 196, Trees and House patt., a cylindrical body w/a widely flaring & rolled rim, decorated w/a wide central landscape band in black, orange & green against an ivory ground, marked..... **1,100**

**Vase,** 7" h., flattened ovoid body w/a lightly scalloped rim, molded up from the base & around the rim w/vine, leaves & clouds in relief in green, brown & gold on a beige ground, marked .................................. **230**

**Vase,** 7" h., 4 1/2" h., "Fantasque" ware, slightly tapering cylindrical body w/a closed rim & thick footring, decorated w/a stylized landscape in shades of blue, green, yellow & rose on an ivory ground, marked (ILLUS. top next page) ................... **770**

**Vase,** 7 1/2" h., 5 1/2" d., "Bizarre" ware, Inspiration patt., decorated in mottled blues, greens & purples, stamped mark ...... **950**

**Vase,** 8" h., "Bizarre" ware, Isis shape, Caprice patt., stylized landscape w/hills, arch & tall trees in lavender, blue, yellow, green & brown (ILLUS. right w/bowl).. **3,800**

*Clarice Cliff "Fantasque" Vase*

**Vase,** 8" h., "Bizarre" ware, Nasturtium patt., footed ovoid body w/a flaring rolled rim, decorated w/vivid orange, red & yellow blossoms w/black, red, yellow & green leaves atop a mottled caramel & tan ground against a white background, marked "Nasturtium - Bizarre by Clarice Cliff - Hand painted - England"..................... **900**

**Vase,** 8" h., "Bizarre" ware, Shape No. 358, bulbous ovoid lower body tapering to a heavily ringed tapering neck, Blue Chintz patt., stylized blue, green & pink blossom forms w/blue border band (ILLUS. right w/plate) ............................... **2,800**

**Vase,** 8" h., "Bizarre" ware, Shape No. 362, ovoid upper body above a heavy ringed & waisted base, Delecia Citrus patt., brightly painted fruits on a cream ground (ILLUS. center w/cracker jar) ................... **1,200**

*Crocus Pattern Vase*

**Vase,** 8" h., "Bizarre" ware, Shape No. 386, swelled cylindrical base below the angled shoulder & tall gently flaring neck, Crocus patt., a yellow rim band & brown bottom section below a cluster of colorful crocus blossoms on a cream ground (ILLUS.)........................................ **1,500**

# COORS

*It was in 1908 that John J. Herold, formerly of the Owens and Roseville potteries, relocated to Golden, Colorado and, together with the Adolph Coors family, founded the Herold Pottery Com-*

*pany. Mr. Herold remained with the company for just two years but the firm's name didn't change until 1920 when it became the Coors Porcelain Company. One of Coors' most popular patterns, Rosebud, is widely sought by collectors today and there are several variations available but generally collectors seek them all. Original glaze colors included green, orange, rose, white (ivory), yellow and blue and today the ivory glaze seems hardest to find.*

*Still operating today, the Coors Ceramic Division produces items for use in chemical laboratories.*

*Coors Marks*

**Apple baker,** cov., Rosebud patt., blue, 4 3/4" d., 12 oz. ............................................. **$70**

**Ashtray,** square, w/advertising "COORS, GOLDEN, MALTED MILK," w/bull heads & barley decoration on corners, beige ......... **140**

**Ashtray,** triangular, Anholtz design ..................... **3**

**Bank,** figural clown head, sitting or hanging-type, white, each .................................... **175**

**Cake plate,** Rosebud patt., orange, 11" d. ......... **65**

**Cake plate,** thermo-porcelain, Hawthorne decal, 11 1/4" d. ............................................. **75**

**Cake server,** Rosebud patt., yellow, 10".......... **160**

**Cake server,** thermo-porcelain, Floree patt., 10"......................................................... **130**

**Casserole,** cov., individual, Coorado line, orange, 2 x 2 .................................................. **45**

**Casserole,** cov., Rosebud patt., blue, 2 pt......... **50**

**Coffee maker,** percolator-type, thermo-porcelain, Tulip patt., four-part w/brewing insert....................................................... **250**

**Creamer,** Rosebud patt., orange, 3" d., 7 1/2 oz. ................................................................ **30**

**Creamer & sugar bowl,** porcelain w/h.p. "Herold, Gem of the Rockies," pre-1920, pr. ................................................................ **300**

**Cup & saucer,** Rosebud patt., white, cup 8 oz. ................................................................ **65**

**Custard cup,** Rosebud patt., maroon, 4" d., 7 oz. ..................................................... **15**

**Custard cup,** thermo-porcelain, Gazebo patt., 4" d. ................................................... **25**

**Egg cup,** Rosebud patt., orange, 3" d., 6 oz. ................................................................ **45**

**Figure of monk,** laughing or crying, orange, 6" h., each ...................................... **325**

**Gravy boat,** Rockmount line, red ...................... **50**

**Honey pot,** cov., Rosebud patt., yellow, no spoon .......................................................... **300**

**Honey pot spoon/ladle,** Rosebud patt., turquoise ....................................................... **150**

**Loaf pan,** Rosebud patt., blue, 2 x 5 x 9 ............ 65
**Malted milk crock,** cylindrical w/aluminum
lid, reads "COORS PURE MALTED
MILK" ......................................................... 250
**Mixing bowl w/spout & handle,** Rosebud
patt., yellow, 3 1/2 pt. ..................................... 65
**Muffin plate,** cov., Rosebud patt., tur-
quoise, 5 1/2" d. .......................................... 350
**Pie plate,** Coorado line, yellow ........................... 60
**Pitcher,** cov., Rosebud patt., turquoise, 14
oz. ............................................................... 175
**Pitcher,** cov., Rosebud patt., maroon, 3 pt. ..... 225
**Pitcher,** cov., jug-type, thermo-porcelain,
Open Window decal, 3/4 pt. ........................... 75
**Pitcher,** cov., jug-type, thermo-porcelain,
Chrysanthemum patt., 3 1/4 pt. .................... 110
**Plate,** dessert, 6 1/4" d., Rosebud patt.,
orange ......................................................... 15
**Plate,** 9 1/4" d., Mello-tone line, all colors,
each ............................................................... 9
**Plate,** dinner, small, 9 1/4" d., Rosebud
patt., yellow ................................................... 28
**Plate,** dinner, large, 10 1/4" d., Rosebud
patt., blue ..................................................... 36
**Platter,** 12" l., Rosebud patt., yellow ................. 45
**Ramekin,** handled, Rosebud patt., maroon,
4 1/4" d., 9 oz. .............................................. 35
**Refrigerator set,** Rosebud patt., two bases
w/lid, 2 x 5 x 5" ........................................... 250
**Salt & pepper shakers,** Rosebud patt.,
blue, 2 1/2" h., pr. .......................................... 50
**Salt & pepper shakers,** thermo-porcelain,
Tulip patt., 4 1/4" h., pr. .................................. 75
**Salt & pepper shakers,** Rosebud patt.,
orange, 4 1/2" h., pr........................................ 60
**Salt shaker,** beer bottle shape w/decal
advertising Coors .......................................... 22
**Sauce dish,** Rosebud patt., yellow, 5" d. ........... 18
**Soup plate w/flanged rim,** Rosebud patt.,
yellow, 8" d. .................................................. 45
**Sugar bowl,** cov., Rosebud patt., maroon,
4" d. .............................................................. 45
**Teapot,** cov., Rosebud patt., orange, 2-cup..... 275
**Teapot,** cov., thermo-porcelain, Open Win-
dow decal, 5-cup ........................................... 175
**Teapot,** cov., Rosebud patt., blue, 6-cup ......... 225
**Tumbler,** footed, Rosebud patt., yellow,
3" d., 12 oz. ................................................. 225
**Utility jar,** w/rope handles, Rosebud patt.,
4 1/2" d., 2 1/2 pt. ......................................... 85
**Vase,** 6" h., grapevine design, marked
"Coors Beer, Colorado State Fair, 1939,"
matte white ................................................... 75
**Vase,** 6" h., Greek key design ........................... 55
**Vase,** bud, 8" h., bulbous shouldered base
w/tall slender cylindrical neck & flared
rim ................................................................ 30
**Vase,** 10" h., Golden shape, handles form
circle from rim to base.................................... 75
**Vase,** 12" h., classic form w/rope handles........ 125
**Vase,** 12" h., two-handled, Art Deco style ....... 160

# COWAN

*R. Guy Cowan opened his first pottery studio in
1912 in Lakewood, Ohio. The pottery operated
almost continuously, with the exception of a break
during the war, at various locations in the Cleveland
area until it was forced to close in 1931 due to
financial difficulties.*

*Many of this century's finest artists began with
Cowan and its associate, the Cleveland School of
Art. This fine art pottery, particularly the designer
pieces, are highly sought after by collectors.*

*Many people are unaware that it was due to R.
Guy Cowan's perseverance and tireless work that
art pottery is today considered an art form and
found in many art museums.*

*Cowan Marks*

**Ashtray,** center relief-molded unicorn decoration, caramel glaze, designed by
Waylande Gregory, w/footed foliate
metal stand, Shape No. 925, 3/4 x 5 1/2"..... **$90**
**Ashtray/nut dish,** ivory glaze, Shape No.
769, 1"............................................................. 25

*Cowan Clown Ashtrays & Vases*

**Ashtray/nut dish,** figural clown Periot, blue
or ivory glaze, designed by Elizabeth
Anderson, Shape No. 788, 2 1/2 x 3",
each (ILLUS. lower center) ......................... 150
**Book end,** figural, modeled as a large
rounded stylized elephant w/trunk
curved under, standing on a stepped
rectangular base, overall Oriental Red
glaze, designed by Margaret Postgate,
Shape No. E-2, impressed mark, 5" l.,
7 1/2" h........................................................... 1,210
**Book ends,** figural Art Deco style elephant,
push & pull, tan glaze, designed by
Thelma F. Winter, one Shape No. 840 &
one Shape No. 841, 4 3/4" h., pr................. 250
**Book ends,** figural, model of a seated polar
bear, front paws near face, ivory glaze,
designed by Margaret Postgate, 6" h.,
pr. (ILLUS. left, top next page) .................. 1,600
**Book ends,** figural, a little girl standing
wearing a large sunbonnet & full ruffled
dress, verde green, designed by Kat.
Barnes Jenkins, Shape No. 521, 7" h.,
pr. .............................................................. 450

*Cowan Book Ends & Model of Horse*

*Elephant Book Ends & Paperweights*

**Book ends,** figural, modeled as a large rounded stylized elephant w/trunk curved under, standing on a stepped rectangular base, overall Oriental Red glaze, designed by Margaret Postgate, Shape No. E-2, 7 1/4" h., pr. (ILLUS. top center & lower left) .................................... **2,000**

**Book ends,** "Pierette," stylized figure of young woman wearing a short flaring skirt & holding a scarf behind her, russet & salmon glaze, designed by Elizabeth Anderson, Shape No. 792, 8 1/4" h. (ILLUS. center) ...................................... **1,800**

*Cowan Bowl & Vases*

**Bowl,** 5 1/4" d., individual, green & black, designed by Arthur E. Baggs (ILLUS. right) .......................................... **3,000**

**Bowl,** 7 1/2" w., octagonal, the alternating side panels hand-decorated w/floral design, brown & yellow glaze, Shape No. B-5-B .................................. **375**

**Bowl,** 2 1/2 x 9 1/4", Egyptian blue glaze, designed by R.G. Cowan, Shape No. B-12 ................................. **75**

**Bowl,** 3 x 11 1/4", designed to imitate hand molding, two-tone blue glaze, Shape No. B-827............................ **300**

**Bowl,** 2 3/4 x 11 1/2 x 15", Oriental Red glaze, designed by Waylande Gregory, Shape No. B-4............................ **200**

**Bust of a woman,** Art Deco style, tall elongated form, the head w/long hair tilted to one side against her shoulder, designed by Wayland Gregory, overall smooth gunmetal glaze, impressed mark, 3 1/2" w., 10" h. ....................... **31,900**

*Cowan Bust*

**Bust of a woman,** close-cut hair in ringlets, original sculpture by Jose Martin, terra cotta, 13 1/2" h. (ILLUS.)............ **5,000**

**Candelabrum,** "Pavlova," porcelain, two-light, Art Deco style, a footed squatty tapering central dish issuing at each side a stylized hand holding an upturned cornucopia-form candle socket, the center fitted w/a figure of a nude female dancer standing on one leg w/her other leg raised, her torso arched over & holding a long swirled drapery, Special Ivory glaze, stamped mark, 10" l., 7" h. (chip under rim of one bobeche) ........................... **248**

**Candleholder,** flaring base w/flattened rim, black & silver, Shape No. 870, 1 1/2" h. ......... **50**

**Candleholder,** figural, model of a viking ship prow, green glaze, Shape No. 777, 5 1/4" h. ......................................... **25**

**Candleholders,** ivory glaze, Shape No. 692, 2 1/4" h., pr. ...................................... **30**

**Candlestick,** figural, a model of a seated beaver beside a slender tree trunk candle shaft & holding upright a tall open book reading "Light See High Light Doth Light of Light Beguile," overall forest green glaze, designed by Frank N. Wilcox, number 137 of 156, 9" h. .................. **1,700**

**Candlestick,** figural, semi-nude female standing before figural branches on round base w/flared foot, one arm across her body & the other raised overhead, shaded tan & green glaze, designed by R.G. Cowan, Shape No. 744-R, 12 1/2" h. (ILLUS. below) .............. **1,000**

*Cowan Figural Nude Candlestick*

**Centerpiece set,** 6 1/4" h. trumpet-form vase centered on 8" sq. base w/candle socket in each corner, Princess line, vase Shape No. V-1, Mark No. 8, candelabra Shape No. S-2, Mark No. 8, black matte, 2 pcs., together w/four nut dishes/open compotes, green glaze, Shape No. C-1, Mark No. 8, the set ............. **750**

**Cigarette holder,** w/wave design, Oriental Red glaze, designed by Waylande Gregory, Shape No. 927-J, 3 1/4" ...................... **100**

**Cigarette/matchholder,** flared foot w/relief-molded sea horse decoration, orange glaze, Shape No. 72, 3 1/2" h. ........... **30**

**Comports,** open, April green, Shape No. C-1, 6 1/4" d., 1 1/4" h., set of 4 ................... **125**

**Console bowl,** octagonal, stand-up-type, verde green, Shape No. 689, 3 x 8 x 8 1/2" ................................................. **95**

**Console bowl,** footed, flaring fluted sides, white glaze exterior, blue glaze interior, Shape No. 713-A, 3 1/2 x 7 1/4 x 10 1/2" ....... **90**

**Console bowl,** April green, Shape No. B-1, 11 1/2" l., 2 1/4" h. ......................................... **95**

**Console bowl,** turquoise & dark mate blue, Shape No. 690, 3 1/2 x 8 x 16" ................... **120**

**Console bowl,** ivory & pink glaze, Shape No. 763, 3 1/4 x 9 x 16 1/2" ............................ **80**

**Console bowl,** w/wave design, verde green, designed by Waylande Gregory, 2 3/4 x 9 x 17 1/2" ........................................ **400**

**Console set:** 9" d. bowl & pair of 4" h. candleholders; ivory & purple glaze, Shape Nos. 733-A & 734 ........................................ **150**

**Figurine,** kneeling female nude, almond glaze, 9" h. .................................................... **350**

**Figurine,** "Persephone," standing female nude holding a long scarf out to one side and near her shoulder, ivory glaze, designed by Waylande Gregory, Shape No. D-6, 15" h. (ILLUS. top next column).. **3,000**

*"Persephone" Figurine*

**Figurines,** "Spanish Dancers," Art Deco angular poses, the shirtless man pulling a dagger from the sheath at his waist, the female wearing a long pleated dress, walking & carrying a large bundle under one arm, polychrome glazes, by Elizabeth Anderson, 1938, impressed mark, 6 1/2" l., 9" h., pr ..................................... **1,320**

**Finger bowl,** Egyptian blue, Shape No. B-19, 3" ................................................................. **80**

**Flower frog,** model of an artichoke, light green, Shape No. 775, 3" h. ........................... **90**

*Various Cowan Flower Frogs*

**Flower frog,** figural, "Repose," Art Deco style, a semi-nude sinewy lady standing & slightly curved backward, her arms away from her sides holding trailing drapery, in a cupped blossom-form base, ivory glaze, designed by R.G. Cowan, Shape No. 712, 6 1/2" h. (ILLUS. lower center) ................................. **450**

**Flower frog,** figural, "Scarf Dancer," Art Deco style nude dancing lady in a curved pose standing on one leg & holding the ends of a long scarf in her outstretched hands, ivory glaze, designed by R.G. Cowan, Shape No. 686, 7" h. (ILLUS. top) ................................. 350

**Flower frog,** figural, Art Deco style, two nude females partially draped in flowing scarves, each bending backward away from the other w/one hand holding the scarf behind each figure & their other hand joined, on an oval base w/flower holes, ivory glaze, designed by R.G. Cowan, Shape No. 685, 7 1/2" h. (ILLUS. lower right) ..................................... 680

**Flower frog,** figural "Marching Girl," Art Deco style, a nude female partially draped w/a flowing scarf standing & leaning backward w/one hand on her hip & the other raising the scarf above her head, on an oblong serpetine-molded wave base w/flower holes, ivory glaze, designed by R.G. Cowan, Shape No. 680, 8" h. (ILLUS. lower left) ...................... 300

**Flower frog,** a standing semi-nude Art Deco lady, posed w/one leg kicked to the back, her torso bent back w/one arm raised & curved overhead, the other arm curved around her waist holding a long feather fan, a long drapery hangs down the front from her waist, on a rounded incurved broad leaf cluster base, overall Original Ivory glaze, designed by R. G. Cowan, Shape No. 806, stamped mark, 4" w., 9 1/2" h. ........................... 1,650

**Flower frog,** figural, "Triumphant," figure of a standing semi-nude Art Deco lady w/one leg raised, leaning back w/one arm raised above her head & the other on her hip, a clinging drapery around her lower body, standing on a round incurved leaf cluster base, overall Original Ivory glaze, stamped mark, 4 1/2" w., 15" h. ....................................... 2,310

**Ginger jar,** cov., blue lustre, Shape No. 513, 6 3/4" h. ................................. 300

**Lamp,** foliage decoration, 9" h. ........................ 175

**Lamp,** girl w/deer decoration, ivory, 18" h. ....... 300

**Model of a horse,** standing animal on an oblong base, Egyptian blue glaze, designed by Viktor Schreckengost, 7 3/4" h. (ILLUS. right w/bookends) .......... 2,500

**Model of elephant,** standing on square plinth, head & trunk down, rich mottled Oriental Red glaze, designed by Margaret Postgate, ca. 1930, faint impressed mark on plinth & paper label reading "X869 Elephant designed by M....et P....," 10 1/2" h. .......................................... 4,620

**Paperweight,** figural, modeled as a large rounded stylized elephant w/trunk curved under, standing on a stepped rectangular base, ivory glaze, designed by Margaret Postgate, Shape No. D-3, 4 3/4" h. (ILLUS. lower center) ..................... 400

**Paperweight,** figural, modeled as a large rounded stylized elephant w/trunk curved under, standing on a stepped rectangular base, blue glaze, designed by Margaret Postgate, Shape No. D-3, 4 3/4" h. (ILLUS. lower right) ...................... 450

**Paperweight,** figural, modeled as a large rounded stylized elephant w/trunk curved under, standing on a stepped rectangular base, overall Oriental Red glaze, designed by Margaret Postgate, Shape No. D-3, 4 3/4" h. (ILLUS. top right) ................... 500

**Plaque,** seascape decoration, designed by Thelma Frazier Winter, 11 1/2" d. ................ 900

**Plaque,** hand-decorated by Alexander Blazys, Egyptian blue, artist-signed, 2 1/2 x 12 1/2" ......................................... 2,500

**Strawberry jar w/saucer,** light green, designed by R.G. Cowan, Shape No. SJ-6, 6" h., 2 pcs. ........................................ 200

**Trivet,** round, center portrait of young woman's face encircled by a floral border, white on blue ground, impressed mark & "Cowan," 6 5/8" d. (minor staining from usage) ...................................... 303

**Urn,** classical form w/trumpet foot supporting a wide bulbous ribbed body w/a wide short cylindrical neck flanked by loop handles, overall Peacock blue glaze, stamped mark, 8" d., 9 1/2" h. ........................ 88

*Cowan Urn w/Figural Grape Handles*

**Urn,** cov., black w/gold trim & figural grape cluster handles, Shape No. V-95, 10 1/4" h. (ILLUS.) ........................................ 450

**Vase,** 3 1/4" h., footed, baluster-form, Feu Rouge glaze, Shape No. 533 ...................... 100

**Vase,** 4 3/4" h., bulbous body w/horizontal ribbing, wide cylindrical neck, green glaze, Shape No. V-30 (ILLUS. lower left w/ashtrays) ...................................... 90

**Vase,** 5 1/4" h., Lakeware, melon-lobed shape ..................................................... 90

**Vase,** 5 1/2" h., Lakeware, bulbous base w/wide shoulder tapering to wide cylindrical neck, blue glaze, Shape No. V-72 ........ 90

**Vase,** 6 1/4" h., experimental, polychrome, designed by Arthur E. Baggs, Shape No. 15-A ................................................... 1,500

**Vase,** bud, 6 1/4" h., flaring domed foot below ovoid body taperint to cylindrical neck w/flaring rim, plum glaze, Shape No. 916 ....................................................... 80

**Vase,** 6 1/2" h., blue & green, Shape No. V-55 ......................................................... 160

*Cowan Decorated Vases*

**Vase,** 6 1/2" h., bulbous body w/short molded rim, black w/Egyptian blue bands & center decoration, designed by Whitney Atchley, Shape No. V-38 (ILLUS. right) ............................................ **1,600**

**Vase,** 6 1/2" h., mottled dark blue & green, Shape No. V-55.................................... **160**

**Vase,** 6 1/2" h., spherical body w/flaring cylindrical neck flanked by scroll handles, Egyptian blue, designed by Viktor Schreckengost, Shape No. V-99 (ILLUS. center w/bowl) ........................................ **550**

**Vase,** 7 1/4" h., footed slender ovoid body w/flaring rim, Oriental Red glaze, Shape No. V-12 ....................................................... **175**

**Vase,** 7 1/2" h., baluster-form w/trumpet-form neck, blue rainbow lustre, Shape No. 631 ............................................................ **90**

**Vase,** 7 1/2" h., footed, tapering cylindrical body, green drip over yellow glaze, Shape No. 591, 8" h. (ILLUS. far right w/ashtrays) ....................................................... **275**

**Vase,** 5 1/4 x 7 3/4", flared tulip-shaped body, squared feet, blue.................................... **80**

**Vase,** 8" h., blue lustre, Shape No. 615............ **100**

**Vase,** 8" h., bulbous body tapering to cylindrical neck w/flaring rim, verde green, Shape No. V-932 ........................................ **100**

**Vase,** 8" h., bulbous body tapering to cylindrical neck w/flaring rim, black drip over Feu Rouge (red) glaze Shape No. V-932 (ILLUS. top w/ashtrays) ........................ **550**

**Vase,** 8" h., cylindrical body, black w/overall turquoise blue decoration, triple-signed (ILLUS. above left)........................ **1,000**

**Vase,** 8" h., 8" d., wide bulbous body w/narrow molded rim, embossed w/a band of stylized leaves and covered in Egyptian blue glaze, designed by Paul Bogatay, Shape No. V-61 ......................................... **750**

**Vase,** 8 1/4" h., "Logan," footed, compressed bulbous base w/trumpet-form neck, flattened sides w/notched corners, decorative side handles, designed by R.G. Cowan, verde green glaze, Shape No. 649-B ........................................ **225**

**Vase,** cov., 8 1/2" h., Egyptian blue, Shape No. V-91 .......................................................... **650**

**Vase,** 9" h., footed bulbous ovoid body w/slightly flaring rim, copper lustre, Shape No. 585 ............................................. **250**

**Vase,** 9" h., 6 1/2" d., footed trumpet-form, the sides w/horizontal ribbing, overall Russet Brown glaze, stamped mark ............ **138**

**Vase,** 10 1/2" h., footed bulbous ovoid body, Star patt., decorated w/relief-molded foliage, orange glaze, designed

by Waylande Gregory, Shape V-32, mark No. 8 & 9 (ILLUS. left w/bowl) ............ **600**

**Vase,** 11 1/4" h., Chinese Bird patt., footed urn shape w/relief-molded birds at base, tan & brown crystalline glaze, impressed mark , Shape No. V-747 (small stilt pull on bottom not visible from side) ................... **880**

**Vase,** 11 1/2" h., bulbous base tapering to tall slender cylindrical neck, blue lustre, Shape No. 554-B................................................ **100**

**Vase,** 11 1/2" h., 6 1/2" w., Chinese Bird patt., a fanned & lightly ribbed upper body above a large stylized exotic long-tailed bird at the bottom resting on an oblong scalloped foot, covered in in a Jade Green glaze, stamped mark ................ **495**

**Vase,** 11 3/4" h., wine & yellow glaze, Shape No. V-15................................................ **500**

**Vase,** 12" h., footed ovoid body, mother-of-pearl finish, Shape No. 847 ......................... **300**

**Wall plate,** flat, blue, 11 1/4" d. ........................ **150**

**Wall plate,** cupped, blue, 11 1/2" d. ................. **150**

# DOULTON & ROYAL DOULTON

*Doulton & Co., Ltd., was founded in Lambeth, London, about 1858. It was operated there till 1956 and often incorporated the words "Doulton" and "Lambeth" in its marks. Pinder, Bourne & Co., Burslem was purchased by the Doultons in 1878 and in 1882 became Doulton & Co., Ltd. It added porcelain to its earthenware production in 1884. The "Royal Doulton" mark has been used since 1902 by this factory, which is still in production. Character jugs and figurines are commanding great attention from collectors at the present time.*

*Royal Doulton Mark*

## CHARACTER JUGS

**'Ard of 'Earing,** large, D 6588, 7 1/2" h. ..... **$1,210**

**Captain Hook,** large, D 6597, 7 1/4" h............. **570**

**Granny,** large, toothless, D 5521, 6 1/4" h. ...... **880**

**Regency Beau,** large, D 6559, 7 1/4" h. .......... **915**

**Scaramouche,** large, first version, D 6558, 7" h. ........................................................... **935**

## DICKENSWARE

**Plates,** 10 3/8'" d., each w/a color scene, one titled "Alfred Jingle," the other "Sergeant Buzfuz," pr. ......................................... **165**

## FIGURINES

**April,** HN 2708, white dress w/flowers, Flower of the Month series, 1987 ................. **125**

**Ascot,** HN 2356, green dress w/yellow shawl, 1968 to present ................................. 150

**Autumn Breezes,** HN 1934, red, 1940 to present ........................................................ 227

**Ballerina,** HN 2116, lavender, 1953-73 .......... 230

**Bess,** HN 2003, purple cloak, 1947-50 ..... 525-550

**Biddy Penny Farthing,** HN 1843, green & lavender, 1938 to present ........................... 162

**Bluebeard,** HN 2105, purple, green & brown, 1953-92 ........................................ 438

**Boatman (The),** HN 2417, yellow, 1971-87 ..... 170

**Carol,** HN 2961, white, 1982 to present ......... 135

**Cavalier,** HN 2716, brown & green, 1976-82 ............................................................ 195

**Centurian,** HN 2726, grey & purple, 1982-84 ............................................................ 173

**Christine,** HN 2792, flowered blue & white dress, 1978 to present ................................ 225

*Christmas Morn*

**Christmas Morn,** HN 1992, red & white, 1947- (ILLUS.) ...................................... 198

**Christmas Time,** HN 2110, red w/white frills, 1953-67 .......................................... 376

**Clarissa,** HN 2345, green dress, 1968-81 ....... 168

**Clown (The),** HN 2890, gold & grey, 1979-1988 .................................................. 175

**Debbie,** HN 2385, blue & white dress, 1969-82 .............................................. 83

**Delphine,** HN 2136, blue & lavender, 1954-67 ........................................................ 250-300

**Doctor,** HN 2858, black & grey, 1979-92 ........ 190

**Elegance,** HN 2264, green dress, 1961-85 ...... 193

**Eventide,** HN 2814, blue, white, red, yellow & green, 1977-91 ................................... 165

**Fair Lady,** HN 2835, coral pink, 1977 to present .................................................. 175

**Fragrance,** HN 2334, blue, 1966 to present..... 175

**Grand Manner,** HN 2723, lavender-yellow, 1975-81 .......................................... 225

**Harlequin,** HN 2186, blue, 1957-69 ................ 250

**HRH Prince Phillip, Duke of Edinburgh,** HN 2386, black & gold, 1981, limited edition of 1,500 ......................................... 438

**HRH the Prince of Wales,** HN 2883, purple, white & black, limited edition of 1,500, 1981 .............................................. 450

**Janine,** HN 2461, turquoise & white, 1971 to present ...................................... 195

**Jersey Milkmaid (The),** HN 2057, blue, white & red, 1950-59 ............................ 150

**Lady Pamela,** HN 2718, purple, 1974-81 ........ 200

**Laird (The),** HN 2361, green & brown, 1969 to present ...................................... 150

**Lisa,** HN 2310, violet & white dress, 1969-82 .................................................. 175

**Little Nell,** HN 540, pink dress, 1922-32 ........... 93

**Loretta,** HN 2337, rose-red dress, yellow shawl, 1966-80 ...................................... 175

**Lunchtime,** HN 2485, brown, 1973-80 ............. 175

**Mask Seller,** HN 2103, green coat, black hat, 1953 to present ............................. 175

**Maureen,** HN 2481, white dress w/purple flowers, 1987 to present .......................... 165

**Melanie,** HN 2271, blue, 1965-81 .................... 150

*The Orange Lady*

**Orange Lady (The),** HN 1759, pink, 1936-75 (ILLUS.) ......................................... 225

**Potter (The),** HN 1493, multicolored jugs & jars, dark brown & red robe & hood, 1932 to present ...................................... 450

**Punch & Judy Man,** HN 2765, green & yellow, 1981-90 ...................................... 255

**Rest Awhile,** HN 2728, blue, white & purple, 1981-84 ...................................... 150

**Reverie,** HN 2306, peach dress, 1964-81 ........ 225

**Romance,** HN 2430, gold & green dress, 1972-81 .......................................... 165

**Rose,** HN 1368, pink-red dress, 1930 to present .................................................. 70

**Royal Governor's Cook,** HN 2233, dark blue, white & brown, Figures of Williamsburg Series, 1960-83 ........................ 392

**Silversmith of Williamsburg,** HN 2208, green jerkin, 1960-83 ............................ 150

**Stephanie,** HN 2807, yellow gown, 1977-82 ............................................................ 150

**Stitch in Time (A),** HN 2352, 1966-81 ............. 175

**Taking Things Easy,** HN 2677, blue, white & brown, 1975-87 ................................ 178

**Thanksgiving,** HN 2446, blue overalls, 1972-76 .......................................... 200

**Top o' the Hill,** HN 1834, orange dress, green & red scarf, 1937 to present .............. **207**
**Votes For Women,** HN 2816, 1978-81 ........... **195**
**Wigmaker of Williamsburg,** HN 2239, white & brown, 1960-83 .............................. **177**

## MISCELLANEOUS
**Bowl,** 8 7/8" d., 3 3/4" h., wide shallow rounded form, interior w/transfer-printed polychrome fox hunt scenes, green vintage border w/gilt trim, early 20th c. ............. **138**

*Royal Doulton Scenic Cabinet Plates*

**Cabinet plates,** 10 1/4" d., each w/a different English garden view within a narrow acid-etched gilt border, transfer-printed & painted by J. Price, ca. 1928, artist-signed, green printed lion, crown & circle mark, impressed year letters, painted pattern numbers "H3587," set of 12 (ILLUS. of part) ....................................... **5,750**
**Candlestick,** "Old Moreton" series, low flaring round foot & slightly swelled cylindrical shaft below widely flaring flattened socket rim, color transfer of 16th c. gentleman titled "Old Moreton," impressed "7277," 6 3/8" h.............................................. **83**
**Chop plate,** round w/flanged rim, "Old Moreton" series, black transfer-printed design decorated in polychrome, a large center interior scene titled "Queen Elizabeth at Old Moreton 1589," early 20th c., 12 3/4" d. ...................................................... **110**
**Lamp base,** slender ovoid ceramic body w/a tapering neck supporting electric lamp fittings, base decorated w/daffodils in greens, blue, white & yellow, fine brass round base mount w/a ring on the backs of four tiny figural turtles resting on a round disk on small ball feet, early 20th c., overall 28 1/2" h. (minor damage to body) ......................................... **578**
**Loving cup,** stoneware, cylindrical body w/low tapering base & wide short flaring rim, the wide tooled central band in band w/enameled floral designs in white & green flanked by thin brown stripes,

three applied ear-form loop handles, handles, top & base in blue, marked "Doulton Lambeth," 6 1/8" h. ........................ **275**

*"Robin Hood" Series Plate*

**Plate,** 7 1/2" sq., "Robin Hood" series (Friar Tuck Joins Robin Hood) natural-colored scene of Robin Hood & Friar Tuck standing & talking under large tree (ILLUS.) ........... **85**
**Plates,** 10 1/4" d., series-type, color transfer-printed scenes on a tan speckled ground, one titled "The Battle," the other "The Press Gang," pr. ................................. **138**
**Vase,** 5 3/4" h., 3 3/4" d., baluster-form w/short flaring neck, slip-decorated in color w/celadon green fish & kelp on a dark brown ground, stamped "Doulton-Lambeth - 1883 - GTH - WP (?) - 593" ........ **440**
**Vase,** 6" h., 3" d., Sung Ware, footed simple ovoid body tapering to a small trumpet neck, bright red & blue Flambé glaze, marked "Royal Doulton - Flambé - Sung - Noke".............................................. **248**
**Vase,** 6 3/4" h., Sung Ware, tapering cylindrical body w/flared foot & incurved rim, scene of water fowl standing among tall reeds in a range of colors including Flambé reds & blues, decorated by A. Eaton & glazed by Charles Noke, Royal Doulton Flambé ink stamp mark & "No. 2836 Sung Noke" in black slip, ca. 1920s (two tight cracks at rim) ................................ **358**
**Vase,** 6 3/4" h., wide shoulder tapering toward the base, extended neck, decorated w/white daffodils w/blue centers outlined w/white slip on a mottled light olive green ground, impressed mark "t - 1898" & inscribed "MW" .............................. **173**
**Vase,** 7" h., Flambé Ware, footed wide bulbous body w/wide shoulder tapering to short cylindrical neck w/molded rim, rich red glaze w/swirling mottled grey, black, blue & cream, artist-signed, Charles Noke, ink stamp & Doulton paster on bottom ......................................................... **358**
**Vase,** 7 3/4" h., Art Deco style baluster-form decorated w/alternating vertical green & black panels, horizontal black & white panels on shoulder, impressed "Royal Doulton Lambeth England,"

"8190" w/"S" in black slip, artist's monogram incised in bottom .................................. **468**

**Vase,** 8 7/8" h., dome footed w/wide cylindrical body, the narrow shoulder tapering to wide waisted cylindrical neck decorated w/sprays of prunus & flanked by bronzed elephant head handles, flat rim, decorated in the style of Japanese lacquerwork w/wading birds among reeds between printed gilt borders of mons & ruyi-head forms in gold, platinum & red on brown ground, impressed & gilt-printed "DOULTON, BURSLEM - 863 - AP," ca. 1882 (tiny chip to underside rim of foot) ....................................... **3,737**

**Vase,** 12 1/2" h., Sung Ware, very wide bulbous ovoid body w/narrow cylindrical neck, stylized red, green & purple cherry blossoms interspersed w/lustered green, blue, red & tan drip glazes, decorated by Charles Noke, "Sung" & "Noke" in black slip & "7163," "4," & "46" impressed on bottom (restored drill hole in bottom) ....... **1,870**

**Wash bowl & pitcher set,** deep rounded wide bowl & tall slightly tapering tankard-form pitcher w/gently arched rim & angled handle, blue, white & gold-trimmed Art Nouveau-style "Aubery" patt., ca. 1910, bowl 16" d., pitcher 13 1/2" h., the set ........................................ **550**

**Wash bowl & pitcher set,** Royal Mail series, early English coaching scenes around the sides of each, four in polychrome, early 20th c., bowl 11 7/8" d., pitcher 7 3/8" h., pr. ..................................... **193**

**Whiskey jug w/figural stopper,** 'Kingsware,' bulbous ovoid body w/a loop shoulder handle, the body in overall dark brown, the stopper in the shape of a stout 18th c. man wearing a tricorn hat & painted in polychrome, 8 1/4" h. .................... **110**

**Whiskey jug w/stopper,** stoneware, advertising-type, bulbous ovoid body w/a wide shoulder centered by a small cylindrical neck w/tiny knobbed stopper, small loop shoulder handle, brown neck & handle shaded to tan below, the front w/applied ship & label reading "Special Highland Whiskey" in olive green & cream, stopper w/"Dewar's Whiskey," 7 1/8" h. ...................................................... **138**

# FIESTA (HOMER LAUGHLIN CHINA CO. -HLC)

*Fiesta Mark*

Fiesta dinnerware was made by the Homer Laughlin China Company of Newell, West Virginia, from the 1930s until the early 1970s. The brilliant colors of this inexpensive pottery have attracted numerous collectors. On February 28, 1986, Laughlin reintroduced the popular Fiesta line with minor changes in the shapes of a few pieces and a contemporary color range. The effect of this new production on the Fiesta collecting market is yet to be determined.

*Fiesta Carafe*

**Ashtray**
    cobalt blue ............................................. **$55-60**
    ivory ........................................................ **55-60**
    red........................................................... **55-60**
    turquoise ................................................. **50-55**
    yellow...................................................... **48**

**Bowl,** cream soup
    cobalt blue ............................................. **60-65**
    ivory ........................................................ **56**
    red .......................................................... **65-70**
    turquoise ................................................. **47**
    yellow...................................................... **44**

**Bowl,** dessert, 6" d.
    ivory ........................................................ **45-50**
    turquoise ................................................. **40**
    cobalt blue ............................................. **45-50**
    red .......................................................... **55**
    yellow...................................................... **38**

**Bowl,** individual fruit, 5 1/2" d.
    ivory ........................................................ **33**
    turquoise ................................................. **25**
    yellow...................................................... **25**

**Bowl,** nappy, 8 1/2" d.
    ivory ........................................................ **53-56**
    turquoise ................................................. **42**
    red........................................................... **55**
    yellow...................................................... **44**
    cobalt blue ............................................. **55-60**

**Bowl,** nappy, 9 1/2" d.
    ivory ........................................................ **65-70**
    turquoise ................................................. **50-55**
    cobalt blue ............................................. **65-75**
    red........................................................... **70-75**
    yellow...................................................... **50-60**

**Bowl,** salad, large, footed
    cobalt blue ............................................. **375-400**
    red........................................................... **350-375**
    turquoise ................................................. **335-380**
    yellow...................................................... **350-385**

**Candleholders,** bulb-type, pr.
    cobalt blue ............................................. **120-125**
    ivory ........................................................ **115-120**
    red........................................................... **115-120**
    turquoise ................................................. **100-105**
    yellow...................................................... **100-105**

**Carafe,** cov.
    cobalt blue ............................................. **325-340**

ivory ...................................................... 300-330
red ......................................................... 295-310
turquoise ............................................ 280-295
**Carafe,** cov. yellow (ILLUS.)...................... 270-280
**Casserole,** cov., two-handled, 10" d.
  cobalt blue ......................................... 200-210
  ivory ...................................................... 195-205
  red ......................................................... 195-200
  turquoise ............................................ 130-140
  yellow................................................... 155-160
**Coffeepot,** cov.
  cobalt blue ......................................... 235-245
  ivory ...................................................... 230-240
  red ......................................................... 225-250
  turquoise ............................................ 200-205
  yellow................................................... 175-185
**Coffeepot,** cov., demitasse, stick handle
  cobalt blue ......................................... 475-500
  ivory ...................................................... 500-535
  red ......................................................... 525-575
  turquoise ............................................ 620-665
  yellow................................................... 425-465
**Compote,** 12" d., low, footed
  cobalt blue ......................................... 170-180
  ivory ...................................................... 165-170
  red ......................................................... 180-190
  turquoise ............................................ 150-160
  yellow................................................... 155-160
**Compote,** sweetmeat, high stand
  cobalt blue ............................................. 90-95
  ivory ........................................................ 83-88
  red ........................................................ 90-100
  turquoise ................................................ 75-80
  yellow..................................................... 75-85
**Creamer**
  cobalt blue ................................................... 35
  ivory ............................................................. 30
  red ........................................................... 30-35
  turquoise ...................................................... 24
  yellow.......................................................... 25
**Cup,** demitasse, stick handle
  cobalt blue ................................................... 75
  ivory ........................................................ 75-80
  red ............................................................... 80
  turquoise ................................................ 71-75
  yellow..................................................... 55-60
**Cup,** ring handle
  cobalt blue ............................................. 26-28
  ivory ...................................................... 28-30
  red ......................................................... 25-30
  turquoise ...................................................... 24
  yellow.......................................................... 23
**Cup & saucer,** demitasse, stick handle
  cobalt blue ................................................... 95
  ivory ...................................................... 90-100
  red ....................................................... 100-105
  turquoise .............................................. 90-100
  yellow..................................................... 75-80
**Cup & saucer,** ring handle
  cobalt blue ................................................... 35
  ivory ...................................................... 30-35
  red ......................................................... 35-40
  turquoise ...................................................... 30
  yellow..................................................... 25-30

**Egg cup**
  cobalt blue .............................................. 74-78
  ivory ........................................................ 72-75
  red............................................................ 75-80
  turquoise ................................................ 55-60
  yellow...................................................... 60-65
**Fork** (Kitchen Kraft)
  cobalt blue .......................................... 155-170
  light green ........................................... 115-125
  red.......................................................... 145-160
  yellow.................................................... 145-165
**Gravy boat**
  cobalt blue .............................................. 70-73
  ivory ........................................................ 69-71
  red............................................................ 75-85
  turquoise ................................................ 40-45
  yellow...................................................... 40-45
**Marmalade jar,** cov.
  cobalt blue .......................................... 320-345
  ivory ...................................................... 315-345
  red.......................................................... 325-345
  turquoise .............................................. 310-340
  yellow.................................................... 245-265
**Mixing bowl,** nest-type, size No. 1, 5" d.
  cobalt blue .......................................... 265-285
  ivory ...................................................... 250-265
  red.......................................................... 215-235
  turquoise .............................................. 240-260
  yellow.................................................... 195-215
**Mixing bowl,** nest-type, size No. 2, 6" d.
  cobalt blue .......................................... 120-130
  ivory ...................................................... 145-160
  red.......................................................... 125-135
  turquoise .............................................. 135-145
  yellow.................................................... 125-135
**Mixing bowl,** nest-type, size No. 3, 7" d.
  cobalt blue .......................................... 155-165
  ivory ...................................................... 150-160
  red.......................................................... 145-155
  turquoise .............................................. 145-155
  yellow.................................................... 130-140
**Mixing bowl,** nest-type, size No. 4, 8" d.
  cobalt blue .......................................... 150-165
  ivory ...................................................... 170-180
  red.......................................................... 140-155
  yellow.................................................... 120-130
**Mixing bowl,** nest-type, size No. 5, 9" d.
  cobalt blue .......................................... 200-210
  ivory ...................................................... 190-205
  red.......................................................... 190-200
  turquoise .............................................. 170-180
  yellow.................................................... 140-150
**Mixing bowl,** nest-type, size No. 6, 10" d.
  cobalt blue .......................................... 295-320
  ivory ...................................................... 280-305
  red.......................................................... 285-300
  turquoise .............................................. 280-310
  yellow.................................................... 230-260
**Mixing bowl,** nest-type, size No. 7, 11 1/2" d.
  cobalt blue .......................................... 380-420
  ivory ...................................................... 425-465
  red.......................................................... 410-455
  turquoise .............................................. 335-370
  yellow.................................................... 355-395
**Mug** red ...................................................... 80
**Mug,** Tom & Jerry style
  cobalt blue .............................................. 70-75
  ivory/gold .............................................. 75-80
  red............................................................ 75-80
  turquoise ................................................ 50-55
  yellow........................................................... 57

**Mustard jar,** cov.
  cobalt blue ........................................ **290-305**
  ivory ................................................... **270-285**
  light green.......................................... **293**
  red ..................................................... **300-310**
  turquoise........................................... **230-250**
  yellow................................................. **260-275**

*Fiesta Onion Soup Bowl*

**Onion soup bowl,** cov. turquoise (ILLUS.). **11,000**
**Pie server** (Kitchen Kraft)
  cobalt blue ........................................ **155-170**
  light green.......................................... **140-155**
  red ..................................................... **175-190**
  yellow................................................. **130-145**
**Pitcher,** water, disc-type
  chartreuse.......................................... **295**
  cobalt blue ........................................ **155-160**
  forest green ....................................... **343**
  vory.................................................... **155-165**
  medium green..................................... **1,867**
  red ..................................................... **150-160**
  turquoise........................................... **115-120**
  yellow................................................. **115-120**
**Plate,** 10" d.
  cobalt blue ........................................ **41-42**
  ivory ................................................... **40**
  light green.......................................... **29**
  medium green..................................... **168**
  red ..................................................... **44**
  turquoise........................................... **29**
  yellow................................................. **28-30**
**Plate,** 6" d.
  cobalt blue ........................................ **8**
  ivory ................................................... **7**
  red ..................................................... **7**
  turquoise........................................... **7**
  yellow................................................. **7**
**Plate,** 7" d.
  cobalt blue ........................................ **11**
  ivory ................................................... **10**
  red ..................................................... **12**
  turquoise........................................... **9**
  yellow................................................. **9**
**Plate,** 9" d.
  cobalt blue ........................................ **17-18**
  ivory ................................................... **16**
  red ..................................................... **17-18**
  turquoise........................................... **13**
  yellow................................................. **13**
**Plate,** chop, 13" d.
  cobalt blue ........................................ **45-50**
  ivory ................................................... **43-47**
  red ..................................................... **45-50**
  turquoise........................................... **40-45**
  yellow................................................. **38**

**Plate,** chop, 15" d.
  cobalt blue ........................................ **75-80**
  ivory ................................................... **64-67**
  red..................................................... **75-80**
  turquoise........................................... **50-55**
  yellow................................................. **47**
**Plate,** grill, 10 1/2" d.
  cobalt blue ........................................ **45**
  ivory ................................................... **45-50**
  red..................................................... **60-70**
  rose.................................................... **74**
  turquoise........................................... **43**
  yellow................................................. **40-43**
**Platter,** 12" oval
  cobalt blue ........................................ **45-48**
  ivory ................................................... **35-40**
  red..................................................... **52**
  turquoise........................................... **35-40**
  yellow................................................. **36**
**Relish tray w/five inserts**
  cobalt blue ........................................ **300-375**
  ivory ................................................... **375-400**
  red..................................................... **370-380**
  turquoise........................................... **345-365**
  yellow................................................. **325-350**
**Salt & pepper shakers,** pr.
  cobalt blue ........................................ **32**
  ivory ................................................... **30-35**
  red..................................................... **30-35**
  turquoise........................................... **26**
  yellow................................................. **25**
**Soup plate,** w/flanged rim, 8" d.
  ivory ................................................... **54**
  red..................................................... **55-60**
  turquoise........................................... **39**
  yellow................................................. **36**
**Sugar bowl,** cov.
  cobalt blue ........................................ **55-60**
  ivory ................................................... **55-60**
  medium green..................................... **265**
  red..................................................... **55-60**

*Fiesta Sugar Bowl*

  turquoise (ILLUS.)............................... **46**
  yellow................................................. **42**
**Teapot,** cov., medium size (6 cup)
  cobalt blue ........................................ **215-225**
  ivory ................................................... **200**
  red..................................................... **195-200**
  turquoise........................................... **160-165**
  yellow................................................. **155-160**
**Tumbler,** water, 10 oz.
  cobalt blue ........................................ **73-75**
  ivory ................................................... **69-72**
  red..................................................... **72**
  turquoise........................................... **62**
  yellow................................................. **60-65**

**Utility tray**
cobalt blue ........................................... 45-50
ivory ....................................................... 35-40
red ......................................................... 45-50
turquoise.................................................... 40
yellow........................................................ 42
**Vase,** 8" h.
cobalt blue ......................................... 720-740
ivory ................................................... 750-770
red ..................................................... 760-780
turquoise............................................ 550-600
yellow................................................. 525-585
**Vase,** bud, 6 1/2" h.
cobalt blue ......................................... 100-105
ivory ................................................... 105-110
red ....................................................... 90-100
turquoise.............................................. 90-100
yellow.................................................... 85-90

# FRANCISCAN WARE

*A product of Gladding, McBean & Company of Glendale and Los Angeles, California, Franciscan Ware was one of a number of lines produced by that firm over its long history. Introduced in 1934 as a pottery dinnerware, Franciscan Ware was produced in many patterns including "Desert Rose," introduced in 1941 and reportedly the most popular dinnerware pattern ever made in this country. Beginning in 1942 some vitrified china patterns were also produced under the Franciscan name.*

*After a merger in 1963 the company name was changed to Interpace Corporation and in 1979 Josiah Wedgwood & Sons purchased the Gladding, McBean & Co. plant from Interpace. American production ceased in 1984.*

*Franciscan Mark*

**Ashtray,** Apple patt., 4 1/2 x 9" oval.............. $105
**Ashtray,** Desert Rose patt., 4 3/4 x 9" oval........ 85
**Ashtray,** Desert Rose patt., square ................. 325
**Ashtray,** El Patio tableware, coral satin glaze............................................................. 8
**Ashtray,** individual, Desert Rose patt., 3 1/2" d. ................................................... 24
**Ashtray,** individual, Apple patt., apple-shaped, 4" w., 4 1/2" l. .................................. 19
**Ashtray,** individual, Ivy patt., leaf-shaped, 4 1/2" l. .................................................... 27
**Baking dish,** Apple patt., 1 qt. ...................... 275
**Baking dish,** Desert Rose patt., 1 qt. ............. 223
**Baking dish,** Meadow Rose patt., 9 x 14", 1 1/2 qt. .................................................... 125
**Bank,** figural pig, Desert Rose patt. ................ 265
**Bell,** Desert Rose patt., Danbury Mint, 4 1/4" h. .................................................. 130
**Bell,** dinner, Franciscan.................................... 150
**Bowl,** bouillon soup, cov., 4 1/2" d., Desert Rose patt.................................................... 275

**Bowl,** fruit, 5 1/4" d., Desert Rose patt. .............. 15
**Bowl,** cereal, 6" d., Desert Rose patt. ................ 18
**Bowl,** 7" d., Picnic patt. .................................... 8
**Bowl,** cereal, 7" d., October patt. ...................... 18
**Bowl,** salad, 10" d., Desert Rose patt. ............. 120
**Bowl,** salad, 11" d., Daisy patt. ......................... 90
**Bowl,** fruit, Arden patt. ..................................... 12
**Box,** cov., Desert Rose patt., heart-shaped, 4 1/2" l., 2 1/2" h.......................... 195
**Box,** cov., egg-shaped, 1 1/2 x 4 3/4", Desert Rose patt........................................ 200
**Box,** cov., round, Desert Rose patt., 4 3/4" d., 1 1/2" h............................................ 195
**Box,** cov., Twilight Rose patt., heart-shaped ...................................................... 225
**Butter dish,** cov., Desert Rose patt. .................. 55
**Candleholders,** Desert Rose patt., pr............... 95
**Candleholders,** Starburst patt., pr.................. 150
**Casserole,** cov., Desert Rose patt., 1 1/2 qt., 4 3/4" h.............................................. 95
**Casserole,** cov., Desert Rose patt., 2 1/2 qt. .......................................................... 225
**Cigarette box,** cov., Desert Rose patt., 3 1/2 x 4 1/2", 2" h................................... 150
**Coaster,** Apple patt., 3 3/4" d. ........................... 53
**Coffee server,** El Patio tableware, turquoise glossy glaze.................................... 40
**Coffeepot,** cov., Desert Rose patt., 7 1/2" h. .............................................. 140
**Coffeepot,** cov., 10" h., Daisy patt. .................... 85
**Coffeepot,** cov., demitasse, Coronado Table Ware, coral satin glaze........................ 90
**Coffeepot,** individual, cov., Desert Rose patt. ................................................... 425
**Compote,** open, Desert Rose patt., 8" d., 4" h. ....................................................... 77
**Compote,** open, Meadow Rose patt., 8" d., 4" h. ....................................................... 85
**Cookie jar,** cov., Desert Rose patt. .................. 325
**Creamer,** individual, Desert Rose patt., 3 1/2" h. ............................................. 45
**Creamer,** Ivy patt., 4" h. .................................... 30
**Creamer,** Desert Rose patt., 4 1/4" h. ................ 28
**Creamer,** October patt. ..................................... 24
**Creamer & cov. sugar bowl,** Daisy patt., pr. ............................................................. 58
**Creamer & open sugar bowl,** Tiempo patt., lime green, pr. ..................................... 25
**Creamer & open sugar bowl,** individual, Desert Rose patt. ....................................... 115
**Creamer & open sugar bowl,** individual, El Patio Nuevo patt., orange, pr. .................... 50
**Cup & saucer,** Arden patt. ................................ 15
**Cup & saucer,** coffee, Desert Rose patt. .......... 22
**Cup & saucer,** Desert Rose patt., jumbo size.......................................................... 75
**Cup & saucer,** tall, Desert Rose patt. ............... 55
**Cup & saucer,** tea, Desert Rose patt. ............... 18
**Cup & saucer,** demitasse, Apple patt. .............. 55
**Cup & saucer,** demitasse, Desert Rose patt. ...................................................... 65
**Cup & saucer,** demitasse, El Patio tableware, golden glow glossy glaze .................... 20
**Cup & saucer,** demitasse, El Patio tableware, Mexican blue glossy glaze ................... 20
**Cup & saucer,** demitasse, El Patio tableware, turquoise glossy glaze........................ 20
**Egg cup,** Desert Rose patt., 2 3/4" d., 3 3/4" h. .................................................. 48

**Egg cup,** Meadow Rose patt., 2 3/4 d., 3 3/4" h. ................................... **19**

**Egg cup,** Twilight Rose patt., 2 3/4" d., 3 3/4" h. .................................. **350**

**Egg cup,** Apple patt., double ............................ **32**

**Goblet,** footed, Desert Rose patt., 6 1/2" h. ..... **210**

**Goblet,** Meadow Rose patt., 6 1/2" h. ............... **85**

**Goblet,** Picnic patt., 6 1/2" h. .......................... **20**

**Gravy boat,** Desert Rose patt. .......................... **45**

**Hurricane lamp,** Desert Rose patt. ................. **325**

**Jam jar,** cov., Desert Rose patt. ...................... **125**

**Microwave dish,** oblong, Desert Rose patt., 1 1/2 qt. ...................................... **295**

**Mixing bowls,** Desert Rose patt., 3 pc. set ...... **550**

**Mug,** Desert Rose patt., 10 oz. ......................... **145**

**Mug,** Desert Rose patt., 12 oz. .......................... **65**

**Napkin ring,** Desert Rose patt. .......................... **60**

**Napkin ring,** Meadow Rose patt. ....................... **19**

**Pepper mill,** Duet patt. .................................... **125**

**Pepper mill,** Starburst patt. ............................. **165**

**Pickle dish,** Desert Rose patt., 4 1/2 x 11" ...... **42**

**Pickle/relish boat,** Desert Rose patt., interior decoration, 4 1/2 x 11" .................. **350**

**Pitcher,** milk, 6 1/2" h., Desert Rose patt., 1 qt. ...................................... **110**

**Pitcher,** milk, 8 1/2" h., Daisy patt. ..................... **78**

**Plate,** dinner, Arden patt. .................................. **15**

**Plate,** luncheon, Arden patt. ............................. **12**

**Plate,** salad, Arden patt. ...................................... **8**

**Plate,** bread & butter, 6 1/4" d., Ivy patt. ............ **10**

**Plate,** bread & butter, 6 1/2" d., October patt. ................................................. **7**

**Plate,** bread & butter, 6 1/2" d., Wildflower patt. ............................................ **50**

**Plate,** side salad, 4 1/2 x 8", crescent-shaped, Apple patt. ................................ **38**

**Plate,** side salad, 4 1/2 x 8", crescent-shaped, Ivy patt. ................................... **49**

**Plate,** side salad, 4 1/2 x 8, crescent-shaped, Meadow Rose patt. ................... **29**

**Plate,** child's, divided, 7 1/4 x 9", Apple patt. ............................................... **169**

**Plate,** luncheon, 9 1/2" d., Desert Rose patt. ................................................. **28**

**Plate,** coupe, party w/cup well, Desert Rose patt., 10 1/2" d. ........................... **160**

*Dessert Rose Dinner Plate*

**Plate,** dinner, 10 1/2" d., Desert Rose patt. (ILLUS.). ......................................... **24**

**Plate,** T.V. w/cup well, 8 x 13 1/2", Ivy patt. ........ **85**

**Plate,** T.V. w/cup well, 14" l., Desert Rose patt. ................................................ **144**

**Plate,** T.V. w/cup well, 8 1/4 x 14", Starburst patt. ........................................ **75**

**Plate,** chop, 11 1/2" d., Desert Rose patt. .......... **55**

**Plate,** chop, 14" d., Desert Rose patt. .............. **195**

**Plate,** coupe, steak,11" l., Apple patt. .............. **138**

**Plate,** coupe, steak, 11" l., Desert Rose patt. ................................................ **125**

**Plate,** grill or buffet, 11" d., Desert Rose patt. ................................................. **96**

**Platter,** 11" l., oval, Arden patt. ....................... **35**

**Platter,** 11 1/4" l., Ivy patt. ............................... **65**

**Platter,** 12 3/4" l., Apple patt. ........................... **50**

**Platter,** 10 1/4 x 14" oval, Apple patt. ............... **45**

**Platter,** 19" l., oval, Apple patt. ...................... **207**

**Relish dish,** oval, Desert Rose patt. ................. **45**

**Relish/pickle dish,** Wildflower patt., interior design, 4 1/4 x 12" oval .................. **525**

**Salt & pepper shakers,** figural rose bud, Desert Rose patt., pr. ........................ **28**

**Salt & pepper shakers,** October patt., pr. ......... **35**

**Salt & pepper shakers,** Strawberry Time patt., 3" h., pr. .................................... **35**

**Salt shaker & pepper mill,** Daisy patt., pr. ....... **135**

**Salt shaker & pepper mill,** Desert Rose patt., 6" h., pr. ..................................... **325**

**Sherbet,** Desert Rose patt., footed, 4" d., 2 1/2" h. ............................................ **23**

**Sherbet,** Ivy patt., footed, 4" d., 2 1/2" h. .......... **30**

**Sherbet,** Coronado Table Ware, ivory glaze ............................................... **12**

**Soup bowl,** footed, Desert Rose patt. ............... **35**

**Soup bowl,** rimmed, Desert Rose patt. ............. **35**

**Soup plate w/flanged rim,** Arden patt. .............. **15**

**Soup tureen,** cov., Desert Rose patt. ............... **525**

**Soup tureen,** cov., Fresh Fruit patt., made in England ....................................... **200**

**Sugar bowl,** cov., Coronado Table Ware, glossy coral glaze ............................ **14**

**Sugar bowl,** cov., Desert Rose patt. ................. **38**

**Sugar bowl,** cov., Strawberry Time patt. .......... **30**

**Syrup pitcher,** Desert Rose patt., 1 pt., 6 1/2" h. ............................................ **95**

**Tea canister,** cov., Desert Rose patt. .............. **282**

**Teapot,** cov., Arden patt. ................................. **125**

**Teapot,** cov., Desert Rose patt., 6 1/2" h. .......... **95**

**Thimble,** Desert Rose patt., 1" h. ..................... **45**

**Trivet,** tile, Desert Rose patt. .......................... **195**

**Tumbler,** Desert Rose patt., 10 oz., 5 1/4" h. ........................................... **38**

**Vase,** bud, 6" h., Meadow Rose patt. ................. **50**

**Vegetable bowl,** open, oval, Arden patt., large ............................................... **45**

**Vegetable bowl,** Daisy patt., 6 3/4 x 13 3/4", 2 1/4" h. ........................ **38**

**Vegetable dish,** Desert Rose patt., 8" l. ............ **35**

**Vegetable dish,** Desert Rose patt., 9" l. ............ **45**

# FRANKOMA

*John Frank began producing and selling pottery on a part-time basis during the summer of 1933 while he was still teaching art and pottery classes at the University of Oklahoma. In 1934, Frankoma Pottery became an incorporated business that was successful enough to allow him to leave his teaching position in 1936 to devote full time to its growth. The pottery was moved to Sapulpa, Oklahoma in 1938 and a full range of art pottery and dinnerwares* were eventually offered. In 1953 Frankoma switched from Ada clay to clay found in Sapulpa. Since John Franks' death in 1973, the pottery has been directed by his daughter, Janiece. In early 1991 Richard Bernstein became owner and president of Frankoma Pottery which was renamed Frankoma Industries. Janiece Frank serves as vice president and general manager. The early wares and limited editions are becoming increasingly popular with collectors today.

*Frankoma Mark*

John Frank studied at the Chicago Art Institute and was fortunate to train under two noted ceramic artists: Mrs. Myrtle Merritt French and Dr. Charles F. Binns. When a Dr. Jacobsen asked Professor French to find someone to begin a new ceramic art department at the University, she highly recommended John Frank. That position enabled him to study and formulate various glazes. From these experiments he was able to create a beautiful rutile glaze that had been used only sparingly in the past.

When he founded Frankoma Potteries in 1933 Mr. Frank almost always used the rutile technique which helped to create beautiful glazes for his pottery.

With his family, Mr. Frank moved his operation from Norman, Oklahoma to Sapulpa, Oklahoma. He felt he had come home. The family and its company have remained in Sapulpa since that time.

Over the years Frankoma products have been marked in a variety of ways. The "pot and leopard" mark was used from 1935-1938 when a fire on November 11, 1938 destroyed everything including the mark.

A creamy looking clay known as "Ada" is highly collectible today but it was discontinued in 1953. Frankoma then began using the clay from Sapulpa which resulted in a red brick color.

In May 1970 John Frank was contacted by a writer and in response to his questions Mr. Frank personally sent the writer the answers. There has been much controversy over the actual date when John Frank changed from Ada clay (which is more valuable) to Sapula clay. Below is a paragraph from John Frank's letter to the writer, signed by him, that explains the date. You can find the entire letter printed beginning on page 13 of the "Collectors Guide to Frankoma Pottery," Book II, by Susan N. Cox.   "...We have always used an Oklahoma clay as the base of all our pottery. The first clay came from Ada, and we used it until 1953 when we

switched over to a local brick shale that we dig right here in Sapulpa. Using this as a base we add other earths and come up with what we call our Frankoma Pottery. Peculiar in itself, and it is not available anywhere else, nor is it used by any other pottery, it fires a brick red and we are able to temper it in the cooling so that all of our ware is guaranteed oven proof."

When Richard Bernstein purchased Frankoma in 1991 a new era began resulting in different products and glazes. True Frankoma collectors search for the products made before 1991 and certainly those made before 1953. Lucky ones can find pot and leopard-marked pieces and those marked "Frank Potteries."

**Baker,** Westwind patt., Model No. 6vs, Peach Glow glaze, 1 1/2 pt. ......................... **$24**
**Book ends,** Bucking Bronco, Model No. 423, Prairie Green glaze, 5 1/2" h., pr......... **400**

*Frankoma Leopard Book End*

**Book ends,** model of leopard, Pompeian Bronze glaze, Model No. 431, 9" l., 5 1/2" h., pr. (ILLUS. of one) ....................... **900**
**Book ends,** seated figure, Ivory glaze, Model No. 425, 1934-38, 5 3/4" h., pr. ...... **1,000**

*Ocelot Book Ends*

**Book ends,** Walking Ocelot on a two-tiered oblong base, black high glaze, Model No. 424, signed on reverse of tiered base "Taylor" denoting designer Joseph Taylor, pot & leopard mark on bottom, 7" l., 3" h., pr. (ILLUS.) ............................ **1,015**
**Bottle-vase,** V-1, 1969, limited edition, 4,000 created, small black foot w/Prairie Green body, 15" h. ...................................... **125**
**Bottle-vase,** V-7, limited edition, 3,500 created, Desert Gold glaze, body w/coffee glazed stopper & base, signed by Joniece Frank, 13" h. ................................... **100**
**Bowl,** 11" l., divided, Lazybones patt., Brown Satin glaze, Model No. 4qd................. **18**
**Brooch,** four-leaf clover-shape, Desert Gold glaze, w/original card, 1 1/4" h.............. **40**
**Canteen,** Indian Thunderbird decoration, Prairie Green glaze, incised mark, No. 59, 6 1/2" h. ...................................................... **60**
**Catalog,** 1953, unnumbered sixteen pages, dated July 1, 1953, two versions for

color cover, one w/photograph of Donna Frank or one w/photograph of Grace Lee Frank, each ...................................................... **45**

**Christmas card,** 1969........................................ **44**

**Christmas card,** figural fish tray, Woodland Moss glaze, marked, "1960 the Franks, Frankoma Christmas Frankoma," 4" l. ............................................ **75**

**Christmas card,** "Statue of Liberty Torch," White Sand glaze, created by Grace Lee Frank Smith for her & Dr. A. Milton Smith's friends, 1986, 3 1/2" l. ...................... **75**

*Bronze Green Cigarette Box*

**Cigarette box,** cov., rectangular, cover w/single raised & hard-to-find curved leaf handle, Bronze Green glaze, Ada clay, marked "Frankoma," 4 x 6 3/4", 3 1/2" h. (ILLUS.)........................................ **150**

**Figure of Fan Dancer,** seated, No. 113, Ivory glaze, Ada clay, 14" l., 9" h.................. **800**

**Figure of farmer boy,** wearing dark blue overalls, light blue short-sleeved shirt, black scarf tied around neck, yellow hair & ivory wide-brim hat w/only brim showing from front, black shoes, bisque arms, hands, face & neck, marked "Frankoma 702," 6 3/4" h................................. **125**

**Figure of gardener girl,** holding pale green apron to form a basket in front of her, light blue dress w/short puffed sleeves & scooped neckline, long yellow hair w/dark blue bow on top, bisque face, neck, arms & hands, marked "Frankoma 701," 5 3/4" h. ........................... **125**

*Frankoma Indian Chief Figure*

**Figure of Indian Chief,** No. 142, Desert Gold glaze, Ada clay, 7" h. (ILLUS.).............. **165**

**Mug,** 1968, (Republican) elephant, white........... **80**

**Mug,** 1970, (Republican) elephant ..................... **60**

**Mug,** 1971, (Republican) elephant ..................... **55**

**Mug,** 1973, (Republican) elephant ..................... **40**

**Mug,** 1974, (Republican) elephant ..................... **30**

**Mug,** 1977, Elephant & Donkey, Dusty Pink glaze............................................................. **18**

**Pitcher,** Wagon Wheel patt., Model No. 94d, Prairie Green glaze, Ada clay, 2 qt. ....... **45**

**Plate,** 8 1/2" d., Bicentennial Series, Limited Edition No. 1, "Provocations," eleven signers of the Declaration of Independence, White Sand glaze, 1972, mispelling of United States as "Staits" ......... **155**

**Plate,** 8 1/2" d., Christmas, 1971, "No Room in the Inn"............................................. **30**

**Plate,** 7" d., Wildlife Series, Limited Edition No. 1, Bobwhite quail, Prairie Green glaze, 1,000 produced.................................. **125**

**Plate,** 7 1/2" d., Easter 1972, "Jesus Is Not Here...He Is Risen," scene of Jesus' tomb ........................................................... **20**

**Plate,** 8 1/2" d., Bicentennial Series, Limited Edition No. 1, "Provocations," eleven signers of the Declaration of Independence, White Sand glaze, 1972 ........ **95**

**Plate,** 8 1/2" d., Christmas 1968, "Flight into Egypt"........................................................ **45**

**Plate,** 10" d., Mayan Aztec patt., Woodland Moss glaze, Model No. 7fl.............................. **12**

**Political chip,** John Frank's profile on front surrounded by the words, "Honest, Fair, Capable," & at bottom "Elect John Frank Representative 1962," obverse w/outline of Oklahoma state w/"One Frank" inside it, around it "Oklahomans deserve outstanding leadership" & "For statesmanship vote Republican," unglazed red brick color, 1 3/4" d., 1/8" h. ........................ **25**

**Postcard,** color photograph of Joniece Frank sitting w/various Frankoma products used to show the current Frankoma glazes, 5 1/2 x 6 1/2"...................................... **10**

**Salt & pepper shakers,** model of a Dutch shoe, Desert Gold glaze, Model No. 915h, ca. 1957-60, 4" l., pr. ........................... **50**

**Salt & pepper shakers,** model of an elephant, Desert Gold glaze, No. 160h, produced in 1942 only, Ada clay, 3" h., pr........ **135**

*John Frank Tournament Stein*

**Stein,** footed, advertising-type, for John Frank Memorial Charity Gold Tournament, Blue, 150 created, 1973 (ILLUS.)......... **16**

**Teapot,** cov., Wagon Wheel patt., Model No. 94j, Desert Gold glaze, Ada clay, 2 cup .............................................................. 35

**Trivet,** Eagle sitting on branch, large wings fill up most of the trivet, Peach Glow glaze, Model No. 2tr, 6" sq. ........................... 65

**Trivet,** Eagle, undated, Woodland Moss glaze, Model No. AETR, 6" d. ...................... 25

**Trivet,** Lazybones patt., Model No. 4tr, produced in 1957 only, hard-to-find, 6" d. ........... 65

**Trivet,** Spanish Iron patt., created by Joniece Frank, Woodland Moss glaze, produced 1966-1989, 6" sq. .......................... 25

**Tumbler,** juice, Plainsman patt., Model No. 51c, Autumn Yellow glaze, 6 oz. ..................... 7

**Vase,** 10" h., leaf-handled, Sapulpa clay, No. 71 .............................................................. 75

**Vase,** 6" h., Prairie Green glaze, Ada clay, No. 28 .............................................................. 60

**Vase,** 6" h., Prairie Green glaze, Ada clay, No. 38 .............................................................. 50

**Vase,** 3 1/2" h., round foot rising to bulbous body w/short neck & rolled lip, unusual high gloss deep blue, marked "Frank Potteries" ..................................................... 550

**Vase,** 4" h., small foot rising to a flat, narrow body w/tab handle on each side, Ivory glaze, marked "Frankoma" ................... 70

**Vase,** 4" h., small foot rising to a flat, narrow body w/tab handle on each side, Ivory glaze, pot & leopard mark .................. 155

**Vase,** 6" h., square-shaped w/relief-molded flying goose, relief-molded reed decoration on reverse, No. 60B .............................. 35

**Vase,** 7" h., Art Deco-style w/round foot w/panel on each side at base, rising to a plain, flat body w/stepped small elongated handles, Jade Green glaze, Model No. 41, pot & leopard mark ......................... 195

**Wall masks,** bust of Oriental man, No. 135 & Oriental woman, No. 133, Jade Green glaze, pot & leopard mark, Ada clay, man 5 1/2" h., woman 4 3/4" h., pr. .............. 385

# GEISHA GIRL WARES

*Geisha Girl Porcelain features scenes of Japanese ladies in colorful kimonos along with the flora and architecture of turn of the century Japan. Although bearing an Oriental motif, the wares were produced for Western use in dinnerware and household accessory forms favored during the late 1800s through the early 1940s. There was minimal production during the Occupied Japan period. Less ornate wares were distributed through gift shops and catalogs during the 1960s-70s; some of these are believed to have been manufactured in Hong Kong. Beware overly ornate items with fake Nippon marks which are in current production today, imported from China. Over a hundred porcelain manufacturers and decorating houses were involved with production of these wares during their heyday.*

*Prices cited here are for excellent to mint condition items. Enamel wear, flaking, hairlines or missing parts all serve to lower the value of an item. Prices in your area may vary.*

*Over 275 Geisha Girl Porcelain patterns and pattern variations have been catalogued; others are still coming to light.*

*The most common patterns include:*

*Bamboo Tree*

*Battledore*

*Child Reaching for Butterfly*

*Fan series*

*Garden Bench series*

*Geisha in Sampan series*

*Meeting series*

*Parasol series*

*Pointing series*

*The rarest patterns include:*

*.. And They're Off*

*Bellflower*

*Bicycle Race*

*Capricious*

*Elegance in Motion*

*Fishing series*

*Foreign Garden*

*In Flight*

*Steamboat*

*The most popular patterns include:*

*Boat Festival*

*Butterfly Dancers*

*By Land and By Sea*

*Cloud series*

*Courtesan Processional*

*Dragonboat*

*Small Sounds of Summer*

*So Big*

*Temple A*

*A complete listing of patterns and their descriptions can be found in The Collector's Encyclopedia of Geisha Girl Porcelain. Additional patterns discovered since publication of the book are documented in The Geisha Girl Porcelain Newsletter.*

*References: Litts. E., Collector's Encyclopedia of Geisha Girl Porcelain, Collector Books, 1988; Geisha Girl Porcelain Newsletter, P. O. Box 3394, Morris Plains, NJ 07950.*

*Bamboo Trellis Basket Vase*

**Basket-vase,** 8 1/2" h., Bamboo Trellis patt., apple green around handle, brown around base, both w/gold lacing (ILLUS.) .................................................... **$125**

*Carp A Biscuit Jar*

**Biscuit jar,** cov., 6" h., tri-footed, Carp A patt., orange w/gold lacing (ILLUS.) ............... **65**
**Biscuit jar,** cov., Battledore patt., apple green w/gold lacing & white & yellow mums, marked "Japan," 6 1/2" h. ................. **50**

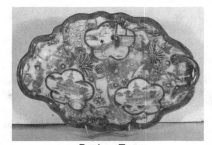

*Bonbon Tray*

**Bonbon tray,** Bow B patt., orange w/gold radiations, three large plum blossom reserves, one w/subject pattern & two scenic, backdrop of flowers, wheat & stippled highlights, 5 x 7 1/4" (ILLUS.) ........... **28**
**Bowl,** 7 1/2" d., Cherry Blossom patt., red edge ............................................................. **45**
**Bowl,** 8" d., Festival Dance patt., pale blue w/gold lacing below (ILLUS.) ......................... **40**

*Festival Dance Bowl*

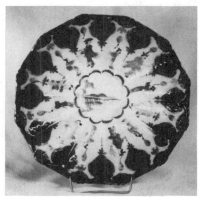

*Daikoku Bowl*

**Bowl,** 8 5/8" d., Daikoku patt., cobalt blue extending inward to form alternating clover & scallop patterns over the lobes, pattern circles around side of bowl, center has chrysanthemum-shaped reserve of hand-painted scenery (ILLUS.) ................. **75**
**Bowl,** 8 3/4" d., raised footrim, Cat, Garden Bench K & Parasol H patterns in reserves on a background diaper of butterflies & peonies, mint green w/gold lacing, red & gold leaves on exterior ................. **65**

*Boys' Processional Bowl*

**Bowl,** 9 1/2" d., Boys' Processional patt., red-orange w/yellow lacing (ILLUS.) .............. **55**

*Boat Festival Cake Platter*

**Cake platter,** 11" d., Boat Festival patt., scalloped blue w/interior band of gold lace, plum blossom & "Japan" mark (ILLUS.) ......................................................... **35**

*Foreign Garden Celery Tray*

**Celery tray,** Foreign Garden patt., cobalt blue rim band (ILLUS.) ...................................... **45**
**Celery tray,** Painting D patt., scalloped red-orange w/gold lacing, rich maroon coloring ................................................................... **45**

*Courtesan Processional Chamberstick*

**Chamberstick,** Courtesan Processional patt., cobalt blue w/gold lacing (ILLUS.).......... **70**

*Battledore Chocolate pot*

**Chocolate pot,** cov., Battledore patt., red w/gold cherry blossoms around rim & spout, handle red w/gold vines, pattern in wavy panel alternating w/linear diaper stencil covered w/apple green wash topped by pink, yellow & maroon cherry blossoms, signed in Japanese, 7 1/4" h. (ILLUS.)......................................................... **75**
**Chocolate pot,** cov., Battledore patt., apple green w/gold lacing, 9 1/2" h. .............. **60**
**Condensed milk jar w/drip plate,** Temple B patt., red w/gold striations ......................... **55**

*Bellflower Lemonade Set*

**Lemonade set:** pitcher & five handled mugs; Bellflower patt., brown w/green band & beading, marked "Japan" (ILLUS.)....................................................... **150**
**Match holder,** Garden Bench A patt., blue-green, striker on base .................................... **37**
**Match holder,** Lantern B patt., red-orange w/apple green circles, strikers on both sides, 1 1/4 x 2 1/2 x 2 1/2" .......................... **45**
**Mayonnaise set:** bowl, drip plate & ladle; Duck Watching A patt., gold border, black stencil, yellow background, marked "Made in Japan" ............................... **40**
**Mug,** child size, Wait for Me patt., red trim ........ **28**
**Mustard pot,** cov., w/attached drip plate, Rendezvous patt., multicolor geometric border.......................................................... **35**

*So Big Pancake Server*

**Pancake server,** cov., So Big patt., floriate-edged dish w/upward reaching rim, multi-banded border, red w/gold lacing, beige w/gold chrysanthemums, tan w/gold circles & netting, red w/gold scalloped lines & semicircles, dome cover w/squared handle & six steam holes, red & gold handle, signed "Kutani," 3 1/2 x 9 1/2" (ILLUS.) .................................. **150**

**Perfume bottle w/stopper,** Prayer Ribbon patt., red-orange stopper & neck overlaid by intertwined gold circles ...................... **75**

*Kakemono Pin Tray*

**Pin tray,** Kakemono patt., blue-green (ILLUS.) ......................................................... **22**

**Pitcher,** 8 1/2" h., Temple B patt., red-orange w/interior band of gold lace .............. **75**

*Birdcage Child's Plate*

**Plate,** child's, Birdcage patt., pine green w/white ribbon (ILLUS.) .................................. **15**

*Chinese Coin Plate*

**Plate,** 6" d., Chinese Coin patt., green coins & gold cherry blossoms on red serve as backdrop for three reserves; one w/geisha, the others noting scenes from Boone Island, York, Maine & Young's Hotel, York Beach, Maine (ILLUS.) ......................................................... **35**

**Plate,** 6" d., Temple Vase patt., wavy red-orange w/yellow lacing, second border of wavy pink diaper of stylized clouds, waves & flowers, interior border of cobalt blue, red & violet w/yellow cherry blossoms ......................................................... **20**

**Plate,** 7" d., Butterfly Dancers patt., scalloped red-orange w/gold lacing ...................... **25**

*Rivers Edge Sugar Bowl & Creamer*

**Sugar bowl, cov., & creamer,** Rivers Edge patt., geometric red & turquoise green border w/gold, handles red w/gold, spout red w/gold chrysanthemums, upper edge of body is red w/gold band, centered below which are two turquoise triangles surrounding golden form encompassing blue & yellow butterfly, forms look like miniature chocolate pot & jam jar, signed "Kutani," 4" h., pr. (ILLUS.) ......................................................... **50**

**Sugar shaker,** handled & pleated, To the Teahouse patt., beige top, red w/gold neck, multicolored floral shoulder, signature worn, 4 3/4" h. ......................................... **85**

*Rivers Edge Sweetmeat Set*

**Sweetmeat set,** Rivers Edge patt., gold edged, nine pieces in lacquered box (ILLUS.) ......................................................... **85**

**Teapot,** cov., Fan A, Fan Dance A & scenic patterns in reserves on pink background w/red ribbons & large gold plum blossoms, signed "Kutani" ................................. **125**

*Geisha in Cards Teapot*

**Teapot,** cov., Geisha in Cards patt., scalloped cobalt blue, advertising premium marked "Cafe Martin, New York," 3" h. (ILLUS.).......................................................... **40**

*Feather Fan Trivet*

**Trivet,** Feather Fan patt., grey w/gold lacing interrupted by red-orange outlined beige segments w/gold dots & stylized pink & gold chrysanthemums w/cobalt blue stylized leaves, marked "Royal Kaga Nippon" (ILLUS.)................................... **55**

*Cricket Cage Vase*

**Vase,** 3 1/2" h., Cricket Cage patt., red-orange (ILLUS.)............................................... **20**

*Parasol C Bud Vase*

**Vase,** bud, 3 1/2" h., tri-footed, Parasol C patt., red-orange w/single gold bud (ILLUS.)......................................................... **28**
**Vase,** 5" h., Temple A patt., red & gold edge, interior band of beige w/flowers, signed "Kutani" ............................................. **55**
**Vase,** 8" h., Fan A patt., cobalt blue, five reserves; one large & three small pinched corner rectangles w/Court Lady patt., four-lobed w/Garden Bench H & stylized fan w/subject pattern backdrop of dots, phoenix, water & mums .................. **140**
**Wall pocket,** Waterboy patt., pine green, Torii mark ...................................................... **65**
**Water jar,** child's, Pointing A patt. red-orange w/yellow beading, 2 1/4" h. ............... **25**

# GRUEBY

*Some fine art pottery was produced by the Grueby Faience and Tile Company, established in Boston in 1891. Choice pieces were created with molded designs on a semi-porcelain body. The ware is marked and often bears the initials of the decorators. The pottery closed in 1907.*

# GRUEBY

*Grueby Pottery Mark*

**Bowl,** 4 3/4" d., 3 3/4" h., coupe-form, the deep half-round bowl raised on a low funnel foot, mottled matte green glaze w/glossy interior, impressed flower mark ... **$495**
**Bowl,** 7" d., 3 1/2" h., deep flaring floriform five-lobed sides w/tooled buds on slender stems, fine curdled matte green glaze on exterior, glossy green interior glaze, circular pottery mark & "RE 339-2".. **2,750**
**Candlestick,** tall slender corseted form w/flaring foot & bulbed neck below the flaring socket rim, tooled & applied leaves around the sides, leathery dark greenish blue matte glaze, paper label, 4" d., 8 1/2" h. ......................................... **2,530**
**Paperweight,** figural, oblong model of a scarab beetle, overall white curdled glaze, impressed pottery mark, 4" l., 2 3/4" h. ...................................................... **880**
**Vase,** 3 3/4 x 4", footed squatty bulbous body w/flared rim, modeled w/stylized

leaf design under a rich dark blue matte glaze, impressed pottery mark & "DS" ..... **1,980**

**Vase,** 4 1/2" h., 4 1/4" d., bulbous ovoid body w/a rounded shoulder centering a short rolled neck, crisply tooled & applied wide pointed leaves alternating w/yellow buds around the shoulder, leathery matte green glaze, no visible mark (minor touch-ups to edges, restoration to small rim chips) .......................... **5,225**

**Vase,** 5" h., 3 1/2" d., footed bulbous body w/slightly flaring rim, semi-matte leathery green glaze, impressed mark (small chips to rim)................................................. **880**

**Vase,** 6" h., 8 1/4" d., wide squatty tapering bulbous body, the wide shoulder centering a wide short cylindrical neck, wide applied pointed leaves alternating w/small buds around the shoulder, fine matte green glaze, impressed round pottery mark, by Florence Liley ..................... **5,500**

**Vase,** 7" h., footed cylindrical body, the rounded shoulder tapering to flared rim, covered in a thick honey matte glaze, stamped pottery mark ............................... **1,870**

**Vase,** 7 1/2" h., swelled cylindrical body w/a pentagonal rim, molded w/five alternating leaf & bud designs, matte green glaze, modeled by Gertrude Priest, signed, ca. 1905 (minor chips, restoration to chip at top of rim)........................... **1,955**

**Vase,** 7 1/2" h., 4" d., footed nearly spherical lower body tapering to a tall gently flaring neck, the base w/applied rounded leaves, rare celadon green semi-matte glaze, faintly impressed round mark ......... **1,980**

**Vase,** 7 1/2" h., 4 1/2" d., ovoid body tapering to a wide cylindrical neck, the lower two-thirds of the body w/applied broad oblong leaves alternating w/slender stems w/buds around the rim, matte green glaze, circular stamp (small flecks to leaf edges) ............................................. **4,400**

**Vase,** 7 3/4" h., 4" d., slightly swelled cylindrical form w/a ruffled floriform rim, tooled & applied w/full-length broad pointed leaves, leathery matte green glaze, circular Faience mark .................... **2,640**

**Vase,** 8" h., squatty bulbous base w/shoulder tapering sharply to tall cylindrical neck w/slightly flaring rim, tooled & applied rounded leaves at the base, covered in matte green glaze, impressed circular "Faience" mark (touch-up to minor nicks at edges of leaves)................ **2,860**

**Vase,** 8 1/4" h., 7 1/2" d., flat-bottomed spherical body w/horizontal ridges, tapering to a slender short trumpet neck w/flattened rim, overall matte green glaze, impressed Faience mark (rim chip restoration)................................................ **3,850**

**Vase,** 8 3/4" h., 7" d., bulbous ovoid body w/a wide flat molded mouth, tooled slender matte green leaves against a mustard yellow ground, by Ruth Erikson, impressed pottery mark & "RE - 9 - 22 - 37" (stilt pulls on base) ............................. **5,500**

**Vase,** 9" h., tapering ridged cylindrical body, slightly rounded at the base, rich

matte cucumber green glaze, impressed circular "Pottery" mark ............................... **1,540**

*Large Rare Grueby Vase*

**Vase,** 20" h., bulbous ovoid body w/tapering neck, flat rim, decorated w/tooled & applied waterlily blossoms in yellow & red & large curled leaves under a rich thick matte green glaze, impressed circular mark, some color run (ILLUS.) ....... **22,000**

# HALL CHINA

*Founded in 1903 in East Liverpool, Ohio, this still-operating company at first produced mostly utilitarian wares. It was in 1911 that Robert T. Hall, son of the company founder, developed a special single-fire, lead-free glaze which proved to be strong, hard and non-porous. In the 1920s the firm became well known for their extensive line of teapots (still a major product) and in 1932 they introduced kitchenwares followed by dinnerwares in 1936 and refrigerator wares in 1938.*

*The imaginative designs and wide range of glaze colors and decal decorations have led to the growing appeal of Hall wares with collectors, especially people who like Art Deco and Art Moderne design. One of the firm's most famous patterns was the "Autumn Leaf" line, produced as premiums for the Jewel Tea Company. For listings of this ware see "Jewel Tea Autumn Leaf."*

*Helpful books on Hall include, The Collector's Guide to Hall China by Margaret & Kenn Whitmyer, and Superior Quality Hall China - A Guide for Collectors by Harvey Duke (An ELO Book, 1977).*

HALL CHINA

*Hall Marks*

**Ashtray,** triangular, deep, No. 683, turquoise............................................................. $15
**Ashtray w/match holder,** closed sides, No. 618 1/2, cobalt.................................... 20
**Baker,** fluted, French shape, Yellow Rose patt............................................................. 25
**Batter jug,** Sundial shape, Blue Garden patt............................................................. 250
**Bean pot,** cov., New England shape, No. 4, Blue Blossom patt. ................................. 225
**Bean pot,** cov., New England shape, No. 4, Shaggy Tulip patt. ................................. 275
**Bean pot,** cov., New England shape, No. 488 patt. ................................................... 275
**Bean pot,** cov., New England shape, Wild Poppy patt............................................. 205
**Bean pot,** cov., tab-handled, Pert shape, Rose Parade patt. ................................... 125
**Bowl,** 6" d., Radiance shape, No. 4, Crocus patt...................................................... 28
**Bowl,** 6" d., Radiance shape, Yellow Rose patt......................................................... 20
**Bowl,** 7 1/2" d., straight-sided, Rose White patt.......................................................... 18
**Bowl,** 8 1/2" d., Thick Rim shape, Tulip patt........ 25
**Bowl,** 8 3/4" d., Five Band shape, Cactus patt............................................................ 35
**Bowl,** 9" d., salad, Serenade patt....................... 20
**Bowl,** 10" d., Medallion line, lettuce green ......... 30

*Primrose Cake Plate*

**Cake plate,** Primrose patt. (ILLUS.) ................... 20
**Canister,** cov., Radiance shape, Chinese red ............................................................... 175
**Casserole,** cov., Five Band shape, Flamingo patt. ............................................................. 75
**Casserole,** cov., Radiance shape, Blue Bouquet patt...................................................... 55
**Casserole,** cov., Radiance shape, Crocus patt. ................................................................ 80
**Casserole,** cov., Ribbed line, russet ................. 35
**Casserole,** cov., round, No. 76, Wild Poppy patt., 10 1/2" d. ............................................... 75
**Casserole,** cov., Sundial shape, No. 4, Chinese red ............................................................... 65
**Coffeelator,** cov., cobalt blue........................... 125
**Coffeepot,** cov., Drip-O-Later, Duse shape ....... 50
**Coffeepot,** cov., Drip-O-Later, Sash shape, red ................................................................... 70
**Coffeepot,** cov., Drip-O-Lator, Jerry shape (ILLUS. left, top next column)........................ 50
**Coffeepot,** cov., Drip-O-Lator, Waverly shape ............................................................ 35

**Coffeepot,** cov., Drip-O-Lator, Scoop shape w/Wildflower patt. ................................. 40

*Hall Coffeepots*

**Coffeepot,** cov., drip-type, all-china, Jordan shape, Morning Glory patt. .................... 275

*Crocus Pattern Coffeepot*

**Coffeepot,** cov., drip-type, all-china, Kadota shape, Crocus patt. (ILLUS.) ........... 350
**Coffeepot,** cov., drip-type, all-china, Medallion line, lettuce green ........................ 175
**Coffeepot,** cov., drip-type w/basket, Crocus patt. ............................................................ 90
**Coffeepot,** cov., electric percolator, Game Birds patt. ..................................................... 103

*Ansel Shape Tricolator Coffeepot*

**Coffeepot,** cov., Tricolator, Ansel shape, yellow art glaze (ILLUS.) ............................... 75
**Coffeepot,** cov., Tricolator, Coffee Queen, Ritz shape, Chinese red (ILLUS. right w/Jerry Drip-O-Lator) .................................... 135

*Coffee Queen Tricolator Coffeepot*

Coffeepot, cov., Tricolator, Coffee Queen, yellow (ILLUS.) .............................................. 35

Cookie jar, cov., Five Band shape, Chinese red (marks on paint) .............................. 98

*Meadow Flower Cookie Jar*

Cookie jar, cov., Five Band shape, Meadow Flower patt. (ILLUS.) ..................... 260

Cookie jar, cov., Grape design, yellow, gold band .................................................... 60

Cookie jar, cov., Owl, brown glaze ................. 120

Cookie jar, cov., Red Poppy patt. ...................... 50

Cookie jar, cov., Sundial shape, Blue Blossom patt. ...................................................... 350

Cookie jar, cov., Zeisel, gold dot design ............ 85

Creamer, Art Deco style, Crocus patt. .............. 25

Creamer, Medallion shape, Silhouette patt. ....... 18

Creamer, modern, Red Poppy patt. ................... 35

Creamer, individual, Sundial shape, Chinese red, 2 oz. ......................................... 65

Creamer, Sundial shape, Chinese red, 4 oz. ........................................................... 45

Creamer & cov. sugar bowl, Blue Bouquet patt., pr. ...................................... 40

Custard, straight-sided, Rose Parade patt. ........ 32

Custard cup, Medallion line, lettuce green ....... 12

Custard cup, Radiance shape, Serenade patt. .................................................. 20

Custard cup, straight sides, Rose White patt. .................................................. 20

Custard cup, Thick Rim shape, Meadow Flower patt. ................................................ 35

*Radiance Shape Drip Jar*

Drip jar, cov., Radiance shape, Chinese red (ILLUS.) ................................................. 60

Drip jar, cov., Thick Rim shape, Royal Rose patt. ...................................................... 25

Drip jar, open, No. 1188, Mums patt. ................. 35

Gravy boat, Red Poppy patt. ........................... 110

Gravy boat, Springtime patt. ............................. 30

Leftover, cov., loop handle, Blue Blossom patt. ...................................................... 150

Leftover, cov., rectangular, Blue Bouquet patt. ...................................................... 65

Leftover, cov., square, Crocus patt. .................... 85

*Fantasy Leftover*

Leftover, cov., Zephyr shape, Fantasy patt. (ILLUS.) .......................................... 195

Mug, beverage, Silhouette patt. .......................... 60

Mug, flagon shape, Monk patt. ........................... 45

Mug, Tom & Jerry, Red Dot patt. ........................ 15

*Orange Poppy Pie Plate*

Pie plate, Orange Poppy patt. (ILLUS.) ............. 45

Pitcher, ball-shape, No. 3, Chinese Red............ 90

Pitcher, ball-shape, No. 3, Delphinium............... 35

*Hall Ball-type Pitcher*

Pitcher, ball-shape, No. 3, orchid (ILLUS.) ........ 75

Pitcher, cov., jug-type, Radiance shape, No. 488 patt., No. 4 ...................................... 95

Pitcher, jug-type, Doughnut shape, cobalt......... 65

**Pitcher,** jug-type, loop handle, Blue Blossom patt. ........................................ 195
**Pitcher,** jug-type, loop handle, emerald green........................................................ 65
**Pitcher,** jug-type, Medallion line, Silhouette patt., No. 3...................................... 35
**Pitcher,** jug-type, No. 628, maroon ................... 90
**Pitcher,** jug-type, Nora, yellow ........................... 20
**Pitcher,** jug-type, Pert shape, Rose Parade patt. ....................................................... 62
**Pitcher,** jug-type, Streamline shape, Canary...................................................... 55
**Pitcher,** Radiance shape, Wildfire patt., No. 5................................................... 45
**Pitcher,** Rose White patt., large ........................ 35

*Tankard-type Pitcher*

**Pitcher,** tankard-type, black (ILLUS.) ................. 65
**Plate,** salad, 8 1/4" d., No. 488 patt.................... 15
**Plate,** dinner, 9" d., Silhouette patt. .................... 15
**Plate,** dinner, 10" d., Wildfire patt. ..................... 45
**Platter,** 11 1/4" l., oval, Springtime patt. ............. 20
**Platter,** 13 1/4" l., oval, Mums patt. ................... 35
**Pretzel jar,** cov., Pastel Morning Glory patt...... 125
**Punch set:** punch bowl & 10 punch cups; Old Crow, punch bowl reads "May YOU always - have an eagle in your pocket ...a turkey on your table - and Old Crow in your glass," the set ................................. 175
**Salt & pepper shakers,** Five Band shape, Blue Blossom patt., pr. .............................. 90
**Salt & pepper shakers,** Medallion line, lettuce green, pr. ................................................ 55
**Salt & pepper shakers,** Novelty Radiance shape, Orange Poppy patt., pr. ...................... 95
**Salt & pepper shakers,** Radiance shape, canister-style, Chinese red, pr. .................. 120
**Salt & pepper shakers,** Teardrop shape, Blue Bouquet patt., pr. ................................. 35
**Soup tureen,** cov., Crocus patt., clover lid....... 350
**Soup tureen,** Thick Rim shape, Blue Bouquet patt. ....................................................... 300
**Stack set,** Medallion line, lettuce green ............. 95
**Stack set,** Radiance shape, Carrot patt. .......... 125
**Sugar bowl,** cov., Art Deco style, Crocus patt. ...................................................... 35
**Sugar bowl,** cov., Medallion line, Silhouette patt. ...................................................... 25
**Sugar bowl,** cov., Red Poppy patt., modern ...................................................... 40
**Tea tile,** octagonal, art glaze blue & white ......... 45

**Tea tile,** round, Chinese red............................... 50
**Tea tile,** round, cobalt w/gold trim ..................... 50
**Tea tile,** round, Silhouette patt. ......................... 150
**Tea tile,** round, Wild Poppy patt. ...................... 125
**Teapot,** cov., Airflow shape, cobalt blue w/gold trim, 6-cup.......................................... 90
**Teapot,** cov., Airflow shape, yellow w/gold trim, 6-cup ......................................... 95
**Teapot,** cov., Aladdin shape, cobalt blue w/gold trim, 6-cup.......................................... 95
**Teapot,** cov., Aladdin shape, Crocus patt. ....... 925
**Teapot,** cov., Aladdin shape, oval opening, w/infuser, cobalt blue w/gold trim ................ 110
**Teapot,** cov., Aladdin shape, round opening, cadet blue w/gold trim ............................ 65

*Serenade Teapot*

**Teapot,** cov., Aladdin shape, w/infuser, Serenade patt. (ILLUS.) ............................... 350
**Teapot,** cov., Albany shape, emerald green w/"special gold" decoration .......................... 50
**Teapot,** cov., Art Deco style, Adele shape, olive green ................................................... 200
**Teapot,** cov., Art Deco style, Damascus shape, blue............................................... 175
**Teapot,** cov., Art Deco style, Danielle shape, maroon ............................................ 175
**Teapot,** cov., Automobile shape, Chinese red ............................................................ 900
**Teapot,** cov., Baltimore shape, Gold Label line, ivory, ................................................... 80
**Teapot,** cov., Baltimore shape, green w/gold.......................................................... 195
**Teapot,** cov., Basket shape, cadet blue w/platinum decoration ................................. 150
**Teapot,** cov., Basketball shape, cobalt blue..... 750

*Orange Poppy Teapot*

**Teapot,** cov., Bellevue shape, Orange Poppy patt. (ILLUS.)................................. 1,600
**Teapot,** cov., Birdcage shape, yellow, "Gold Special" decoration (ILLUS. top next page) ................................................... 500
**Teapot,** cov., Blue Garden patt., morning set ............................................................ 400

*Birdcage Teapot*

**Teapot,** cov., Boston shape, cobalt blue w/gold Trailing Aster design, 6-cup .............. 150
**Teapot,** cov., Boston shape, Crocus patt. ........ 225
**Teapot,** cov., Boston shape, Golden Fruit patt. band .................................................. 150

*Bowling Ball Teapot*

**Teapot,** cov., Bowling Ball shape, turquoise (ILLUS.)....................................................... 375
**Teapot,** cov., Cleveland shape, turquoise w/gold decoration ............................................. 45
**Teapot,** cov., Football shape, maroon.............. 600
**Teapot,** cov., French shape, maroon w/gold decoration, 6-cup ............................... 45
**Teapot,** cov., French shape, old rose w/gold French Flower decoration, 6-cup ........ 50
**Teapot,** cov., French shape, Royal Rose patt. ................................................................ 100
**Teapot,** cov., Globe shape, No-Drip, Addison grey w/gold decoration, 6-cup ................ 90
**Teapot,** cov., Hollywood shape, Indian red ..... 150
**Teapot,** cov., Illinois shape, maroon w/gold decoration ................................................. 175
**Teapot,** cov., Kansas shape, ivory w/gold decoration ................................................. 300
**Teapot,** cov., Los Angeles shape, emerald green w/gold decoration, 6-cup ................ 85
**Teapot,** cov., Manhattan shape, side handle, cobalt blue, 2-cup ................................... 95
**Teapot,** cov., Manhattan shape, warm yellow, 6-cup .................................................. 85
**Teapot,** cov., Manhattan shape, Wild Poppy patt. .................................................. 220
**Teapot,** cov., McCormick shape, turquoise ........ 50
**Teapot,** cov., Melody shape, Chinese red ........ 305

*Moderne Teapot*

**Teapot,** cov., Moderne shape, marine blue (ILLUS.)....................................................... 85
**Teapot,** cov., musical-type, blue, 6-cup........... 150
**Teapot,** cov., New York shape, Crocus patt. ................................................................ 275
**Teapot,** cov., New York shape, Gold Label line, ivory w/flower decoration, 6-cup ............. 50

*Ohio Teapot*

**Teapot,** cov., Ohio shape, pink, gold dot decoration (ILLUS.) ....................................... 250
**Teapot,** cov., Parade shape, black.................... 65
**Teapot,** cov., Pert shape, Chinese red, 4-cup ................................................................ 60
**Teapot,** cov., Pert shape, Chinese red & white, 2-cup.................................................. 75
**Teapot,** cov., Philadelphia shape, blue w/hearth scene patt. ................................... 75
**Teapot,** cov., Radiance shape, Acacia patt. ..... 225
**Teapot,** cov., Rhythm shape, cobalt blue ......... 110

*Fantasy Teapot*

**Teapot,** cov., Streamline shape, Fantasy patt. (ILLUS.)............................................... 400
**Teapot,** cov., Surfside shape, canary yellow .............................................................. 185

*Tea-for-Two Teapot*

Teapot, cov., Tea-for-Two shape, pink
w/gold decoration (ILLUS.)........................... 200
Teapot, cov., Tea-for-Two shape, Stock
brown w/gold decoration .............................. 100
Teapot, cov., Tea-for-Two shape, Stock
green ............................................................. 125
Teapot, cov., Thorley series, Apple design,
black w/gold decoration.................................. 95
Teapot, cov., Thorley series, Grape shape,
yellow w/gold band......................................... 75
Teapot, cov., Thorley series, Regal shape,
apple green, gold decoration w/rhine-
stones............................................................ 125
Teapot, cov., Thorley series, Royal shape,
ivory ................................................................ 85
Teapot, cov., Thorley series, Starlight
shape, pink w/gold & rhinestone decora-
tion ................................................................ 125
Teapot, cov., Thorley series, Windcrest
shape, lemon yellow w/gold decoration ......... 95
Teapot, cov., Tip-Pot, twinspout, emerald
green .............................................................. 95
Teapot, cov., Victorian series, Benjamin
shape, warm yellow...................................... 100

*Birch Teapot*

Teapot, cov., Victorian series, Birch shape,
blue w/gold decoration (ILLUS.)................... 175
Teapot, cov., Victorian series, Bowknot
shape, pink.................................................... 50
Teapot, cov., Victorian series, Murphy
shape, blue..................................................... 45
Teapot, cov., Windshield shape, Camellia
w/gold decoration ......................................... 40
Teapot, cov., Windshield shape, Carrot
patt. .............................................................. 160
Twin-Tee set: cov. teapot, cov. hot water
pot & matching divided tray; art glaze
green ............................................................ 125

Twin-Tee set: cov. teapot, cov. hot water
pot & matching divided tray; Pansy patt....... 185
Vase, Edgewater, No. 630, cobalt ..................... 25
Vase, bud, Trumpet, No. 631, Chinese red ....... 35
Vase, bud, No. 631 1/2, maroon......................... 15
Vase, bud, No. 641, canary ............................... 10

*Blue Garden Water Bottle*

Water bottle, cov., refrigerator ware line,
Zephyr shape, Blue Garden patt.
(ILLUS.)....................................................... 750
Water bottle, cov., refrigerator ware line,
Zephyr shape, Chinese red.......................... 300
Water server, cov., Montgomery Ward
refrigerator ware, delphinium blue................. 55
Water server, Plaza shape, Chinese red......... 135
Water server w/cork stopper, Hotpoint
refrigerator ware, Dresden blue .................... 75

# HARKER POTTERY

*Harker Pottery was in business for over 100
years (1840-1972) in the East Liverpool area of
eastern Ohio. One of the oldest potteries in Ohio, it
advertised itself as one of the oldest in America.
The pottery produced two lines that are favorites of
collectors: ovenware under the BakeRite and HotO-
ven brands and Cameoware. However, Harker also
produced many other lines as well as Rockingham
reproductions, souvenir items and a line designed
by Russel Wright that are gaining popularity with
collectors. Harker was marketed under dozens of
backstamps in its history.*

*Harker Marks*

## ADVERTISING, NOVELTY & SOUVENIR PIECES

**Ashtrays,** w/advertising, each.................... $10-20

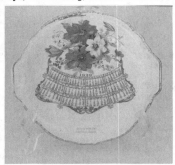

*Harker 1929 Calendar Plate*

**Calendar plates,** 1907 to 1930, later dates of lower value, each (ILLUS. of 1929 plate) ............................................................ 30-50
**Souvenir plates,** 6" d., each ......................... 20-25
**Trivet,** "Townsend Plan"................................ 35-50

## AUTUMN LEAF

*Harker made some Autumn Leaf for Jewel Tea before Hall China received the exclusive contract. The design is larger than that used on later ware and no mark has been found.*

**Cake plate,** Virginia shape ......................... 200-250
**Casserole,** cov. ............................................ 75-100

## BAKERITE, HOTOVEN

*Harker was one of the first American potteries to produce pottery that could go from the oven to the table. Most of this ware, made from the late 1920s to 1970, features brightly colored decals that are popular with collectors today. Prices vary depending upon the decal pattern. Among the most popular designs are Amy, Colonial Lady, Countryside, red and blue Deco Dahlia, Fireplace, Ivy, Lisa, Mallow, Monterey, Oriental Poppy, Petit Point, Red Apple and Tulips.*

**Au gratin/casserole,** cov............................... 25-35
**Batter bowl,** w/pouring lip ............................ 40-50
**Batter jug,** cov., Ohio shape ......................... 30-40
**Batter set,** two batter jugs, lifter & utility plate, the set..................................................... 100-150
**Bean pot,** Calico Tulip patt., w/original wire rack ................................................................... 65

*Various Petit Point Pattern Pieces*

**Bean pot,** individual, Petit Point patt. (ILLUS. top row, center front) ..................... 8-10
**Bowl,** 6" d., Red Apple I patt., Zephyr shape (ILLUS. front row, second from right w/casserole) ...................................... 20
**Bowl,** 9" d., Petit Point Rose patt. ..................... 15
**Butter dish,** cov., Petit Point patt., 1 lb. ............. 40
**Butter tray,** cov. .......................................... 30-50
**Cake/pie lifter** ............................................ 10-20
**Casserole,** cov., Petit Point patt., Zephyr shape (ILLUS. top row, left w/bean pot)......... 35
**Casserole,** cov., Red Apple I patt., Zephyr shape .............................................................. 35
**Casserole,** cov., stacking-type .................... 10-20
**Cheese bowl,** cov. ...................................... 30-40
**Cheese tray,** Zephyr shape ........................ 15-20
**Coffeepot,** cov., Petit Point patt, Zephyr shape, no brewer (ILLUS. top row, right w/bean pot) ..................................................... 50
**Coffeepot,** cov., w/basket ............................ 65-80
**Condiment jar,** cov., individual ..................... 10-15
**Condiment set,** three jars in a holder, the set ................................................................. 50-60
**Cookie jar,** cov., Modern Age shape ............ 25-30
**Cookie jar,** cov., Zephyr shape .................... 40-50
**Cup & saucer,** jumbo size............................. 20-30
**Custard cup,** individual ................................ 8-10
**Custard cup set,** six cups in a rack, the set.. 60-75
**Grease jar,** cov., D'Ware shape.................... 20-25
**Grease jar,** cov., Hi-Rise shape ................... 15-25
**Hot plate,** Petit Point Rose patt........................ 40
**Mixing bowl,** medium.................................. 15-20
**Mixing bowl,** Petit Point patt., large ............ 25-50
**Mixing bowl,** Petit Point patt., medium (ILLUS. middle row, center w/bean pot)......... 20
**Pie baker** .................................................... 15-25
**Pie plate,** Amy patt....................................... 16
**Pie plate,** Petit Point Rose patt. ...................... 15
**Pitcher,** jug-type, Arches patt....................... 20-30
**Pitcher,** jug-type, Hi-Rise shape ................ 50-125
**Pitcher,** jug-type, Regal shape...................... 25-40
**Plate,** dinner, Petit Point patt. ......................... 15
**Plate,** dinner, Red Apple II patt. (ILLUS. back row, center w/casserole)......................... 15
**Rolling pin** ................................................ 75-125
**Rolling pin,** Petit Point patt. (ILLUS. front left w/bean pot)............................................... 125
**Rolling pin,** Silhouette patt. .......................... 115
**Salad fork or spoon,** Petit Point patt., each (ILLUS. front row, right w/bean pot)....... 20
**Salt & pepper shakers,** Hi-Rise shape, pr. .. 15-25
**Scoop** ....................................................... 50-150
**Syrup pitcher,** cov., Ohio shape.................. 15-25
**Tea tile,** octagonal, Petit Point patt. (ILLUS. top row, center back)........................................ 25
**Teapot,** cov., Red Apple II patt., Zephyr shape.. 50
**Teapot,** cov., w/basket .................................. 65-85
**Utility bowl,** Petit Point patt., Zephyr shape, 3" d. (ILLUS. middle row, left)............... 8
**Utility bowl,** Red Apple I patt. .......................... 10
**Utility plate,** Calico Tulip patt., Virginia shape, 12" w. .................................................... 28
**Utility plate,** Virginia shape........................... 10-25

## CAMEOWARE

*Created in the early 1930s and based on a European process, the sky blue ware with its white design that seems to be etched into the surface is Harker's most widely collected pattern. The process was first tried by Bennett Pottery but when*

Bennett closed, the Cameoware line was taken over by Harker. After the blue intaglios met with great success, Harker also made pink, which was much less popular and rare today, and yellow, which never went into full production. Because of its rarity and its bright contrast to the blue engobe, the yellow ware is highly prized and highly priced today. Prices given are for pink or blue. Yellow prices are almost double or more, depending upon the item.

In addition, Harker also manufactured a line of blue and pink intaglio ware for Montgomery Ward with the name "White Rose." Not so common as the design called "Dainty Flower," White Rose has its own devoted fans.

**Ashtray,** Dainty Flower patt., Swirl or
  Zephyr shape, each .................................... 5
**Ashtray,** Modern Age shape, blue Dainty
  Flower patt., (ILLUS. far left) ........................ 20
**Au gratin/casserole,** cov., Zephyr shape ..... 25-45
**Berry/salad set,** serving bowl & six individ-
  ual dishes, the set .................................... 40-50
**Bowl,** cereal, Shellware shape ...................... 8-10
**Bowl,** salad, Pear patt., Swirl shape ................ 20
**Cake/pie lifter** .......................................... 15-20
**Casserole,** cov., square, blue ......................... 65
**Coffeepot or teapot,** cov., each .................. 30-50
**Cookie jar,** cov., blue Dainty Flower patt.,
  Zephyr shape (ILLUS. far right w/ash-
  tray) ......................................................... 50
**Creamer** ................................................. 10-25
**Cup & saucer,** Swirl shape, blue ..................... 16
**Custard cup** ............................................. 8-10
**Demitasse cup & saucer** .......................... 25-30
**Fork or spoon,** each ................................. 15-20

*A Variety of Dainty Flower Pieces*

**Fruit dish,** blue Dainty Flower patt., Vir-
  ginia shape (ILLUS. top, far right) ................... 5
**Gravy boat** .............................................. 30-35
**Grease jar,** cov., D'Ware shape ................... 15-30
**Grease jar,** cov., Hi-Rise shape .................. 10-25
**Mixing bowl** ............................................ 25-45
**Pitcher,** jug-type, Hi-Rise shape ................ 75-150
**Pitcher,** jug-type, round ............................. 30-50
**Pitcher,** jug-type, square ........................... 30-50
**Plate,** 6" d., Swirl shape ............................... 5-8
**Plate,** 6" sq., blue Dainty Flower, Virginia
  shape (ILLUS. top row, far left w/fruit
  dish) ........................................................... 8

**Plate,** 7" d., luncheon, blue Dainty Flower
  patt., Swirl shape (ILLUS. back row, left
  w/ashtray)................................................... 10
**Plate,** 7" sq., Zephyr shape ....................... 12-15
**Plate,** 9" d. ............................................. 12-15
**Platter,** oval, plain .................................... 15-35
**Platter,** rectangular................................... 20-40
**Rolling pin,** blue or pink........................... 100-125
**Salt & pepper shakers,** D'Ware shape, pr. .. 20-25
**Salt & pepper shakers,** Dainty Flower
  patt., Hi-Rise shape, stained, pr. (ILLUS.
  top row, center front w/fruit dish)..................... 6
**Salt & pepper shakers,** Hi-Rise shape,
  perfect, pr. ............................................... 25-30
**Salt & pepper shakers,** Modern Age
  shape, pr. ................................................ 10-20
**Soup plate,** flat rim, square ....................... 10-15
**Sugar bowl,** cov.......................................... 10-25
**Tea tile** .................................................. 20-30
**Utility plate,** blue Dainty Flower patt., Vir-
  ginia shape, 12" w. (ILLUS. back row,
  center w/fruit dish)...................................... 25
**Vegetable bowl,** blue Dainty Flower patt.,
  Virginia shape (ILLUS. bottom w/fruit
  dish) ......................................................... 20

## CHILDREN'S WARE

Harker's Kiddo sets were made in pink and blue with an occasional rare teal. Their etched classic designs of ducks, elephants, kittens and toy soldiers are loved by many collectors. Harker also made hot water feeders.

**Bowl** ....................................................... 25-30
**Hot water feeder,** child's........................... 40-60

*Child's Mug & Plate*

**Mug,** toy soldier decoration, Kiddo set
  (ILLUS. bottom)........................................... 15
**Plate,** Teddy bear w/balloon decoration,
  Kiddo set (ILLUS. top).................................... 30

## LATER INTAGLIOS

Although highly popular during their time and thus so abundant, the later intaglios produced by Harker are not so in demand today. Therefore the prices are about half of those of Dainty Flower.

Often labeled "Cameoware" by dealers, the green, pink-cocoa, yellow and robin's-egg blue ware do not carry the Cameoware backstamp. Popular designs include Brown-Eyed Susan, Cock O'Morn, Ivy Wreath, Petit Fleur, Springtime, Wild Rice and Wild Rose.

| | |
|---|---|
| Creamer & sugar bowl, pr. | 10-15 |
| Cup & saucer | 5-8 |
| Plate, dinner | 5-10 |
| Platter | 10-20 |

## MODERN AGE/MODERN TULIP

Created to resemble and compete with Jewel Tea's Autumn Leaf, Modern Tulips' orange and brown pattern was primarily used on Harker's Modern Age shape, easily identified by its flattened oval, "Life-Saver" finials and the impressed arrow fletchings. Unfortunately, Modern Tulip has yet to be discovered by collectors.

| | |
|---|---|
| Cake plate | 15-20 |
| Cookie jar, cov. | 30 |
| Creamer | 10 |
| Custard cup | 5 |
| Pie baker | 15 |
| Pitcher, cov., square, jug-type | 25 |
| Plate, 6" d. | 5 |
| Sugar bowl | 10-15 |
| Teapot, cov. | 20 |
| Utility bowl, 4" d. | 8 |

## ROCKINGHAM

The dark brown Rockingham glazed pieces were reproduced by Harker in the early 1960s. Because they are often impressed with the date of Harker's founding—"1840"—some confusion among collectors and dealers has arisen. Most items are marked as reproductions, but some are not. Many collectors find the honey-brown and bottle green items more desirable.

| | |
|---|---|
| Ashtray, model of a tobacco leaf | 15-20 |
| Bread tray | 20-35 |
| Mug, figural, Daniel Boone head | 20-30 |
| Mug, figural hound handle | 25-30 |
| Mug, figural Jolly Roger head | 15-25 |

*Hound-handled Pitcher*

Pitcher, jug-type w/figural hound handle (ILLUS.) ............ 50

Plate, relief-molded American Eagle (Great Seal of the U.S.) ............ 10-25

## ROYAL GADROON/CHESTERTON (GREY) OR CORINTHIAN (TEAL)

With its distinctive scalloped edge, the Gadroon line was extremely popular. In the days of bright decals, it was a perfect foil for classic designs like Bridal Rose, Currier & Ives, Cynthia, Forget-me-not, Game Birds, Godey, Ivy, Margaret Rose, Morning Glories, Royal Rose, Violets, White Thistle and Wild Rose.

The classic grey and deep teal of Chesterton and Corinthian, create an elegant backdrop. Still popular today, these two gadroon patterns are frequently marked "Pate sur Pate."

| | |
|---|---|
| Bowl, cereal or soup, lug handles, Vintage patt. | 8 |
| Bowl, cereal/soup, lug handles | 8-10 |
| Cake plate, Wild Rose patt., 10" d. | 15 |
| Cake set: cake plate w/six matching serving plates & cake server; Currier & Ives patt., 8 pcs. | 35 |
| Cake/pie lifter | 10-20 |
| Casserole, cov. | 40-50 |
| Cup & saucer | 10-15 |
| Fork or spoon, each | 15-25 |
| Fruit dish | 3-5 |
| Fruit dish, St. John's Wort patt. | 3 |
| Gravy boat | 15-25 |
| Nappy | 15-20 |
| Party set, cup & plate, 2 pcs. | 10-15 |
| Pickle dish | 8-10 |
| Plate, 6" d., luncheon, Bermuda patt. | 8 |
| Plate, 6" d., Game Birds patt. | 6 |
| Plate, 9" d. | 12-15 |
| Plate, 9" d., dinner, Magnolia patt. | 10 |
| Plate, 9" d., dinner, Violets patt. | 8 |
| Platter | 20-25 |
| Platter, 15" l., oval, Vintage patt. | 20 |
| Rolling pin | 85-125 |
| Salt & pepper shakers, pr. | 10-20 |
| Soup plate, flat | 10-15 |
| Teapot, cov., Ivy Vine patt. | 50 |
| Teapots, cov., each | 30-50 |

## RUSSEL WRIGHT

White Clover intaglio on green, charcoal, coral or gold.

| | |
|---|---|
| Clock, original works | 75-100 |
| Plate | 10-20 |

## STONE CHINA

Made of genuine Stone China clay, this heavy ware with its pink, blue, white and yellow engobe over a grey body was manufactured in the 1950s and 1960s. The engobe (colored clay) was mixed with tiny metallic chips. Later, Harker added hand-decorated designs like Seafare and used its patented intaglio process to create many other designs.

| | |
|---|---|
| Bowl, cereal/soup | 5-8 |
| Bowl, fruit | 2-3 |
| Butter tray, cov. | 10-15 |
| Casserole, cov. | 25-30 |
| Coffeepot, cov. | 15-25 |
| Cookie jar, cov. | 20-30 |

Creamer & sugar bowl, pr. .......................... 15-20
Cruet set ................................................. 30-45
Cup & saucer ............................................ 5-10
Nappy ..................................................... 10-15
Nappy, divided ........................................... 8-12
Pitcher, jug-type ....................................... 15-20
Plate, 9" d. ................................................. 5-10
Platter .................................................... 15-20
Rolling pin ............................................. 100-150
Salt & pepper shakers, D'Ware shape, pr. .. 10-15
Teapot, cov. ............................................ 15-25
Tidbit tray ............................................... 15-25

# HARLEQUIN

*The Homer Laughlin China Company, makers of the popular "Fiesta" pottery line, also introduced in 1938 a less expensive and thinner ware which was sold under the "Harlequin" name. It did not carry the maker's trade-mark and was marketed exclusively through F. W. Woolworth Company. It was produced in a wide range of dinnerwares in assorted colors until 1964. Out of production for a number of years, in 1979 Woolworth requested the line be reintroduced using an ironstone body and with a limited range of pieces and colors offered. Collectors also seek out a series of miniature animal figures produced in the Harlequin line in the 1930s and 1940s.*

Ashtray, regular, maroon ........................... $68-76
Ashtray, regular, mauve blue ..................... 48-54
Ashtray, regular, red ................................ 63-71
Ashtray, regular, spruce green ................... 60-69
Ashtray, regular, yellow ............................ 38-46
Bowl, 36s, cereal, 6 1/2" d., maroon ......... 84-120
Bowl, 36s, cereal, 6 1/2" d., mauve blue .......... 22
Bowl, 36s, cereal, 6 1/2" d., red ................. 18-20
Bowl, 36s, oatmeal, 6 1/2" d., spruce green .. 73-99
Bowl, 36s, oatmeal, 6 1/2" d., yellow ........... 16-18
Bowl, individual salad, 7" d., mauve blue .......... 33
Bowl, individual salad, 7" d., red ................. 40-45
Bowl, individual salad, 7" d., spruce green ... 33-40
Bowl, individual salad, 7" d., yellow ............. 29-32
Candleholders, maroon, pr. .................... 365-390
Candleholders, mauve blue, pr. .............. 315-360
Candleholders, red, pr. ......................... 300-310
Candleholders, spruce green, pr............. 335-370
Candleholders, yellow, pr. ..................... 265-285
Cream soup, handled, maroon ................... 36-39
Cream soup, handled, mauve blue .................. 31
Cream soup, handled, red ........................ 33-35
Cream soup, handled, spruce green .......... 34-36
Cream soup, handled, yellow ..................... 23-26
Creamer, individual size, maroon.................... 35
Creamer, individual size, mauve blue ............... 29
Creamer, individual size, red........................ 28
Creamer, individual size, spruce green ......... 24-28
Creamer, individual size, yellow..................... 25
Creamer, maroon...................................... 25
Creamer, mauve blue................................. 21
Creamer, novelty, ball-shaped, maroon ........ 49-53
Creamer, novelty, ball-shaped, mauve blue.. 39-42
Creamer, novelty, ball-shaped, red ............. 38-41
Creamer, novelty, ball-shaped, spruce green ........................................... 46-54
Creamer, novelty, ball-shaped, yellow ......... 29-31
Creamer, red........................................... 23
Creamer, spruce green ............................... 27
Creamer, yellow ...................................... 13

Cup & saucer, maroon .................................. 20
Cup & saucer, mauve blue ......................... 13-17
Cup & saucer, red ................................... 16-18
Cup & saucer, spruce green........................ 17-19
Cup & saucer, yellow................................. 14-16
Egg cup, maroon........................................ 38
Egg cup, mauve blue ............................... 32-35
Egg cup, red .......................................... 34-36
Egg cup, spruce green ............................. 33-37
Egg cup, yellow...................................... 27-29
Gravy boat, maroon................................. 41-44
Gravy boat, mauve blue ........................... 30-33
Gravy boat, red ..................................... 30-32
Gravy boat, spruce green .......................... 41-44
Gravy boat, yellow ................................. 23-25
Marmalade jar, cov., maroon................... 335-355
Marmalade jar, cov., mauve blue ............ 265-300
Marmalade jar, cov., red.......................... 285-300
Marmalade jar, cov., spruce green .......... 325-380
Marmalade jar, cov., yellow .................... 210-230
Nappy, maroon....................................... 44-49
Nappy, mauve blue ................................. 34-37
Nappy, red............................................ 33-37
Nappy, spruce green ................................ 47-51
Nappy, yellow........................................... 31
Nut dish, individual size, basketweave interior, maroon .................................... 21-23
Nut dish, individual size, basketweave interior, mauve blue............................... 18-20
Nut dish, individual size, basketweave interior, red ........................................ 19-21
Nut dish, individual size, basketweave interior, spruce green ................................ 23
Nut dish, individual size, basketweave interior, yellow ......................................... 17
Pitcher, 9" h., ball-shaped w/ice lip, maroon ............................................ 110-115
Pitcher, 9" h., ball-shaped w/ice lip, mauve blue ............................................ 75-85
Pitcher, 9" h., ball-shaped w/ice lip, red........ 85-90
Pitcher, 9" h., ball-shaped w/ice lip, spruce green ............................................ 91-98
Pitcher, 9" h., ball-shaped w/ice lip, yellow ... 65-70
Plate, 6" d., maroon...................................... 7
Plate, 6" d., mauve blue ................................. 7
Plate, 6" d., red .......................................... 7
Plate, 6" d., spruce green ............................... 7
Plate, 6" d., yellow ....................................... 5
Plate, 7" d., maroon..................................... 12
Plate, 7" d., mauve blue ................................ 10
Plate, 7" d., red .......................................... 10
Plate, 7" d., spruce green .............................. 11
Plate, 7" d., yellow ....................................... 8
Plate, 9" d., maroon................................. 16-18
Plate, 9" d., mauve blue ................................ 14
Plate, 9" d., red .......................................... 15
Plate, 9" d., spruce green .............................. 16
Plate, 9" d., yellow ...................................... 11
Plate, 10 "d., maroon............................... 42-44
Plate, 10 "d., mauve blue .............................. 30
Plate, 10 "d., red...................................... 38-40
Plate, 10 "d., spruce green ........................ 40-43
Plate, 10 "d., yellow................................. 25-28
Platter, 11" l., oval, maroon........................ 30-33
Platter, 11" l., oval, mauve blue ................... 24-26
Platter, 11" l., oval, red.............................. 26-28
Platter, 11" l., oval, spruce green ................. 28-31
Platter, 11" l., oval, yellow.......................... 20-22
Platter, 13" l., oval, maroon......................... 37-41

Platter, 13" l., oval, mauve blue ................... 31-35
Platter, 13" l., oval, red................................. 38-41
Platter, 13" l., oval, spruce green ................. 37-41
Platter, 13" l., oval, yellow............................ 26-29
Salt & pepper shakers, maroon, pr............. 28-31
Salt & pepper shakers, mauve blue, pr. ..... 24-28
Salt & pepper shakers, red, pr................... 31-33
Salt & pepper shakers, spruce green, pr. .... 33-36
Salt & pepper shakers, yellow, pr.............. 17-19
Soup plate w/flanged rim, maroon ............. 33-37
Soup plate w/flanged rim, mauve blue........ 26-28
Soup plate w/flanged rim, red .................... 30-32
Soup plate w/flanged rim, spruce green ..... 28-32
Soup plate w/flanged rim, yellow ............... 18-20
Sugar bowl, cov., maroon............................ 36-39
Sugar bowl, cov., mauve blue .................... 25-27
Sugar bowl, cov., red.................................. 31-35
Sugar bowl, cov., spruce green................... 41-44
Sugar bowl, cov., yellow.............................. 16-18

## ANIMALS

Model of a cat, mauve blue ............................ 292
Model of a cat, spruce green.......................... 225
Model of a cat, yellow..................................... 223
Model of a donkey, maroon ............................ 298
Model of a donkey, mauve blue...................... 350
Model of a donkey, spruce green ................... 250
Model of a duck, maroon .......................... 225-250
Model of a duck, mauve blue .................... 245-265
Model of a duck, spruce green................. 225-250
Model of a duck, yellow............................ 200-225
Model of a fish, maroon .................................. 350
Model of a fish, spruce green.......................... 273
Model of a penguin, maroon........................... 237
Model of a penguin, yellow ............................. 263

## HAVILAND

*Haviland porcelain was originated by Americans in Limoges, France, shortly before the mid-19th century and continues in production. Some Haviland was made by Theodore Haviland in the United States during the last World War. Numerous other factories also made china in Limoges. Also see LIMOGES.*

H&C°     ʰᵃᵛⁱˡᵃⁿᵈ ₛ꜀ₒ Limogea.

*Haviland Marks*

Basket, mixed floral decoration w/blue trim,
    Blank No. 1130, 5 x 7 1/2".......................... $154
Bone dishes, No. 146 patt., Blank No. 133,
    set of 4 ........................................................ 66
Bouillon cups & saucers, No. 72 patt.,
    Blank No. 22, ten sets ................................ 226
Bowl, 8 3/8 x 10 3/8", 3 1/2" h., Christmas
    Rose patt., Blank No. 418 ......................... 1,100
Butter dish, cov., No. 133 patt...................... 110
Butter dish, cov., No. 271A patt., Blank
    No. 213........................................................ 187
Cake plate, handled, 87C patt., Blank No.
    2, 10 1/2" d. ................................................ 61
Cake plate, handled, No. 72 patt., Blank
    No. 22.......................................................... 105
Cake plate, handled, Ranson blank No. 1 ....... 132

Candlesticks, Marseille blank, h.p. floral
    decoration, 6 3/4" h., pr........................... 193
Celery tray, Baltimore rose patt., Blank No.
    207, 5 5/8 x 12"......................................... 110
Celery tray, Blank No. 305, titled "Her Maj-
    esty," 13" l. ............................................... 66
Chocolate set: cov. pot & eight cups &
    saucers; decorated w/pink & blue flow-
    ers w/green stems, Blank No. 1, the set ...... 468

*Haviland Chocolate Set*

Chocolate set: individual cov. 5" h. choco-
    late pot, creamer & sugar bowl; No.
    237C patt., Blank No. 9, the set (ILLUS.)..... 468
Coffee set: cov. coffeepot, creamer, sugar
    bowl & twelve cups & saucers; Ranson
    blank No. 1, the set ..................................... 523
Coffeepot, cov., demitasse, Osier, Blank
    No. 211, impressed "Haviland & Co. -
    Limoges - France" & English mark.............. 187
Comport, divided, shell-shaped, white
    w/green trim, full-bodied red lobster at
    center, non-factory decor of red, green &
    black........................................................... 550
Compote, Meadow Visitors patt., smooth
    blank, 5 1/8" h., 9 7/8" d. ........................... 165
Cracker jar, cov., floral decoration, cobalt,
    gold & blue bells, 1900 & decorator's
    marks ......................................................... 330
Cracker jar, cov., Marseille blank (small
    repair on base rim & inner rim of cover)....... 110
Creamer, Moss Rose patt., gold trim,
    5 1/2" h....................................................... 50
Creamer & sugar bowl, Mont Mery
    patt., ca. 1953 ............................................ 94
Cup & saucer, breakfast, Moss Rose patt.
    w/gold trim.................................................. 33
Cup & saucer, demitasse, Papillon Butter-
    fly patt., floral by Pallandre ......................... 121
Cups & saucers, Papillon butterfly handles
    w/Meadow Visitors decoration, six sets ... 1,320
Cuspidor, smooth blank, bands of roses
    decorating rim & body, 6 1/2" h. .................. 193
Cuspidor, Moss Rose patt, smooth blank,
    8" d., 3 1/4" h.............................................. 248
Dessert set: 8 1/2 x 15" tray & four 7 1/4"
    dishes; Osier Blank No. 637, fruit & floral
    decoration, the set...................................... 110
Dessert set: 9 x 15" oblong tray w/twelve
    7" square matching plates; centers dec-
    orated w/Meadow Visitors patt. & bor-
    dered in rich cobalt blue w/gold trim,
    commissioned for Mrs. Wm. A. Wilson,
    13 pcs........................................................ 3,520
Dessert set: large cov. coffeepot, creamer,
    sugar bowl, eight cups & saucers, cake
    plate & eight dessert plates; cable
    shape, Moss Rose decoration w/blue
    trim, the set ................................................ 248

*Haviland Scenic Dish*

**Dish,** shell-shaped, incurved rim opposite pointed rim, h.p. scene of artist's water side studio, decorated by Theodore Davis, front initialed "D," back w/presidential seal & artist's signature, part of Hayes presidential service, 8 x 9 1/2" (ILLUS.) ....................................................... **1,925**

**Dresser tray,** h.p. floral decoration, 1892 mark ............................................................. **55**

**Egg cup,** footed, No. 69 patt. on blank No. 1 ........................................................................ **72**

**Egg cups,** footed, No. 72 patt., Blank No. 22, pr. .................................................................. **165**

**Fish set:** 23" l. platter & six 9" d. plates; each w/different fish scene, dark orange & gold borders, Blank No. 1009, 7 pcs. ......... **495**

**Fish set:** 22" l. oval platter & twelve 8 1/2" d. plates; each piece w/a different fish in the center, the border in two shades of green design w/gold trim, h.p. scenes by L. Martin, mark of Theodore Haviland, 13 pcs. ..................................... **2,750**

**Fish set:** 23 1/4" l. platter & twelve 7 3/8" plates; Empress Eugenie patt., No. 453, Blank No. 7, 13 pcs. ................................... **413**

**Gravy boat w/attached underplate,** No. 98 patt., Blank No. 22 .................................... **77**

**Gravy boat w/attached underplate,** No. 98 patt., Blank No. 24 .................................. **116**

**Hair receiver,** cov., squatty round body on three gold feet, h.p. overall w/small flowers in blues & greens w/gold trim, mark of Charles Field Haviland ........................... **150**

**Ice cream set:** tray & 6 individual plates, Old Pansy patt. on Torse blank, 7 pcs. ........ **303**

**Jam jar w/underplate,** cov., No. 577 patt., smooth blank ................................................ **193**

**Match box,** gold trim, 1882 & decorator's marks ......................................................... **99**

**Mayonnaise bowl w/underplate,** cov., leaf-shaped, Blank No. 271A ...................... **166**

**Moustache cup & saucer,** No. 270A patt., Blank No. 16 .............................................. **88**

**Muffin server,** No. 31 patt., Blank No. 24 ........ **187**

**Mustard pot,** cov., No. 266 patt. on Blank No. 9 .......................................................... **220**

**Nut dish,** footed, No. 1070A patt. ...................... **55**

**Olive dish,** No. 257 patt. .................................... **99**

**Oyster plates,** four-well, all white w/relief-molded scrolled design, 7 1/2" d., pr. ........... **132**

**Oyster plates,** five-well, 72C patt., Blank No. 24??, center indent for sauce, 9" d., pr. ............................................................... **241**

**Oyster tureen,** Henri II Blank, decorated by Dammouse ............................................. **1,050**

**Pancake server,** decorated w/yellow flowers w/pale green stems, smooth blank, 1892 & decorator marks ........................... **154**

**Pickle dish,** shell-shaped w/gold trim, leaf mold, 8 3/4" l. .......................................... **110**

**Pitcher,** 8 5/8" h., Ranson blank No. 1 ............ **318**

**Pitcher,** 7" h., milk-type, tankard style w/tapering cylindrical white body w/a large relief-molded anchor under the heavy ropetwist loop handle, bright gold trim, old Haviland & Co. mark ................... **175**

**Pitcher,** 8 3/8" h., Ivy patt. w/gold trim ............ **121**

**Pitcher,** 9" h., tankard-shaped lemonade-type, Ranson blank, delicate floral band around the upper body trimmed in gold, gold handle & trim bands, factory-decorated, Haviland & Co. mark ........................ **225**

**Pitcher,** 9 1/2" h., No. 279 patt., Blank No. 643 ............................................................ **210**

**Plate,** dinner, No. 9 patt., set of 10 .................. **220**

**Plate,** 6 1/2" d., bread & butter, Paisley patt., smooth blanks w/gold edge, brownish red ground w/flowers in yellow, bright blue, green & white border design w/yellow flowers & bright blue leaves, turquoise scroll trim, Haviland & Co. mark ............................................................... **26**

**Plate,** coupe salad, 7 1/2" d., Baltimore Rose patt, Blank No. 207, set of 8 .............. **220**

**Plate,** 8 1/2" d., cobalt & gold Pallandre patt. ........................................................... **110**

**Plate,** 7 1/2 x 8 1/2", heart-shaped, Baltimore Rose patt. ........................................ **275**

**Plate,** 9 3/4" d., portrait of lady in forest scene, artist-signed, Blank No. 116 ............ **193**

**Plate,** chop, 11 1/4" d., 33A patt., Blank No. 19 ........................................................... **61**

**Plates,** luncheon, 8 3/8" d., Club Ware, Meadow Visitors patt. & various fruits, set of 8 ....................................................... **242**

**Plates,** dinner, No. 271A, Blank No. 213, set of 8 ....................................................... **187**

**Plates,** salad, Meadow Visitors patt., smooth blank, set of 10 ............................... **165**

**Platter,** 12 1/4 x 18" oval, Moss Rose patt. w/blue trim, smooth blank ........................... **66**

**Platter,** 14 x 20", Ranson blank No. 1 .............. **413**

**Punch bowl,** Baltimore Rose patt. ................. **1,210**

**Punch bowl,** tapering scalloped pedestal foot supporting wide shallow cup bowl, decorated w/flowers in shades of green w/some pink flowers & green leaves, variation of Schleiger No. 249B on Blank 17, Haviland & Co. mark, 4" h. ................ **75**

**Ramekins & underplates,** Ranson Blank No. 1, set of 12 .......................................... **413**

**Sauce dishes,** Meadow Visitors patt., smooth blank, 4 3/4" d., set of 8 ................. **176**

**Sauce tureen w/attached underplate,** No. 146 patt., Blank No. 133, 7" d. underplate, bowl 5 1/4" d. ................................... **110**

**Sauceboat & undertray,** footed double-spouted boat-shaped sauceboat w/looped side handles w/molded rope trim, matching dished undertray, heavy gold trim on white, old Haviland & Co. mark, 2 pcs. (ILLUS. below) ........................ 150

*Double-spouted Sauceboat & Tray*

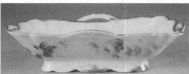

*Haviland Serving Dish with Poppies*

**Serving dish,** scalloped rectangular form w/a scalloped footring below the flaring side w/low open side handles, decorated w/pale yellowish green to dark green poppies & pale pink shadows, gold trim, variation of Schleiger No. 665, Haviland & Co. mark, 8 x 10" (ILLUS.) ........................ 175

**Soup bowls,** No. 271A patt., Blank No. 213, set of 8 ................................. 209

**Soup tureen,** cov., pink Drop Rose patt., on Blank No. 22 ........................................ 385

**Sugar bowl,** cov., large cylindrical form w/small loop side handles & inset flat cover w/arched handle, white ground decorated w/sprays of pink daisies touched w/yellow & greyish brown leaves, variation of Schleiger No. 1311, 1 lb. size, Charles Field Haviland, marked "CFH/GDM" ........................................ 75

**Tea set:** cov. teapot, creamer & sugar bowl, floral & leaf mold w/gold trim, 3 pcs. ............................................................ 204

**Tea set:** small cov. teapot, creamer & sugar bowl, six cups & saucers, No. 19 patt., 15 pcs. ............................................. 1,320

**Tea set:** cov. teapot & ten large cups & saucers; No. 19 patt., 21 pcs. ................... 1,045

**Tea set:** large cov. teapot, creamer, sugar bowl & twelve cups & saucers, No. 956 patt., Blank No. 19, 27 pcs. ........................ 325

**Tea & toast tray & cup,** No. 482 patt., Blank No. 208, pr. ..................................... 105

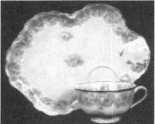

*Haviland Tea & Toast Set*

**Tea & toast tray & cup,** Pink Drop Rose patt., gold border w/wreath, the set (ILLUS.) ............................................................ 165

*Butterfly-handled Cup and Saucer*

**Teacup & saucer,** cup w/tapering cylindrical bowl & figural butterfly handle, h.p. grey band design on rim & border, Haviland & Co. (ILLUS.) ..................................... 125

**Teapot,** Henri II Blank w/gold & silver decoration (inner rim restored) ........................... 138

**Toothbrush box,** cov., Moss Rose patt. w/gold trim, smooth blank, ca. 1860s-70s, 8" l. ..................................................... 110

**Vegetable dish,** cov., Marseille patt., Blank No. 9, 9 1/2" l. ....................................... 72

**Vegetable dish,** cov., decorated w/small orange roses, Blank No. 24, 10" d. ............... 61

**Wash pitcher,** Moss Rose patt. w/gold trim, smooth blank, 12" h. ............................. 303

# HEAD VASE PLANTERS

Head Vase Planters were most popular and most abundant during the 1950s. Whereas some could be found prior to this period, the majority were Japanese imports and a direct product of Japan's post war industrial boom. Coming in all sizes, shapes, styles and quality, these factors varied according to importer. American manufacturers did produce some head vase planters during this time, but high quality standards and production costs made it hard to compete with the less expensive imports.

**Ardalt,** No. 6039, Madonna w/both hands holding roses, pastel coloring in glossy bisque, planter, paper label, 6" h. ................... $22

**Ardco,** No. C1248, high bouffant hair, dark green dress, earrings, necklace, paper label, 5 1/2" h. .......................................... 33

**Brinn,** No. TP2071, molded blonde hair, painted eyes, earrings, right hand near face, 6" h. ........................................... 77

**Inarco,** King w/full grey beard, red, yellow & black w/gold trim, 4 3/4" h. (small base flake) ...................................................... 72

**Inarco,** No. E1062, 1963, head turned to the right, gold clasps on black gown, earrings, necklace, closed eyes w/big lashes, paper label & stamp, 5 1/4" h. ............ 44

**Inarco,** No. E1062, 1963, ringlet hair, earrings, closed eyes w/big lashes, black gloved right hand holding gilt decorated fan under right cheek, paper label & stamp, 6" h. ................................................. 105

**Inarco,** No. E1611, 1964, closed eyes w/big lashes, earrings, gold painted bracelet, left hand under face on right, 5 1/2" h. ...................................................... **275**

**Inarco,** No. E1756, "Lady Aileen," gold & green tiara & matching painted necklace, paper label, 5 1/2" h. ............................ **176**

*Inarco Jackie Kennedy*

**Inarco,** No. E1852, Jackie Kennedy wearing black dress & glove w/hand to cheek, paper label, 6" h. (ILLUS.). ............................ **253**

**Inarco,** No. E193/M, 1961, applied pink rose in hair, light green dress, earrings, necklace, right hand on cheek, closed eyes w/big lashes, 5 1/2" h. ............................ **39**

**Inarco,** No. E2254, black dress, pearl finish on hair, earrings, necklace, closed eyes w/big lashes, paper label, 6" h. ...................... **55**

**Inarco,** No. E2322, black dress, black open-edged hat w/white ribbon, gloved hand by right cheek, earrings, necklace, paper label, 7 1/4" h. .................................... **116**

**Inarco,** No. E2523, child w/blue scarf & dress, pigtails, painted eyes, high gloss, stamped, 5 1/2" h. ......................................... **61**

*Inarco Soldier Boy*

**Inarco,** No. E2735, soldier boy w/bayonet, closed eyes, stamped, 5 3/4" h. (ILLUS.). ....... **55**

**Inarco,** No. E5624, pink hat & blue dress, earrings, painted eyes, paper label & stamp, 5 1/2" h. ............................................. **83**

**Inarco,** No. E779, 1962, applied blonde hair & peach rose, peach dress, earrings, necklace, right hand by cheek, paper label & stamp, 6" h. .............................. **44**

**Inarco,** No. E969/6, 1963, mint green hat & dress, painted closed eyes w/big lashes, 4 1/2" h. ....................................................... **25**

**Japan,** No. 2261, black dress w/white collar, black bow in blonde hair, painted eyes, earrings, glazed finish, 7" h. .............. **132**

**Lefton,** No. 1086, white iridescent blouse, necklace, paper label, 6" h. .......................... **44**

**Lefton,** No. 1343A, applied flowers on large brimmed hat & collar, painted features, raised right hand, paper label, glossy finish, 6" h. .......................................... **61**

**Lefton,** No. 2536, flower in hair, earrings & necklace, gloved right hand under chin, 5 1/4" h. ................................... **72**

**Lefton,** No. 2796, blue blouse, blue sash on head, paper label, 6" h. ............................ **61**

**Lefton,** No. 2796, pink blouse, pink sash on head, paper label, 6" h. ............................ **61**

**Lefton,** No. 4596, green hat, scarf & coat, earrings, painted eyes, black gloved hand under cheek, partial Lefton's label, 5 1/2" h. ........................................................ **110**

**Lefton,** No. 611B, Lefton paper label & Geo. Z. Lefton stamp, bird on pink floral hat, high collar, closed painted eyes, glossy finish, 6 1/4" h. ................................... **50**

**Manchu,** Ceramic Arts Studio of Madison, WI, 7 1/2" h. .................................................... **132**

**Napco,** No. A5120, large pink hat, fur trimmed pink dress w/blue daisy, closed eyes w/big lashes, paper label, 5" h. .............. **31**

**Napco,** No. A5120, orange bonnet w/bow & matching lace-trimmed dress, paper label, 5 1/4" h. ................................................ **28**

**Napco,** No. C1775A, 1956, green striped hat w/bow on top right, jeweled green dress, hand by check, big lashes, stamped, 7 1/4" h. ................................... **77**

**Napco,** No. C2589A, 1956, wearing black dress & feather hat, gold painted earring, closed eyes w/big lashes, right hand under right side of chin, bracelet, paper label & stamp, 5" h. ...................................... **50**

*Napco No. C2632C*

**Napco,** No. C2632C, large lavender hat w/dark trim, matching lavender dress, hand to hat, earring in exposed ear, 7" h. (ILLUS.) ........................................ **176**

*Napco No. C2633C*

**Napco,** No. C2633C, 1956, black hat & dress, gold dots on white hat bow, earrings, necklace, closed eyes w/big lashes, 5 1/2" h. (ILLUS.) .............................. **45**

*Napco No. C2636B*

**Napco,** No. C2636B, 1956, flat white hat w/gold trim, dark green dress, left hand under chin, earrings, necklace, closed eyes w/big lashes, paper label, 6" h. (ILLUS.) ........................................ **55**

**Napco,** No. C2637C, 1956, white round flat hat, black dress, hand under left cheek, painted eyes, earrings, necklace, paper label & stamp, 7" h. ........................................ **77**

**Napco,** No. C264B, baby w/white bonnet, paper label, 5 1/2" h. ...................................... **55**

**Napco,** No. C2683C, 1956, earrings, painted eyes, molded necklace, stamped, 6" h. .............................................. **330**

**Napco,** No. C3205B, wearing crown of gold & white flowers, necklace, paper label, 5 1/2" h. ........................................... **66**

**Napco,** No. C3815, 1959, gold & white trim on blue hat, blue high collar jacket, earrings, closed eyes w/big lashes, paper label, 5 1/2" h. ................................................ **44**

**Napco,** No. C3959A, blue hat w/bow & high collar blouse, real lashes, earrings, paper label, 5 1/2" h. ...................................... **55**

**Napco,** No. C4556C, 1960, child wearing green hat, painted eyes, glossy finish, partial paper label, impressed, 5 1/4" h. .......... **50**

**Napco,** No. C4818C, 1960, black hat w/white & red polka dots, black dress w/white collar, closed eyes w/big lashes, earrings, necklace, 7" h. ................................ **50**

**Napco,** No. C4899C, wearing light purple top & turban hat w/flower, necklace & earrings, paper label, 5 3/4" h. (paint scratches) ......................................... **94**

**Napco,** No. C5675, 1962, white dress w/bow on front, closed eyes w/big lashes, necklace, 6 1/2" h. ............................ **50**

**Napco,** No. C5676, 1962, white dress w/gold dots, flower band on head, painted closed eyes, necklace, 6 1/2" h. ........ **55**

*Napco No. CX2707*

**Napco,** No. CX2707, 1957, Christmas girl, green w/red trimmed hat & dress, painted eyes, right hand under cheek, paper label & stamp, 5 1/2" h. (ILLUS.).......... **77**

*Napco No. CX2708*

**Napco,** No. CX2708, 1957, Christmas girl, holly sprigs in hat, painted cross necklace, gloved right hand away from face, closed eyes w/big lashes, paper label & stamp, 6" h. (ILLUS.).................................... **176**

**Napco,** No. CX2709A, 1957, Christmas child in fur trimmed hat & coat, holding song book, painted eyes, paper label & stamp, 3 1/2" h. (worn paint on back near base) ................................................... **77**

**Napcoware,** No. 8494, gold bow in long hair, gold dress w/white collar, left earring, painted eyes, 7 1/4" h. ........................ **110**

**Napcoware,** No. C6428, three flowers on neck of blue gown, dark gloved hand on left cheek, earrings, closed eyes w/big lashes, stamped mark, 5 1/2" h...................... **39**

*Napcoware No. C6429*

**Napcoware,** No. C6429, molded bouffant hair, white floral collar on blue gown, closed eyes w/big lashes, earrings, dark blue glove, hand by cheek, 7" h. (ILLUS.)....................................................... **110**

**Napcoware,** No. C6985, green dress w/center jewel, closed eyes w/big lashes, earrings, necklace, 8 1/2" h. ............ **165**

**Napcoware,** No. C7472, dark blue blouse, necklace & earrings, paper label, 6" h............ **39**

**Napcoware,** No. C7473, head turned to right, applied floral decoration on right shoulder, earrings, necklace, painted eyes, 7 3/4" h. ................................................. **55**

*Napcoware No. C7474*

**Napcoware,** No. C7474, dark dress w/leaf & pearl decoration on right shoulder, head tilted to right, blonde, open eyes w/slanted lashes, earrings, necklace, paper label, 8 1/2" (ILLUS.)........................... **121**

**Napcoware,** No. C7494, green hat w/large light green bow & matching green collar, earrings, necklace, paper label, 5 3/4" h. (rough hat)..................................................... **33**

**Napcoware,** No. C8493, long hair off to right side, gold bow & dress w/white collar, earring in left ear, painted eyes, 6" h. (ILLUS. top next column) ............................... **88**

**Relpo,** No. 2004, green dress & hair bow, painted eyes, earrings, paper label & stamp, 7" h. ................................................. **165**

*Napcoware No. C8493*

**Relpo,** No. 2089, Marilyn, grey bow in hair on right, black halter dress, earrings, painted eyes, open lips, paper label & stamp, 7" h. (chip on top of bow, minor paint wear on chin & left cheek) ............... **1,100**

**Relpo,** No. 5634, 1965, Christmas girl, hood w/holly, fur trimmed coat, painted eyes, gloved hand near face, Sampson Import Co., impressed, 7 1/2" h.................... **165**

**Relpo,** No. C1811, Nun wearing grey & light blue habit, painted features, stamped, 5 1/2" h. .......................................... **50**

**Relpo,** No. K1053, gold & white flowers on brown hat, gold & white bow & collar, earrings, necklace, painted eyes, paper label & stamp, 6" h. ..................................... **50**

**Relpo,** No. K1054, red hooded coat, closed eyes w/big lashes, right hand away from face, stamped, 5 1/2" h. ................................. **77**

**Relpo,** No. K1175M, wearing hat & matching dress, w/hands folded under chin, open eyes, earrings, necklace, 5 1/2" h. ........ **77**

**Relpo,** No. K1633, Japan, black dress w/white decoration, gloved right hand touching chin & cheek, earring, necklace, painted eyes, 7" h. ............................... **88**

*Relpo No. K1662*

**Relpo,** No. K1662, floral molded green & lavender hat & green dress, painted eyes, earrings, necklace, paper label & stamp, 6" h. (ILLUS.)................................... **105**

**Relpo,** No. K1696, wearing green bow in hair & matching top, earrings, necklace, paper label, 5 1/2" h. ..................................... **55**

**Relpo,** No. K1836, Japan, white hat w/blue edge & bow, blue dress w/white trim, painted eyes, right earring, 6 1/2" h. ........... **467**

**Relpo,** No. K1932, black bows in hair & black high collar dress, earrings, painted eyes, paper label & stamp, 5 1/2" h. ........... **187**

**Ruben,** multicolored clown in green & yellow, closed eyes, 5" h................................... **17**

**Ruben,** No. 4123, white ruffled black dress, earrings, necklace, painted eyes, impression & paper label, 7" h. ...................... **88**

**Ruben,** No. 4129, blonde ponytails, painted eyes, earrings, necklace, paper label, 5 1/2" h. ...................................................... **77**

**Ruben,** No. 4185, braided blonde hair w/flower, green dress w/high white collar, impressed mark, 5 1/2" h. ...................... **110**

**Ruben,** No. 484, heart-shaped grey hat, necklace, earrings, paper label, 5 3/4" h. ...... **132**

**Ruben,** No. 487M, 1963, black hat, painted brooch w/pink center, hand by right cheek, painted eyes, necklace, paper label & stamp, 6 1/4" h. ................................. **55**

**Rubens,** No. 4125, yellow dress w/high collar, unbraided ponytails, closed eyes w/big lashes, paper label, 4" h. ...................... **39**

**Rubens,** No. 4155, blue bow on orange cap & dress, violet flowers in hair, earrings, painted eyes, impressed marking, 5 1/2" h. ...................................................... **132**

*Rubens "Lucy"*

**Rubens,** No. 531, Japan, Lucy in top hat w/horse neck piece, shades of grey, stamped & painted lashes, flake in tie end, 7 1/2" h. (ILLUS.)................................. **275**

**Rubens,** No. 531, Japan, Lucy in top hat w/horse neck piece, yellow & green w/glazed finish, stamped & painted lashes, 7 1/2" h............................................. **253**

*No. S569B*

**S569B,** wearing black pierced hat w/white bow & black gown w/white polka dots, right hand on cheek, closed eyes w/big lashes, stamped, 5 1/8" h. (ILLUS.) .............. **50**

*Ucagco Baby*

**Ucagco,** baby dressed in blue bonnet trimmed w/lace & blue bib, paper label, 6" h. (ILLUS.)................................................. **39**

**Velco,** No. 3688, Japan, pink hair bow & dress, w/hand at cheek, paper label, 5 1/2" h. (missing one earring) ...................... **83**

**Velco,** No. 3749, white bow on grey hat, black dress, rhinestone earrings, closed eyes w/big lashes, left hand near chin, paper label & stamp, 5 3/4" h. ...................... **110**

# HISTORICAL & COMMEMORATIVE WARES

*Numerous potteries, especially in England and the United States, made various porcelain and earthenware pieces to commemorate people, places and events. Scarce English historical wares with American views command highest prices. Objects are listed here alphabetically by title of view.*

*Most pieces listed here will date between about 1820 and 1850. The maker's name is noted at the end of each entry.*

**Almshouse, New York plate,** floral & scroll border, dark blue, 10" d., Andrew Stevenson (small blister, light stains, small chips on table ring) ........................... $385

**Arms of New York plate,** flowers & vines border, dark blue, 10" d., T. Mayer (wear, scratches w/pinpoint flakes) .............. 440

**Arms of Rhode Island plate,** flowers & vines border, dark blue, 8 5/8" d., T. Mayer (worn w/scratches) ........................... 385

**Arms of South Carolina plate,** florals & vines border, dark blue, 7 1/2" d., T. Mayer (rim wear, small flakes on table ring) ................................................................ 550

**Baltimore & Ohio Railroad, level (The) plate,** shell border, dark blue, 10 1/8" d., E. Wood (stains, minor roughness on table ring) ................................................................ 990

**Baltimore & Ohio Railroad, level (The) soup plate,** shell border, dark blue, 10" d. (E. Wood) ....................................... 953

**Battery, New York (Flagstaff Pavilion) plate,** vine leaf border, dark blue, 7 1/8" d., R. Stevenson (wear, scratches)................................................................ 220

**Battle of Chapultepec plate,** 9 1/2" d., Texian Campaign series, symbols of war & a "goddess-type" seated border, green, Shaw (light facial wear).................... 532

**Boston and Bunker's Hill platter,** 19" l., well & tree, Catskill Moss series, bunches of moss on a network of moss, light blue (Ridgway)....................................... 420

**Boston Harbor waste bowl,** flowers, foliage & scrolls border, spread-winged eagle w/shield in foreground w/Boston harbor in background, 7" d., 3 5/8" h., Rogers (wear, hairline)................................ 825

**Boston State House pitcher,** 5 3/4" h., Rose Border series, fully opened roses w/leaves border, dark blue, Stubbs (half the spout w/old restoration, slightly discolored) ................................................................ 202

**Boston State House plate,** floral border, medium blue, unmarked, 8 1/2" d. , Wood (wear & scratches)........................... 110

**Boston State House sauce tureen, cover & undertray,** floral border, medium blue, 8 3/8" l., Wood, the set (stains, table ring chips on undertray) ................................... 715

**Boston State House soup plate,** floral border, dark medium blue, 10" d. (Wood)..... 364

**Boston State House tile,** rectangular, floral border, dark medium blue, 6" l., Minton (several very minor flakes along rim) ................................................................ 190

**Capitol, Washington (The) cake plate,** footed, Beauties of America series, flowers within medallions border, dark blue, 10 1/2" d., 2 1/2" h., Ridgway (few hard-to-find internal hairlines & minor stain)...... 3,080

**Capitol, Washington (The) plate,** shell border, dark blue, 7 1/2" d. (E. Wood).......... 715

**Capitol, Washington (The) plate,** vine border, dark blue, 10" d., Stevenson (flake on table ring) ....................................... 550

**Capitol, Washington (The) plate,** vine border, embossed white rim, dark blue, 10 1/8" d., Stevenson (minor wear).............. 413

**Chief Justice Marshall, Troy plate,** shell border, dark blue, 8 1/2" d., E. Wood (minor edge wear) ........................................ 495

**Christianburg Danish Settlement on the Gold Coast, Africa platter,** shell border, well-and-tree center, dark blue, 18 3/4" l., E. Wood (wear, small glaze flakes, hairline) ........................................ 1,265

**City Hall, New York - Insane Asylum, New York pitcher,** flowers & foliage border, jug-type, dark blue, 6 1/4" h., Clews (rim & spout edge wear, circular hairline in bottom) ........................................ 550

**City Hall, New York plate,** flowers within medallions border, dark blue, 9 7/8" d. (Ridgway) ................................................ 330

**City of Albany, State of New York plate,** shell border, dark blue, 10 1/4" d., E. Wood (minor scratches) .............................. 660

**City of Montreal platter,** 18" l., well & tree, flowers border, light blue, Davenport (professional restoration to hairline from rim half way into center) ........................ 672

**Columbia College, New York plate,** acorn & oak leaves border, medium blue, 6 3/8" d., R. Stevenson (flake at table ring & pinpoints on rim) ........................ 385

**Columbia College, New York plate,** floral & scroll border, dark blue, 7 1/2" d., Andrew Stevenson (rim chip) ...................... 660

**Commodore MacDonnough's Victory plate,** irregular shells border, dark blue, 10 1/8" d., Wood (minor wear, light scratches)................................................................ 605

**Dam & Water Works (The), Philadelphia plate,** fruit & flower border, dark blue, 9 3/4" d., Henshall, Williamson & Co. (few face scratches) ................................. 440

**Dam & Water Works (The), Philadelphia (Sidewheel Steamboat) soup plate,** fruit & flowers border, dark blue, 9 3/4" d., Henshall, Williamson & Co. (wear)................................................................ 660

**Dam & Water Works (The), Philadelphia (Stern Wheeler Steamboat) plate,** fruit & flower border, dark blue, 10" d., Henshall, Williamson & Co. (chips on table ring, some wear & scratches)...................... 660

**Detroit platter,** 18 3/4" d., Cities series, groups of flowers & scrolls border, dark blue, Davenport (professional repair of line through left part of transfer) .............. 2,800

**Entrance of the Erie Canal into the Hudson at Albany plate,** floral border, dark blue, 10" d., E. Wood (minor wear, pinpoint flakes, spider crack) ........................... 880

**Fair Mount Near Philadelphia bowl,** spread-eagle border, dark blue, 9 1/4" d., Stubbs (wear, light crazing, chip on table ring, several shallow chips on beaded rim) ....................................... 550

**Fair Mount Near Philadelphia plate,** spread-eagle border, dark blue, 10 1/4" d., Stubbs (minor scratches)............ 275

**Fair Mount Near Philadelphia plate,** spread-eagle border, medium blue, 10 1/4" d., Stubbs (minor scratches)............ 149

**Fall of Montmorenci, Near Quebec plate,** shell border, dark blue, 8 3/8" d., Wood (wear, scratches).......................................... 165

**From Fishkill, Hudson River platter,** Picturesque Views series, birds, flowers & scrolls border, black, 15 1/2" l., Clews (light wear on face, seen only when tilted) .............................................................. 476

**Harvard College soup plate,** acorn & oak leaves border, dark blue,10" d., Stevenson & Williams (wear, scratches) .................. 165

**Lafayette & Washington Busts plate,** black transfer-print central reserve w/pair of portraits below a spreadwinged American eagle, plain background w/black rim band, ca. 1825, 6 3/4" d., Wood (wear) .................................. 605

**Landing of General Lafayette at Castle Garden, New York, 16 August 1824 gravy underplate,** primrose & dogwood border, dark blue, 9 3/4" l., Clews ................ 963

**Landing of General Lafayette at Castle Garden, New York, 16 August 1824 pitcher,** floral & vine border, jug-type, dark blue, 7 7/8" h., Clews (spider crack in foot, wear, glaze flakes) ........................ 1,100

*Landing of General Lafayette Plate*

**Landing of General Lafayette at Castle Garden, New York, 16 August 1824 plate,** primrose & dogwood border, dark blue, 8 3/4" d., Clews (ILLUS. left) .............. 310

**Landing of General Lafayette at Castle Garden, New York, 16 August 1824 plate,** floral & vine border, dark blue, 10 1/4" d., Clews ...................................... 432

**Landing of General Lafayette at Castle Garden, New York, 16 August 1824 platter,** floral & vine border, dark blue, 15 1/4" l., Clews (small edge flakes) ......... 1,760

**Landing of General Lafayette at Castle Garden, New York, 16 August 1824 toddy plate,** floral & vine border, dark blue, 5 1/2" d., Clews ................................... 413

**Landing of General Lafayette at Castle Garden, New York, 16 August 1824 tureen,** cov. w/cut out for ladle, floral & vine border, dark blue, 8 1/2" l., lid is a close fitting mismatch w/edge chips, Clews (ILLUS. right) .................................... 660

**Landing of General Lafayette at Castle Garden, New York, 16 August 1824 wash bowl,** floral & vine border, dark blue, 12 1/8" d., 4 1/2" h., Clews (wear, chip on table rim, two rim hairlines).......... 1,210

**Mitchell & Freeman's China and Glass Warehouse, Chatham Street, Boston plate,** foliage border, dark blue, 9" d., Adams (wear, scratches, chip on rim back) .......................................................... 385

**Mitchell & Freeman's China and Glass Warehouse, Chatham Street, Boston plate,** foliage border, dark blue, 10 1/4" d., Adams (very minor wear)........ 1,100

**Mount Vernon, The Seat of the Late Gen'l. Washington cup & saucer,** large flowers border, dark blue, maker unknown, 5 1/2" d., 2 1/2" h. (light wear on saucer, small chip on foot of cup) .......... 364

**Nahant Hotel, Near Boston plate,** spreadeagle border, dark blue, 8 7/8" d. (Stubbs)........................................................ 413

**Narrows from Fort Hamilton (The) platter,** 17 1/2" l., American Scenery series, long-stemmed roses border, black, Ridgway (light wear) ........................................... 308

*New York from Brooklyn Heights Platter*

**New York From Brooklyn Heights platter,** flowers between leafy scrolls border, dark blue, 16 1/4" l., minor wear & small rim flake, Stevenson (ILLUS.) .................. 6,050

**New York from Weehawk platter,** floral border, dark blue, 18 3/4" l., Stevenson (knife scratches, hairline) .......................... 1,210

**Niagara Falls From the American Side platter,** shell border, dark blue, 14 7/8" l., Wood & Sons (wear, scratches)................................................. 2,640

**Octagon Church, Boston soup plate,** flowers within medallions border, dark blue, 9 3/4" d. (Ridgway) .............................. 385

**Picturesque View, Little Falls at Luzerne, Hudson River platter,** floral & scroll border, black, 17 1/2" l., Clews (wear, knife scratches, small flakes) ...................... 440

**President's House, Washington plate,** four medallion - floral border, purple, 10 3/8" d. (E. Wood)...................................... 248

*Sandusky Platter*

**Sandusky (Ohio) platter,** floral border, medium dark blue, harbor scene w/steamship "Henry Clay" & other ships, shoreline in background w/several buildings, 16 1/2" l., minor wear & short scratches, retailer's mark "I.M. Thompson & Co. Wheeling Va.," Clews (ILLUS.)...................................................... **8,250**

**State House, Boston gravy boat,** flowers within medallions border, dark blue, 6 1/2" l., Ridgway (minor stains at interior pinpoints) .............................................. **330**

**State House, Boston platter,** spreadeagle border, dark blue, 14 5/8" l., Stubbs (minor scratches, spider crack)..... **1,045**

**States series plate,** two-story building w/curved drive, border w/names of fifteen states in festoons separated by five-point stars border, dark blue, 7 3/4" d., Clews (small rim bruise) .............. **358**

**States series plate,** building, sheep on lawn, border w/names of fifteen states in festoons separated by five-point stars border, dark blue, 8 3/4" d., Clews (rim w/area of glaze flakes, stain)........................ **303**

**Table Rock, Niagara plate,** shell border - circular center, dark blue, 10 1/8" d., E. Wood (minor wear & scratches)................... **413**

**Transylvania University, Lexington plate,** shell border, dark blue, 9 1/4" d., Wood (wear)................................................ **385**

**United States Hotel, Philadelphia plate,** 10" d., foliage w/grotto center border, dark blue, Tams (large in-the-making spider to left of ladies) ................................ **532**

**View of Trenton Falls---Three People Rock plate,** shell w/circular center w/trailing vine around outer edge of center border, dark blue, 7 3/4" d., Wood (light wear) ..................................................... **280**

# HOMER LAUGHLIN CHINA COMPANY

*It was after the Civil War that Homer Laughlin journeyed to East Liverpool, Ohio and set up his first short-lived stoneware pottery. In 1870 Homer and his brother Shakespeare opened another pottery which produced yellowwares and Rockingham-glazed utilitarian pieces. Some years later the firm added whiteware to the production as well as fine white ironstone china.*

*By the early 20th century the firm had grown tremendously and although Homer Laughlin sold out his interest in the company to the W.E. Wells family in 1898, the company name continued as the Homer Laughlin China Company. During the 1920s numerous additional production factories were opened and a wide range of dinnerwares became the main focus of their output. In the 1930s the famous Fiesta, Harlequin (which see) and Riviera lines were produced and met with great public success. Today the Homer Laughlin firm continues in operation as one of this country's longest continually running potteries.*

*The products of Homer Laughlin are well marked and often carry a dating code as well as the trademark. A wide range of factory-named dinnerware*

shapes were made by the company, however, many of the patterns they used were only given numbers, which makes collecting by pattern a little more difficult today. The following is a brief listing of Homer Laughlin dinnerware lines and patterns.

*Helpful references in this field are The Collector's Encyclopedia of Homer Laughlin China by Joanne Jasper (Collector Books, 1993) and The Collector's Encyclopedia of Fiesta, Plus Harlequin, Riviera and Kitchen Kraft, by Bob & Sharon Huxford (Collector Books, 1992). Information here was provided by the Homer Laughlin China Collectors Association. Also refer to their book Fiesta, Harlequin and Kitchen Kraft: The Homer Laughlin China Collectors Association Guide (summer 2000).*

*Value Guide: low end vs high end pricing is dependent on market availability and collector demand at any given moment. Generally there are harder-to-find colors in each of the lines and those would be reflected in the high end pricing. However, those colors may be different for different collectors. This is meant as a guide only. Condition of the items is representative of what prices would be without any chips, cracks, dings, scratches, etc. The smallest flaw can and does drastically lower the value accordingly.*

**Creamer & cov. sugar bowl,** Bluebird patt., pr. ...................................................... **$55**

**Cup & saucer,** Kitchen Kraft line, Mexicana patt. ................................................................ **22**

**Dinner service:** 15 each dinner plates, bread & butter plates, 10 each salad bowls, dessert bowls, cups, 7 saucers, 4 soup/cereal bowls; Casualtone Coventry, the set ......................................... **175**

**Dinner service:** 8 cups & saucers, ten each dinner plates & bread & butter plates, 6 fruit/dessert bowls & 1 vegetable bowl; Cavalier shape, Romance patt., the set ......................................... **175**

**Fork,** Kitchen Kraft line, Mexicana patt.............. **85**

**Pie server,** Kitchen Kraft line, Mexicana patt. ................................................................ **85**

**Plate,** 7" d., Kitchen Kraft line, Mexicana patt. ................................................................ **14**

**Plate,** 9" d., Kitchen Kraft line, Mexicana patt. ................................................................ **22**

**Salt & pepper shakers,** Kitchen Kraft line, Mexicana patt., pr........................................ **85**

**Soup plate w/flanged rim,** Kitchen Kraft line, Mexicana patt. ....................................... **42**

## CARNIVAL LINE
*Colors: light green, red (orange), Harlequin yellow, grey, forest green, ivory, cobalt blue*

**Bowl,** fruit .............................................................. **4-8**
**Bowl,** oatmeal ...................................................... **5-9**
**Plate,** 6 1/2" d. ..................................................... **2-4**
**Saucer,** ................................................................. **2-3**
**Tea cup** ................................................................ **3-6**
**Tea cup,** cobalt blue glaze .............................. **15+**

## OVENSERVE LINE
*Colors: pink, turquoise, forest green, dark brown, rust*

**Baking dish,** oval............................................... **6-9**

**Casserole,** French-style .................................... 5-8
**Custard cup** ..................................................... 4-6
**Pie plate,** individual ........................................ 9-13
**Ramekin,** round ................................................. 6-8

## RIVIERA LINE

*Colors: light green, mauve blue, red (orange), Harlequin yellow & ivory.*

**Bowl,** 7 1/4" d., nappy ................................... 25-32
**Bowl,** 5 1/2" d., fruit ...................................... 10-14
**Casserole,** cov. ............................................. 90-145
**Plate,** 10" d., dinner ...................................... 45-65
**Tea cup & saucer,** the set ............................. 8-12
**Teapot,** cov. ............................................... 125-175
**Tumbler,** handled .......................................... 55-80
**Tumbler,** handled, ivory glaze ...................... 140+

## WELLS ART GLAZE LINE

*Colors: rust, peach, green, yellow*

**Bowl,** 8" d., nappy ......................................... 18-24
**Creamer** ........................................................ 15-24
**Pitcher,** cov., 9" h., jug-form ....................... 90-125
**Plate,** 9" d. ................................................... 11-16
**Platter,** 11 1/2" .............................................. 19-27
**Syrup pitcher** .............................................. 75-110

## HULL

*This pottery was made by the Hull Pottery Company, Crooksville, Ohio, beginning in 1905. Art Pottery was made until 1950 when the company was converted to utilitarian wares. All production ceased in 1986.*

*Reference books for collectors include Roberts' Ultimate Encyclopedia of Hull Pottery by Brenda Roberts (Walsworth Publishing Company, 1992), and Collector's Guide to Hull Pottery - The Dinnerware Lines by Barbara Loveless Gick-Burke (Collector Books, 1993).*

*Hull Marks*

**Ashtray,** Ebb Tide patt., E8 ........................... $225
**Ashtray,** Butterfly patt., B3, 7" l. ..................... 55
**Ashtray,** Continental patt., No. A1, 8" .............. 50
**Ashtray,** Serenade patt., No. S23, 10 1/2 x 13" .................................................. 95
**Ashtray** Parchment & Pine patt., No. S-14, 14" l. ................................................................ 150
**Bank,** Corky Pig, colored ................................ 125
**Bank,** figural Corky Pig, pink, white & blue, 5" ................................................................... 100
**Basket,** Parchment & Pine patt., No. S-3, 6" h. ................................................................ 75
**Basket,** Sueno Tulip patt., No. 102-33-6", 6" h. ................................................................ 350
**Basket,** Open Rose (Camellia) patt., No.142, 6 1/4" h. ......................................... 350
**Basket,** Sun Glow patt., No. 84, 6 1/2" h. .......... 75

**Basket,** Serenade patt., bonbon-type, blue ground, No. S5, 6 3/4" h. ............................... 93
**Basket,** Orchid patt., No. 305, 7" h. ............... 550
**Basket,** Rosella patt., No. R-12, 7" h. ............ 185
**Basket,** Mardi Gras/Granada patt., No. 32, 8" h. ................................................................ 125
**Basket,** Morning Glory patt., No. 65-8, 8" h. ................................................................ 150
**Basket,** Blossom Flite patt., No. T4, 8 1/2" h. ........................................................... 125
**Basket,** Royal Woodland patt., No. W9, 8 3/4" h. ........................................................... 50
**Basket,** Woodland Matte patt., fan-shaped w/center handle, pink & green, W9-8 3/4", 8 3/4" h. .......................................... 143
**Basket,** Woodland Matte patt., fan-shaped w/center handle, yellow & green, W9-8 3/4", 8 3/4" h. .......................................... 223
**Basket,** Poppy patt., No. 601, 9" h. ................. 750
**Basket,** Ebb Tide patt., E5, 9 1/8" h. ............... 125
**Basket,** Wildflower patt., No. 79, 10 1/4" h. .... 2,000
**Basket,** Butterfly patt., three-handled, No. B17, 10 1/2" h. ............................................ 350
**Basket,** Magnolia Gloss patt., No. H-14, 10 1/2" h. ........................................................ 250
**Basket,** Magnolia Matte patt., No. 10, 10 1/2" h. ........................................................ 325
**Basket,** Royal Woodland patt., No. W22, 10 1/2" h. ........................................................ 135
**Basket,** Tokay patt., round "moon" form, No. 11, 10 1/2" h. .......................................... 125
**Basket,** Wildflower patt., No. W-16-10 1/2", 10 1/2" h. ........................................................ 375
**Basket,** Poppy patt., No. 601, 12" h. ............. 1,300
**Basket,** Serenade patt., yellow ground, ruffled sides, No. S14, 12" h. ........................... 300
**Basket,** Ebb Tide patt., model of a large shell w/long fish handle, No. E-11, 16 1/2" l. ........................................................ 248
**Bonbon,** Butterfly patt., No. B4, 6" d. .............. 40
**Book ends,** Orchid patt., No. 316, 7" h., pr... 1,200
**Bowl,** cereal, 6" d., Floral patt., No. 50 ............ 10
**Bowl,** 6 1/2" d., low, Poppy patt., No. 602 ........ 295
**Bowl,** 7" d., Orchid patt., No. 312 ................... 135
**Bowl,** 8" d., Calla Lily patt., No. 500-32 .......... 135
**Bowl,** fruit, 9 1/2" d., Tokay patt., No. 7 ........... 135
**Bowl,** salad, 10" d., No. 49 .............................. 50
**Bowl,** fruit, 10 1/2" d., Butterfly patt., No. B16 ................................................................ 150
**Candleholders,** Butterfly patt., No. B22, 2 1/2" h., pr. .................................................... 85
**Candleholders,** Ebb Tide patt., No. E-13, 2 3/4" h., pr. .................................................... 75
**Candleholders,** Bow-Knot patt., No. B17, 4" h., pr. ......................................................... 225
**Candleholders,** Dogwood patt., No. 512, 4" h., pr. ......................................................... 160
**Candleholders,** Magnolia Gloss patt., No. H-24, 4" h., pr. ................................................ 85
**Candleholders,** Water Lily patt., No. L-22-4", 4" h., pr. ................................................... 125
**Candleholders,** Serenade patt., No. S16, 6 1/2" h., pr. .................................................. 105
**Candy dish,** Butterfly patt., No. B6, 4 3/4 x 5 1/2" ................................................... 45
**Candy dish,** Continental patt., C62, 8 1/4" h. ........................................................... 45
**Candy dish,** cov., Serenade patt., No. S3C, 8 1/4" h. ................................................. 95

**Candy dish,** cov., Tokay patt., No. 9C,
8 1/2" h. ...... **100**
**Canister,** cov., Little Red Riding Hood
patt., "Salt" ...... **1,100**
**Casserole,** cov., French handle-type &
warmer, House n' Garden line, No. 979,
Mirror Brown, 3 pt., 3 pcs. ...... **125**
**Casserole,** oval w/figural duck cover,
House n' Garden line, Mirror Brown, 2
pt. ...... **95**
**Casserole,** cov., Floral patt., No. 42,
7 1/2" d. ...... **60**

*Sun Glow Pattern Casserole*

**Casserole,** cov., Sun Glow patt., No. 51-
7 1/2", 7 1/2" d. (ILLUS.) ...... **50**
**Casserole,** cov., Serenade patt., No.S20,
9" d. ...... **125**
**Coaster/spoon rest,** Gingerbread Boy
patt., 5" l. ...... **39**
**Compote,** Tokay patt., No. 9 ...... **65**
**Console bowl,** Wildflower patt., No. 69,
4" h., pr. ...... **250**
**Console bowl,** Iris patt., No. 409-12", 12" l. ...... **225**
**Console bowl,** Magnolia Gloss patt., No.
H-23, 13" l. ...... **95**
**Console bowl,** Orchid patt., No. 314, 13" l. ...... **350**
**Console bowl,** Royal Woodland patt., No.
W29, 13" l. ...... **75**
**Console bowl,** Water Lily patt., No. L-21-
13 1/2", 13 1/2" l. ...... **175**
**Console bowl,** shell-shaped, Ebb Tide
patt., E12, 15 3/4" l. ...... **200**
**Console bowl,** Parchment & Pine patt.,
unmarked, No. S-9, 16" l. ...... **78**
**Console set:** 16 1/2" l. console bowl & two
3" h. candleholders; Blossom Flite patt.,
Nos. T10 & T11, 3 pcs. ...... **120**
**Cookie jar,** cov., Barefoot Boy (small chip
inside rim on lid, flake on rim of base) ...... **280**
**Cookie jar,** cov., figural Duck ...... **30**
**Cookie jar,** cov., Floral patt., No. 48,
8 1/4" h. ...... **65**
**Cookie jar,** cov., Gingerbread Boy, blue
w/white trim ...... **390**
**Cookie jar,** cov., Gingerbread Man patt.,
12" h. ...... **550**
**Cookie jar,** cov., Little Red Riding Hood,
open basket, gold stars on apron ...... **395**
**Cornucopia-vase,** Water Lily , pink w/gold,
L7-6 1/2", 6 1/2" h. ...... **115**
**Cornucopia-vase,** Bow-Knot patt., blue &
pink, No. B5-7 1/2, 7 1/2" h. ...... **313**
**Cornucopia-vase,** Parchment and Pine
patt., No. S-2, 7 3/4" h. ...... **45**
**Cornucopia-vase,** Calla Lily patt., No. 570-
33, 8" h. ...... **110**

**Cornucopia-vase,** Poppy patt., No. 604,
8" h. ...... **325**
**Cornucopia-vase,** Magnolia Gloss patt.,
No. H-10, 8 1/2" h. ...... **70**
**Cornucopia-vase,** Royal Woodland patt.,
No. W10, 11" h. ...... **45**
**Cornucopia-vase,** Tokay patt., No. 10,
white ground, 11" l. ...... **58**
**Cornucopia-vase,** Dogwood patt., No.
511, 11 1/2" h. ...... **275**
**Cornucopia-vase,** double, Magnolia Gloss
patt., No. H-15, 12" h. ...... **85**
**Cornucopia-vase,** double, Magnolia Matte
patt., No. 6, 12" h. ...... **165**
**Cornucopia-vase,** double, Water Lily patt.,
No. L-27-12", 12" h. ...... **250**
**Cornucopia-vase,** Parchment & Pine patt.,
No. S-6, 12" ...... **80**

*Bow-Knot Cornucopia-vase*

**Cornucopia-vase,** double, Bow-Knot patt.,
No. B13, 13 1/2" h. (ILLUS.) ...... **295**
**Creamer,** Water Lily patt., No. L-19-5",
5" h. ...... **75**
**Creamer,** Rosella patt., No. R-3, 5 1/2" h. ...... **50**
**Creamer,** Ebb Tide patt., No. E15 ...... **60**
**Creamer,** Royal Woodland patt., No. W28 ...... **25**
**Creamer & cov. sugar bowl,** Little Red
Riding Hood patt., side-pour creamer,
pr. ...... **275**
**Dish,** leaf-shaped, Tokay patt., No. 19,
14" l. ...... **95**
**Ewer,** Open Rose (Camellia) patt., No. 128,
4 3/4" h. ...... **85**
**Ewer,** Magnolia Gloss patt., No. H-3,
5 1/2" h. ...... **45**

*Rosella Pattern Ewer*

**Ewer,** Rosella patt., No. R-9, 6 1/2" h.
(ILLUS.)............................................................ **75**
**Ewer,** Royal Woodland patt., No. W6,
6 1/2" h. ............................................................ **45**
**Ewer,** Iris patt., No. 401-8", cream & rose,
8" h. .................................................................. **175**
**Ewer,** Dogwood patt., No. 505-6 1/2",
8 1/2" h. ............................................................ **250**
**Ewer** Calla Lily patt., No. 506, 10" h. ................ **330**
**Ewer,** Mardi Gras/Granada patt., No. 31,
10" h. ................................................................ **115**
**Ewer,** Morning Glory patt., No. 66-11,
11" h. ................................................................ **450**
**Ewer,** Blossom Flite patt., No. T13,
12 1/2" h. .......................................................... **200**
**Ewer,** Orchid patt., No. 311, 13" h. .................... **675**
**Ewer,** Poppy patt., No. 610, 13" h. .................... **850**
**Ewer,** 13 1/2" h., Serenade patt., No. S13-
13 1/2"............................................................... **363**
**Ewer,** Bow-Knot patt., No. B15, 13 1/2" h. .... **1,300**
**Ewer,** Dogwood patt., No. 519, 13 1/2" h. ........ **800**
**Ewer,** Woodland Gloss patt., No. W24-
13 1/2", 13 1/2" h............................................. **183**
**Flower dish,** Butterfly patt., No. B7,
6 3/4 x 9 3/4" .................................................... **63**
**Flowerpot,** Sun Glow patt., No. 98,
7 1/2" h.............................................................. **45**
**Flowerpot & saucer,** Calla Lily patt., No.
592, 6" h. .......................................................... **125**
**Flowerpot w/attached saucer,** Sueno
Tulip patt., No. 116-33-4 3/4", 4 3/4" h. ........ **135**
**Flowerpot w/attached saucer,** Woodland
patt., No. W11, 5 1/2" h. ...................... **150-175**
**Grease jar,** cov., Sun Glow patt., No. 53,
5 1/4" h. ............................................................ **45**
**Jardiniere,** Dogwood patt., No. 514, 4" h......... **110**
**Jardiniere,** Poppy patt., No. 603, 4 3/4" h........ **175**
**Jardiniere,** Woodland Matte patt., pink &
yellow, No. W7-5 1/2", 5 1/2" h. .................... **145**
**Jardiniere,** Woodland patt., dark green &
blue, No. W7-5 1/2", 5 1/2" h.......................... **96**
**Jardiniere,** Orchid patt., No. 310, 6" h. ............ **225**
**Jardiniere,** Calla Lily patt., No. 591, 7" h. ........ **300**
**Lamp base,** Rosella patt., No. 63-4", 4" h........ **300**
**Lamp base,** Sueno Tulip patt., 6 1/2" h............ **600**
**Lamp base,** Orchid patt., No. 303, 10" h............ **600**
**Lamp base,** Iris patt., No. 414, 16" h. .............. **750**
**Mug,** Serenade patt., No. S22, 8 oz. .................. **55**
**Pitcher,** 7 1/2" h., Sun Glow patt., No. 55 .......... **85**
**Pitcher,** 8" h., Sueno Tulip patt., No. 109-
33-8".................................................................. **235**
**Pitcher,** 8 1/2" h., Blossom Flite patt., No.
T3 ...................................................................... **90**
**Pitcher,** 8 1/2" h., Magnolia Gloss patt.,
No. H-11 ............................................................ **85**
**Pitcher,** 13" h., Sueno Tulip patt., No. 109-
33-13"................................................................ **400**
**Pitcher,** 14" h., Tokay patt., No. 21 .................. **225**
**Pitcher,** Floral patt., No. 46, 1 qt. ...................... **50**
**Pitcher,** Serenade patt., No. S21, 1 1/2 qt. ...... **125**
**Planter,** baby w/pillow, pink w/gold trim,
No. 92, 5 1/2" h. ................................................ **35**
**Planter,** model of two Siamese cats, No.
63, 5 3/4" l. ........................................................ **85**
**Planter,** model of lovebirds, pink & brown,
Novelty line, No. 93, 6" h. ................................ **40**
**Planter,** model of a parrot pulling a flower
blossom-form cart, Novelty line, No. 60,
9 1/2" l., 6" h..................................................... **50**

**Planter,** model of a Dachshund dog, 14" l.,
6" h. .................................................................. **110**
**Planter,** bust of the Madonna, yellow, No.
24, 7" h. ............................................................ **35**
**Planter,** model of twin geese, Novelty line,
No. 95, 7 1/4" h. ................................................ **50**
**Planter,** model of a kitten, No. 61, pink,
7 1/2" h. ............................................................ **50**
**Planter,** model of a standing lamb, No.
965, 7 1/2" h. .................................................... **65**

*Basket Girl Planter*

**Planter,** Basket Girl, No. 954, 8" h.
(ILLUS.)............................................................ **40**
**Planter,** model of a pheasant, No. 61,
6 x 8" ................................................................ **50**

*Figural Swan Planter*

**Planter,** model of a swan, yellow glossy
glaze, Imperial line, No. 69,
8 1/2 x 10 1/2", 8 1/2" h. (ILLUS.).................... **50**
**Planter,** model of Bandanna Duck, Novelty
line, No. 74, 9" h. .............................................. **50**
**Planter,** Blossom Flite patt., No. T12,
10 1/2" l. ............................................................ **95**
**Rose bowl,** Iris patt., No. 412-7", 7" l. .............. **188**
**Salt & pepper shakers,** Sun Glow patt.,
No. 54, 2 3/4" h., pr. .......................................... **20**
**Salt & pepper shakers,** Floral patt., No.
44, 3 1/2" h., pr. ................................................ **25**
**Serving tray,** three-part w/butterfly handle,
Butterfly patt., gold-trimmed scalloped
rim, B23, 11 1/2" l. ............................................ **200**

**Sugar bowl,** cov., Rosella patt., No. R-4, 5 1/2" h. ............................................. **60**

**Tea set,** cov. teapot, creamer & cov. sugar bowl, Butterfly patt., Nos. B18, B19 & B20, 3 pcs. ................................................. **275**

**Tea set:** cov. teapot No. S-11, cov. sugar bowl No. S-13 & creamer No. S-12; Parchment and Pine patt., 3 pcs. ................ **135**

**Tea set:** cov. teapot W26, cov. sugar bowl W28 & creamer W27; Woodland Gloss patt., teapot 6 1/2" h., 3 pcs. ................ **275**

**Teapot,** cov., Serenade patt., No. S17, 5" h., 6-cup ................................................ **175**

**Teapot,** cov., Dogwood patt., No. 507, 5 1/2" h. ............................................... **350**

**Teapot,** cov., Mardi Gras/Granada patt., No. 33, 5 1/2" h. ......................................... **200**

**Teapot,** cov., House n' Garden line, Mirror Brown, 6" h. ................................................ **35**

**Teapot,** cov., Parchment & Pine patt., No. S-11, 6" h. ................................................ **125**

**Teapot,** cov., Ebb Tide patt., No. 14, 6 1/2" h. ............................................... **200**

**Teapot,** cov., Magnolia Gloss patt., gold trim, No. H-20, 6 1/2" h. ............................. **175**

*Blossom Flite Pattern Teapot*

**Teapot,** cov., Blossom Flite patt., No. T14, 8" h. (ILLUS.)...................................... **100**

**Teapot,** cov., Wildflower patt., No. 72, 8" h. ... **1,200**

**Teapot,** cov., Royal Woodland patt., No. W26, 8-cup ................................................ **95**

**Tray,** Mirror Brown patt., 10 x 10" ...................... **75**

**Vase,** 5 1/2" h., Water Lily patt., No. L-2-5 1/2" ................................................ **48**

**Vase,** 6" h., Sueno Tulip patt., No. 110-33-6" ................................................ **150**

**Vase,** 6 1/2" h., Bow-Knot patt., No. B4-6 1/2" ................................................ **213**

**Vase,** 6 1/2" h., Rosella patt., No. R-6-6 1/2" ................................................ **40**

**Vase,** 6 1/2" h., Royal Woodland patt., No. W4 ................................................ **35**

**Vase,** bud, 6 1/2" h., Serenade patt., No. S1-6 1/2" ................................................ **63**

**Vase,** 6 1/2" h., Sueno Tulip patt., blue & pink, 106-33-6 ........................................ **163**

**Vase,** bud, 6 3/4" h., Orchid patt., No. 306 ...... **145**

**Vase,** 7" h., Butterfly patt., No. B10-7" ............... **55**

**Vase,** bud, 7" h., Ebb Tide patt., No. E1 ........... **75**

**Vase,** bud, 7" h., Open Rose (Camellia) patt., No. 129................................................ **145**

**Vase,** 7 1/2" h., Royal Woodland patt., No. W8................................................ **40**

**Vase,** 8" h., Calla Lily patt., No. 500-33 ........... **145**

**Vase,** 8 1/2" h., Iris patt., No. 407-8 1/2" .......... **150**

**Vase,** 8 1/2" h., Magnolia Gloss patt., gold trim, No. H-8 ........................................ **70**

**Vase,** 8 1/2" h., Magnolia Matte patt., pink & blue, No. 1-8 1/2" ...................................... **173**

*Open Rose Vase*

**Vase,** 8 1/2" h., Open Rose (Camellia) patt., No. 126 (ILLUS.) ................................ **325**

**Vase,** 8 1/2" h., Woodland Matte patt., pink ground, No. W16-8 1/2"................................ **218**

**Vase,** 9" h., Morning Glory patt., No. 215-9"....... **55**

**Vase,** 10" h., Calla Lily patt., No. 520-33 .......... **350**

**Vase,** 10" h., Orchid patt., No. 302 ................ **325**

**Vase,** 10 1/2" h., Butterfly patt., No. B14-10 1/2" ................................................ **100**

**Vase,** 10 1/2" h., Iris patt., No. 403-10 1/2" ...... **325**

**Vase,** 10 1/2" h., Magnolia Matte patt., dusty rose & yellow, bulbous baluster-form body w/high forked & fanned rim, pointed loop shoulder handles, No. 2-10 1/2"................................................ **104**

**Vase,** 10 1/2" h., Magnolia Matte patt., No. 8-10 1/2"................................................ **143**

**Vase,** 10 1/2" h., Poppy patt., No. 605 ............ **450**

**Vase,** 10 1/2" h., Wildflower patt., yellow & rose, No. 59-10 1/2" ...................................... **285**

**Vase,** 12" h., handled, Tokay patt., No. 12-12"................................................ **475**

**Vase,** 12" h., Open Rose (Camellia) patt., No. 124-12" ........................................ **400**

**Vase,** 12 1/2" h., Magnolia patt., No. 22-12 1/2" ................................................ **250**

**Vase,** 12 1/2" h., Water Lily patt., No. L-16-12 1/2" ................................................ **395**

**Vase,** 12 1/2" h., wing-shaped handles, No. H-16-12/12"................................................ **225**

**Vase,** 15" h., Continental patt.,No. C60-15" ..... **150**

**Wall pocket,** model of a flying goose, Novelty line, No. 67, 6" h. ............................. **45**

**Wall pocket,** model of an iron, Sun Glow patt., unmarked, 6" h. ................................ **65**

**Wall pocket,** model of a cup & saucer, Sun Glow patt., No. 80, 6 1/4" h. ...................... **75**

**Wall pocket,** Rosella patt., No. R-10, 6 1/2" h. ............................................... **85**

**Wall pocket,** Royal Woodland patt., shell-shaped, No. W13, 7 1/2" l. ............................. **50**

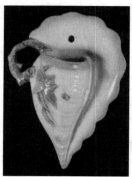

*Woodland Gloss Pattern Wall Pocket*

**Wall pocket,** Woodland Gloss patt., conch shell shape, No. W13-7 1/2", 7 1/2" l. (ILLUS.)............................................................. 93
**Wall pocket,** Woodland Matte patt., No. W13-7 12", 7 1/2" l. ..................................... 190
**Wall pocket,** Bow-Knot patt. ............................ 250
**Window box,** Dogwood patt., No. 508, 10 1/2" l. ............................................................ 195
**Window box,** Parchment & Pine patt., No. S-5, 10 1/2" l. ............................................... 85
**Window box,** Butterfly patt., No. B8, 12 3/4" l. .......................................................... 50

# HUMMEL FIGURINES & COLLECTIBLES

*The Goebel Company of Oeslau, Germany, first produced these porcelain figurines in 1934 having obtained the rights to adapt the beautiful pastel sketches of children by Sister Maria Innocentia (Berta) Hummel. Every design by the Goebel artisans was approved by the nun until her death in 1946. Though not antique, these figurines with the "M.I. Hummel" signature, especially those bearing the Goebel Company factory mark used from 1934 and into the early 1940s, are being sought by collectors though interest may have peaked some years ago.*

*Hummel Marks*

**A Fair Measure,** 4 3/4" h., Trademark 5 ........ $390
**A Stitch in Time,** 6 3/4" h., Trademark 6 ......... 350
**Accordion Boy,** 5 1/4" h., Trademark 5........... 300
**Accordion Boy,** 5 1/4" h., Trademark 6........... 240
**Adoration,** 6 1/4" h., Trademark 3 ................... 575
**Adoration,** 6 1/4" h., Trademark 6 ................... 420
**Angel Duet font,** 2 x 4 3/4" h., Trademark 4 ................................................................... 80

**Angel Lights candleholder,** 8 1/3 x 10 1/3", Trademark 6......................................... 350
**Angel Serenade,** angel standing, part of Nativity scene, 3" h., Trademark 3 .............. 145
**Angel Serenade,** angel standing, part of Nativity scene, 3" h., Trademark 4 .............. 125
**Angel with Accordion,** 2 1/2" h., Trademark 4 .................................................................. 100
**Angel with Birds font,** 2 3/4 x 3 1/2" h., Trademark 1...................................................... 325
**Angel with Lute,** 2 1/2" h., Trademark 4 ......... 100
**Angelic Sleep candleholder,** 3 1/2 x 5", Trademark 2...................................................... 425
**Angelic Song,** 4" h., Trademark 6 ................... 180
**Apple Tree Boy,** 4" h., Trademark 1 ............... 225
**Apple Tree Boy,** 4" h., Trademark 4 ............... 225
**Apple Tree Boy,** 6" h., Trademark 3............... 450
**Apple Tree Boy,** 6" h., Trademark 4 ............... 425
**Apple Tree Boy,** 6" h., Trademark 6............... 350
**Apple Tree Boy & Apple Tree Girl book ends,** 5 1/4" h., Trademark 4, pr. ................. 425
**Apple Tree Boy table lamp,** 7 1/2" h., Trademark 2........................................... 1,000
**Apple Tree Girl,** 4" h., Trademark 1 ............... 500
**Apple Tree Girl,** 4" h., Trademark 3 ............... 250
**Apple Tree Girl,** 4" h., Trademark 4 ............... 225
**Apple Tree Girl,** 6" h., Trademark 1 ............... 900
**Apple Tree Girl,** 6" h., Trademark 4 ............... 425
**Artist (The),** 5 1/2" h., Trademark 4 ............. 1,200
**Auf Wiedersehen w/Tyrolean cap,** 5 1/4" h., Trademark 2.............................. 4,000
**Ba-Bee Ring plaque,** 5" d., Trademark 1 ........ 700
**Baker,** 4 3/4" h., Trademark 4 .......................... 300
**Band Leader,** 5" h., Trademark 1 .................... 750
**Barnyard Hero,** 4" h., Trademark 3 ................. 300
**Be Patient,** 4 1/4" h., Trademark 3................... 350
**Be Patient,** 6 1/4" h., Trademark 4................... 475
**Bird Duet,** 4" h., Trademark 3 .......................... 230
**Birthday Serenade,** 4 1/4" h., Trademark 4..... 260
**Birthday Serenade,** reverse mold, 4 1/4" h., Trademark 4.............................. 550
**Blessed Event,** 5 1/4" h., Trademark 4............ 600
**Book Worm,** 4" h., Trademark 4 ...................... 350
**Book Worm,** 5 1/2" h., Trademark 4 ................ 350
**Book Worm book ends,** 5 1/2" h., Trademark 4, pr. ............................................... 600
**Boots,** 5 1/2" h., Trademark 1 .......................... 700
**Boots,** 5 1/2" h., Trademark 3 .......................... 325

*Boy with Toothache*

Boy with Toothache, 5 1/2" h., Trade-
mark 4 (ILLUS.) ............................................ 320
Builder, 5 1/2" h., Trademark 4 ...................... 375
Candlelight, 6 3/4" h., Trademark 4 ................. 350
Chef, Hello, 6 1/4" h., Trademark 3 ................. 400
Chef, Hello, 6 1/4" h., Trademark 4 ................. 350

*Chick Girl*

Chick Girl, 3 1/2" h., Trademark 1 (ILLUS.) ..... 650
Christ Child, from Nativity set,
1 1/2 x 3 3/4", Trademark 3 ............................ 95
Congratulations, 6" h., Trademark 3, (no
socks) ........................................................... 325
Culprits, 6 1/4" h., Trademark 1 ..................... 1,100
Doctor, 4 3/4" h., Trademark 3 ........................ 275
Doll Mother, 4 3/4" h., Trademark 3 ................. 350
Duet, 5 1/4" h., Trademark 3 ............................ 450
Farewell, 4 3/4'" h., Trademark 1 .................... 1,000
Farewell, 4 3/4" h., Trademark 2 ...................... 475
Farm Boy, 5 1/4" h., Trademark 4 .................... 350
Favorite Pet 4 1/4" h., Trademark 4 ................. 450
Favorite Pet 4 1/4" h., Trademark 6 ................. 345
Feeding Time, 5 3/4" h., Trademark 1 .......... 1,000
Feeding Time, 5 3/4" h., Trademark 2 ............. 625
Festival Harmony, angel w/flute, 8" h.,
Trademark 3 .................................................. 650
Festival Harmony, angel w/mandolin,
8" h., Trademark 4 ........................................ 475
Festival Harmony, angel w/flute,
10 3/4" h., Trademark 3 ................................ 800
Flower Madonna, 8 1/4" h., Trademark 4,
color ............................................................. 575
For Father, 5 1/2" h., Trademark 3 ................. 375

*Forest Shrine*

Forest Shrine, 9" h., Trademark 6 (ILLUS.) ..... 650
Girl with Doll, 3 1/2" h., Trademark 4 ............. 100
Globe Trotter, 5" h., Trademark 3 ................... 350
Going to Grandma's, 4 3/4" h., Trademark
1 ................................................................. 1,000
Going to Grandma's, 6" h., Trademark 1 ..... 1,500
Going to Grandma's, 6" h., Trademark 3 ........ 800
Good Friends, 4" h., Trademark 1 ................... 750
Good Friends table lamp, 7 1/2" h.,
Trademark 4 ................................................. 475
Good Hunting, 5 1/4" h., Trademark 4 ............ 425
Good Hunting, 6 1/4" h., Trademark 3 ............ 425
Goose Girl, 4" h., Trademark 4 ....................... 250
Goose Girl, 4 3/4" h., Trademark 1 ................. 800
Goose Girl, 7 1/2" h., Trademark 1 .............. 1,300

*Happiness*

Happiness, 4 3/4" h., Trademark 3
(ILLUS.) ...................................................... 225
Happy Birthday, 5 1/2" h., Trademark 4 .......... 450
Happy Days, 4 1/4" h., Trademark 4 ............... 250
Happy Days, 5 1/4" h., Trademark 3 ............... 475
Happy Days, 5 1/4" h., Trademark 4 ............... 225
Happy Days, 6" h., Trademark 1 ................... 1,550
Happy Pastime, 3 1/2" h., Trademark 3 .......... 275
Hear Ye, Hear Ye, 5" h., Trademark 1 ............. 750
Hear Ye, Hear Ye, 7 1/2" h., Trademark 3 ....... 750
Heavenly Protection, 9 1/4" h., Trademark
3 ............................................................... 1,200
Herald Angels candleholder, 2 14 x 4",
Trademark 3 ................................................. 275
Just Resting, 3 3/4" h., Trademark 3 ............... 250
Just Resting, 5" h., Trademark 1 .................... 800
Kiss Me, 6" h., Trademark 4, w/socks ............. 950
Kiss Me, 6" h., Trademark 4, without socks ..... 450
Latest News, 5 1/4" h., Trademark 3 ............... 500
Let's Sing, 3 1/4" h., Trademark 3 ................. 225
Letter to Santa Claus, 7" h., Trademark 4 ... 1,000
Little Band candleholder music box,
4 3/4 x 5", Trademark 4 ................................ 500
Little Cellist, 8" h., Trademark 4 .................... 650
Little Fiddler, 4 3/4" h., Trademark 1 .............. 800
Little Fiddler, 4 3/4" h., Trademark 4 .............. 325
Little Fiddler, 7 1/2" h., Trademark 4 .............. 550
Little Fiddler, 11" h., Trademark 1 ............... 3,500
Little Gardener, 4 1/4" h., Trademark 1 .......... 500
Little Goat Herder, 4 3/4" h., Trademark 1 ...... 500
Little Goat Herder, 4 3/4" h., Trademark 3 ...... 325
Little Guardian, 3 3/4" h., Trademark 1 .......... 525
Little Hiker, 5 1/2" h., Trademark 1 ................. 750
Lost Stocking, 4 3/8" h., Trademark 4 ......... 1,500

**Mail Is Here (The),** 4 1/4 x 6", Trademark 3.. **1,000**
**Max & Moritz,** 5 1/4" h., Trademark 1 .............. **800**

*Meditation*

**Meditation,** 5 1/4" h., Trademark 1
(ILLUS.)....................................................... **850**
**Meditation,** 7" h., Trademark 1 ..................... **5,000**
**Merry Wanderer,** 4 3/4" h., Trademark 1 ........ **700**
**Mountaineer,** 5 1/4" h., Trademark 4 .............. **400**

*Out of Danger*

**Out of Danger,** 6 1/4" h., Trademark 2
(ILLUS.)....................................................... **650**
**Playmates,** 4" h., Trademark 1 ....................... **650**
**Playmates,** 4 1/2" h., Trademark 4 ................. **400**
**Postman,** 5 1/4" h., Trademark 3 .................... **325**
**Prayer Before Battle,** 4 1/4" h., Trademark
1 .................................................................. **650**
**Quartet plaque,** 6 x 6", Trademark 3 .............. **625**
**School Boy,** 4" h., Trademark 1 ...................... **600**
**School Boy,** 5 1/2" h., Trademark 1 ............... **750**
**School Boys,** 10 1/4" h., Trademark 4 ........ **2,150**
**Sensitive Hunter,** 4 3/4" h., Trademark 3 ........ **350**
**Sensitive Hunter,** 4 3/4" h., Trademark 4 ........ **325**
**Sensitive Hunter,** 5 1/2" h., Trademark 4 ....... **375**
**She Loves Me,** 4 1/4" h., Trademark 4 ........... **290**
**Signs of Spring,** 4" h., Trademark 2, two
shoes on.................................................... **1,500**
**Silent Night candleholder,** 5 1/2" l.,
4 3/4" h., Trademark 1.............................. **1,100**
**Silent Night candleholder,** 5 1/2" l.,
4 3/4" h., Trademark 4............................... **475**
**Sister,** 5 3/4" h., Trademark 2 ......................... **175**

**Skier,** 5 1/4" h., Trademark 1 .......................... **850**
**Skier,** 5 1/4" h., Trademark 3 .......................... **350**
**Smart Little Sister,** 4 3/4" h., Trademark 4 ..... **375**
**Soldier Boy,** 6" h., Trademark 4 ...................... **650**
**Soloist,** 4 3/4" h., Trademark 1 ....................... **500**
**Soloist,** 4 3/4" h., Trademark 4 ....................... **200**
**Spring Cheer,** 5" h., Trademark 1 ................... **650**
**Spring Cheer,** 5" h., Trademark 3.................... **325**
**Spring Cheer,** 5" h., Trademark 4 (yellow
dress) ......................................................... **300**
**St. Joseph,** 7 1/2" h., Trademark 3 ................. **285**
**Street Singer,** 5" h., Trademark 3 ................... **350**
**Strolling Along,** 4 3/4" h., Trademark 1 ......... **950**
**Strolling Along,** 4 3/4" h., Trademark 3 ......... **350**
**Surprise,** 5 1/2" h., Trademark 1 ..................... **950**
**Sweet Music,** 5 1/4" h., Trademark 3.............. **325**
**Telling Her Secret,** 5 1/4" h., Trademark 4..... **450**
**Telling Her Secret,** 6 3/4" h., Trademark 3...... **550**
**To Market,** 5 1/2" h., Trademark 1 ................ **1,000**
**To Market,** 5 1/2" h., Trademark 3 .................. **450**
**To Market,** 5 1/2" h., Trademark 4 .................. **425**
**Umbrella Boy,** 5" h., Trademark 4 ................... **850**
**Umbrella Boy,** 8" h., Trademark 3 ................ **2,000**
**Umbrella Girl,** 4 3/4" h., Trademark 3.......... **1,000**
**Umbrella Girl,** 8" h., Trademark 3................. **2,000**
**Village Boy,** 5" h., Trademark 3...................... **400**
**Volunteers,** 5" h., Trademark 3 ....................... **400**
**Volunteers,** 5 1/2" h., Trademark 1 .............. **1,100**
**Wash Day,** 5 3/4" h., Trademark 4 .................. **450**
**Wayside Devotion,** 7 1/2" h., Trademark 3 ..... **700**
**Worship,** 5" h., Trademark 3 ............................ **275**

## IRONSTONE

*The first successful ironstone was patented in 1813 by C. J. Mason in England. The body contains iron slag incorporated with the clay. Other potters imitated Mason's ware and today much hard, thick ware is lumped under the term ironstone. Earlier it was called by various names, including graniteware. Both plain white and decorated wares were made throughout the 19th century. Tea Leaf Lustre ironstone was made by several firms.*

### GENERAL

**Bowl,** 7 1/4" d., 2 3/4" h., scalloped rim, all-
white, ca. 1890s, Maddock & Co............. **$20-25**
**Bowl,** 8 1/2" d., 3" h., large ribs w/scalloped
rim, all-white, ca. 1890s, J. & G. Meakin... **40-50**
**Bowl,** 12" d., 3" h., wide flanged rim,
"gaudy" Imari-style decoration w/blue
transfer design highlighted w/red enameling, printed mark "Mason's Patent Ironstone China" (interior wear, rim hairline,
minor crazing) ............................................. **220**
**Bread plate,** "Give Us This Day, Our Daily
Bread" embossed on outer rim, all-white,
unmarked, 12" l. ..................................... **155-175**
**Butter dish, cover & drain,** Corn & Oats
shape, all-white, ca. 1863, 6" d. ............ **200-220**
**Cake stand,** scalloped apron & fluted pedestal, all-white, by J.F., 9 3/4" d.,
4 1/2" h. ................................................. **245-275**
**Cheese dish,** cov., "gaudy" style, molded
C-scrolled edging trimmed in cobalt blue
on the slant lid, decorated w/orange
flowers, late 19th c. .................................... **204**
**Cheese dish,** cov., "gaudy" style, slanted
cover & underplate in the Derby patt., S.
Fielding & Co., England ................................ **132**

*Dudson Cheese Keeper*

**Cheese keeper,** cov., dome & stand w/high relief clusters of grapes, wheat & hops, all-white, ca. 1870s, 13" d., 10" h., Dudson (ILLUS.) .......................................... **550-600**

**Coffeepot,** cov., "gaudy," ovoid body raised on tab feet, wide trumpet neck w/inset domed cover, swan's-neck spout & C-scroll handle, blue transfer-printed War Bonnet patt. trimmed in red, orange & yellow, marked "Ironstone China," 19th c., 10" h. (minor wear & hairline in spout) ................................................ **220**

**Compote,** open, 5 3/4" d., 3 3/4" h., One Big and Two Little Ribs shape, all-white, ca. 1860s, Elsmore & Forster ..... **135-150**

*Ironstone Fruit Garden Compote*

**Compote,** open, 12" d., 6 3/4" h., Fruit Garden patt., all-white, ca. 1860s, Jacob Furnival (ILLUS.) .................................... **235-250**

**Cup & saucer,** handled, Berlin Gothic shape, all-white, ca. 1840s, T.J. & J. Mayer ....................................................... **80-85**

**Cup & saucer,** handled, Pomegranate shape, all-white, ca. 1850s, Jacob Furnival ................................................................. **45-50**

**Dinner service:** thirty-nine 9 1/2" d. plates, seventeen 8 1/8" d. plates, sixteen 9 1/2" d. soup plates, eight 6 1/8" d. plates, eleven serving platters, 9 1/4" l., & 10" l., two 12" l. platters, five platters 14 1/8" l., 18" l., 19 3/4" l., three rectangular-form cov. vegetable dishes, two cov. sauce tureens w/underplates, oval gravy boat, a bone dish, two oval serving bowls & a cov. 13 1/2" l. cov. soup tureen; polychrome decorated bird & floral design, 19th c., Davenport, the set (ILLUS. of part, top next column) .............. **8,625**

*Ironstone Dinner Service*

**Dinner service:** twelve each 10 1/4" d. dinner plates, 9 1/4" d. luncheon plates, 9 1/4" d. soup plates & 7" d. salad plates; black transfer-printed Oriental design w/polychrome enamel trim, marked "Mason's Ironstone China," 19th c., the set (minor enamel & edge flaking)..... **495**

**Ewer,** Atlantic shape, all-white, ca. 1858, T. & R. Boote, 12" h.................................. **195-220**

**Ewer,** Girard shape, all-white, ca. 1846, Ridgway, Bates & Co., 12" h................. **175-190**

**Ewer,** Late Victorian w/fluted rim & ornate handle & scalloped foot, all-white, ca. 1890s, Alfred Meakin .............................. **90-100**

**Ewer,** plain w/loop handle, all-white, ca. 1870s, Clementson Bros., 11 3/4" h...... **110-125**

**Foot bath,** Classic Gothic shape, all-white, ca. 1850, John Alcock........... **1,300-1,400**

*Scalloped Decagon Foot Bath*

**Foot bath,** Scalloped Decagon/Cambridge shape, all-white, ca. 1852, Davenport (ILLUS.)......................................... **1,000-1,200**

**Gravy boat,** Long Octagon shape, all-white, ca. 1847, T.J. & J. Mayer .......... **125-140**

**Inhaler,** squatty bulbous body tapering to a cylindrical neck fitted w/a slender cylindrical glass mouthpiece, blue marbleized decoration & black shield transfer marked "Mfg. by S. Mawson & Thompson," England, 19th c., 11" h. (shallow chip on rim spout)........................................ **275**

*Grape Octagon Ladle*

**Ladle,** Grape Octagon shape, all-white, ca. 1970s, Red Cliff (ILLUS.) .......................... **30-40**

**Ladle,** Hyacinth shape, all-white, unmarked, soup tureen size.................... **90-100**

**Mug,** Basketweave with Band patt., all-white, Alfred Meakin.............................. **65-70**

**Mug,** Gothic patt., all-white, ca. 1840s, James Edwards ................................... **120-130**

**Mug,** Gothic shape, all-rare, ca. 1847, T.J. & J. Mayer, rare.................................. **100-120**

**Mug,** Laurel Wreath patt., all-white, ca. 1867, Elsmore & Forster, 4 5/8" d., 3 1/4" h...................................... **75-85**

**Mug,** Royal shape (Lion's Head), all-white, ca. 1870s, 4 1/2" d., 3 3/8" h.......... **45-50**

**Pitcher,** 8" h., "gaudy," paneled cylindrical lower body below the tapering shoulder & flared neck w/pointed spout, looped dragon handle, printed w/an Imari-style design in underglaze-blue w/red, green & copper lustre trim, impressed "Mason's Patent Ironstone China," 19th c. (minor flaking)......................................... **688**

**Soup plate,** Sydenham shape, decagon, all-white, ca. 1853, T. & R. Boote, 9 1/2" d...................................... **50-70**

**Soup tureen,** cov., oval body raised on scrolled feet, molded end handles, stepped & domed cover w/scrolled ring finial, decorated w/floral sprays & banding design, ca. 1870, 13 1/2" l., 11" h........ **1,064**

**Soup tureen, cover, ladle & underplate,** Grape Octagon shape, all-white, ca. 1960s, Red Cliff, 14 1/2" d., 13" h., 4 pcs......................................................... **140-160**

**Soup tureen, cover, ladle & underplate,** Stafford shape, all-white, ca. 1854, S. Alcock & Co., 4 pcs. ............................ **750-800**

*Wedgwood Soup Tureen w/Underplate*

**Soup tureen, cover & underplate,** Gothic Octagon shape, all-white, ca. 1840s, J. Wedgwood (ILLUS.).............................. **700-750**

**Sugar bowl,** cov., Chinese shape, all-white, ca. 1858, T. & R. Boote, 7 3/4" h. .... **85-95**

**Sugar bowl,** cov., Grape Octagon shape, all-white, Livesley & Powell ...................... **75-85**

**Sugar bowl,** cov., Plain Uplift, all-white, ca. 1880s, Cockson, Chetwynd & Co. ............ **60-70**

**Syllabub cup,** 1851 shape w/loop handle, all-white, T. & R. Boote ............................ **30-35**

**Syllabub cup,** Tulip shape, all-white, ca. 1855, Elsmore & Forster ........................... **20-25**

**Tea set:** child's, cov. teapot, creamer & cov. sugar bowl; Lily-of-the-Valley patt., all-white, James Edwards, the set......... **220-250**

**Tea set:** child's, cov. teapot, creamer, cov. sugar bowl, waste bowl & six cups & saucers; plain, all-white, unmarked, ca. 1880s, the set....................................... **180-200**

*Furnival Teapot*

**Teapot,** cov., Classic Gothic shape, all-white, ca. 1850, Jacob Furnival, 8 1/2" h. (ILLUS.)................................................ **210-230**

**Teapot,** cov., Grape Octagon body decorated w/blackish purple transfer-printed design of large roses & morning glories w/polychrome enamel trim, mid-19th c., 9" h. (spout chips) ...................................... **165**

**Teapot,** cov., Laurel Wreath patt., black transfer-printed bust portrait of George Washington inside wreath on each side, English diamond registry mark & "Elsmore & Forster, Tunstall," mid-19th c., 9 3/4" h. ..................................................... **440**

*Edwards Teapot*

**Teapot,** cov., Lily-of-the-Valley, all-white, ca. 1863, James Edwards, 8" h. (ILLUS.)................................................. **195-215**

**Teapot,** cov., Memnon shape, six panels w/branch handle & bud finial, all-white, ca. 1850s, John Meir & Son, 8 3/4" h. ............................................. **150-165**

*Panelled Grape Teapot*

**Teapot,** cov., Paneled Grape shape, all-white, ca. 1960s, Red Cliff, 8" h. (ILLUS.)............................................ **60-70**

**Toddy bowl,** cov., Gothic Paneled, all-white, ca. 1860s, Elsmore & Forster, 10 1/2" d. .......................................... **250-275**

**Toddy plate,** paneled shape, "gaudy" Floral w/Eye patt., underglaze-blue trimmed w/red, green & copper lustre, impressed "Pearl White," 6 3/8" w. (wear, crazing, stains)................................................... **138**

**Toothbrush box,** cov., Gothic Octagon shape, all-white, ca. 1852, Davenport, 3 1/2 x 8", 3 1/4" h. .............................. **135-150**

**Toothbrush box,** cov., Vintage shape, all-white, ca. 1865, E. & C. Challinor ............. **75-85**

**Vegetable dish,** cov., a flanged scalloped foot supporting an oval flared body w/a wide flattened flanged rim, inset high stepped & domed cover w/a blossom finial, colorful Imari-style transfer decoration trimmed in polychrome & gilt, lion & unicorn mark w/"Stone China LIV," mid-19th c., 13 1/2" l. (hairline in cover)............. **303**

*Cable & Ring Vegetable Dish*

**Vegetable dish,** cov., Cable & Ring shape, all-white, ca. 1875, J. & G. Meakin, 10 3/4" l. (ILLUS.)................................. **60-75**

**Vegetable dish,** cov., Ceres shape w/cable & rope border, all-white, ca. 1859, Elsmore & Forster, 10" l. ............................ **240**

**Vegetable dish,** cov., octagonal flared footring below the flaring octagonal bowl w/a flattened scalloped flanged rim, octagonal tapering domed cover w/blos-

som finial, Imari-style transfer decoration w/polychrome decoration & gilt trim, mid-19th c., 11 1/2" l. (chips on inner cover flange) ........................................... **440**

*President Shape Vegetable Dish*

**Vegetable dish,** cov., President shape, all-white, ca. 1856, John Edwards, 12" l. (ILLUS.)................................................ **165-195**

**Vegetable dish,** cov., Scotia (Poppy) shape, oval, all-white, ca. 1870, F. Jones & Co., 9" l. ..................................... **85-95**

**Wash bowl & pitcher,** Paneled Grape, all-white, Jacob Furnival, 2 pcs................... **180-200**

**Wash bowl & pitcher,** Plain Berlin patt., all-white, ca. 1862-70, Liddle, Elliot & Son, 2 pcs. ........................................... **150-160**

*Boote's Waste Bowl*

**Waste bowl,** Sydenham shape, all-white, ca. 1853, T. & R. Boote, 5 3/8" d., 3 3/4" h. (ILLUS.)................................... **115-125**

**Waste bowl,** Trent shape, all-white, ca. 1855, John Alcock ..................................... **85-90**

## TEA LEAF IRONSTONE

**Bone dish,** crescent-shaped, Chelsea patt., A. Meakin .............................................. **40**

**Bone dish,** plain crescent shape, A. Meakin......................................................... **40**

**Bone dish,** scalloped crescent shape, A. Meakin......................................................... **25**

**Boston egg cup,** Ruth Sayers decoration ....... **115**

**Butter dish, cover & insert,** Basketweave patt., A. Shaw (some glaze wear on insert) ................................................................ **375**

**Cake plate,** Bamboo patt., A. Meakin ............... **70**

**Cake plate,** Daisy 'n Chain patt., Wilkinson ..... **190**

**Cake plate,** Daisy patt., A. Shaw (fine crazing, tiny edge chip) ....................................... **130**

**Cake stand,** square, low pedestal base, handled, Square Ridged patt., Red Cliff, ca. 1970 ............................................... **170**

**Chamberpot,** cov., Fish Hook patt., A. Meakin............................................................ **300**

**Chamberpot,** cov., Lion's Head patt., Mellor, Taylor & Co. ............................................ 175

**Coffeepot,** cov., Scroll patt., A. Meakin .......... 185

**Cookie jar,** cov., round, Kitchen Kraft line, gold Tea Leaf, Homer Laughlin, ca. 1950s ............................................................... 175

**Creamer,** Bamboo patt., A. Meakin, 5 1/4" h. .......................................................... 195

**Creamer,** Cable patt., A. Shaw, 7" h. (manufacturing flaw on lower side) ...................... 280

**Creamer,** Iona patt., gold Tea Leaf, Powell & Bishop, 4 1/2" h. .................................... 70

**Creamer,** Lily of the Valley patt., Anthony Shaw ................................................................ 375

**Creamer,** Square Ridged patt., Wedgwood (slight wear) .................................................. 90

**Cup plate,** Niagara Fan patt., A. Shaw, 4 5/8" d. ............................................................ 60

**Cup plate,** Niagara patt., A. Shaw, 4 5/8" d. ....... 60

**Cup plate,** plain, A. Meakin, 3 1/2" d. ................. 45

**Cup plate,** Rondeau patt., Davenport, 3 7/8" d. ......................................................... 120

**Cup & saucer,** handled, Chelsea patt., A. Meakin ........................................................... 60

**Cup & saucer,** handled, child's, plain round, Wilkinson .......................................... 200

**Egg cup,** Empress patt., Micratex by Adams, ca. 1960s ...................................... 200

**Gravy boat,** Aladdin lamp-style, Cumbow decoration ..................................................... 60

**Gravy boat,** Basketweave patt., Anthony Shaw ............................................................. 140

**Gravy boat,** Chinese patt., A. Shaw ................. 230

**Gravy boat,** Golden Scroll patt., Bishop & Stonier ........................................................ 45

**Ladle,** soup-type, large, unmarked ................... 625

**Mug,** hot water-type, Daisy patt., twelve-sided, A. Shaw ............................................. 275

**Oyster bowl,** pedestal foot, Edwards ................ 55

**Pitcher,** 6 3/4" h., Plain Round patt., gold Tea Leaf, J.M. & Co. (some lustre wear) ....... 50

**Pitcher,** 7" h., Empress patt., Micratex by Adams, ca. 1960s ....................................... 80

**Pitcher,** 7 1/2" h., milk-type, Hanging Leaves patt., A. Shaw ................................. 375

**Pitcher,** 8" h., Fish Hook patt., Alfred Meakin ........................................................... 225

**Pitcher,** 8" h., Maidenhair Fern patt., Wilkinson ...................................................... 900

**Pitcher,** 8" h., water-type, Lion's Head patt., Mellor, Taylor & Co. .......................... 150

**Platter,** 12" l., oval, Chelsea patt., A. Meakin ........................................................... 55

**Punch bowl,** footed deep rounded bowl, A. Meakin, 9" d. ......................................... 650

**Relish dish,** Maidenhair Fern patt., Wilkinson ...................................................... 250

**Relish dish,** mitten-style, Hawthorn patt., Wilkinson (small glaze flaw on foot rim) ....... 275

**Sauce tureen, cover & ladle,** Maidenhair Fern patt., Wilkinson (hairline & chip on base, small hairline on foot) ...................... 400

**Sauce tureen, cover, ladle & undertray,** Square Ridged patt., Red Cliff, ca. 1960s, the set .............................................. 175

**Sauce tureen, cover & undertray,** Basketweave patt., A. Shaw, the set (flake at ladle opening, under rim flaws) ................... 500

**Sauce tureen, cover, undertray & ladle,** Cable patt., A. Shaw, the set (discoloration on handle) ............................................. 500

**Sauce tureen, cover, undertray & ladle,** Fish Hook patt., A. Meakin, plain white ladle, the set (small inner rim chip on base) ............................................................ 350

**Serving dish,** oval, Brocade patt., A. Meakin, 7" l. (tiny discolored spot) ............... 190

**Shaving mug,** Chinese patt., Anthony Shaw ............................................................. 110

**Shaving mug,** Maidenhair Fern patt., Wilkinson (professional repair to outside rim chip) ..................................................... 500

**Soap dish,** cov., Cable patt., A. Shaw (inside lid rim chip) .................................... 150

**Soap dish,** cov., Square Ridged patt., Mellor, Taylor & Co. ........................................ 325

**Soap dish, cover & insert,** Bamboo patt., A. Meakin ......................................................... 260

**Soup plate w/flanged rim,** Clementson, 9" d. ............................................................... 70

**Soup tureen, cover, undertray & ladle,** Square Ridged patt., Red Cliff, ca. 1970, the set ....................................................... 425

**Tea set:** cov. teapot, cov. sugar bowl & creamer; Empress patt., Micratex by Adams, ca. 1960s, the set ........................ 165

**Teapot,** cov., Bamboo patt., A. Meakin ........... 150

**Teapot,** cov., Cable patt., A. Shaw ................. 250

**Teapot,** cov., Daisy 'n Chain patt., Wilkinson ............................................................. 120

**Teapot,** cov., Hanging Leaves patt., A. Shaw (slight roughness inside lid) .............. 600

**Teapot,** cov., Simple Square patt., Wedgwood ........................................................... 120

**Toothbrush vase,** cylindrical w/scalloped rim, Alfred Meakin .................................... 250

**Toothbrush vase,** Heavy Square patt., Clementson (some crazing, small spider crack) ........................................................... 350

**Vegetable dish,** cov., Bamboo patt., A. Meakin, 10" l. (some glaze wear) ................ 80

**Vegetable dish,** cov., Iona patt., gold Tea Leaf, Bishop & Stonier, 12" l. .................... 50

**Vegetable dish,** cov., oval, Basketweave patt., A. Shaw, 10 1/4" l. ............................. 230

**Vegetable dish,** cov., oval, Brocade patt., A. Meakin, 10" l. ...................................... 150

**Vegetable dish,** cov., oval, Chelsea shape, A. Meakin ................................................. 120

**Vegetable dish,** cov., rectangular, Bamboo patt., A. Meakin, 12" l. ............................. 90

**Vegetable dish,** cov., square, Bullet patt., A. Shaw, 12" w. ...................................... 95

**Vegetable dish,** cov., square, Fish Hook patt., A. Meakin ...................................... 120

**Vegetable dish,** cov., Square Ridged patt., Mellor, Taylor & Co., 12" l. ..................... 130

**Vegetable dish,** cov., Square Ridged patt., Wedgwood, 10" l. .................................. 80

**Wash bowl & pitcher,** Brocade patt., A. Meakin (spider crack in bowl) ...................... 275

**Wash pitcher,** Cable patt., A. Shaw .................. 170

**Wash pitcher,** Daisy 'n Chain patt., Wilkinson ............................................................. 130

**Wash pitcher,** Daisy patt., A. Shaw .................. 160

**Wash pitcher,** Square Ridged patt., Wedgwood (small hairline in bottom) .................... 210

**Waste bowl,** Plain Round patt., T. Hughes........ 40

## TEA LEAF VARIANTS

**Chamber pot,** cov., Morning Glory patt.,
Portland shape, Elsmore & Forster ............. 525

**Creamer,** child's, Teaberry patt., Scalloped Treasure shape, Clementson ............ 525

**Creamer,** Pinwheel patt., Full Paneled
Gothic shape, unmarked ............................ 450

**Creamer,** Pre-Tea Leaf patt., Niagara
shape, E. Walley ...................................... 500

**Creamer,** Teaberry patt., Heavy Square
shape, Clementson ................................... 450

**Cup & saucer,** handled, child's, Teaberry
patt., Plain Round shape, Clementson
(minor damage) ........................................ 275

**Cup & saucer,** handleless, Tobacco Leaf
patt., Fanfare shape, Elsmore & Forster...... 120

**Gravy boat,** Morning Glory patt., Richelieu
shape, Wileman (wear on spout, interior
small pits) ................................................ 100

**Mug,** Sydenham shape, lustre band trim,
large, unmarked ....................................... 225

**Pitcher,** 7 1/8" h., milk-type, Morning Glory
patt., Portland shape, Elsmore & Forster..... 450

**Pitcher,** 7 1/2" h., milk-type, Teaberry patt.,
Heavy Square shape, Clementson .............. 600

**Pitcher,** 8" h., Lustre Scallops patt.,
Wrapped Sydenham shape, E. Walley
(slight glaze wear, manufacturing flaw)........ 475

**Pitcher,** 9 1/2" h., Teaberry patt., Heavy
Square shape, Clementson (crazing,
glaze hairline, small base nick) ................... 500

**Plate,** 11" d., Teaberry patt., New York
shape .................................................... 50

**Platter,** 16" oval, Laurel Wreath patt., lustre
trim ....................................................... 400

**Relish dish,** Laurel Wreath shape, lustre
trim, Elsmore & Forster ............................. 400

**Relish dish,** Pre-Tea Leaf patt., Niagara
shape, E. Walley (small foot rim chip).......... 600

**Relish dish,** Teaberry patt., Quartered
Rose shape, J. Furnival ............................. 675

**Sauce tureen, cover & ladle,** Laurel
Wreath patt., lustre trim, plain white
ladle, Elsmore & Forster, the set (ladle
repair, small rim chip & spider crack) .......... 500

**Soap dish,** cov., Morning Glory patt., Portland shape, Elsmore & Forster (profes-
sional repair to lower rim crack) ................. 425

**Sugar bowl,** cov., Pre-Tea Leaf patt., Hyacinth shape, Cochran & Co. ....................... 550

**Teapot,** cov., Ceres shape, lustre trim,
Elsmore & Forster .................................... 425

**Teapot,** cov., Chelsea Grape patt., Primary
shape, unmarked, 9 1/2" h. ........................ 175

**Teapot,** cov., Morning Glory patt., Portland
shape, Elsmore & Forster .......................... 275

**Teapot,** cov., Pre-Tea Leaf patt., Niagara
shape, E. Walley ...................................... 700

**Vegetable dish,** cov., New York shape,
lustre & blue sprig trim (small hairline) ........ 500

**Vegetable dish,** cov., oval, Tobacco Leaf
patt., Elsmore & Forster ............................ 375

**Vegetable dish,** cov., Pomegranate patt.,
Prairie Flowers shape, Powell & Bishop,
9" l. ....................................................... 550

**Vegetable dish,** cov., Pre-Tea Leaf patt.,
Niagara shape, E. Walley............................ 700

**Waste bowl,** Pre-Tea Leaf patt., Niagara
shape, E. Walley ....................................... 300

**Waste bowl,** Teaberry patt., plain round,
unmarked (some glaze wear)...................... 195

## LEFTON

*The Lefton China Company was the creation of
Mr. George Zoltan Lefton who migrated to the
United States from Hungary in 1939. In 1941 he
embarked on a new career and began shaping a
business that sprang from his passion for collecting
fine china and porcelains. Though his funds were
very limited, his vision was to develop a source
from which to obtain fine porcelains by reviving the
postwar Japanese ceramic industry, which dated
back to antiquity. As a trailblazer, George Zoltan
Lefton soon earned the reputation as "The China
King".*

*Counted among the most desirable and sought
after collectibles of today, Lefton items such as
Bluebirds, Miss Priss, Angels, all types of dinnerware and tea-related items are eagerly acquired by
collectors. As is true with any antique or collectible,
prices may vary, depending on location, condition
and availability.*

*For additional information on the history of
Lefton China, its factories, marks, products and values, readers should consult Collector's Encyclopedia of Lefton China, Books I and II and The Lefton
Price Guide by Loretta DeLozier.*

*Lefton "Pin Money" Bank*

**Bank,** porcelain, model of a coin purse,
white decorated w/rhinestones & applied
flowers & marked "Pin Money," No.
90256, 5" h. (ILLUS.) ............................... **$60**

**Bank,** model of a lion, wearing glasses, No.
13384, 6" h. ........................................... 55

**Bank,** model of a cat, No. 1564, 6 3/4" h............ 30

*Various Lefton Christy Items*

**Box,** cov., candy, round footed, Christy decoration, No. 442, 5" (ILLUS. left) ............. **35**

*Lefton Americana Cake Plate*

**Cake plate,** Americana patt., No. 980, 12 1/4" d. (ILLUS.)........................................... **75**

*Lefton Brown Heritage Floral Coffeepot*

**Coffeepot,** cov., Brown Heritage Floral patt., No. 062 (ILLUS.) ................................... **200**
**Coffeepot,** cov., Eastern Star patt. .................... **75**

*Festival Coffeepot*

**Coffeepot,** cov., Festival patt., No. 2935 (ILLUS.)........................................................ **145**

**Coffeepot,** cov., Forget-Me-Not patt., No. 4174, 6-cup ................................................. **95**
**Coffeepot,** cov., Garden Daisy patt., No. 1506 ............................................................ **50**
**Coffeepot,** cov., Green Heritage patt., No. 3065 ............................................................ **165**

*Lefton Blue Paisley Compote*

**Compote,** open, footed, Blue Paisley patt., lattice edge, No. 2341, 7" (ILLUS.)................ **18**
**Cookie jar,** cov., white, decorated w/relief-molded cookies, No. 102................................ **45**
**Creamer & cov. sugar bowl,** Eastern Star patt., No. 102, pr. .......................................... **25**

*Figural Cow Creamer & Sugar Bowl*

**Creamer & cov. sugar bowl,** figural Bossie the Cow, No. 6512, pr. (ILLUS.) ......... **35**

*Rose Heirloom Creamer & Sugar*

**Creamer & cov. sugar bowl,** Rose Heirloom patt., No. 1075, pr. (ILLUS.) .................. **85**
**Cup & saucer,** demitasse, Eastern Star patt. ............................................................... **20**
**Cup & saucer,** Eastern Star patt., No. 2337....... **15**
**Dish,** deviled egg, Country Squire patt., No. 1601, 12 1/2" d. (ILLUS. top next page)......... **28**

**Figure group,** Bride & Groom in Honeymoon Boat, white w/pink, No. 990, 6 1/4" h. ........................................... **175**

*Country Squire Deviled Egg Dish*

**Figure group,** Provincial Girl w/bird in cage, No. 5263, 8" h. .................................... **135**
**Figurine,** angel w/hearts on dress, No. 7699 ................................................................ **10**
**Figurine,** clown, No. 01881, 3 3/4" ..................... **22**
**Figurine,** flower girl, No. 125, 4 1/2" h. (3 different figures), each ................................... **42**

*Gay Nineties Figurine*

**Figurine,** Gay Nineties, white w/gold trim, No. 1573, 7 1/2" h. (ILLUS.) ......................... **150**

*Figure of George Washington*

**Figurine,** George Washington, No. 1108, 8" h. (ILLUS.) ................................................ **85**

**Figurine,** Kewpie, No. 02132, 3" ...................... **20**
**Figurine,** Lady w/chintz rose dress, No. 780, 8 1/2" ................................................... **145**

*Lefton Lady Figurine*

**Figurine,** lady w/flowers in apron, blue & white, No. 5604, 6" h. (ILLUS.) ...................... **55**

*Lefton Madonna with Child*

**Figurine,** Madonna w/Child, No. 1057, 8 1/2" h. (ILLUS.) ........................................... **95**
**Figurine,** Miss January, No. 5146 ..................... **22**
**Figurine,** Miss Murray, Old Masters series, No. 3987, 7 1/4" h. ....................................... **75**

*Angel in Frame*

**Figurine,** Saturday, square frame, No.
6883, 3 1/4 x 4" (ILLUS.)............................... **28**

*Lefton Colonial Couple*

**Figurines,** Colonial couple, Norman &
Elaine, No. 3045, 7" h., pr. (ILLUS.)............. **150**

*Lefton Jam Jar*

**Jam jar,** cov., square w/relief-molded basketweave base, cover w/molded green
leaves, fruit section finial, No. 5108,
5 1/2" h. (ILLUS.)............................................ **12**
**Jam jar w/spoon,** cov., figural pear, No.
1071 ............................................................... **15**
**Lady head vase,** pink, No. 1343, 6 1/2" h......... **22**
**Model,** Country Post Office, Colonial Vil-
lage series, No. 07341 ................................. **65**
**Model of a bird,** Parakeet, No. 395, 5"............. **35**
**Model of a bird,** Waxwing, No. 6609,
4 1/2"............................................................... **18**
**Model of a dog,** Pekinese, No. 7328, 4"............ **40**
**Model of a duck,** Mallard, No. 2070, 4"............. **35**
**Model of a hand,** bisque, lady's w/applied
porcelain flower bracelet, No. KW2933.......... **45**
**Model of a horse,** hunter, matte finish, No.
1006, 7" ......................................................... **80**
**Model of a horse,** No. 547, 4 1/2", three
different figures, each..................................... **30**
**Model of a squirrel,** bisque, No. 4749, 5" ......... **30**
**Model of a tiger,** black, white & gold, No.
8743, 8 1/2" l. (ILLUS. top next column) ....... **85**
**Model of an eagle,** No. 802, 11" h. ................. **100**
**Model of an elephant,** w/raised trunk &
tusks, No. 075, original paper label, 5" h........ **70**

*Lefton Tiger*

**Models of a cat,** grey, No. 2013, 2 1/2", set....... **18**
**Models of a deer,** No. 4217, 6", pr. .................. **32**
**Models of a hen & a rooster,** black &
white, No. 926, 11 1/2" h., pr......................... **95**
**Models of swan w/baby,** No. 841, 3 1/2",
pr. ................................................................... **55**
**Mug,** Christy decoration, No. 447, 7" h.
(ILLUS. right)................................................... **8**
**Planter,** bisque, ice pink, No. 1030, 4" .............. **15**
**Planter,** Humpty Dumpty, No. 065, 7" (two
different), each ................................................ **22**
**Salt & pepper shakers,** pig wearing over-
alls, No. 3079, 3" h., pr.................................. **20**
**Salt & pepper shakers,** rabbit, No. 2197,
3 1/2" h., pr..................................................... **18**
**Tea bag holder,** Miss Priss, No. 1506 .............. **55**

*Dainty Miss Tea Bag Holder*

**Tea bag holder,** teapot shape, Dainty Miss
w/green polka dots, No. 648 (ILLUS.) ............ **50**

*Lefton Violet Chintz Tidbit Tray*

**Tidbit tray,** Single Violet chintz, No. 651
(ILLUS.)........................................................... **35**
**Vase,** 5 1/2" h., bisque, figural hands
w/applied flowers, No. 4198 ........................... **28**

**Vase,** 5 1/2" h., flower-shaped, No. 1548 .......... **18**
**Vase,** 6 1/4" h., cylindrical w/Christy decoration & gold trim, No. 438 (ILLUS. center) .................................................................... **15**
**Vase,** 7" h., pink w/Forget-Me-Not decoration, No. 7633 .......................................... **65-76**

*Hot Air Balloon Wall Plaque*

**Wall plaque,** hot air balloon w/two kittens in basket, tan, white, pink & blue, No. 3709, 4 1/2" (ILLUS.) ...................................... **30**

*Lefton Two Piece Wall Plaque*

**Wall plaques,** figural girl w/blond hair, white, pink & blue dress, holding watering can together w/pink & yellow flowers & green leaves in blue flowerpot, No. 2630, girl 7" h., the set (ILLUS.) ................... **125**

*Ornate Lefton Wall Plaques*

**Wall plaques,** ornate scrolled & relief-molded forms w/a boy & a girl leaning on

wall above leafy vines w/grape clusters, No. 350, 8 1/2", pr. (ILLUS.) ........................ **100**

# LURAY PASTELS

*LuRay Pastels, made by The Taylor, Smith & Taylor Co. of Chester, West Virginia from 1938 until 1961, was a line available in four colors - Windsor Blue, Surf Green, Persian Cream and Sharon Pink. No one original color seems to be more desirable than the others. A fifth color, Chatham Gray, ran from 1949 until 1952. Collectors refer to the early-shaped A/D sets as "Chocolate Sets." Decal-decorated LuRay sets were produced but are very rare. No known examples of the handleless sugar, 7" mini platter or gray salad bowl have been found with the LuRay backstamp. An asterisk (\*) indicates an older original mold shape.*

*Original Style After-Dinner Service*

**After-dinner coffee cup,** four original colors, each (ILLUS. front) .......................... **$20-25**
**After-dinner coffee cup,** gray ................... **75-100**
**After-dinner coffeepot,** cov., four original colors, each (ILLUS. back) ................... **150-200**
**After-dinner individual sugar bowl,** cov., four original colors, each (ILLUS. right) ..... **50-75**
**After-dinner inidividual creamer,** four original colors, each (ILLUS. left) ............. **45-65**
**After-dinner saucer,** four original colors, each (ILLUS. front) ...................................... **7-12**
**After-dinner saucer,** gray ............................ **15-25**

*Various LuRay Bowls*

**Bowl,** 5" d., fruit, four original colors, each (ILLUS. front) ................................................. **5-8**
**Bowl,** 5" d., fruit, gray ............................... **10-15.99**
**Bowl,** 6 1/4" d., grapefruit, rare, four original colors, each (ILLUS. left w/fruit bowl) ....................................................... **350-400**

*LuRay 36's & Lug Soup Bowls*

**Bowl,** 36's bowl (oatmeal), four original colors, each (ILLUS. left) .............................. **50-75**
**Bowl,** 36's bowl (oatmeal), gray ............... **250-300**
**Bowl,** coupe soup, flat, four original colors, each (ILLUS. right w/fruit bowl) ................ **15-20**
**Bowl,** coupe soup, flat, gray ......................... **30-40**

*LuRay Cream Soup Bowl & Saucer*

**Bowl,** cream soup, four original colors, each (ILLUS.) ........................................... **75-95**
**Bowl,** lug soup (tab cereal), four original colors, each (ILLUS. right) ........................ **20-25**
**Bowl,** lug soup (tab cereal), gray ................. **40-50**

*Various LuRay Items*

**Butter dish,** cov., four original colors, each (ILLUS. center) ......................................... **50-75**
**Butter dish,** cov., gray ............................. **150-225**

*Luray Cake Plate*

**Cake plate,** 11" d., four original colors, each (ILLUS.) ........................................... **65-95**

*LuRay Calendar Plate*

**Calendar plate,** 8", 9" or 10" d., each (ILLUS. of 10" d)...................................... **50-75**

*LuRay Covered Casserole*

**Casserole,** cov., four original colors, each (ILLUS.)................................................. **125-175**
**"Chocolate set" A/D creamer*,** four original colors, each (ILLUS. left) ................. **400-500**

*Modern Style "Chocolate Set"*

**"Chocolate set" A/D cup*,** four original colors, each (ILLUS. front) ..................... **75-100**
**"Chocolate set" A/D pot*,** cov., four original colors, each (ILLUS. back) ........ **1,000-1,500**
**"Chocolate set" A/D saucer*,** four original colors, each (ILLUS. front) ........................ **25-35**
**"Chocolate set" A/D sugar bowl*,** cov., four original colors, each (ILLUS. right) ........................................................ **500-600**
**Chop plate,** 15" d., four original colors, each (ILLUS. top next page) .................... **30-40**
**Chop plate,** 15" d., gray ........................... **350-450**

*LuRay Chop Plate*

*LuRay Coaster/Nut Dish*

**Coaster (nut dish),** four original colors, each (ILLUS.) ........................................... **75-95**

*Compartment (Grill) Plate*

**Compartment (grill) plate,** four original colors, each (ILLUS.) ............................... **25-30**
**Compartment (grill) plate,** gray .............. **100-125**
**Cream soup saucer,** four original colors, each (ILLUS. w/bowl) ............................... **20-25**
**Creamer,** four original colors, each .............. **10-15**

*LuRay Creamer*

**Creamer,** gray (ILLUS.) ................................. **30-45**
**Egg cup,** double, four original colors, each (ILLUS. left w/butterdish) ........................... **15-25**
**Egg cup,** double, gray ................................. **75-100**

*LuRay Epergne & Vases*

**Epergne (flower vase),** four original colors, each (ILLUS. center) ...................... **125-150**

*Various LuRay Jugs*

**Jug,** juice, four original colors, each (ILLUS. left) ............................................ **175-225**
**Jug,** water, flat, four original colors, each (ILLUS. right) .............................................. **75-95**
**Jug,** water, footed*, four original colors, each (ILLUS. center) ............................ **100-125**
**Mixing bowl,** 7" d., four original colors, each .................................................... **125-175**
**Mixing bowl,** 8 3/4" d., four original colors, each .................................................... **125-175**
**Mixing bowl,** 10 1/4" d., four original colors, each ............................................... **125-175**

*Luray Muffin Cover & Plate*

**Muffin cover,** four original colors, each
(ILLUS. w/an 8" plate) ........................... **175-225**
**Pepper shaker,** four original colors, each
(ILLUS. right w/butterdish) ....................... 10-15
**Pepper shaker,** gray ...................................... **20-30**
**Pickle (celery) dish,** four original colors,
each ..................................................... **35-45**

*LuRay 6" to 10" Plates*

**Plate,** 6" d., four original colors, each
(ILLUS.)......................................................... **4-6**
**Plate,** 6" d., gray ............................................. **8-12**
**Plate,** 7" d., four original colors, each
(ILLUS.)......................................................... **10-15**
**Plate,** 7" d., gray ........................................... **20-30**
**Plate,** 8" d., four original colors, each............. **20-25**
**Plate,** 8" d., gray (ILLUS.).............................. **40-50**
**Plate,** 9" d., four original colors, each
(ILLUS.)......................................................... **10-15**
**Plate,** 9" d., gray ........................................... **20-30**
**Plate,** 10" d., four original colors, each
(ILLUS.)......................................................... **15-20**
**Plate,** 10" d., gray ......................................... **30-40**

*LuRay Platters*

**Platter,** 7" l., mini size, four original colors,
each (ILLUS. top) ................................... **200-250**
**Platter,** 11 1/2" l., four original colors, each
(ILLUS. center)......................................... **15-20**
**Platter,** 11 1/2" l., gray ................................. **45-75**
**Platter,** 13" l., four original colors, each
(ILLUS. bottom) ...................................... **15-25**
**Platter,** 13" l., gray......................................... **45-75**

*LuRay Relish Dish*

**Relish dish,** four-part, four original colors,
each (ILLUS.) ........................................ **125-175**
**Salad bowl,** four original colors, each........... **50-75**
**Salad bowl,** gray ....................................... **300-400**
**Salt shaker,** four original colors, each .......... **10-15**
**Salt shaker,** gray ........................................... **20-30**
**Sauceboat,** four original colors, each ........... **30-40**
**Sauceboat,** w/fixed stand, four original col-
ors, each ................................................ **25-35**
**Sugar bowl,** cov., four original colors, each.. **15-20**

*LuRay Sugar Bowls*

**Sugar bowl,** cov., gray (ILLUS. left).............. **45-60**
**Sugar bowl,** cov., handleless, four original
colors, each (ILLUS. right) ..................... **75-125**

*LuRay Teapots & Tea Cup & Saucer*

**Tea cup,** four original colors, each (ILLUS.).... **7-12**
**Tea cup,** gray ................................................ **15-25**
**Tea saucer,** four original colors, each
(ILLUS. w/cup) ............................................. **3-5**
**Tea saucer,** gray ............................................. **7-10**
**Teapot,** cov., curved spout, four original
colors, each (ILLUS. left w/tea cup) .......... **75-95**
**Teapot,** cov., curved spout, gray................ **300-400**
**Teapot,** cov., flat spout*, four original col-
ors, each (ILLUS. right w/tea cup)......... **150-200**
**Tidbit tray,** three-tier, four original colors,
each ........................................................ **95-125**
**Tidbit tray,** two-tier, gray......................... **150-200**

*LuRay Tumblers*

**Tumbler,** juice, four original colors,
3 1/2" h., each (ILLUS. left) ...................... **45-65**
**Tumbler,** water, four original colors,
4 1/4" h., each (ILLUS. right).................. **75-100**
**Vase,** bud, four original colors, each
(ILLUS. right w/epergne) ...................... **250-350**
**Vase,** urn-type, four original colors, each
(ILLUS. left w/epergne) ........................ **250-350**

Vegetable bowl (baker), oval, four original
  colors, each................................................ **20-25**
Vegetable bowl (baker), oval, gray ............. **60-75**
Vegetable bowl (nappy), round, four origi-
  nal colors, each......................................... **20-25**
Vegetable bowl (nappy), round, gray ......... **60-75**

# MAJOLICA

*Majolica, a tin-enameled glazed pottery, has
been produced for centuries. It originally took its
name from the island of Majorca, a source of
figuline (potter's clay). Subsequently it was widely
produced in England, Europe and the United
States. Etruscan majolica, now avidly sought, was
made by Griffen, Smith & Hill, Phoenixville, Pa., in
the last quarter of the 19th century. Most majolica
advertised today is 19th or 20th century. Once
scorned by most collectors, interest in this colorful
ware so popular during the Victorian era has now
revived and prices have risen dramatically in the
past few years. Also see SARREGUEMINES and
WEDGWOOD.*

Majolica Etruscan Mark

### ETRUSCAN

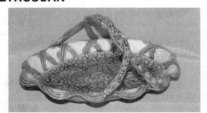

Begonia Pattern Basket

Basket, wicker-handled, Begonia patt.
  (ILLUS.)...................................................... **$660**
Bowl, 8 3/8" d., Shell & Seaweed patt.,
  glazed in pink, brown, bluish grey &
  green, impressed mark (rim wear, firing
  marks in glaze)............................................ **316**
Butter pat, Leaf on Plate patt. .......................... **85**
Cake stand, Shell & Seaweed patt., upright
  shell-form pedestal, in pink, brown, bluish grey & green glazes, impressed
  mark, 4 7/8" h. (rim chips) ............................ **489**
Compote, shell, triple dolphin-footed
  (ILLUS. top next column) .......................... **4,950**
Compote, Daisy patt. in yellow, pink &
  blue, mark for Griffen, Smith & Co., hair-
  lines, 9" d., 5 3/8" h. ................................... **193**
Holy water font, domed cylindrical body
  w/shell decorated cup-shaped top, decorated w/portrait of Virgin Mary, Rose of
  Sharon & Tree of Life, pat. date Nov. 6,
  1883, 6 1/2" h. (ILLUS center next col-
  umn) ........................................................ **8,800**

Pitcher, 6" h., Shell & Seaweed patt. ............... **195**

Shell Dolphin-footed Compote

Rare Etruscan Holy Water Font

Baseball & Soccer Pitcher

Pitcher, 7 3/4" h., jug-type, decorated
  w/multicolored scene of baseball & soc-
  cer players (ILLUS.) ................................. **3,025**

Lily Pattern Punch Set

**Punch set:** punch bowl & six matching cups; Lily patt., the set (ILLUS.) ............... **2,970**

*Strawberry Serving Tray*

**Serving tray,** spade-shaped dish, Strawberry patt., cobalt blue, missing creamer & sugar bowl (ILLUS.) ............................... **1,760**

*Etruscan Soap Dish & Vases*

**Soap dish,** cov., Star of David finial, blue (ILLUS. far right) ...................................... **2,200**
**Syrup pitcher w/metal lid,** Sunflower patt., cobalt blue ground ...................................... **495**
**Vase,** bud, 4" h., Corn patt. (ILLUS. far left) ..... **660**
**Vase,** 4 3/4" h., Oak Leaf & Acorn patt. (ILLUS. second from left) ........................... **550**
**Vase,** 6 1/2" h., flaring foot below baluster-form body w/wide cylindrical neck, cobalt blue & yellow w/brown figural lion head at shoulder, lion leg handles (ILLUS. second from right) ..................................... **1,210**

*Butterfly Wall Pocket*

**Wall pocket,** butterfly-shaped, ivory, yellow, green & cobalt blue (ILLUS.) ............. **3,850**

## GENERAL

**Bowl,** cov., 7 1/4" d., figural artichoke w/attached underplate, bird finial ................. **295**
**Box,** cov., modeled in the form of a turquoise-glazed cushion tied w/yellow cord & surmounted by a white dog knop, the pink-glazed interior fitted w/three rectangular & two oval wells, George Jones, England, ca. 1870s, 10 5/8" l. ........ **4,312**
**Cake set:** 12" handled server & six matching plates; deep red florals on a gold basketweave ground, the set ...................... **165**
**Candelabrum,** three-light, urn-form nozzles supported on a shaped crossbar above a flower-filled urn raised on a fluted pedestal flanked by two scantily-clad cherubs on an oval base raised on four bracket feet, impressed marks, Minton, England, ca. 1869, 16 1/8" h. (seated cherub w/restored leg & foot, small chip to bracket foot at back of base) ......................................................... **5,462**
**Center bowl,** figural, deep oblong form w/broad openwork basketweave sides & undulating rim flanked by a large figural putto at each end w/a large oval medallion joined by foliate festoons at the sides below the basketweave, flaring scalloped & molded base, impressed Minton mark, England, 1868, 11" l. .......... **2,875**

*Minton Rabbit Centerpiece*

**Centerpiece,** modeled as a large turquoise cabbage leaf supported by green ferns flanked by two white & black crouched rabbits, Minton (ILLUS.) .......................... **9,075**

*Minton Majolica Centerpiece*

**Centerpiece,** modeled as a basket raised on a clump of reeds & supported by three putti, on shaped Neoclassical base, impressed "Minton" date code for

1863 & design number 874, 11 1/2" h. (ILLUS.)....................................................... **4,887**

**Centerpieces,** figural, the top wide round bowl modeled in a green & tan basketweave design w/a rim border band of white florettes, supported on the heads of standing bacchanalian putti, one carrying a tambourine, the other a Pan flute, standing on circular bases molded w/leaves & rockwork, impressed Minton ermine marks & date cyphers for 1860, 20" h., pr...................................................... **10,925**

**Charger,** center decorated w/polychrome classical scene bordered w/musical instruments, mythological figures & animals, 19th c., Italy, 18" d. ........................... **633**

**Cheese dish,** cov., tall cylindrical cover w/flat top centered by an arched branch handle & molded prunus branches & blossoms, matching large blossoming branches molded around the sides on an argenta ground, Wedgwood impressed mark, ca. 1882, 8 1/4" h. (slight stains)........ **690**

**Compote,** open, the pedestal composed of three figural standing herons on a tripartite base, supporting a wide shallow rounded dish composed of a band of large lily pad leaves, late 19th c. .................. **440**

**Cup & saucer,** Bird & Fan patt........................... **195**

**Dish,** oval, Palissy-style, center w/relief-molded Venus & Cupid on mottled grey ground, the rim molded w/eight shallow wells alternating w/satyr & angel masks within ochre strapwork borders, impressed marks, Minton, England, ca. 1875, 19 1/2" l. ......................................... **3,450**

**Figurines,** figural vintager modeled as a cherub draped in either ivy or ears of wheat, tugging at a rope wrapped around a tall flared basket to one side, a discarded quiver of arrows beneath their feet, impressed marks, Minton, England, ca. 1863 & 1864, one w/incised "405," 10 3/4" h., pr. (one w/minor restoration to edge of basket)...... **6,037**

*George Jones Game Dish*

**Game dish,** cov., two-handled, game bird nestled in grassy setting on cover, the sides decorated w/rabbits amid ferns, George Jones, England, 13" w., 7" h. (ILLUS.)................................................. **19,250**

**Game dish,** cov., oval, molded around the sides w/game birds & swags of brown netting on pink ground, the cover molded w/a fox crouching before a bird on a bed

of green fern leaves on brown glaze, George Jones, England, 1875, 11" l. ........ **6,800**

**Patch box,** cov., modeled as a butterfly, browns, white, yellow & blue lid, green & white floral decoration around sides, George Jones, England ........................... **6,600**

**Pedestal,** Louis XVI-Style, the fluted baluster-form w/a square top, elaborately molded w/acanthus leaves & formalized foliage, glazed in shades of green, blue, brown, orange & gold on a yellow ground, impressed & printed Rorstrand marks, ca. 1900, 46" h. .............................. **2,645**

**Pitcher,** 7" h., white background molded w/a green lily pad & colored flower, late 19th c. ........................................................... **248**

**Pitcher,** 8" h., flat-sided w/a circular body molded in relief w/fish, molded bamboo-form handle, Holdcroft, England, 1877......... **978**

*George Jones Underwater Pitcher*

**Pitcher,** 8" h., tapering cylindrical form w/C-form handle, greenish blue ground on lower part w/underwater scene of fish, crabs & plant life, dark blue handle & wide band around top w/relief-molded sea gulls, George Jones, England (ILLUS.).................................................... **13,200**

**Pitcher,** 8 1/4" h., Fish on Waves, squatty bulbous body, angled handle ...................... **275**

**Pitcher,** 8 1/4" h., Sharkskin & Floral Bow decoration ........................................................ **85**

**Pitcher,** 9" h., figural monkey ........................... **800**

**Pitcher,** 9 1/4" h., Birds Nest decoration, bulbous ovoid form w/tree knurls protruding around base, angled branch handle .................................................................... **95**

**Pitcher,** 10" h., figural, seated cat, green interior, ivory exterior w/brown floral trim above eyes, brown tail forms handle, leafy green base, Minton (ILLUS. top next page) ................................................. **9,350**

**Pitcher,** 13" h., jug-form, hinged shell-form pewter lid w/figural jester head knop, modeled as an ivy-clad rustic stone tower w/four dancing figures wearing colorful medieval-style costumes, impressed marks & dated 1869, Minton, England (cover & handle restored) ........... **1,610**

**Platter,** oval, 25" l., molded in low relief w/a naturalistically-colored salmon resting on a bed of green fern leaves on a turquoise ground, the reeded rim glazed in greyish green, impressed marks, year & "QIG," painted shape number "M 2164," Wedgwood, England (very minor haircrack) ................................................. **4,887**

*Minton Figural Cat Pitcher*

**Potpourri bowl, cover & pedestal base,** wide squatty classical-form bowl w/molded grotesque heads joined by leafy swags around the rim above the rounded paneled sides, a high stepped & domed scroll-pierced cover w/acorn finial, raised on a baluster-form pedestal molded w/small grotesque heads & swags above a domed scroll-pierced foot on a ringed flaring molded foot, impressed Minton mark, ca. 1870, 10" h... **3,738**

**Sardine box,** cov., rectangular, molded w/band of green leaves on turquoise ground, the cover w/three grey sardines on a bed of seaweed, interior & cover w/pink glaze, George Jones, England, ca. 1870, 5 3/4" l. ...................... **1,840**

**Strawberry server,** molded w/strawberry leaves on blue & white napkin ground & fitted w/a creamer & sugar bowl, George Jones, 13" l. ............................................... **600**

**Sugar bowl,** cov., Bird & Fan patt. ................... **250**

**Tea set:** cov. teapot, cov. sugar bowl, creamer & tray; the oblong keyhole-form tray w/a blossom sprig border band, serving pieces of simple ovoid form w/the lower body w/a molded brown basketweave design, the upper body molded w/white blossoms on leafy twigs against a blue ground, George Jones, England, late 19th c., the set..................... **4,400**

**Teapot,** cov., Chinese man finial..................... **250**

**Teapot,** cov., figural, naturalistically modeled as a large fish in pale blue & pink & set w/green seaweed handle w/turquoise spout protruding from mouth, Minton, England, molded diamond registration mark, gilt-printed Minton crowned globe mark, 7 3/8" h. (green enamel flaked) ............................................................ **1,495**

**Vase,** 6 1/2" h., model of a large inverted straw bonnet, leghorn-shape w/basketweave ground molded w/long ribbons, flowers & a feather against the sides w/alternating dark & light bands of color, impressed Wedgwood mark, ca. 1882 (slight hairlines) .................................... **575**

*Minton Majolica "Queen's" Vase*

**Vases,** 28" h., "Queen's" footed slender ovoid form tapering to cylindrical neck w/flared rim, molded w/fruiting vine & berried ivy branches on ochre ground beneath twig handles tied w/pale blue ribbon & set on each shoulder w/the head of a cat, green bands of molded fluting around lower body & neck, impressed "1857," Minton, England, repair to one rim & handle, chips to cats' ears, one w/chip to foot, pr. (ILLUS. of one) ......................................................... **25,875**

*Minton Satyr Wall Bracket Shelves*

**Wall bracket shelves,** conical form w/relief-molded satyr figures, Minton, 18" h., pr. (ILLUS.) ................................. **17,600**

# MCCOY

*Collectors are now seeking the art wares of two McCoy potteries. One was founded in Roseville, Ohio, in the late 19th century as the J.W. McCoy Pottery, subsequently becoming Brush-McCoy Pottery Co., later Brush Pottery. The other was also founded in Roseville in 1910 as Nelson McCoy Sanitary Stoneware Co., later becoming Nelson McCoy Pottery. In 1967 the pottery was sold to D.T. Chase of the Mount Clemens Pottery Co. who sold his interest to the Lancaster Colony Corp. in 1974.*

*The pottery shop closed in 1985. Cookie jars are especially collectible today.*

*A helpful reference book is The Collector's Encyclopedia of McCoy Pottery, by the Huxfords (Collector Books), and McCoy Cookie Jars From the First to the Latest, by Harold Nichols (Nichols Publishing, 1987).*

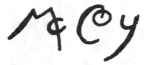

*McCoy Mark*

**Book end/planter,** model of a violin, ca. 1959, 10" h., pr. .................................... **$100-150**
**Book ends,** decorated w/swallows, ca. 1956, 5 1/2 x 6" .................................... **125-150**
**Book ends,** Lily Bud line, ca. 1940s, 5 3/4" h., pr. .......................................... **150-200**
**Book ends,** model of a bird, ca. 1940s, marked "NM," pr. ................................... **175-225**
**Cache pot,** double w/applied bird ................. **35-45**
**Cookie jar,** Bunch of Bananas, ca. 1948 .. **125-150**
**Cookie jar,** Chipmunk, ca. 1960 .............. **100-125**
**Cookie jar,** Grandfather Clock, ca. 1962 .... **80-150**
**Cookie jar,** Grandma (Granny), ca. 1972 ... **90-110**
**Cookie jar,** Happy Face, ca. 1972 .............. **60-80**
**Cookie jar,** heart-shaped, Hobnail line, ca. 1940 ...................................................... **400-500**

*Indian Head Cookie Jar*

**Cookie jar,** Indian Head, ca. 1954 (ILLUS.) ................................................. **325-425**
**Flower bowl ornament,** model of a peacock, 4 3/4" h. ........................................ **100-125**
**Flower holder,** figural, model of a turtle, 4 1/4" l. ...................................................... **50-100**
**Iced tea server,** El Rancho Bar-B-Que line, ca. 1960, 11 1/2" h. ........................ **250-300**
**Jardiniere,** swallows decoration, 7" h. ....... **85-125**
**Jardiniere,** fish decoration, ca. 1958, 7 1/2" h. .................................................. **350-400**
**Jardiniere & pedestal base,** basketweave design, overall 21", 2 pc. ....................... **250-350**
**Jardiniere & pedestal base,** sand butterfly decoration, shaded brown & green ground, overall 21" h., 2 pc. (ILLUS. top next column) .......................................... **250-350**

*Sand Butterfly Jardiniere & Pedestal*

*Cowboy Boots Lamp*

**Lamp w/original shade,** model of pair of cowboy boots base, ca. 1956 (ILLUS.) ................................................. **150-200**
**Mug,** "Happy Face," ca. 1971, 4" ................. **15-20**

*Large Oil Jar*

**Oil jar,** bulbous ovoid body w/slightly flaring rim, angled shoulder handles, red sponged glaze, 18" h. (ILLUS.) ............ **300-400**
**Pitcher,** 10" h., Butterfly line ..................... **150-225**
**Pitcher-vase,** 7" h., figural parrot, ca. 1952 ...................................................... **150-200**
**Planter,** divided, Butterfly line, white, 5 1/2 x 7 1/2" ....................................... **125-150**
**Planter,** figural, clown riding pig, white w/blue & red trim, 8 1/2" l. ...................... **80-100**
**Planter,** figural, Madonna, white, 6" h. ...... **250-300**
**Planter,** model of a baby scale, ca. 1954, 5 x 5 1/2" .............................................. **60-75**
**Planter,** model of a backward bird, ca. early 1940s, 4" h. ..................................... **50-60**
**Planter,** model of a barrel, Calypso line, ca. 1959, 5 x 7 1/2" .................................... **100-140**

*Figural Bear Planter*

**Planter,** model of a bear w/ball, yellow w/black trim, red ball, 5 1/2 x 7" (ILLUS.) .............................................. **100-125**
**Planter,** model of a bird dog, ca. 1959, 7 3/4" l. ................................................. **125-175**
**Planter,** model of a carriage, ca. 1955, 8 x 9" .................................................... **150-200**

*Fish Planter*

**Planter,** model of a fish, pink & green, 7 x 12" (ILLUS.) ................................. **900-1,200**
**Planter,** model of a lemon, 5 x 6 1/2" .......... **75-100**
**Planter,** model of a rabbit w/carrot, white w/black trim, orange & green carrot, 7 1/4" h. ................................................. **100-125**
**Planter,** model of a rooster on wheel of wheelbarrow, 10 1/2" l. .......................... **100-125**
**Planter,** model of a snowman, 4 x 6" ........... **50-60**
**Planter,** model of a stork, ca. 1956, blue & pink, 7 x 7 1/2" (ILLUS. top next column) ................................................... **60-75**
**Planter,** model of a trolley car, ca. 1954, 3 3/4 x 7" .............................................. **80-100**
**Planter,** model of a wagon wheel, ca. 1954, 8" h. .......................................................... **30-40**

**Planter,** model of a wishing well, ca. 1950, 6" h. or 7" h. ................................................ **20-30**

*Figural Stork Planter*

**Planter,** model of an apple, 5 x 6 1/2" ......... **75-100**
**Planter,** model of Liberty Bell, cold painted black bell, base embossed "4th July 1776," 8 1/4 x 10" ................................. **200-300**
**Planter,** model of "stretch" dachshund, 8 1/4" l. ...................................................... **175-200**
**Planter,** pansy ring, ca. 1950 ........................ **65-75**
**Planter,** rectangular, relief-molded golf scene, ca. 1957, 4 x 6" .......................... **150-200**
**Planter,** rectangular, relief-molded scene w/three fawns, tan, brown & green, ca. 1954, 8 x 12" ........................................ **250-300**
**Planting dish,** model of a swan, 10 1/2" l. ............................................... **200-250**
**Planting dish,** rectangular, front w/five relief-molded Scottie dog heads, white, brown & green, ca, 1949, 8" l. .................. **40-50**
**Platter,** 14" l., Butterfly line ..................... **250-400**
**Spoon rest,** Butterfly line, 4 x 7 1/2" ......... **100-150**
**Sprinkler,** model of a turtle, green w/yellow trim, ca. 1950, 5 1/2 x 10" ......................... **60-80**
**Strawberry jar,** w/relief-molded peacock, 8" h. .......................................................... **35-50**
**Tea set:** cov. teapot, creamer & open sugar bowl; Pine Cone patt., ca. 1946, 3 pcs.... **75-100**
**TV lamp,** model of a fireplace, ca. 1950s, 6 x 9" ...................................................... **75-100**
**Vase,** 6" h., heart-shaped, ca. 1940s ............ **50-70**
**Vase,** 6" h., Hobnail line, Castlegate shape ................................................... **150-200**
**Vase,** 6 1/2" h., figural lower tulip, ca. 1953 ...................................................... **100-125**
**Vase,** 8" h., figural chrysanthemum, ca. 1950 ...................................................... **100-125**

*Magnolia Vase*

**Vase,** 8 1/4" h., figural magnolia, ca. 1953, pink, white, brown & green (ILLUS.) .... **150-175**

*Wide Lily Vase*

**Vase,** 8 1/2" h., figural wide lily-form, ca. 1956, white, brown & green (ILLUS.) .... **350-400**
**Vase,** 9" h. or 10" h., figural lizard handles.................................................. **300-400**
**Vase** 10" h., "Blades of Grass," fan-shaped .......................................... **250-350**
**Vase,** 14" h., Antique Curio line, ca. 1962... **75-100**
**Vase,** 14 1/2" h., fan-shaped, ca. 1954 ..... **150-200**
**Wall pocket,** Butterfly line, 6 x 7" ........... **200-400**

*Clown Wall Pocket*

**Wall pocket,** figural, clown, white w/red & black trim, 8" l. (ILLUS.) ....................... **100-150**
**Wall pocket,** Lily Bud line, marked "NM," 8" l. ..................................................... **200-250**
**Wall pocket,** model of a bird bath, 5 x 6 1/2" .............................................. **85-100**
**Wall pocket,** model of a cuckoo clock, 8" l. ..................................................... **125-150**
**Wall pocket,** model of a Dutch shoe, 7 1/2" l. ................................................... **40-50**
**Wall pocket,** model of a fan, blue, 8 x 8 1/2" .............................................. **75-90**
**Wall pocket,** model of a pear........................ **65-80**
**Wall pocket,** model of an apple ................... **50-60**
**Wall pocket,** model of bellows, 9 1/2" l. .... **80-100**
**Wall pocket,** model of lovebirds on trivet, 8 1/2" l. ................................................... **75-90**

# MEISSEN

*Meissen Mark*

The secret of true hard paste porcelain, known long before to the Chinese, was "discovered" accidentally in Meissen, Germany by J.F. Bottger, an alchemist working with E.W. Tschirnhausen. The first European true porcelain was made in the Meissen Porcelain Works, organized about 1709. Meissen marks have been widely copied by other factories. Some pieces listed here are recent.

*Meissen Dish*

**Candelabra,** four-light, each modeled w/a man or woman seated on high domed base painted w/birds & insects, each figure holding a child on their lap & supporting a scroll-molded candleholder fitted w/three flower-encrusted branches, ca. second half 19th c., underglaze-blue crossed swords mark & incised "D 176" & "D 177," 18 5/8" h., pr. (one damaged, minor chips, losses & restoration to candelabra) ..................... **$2,875**
**Centerpiece,** a pierced shallow basket supported on a foliate stem above a rocky base applied w/four dancing figures, shaded pink enamel & gilding, gilt trim, interior w/stylized flower meander, underglaze-blue crossed swords mark, 12 1/8" h. (stem restored & minor crack to basket) ................................................... **1,725**
**Clock,** shelf or mantel, a round clock dial w/Roman numerals enclosed in a footed scroll-molded body in pale pink, turquoise & gilding w/four applied figures of putti, each allegorical of one of the Four Seasons, colorful applied flowers &

leaves, second half 19th c., underglaze-blue crossed swords, 18 3/8" h. ............... **4,600**

**Dessert service:** five 8" d. plates w/pierced rims & two compotes; the plates w/basketweave edges w/three pink flower-filled reserves, a large wreath of pink flowers around the center, each compote w/a domed gadrooned round foot & tall ringed pedestal supporting a shallow flaring dish w/a reticulated border & centered by a standing figure of a young boy flower seller or a young girl flower seller, gilt trim, early 20th c., compotes 11 1/2" h., the set ...................................... **1,840**

**Dish,** deep w/flanged rim, scalloped border, slip decorated w/raised foliate & scrolled cartouches & enameled floral sprays, early 19th c., Germany, 15 1/4" d. (ILLUS.)..................................... **1,265**

**Figure group,** a man, woman & child in 18th c. attire, she seated in front of a small fruiting tree, the man standing to the left holding fruit, the child behind her & beside the tree, a basket of flowers on the ground beside her, all on an oval base w/an acanthus-molded border band, late 19th - early 20th c., 9 1/2" h. .... **1,840**

**Figure group,** "The Good Mother," a lady in 18th c. costume seated in an armchair surrounded by three small children, Model E69, late 19th - early 20th c., 8 3/4" h. (losses) ...................................... **2,415**

**Figure of a gardener,** standing in 18th c. attire, colored enamel & gilt trim, leaning on a shovel & holding flowers, incised "C69," late 19th c., 7 1/2" h. ......................... **575**

**Plate,** 9 5/8" d., gilt-decorated pink & burgundy border w/an enamel-decorated center scene of a cupid & female in a wooded landscape, titled on back "Lei wiedergut," late 19th c. ............................... **489**

**Platter,** Blue Onion patt., 1814-60, crossed swords mark................................................. **250**

*Tea Set w/Miner Decoration*

**Tea set:** cov. 3 1/2" h. teapot, cov. 5" h. tea canister, six cups & 4 3/4" d. saucers; each w/scrolled gilt trim & central enamel decorations of miners at work,

18th c., Germany, the set (ILLUS. of part)......................................................... **13,800**

**Tray,** oval, raised border of molded laurel leaves & grapes, an ornate gilt-framed central cartouche enamel-decorated w/a detailed landscape w/buildings & 18th c. figures, late 18th - early 19th c., 10 x 13 3/8" ............................................. **1,840**

**Urns,** tall classical baluster-form, flaring round fluted pedestal foot tapering to a flared ring below the body w/a band of fluting below the wide dark blue-glazed body, the shoulder w/a narrow molded white band below the flaring dark blue neck w/a rolled molded white band, arched entwined white snake handles from the shoulder to the rim & down to the base of the neck, gilt trim on the white, late 19th c., 10 3/4" h., pr............... **1,610**

## METLOX POTTERIES

METLOX       Miniatures
MADE IN       by METLOX
U. S. A.      MANHATTAN BEACH
              CALIFORNIA

C Romanelli

*Metlox Marks*

Technically, Metlox Potteries began business in 1921 but it was not until the 1970s that collectors began to take notice of the varied and high quality items produced by them. It was in 1932 that Metlox began producing dishes for everyday use and within two years the now well-known Poppytrail came on the market. Metlox continued to grow, putting out decorated dinnerwares, a very successful line designed by Carl Romanelli called Modern Masterpieces, Nostalgia line and the Poppets group.

When Carl Romanelli, a sculptor, joined Metlox he was the first artware designer Metlox hired. Romanelli was known for his miniature animals, Zodiac series and novelties. However, a majority of artware collectors prefer his nudes and nudes with vases.

Collectors seem to prefer a Metlox "line" rather than a Metlox assortment. The company made a large amount of dinnerware which is still inexpensive today. They also turned out their share of cookie jars. Besides the lines already mentioned, Vernonware has always been a popular collectible. Their giftware line of the 1980s, which is beginning to catch collectors' interest, included animals, clocks (which were difficult to make so few left the factory), flowerpots and so on. American Royal Horses was part of the Nostalgia line and is being noticed by collectors today.

In 1946 Evan Shaw purchased Metlox from Willis Prouty. Shaw had owned the American Pottery which was destroyed by fire just before he bought

*Metlox. Many researchers credit Evan Shaw with the tremendous success of the company. When he died ih 1980 Kenneth Avery headed the company. Operations ceased in 1989.*

**Ashtray,** Homestead Provincial patt., 8 1/4" d. ............................................... **$60**
**Ashtray,** Sombrero patt., 2 3/4 x 6" ................... 30
**Ashtray,** Red Rooster patt., Provincial shape, 8" sq. ....................................... 38
**Ashtray,** Red Rooster patt., Provincial shape, 10" sq. ...................................... 65
**Bowl,** individual soup, 5" d., lug-handled, California Provincial patt. ..................... 45
**Bowl,** individual soup, 5" d., lug-handled, Provincial Rose patt. ........................... 17
**Bowl,** individual soup, 5" d., lug-handled, Red Rooster patt. .................................. 23
**Bowl,** individual soup, 5" d., lug-handled, Red Rooster patt., Provincial shape.............. 10
**Bowl,** fruit, 6" d., Red Rooster patt., Provincial shape ............................................. 5
**Bowl,** cereal, 7 1/8" d., Vernonware, Della Robbia shape ....................................... 10
**Bowl,** soup, 8 1/8" d., Sculptured Grape patt. .................................................... 14
**Bowl,** 11" d., low flower-type, round w/ruffled rim, No. 736............................... 27
**Bowl,** salad, 11 1/8" d., Red Rooster patt., Provincial shape ................................... 75
**Butter dish,** cov., Provincial Rose patt. ............ 50
**Butter dish,** cov., Sculptured Grape patt. .......... 45
**Butter dish,** cov., Vernonware, Della Robbia shape................................................ 60
**Candleholder,** Provincial Blue patt. ................... 35
**Canister,** cov., model of broccoli stalks, "Vegetable" line, green glaze w/darker green cover, 1 1/2 qt. ........................... 130
**Canister set,** Happy Time patt., Provincial shape, set of 4 ............................... 175
**Casserole,** cov., basketweave base w/figural chicken lid, Red Rooster patt., Provincial shape, 1 qt., 10 oz. ................... 150
**Casserole,** cov., hen on nest, California Provincial patt., 1 qt., 10 oz. ................ 215
**Coffee carafe,** cov., & metal warmer, California Provincial patt., 7 cup, 44 oz. ...... 275
**Coffeepot,** cov., California Provincial patt., green, 42 oz. ..................................... 90
**Coffeepot,** cov., Homestead Provincial patt. .................................................. 90
**Coffeepot,** cov., Provincial Blue patt.............. 100
**Coffeepot,** cov., Provincial Rose patt. ............. 70
**Coffeepot,** cov., Vernonware, Della Robbia shape ................................................ 50
**Cookie jar,** Ballerina Bear.............................. 110
**Cookie jar,** Bear w/Blue Sweater..................... 105
**Cookie jar,** Chef Pierre ................................... 100
**Cookie jar,** cov., Provincial Blue patt. .............. 225
**Cookie jar,** cov., Provincial Rose patt.............. 80
**Cookie jar,** Drummer Boy (ILLUS. top next column) ....................................... 750
**Cookie jar,** Parrot, seated on a short brown tree stump, green & yellow, Model No. 555 ................................................. 425
**Cookie jar,** Pine Cone w/grey squirrel finial, Model No. 509, 11" h. ................... 95
**Cookie jar,** Rex, dinosaur, white..................... 110

*Rare Drummer Boy Cookie Jar*

*Rose Blossom Cookie Jar*

**Cookie jar,** Rose Blossom, pale pink w/green leaves at bottom, Model No. 513, 2 3/4 qt. (ILLUS.) ................................... **380**
**Cookie jar,** Tulip, yellow & green ................... 425
**Creamer,** Antique Grape patt., Traditional shape ................................................. 17
**Creamer,** Sculptured Grape patt., Traditional shape ......................................... 16
**Cruet set,** 2 pcs. on wood tray, Red Rooster patt., Provincial shape, the set ........ 70
**Cruet set,** 5-piece, Provincial Rose patt........... 150
**Cup & saucer,** Antique Grape patt., Traditional shape ........................................ 10
**Cup & saucer,** California Provincial patt. .......... 16
**Cup & saucer,** Heavenly Days patt., Anytime shape........................................... 12
**Cup & saucer,** Pintoria patt., rectangular shaped saucer w/round depression for round cup, Poppy Orange gloss, scarce pattern, set ................................... 95
**Cup & saucer,** Sculptured Grape patt., blue fruit w/green leaves & brown twigs, set .................................................. 19
**Cup & saucer,** Sculptured Grape patt., Traditional shape.................................. 10
**Figure,** Poppet series, "Louisa," w/hands in a muff & hat tied under her chin, 8 1/2" h. ........................................... 70
**Figure,** Poppets series, "Cigar Store Indian," w/basket without handles attached to body from left foot to below waist, full headdress, blanket around shoulders, white & brown, 8 3/4" h.............. 105

*"Grover" Poppets Figure*

**Figure,** Poppets series, "Grover," bass drum man, blue coat & hat, black shoes, drum w/white front & "Rejoice" in blue, 6 3/4" h. (ILLUS.) ............................................. **95**

*Man & Woman in Surrey*

**Figure of a man,** seated, shelf-sitter, "Papa," Model No. 653, 5 1/4" h. (ILLUS. right in surrey) ............................................. **110**
**Figure of a woman,** seated, shelf-sitter, "Mama," Model No. 652, 5" h. (ILLUS. left in surrey) ............................................. **110**
**Figure of a woman,** standing on oval base, one leg bent to other knee, head back, hair cascading to base, both arms stretched upward holding two birds, satin ivory glaze, "C. Romanelli," signed on base rim, Model No. 1825, 10 3/4" h. ....... **250**
**Gravy boat,** California Provincial patt., 1 pt. ....... **75**
**Gravy boat,** Fastand, Antique Grape patt., Traditional shape ............................................. **30**
**Gravy boat,** Provincial Rose patt. ...................... **28**
**Gravy boat,** Vernonware, Della Robbia shape ............................................. **45**
**Gravy bowl w/attached underplate,** Sculptured Grape patt. ............................................. **30**
**Hen on Nest,** California Provincial patt. ........... **105**
**Jam & jelly dish,** California Ivy patt. .................. **30**
**Jam/mustard jar,** cov., Homestead patt. ........... **65**
**Match box,** hanging-type, Homestead Provincial patt. ............................................. **95**

**Model of a surrey w/metal fringe,** pale green, Nostalia Line, 10 1/2" l., 9" h. (ILLUS. with figures) ...................... **130**
**Model of horse,** large Thoroughbred, brown glaze, Nostalgia line, American Royal Horses, 8 3/4" l., 8 1/2" h. .................. **125**
**Mug,** Provincial Rose patt. ............................... **25**
**Mug,** cocoa, California Provincial patt., 8 oz. ............................................. **35**
**Pitcher,** large, w/ice lip, Provincial Rose patt. ............................................. **60**
**Pitcher,** small, Provincial Rose patt. .................. **35**
**Planter,** model of three owls seated on a log w/mama on left, papa on right & baby in front, blue & white w/black accents & yellow eyes, 5 3/4" h. ............................................. **60**
**Plate,** bread & butter, 6 1/4" d., Heavenly Days patt., Anytime shape ............................... **5**
**Plate,** salad, 7 1/2" d., Antique Grape patt., Traditional shape ............................................. **8**
**Plate,** salad, 7 1/2" d., Heavenly Days patt., Anytime shape ............................................. **8**
**Plate,** salad, 7 1/2" d., Sculptured Grape patt., Traditional shape ............................... **10**
**Plate,** salad, 7 5/8" d., Vernonware, Della Robbia shape ............................................. **8**
**Plate,** dinner, 10 5/8" d., Vernonware, Della Robbia shape ............................................. **9**
**Plate,** chop, 12 1/4" d., California Provincial patt. ............................................. **70**
**Plate,** chop, 13" d., Heavenly Days patt., Anytime shape ............................................. **22**
**Platter,** 9 5/8" oval, Antique Grape patt., Traditional shape ............................................. **30**
**Platter,** 11" oval, California Provincial patt. ........ **52**
**Platter,** 13" l., Provincial Rose patt. .................. **40**
**Platter,** 13 1/4" l., oval, California Ivy patt. ......... **38**
**Platter,** 13 1/2" oval, California Provincial patt. ............................................. **35**
**Platter,** 14 1/4" oval, Antique Grape patt., Traditional shape ............................................. **38**
**Salt & pepper shakers,** Antique Grape patt., Traditional shape, pr. ............................... **18**
**Salt shaker & pepper mill,** California Provincial patt., green, pr. ............................... **65**
**Soup tureen,** cover & ladle, Red Rooster patt., Provincial shape, 3 pcs. ...................... **440**
**Sugar bowl,** cov., Antique Grape patt., Traditional shape ............................................. **20**
**Sugar bowl,** cov., Sculptured Grape patt., Traditional shape ............................................. **22**
**Sugar bowl,** cov., Vernonware, Della Robbia shape ............................................. **20**
**Teapot,** cov., Red Rooster patt., Provincial shape, 42 oz., 7-cup ............................................. **110**
**Vegetable bowl,** cov., Antique Grape patt., Traditional shape, 1 qt. ............................... **50**
**Vegetable bowl,** cov., Antique Grape patt., Traditional shape, 2 qt. ............................... **65**
**Vegetable bowl,** cov., California Ivy patt., 11" l. ............................................. **60**
**Vegetable bowl,** cov., Provincial Rose patt. ............................................. **70**
**Vegetable bowl,** open, Antique Grape patt., Traditional shape, 8 1/2" d. ............................... **32**
**Vegetable bowl,** open, divided, Antique Grape patt., Traditional shape, 8 1/2" d. ........ **30**
**Vegetable bowl,** open, Sculptured Grape patt., Traditional shape, 8 1/2" d. .................. **20**

**Vegetable bowl,** open, California Ivy patt.,
9" d. .................................................................. **30**
**Vegetable bowl,** open, divided, Antique
Grape patt., Traditional shape, 9 1/2" d. ........ **34**
**Vegetable bowl,** open, Sculptured Grape
patt., Traditional shape, 9 1/2" d. ................... **25**
**Vegetable bowl,** open, Vernonware, Della
Robbia shape, 10 5/8" d. ................................ **35**
**Vegetable bowl,** open, divided, Vernon-
ware, Della Robbia shape, 12 1/8" oval ......... **45**

# MOORCROFT

*William Moorcroft became a designer for James
Macintyre & Co. in 1897 and was put in charge of
their art pottery production. Moorcroft developed a
number of popular designs, including Florian Ware
while with Macintyre and continued with that firm
until 1913 when they discontinued the production of
art pottery.*

*After leaving Macintyre in 1913, Moorcroft set up
his own pottery in Burslem and continued producing the art wares he had designed earlier as well as
introducing new patterns. After William's death in
1945, the pottery was operated by his son, Walter.*

**MOORCROFT**

*Moorcroft Marks*

**Bowl,** 4" d., Dawn Landscape patt., stylized
design w/trees in matte blue glaze, artist-signed, impressed mark, ca. 1928 ........ **$345**

*Hibiscus Pattern Covered Bowl*

**Bowl,** cov., 5 1/2" d., 3 1/2" h., bulbous
body, button finial, Hibiscus patt., red &
yellow blossoms on dark blue ground,
incised "Made in England - Moorcroft" &
stamped label "#222 By Appointment W.
Moorcroft Potters to the Queen," artist-
initialed (ILLUS.) ......................................... **380**
**Ginger jar,** cov., Clematis patt., dark blue,
rose & yellow flowers & green leaves on
cobalt blue ground, incised stamp "Made
in England," 6" h. (ILLUS. top next col-
umn) ............................................................. **870**
**Vase,** 4" h., deep blue ground decorated
w/purple plums, grapes & green leaves ....... **220**

**Vase,** 4 1/8" h., footed bulbous ovoid body
tapering to rolled rim, Poppy patt., red
blossom, green leaves on cobalt blue
shading to green ground, cobalt blue
interior, incised "Made in England - Pot-
ters H.M. Queen" in blue ............................. **200**

*Clematis Pattern Ginger Jar*

*Blackberry Pattern Vase*

**Vase,** 6 1/8" h., footed baluster form
w/flared rim, Blackberry patt., purple &
red fruit & leaves on shaded dark & light
blue & green ground, cobalt blue interior,
incised "Made in England - Potter to the
Queen" (ILLUS.) ........................................... **340**
**Vase,** 6 1/4" h., 3 1/2" d., baluster-form
w/widely flaring rim, Pansy patt., large
red & purple blossoms & yellow leaves
on a dark blue ground, fitted into a hammered pewter footed base marked
"Made In England - Tudric - Moorcroft -
01516 - Made By Liberty & Co." ................... **880**
**Vase,** 6 3/4" h., 3" d., slender baluster-form
w/short flared neck, decorated overall
w/clusters of blue & pink flowers & green
leaves on a white ground, Macintyre
stamp, Moorcroft signature ....................... **1,980**
**Vase,** 7 1/4" h., footed bulbous ovoid body
tapering to flared neck, Poppy patt., red
& white blossoms & green leaves on
dark blue ground, printed mark "Made in
England," artist-initialed (ILLUS. top next
page) .......................................................... **700**

*Poppy Pattern Vase*

# NEWCOMB COLLEGE POTTERY

*This pottery was established in the art department of Newcomb College, New Orleans, Louisiana, in 1897. Each piece was hand-thrown and bore the potter's mark & decorator's monogram on the base. It was always a studio business and never operated as a factory and its pieces are therefore scarce, with the early wares being eagerly sought. The pottery closed in 1940.*

*Newcomb College Pottery Mark*

**Bowl,** 7" d., 2 1/2" h., footed wide squatty bulbous form w/a wide flat mouth, the shoulder decorated w/pairs of large pink blossoms w/yellow centers joined by slender green leaves all against a dark blue ground, matte glaze, impressed mark, "H. Bailey - #IZ31" ............................ **$990**

*Early Newcomb College Bowl*

**Bowl,** 8 1/2" d., 3 1/4" h., low round body w/incurved sides & narrow flat rim, incised stylized white & yellow blossoms on a glossy cobalt & green ground, by Henrietta Bailey, 1904, two hairlines at rim, impressed "NC - HB - ZZ74" (ILLUS.).................................................. **4,950**

**Bowl-vase,** footed squatty round bulbous body incised around top w/a band of white & yellow roses on a bluish green ground, by Henrietta Bailey, 1914, impressed "NC - HB - GT32 - JM - 256" 31/4 x 6 1/4" ..................................... **1,870**

**Bowl-vase,** bulbous body w/deeply-colored landscape scene of a live oak w/Spanish moss w/full moon in background, by Sadie Irvine, ca. 1932, impressed "NC - SI - KS - UB46," 5 1/2" d., 3 3/4" h. .......... **2,090**

**Bowl-vase,** squatty bulbous body w/short cylindrical neck, decorated w/light blue & yellow daffodils on a faded blue ground, by Sadie Irvine, ca. 1922, impressed "NC - SI - JM - MI38 - 212," 7" d., 4 1/4" h. ...................................................... **1,980**

**Mug,** slightly tapering waisted form w/loop handle, decorated w/a wide upper band of stylized landscape in bluish green above a wide blue-washed lower band, glossy glaze, painted by Desiree Roman & Marie Delavigne, 1901, impressed "NC - DR - MD - G73X - Q - JM," 5" w., 4" h............................................................ **3,575**

**Pitcher,** 5" h., 4 1/2" d., gently flaring cylindrical body w/a pinched rim spout & loop handle, decorated w/an upper band in the Espanol geometric patt., on a dark blue matte ground, impressed "207" ......... **1,320**

**Pitcher,** cov., milk, 5 1/4" h., cylindrical body w/pinched spout, flat inset lid & button finial, large loop handle, the top decorated w/a band of incised stylized blossoms in orange, dark blue & bluish green against a light blue ground, orange spout, rim & narrow band on lid, decorated by Charlotte Payne, 1905, impressed "NC - CP - AT44" ................... **3,850**

**Pitcher,** 8" h., 6" d., tall ovoid tapering to a short waisted neck w/angled handle from rim to shoulder, decorated around the neck w/a carved band of pink nasturium blossoms & green leaves on a matte dark blue ground, by Sadie Irvine, 1924, incised "NC - SI - 230 - OB65" ........ **2,310**

*Early Newcomb College Vase*

**Vase,** 4 1/4" h., 4 1/2" d., footed squatty bulbous body, the wide shoulder tapering to cylindrical neck w/flat rim, decorated w/h.p. yellow sunflower petals & blue seeds, outlined in blue, on ivory ground, by S. Massegali, artist-signed & impressed "NC - P," stilt pull to base (ILLUS.) ..................................................... **4,950**

**Vase,** 4 1/2" h., 2 1/2" d., bud-type, waisted cylindrical form decorated up the sides w/sprigs of wide flowers & green long leaves on a bluish green ground, by Henrietta Bailey, 1915, impressed "NC - KB82 - HB - 212" ........................................ **1,870**

**Vase,** 5 1/4" h., bulbous ovoid form w/flat rim, incised w/yellow daisies on an ivory & light blue ground, by Desiree Roman, 1903, impressed "NC - D.R. - JM - Q - JJ79," (two tight hairlines to rim) .............. **7,150**

*Newcomb College Vase w/Sailboats*

**Vase,** 5 3/4" h., 5 3/4" d., wide expanding cylindrical body w/flat rim, carved & decorated w/a continuous band of blue sailboats w/clouds in background, glossy blue, white & green glaze, decorated by Desiree Roman, ca. 1903, impressed "NC - W - D.R. - X37 -JM" (ILLUS.) ........ **13,750**

**Vase,** 6" h., bulbous body tapering to wide cylindrical neck w/closed rim, decorated w/light blue irises w/green leaves on faded blue ground, by C. Chalaron, ca. 1925, impressed "NC - JM - 26ON33 - CMC" .......................................................... **2,420**

**Vase,** 6" h., footed cylindrical body tapering above a shoulder to a flat molded rim, incised decoration of cotton plants in white on a light blue ground w/blue band around base & rim, by Mazie T. Ryan, 1904, impressed "NC - JM - MTRyan, 1904 - NN1" ................................................ **6,325**

**Vase,** 6" h., hand-thrown, a wide three-lobed lip on the wide cylindrical neck w/carved vertical fine ribs above the wide squatty bulbous lower body, brown clay body decorated w/pale blue interior & white thick drippy glaze down the sides, incised "NC - HB - M," by L. Nicholson ...................................................... **880**

**Vase,** 6" h., slightly swelled cylindrical form tapering slightly to a short cylindrical neck, carved & painted around the shoulder w/large light blue flowers w/ivory & green centers & green leaves against a dark blue matte ground, impressed mark, "#OY14 - #19 -Sadie Irvine" ....................................................... **1,320**

**Vase,** 6" h., 3 1/4" d., simple ovoid form w/a tapering neck & flattened rim, crisply modeled w/a landscape of live oak trees & Spanish moss in shades of dark & light blue w/pale green, by Anna F. Simpson, 1930, matte glaze, impressed "NC - AFS - JH -78 - SG85" ..................................... **4,400**

# NILOAK POTTERY

*This pottery was made in Benton, Arkansas and featured hand-thrown varicolored swirled clay decoration in objects of classic forms. Designated Mission Ware, this line is the most desirable of Niloak's production which was begun early in this century. Less expensive to produce, the cast Hywood Line, finished with either high gloss or semi-matte glazes, was introduced during the economic depression of the 1930s. The pottery ceased operation about 1946.*

## Niloak

*Niloak Pottery Mark*

**Ashtray/match holder,** Mission Ware, shallow round form w/rim rests centered by cylindrical match holder, swirled brown, orange & cream clays, paper label, 2 1/4 x 4 3/4" .................................... **$440**

**Bowl-vase,** Mission Ware, wide flat-bottomed form w/rounded bottom & tapering cylindrical sides to the wide flat mouth, dark brown, beige & dark terra cotta swirled clays, stamped mark, 8" d., 6" h. ...................................................... **440**

**Candlesticks,** Mission Ware, widely flaring funnel base tapering to a molded cylindrical shaft topped by a wide cupped socket, swirled brown, blue, terra cotta & sand clays, stamped mark, 5" d., 8" h., pr. ...................................... **330**

**Chamber pot,** child's, Mission Ware, footed squatty bulbous form w/wide flared rim & C-form handle, swirled cream & brown clays, 5 1/2" d. ................... **550**

**Chamberstick,** Mission Ware, flaring base w/loop handle, swirled tan, brown, orange & cream clays, 4 1/2" h. .................. **253**

**Cigarette jar,** cov., Mission Ware, cylindrical w/inset lid & bud finial, swirled blue, cream & brown clays, 4 3/4" h. ...................... **825**

**Compote,** open, Mission Ware, flared foot, shallow, round w/incurved sides & rim, swirled grey, tan, orange & cream clays, 5" h., 10" d. .............................................. **825**

**Decanter w/original stopper,** Mission Ware, swirled tan, orange, grey & cream clays, 10 1/2" h. (chips to top of decanter) .......................................................... **880**

**Figurine,** Southern Belle, Hywood Line, standing, wearing hat, pink & aqua matte glaze, 7" h. ................................................... **110**

**Flower bowl,** Mission Ware, squatty bulbous body w/center opening & pierced rim, swirled brown, cream & orange clays, 3 x 5 1/2" (one line, probably in making) ............................................................ **198**

**Flower frogs,** Mission Ware, round, swirled multicolored clays, largest 4 1/2" w., set of 3 (ILLUS. front, top nxet page) .......................................................... **121**

**Flowerpot w/undertray,** Mission Ware, expanding cylindrical form w/flat rim, hole in bottom for drainage, swirled

brown, tan, grey & cream clays, 9" d.,
10" h. .......................................................... **1,045**

*Niloak Flower Frogs & Umbrella Stand*

**Humidor,** cov., Mission Ware, wide
waisted cylinder w/inset lid & large round
flat finial, swirled cream, tan & light
brown clays, 6 1/2" h. ............................... **1,430**

**Jardiniere,** Mission Ware, bulbous ovoid
w/collared rim, swirled brown clays,
10" h. ........................................................ **1,210**

**Model of dog,** bulldog w/collar, Hywood
Line, red matte glaze, 4" h. ......................... **110**

**Mug,** Mission Ware, cylindrical w/C-form
handle, swirled multicolored clays, 5" h. ...... **253**

**Mugs,** Mission Ware, tapering cylindrical
form w/C-form handles, swirled light &
dark brown clays, patent pending mark,
4" h., set of 6 ............................................. **990**

**Necklace,** Mission Ware, alternating small
& tiny stones suspending a pendent consisting of a group of long & round swirled
light clay stones, 18" l. ............................... **825**

**Pedestal base,** Mission Ware, short wide
waisted cylindrical form, swirled cream,
tan, brown & grey clays, 7" h. (bruise to
bottom) ...................................................... **358**

**Pitcher,** 9" h., Hywood Line, footed spherical body w/relief-molded circles, C-form
shoulder handle opposite collared rim
w/pointed spout, blue & mustard matte
glaze .......................................................... **99**

**Pitcher,** 9" h., Mission Ware, bulbous ovoid
body w/flaring rim & C-form handle,
swirled grey, tan, brown, orange &
cream clays, paper label ........................... **1,045**

**Pitcher,** 11" h., Mission Ware, tall slender
ovoid body w/rim spout & rim turned up
above large C-form handle, large swirls
of brown, tan, cream & grey clays ............. **1,320**

**Powder bowl,** cov., Mission Ware, footed
bulbous body, flat inset lid w/small button finial, swirled grey, tan & cream
clays, 6" w., 3 1/2" h. ................................. **523**

**Punch bowl,** Mission Ware, pedestal foot,
deep rounded sides w/molded rim,

swirled cream, tan & brown clays, 13" d.,
9" h. .......................................................... **2,640**

**Shot glasses,** Mission Ware, tapering
cylindrical form, swirled multicolored
clays, 2 1/4" h., set of 6 (one chip) .............. **468**

**Tankard set:** Mission Ware, cylindrical
10 1/2" h. tankard & twelve 2" h. cylindrical mugs; tan pitcher w/zig-zag swirls in
cream & brown, multicolored swirled
mugs, pitcher w/hairline, two mugs
w/flaws, the set ......................................... **1,760**

**Tray,** Mission Ware, round w/straight sides,
swirled orange, cream, grey & brown
clays, 13" d. ............................................... **1,045**

**Umbrella stand,** Mission Ware, wide cylindrical body w/flared foot & rim, swirled
multicolored clays, 20" h. (firing crack in
base) ......................................................... **2,310**

**Umbrella stand,** Mission Ware, cylindrical
w/flared foot & rim, swirled cream, tan,
blue & brown clays, crack to base, 21" h.
(ILLUS. w/flower frogs) .............................. **1,650**

**Vase,** 5 1/2" h., Mission Ware, cylindrical,
swirled multicolored clays ........................... **132**

**Vase,** 5 3/4" h., 7" d., Mission Ware,
squatty spherical form w/closed rim,
swirled brown, blue, terra cotta & sand
clays, stamped mark & paper label ............. **248**

**Vase,** 7" h., Mission Ware, fan-type, swirled
orange, grey, blue & cream clays................ **319**

**Vase,** bud, 7" h., Mission Ware, flared base
tapering to slender cylinder w/flat rim,
swirled multicolored clays ........................... **154**

**Vase,** 8 1/2" h., 4 1/2" d., Mission Ware, tall
trumpet-form body on a flaring disk foot,
swirled brown, blue & terra cotta clays,
stamped mark ............................................ **165**

**Vase,** 9 1/2" h., 5" d., Mission Ware, baluster-form w/short flared neck, banded
swirls of brown, blue, terra cotta & sand
clays, stamped mark ................................... **303**

**Vase,** 9 1/2" h., 5 1/2" d., Mission Ware,
footed bulbous base tapering to a tall
wide trumpet neck, swirled brown, blue,
terra cotta & purple clays, stamped mark..... **358**

**Vase,** 9 3/4" h., 4 3/4" d., Mission Ware,
footed elongated pear-form body tapering to a short cylindrical neck w/flattened
flaring rim, swirled brown, blue, terra
cotta & sand clays, stamped mark .............. **385**

**Vase,** 10" h., 4 1/2" d., Mission Ware, tall
corseted form, brown, blue & terra cotta
swirled clays, stamped mark ....................... **220**

**Vase,** 10" h., 4 1/2" d., Mission Ware, tall
cylindrical body w/flaring foot, swirled
brown, blue & reddish terra cotta clays,
stamped mark & paper label ....................... **385**

**Vase,** 12" h., 7 1/2' d., Mission Ware, tall
ovoid body tapering to a short flaring
neck, finely swirled brown, ivory & terra
cotta clays, stamped mark & paper label ..... **495**

**Vase,** 12 1/4" d., 5 1/2" d., Mission Ware,
tall slender corseted form, swirled
brown, blue, terra cotta & purple clays,
stamped mark ............................................ **330**

**Vase,** 14" h., 7" d., Mission Ware, tall
footed swelled cylindrical form w/a narrow shoulder tapering to a thick molded
rim, finely swirled brown, blue, terra

cotta & purple clays, stamped mark & paper label .................................................. **880**

**Wall pocket,** Mission Ware, conical w/flat rim, swirled brown, orange, grey & cream clays, paper label, 7 1/2" l. ................ **440**

**Whiskey jug,** Mission Ware, four-sided centered by cylindrical neck w/molded rim, wide shoulder w/loop handle, swirled blue, grey & cream clays, 6" h. ..... **2,750**

# NIPPON

*"Nippon" is a term which is used to describe a wide range of porcelain wares produced in Japan from the late 19th century until about 1921. It was in 1891 that the U.S. implemented the McKinley Tariff Act which required that all wares exported to the United States carry a marking indicating the country of origin. The Japanese chose to use "Nippon," their name for Japan. In 1921 the import laws were revised and the words "Made in" had to be added to the markings. Japan was also required to replace the "Nippon" with the English name "Japan" on all wares sent to the U.S.*

*Many Japanese factories produced Nippon porcelains and much of it was hand-painted with ornate floral or landscape decoration and heavy gold decoration, applied beading and slip-trailed designs referred to as "moriage." We indicate the specific marking used on a piece, when known, at the end of each listing below. Be aware that a number of Nippon markings have been reproduced and used on new porcelain wares.*

*Important reference books on Nippon include: The Collector's Encyclopedia of Nippon Porcelain, Series One through Three, by Joan F. Van Patten (Collector Books, Paducah, Kentucky) and The Wonderful World of Nippon Porcelain, 1891-1921 by Kathy Wojciechowski (Schiffer Publishing, Ltd., Atglen, Pennsylvania).*

*Rare Nippon Tapestry Basket*

**Basket,** "tapestry," moon-shaped, flattened round form w/a large kidney-shaped opening for the handle, on a flat gold base, decorated w/an autumnal landscape w/swans on a lake, 9" h., blue "Maple Leaf" mark (ILLUS.)...................... **$1,870**

**Celery dishes,** long oval form w/end handles pierced in the form of a Native American chieftain's head, the interior painted w/a lakeside landscape at sun-

set, 8 1/4" l., pr. (green "M" in Wreath mark) ...................................................... **104**

*Nippon Scenic Chamberstick*

**Chamberstick,** saucer-form base decorated w/scene of house by lake w/trees & mountains, natural colors, 4 1/4" d., 2" h., green "M" in Wreath mark (ILLUS.) ..... **125**

**Charger,** round, "tapestry," a fine linen finish on a design of large pink roses & green leaves against a shaded tan ground, raised gold rim band, 12" d., blue "Maple Leaf" mark .......................... **2,640**

**Chocolate set:** cov. pot & five cups & saucers; cylindrical w/angled gold handles, each piece w/h.p. lakeside landscape scene w/tall slender leafy trees silhouetted in the foreground, the set (green "M" in Wreath mark) .................................... **173**

**Condiment set:** square form salt & pepper shakers, tapering square form cov. mustard jar & rectangular tray; all decorated w/h.p. dragon motif in green & gold w/gold handles & finial on mustard jar, 4 pcs........................................................................... **66**

**Humidor,** cov., hexagonal footed form w/inset domed cover & angular button finial, the sides decorated w/pairs of tall pale green & brown upright lily blossoms on stems w/brown leaf bands at the top & bottom, the blossoms dividing a background Egyptian river sunset scene w/sailing ships, matching brown bands on the cover, 6 1/2" h. (green "M" in Wreath mark) .............................................. **425**

*Nippon Wedgwood-style Loving Cup*

**Loving cup,** Wedgwood-style, deep tapering bowl on a flaring funnel foot, long loop handles at the sides, blue ground w/overall white slip decoration including bands of scrolls, Greek key and tall stems of flowers around the body,

5 1/2" h., green "M" in Wreath mark (ILLUS.) ...................... **303**

**Mug,** cylindrical w/incurved rim & angled gold handle, the center w/a wide red band & round reserve h.p. w/various gambling designs including dice & cards, against a dark charcoal mottled ground, 5" h. (green "M" in Wreath mark) ................. **144**

**Nut dish,** trefoil shape w/three handles, fine moriage decoration w/acorns, 7" d. (green "M" in Wreath mark) ......................... **110**

**Plaque,** pierced to hang, round, h.p. green leafy branches w/small red berries across the top & lower border, a large bluish white moriage decorated bird perched on the upper branch, 7 3/4" d. (blue "Maple Leaf" mark) .............................. **86**

**Plaque,** pierced to hang, round, h.p. desert scene w/three men on camels near an oasis, shaded deep rose to lavender ground w/purple mountains in the distance, beaded rim, 9" d. (green "M" in Wreath mark) ............................................. **150**

*Scenic Nippon Tapestry Vase*

**Vase,** 5" h., "tapestry," wide ovoid body tapering to a short flared neck flanked by small looped shoulder handles, decorated w/a wide h.p. central landscape scene in autumn colors, decorative gold bands around the neck & base, gold handles, green "Maple Leaf" mark (ILLUS.) ..................................................... **688**

**Vase,** 5 1/4" h., simple ovoid body w/a short upright scalloped mouth flanked by ornate scroll handles, the body h.p. w/large white apple blossoms & green leaves on a dark to light shaded blue ground, enameled rim & handles (blue "Sendai" mark) ............................................... **58**

**Vase,** 12" h., decorated w/colorful h.p. poppies on shaded matte brown ground, delicate slip-trailed decorated neck, handles & base ................................................ **265**

**Vase,** 12" h., pillow-style w/flattened ovoid body on a flared scrolling foot, wide rounded shoulders centered by a short flaring deeply ruffled neck, double loop gilt shoulder handles, decorated w/a central reserve showing a mountainous lakeside landscape w/a heavy gold border, ornate gilt scrolling w/turquoise jeweling above & below scene, gilt neck & foot bands & gilt handles, marked

"Hand-painted Morimura Nippon" (ILLUS. below) .............................................. **770**

*Nippon Pillow Vase with Landscape*

*Large Ornate Nippon Landscape Vase*

**Vase,** 17 1/2" h., tall slender swelled cylindrical form tapering to a molded rim, a wide continuous finely painted mountainous landscape scene on a satin ground, cobalt blue rim & base bands heavily decorated w/gilt scrolling & turquoise jeweling, blue "Maple Leaf" mark (ILLUS.) ................................................ **7,480**

**Vases,** 13 1/2" h., tall slender triangular baluster-form body w/a wide rounded shoulder centering a short widely flaring tricorner mouth, decorated overall w/large h.p. red roses among large heavy gold acanthus leaves, raised on short flaring spade-shaped feet, unmarked, pr. .............................................. **690**

**Wall plaque,** round, molded in relief w/lion & lioness in a rocky landscape, natural coloration, 10 1/2" d., green "M" in Wreath mark (ILLUS. top next page) .......... **440**

*Wall Plaque with Lions*

**Wall plaque,** round, molded in relief w/a scene of a Native American racing on horseback & pointing a rifle, natural coloration, 10 1/2" d., green "M" in Wreath mark ............................................................ 990

**Whiskey jug w/stopper,** wide square form w/slightly flaring sides below the wide rounded shoulder centered by a small cylindrical neck w/rim spout & angled handle, bulbous mushroom stopper, one side w/a valley landscape, other panels w/bands of stylized leafy scrolls on orangish brown against a cream ground, edges, shoulder & neck w/a black or orangish tan ground decorated w/stylized leafy scrolls & classical motifs, 7 1/2" h., green "M" in Wreath mark ............ 770

*Ornate Nippon Whiskey Jug*

**Whiskey jug w/stopper,** wide swelled cylindrical body w/a wide shoulder centered by a small cylindrical neck w/a spout & flared edges, angled handle, decorated w/bands of Egyptian designs on a white ground, gold handle & trim, w/advertising for E.M. Higgins Old Velvet, 6 1/2" h., green "M" in Wreath mark (ILLUS.) ......................................................... 825

# NORITAKE

*Noritake china, still in production in Japan, has been exported in large quantities to this country since early in this century. Though the Noritake Company first registered in 1904, it did not use "Noritake" as part of its backstamp until 1918. Interest in Noritake has escalated as collectors now seek out pieces made between the "Nippon" era and World War II (1921-41). The Azalea pattern is also popular with collectors.*

*Noritake Mark*

**Ashtray,** center Queen of Clubs decoration, 4" w. ..................................................... $40
**Ashtray,** center Indian head decoration, 5 1/2" w. ...................................................... 215
**Ashtray,** figural nude lady seated at edge of lustered flower form tray, 7" w. ................ 595

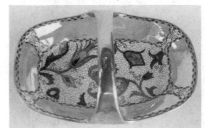

*Noritake Basket*

**Basket,** oblong w/center handle, gold lustre ground, interior w/center stylized floral decoration & geometric design in each corner & around rim, 7 3/4" l., 3" h. (ILLUS.) ......................................................... 80
**Basket,** Roseara patt. ..................................... 90
**Basket-bowl,** footed, petal-shaped rim, 6 1/2" w. ......................................................... 90
**Basket-vase** 7 1/2" h. ...................................... 110
**Berry set:** master bowl & 6 sauce dishes; decal & h.p. purple orchids, green leaves & pods decoration on green ground, 7 pcs. ...................................... 80
**Bonbon,** raised gold decoration, 6 1/4" w. ......... 25
**Bonbon dish,** Azalea patt. ............................... 40
**Bowl,** 6" sq., flanged rim w/pierced handles, orange lustre ground decorated w/h.p. scene w/large tree in foreground (ILLUS. top next page) .................................... 80
**Bowl,** 6 1/2" d., 2" h., fluted sides of alternating light & dark grey panels w/pointed rims, center w/Art Deco floral decoration (ILLUS. center left, next page) ..................... 155
**Bowl,** 8 3/4" d., 2" h., Art Deco style orange & white checkerboard ground decorated

w/stylized dark brown rose buds & leaves outlined in grey & grey stems .......... **175**

*Noritake Scenic Bowl*

*Art Deco Bowl*

**Bowl,** 9" d., footed, scenic interior decoration, lustre finish exterior ................................ **50**
**Bowl,** shell-shaped, three-footed, Tree in Meadow patt. ............................................... **295**
**Bowl,** soup, Azalea patt. .................................. **20**
**Butter dish, cover & drain insert,** Azalea patt., 3 pcs. .................................................. **85**
**Cake plate,** Sheridan patt., 9 3/4" d. ................. **25**

*Noritake Cake Plate*

**Cake plate,** rectangular, open-handled, turquoise border w/oval center Oriental scene on black ground, 10" l. (ILLUS.) ......... **110**
**Cake plate,** open-handled, Tree in Meadow patt. ................................................... **33**

**Cake set:** 10" d. handled master cake plate & 6 serving plates; fruit bowl medallions center, blue lustre rims, 7 pcs. ...................... **90**
**Cake set:** 14 x 6 1/4" oblong tray w/pierced handles & six 6 1/2" d. serving plates; white w/pale green & gold floral border, 7 pcs. ...................................................... **90**
**Candlesticks,** Indian motif decoration, 3 1/4" h., pr. ................................................. **110**
**Candy dish,** octagonal, Tree in Meadow patt. ....................................................... **365**
**Candy dish,** cov., figural bird finial, scalloped rim, blue lustre finish, 6 1/2 x 7 1/4" ........................................... **120**
**Celery set:** celery tray & 6 individual salt dips, decal & h.p. florals & butterflies decoration, 7 pcs. .................................... **85**
**Celery tray,** Azalea patt. ................................... **45**

*Figural Swan Cigarette Holder*

**Cigarette holder,** footed, figural swan, orange lustre w/black neck & head, black outlining on wing feathers & tail, 3" w., 4 1/2" h. (ILLUS.) ................................. **120**
**Cigarette holder,** bell-shaped w/bird finial, 5" h. ............................................................. **350**
**Cigarette holder/playing card holder,** pedestal foot, gold lustre ground decorated w/scene of golfer, 4" h. ...................... **275**

*Art Deco Style Cigarette Jar*

**Cigarette jar,** cov., bell-shaped cover w/bird finial, Art Deco style silhouetted scenic decoration of woman in chair & man standing, both holding cigarettes, 4 3/4" h., 3 1/2" d. (ILLUS.) .......................... **380**
**Coffee set:** cov. coffeepot, creamer, cov. sugar bowl & four cups & saucers; grey-

ish blue butterfly, pink florals & grey leaves decoration, 11 pcs. ........................... **225**

**Cologne bottle w/flower cluster stopper,** Art Deco man wearing checkered cape & lustered sides, 6 3/4" h. ........................... **295**

**Cologne bottle w/stopper,** two-handled, Art Deco lady decoration............................. **375**

*Noritake Condiment Set*

**Condiment set:** cov. mustard jar & pr. salt & pepper shakers on handled tray; blue lustre w/tops decorated w/flowers, 7" w. tray, the set (ILLUS.) .................................... **240**

*Noritake Cracker Jar*

**Cracker jar,** cov., footed spherical body decorated w/a black band w/white swords & shields design & center oval yellow medallion w/scene of white sail- boat on lake, white clouds in distance & blue stylized tree in foreground, black & white geometric design bands around rim & cover edge, orange lustre ground, 7" h. (ILLUS.)............................................... **250**

**Creamer,** Azalea patt. ......................................... **25**

**Creamer,** Tree in Meadow patt. .......................... **20**

**Creamer & cov. sugar bowl,** Azalea patt., pr. ....................................................................... **85**

**Creamer & cov. sugar bowl,** blue scenic decoration, brown borders, pr. ...................... **70**

*Art Deco Style Creamer & Sugar Bowl*

**Creamer & open sugar bowl,** Art Deco style checked decoration in black, blue, brown & white, orange lustre interior basket-shaped sugar bowl w/overhead handle, creamer 3" h., sugar bowl 4 1/2" h., pr. (ILLUS.) .................................... **110**

*Scenic Berry Creamer & Sugar Shaker*

**Creamer & sugar shaker,** berry set-type, decorated w/a scene of a gondola, orange lustre ground, pr. 6 1/2" h. (ILLUS.)............................................................. **75**

**Creamer & sugar shaker,** berry set-type, orange lustre interior, scenic decoration w/cottage, bridge & trees above floral cluster, blue lustre ground, 6 1/2" h., pr. ....... **80**

**Creamer & sugar shaker,** berry set-type, raised gold decoration, 5 3/4" h. creamer & 6 1/4" h. sugar shaker, pr............................ **80**

*Noritake Cruet Set*

**Cruet set w/original stoppers,** the two conjoined globular bottles set at angles & joined w/a handle at the shoulder, shaded orange lustre ground decorated w/green & yellow clover leaves & stems, 6" l., 3 1/2" h. (ILLUS.).................................... **125**

**Cruets,** conjoined oil & vinegar, Tree in Meadow patt..................................................... **295**

**Cup & saucer,** Azalea patt.................................. **20**

**Cup & saucer,** demitasse, Tree in Meadow patt. ................................................................... **35**

**Cup & saucer,** Tree in Meadow patt................. **15**

**Desk set:** heart-shaped tray w/pen rack at front & two cov. jars w/floral finials; decal & h.p. florals, 6 1/2" w. ................................. **275**

**Dinner bell,** figural Chinaman, 3 1/2" h. ........... **310**

**Dish,** blue lustre trim, 5" sq. .............................. **20**

**Dresser box,** cov., figural lady on lid, lustre finish, 5" h..................................................... **600**

**Figurine,** maiden carrying a bundle of sticks on her head ...................................... **140**

**Fish plates,** h.p. & decal w/h.p. center fish decoration, gold borders, 8 1/2" d., pr. ......... 110

**Flower holder,** model of bird on stump, base pierced w/four flower holes, 4 1/2" h. ........................................................ 95

*Art Deco Style Hair Receiver*

**Hair receiver,** cov., Art Deco style, geometric design on gold lustre ground, 3 1/2" d. (ILLUS.) .......................................... 160

**Humidor,** cov., playing cards decoration, figural dog finial, 5 1/4" h. ........................... 575

**Humidor,** cov., relief-molded & h.p. eagle decoration, 6 3/4" h. .................................... 600

**Humidor,** cov., model of an owl w/head as cover, lustre finish, 7" h. ............................. 750

**Humidor,** cov., relief-molded & h.p. horse head, 7" h. ................................................... 650

**Humidor,** cov., four panels of decal & h.p. yellow roses & black leaves on orange ground within h.p. black oval borders, 7 1/2" h. ....................................................... 450

**Inkwell,** model of an owl, Art Deco style, 3 1/2" h. ...................................................... 240

**Jam jar, cover & underplate,** melon-shaped, pink ground w/grey leaves, handle & leaf-shaped underplate, 5 3/4" l., 4 1/4" h., the set ......................................... 115

**Lemon plate,** Azalea patt. ................................ 35

**Lobster set:** sauce bowl, underplate & ladle; molded lotus form, petals w/highlights & lobster decoration on 10 3/4" d. underplate ...................................................... 195

**Marmalade jar, cover, underplate & ladle,** flower bud finial, 5 1/4" h. .................. 70

**Mayonnaise set,** Azalea patt., 3 pcs. ............... 45

**Night light,** figural lady, 9 1/4" h., 2 pc. ........ 2,000

**Nut bowl,** tri-lobed bowl w/figural squirrel seated at side eating nut, 7 1/2" w. .............. 120

**Nut bowl,** molded nut shell form w/three relief-molded nuts & side h.p. w/walnuts & green ferns decoration ............................... 75

**Plaque,** pierced to hang, silhouetted Art Deco style scene of woman in gown w/full ruffled skirt, sitting on couch & holding mirror, white lustre ground, 8 3/4" d. (ILLUS. top next column) .............. 325

**Plaque,** pierced to hang, relief-molded & h.p. double Indian portraits, 10 1/2" d. ...... 500

**Plate,** 6 1/2" d., Azalea patt. .............................. 12

**Plate,** 6 1/2" d., Tree in Meadow patt. ................ 16

**Plate,** 7 1/2" d., Azalea patt. .............................. 13

**Plate,** 8 1/2" d., Tree in Meadow patt. ................ 14

**Plate,** 9 1/2" d., pierced handles, gondolas decoration on orange shaded to yellow ground .......................................................... 45

**Plate,** dinner, Azalea patt. ................................... 35

**Platter,** 10" l., Tree in Meadow patt. ................ 100

*Scenic Noritake Plaque*

**Platter,** 14" l., Tree in Meadow patt. .................... 60

**Powder box,** cov., figural bird finial, 3 1/2" d. .................................................... 110

**Powder box,** cov., Art Deco decoration, 4" d. ............................................................ 550

**Powder box,** cov., figural Colonial lady forms cover, 6 1/2" h. ................................ 595

**Powder box,** cov., figural woman w/red hair finial ................................................... 450

**Powder puff box,** cov., disk-form, stylized floral decoration in red, blue, white & black on a white iridized ground w/blue lustre border, 4" d. ..................................... 195

**Relish dish,** Azalea patt., 8" l ........................... 25

**Ring holder,** model of a hand ............................ 40

**Salt & pepper shakers,** Tree in Meadow patt., pr. ................................................... 20

**Sauce dish,** Azalea patt. .................................... 15

**Shaving mug,** landscape scene w/tree, birds & moon decoration ................................ 65

**Smoke set:** handled tray, cigar & cigarette jars & match holder; cigars, cigarettes & matchsticks decoration, the set ................... 325

*Noritake Double Spoon Holder*

**Spoon holder,** double tray-form, oblong shape w/gold angular center handle, orange lustre interior, exterior decorated w/flowers & butterfly on black ground, 6 1/2" l., 2 1/2" h. (ILLUS.) ....................... 95

**Sugar bowl,** cov., Azalea patt. ........................... 60

**Sugar shaker,** lavender & gold decoration, blue lustre trim ...................................... 45

**Syrup jug,** Azalea patt. ...................................... 60

**Tea strainer w/footed rest,** cov., Azalea patt. decal & h.p. red roses & gold trim on green ground, 2 pcs. ............................. 85

**Toast rack,** two-slice, blue & yellow decoration .................................................... 60

**Tray,** pierced handles, decal & h.p. fruit border, lustre center, 11" w. ....................... 85

**Tray,** rectangular, pierced end handles, floral decoration on white ground, green edge trim w/brown trim on handles, 17 1/2" l. .......................................................... 95

*Scenic Noritake Vase*

**Vase,** 4 1/4" h., 5 1/4" d., footed bulbous body w/figural leaf & grape cluster handles, gold & blue lustre ground decorated w/scene of trees & children (ILLUS.)...................................................... 275
**Vase,** 5 1/2" h., orange & gold rim & handles, h.p. tree & cottage lakeside scene......................................................... 65
**Vase,** 5 1/2" h., two-handled, imitative of Wedgwood's jasper ware ............................ 110
**Vase,** 6 1/4" h., six-sided, scenic decoration ................................................................. 145

*Noritake Fan-shaped Vase*

**Vase,** 6 1/2" h., footed, fan-shaped, colorful Art Deco floral design on orange ground (ILLUS.)...................................................... 225
**Vase,** 7" h., fan-shaped w/ruffled rim, fruit & vines decoration, green & blue base.............. 70
**Vase,** 8" h., footed ovoid body w/squared rim handles, butterfly decoration on shaded & streaked blue & orange ground ......................................................... 195
**Vase,** 8 1/4" h., 5 1/4" d., footed ovoid body w/scalloped rim & scrolled rim handles, blue interior, exterior base w/blue, brown & black vertical lines on white, black band on upper body decorated w/stylized flowers in yellow, purple, brown & blue w/green & brown leaves (ILLUS. top next column) ........................................ 550
**Vase,** 8 1/4" h., Indian motif & lustre decoration ......................................................... 130
**Vase,** 8 1/2" h., ribbed body, ornate handles, decal & h.p. landscape scene decoration ......................................................... 190
**Vase,** 9" h., blackbirds decoration on yellow ground, pr...................................................... 125

*Stylized Noritake Vase*

**Vase,** 10 1/4" h., scenic decoration .................. 120
**Vegetable bowl,** open, round, Tree in Meadow patt.................................................... 45
**Vegetable dish,** cov., round, Azalea patt........... 90
**Wall pocket,** double, relief-molded floral cresting backplate, stylized florals & bird of paradise decoration, lustre border, 8" l. ................................................................. 160
**Wall pocket,** single, h.p. tree & cottage lakeside scene on blue lustered ground, 8" h. ................................................................ 110
**Waste bowl,** Azalea patt. .................................. 60

# OHR (GEORGE) POTTERY

*George Ohr, the eccentric potter of Biloxi, Mississippi, worked from about 1883 to 1906. Some think him to be one of the most expert throwers the craft will ever see. The majority of his works were hand-thrown, exceedingly thin-walled items, some of which have a crushed or folded appearance. He considered himself the foremost potter in the world and declined to sell much of his production, instead accumulating a great horde to leave as a legacy to his children. In 1972 this collection was purchased for resale by an antiques dealer.*

**GEO. E. OHR**
**BILOXI, MISS.**

*Ohr Pottery Marks*

**Bowl,** 3 1/2 x 7 1/2", footed, bisque-fired free-form shape assymetrically pinched & folded, red & ivory marbleized clay, incised signature (one chip to edge) ....... **$4,400**
**Bowl,** 4 3/4" d., 3 1/2" h., free-form collapsed body w/closed-in rim, covered in a speckled black & brown glaze, die-stamped "G.E. OHR - Biloxi, Miss."........... 2,530
**Bowl,** 5" d., 3" h., footed irregular rounded sides in pinched & folded bisque red scroddled clay, incised script signature (minute nick on one fold)........................... 2,310
**Bowl-vase,** footed squatty bulbous form w/the top sides heavily dimpled & folded toward the center, overall aventurine glaze, impressed "G.E. OHR - Biloxi, Miss.," 4" d., 3" h. ...................................... 2,310

**Bowl-vase,** footed oblong upright sides w/deeply pinched & folded sides, bisque scroddled clay, incised script signature, 6" w., 4" h. .................................................... **3,190**

**Chamberstick,** a round cushion base tapering to a short cylindrical stem w/a cupped socket, a low fanned handle on the base, mottled greenish brown glaze, impressed "GEO E OHR Biloxi," 3" h. .......... **460**

**Chamberstick,** wide footed domed bulbous base w/a deep in-body twist, tapering to a cylindrical neck w/flared rim, applied angular handle from the neck to the base, gunmetal & green exterior glaze, matte ochre interior glaze, incised "G.E. OHR," 3 1/2" d., 4" h. ...................... **2,310**

**Cup,** footed deep gently flaring sides w/deep vertical dimples, small applied loop handle, glossy green & purple exterior glaze, matte red interior, original price tag on bottom, marked in black glaze "LG606," 4 3/4" d., 3" h. ................... **2,860**

**Mug,** footed bulbous angled ovoid body w/a squared tab handle pierced w/three openings, brown gunmetal glaze, impressed "G.E. OHR. - Biloxi, Miss.," 5 1/4" w., 3 1/2" h. ..................................... **2,090**

**Mug,** Joe Jefferson-type, cylindrical form w/pinched handle, covered in an unusual salmon pink & green glossy glaze, inscribed "Hers (sic) your good health and all your family's - may they all live long and prosper - J.Jefferson," die-stamped "G.E. OHR - Biloxi, Miss. - 8-18-1896," 4" h. ........................................... **1,210**

**Pitcher,** 6 1/2" h., 4" d., footed bulbous base below a double-funnel form body w/tapering sides below the tall flaring neck w/pinched rim spout, applied looped strap handle, bright pink, green, red & white sponged matte glaze, impressed "G.E.OHR - Biloxi, Miss." ......... **7,700**

**Pitcher,** puzzle-type, 6 1/2" h., 5 3/4" d., wide globular body incised w/a branch & medallion design, gently tapering shoulder above incised band, tall slender cylindrical neck w/flat rim, textured twig-shaped handle from center of neck to base, covered w/speckled glossy ocher & mahogany glazes, impressed "GEO. E. OHR - BILOXI. MISS." ......................... **2,530**

*Large Ohr Pitcher*

**Pitcher,** 10" h., 7" d., footed tapering ovoid dimpled body w/a folded side & single looped ribbon handle, red, pink, cobalt blue, green, yellow & white sponged glaze, one chip & several minor nicks at rim, one small base chip, impressed "G.E. Ohr - Biloxi, Miss." & script signature (ILLUS.)............................................. **44,000**

**Vase,** 3" h., 4" d., footed squatty bulbous compressed base, the sides tapering sharply to a wide cylindrical neck w/flat rim, covered in indigo & green sponged pattern on a raspberry ground, overglazed in white, die-stamped "GEO. E. OHR - BILOXI, MISS." ............................. **1,870**

**Vase,** 4" h., 2 3/4" d., footed tapering cylindrical body w/rounded base, molded rings at neck, covered in a fine & unusual sponged raspberry, red & black matte & glossy glaze, die-stamped " G.E. OHR - Biloxi, Miss" ........................... **2,090**

**Vase,** 4" h., 3 1/4" d., footed, bulbous base w/pinched & folded rim, covered in fine & unusual sponged cobalt, raspberry, ochre & green glossy glaze, die-stamped "G.E. OHR - Biloxi, Miss" (two glaze flecks to rim) .................................... **2,970**

**Vase,** 4" h., 4 1/4" d., tapering cylindrical form w/flat flared rim w/an inset four-sided top w/pinched corners, covered in a marbleized brown & yellow glossy glaze, die-stamped "G.E. OHR - BILOXI, MISS." ....................................................... **2,970**

**Vase,** 4 1/4" h., round footing below the spherical body tapering to an upright pinched & folded cross-shaped rim, bisque scroddled clay, incised script signature ....................................................... **1,100**

**Vase,** 5" h., 5 1/4" d., footed squatty bulbous lower body below the tall flaring neck pinched in the center to form two folded lobes, two incised lines around the shoulder, bisque scroddled clay, incised script signature (few minor flakes at rim) ....................................................... **2,090**

**Vase,** 5 1/2" h., 3 1/2" d., ovoid body below a slightly flaring neck w/an exaggerated labial rim, green & gunmetal mottled glaze, unusual script signature w/"Biloxi" (restoration to stilt pulls at base) .............. **1,650**

**Vase,** 6" h., flared foot below bulbous base w/deep in-body twists at shoulder, tapering to wide cylindrical neck, covered in limpid mirrored mahogany speckled glaze, die-stamped "G.E. OHR - Biloxi, Miss" ........................................................ **2,090**

**Vase,** 6" h., 4" d., footed ovoid body tapering to a wide short cylindrical neck w/a tightly crimped upright rim, raspberry, green, blue & grey sponged glaze, stamped "G.E. OHR - Biloxi, Miss." (touch-ups to nick on two rim tips) ............ **4,400**

**Vase,** 6 1/4" h., 5 1/2" d., footed wide bulbous body w/deep in-body twist near wide flaring rim, covered in a speckled gunmetal & khaki glaze, stamped "G.E. OHR - Biloxi, Miss." ................................... **1,980**

*Ohr Pinched Neck Vase*

**Vase,** 6 3/4" h., bulbous base w/tall upright tightly pinched neck, covered in a brown & caramel marbleized glossy glaze, die-stamped "G.E. OHR - Biloxi, Miss." (ILLUS.)..................................................... **2,200**

# OLD IVORY

*Old Ivory china was produced in Silesia, Germany, in the late 1800s and takes its name from the soft white background coloring. A wide range of table pieces was made with the various patterns usually identified by a number rather than a name.*

*The following prices are averages for Old Ivory at this time. Rare patterns will command higher prices and there is some variance in prices geographically. These prices are also based on the item being perfect. Cups are measured across the top opening.*

**Basket,** handled, No. U2, Deco patt.............. **$400**
**Berry set:** 10 1/2" d. master bowl & six small berries; No. 15, Clairon patt., the set ............................................................ **285**
**Berry set:** 9 1/2" master bowl & six small berries; No. 84, Empire patt., the set .......... **250**
**Bonbon,** inside handle, No. 62, Florette patt., rare, 6" l. ...................................... **450**
**Bone dish,** No. 16, Worcester patt., rare ........ **400**
**Bouillon cup & saucer,** No. 16, Clairon patt., 3 1/2" d. ............................................. **250**
**Bowl,** 5 1/2" d., No. 7, Clairon patt. .................... **45**
**Bowl,** 6 1/2" d., No. 22, Clairon patt. ............... **100**
**Bowl,** 9" d., No. 34, Empire patt. ...................... **150**
**Bowl,** 9" d., No. 69, Florette patt. .................... **200**
**Bowl,** 10" d., No. 11, Clairon patt. .................... **125**
**Bowl,** 10" d., No. 16, Clairon patt. .................... **125**

*Old Ivory Bun Tray*

**Bun tray,** oval w/open handles, No. 122, Alice patt., 10" l. (ILLUS.) ............................ **300**
**Butter pat,** No. 15, Mignon patt., 3 1/4" d. ...... **150**
**Cake plate,** open-handled, No. 200, Deco patt., 9 1/2" h. ............................................. **125**
**Cake plate,** tab-handled, No. U15, Florette patt., 9 1/2" d. .......................................... **185**
**Cake plate,** open-handled, No. 10, Clairon patt., 10 1/2" d. .......................................... **150**
**Cake plate,** open-handled, No. 17, Clairon patt., 10 1/2" d. .......................................... **400**
**Cake plate,** tab-handled, No. 137, Rivoli patt., 10 1/2" d. .......................................... **185**
**Cake plate,** tab-handled, No. 57, Florette, 10 1/2" d. ................................................... **195**

*Florette Cake Plate*

**Cake plate,** tab-handled, No. 75, Florette patt. (ILLUS.) ......................................... **250-300**
**Cake set:** 10 1/2" d. cake plate & six small serving plates; No. 69, Florette patt., the set ................................................................ **450**
**Celery dish,** No. 28, Clairon patt., 11 1/4" l. ..... **150**
**Center bowl,** No. 84, Deco Variant patt., 12 1/2" d. .................................................... **500**
**Charger,** No. 16, Clairon patt., 13" d. .............. **300**
**Charger,** No. 44, Florette patt. ................. **500-650**
**Chocolate pot,** cov., No. 44, Florette patt., rare, 9 1/2" h. ........................................ **600-700**
**Chocolate set:** 9 1/2" h. cov. pot & six cups & saucers; No. 53, Empire patt., rare, the set ............................................. **1,500**
**Chocolate set:** 9 1/2" h. cov. pot & six cups & saucers; No. 75, Empire patt., the set .......................................................... **900**
**Chowder cup & saucer,** No. U29, Eglan-tine patt., 4" d. ......................................... **300**
**Cider cup & saucer,** No. 16, Clairon patt., 3" d. ......................................................... **150**
**Coffeepot,** cov., No. 84, Deco variant patt., 9" h. ....................................................... **1,200**
**Coffeepot,** cov., demitasse, No. 123, Empire patt. (ILLUS. top next page) ...... **500-650**
**Compote,** 9" d., open, No. U11, Alice patt., rare ........................................................... **600**
**Cracker jar,** cov., No. 33, Empire patt., 5 1/2" h. ..................................................... **500**
**Cracker jar,** cov., No. 39, Empire patt., very rare, 5 1/2" h. ..................................... **900**
**Cracker jar,** cov., No. 15, Clairon patt., 8 1/2" h. ..................................................... **500**
**Cracker jar,** No. 44, Florette patt. ......... **850-1,000**

*Empire Pattern Demitasse Coffeepot*

**Creamer & cov. sugar bowl,** No. 122,
Alice patt., pr. ................................................ 250
**Creamer & cov. sugar bowl,** No. 11,
Clairon patt., 5 1/2" h., pr. ........................... 175
**Creamer & cov. sugar bowl,** No. 202,
Deco patt., pr. ............................................... 185
**Creamer & cov. sugar bowl,** service size,
No. 84, Deco Variant patt., pr. ..................... 400
**Creamer & cov. sugar bowl,** service size,
No. U17, Eglantine patt., pr. ......................... 500
**Creamer & cov. sugar bowl,** No. 39,
Empire patt., rare, 3 1/2" & 5 1/2" h., pr. ...... 400
**Creamer & cov. sugar bowl,** No. 99,
Empire patt., rare, 5 1/2" h., pr. ................... 450

*Louis XVI Pattern Creamer & Sugar Bowl*

**Creamer & cov. sugar bowl,** No. 76, Louis
XVI patt., rare, pr. (ILLUS.) ................... 300-400
**Cup & saucer,** cov., bouillon-type, No. 73,
Alice patt., rare, 3 1/2" d. ............................. 350
**Cup & saucer,** No. U30, Alice variant w/Y
border ....................................................... 65-75
**Cup & saucer,** No. 16, Clairon patt.,
3 1/4" d. ......................................................... 75

*Clairon Pattern Cup & Saucer*

**Cup & saucer,** No. 90, Clairon patt.
(ILLUS.) ................................................... 75-95

**Cup & saucer,** No. 203, Deco patt.,
3 1/4" d. ......................................................... 95
**Cup & saucer,** No. 82, Empire patt. ............. 75-95
**Cup & saucer,** No. 84, Empire patt.,
3 1/4" d. ......................................................... 75
**Cup & saucer,** 5 o'clock-type, No. 28,
Empire patt., 3" d. ......................................... 85

*Florette Pattern Cup & Saucer*

**Cup & saucer,** No. 62, Florette patt.
(ILLUS.) ................................................. 150-250
**Demitasse cup & saucer,** No. 16, Clairon
patt., 2 1/2" d. .............................................. 125
**Demitasse cup & saucer,** No. 22, Clairon
patt., 2 1/2" d. .............................................. 200

*Deco Pattern Cup & Saucer & Teapot*

**Demitasse cup & saucer,** No. 75, Deco
Variant patt. (ILLUS. left) ...................... 125-140
**Demitasse cup & saucer,** No. 5, Elysee
patt., rare, 2 1/2" d. ...................................... 175
**Demitasse pot,** cov., No. 73, Clairon patt.,
7 1/2" h. ........................................................ 525
**Demitasse pot,** cov., No. 33, Empire patt.,
7 1/2" h. ........................................................ 500
**Demitasse pot,** cov., No. 62, Florette patt.,
very rare, 7 1/2" h. ..................................... 1,200
**Demitasse pot,** No. 44, Florette patt. ....... 800-900
**Dish,** tri-lobed, No. 202, Deco patt., 6" w. .......... 95
**Dish,** tri-lobed, No. 204, Rivoli patt., 6" w. ........ 175
**Dresser tray,** No. 90, Clairon patt.,
11 1/2" l. ...................................................... 250
**Dresser tray,** No. 34, Empire patt. ................. 250
**Egg cup,** No. 84, Eglantine patt., very rare,
2 1/2" h. ........................................................ 500
**Ice cream bowl,** No. 6, Eglantine patt.
(ILLUS. top next page) .......................... 300-400
**Jam dish,** individual, No. 28, Alice patt. ........... 150
**Jam jar,** cov., No. 137, Deco patt., 3 1/2" h. ...... 250
**Mayonnaise set,** No. 10, Empire patt.,
6 1/2" d., the set .......................................... 275
**Muffineer,** No. 73, Louis XVI patt., 4" h. .......... 485

*Eglantine Pattern Ice Cream Bowl*

*Louis XVI Muffineer & Salt & Peppers*

**Muffineer,** No. 84, Louis XVI patt. (ILLUS. left) ......................................... **350-450**

**Mustache cup & saucer,** No. 4, Elysee patt., 3 1/2" d. ....................................... **450**

**Mustard pot,** cov., No. 84, Carmen patt., 3 3/4" h. ........................................... **325**

**Olive dish,** No. 20, Florette patt., rare, 6 1/2" l. .............................................. **195**

**Pickle dish,** No. 32, Empire, 8 1/2" l. ................ **75**

**Pin tray,** No. U22, Eglantine patt. .................... **350**

*Acanthus Pattern Water Pitcher*

**Pitcher,** water, No. 84, Acanthus patt. (ILLUS.) ........................................... **1,000-1,200**

**Pitcher,** 8" h., water, No. 11, Acanthus patt. ................................................. **1,200**

**Plate,** 8 1/2" d., No. 60, Alice patt. ...................... **85**

**Plate,** 6 1/2" d., No. 10, Clairon patt. .................. **45**

**Plate,** 7 1/2" d., No. 12, Clairon patt. .................. **85**

**Plate,** 8 1/2" d., No. 8, Clairon patt. .................... **85**

**Plate,** 9 1/2" d., dinner, No. 21, Clairon patt., rare .......................................... **300**

**Plate,** 8 1/2" d., No. 200, Deco patt. ................... **75**

**Plate,** 7 1/2" d., No. 4, Elysee patt. ..................... **65**

**Plate,** 8 1/2" d., No. 15, Empire patt. ................... **75**

**Plate,** 8 1/2"d., No. 53, Empire patt. ................ **125**

**Plate,** 9 1/2" d., dinner, No. 40, Empire patt., rare ...................................... **300**

**Plates,** 6 1/4" d., No. 40, set of 5 ..................... **127**

**Platter,** 11 1/2" l., No. 22, Clairon patt. ............. **325**

**Platter,** 13 1/2" l., No. 75, Alice patt. ................ **300**

**Porringer,** No. 82, Empire patt., 6 1/4" d. ........ **175**

**Powder jar,** cov., No. U22, Eglantine patt., rare ............................................. **450**

**Ramekin & underplate,** No. 11, Quadrille patt., rare, 4 1/2" d., 2 pcs. ................... **500**

**Salt & pepper shakers,** No. 44, Florette patt. .......................................... **150-250**

**Salt & pepper shakers,** No. 15, Louis XVI patt., pr. (ILLUS. right) ..................... **100-125**

**Salt & pepper shakers,** No. 76, Louis XVI patt., 2 3/4" h., pr. .............................. **200**

**Shaving mug,** No. 22, Clairon patt., rare, 3 1/4" h. ......................................... **1,000**

**Soup tureen,** cov., No. 84, Deco Variant patt., rare, 13" l. ................................ **2,500**

**Spoon rest,** lay-down type, No. 204, Deco patt., 8 1/4" l. ..................................... **250**

**Spooner,** No. 40, Carmen patt., 4" h. .............. **400**

**Tazza,** No. U2, Rivoli patt., rare, 9" d. ............. **600**

**Tea cup & saucer,** No. 4, Elysee patt., 3 1/4" d. ......................................... **95**

**Tea tile,** No. 15, Alice patt., 6" sq. .................... **225**

**Teapot,** cov., No. 200, Deco patt., 8 1/2" l. ...... **500**

**Teapot,** cov., No. 75, Deco Variant patt. (ILLUS. right) ............................. **500-600**

**Toothpick holder,** No. 15, Clairon patt., 2 1/4" h. ........................................... **295**

**Vase,** 5" h., No. 134, Deco Variant patt. ........... **385**

**Vegetable dish,** cov., No. 15, Clairon patt., 10 1/2" l. ....................................... **1,000**

**Waste bowl,** No. 28, Worcester patt., 5" d. ...... **295**

# OWENS

*Owens Pottery Mark*

Owens pottery was the product of the J.B. Owens Pottery Company, which operated in Ohio from 1890 to 1929. In 1891 it located in Zanesville and produced art pottery from 1896, introducing "Utopian" wares as its first art pottery. The company switched to tile after 1907. Efforts to rebuild after the factory burned in 1928 failed and the company closed in 1929.

**Bowl,** 3 1/2 x 11", Aborigine line, rounded sides w/flat rim, tan earthenware w/dark brown stripes & light & brown zigzag lines, interior w/dark brown glaze, incised "JBO" & mark No. 10 .................... **$150**

**Ewer,** Utopian line, decorated w/yellow roses on a brown, green & amber ground, decorated by Sarah Timberlake, artist-initialed & impressed "Utopia, J.B. Owens, 181," minor crazing, 9 3/8" h. (ILLUS. top next page) ............... **303**

*Owens Ewer*

*Owens Alpine Line Humidor*

**Humidor,** cov., Alpine line, squatty bulbous body, cover w/molded rim & large domed finial, decorated w/h.p. scene of pipe & bag of tobacco, shaded brown ground, mark No. 13, 5 7/8" h.(ILLUS.)........ **750**

*Owens Art Nouveau Jardiniere*

**Jardiniere,** Art Nouveau line, footed, wide tapering cylindrical body w/flaring rim, under-glaze gold swirl decoration on dark brown ground, impressed "J.B. Owens" & "Art Nouveau," shape No. 1005, 7 1/2" h. (ILLUS.)................................ **350**
**Jardiniere,** Cyrano line, footed waisted cylindrical body, squeeze bag applied filigree designs & beading at rim, dark brown glossy ground, unmarked, 8 1/4" h. ........................................................ **350**
**Jardiniere,** Delft line, footed bulbous body w/slightly flaring rim, decorated w/typical Holland scene of a young girl & her mother standing near the water, a ship in the background, shaded blue ground, unmarked, 10 1/2" h. ................................... **750**

**Jug,** Aborigine line, squatty bulbous base tapering to cylindrical neck & loop handle, tan & brown earthenware exterior, incised "JBO," shape No. 31, 5 1/8" h. ........ **200**

*Corona Line Model of Dog*

**Model of a dog,** Whippet or Greyhound, sitting, wearing collar, glass eyes, shaded grey, Corona line, unmarked (ILLUS.)...................................................... **5,000**
**Model of a rabbit,** sitting animal w/raised ears, glass eyes, shaded grey & tan, Corona line, marked "Corona," shape No. 8873, 13 x 15".................................... **3,500**
**Mug,** Feroza line, cylindrical body w/C-form handle, molded uneven ground in iridescent deep red, shape No. 1108, 4 7/8" h. ..... **450**
**Pitcher,** Embossed Lotus line, tapering cylindrical form w/incurved rim, pinched spout & C-form handle, cream ground decorated w/embossed & slip-painted berries & leaves, marked "Lotus," shape No. X236, mark No. 10, 3" h. ...................... **250**

*Owens Feroza Line Pitcher*

**Pitcher,** tankard, 11 1/4" h., Feroza line, uneven molded ground w/mottled dark brownish iridescent finish, shape No. 1109 (ILLUS.).............................................. **850**
**Pitcher,** tankard, 17" h., Onyx line, tapering cylindrical form w/ringed base, long D-form angled handle, shape No. 819, mark No. 8................................................... **650**

**Teapot** cov., Lotus line, Aladdin-type, domed cover w/button finial, shaded green w/floral decoration in green, pink & white, marked "Owens" & "Denny," shape No. 1255, 3 1/4 x 7" ......................... **450**

**Vase,** 12 1/4" h., Alpine line, footed bulbous ovoid body w/trumpet-form neck, shaded brown w/free-hand overglaze white slip floral decoration, matte finish, artist-initialed, shape No. 1122, mark No. 13............................................................ **1,000**

**Vase,** 15 1/8" h., creamware, footed bulbous ovoid body tapering to slender cylindrical neck w/small bulbous top & flat rim, overall cream ground, shape No. 1126, mark No. 10........................................ **650**

**Vase,** 16 1/2" h., Lotus line, compressed bulbous base tapering to tall cylindrical body w/slightly tapering neck & closed rim, decorated w/irises in rose, pink, purple & yellow w/green leaves against an ivory, grey & peach ground, artist-signed, impressed mark (harmless glaze flaws to top) ............................................... **1,540**

**Wall pocket,** Green Ware line, cornucopia-shaped w/scalloped rim, decorated w/relief-molded flowers & ribbon, marked "Owensart," 11" l. ........................... **400**

# PENNSBURY POTTERY

*Pennsbury*
*Pottery*

*Pennsbury*
*Pottery*

*morrisville, Pa.*

### Pennsbury Pottery Marks

*Henry Below and his wife Lee founded the Pennsbury Pottery in Morrisville, Pennsylvania in 1950. The Belows chose the name because William Penn's home was nearby. Lee, a talented artist who designed the well-known Rooster pattern, almost the entire folk art designs and the Pennsylvania German blue and white hand-painted dinnerware, had been affiliated with Stangl Pottery of Trenton, New Jersey. Mr. Below had learned pottery making in Germany and became an expert in mold making and ceramic engineering. He, too, had been associated with Stangl Pottery and when he and Lee opened Pennsbury Pottery, several workers from Stangl joined the Belows. Mr. Below's death in 1959 was unexpected and Mrs. Below passed away in 1968 after a long illness. Pennsbury filed for bankruptcy in October, 1970. In 1971 the pottery was destroyed by fire.*

*During Pennsbury's production years, an earthenware with a high temperature firing was used. Most of the designs are a sgraffito-type similar to Stangl's products. The most popular coloring, a characteristic of Pennsbury, is the smear-type glaze of light brown after the sgraffito technique has been used. Birds are usually marked by hand and most often include the name of the bird. Dinnerware followed and then art pieces, ashtrays and*

*teapots. The first dinnerware line was Black Rooster followed by Red Rooster. There was also a line known as Blue Dowry which had the same decorations as the brown folk art pattern but the decorations were done in cobalt.*

**Canister,** cov., Black Rooster patt., w/black rooster finial, front reads "Flour," 9" h......... **$185**

### Rooster Cup & Saucer

**Cup & saucer,** Black Rooster patt., cup 2 1/2" h., saucer 4" d. (ILLUS.)...................... **55**

**Desk basket,** Two Women Under Tree patt., 5" h. ...................................................... **75**

**Model of chickadee,** head down, on irregular base, model no. 111, signed R.B., 3 1/2" h. ......................................................... **140**

**Mug,** beer-type, Barber Shop Quartet patt. ........ **35**

**Mug,** beer, Amish patt., dark brown rim & bottom w/dark brown applied handle, 5" h. ................................................................. **38**

### Commemorative Pie Plate

**Pie plate,** Dutch Haven commemorative, birds & heart in center, inscribed around the rim "When it comes to Shoo-Fly Pie - Grandma sure knew how - t'is the Kind of Dish she used - Dutch Haven does it now," 9" d. (ILLUS.)..................................... **125**

**Pitcher,** 5" h., Delft Toleware patt., fruit & leaves, white body w/fruit & leaves outlined in blue, blue inside ............................... **95**

**Pitcher,** 7 1/4" h., Amish patt. w/interlocked pretzels on reverse (ILLUS. top next page) .......................................................... **105**

**Plaque,** commemorative, "What Giffs, what ouches you?," reverse marked "NFB-

PWC Philadelphia, PA 1960," drilled for hanging, 4" d. (ILLUS. center this column) ............................................................. **30**

*Amish Pattern Pitcher*

*Commemorative Plaque*

*Plaque with Rooster*

**Plaque,** Rooster patt., "When the cock crows the night is all," drilled for hanging, 4" d. (ILLUS.) ................................................. **40**
**Plaque,** shows woman holding Pennsbury cookie jar, marked "It is Whole Empty," drilled for hanging, 4" d. ................................. **35**

*Plaque with Amish Couple Kissing*

**Plaque,** Amish man & woman kissing over cow, drilled for hanging, 8" d. (ILLUS.) ........... **87**
**Plate,** 6" d., Black Rooster patt. ......................... **25**

*Plate with Courting Buggy*

**Plate,** 8" d., Courting Buggy patt. (ILLUS.) ......... **75**

*Plate with Red Rooster Pattern*

**Plate,** 10" d., Red Rooster patt. (ILLUS.) ........... **48**
**Relish tray,** Black Rooster patt., five-section, each w/different scene, Christmas-tree shape, 14 1/2" l., 11" w ......................... **220**

*Donkey & Clown Wall Pocket*

**Wall pocket,** donkey & clown w/dark green
border, ivory center, 6 1/2" sq. .................... **105**

# PIERCE (HOWARD)
# PORCELAINS

Howard Pierce was born in Chicago, Illinois in 1912. He attended the university there and also the Chicago Art Institute but by 1935 he wanted a change and came to California. That move would alter his life forever. He settled in Claremont and attended the Pomona College. William Manker, a well-known ceramist, hired Mr. Pierce in 1936 to work for him. That liaison lasted about three years. After leaving Manker's employment Howard opened a small studio in Laverne, California and, not wishing to be in competition with Manker, began by creating miniature animal figures, some of which he made into jewelry. In 1941, he married Ellen Voorhees who was living in National City, California. In the 1950s, Mr. Pierce had national representation through the N.S. Gustin Company. Polyurethane animals are high on collectors lists as Howard, after creating in the early years only a few pieces using this material, realized he was allergic to it and had to discontinue its use. Pierce was a man of many talents and a great deal of curiosity. He experimented with various mediums such as a Wedgwood Jasper Ware type body, then went into porcelain bisque animals and plants that he put close to or in open areas of high-gloss vases. When Mt. St. Helens volcano erupted, Pierce was one of the first to experiment with adding the ash to his silica which produced a rough-textured glaze. Lava, while volcano associated, was a glaze treatment unrelated to Mt. St. Helens. Howard described Lava as "...bubbling up from the bottom..." Pierce also created some pieces in gold leaf which are harder to find than the gold treatment he formulated in the 1950s for Sears. They had ordered a large number of pieces and wanted all of them produced in the gold treatment. Many of these pieces are not marked. Howard also did what he termed 'tipping' in relation to glazes. A piece would be high-gloss overall but, then the tops, bottoms, sides, etc. would be brushed, speckled or mottled with a different glaze, most often brown, black or grey. For example, a set of three fish made in the late 1950s or early 1960s were on individual bases that were 'tipped' as were the fins with the bodies being a solid brown or black. Toward the late 1970s, Mr. Pierce began putting formula numbers on his pieces and recording the materials used to create certain glazes. In November 1992, because of health problems, Howard and Ellen Pierce destroyed all the molds they had created over the years. Mr. Pierce began working on a limited basis producing miniature versions of past porcelain wares. These pieces are simply stamped "Pierce." Howard Pierce passed away in February, 1994.

*Howard Pierce Ceramics Marks*

**Bowl,** 7 1/4" d., 4 1/4" h., fluted body flaring to a fluted rim, Manker influence, pale & deep blue w/black accents, incised mark, "Pierce 1983" in script ..................... **$100**

*Howard Pierce Bowl*

**Bowl,** 13" l., 2" h., free-form, black outside, speckled black & white inside, 1950s (ILLUS.) ......................................................... **75**
**Candleholders,** comma-shaped, high gloss grey glaze, 2 3/4" h., pr. ...................... **100**
**Figure group,** boy standing w/head bent & left arm extended to feed dog seated at his left side, nondescript mottled brown glaze, marked "Howard Pierce," 5" h. ............ **85**
**Figure group,** three monkeys stacked on top of one another, black, one-piece, Model No. 300P, 15" h. ................................. **275**

*Pierce Owls in a Tree*

**Figure group,** two owls in a tree, seated on branches, three open branches for small flowers, dull dark brown tree, light & dark brown owls, larger, unusual size for Pierce owls in tree, stamp mark "Howard Pierce," tree, 6" w., 13" h., large owl, 6" h., small owl, 3 1/2" h. (ILLUS.) .............. **240**

**Figure of native woman,** w/long body, short legs, arms behind her back, dark brown glaze w/mottled brown skirt, hard-to-find, 3 1/2" w., 16 1/2" h. .......................... **285**

**Figures of Hawaiian boy & girl,** overall black bodies w/green mottled pants on boy, green mottled grass skirt on girl, both w/hands in Hula dance position, 1950s, boy, 7" h., girl, 6 3/4" h., pr. .............. **185**

**Jug,** bulbous body w/small pouring spout & small finger hold, brown mottled rough-textured glaze, stamp mark "Howard Pierce," 5 3/4' h. ............................................. **110**

**Magnet,** model of a dinosaur, gloss grey glaze, 3" l., 1 1/2" h. ................................. **75**

**Model of bear,** brown, 7" l. ................................. **85**

**Model of circus horse,** head down, tail straight, leaping position w/middle of body supported by small, round center base, light blue w/cobalt accents, experimental glaze, 7 1/2" l., 6 1/2" h. .................. **185**

**Model of deer,** seated, brown & white glaze .................................................................. **50**

**Model of hen & rooster,** brown, pr. .................... **75**

*Howard Pierce Hippopotamus*

**Model of hippo,** standing, short tail, bulbous body, large nose & mouth, small ears & eyes, very distinct features, dark grey bottom, mottled grey top, 1950s, stamp marked "Howard Pierce Porcelain," 9 3/4" l., 3" h. (ILLUS.) ......................... **185**

**Model of owl,** shades of grey, 5" h. .................... **50**

**Model of panther,** pacing position, brown glaze, 11 1/2" l., 2 3/4" h. ............................. **250**

**Model of skunk,** rough textured matte glaze, 6" h. ................................................... **125**

**Models of birds,** seated, heads up, nondescript bodies except for eyes & beaks, black satin-matte glaze w/orangish red breasts, stamp mark "Howard Pierce," large, 4 1/2" h., medium, 3" h., small, 1 3/4" h., the set ......................................... **165**

**Models of dogs w/drooping ears,** dark & light brown, 8" h., & 6" h., pr. (ILLUS. top next column) .......................................................... **175**

**Models of fish,** each on a half-circle base, dark brown bodies w/speckled bases & fins, large fish, 6" h., medium fish, 4 3/4" h., small fish, 3" h., the set ................ **165**

**Models of giraffes,** brown & white, 1950s, 9" h., 10" h., pr. ......................................... **215**

*Howard Pierce Dogs w/Drooping Ears*

**Models of monkeys,** grey, pr. ......................... **165**

**Models of mother quail & two chicks,** brown & white, the set .................................. **65**

**Pencil holder,** nude women in relief around outside, tan & brown glaze, one year limited production, 1980, 3 1/2" d., 4 1/4" h. .......................................................... **160**

**Planter,** half-circle alcove in gold leaf w/white bisque angel holding songbook & standing in alcove, hard-to-find, 7" h. ....... **175**

*Howard Pierce Sugar Bowl*

**Sugar bowl,** open, Wedgwood-type white bisque lamb motif, pale blue matte handle & outer edges, produced in 1950s, 2 3/4" h. (ILLUS.) ............................................. **60**

**Vase,** 9" h., tapering body w/a flaring neck & stretched rim, brown bottom half of body & neck, yellow mid-section of body & interior, stamp mark, "Howard Pierce," & copyright symbol, hard-to-find color combination ..................................................... **90**

**Vase,** rectangular, 5 x 9", Viking boat design, brown ................................................ **25**

**Vase,** rectangular, 7 x 9 1/4", glossy forest green w/white bisque horse & tree in insert .......................................................... **65**

**Wall plaque,** rectangular, modernistic birds in relief, pale green background w/darker green birds, cement, 19" l., 1/2" deep, 6 1/4" h. .............................................. **250**

**Whistle,** bird-shaped w/hole at tail, grey w/white textured glaze, 3 1/2" h. .................. **100**

**Whistle,** snake crawling w/body forming an "M" shape, brown w/white glaze, 3 1/4" l., 2 3/4" h. .......................... **125**

# QUIMPER

*This French earthenware pottery has been made in France since the end of the 17th century and is still in production today. Because the colorful decoration on this ware, predominantly of Breton peasant figures, is all hand-painted and each piece is unique, it has become increasingly popular with collectors in recent years. Most pieces offered today date from about the mid-19th century to the present. Modern potteries continue to operate today and contemporary examples are available in gift shops.*

*Quimper Marks*

*Delft-style Bonboniere*

**Bonboniere (candy dish),** cov., long low rectangular form w/cut corners, overall blue on white Delft-style floral & leaf decoration, Henriot Quimper marked in blue, mint, 5 x 10 1/2", 4 1/2" h. (ILLUS.) ........... **$500**

**Bowls,** 5 1/4" d., berry, center decorated w/a traditional peasant man or lady surrounded by a border band of floral sprig garland, HB Quimper cz 176, mint, set of 6 ................... **250**

**Brandy set:** 6 1/2 x 7" keg supported on a wooden frame w/six small cups hanging from frame; "Ivoire Corbeille" patt., keg decorated w/a bust portrait of a man on one side & a lady on the other, Henriot Quimper 101, mint, the set ........... **70**

**Bust of a baby,** Modern Movement, modeled sipping from a bowl, crest of the town of Brest on interior of bowl, Henriot Quimper & C. Maillard marks, mint, 5" w., 2 1/2" h. ........................... **160**

**Butter knife,** stainless steel blade, handle decorated w/a peasant lady on one side & a reserve of florals on the other, unsigned, mint, 4 1/2" l. ................ **30**

**Calottes (flat European soup plates),** each decorated in various shades of blue on a cream ground in a geometric

"snowflake" style design, Henriot Quimper 90, overall excellent, 9" d., set of 4 (ILLUS. below) ................... **100**

*Set of Quimper Soup Plates*

*Figural Quimper Candlesticks*

**Candlesticks,** figural, Modern Movement, each in the form of a standing man posing w/a pot atop his head forming the candle socket, yellow-glazed ground w/green-dotted shirt, HB Quimper France, excellent, 7 3/4" h., pr. (ILLUS.) ...... **325**

**Charger,** wooden, round w/serrated rim, decorated w/an interior cottage scene of a lady making crepes over an open fire, rich Modern Movement colors in traditional Paul Fouillen palette, by Paul Fouillen, excellent, rare large size, 15 3/4" d. ................................... **750**

*Quimper Faience Charger*

**Charger,** faience central polychrome landscape scene w/figures playing Bocce, floral banded borders, signed "d'apres Deyrolle and Henriot Quimper," ca. 1930, France, 18" d. (ILLUS.) .................. **1,035**

**Christmas ornament,** round ball decorated w/a peasant lady & florals, dated 1986, HB-Henriot mark, mint........................... **20**

**Cigarette holder,** special commission from "Camel" cigarettes, features a brown camel on each side w/palm trees on the corners, Henriot Quimper France 96, very good, 3 1/2" l., 3" h. (fine hairline) ....... **275**

**Coffeepot,** cov., yellow ground decorated w/a peasant man & lady w/floral sprays, Macy's (in a star) indicating a commissioned piece, 8" h. (finial broken & reglued) ......................................................... **100**

**Dish,** shell-shaped, Demi-Fantasie patt., scene of full-facing man leaning on a walking stick w/floral sprays at either side, HR Quimper mark, 5 x 7 1/2" (small piece off corner reglued)...................... **55**

**Doll dishes,** decorated w/peasants w/florals on either side, HB Quimper France w/ artist's initials, mint, 6" d., set of 6 .......... **125**

*Doll Dishes with Rooster Decoration*

**Doll dishes,** each piece w/a pink glaze decorated w/a colorful rooster in the center & a blue sponged rim, unsigned but attributable to Henriot, excellent, set of 9 pcs. (ILLUS.) ............................................... **100**

*Breton Dancers Figure Group*

**Figure group,** Modern Movement, a young Breton couple dancing the folk dance "gavotte," by artist Micheau-Vernez,

Henriot Quimper plus the artist's mark, mint, 12 1/2" h. (ILLUS.).............................. **450**

**Figure of a peasant lady,** Modern Movement, standing holding a basket over her arm, bright colors, Henriot Quimper France, mint, 4" h. ........................................ **190**

*Figure of Breton Boy*

**Figure of boy,** Modern Movement, little Breton boy wearing a black hat, blue jacket, black vest, brown pants & yellow clogs, by Berthe Savigny, HB Quimper py F.822 & Savigny signature, mint, 10 1/4" h. (ILLUS.)....................................... **250**

**Figure of St. Anne,** standing wearing a yellow robe w/black ermine tail design & a blue mantle, the child Mary stands nestled next to her mother, HB-Henriot Quimper France, recent vintage, mint, 5" h. ...................................................... **55**

**Figure of The Virgin & Child,** "Vierge et l'Enfant," Mary standing wearing a crown & cradling the Baby Jesus in her arms & holding a flower in her right hand, unusual & rare mold w/much detail work on the robes, Henriot Quimper France, mint, 11 1/2" h. ........................................... **500**

*Quimper Fish Platter with Couple*

**Fish platter,** oval, "Ivoire Corbeille" patt., center decorated w/busts of a young couple surrounded by swags of blue-sponged circlets, Henriot Quimper 79, pierced to hang, excellent, 10 1/4 x 21" (ILLUS.)....................................................... **650**

**Inkwell,** heart-shaped, decorated w/a facing peasant couple w/floral sprays around the sides, complete w/insert & lid, Henriot Quimper, excellent, 3 x 3 1/2" (one tiny rim flake)........................ **250**

*Fine Quimper Jardiniere*

**Jardiniere,** low oval form w/upright sides w/flared rim & base bands supported on four paw feet, figural satyr head end handles, "Decor Riche" patt., front w/oval reserve of a seated courting couple w/blue acanthus panels & border, the reverse w/a reserve w/intricate colored flower blossoms, HB Quimper, excellent, one foot professionally repaired, 8 1/2 x 16", 5 3/4" h. (ILLUS.) .................. **1,250**

**Knife rest,** triangular w/flared ends, in the "Bluets" (blue Forget-me-nots) patt., unsigned but attributable to AP, late 19th c., good condition w/some glaze edge wear, 3 1/2" l. ............................................... **50**

**Knife rests,** long triangular form w/flared ends, hollow center, one decorated w/a standing peasant man, the other w/a standing peasant woman, florals on the other two sides, HR Quimper, excellent w/a couple of tiny flakes, 3 1/4" l., matched pr. ................................................... **65**

*Figural Quimper Lamp*

**Lamp,** table model, figural, Modern Movement, figure of a Breton lady standing w/her arms extended out supporting large shallow baskets of colorful flowers, socket shafts issuing from flowers, on a square foot, by C. Maillard, Henriot Quimper France & C. Maillard mark, 13" h. (ILLUS.)............................................. **850**

**Pitcher,** figural, Modern Movement, model of a peasant man's head, the streamers from his hat forming the handle, his hat brim serving as the spout, Henriot Quimper France w/a.g. 159, mint................. **250**

**Pitcher,** 4 3/4" h., bulbous body, decorated w/a traditional peasant lady w/floral sprays, Henriot Quimper France beneath handle, excellent (tiny wear spot on lip)................................................... **100**

**Pitcher,** 5 1/2" h., cylindrical neck, decorated w/a traditional peasant man & floral sprays, HR Quimper 38 France beneath handle, mint.............................. **125**

**Plate,** 6 1/2" l., oval w/scalloped rim, Flower patt., brown sponged border trim on a cream-glazed ground, HB Quimper France x.xx, excellent ............................. **35**

**Plate,** 7" d., "suject ordinaire" decoration, a blue background glaze w/a peasant lady surrounded by concentric yellow & cobalt blue bands, Henriot Quimper France 125 (tiny amounts of glaze wear on rim) ..................................................... **60**

**Plate,** 9" d., "faience populaire," decorated w/a hen surrounded by a single brush stroke border, early 20th c., HR only, mint ................................................................ **200**

*Porquier-Beau Botanical Plate*

**Plate,** 9 1/4" d., lightly scalloped flanged rim w/yellow edge band, h.p. blackberry canes w/berries, First Period Porquier-Beau Botanical, intersecting PB mark, excellent condition (ILLUS.) ..................... **1,000**

**Plate,** 9 1/4" d., "Scene Breton" design w/a group scene of a family praying at a wayside shrine, First Period Porquier-Beau, intersecting PB mark, mint................. **875**

**Plate,** 9 1/4" d., "Scene Breton" design w/two tipsy men leaning against each other after a drinking bout, First Period Porquier-Beau, intersecting PB mark, mint ..................................................................... **675**

**Plate,** 9 1/2" d., colorful rooster on fence center scene, blue, green, brown & white geometric border, unsigned, late 19th c., mint ...................................................................... **250**

**Plate,** 9 1/2" d., "Croisille" patt., center w/a lady holding a basket & facing forward, surrounded by a border which alternates blue criss-cross lattice & a stylized dogwood blossom, Henriot Quimper, very good (dust adhering to glaze from manufacturing) ...................................................... **200**

**Plate,** 9 1/2" d., Modern Movement, geometric decoration in vibrant colors of cobalt blue, rose, tan, orange & brown

w/a stylized star in the center, HB
Quimper 176 C.C., mint ............................. **125**

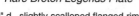

*Rare Breton Legends Plate*

**Plate,** 10" d., slightly scalloped flanged rim,
Breton Legends patt., large color scene
of a bagpiper surrounded by goblins
dancing beneath a quarter moon, Hen-
Riot Quimper France 117, rare, mint
(ILLUS.)......................................................... **700**

**Plate,** 10 1/2" l., fish-shaped, "soleil" yellow
glaze decorated w/a peasant man,
stamped mark "entierement decor main,"
w/HB Quimper, mint ...................................... **15**

*Quimper Plates with Figures*

**Plates,** 9 1/4" d., traditional decoration, one
w/a man standing holding a pipe, the
other w/a facing lady standing holding a
flower, each figure flanked by colorful
bushes all within a brush stroke border
garland, HR Quimper beneath the fig-
ures, mint, pr. (ILLUS.) ................................. **325**

**Platter,** 7 3/4 x 11 1/4", oval w/scalloped
rim, decorated w/a standing peasant
lady w/floral sprays on each side of her,
floral garland border band, HB Quimper
207 p.y., mint................................................. **110**

**Platter,** 7 1/2 x 11 3/4", oval w/scalloped
rim, central color scene of a native peasant lady seated on a stump w/an "a la
touche" floral border, unsigned, mid-19th
c., mint (ILLUS. top next column)................. **150**

**Platter,** 9 1/4 x 12", oval w/slightly scalloped rim, center decoration of a profiled
peasant man w/walking stick surrounded
by a floral garland border, HR Quimper
beneath the figure, mint ............................... **200**

*Early Quimper Oval Platter*

*Croisille Pattern Quimper Platter*

**Platter,** 10 1/2 x 13 1/2", oval w/scalloped
rim, "Croisille" patt., Demi-Fantasie style
peasant couple in the center surrounded
by a border of blue criss-cross latticework (croisille) & stylized dogwood flowers, Henriot Quimper 159 in blue w/an
impressed 3, excellent w/vibrant colors
(ILLUS.)......................................................... **900**

**Platter,** 11 1/4 x 15", oval w/scalloped rim,
yellow-glazed ground decorated in the
center w/a standing peasant man
w/walking stick flanked by tall floral
bushes, colored leafy band border, Henriot Quimper France 447, half inch chip
on rim .............................................................. **75**

**Porringer,** round bowl, decorated w/tradi-
tional peasant man w/floral sprays &
blue handles, Henriot Quimper France
42, excellent, overall 5 1/2" l. ........................ **35**

**Salt basket,** figural, double-type w/two
kissing swans, black & yellow sponging
on necks & bodies w/blue wings, Henriot
Quimper, mint, 3 1/2 x 3 1/2"......................... **65**

**Salt dip,** open, decorated w/a floral garland
on the exterior rim, HB Quimper, mint,
2" d. ................................................................ **25**

**Salt & pepper cellar,** oblong double open chambers w/a central ring handle, "Suject ordinaire" patt., a peasant man & flowers surrounded by yellow & blue concentric bands, Henriot Quimper France 595, mint, 5 1/4" l. ............................. 35

**Salt & pepper shakers,** tapering paneled shape, decorated w/a peasant man or peasant woman w/yellow & blue sponged tops & florals on the sides, HB Quimper 475 p.9, mint w/original cork stoppers, 3 1/2" h., pr. ................................... 30

*Quimper Sectioned Serving Dish*

**Serving dish,** rectangular w/rounded corners & six shallow sections, yellow-glazed ground w/each section decorated w/a peasant or floral cluster, Henriot Quimper France 72, excellent, 9 x 15" (ILLUS.)..................................................... 100

**Snuff bottle,** figural, model of a small book, decorated w/a rooster & the phrase "Quand ce cog chantera, mon amour finira," reverse sides decorated w/a peasant man, HB only, late 19th c., mint, 3" l. ................................................................ 300

**Tea set, child's:** cov. teapot, cov. sugar bowl, creamer & three cups & saucers; white background glaze w/blue sponged trim & "a la touche" flower sprigs w/rose-colored buds & green leaves, unsigned but attributable to Henriot, ca. 1950s-60s, the set (one cup broken & reglued) ........ 75

**Teabag holder,** figural, model of a bagpipe, "Bruyere" (pink bleeding heart flower) patt., black & yellow sponged border trim & a pink bow handle, Henriot Quimper 138, mint, 4" l.................................. 20

*Quimper Tray with Ropetwist Handles*

**Tray,** rectangular w/notched corners & ropetwist end handles, Demi-Fantasie patt., center decoration of a peasant woman standing & holding a distaff flanked by tall colorful flowering bushes,

dark blue border band & handles, Henriot Quimper France 100, mint, 8 1/2 x 13 1/4" (ILLUS.)................................. 250

**Tray,** round, "Broderie Bretonne" patt., center scene of a seated lady holding a water jar surrounded by an intricate raised-to-the-touch border based on Breton embroidery work, HB Quimper Pk 604, mint, 7 3/4" d. ................................. 110

**Trivet,** footed, yellow ground decorated w/a peasant man w/florals & a red "S" link chain border, Macy's Quimper France x, excellent, 5 3/4" sq. ...................................... 85

**Vase,** 5" h., 7 1/2" w., fan-shaped, decorated w/a traditional peasant couple w/florals & a red lattice fan case w/blue butterfly figural feet, Henriot Quimper France 80, very good (faint 1" hairline) ........ 300

*Vase with Demi-Fantasie Pattern*

**Vase,** 11" h., baluster-form w/flared foot, short cylindrical neck & loop handles from rim to shoulder, h.p. Demi-Fantasie patt., a crest of Brittany on the shoulder band above a color scene of two courting peasants, upper & lower borders festooned w/bleeding hearts & wild gorse, HR Quimper mark, one flat chip of bottom (ILLUS.)` ............................................ 1,100

**Vase,** 12 1/2" h., "Decor Riche" patt., the front w/a color scene of a young couple courting surrounded by bleeding hearts & wild gorse blossoms, the reverse shows the Crest of Brittany, blue acanthus scrolled borders around the rim & base, HenRiot Quimper France 159, mint ............................................................. 550

**Vases,** 9" h., 8" d., bulbous flat-bottomed shape tapering to a short rolled neck, "Broderie Bretonne" patt., each w/a cartouche framing a colored scene, one w/a seated peasant lady, the other w/a facing seated man w/pipe, raised yellow detailed wisteria vines on a dark blue ground around the sides, HB Quimper 524 Pi & Pj marks, mint, pr. ..................... 2,000

**Wall plaque,** rectangular w/cut corners, a large bas-relief courting couple in the center under the words "Au dud névez," & "Ploare" (their village name) below, zigzag geometric border in terra cotta, black & cream, First Period Porquier-Beau, signed & w/intersecting PB, late

19th c., superb, 15 x 18 1/4" (ILLUS. below)........................................................ **1,200**

*Fine Quimper Wall Plaque*

**Wall pocket,** figural, in the shape of an open envelope, decorated w/a traditional peasant man w/floral sprays & blue latticework, one side unglazed w/match striker, HR Quimper, 4 1/4" w., 4 1/4" h. (one tiny back corner flake).......................... **175**

**Wall pockets,** cone-shaped, decorated w/the "Demi-Fantasie" patt., profiled peasant lady holding a folded umbrella on one, the other w/a three-quarters portrait of a facing man w/hand on his hip & holding a pipe to his lips, HR Quimper beneath the figures, mint, 10 1/4" l., pr. ....... **350**

# REDWARE

*Red earthenware pottery was made in the American colonies from the late 1600s. Bowls, crocks and all types of utilitarian wares were turned out in great abundance to supplement the pewter and handmade treenware. The ready availability of the clay, the same used in making bricks and roof tiles, accounted for the vast production. The lead-glazed redware retained its reddish color though a variety of colors could be obtained by adding various metals to the glaze. Interesting effects occurred accidentally through unsuspected impurities in the clay or uneven temperatures in the firing kiln which sometimes resulted in streaks or mottled splotches.*

*Redware pottery was seldom marked by the maker.*

**Apple butter jar,** bulbous ovoid body w/applied handle & tooled lines, brown splotches on deep orange ground, 5" h. .... **$578**

**Bowl,** 5 1/4" d., 2 1/2" h., footed w/rounded sides & flat rim, dark greenish orange ground w/brown spots, bottom incised "B" (minor glaze flakes on interior) .............. **303**

**Bowl,** 10 1/2" d., 7" h., deep sides w/light green glaze splotches, 19th c. (chips).......... **460**

**Bust of man,** full bottomed wig, wheel thrown & hand-molded & tooled, brown glaze, 10" h. (minor chips)............................ **770**

**Chamberstick,** cylindrical w/saucer base & applied handle, brown & green glaze on orange ground, 3" h. (base glued)............... **176**

**Creamer,** cylindrical w/reeded base & applied handle, green & mottled brown glaze on orange ground, 2 1/8" h. (edge chips)............................................................. **303**

**Dish,** orange ground w/brown sponged rim, 6 1/2" d. (wear & chips) ............................... **440**

**Dish,** coggled rim, greenish pinkish grey mottled glaze, 7" d. (small chips) ................. **110**

**Dish,** orange glazed interior, exterior & rim w/black patina, 7 1/2" d. (wear & hairline) ............................................................. **303**

*Redware Dish*

**Dish,** oblong, shallow canted sides w/flat narrow rim, orange ground w/brown & green spots, 11 3/4" l. (ILLUS.) .................. **660**

**Doorstop,** square form decorated w/molded starflower, yellow & brown glaze, 3 x 4 3/4 x 5" .................................... **330**

**Figure of Uncle Sam,** standing full-figure, polychrome, 4" h. (worn & flaked polychrome) ........................................................ **275**

**Flask,** ovoid body tapering to small molded rim, deep orangish ground w/dark brown splotches, 7" h. (wear & minor chips)........... **385**

**Flowerpot w/attached saucer,** tapering cylindrical form, tooled lines at base & rim, yellow slip & mottled brown, orange & cream glaze, wear, flakes & short hairlines, 5" h. .................................................... **358**

**Flowerpot w/saucer,** tapering cylindrical form w/narrow rolled rim, brown running glaze on orange ground, impressed "John W. Bell, Waynesboro, Pa.," 4 3/8" h. (chips) ............................................ **385**

*Redware Ram-form Footwarmer*

**Footwarmer,** figural recumbent ram, 19th c., very minor chips, 6 3/4" h., 13 1/2" l. (ILLUS.)...................................................... **518**

**Jar,** cov., cylindrical w/molded base & rim bands, eared handles, fitted cover w/small knob finial, mottled burnt orange w/greenish & brown splotches, 8" h. ........... **825**

**Jar,** ovoid body w/wide molded rim, greenish mottled glaze w/amber spots, 5 1/2" h.................................................... **248**

**Jar,** bulbous ovoid body w/applied ribbed strap handle & tooled bands, brown sponging on burnt orange ground, 6" h........ **165**

**Jar,** bulbous ovoid body tapering to slightly flared rim, dark brown pattern on orangish brown ground, 6 3/8" h. (short hairline in base, minor flakes) ........................... **275**

**Jar,** footed bulbous ovoid body tapering to a wide slightly flaring rim, dark brown splotches on orange ground w/mottled green glaze, 7 3/8" h. (chips) ....................... **825**

**Jar,** wide cylindrical body w/flared rim, net like pattern of dark brown over burnt orange ground, 7 1/2" h. (wear & small chips)................................................. **523**

**Jar,** cov., wide cylindrical body w/shoulder tapering to flared rim, inset cover w/tiny cylindrical finial, dark brown daubs on greenish glaze w/mottled amber, yellow & green, 8" h. (chips)................................. **1,485**

**Jar,** cylindrical, greenish glaze w/amber spots & brown brushed spirals, 8 5/8" h. (wear & chips) ......................................... **853**

**Jar,** ovoid body w/strap handle, green glaze w/orange spots, 8 3/4" h. (glazed over rim hairline, chips) ............................... **220**

**Jar,** bulbous ovoid form w/tooled lines, dark brown splotches & flecks on dark orange ground, 9 1/8" d. (wear & old chips)................................................. **220**

**Jug,** globular w/ribbed strap handle & tooled lines, amber ground w/brown splotches & green mottled glaze, 3 5/8" h...................................................... **4,510**

**Jug,** bulbous ovoid body w/applied ribbed handle, brown flecks on a metallic deep amber ground, 7 1/4" h. (wear & surface & edge chips) ......................................... **193**

**Jug,** bulbous ovoid body w/applied strap handle, dark glaze w/black splotches, 8 3/4" h (chips on base) ............................. **303**

**Jug,** semi-ovoid body w/applied strap handle, brown & green glaze w/amber & brown spots, 9 1/4" h. (minor chips)............. **605**

**Jug,** bulbous ovoid, brown running glaze on deep orange ground, glazed over handle attachment, 12" h. (wear & old chips)................................................. **110**

**Jug,** bulbous ovoid body w/applied strap handle, deep reddish tan, 12 1/4" d. (wear & minor glaze flakes)........................... **550**

**Model of dog,** seated Spaniel w/molded & hand-tooled features including a neck chain & padlock, clear glaze w/brown streaking, 19th c., 8 1/4" h. (edge chips, glaze flakes, old repair, black paint on bottom edge)................................................. **358**

**Mold,** food, fluted interior, dark brown sponging on deep orange ground, 4 1/4" d. (hairline)...................................... **110**

**Mold,** food, Turk's turban-style, divided & fluted, dark brown glaze wbrown sponged scalloped rim, 7 3/4" d. (small flakes).................................................... **138**

**Mold,** food, Turk's turban-style, swirled design w/running brown glaze on orange ground, impressed label "John W. Bell, Waynesboro, Pa.," 8 3/4" d., 4 1/8" h. (hairline) ................................................. **495**

**Mug,** footed bulbous body w/molded ribs & applied handle, brown sponging w/mottled green glaze on orange ground, 3" h. ...... **275**

**Mug,** barrel form w/tooled band & applied handle, dark brown glaze, 3 5/8" h. (chips) ................................................... **121**

**Mug,** cylindrical w/applied ribbed handle & tooled bands, dark burnt orange ground w/brown streaks, 4 7/8" h. (chips) ............ **138**

**Mush mug,** footed squatty bulbous body w/applied ribbed handle, dark greenish amber glaze, 3 1/2" h. (chips) ....................... **88**

**Pepper pot,** waisted cylindrical base w/top tapering sharply to mushroom-shaped top pierced w/holes, brown sponging on green & light brown glaze, 5 1/2" h. ............. **495**

**Pie plate,** brown brushed & sponged design on burnt orange ground, 7 3/8" d. (minor chips & short hairline) ....................... **220**

**Pie plate,** orange glaze w/dark brown splotches, 8 1/4" d. ................................... **1,155**

**Pitcher,** 6 3/4" h., squatty ovoid body tapering to tall slightly flared rim w/pinched spout & applied ribbed strap handle, brown splotches & flecks on lighter brown ground ................................... **220**

**Pitcher,** 7 5/8" h., bulbous ovoid body w/tooled band, gallery rim lip, pinched spout & ribbed strap handle, dark brown splotches & flecks on orange ground (wear & chips) ........................................... **660**

**Pitcher,** 8" h., bulbous ovoid body w/applied ribbed handle & tooled lines, brown flecked glaze (chips).......................... **193**

**Pitcher,** 8" h., footed spherical body, tapering cylindrical neck w/tooled band w/reeded lip, applied C-form handle, marbleized white, green, brown & blue glaze w/white slip interior (chips) ................. **550**

**Stove leveler,** flaring cylindrical form w/molded top, brown splotches on orange ground, 2 3/4" h. (chips).................. **176**

**Teapot,** cov., cylindrical form w/an engine-turned body in an overall optic block design, straight angled spout, large loop handle, slightly domed cover w/knob finial, impressed pseudo-Chinese mark, England, ca. 1770, 6" h. (restored chip on spout lip, nicks to rims)........................... **748**

# RED WING

*Various potteries operated in Red Wing, Minnesota from 1868, the most successful being the Red Wing Stoneware Co., organized in 1878. Merged with other local potteries through the years, it became known as Red Wing Union Stoneware Co. in 1894, and was one of the largest producers of* utilitarian stoneware items in the United States. After a decline in the popularity of stoneware products, an art pottery line was introduced to compensate for the loss and this was reflected in a new name for the company, Red Wing Potteries, Inc., in 1930. Stoneware production ceased entirely in 1947, but vases, planters, cookie jars and dinnerwares of art pottery quality continued in production until 1967 when the pottery ceased operation altogether.

*Red Wing Marks*

## CONVENTION COMMEMORATIVES

*Red Wing Commemorative Feeder*

**Buttermilk feeder,** & chicken drinking font, 1993 Red Wing Collectors Society Commemorative, maker produced 4,820 (ILLUS.)...................................................... **$95**
**Jar,** pantry, 1991 Red Wing Collectors Society Commemorative, maker produced 3,560 ................................................. **115**
**Jug,** fancy, 1990 Red Wing Collectors Society Commemorative, maker produced 3,550 ................................................. **95**

## DINNERWARES & NOVELTIES

**Basket,** yellow & grey, marked "Red Wing USA #348," w/75th Anniversary Stamp, 7" h. ...................................................... **50**
**Bowl,** salad, 12" d., Tampico patt...................... **75**
**Casserole,** cov., Village Green patt. ................. **33**
**Cookie jar,** cov., figural French Chef, blue glaze....................................................... **250**
**Cookie jar,** cov., green rooster, marked "Red Wing #249," 9 1/4" l. (ILLUS. top next column)............................................... **145**
**Cookie jar,** cov., yellow grapes, marked "Red Wing USA," 10" h. ............................... **80**
**Cup & saucer,** Provincial patt. ........................... **10**

**Figurine,** green swan, marked "Red Wing USA #259," 5 1/8" h. ...................................... **55**
**Figurine,** grey lined rooster, marked "Red Wing #M-1438," 9 1/4" h. .............................. **85**

*Red Wing Rooster Cookie Jar*

**Planter,** grey donkey w/side baskets, unmarked, rare, 6 1/4" h.............................. **145**

*Red Wing Goose Planter*

**Planter,** goose, flecked, Nile blue, marked "Red Wing USA #439," 9 1/2" l. (ILLUS.) ..... **105**

*Red Wing Canoe Shaped Planter*

**Planter,** canoe-shaped, white birch pottery, marked "Red Wing #733," 17" l. (ILLUS.)..... **250**
**Plate,** 6" d., bread & butter, Provincial patt........... **4**
**Syrup pitcher,** Provincial patt. ........................... **15**

*Red Wing Bud Vase*

**Vase,** green bud vase, stamped "Red Wing Art Pottery," rare, 8 7/8" h. (ILLUS.) ............. **150**

## STONEWARE & UTILITY WARES

*Bean Pot w/Peter Bootzin Advertising*

**Bean pot,** cov., white & brown glaze, w/advertising "Peter Bootzin, The Corner Store, Medford, Wisc." (ILLUS.) ..................... **85**

**Bean pot,** cov., white & brown glaze, w/advertising "Sheffield Brick & Tile Co., Sheffield, Iowa" ........................................... **80**

*Stoneware Beater Jar*

**Beater jar,** white glaze w/blue band, w/advertising "Huemoeller Bros., Northrop-Truman, Minnesota " (ILLUS.) ...... **150**

**Beater jar,** white glaze w/blue band, w/advertising "Schulenburg & Thom, Wells, Minn." ............................................. **145**

**Bowl,** 6" d., saffronware, yellowware .............. **140**

**Bowl,** 7" d., Dunlap bowl, brown & white, w/advertising "Columbia Metal Products Co., Chicago, IL." ........................................... **55**

**Bowl,** 7" d., genuine Dunlap bowl, brown.......... **45**

**Butter Crock,** white glazed stoneware, bottom signed "Red Wing Stoneware," 10 lbs................................................................. **65**

**Churn,** white glazed stoneware, birch leaf with ski oval mark, 3 gal. ............................. **290**

**Churn,** salt glazed stoneware, cobalt markings, unsigned, 4 gal. .................................... **845**

**Crock,** white glazed stoneware, two "elephant ears," no oval stamp, eared handles, 11" d., 4 gal. (ILLUS. top next column) ........................................................... **95**

**Crock,** white glazed stoneware, 4" wing, Red Wing oval stamp, 13" d., 6 gal. ........ **110**

**Crock,** white glazed stoneware, 4" wing, Red Wing oval stamp, bail handles, 13 3/4" d., 8 gal. ......................................... **105**

*Crock w/Elephant Ears Marking*

**Crock,** white glazed stoneware, two birch leaves, Union oval stamp, eared handles, 15 1/2" d., 10 gal. ................................. **145**

**Crock,** white glazed stoneware, two birch leaves, no oval stamp, eared handles, 16" d., 12 gal. .............................................. **125**

**Crock,** white glazed stoneware, two birch leaves, Union oval stamp, eared handles, 16 3/4" d., 15 gal................................. **145**

**Crock,** white glazed stoneware, 6" wing, Red Wing oval stamp, no handles, 19 1/4." d., 20 gal. ......................................... **125**

**Fruit jar,** screw-on metal lid, "Stone Mason Fruit Jar," 2 qt., blue mark ............................ **275**

*Red Wing Jar w/Ball Lock*

**Jar,** cov., ball lock, brown & white glazed stoneware, no wing, Red Wing oval stamp, 3 gal. (ILLUS.) ................................... **135**

**Jar,** cov., white glazed stoneware, stamped "Red Wing Refrigerator Jar" ......................... **265**

**Jug,** syrup, shouldered, white glazed stoneware, signed "Minnesota Stoneware, Red Wing, Minn.," 1 gal. ..................... **145**

**Jug,** white glazed stoneware, w/advertising "Creamery & Dairy Supplies, Minneapolis, Minn.," 1 gal. ........................................... **105**

**Jug,** beehive-shaped, white glazed stoneware, two birch leaves, Union oval stamp, 3 gal. .................................................. **400**

**Jug,** beehive-shaped, white glazed stoneware, two birch leaves, no oval stamp, 4 gal. .................................................................. **550**

*Red Wing Beehive-Shaped Jug*

**Jug,** beehive-shaped, white glazed stoneware, 4" wing, Red Wing oval stamp, 5 gal. (ILLUS.) ................................................ **385**

**Jug,** shouldered, brown & white glazed stoneware, 4" wing, no oval stamp, 5 gal. .............................................................. **450**

**Jug,** shouldered, white glazed stoneware, two birch leaves, no stamp, bottom signed, 5 gal. ............................................... **195**

*Red Wing "Koverwate"*

**"Koverwate,"** white glazed stoneware, stamped "Koverwate, Red Wing, Minn.," 10 gal. size (ILLUS.) ................................... **225**

*Red Wing Poultry Waterer*

**Poultry waterer,** cov., ball lock, white glazed stoneware, marked "Vacuum Poultry Waterer, Red Wing Potteries," wire handle, 5 gal. (ILLUS.) ........................ **275**

*5 Gallon Stoneware Water Cooler*

**Water cooler,** cov., white glazed stoneware, bail handles, small wing, 5 gal. (ILLUS.) ..................................................... **425**

**Water cooler,** cov., white glazed stoneware, bail handles, large wing, 10 gal. ........ **700**

# ROCKINGHAM WARES

*The Marquis of Rockingham first established an earthenware pottery in the Yorkshire district of England around 1745 and it was occupied afterwards by various potters. The well-known mottled brown Rockingham glaze was introduced about 1788 by the Brameld Brothers and became immediately popular. It was during the 1820s that the production of true porcelain began at the factory and continued to be made until the firm closed in 1842. Since that time the so-called Rockingham glaze has been used by various potters in England and the United States, including some famous wares produced in Bennington, Vermont. However, very similar glazes were also used by potteries in other areas of the United States including Ohio and Indiana and only wares specifically attributed to Bennington should use that name. The following listings will include mainly wares featuring the dark brown mottled glaze produced at various sites here and abroad.*

*Rockingham-glazed Dog*

**Flask,** flattened ovoid form tapering to a short molded neck, the front & back molded in relief w/scenes of hunting dogs, mottled dark brown glaze, 7 1/4" h. (hairline in bottom) ...................... **$330**

**Model of a dog,** seated Spaniel facing viewer, on a thick oblong base, free-standing front legs, molded deer &

hounds around the base mottled dark brown glaze, 19th c., 10 1/2" h. ..................... **399**

**Model of a dog,** seated Spaniel w/molded details & free-standing front legs, on a thick rectangular base w/notched corners, overall mottled dark brown glaze, 10 3/4" h. (wear, small chips) ...................... **303**

**Model of a dog,** seated Spaniel on thick irregular-shaped base, freestanding front legs, mottled dark brown glaze, wear on nose, hairlines in front legs & small chips on base, 10 3/4" h. (ILLUS.) ...... **330**

*Rockingham Lion*

**Model of a lion,** recumbent animal w/curly mane, on rectangular stepped base, mottled dark brown glaze, minor chips on base, 9 3/8" l. (ILLUS.) ........................... **880**

**Pitcher,** 9" h., ovoid body tapering to a wide rolled spout & branch handle, the sides molded w/a scene of a hunter & dog, dark brown mottled brown glaze on yellowware, late 19th c. .............................. **175**

*Rockingham Pitcher*

**Pitcher,** 10" h., gourd-form w/arched rim spout & scrolled handle, swirled alternate rib pattern, overall mottled brown Rockingham glaze, chip on base caused by stilt (ILLUS.) .......................................... **504**

# ROOKWOOD

*Considered America's foremost art pottery, the Rookwood Pottery Company was established in Cincinnati, Ohio in 1880, by Mrs. Maria Nichols Longworth Storer. To accurately record its development, each piece carried the Rookwood insignia, or mark, was dated, and, if individually decorated, was* *usually signed by the artist. The pottery remained in Cincinnati until 1959 when it was sold to Herschede Hall Clock Company and moved to Starkville, Mississippi, where it continued in operation until 1967.*

*A private company is now producing a limited variety of pieces using original Rookwood molds.*

*Rookwood Mark*

**Basket,** hanging-type, bulbous bullet form, green Matte glaze, No. S1732, 1905, 10" d., 9" l. (minute flakes) ........................ **$440**

**Basket,** gondola-shaped w/curved & pointed ends, decorated w/slip-painted daisies in yellow on a shaded green ground, Standard glaze, No. 374, 1888, K. Shirayamadani, 15 1/2" l., 8" h................ **660**

**Book ends,** figural, model of a squirrel seated on a log holding up & eating a nut, greyish green Matte glaze, No. 6025, 1928, Sallie Toohey, 4 1/4" h., pr. ...... **748**

**Book ends,** figural, modeled as a blue jay, w/oak leaves & acorns, creamy Matte glaze, No. 2829, 1929, 5 3/8" h., pr.............. **316**

**Book ends,** figural, one w/Dutch girl dressed in blue & white, the other w/Dutch boy w/blue hat & lavender vest, leaning on dark brown stone wall behind a stand of pink tulips, Matte glaze, No. 6022, 1928, Sallie Toohey, 6" h., pr. ............ **523**

**Bowl,** 7" w., deep square, slightly rounded body w/indented corners on square foot, Limoges-style decoration w/two butterflies in brown tones soaring against a peach, green & white smeared ground w/gold highlights & black reeds, painted gold accents at rim, kiln mark, No. 166, 1883, N.J. Hirschfeld.................................. **413**

*Unusual Rookwood Bowl*

**Bowl,** 12" l., oval w/incurved sides forming openings at each end, decorated w/detailed flowers in green & blue w/white centers against an ivory, light blue & medium blue ground, gold geometric & floral designs, No. 344B, 1887, Kataro Shirayamadani (ILLUS.) ............ **1,540**

**Bowl-vase,** bulbous body w/incurved rim, the upper body decorated w/pink flowers w/green centers on a light blue ground, the lower body darker blue w/scalloped edge, impressed "V" & signature, No. 214E, 1915, E.H. McDermott, 4 1/2" d. ........ **358**

**Card holder,** rectangular form on pedestal base, paneled design w/ribbed top, blue crystalline glaze, No. 2952, 1927, 3" w., 3 1/2" h. ........................................................ **220**

**Clock,** relief-molded panther on base, gunmetal glaze, No. 7039, 1950, 7 1/2" h. ......... **286**

**Compote,** shallow oblong form w/crimped rim, floral medallion in center, pedestal base, glossy red glaze, No. S2205, 1955, marked w/Rookwood anniversary triangle, 6" d., 4 1/2" h. ................................ **231**

**Cup & saucer,** cylindrical w/D-form handle, painted & incised cherry blossoms on olive ground, saucer 5" d., cup 3" h., No. 208, 1886, Anna M. Bookprinter ................. **275**

*Rookwood Silver Overlay Ewer*

**Ewer,** footed, baluster-form w/a widely flaring rolled tricorner rim, slender S-scroll handle, decorated w/yellow blossoms on green leaves trimmed w/silver overlay flowering vines up the sides & beneath the handle w/a silver overlaid rim, handle & base, Standard glaze, No. 510, 1892, silver marked by Gorham Co., No. R198, Harriet R. Strafer, insignificant break in silver & fracture to base not visible from top or outside, 7" h. (ILLUS.) ................... **3,850**

**Ewer,** flattened spherical body tapering to a slender tall neck w/a tricorner rim, a long C-form handle from rim to shoulder, decorated w/yellow flowers & green leaves on a dark brown to green ground, Standard glaze, No. 715D, No. X272X, 1898, Josephine Zettel, 7 1/2" h. ........................... **660**

**Ewer,** squatty bulbous base on a narrow footring tapering to slender cylindrical neck w/flaring rim & pinched spout w/long arched handle, decorated w/yellow dogwood w/black centers on brown stems & green leaves on a dark brown, orange & green ground, Standard glaze, No. 495B, 1899, Mary Nourse, 9" h. ............ **770**

**Ewer,** oviform w/an elongated neck & floriform spout, in a Standard glaze, decorated w/a mustard yellow & olive green

branch of prunus, applied w/a C-scroll handle, No. 450 W, 1892, Albert R. Valentien, 17" h. .............................................. **1,150**

**Flower frog,** figural satyr w/turtle, brown Matte glaze, No. 2336, 1921, 7" h. .............. **468**

**Inkwell,** flat oval form w/flared rim, decorated w/feather among yellow & green clover, centered w/spherical well adorned w/silver overlay in elaborate scrolled design w/hammered silver top, Standard glaze, No. 586C, 1899, silver marked by Gorham Co., Constance Baker, 10" l. (minor flaws underneath base, probably in firing) ............................ **1,760**

**Jar,** cov., wide squatty compressed body raised on tiny peg feet, the wide shoulder centered by a low, wide domed cover, incised rectangular panels, fine dark red & dusty green Matte glaze, No. 1349, 1908, 6" d. (minor inner rim flake) ...... **413**

**Model of an egret,** head up & turned to the side, glossy black glaze, No. 6992, 1948, 8 1/2" h. ................................................. **187**

**Mug,** tapering cylindrical body w/compressed base, decorated w/painted & molded clover in pink & green against a green to ivory ground, Vellum glaze, w/silver overlay C-form handle & rim, 1905, impressed signature & "Commercial Club of Cincinnati," Sara Sax, 5 1/2" h. ................................................. **770**

**Paperweight,** figural seated female nude on rectangular base, ivory Matte glaze, impressed signature, No. 2868, 1928, 4" h. ...................................................... **330**

**Pilgrim flask,** spherical body w/narrow cylindrical neck, applied handle from neck to shoulder, Limoges-type, decorated w/scene of white geese in flight & white, orange & black water fowl wading in pool against smeared ground in olive green & white w/gold accents & black reeds, 1882, A.R. Valentien, 7" h. ............... **880**

**Pin tray,** shallow oval form w/rolled rim, figural molded reclining nude female at one end, glossy green glaze, No. 2595, 1949, 4 1/2" w. ...................................... **176**

**Plaque,** rectangular, a scene depicting tall leafy birch trees by a lake at dusk in shades of blue & grey w/touches of pink & brown, Vellum glaze, 1921, Ed Diers, framed, 5 3/4 x 8" .................................... **2,415**

**Plaque,** rectangular, a wide landscape scene of trees along a riverbank, unusual red leaves on brown trunks w/green grass along light blue body of water, Vellum glaze, incised "V" & painted signature, 1915, original frame, E.T. Hurley, 5 1/2 x 9 1/2" ........................ **2,860**

**Plaque,** rectangular, a winter landscape depicting a wind-swept evergreen tree in the snow silhouetted against a pink sky, Vellum glaze, 1915, E.F. McDermott, original wooden frame, 8 1/2 x 11" ........... **4,675**

**Plaque,** rectangular, large landscape of an autumn scene w/birch trees by a pond, Vellum glaze, original molded frame, 1940s, w/paper label & artist's initials, E.T. Hurley, 11 x 13" .............................. **11,000**

*Rookwood Tea Set*

**Tea set:** cov. 7 1/2" d., 5" h. teapot, 5" d. creamer & 6" d. cov. sugar bowl; each w/squatty bulbous bodies, decorated w/wild roses in salmon & white w/brown stems, thorns & leaves against a peach to ivory ground, Cameo glaze, the creamer w/C-form handle & pinched spout, the sugar bowl w/C-form handles & domed lip w/butterfly finial, the teapot w/swan's-neck spout, domed cover w/butterfly finial & rattan-wrapped swing bail handle, No. 404, 1891, H.E. Wilcox, teapot lid has crack & small flake to creamer, the set (ILLUS.) ............................. **660**

**Tile,** carved & painted stylized floral design in brown & green w/blue background, framed, 4" sq. ............................................. **286**

**Tile,** geometric design of squares in tan, blue & purple, framed, 4" sq. ....................... **187**

**Tile,** deeply incised & painted decoration of windmill on hillside w/trees in green on a rose ground, framed, 6" sq. ........................ **231**

**Tile,** squeezebag technique decoration of white windmill, dark blue trees against a light blue sky, 1919, artist-signed, framed, 6" sq. .............................................. **330**

**Tray,** molded design of a peacock feather, black & blue Matte glaze, No. 1668, 1922, 6 1/2" l. .............................................. **165**

*Rookwood Floral Decorated Urn*

**Urn,** cov., porcelain, wide bulbous ovoid body w/high domed cover w/button finial, decorated w/elaborate overall floral design w/swirling blossoms & leaves in red, green, blue, yellow & brown against an ivory ground, decorated inner lid & decorated & pierced exterior top, No. 2448, 1921, Arthur Conant, harmless line in body, 14 1/2" h. (ILLUS.) ............... **6,600**

**Vase,** 3" h., bulbous rounded body w/a four-sided wide neck incised w/a band of short pickets, shaded dark blue to moss green Matte glaze, No.1186, 1905 .............. **440**

**Vase,** 4 3/4" h, 3" w., pentagonal, each panel w/embossed rook at base, embossed foliate design near rim, blue Matte glaze, production vase, No. 1795, 1927 ......................................................... **358**

**Vase,** 5 3/4" h., short trumpet-form w/wide flaring rim, decorated w/cherry blossoms in white & pink under an orange to blue shaded ground w/yellow interior, Vellum glaze, No. 22643, 1925, Lenore Asbury ....... **990**

**Vase,** 6" h., ovoid body w/wide shoulder tapering to short cylindrical neck, painted stylized papyrus decoration in red, yellow & green on a grey ground, yellow leaf design outlined in blue on shoulder, Matte glaze, No. 1926, 1921, C.S. Todd ................................................. **2,420**

**Vase,** 6" h., 4 3/4" d., bulbous nearly spherical body tapering to a short flaring trumpet neck, decorated w/white hydrangea on an opalescent dark blue & green ground, Sea Green glaze, No. 402, 1902, Sara Sax ...................................... **5,225**

**Vase,** 6" h., 5 1/2" d., Jewel Porcelain, wide bulbous body w/narrow rolled rim, decorated w/Art Deco flowers in pink, green & blue, No. 6180, 1930, Sara Sax ............... **2,310**

**Vase,** 6 1/4" h., tapering ovoid form w/a wide flat mouth, molded around the shoulder w/a band of stylized flowers, Matte Green glaze, No. 2208, 1928 ............ **489**

**Vase,** 7" h., bulbous ovoid body tapering very slightly to wide closed rim, overall decoration of bushy green palms & a flock of birds on salmon ground, Vellum glaze, No. 942C, 1906, E.T. Hurley .......... **1,760**

**Vase,** 8 1/4" h, gently flaring cylindrical body w/flat rim, thickly enameled antelopes & stylized foliage in white & brown under a matte yellow Butterfat glaze, No. 6112, 1929, William Hentschel ................. **4,950**

**Vase,** 8 1/2" h., shouldered cylindrical body tapering slightly to short neck w/molded rim, decorated w/pink poppies on a shaded grey ground, Vellum glaze, No. 944D, 1907, Elizabeth Lincoln .................... **523**

**Vase,** 8 3/4" h., 4" d., cylindrical w/incurved rim, decorated w/a wide upper band painted w/pale purple irises & green leaves & stems on an ivory ground, lavender background, Iris glaze, No. 952, 1909, Lenore Asbury ................................. **1,980**

**Vase,** 9" h., footed trumpet form w/handles at base, decorated w/molded design of two ladies & stars, glossy grey glaze, No. 6539, 1935............................................. **385**

*Rare Black Iris Vase*

**Vase,** 9" h., slender ovoid body tapering to a short wide slightly rolled neck, decorated w/broad purple & pink irises w/yellow beards on green to blue stems w/green to blue leaves surrounding vase, two unopened buds in purple & yellow on a ground shading from peach, purple & light green to black, Black Iris glaze, No. 907E, 1907, Constance Baker (ILLUS.) .......................................... **7,700**

**Vase,** 9" h., slender ovoid form decorated w/large red & white lotus blossoms w/yellow centers, brown stems & leaves on a shaded yellow ground, Wax Matte glaze, No. 951D, 1941, K. Shirayamadani ...................... **2,640**

**Vase,** 9 1/8" h., tapered oviform w/raised riim, decorated w/a large iris blossom in dark blue & olive green on a mustard yellow & brown ground, Standard glaze, No. 94 DO, 1903, Sallie E. Coyne (crazing) .............................................................. **518**

**Vase,** 9 1/4" h., gently tapering cylindrical body w/flat rim, decorated w/green branches on a brown ground, Carved Matte glaze, No. 950C, 1905, Sallie Toohey .......................................................... **1,430**

**Vase,** 9 1/4" h., 3 3/4" d., tall slightly swelled cylindrical body tapering slightly to a short cylindrical neck, decorated w/large pale purple irises & dark green leaves & stems on a dark grey to white ground, Iris glaze, No. 907D, 1906, Sara Sax .................................................................. **4,125**

**Vase,** 9 1/2" h., 4 3/4" d., Jewel Porcelain, swelled cylindrical body w/a thick molded rim, decorated w/stylized reclining nudes in ivory on a flowing brown & cobalt blue ground, No. 1121C, 1931, Jens Jensen ............................................. **6,600**

**Vase,** 10 1/4" h., 5 3/4" d., simple tall ovoid form w/short flared rim, decorated w/an autumnal landscape w/elm trees in yellow, brown & polychrome against cream & blue, Wax Matte glaze, No. 892C, 1938, Mary Helen McDonald ................... **3,850**

**Vase,** 10 1/2" h., 4" d., tapering cylindrical body decorated w/purple lilacs against a

grey to ivory ground, Iris glaze, No. S1771, 1904, Ed Diers (restoration to top) ............................................................ **550**

**Vase,** 11 3/4" h., 6 1/2" d., footed ovoid body tapering gently to a flaring neck, decorated w/large fleshy magnolias in lavender & white on a pale purple to blue ground, Vellum glaze, No. 827, 1927, Lenore Asbury ......................................... **6,050**

**Vase,** 15" h., 7 1/2" d., gently flaring cylindrical form w/a wide flat rim, boldly decorated w/stylized blue iris & green leaves on a pink ground, Wax Matte glaze, No. 1369, 1925, Sallie Coyne ......................... **3,575**

**Vase,** 26" h., 11" d., floor-type, tall ovoid body tapering to a flaring trumpet neck, a wide embossed stylized geometric band in yellow around the neck, overall frothy Matte green glaze, No. 306, 1916 ... **3,575**

**Wall pocket,** conical w/flared & scalloped rim, two loop handles near rim, blue Matte glaze, No. 2965, 1928, 6" h. .............. **330**

**Wall sconce,** rectangular plaque-form deeply embossed w/a pair of owls under a green & brown Matte glaze, candle socket at the bottom edge, No. 1688, 1910, 6 x 11 1/4" (minor restoration to candleholder & sides)................................. **660**

**Water jug,** Turkish style, bulbous ovoid body tapering to closed flat mouth w/overhead loop handle, tapering cylindrical spout on one end w/short flaring cylindrical filling spout on the other, die impressed design at top, shoulder & base covered in gold w/gold trim on spouts & handle, body decorated w/two painted butterflies in tones of brown above black reeds & grasses on matte finish ground of cream & shaded blue, No. 41, 1886, Matt Daly, 9 1/2" h. ............. **1,210**

# ROSEMEADE

*Rosemeade Mark*

*Laura Taylor was a ceramic artist who supervised Federal Works Projects in her native North Dakota during the Depression era and later demonstrated at the potter's wheel during the 1939 New York World's Fair. In 1940, Laura Taylor and Robert J. Hughes opened the Rosemeade-Wahpeton Pottery, naming it after the North Dakota county and town of Wahpeton where it was located. Rosemeade Pottery was made on a small scale for only about twelve years with Laura Taylor designing the items and perfecting colors. Her animal and bird figures are popular among collectors. Hughes and Taylor married in 1943 and the pottery did a thriving business until her death in 1959. The pottery closed in 1961 but stock was sold from the factory sales-room until 1964.*

**Model of bear,** solid black glaze, 3" l. ............ **$395**
**Salt & pepper shakers,** model of Bob-
white quail, pr. ................................................. 60
**Salt & pepper shakers,** model of Brussel
sprout, pr. ....................................................... 20
**Salt & pepper shakers,** model of duck,
yellow glaze, pr. ............................................. 50
**Salt & pepper shakers,** model of ele-
phant, rose, pr. ............................................... 95
**Salt & pepper shakers,** model of Flicker-
tail, pr. ............................................................. 62
**Salt & pepper shakers,** model of grouse,
pr. ................................................................... 50
**Salt & pepper shakers,** model of hen &
rooster, pr. ...................................................... 55
**Salt & pepper shakers,** model of Mallard
duck, pr. .......................................................... 75
**Salt & pepper shakers,** model of mocca-
sin, pr. ............................................................. 50
**Salt & pepper shakers,** model of pheas-
ant, miniature, pr. ........................................... 44
**Salt & pepper shakers,** model of rose, pr. ....... 33
**Salt & pepper shakers,** model of skunk,
large, pr. .......................................................... 68
**Salt & pepper shakers,** model of skunk,
small, pr. .......................................................... 60
**Salt & pepper shakers,** model of tulip
blossom, pr. ..................................................... 43
**Salt & pepper shakers,** model of turkey,
small, pr. .......................................................... 83
**Sugar bowl,** model of a Mallard duck ............... 75

# ROSEVILLE

*Roseville Pottery Company operated in Zanesville, Ohio, from 1898 to 1954 after having been in business for six years prior to that in Muskingum County, Ohio. Art wares similar to those of Owens and Weller Potteries were produced. Items listed here are by patterns or lines.*

*Roseville*

*Roseville Mark*

## AZTEC (1915)
*Muted earthy tones of beige, grey, brown, teal, olive, azure blue or soft white with slip-trailed geometric decoration in contrasting colors.*

**Pitcher,** 5" h., footed w/round curved sides
tapering to wide flaring rim, grey & white
design on blue ground.............................. **$193**
**Vase,** 8" h., tapering cylinder swelling
slightly at top, squeeze-bag decoration
of lacy loops & swags in white & yellow
against a blue ground, artist-initialed .......... 495

**Vase,** 10" h., flared foot w/expanding cylindrical body & flared rim, white & tan decoration against a blue ground, artist-
signed............................................................. 248

## BANEDA (1933)
*Band of embossed pods, blossoms and leaves on green or raspberry pink ground.*

**Jardiniere,** two-handled, green ground,
No. 626-7", 7" h. ............................................ 413
**Jardiniere & pedestal base,** raspberry
pink ground, No. 626-8", 8" h., 2 pcs ......... 1,870
**Urn,** small rim handles, footed bulbous
body w/flat rim, raspberry pink ground,
No. 606-7", 7" h. ............................................ 770
**Vase,** 4" h., footed bulbous body
w/incurved flat rim, flat shoulder han-
dles, green ground, No. 587-4" ................... 275
**Vase,** 4" h., footed, wide squatty bulbous
base tapering sharply to small molded
mouth, tiny rim handles, raspberry pink
ground, No. 603-4" ........................................ 495
**Vase,** 5" h., footed, pear-shaped w/small
loop handles near rim, green ground,
No. 601-5" ..................................................... 550
**Vase,** 7" h., footed swelled cylindrical body
tapering to a short, wide cylindrical neck
flanked by small down-curved loop han-
dles, green ground, No. 590-7" ................... 525
**Vase,** 7" h., footed swelled cylindrical body
tapering to a short, wide cylindrical
neck flanked by small down-curved
loop handles, raspberry pink ground,
No. 590-7" ..................................................... 550
**Vase,** 7" h., footed wide cylindrical body
tapering to short wide cylindrical neck,
small loop handles, raspberry pink
ground, No. 592-7" ........................................ 504
**Vase,** 7" h., footed wide cylindrical body
tapering to short wide cylindrical neck,
small loop handles, green ground, No.
592-7" ......................................................... 1,650
**Vase,** 7" h., trumpet-shaped w/handles
from base to mid-section, green ground,
No. 604-7" .............................................. 350-400
**Vase,** 7" h., footed wide cylindrical body
w/wide collared rim, small loop handles
from shoulder to rim, green ground, No.
610-7" ............................................................ 660
**Vase,** 9" h., cylindrical w/short collared
neck, handles rising from shoulder to
beneath rim, green ground, No. 594-9" ...... 990
**Vase,** 9" h., bulbous body tapering to short
wide cylindrical rim, handles from mid-
base to below rim, raspberry pink
ground, No. 596-9" (small chip to base) ...... 825
**Vase,** 9" h., bulbous body tapering to short
wide cylindrical rim, handles from mid-
base to below rim, green ground, No.
596-9" ............................................................ 853
**Vase,** 12" h., expanding cylinder w/small
rim handles, raspberry pink ground, No.
599-12" (repairs to rim, handles & base) ...... 770

## BITTERSWEET (1940)
*Orange bittersweet pods and green leaves on a grey blending to rose, yellow with terra cotta, rose with green or solid green bark-textured ground; brown branch handles.*

Basket, hanging-type, green ground ............... 244
Basket w/pointed overhead handle,
green ground, No. 809-8", 8" h. ................... 242
Cornucopia-vase, green ground, No. 882-
8", 8" h. ................................................................ 185
Creamer, yellow ground, No. 871-C ................ 100
Jardiniere, green ground, 4" h., No. 400-
4" ......................................................................... 130
Jardiniere, pink ground, No. 842-7", 7" h. ....... 165
Jardiniere & pedestal base, yellow
ground, No. 802-8", 8" h., 2 pcs. (chip to
bottom ring of jardiniere) ............................. 880
Jardiniere & pedestal base, green
ground, overall 24" h., 2 pcs. ..................... 1,295
Planter, curved shaped sides, grey ground,
No. 828-10", 10 1/2" l. ................................. 110
Teapot, cov., yellow ground, No. 871-P .......... 225
Vase, double bud, 6" h., green ground, No.
873-6" .................................................................. 235
Vase, 8" h., asymmetrical handles, bulging
cylindrical form, grey ground, No. 883-8" ..... 135
Candleholders, handles rising from conical
base to midsection of nozzle, green
ground, No. 851-3", 3" h., pr. ....................... 125

## BLEEDING HEART (1938)
*Pink blossoms and green leaves on shaded
blue, green or pink ground.*

Basket w/pointed overhead handle,
w/flower frog, green ground, No. 361-
12", 12" h., 2 pcs. ......................................... 358
Book ends, book-shaped, pink ground, No.
6, pr. .................................................................. 385
Candlesticks, pink ground, 1139-4 1/2",
4 1/2" h., pr. ................................................... 165
Console bowl, pink ground, No. 382-10",
10" l. .................................................................. 250
Console bowl, pink ground, No. 383-14",
14" l. .................................................................. 450
Flower frog, round base, scalloped edge,
overhead handle, blue ground, No. 40,
3 1/2" h. ........................................................... 220
Jardiniere, blue ground, No. 651-5", 5" h. ....... 413
Jardiniere, green ground, No. 651-6", 6" h.
(small glaze chip to handle) ........................ 248
Jardiniere & pedestal base, pink ground,
jardiniere 8" h., No. 651-8", 2 pcs. ........... 1,045
Vase, 12" h., expanding cylinder w/small
handles at shoulder, blue ground, No.
974-12" .............................................................. 660
Vase, 12" h., expanding cylinder w/small
handles at shoulder, green ground, No.
974-12" (tiny glaze nick off one handle) ....... 468

## CARNELIAN I (1910-15)
*Matte glaze with a combination of two colors or
two shades of the same color with the darker dripping over the lighter tone or heavy and textured
glaze with intermingled colors and some running.*

Vase, 7" h., footed bulbous ovoid w/shoul-
der tapering to wide molded rim, handles
from shoulder to rim, light & dark blue,
No. 331-7" ......................................................... 176
Vase, 10" h., semi-ovoid base & long wide
neck w/rolled rim, ornate handles, grey &
mauve, black label, No. 337-10" .................... 413
Vase, 12" h., bulbous ovoid body w/wide
cylindrical neck, scrolled shoulder handles, grey & mauve, No. 338-12" ................. 440

Wall pocket, ornate side handles, flaring
rim, turquoise blue & aqua, 8" h. ............... 450
Wall pocket, ornate side handles, flaring
rim, mustard over light green, No. 1249-
9", 9" h. .............................................................. 245

## CARNELIAN II (1915)
*Intermingled colors, some with a drip effect.*

Bowl, 10" d., low faceted body, mottled
pink & green glaze ...................................... 495
Bowl, 14" d., short pedestal foot below
compressed round body w/incurved
sides & wide flaring rim, scrolled han-
dles, mottled pink & green glaze ................. 550
Lamp base, footed spherical body w/wide
cylindrical neck & scrolling angled handles, raspberry & green mottled matte
glaze, metal fittings, 8" h. (bruise to one
handle) ............................................................. 330
Urn, squatty bulbous body w/wide flaring
rim, scrolled handles, 5" h. ......................... 303
Urn, globular body tapering to flaring rim,
scrolled shoulder handles, rose, green &
grey ground, 6" h. .......................................... 660
Urn, footed, compressed globular form
w/short molded neck, ornate scrolled
handles, mottled pink, yellow & green
glaze, 7" h. ...................................................... 358
Urn, bulbous body w/wide cylindrical neck
& slightly flaring rim, scrolled shoulder
handles, mottled pink & green glaze,
7 1/4" h. ........................................................... 330
Urn, globular body w/tapering wide cylindri-
cal neck & molded rim, scrolled angular
handles from shoulder to rim, mottled
pink, yellow & green glaze, 8" h. ................. 935
Urn, ornate handles, compressed globular
form, purple & rose, 9" d., 8" h. ................. 825
Urn, bulbous body w/wide cylindrical neck,
ornate scrolled handles from shoulder to
rim, mottled pink, yellow & green glaze,
9 3/4" h. ........................................................... 770
Vase, 7" h., footed, bulbous base tapering
to wide cylindrical neck w/rolled rim,
ornate handles from shoulder to below
rim, mottled rose, grey & green glaze
(customary grinding chips to base & tight
line to one handle) ........................................ 239
Vase, 9" h., bulbous ovoid body w/short
collared mouth, angled shoulder han-
dles, mottled pink, yellow & green glaze ...... 715
Vase, 9" h., ovoid body tapering to cylindrical neck w/molded rim, mottled pink &
green glaze ...................................................... 440
Vase, 10" h., compressed globular base
w/trumpet form neck, ornate handles
from base to midsection, mottled pink,
amber & green glaze ..................................... 605
Vase, 10" h., compressed globular form
w/angled handles from mid-section to
rim, mottled rose & green glaze ............... 1,100
Vase, 10" h., footed wide tapering cylindrical body w/wide slightly flaring neck,
mottled pink & green glaze ........................... 523
Vase, 12" h., bulbous ovoid body w/wide
flaring rim flanked by buttressed handles, rose, mauve & green mottled
glaze, No. 445-12" (restoration to drill
hole at base) ................................................. 1,650

**Vase,** 12" h., flaring foot below wide bulbous body w/shoulder tapering to wide flaring cylindrical neck, rose, yellow, blue, violet & green mottled matte glaze, No. 446-12" ...................................................... **2,860**

**Vase,** 13 1/2" h., ovoid body w/slightly flaring rim, mottled pink & green glaze (bruise to base) .......................................... **990**

**Vase,** 15" h., floor-type, footed balusterform w/angled handles from shoulder to below rim, mottled grey, blue & green matte glaze................................................ **1,540**

**Vase,** 18" h., floor-type, tall ovoid body w/ringed base and flaring foot, molded rim & scrolled shoulder handles, mottled pink & green glaze ...................................... **1,815**

## CHERRY BLOSSOM (1933)
*Sprigs of cherry blossoms, green leaves and twigs with pink fence against a combed blue-green ground or creamy ivory fence against a terra cotta ground shading to dark brown.*

**Bowl,** 4" h., two-handled, canted sides, terra cotta ground......................................... **275**

**Jardiniere,** shoulder handles, terra cotta ground, 6" h., No. 627-6"............................ **358**

**Planter,** rectangular w/two small handles, terra-cotta ground, No. 240-8", 3 x 11", 7" l............................................................. **303**

**Vase,** 5" h., two-handled, slightly ovoid, terra cotta ground, No. 619-5"...................... **275**

**Vase,** 6" h., bulbous body, shoulder tapering to wide molded mouth, small loop shoulder handles, terra cotta ground, No. 621-6 ............................................... **354**

**Vase,** 6" h., bulbous body, shoulder tapering to wide molded mouth, small loop shoulder handles, blue-green ground, No. 621-6 ............................................... **605**

**Vase,** 7 1/2" h., two-handled, footed cylindrical body, terra cotta ground, No. 620-7"....................................................... **343**

**Vase,** 15" h., floor-type, bulbous ovoid w/wide molded mouth, small loop shoulder handles, blue-green ground, No. 628-15" (few minute flecks to decoration, glazed-over chip to branch & few minor chips to base)........................................... **3,575**

## CLEMATIS (1944)
*Clematis blossoms and heart-shaped green leaves against a vertically textured ground — white blossoms on blue, rose-pink blossoms on green and ivory blossoms on golden brown.*

*Clematis Hanging-Type Basket*

**Basket,** hanging-type, brown ground, No. 470-5", 5" h. (ILLUS.) ................................... **175**

**Basket,** hanging-type, green ground, No. 470-5", 5" h. .......................................... **175-200**

**Basket,** waisted cylindrical body, green ground, No. 387-7" ..................................... **134**

**Basket,** blue ground, No. 388-8" .................... **160**

**Basket w/ornate circular handle,** waisted cylindrical body, brown ground, No. 387-7", 7" h....................................................... **170**

**Basket w/overhead handle,** pedestal base, green ground, No. 389-10", 10" h............................................... **175-200**

**Bowl,** 10" d., green ground, No. 6-10"........... **250**

**Candleholders,** bulbous w/tiny pointed handles, brown ground, No. 1158-2", 2" h., pr............................................................ **98**

**Console bowl,** brown ground, end handles, 17 1/2" l............................................ **132**

**Cookie jar,** cov., brown ground, No. 3-8", 8" h................................................................ **427**

**Cookie jar,** cov., green ground, No. 3-8", 8" h................................................................ **550**

**Creamer & open sugar bowl,** green ground, No. 5S & 5C, pr. ......................... **155**

**Ewer,** blue ground, No. 17-10", 10" h.......... **173**

**Ewer,** green ground, No. 17-10", 10" h............. **245**

**Ewer,** blue ground, No. 18-15", 15" h.......... **365**

**Ewer,** brown ground, No. 18-15", 15" h.......... **290**

**Flower frog,** green ground, No. 50, 4 1/2" h................................................................ **28**

**Flower frog,** green ground, No. 192-5", 5" h................................................................ **115**

**Jardiniere,** blue ground, No. 667-8", 8" h. ....... **322**

**Tea set:** cov. teapot, creamer & open sugar bowl, green ground, No. 5, 3 pcs. ................. **325**

**Vase,** 6" h., two-handled, urn-form, brown ground, No. 188-6".................................... **105**

**Vase,** 7" h., brown ground, No. 105-7".............. **99**

**Vase,** 7" h., brown ground, No. 105-7"............. **150**

**Vase,** bud, 7" h., angular handles rising from flared base to slender neck, green ground, No. 187-7".................................... **150**

**Vase,** 8" h., two-handled, blue ground, No. 107-8"........................................................ **90-100**

**Vase,** 8" h., two-handled, globular base w/high collared neck, green ground, No. 108-8"................................................................ **90**

**Vase,** 8" h., footed baluster-form w/flaring mouth & angled shoulder handles, blue ground, No. 122-8" ...................................... **185**

**Vase,** 10" h., two-handled, brown ground, No. 111-10".................................................. **210**

**Wall pocket,** angular side handles, brown ground, No. 1295-8", 8 1/2" h...................... **138**

## COLUMBINE (1940s)
*Columbine blossoms and foliage on shaded ground — yellow blossoms on blue, pink blossoms on pink shaded to green and blue blossoms on tan shaded to green.*

**Basket,** elaborate handle rising from midsection, pink ground, No. 365-7", 7" h......... **220**

**Basket,** hanging-type, pink ground, 8" h. ......... **220**

**Basket,** blue ground, No. 367-10", 10" h.......... **220**

**Basket,** pointed handle rising from flat base, ovoid w/boat-shaped top w/shaped rim, pink ground, No. 368-12", 12" h.......................................................... **350**

**Basket w/overhead handle,** footed, bulbous ovoid body w/irregular rim, brown ground, 610-12", 12" h. (small chip to base) .................................................................. **275**

**Bowl,** 6" d., two-handled, squatty bulbous body w/small angled shoulder handles, blue ground, No. 400-6" .............................. 220

**Jardiniere,** squatty w/small handles at shoulder, tan ground, No. 655-3", 3" h. .......... 90

**Jardiniere,** two-handled, pink ground, No. 655-6", 6" h. .............................................. 138

**Jardiniere,** two-handled, tan ground, No. 655-6", 6" h. (restoration to rim chip) ............. 99

**Jardiniere,** two-handled, blue ground, No. 655-10" 10" h. ............................................ 413

**Rose bowl,** bulbous body flanked by angled handles, wide slightly flared & shaped rim, pink ground, No. 399-4", 4" h. ............... 150

**Vase,** 4" h., ovoid body w/wide flared & shaped rim flanked by small angled handles, pink ground, No. 12-4" ........................ 135

**Vase,** 4" h., blue ground, No. 657-4" ............... 250

**Vase,** 6" h., blue ground, No. 13-6" ................ 110

**Vase,** 6" h., pink ground, No. 14-6" ............... 132

**Vase,** 7" h., blue ground, No. 16-7" ............... 108

**Vase,** 7 1/2" h., two-handled, ovoid w/slightly flaring mouth, pink ground, No. 17-7" (small chip to handle)........................... 88

**Vase,** 7" h., blue ground, No. 18-7" ................ 225

**Vase,** 9" h., two-handled, blue ground, No. 21-9" ...................................................... 220

**Vase,** 10" h., ovoid body w/angular handles rising from base to midsection, blue ground, No. 24-10" ..................................... 285

**Vase,** 10" h., ovoid body w/angular handles rising from base to midsection, tan ground, No. 24-10" ..................................... 295

*Columbine Vase*

**Vase,** 12" h., swelled ovoid body w/flaring rim, angular handles at midsection, flat disc base, pink ground, No. 25-12 (ILLUS.)...................................................... 468

**Vase,** 14" h., floor-type, slender ovoid body tapering to a flared & shaped rim, pointed angular handles at midsection, flat disc base, tan ground, No. 26-14" .......... 463

**Wall pocket,** squared flaring mouth, conical body w/curled tip, blue ground, No. 1290-8" ...................................................... 625

## DAHLROSE (1924-28)
*Band of ivory daisy-like blossoms and green leaves against a mottled tan ground.*

**Jardiniere & pedestal base,** No. 614-10", 10" h., 2 pcs. (re-glued base chip to jardiniere) ......................................................... 935

**Vase,** 6" h., cylindrical w/small pointed handles at the shoulder, No. 363-6" ................... 139

**Vase,** 10" h., footed tapering square form, paper label ...................................................... 330

**Vase,** 12" h., footed wide ovoid w/wide flaring rim, angled handles from shoulder to rim, No. 370-12" ........................................ 523

**Wall pocket,** conical w/molded rim, tiny rim handles, No. 1258-8", 8" h. .......................... 550

**Candleholders,** angular handles rising from low slightly domed base, 3 1/2" h., pr. ...................................................................... 95

## DAWN (1937)
*Incised spidery flowers on green ground with blue-violet tinted blossoms, pink or yellow ground with blue-green blossoms, all with yellow centers.*

*Dawn Vase*

**Vase,** 6" h., cylindrical w/tab handles below rim, square foot, green ground, No. 826-6" (ILLUS.)..................................................... 110

**Vase,** 6" h., tab handles at rim, semi-ovoid, square foot, green ground, No. 827-6" ........ 200

**Vase,** 10" h., bulbous ovoid body on square foot, buttressed shoulder handles, yellow ground, No. 832-10" (glaze flakes to base & handle) ............................................. 358

## DOGWOOD I (1916-18)
*White dogwood blossoms and brown branches against a textured green ground.*

**Basket w/overhead handle,** 8" h. ................... 440

**Vase,** 6" h., bulbous ovoid body, No. 300-6"..... 275

**Vase,** 9" h., ovoid body w/flaring rim, No. 303-9"........................................................ 385

**Wall pocket,** cone-shaped, 9 1/2" h., No. 1245-9"...................................................... 358

## DOGWOOD II (1928)
*White dogwood blossoms & black branches against a smooth green ground.*

**Basket,** hanging-type ....................................... 275

**Basket,** 8" h. .................................................... 214

**Vase,** 8" h., ovoid body tapering to wide cylindrical neck, No. 135-8" (couple of burst bubbles to neck & body)..................... 110

## EARLAM (1930)
*Mottled glaze on various simple shapes. The line includes many crocus or strawberry pots.*

**Bowl,** 4" h., canted sides w/scroll handles, bluish green glaze on exterior & salmon interior, unmarked, No. 217-4" ..................... 248
**Bowl,** 4" d., blue ground, No. 515-4" ............... 188
**Planter,** rectangular w/shaped rim, blue ground, No. 88-6 x 10" .................................. 295
**Planter,** two-handled, rectangular w/shaped rim, curved end handles, mottled green glaze, No. 89-8", 5 x 10 1/2" ...... 275
**Strawberry pot w/saucer,** four pockets, mottled green glaze, No. 91-8", 8" h. ........ 1,045
**Urn-vase,** two-handled, mottled blue-green, No. 521-7", 7" h............................... 440
**Vase,** 6" h., two-handled, semi-ovoid, mottled blue-green glaze, No. 518-6"................ 220
**Vase,** 7" h., bulbous ovoid w/large loop handles, orange, green & blue matte glaze, No. 519-7" (minute burst bubble ar rim & small flat chip inside bottom ring) ................................................................ 413
**Vase,** 7" h., globular w/handles at shoulder, mottled blue & green glaze, No. 521-7" ....... 375

## EARLY EMBOSSED PITCHERS (Pre-1916)
**Boy w/horn** ................................................. 550
**The Bridge,** 6" h. ......................................... 258
**The Cow,** 6 1/2" h............................................ 399
**The Owl,** 6 1/2" h............................................ 599

## FALLINE (1933)
*Curving panels topped by a semi-scallop separated by vertical peapod decorations; blended backgrounds of tan shading to green and blue or tan shading to darker brown.*

**Vase,** 6" h., footed cylindrical body w/large loop handles from midsection to rim, tan shading to blue & green, No. 642-6" ........... 990
**Vase,** 6" h., two-handled, ovoid, tan shading to blue & green, No. 643-6" .................... 935
**Vase,** 6" h., globular body w/a narrow swelled shoulder below the wide short cylindrical neck, C-scroll handles from the neck to the top of the body, green "pods" on a light shaded to dark brown ground, No. 644-6", gold foil label ............... 798
**Vase,** two-handled, tan shading to darker brown, 6" h., No. 650-6" ........................... 660
**Vase,** 6 1/2" h., bulbous ovoid w/large loop handles, blue ground, No. 645-6 1/2" .......... 928
**Vase,** 6 1/2" h., bulbous ovoid w/large loop handles, tan shading to darker brown ground, No. 645-6 1/2" .............................. 660
**Vase,** 7" h., globular body tapering to stepped shoulder & wide cylindrical neck w/shoulder loop handles, shaded brown body, No. 648-7" ...................................... 1,045
**Vase,** 7 1/2" h., two-handled, slightly rounded cylinder, tan shading to brown, No. 647-7" ...................................................... 715
**Vase,** 7 1/2" h., two-handled, slightly rounded cylinder, tan shading to blue & green, No. 647-7" ......................................... 758
**Vase,** 9" h., two large handles rising from midsection to neck, horizontally ribbed lower section, shaded brown, No. 652-9" ..... 963

## FOXGLOVE (1940s)
*Sprays of pink and white blossoms embossed against a shaded matte-finish ground.*

**Basket,** hanging-type, blue ground, No. 466-5", 6 1/2" h...................................... 300-350
**Basket,** hanging-type, green ground, No. 466-5", 6 1/2" h...................................... 250-300
**Basket w/circular overhead handle,** conical body w/asymmetric & shaped rim on round disc base, No. 373-8", 8" h................ 225
**Basket w/circular overhead handle,** footed conical body w/widely flaring rim, green ground, No. 374-10", 10" h................ 495
**Basket w/circular overhead handle,** footed conical body w/widely flaring rim, pink ground, No. 374-10", 10" h. ................. 220
**Basket w/circular overhead handle,** footed fan-shape w/shaped rim, pink ground, No. 375-12", 12" h........................... 330
**Book ends,** blue ground, No. 10, pr................ 250

*Foxglove Book Ends*

**Book ends,** pink ground, No. 10, minor glaze nick back edge of one, pr. (ILLUS.)..... 308
**Candleholders,** disk base, conical w/angled handles from midsection to base, pink ground, No. 159-5", 5" h., pr. ...... 193
**Console bowl,** boat-shaped w/angled end handles, blue ground, No. 421-10", 10" l...... 141
**Console bowl,** boat-shaped w/angled end handles, green ground, No. 421-10", 10" l. ................................................................ 210
**Console bowl,** boat-shaped w/angled end handles, pink ground, No. 421-10", 10" l...... 205
**Console bowl,** oval w/cut-out rim & pointed end handles, blue ground, No. 422-10", 10" l................................................. 160
**Cornucopia-vase,** snail shell-type, pink ground, No. 166-6"...................................... 135
**Cornucopia-vase,** green ground, No. 164-8", 8" h.............................................................. 275
**Ewer,** pink ground, No. 4-6 1/2", 6 1/2" h. ........ 218
**Flower frog,** cornucopia-shaped, pink ground, No. 46, 4" h. .................................. 165
**Jardiniere,** two-handled, blue ground, No. 659-3", 3" h............................................ 100
**Jardiniere,** two-handled, green ground, No. 659-5", 5" h. ........................................ 160
**Jardiniere,** two-handled, blue ground, No. 659-8", 8" h. ........................................ 220
**Model of a conch shell,** green ground, No. 426-6", 6" l. ......................................... 225
**Model of a conch shell,** pink ground, No. 426-6", 6" l. ........................................... 175
**Pedestal base,** large, blue ground.................. 385
**Tray,** single open handle, leaf-shaped, green ground, 8 1/2" w. ......................... 100-125
**Tray,** open rim handles, shaped oval, blue ground, 11" l. ................................................ 150

**Urn-vase,** pink ground, No. 162-8", 8" h. ......... **248**
**Vase,** 4" h., squatty bulbous base w/wide
cylindrical neck, angular side handles,
pink ground, No. 42-4" ................................. **110**
**Vase,** 4" h., squatty bulbous base w/wide
cylindrical neck, angular side handles,
blue ground, No. 42-4" ................................. **145**
**Vase,** 5" h., three-section pillow-type, pink
& green, No. 165-5"...................................... **180**
**Vase,** 6 1/2" h., ovoid body w/flared rim,
double angled handles from base to rim,
pink ground, No. 44-6" ........................... **125-150**
**Vase,** 7" h., semi-ovoid w/long slender
angled side handles, blue ground, No.
45-7".......................................................... **231**
**Vase,** 7" h., semi-ovoid w/long slender
angled side handles, green ground, No.
45-7" .......................................................... **165**
**Vase,** 7" h., semi-ovoid w/long slender
angled side handles, pink ground, No.
45-7" .......................................................... **138**
**Vase,** 7" h., two-handled, blue ground, No.
46-7" (minute glaze miss to handle)............. **165**
**Vase,** 9" h., footed spherical body tapering
to wide cylindrical neck w/flaring rim,
small angled shoulder handles, No. 50-
9".............................................................. **297**
**Vase,** 10" h., angular handles rising from
base to below flaring rim, pink ground,
No. 51-10".................................................. **330**
**Vase,** 14" h., conical w/flaring mouth, four
short handles rising from disc base, blue
ground, No. 53-14"...................................... **660**
**Vase,** 15" h., footed ovoid body, two-han-
dled, green ground, No. 54-15" ................... **468**
**Vase,** 15" h., footed ovoid body, two-handled, pink ground, No. 54-15"..................... **895**
**Vase,** 16" h., pear-shaped body w/closed
rim, angled handles from lower body to
shoulder, green ground, No. 55-16"............ **605**
**Vase,** 18" h., floor-type, two-handled,
footed baluster-form w/narrow flared rim,
blue ground, No. 56-18" ........................ **725-750**
**Vase,** 18" h., floor-type, two-handled,
footed baluster-form w/narrow flared rim,
pink ground, artist-initialed, No. 56-18" ........ **715**
**Wall pocket,** conical w/flaring rim, loop
handles, green ground, No. 1292-8",
8" h. ........................................................... **400**

## FREESIA (1945)

*Trumpet-shaped blossoms and long slender
green leaves against wavy impressed lines — white
and lavender blossoms on blended green; white
and yellow blossoms on shaded blue or terra cotta
and brown.*

**Basket,** hanging-type, blue ground, No.
471-5"......................................................... **300**
**Basket,** hanging-type, terra cotta ground,
No. 471-5" .................................................. **259**
**Basket,** green ground, No. 390-7", 7" h. .......... **220**
**Basket,** terra cotta ground, No. 390-7",
7" h............................................................. **160**
**Basket,** terra cotta ground, No. 392-10",
10" h. ......................................................... **275**
**Basket w/low overhead handle,** green
ground, No. 310-10", 10" h........................... **250**
**Basket w/overhead handle,** terra-cotta
ground, No. 391-8", 8" h.............................. **143**

**Book ends,** blue ground, No. 15, 5 1/4" h.,
pr................................................................. **248**
**Bowl,** 6" d., green ground, No. 464-6"............. **135**
**Bowl,** 11" d., two-handled, terra cotta
ground, No. 465-8".................................... **135**
**Candleholders,** tiny pointed handles,
domed base, green ground, No. 1160-
2", 2" h., pr.................................................... **90**
**Candlestick,** disc base, cylindrical w/low
handles, green ground, No. 1161-4 1/2",
4 1/2" h. ....................................................... **75**
**Candlesticks,** disc base, cylindrical w/low
handles, blue ground, No. 1161-4 1/2",
4 1/2" h., pr. ............................................... **150**
**Candlesticks,** disc base, cylindrical w/low
handles, green ground, No. 1161-4 1/2",
4 1/2" h., pr. ............................................... **125**
**Candlesticks,** disc base, cylindrical w/low
handles, terra cotta ground, No. 1161-
4 1/2", 4 1/2" h., pr................................. **120-130**
**Console bowl,** oval w/angled end handles,
green ground, No. 7-10", 10"...................... **250**
**Console bowl,** low, round, green ground,
No. 465-8", 8" d. ........................................ **175**
**Console bowl,** oval w/shaped flaring rim &
angled end handles, green ground, No.
469-14", 16 1/2" l......................................... **208**
**Console bowl,** oval w/shaped flaring rim &
angled end handles, terra cotta ground,
No. 469-14", 16 1/2" l. ................................ **135**
**Cookie jar,** cov., bulbous ovoid body
w/angled shoulder handles, slightly
domed lid w/knob finial, terra cotta
ground, No. 4-8", 8" h................................. **438**
**Cookie jar,** cov., bulbous ovoid body
w/angled shoulder handles, slightly
domed lid w/knob finial, blue ground, No.
4-8", 8" h. ................................................... **550**
**Creamer,** green ground, No. 6C...................... **100**
**Ewer,** blue ground, No. 19-6", 6" h. ................ **139**
**Ewer,** terra cotta ground, No. 19-6", 6" h........ **260**
**Ewer,** blue ground, No. 20-10", 10" h. ............ **300**
**Ewer,** blue ground, No. 21-15", 15" h. ............ **248**
**Ewer,** terra cotta ground, No. 21-15", 15" h...... **750**
**Jardiniere,** tiny rim handles, terra cotta
ground, No. 669-4", 4" h........................ **75-100**
**Jardiniere,** rim handles, blue ground, No.
669-8", 8" h................................................. **425**
**Jardiniere & pedestal base,** green
ground, No. 669-8", 2 pcs. ......................... **805**
**Jardiniere & pedestal base,** terra cotta
ground, No. 669-8", 2 pcs. ...................... **1,000**
**Pitcher,** 10" h., tankard, footed slender
ovoid body w/wide spout & pointed
arched handle, terra cotta ground, No.
20-10"................................................... **150-200**
**Pitcher,** 10" h., tankard, footed slender
ovoid body w/wide spout & pointed
arched handle, green ground, No. 20-10" ..... **450**
**Tea set:** cov. teapot, creamer & open sugar
bowl; blue ground, Nos. 6, 6C & 6S, 3
pcs. (ILLUS. of teapot, top next page) ......... **605**
**Tea set:** cov. teapot, creamer & open sugar
bowl; Nos. 6, 6C & 6S, terra cotta
ground, 3 pcs. ............................................. **450**
**Teapot,** cov., terra cotta ground, No. 6............. **200**
**Urn-vase,** two-handled, bulbous body
tapering to wide cylindrical neck, green
ground, No. 196-8", 8" h.............................. **209**

*Freesia Teapot*

**Vase,** bud, 7" h., handles rising from compressed globular base, long slender tapering neck, terra cotta ground, No. 195-7" .......... **83**

**Vase,** 6" h., footed squatty bulbous base w/wide cylindrical neck, large angled handles, terra cotta ground, No. 118-6" ......... **88**

**Vase,** 6" h., two-handled, wide fan-shaped body, terra cotta ground, No. 199-6" ........... **135**

**Vase,** 7" h., base handles, long cylindrical neck, terra cotta ground, No. 119-7" ...... **75-125**

**Vase,** 7" h., two-handled, slightly expanding cylinder, blue ground, No. 120-7" .......... **140**

**Vase,** 7" h., two-handled, slightly expanding cylinder, green ground, No. 120-7" ......... **161**

**Vase,** bud, 7" h., handles rising from compressed globular base, long slender tapering neck, green ground, No. 195-7" ........................................ **95-100**

**Vase,** 7" h., two-handled, fan shaped, blue ground, No. 200-7" ....................................... **150**

**Vase,** 8" h., footed ovoid body flanked by D-form handles, terra cotta ground, No. 121-8" .................................................... **150**

**Vase,** 8" h., globular base & flaring rim, handles at midsection, blue ground, No. 122-8" ........................................ **125-150**

**Vase,** 8" h., globular base & flaring rim, handles at midsection, terra cotta ground, No. 122-8" ...................................... **110**

**Vase,** 9" h., two angular handles at base, cylindrical top w/flaring rim, terra cotta ground, No. 124-9" ...................................... **110**

**Vase,** 9" h., two angular handles at base, cylindrical top w/flaring rim, blue ground, No. 124-9" ...................................... **190**

**Vase,** 9 1/2" h., a short ringed pedestal base supporting a flaring half-round base w/an angled shoulder tapering slightly to a tall, wide cylindrical neck, down-curved angled loop handles from center of neck to rim of lower shoulder, terra cotta ground, No. 123-9" ..................... **180**

**Vase,** 9 1/2" h., a short ringed pedestal base supporting a flaring half-round base w/an angled shoulder tapering slightly to a tall, wide cylindrical neck, down-curved angled loop handles from center of neck to rim of lower shoulder, blue ground, No. 123-9 ............................... **185**

**Vase,** 10" h., two-handled, spherical base w/wide cylindrical neck & flat rim, terra cotta ground, No. 126-10" (ILLUS. top next column)................................................. **165**

**Vase,** 10" h., two-handled, spherical base w/wide cylindrical neck & flat rim, blue ground, No. 126-10" ...................................... **230**

**Vase,** 10 1/2" h., two-handled, trumpet-form body, green ground, No. 125-10" (professional repair) ..................................... **175**

*Freesia Vase*

**Vase,** 15" h., tall slender ovoid body tapering to narrow cylindrical neck w/wide flaring rim, pointed shoulder handles, blue ground, No. 128-15" ............................. **660**

**Vase,** 18" h., floor-type, tall slender ovoid body w/slightly flared rim, angled shoulder handles, green ground, No. 129-18" ...... **550**

**Vase,** No. 129-18"18" h., floor-type, tall slender ovoid body w/slightly flared rim, angled shoulder handles, blue ground, No. 129-18" ............................................ **495**

**Wall pocket,** waisted long body w/small angled side handles, green ground, No. 1296-8", 8 1/2" h............................................. **237**

**Wall pocket,** waisted long body w/small angled side handles, terra cotta ground, No. 1296-8", 8 1/2" h. ................................... **295**

**Window box,** two-handled, green ground, No. 1392-8", 10 1/2" l. ............................. **150**

**Window box,** two-handled, terra cotta ground, No. 1392-8", 10 1/2" l. ..................... **125**

**Candleholders,** tiny pointed handles, domed base, terra cotta ground, No. 1160-2", 2" h., pr. ......................................... **100**

## FUTURA (1928)
*Varied line with shapes ranging from Art Deco geometrics to futuristic. Matte glaze is typical although an occasional piece may be high gloss.*

**Bowl w/flower frog,** 8" d., collared base, shaped flaring sides w/relief decoration, orange glaze w/polychrome geometric design, Nos. 187-8" & 15-3 1/2", 2 pcs. (professional repair to rim) .......................... **330**

**Bowl-planter,** 5 1/2" h., square w/flared rim, raised on four feet, grey & green glaze, No. 190-3 1/2 - 6" ............................. **286**

**Candleholders,** conical base w/square handles, widely flaring shallow socket, green & orange glaze, No. 1072-4", 4" h., black paper label on one, pr............... **711**

**Jardiniere,** angular handles rising from wide sloping shoulders to rim, sharply canted sides, aqua & green w/pink leaves, No. 616-6", 6" h............................... **275**

**Jardiniere,** angular handles rising from wide sloping shoulders to rim, sharply canted sides, terra cotta ground, No. 616-7", unmarked, 7" h. .............................. **413**

**Jardiniere,** angular handles rising from wide sloping shoulders to rim, sharply canted sides, pink & purple heart-shaped leaves on a greyish-purple ground, No. 616-9", 9" h. (three hairlines to base & up side, 3" & less) ...................... **275**

**Jardiniere,** angular handles rising from wide sloping shoulders to rim, sharply canted sides, terra cotta ground, No. 616-9", 9" h. ............................................... **358**

**Jardiniere,** angular handles rising from wide sloping shoulders to rim, sharply canted sides, terra cotta ground, No. 616-14", 14" h. ......................................... **440**

**Vase,** 4" h., square mounted cone-shaped body w/four vertical supports extending down from mid-point of sides to corners of square disc base, purple, No. 430-9" (tight rim crack & chip off one foot) ............. **413**

**Vase,** 4 1/2" h., 6 1/2" w., straight handles rising from sharply canted low base to rim, upper portion square w/cut corners & canted sides, low-relief curving design on sides & base, terra cotta, No. 85-4" ....... **289**

**Vase,** 5" h., flaring squared footed & slightly flaring squared sides, embossed green leaf decoration on foot, shaded brown & gold, No. 421-5" ........................... **303**

**Vase,** 5" h., 5" w., 1 1/2" d., stepped base, incised fan effect, light & darker blue glaze, No. 81-5", ........................................ **289**

**Vase,** 6" h., flat flaring body in a mottled blue over orange glaze w/a green geo-metric pattern on the shoulders, low rect-angular mouth, No. 82-6", unmarked .......... **366**

**Vase,** 6" h., footed, wide bulbous form, brown & blue ground, No. 137-6" ................. **660**

**Vase,** 7" h., 5 1/2" d., high domed & stepped beehive-form body below a wide & flaring neck joined by two short strap handles to the shoulder, shaded cream to blue body w/green leaves around the body, unmarked, No. 403-7" ...... **880**

**Vase,** 7" h. ringed ovoid body w/closed rim flanked by four stepped buttresses, light & dark blue glaze, No. 405-7" ..................... **750**

**Vase,** 7" h., footed ringed-ovoid body w/short flaring wide mouth, yellow, green & blue glaze, No. 424-7" (professional repair of small glaze nicks off foot) .............. **440**

**Vase,** 8" h., spherical body on polyhedron base, tiny cylindrical neck, blue ground w/green design (restored base) .................. **495**

**Vase,** 8" h., bottle-shaped w/stepped back bands, grey-blue & pink, No. 384-8" ............ **495**

**Vase,** 8" h., square buttressed body flaring slightly at neck, orange, green & taupe glaze, No. 402-8" ...................................... **935**

**Vase,** 8" h., squared form w/angled but-tress corners & flared rim, shaded green, No. 402-8" ................................................ **550-600**

**Vase,** 8" h., cylindrical base expanding to bulbous ringed top, four green & blue Art Deco design feet, blue matte ground w/green shoulder design, No. 405-7 1/2" ..... **935**

**Vase,** 8" h., high domed & stepped bee-hive-form, shaded tan w/green leaves around the body, unmarked, No. 406-8" ...... **825**

**Vase,** 8" h., square, slightly tapering body twisting toward the rim, pink ground, No. 425-8" ................................................... **537**

**Vase,** 8" h., semi-ovoid, flaring foot, flat closed handles from midsection to neck, molded trailing florals on side, purple & mauve, No. 427-8" (professional repair to small chips) ............................................. **248**

**Vase,** 8" h., globular w/low canted foot & short collared neck, brown shading to tan, embossed cluster of small flowers & leaves at shoulder & three rings around middle, No. 428-8" ................................... **440**

**Vase,** 8" h., globular w/low canted foot & short collared neck, pink-beige shading to sand white, embossed cluster of small flowers & leaves at shoulder & three rings around middle, No. 428-8" .................. **262**

**Vase,** 9" h., a wide low domed foot below four short, narrow side buttresses flank-ing the tall gently flaring trumpet-form body decorated w/crocuses, purple, No. 429-9" ..................................................... **875**

**Vase,** bud, 10" h., stacked conical form w/gold, green & purple scattered design against a cobalt blue ground, No. 390-10" ......................................................... **880**

**Vase,** bud, 10" h., stacked conical form w/ivory, green & lavender scattered design against an orange ground, No. 390-10" ......................................................... **605**

**Vase,** 10" h., 6" d., a narrow flaring foot below the wide ovoid body tapering to a wide, deep flaring neck flanked by small straight handles down to the shoulder, small molded brown pine cones & dark green pine sprigs on the neck & shoul-der on the mottled green crystalline glaze, No. 433-10" ........................... **1,000-1,200**

**Vase,** 12" h., wide ovoid body on a footring, the neck composed of tapering bands, smooth sides, turquoise glaze w/gun-metal shading, No. 394-12" ......................... **807**

**Vase,** 12" h., stepped domed base, expanding cylindrical body flanked by buttressed handles, chevron pattern in green on orange ground, No. 410-12" (1/4" chip to rim, very short & tight line opposing) ............................................. **1,045**

**Vase,** 12" h., slightly tapering tall cylindrical body w/flat flared rim, flanked by long tapering buttress handles, No. 437-12" ..... **1,288**

## GARDENIA (1940s)
*Large white gardenia blossoms and green leaves over a textured impressed band on a shaded green, grey or tan ground.*

**Basket,** hanging-type, green ground, 8".......... **220**

**Book ends,** brown ground, No. 659, 5 1/2" h., pr...................................................... **275**

**Book ends,** green ground, No. 659, 5 1/2" h., pr...................................................... **250**

**Bowl,** 10" d., grey ground, No. 628-10"............ **120**

**Candleholders,** grey ground, No. 651-2", 2" h., pr............................................................ **75**

**Candleholders,** grey ground, No. 652-4", 4 1/2" h., pr...................................................... **115**

**Ewer,** ovoid base, green ground, No. 617-10", 10" h.................................................... **180**

**Ewer,** ovoid base, grey ground, No. 617-
10", 10" h............................................................ **150**
**Jardiniere,** grey ground, No. 603-10" (2
small petal nicks)........................................... **350**
**Jardiniere,** footed wide bulbous body
tapering to a scalloped rim flanked by
two small shoulder handles, No. 641-5",
5" h.......................................................................... **92**
**Vase,** 8" h., handles rising from base to
midsection, cylindrical body, tan ground,
No. 683-8"............................................................. **125**
**Vase,** 8" h., handles rising from base to
midsection, cylindrical body, grey
ground, No. 683-8".......................................... **165**
**Vase,** 8" h., tan ground, No. 684-8"................... **165**
**Vase,** 10" h., tall ovoid body w/fanned rim,
base handles, grey ground, No. 685-10"...... **237**
**Vase,** 10" h., two-handled, tan ground, No.
924-9"..................................................................... **325**
**Vase,** 12" h., handles rising from low base
to midsection, tan ground, No. 687-12"
(glaze flakes to bottom).............................. **138**
**Vase,** 14 1/2" h., floral-type, two handles
rising from midsection to below rim, tan
ground, No. 689-14"..................................... **375**
**Wall pocket,** brown ground, No. 662-8",
8" h....................................................................... **280**
**Wall pocket,** large handles, green ground,
No. 666-8", 9 1/2" h....................................... **260**
**Window box,** green ground, No. 668-8",
8" l........................................................................... **95**
**Window box,** green ground, No. 669-12",
14" l....................................................................... **150**
**Window box,** grey ground, No. 669-12",
14" l....................................................................... **115**

## IRIS (1938)

*White or yellow blossoms and green leaves on
rose blending with green, light blue deepening to a
darker blue or tan shading to green or brown.*

**Basket,** tan ground, 10" d., 8 1/2" h. ............... **295**
**Basket w/pointed overhead handle,** com-
pressed ball form, blue ground, No. 354-
8", 8" h.................................................................. **303**

*Iris Basket*

**Basket w/semicircular overhead handle,**
rose ground, No. 355-10", 9 1/2" h.
(ILLUS.)............................................................. **468**
**Bowl-vase** squatty bulbous body
w/stepped shoulder handles, blue
ground, No. 357-4", 4" h. ............................ **110**
**Bowl-vase** squatty bulbous body
w/stepped shoulder handles, rose
ground, No. 357-4", 4" h.............................. **105**

**Candlesticks,** flat disc base, cylindrical
nozzle flanked by elongated open handles, rose ground, No. 1135-4 1/2",
4 1/2" h., pr....................................................... **175**
**Console bowl,** 8" d., tan ground, No. 361-
8"........................................................................... **150**
**Cornucopia-vase,** blue ground, No. 130-
4", 4" h................................................................... **75**
**Cornucopia-vase,** rose ground, No. 131-
6", 6" h., silver foil label ............................. **138**
**Ewer,** rose ground, No. 926-10", 10" h. .... **225-275**
**Flower frog,** blue ground, No. 38.................... **125**
**Flower frog,** rose ground, No. 38.................... **130**
**Flowerpot,** brown ground, No. 648-5" ............. **90**
**Jardiniere,** two-handled, rose ground, No.
647-3", 3" h.......................................................... **70**
**Jardiniere,** two-handled, rose ground, No.
647-4", 4" h....................................................... **154**
**Jardiniere,** two-handled, pink ground, No.
647-5", 5" h. (shallow spider-line at
base, not thru) ............................................... **380**
**Rose bowl,** rose ground, No. 356-6", 6" h. ...... **185**
**Vase,** 4" h., base handles, tan ground, No.
914-4"..................................................................... **110**
**Vase,** 5" h., ovoid body on flat circular
base, rim handles, blue ground, No. 915-
5"............................................................................. **125**
**Vase,** 6" h., tan ground, No. 917-6" ................. **165**
**Vase,** 6 1/2" h., two handles rising from
shoulder of globular base to midsection
of wide neck, rose ground, No. 917-6".. **150-175**
**Vase,** 6 1/2" h., two handles rising from
shoulder of globular base to midsection
of wide neck, blue ground, No. 917-6" ......... **152**
**Vase,** bud, 7" h., two-handled, blue ground,
No. 918-7" ........................................................ **231**
**Vase,** 7" h., blue ground, No. 919-7" .............. **175**
**Vase,** 8" h., bulbous base w/short shoulder
tapering to wide cylindrical neck & flat
rim, handles from shoulder to middle of
neck, tan shading to brown ground, No.
921-8".................................................................. **175**
**Vase,** 8" h., tan ground, No. 923-8" ............... **225**
**Vase,** 8" h., urn-form w/pedestal base, tan
ground, No. 923-8" ....................................... **215**
**Vase,** 10" h., two-handled, rose ground,
No. 924-9" ........................................................ **344**
**Vase,** 10" h., rose ground, No. 927-10"........... **475**
**Vase,** 12 1/2" h., semi-ovoid base w/two
handles rising from shoulder to beneath
rim of short, wide mouth, brown ground,
No. 928-12" ..................................................... **350**
**Vase,** 15" h., two large handles rising from
shoulder to rim, blue ground, No. 929-
15"......................................................................... **950**
**Wall shelf,** rose ground, No. 2, 8" h. ............... **450**

## LAUREL (1934)

*Laurel branch and berries in low relief with
reeded panels at the sides. Glazed in deep yellow,
green shading to cream or terra cotta.*

**Bowl,** 6" d., squatty bulbous body
w/incurved rim & angled shoulder han-
dles, yellow ground, No. 250-6 1/4" ............ **248**
**Vase,** 6" h., angular shoulder handles,
green ground, No. 668-6"............................. **358**
**Vase,** 7" h., green ground ............................. **350**
**Vase,** 8" h., deep yellow & black, No. 673-
8" (minor chip repair to base) ...................... **163**

**Vase,** 9" h., short cylindrical bottom w/wide slightly flaring neck, closed handles at midsection, terra cotta, No. 675-9", each ..... **358**

**Vase,** 9 1/4" h., angular side handles, globular base w'wide stepped mouth, terra cotta, No. 674-9 1/4" (repaired chips) .......... **110**

**Vase,** 14 1/2" h., base handles rising from stepped disc base to midsection of slightly flaring cylindrical body, green ground, No. 678-14 1/2" (chip to rim) .......... **880**

## MAGNOLIA (1943)
*Large white blossoms with rose centers and black stems in relief against a blue, green or tan textured ground.*

**Basket,** hanging-type, tan ground, No. 469-5" ..................... **149**

**Basket w/ornate overhead handle,** blue ground, No. 383-7" .................. **132**

**Basket w/ornate overhead handle,** blue ground, No. 384-7", 7" h. ............... **83**

**Book ends,** tan ground, No. 13, 5 1/2" h., pr. .......... **198**

**Bowl,** 10" l., two-handled, tan ground, No. 450-10" .......... **175**

**Cookie jar,** cov., shoulder handles, tan ground, No. 2-8", overall 10" h. .......... **450**

**Jardiniere & pedestal base,** blue ground, No. 665-8", 2 pcs. .......... **950**

**Model of a conch shell,** green ground, No. 453-7", 6 1/2" w. .......... **187**

**Pitcher,** blue ground, No. 1327 .......... **335**

**Planter,** angular end handles, tan ground, No. 388-6", 8 1/2" l. .......... **125**

**Tea set:** cov. teapot, creamer & sugar bowl; blue ground, Nos. 4, 4C & 4S, 3 pcs. (very shallow & small chip to bottom of lid, minor bruise to base of creamer & petal on sugar bowl) .......... **220**

**Teapot,** cov., green ground, No. 4 .......... **330**

**Vase,** 5" h., blue ground, No. 182-5" .......... **121**

**Vase,** 8" h., globular w/large angular handles, green ground, No. 91-8" .......... **263**

**Vase,** 9" h., two-handled, tan ground, No. 93-9" (chipped) .......... **110**

**Wall pocket,** overhead handle w/pointed ends, brown ground, No., 1294-8 1/2", 8 1/2" h. .......... **222**

**Wall pocket,** overhead handle w/pointed ends, blue ground, No. 1294-8 1/2", 8 1/2" h. .......... **375**

## MING TREE (1949)
*High gloss glaze in mint green, turquoise, or white is decorated with ming branch: handles are formed from gnarled branches.*

**Basket,** hanging-type, blue ground, 6" .......... **200**

**Basket,** hanging-type, green ground, 6" .......... **295**

**Basket,** hanging-type, blue ground, No. 505-8", 8" h. .......... **220**

**Basket,** overhead branch handle, rounded body w/shaped rim, blue ground, No. 508-8", 8" h. .......... **125**

**Basket,** white ground, No. 510-14", 14" .......... **275**

**Candleholders,** squat melon-ribbed body w/angular branch handles at shoulder, blue ground, No. 551, pr. .......... **98**

**Console bowl,** blue ground, No. 528-10", 10" l. .......... **165**

**Console bowl,** green ground, No. 528-10", 10" l. .......... **110**

**Ewer,** white ground, No. 516-10", 10" h. .......... **163**

**Vase,** 8" h., asymmetrical branch handles, green ground, No. 582-8" .......... **110**

**Vase,** 14" h., green ground, No. 585-14" .......... **525**

**Wall pocket,** overhead branch handle, white ground, No. 566-8", 8 1/2" h. .......... **275**

**Wall pocket,** overhead branch handle, green ground, No. 566-8", 8 1/2" h. .......... **275**

## MOSS (1930s)
*Green moss hanging over brown branch with green leaves; backgrounds are pink, ivory or tan shading to blue.*

**Bowl,** 7" d., footed w/rounded sides & small angled side handles, pink ground, No. 291-7" .......... **143**

**Bowl,** 8" d., footed, round sides & small angled handles, pink shading to blue, No. 291-8" .......... **143**

**Bowl,** 10" l., oblong w/end handles, No. 293-10" .......... **210**

**Bowls,** 5" d., footed, round sides & small angled handles, pink shading to blue, No. 291-5", pr. .......... **358**

**Candleholders,** flat disc base, ball-shaped, pink ground, No. 1109-2", 2" h., pr. .......... **220**

**Vase,** 6" h., footed, expanding cylinder w/angled handles, pink shading to blue, No. 775-6" (restored small chip to bottom ring) .......... **220**

**Vase,** 8" h., ovoid w/slightly flaring rim, ornate angular side handles, pink ground, No. 780-8" .......... **330**

**Vase,** 8 1/2" h., flared foot, bulbous body w/wide flaring rim, blue ground, No. 779-8" .......... **220**

**Vase,** 10" h., two-handled, footed ovoid body w/flaring rim, tan shading to blue, No. 784-10" .......... **660**

## MOSTIQUE (1915)
*Indian designs of stylized flowers and arrowhead leaves, slip decorated on bisque, glazed interiors. Occasional bowl glazed on outside as well.*

**Bowl,** 7" d., stylized flowers, grey ground, No. 131-7" .......... **122**

**Jardiniere,** geometric design, grey ground, 6" h. .......... **150**

**Jardiniere,** geometric floral design w/arrowhead leaves, tan ground, No. 606-6", 6" h. .......... **250**

**Jardiniere,** bulbous nearly spherical body w/a wide flat mouth flanked by small arched loop handles, a terra cotta ground decorated w/large geometric white & gold blossoms on tall brown stems w/white & blue angular leaves down the sides, triple dark brown bands under the blossoms near the rim, 8" h. ..... **1,430**

**Jardiniere,** green, blue, yellow & brown geometric design on grey ground, No. 622-8", 8" h. .......... **523**

**Umbrella stand,** tall slightly waisted cylindrical form w/large incised squared four-petal white blossoms above forked & spearpoint dark green stylized leaves

around the rim, light green incised rim &
base bands, all on a light terra cotta
ground, marked, 21" h. (harmless tight
line in top) .................................................. **1,045**
**Vase,** 6" h., two-handled, brown ground .......... **185**
**Vase,** 6" h., tapering cylinder, geometric
floral design, tan ground, No. 164-6" ........... **154**
**Vase,** 15" h., floor-type, arrowhead design,
grey ground, No. 164-15" ............................ **643**
**Vase,** 15" h., 8" w., floral & geometric
design, grey ground ..................................... **648**
**Wall pocket** .................................................. **395**

## ORIAN (1935)
*Characterized by handles formed on blade-like
leaves with suggestion of berries at base of handle,
high-gloss glaze; blue or tan with darker drip glaze
forming delicate band around rim, or in plain yellow
with no over drip.*

**Bowl,** 11" d., flared foot, sharply canted
sides w/wide flared rim, turquoise , No.
272-10" ....................................................... **143**
**Urn,** two handled, footed spherical body
w/closed rim, shaded red glossy exterior
& green interior glaze, unmarked, No.
274-6", 6" h. ............................................... **220**
**Vase,** 9" h., slender handles rising from
compressed ringed base to middle of
long wide neck, turquoise w/beige inte-
rior, No. 739-9" ........................................... **231**

## PANEL (1920)
*Background colors are dark green or dark
brown; decorations embossed within the recessed
panels are of natural or stylized floral arrangements
or female nudes.*

**Vase,** 6" h., fan-shaped, female nudes,
dark green ground ....................................... **825**
**Vase,** 6" h., pillow-shaped, dark brown
ground .......................................................... **358**
**Vase,** 7" h., footed ovoid body w/short
cylindrical neck, embossed flowers &
leaves on dark green ground ...................... **358**
**Vase,** 8" h., fan-shaped, nude in panel,
dark green ground ....................................... **605**
**Vase,** 8" h., compressed bulbous base
tapering to wide cylindrical neck, handles from base to mid-section of neck,
blue ground, No. 842-8", 8" h. (small
chip to base) ............................................... **275**
**Vase,** 10 1/4" h., 4 1/4" d., tall ovoid body
w/widely flaring rim, female nudes, dark
green ground, No. 296-10" (small glaze
chip to base, possibly in making) ........... **1,430**
**Vase,** 11" h., footed conical form. nude in
panel, dark brown ground, No. 298-11"
(drill hole to bottom) ................................... **605**
**Vase,** 11" h., footed conical form. nude in
panel, dark green ground, No. 298-11" ..... **1,870**
**Vase,** 12" h., embossed flowers & leaves
on dark green ground, No. 299-12 ............ **1,045**
**Wall pocket,** conical form, curved backplate w/pointed center w/hanging hole,
nude, green ground, 9" h. ............................ **297**

## PEONY (1942)
*Floral arrangement with green leaves on tex-
tured, shaded backgrounds in yellow with brown,
pink with blue, and green.*

**Ashtray,** gold ground, No. 27 ...................... **155**
**Basket,** green ground, No. 377-8", 8" h. .......... **185**
**Basket w/angular overhead handle,**
shaped rim, disc foot, gold ground, No.
379-12", 11" h. (chip & bruise to base) ......... **110**
**Basket w/overhead handle,** hanging-type,
green ground, No. 467-5" ............................ **225**
**Basket w/overhead handle,** hanging-type,
green ground, No. 376-7", 7" h. .................. **187**
**Basket w/overhead handle,** hanging-type,
pink ground, No. 376-7", 7" h. .................... **185**
**Basket w/overhead handle,** gold ground,
No. 378-10", 10" h. ..................................... **185**
**Bowl,** 10" l., two-handled, irregular rim,
green ground, No. 430-10" .......................... **125**
**Bowl,** 10" l., two-handled, irregular rim,
pink ground, No. 430-10" ............................ **150**
**Cornucopia-vase,** double, rose ground,
No. 172 ........................................................ **110**
**Ewer,** green ground, No. 7-6", 6" h. .............. **112**
**Ewer,** pink ground, No. 8-10", 10" h. .............. **225**
**Ewer,** rose ground, No. 9-15", 15" h. ............. **600**
**Jardiniere,** tiny rim handles, green ground,
No. 661-3", 3" h. .......................................... **100**
**Jardiniere & pedestal,** green & gold,
30" h., 2 pcs. ............................................... **950**
**Model of a conch shell,** gold ground, No.
436, 9 1/2" w. ............................................... **198**
**Tea set:** cov. teapot, creamer & open
sugar; green ground, No. 3, 3 pcs ............... **300**
**Vase,** 18" h., floor-type, green ground, No.
70-18" .......................................................... **523**
**Vase,** 6 " h., two-handled, green ground,
No. 58-6" ...................................................... **90**
**Vase,** double bud, 4" h., gold & green
ground, No. 167-4 1/2" ................................. **99**
**Vase,** bud, 6" h., pink ground, No. 173-6" ........ **125**
**Vase,** 15" h., floor-type, gold ground, No.
69-15" .......................................................... **440**
**Vase,** 15" h., floor-type, pink ground, No.
69-15" .......................................................... **470**
**Vase,** 18" h., floor-type, gold ground, No.
70-18" .......................................................... **465**
**Wall pocket,** gold ground .............................. **325**

## PINE CONE (1931)
*Realistic embossed brown pine cones and green
pine needles on shaded blue, brown or green
ground. (Pink is extremely rare.)*

**Ashtray,** blue ground, No. 499, 4 1/2" l. ........... **225**
**Basket,** hanging-type, squatty bulbous
body tapering slightly toward the base,
w/a short wide cylindrical neck flanked
by tiny branch hanging handles, brown
ground, No. 352-5", 7" d., 5 1/2" h. ........... **450**
**Basket,** w/overhead branch handle, asymmetrical body, brown ground, No. 408-
6", 6" h. ........................................................ **347**
**Basket,** w/overhead branch handle, disc
base, flaring rim, green ground, No. 338-
10", 10" h. .................................................... **379**
**Basket,** w/overhead branch handle, boat-
shaped, blue ground, No. 410-10",
10" h. ............................................................ **398**
**Bowl,** boat-shaped, 8" l., brown ground,
No. 427-8" .................................................... **325**
**Bowl,** 8", blue ground, No. 428-8" .................... **325**
**Bowl,** boat-shaped, 10" l., brown ground,
No. 429-10" .................................................. **500**

**Console bowl,** blue ground, No. 322-12", 12" l. ...................................................... 385
**Cornucopia-vases,** blue ground, No. 126-6", 6" h. pr. ............................................. 385
**Dish,** divided w/tall center handle, blue ground, No. 462, 6 1/5 x 13" ...................... 550
**Ewer,** brown ground, No. 851-15", 15" h.,..... 1,045
**Fruit bowl,** footed bulbous form w/side handles, one extending over rim, blue ground, No. 262-10" ................................... 880
**Jardiniere,** brown ground, No. 632-3", 3" h...... 162
**Jardiniere,** green ground, two-handled, No. 632-5", 5" h. ............................................ 270
**Jardiniere,** brown ground, No. 632-5", 5" h...... 195
**Jardiniere,** brown ground, No. 642-6", 6" h...... 313
**Jardiniere & pedestal base,** brown ground, No. 632-8", 8" h, 2 pcs., (small nick to rim of jardiniere) ............................ 1,760
**Mug,** brown ground, No. 960-4", 4" h. .............. 275
**Pitcher,** 9" h., green ground, No. 415-9" .......... 358
**Pitcher,** 9 1/2" h., ovoid, small branch handle, green ground, No. 708-9" ...................... 440
**Sand jar,** green ground, No. 776-14", 14" h. ................................................................ 1,500
**Tray,** blue ground, No. 430-12", 12" l. ............. 330
**Umbrella stand,** blue ground, No. 777-20", 20" h. ................................................................ 3,565
**Umbrella stand,** brown ground, No. 777-20", 20" h. ...................................................... 2,334
**Urn-vase,** asymmetrical handles, footed, brown ground, No. 121-7", 7" h. ................... 233
**Urn-vase,** brown ground, No. 908-8", 8" h. ...... 355
**Vase,** 6" h., bulbous base w/wide cylindrical neck, handles from shoulder to midsection of neck, blue ground, No. 839-6" ..... 385
**Vase,** 6" h., footed tapering cylindrical body w/asymmetric handles, blue ground, No. 748-6" ................................................................. 275
**Vase,** 6" h., bulbous base w/wide cylindrical neck, handles from shoulder to midsection of neck, brown ground, No. 839-6" ........................................................... 182
**Vase,** 6" h., trumpet-shaped, brown ground, No. 906-6" ................................ 150-200
**Vase,** bud, 7" h., blue ground, No. 112-7" ....... 243
**Vase,** bud, 7" h., brown ground, No. 112-7" ..... 246
**Vase,** 7" h., two-handled, footed wide cylinder, brown ground, No. 704-7" ..................... 220
**Vase,** 7" h., two-handled, footed wide cylinder, green ground, No. 704-7"..................... 203
**Vase,** triple bud, 8" h., blue ground, No. 113-8" .............................................................. 405
**Vase,** 8" h., double, brown ground, No. 473-8" ........................................................ 275-350
**Vase,** 8" h., footed cylindrical form w/flaring rim, asymmetric handles, brown ground, No. 746-8 ............................................................. 330
**Vase,** 8" h., compressed bulbous base tapering to wide cylindrical neck, handles from base to mid-section of neck, blue ground, No. 842-8", 8" h. ...................... 413
**Vase,** 9" h., slender conical body on wide flaring foot, blue ground, No. 705-9" .... 350-400
**Vase,** 9" h., slender conical body on wide flaring foot, brown ground, No. 705-9" ....... 220
**Vase,** 9" h., footed ovoid body w/wide flared rim, asymmetrical handles, blue ground, No. 707-9" ...................................... 220
**Vase,** 9" h., brown ground, No. 847-9" ............. 310

**Vase,** 10" h., blue ground, No. 485-10" (couple burst bubbles to handle) ................. 770
**Vase,** 10" h., expanding cylinder, brown ground, No. 709-10" .................................... 453
**Vase,** 10" h., expanding cylinder, green ground, No. 709-10" .................................... 345
**Vase,** 10" h., footed cylindrical body w/flaring rim, branch handles from midsection to base, brown ground, No. 804-10" ........... 303
**Vase,** 10" h., footed, two-handled bulbous body tapering to wide tall cylindrical neck w/irregular cut-out rim, brown ground, No. 848-10" ....................................................... 458
**Vase,** 10" h., footed, two-handled bulbous body tapering to wide tall cylindrical neck w/irregular cut-out rim, blue ground, No. 848-10" ....................................................... 743
**Vase,** 10 1/2" h., flaring foot beneath an expanding conical body flanked by long handles from base to mid-section in the form of pine needles & pine cone, blue ground, No. 747-10" ........................... 450-525
**Vase,** 10 1/2" h., flaring foot beneath an expanding conical body flanked by long handles from base to mid-section in the form of pine needles & pine cone, brown ground, No. 747-10" .................................... 416
**Vase,** 12" h., blue ground, No. 711-12" .......... 950
**Vase,** 12" h., corseted form w/asymmetric branch handles, blue ground, No. 712-12"................................................................... 355
**Vase,** 12" h., corseted form w/asymmetric branch handles, green ground, No. 712-12"................................................................... 522
**Vase** 18" h., floor-type, footed ovoid body tapering to flaring cylindrical neck, shoulder handles, brown ground, No. 913-18" .. 1,870
**Wall pocket,** triple, brown ground, No. 466, 8 1/4" h. ............................................................ 605
**Wall pocket,** double, two flaring conical containers joined by an arched pine cone & needle top handle, brown ground, No. 1273-8", 8 1/2" h. ............... 400-425
**Wall pocket,** double, two flaring conical containers joined by an arched pine cone & needle top handle, green ground, No. 1273-8", 8 1/2" h. ................................... 440
**Window box,** rectangula w/low center handle, blue ground, No. 469-12", 12" l. (fleck to base & under rim (in making) & to handle) ....................................................... 385

## ROZANE (1900)

*Dark blended backgrounds; slip decorated underglaze artware.*

**Vase,** 4 5/8" h., footed bulbous base tapering to wide cylindrical neck w/flaring rim, rose hip decoration, Greek key handles from shoulder to rim, No. 847 (repair to foot) ................................................................. 165
**Vase,** 11 1/4" h., slender cylindrical body tapering to narrow cylindrical neck w/flaring rim, brown, green & orange ground w/decoration of wild roses, artist-signed ............................................................... 385

## RUSSCO (1930s)

*Octagonal rim openings, stacked handles, narrow perpendicular panel front and back. One type glaze is solid matte color; another is matte color with lustrous crystalline over glaze, some of which shows actual grown crystals.*

**Urn-vase,** angular handles, blue, No. 108-6, 7" h. .......................................................... **128**
**Vase,** 8 1/2" h., flared foot, slender trumpet form w/curved base handles, cream w/green crystalline overglaze, No. 695-8" ................................................................. **242**
**Vase,** 10" h., footed baluster form w/flaring rim & slender scrolled handles, orange glaze, No. 700-10" ..................................... **358**

## SILHOUETTE (1952)
*Recessed area silhouettes nature study or female nudes. Colors are rose, turquoise, tan and white with turquoise.*

**Basket,** curved rim & asymmetrical handle, florals, rose ground, No. 710-10", 10" h. ...... **183**
**Basket w/overhead handle,** tan, No. 708-6", 6" h. ........................................................ **113**
**Planter,** florals, rose ground, No. 769-9", 9" l. ........................................................... **210**
**Vase,** 9" h., double, base w/canted sides supporting two square vases w/sloping rims, joined by a stylized branch-form center post, florals, orange shading to brown ground, No. 757-9" ............................ **165**
**Vase,** 12" h., florals, rose ground, No. 788-12" ................................................................. **253**
**Vase,** 12" h., florals, white ground, No. 788-12" ................................................................. **99**

## SNOWBERRY (1946)
*Brown branch with small white berries and green leaves embossed over spider-web design in various background colors (blue, green and rose).*

**Basket,** w/asymmetrical overhead handle, shaded rose ground, No. 1BK-8", 8" h. ........ **149**
**Basket w/curved overhead handle,** disc base, shaded green ground, No. 1BK-10", 10" h, ................................................... **165**
**Book ends,** shaded green ground, No. 1BE, pr. ........................................................ **231**
**Candleholders,** squatty w/angular handles at shoulder, shaded rose ground, No. 1CS1-2", 2" h., pr. ................................... **115**
**Console bowl,** shaded rose ground, No. 1BL-8", 11" l. ...................................................... **115**
**Ewer,** shaded green ground, No. 1TK-6", 6" h. ................................................................. **118**
**Ewer,** shaded rose ground, No. 1TK-6", 6" h. ................................................................. **127**
**Ewer,** shaded green ground, No. 1TK-10, 10" h. ................................................................. **240**
**Ewer,** flaring base, oval body, shaded rose ground, No. 1TK-15", 16" h. ......................... **319**
**Tea set:** cov. teapot, open sugar bowl & creamer; shaded green ground, Nos. 1TP, 1S & 1C, 3 pcs. ......................................... **360**
**Tea set:** cov. teapot, open sugar bowl & creamer; shaded blue ground, Nos. 1TP, 1S & 1C, the set ........................................... **303**
**Vase,** 6 1/2" h., pillow-type, shaded blue ground, No. 1FH-6" ..................................... **110**
**Vase,** 7" h., two-handled, shaded rose ground, No. 1V1-7" ....................................... **103**

**Vase,** 10" h., shaded rose ground, No. 1V2-10" ................................................................. **242**
**Vase,** 18" h., shaded blue ground, No. 1V-18 ..................................................................... **450**
**Vase,** 18" h., shaded rose ground, No. 1V-18" ................................................................... **440**
**Wall pocket,** wide half-round form tapering to a pointed base, low angled handles along the lower sides, shaded blue ground, No. 1WP-8", 8" w., 5 1/2" h. ..... **250-300**
**Wall pocket,** wide half-round form tapering to a pointed base, low angled handles along the lower sides, shaded rose ground, No. 1WP-8", 8" w., 5 1/2" h. ............ **237**

## SUNFLOWER (1930)
*Tall stems support yellow sunflowers whose blooms form a repetitive band. Textured background shades from tan to dark green at base.*

**Basket,** hanging-type, 8" d., 5" h. ...................... **935**
**Bowl,** 5" d., No. 208-5" .................................... **748**
**Jardiniere,** No. 619-8", 8" h., unmarked (two hairlines from rim, straight 1" & T-shaped 1/1/2") ............................................ **1,100**
**Jardiniere,** No. 619-10", unmarked (restoration to opposing hairlines, small chip to edge of leaf) ............................................ **1,045**
**Jardiniere,** No. 619-12" (minor scrape inside rim, stress fracture to base) ............ **2,530**
**Vase,** 5" h. ....................................................... **382**
**Vase,** 6" h., squatty bulbous body, wide shoulder w/short cylindrical neck, No. 488-6" (bruise to rim, abrasion to one flower) ............................................................ **770**
**Vase,** 7" h., bulbous base below expanding cylindrical neck w/wide flaring flat rim (crack from rim) .......................................... **413**
**Vase,** 7" h., waisted cylindrical form w/wide flaring mouth, No. 487-7" ............................. **990**

## TEASEL (1936)
*Embossed decorations of long-stems gracefully curving with delicate spider-like pods. Colors and glaze treatments vary from monochrome matte to crystalline. Colors are beige to tan, medium blue highlighted with gold, pale blue and deep rose (possibly others).*

**Bowl,** 4" d., pale blue ground, No. 342-4" ........ **187**
**Bowl,** 8" d., blue ground, No. 344-8" ................ **175**
**Candleholders,** shaded blue ground, No. 1131, 2" h., pr. ............................................... **165**
**Jardiniere,** brown ground, footed squatty bulbous body w/a wide cylindrical neck, small angled shoulder handles, No. 644-4", 4" h. ............................................................. **150**
**Jardiniere,** peach matte ground, footed squatty bulbous body w/a wide cylindrical neck, small angled shoulder handles, No. 644-4", 4" h. ............................................... **165**
**Jardiniere,** footed spherical body w/a wide closed rim & small tab shoulder handles, blue ground, No. 343-6", 6" h. ................. **178**
**Rose bowl,** footed spherical body w/a wide closed rim & small tab shoulder handles, beige shading to tan ground, No. 343-6", 6" h. ................................................................. **132**
**Vase,** 6" h., closed handles at midsection, cut-out rim, beige shading to tan ground, No. 881-6" ........................................................ **150**

**Vase,** 6" h., closed handles at midsection, cut-out rim, mottled blue ground, No. 881-6" ......................................................... **165**

**Vase,** 6" h., closed handles at rim, beige shading to tan ground, No. 882-6" .............. **176**

**Vase,** 6" h., closed handles at rim, deep rose, No. 882-6" ......................................... **138**

*Teasel Vase*

**Vase,** 8" h., closed handles at shoulder, low foot, blue ground, No. 884-8" (ILLUS.) ...................................................... **193**

**Vase,** 8" h., blue ground, rectangular foot below flaring rectangular body w/stepped rim ends, shaped low buttress side handles, No. 885-8" ................... **190**

**Vase,** 9" h., closed handles at base, flaring mouth, beige shading to tan, No. 886-9" ...... **330**

## TOURMALINE (1933)

*Although the semi-gloss medium blue, highlighted around the rim with lighter high gloss and gold effect, seems to be accepted as the standard Tourmaline glaze, the catalogue definitely shows this and two other types as well. One is a mottled overall turquoise, the other a mottled salmon that appears to be lined in the high gloss but with no over run to the outside.*

**Bowl,** 7" d., shallow w/sharply canted sides, intermingled blue crystalline mat glaze, No. 152-7 ........................................ **495**

**Bowl,** 7" d., shallow w/sharply canted sides, mottled blue semi-gloss glaze, No. 152-7 ........................................................ **165**

**Candlesticks,** flared ribbed base, flaring nozzle, mottled blue ground, gold labels, No. 1089-4 1/2", 4 1/2" h., pr ....................... **165**

**Urn-vase,** compressed globular base w/short collared neck, mottled blue, No. A-200-4", 4 1/2" h. ................................. **253**

**Vase,** 5 1/2" h., globular w/loop handles rising from midsection to rim, mottled turquoise blue, No. A-517-6" ........................ **112**

**Vase,** 6" h., pillow-type, mottled blue glaze ........ **75**

**Vase,** 6" h., mottled blue ground, No. A517-6" ............................................................... **175**

**Vase,** 7" h., cylindrical w/low flaring foot, slightly flared rim, mottled blue, No. 308-7" ..................................................... **121**

**Vase,** 7" h., shaded orange glaze, No. 318-7" ..................................................... **143**

*Tourmaline Vase*

**Vase,** 8" h., hexagonal twisted form, mottled pink & green semi-gloss glaze, large gold foil label (ILLUS.) .................................. **220**

**Vase,** 8" h., twisted paneled effect, mottled blue, No. A-425-8" ........................................ **385**

**Vase,** 9" h., flared foot below buttressed base, trumpet-form body, mottled turquoise glaze, No. A-429-9" ........................... **413**

**Vase,** 10" h., squatty bulbous base w/wide cylindrical neck w/horizontally ribbed lower half & slightly flaring rim, mottled blue mat over blue-yellow glossy glaze, gold foil label ............................................... **468**

## VISTA (1920s)

*Embossed green coconut palm trees & lavender blue pool against grey ground.*

**Basket,** hanging-type, wide low-sided cylindrical form w/three low strap handles along the sides, 8" d., 4" h. (abrasion to bottom, glaze scaling to edge & rim, tough-up to a couple of points) .................... **385**

**Basket w/pointed overhead handle,** tapering square form w/pointed side rim, 5 1/2 x 6 1/2" ................................................. **454**

**Jardiniere,** 9" h. ............................................... **465**

**Jardiniere & pedestal base,** 12" h., jardiniere, overall 36" h., 2 pcs. (two glaze flakes to rim & "T"-shaped hairline to base of jardiniere which crawls up side & spreads 4" ................................................ **2,200**

**Planter,** rectangular w/curved sides & end handles, 4 1/2 x 11 1/2", 6" h. (bruise to corner of base, shallow line to bottom that does not go through, small chip to inner rim, minor glaze scaling) .................... **715**

**Vase,** 10" h., bulbous base tapering to cylindrical neck flanked by buttressed handles (restoration to rim chip) .................. **523**

**Vase,** 10" h., tapering cylindrical body w/flaring base ............................................. **660**

**Vase,** 12" h., ovoid body tapering to round base ...................................................... **660**

**Vase,** 12" h., wide cylindrical form expanding slightly at top flanked by buttressed handles ............................................... **823**

**Vase,** 12" h., 4 3/4" d., footed, bulbous base tapering to tall wide cylindrical neck w/flat rim ......................................................... **715**

**Vase,** floor-type, 14" h., footed tapering cylindrical form ........................................... **915**

**Vase,** 15" h., tall tapering cylindrical body w/flaring foot & bulbous top w/closed rim (bruise to rim) ............................................ **1,100**

## WATER LILY (1940s)

*Water lily and pad in various color combinations: tan to brown with yellow lily, blue with white lily, pink to green with pink lily.*

**Basket,** conch shell-shaped w/high arched handle, gold shading to brown ground, No. 381-10", 10" h. ................................. **220**

**Basket,** w/asymmetrical overhead handle, curved & sharply scalloped rim, pink shading to green ground, No. 382-12", 12" h. ................................................ **275**

**Basket w/pointed overhead handle,** cylindrical w/flaring rim, pink shading to green ground, No. 380-8", 8" h. .................. **150**

**Cookie jar,** cov., angular handles, blended blue ground, No. 1-8", 8" h. ...................... **392**

**Cookie jar,** cov., angular handles, gold shading to brown ground, No. 1-8", 8" h. ..... **555**

**Cornucopia-vase,** gold shading to brown ground, No. 176-6", 6" h. ............................ **139**

**Cornucopia-vase,** blue ground, No. 178-8", 8" h. ................................................... **195**

**Cornucopia-vases,** pink ground, No. 177-6", 6" h., pr. ........................................... **295**

**Ewer,** blue ground, No. 12-15", 15" h. .............. **450**

**Flower holder,** two-handled, fan-shaped body, pink shading to green ground, No. 48, 4 1/2" h. ......................................... **118**

**Jardiniere,** blended blue ground, No. 663-8", 9" d., 8" h. ...................................... **248**

**Model of a conch shell,** blended blue ground, No. 438-8", 8" h. ............................ **203**

**Model of a conch shell,** pink shading to green ground, No. 438-8", 8" h. .................. **175**

**Rose bowl,** two-handled, gold shading to brown ground, No. 437-6", 6" d. .................. **176**

**Vase,** 4" h., gold shading to brown ground, No. 71-4" ............................................ **65**

**Vase,** 6" h., shaded blue ground, No. 174-6" ............................................................ **135**

**Vase,** 8" h., footed w/squatty bulbous bottom section below a wide cylindrical body flanked by long arched handles, blue ground, No. 76-8" .......................... **104**

**Vase,** 14" h., angular side handles, blended blue ground, No. 82-14" ............................. **303**

**Vase,** 14" h., angular side handles, gold shading to brown ground, No. 82-14" ........ **303**

**Vase,** 14" h., angular side handles, pink shading to green ground, No. 82-14" (small chip to bottom ring) ........................... **303**

**Vase,** 15" h., pink shading to green ground, No. 83-15" ............................................. **459**

**Vase,** 15" h., two-handled, gold shading to brown ground, No. 83-15" ...................... **413**

**Vase,** 18" h., floor-type, tall baluster-form w/pointed shoulder handles, pink shading to green ground, No. 85-18" .................. **587**

## WHITE ROSE (1940)

*White roses and green leaves against a vertically combed ground of blended blue, brown shading to green or pink shading to green.*

**Console bowl,** pink shading to green ground, No. 391-10", 10" l. ........................... **175**

**Vase,** 5" h., footed trumpet-form body w/notched rim & asymmetrical base loop handles, pink shading to green ground, 980-6" ............................................................ **99**

**Vase,** 7" h., pink shading to green ground, No. 983-7" ................................................ **154**

**Vase,** 8" h., flattened ovoid body on a rectangular foot, small pointed shoulder handles, brown shading to green ground, No. 984-8" ..................................... **222**

## WINCRAFT (1948)

*Revived shapes from older lines such as Pine Cone, Bushberry, Cremona, Primrose and others. Vases with animal motifs, contemporary shapes in high gloss of blue, tan, lime and green.*

**Basket,** hanging-type, lime green ground, 8" h. ............................................................. **175**

**Basket,** hanging-type, tan ground, 8" h. ......... **165**

**Basket,** footed half-round form w/arched rim & angled overhead handle, lime green ground, No. 208-8", 8" h. ................ **190**

**Basket,** footed half-round form w/arched rim & angled overhead handle, tan ground, No. 208-8", 8" h. ...................... **154**

**Cigarette box,** cov., shaded blue ground, No. 240, 4 1/2" l. ...................................... **121**

**Console bowl,** rectangular foot supporting a long, low serpentine bowl w/pointed ends, green ground, No. 227-10", 13 1/2" l., 4" h., .................................... **49**

**Cornucopia-vase,** florals in relief on shaded green ground, No. 222-8", 8" h. ......... **95**

**Ewer,** bell-form body below a tall neck w/upright tall spout & angled shoulder handle, chartreuse ground, No. 216-8", 8" h. ............................................................. **115**

**Flowerpot,** blue ground, No. 265-5", 5" h. ........ **80**

**Jardiniere,** pink ground, No. 635-6", 6" h. ........ **330**

**Teapot,** cov., brown & yellow ground, No. 271-P ............................................................ **265**

**Vase,** 6" h., asymmetrical fan shape, pine cones & needles in relief on lime ground, No. 272-6" ....................................... **115**

**Vase,** 8" h., blue ground w/arrow leaf design, No. 273-8" .................................... **125**

**Vase,** 8" h., flowing lily form w/asymmetrical side handles, tulip & foliage in relief on glossy green & yellow ground, No. 282-8" ............................................................ **150**

**Vase,** 8" h., brown ground, No. 283-8" ............. **165**

**Vase,** 10" h., ovoid base & long cylindrical neck w/wedge-shaped closed handle on one side & long closed column-form handle on the other, shaded green ground, No. 284-10" ................................. **176**

**Vase,** 10" h., cylindrical, tab handles, black panther & green palm trees in relief on blue ground, No. 290-10" .......................... **605**

**Vase,** 12" h., yellow, No. 275-12" ................... **605**

**Vase,** 12" h., fan-shaped, glossy gold ground, No. 287-12" .................................. **99**

**Wall pocket,** tan ground, No. 267-5" .............. **295**

**Wall pocket,** rectangular box-like holders w/horizontal ribbing & ivy leaves as rim handle, brown ground, No. 266-4", 8 1/2" h. ......................................................... **250**

## WINDSOR (1931)

*Brown or blue mottled glaze, some with leaves, vines and ferns, some with a repetitive band arrangement of small squares and rectangles in yellow and green.*

**Vase,** 6" h., canted sides, handles rising from shoulder to rim, geometric design against mottled terra cotta ground, No. 546-6"........................ 440

**Vase,** 6" h., canted sides, handles rising from shoulder to rim, geometric design against mottled blue ground, No. 546-6"...... 440

**Vase,** 7" h., large handles, globular base, stylized ferns against mottled terra cotta ground, No. 548-7" (restoration to base chip) ........................ 330

**Vase,** 7" h., large handles, globular base, stylized ferns against mottled blue ground, No. 548-7"........................ 715

**Vase,** 7" h., trumpet-shaped w/long loop handles from rim to midsection, green leaves on terra cotta ground, NO. 550-7"..... 495

## WISTERIA (1933)
*Lavender wisteria blossoms and green vines against a roughly textured brown shading to deep blue ground, rarely found in only brown.*

**Bowl-vase,** squatty bulbous form tapering sharply to a flat mouth flanked by small loop handles, brown ground, No. 242-4", 4" h................ 382

**Bowl-vase,** squatty bulbous form tapering sharply to a flat mouth flanked by small loop handles, blue ground, No. 242-4", 4" h................ 463

**Urn,** bulbous body w/wide flat mouth, small loop shoulder handles, brown ground, 8" h................ 880

**Urn-vase,** small rim handles, straight sides, No. 632-5", 5" h........................ 550

**Urn-vase,** small rim handles, straight sides, No. 632-5", 5" h. (glaze scrape to base, few minor flecks to decoration) .................. 330

**Vase,** 4" h., squatty, angular handles on sharply canted shoulder, blue ground, No. 629-4", silver foil label............ 550

**Vase,** 4" h., squatty, angular handles on sharply canted shoulder, brown ground, No. 629-4", silver foil label............ 315

**Vase,** 6 1/2" h., 4" d., bulbous ovoid body w/a wide shoulder tapering up to a small mouth, small angled shoulder handles, mottled blue & blue ground, No. 630-6" ....... 523

**Vase,** 6" h., ovoid body tapering to short cylindrical neck flanked by small loop handles, blue ground, No. 631-6"................ 560

**Vase,** 6 1/2" h., 4" d., bulbous ovoid body w/a wide shoulder tapering up to a small mouth, small angled shoulder handles, mottled blue & brown ground, No. 630-6"..... 504

**Vase,** 7" h., bulbous waisted ovoid body w/small pointed shoulder handles, brown ground, No. 634-7" .................. 547

**Vase,** 8" h., pear-shaped body w/short cylindrical neck & tiny angled shoulder handles, blue ground, No. 636-8".......... 870

**Vase,** 8" h., 6 1/2" d., wide tapering cylindrical body w/small angled handles flanking the flat rim, brown ground, No. 633-8"........................ 653

**Vase,** 8 1/2" h., bulbous ovoid body tapering to a short cylindrical neck w/a wide flat rim, pointed angled handles from the neck to the shoulder, blue ground............ 2,090

**Vase,** 8 1/2" h., slender base handles, conical body bulging slightly below rim, brown ground, No. 635-8" ........................ 509

**Vase,** 8 1/2" h., slender base handles, conical body bulging slightly below rim, blue ground, No. 635-8"........................ 867

**Vase,** 9 1/2" h., cylindrical ovoid body w/angular handles rising from shoulder to midsection of slender cylindrical neck, brown ground, No. 638-9", partial paper label........................ 523

**Vase,** 10" h., corseted form w/flaring rim, angled mid-section handles, brown ground (hairline & small chip to rim, one chip per handle & one to base) .................. 385

**Vase,** 10" h., cylindrical body w/closed rim, angled shoulder handles, brown ground, No. 639-10"........................ 605

**Vase,** 10" h., cylindrical body w/closed rim, angled shoulder handles, blue ground, No. 639-10" ........................ 1,870

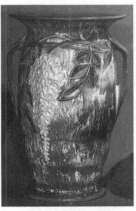

*Tall Wisteria Vase*

**Vase,** 12" h., two-handled, expanding cylinder w/flaring rim, brown ground, No. 640-12" (ILLUS.) ........................ 1,650

**Vase,** 15" h., bottle-shaped w/angular handles at shoulder, blue ground, No. 641-15" (restoration to rim & handles, small flakes to a few petals) ........................ 2,310

## ZEPHYR LILY (1946)
*Tall lilies and slender leaves adorn swirl-textured backgrounds of Bermuda Blue, Evergreen and Sienna Tan.*

**Basket,** footed half-round body w/curled-in rim tabs & high arched handle, terra cotta ground, No. 393-7", 7" h. .................. 188

**Cookie jar,** cov., blue ground, No. 5-8", 10" h........................ 358

**Jardiniere,** terra cotta ground, No. 671-8", 8" h........................ 193

**Jardiniere,** two-handled, green ground, No. 679-9", 9" h. ........................ 385

**Tea set:** cov. teapot, creamer & open sugar bowl; terra cotta ground, 3 pcs. .................. 413

**Vase,** 9" h., conical w/flaring buttressed base, blue ground, No. 136-9" .................. 110

# ROYAL BAYREUTH

*Good china in numerous patterns and designs has been made at the Royal Bayreuth factory in Tettau, Germany since 1794. Listings below are by the company's lines, plus miscellaneous pieces. Interest in this china remains at a peak and prices continue to rise. Pieces listed carry the company's blue mark except where noted otherwise.*

*Royal Bayreuth Mark*

## CORINTHIAN

**Cake plate,** classical figures on black ground, 10" d.................................**$125-150**
**Creamer,** classical figures on green ground....... 50
**Creamer & cov. sugar bowl,** classical figures on black ground, pr. ........................... 100
**Pitcher,** milk, classical figures on green ground............................................................. 125

*Corinthian Pitcher*

**Pitcher,** tankard, 6 7/8" h., 3 3/4" d., orange inside top, classical figures on black satin ground gold bands w/black & white geometric design around neck & base (ILLUS.) ............................................ 125
**Planter,** classical figures on red ground........... 100
**Toothpick holder,** classical figures on black ground, 2 1/4" h. ......................... **175-200**

## DEVIL & CARDS

**Ashtray** ................................................................ 150
**Ashtray,** two cards ............................................. 325
**Ashtray w/match holder** ................................. 250
**Candleholder** .................................................... 550
**Creamer,** figural red devil, 3 1/2" h............ **300-400**
**Creamer,** 3 3/4" h. ........................................ **250-325**
**Creamer,** figural red devil, 4 1/2" h........... **375-475**
**Match holder,** hanging-type, 4" w., 5" h. .. **500-600**
**Mug,** 4 3/4" h. ............................................ **400-500**
**Mug,** w/blue rim ................................................ 395
**Pitcher,** milk, 5" h. ..................................... **450-600**

*Devil & Cards Pitcher*

**Pitcher,** water, 7 1/4" h. (ILLUS.) .............. **700-850**
**Plate,** 6" d. ....................................................... 500
**Salt dip,** master size ........................................ 325
**Salt shaker** ....................................................... 175
**Stamp box,** cov., 3 1/2" l. ................................. 595
**Sugar bowl,** cov. ............................................... 400
**Sugar bowl,** open, short ................................... 350

## MOTHER-OF-PEARL

**Ashtray,** Murex Shell patt. ................................. 80
**Basket,** reticulated rim, ornate handle, rose decoration, 3 3/4 x 4" oval, 4 1/4" h............. 150
**Bowl,** 3 1/2" octagonal, white w/green highlights, pearlized finish ..................................... 65
**Bowl,** 5 1/2" d., grape cluster mold, pearlized white finish............................................ 150
**Bowl,** 6 1/2 x 9", oak leaf-shaped, footed, pearlized finish w/gold trim .......................... 850
**Bowl,** 10" oval, handled, figural poppy mold, apricot satin finish............................. 600
**Cake plate,** decorated w/roses, 10 1/2" d. ....... 125
**Compote,** open, 4 1/2" d., 4 1/2" h., reticulated bowl & base, decorated w/delicate roses, pearlized finish ................................. 140
**Compote,** open, decorated w/roses, pearlized finish, small........................................... 49
**Creamer,** grape cluster mold, pearlized white, 3 3/4" h............................................... 175
**Creamer,** Murex Shell patt., white pearlized finish, 4 1/2" h. ................................... **150-200**
**Creamer,** boot-shaped, figural Spiky Shell patt., 4 3/4" h....................................... **250-275**
**Creamer,** Murex Shell patt., spiky form............. 95
**Creamer & cov. sugar bowl,** grape cluster mold, pearlized yellow, colorful foliage, pr. ........................................................................ 375
**Cup & saucer,** demitasse, footed, figural Spiky Shell patt., pearlized finish ................. 150
**Cup & saucer,** demitasse, Oyster & Pearl mold ..................................................................... 350
**Dish,** cov., Murex Shell patt., large................. 175
**Hatpin holder,** figural poppy mold, pearlized white finish........................................... 575
**Hatpin holder,** white pearlized finish .............. 160
**Humidor,** cov., Murex Shell patt..................... 850
**Mustard jar,** cov., Murex Shell patt. white pearlized finish, 3 1/2" h. ...................... **200-250**
**Nappy,** grape cluster mold, pearlized white finish, 6" x 7".................................................. 175
**Nappy,** handled, figural poppy mold, pearlized satin finish.................................... **150-250**
**Pitcher,** milk, boot-shaped, figural Spiky Shell patt., pearlized finish, 5 1/2" h. ........... 375

**Sugar bowl,** cov., footed, figural Spiky
Shell patt., pearlized finish, 3 1/2" h. ............ **325**
**Toothpick holder,** Murex Shell patt. ................ **110**
**Toothpick holder,** Murex Shell patt., pearl-
ized finish ....................................................... **175**
**Wall pocket,** figural grape cluster, pearl-
ized finish, 9" h. ..................................... **400-600**

## OLD IVORY
**Basket,** 3" h., 7 3/4" l. ................................. **200-250**
**Bowl,** 4 x 6" .................................................. **200-250**
**Pitcher,** water, 9" h. ................................. **800-1,000**
**Toothpick holder** ..................................... **375-425**

## ROSE TAPESTRY
**Basket,** two-color roses, 3" h. .......................... **350**
**Basket,** two-color roses, 4 1/4" w., 3 3/4" h. ...... **450**
**Basket,** miniature, rope handle, tiny pink
roses frame the rim, small bouquet of
yellow roses on each side & yellow
roses on the interior, shadow green
leaves, 2 1/2 x 4 1/4 x 4 1/2" ........................ **325**
**Basket,** three-color roses, 4 3/4 x 5 1/4" .......... **425**
**Basket,** miniature, two color roses on yel-
low ground, braided decoration around
rim ...................................................................... **375**
**Bell,** pink American Beauty roses, 3" h. .... **450-550**
**Bell,** gold loop handle, three-color roses,
3 1/4" h. ............................................................. **400**

*Rose Tapestry Bowl*

**Bowl,** 10 1/2" d., gently scalloped rim
w/four shell-molded gilt-trimmed han-
dles, three-color roses (ILLUS.) ......... **900-1,100**
**Bowl,** 10 1/2" d., shell- & scroll-molded rim,
three-color roses ............................................ **995**
**Box,** cov., pink & white roses, 2 1/2" sq. .......... **175**
**Box,** cov., two-color roses, 1 1/2 x 2 1/2" ......... **165**
**Box,** cov., three-color roses, 2 1/2 x 4 1/2",
1 3/4" h. ............................................................. **295**
**Box,** w/domed cover, three-color roses,
4 1/2" d., 2 3/4" h. ............................................ **400**
**Box,** cov., shell-shaped, 3 x 5 1/2" .................. **375**
**Cake plate,** three-color roses, free-form
fancy rim w/gold beading, 9 1/2" w. .............. **425**
**Cake plate,** pierced gold handles, three-
color roses, 10 1/2" d. ............................ **450-500**
**Candy dish,** three-color roses, 8" oval ............ **350**
**Chamberstick,** a shaped & flattened base
centered by a waisted cylindrical short
standard supporting the dished socket

w/three rim points, an ornate C-scroll
handle down the side, three-color roses,
4 1/4" h. ..................................................... **850-950**
**Chocolate set:** cov. chocolate pot w/four
matching cups & saucers, three-color
roses, 9 pcs. ..................................... **2,000-2,400**
**Clock,** table-model, three-color roses,
upright rectangular case w/a flaring base
& domed top ............................................... **1,000**
**Creamer,** wide cylindrical body slightly flar-
ing at the base & w/a long buttress spout
& gilt angled handle, two-color roses on
a rose ground, 3" h. ......................................... **385**
**Creamer,** ovoid body w/flared base & long
pinched spout, three-color roses,
3 1/2" h. ..................................................... **175-200**
**Creamer,** corset-shaped, three-color roses,
3 3/4" h. ..................................................... **250-300**
**Creamer,** two-color roses, 3 1/2" d., 4" h. ........ **375**
**Creamer,** pinched spout, two-color roses ......... **355**
**Creamer & cov. sugar bowl,** pink & white
roses, pr. .......................................................... **675**
**Creamer & cov. sugar bowl,** two-color
roses, pr. .......................................................... **575**
**Cups & saucers,** demitasse, three-color
roses, 2 sets .................................................... **300**
**Dessert set:** large cake plate & six match-
ing small serving plates; three-color
roses, 7 pcs. ................................................ **1,100**
**Dish,** three-color roses, 2" w., 4 1/2" l,
1 1/2" h. ............................................................. **195**
**Dish,** handled, clover-shaped, decorated
w/yellow roses, 5" w. ....................................... **225**
**Dish,** leaf-shaped, three-color roses,
5" l. ............................................................ **225-250**
**Dresser box,** cov., kidney-shaped, double
pink roses, 2 x 5 1/4" ................................ **375-400**
**Flowerpot & underplate,** three-color
roses, 3 x 4", 2 pcs. ........................................ **295**

*Rose Tapestry Hair Receiver*

**Hair receiver,** cov., footed, two-color
roses, 4" d., 2 1/2" h. (ILLUS.) ...................... **375**
**Hatpin holder,** two-color roses, scroll-
molded reticulated gilt-trimmed foot
below the baluster-form body w/a flaring
gilt-trimmed rim, 4 1/2" h. ....................... **550-650**
**Match holder,** hanging-type, three-color
roses ................................................................. **460**
**Match holder,** wall hanging-type, a bul-
bous rounded pouch w/a wide arched
backplate w/hanging hole, white & pink
roses ................................................................. **375**
**Model of a high-top lady's shoe,** pink
roses w/a band of green leaves around
top, 3 1/2" h. .............................................. **500-700**
**Model of a shoe,** decorated w/pink roses &
original shoe lace ...................................... **450-475**

**Model of a Victorian lady's high-heeled shoe,** three-color roses ................................. 400

**Nappy,** tri-lobed leaf shape, decorated w/orange roses, 4 1/2" l................................ 200

**Nappy,** open-handled, three-color roses, 5" d. ................................................... 225

**Nut set:** master footed bowl & six small footed bowls; decorated w/pink roses, 7 pcs.................................................... 1,250-1,275

**Pitcher,** 5" h., wide cylindrical body tapering slightly toward rim, three-color roses, 24 oz. ................................................ 375

*Rose Tapestry Planter*

**Planter,** squatty bulbous base below wide gently flaring sides w/a ruffled rim, small loop handles near the base, three-color roses, 2 3/4" h. (ILLUS.)................................ 280

**Plaque,** pierced to hang, large pink roses........ 575

**Plate,** 6" d. ............................................ 200-250

**Plate,** 7" d., three-color roses ......................... 275

**Plate,** 7 1/2" d., round w/slightly scalloped rim & four sections of fanned ruffles spaced around the edge, three-color roses ................................................... 300-400

**Plate,** 10 1/2" d., overall colorful roses w/four gilded scrolls around the rims .... 175-200

**Powder box,** cov., footed, three-color roses, 4" d., 2 1/2" h. ............................... 350-450

**Powder jar,** cov., footed squatty rounded base w/a squatty domed cover, three-color roses, 3" d., 2 1/2" h. .................... 425-525

**Relish dish,** open-handled, three-color roses, 4 x 8" ......................................... 300-350

**Relish dish,** oblong w/gilt-trimmed scalloped rim, decorated w/large pink roses, 4 3/4" w., 8" l. ...................................... 325-375

**Salt dip,** ruffled rim, 3" d................................. 280

**Salt & pepper shakers,** three-color roses, pr. ............................................... 495

**Salt shaker,** pink roses .................................. 250

**Sugar bowl,** cov., two-handled one-color rose, 3 1/2" d., 3 1/4" h............................... 350

**Vase,** 4 1/4" h., footed swelled base tapering to cylindrical sides, two-color roses........ 345

**Vase,** 4 1/2" h., decorated w/American Beauty roses ............................................ 375

**Vase,** 4 3/4" h., slightly swelled slender cylindrical body w/a short rolled neck, three-color roses in pink, yellow & white ..... 288

**Vase,** 6 1/2" h., decorated w/roses & shadow ferns......................................... 350-425

**Vase,** 7" h., bulbous ovoid body tapering to a short tiny flared neck .......................... 300-375

**Wall pocket,** three-color roses, 5 x 9".......... 1,300

## SAND BABIES

**Trivet** ...................................................... 125-150

## SNOW BABIES

**Creamer** .................................................. 150-175

**Pitcher,** 3 1/2" h. ......................................... 125

**Salt shaker** ................................................ 120

**Tea tile** ..................................................... 145

**Trivet,** ...................................................... 150

## SUNBONNET BABIES

**Ashtray,** babies cleaning ............................... 275

**Bell,** babies sewing, unmarked ................. 400-450

**Candlestick,** babies washing, 5" d., 1 3/4" h.................................................... 275

**Creamer,** babies ironing, 3" h.......................... 250

**Creamer & open sugar bowl,** babies sewing, pr. ...................................................... 475

**Creamer & open sugar bowl,** boat-shaped, babies fishing on sugar, babies cleaning on creamer, pr. ...................... 500

**Cup & saucer,** babies washing........................ 350

**Dish,** diamond-shaped .................................. 200

**Dish,** heart-shaped........................................ 200

**Mug,** babies washing..................................... 350

**Pitcher,** milk, 4 1/4" h., babies washing .......... 325

*Sunbonnet Babies Plate*

**Plate,** 6" d., babies washing (ILLUS.)........ 250-325

**Saucer,** babies fishing.................................... 75

**Tea set,** child's ....................................... 700-800

**Toothpick holder,** babies mending .......... 450-550

**Vase,** 3" h., babies fishing ............................. 235

## TOMATO ITEMS

**Tomato bowl,** berry....................................... 50

**Tomato bowls,** 5 3/4" d., set of 4.................... 145

**Tomato box,** cov., w/green & brown finial, 3" d. ...................................................... 45

**Tomato creamer,** cov., large ......................... 200

**Tomato creamer,** cov., small...................... 45-50

*Tomato Creamer & Sugar Bowl*

**Tomato creamer & cov. sugar bowl,** creamer 3" d., 3" h., sugar bowl 3 1/2" d., 4" h. pr. (ILLUS.) .......................... 125

**Tomato cup & saucer,** demitasse.................. 125

**Tomato mustard jar,** cover & figural leaf spoon, 3 pcs.............................................. 125

**Tomato pitcher,** milk, 4 1/2" h. .................. 250-350

**Tomato plate,** 4 1/4" d., ring-handled, figural lettuce leaf.......................................... 19

**Tomato plate,** 5 1/2" d., ring-handled, figural lettuce leaf w/molded yellow flowers ....... **29**

**Tomato plate,** 7" d., ring-handled, figural lettuce leaf w/molded yellow flowers ............. **38**

**Tomato salt & pepper shakers,** pr. ................ **150**

**Tomato tea set,** cov. teapot, creamer & cov. sugar bowl, 3 pcs .................................. **325**

**Tomato teapot,** cov., small ............................. **350**

# MISCELLANEOUS

**Ashtray,** figural elk ......................................... **275**

**Ashtray,** figural lobster .................................... **150**

**Ashtray,** figural, oyster & pearl design, 4" l ..................................................... **275-325**

**Ashtray,** figural shell, 4 1/2 x 4 1/2" ................. **45**

**Ashtray,** mountain goat decoration, 5 1/2" l. ................................................. **350-450**

**Ashtray,** scenic decoration of Dutch lady w/basket, 5 1/2" d ......................................... **60**

**Ashtray,** stork decoration, artist-signed, 4 1/2" l. ................................................... **60**

**Ashtray,** stork decoration on yellow ground, 3 1/4 x 5", 1 1/4" h .......................... **125**

**Basket,** miniature, scene w/cows, unmarked ..................................................... **59**

**Basket,** "tapestry," footed, bulbous body w/a ruffled rim & ornate gold-trimmed overhead handle, portrait of lady w/horse, 5" h. ........................................... **595**

**Basket,** handled, boy & donkey decoration, artist-signed, 5 3/4" h. ................................ **175**

**Basket** w/reticulated handles, decorated w/white roses, 7 3/4" l., 3 1/2" h. ............. **125**

**Bell,** musicians scene, men playing a cello & mandolin ............................................ **275-325**

**Bell,** nursery rhyme decoration w/Jack & the Beanstalk .......................................... **400-450**

**Bell,** nursery rhyme decoration w/Little Bo Peep ...................................................... **350-400**

**Bell,** w/original wooden clapper, decorated w/scene of ocean liner being brought into harbor by tugboats ............................... **275**

**Bell,** peacock decoration, 2 1/2" d., 3" h. ......... **275**

**Berry set:** 9 3/4" d. bowl & four 5" d. sauce dishes; decorated w/musicians scene, 5 pcs. ............................................... **350-450**

**Berry set:** 9 1/2" d. bowl & six 5" d. sauce dishes; portrait decoration, 7 pcs. ......... **650-750**

**Bowl,** 5 3/4" d., nursery rhyme scene w/Jack & Jill .................................................. **125**

**Bowl,** 6" d., figural conch shell ......................... **75**

**Bowl,** 6 7/8" d., 2 1/2" h., footed, shallow slightly scalloped sides, Cavalier Musicians decoration, gold trim on feet .............. **110**

**Bowl,** 8" l., 4" h., figural lobster ....................... **250**

**Bowl,** 6 1/4 x 8 1/2", shell-shaped ............. **400-450**

**Bowl,** 9 1/2" d., figural poppy .......................... **135**

**Bowl,** 10" d., decorated w/gold roses ........ **150-200**

**Bowl,** 10" d., decorated w/pink roses ........ **125-150**

**Bowl,** 5 x 10", footed, handled, figural poppy, apricot satin finish ............................ **700**

**Bowl,** 10 1/2" d., floral decoration, blown-out mold .............................................. **250-300**

**Bowl,** 10 1/2" d., "tapestry," decorated w/Colonial scene ............................. **1,100-1,300**

**Box,** cov., four-footed ring base, scenic decoration of Dutch children ....................... **125**

**Box,** cov., shell-shaped, nursery rhyme scene, Little Boy Blue decoration ................ **225**

**Box,** cov., square, desert scene decoration on cover, Arabs w/camels on background colors of pink & brown, unmarked, 2 x 2 1/2", 1 3/4" h. ...................... **65**

*Royal Bayreuth Heart-shaped Box*

**Box,** cov., heart-shaped decorated w/scene of two brown & white cows & trees in pasture, green & yellow background, unmarked, 2 x 3 1/4", 1 1/2" h. (ILLUS.) ................................................... **65**

**Box,** cov., scene of woman on horse, woman & man w/rake watching, 4 1/4" d., 2 1/4" h .................................. **200-225**

**Box,** cov., figural turtle, 2 3/4 x 5" ................. **1,500**

**Box,** cov., shell-shaped, Little Jack Horner decoration, 5 1/2" d. .................................... **250**

**Cake plate,** decorated w/scene of men fishing ............................................... **175-225**

**Candleholder,** figural rose ...................... **550-650**

**Candleholder,** penguin decoration ................. **335**

**Candlestick,** figural bassett hound, brown, 4" h ..................................................... **500-550**

**Candlestick,** decorated w/scene of cows, 4" h. .................................................... **75-100**

**Candlestick,** elks scene, 4" h. .......................... **145**

**Candlestick,** decorated w/frog & bee, 6 1/2" h .............................................. **475-525**

**Candlestick,** figural clown, red, 4 1/2 x 6 1/2" .............................................. **575**

**Candlestick,** w/match holder, figural clown, 7" h. ................................................ **1,300**

**Candlestick,** oblong dished base w/a standard at one edge flanked by downswept open handles, tulip-form socket w/flattened rim, interior of dished base decorated w/scene of hunter & dogs ............ **275-325**

**Candy dish,** figural lobster ................................ **125**

**Candy dish w/turned over edge,** nursery rhyme scene w/Little Miss Muffet ................ **125**

**Celery dish,** figural lobster ............................... **150**

**Chamberstick,** wide deeply dished, round pinched sides, central cylindrical socket w/flattened rim, S-scroll handle from side of dish to socket, dark brick red ground, decorated w/"Dancing Frogs" & flying insects, rare ................................. **1,200-1,500**

**Cheese dish,** miniature, scenic decoration ........................................... **400-500**

**Chocolate pot,** cov., figural poppy, tall pink blossom w/ruffled rim, figural poppy on cover, light green & white leafy footed base & large leaf & stem handle, 8 1/2" h. (ILLUS. top next page) ...... **1,400-2,000**

**Cracker jar,** cov., figural lobster ...................... **600**

*Poppy Pattern Chocolate Pot*

**Cracker jar,** cov., figural poppy, 6" h......... **700-900**
**Creamer,** Arab scene decoration ...................... **95**
**Creamer,** Brittany Girl decoration...................... **75**
**Creamer,** cobalt blue, Babes in Woods
   decoration (unmarked) ................................. **250**
**Creamer,** decorated w/man in fishing boat
   scene......................................................... **145**
**Creamer,** figural alligator, 4 1/2 " h............. **350-400**
**Creamer,** figural apple............................. **150-225**
**Creamer,** figural apple, all-green.............. **200-250**
**Creamer,** figural bear, 4 1/4" h. ................ **800-900**
**Creamer,** figural Bird of Paradise,
   3 3/4" h. ................................................. **450-500**
**Creamer,** figural black cat ....................... **250-300**
**Creamer,** figural bull, brown ..................... **275-325**
**Creamer,** figural bull, grey ........................ **250-325**
**Creamer,** figural bull head, 4" h. ............... **175-225**
**Creamer,** figural butterfly, open wings ..... **350-450**
**Creamer,** figural cat handle, 4" h. ............. **400-450**
**Creamer,** figural chimpanzee, 4" h........... **400-450**
**Creamer,** figural clown, orange outfit,
   3 5/8" h. (minor enamel flakes) ............. **375-425**
**Creamer,** figural clown, red suit ............... **450-500**
**Creamer,** figural coachman, 4 1/4" h........ **275-300**
**Creamer,** figural cockatoo, 4" h................ **400-500**
**Creamer,** figural crow, black, 4 1/2" h. ...... **150-200**
**Creamer,** figural crow, black & white........ **150-200**
**Creamer,** figural crow, brown beak .......... **150-200**
**Creamer,** figural crow, brown bill & eyes
   (rare) ......................................................... **250**
**Creamer,** figural dachshund .................... **300-400**
**Creamer,** figural duck...................................... **315**

*Eagle Creamer*

**Creamer,** figural eagle, grey (ILLUS.) ....... **400-450**
**Creamer,** figural fish head, grey ...................... **250**
**Creamer,** figural flounder, 4 1/4" h. ........... **600-800**

**Creamer,** figural frog .................................. **160-175**
**Creamer,** figural geranium, 4" h. .............. **450-550**
**Creamer,** figural girl w/basket, 4 1/4" h. .... **550-650**
**Creamer,** figural girl w/pitcher, red .................. **895**
**Creamer,** figural grape cluster, light green....... **128**
**Creamer,** figural grape cluster, lilac.................. **95**
**Creamer,** figural grape cluster, white ........ **100-150**
**Creamer,** figural grape cluster, yellow
   (unmarked)................................................... **175**
**Creamer,** figural hawk, 4 3/4" h. ............... **450-500**
**Creamer,** figural ibex head w/trumpet-form
   bowl, stirrup-type, 4 1/4" h...................... **700-800**
**Creamer,** figural lady bug, 4" h.............. **900-1,100**
**Creamer,** figural lamplighter ..................... **250-300**
**Creamer,** figural lemon ............................. **200-225**
**Creamer,** figural leopard .................... **3,200-3,600**

*Figural Lobster Creamer*

**Creamer,** figural lobster (ILLUS.) ............. **125-175**
**Creamer,** figural Man of the Mountain,
   3 1/2" h. ................................................. **110-125**
**Creamer,** figural maple leaf, 4" h.............. **250-325**
**Creamer,** figural milk maid, red dress,
   4 3/4" h. ................................................. **700-800**
**Creamer,** figural monk, brown, 4 1/2" h..... **600-800**
**Creamer,** figural monkey, brown .............. **425-450**
**Creamer,** figural monkey, green................. **575**
**Creamer,** figural mountain goat ................ **275-375**
**Creamer,** figural Murex shell, colored
   glaze, 3 3/4" h. ...................................... **200-300**
**Creamer,** figural oak leaf................................ **225**
**Creamer,** figural oak leaf, white w/orchid
   highlights.................................................... **275**
**Creamer,** figural orange ........................... **200-250**
**Creamer,** figural pansy, purple, 4" h......... **250-300**
**Creamer,** figural parakeet ........................ **350-500**
**Creamer,** figural parakeet, green ............ **275-325**
**Creamer,** figural pear ............................... **535-550**
**Creamer,** figural pig, blue................................ **775**
**Creamer,** figural pig, grey......................... **550-600**
**Creamer,** figural pig, red, 4 1/4" h. ........... **600-800**
**Creamer,** figural platypus, 4" h............ **1,000-1,200**
**Creamer,** figural poodle, black ................. **250-300**
**Creamer,** figural poodle, black & white............ **250**
**Creamer,** figural poodle, red, 4 1/2" h. ...... **500-600**
**Creamer,** figural poppy, peach iridescent........ **425**
**Creamer,** figural robin, 4" h. ..................... **175-225**
**Creamer,** figural rooster ........................... **400-450**
**Creamer,** figural rose, pink, 3" h................ **350-400**
**Creamer,** figural Santa Claus, attached
   handle, red, 4 1/4" h. ...................... **3,200-3,600**
**Creamer,** figural seal ................................ **325-400**
**Creamer,** figural shell w/coral handle.............. **185**
**Creamer,** figural shell w/lobster handle,
   unmarked, 2 1/2" h. ........................................ **75**

**Creamer,** figural snake................................... **1,000**
**Creamer,** figural Spiky Shell, white satin
finish, 4 1/4" h.............................. **75-125**
**Creamer,** figural St. Bernard, brown .............. **250**
**Creamer,** figural strawberry, 3 3/4" h. ....... **250-300**
**Creamer,** figural water buffalo.................. **275-325**

*Water Buffalo Creamer*

**Creamer,** figural water buffalo, black &
white (ILLUS.) .............................. **175**
**Creamer,** figural water buffalo, souvenir of
Portland, Oregon............................ **300**
**Creamer,** figural watermelon........................... **395**
**Creamer,** flow blue, Babes in Woods deco-
ration ................................................ **325**
**Creamer,** miniature, "tapestry" scene of girl
& horse.............................................. **275**
**Creamer,** scene of girl w/basket, salmon
color ...................................... **800-1,000**
**Creamer,** stirrup-type, figural ibex head.......... **625**
**Creamer,** "tapestry," Scottish highland
goats scene................................... **350**
**Creamer,** pasture scene w/cows & trees,
3 1/4" h............................................. **95**
**Creamer,** figural clown, green, 3 1/2" h........... **400**
**Creamer,** left-handled, scene of two girls
under umbrella, 3 1/2" h. .............................. **380**
**Creamer,** blue cylindrical body w/flared
base & figural brown & grey cat handle,
3 3/4" h.............................................. **395**
**Creamer,** figural seashell, boot-shaped,
3 3/4" h............................................. **195**
**Creamer,** "tapestry," footed ovoid body
tapering to a wide rounded & flaring
neck w/a pinched spout & small C-scroll
handle, sheep in the meadow decora-
tion, 3 3/4" h. ......................... **300-350**
**Creamer,** pinched spout, "tapestry," goats
decoration, 4" h. ...................................... **350**
**Creamer,** crowing rooster & hen decora-
tion, 4 1/4" h. ...................................... **125**
**Creamer,** figural elk head, shades of brown
& cream, 3 1/2" d., 4 1/4" h. ........................ **225**
**Creamer,** figural lamplighter, green,
4 1/2" h.............................................. **275**
**Creamer,** figural crow, black, 4 3/4" h. ............. **225**
**Creamer,** "tapestry," wide ovoid body w/a
flaring foot & a long pinched spout,
ornate gilt D-form handle, "The Bathers"
landscape scene, 3 1/2" h. ..................... **375-425**
**Creamer & cov. sugar bowl,** figural apple,
pr. ........................................................ **350-400**
**Creamer & cov. sugar bowl,** figural grape
cluster, purple, pr. .......................................... **225**
**Creamer & cov. sugar bowl,** figural pansy,
lavender, pr. ...................................................... **375**

**Creamer & cov. sugar bowl,** figural
poppy, pr. ........................................................ **300**
**Creamer & cov. sugar bowl,** figural
rooster, pr. ...................................................... **350**
**Creamer & cov. sugar bowl,** figural straw-
berry, unmarked, pr. ...................................... **500**
**Creamer & open sugar bowl,** each deco-
rated w/a mountain landscape w/a boy &
donkey, 3" h., pr. .................................... **250-350**
**Creamer & open sugar bowl,** figural
poppy, pr. ...................................................... **400-500**
**Creamer & open sugar bowl,** figural
poppy, white satin finish, pr. ......................... **525**
**Creamer & open sugar bowl,** figural
rooster, creamer w/multicolored feathers
& sugar bowl in black, pr. ............................ **1,200**
**Creamer & open sugar bowl,** figural
strawberry, unmarked, pr. ....................... **500-600**
**Creamer & open sugar bowl,** "tapestry,"
barrel-shaped, the creamer w/a long
pinched spout, creamer w/goose girl
scene, sugar w/Alpine village scene,
sugar bowl 3 7/8" h., creamer 4 1/4" h.,
pr. ...................................................... **675**
**Cup & saucer,** decorated w/hunting scene
of man & dog........................................ **100-125**
**Cup & saucer,** figural rose........................ **150-200**
**Cup & saucer,** floral decoration on the
inside & outside, gold handle on cup,
scalloped standard saucer, ca. 1916 ....... **35-75**
**Cup & saucer,** scene of man w/turkeys........... **125**
**Cup & saucer,** "tapestry," floral
decoration ......................................... **200-250**
**Cup & saucer,** demitasse, Castle scene
decoration, artist-signed............................ **140**
**Cup & saucer,** demitasse, figural apple.... **100-150**
**Cup & saucer,** demitasse, figural grape
cluster...................................................... **200-250**
**Cup & saucer,** demitasse, figural orange ........ **150**
**Dish,** leaf-shaped, nursery rhyme decora-
tion w/Little Miss Muffet............................... **155**
**Dish,** leaf-shaped, "tapestry," scenic Lady
& Prince decoration...................................... **125**
**Dresser tray,** rectangular, "tapestry," Lady
& Prince scenic decoration, 7 x 9 1/4"... **450-550**

*Boy & Donkeys Dresser Tray*

**Dresser tray,** rectangular w/rounded corners, scene of boy & three donkeys in
landscape, 8 x 11" (ILLUS.) .................. **175-250**
**Dresser tray,** rectangular w/rounded corners, "tapestry" decoration of a young
courting couple wearing early 19th c.
attire, 11 1/2" l. ...................................... **500-600**
**Dresser tray,** decorated w/hunting
scene................................................... **200-275**

**Ewer,** scene of hunter w/dog, 4 1/2" h.............. 225
**Ewer,** cobalt blue, Babes in Woods decoration, 6" h. ......................................................... 650
**Flower holder w/frog-style cover,** hunt scene decoration, 3 3/4" h..................... **200-225**
**Gravy boat** w/attached liner, decorated w/multicolored floral sprays, gadrooned border, gold trim, cream ground...................... 45
**Gravy boat & underplate,** figural poppy, satin finish, 2 pcs.......................................... 250
**Hair receiver,** cov., decorated w/scene of boy & donkey ........................................ **125-150**
**Hair receiver,** cov., "tapestry," scene of farmer w/turkeys.......................................... 300
**Hair receiver,** cov., three-footed, scene of dog beside hunter shooting ducks .............. 335
**Hair receiver,** cov., decorated w/a scene of a Dutch boy & girl, 3 1/4" h......................... 150
**Hatpin holder,** figural owl ................................ 850
**Hatpin holder,** footed baluster-form body w/a scalloped rim & top pierced w/holes, "tapestry" design of a youth & maiden in early 19th c. costume, 4 1/2" h. ............ **450-575**
**Hatpin holder,** hexagonal shape, decorated w/pink & white roses, green leaves & gold trim on rim, satin finish ...................... 350
**Humidor,** cov., figural elk ............................... 950
**Humidor,** cov., figural gorilla, black............... **1,750**
**Humidor,** cov., tapering cylindrical body w/elk head handles, figural antlers on lid, brown, 6 1/4" h. ..................................... **600-800**
**Humidor,** cov., 7 3/4" h. ......................... **900-1,200**
**Humidor,** cov., Arab scene decoration, grey ...................................................... **500-600**
**Humidor,** cov., purple & lavender floral decoration ................................................... 325

*Royal Bayreuth Lamp Base*

**Lamp base,** "tapestry," slender ovoid body decorated w/"The Chase" scene, hounds after stag in water, raised on a metal ring support w/four short legs w/paw feet, set on an octagonal metal base w/molded swirled leafy stems, fitted for electricity, overall 21" h. (ILLUS.) ...................... **900-1,100**

**Match holder,** hanging-type, figural elk .......... 575
**Match holder,** hanging-type, figural shell.. **275-325**
**Match holder,** hanging-type, figural spiky shell................................................................ 275
**Match holder,** hanging-type, scene of Arab on horseback................................................. 300
**Match holder,** hanging-type, scene of fishermen in boat ....................................... **325-350**
**Match holder,** hanging-type, stork decoration on yellow ground ......................... **325-350**
**Match holder,** hanging-type, "tapestry," sheep in landscape scene, 4 1/2" l.............. 485
**Match holder w/striker,** decorated water scene w/brown "Shadow Trees" & boats on orange & gold ground, unmarked, 3 1/4" d., 2 1/2" h. ...................................... 65
**Mint dish,** ruffled, w/Dutch girl decoration, 4 1/2" d............................................................. 125
**Model of a man's high top slipper** ............... 250
**Model of a man's shoe,** black oxford............. 150
**Mug,** beer, figural elk ................................ **400-450**
**Mug,** figural clown ......................................... 550
**Mug,** decorated w/cavalier scene, 4 1/2" h................................................... **125-150**
**Mug,** candle lady decoration, 5" h. ............ **300-375**

*Figural Elk Beer Mug*

**Mug,** beer, figural elk, 5 3/4" h. (ILLUS.) .......... 650
**Mustard jar,** cov., figural grape cluster, yellow.................................................................. 175
**Mustard jar,** cov., figural lobster ...................... 225
**Mustard jar,** cov., figural rose .......................... 550
**Mustard jar,** cov., figural shell.................. **100-160**
**Mustard jar,** cov., figural pansy, 3 1/4" h. . **400-600**
**Mustard jar, cover & spoon,** figural poppy, red, green spoon, 3 pcs.................... 300
**Nappy,** handled, figural poppy ......................... 150
**Nut set:** large pedestal-based open compote & six matching servers; each decorated w/a colorful pastoral scene w/animals, 7 pcs.......................................... 450
**Pin dish,** decorated w/Arab scene ............. **75-100**
**Pin tray,** triangular, "tapestry" portrait decoration of lady wearing large purple plumed hat, 5 x 5 x 5".................................... 250
**Pincushion,** figural elk head ........................... 350
**Pipe holder,** figural Bassett hound, black **450-550**
**Pitcher,** 2 1/2" h., scene w/cows ..................... 170
**Pitcher,** 3 1/8" h., 2 3/8" w., squared waisted body w/short, wide spout & angled gilt handle, scene of Arab on horse (ILLUS. right, top next page) .............. 125

*Royal Bayreuth Pitcher & Vase*

*Cavalier Pitcher*

**Pitcher,** 3 1/4" h., 2" d., decorated w/Cavalier scene, two Cavaliers drinking at a table, grey & cream ground, unmarked (ILLUS.) .......................................................... 55
**Pitcher,** 3 1/2" h., nursery rhyme scene w/Little Boy Blue............................................ 210
**Pitcher,** 3 1/2" h., scenic decoration of Arab on horse................................................ 95

*Pitcher with Musicians Scene*

**Pitcher,** 3 1/2" h., 2 1/4" d., scene of musicians, one playing bass & one w/mandolin, unmarked (ILLUS.) .................................... 55
**Pitcher,** 3 3/4" h., corset-shaped, Colonial Curtsey scene w/a couple ............................ 165
**Pitcher,** miniature, 4 1/2" h., scene of a skiff w/sail..................................................... 125
**Pitcher,** 5" h., Arab w/horse decoration .......... 140
**Pitcher,** 5" h., double handles, scene of fisherman in boat w/sails ...................... 150-200
**Pitcher,** 5" h., figural crow ............................... 165
**Pitcher,** 5" h., scene of an Arab on white horse w/brown horse nearby........................ 150

**Pitcher,** squatty, 5" h., 5" d., decorated w/hunting scene ........................................... 100
**Pitcher,** 5 1/4" h., pinched spout, "tapestry," scene of train on bridge over raging river ................................................................. 550
**Pitcher,** 6" h., decorated w/hunting scene................................................. 125-150
**Pitcher,** 6 3/4" h., wide ovoid body w/a flaring lightly scalloped base & a long pinched spout, "tapestry" finish w/a color landscape "Don Quixote" scene ........... 525-575
**Pitcher,** lemonade, 6 3/4" h., wide ovoid body w/flat foot & long pinched spout, ornate D-shape handle, dark brick red ground w/green "Dancing Frog" & flying insects decoration .......................... 1,200-1,500
**Pitcher,** lemonade, 7 1/2 " h., figural apple ...................................................... 900-1,100
**Pitcher,** lemonade, 7 1/2 " h., figural lemon ................................................. 1,000-1,200
**Pitcher,** milk, babies mending.................. 375-400
**Pitcher,** milk, figural coachman...................... 750

*Lobster Milk Pitcher*

**Pitcher,** milk, figural lobster (ILLUS.) .............. 250
**Pitcher,** milk, figural oak leaf............................ 500
**Pitcher,** milk, figural poppy............................... 350
**Pitcher,** milk, figural red & white parrot handle ............................................................. 550
**Pitcher,** milk, figural St. Bernard dog, unmarked ...................................................... 400
**Pitcher,** milk, Goose Girl decoration ............... 150
**Pitcher,** milk, musicians decoration.................. 150
**Pitcher,** milk, 3" h., figural shell w/lobster handle ............................................................. 150
**Pitcher,** milk, 4" h., figural St. Bernard ...... 450-600
**Pitcher,** milk, 4 1/4" h., figural rose ........... 600-800
**Pitcher,** milk, 4 1/2" h., figural poppy ........ 350-400
**Pitcher,** milk, 4 1/2" h., nursery rhyme scene w/Jack & the Beanstalk .................... 325
**Pitcher,** milk, 4 3/4" h., figural clown, yellow ................................................... 900-1,100
**Pitcher,** milk, 4 3/4" h., figural coachman . 350-425
**Pitcher,** milk, 4 3/4" h., figural cockatoo........... 695
**Pitcher,** milk, 4 3/4" h., figural eagle ......... 550-600
**Pitcher,** milk, 4 3/4" h., figural shell w/seahorse handle ......................................... 315-350
**Pitcher,** milk, 5" h., figural dachshund ...... 600-700
**Pitcher,** milk, 5" h., figural fish head.......... 450-500
**Pitcher,** milk, 5" h., figural owl, brown ...... 400-600
**Pitcher,** milk, 5 1/4" h., figural elk.............. 275-325
**Pitcher,** milk, 5 1/2" h., figural fish head........... 300
**Pitcher,** milk, 5 1/2" h., figural lamplighter, green ...................................................... 400-500

**Pitcher,** milk, tankard, 9 1/2" h., h.p. pastoral cow scene ........................................ **200-250**
**Pitcher,** water, 6" h., figural apple ............ **700-900**
**Pitcher,** water, 6" h., figural pelican .......... **700-900**
**Pitcher,** water, 6" h., figural Santa Claus, red ................................................... **7,000-9,000**
**Pitcher,** water, 6 1/4" h., figural oak leaf............................................ **1,700-2,000**
**Pitcher,** water, 6 1/2" h., figural strawberry ................................. **900-1,100**
**Pitcher,** water, 6 3/4" h., figural lobster .......... **395**
**Pitcher,** water, 6 3/4" h., figural robin ...... **800-900**
**Pitcher,** water, 7" h., figural coachman ............ **800**
**Pitcher,** water, 7" h., figural duck .......... **800-1,000**
**Pitcher,** water, 7" h., figural elk ................. **500-700**
**Pitcher,** water, 7" h., figural orange.......... **800-900**
**Pitcher,** water, 7" h., figural rooster, multicolored.................................... **3,200-3,600**
**Pitcher,** water, 7" h., figural seal ......... **3,600-4,000**
**Pitcher,** water, 7 1/4" h., decorated w/frog & bee ........................................... **900-1,000**
**Pitcher,** water, 7 1/4" h., pinched spout, scenic decoration of cows in pasture .... **257-300**
**Pitcher,** water, 7 1/2" h., figural conch shell, brownish amethyst & yellow mottled body, orange angled coral handle ......... **500-700**
**Pitcher,** water, 7 3/4" h., 6" d., figural lobster, red shaded to orange w/green handle ............................................................ **525**
**Pitcher,** decorated w/scene of hunter & dog ......................................................... **125-175**
**Pitcher,** sheep scene ...................................... **150**
**Plaque,** decorated w/scene of Arab on horse, 9 1/2" d. ...................................... **125-150**

*Royal Bayreuth "Tapestry" Plaque*

**Plaque,** pierced to hang, "tapestry," round w/a scroll-molded gilt-trimmed border, center portrait of woman leaning on horse, 9 1/2" d. (ILLUS.)........................ **775-825**
**Plate,** 5 1/4" d., leaf-shaped, decorated w/small yellow flowers on green ground, green curved handle ..................................... **38**
**Plate,** 6" d., decorated w/soccer scene ..... **175-200**
**Plate,** 6" d., handled, figural leaf & flower.......... **85**
**Plate,** 7" d., decorated w/scene of girl walking dog ......................................................... **100**
**Plate,** 7 1/2" d., nursery rhyme scene w/Little Bo Peep.......................................... **125**
**Plate,** 8" d., decorated w/pink & yellow flowers, gold rim, pink ground, blue mark.. **50-75**
**Plate,** 8" d., scene of man hunting................... **125**

**Plate,** 8 1/2" d., scene of man fishing ............... **125**
**Plate,** 8 1/2" d., scene of man hunting............... **125**
**Plate,** 9" d., candle girl decoration............ **150-175**
**Plate,** 9" d., Cavalier Musicians scene ..... **225-275**
**Plate,** 9" d., figural ear of corn ......................... **495**
**Plate,** 9" d., scene of man smoking pipe ... **150-175**
**Plate,** 9 1/2" d., nursery rhyme scene w/Jack & the Beanstalk ......................... **250-300**
**Plate,** 9 1/2" d., scroll-molded rim, "tapestry," toasting Cavalier scene........................ **825**
**Plate,** 9 1/2" d., "tapestry," lady w/horse scene................................................... **770-800**
**Plate,** 9 1/2" d., "tapestry," landscape scene w/deer by a river .............................. **250**
**Playing card box,** cov., decorated w/a sailing ship scene ..................................... **195-250**
**Powder box,** cov., Cavalier Musicians scene ................................................................ **175**
**Powder box,** cov., round, "tapestry," scenic Lady & Prince decoration ..................... **150-175**
**Powder jar,** figural pansy, 4 1/4" h............ **500-600**
**Relish dish,** open-handled, footed, ruffled edge, cow scene decoration, 8" l. ............... **175**
**Relish dish,** figural cucumber, 5 1/4 x 12 1/2"................................................... **150-250**
**Relish dish,** figural Murex Shell............... **200-300**
**Salt & pepper shakers,** figural conch shell, unmarked, pr. ................................................ **100**
**Salt & pepper shakers,** figural ear of corn, pr. .............................................................. **600-800**
**Salt & pepper shakers,** figural grape cluster, purple, pr. ...................................... **150-175**
**Salt & pepper shakers,** figural poppy, red, pr. .............................................................. **300-400**
**Salt & pepper shakers,** figural shell, pr.... **125-150**
**Salt shaker,** figural elk ..................................... **135**
**Shaving mug,** figural elk head.................. **500-600**
**Stamp box,** cov., colorful scene of Dutch children................................................................ **125**
**Stamp box,** cov., "tapestry," Cottage by Water Fall scene ........................................... **225**
**String holder,** hanging-type, figural rooster head ........................................................ **550-650**
**Sugar bowl,** cov., Brittany Girl decoration ....... **100**
**Sugar bowl,** cov., figural lemon (small finial flake) ................................................................ **175**
**Sugar bowl,** cov., figural pansy, purple (tiny rim flake)....................................... **225-250**
**Sugar bowl,** cov., figural poppy, red ......... **225-250**
**Sugar bowl,** cov., figural rose .................. **300-400**
**Sugar bowl,** cov., figural shell w/lobster handle ............................................................. **200**
**Sugar bowl,** cov., figural lobster, 3 3/4" h. **110-150**
**Tea strainer,** figural pansy, 5 3/4" l. .......... **350-400**
**Tea strainer,** figural red poppy, 5 3/4" l..... **350-400**
**Teapot,** cov., child's, decorated w/a scene of hunters, 3 3/4" h. ................................... **125**
**Teapot,** cov., child's, boy & donkey decoration, green, unmarked, 4" h. ......................... **225**
**Teapot,** cov., demitasse, decorated w/scene of rooster & hen ..................... **250-300**
**Teapot,** cov., figural orange, 6 1/2" h. ...... **425-500**
**Teapot,** cov., figural poppy, red...................... **350**
**Toothpick holder,** ball-shaped w/overhead handle, "tapestry," lady w/horse scene ........ **475**
**Toothpick holder,** Bird of Paradise decoration ....................................................... **225-250**
**Toothpick holder,** decorated w/scene of girl w/two chickens ..................................... **100**

**Toothpick holder,** figural bellringer, 3 1/2" h................................................ **175-225**
**Toothpick holder,** figural elk head, 3" h. .. **225-250**
**Toothpick holder,** figural Murex Shell............ **175**
**Toothpick holder,** figural poppy, red.............. **300**
**Toothpick holder,** man hunting turkeys scene................................................ **200**
**Toothpick holder,** rooster & hen decoration, 2 1/2" h. ...................................... **200-250**
**Toothpick holder,** round, one side handle, decorated w/scene of man tending turkeys...................................................... **250-275**
**Toothpick holder,** "tapestry," scene of woman w/pony & trees, 2 2/5" h............ **450-550**
**Toothpick holder,** three-handled floral decoration, 2 1/4" h. ............................. **175-200**
**Toothpick holder,** three-handled, Harvest scene decoration......................................... **150**

*Toothpick Holder with Hunt Scene*

**Toothpick holder,** three-handled, Hunt scene decoration, 3" h. (ILLUS.) .................. **265**
**Toothpick holder,** three-handled, scene of horse & wagon ............................................ **150**
**Toothpick holder,** three-handled, three feet, nursery rhyme decoration w/Little Boy Blue................................................. **225-250**
**Toothpick holder,** two-handled, four-footed, scene of horsemen, unmarked.......... **75**
**Tray,** club-shaped, scene of hunter w/dog ....... **150**

*Tray with Girl & Geese Scene*

**Tray,** decorated w/scene of girl w/geese, molded rim w/gold trim, 9 x 12 1/4" (ILLUS.)...................................................... **425**
**Tray,** "tapestry," scene of train on bridge over raging river, 7 3/4 x 11" ........................ **800**
**Vase,** miniature, 2 3/4" h., conical body on three tab feet, tapering to a short flaring neck, small knob handles at shoulders, decorated w/a scene of cows...................... **125**

**Vase,** 3" h., basket-shaped w/overhead handle, square rim, Babes in Woods decoration ............................................. **325-350**
**Vase,** 3" h., scene of children w/St. Bernard dog ....................................................... **125**
**Vase,** 3 1/4" d., footed, baluster-form body w/angled shoulder handles, short cylindrical silver rim, Cavalier Musicians scene on grey ground ........................... **75-125**
**Vase,** 3 1/4" h., 1 7/8" d., footed, conical body tapering to a silver rim, small tab handles, decorated w/scene of white & brown cows w/green & brown ground (ILLUS. left, with pitcher)......................... **75-125**
**Vase,** 3 1/2" h., Cavalier Musicians decoration ........................................................ **125**
**Vase,** 3 5/8" h., footed conical body tapering to a swelled neck flanked by four loop handles, decorated w/hunting scene, man & woman on horses, unmarked ................................................. **45-50**
**Vase,** 3 3/4" h., handled, flow blue, Babes in Woods decoration, scene of girl curtseying............................................................. **370**
**Vase,** 4" h., Babes in Woods scene .......... **250-300**
**Vase,** 4" h., ovoid body w/a tiny, short flaring neck, "tapestry," scene of two cows, one black & one tan ...................................... **475**
**Vase,** 4" h., two-handled, decorated w/long-tailed Bird of Paradise ............... **225-300**
**Vase,** 4 1/2" h., sailing scene decoration... **135-150**
**Vase,** 4 1/2" h., "tapestry," courting couple decoration ................................................. **525**
**Vase,** bud, 4 1/2" h., two handles, Babes in Wood scene, cobalt blue & white ......... **225-325**
**Vase,** 4 3/4" h., handled, Babes in Woods decoration, girl holding doll ................... **500-550**
**Vase,** bud, 4 3/4" h., "tapestry," rounded body w/a thin tall neck, Lady & Prince scenic decoration ............................... **120-200**
**Vase,** 5" h., "tapestry," bulbous ovoid body tapering to a short slender flaring neck, cottage by a waterfall landscape .......... **295-350**
**Vase,** 5" h., "tapestry," bulbous ovoid body tapering to a short slender flaring neck, 'Castle by the Lake' landscape scene ......... **365**
**Vase,** 5 1/4" h., ovoid body w/short cylindrical neck, medallion portrait framed w/gold band in incised leaf design w/enamel trim.............................................. **200**
**Vase,** 5 1/2" h., decorated w/brown & white bust portrait of lady on dark green ground, artist-signed .................................... **475**
**Vase,** 5 1/2" h., portrait decoration ........... **250-300**
**Vase,** 5 1/2" h., teardrop-shaped, colorful floral decoration............................................ **125**
**Vase,** 6" h., "tapestry," decorated w/a scene of an elk & three hounds in a river..... **475**
**Vase,** 7" h., decorated w/Arab scene ........ **125-150**
**Vase,** 7" h., decorated w/portrait of a lady.................................................. **275-350**
**Vase,** 7" h., "tapestry," a bulbous ovoid body w/the rounded shoulder centering a tiny flared neck, a shaded pastel ground centered on one side w/a three-quarters length portrait of a lady in 18th c. attire w/a large feathered hat & large muff, the reverse w/a landscape scene................................................ **550-650**

**Vase,** 7 3/4" h., mercury & floral finish, ca. 1919, artist-signed & signed "Kgl. Priv. Tettan"......................................................... **175**

**Vase,** 8" h., decorated w/scene of hunter & dogs .................................................... **200-225**

**Vase,** 8 1/4" h., footed squatty bulbous bottom tapering to a tall waisted base w/a gently scalloped flaring rim, polychrome boy & two donkeys decoration ............. **250-300**

**Vase,** 8 1/4" h., "tapestry," slender ovoid body w/a short cylindrical flaring neck, "The Bathers" landscape scene .......... **435-550**

**Vase,** 9" h., tall slender waisted cylindrical body w/a gently scalloped flaring rim, three long green scroll & bead loop handles down the sides, the top body w/a band decorated w/a toasting Cavaliers scene in color on one side & "Ye Old Bell" scene on the other, the lower body all in dark green, ca. 1902 .................... **250-300**

*Vase with Peacock*

**Vase,** 9 1/2" h., peacock decoration, openwork on neck & at base, ornate scroll handles, lavish gold trim (ILLUS.) ............... **740**

**Vase,** 11 1/2" h., polar bear scene ................... **850**

**Vase,** double-bud, ovoid body w/two angled short flaring necks joined by a small handle, scene of Dutch children ......... **125**

**Vase,** miniature, ball-shaped, footed, silver rim, Arab scene decoration ......................... **150**

**Vases,** 2 1/2" h., decorated w/sunset scene of a ship, pr. ......................................... **100-125**

*Small Royal Bayreuth Vases*

**Vases,** 3 1/8" h., 2 5/8" d., squatty bulbous lower body below the tall tapering sides ending in a ringed neck & flanked by loop handles, one w/scene of Dutch boy & girl playing w/brown dog & the other w/scene of Dutch boy & girl playing w/white & brown dog, green mark, pr. (ILLUS.)............................................................ **110**

**Wall pocket,** figural grape cluster, purple ........ **350**

**Wall pocket,** figural grape cluster, yellow ........ **350**

**Wall pocket,** depicts a jester & "Many Kiss the Child for the Nurses SAKE," green ground, signed "NOKE," 9" h. ..................... **750**

**Wall pocket,** figural red poppy, 9 1/2" l. .... **650-700**

# ROYAL COPENHAGEN

*This porcelain has been made in Copenhagen, Denmark, since 1715. The ware is hard paste.*

*Royal Copenhagen Mark*

**Dish,** shallow rounded shell-shaped molded in high-relief along one side w/a large blue lobster on a pearl grey ground, stamped "Royal Copenhagen - UD," 7 1/2" d., 2" h. .....................................**$220**

**Figure group,** witch w/soldier, No. 1112, 8" h.............................................................. **495**

**Figure group,** Pan clinging to mountain goat, No. 737, 8 x 8".................................... **225**

*Royal Copenhagen Bricklayer*

**Figure of bricklayer,** standing man in work outfit, holding tray of mortar, No. 4377, 10" h. (ILLUS.)............................................... **225**

**Figure of Fanoe girl,** seated w/apron fanned out to form pin tray or bonbon dish, No. 1315, 5 1/2" w., 5" h. (ILLUS. top nrxt page) ..................................................... **200**

**Figure of girl,** nude, reclining on her stomach holding a blue cloth to her chin, No. 4706, 6 1/2" l., 4" h. ..................................... **200**

**Figure of Little Mermaid,** No. 5689, 5" w., 5" h. (ILLUS. center left next page)............. **175**

*Royal Copenhagen Fanoe Girl*

*Royal Copenhagen Little Mermaid*

*Royal Copenhagen Rosebud*

**Figure of Rosebud,** curled up sleeping child, No. 3009, 5 1/2" l., 5 1/2" h. (ILLUS.) ........................................ **225**

**Figure of Thumbelina,** tiny girl in half a nut shell, No. 4374, 3 1/2" h. ........................... **125**

**Figurine,** girl holding doll, No. 1938, ca. 1920s, 5" h. .................................................. **300**

**Model of Barn Owl,** shades of brown, black & cream on white base, No. 273, 8 3/4" h. (ILLUS. top next column) .............. **275**

**Model of Elk (moose),** recumbent pose, No. 2813, 10" l., 9" h. .................................. **500**

*Royal Copenhagen Barn Owl*

*Royal Copenhagen Hooded Crow*

**Model of Hooded Crow,** shades of blues & grey, No. 365, 14" l., 6 1/2" h. (ILLUS.) ........ **400**

*Royal Copenhagen Leopard*

**Model of Leopard (panther),** seated w/head down, No. 2555, 8" l., 8" h. (ILLUS.) ...................................................... **600**

**Model of Pointer Puppy,** white w/black markings, No. 259, 6 3/4" l., 7 1/2" h. .......... **200**

**Model of Rabbit,** large, white w/black markings, red eyes, No. 4676, 6" w., 6" h. .......................................................... **200**

**Model of Sea Lion,** head raised, shades of tan & grey, No. 14341, 4" w., 5" H. .............. **100**

*Royal Copenhagen Tiger*

**Model of Tiger,** recumbent position, No. 714, 12" l., 5 1/2" h. (ILLUS.) ........................ **450**

## ROYAL COPLEY

Royal Copley was a trade name used by the Spaulding China Company of Sebring, Ohio during the 1940s and 1950s for a variety of ceramic figurines, planters and other decorative pieces. Similar pieces were also produced under the trade name "Royal Windsor" as well as the Spaulding China mark.

The Spaulding China Company stopped producing in 1957 but for the next two years other potteries finished production of their outstanding orders. Today these originally inexpensive wares are developing a dedicated collector following.

**Ashtray,** heart-shaped w/two love birds sitting at top of heart, signed "Royal Copley," rose w/blue or yellow w/blue, 5 1/2", each ........................................................ **$35-50**

*Figural Pig Bank*

**Bank,** model of a pig, standing & smiling, two small holes in bottom, bank must be broken to retrieve money, 4 1/2" h. (ILLUS.).................................................... **35-50**

*"Farmer Pig" Bank*

**Bank,** model of a pig, "Farmer Pig," standing & wearing neck scarf, brown w/tan scarf, pink w/blue scarf, blue w/green scarf & brown & green w/brown scarf, two small holes in bottom, bank must be broken to retrieve money, brown w/green scarf is hardest to find, pink is most desirable color, 5 1/2" h., each (ILLUS.).................................................... **75-125**

*Teddy Bear Bank & Planters*

**Bank,** model of Teddy bear, white w/black & gold trim, red bow at neck, two small holes in bottom, bank must be broken to retrieve money, 7 1/4" h. (ILLUS. left)... **175-200**

*Figural Rooster Banks*

**Bank,** model of rooster, one, two, three or four small holes in bottom, bank must be broken to retrieve money, three colorations available, 7 1/2" h., each (ILLUS. of two) ........................................................ **75-85**
**Bank,** model of Teddy bear, brown, two small holes in bottom, bank must be broken to retrieve money, 7 1/2" h. ............ **150-160**
**Creamer & sugar bowl,** w/leaf handles, yellow & brown, grey & pink or tricolored, marked "Royal Copley" on bottom, tricolored & grey & pink are equally hard to find, 3" h., pr., each set ............................ **50-75**

*Figure of Dancing Lady*

**Figurine,** dancing lady, wearing hat & long full-skirted dress, one hand holding her

hat in place while wind blows at her
dress, four colorations, unmarked, 8" h.,
each (ILLUS.) ...................................... **135-150**

**Head vase planter,** "Island Lady," jet black
w/white turban, earrings, signed "Royal
Windsor" on back, three runners on bot-
tom of base, 8" h. ........................................ **100**

**Lamp base,** model of pig, decorated w/pink
or blue stripes, factory-drilled on top &
bottom, unmarked, extremely hard to
find, pink is easier to locate, 6 1/2" h.,
each ..................................................... **200-225**

*Figural Cocker Spaniel Lamp Base*

**Lamp base,** model of a dog, Cocker Spaniel, sitting in begging position, brown or
black, black is more rare than brown,
10" h. (ILLUS.)....................................... **125-150**

**Model of bear,** Teddy bear, eyes closed &
playing concertina, brown, unmarked,
7 1/2" h. (hard to find in mint condition)... **90-100**

**Model of bird,** Swallow w/extended wings,
cobalt, rose or yellow, blue is hardest,
choicest & priciest coloration, 7" h.,
each ...................................................... **75-150**

**Model of bird,** Hunt's Swallow, female flying toward ground, male flying upward,
four colorations, some are hand-decorated, cobalt pair & females hardest to
find, 8" h., pr. (ILLUS. of female, right
w/Jay bird)............................................. **150-250**

*Spaulding Jay Bird & Hunt Swallow*

**Model of bird,** Jay bird, various colors,
Spaulding mark, hand-decorated birds
bring higher prices, 8" h. (ILLUS. left) ..... **75-100**

**Model of cockatoo,** signed "Royal Cop-
ley," rose or green, 8 1/4" h., each .......... **45-50**

**Model of dog pulling wagon,** sitting dog,
brown w/black & white spots, wagon
imprinted "FLYER" on side, unmarked,
5 1/4" h. .................................................. **35-50**

**Model of drake & duck,** Gadwells, Game
Bird series, signed "A.D. Priollo" on
base, Royal Windsor mark, series consists of Gadwells, Teals & Mallards,
Gadwells & Teals are hardest to find,
sizes vary, pr. ...................................... **150-250**

**Model of hen & rooster,** black & white
w/red trim, green base, 5 1/2" h. & 6" h.,
pr. (rooster is harder to find)................. **350-400**

**Model of hen & rooster,** black & white
w/red trim, green base, 7" h. & 8" h.,
pr. ...................................................... **200-225**

**Model of hen & rooster,** brown breast,
Royal Windsor mark, 10" h. & 10 1/2" h.,
pr. (hens are harder to find) ................. **300-350**

**Model of hen & rooster,** teal breast, Royal
Windsor mark, 10" h. & 10 1/4" h., pr.
(hens are harder to find)....................... **350-400**

**Model of kitten,** brown to brown grey,
8" h., each (colors hard to match) ........ **100-125**

**Model of rooster,** all-white, 10" h. .................. **129**

*Models of Kingfishers*

**Models of birds,** Kingfishers, one on leaf
base w/wings extended, the other flying
downward, blue, rose or yellow, blue is
hardest to find, rose pairs are hard to
match, 5" h., pr., each (ILLUS.)............. **100-150**

*Models of Kittens*

**Models of kittens,** black & white w/red
bow at neck, sitting, one looking up &
one looking down, one shown on left is
harder to find, 8" h., each (ILLUS.)............ **75-85**

**Pitcher,** 8" h., Pome Fruit patt., stamped
or incised "Royal Copley" on bottom, five
colorations, each (blue is most popular &
priciest)..................................................... **45-85**

**Planter,** figure of Madonna w/side planter,
marked w/raised letters on bottom,

Royal Windsor mark, pale blue, pale rose or solid white, 6 1/4" h., each (solid white is most difficult color to locate)......... **40-55**
**Planter,** model of bird on birdhouse, 8" h.. **135-150**
**Planter,** model of cat, recumbent, white, 7 1/2" l., 5 1/2" h. .................................... **135-150**
**Planter,** model of Cocker-type dog standing on a log & playing a large bass fiddle, unmarked, 7" h. (premium item, very difficult to find) ....................................... **165-175**
**Planter,** model of dog, recumbent Poodle wearing collar, grey, pink or white, grey is hardest to find, pink is most common color, 8 1/2" l., 6 1/2" h., each .................. **60-85**

*Hummingbird & Wall Pocket Planter*

**Planter,** model of Hummingbird on flower, blue or red & white bird, red flower, green leaves form base, blue bird brings higher price, 5 1/4" h. (ILLUS. left) ............ **50-75**
**Planter,** model of kitten in cradle, 7 1/2" h. ................................................. **175-195**
**Planter,** model of kitten w/birdhouse, 8" h. ...................................................... **150-175**
**Planter,** model of kitten w/cello, black & white, unmarked, 7 1/2" h. ..................... **125-135**
**Planter,** model of puppy w/mailbox, black & white, runners on underside, unmarked, 8 1/2" h. (premium item)......................... **75-100**

*Rooster Planter*

**Planter,** model of rooster on wheelbarrow, 8" h. (ILLUS.)......................................... **100-125**
**Planter,** model of Teddy bear w/basket on back, brown w/blue, pink or yellow basket, runners on bottom, unmarked, 6 1/4" h., each .......................................... **65-75**
**Planter,** model of Teddy bear, white w/black trim & red bow at neck, 8" h. (ILLUS. center)......................................... **75-85**

*Siamese Cats Planter*

**Planter,** model of two Siamese cats, one sitting & one recumbent, white w/black trim, blue eyes, green or rust woven basket, green is more desirable, 8" h., each (ILLUS.)................................................. **175-200**
**Planter/book ends,** model of ram's head, pr. .................................................................. **55**
**Vase,** 8 1/2" h., figural, model of mare nuzzling her foal, signed "Royal Copley," medium rusty brown.................................. **35-50**
**Vase,** 10" h., pink & green floral decal decoration on butterscotch or white ground, three distinct classic styles, marked "Spaulding" in gold on underside, each (collectors prefer butterscotch finish) ...... **75-100**
**Wall pocket,** model of rooster, full figure walking bird, black & white w/green background or brown w/green background, signed "Royal Copley," 5 1/2" h., each (black & white version is more prized by collectors) ................................. **45-60**
**Wall pocket,** figural, "Pigtail Girl," bust of girl w/ruffled collar & bonnet, grey, deep red, turquoise, pink & deep blue, marked "Royal Copley," deep red & blue are the most desired & therefore harder to find & costlier, 7" h., each (ILLUS. right w/Hummingbird planter) ....................................... **75-125**
**Wall pocket,** figural, full face pirate head w/ruddy complexion, grey or red bandanna, signed "Royal Copley," 8" h., each ......................................................... **45-60**
**Wall pockets,** figural, head of old man & old woman w/grey hair & old-style hat, deep rose & miscellaneous other colors, signed "Royal Copley," 8" h., each pr...... **80-100**

# ROYAL VIENNA

*Royal Vienna Mark*

The second factory in Europe to make hard paste porcelain was established in Vienna in 1719 by Claud Innocentius de Paquier. The factory underwent various changes of administration through the years and finally closed in 1865. Since then, however, the porcelain has been reproduced by various factories in Austria and Germany, many of which have also reproduced the early beehive mark. Early pieces, naturally, bring far higher prices than the later ones or the reproductions.

*Royal Vienna Cabinet Plates*

**Cabinet plate,** 9 1/2" d., h.p. center scene of maiden clad in white drapery standing in a garden below falling blossoms, pale blue & maroon border gilt w/vignettes of animals & scrollwork panels, ca. 1900, artist-signed, underglaze-blue shield mark, small ground out chip to rim (ILLUS. right) ............................................ **$805**

**Cabinet plate,** center free-form enamel decorated panel depicting a nude female in landscape, border w/gilt foliate design on deep burgundy ground, late 19th c., 9 1/2" d. .................................................. **1,840**

**Cabinet plate,** central figural scene "Mione & Amor," gilt foliate design on cobalt border, late 19th c., 9 1/2" d. ........................... **518**

**Cabinet plate,** 9 5/8" d., h.p. center portrait of Angelina, a young dark-haired woman wearing an off the shoulder gown, a flower in her hair, within a maroon, yellow, pink & green ground border gilt w/foliate scrollwork, shield mark in underglaze-blue, artist-signed & title painted in black on reverse (ILLUS. center) ..................................................... **1,380**

**Cabinet plate,** 9 3/4" d., h.p. center scene of maiden guiding two soldiers towards a woodland lake w/blue ground border decorated w/stylized foliage & flower medallions, gold trim, late 19th c., underglaze-blue shield mark (ILLUS. left) ............. **690**

**Cabinet plates,** 9 1/2" d., each decorated in center w/scene of three maidens or a young woman w/a cupid, each on a terrace and within a gilt scroll cartouche, reserved on cobalt ground & surrounded by three panels of cupids amongst clouds separated by tooled gilt oblong panels & foliate scrollwork within a gilt edged rim, shield marks in underglaze-blue, titles in black script, signed Mohau, early 20th c., the pair.................................. **1,495**

**Plaque,** round w/central enamel decorated bust portrait depicting Queen Elizabeth of England, scrolled gilt foliate decorated ruby red border, titled in German on reverse, 19th c, 16 1/2" d. (ILLUS. top next column)............................................. **2,300**

**Plate,** 10 1/8" d., gilt-trimmed cobalt blue border, center w/a colored enamel bust portrait of a female, late 19th c..................... **316**

*Royal Vienna Portrait Plaque*

*Royal Vienna Scenic Plate*

**Plates,** 11 1/2" d., the center decorated w/colorful scene of seated woman & man standing near, titled "Maiden and Shepherd Boy," gilt designs on wide green ground, ca. 1864, beehive mark under glaze & over glaze (ILLUS.) ........... **1,200**

*Royal Vienna Covered Urn*

**Urn,** cov., decorated w/two continuous figural scenes, one titled "Hector Abschied" & the other "Alexander und die Familie des Darius" on a gilt ground flanked by loop handles, raised on a circular base w/figural panels, pseudo shield mark in blue enamel & decorator mark of Dorfl Franz, late 19th c., 21" h. (ILLUS.)............ **4,887**

# ROYAL WORCESTER

*This porcelain has been made by the Royal Worcester Porcelain Co. at Worcester, England, from 1862 to the present. For earlier porcelain made in Worcester, see WORCESTER. Royal Worcester is distinguished from wares made at Worcester between 1751 and 1862 that are referred to as only Worcester by collectors.*

*Royal Worcester Marks*

*Royal Worcester Bowl*

**Bowl,** 7 1/2 x 8 1/2", 4" h., basketweave exterior, open gold handles, interior w/multicolored flowers, beige bisque ground, ca. 1903 (ILLUS.) .......................... **$295**

*Royal Worcester Scenic Plates*

**Cabinet plates,** 10 1/2" d., each w/a different English rural scene within a narrow acid-etched gilt border, artist-signed, printed mark, ca. 1929, set of 12 (ILLUS. of part) ...................................................... **5,750**

**Candlestick,** figural, a young woodsman w/an ax over his shoulder standing to one side of a tall slender tree trunk topped by the candle socket, a large ovoid wicker basket standing on the other side of the tree, a green & cream colored ground w/gilt trim, Shape 1793, ca. 1895, printed mark, 11 7/8" h. ...... **633**

**Cups & saucers,** cream-colored ground w/gilt highlighted enameled floral designs, ca. 1900, saucers 5 3/8" d., two extra saucers, set of 10 ............................... **374**

**Ewer,** bulbous basketweave-molded body w/tall neck, applied w/a realistic gilt lizard wrapped around the sides & forming the handle, late 19th c., 6" h. ........................ **460**

**Ewer,** Chelsea-style, large ovoid body raised on a short round pedestal on a square foot, a short ringed cylindrical neck flaring to a long arched ruffled & crimped spout & continuing into a high looped handle ending in a satyr mask, gilt neck, handle & base, the ivory body decorated w/a large color-enameled leafy blossom branch trimmed w/gilt, Shape 1144, ca. 1892, 10 3/4" h. ................. **575**

**Ewer,** classical baluster-form, a ringed & stepped round pedestal base supporting a wide ovoid body w/a wide shoulder tapering to a short ringed neck w/a rolled tricorner rim continuing into an ornate scrolled arched handle from rim to triple-branched ends at the shoulder, cream ground decorated on the sides w/large green & gilt ferns w/heavy gilt trim on the neck, spout, handle & base, Shape 1309, ca. 1890, printed mark, 10 1/2" h. ...... **633**

**Ewer,** footed tapering melon-lobed body w/a flaring neck w/shell-scalloped rim, large gilt twig handle & small gilt twig handles around the waist, decorated w/multicolored foliage on the cream ground, No. 1507, 1902, 9" h. ...................... **316**

**Figure group,** "Hide and Seek," modeled as a young boy & girl hiding amid three tree stump-form vases, set on an oval rockwork base, Shape 825, printed mark, ca. 1881, 6 1/2" h. (gilt wear, line in base) ............................................................. **489**

**Inkstand,** figural, a fluted round well & domed cover w/a seated putto finial, the sides w/applied seaweed, supported by a stand w/three shell-form dishes alternating w/three nude female sphinx figures, enameled decoration, ca. 1877, printed mark, 7 1/4" h. (restored headdress, hairline in one shell dish, gilt rim wear) .............................................................. **920**

**Jardiniere,** Oriental-style, wide bulbous spherical body w/a low wide ring neck, raised on scrolled-under legs & pierced scrolls in gilt & bronze enamel, the sides molded in bold relief w/lily pads in bronze enamel & gilt leaves, cream ground, ca. 1882, printed mark, 6 1/2" h. (gilt wear) ......................................................... **374**

**Plates,** 9 1/4" d., blue enamel & gilt floral trim w/bird centers, ca. 1886, set of 10 ........ **259**

**Vase,** 3 1/4" h., double-walled, ovoid body w/a short rolled neck, the outer cellwork body pierced around lobed cartouches decorated w/gilt-decorated landscapes on the inner body wall, gilt jeweling on the outer cellwork, printed mark, ca. 1887 .................................................... **1,150**

**Vase,** cov., 7 3/4" h., handled, the body decorated in prismatic enamels w/florals, late 19th c........................................................ **259**

**Vase,** 8 7/8" h., Sabrina Ware, a thin footring supporting the tapering cylindrical body w/a rounded base & ending in a bulbed cylindrical neck, mottled blue, iron-red & white mottled glaze, printed mark, ca. 1902 ........................................... **230**

**Vase,** 10 1/4" h., a flaring round pedestal base supporting a squatty wide halfround lower body w/a wide flattened shoulder tapering to a tall slender neck w/molded, flared mouth, a small rectangular neck panel flanked by long scrolled foliate handles down to the shoulder, molded swirled flutes up the neck, the creamy ground decorated w/color-enameled leafy flowers & gilt trim, printed mark, Shape 1491, ca. 1982 ....................... **633**

*Royal Worcester Vase*

**Vase,** 11 5/8" h., gilt square base below ovoid body w/flared rim, decorated on front w/a colorful spray of flowers within a gilt square frame & flanked by burnished gilt scroll handles, cobalt ground between gilt borders & pedestal foot, top of pedestal & corner of base restored, some crackling to glaze & wear to gilding, factory mark in iron red script (ILLUS.) ....................................................... **1,082**

**Vase,** 14 1/4" h., classical baluster-form, a short ringed pedestal base supporting the tall ovoid body tapering to a slender waisted neck w/rolled rim, griffin head figural shoulder handles, large side panels decorated in color w/scenes of polar bears & ice-capped mountains, molded trim on cream ground w/gilt trim, Shape 1764, ca. 1903 (missing cover) .............. **16,100**

**Vases,** 8" h., wide bulbous ovoid body w/an embossed basketweave design in ivory, raised on four gilt twig-form short legs continuing up the sides as gilt & red twigs w/leaves, small gilt loop shoulder handles & a short cylindrical flat neck w/a gilt Greek key design, Shape 357, printed mark, ca. 1882, pr. (gilt wear) .......... **460**

**Vases,** cov., 9 1/4" h., a footring supporting a wide half-round lower body below a wide sloped shoulder centered by a short tapering ribbed neck w/a pointed domed cover pierced w/trefoils & topped by a pointed button finial, upright paneled & scrolled gilt shoulder handles, the body w/gilt-trimmed narrow ribbed bands at the foot & shoulder, the body w/a ivory ground decorated w/color-enameled & gilt flowers, w/inner lids, Shape 1256, printed mark, ca. 1889, pr. (one cover w/hairline) .................................................. **2,415**

# R.S. PRUSSIA
# & RELATED WARES

*R.S. Prussia & Related Marks*

Ornately decorated china marked "R.S. Prussia" and "R.S. Germany" continues to grow in popularity. According to the Third Series of Mary Frank Gaston's Encyclopedia of R.S. Prussia (Collector Books, Paducah, Kentucky), these marks were used by the Reinhold Schlegelmilch porcelain factories located in Suhl in the Germanic regions known as "Prussia" prior to World War I, and in Tillowitz, Silesia, which became part of Poland after World War II. Other marks sought by collectors include "R.S. Suhl," "R.S." steeple or church marks, and "R.S. Poland."

The Suhl factory was founded by Reinhold Schlegelmilch in 1869 and closed in 1917. The Tillowitz factory was established in 1895 by Erhard Schlegelmilch, Reinhold's son. This china customarily bears the phrase "R.S. Germany" and "R.S. Tillowitz." The Tillowitz factory closed in 1945, but it was re-opened for a few years under Polish administration.

Prices are high and collectors should beware of the forgeries that sometimes find their way onto the market. Mold names and numbers are taken from Mary Frank Gaston's books on R.S. Prussia.

The "Prussia" and "R.S. Suhl" marks have been reproduced so buy with care. Later copies of these marks are well done but quality of porcelain is inferior to the production in the 1890-1920 era.

*Collectors are also interested in the porcelain products made by the Erdmann Schlegelmilch factory. This factory was founded by three brothers in Suhl in 1861. They named the factory in honor of their father, Erdmann Schlegelmilch. A variety of marks incorporating the "E.S." initials were used. The factory closed circa 1935. The Erdmann Schlegelmilch factory was an earlier and entirely separate business from the Reinhold Schlegelmilch factory. The two were not related to each other.*

## R.S. GERMANY

**Berry set:** 9" master bowl & six matching 5 1/2" sauce dishes, Iris mold, decorated w/large red roses, 7 pcs. ..................... **$500-550**

**Bowl,** 8" h., handled, decorated w/scene of two colorful parrots, green highlights .... **275-325**

**Bowl,** 10" d., decorated w/wild roses, raspberries, & blueberries, glossy glaze ...... **125-175**

**Bowl,** 10 1/2", handled, Lebrun portrait, Tiffany finish, artist's palette, paint brush ............................................. **1,800-2,000**

**Bowl,** large, Lettuce mold, floral decoration. lustre finish ................................... **300-350**

*R.S. Germany Cake Plate*

**Cake plate,** double-pierced small gold side handles, decorated w/a scene of a maiden near a cottage at the edge of a dark forest, 10" d. (ILLUS.)................... **275-325**

**Coffeepot,** cov., demitasse, Ribbon & Jewel mold, rose garland decoration .... **400-450**

**Creamer,** Mold 640, decorated w/roses, gold trim on ruffled rim & ornate handle .... **35-50**

*R.S. Germany Cup & Saucer*

**Cup & saucer,** decorated w/blue, black & white bands on beige lustre ground, cup w/center silhouette of Art Deco lady in blue dancing w/blue scarf, cup 3 1/2" d., 2 1/4" h., saucer 5 3/4" d. (ILLUS.)........ **100-150**

**Cup & saucer,** demitasse, ornate handle, eight-footed .............................................. **75-100**

**Gravy boat w/underplate,** poppy decoration ......................................................... **75-100**

**Mustard jar,** cov., calla lily decoration......... **65-100**

**Pitcher,** 9" h., Mold 343, floral decoration w/overall gilt tracery on cobalt blue (red castle mark).......................................... **700-800**

**Plate,** 7 1/4" d., poppy decoration .............. **30-50**

**Plate,** 8" d., decorated w/scene of colorful parrots, gold rim ................................... **250-300**

**Salad set,** 10 1/2" d. lettuce bowl & six 8" matching plates, Mold 12, Iris decoration on pearl lustre finish, 7 pcs. ........ **300-350**

**Toothpick holder,** two-handled, decorated w/roses & gold trim, artist-signed... **75-125**

**Tray,** handled, decorated w/large white & green poppies, 15 1/4" l. ....................... **275-300**

## R.S. PRUSSIA

**Bell,** tall trumpet-form ruffled body w/twig handle, decorated w/small purple flowers & green leaves on white ground, unmarked, 3 1/2" l. ................................. **300-350**

**Berry set:** master bowl & six sauce dishes; five-lobed, floral relief rim w/forget-me-nots & water lilies decoration, artist-signed, 7 pcs. ........................................ **400-450**

*Ribbon & Jewel Melon Eaters Berry Set*

**Berry set:** master bowl & six sauce dishes; Ribbon & Jewel mold w/Melon Eaters decoartion, 7 pcs. (ILLUS) .............. **3,500-3,800**

**Bowl,** 7" d., decorated w/roses, satin finish ............................................................ **150-200**

**Bowl,** 9 3/4" d., Iris variant mold, rosette center & pale green floral decoration .... **250-300**

**Bowl,** 10" d., floral decoration in black & gold ...................................................... **150-175**

**Bowl,** 10" d., Icicle mold (Mold 7), red & gold border around the creamy satin interior decorated w/large gold roses ... **450-525**

**Bowl,** 10" d., Iris mold, Spring Season portrait decoration ................................. **2,200-2,400**

**Bowl,** 10" d., Mold 202, gold beaded rim, double swans center scene in shades of beige & white, unmarked ...................... **200-225**

**Bowl,** 10" d., Mold 85, Summer Season portrait w/mill scene in background (ILLUS. top next page) ................... **2,000-2,400**

**Bowl,** 10 1/4" d., center decoration of pink roses w/pearlized finish, border in shades of lavender & blue w/satin finish, lavish gold trim (unlisted mold).............. **400-450**

*Summer Season Portrait Bowl*

**Bowl,** 10 1/4" d., Mold 251, apple blossom decoration, satin finish .......................... **250-300**

**Bowl,** 10 1/2" d., Countess Potocka portrait decoration, heavy gold trim ............. **4,000-4,300**

**Bowl,** 10 1/2" d., decorated w/pink roses & carnations on white shaded to peach ground, iridescent Tiffany finish ................... **595**

**Bowl,** 10 1/2" d., decorated w/scene of Dice Throwers, red trim...................... **850-1,000**

**Bowl,** 10 1/2" d., handled, four-lobed, decorated w/Art Nouveau relief-molded scrolls & colorful sprays on shaded green ground........................................ **200-250**

**Bowl,** 10 1/2" d., Iris mold, poppy decoration .......................................... **350-400**

**Bowl,** 10 1/2" d., Mold 101, Tiffany finish around rim, orchid & cream trim on molded border blossoms, central bouquet of pink, yellow & white roses w/green leaves ..................................... **250-300**

**Bowl,** 10 1/2" d., Point & Clover mold (Mold 82), decorated w/forget-me-nots & roses, satin finish, artist-signed............. **300-350**

**Bowl,** 10 1/2" d., Point & Clover mold (Mold 82), decorated w/pink roses & green leaves w/shadow flowers & a Tiffany finish..................................................... **250-300**

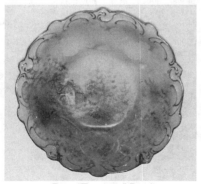

*Rare "Tapestry" Bowl*

**Bowl,** 10 3/4" d., Mold 217, "tapestry" center mill scene, gilt scroll border (ILLUS.)........................................... **1,100-1,400**

**Bowl,** 11" d., 3" h., Sunflower mold, satin finish................................................... **450-500**

**Bowl,** 11" d., Mold 155, Sheepherder scene decoration in shades of green w/gold & pink........................................ **350-400**

**Bowl,** 11" d., Mold 22, four large jewels, satin finish........................................ **250-300**

**Bowl,** 11" d., 3" h., Fishscale mold, decorated w/white lilies on purple & orange lustre ground, artist-signed................... **325-375**

**Bread tray,** Mold 428, wide oval form w/low flared sides w/a narrow flanged rim, pierced end rim handles, decorated w/a large cluster of roses in peach, pink & green, traces of gold edging, 9 x 12 1/2"..................................................... **175-225**

**Butter dish, cover & insert,** Mold 51, floral decoration, unmarked ........................... **200-250**

*Floral Decorated Cake Plate*

**Cake plate,** open handled, decorated w/pink & white flowers, green leaves, pink & yellow ground, gold trim, 9 3/4" d. (ILLUS.)....................................................... **195**

**Cake plate,** open-handled, Fleur-de-Lis mold, Spring Season portrait, 9 3/4" d......................................... **1,300-1,600**

**Cake plate,** open-handled, Mold 155, hanging basket decoration, 10" d......... **325-350**

**Cake plate,** open-handled, Mold 259, decorated w/pink & yellow roses, pearl button finish, 10" d..................................... **350-400**

**Cake plate,** open-handled, Fleur-de-Lis mold, decorated w/a castle scene in rust, gold, lavender & yellow, 10 1/4" d... **1,000-1,300**

**Cake plate,** open-handled, Medallion mold, center Flora portrait, Tiffany finish w/four cupid medallions, unmarked, 10 1/2" d............................................. **900-1,000**

**Cake plate,** Iris mold, yellow poppy decoration, 11" d. ............................................ **250-300**

**Cake plate,** open-handled, Carnation mold (Mold 28), dark pink roses against teal & green w/gold trim, 11" d. ........................ **250-300**

**Cake plate,** open-handled, modified Fleur-de-Lis mold, floral decoration, beaded, satin finish, artist-signed, 11" d. ........... **175-225**

**Cake plate,** Hidden Image mold, light blue highlights, 11 1/2" d.......................... **450-500**

**Cake plate,** open handles, Mold 256, satin ground decorated w/flowers in blue, pink & white w/gold trim, 11 1/2" d. .............. **120-150**

**Cake plate,** open-handled, Mold 330, decorated w/snapdragons on pastel ground, artist-signed, 11 1/2" d. ......................... **350-375**

**Cake plate,** open-handled, Mold 343, Winter figural portrait in keyhole medallion, cobalt blue inner border, gold outer border, 12 1/2" d. ..................................... **400-450**

**Cake plate,** Bow-tie mold, pink & gold ...... **500-600**

**Cake plate,** open-handled, Carnation mold, decorated w/multicolored roses ............ **300-350**

**Celery dish,** Carnation mold, carnations & pink roses decoration on white shaded to peach ground, iridescent Tiffany finish, 9" ..................................................... **375**

**Celery dish,** Hidden Image mold, colored hair, 5 x 12" ........................................... **400-450**

**Celery dish,** Mold 25, oblong, pearlized finish w/Surreal Dogwood blossoms w/gold trim, 6 x 12 1/4" ..................................... **75-125**

**Celery tray,** Mold 254, decorated w/green & pink roses, lavish gold tracery, artist-signed, 12" l. ........................................... **275-325**

**Celery tray,** Ribbon & Jewel mold (Mold 18), pink roses & white snowball blossoms within a wide cobalt blue border w/gilt trim, 12" l. ...................................... **250-300**

**Celery tray,** Mold 255, decorated w/Surreal Dogwood decoration, pearlized lustre finish, artist-signed, 12 1/4" l. ............... **200-225**

**Celery tray,** open-handled decorated w/soft pink & white flower center w/lily-of-the-valley, embossed edge of ferns & pastel colors w/gold highlights, 12 1/2" l. ..................................................... **200-250**

**Celery tray,** Carnation mold, decorated w/pink & yellow flowers on lavender satin finish, 6 1/2 x 13 1/4" .................... **300-350**

**Centerpiece bowl,** Carnation mold, decorated w/pink & yellow roses, 15 1/2" d. ................................ **2,000-2,500**

**Chocolate cup & saucer,** decorated w/Castle scene ...................................... **125-150**

**Chocolate cup & saucer,** footed, egg-shaped cup, pink & white poppies decoration ................................................... **100-150**

**Chocolate pot,** cov., Hidden Image mold image on both sides, light green, 9 3/4" h. ............................................ **1,000-1,100**

**Chocolate pot,** cov., peacock & pine trees decoration ............................................... **650-750**

**Chocolate pot,** cov., Swag & Tassel mold, decorated w/scene of sheepherder & swallows............................................... **900-1,000**

**Chocolate set,** cov. pot & four cups & saucers, sunflower decoration, the set ....... **700-750**

**Chocolate set:** 10" h. cov. chocolate pot & four cups & saucers; Mold 729, pansy decoration w/gold trim, the set .............. **900-975**

**Chocolate set:** 10" h. cov. chocolate pot & four cups & saucers; Ribbon and Jewel mold, scene of Dice Throwers decoration on pot & single Melon Eater scene on cups, the set................................ **4,500-5,000**

**Chocolate set:** tankard-style covered pot & six cups & saucers; Mold 510, laurel chain decoration, the set ................ **1,000-1,300**

**Chocolate set:** 10" h., cov. chocolate pot & six cups & saucers; Mold 517, Madame Lebrun portrait decoration, the set (ILLUS.)........................................... **7,200-8,000**

*Lebrun-decorated Chocolate Set*

**Coffeepot,** cov., Mold 517, raised floral designs as part of border, unmarked .... **250-300**

**Cracker jar,** cov., Mold 540a, beige satin ground w/floral decoration in orchid, yellow & gold, 9 1/2" w. handle to handle, overall 5 1/2" h. ................................... **300-350**

**Cracker jar,** cov., Mold 634, molded feet, surreal dogwood blossoms decoration on pearlized lustre finish, 8" d., 6 1/2" h. **250-300**

**Cracker jar,** cov., Mold 704, grape leaf decoration, 7" h. ................................... **450-500**

**Cracker jar,** cov., decorated w/hanging basket of flowers, satin finish, 6 x 9 1/2" **325-375**

**Cracker jar,** cov., Hidden Image mold, image on both sides, green mum decoration ................................................ **900-1,000**

**Cracker jar,** cov., Lebrun portrait decoration, no hat, satin finish .................. **1,500-2,000**

**Creamer & cov. sugar bowl,** floral decoration, green highlights, pr. ...................... **125-150**

**Creamer & cov. sugar bowl,** Mold 505, pink & yellow roses, pr. ....................... **125-175**

*Melon Eaters Creamer & Sugar*

**Creamer & cov. sugar bowl,** Ribbon & Jewel mold, single Melon Eaters decoration, pr. (ILLUS.)............................ **1,500-1,800**

**Creamer & cov. sugar bowl,** satin finish, Tiffany trim, pr. ..................................... **175-200**

**Cup & saucer,** decorated w/pink roses, peg feet & scalloped rim, cup 1 3/4" h., saucer 4 1/4" d., pr. .............................. **125-175**

**Dessert set:** 9 1/2" d. cake plate & six 7" d. individual plates; Carnation mold, decorated w/carnations, pink & white roses, iridescent Tiffany finish on pale green, the set ................................................... **995**

**Dessert set:** pedestal cup & saucer, creamer & sugar bowl, two 9 3/4" d., handled plates, eleven 7 1/4" d. plates, nine cups & saucers, oversized creamer & sugar bowl, plain mold, decoration w/pink poppies w/tints of aqua, yellow & purple, all pieces are matching, the set ................................................ **2,200-2,500**

**Dresser tray,** decorated w/mill scene, shaded green ground, 7 x 11" ............... **350-450**

**Dresser tray,** Icicle mold, scenic decoration, Man in the Mountain, 7 x 11 1/2"... **600-700**

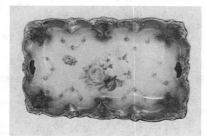

*Mold 404 Dresser Tray*

**Dresser tray,** rectangular w/pierced end handles, Mold 404, decorated w/pink & white roses, Tiffany border w/gold clover leaves (ILLUS.) ..................................... **250-300**

**Ferner,** six vertical ribs, scalloped, decorated w/lilies-of-the-valley on shaded pastel ground, artist-signed, 3 7/8 x 8 1/4" .................................................. **200-250**

**Hair receiver,** cov., Mold 814, Surreal Dogwood decoration ................................... **150-175**

**Match holder w/striker,** floral decoration ........................................... **100-125**

**Model of a lady's slipper,** embossed scrolling on instep & heel & embossed feather on one side of slipper, a dotted medallion w/roses & lily-of-the-valley on the other, shaded turquoise blue w/fancy rim trimmed w/gold, 8" l......................... **250-300**

**Mug,** Lily mold, Lebrun portrait decoration (no hat)................................................. **200-250**

**Mug,** rose decoration on pink satin finish .. **125-175**

**Mustache cup,** Mold 502 .......................... **250-300**

**Mustard pot,** cov., Mold 509a, decorated w/white flowers, glossy light green ground ...................................................... **150-175**

**Mustard pot,** cov., Mold 521, pink rose decoration, satin finish .......................... **150-200**

**Nut bowl,** footed, Point & Clover mold, decorated w/ten roses in shades of salmon, yellow & rose against a pink, green & gold lustre-finished bround, 6 1/2" d.................................................... **150-200**

**Nut dish,** Carnation mold (Mold 28), floral decoration w/pearlized finish ................ **200-250**

**Pin dish,** cov., Hidden Image mold, floral decoration, 2 3/4 x 4 3/4" ...................... **350-450**

**Pitcher,** cider, 7" h., iris decoration w/green & gold background ................................ **250-300**

**Pitcher,** lemonade, 6" h., Mold 501, relief-molded turquoise blue on white w/pink Surreal blossoms & fans around scalloped top & base, unmarked ................. **250-300**

**Pitcher,** tankard, 10" h., Mold 584, decorated w/hanging basket of pink & white roses ............................................... **700-750**

**Pitcher,** tankard, 11" h., Carnation Mold, overall decoration of pink poppies & carnations, white ground, iridescent Tiffany finish.............................................. **1,100**

**Pitcher,** tankard, 12" h., Mold 538, decorated w/Melon Eaters scene (ILLUS. left) .................................... **3,500-4,000**

*R. S. Prussia Tankard Pitchers*

**Pitcher,** tankard, 13" h., decorated w/poppies...................................................... **600-650**

**Pitcher,** tankard, 13" h., decorated w/scene of Old Man in Mountain & swans on lake (ILLUS. right) ........... **4,000-4,500**

**Pitcher,** tankard, 13 1/4" h., Stippled Floral mold (Mold 525), roses decoration, unmarked ............................................ **625-675**

**Pitcher,** tankard, 13 1/2" h., Carnation Mold, pink poppy decoration, green ground ................................................ **750-850**

**Pitcher,** water, 8 3/4" h., Carnation mold ......... **660**

**Plaque,** decorated w/scene of lady w/dog, 9 1/4 x 13" ...................................... **2,000-2,500**

**Plate,** 7" d., Fleur-de-Lis mold, Summer Season Portrait decoration.................... **450-500**

**Plate,** 7 1/2" d., Carnation mold, decorated w/pink roses, lavender ground, satin finish.................................................... **200-250**

**Plate,** 7 1/2" d., Carnation mold, decorated w/pink roses, pink ground, unmarked .......... **175**

**Plate,** 8 1/2" d., Gibson Girl portrait decoration, maroon bonnet .............................. **500-550**

**Plate,** 8 1/2" d., Medallion mold (Mold 14), Reflecting Lilies patt. ............................ **125-150**

**Plate,** 8 1/2" d., Mold 263, pink & white roses decoration.................................... **175-200**

**Plate,** 8 1/2" d., Mold 300, beaded gold band around the lobed rim, Old Mill Scene decoration in center against a shaded dark green to yellow & blue ground ................................................ **150-200**

**Plate,** 8 3/4" d., Mold 278, center decoration of pink poppies on white ground, green border......................................... **150-175**

*Mold 91 Rose-decorated Plate*

**Plate,** 8 3/4" d., Mold 91, yellow roses decoration on pink ground, shiny yellow bor-
der (ILLUS.)............................................ **150-200**
**Plate,** 9" d., Mold 343, spring figural scenic
decoration in keyhole medallion, iridescent Tiffany purple finish at base of figure, gold finish around portrait
decoration w/small pink roses......... **1,800-2,100**
**Plate,** 9 3/4" d., Icicle mold, swan
decoration ............................................ **800-900**
**Plate,** 11" d., decorated w/carnations &
roses w/gold trim, white shading to
peach ground, iridescent Tiffany finish
(slight gold wear)...................................... **250**
**Plate,** 11" d., Point & Clover mold, Melon
Eater decoration.............................. **900-1,100**
**Plate,** dessert, Mold 506, branches of pink
roses & green leaves against a shaded
bluish green to white ground w/shadow
flowers & satin finish ............................ **100-125**
**Relish dish,** Fleur-de-Lis mold, basket of
flowers decoration w/shadow flowers,
8" l. ...................................................... **100-125**
**Relish dish,** scene of masted ship,
4 1/2 x 9 1/2" ...................................... **250-300**
**Relish dish,** Icicle mold, scene of swans
on lake.................................................. **450-500**
**Relish dish,** Mold 82, decorated w/forget-
me-nots & multicolored carnations, six
jeweled domes ..................................... **125-175**
**Shaving mug,** Hidden Image mold, floral
decoration ............................................ **175-225**
**Spooner/vase,** Mold 502, three-handled,
decorated w/delicate roses & gold trim,
unsigned, 4 1/4" h. ............................. **75-100**
**Syrup pitcher,** Mold 512, dogwood & pine
decoration ................................................. **175**
**Syrup pitcher & underplate,** Mold 507,
white & pink roses on a shaded brown to
pale yellow ground, 2 pcs...................... **200-250**
**Tea set:** child's, cov. teapot & four cups &
saucers; decorated w/roses, the set ..... **650-700**
**Tea set:** cov. teapot, creamer & cov. sugar
bowl; floral decoration, the set ............. **300-350**
**Tea set:** cov. teapot, creamer & cov. sugar
bowl, mill & castle scene, shaded brown
ground, 3 pcs. .................................... **900-1,000**
**Tea set:** cov. teapot, creamer & cov. sugar
bowl; pedestal base, scene of Colonial
children, 3 pcs. .................................... **600-700**
**Tea strainer,** floral decoration................... **200-250**
**Toothpick holder,** ribbed hexagonal shape
w/two handles, decorated w/colorful
roses .................................................. **265-300**
**Toothpick holder,** Stippled Floral mold
(Mold 23), white floral decoration ......... **150-175**
**Toothpick holder,** three-handled, decorated w/white daisies on white ground,
gold handles & trim on top ................... **150-175**
**Toothpick holder,** urn-shaped, floral decoration, molded star mark ...................... **150-175**
**Tray,** pierced handles, Mold 82, decorated
w/full blossom red & pink roses,
8 x 11 1/8" (gold Royal Vienna mark).... **250-300**
**Tray,** rectangular, pierced handles, Mold
404, decorated w/pink & white roses, Tiffany border w/gold clover leaves........... **250-300**
**Vase,** 4" h., salesman's sample, handled,
Mold 914, decorated w/large lilies &

green foliage, raised beading around
shoulder, gold handles, shaded green
ground, artist-signed ............................ **150-175**
**Vase,** 4 1/2" h., Mold 910, decorated w/pink
roses, satin finish w/iridescent Tiffany
finish around base................................ **250-275**
**Vase,** 5 1/2" h., cottage & mill scene decoration, cobalt trim................................. **550-650**
**Vase,** 6 1/4" h., castle scene decoration,
brown tones w/jewels ........................... **450-500**
**Vase,** 6 1/4" h., decorated w/brown &
cream shadow flowers .......................... **75-100**
**Vase,** 6 1/4" h., decorated w/mill scene,
brown w/jewels..................................... **450-500**
**Vase,** 8" h., cylindrical body w/incurved
angled shoulder handles, decorated
w/parrots on white satin ground,
unmarked ...................................... **2,200-2,600**

*R.S. Prussia Vases with Animals*

**Vase,** 8" h., ovoid body w/wide shoulder
tapering to cylindrical neck w/flared rim,
decorated w/scene of black swans
(ILLUS. left) .................................... **1,200-1,500**
**Vase,** 10" h., ovoid body decorated
w/scene of two tigers, pastel satin finish
(ILLUS. right).................................. **5,000-6,000**

*R.S. Prussia Ovoid Vase w/Parrots*

**Vase,** two handled, tall slender ovoid body
w/colorful scene of two parrots, shaded
brown foliage, unmarked (ILLUS.) .. **1,800-2,000**

*Rare Melon Eaters Vases*

**Vases,** 11 3/4" h., Mold 901, footed slightly tapering cylindrical body w/a high flaring cupped deeply fluted neck w/jewels, beading & jewels around the shoulder & foot, ornate scrolled gilt handles, Melon Eaters decoration against a shaded dark green ground, pr., each (ILLUS.) .... **1,800-2,000**

## OTHER MARKS

**Bowl,** 10" d., Cabbage mold w/center rose decoration (R.S. Tillowitz) .................... **250-300**

**Bowl,** 10" d., shallow w/very ornate, large Flora portrait, front pose past waist, floral garland, veiling, four different cameo portraits of Flora, wide Tiffany border, lavish gold (E.S. Prov. Saxe) .......... **1,100-1,300**

**Chocolate pot,** cov., Art Nouveau decoration, glossy finish (R.S. Tillowitz - Silesia) ................ **55**

**Chocolate pot,** cov., lemon yellow ground w/Art Deco decoration & gold trim (R.S. Tillowitz - Silesia) ........................................ **150**

**Coffee set:** 6 5/8" l., 3 1/4" d., cov. ovoid coffeepot & two cups & saucers; each piece decorated w/a color oval reserve w/a different romantic scene within a thin gilt border & a deep burgundy panel against a creamy white ground trimmed w/gilt scrolls, a wide red & narrow dark green border band on each, saucers 2 3/4" d., cups 2 1/4" h., blue beehive & R.S. Suhl marks, the set ............................ **650**

**Fernery,** pedestal base, decorated w/pink & white roses, mother-of-pearl finish (R.S. Poland)................................................ **450**

**Match holder,** hanging-type on attached backplate decorated w/a scene of a man w/mug of beer & pipe (E.S. Prov. Saxe).................................................... **175-200**

**Plate,** 7" d., scene of girl w/rose, trimmed w/gold flowers, beading & a burgundy border ................................................. **100-125**

**Plate,** 7 3/4" d., Sunflower mold, rose pink & yellow roses w/Tiffany finish (Wheelock Prussia) .............................. **125-150**

**Plate,** 8" d., peafowl decoration (R.S. Tillowitz - Silesia) ................................. **150-200**

**Plate,** 10 1/2" d., lovely center portrait of Madame DuBarry, four cameos in different poses on a deep burgundy lustre border band (E.W. Prov. Saxe) ............. **500-600**

**Relish dish,** woman's portrait w/shadow flowers & vine border on green ground, 8" l. (E.S. Germany Royal Saxe)........... **100-125**

*E. Schlegelmilch Handled Server*

**Server,** center-handled, decorated w/orange, white & pink poppies on a shaded bluish grey ground, w/a narrow gilt border band, 8 1/2" d., 3 3/4" h., E. Schlegelmilch - Thuringia (ILLUS.) ....... **100-150**

**Serving dish,** center-handled, decorated w/lavender & pink roses, gold trim, 11" d. (R.S. Poland) ............................. **500-550**

**Tray,** rectangular, open-handled, bright colored bird decoration, 5 x 14" (R.S. Tillowitz) ................................................. **75-100**

**Vase,** miniature, 3 1/2" h., cylindrical body w/a rounded shoulder tapering to a tiny rolled neck, decorated w/a colored scene of crowned cranes (R.S. Poland)........................................ **375-425**

*Melon Eaters Vase*

**Vase,** 6 3/8" h., 3" d., wide ovoid shouldered body tapering to slender flaring cylindrical neck, Melon Eater decoration surrounded by gold border w/reverse decorated w/heart-shaped area w/dainty pink roses on pastel ground, two-thirds of vase covered in purplish lustre w/fine gold leaves & flowers overall, neck in off white w/fine gold floral decoration, artist-signed in gold, Red Crown "Viersa" mark, Suhl or Tillowitz (ILLUS.) ............ **350-400**

*R.S. Poland Vase w/Geese*

**Vase,** 7" h., footed urn-form w/scrolled handles, decorated w/scene of two geese, R.S. Poland (ILLUS.)...................... **1,500-1,800**

**Vase,** 7 1/2" h., wide squatty bulbous base tapering sharply to a tall slender cylindrical neck w/an upturned four-lobed rim, long slender gold handles from rim to shoulder, decorated w/a center reserve of a standing Art Nouveau maiden w/her hands behind her head & a peacock behind her framed by delicate gold scrolls & beading & floral bouquets all on a pearl lustre ground (Prov. Saxe - E.W. Germany) ............................................. **375-425**

**Vase,** 9" h., 3" d., tall slender ovoid body tapering to a tall slender trumpet neck, a wide band around the body decorated w/a colored scene of "The Melon Eaters" between narrow gold & white bands, the neck & lower body in deep rose decorated w/gilt leaf sprigs (R.S. Suhl) ..... **800-1,000**

**Vase,** 9 1/4" h., gently tapering cylindrical body w/a wide cupped scalloped gilt rim, pierced gold serpentine handles from rim to center of sides, decorated around the body w/large blossoms in purple, pink, yellow & green on a shaded brownish green ground (Prove. Saxe) ............ **125-150**

**Vase,** 9 1/2" h., portrait of "Lady with Swallows," gold beading, turquoise on white ground (Prov. Saxe - E.S. Germany) ... **500-550**

**Vase,** 10" h., gold Rococo handles, scene of sleeping maiden w/cherub decoration (E.S. Royal Saxe)................................. **350-400**

**Vase,** 13 1/2" h., portrait of "Lady with Swallows," gold beaded frame, green pearl lustre finish w/gold trim (Prov. Saxe - E.S. Germany) ......................... **600-650**

**Vase,** 13 1/2" h., twisted gold handles, portrait of "Goddess of Fire," iridescent burgundy & opalescent colors w/lavish gold trim (Prov. Saxe, E.S. Germany)........... **650-700**

**Vases,** 10" h., gently swelled body tapering to narrow rounded shoulders & a short flaring scalloped neck, ornate C-scroll gilt shoulder handles, gold neck band, the body decorated w/a colored scene of a sheepherder leading his flock toward a mill in the background, trees overhead, the second identical except w/a cottage

scene, R.S. Poland, pr. (ILLUS. of one, below).................................................. **350-1,400**

*R.S. Poland Landscape Vase*

# RUSSEL WRIGHT DESIGNS

*The innovative dinnerwares designed by Russel Wright and produced by various companies beginning in the late 1930s were an immediate success with a society that was turning to a more casual and informal lifestyle. His designs, with their flowing lines and unconventional shapes, were produced in many different colors which allowed the hostess to arrange a creative table.*

*Although not antique, these designs, which we list below by line and manufacturer, are highly collectible. In addition to dinnerwares, Wright was also known as a trend-setter in the design of furniture, glassware, lamps, fabric and a multitude of other household goods.*

*Russel Wright Marks*

## AMERICAN MODERN (STEUBENVILLE POTTERY CO.)

*Group of American Modern Pieces*

**Baker,** cov., glacier blue, small......................... **$55**
**Baker,** cov., granite grey, small........................... 30
**Bowl,** child's, black chutney ................................ 85

**Bowl,** child's, chartreuse ..................................... 60
**Bowl,** fruit, lug handle, cedar green ................... 20
**Bowl,** fruit, lug handle, chartreuse (ILLUS. left) ................................................................. 20
**Bowl,** fruit, lug handle, glacier blue ................... 28
**Bowl,** salad, cedar green ................................... 85
**Bowl,** salad, white ........................................... 165
**Bowl,** soup, lug handle, bean brown ................. 22
**Bowl,** soup, lug handle, coral ........................... 13
**Butter dish,** cov., granite grey ......................... 255
**Butter dish,** cov., white .................................. 365
**Carafe,** granite grey (no stopper) ..................... 185
**Carafe w/stopper,** bean brown ....................... 500
**Casserole,** cov., stick handle, black chutney ............................................................. 45

*Black Chutney Celery Tray*

**Celery tray,** black chutney, 13" l. (ILLUS.) ......... 30
**Coaster,** granite grey ........................................ 15
**Coaster,** white ................................................. 30
**Coffee cup cover,** black chutney..................... 175
**Coffee cup cover,** coral ................................. 110
**Coffeepot,** cov., cedar green .......................... 200
**Coffeepot,** seafoam blue ................................ 185
**Coffeepot,** cov., demitasse, chartreuse ............. 95
**Coffeepot,** cov., demitasse, coral ................... 118
**Creamer,** cedar green ...................................... 20
**Creamer,** white ................................................ 30
**Cup & saucer,** coffee, seafoam blue ............... 15
**Cup & saucer,** demitasse, cantaloupe.............. 50
**Cup & saucer,** demitasse, chartreuse .............. 25
**Gravy boat,** chartreuse ..................................... 20
**Hostess plate & cup,** cedar green, pr. .............. 95

*American Modern Hostess Set*

**Hostess plate & cup,** white, pr. (ILLUS.) ........ 200
**Ice box jar,** cov., black chutney ....................... 225
**Ice box jar,** cov., coral .................................. 185
**Mug (tumbler),** black chutney.......................... 125
**Mug (tumbler),** cedar green.............................. 85
**Pickle dish,** seafoam blue ................................ 18
**Pickle dish,** white............................................ 28
**Pitcher,** cov., water, cedar green ..................... 235
**Pitcher,** cov., water, white............................... 325
**Pitcher,** water, 12" h., bean brown.................. 150

**Pitcher,** water, 12" h., granite grey ................. 105
**Plate,** bread & butter, 6 1/4" d., coral ................. 6
**Plate,** salad, 8" d., seafoam blue...................... 12
**Plate,** salad, 8" d., white .................................. 20
**Plate,** dinner, 10" d., cantaloupe ...................... 20
**Plate,** dinner, 10" d., granite grey ..................... 10
**Plate,** chop, 13" sq., chartreuse ....................... 25
**Plate,** chop, 13" sq., seafoam blue.................... 50
**Plate,** child's, coral ......................................... 60
**Plate,** child's, seafoam blue.............................. 75
**Platter,** 13 3/4" l., oblong, granite grey.............. 40
**Platter,** 13 3/4" l., oblong, white ....................... 65
**Ramekin,** cov., individual, bean brown............. 250
**Ramekin,** cov., individual, granite grey .............. 188
**Relish dish,** divided, raffia handle, coral........... 175
**Relish dish,** divided, raffia handle, white ......... 300
**Relish rosette,** granite grey .............................. 175
**Relish rosette,** seafoam blue ........................... 225
**Salad fork & spoon,** coral, pr. ......................... 135
**Salad fork & spoon,** white, pr.......................... 275
**Sauceboat,** bean brown ................................... 75
**Sauceboat,** coral.............................................. 40
**Shaker,** single, chartreuse ................................. 6
**Shaker,** single, glacier blue .............................. 12
**Stack server,** cov., cedar green (ILLUS. back, with fruit bowl)............................. 100-120
**Stack server,** cov., chartreuse......................... 170
**Stack server,** cov., granite grey....................... 300
**Sugar bowl,** cov., chartreuse.............................. 8
**Sugar bowl,** cov., granite grey.......................... 10
**Teapot,** cov., cedar green ............................... 150
**Teapot,** cov., seafoam blue............................. 135
**Tumbler,** child's, cedar green............................ 85
**Tumbler,** child's, granite grey............................ 60
**Vegetable bowl,** cov., cedar green, 12" l........... 75
**Vegetable bowl,** cov., coral, 12" l. .................... 63
**Vegetable dish,** open, divided, black chutney ............................................................ 105
**Vegetable dish,** open, divided, cedar green (ILLUS. right front, with fruit bowl)........ 95
**Vegetable dish,** open, oval, cantaloupe, 10" l. ................................................................. 45
**Vegetable dish,** open, oval, granite grey, 10" l. ................................................................. 25

# CASUAL CHINA (IROQUOIS CHINA COMPANY)

*Casual Creamer, Pitcher & Coffeepot*

**Bowl,** 5" d., cereal, redesigned ......................... 15
**Bowl,** 5" d., cereal, ripe apricot ........................ 15
**Bowl,** 5 1/2" d., fruit, ice blue, 9 1/2 oz.............. 15
**Bowl,** 5 3/4" d., fruit, redesigned, oyster grey ................................................................ 16
**Bowl,** 10" d., salad, pink sherbet, 52 oz. ........... 40
**Butter dish,** cov., brick red, 1/4 lb................ 1,000
**Butter dish,** cov., white, 1/2 lb. ...................... 150

**Carafe,** cov., charcoal ...................................... 265
**Carafe,** cov., oyster grey ................................ 300
**Casserole,** cov., lettuce green, 8" d., 2 qt. ........ 45
**Casserole,** deep tureen, lemon yellow............ 250
**Casserole,** deep tureen, white ........................ 260
**Coffeepot,** cov., nutmeg brown........................ 150
**Coffeepot,** cov., oyster grey (ILLUS. right) **125-150**
**Coffeepot,** cov., sugar white ............................ 200
**Coffeepot,** cov., demitasse, lemon yellow ....... 125
**Cover for casserole,** oyster grey, 4 qt. ............ 30
**Cover for cereal/soup bowl** ............................ 25
**Cover for vegetable bowl,** open/divided........... 35
**Cover for water pitcher** .................................. 50
**Creamer,** family-style, oyster grey (ILLUS.
    left) .............................................................. 40-45
**Creamer,** family-style, pink sherbet.................. 58
**Creamer,** stacking-type, ice blue...................... 20
**Cup & saucer,** coffee, oyster grey (ILLUS.
    front center)............................................... 15-20
**Cup & saucer,** redesigned, avocado yellow....... 18
**Cup & saucer,** tea, charcoal ............................ 15
**Cup & saucer,** tea, lemon yellow...................... 25
**Cup & saucer,** tea, lemon yellow (ILLUS.
    left front)...................................................... 10-15

*Casual Cups & Saucers & Shakers*

**Cup & saucer,** demitasse (after dinner),
    avocado yellow (ILLUS. front right) ....... **150-175**
**Cup & saucer,** demitasse (after dinner),
    pink sherbet................................................. 200
**Cup & saucer,** demitasse (after dinner),
    sugar white .................................................. 175
**Gravy,** redesigned w/cover which becomes
    stand, ripe apricot........................................ 185
**Gravy,** redesigned w/cover which becomes
    stand, sugar white........................................ 200
**Gravy bowl,** 5 1/4", 12 oz. ................................ 25
**Gravy stand,** ice blue...................................... 20
**Gravy stand,** oyster grey .................................. 30
**Gravy w/attached stand,** avocado yellow......... 75
**Gravy w/attached stand,** nutmeg brown......... 100
**Gumbo soup bowl,** handled, charcoal,
    21 oz. ........................................................... 45
**Gumbo soup bowl,** handled, ice blue,
    21 oz. ........................................................... 40
**Hostess set:** plate w/well & matching cup;
    sugar white, 2 pcs. ..................................... 75-85
**Mug,** pink sherbet, 13 oz. .................................. 85
**Mug,** restyled, aqua......................................... 135
**Mug,** restyled, ice blue .................................... 55
**Party (hostess) plate w/cup,** pr., each ........... 115
**Pepper mill,** lemon yellow............................... 300
**Pitcher,** cov., charcoal, 1 1/2 qt. ...................... 175
**Pitcher,** cov., ice blue, 1 1/2 qt........................ 155
**Pitcher,** redesigned, nutmeg brown ................. 185
**Pitcher,** redesigned, ripe apricot (ILLUS.
    center with coffeepot)............................ 150-200

**Plate,** bread & butter, 6 1/2" d., lettuce
    green ............................................................. 8
**Plate,** salad, 7 1/2" d. ...................................... 15
**Plate,** luncheon, 9 1/2" d., pink sherbet.............. 10
**Plate,** dinner, 10" d., oyster grey ...................... 15
**Plate,** chop, 13 7/8" d., ice blue ........................ 55
**Plate,** chop, 13 7/8" d., parsley green ............... 60
**Platter,** 10 1/4" oval, individual, lettuce
    green ............................................................. 85
**Platter,** 12 3/4" oval, brick red ........................ 55
**Platter,** 12 3/4" oval, parsley green .................. 35
**Platter,** 14 1/2" oval, sugar white ...................... 45
**Salt & pepper shakers,** stacking-type, ice
    blue, pr. ........................................................ 25
**Salt & pepper shakers,** stacking-type,
    parsley green & oyster grey , pr. (ILLUS.
    left rear, with cups).................................... 20-25
**Salt & pepper shakers,** stacking-type,
    parsley green, pr. .......................................... 30
**Salt shaker,** single, redesigned ...................... 200
**Salt shaker & pepper mill,** redesigned,
    lemon yellow, pr. (ILLUS. right rear, with
    cups) ...................................................... 200-300
**Soup,** 11 1/2 oz. ............................................... 22
**Soup,** redesigned, 18 oz. .................................. 25
**Sugar,** redesigned, aqua .................................. 350
**Sugar,** stacking-type, brick red......................... 450
**Sugar,** stacking-type, pink sherbet.................... 20
**Sugar,** stacking-type, sugar white, family
    size................................................................ 40
**Teapot,** cov., restyled, aqua .......................... 2,000
**Tumbler,** ice tea, Pinch patt., seafoam
    blue, Imperial Glass Co., 14 oz. .................... 45
**Tumbler,** water, Pinch patt., brick red,
    Imperial Glass Co., 11 oz. ............................ 110
**Vegetable dish,** open, cantaloupe, 81/8",
    36 oz. ............................................................ 55
**Vegetable dish,** open, nutmeg brown,
    81/8", 36 oz. .................................................. 35
**Vegetable dish,** open or divided (casse-
    role), 10", sugar white ................................... 50

## IROQUOIS CASUAL COOKWARE

**Casserole,** 3 qt.................................................. 225
**Dutch oven** ..................................................... 500
**Fry pan,** cov. ................................................... 500
**Sauce pan,** cov. ............................................... 500
**Serving tray,** electric, 12 3/4 x 17 1/2".......... 2,000

## SCHOOP (HEDI) ART CREATIONS

Hedi Schoop escaped from Germany in 1930 then immigrated to Hollywood, California in 1933. She began producing ceramics of her own designs in 1940. Schoop turned out as many as 30,000 pieces per year once her production was running smoothly. A fire destroyed the pottery in 1958 and Hedi did free-lance work for several California companies. She retired from working full-time in the early 1960s but her talents would not let her quit completely. She died in 1996 and had painted, although sparingly, until then.

There were a variety of marks ranging from the stamped or incised Schoop signature to the hard-to-find Hedi Schoop sticker. The words "Hollywood, Cal." or "California" can also be found in conjunction with the Hedi Schoop name. You can find items with a production number, artists' names or initials.

*Schoop was imitated by many artists especially some decorators who opened businesses of their own after working with Schoop. Mac and Yona Lippen owned Yona Ceramics and Katherine Schueftan owned Kim Ward Studio. They used many of Schoop's designs and today they have their own following among collectors. There were others but Schueftan lost a lawsuit Hedi had brought against her in 1942 for design infringements. It is important to buy pieces marked Hedi Schoop or buy from a reputable dealer if you want to be sure you have the real thing.*

*Considering the number of products created, it would be easy to assume that Schoop pieces are plentiful. This would be an erroneous assumption. Collectors will indeed be fortunate to find any Schoop figurines for less than $100.00 and to amass many of her products takes dedication and determination.*

Hedi
Schoop

HEDI SCHOOP
HOLLYWOOD.CALIF.

Hedi Schoop
HOLLYWOOD CAL.

### Hedi Schoop Marks

**Candleholder,** figural, a mermaid holding a single candle socket in each hand above her head, rare, ca. 1950, 13 1/2" h. ............ **$600**

**Figure of a ballerina dancer,** on a thin round base, long skirt flared upward revealing right foot, right arm extended & holding up skirt, left arm extended forward w/head turned to front, bluish grey w/silver overtones, impressed mark "Hedi Schoop," 9 1/4" h. ................ 110

### Hedi Schoop Chinese Woman Figure

**Figure of a Chinese woman,** standing on a round black base, white floor-length skirt, black, white & green blouse w/long sleeves flaring at wrists, a white flower in black hair above each ear, right fingers bent to hold a pot w/black cloth handle & in same colors as blouse, right leg bent at knee, woman 9" h., pot 2 1/2" h., 2 pcs. (ILLUS.) ................ 125

**Figure of a clown,** standing w/one leg crossed over the other, one hand to head, other hand to mouth, bucket & mop at his side, 10 1/2" h. ............ 155

**Figure of a girl,** standing & holding handmade flowers in both arms, "Debutante," rough textured finish, ca. 1943, 12 1/2" h. ............ 185

**Figure of a girl,** standing on cobalt blue-glazed round base, legs slightly apart, arms stretched out to sides, hands folded to hold jump rope, rough textured black hair w/pigtails out to sides & held in place w/cobalt blue glossy ties, light blue long sleeved shirt, cobalt blue overblouse w/straps, rough textured cobalt blue short skirt & socks, inkstamp on unglazed bottom, "Hedi Schoop Hollywood, Cal.," 8 1/2" h. ................ 165

**Figure of a girl,** standing w/a poodle, on round base, 1950s, 9" h. ............ 175

**Figure of a girl standing,** bell-shaped skirt w/scalloped edges, sunflower-shaped face & yellow hair, green blouse, yellow skirt, Model No. 703, 9" h. ............ 105

### Schoop Jardiniere with Chinese Scene

**Jardiniere,** cylindrical, incised stylized design of a kneeling Chinese woman w/ming trees & animals, base & design in gold glaze on a light green body, 7" h. (ILLUS.) ................ 125

**Lamp,** figural, TV-type, Comedy & Tragedy masks on a base w/full Comedy, part Tragedy conjoined, dark green w/gold trim, ca. 1954, 10 3/4" l., 12" h. ................ 275

**Model of a cat lying down,** head up, tail wrapped around side, paws tucked under body, brown collar around neck w/two yellow bells & two small brown pots attached, white rough textured body, inkstamp under glaze, "Hedi Schoop Hollywood, Cal.," 6 3/4" l., 6 1/2" h. ................ 115

**Planter,** model of a horse, rough textured mane & tail, white glossy glazed body w/mint green face accents, saddle, bows in assorted areas & scalloped edging at the base, inkstamp mark "Hedi Schoop," 7 1/2" h. ................ 100

**Vase,** 9" h. at highest point, 4 1/2" h., at lowest point, 9" l., seashell-form, footed oval base, fluted edge rising from the low end to the higher end, dark green base w/dark green & gold fading to light green, rim trimmed in gold, transparent textured glossy glaze, marked w/a silver label w/red block letters, "Hedi Schoop Hollywood, Calif." on two lines ...................... **85**

## SEVRES & SEVRES-STYLE

*Some of the most desirable porcelain ever produced was made at the Sèvres factory, originally established at Vincennes, France, and transferred, through permission of Madame de Pompadour, to Sèvres as the Royal Manufactory about the middle of the 18th century. King Louis XV took sole responsibility for the works in 1759 when production of hard paste wares began. Between 1850 and 1900, many biscuit and soft-paste pieces were made again. Fine early pieces are scarce and high-priced. Many of those available today are late productions. The various Sèvres marks have been copied and pieces listed as "Sèvres-Style" are similar to actual Sèvres wares, but not necessarily from that factory. Three of the many Sèvres marks are illustrated below.*

*Sevres Marks*

**Center bowl,** the sides painted w/reserves of a courting couple & a landscape, on a cobalt blue ground, artist-signed, gilt-metal mounts, ca. 1900, 12 3/4" l ............. **$403**

*Bronze-mounted Sevres Centerpiece*

**Centerpiece,** a gilt-bronze mounted porcelain bulbous body w/continuous putto decorated figural band within 'jewel' & gilt decorated borders on a bleu celeste ground flanked by angular handles fitted w/winged putti, on a drapery-cast reeded base, late 19th c., lacking lid, 14 1/2" h. (ILLUS.) .................................................... **8,625**

**Cup & saucer,** cobalt blue ground w/gilt framed oval cartouche on the cup,

enamel-decorated w/flowers, 19th c., cup 3 1/8" h. ................................................. **230**

*Sevres Jewelled Cup & Saucer*

**Cup & saucer,** the cup finely painted w/three royal portraits within a border of red jewels reserved on a deep blue ground gilt & jewelled w/foliate scrollwork, the saucer h.p. w/a coat-of-arms within a similarly decorated border, second half 19th c., pseudo Sevres marks in blue, the cup w/painted titles "Gabrielle d' Estrées," "Marguerite de Navarre" & "Henri IV," minor losses to jewelling, cup 3" h. (ILLUS.) ............................................. **2,587**

**Figure of a huntsman,** bisque, finely modeled as a young man standing before a tree stump on a shaped base & blowing a large hunting horn, 19th c., impressed factory mark & incised "AD98," horn & right hand restored, 15" h. .......................... **920**

**Lamp base,** the wide ovoid body raised on a bronze grooved & draped pedestal, enamel decorated figural & floral cartouches on blue ground, late 18th - early 19th c., 13 1/4" h. .................................... **1,840**

**Patch box,** cov., the cover decorated w/a Napoleonic scene in color, the sides w/landscape panels, all on a cobalt blue ground, gilt scroll trim, late 19th c., 6" l. ....... **978**

*Sevres Plaque*

**Plaque,** round, decorated w/scene depicting a Napoleonic battle within a tied laurel band on a bleu celeste ground, marked w/interlacing "Ls" in red enamel, late 19th c., mounted in a round wood frame, 21" d. (ILLUS.) .............................. **3,220**

*Ornate Sevres Urns*

**Urns,** circular gilt-decorated foot w/square base supporting a swelled pear-shaped body w/tall cylindrical neck, berried laurel wreath shoulder handles, each decorated w/opposing figural & landscape panels within gilt-decorated foliate borders reserved on a gilt-trimmed cobalt blue ground, marked w/interlacing "Ls" enclosing the letter B in underglaze-blue, late 19th c., missing lids, 20 1/2" h., pr. (ILLUS.) ............................ **6,325**

*Unusual Sevres-style Vanity Set*

**Vanity set,** porcelain, comprising wash basin & pitcher, scent bottle w/stopper, cup & cov. rectangular box, each h.p. w/scene of courting couples within silver overlaid cartouches, ca. 1860, 5 pcs. (ILLUS.)..................................................... **3,450**

**Vase,** cov., 11" h., a tall slightly tapering cylindrical body w/rounded bottoms fitted w/an ormolu rim & scrolled handles, fitted w/a domed cover w/ormolu flame finial, the body raised on a slender pedestal w/an ormolu connector & ending on a stepped ormolu base w/paneled rim, the body decorated w/a large reverse decorated in color w/a scene of a young lady & cherub sitting in a garden, blue bands at top of neck & edge of cover, overall gilt trim, artist-signed, late 19th c., ......................................... **440**

**Vase,** 24" h., wide ovoid body w/narrow shoulder tapering to short wide cylindrical neck flanked w/long slender ornate handles, bronze pedestal & shaped foot, decorated w/gilt-scrolled foliate framed rectangular panels h.p. w/classical figures & floral bouquet on a cobalt blue ground, artist-signed, 19th c. .................... **2,760**

## SHAWNEE

*The Shawnee Pottery Company of Zanesville, Ohio opened its doors for operation in 1936 and, sadly, closed in 1961. The pottery was inexpensive for its quality and was readily purchased at dimestores as well as department stores. Sears-Roebuck, Butler Bros., Woolworths and S. Kresge were just a few of the companies that were long-time retailers of this fine pottery.*

*Shawnee Pottery Company had a wide array of merchandise to offer from knick-knacks to dinnerware, though Shawnee is quite often associated with colorful pig cookie jars and dazzling "Corn King" line dinnerware. Planters, miniatures, cookie jars & corn line are much in demand by today's avid collectors. Factory seconds were purchased by outside decorators and trimmed with gold, decals and unusual hand painting which made those pieces extremely desirable in today's market and also enhances the value considerably.*

*Shawnee Pottery has become the most sought-after pottery in today's collectible market.*

*Reference books available are Mark E. Supnick's book, Collecting Shawnee Pottery, The Collector's Guide to Shawnee Pottery by Duane and Janice Vanderbilt or Shawnee Pottery---An Identification & Value Guide by Jim and Bev Mangus.*

*The Shawnee Pottery operated in Zanesville, Ohio, from 1937 until 1961. Much of the early production was sold to chain stores and mail-order houses including Sears, Roebuck, Woolworth and others. Planters, cookie jars and vases, along with the popular "Corn King" oven ware line, are among the collectible items which are plentiful and still reasonably priced. Reference numbers used here are taken from Mark E. Supnick's book, Collecting Shawnee Pottery, The Collector's Guide to Shawnee Pottery by Duane and Janice Vanderbilt, or Shawnee Pottery - An Identification & Value Guide by Jim and Bev Mangus.*

*Shawnee*
*U.S.A.*

*Shawnee Mark*

*Shawnee Figural Banks*

**Bank,** figural Bulldog, 4 1/2" h., unmarked
(ILLUS. left) ......................................... **$175-200**
**Bank,** figural Tumbling Bear, unmarked,
4 3/4" h. (ILLUS. right)........................... **175-200**

*Figural Howdy Doody Bank*

**Bank,** figural, Howdy Doody riding a pig,
marked "Bob Smith U.S.A.," 6 3/4" h.
(ILLUS.)................................................. **500-550**
**Bank - cookie jar,** figural Winnie Pig,
chocolate or butterscotch, marked "Patented: Smiley Shawnee 60 U.S.A." or
"Patented: Smiley Shawnee 61 U.S.A."
10 1/2" h., each ..................................... **450-500**
**Book ends,** figural dog head, Setter,
marked "U.S.A.," 3 3/4" h., pr. .................. **65-75**

*Shawnee Figural Book Ends*

**Book ends,** figural, full-figure of a man at
potter's wheel, brown, marked "Crafted
by Shawnee Potteries Zanesville, Ohio
1960," 9" h., pr. (ILLUS.) ...................... **400-500**
**Casserole,** cov., Corn King patt., No. 74 .......... **85**
**Cigarette box,** cov., embossed Indian
arrowhead on lid, brown, marked "Shaw-
nee," 3 1/4 x 4 1/2" .............................. **400-500**
**Coffeepot,** cov., Pennsylvania Dutch patt,
marked "U.S.A. 52," 42 oz..................... **195-225**
**Coffeepot,** cov., Sunflower patt, marked
"U.S.A.," 42 oz...................................... **195-225**
**Coffeepot,** cov., Valencia line, tangerine
glaze, 7 1/2" h. (ILLUS. top
next column).......................................... **95-125**
**Cookie jar,** figural Cottage, marked "U.S.A.
6," 7" h.............................................. **800-1,000**
**Cookie jar,** figural Cinderella, unmarked ......... **125**
**Cookie jar,** figural Drum Major, marked
"U.S.A. 10," 10" h. ................................ **275-300**

*Valencia Line Coffeepot*

**Cookie jar,** figural Dutch Boy (Jack), paint
under glaze, striped pants, marked
"U.S.A.," 11" h. .................................... **125-150**
**Cookie jar,** figural Dutch Girl (Jill), paint
under glaze, marked "U.S.A.,"
11 1/2" h. .......................................... **125-150**

*Great Northern Boy Cookie Jar*

**Cookie jar,** figural Great Northern Boy,
marked "Great Northern U.S.A. 1025,"
9 3/4" h. (ILLUS.)................................... **350-400**
**Cookie jar,** figural Great Northern Girl,
marked "Great Northern U.S.A. 1026,"
10" h. ................................................. **375-425**
**Cookie jar,** figural Jo-Jo the Clown,
marked "Shawnee U.S.A. 12," 9" h. ...... **275-350**

*Muggsy Cookie Jar*

**Cookie jar,** figural Muggsy Dog, blue bow,
gold trim & decals, marked "Patented
Muggsy U.S.A.," 11 3/4" h. (ILLUS.) ..... **850-950**
**Cookie jar,** figural Smiley Pig, w/clover
blossom, marked "Patented Smiley
U.S.A.," 11 1/2" h. ................................ **500-575**

**Cookie jar,** figural Winnie Pig, clover blossom decoration, marked "Patented Winnie U.S.A.," 12" h................................. **500-575**

*Dutch Style Red Feather Creamer*

**Creamer,** ball-type, Dutch Style, decorated w/red feather, marked "U.S.A. 12," 4 1/2" h. (ILLUS.)..................................... **95-125**

*Pennsylvania Dutch Creamer & Sugar Bowl*

**Creamer,** ball-type, Pennsylvania Dutch patt., marked "U.S.A. 12," 4 1/2" h. (ILLUS. right)............................................... **75-95**
**Creamer,** ball-type, Sunflower patt., marked "U.S.A.," 4 1/2" H......................... **45-65**
**Creamer,** Corn King patt., No. 70...................... **31**
**Creamer,** figural Elephant, marked "Patented U.S.A.," 4 3/4" h. ............................ **35-50**
**Creamer,** figural Puss 'n Boots, marked "Patented Puss N Boots U.S.A.," 4 1/2" h............................................................... **45-65**
**Creamer,** figural Smiley Pig, decorated w/embossed peach flower, marked "Patented Smiley U.S.A.," 4 1/2" h. ............. **125-150**
**Creamer,** "King Corn" line, marked "Shawnee U.S.A. 70," 5" h. ................................. **35-45**
**Creamer,** Lobster Ware, figural lobster handle, charcoal grey, marked "U.S.A. 909," 4 1/2" h............................................. **65-85**

*Valencia Line Dealer's Display Sign*

**Dealer's display sign,** figural Spanish dancers, "Valencia" embossed across

base, tangerine glaze, 11 1/4" h. (ILLUS.)................................................. **400-450**
**Head vase** Polynesian woman, marked "Shawnee U.S.A. 896," 5 3/4" h. .............. **75-95**
**Lamp base,** figural Deer, 4 1/2" h., unmarked................................................. **35-45**
**Lamp base,** figural Mother Goose, 6 1/2" h., unmarked................................. **75-85**
**Lamp base,** figural Rabbit eating ear of corn, 6 1/2" h., unmarked......................... **75-85**

*Shawnee Fern Pattern Matchbox Holder*

**Matchbox holder,** embossed Fern patt., marked "U.S.A.," 5 1/2" h. (ILLUS.)......... **75-100**
**Mixing bowl,** Corn King line, marked "Shawnee 6," 6" d........................................... **50**
**Mixing bowl,** Corn King line, marked "Shawnee 8," 8" d........................................... **65**
**Pitcher,** ball-type, 7" h., Valencia line, marked "U.S.A." ...................................... **45-65**
**Pitcher,** ball-type, 7 1/4" h., Pennsylvania Dutch patt., marked "U.S.A." .................. **95-125**
**Pitcher,** ball-type, 7 1/4" h., Sunflower patt., marked "U.S.A." ............................ **95-125**

*Figural Bo Peep Pitcher*

**Pitcher,** 7 1/2" h., figural Bo Peep, marked "Shawnee U.S.A. 47" (ILLUS.) ............... **95-125**
**Pitcher,** 7 1/2" h., figural Boy Blue, gold trim, marked "Shawnee U.S.A. 46" ...... **200-245**
**Pitcher,** 7 1/2" h., figural Chanticleer Rooster, marked "Patented Chanticleer U.S.A." ...................................................... **75-85**
**Pitcher,** 7 3/4" h., figural Smiley Pig, peach flower decoration, marked "Patented Smiley U.S.A." ...................................... **165-185**
**Pitcher,** 8" h., figural Bo Peep w/blue & peach trim, marked "Patented Bo Peep U.S.A." ...................................................... **85-95**

**Planter,** model of a bicycle built for two, marked "Shawnee U.S.A. 735," 6" h. ........ **65-75**
**Planter,** model of a canopy bed, marked "Shawnee U.S.A. 734," 7 3/4" h. .............. **75-95**

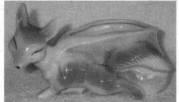

*Fox & Bag Planter*

**Planter,** model of a fox & bag, marked "U.S.A.," 4 1/2" h. (ILLUS.)...................... **50-75**
**Planter,** model of a highchair & kitten, pink or blue, marked "U.S.A. 727," each.......... **75-85**
**Planters,** models of train engine, coal car, boxcar & caboose, white, decorated, Nos. 550, 551, 552, 553, 4 pcs. .............. **85-125**

*Flower & Fern Salt Box*

**Salt box,** cov., Flower & Fern patt., yellow, marked "U.S.A.," 4 3/4" h. (ILLUS.)......... **95-125**
**Salt & pepper shakers,** figural Corn King, No. 77, pr. ........................................ **37**
**Salt & pepper shakers,** figural Cottage, pr..... **275-325**
**Salt & pepper shakers,** figural Duck, pr....... **45-55**
**Salt & pepper shakers,** figural Flower Clusters, pr............................................... **45-55**
**Salt & pepper shakers,** figural Milk Can, pr. ...................................................... **75-95**
**Salt & pepper shakers,** figural Muggsy Dog, large pr. ...................................... **100-150**
**Salt & pepper shakers,** figural Puss 'n Boots, pr................................................ **30-40**
**Salt & pepper shakers,** figural Smiley Pig & Winnie Pig, clover blossom decoration, large, pr. ..................................... **225-275**

*Figural Smiley & Winnie Shakers*

**Salt & pepper shakers,** figural Smiley Pig & Winnie Pig, clover blossom decoration, small, pr. (ILLUS.) ............................. **75-95**
**Salt & pepper shakers,** figural Smiley Pig & Winnie Pig, heart decoration, large, pr.......................................................... **100-125**
**Salt & pepper shakers,** figural Smiley Pig & Winnie Pig, heart decoration, small, pr... **45-55**
**Salt & pepper shakers,** Valencia line, pr...... **20-25**
**Snack jar/bean pot,** cov., tab-handled, Lobster Ware, figural lobster finial on lid, marked "Kenwood U.S.A. 925." 8" h. .... **375-400**
**Sugar bowl,** cov., figural Cottage, marked "U.S.A. 8," 4 1/2" h. ............................. **375-425**
**Sugar bowl,** open, Pennsylvania Dutch patt., marked "U.S.A.," 2 3/4" h. (ILLUS. left w/creamer) .......................................... **85-95**

*Clover Bud Teapot*

**Teapot,** cov., Clover Bud embossed decoration, marked "U.S.A.," 6 1/2" h. (ILLUS.)................................................ **200-275**
**Teapot,** cov., "Corn King" line, marked "Shawnee 75," 30 oz. ............................... **75-95**
**Teapot,** cov., figural Cottage, marked "U.S.A. 7," 5 1/2" h. ............................. **375-450**
**Teapot,** cov., figural Granny Ann, peach & blue, marked "Patented Granny Ann, U.S.A.," 8" h. ...................................... **100-125**
**Teapot,** cov., figural Piper's Son, marked "Tom the Piper's Son patented U.S.A. 44," 7" h. .............................................. **100-125**
**Teapot,** cov., Pennsylvania Dutch patt., marked "U.S.A. 18," 18 oz........................ **65-85**
**Teapot,** cov., Sunflower patt., marked "U.S.A.," 6 1/4" h. ..................................... **75-95**
**Utility basket,** cov., oval, marked "U.S.A.," 4 3/4" h. .................................................. **85-95**
**Utility bucket,** cov., marked "U.S.A.," 5" h. .. **45-55**

*Scotty Dog Wall Pocket*

**Wall pocket,** Scotty Dog head, 9 1/2" h.,
unmarked (ILLUS.) .................................... **65-95**
**Wall pocket,** Sunflower patt., marked
"U.S.A.," 6 3/4" h. .................................. **35-45**

*Tropical Fruit Wall Pocket*

**Wall pocket,** Tropical Fruit, pink, marked
"U.S.A.," 6 1/2" h. (ILLUS.) ....................... **35-45**

## SHELLEY CHINA

*Shelley Mark*

Members of the Shelley family were in the pottery business in England as early as the 18th century. In 1872 Joseph Shelley formed a partnership with James Wileman of Wileman & Co. who operated the Foley China Works. The Wileman & Co. name was used for the firm for the next fifty years, and between 1890 and 1910 the words "The Foley" appeared above conjoined "WC" initials.

Beginning in 1910 the Shelley family name in a shield appeared on wares, although the firm's official name was still Wileman & Co. The company's name was finally changed to Shelley in 1925 and then Shelley China Ltd. after 1965. The firm changed hands in the 1960s and became part of the Doulton Group in 1971.

At first only average quality earthenwares were produced but in the late 1890s new shapes and better quality decorations were used.

Bone china was introduced at Shelley before World War I and these fine dinnerwares became very popular in the United States and are increasingly popular today with collectors. Thin "eggshell china" teawares, miniatures and souvenir items were widely marketed during the 1920s and 1930s and are sought-after today.

**Ashtray,** advertising-type, "Greer's O.V.H." ... **$100**
**Ashtray,** Dainty Blue patt. .......................... **50**
**Ashtray-match holder,** advertising-type,
horseshoe-shaped, "White Horse"
(ILLUS. top next column) ........................... **125**
**Backbar water pitcher,** "White Horse" ........... **500**

*"White Horse" Advertising Ashtray*

**Bowl,** berry, Blue Rock patt. .......................... **30**
**Bowl,** 8" w., lustre glaze, signed "Walter
Slater" ................................................. **800**
**Breakfast set:** two-cup cov. coffeepot,
creamer, open sugar bowl, two 8" d.
plates, two 6" d. plates, two 5 1/2" d.
bowls & one cov. pancake dish; Stocks
patt., Dainty shape, the set ...................... **875**
**Butter dish,** cov., Dainty White patt. .............. **48**
**Butter dish,** cov., round, Blue Rock patt. ......... **175**
**Butter pat,** Primrose patt. .......................... **95**
**Butter pat,** Tall Trees patt. ......................... **135**
**Butter pat,** Woman & Kitten at Desk patt. ........ **135**
**Cake plate,** handled, square, Dainty Blue
patt. ................................................... **125**
**Cake set:** 10" handled cake plate & six
6" d. plates; Wild Flower patt., the set ......... **210**
**Candlestick,** Art Deco-style, orange glaze,
2 1/2" h. .............................................. **150**

*Cloisonné Pattern Candlestick*

**Candlestick,** flaring round base below the
tapering shaft & bulbed candle socket,
down-curved handle from socket to
base, Cloisonné patt., 6 1/2" h. (ILLUS.) ...... **200**
**Candy dish,** Dainty Pink patt., 4 1/2" l. ........... **65**
**Coffeepot,** cov., Bluebells patt., Vincent
shape .................................................. **200**
**Coffeepot,** cov., Campanula patt., tall
tapering ovoid body w/domed cover,
7" h. .................................................... **300**

*Dainty Blue Coffee, Tea & Water Pots*

**Coffeepot,** cov., Dainty Blue patt., Dainty
shape (ILLUS. right) ...................................... 600
**Coffeepot,** cov., Dainty patt. ............................ 435
**Coffeepot,** cov., Syringa patt., Regent
shape .......................................................... 350
**Coffeepot,** cov., Violets patt., Mayfair
shape .......................................................... 325
**Creamer & open sugar bowl,** Dainty Blue
patt., Dainty shape, pr. ................................. 130

*Dainty Floral Creamer & Sugar Bowl*

**Creamer & open sugar bowl,** Floral patt.,
Dainty shape w/floral-molded handle, pr.
(ILLUS.) ....................................................... 300
**Creamer & open sugar bowl,** Wileman &
Co., pr. ........................................................ 150
**Creamer, open sugar bowl & tray,** Blue
Rock patt., 3 pcs. ......................................... 165
**Creamer & sugar bowl,** Blue Rock patt.,
pr. ............................................................... 110
**Creamer & sugar bowl,** Harebell patt., pr. ........ 85
**Creamer & sugar bowl,** Maytime patt., pr. ...... 175
**Cup & saucer,** Ashbourne patt., Gainsbor-
ough shape ................................................... 200
**Cup & saucer,** Begonia patt., six-flute
shape ............................................................ 78
**Cup & saucer,** Black Dainty patt., Dainty
shape, rare ................................................... 800
**Cup & saucer,** Blue Rock patt., Dainty
shape ............................................................ 65
**Cup & saucer,** Bridal Rose patt., six-flute
shape ............................................................ 75
**Cup & saucer,** Caprice patt., New Cam-
bridge shape ................................................ 100

*Chinoiserie Pattern Cup & Saucer*

**Cup & saucer,** Chinoiserie patt., Ripon
shape (ILLUS.) ............................................. 200
**Cup & saucer,** Countryside (Chintz style)
patt., gold foot & scroll handle ..................... 204
**Cup & saucer,** Countryside patt., Queen
Anne shape ................................................. 185
**Cup & saucer,** Countryside patt., various
Chintz shapes, each ..................................... 200
**Cup & saucer,** Dainty Black patt., Dainty
shape, rare ................................................... 800
**Cup & saucer,** Dainty Blue patt., Dainty
shape ..................................................... 70-100
**Cup & saucer,** Dainty Mauve patt., Dainty
shape .......................................................... 150
**Cup & saucer,** Dainty Pink patt., Dainty
shape .......................................................... 150

*Dainty Cup & Saucer w/Floral Handle*

**Cup & saucer,** Dainty shape, lavender &
cream w/floral-molded handle (ILLUS.) ........ 175
**Cup & saucer,** Dainty shape, solid color ............ 60
**Cup & saucer,** demitasse Acacia patt.,
Regent shape .............................................. 100

*Floral-Handled Cup & Saucer*

**Cup & saucer,** Floral patt., Queen Anne
shape w/floral-molded handle (ILLUS.) ........ 400
**Cup & saucer,** Floral patt., Vogue (Art
Deco style) shape ........................................ 300
**Cup & saucer,** Green Daisy patt., Henley
(Chintz) shape ............................................. 150
**Cup & saucer,** Harebell patt. ............................ 52
**Cup & saucer,** Japan patt., Alexandra
shape, Wileman & Co. .................................. 100
**Cup & saucer,** Marguerite patt. ......................... 65
**Cup & saucer,** Marguerite patt., Queen
Anne shape ................................................... 95
**Cup & saucer,** Marguerite patt., Ripon
(Chintz) shape ............................................. 125
**Cup & saucer,** Melody patt., various Chintz
shapes, each ............................................... 130
**Cup & saucer,** miniature, each set ........... 250-300
**Cup & saucer,** miniature, Lily of the Valley
patt., Westminster shape ............................. 325
**Cup & saucer,** Strawberries patt., Queen
Anne shape ................................................... 95

Cup & saucer, Wildflower patt. .......................... 52
Cup & saucer, Woodland patt. .......................... 55
Cup & saucer, demitasse, Forget-Me-Not patt. ................................................................. 48
Cup & saucer, demitasse, Pansy patt. .............. 48
Cup & saucer, demitasse, Rose Spray patt. ................................................................. 48
Cups & saucers, demitasse, footed, pink w/aqua dots, gold lined, 6 each, 12 pcs. ....... 350
Cups & saucers, Crochet patt., pink & blue flower w/gold trim, set of 6 .......................... 290
Demitasse pot, cov., Wildflowers patt., Dainty shape ............................................... 300
Dessert set: cup & saucer & dessert plate; Campanula patt., 3 pcs. .............................. 165
Dessert set: cup & saucer & dessert plate; Rosebud patt. ........................................... 125
Dessert set, cup & saucer & dessert plate, Rock Garden patt., 3 pcs. ........................... 110
Egg cup, Dainty Shamrock patt. ....................... 55
Hot water pot, cov., Dainty Blue patt., Dainty shape (ILLUS. center) ...................... 600

*Shelley Floral Pattern Invalid Feeder*

Invalid feeder, Floral patt. (ILLUS.) ................. 250
Jam pot, cov., Dainty Blue patt. ....................... 200
Jam pot w/metal cover & holder, Bridal Rose patt., the set ......................................... 175
Jelly mold, French shape, large ....................... 75
Jelly mold, model of a large white chicken ..... 200
Loving cup, Bermuda commemorative, "1609-1959," 4 1/2 x 7" ................................. 100
Luncheon set, 8" d. plate, cup & saucer, Blue Daisy patt., Chintz shape, 3 pcs. .......... 160
Luncheon set: cup, saucer & two plates: Jungle Print patt., Daisy shape, Wileman & Co., the set ........................................... 175
Luncheon set, 8" plate, cup & saucer, Harebell patt., 3 pcs. ..................................... 65
Luncheon set, 8" plate, cup & saucer, Stocks patt., 3 pcs. ....................................... 65

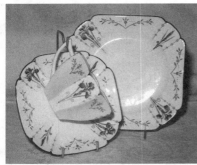

*Blue Iris Luncheon Set*

Luncheon set (trio): cup, saucer & plate: Blue Iris patt., Queen Anne shape, the set (ILLUS.) .................................................. 200
Luncheon set (trio): cup, saucer & plate: Countryside (Chintz) patt., Oleander shape, the set ............................................. 350
Luncheon set (trio): cup, saucer & plate: Crackle patt., Queen Anne shape, the set ..................................................... 190
Luncheon set (trio): cup, saucer & plate: Dainty Black patt., Dainty shape, the set .. 1,075
Luncheon set (trio): cup, saucer & plate: Daisy Cluster patt., Empire shape, Wileman & Co., the set ..................................... 125

*Festoons & Fruit Luncheon Set*

Luncheon set (trio): cup, saucer & plate: Festoons & Fruit patt., Gainsborough shape, the set (ILLUS.) ............................... 125

*Gladiolus Luncheon Set*

Luncheon set (trio): cup, saucer & plate: Gladiolus patt., Eve (Art Deco style) shape, the set (ILLUS.) ............................... 250
Luncheon set (trio): cup, saucer & plate: Hollyhocks patt., Regent shape, the set ....... 135
Luncheon set (trio): cup, saucer & plate: Sunflower & Leaf Border patt., Violet shape, Wileman & Co., the set ................... 225

*Thistle Pattern Luncheon Set*

**Luncheon set (trio):** cup, saucer & plate; Thistle patt., Alexandra shape, Wileman & Co., the set (ILLUS.) .................................. **125**
**Mint dish,** Dainty Blue patt. ................................ **72**

*Shelley Model of a Drake*

**Model of a drake duck,** brown head, grey & black body, Bird Series #12, 4 1/2" h. (ILLUS.) ......................................................... **500**
**Model of a parrot,** Bird Series #3, 7 1/2" h. ...... **500**
**Mug,** decorated w/the coat-of-arms of Wales, 3" h. ................................................... **100**
**Napkin ring,** Harmony patt. ............................... **100**
**Nut dish,** Old England patt., signed by Eric Slater .................................................................. **75**
**Pitcher,** water, jug-form, Blue Dragon patt. ..... **500**
**Plate,** bread & butter, Blue Rock patt. ............... **30**
**Plate,** dinner, Blue Rock patt. ............................ **95**
**Plate,** dinner, Harebell patt. ............................... **45**

*Festoons & Fruit Pattern Plate*

**Plate,** Festoons & Fruit patt., Roseberry shape (ILLUS.) ....................................... **50-100**
**Plate,** Pattern No.11752, florals & butterflies ....................................................... **100-125**
**Plate,** square, Maytime patt. .............................. **125**
**Plate,** 6" d., Rock Garden patt. .......................... **25**
**Plate,** 8" d., Dainty Blue patt. ............................ **65**
**Plate,** 8" d., Harebell patt. .................................. **45**
**Plate,** 8" d., luncheon, Blue Rock patt. .............. **56**
**Plate,** 8" d., Thistle patt. ..................................... **49**
**Plate,** 8 3/4" d., Jacobean patt. (ILLUS. top next column) ................................................ **50-60**
**Plate,** 11" d., dinner, Blue Rock patt. ................. **85**
**Platter,** 10 x 13", meat, Blue Rock patt. ........... **140**
**Platter,** 14 1/2" l., Harebell patt. ....................... **150**
**Reamer & base,** Harmony patt., streaky mottled pink & green glaze, 2 pc. (ILLUS. center next column) ...................... **350**

*Jacobean Pattern Plate*

*Harmony Pattern Two-Piece Reamer*

**Shaving mug,** Harmony patt. ............................. **175**
**Sugar bowl,** open, square, Rock Garden patt. .................................................................. **59**

*Blue Gladiolus Art Deco Tea Set*

**Tea set,** Blue Gladiolus patt., Eve (Art Deco style) shape, 21 pcs. (ILLUS. of part) .......................................................... **2,100**
**Tea set,** Green Lines & Bands patt., Eve (Art Deco style) shape, 21 pcs. ................. **2,000**

*Sun-Ray Art Deco Tea Set*

**Tea set,** Sun-Ray patt., Vogue (Art Deco style) shape, 21 pcs. (ILLUS. of part) ........ **2,500**
**Tea set,** Yellow Phlox patt., Regent shape, teapot & 37 pcs. ......................................... **1,800**

**Teapot,** cov., Begonia patt. .............................. **475**
**Teapot,** cov., Countryside (Chintz-type) patt., Eve (Art Deco style) shape ................ **800**
**Teapot,** cov., Dainty Blue patt., Dainty shape (ILLUS. left) ....................................... **600**
**Teapot,** cov., Dainty Blue patt., large .............. **495**
**Teapot,** cov., Harebell patt. ............................. **325**

*Harmony Drip-Ware Teapot*

**Teapot,** cov., Harmony Drip-Ware, Cambridge shape (ILLUS.) .................................. **600**
**Teapot,** cov., Hollyhocks patt., Regent shape ......................................................... **350**

*Rare Laburnum Pattern Teapot*

**Teapot,** cov., Laburnum patt., Eve (Art Deco style) shape (ILLUS.) .......................... **650**
**Teapot,** cov., Regency patt., Dainty shape ...... **300**
**Teapot,** cov., Rock Garden (Chintz-type) patt., Eve (Art Deco style) shape ................ **775**

*Wildflower Pattern Teapot*

**Teapot,** cov., Wildflower patt., Dainty shape (ILLUS.) ............................................. **450**
**Toast rack,** Harmony Ware patt. ...................... **150**
**Umbrella stand,** advertising-type, columnar form w/molded pilasters flanking arched niches around the side, dark blue ground printed in white w/"Shelley China - Potters to The World," 27" h. (ILLUS. top next column) ...................................... **2,500**

**Vase,** 4 1/2" h., Melody patt. ............................ **200**
**Vase,** 5" h., Balloons & Flashes patt. .............. **125**

*Rare Shelley Umbrella Stand*

**Vase,** 5" h., Cloisonné patt. ............................. **200**
**Vase,** 6" h., New Violettes patt. ....................... **100**

*Harmony Ware Moresque Vase*

**Vase,** 6" h., tall waisted shape, Harmony Ware, Moresque patt., stylized blossoms in orange, pale & dark blue & brown (ILLUS.) ....................................................... **150**
**Vase,** 6 1/2" h., New Fruit patt. ........................ **150**
**Vase,** 7" h., Jazz Circles patt., black & yellow design ..................................................... **175**
**Vegetable bowl,** open, oval, Harebell patt., 9 1/2" l. ........................................................ **145**

## NURSERY WARE BY MABEL LUCIE ATTWELL

*Boo-Boo Cruet Set*

**Baby feeding plate,** color scene inscribed "Fairy Folk with Tiny Wings..." ...................... 350

**Child's set:** cup, saucer & plate; scene of an airplane & Boo-Boos, the set .................. 500

**Cruet set:** three mushroom-shaped covered pots & figural shaker on four-lobed tray; Boo-Boo set (ILLUS.) ........................ 1,000

**Figurine,** Boo-Boo with knapsack ................... 900

**Figurine,** Boo-Boo with mushroom .................. 900

*Rare Diddums Figurine*

**Figurine,** Diddums (ILLUS.) .......................... 2,200

**Figurine,** Golfer ............................................ 2,200

**Figurine,** I's Shy ........................................... 2,200

**Figurine,** Little Mermaid ............................... 2,500

**Mug & saucer,** color duck scene inscribed "Quacky the Sailor," the set .......................... 375

**Mug & saucer,** inscribed "If the Fairies came to Tea," the set .................................. 375

**Platter,** 8" w., duck scene inscribed "Quacky the Sailor" ..................................... 180

*Child's Platter with Duck Scene*

**Platter,** 8" l., squared shape w/molded handles, color scene of mother duck & children, inscribed "Will Somebody Kindly Tell..." (ILLUS.) ............................................. 300

*Boo-Boo Figural Tea Set*

**Tea set:** cov. teapot, creamer & open sugar; Boo-Boo set w/mushroom-shaped open sugar & mushroom house-shaped teapot w/figural Boo-Boo creamer, the set (ILLUS.) .......................... 2,500

## INTARSIO ART POTTERY (1997-99)

*Intarsio Art Pottery Clock*

**Clock,** table model, Art Nouveau-style upright case w/a brown border around a colored central panel w/a dial above a scene of a Medieval couple by a sundial above the inscription "The Days May Come - The Days May Go..."(ILLUS.) ....... 1,500

*Intarsio Art Pottery Cracker Jar*

**Cracker jar,** cov., footed bulbous body w/silver plate rim, cover & bail handle, wide color band decorated w/scenes from Shakespeare plays, 6" h. (ILLUS.) ....... 850

*Caricature Teapot of Lord Salisbury*

**Teapot,** cov., caricature of Lord Salisbury, dark green, black, tan & brown (ILLUS.) ... 1,000

**Teapot,** cov., Cornflower patt., blue ground .. 1,200

*Intarsio Oriental Shape Teapot*

**Teapot,** cov., Oriental shape, wide squatty base centered by an urn-form neck w/domed cover, upright shaped spout & C-scroll handle, dark brown ground decorated w/stylized deep rose & green blossoms & leaves on yellow bands, lighter brown spout & handle (ILLUS.) ...... **1,400**
**Toby mug,** "The Irishman," 7 1/2" h. ................ **850**

*Rare Intarsio Umbrella Stand*

**Umbrella stand,** cylindrical w/flared foot, Flowers patt., white storks flying into a large rising sun in a blue sky, dark water & water lilies around the bottom, 25" h. (ILLUS.).................................................... **8,500**
**Vase,** 8 1/2" h., bulbous body centered by a wide cylindrical neck w/four curved handles from neck to shoulder, decorated w/a central band of brown & white chickens on a blue & green ground, bands of brown scrolls on a green ground above & below & a dark blue neck w/white & yellow flowers & green leaves, green handles ............................ **1,800**
**Wash bowl & pitcher set,** Art Nouveau design w/large stylized flowers in yellow & shaded blue to white on green swirled leafy stems on a dark green & black ground, bowl 18" d., the set (ILLUS. top next column)............................................. **2,200**

*Intarsio Art Nouveau-style Wash Set*

# SLIPWARE

*This term refers to ceramics, primarily redware, decorated by the application of slip, or semi-liquid paste made of clay. Such wares were made for decades in England and Germany and elsewhere on the Continent, and in the Pennsylvania Dutch country and elsewhere in the United States. Today, contemporary copies of early Slipware items are featured in numerous decorator magazines and offered for sale in gift catalogs.*

**Bowl,** 13 " d., 2 1/2" h., wide shallow form, the buff clay decorated on the interior w/an overall combed slip design in white & brown, clear glaze (wear) ................... **$4,180**
**Bowl,** 14 3/4" d., 3 1/2" h., shallow, squiggly white slip decoration on dark brown glaze (wear & old edge chips).................. **1,980**
**Charger,** redware, coggle wheel rim w/yellow slip squiggles & inscription "Pony up the Cash," attributed to Day Pottery, Norwalk, Connecticut, 14" d. (wear, hairline & old rim chips)................................ **18,700**
**Dish,** redware, rectangular, decorated w/a slip-trailed inscription "Chicken Pottry (sic)," American, 19th c., 9 3/4 x 14 1/2" (chips) .......................................................... **460**
**Dish,** redware w/coggled rim, wavy lines of yellow slip w/brown & green, 6 1/2" d. (wear & surface chips) ................................ **413**
**Loaf dish,** redware, rectangular w/coggle wheel rim, yellow three-quill slip decoration, 14" l. (some glaze flaking & edge chips).......................................................... **715**
**Loaf dish,** redware, rectangular w/coggle wheel rim, yellow four-quill slip decoration in center & on each side, 14 1/4" l. (wear, glaze flakes & chips) .......... **770**
**Mold,** food, Turk's turban-style, orange ground w/dark brown splotches & flecks & yellow slip rim, 9" d., 3" h. (wear & small chips) ................................................. **330**
**Pie plate,** w/coggled rim, three-line yellow slip decoration w/green, 7 7/8" d. (minor wear & small chip)...................................... **550**
**Pie plate,** w/coggled rim, yellow slip decoration highlighted in brown & green on greyish amber ground, 7 7/8" d. (wear)........ **550**
**Pie plate,** redware, circular w/coggle wheel rim, three-line yellow slip decoration, 8" d. (wear, surface flakes & hairline) .......... **385**

**Pie plate,** redware w/coggled rim w/three-line slip decoration, 8" d. (wear, hairline & small rim chips) ........................................ **605**

**Pie plate,** redware w/coggled rim, dark brown & green flecked glaze w/white slip wavy lines, attributed to Stahl Pottery, Powder Valley, Lehigh County, Pennsylvania, 8 3/8" d. (minor glaze flakes on rim) ................................................................ **550**

**Pie plate,** redware w/coggled rim, three-line yellow slip decoration, 9" d. (minor wear & old edge chips, short edge hairline) ...................................................................... **385**

**Pie plate,** circular, w/coggle wheel rim, redware w/wavy three-line yellow slip decoration, 9 3/4" d. (cracked) ............................ **385**

**Pie plate,** redware w/coggled rim, decorated w/large yellow slip bird on branch, 10" d. (wear & hairlines) ............................ **3,410**

**Pie plate,** w/coggled rim, yellow slip Seaweed design on blue glaze, 10 1/2" d. (minor wear, edge chips & short hairlines) ................................................................ **1,623**

**Pie plate,** redware w/coggled rim, three-line yellow slip decoration, 11" d. (wear & rim chips) ...................................................... **330**

**Pie plate,** redware w/coggle wheel rim, yellow slip flourish decoration, 12" d. (slip worn & flaked) .......................................... **880**

*Slipware "Lafayette" Plate*

**Plate,** 11 1/2" d., redware w/crimped rim & inscribed "Lafayette" in yellow slip w/yellow slip scrolls above & below inscription, 19th c., Pennsylvania (ILLUS.) .......... **6,900**

# SPATTERWARE

*This ceramic ware takes its name from the "spattered" decoration, in various colors, generally used to trim pieces hand-painted with rustic center designs of flowers, birds, houses, etc. Popular in the early 19th century, most was imported from England.*

*Related wares, called "stick spatter," had freehand designs applied with pieces of cut sponge attached to sticks, hence the name. Examples date from the 19th and early 20th century and were produced in England, Europe and America.*

*Some early spatter-decorated wares were marked by the manufacturers, but not many. 20th century reproductions are also sometimes marked, including those produced by Boleslaw Cybis.*

*Spatterware Creamer*

**Creamer,** bulbous body w/C-form handle & pinched spout, Peafowl patt., free-hand bird in blue, yellow & black, overall strawberry or thumbprint red, green & blue spatter, professional repair, 4" h. (ILLUS.) .................................................. **$5,170**

**Creamer,** footed squatty bulbous base w/tapering wide cylindrical neck, long pinched spout & large C-form handle, red, green & black Holly Berry patt. band around base w/overall blue spatter above, 4" h. .............................................. **660**

**Creamer,** Fort patt. in black, red, grey & green, blue spatter border, 4 1/4" h. (hairline in base & small flakes on rim & spout) ................................................................ **495**

**Creamer,** Rainbow spatter in yellow & lavender, 4 1/4" h. (professional repair) ........... **330**

*Various Spatterware Items*

**Creamer,** bulbous body w/C-form handle & arched spout, Rooster patt., free-hand bird in yellow ochre, red, blue & black, blue border, professional repair, 4 1/2" h. (ILLUS. right) ................................. **880**

**Creamer,** footed paneled bulbous body w/arched spout & angled C-form handle, Peafowl patt., free-hand bird in blue, green, red & black, blue spatter border, 4 1/2" h. .............................................................. **798**

**Creamer,** footed bulbous body w/high arched spout & scrolled C-form handle, Tree patt., free-hand tree in green & black, purple spatter border, 5" h. (stains & base of handle glued) .............................. **990**

**Creamer,** footed paneled bulbous body w/arched spout & angled C-form handle, Clipper Ship patt., free-hand ship in green, red & black, blue spatter border, 5 5/8" h. (ILLUS. left) ................................ **4,840**

**Cup plate,** Peafowl patt. in black, blue & green w/unusual black breast, red spatter background, impressed mark "Opaque Porcelain - Holden," 4" w. (chip on table ring, minor stains) ............................ **550**

**Cup & saucer,** handleless, Acorn & Oak Leaves patt. in two shades of green, brown & black, dark red spatter border (saucer slightly lighter in color & professional repair to cup) .................................. **1,100**

**Cup & saucer,** handleless, Berry & Bird patt., in blue, red, green & black, blue spatter border .............................................. **880**

**Cup & saucer,** handleless, center decoration of eight-point purple star, black spatter border (chip on table ring of saucer) .... **1,100**

**Cup & saucer,** handleless, Christmas Ball patt. in red & green (professional repair to saucer, minor pinpoints on cup) ............ **1,870**

*Spatterware Cup & Saucer*

**Cup & saucer,** handleless, Dove patt., free-hand bird in yellow ochre, blue, green & black, blue spatter border (ILLUS.) .......................................................... **2,750**

**Cup & saucer,** handleless, Drape patt., Rainbow spatter in red & blue ................... **2,090**

*Spatter Handleless Cups & Saucers*

**Cup & saucer,** handleless, Forget-Me-Not patt., free-hand flower in blue, red, green & black, blue spatter border in shape of six-point star on saucer, impressed anchor mark on saucer (ILLUS. bottom row, right) .................................................. **3,190**

**Cup & saucer,** handleless, Fort patt., free-hand fort in blue, black, red & green, red spatter border ............................................ **1,980**

**Cup & saucer,** handleless, Fort patt., free-hand fort in green, black & red, blue spatter border (ILLUS. top row, center) ........ **660**

**Cup & saucer,** handleless, Gooney Bird patt. in red, blue, green & black, blue spatter border, cup w/paneled sides (minor pinpoints on rim of cup) ................. **1,320**

**Cup & saucer,** handleless, Guinea Hen patt. in red, blue, green & black, red spatter border (professional repair to saucer, red varies slightly) ........................ **1,540**

**Cup & saucer,** handleless, Mourning Tulip patt., free-hand flower in yellow, green & black, blue spatter border (pinpoint flakes) .......................................................... **4,290**

**Cup & saucer,** handleless, Pansy patt. in red, blue, green & black, blue spatter border (pinpoints on saucer rim) ............... **3,850**

**Cup & saucer,** handleless, Peacock patt., free-hand bird in yellow, blue, green, red & black, overall light green spatter (ILLUS. top row, right) ............................... **1,650**

**Cup & saucer,** handleless, Peacock patt., free-hand bird in yellow, blue, green, red & black, overall lilac spatter (ILLUS. top row, left) ...................................................... **2,310**

**Cup & saucer,** handleless, Peafowl patt., free-hand bird in blue, yellow & black, green spatter border (professional repair in cup & small edge flakes) .......................... **495**

**Cup & saucer,** handleless, Peafowl patt., free-hand yellow, blue, green & black, red spatter border (pinpoint flakes on table ring of cup, saucer slightly lighter in color) ......................................................... **1,650**

**Cup & saucer,** handleless, Peafowl patt. in red, blue, yellow & black, blue spatter background (firing flaw on saucer) ............... **468**

**Cup & saucer,** handleless, Rainbow spatter border, alternating blue & green .......... **1,485**

**Cup & saucer,** handleless, Rainbow spatter border, alternating blue & yellow (cup slightly lighter in color & has pinpoint flakes) ...................................................... **2,090**

**Cup & saucer,** handleless, Rose patt. in red, green & black, Rainbow spatter border in black & brown (hairline in saucer) ..... **495**

**Cup & saucer,** handleless, Rose patt. in red, green & black, Rainbow spatter border in red & blue ............................................ **660**

**Cup & saucer,** handleless, Rose patt. in red, green & black, red spatter border, saucer impressed "W. Adams & Sons" ...... **550**

**Cup & saucer,** handleless, Schoolhouse patt., red, blue, yellow & black, red spatter border ................................................. **1,760**

**Cup & saucer,** handleless, Schoolhouse patt., red, green & black, blue spatter border, scalloped border on cup, chips on saucer table ring, repair to cup (ILLUS. bottom row, center) .......................... **990**

**Cup & saucer,** handleless, Stag patt. in black, red spatter border .......................... **1,320**

**Cup & saucer,** handleless, Star patt. in blue, green & red, blue spatter border ........ **550**

**Cup & saucer,** handleless, Tree patt. in green & black, blue spatter border ............. **523**

**Cup & saucer,** handleless, Umbrella Flower patt. in red & green, blue spatter border (minor stains, professional repair) ..... **440**

**Cup & saucer,** handleless, Wigwam patt., in red .......................................................... **605**

**Cup & saucer,** handleless, miniature, black & green Rainbow spatter in center & alternating bands on border (small flakes on rim of cup) ........................................... **2,200**

**Pitcher,** 6 1/2" h., paneled body w/blue transfer-printed Eagle & Shield patt. w/red spatter (wear, crazing & dark stains).............................................................. **468**

**Pitcher,** 8" h., paneled body, angled handle, arched pinched spout over molded fan, Peafowl patt., free-hand bird in blue, green, red & black, blue spatter border (professional repair) ..................................... **990**

**Plate,** 6 1/8" d., Adams Rose patt. in red & green, rainbow spatter border in red, blue & green, impressed "Adams" (minor crow's foot & scratches)............................. **935**

**Plate,** 6 1/2" d., Peafowl patt., free-hand bird in blue, yellow, green & black, red & blue spatter rim ........................................ **880**

**Plate,** 6 1/2" d., Wigwam patt., wigwams flanked by blue spatter trees ...................... **440**

**Plate,** 7 1/4" d., Pomegranate patt. in red, blue, black & green, blue spatter border, impressed "F.G. Meakin" (wear & professional repair) ...................................... **440**

**Plate,** 7 3/4" d., Peafowl patt., free-hand blue, black, red & pale yellow, overall green spatter.......................................... **1,650**

**Plate,** 8 3/8" d., paneled edges, Tulip patt. in red, blue, green & black, purple spatter border band (blue flaked in tulip) ........... **550**

**Plate,** 8 5/8" d., Rooster Peafowl patt., free-hand bird in dark blue, pale yellow, red & black, overall dark blue spatter ................. **2,860**

**Plate,** 9 3/8" d., plaid spatterware design in purple, red, blue & green (pinpoint edge flakes)............................................................ **5,170**

**Plate,** 9 1/2" d., Bull's Eye patt., blue & green spatter border (crazing & light scratches)................................................ **1,430**

**Plate,** 9 1/2" d., Bull's Eye patt., purple & black spatter border ................................. **990**

**Plate,** 9 1/2" d., Bull's Eye patt., Rainbow spatter in red & green ................................ **990**

**Plate,** 9 1/2" d., Clover patt. in red, green & black, embossed rim (minor stains) .......... **4,070**

**Plate,** 9 1/2" d., Fort patt. in black, red, grey, green & brown, blue spatter border (minor wear, small rim flake & hairline) ........ **715**

**Platter,** 13 1/2" l., Rainbow spatter in purple & brown .............................................. **2,750**

**Sugar bowl,** cov., Rooster patt., free-hand bird in yellow, blue, red & black, blue spatter border, professional repair, 4 1/4" h. (ILLUS. center with creamers) ....... **880**

**Sugar bowl,** cov., Rainbow spatter in yellow & black, 4 1/2" h. (lid slightly oversize & professionally restored chip, minor crazing) ......................................... **1,210**

**Teapot,** cov., footed bulbous body w/flaring rim, C-form handle & swan's-neck spout, inset stepped & pointed cover w/blossom finial, Tree patt., free-hand tree in green & black, purple spatter border, 6" h. (professional repair) ......................... **1,980**

**Teapot,** cov., footed bulbous body w/flaring rim, C-form handle & swan's-neck spout, Rainbow spatter in blue, red & green, 6 1/4" h. (professional repair to handle) ....... **990**

**Teapot,** cov., creamware, an upright oval cylindrical body w/tapering shoulder to a fitted domed cover w/knob finial, swan's-

neck spout, C-form handle, Rainbow spatter in vertical narrow bands of yellow, goldenrod, blue, green & dark brown, early 19th c., 6 1/2" h. (chips, lid repaired) .................................................... **6,710**

**Teapot,** cov., bulbous body w/narrow shoulder tapering to wide cylindrical neck, C-form handle & swan's-neck spout, domed cover w/button finial, Parrot patt., free-hand bird in red, green & black, blue spatter border, 6 3/4" h. (minor stains & wear, lid professionally repaired) .................................................... **2,530**

**Teapot,** cov., footed paneled body w/scrolled C-form handle, swans' neck spout, domed cover w/blossom finial, Peafowl patt., free-hand bird in blue, green, red & black, overall red spatter, 8 1/2" h. (old yellowed repair at handle).... **1,540**

**Toddy dish,** round, Primrose patt., free-hand flower in red, yellow, green & black, blue spatter border, 5" d. ................... **633**

**Toddy dish,** Wigwam patt., wigwams flanked by blue spatter trees, 5 1/8" d. .......... **495**

**Vegetable dish,** open, footed cartouche-form w/flanged rim & molded end handles, Rose patt. in red, green & black, blue spatter border, 11 1/4" l. (stains, wear, glued foot chip).............................. **468**

**Waste bowl,** Fort patt. in black, red, yellow & green, blue spatter border, 4 1/4" d. ......... **495**

# SPONGEWARE

*Spongeware's designs were spattered, sponged or daubed on in colors, sometimes with a piece of cloth. Blue on white was the most common type, but mottled tans, browns and greens on yellowware were also popular. Spongeware generally has an overall pattern with a coarser look than Spatterwares, to which it is loosely related. These wares were extensively produced in England and America well into the 20th century.*

*Blue Spongeware Batter Pail*

**Batter pail,** cylindrical w/molded rim & rim spout, wire bail handle, blue sponging on white, 5 1/4" d., 4" h. (ILLUS.) .................... **$295**

**Birdhouse,** cylindrical w/conical roof w/knob finial for hanging, overall mottled dark green sponging, 7 1/4" h. (ILLUS. top next page) ............................................. **300**

**Butter crock,** low wide cylindrical form w/molded rim, blue on white w/blue printed "Butter" on front, 9" d., 6" h.............. **303**

*Green Spongeware Birdhouse*

**Canister,** barrel-shaped w/blue sponged bands at top & bottom & thin blue bands flanking center sponging & the name "Rice," 5 3/4" h. .......................................... **500**

*Fine Spongeware Jardiniere*

**Jardiniere,** wide bulbous form w/flared rim, embossed rings of small scrolls trimmed w/rings of blue sponging on white, 9" d., 7 1/2" h. (ILLUS.)......................................... **500**

**Mixing bowls,** yellowware, nesting-type w/overall blue sponging, 3 1/2" to 9 1/4" d., set of 5 (largest does not ring) ...... **295**

**Pitcher,** 7 1/4" h., footed bulbous nearly spherical body tapering to a wide flat flaring neck, thick C-scroll handle, overall heavy blue sponging w/a wide blue band around the bottom flanked by two white bands & two thin blue bands (small chips, hairlines) .......................................... **330**

**Plates,** 9" d. w/flanged scalloped rim, yellowware w/overall fine brown sponging, England, late 18th - early 19th c., pr. (rim chips, one w/rim repair)............................... **440**

**Platter,** 9 3/4 x 13 3/4", oblong, blue sponging on white ..................................... **193**

**Salt crock,** cov., embossed Basketweave and Grapes patt., overall bold blue sponging on white ..................................... **375**

**Salt crock,** cylindrical w/hinged wooden lid, overall brown & greyish sponging, faint worn gilt label "Salt," 6" h. ........................... **137**

**Wash bowl & pitcher,** yellowware 15" d. bowl w/flaring sides & 11 3/4" h. bulbous pitcher, overall blue sponging, 2 pcs. (bowl w/repair & additional damage, worn gilding) ................................................ **275**

# STAFFORDSHIRE FIGURES

*Small figures and groups made of pottery were produced by the majority of the Staffordshire, England potters in the 19th century and were used as mantel decorations or "chimney ornaments," as they were sometimes called. Pairs of dogs were favorites and were turned out by the carload, and 19th century pieces are still available. Well-painted reproductions also abound and collectors are urged to exercise caution before investing.*

**Calf,** recumbent figure w/brush-stroked orange spots on molded greenish brown base, 3" d., 2 1/2" h. (small chip on one ear & light wear) ........................................ **$308**

**Camel,** recumbent figure, brownish tan w/red line on base, 3 1/4" d., 3 1/4" h. (few minute spots of wear) .......................... **616**

*Seated Cat Figure*

**Cat,** seated, black & brown sponging on white, glazed over crack at seam, 4 1/2" h. (ILLUS.)....................................... **275**

**Dog,** seated Mastiff w/open front legs, head turned to the side, boldly spotted fur, on a rectangular enameled pillow base, early 19th c., 4 5/8" h. (chip on pillow corner)......................................................... **633**

**Dog,** seated whippet facing the viewer, on an oval base, decorated w/overall small black dots, black ears & polychrome facial features & neck chain, mid-19th c., 7" h. (wear, chips on base, roughness on nose) ...................................................... **330**

**Dogs,** seated Spaniels in white decorated w/touches of gilt to collar chain & fur, England, 19th c., 13" h., pr. (crazing, minor gilt wear)........................................... **230**

**Dogs,** Whippets in standing position, each w/a rabbit in its mouth, painted in beige & red, 19th c., 11" h., pr. (minor chips)......... **748**

**Figure,** earthenware, rider on horseback, ca. 1880, 11 1/2" h....................... **123**

**Figure group,** a young girl in early Victorian costume & wearing a hat reclining against an oversized recumbent dog, decorated in red & white w/blue, pink & black trim, mid-19th c., 6 1/2" h. (crazing) .......................................................... **1,595**

**Figure of a youth,** standing wearing 18th c. peasant attire, beside a tree trunk, decorated w/overglaze colored enamels, impressed mark, possibly Ralph or Enoch Wedgwood, ca. 1800, 10" h. (restored neck, shallow chip on plinth)......... **690**

**Figure of The Duke of Wellington,** standing wearing a cape atop a square marbleized pedestal, gilt trim, ca. 1840,

13 1/4" h. (restoration to back of shoulders) ............................................................ 345

*Figures of Milton and Shakespeare*

**Figures of Milton & Shakespeare,** pearlware, each modeled holding a quill pen & standing beside a stack of books & manuscripts on & beside a column on a black marbled square base w/green top, ca. 1810-20, chip to upper rim of Milton's base, both w/minor losses & some flaking to enamels, 15 1/2" h., pr. (ILLUS.)...................................................... **1,495**

**Figures of Prudence & Fortitude,** pearlware, each modeled as a young classical maiden wearing a long floral gown, green & yellow or puce & yellow drape & sandals, standing on a black marbled square base, Prudence holding a torch in her left hand & w/a green serpent wrapped around her right wrist, Fortitude leaning against a column, Prudence w/restoration at left shoulder & right wrist, Fortitude w/hairline crack running through the middle, minor flaking to enamels, ca. 1820, 21" h., pr. .................. **4,600**

**Lion,** recumbent animal facing viewer, undecorated, oval base, late 18th c., 4" l. (slight chips) ................................................ **863**

**Match/spill holder,** figural fox w/a swan in his mouth in foreground, colorfully decorated in yellow green, black & orange enamels, 9 3/4" h. (few spots of glaze wear) ............................................................ **672**

**Model of a castle,** squared form w/center tower, Gothic windows & red door flanked by green vines w/pink flowers, blue roofs, two chimneys, cole slaw decoration, 10 3/4" h. (small area of restoration to cole slaw decoration on tower).......... **476**

**Rabbit,** recumbent animal w/black sponge decoration, green & black line on base, 3 3/4" d., 2 1/2" h. (few small spots of wear) ............................................................ **476**

# STONEWARE

*Stoneware is essentially a vitreous pottery, impervious to water even in its unglazed state, that has been produced by potteries all over the world for centuries. Utilitarian wares such as crocks, jugs, churns and the like, were the most common productions in the numerous potteries that sprang into existence in the United States during the 19th century. These items were often enhanced by the application of a cobalt blue oxide decoration. In addition to the coarse, primarily salt-glazed stonewares, there are other categories of stoneware known by such special names as basalt, jasper and others.*

**Betty lamp stand,** waisted cylinder w/flared foot & rim, dark greenish brown glaze, attributed to Zanesville, 3 1/2" h. (minor chips & one large chip on lip)......... **$138**

**Bottle,** cylindrical body w/a conical shoulder tapering to a swelled lip w/cobalt blue trim, impressed mark "F. Gleason - 1853," 9 5/8" h. .............................................. **193**

**Bottle,** cylindrical body w/narrow shoulder tapering to wide, slightly flared neck, brown pebble glaze w/embossed eagle, impressed label "Vitreous Stone Bottle...American Bottle Co. Middlebury, O.," lime coated interior, 5 1/4" h................. **165**

**Bottle,** dark brown Albany slip w/matte finish, impressed label "S. Routson, Wooster, O.," 9 1/8" h. .................................. **605**

**Butter churn,** ovoid body tapering to a cylindrical neck w/molded rim & flanked by eared handles, slip-quilled cobalt blue large scrolling foliate cluster at the front, Worcester, Massachusetts, 19th c., 5 gal., 18 1/4" h. (minor chips, hairlines) ......... **460**

**Butter crock,** cylindrical w/molded rim, cobalt blue stenciled label "Hamilton & Jones, Greensboro, Pa.," 6 3/8" d., 5" h. (chips) ............................................................ **303**

*Stoneware Crock*

**Crock,** slightly tapering cylindrical body w/molded rim, slip-quilled cobalt blue floral decoration, zigzag blue lines & "L.R. Potts - Captina.O," 2 gal. (ILLUS.) ............. **413**

**Crock,** cylindrical w/molded rim, cobalt blue stenciled label arched at the top "Thomas Medford - Stoves - Queensware - etc. - Huntington, W. Va.," freehand blue squiggle band at top & plain band around base, late 19th c., 8 1/4" d., 6 3/4" h. .............................................................. **440**

**Crock,** cylindrical w/molded rim & applied eared handles, decorated w/a slip-quilled cobalt blue house flanked by fencing & a tree, impressed "J & E Norton, Bennington, Vermont," 1850-61, 7 1/4" h. (ILLUS.)...................................... **2,760**

*Bennington Stoneware Crock*

**Crock,** cylindrical w/molded rim & applied eared handles, slip-quilled cobalt blue stylized floral design & impressed label "Underwood & Tenney, Orange, Mass 2.," 9 1/2" h. (stains & chips) ........................ **275**

*Early Stoneware Crock*

**Crock,** ovoid w/wide cylindrical neck, applied loop handles, decorated w/a slip-quilled cobalt blue blooming flower on one side & a wave design on the other, mid-19th c., cracks, minor chips, 4 gal., 14 1/2" h. (ILLUS.) .............................. **173**

*Cylindrical Crock w/Swan Design*

**Crock,** cylindrical w/molded rim & eared handles, brushed blue swan design, ca. 1870, unsigned, attributed to Pottery Works, Little West 12th St., NY, 1 gal., 7 1/2" h. (ILLUS.).......................................... **1,045**

**Crock,** w/molded rim & eared handles, tornado design, "Ottman Bros. & Co., Fort Edward, NY," ca. 1870, 1 gal., 7 1/2" h. ...... **330**

**Crock,** cylindrical w/molded rim & eared handles, brushed cobalt blue flower design, "A.O. Whittemore, Havana, NY," ca. 1870, 2 gal., 8 1/2" h. (kiln burn/stack mark at base in making) ............. **165**

**Crock,** w/molded rim & eared handles, simple slip-quilled flower design & "2", "Geddes, NY," ca. 1860, 2 gal., 9" h. (rim chip & short through line on back, some design fry) ...................................... **143**

**Crock,** cylindrical w/molded rim & eared handles, slip-quilled cobalt blue chicken pecking corn on ground cover, chicken heading downhill, "New York Stoneware Co., Fort Edward, NY," ca. 1880, 2 gal., 9 1/2" h. ...................................... **1,210**

**Crock,** cylindrical w/molded rim & eared handles, slip-quilled cobalt blue decoration of a traveler viewing a direction sign reading "11 miles to Hartford," marked by Seymour Bosworth, Hartford, Connecticut, 3 gal., 10" h. (chips, prefiring dent) ............................................. **690**

**Crock,** cylindrical w/eared handles, brushed flower decoration w/signature, very early, ca. 1850, short-lived Buffalo maker, "P. Mugler & Co., Buffalo, NY," 3 gal., 11" h. (one very minor surface chip at base) ...................................... **330**

*"N. Clark & Co., Mt. Morris" Crock*

**Crock,** ovoid w/eared handles, brushed "3" & accent plume design, very uncommon maker, "N. Clark & Co., Mt. Morris," ca. 1840, few minor rim chips & minor interior lime staining, 3 gal., 12 1/2" h. (ILLUS.)...................................... **303**

**Crock,** cylindrical w/eared handles & slip-quilled cluster of grapes framed w/large leaves & vine, uncommon size for this potter, "W.A. MacQuoid & Co., Pottery Works Little West St.," NY," ca. 1865, 5 gal., 12" h. (hairline at ear on right side) ... **1,320**

*Rare Stoneware Flask*

**Flask,** salt-glazed flattened ovoid body tapering to a short neck w/molded mouth, the sides incised "New York July th4 (sic) 1789" & "I. McKINZIE (sic) July 1789," flanked by cobalt blue leafy branches, one w/flower, attributed to Henry Remmele, New York, ca. 1789 (ILLUS.)...................................................... **12,650**

**Inkwell,** figural bust of old woman wearing bonnet, tan glaze w/brown highlights, 2 1/4" h. (wear & small chips)............ **275**

**Jar,** ovoid body w/thick molded rim & applied eared handles, cobalt blue slip-quilled polka dot bird looking backwards, impressed label "W. Roberts, Binghamton, N.Y. 2," 9 1/2" h.................................... **688**

**Jar,** semi-ovoid body w/applied shoulder handles, cobalt blue brushed floral design w/tulip on one side & flowering tree on the other, impressed "S. Bell 1/1/2," 10 1/4" h. (chips) ........................... **1,210**

**Jar,** cov., eared handles, large signature design bird on plume, heavy cobalt blue w/filled body & leaves, "F.B. Norton & Co., Worcester, Mass.," ca. 1870, 2 gal., 11 1/2" h. (some design fry to thick blue).. **1,100**

**Jar,** semi-ovoid w/molded rim & eared handles, cobalt blue stenciled label "Knox, Haught & Co., Shinnston, W.Va." above leafy sprig w/further free-hand blue leafy bands around the top & "3" at the bottom, late 19th c., 3 gal., 12 3/4" h.............. **1,018**

**Jar,** slightly ovoid w/heavy molded rim & applied eared handles, stenciled cobalt blue front label for "Williams & Reppert, Greensboro, Pa." above a free-hand "3," free-hand blue bands at top & base, late 19th c., 3 gal., 14" h. (rim chips).................. **248**

**Jar,** swelled cylindrical form w/eared shoulder handles, cobalt blue brushed stylized tulip & impressed "T. Reed 3," Tuscarawas County, 14" h. (wear, short hairline & surface chips)............................. **605**

**Jar,** swelled cylindrical body w/heavy molded rim & eared handles, lengthy cobalt blue stenciled label "H.L. Van Matre & Co....Manu'fd by T.P. Reppert, Greensboro, Pa." below a large free-hand "3" near the rim, late 19th c., 3 gal., 14 1/4" h........................................................ **633**

**Jar,** cov., eared handles, unsigned, advertising, slip-quilled w/large dotted bird on top of flower, long tail & filled wing, impressed "Hiram Partridge & Son, #8 Court St. Indigo Paste," attributed to Crafts Factory, Whatley, Mass., ca. 1860, 4 gal., 15 1/2" h. (professional restorations to two tight lines extending from rim)....................................................... **798**

**Jug,** bold ovoid body tapering to a small short tooled neck, applied strap shoulder handle, impressed label "Charlestown," grey salt glaze w/olive bands, early 19th c., 10 1/4" h. (minor edge chips on base, surface chips)............................................... **220**

**Jug,** ovoid w/brushed flower design & very deeply incised w/double snake design, "H. & G. Nash, Utica, NY," ca. 1835, 1 gal., 11" h. extremely rare (minor glaze spider on back) ........................................ **1,000**

**Jug,** ovoid w/faint blue brushed flower design & blue accent at name, early mark, "S. Blair, Cortland," ca. 1830, 2 gal., 13" h. (over glazing & clay discoloration in making)........................................... **176**

**Jug,** bulbous ovoid body w/strap handle, incised figure of woman w/cross-hatched dress & chair, 13 1/2" h. ............................... **358**

*Jug w/Incised Cherries*

**Jug,** ovoid w/incised leaves & blue accented cluster of cherries, blue accents at handle, New York City origin, ca. 1820, unsigned, stack mark/kiln burn in making, 2 gal., 13 1/2" h., rare (ILLUS.) ............................. **880**

**Jug,** semi-ovoid w/cobalt blue signature sunflower design, well-proportioned, "John Burger, Rochester," ca. 1865, 2 gal., 13 1/2" h. (very tight spider line on side) ................................................................ **908**

**Jug,** semi-ovoid, w/slip-quilled ribbed & dotted flower design, very uncommon maker's mark, "E. Selby & Co., Hudson, NY," ca. 1850, 13 1/2" h. (some minor staining).......................................................... **275**

**Jug,** semi-ovoid w/small molded mouth & applied strap handle, cobalt blue brushed floral design & impressed label "Taunton, Mass. 2," 14 3/4" h. ..................... **220**

**Jug,** semi-ovoid w/thick blue slip-quilled tulip decoration, "Burger Brothers, Rochester, NY," ca. 1868, 2 gal., 15" h. ............... **495**

*Jug w/Wooden Stopper*

**Jug,** w/carved wooden stopper, semi-ovoid, cobalt blue leaf & vine design, top to bottom, "Edmands & Co.," ca. 1870, stone ping & long glaze spider lines on side, kiln burn on front in making, 3 gal., 15" h. (ILLUS.)............................................... **220**

**Jug,** tapering cylindrical body w/applied shoulder handles, cobalt blue brushed vintage below Xs & dots, impressed "4," 4 gal., 16" h. (hairlines) ................. **303**

**Jug,** ovoid, two handled, cobalt blue brushed tree design, "I. Seymour Troy Factory," very early maker's mark, ca. 1810, 4 gal., 18" h. (professional restoration to freeze cracks up from base in front) ......................... **715**

**Meat tenderizer,** dated 1877, original handle, 9" l. ...................... **110**

**Milk bowl,** deep slightly flaring cylindrical sides w/wide molded rim, cobalt blue stenciled label "A.P. Donaghho, Parkersburg, W.Va.," 12 3/4" d., 6 1/2" h. (professional repair, slight rim chip)............... **308**

**Pitcher,** 8 1/2" h., unglazed grey clay w/brushed brown Albany slip-quilled decoration, New Geneva Pottery, unsigned, ca. 1860, 1 qt.............. **853**

*Slip-quilled Ovoid Pitcher*

**Pitcher,** 9" h., ovoid, slip-quilled cobalt zigzag, lines & dot decoration, unsigned, probably Albany pottery, ca. 1850, surface chip at base in front and tight line at rim, on side, 1 gal. (ILLUS.) ............. **523**

**Pitcher,** 11" h., handled, w/three beautiful roses on front & blue accents around base and top, Pottery Works, Little West 12th Street NY, unsigned, ca. 1870, 1 gal. ............................ **2,530**

**Pitcher,** 11 1/2" h., bulbous ovoid body w/tall cylindrical neck w/pinched rim spout & applied strap handle, colbalt blue brushed foliage design, impressed label "M. & T. Miller, Newport, Pa." (chips) .......................... **1,540**

**Pitcher,** 13 1/4" h., bulbous ovoid body w/a tall cylindrical neck w/pinched rim spout, applied strap handle, brushed cobalt blue large blossoms, leafy twigs & impressed "2," 2 gal. .................. **880**

**Preserving jar,** cylindrical tapering slightly to a molded rim, cobalt blue stenciled label for A.P. Donaghho, Fredericktown, Pa. above a large spread-winged eagle, 9 1/2" h. ....................... **935**

**Preserving jar,** w/simple brushed plume design repeated four times around jar, unsigned, ca. 1860, 1 gal., 10" h. (some staining from use & surface wear at rim)...... **143**

**Preserving jar,** swelled cylindrical body w/cobalt blue stenciled flowers & "Jas Hamilton & Co., 2," 11" h. (crooked & hairlines) ...................... **248**

*Stenciled Preserving Jar*

**Preserving jar,** w/original lid, eared handles, stenciled sign of friendship - a handshake in thick blue, "Somerset Potters Works," ca. 1880, few rim chips & small tight line over right ear, 4 gal., 14 1/2" h. (ILLUS.)........................ **413**

**Stove leveler,** flaring pedestal below a wide cupped rim, brushed cobalt blue leaf bands, 4 1/2" h. (hairline, chips) ........... **440**

*Water Cooler with Bird on Plume*

**Water cooler,** cov., slip-quilled bird on plume design, body has blue accented deep incised lines, "New York Stoneware Co.," ca. 1870, 4 gal., 15 1/2" h. (ILLUS.)...................................... **1,155**

# TEPLITZ - AMPHORA

*In the late 19th and early 20th centuries numerous potteries operated in the vicinity of Teplitz in the Bohemian region of what was Austria but is now the Czech Republic. They included Amphora, RStK, Stellmacher, Ernst Wahliss, Paul Dachsel, Imperial and lesser-known potteries such as Johanne Maresh, Julius Dressler, Bernard Bloch and Heliosine.*

*The number of collectors in this category is growing while availability of better or rarer pieces is shrinking. Consequently, prices for all pieces are appreciating, while those for better and/or rarer pieces, including restored rare pieces, are soaring.*

*The price ranges presented here are retail. They presume mint or near mint condition or, in the case of very rare damaged pieces, proper restoration. They reflect such variables as rarity, design, quality of glaze, size, and the intangible "in-vogue factor."*

*They are the prices that knowledgeable sellers will charge and knowledgeable collectors will pay.*

*Teplitz-Amphora Marks*

**Bowl,** 10 1/4" w., 5 1/4" h., consisting of two wonderfully detailed high-glazed fish swimming around the perimeter, each executed in the Art Nouveau style w/flowing fins & tails, tentacles drip from their mouths, high-relief w/gold & reddish highlights, rare theme, impressed in ovals "Amphora" & "Austria" w/a crown ...................................................... **$3,500-4,000**

**Bowl,** 14 1/2" w., 4 3/8" h., an exotic Paul Dachsel design of calla lilies growing out of stems which originate at the bottom & gracefully extend around the sides to fully developed calla lilies at each end, in the center on each side are several 'jewels' w/abstract leaves of high-glazed green w/gold overtones, mottled texture w/'jeweled' greenish gold embellishments, stamped over glaze w/intertwined "PD - Turn-Teplitz," handwritten over glaze "0/45" ............................ **4,500-5,500**

*Bust of a Sultry Princess*

**Bust of a woman,** perhaps Sarah Bernhardt in the role of a sultry princess, magnificently finished w/plentiful gold & bronze glazes without excessive fussiness, mounted on a base featuring a maiden on a horse in a forest setting, the bust seemingly supported by stag horns protruding from each side, impressed "Amphora" & "Austria" in a lozenge w/a crown, 1431 & "A" in blue, 13 1/2" w., 18 1/4" h. (ILLUS.)........................... **3,000-4,000**

**Bust of a young woman,** a very young Art Nouveau maiden w/long flowing hair, elegant in her simplicity & beautiful, a 'clean' presentation without the excessive fussiness of many Teplitz busts, manufactured in varying tones, the most desirable being of the soft muted type, semi-rare, impressed "Amphora" in an oval, red "RStK Austria" stamp over the glaze, impressed illegible numbers & "246 - D202" printed in blue over the glaze, 15 1/4" h. ............................. **2,000-2,500**

*Bust of Richard Wagner*

**Bust of Richard Wagner,** the somber looking composer mounted on a pedestal emblazoned "Wagner" on the front, the head w/a beautiful soft flesh-toned Amphora glaze, the pedestal w/a shriveled tan & white glaze w/shades of olive green highlights, one of a rare series of composers, impressed "Amphora" & "Austria" in ovals w/a crown, a circle w/"Imperial Amphora" & "250 -1," 19 3/4" h. (ILLUS.)........................... **2,000-2,500**

**Candlestick,** rare Amphora piece w/many of their special characteristics including jewels, spider webs, butterflies & wonderful soft muted Amphora glazes w/reds, blues & gold, a large handle extends from near the top of the socket, four smaller handles extend up & outward from the base, eleven jewels of various sizes & colors, impressed "Amphora" in an oval & a crown & "28," 14" h. .............................................. **3,500-4,000**

**Centerpiece,** an expansive bowl w/a 'jeweled' effect along the rim, supported by two seated male lions w/fine details, a round base w/a 'jeweled' effect, the underside of the bowl suggests a tropical jungle, a better example of a design featuring animals supporting a bowl, multicolored 'jewels,' lion in a natural brownish glaze, stamped "Amphora - Made in

Czecho-slovakia" in an oval, "734 - 261" in black ink, 12" w., 9 5/8" h. ........... **1,000-1,500**

**Centerpiece,** figural, a long low oblong wave-molded bowl base centered by the large standing figure of an Art Nouveau maiden rising from the waves, wearing a diaphanous gown w/one arm on her hip & enclosing a cluster of blossoms, the other arm above her head supporting an oversized tulip or poppy blossom, pastel coloring, marked "Turn - Teplitz - Bohemia - E. Stellmacher," early 20th c., 28" h. (glaze repair in base) ..................... **1,238**

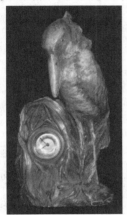

*Fantasy Stork Clock*

**Clock,** table model, a fantasy stork, similar to Martin Bros. birds, stands next to a clock dial framed by Art Nouveau-style leaves, fine detailing, soft brownish tan glaze, rare, raised rectangle w/factory logo & "AK-Turn," impressed "319," 13" h. (ILLUS.)................................. **3,500-4,000**

**Ewer,** an Art Nouveau design w/extraordinary detail combining a reticulated handle suggesting Paul Dachsel & varied circles on the body suggesting Gustav Klimt, a reticulated top, many 'jewels' of different colors & sizes randomly located over the body suggesting a spectrum of stars in the milky way, unusual gold bud spout, high-glazed blue garlands randomly draped about the body, heavy gold trim on the upper part of the handle, top & spout, a subdued gold trim extends down the handle to & around the bottom where there is an abstract tree design, very difficult to produce, rare, impressed "Amphora" in a circle & "40 -537," 14" h. ............................. **4,000-5,000**

**Ewer,** gilt-trimmed ivory ground w/enamel-decorated birds in the paneled sides, Teplitz mark, Czechoslovakia, early 20th c., 10 5/8" h. ................................................. **345**

**Figure group,** a small fine scenic figural group w/a rooster & hen perched side by side overlooking a pond, a small gold frog climbing into the pond, gives a barnyard feeling, soft muted shades of tan w/highlights of gold, a realistic theme &

valuable because of the small size, impressed "Amphora" in an oval & illegible numbers, 6 1/2" w., 7 3/4" h. ........ **750-1,000**

*Unique Figural Humidor*

**Humidor,** cov., figural, a fantasy piece featuring a large globe representing the world being shot from a tiny canon & caught by a jester lying on his back, the jester reputedly represents a prime minister of the time, a hat at the top of the globe forms the handles, soft muted grey Amphora glaze, rare, impressed "Amphora" in an oval & "4216," 14" w., 9" h. (ILLUS.)................................... **3,000-4,000**

**Humidor,** cov., figural, a massive Native American theme composed of three Indian heads w/high-glazed pink & green feathered headdresses, 'jeweled' & draping beaded necklaces on two, a draping necklace of animal teeth on the third, high-glaze green & cobalt blue finial handle on a decorative mixed glazed top, basic color of Campina brown w/much contrasting high-glaze in green, pink, brown & blue, rare, impressed ovals w/"Amphora" & "Austria," a crown & "Imperial - Amphora - Turn" in a circle & "S-1633-46," 10 1/2" h. ............... **2,000-3,000**

**Humidor,** cov., figural, an authentic looking Native American teepee w/an Indian in green feathered headdress, peering out of the bottom, finished in flat Campina brown w/contrasting highlights of high-glaze brown, light blue & cobalt blue, rare, impressed ovals w/"Amphora" & "Austria" & a crown, "Imperial Amphora Turn" in a circle & "S-1738-44," 10 1/2" h. ........................................ **2,000-2,500**

**Model of a bull,** proudly standing & of large stature, realistic colors, on a rocky slope w/his tail extending in an enclosed arch, realistic folds in his skin, prices vary depending on realism of the colors, the more realistic the better, impressed "Amphora" & "Austria" in ovals w/a crown, 18 1/2" l., 15" h. ................... **1,500-3,000**

**Pitcher,** 12" h., cov., footed, modeled as a stylized fish, ribbed body decorated w/gilt outlined yellow flowers, fish scale texture near rim, spout & lid form mouth w/splashes of water at top of lid, stamped "R S + K, Turn-Teplitz, made in Austria" (ILLUS. top next page).................. **316**

*Amphora Fish Pitcher*

**Plaque,** a large oval shape centered by an Art Nouveau lady in high-relief attired in a luminescent pink dress blowing a double-horned musical instrument. She is seated on a rocky ledge. The border of the plaque consists of garlands of flowers & leaves in high-relief, especially the buds, basic color of seafoam green, the surrounding florals in greens & tans, impressed "Ernst Wahliss," 17 x 19 1/2" ............................................. **1,400-1,800**

**Plaque,** terra cotta rectangular form depicting a very stylized beautifully coiffed Art Nouveau lady in profile in high-relief, her unique elegance suggesting a lady of high social stature, the borders are garlanded leaves & buds in high-relief, organic mossy shades of green, soft purples, tans & warm browns, impressed marks "Ernst Wahliss - Made in Austria - Turn - Wien - 157," 11 3/4 x 17" ...... **1,200-1,500**

**Tray,** a desk piece consisting of a ferocious eagle w/wings spread & beak open, staring at a snake draped over the inside & outside of the tray edge, finished in a soft bronzy cast w/contrasting deep brown, unusual theme, impressed signature of artist Klimt, also "BB" in a half circle w/dot in center & "N - 6244," stamped over glaze in black "Crownoakware - Teplitz - Austria," 15" l. overall w/eagle figure 5 1/2" h. ................................. **1,200-1,500**

**Vase,** 5 3/4" h., figural, elegantly executed Paul Dachsel creation w/a greenish cast & numerous vertical ribs extending up from the base, four intertwined gold-bodied dragonflies form a reticulated top, immediately below a series of smaller dragonflies encircle the vase, two multi-layered handles within handles complete the design, stamped over glaze w/intertwined "PD - Turn - Teplitz," impressed "104" ............................................... **2,000-2,500**

**Vase,** 6 3/8" h., spherical base tapering to tall slender cylindrical neck, shoulder loop handles, decorated w/bright yellow & orange irises & green leaves on a chocolate brown ground, by Stellmacher, impressed Stellmacher Teplitz mark, "2820," & "17" w/"2220" in brown slip on base ................................................. **110**

**Vase,** 6 1/2" h., simple ovoid body tapering to a small, flat mouth, painted w/the bust portrait of a young woman in a voluminous hood surmounted by a Byzantine crown surrounded by an aura, above a border of roses, the crown & roses w/applied glass bosses, glazed in shades of bronze, green, pink & black, printed mark "Turn - Teplitz - Bohemian - R. St. - Made in Austria" & impressed "Amphora 2037," ca. 1920 ...................... **1,840**

**Vase,** 7 1/2" h., a playful expression of Amphora w/a pink snake draped around the body of the bulbous vase & extending to the top where its delicate tongue protrudes, a subtle leaf design extends around the bottom, the pink color of the snake distinguishes this piece from more drab versions, impressed in ovals "Amphora" & "Austria," & "4114 - 52" ...................................... **1,500-1,800**

**Vase,** 8 3/4" h., figural, fantasy octopus piece w/head forming the top & mouth & the tentacles extending down around the sides, a dimpled bulbous form, finished in various glazes, the most desirable being a gold-finished octopus contrasting w/a matte background of various colors, impressed "Amphora" in an oval, a crown & "Imperial - Amphora - Turn" in a medallion & "4547 - 32" ................... **2,000-2,500**

**Vase,** 8 3/4" h., four-paneled high-shouldered squared form w/a front-faced Mucha-style Art Nouveau princess portrait, elaborate gold enameling against a landscape decorated w/blue & purple trees w/gold highlights above a base decorated w/Paul Dachsel-style abstract red flowers in a green base, impressed "Amphora" in oval & "579-40," red "RStK Austria" overglaze mark, artist mark "Fr" in gold overglaze ............................ **3,000-3,500**

**Vase,** 10 5/8" h., figural, in the form of a prancing male lion, snarling open mouth, standing on a broad base narrowing at the top, numerous concentric circles form bands around the top & bottom, lion reflects an iridescent gold, green & rose combination of color, body of base in metallic green w/undertones of blues & splotches of reds, impressed "Amphora" & "Austria" in oval, a crown & "500-52," handwritten in black ink over glaze "CB - 613417," estimated value without jewels, $1,500 to 2,000, value w/jewels ...... **2,500-3,500**

**Vase,** 11 1/4" h., figural, a rare Bernard Bloch Austrian Teplitz design consisting of a boy, half-human & half creature of the sea w/scaled fishtail & webbed hands emerging from the water, very expressive face, three beautifully detailed fish in semi-relief swimming about the body of the vase, designed by Schwarz w/name on the side, soft sea green & golden highlights, impressed "BB" & dot in a circle & "P - 3776" ... **1,500-2,000**

**Vase,** 11 1/4" h., figural, an open-mouthed fish w/well-defined teeth swimming around the chimney of the base w/a finely executed tail fin extending up & beyond the vase, a realistic representation produced in various color tones which will determine the price, one w/brighter colors brings more, semi-rare, impressed "Amphora" in an oval, & "4112 - 10".................................... **2,000-3,000**

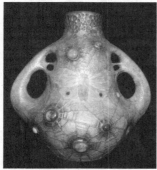

*Ornate Jeweled Art Nouveau Vase*

**Vase,** 11 1/4" h., tapering lobed ovoid form of exceptional Art Nouveau design w/numerous 'jewels,' spider webs & two butterflies w/heavy pierced extended handles suggesting a larger butterfly, 17 'jewels' in varying sizes & colors, red abstract circles drape from the gold-edged top, soft muted tan, red, blue & green glazes w/gold iridescence, impressed "Amphora" & "Austria" in ovals, a crown & "8551 -42," red "RStK Austria" overglaze mark (ILLUS.).... **4,000-5,000**

**Vase,** 11 1/2" h., wicker basket-form w/round loop handles extending up from the rim, large relief-molded iridescent white blossoms, rose leaves & green buds on front w/rose band at rim & base, shaded tan ground w/touches of fired-on gold, impressed marks & "Austria Amphora - 115 - 37" .................................... **550**

**Vase,** 12" h., figural, three standing cockatoos, fully feathered, extend around the body of the vase, their plumes rising over the rim, very detailed w/glossy glaze, subtle color mix of blues, greens & tans w/brown streaks, semi-rare, impressed "Amphora" & "Austria" in ovals, a crown & Imperial circle & "11986 - 56".............................................. **1,500-2,000**

**Vase,** 12 3/4" h., elegant form consisting of four beautifully veined tall leaves forming the funnel of the vase w/the stem of each leaf forming a handle extending into the bottom, each stem issues an additional flat leaf extending across the bottom, leaves finished in a mottled orange w/touches of greens & yellows w/gold overtones, although marked by Ernst Wahliss the design indicates the work of Paul Dachsel who worked at various Amphora factories, rare, stamped over glaze "EW" red mark, impressed "9491," "9786a - 10" in ink over the glaze................................. **3,000-3,500**

**Vase,** 13" h., figural, an exceptional form w/three cherubic children in great detail playing around the basket-like body, the child at the top reaching down in, another child reaching up to the top w/one hand & the third child moving in the direction of the reaching child, w/their arms extended the children reach from the base to the rim & in good proportion, unlike most similar vases there are no added florals or fruits, impressed "Amphora" & "Austria" in oval, a crown & "1397 - 41"..................................... **1,200-1,500**

*Dachsel "Enchanted Forest" Vase*

**Vase,** 13" h., wide-shouldered tapering cylindrical body, a fantasy design by Paul Dachsel worthy of the description "enchanted forest," the design consists of slender molded abstract trees extending from the narrow base to the bulbous top, lovely heart-shaped leaves extend in clusters from the various branches, trees in muted green, the leaves in pearlized off-white w/gold framing, the symbolic sky in rich red extending between the trees from the bottom to the top, rare, intertwined "PD" mark rubbed off (ILLUS.)..................................... **5,500-6,500**

**Vase,** 13 1/8" h., a special creation by Paul Dachsel, perhaps a one-of-a-kind, it may be a commemorative piece honoring an early 20th c. polar expedition, a h.p. polar bear shown standing on a snowy surface, his body outlined by puffy clouds in a blue sky, a soft lustre to the sky, snow & bear w/subtle pink iridescence, below the snow a ring of blue Dachsel circles w/gold inserts extends around the body, a similar design above the sky w/a reddish gold metallic glaze, value hard to estimate to the ultimate Paul Dachsel collectors, stamped over glaze w/intertwined "PD - Turn Teplitz"... **6,000+**

**Vase,** 13 1/2" h., an Amphora creation of Julius Dressler, Arts & Crafts style, mattte green w/majolica highlights, four panels w/the same geometric pattern in each, this type increasing in interest to collectors, marked w/a raised "JBK" & impressed "Austria - 1194".............. **1,000-1,500**

**Vase,** 14" h., figural, a fantasy dragon featuring two flaring wings, one extending practically from the top to the bottom of the body, the other well above & beyond the rim, creature w/a convoluted tail, spine & teeth, the head w/open mouth positioned at top of the vase, bluish green gold iridescence, glazes vary from a flat tan to a variety of very iridescent colors, made in 14" & 17" size, impressed "Amphora" in oval, illegible numbers, large size w/better glazes, $6,500, 14" size w/drab glazes ................. **3,000**

**Vase,** 15 1/2" h., cascades of golden grapes stream down on all sides between four funnel necks, the central funnel projecting skyward, this funnel design suggests Paul Dachsel, especially desirable because the piece is viewable from any angle, metallic purplish glaze w/metallic gold highlights containing numerous little gold circles, marked "Amphora" & "Austria" in ovals, a crown & "3680" ............................... **1,500-2,000**

**Vase,** 15 3/4" h., an Egyptian theme consisting of a vertical mummy case, probably representing King Tut's, surrounded by kneeling slaves, a blue bulbous bottom & narrow slender neck, geometric decorations around top & base, a semi-rare Czech piece, marked in blue stamped underglaze "Amphora - Made in Czecho-slovakia" in an oval, illegible marks w/one in a blue circle w/a logo & another in a red circle.................... **1,000-1,500**

**Vase,** 16" h., bulbous ovoid body tapering to a slender flaring lobed reticulated neck, outswept loop handles at the lower sides, shimmering burnished gold ground w/red touches, adorned randomly w/twenty large variously colored 'jewels,' one handle in red, the other in gold, overall molded vertical ribbing, rare form, impressed "Amphora" in an oval, crown, old "RStK" mark & "3349" ... **7,500-8,000**

**Vase,** 18 1/2" h., slightly flaring cylindrical body w/a bulbous shoulder tapering to a mouth mounted w/a gilt-bronze leaf-cast neck & issuing slender serpentine handles attached to the sides, fitted on a gilt-bronze ring foot w/four flared leaves, the body covered in a light blue, green & ivory crystalline glaze dripping down the buff-colored ground, partial impressed mark "Borsi - Teplitz," base drilled, ca. 1900 ........................................................ **1,150**

**Vase,** 19 3/4" h., figural, a lively form w/two squirrels, one at the base & one at the top, each eagerly pursuing the other w/ears raised in excitement, various finishes, a rare form, impressed & raised "EST" monogram, "Stellmacher - Teplitz" stamped in red, an impressed heart .............................................. **3,500-4,500**

**Vase,** 20" h., footed tall wide cylindrical body w/squatty bulbous base & closed-in rim, mottled mauve glaze w/relief-molded dragon figure in yellow, tan & gilt glaze conforming entirely around body & rim, minor restorations to chips, impressed "AMPHORA" in a lozenge, a crown & "4548 50" (ILLUS. below) .......... **5,750**

*Amphora Dragon Vase*

**Vase,** 20" h., tall slightly tapering cylindrical form w/a widely flared base, boldly molded pine cones hang around the top section from symbolic green trees divided by red indented vertical panels, a Paul Dachsel Secessionist design, rare, stamped over the glaze w/intertwined "PD - Turn - Teplitz" & impressed "2038 - 6" .................................................... **7,000-8,000**

**Vase,** 20 1/4" h., elegant tall form featuring two sunbursts, front & back, two gold handles, reticulated gold circles at the top & several elongated gold 'jewels' rising from the sunbursts, a subtle bluish white w/soft gold tones reflecting the sunbursts, free-form lines in soft green highlighted w/gold extending from the bottom to the top & suggests a randomly built stone wall, rare form, impressed "Amphora" & "Austria" in ovals, a crown, "Imperial" in a circle & "12081 -47" .. **3,000-4,000**

*Massive Amphora Mermaid Vase*

**Vase,** 21" h., 18" w., figural, a wide squatty bulbous base centered by a tall neck, Art Nouveau style w/a mermaid clinging to the top rim, her well-defined body extends down along the side, applied berries, vines & leaves complete the decoration, finished in a matte tan w/gold wash & highlights, bluish berries, red stems, greenish red leaves & a high-glazed gold rim, important & very rare, would be rare even without the applied foliage, impressed "Amphora" in oval & "07 - 7 - 3" (ILLUS.) ........................ **8,000-10,000**

**Vase,** 21 1/2" h., portrait-type, a very large profiled Sarah Bernhardt portrait inspired by Gustav Klimt featuring a majestic bird headdress w/eleven 'jewels' of various sizes & colors, the figure w/long flowing hair streaming from under the headdress to her shoulders, below her neck is a jeweled butterfly, on one side a golden sun rises from the ocean emitting numerous golden rays, bluish green metallic background w/heavy gold detail, impressed "Amphora" & "Austria" in a lozenge, a crown & "02047 - 28" .................................................. **14,000-16,000**

*Somber, Eerie Dragon Vase*

**Vase,** 22" h., figural, a somber swampy-green dragon encircles the tall body several times, his wings spread like a cobra's hood, leering down hungrily at a frog restrained by his tail at the base, this piece can be found finished in other colors including red & tan, this eerie somber look compensates for what the glaze may lack, impressed "Amphora" & "Austria" in ovals, a crown & "4536 - 6" (ILLUS.) .......................................... **4,000-5,000**

**Vase,** 22 1/2" h., figural, an extraordinary dragon w/bat-like wings entwines around the body, numerous golden drops dripping from its open fanged mouth, Art Nouveau stems rise from the bottom to form pink button blossoms, the dragon shows a glitter of silver & gold,

impressed "Amphora" in an oval & "8762 - 52" ........................................ **9,000-9,500**

# TORQUAY POTTERY

TORQUAY
POTTERY

HELE CROSS
POTTERY
TORQUAY

*Torquay Pottery Marks*

In the second half of the 19th century several art potteries were established in the South Devon region of England to take advantage of a belt of fine red clay. The coastal town of Torquay gives its name to this range of wares which often featured incised sgraffito decoration or colorful country-style decoration with mottos.

The most notable potteries operating in the Torquay area were the Watcombe Pottery, The Torquay Terra-cotta Company and the Aller Vale Art Pottery, which merged with Watcombe Pottery in 1901 and continued production until 1962. Other firms whose wares are collectible include Longpark Pottery and The Devonmoor Art Pottery.

Early wares feature unglazed terra cotta items in the Victorian taste including classical busts, statuary and vases and some painted and glazed wares including examples with a celeste blue interior or highlights. In addition to sgraffito designs other decorations included flowers, Barbotine glazes, Devon pixies framed in leafy scrolls and grotesque figures of cats, dogs and other fanciful animals produced in the 1890s.

The dozen or so potteries flourishing in the region at the turn of the 20th century introduced their most popular product, motto wares, which became the bread and butter line of the local industry. The most popular patterns in this line included Cottage, Black and Colored Cockerels and Scandy, based on Scandinavian rosemaling designs. Most of the mottoes were written in English with a few in Welsh. On early examples the sayings were often in Devonian dialect. These motto wares were sold for years at area seaside resorts and other tourist areas with some pieces exported to Australia, Canada and, to a lesser extent, the U.S.A. In addition to standard size tablewares and novelties some miniatures and even oversized pieces were offered.

Production at the potteries stopped during World War II and some of the plants were destroyed in enemy raids. The Watcombe Pottery became Royal Watcombe after the war and Longpark also started up again, but produced simpler patterns. The Dartmouth Pottery started in 1947 and produced cottages similar to those made at Watcombe and also developed a line of figural animals, banks and novelty jugs. The Babbacombe Pottery (1950-59) and St. Marychurch Pottery (ca. 1962-69) were the last two firms to turn out motto wares but these *later designs were painted on and the pieces were lighter in color with less detailing.*

Many books on the various potteries are available and information can be obtained from the products manager of the North American Torquay Society.

**Ashtray,** Motto Ware, Colored Cockerel patt., "A place for ashes," Longpark, 1910, 3 1/2" d. .............................................. **$56**

**Ashtray,** Motto Ware, Cottage patt., "Who burnt the Tablecloth," Royal Watcombe, 3" d. ...................................................................... **35**

**Bank,** figural, model of an owl in brown, nice detailing, Dartmouth, 1960s, 8" h. .......... **63**

**Basket,** B2 Scroll patt., colored scrolls on green, painted by H.M. Exeter, 1930, 3 1/2" h. ............................................................... **113**

**Basket,** hanging-type, Persian patt., decorated overall & on the base, Aller Vale white clay, rare, ca. 1890s, unmarked, 2 5/8" h.(small restoration) ....................... **167**

**Basket,** Motto Ware, Colored Cockerel patt., twisted handle, "No life can be dreary when work's a delight," Watcombe, ca. 1901-20 mark, 3 1/4" h. ....... **129**

**Bowl,** 4 3/8" d., two-handled, Ladybird (Bug) patt., ladybugs in a cream band on a blue ground, Watcombe, ca. 1901-20 mark ................................................................ **129**

**Bowl,** 4 3/8" h., four-handled, Motto Ware, Windmill patt., "Despise school and remain a fool," Crown Dorset Pottery, ca. 1910 ........................................... **126**

**Bowl,** 8" d., advertising-type, Kingfisher patt., "National Association of Master Bakers, Confectioners & Caterers Conference - Torquay 1931" on blue, Watcombe ................................................................ **239**

**Butter tub,** two-handled, Motto Ware, Cottage patt., "Du'ee 'ave zum butter," Watcombe, ca. 1925-35, 4 3/4" w. ................. **90**

*Miniature Motto Ware Pieces*

**Candlestick,** miniature, Motto Ware, Scandy patt., "The night is long that never finds a day," Longpark, ca. 1910, expert restoration, 2 1/2" h. (ILLUS. left) ...... **110**

**Candlestick,** Motto Ware, Colored Cockerel patt., "He who would thrive must rise at five," Longpark Torquay, ca. 1903-09, 8" h. ......................................................................... **156**

**Candy bowl,** cov., advertising-type, "The Stationers Association Conference - Torquay 1930," decoration of an inkwell & quill pen in white on blue, Longpark, 6 1/2" h. .................................................................. **222**

**Cauldron pot,** Motto Ware, Scandy patt., "Well paid, well satisfied," Watcomb, 2 1/2" h. ................................................................. **64**

**Chamberstick,** Motto Ware, Cottage patt., "Many are called but few get up," Watcombe Torquay impressed mark, ca. 1910-27, 2 3/4" h. ............................................ **115**

**Chamberstick,** Motto Ware, Scandy patt., "'Tis the mind that makes the body rich - Shakespeare, Taming of the Shrew," Aller Vale, ca. 1915, 5 1/4" h. ......................... **123**

**Cheese dish,** cov., Motto Ware, Cottage patt., "Don't worry and get wrinkles - Smile and have dimples," also "Cheese," Watcombe, ca. 1930, 6 1/2" d. base, 3 3/4" h. ............................................................. **150**

**Coaster,** advertising-type, "Camwal Table Waters," Watcombe, 1920, 3 7/8" d. ............ **116**

**Coffeepot,** cov., Motto Ware, Cottage patt., "Sow a character, reap a destiny," Watcombe, 8 3/4" h. .......................................... **218**

**Coffeepot,** cov., Motto Ware, Sailboat patt., "Time and tide for no man bide," Longpark, 6 1/4" h. .......................................... **89**

*Scandy Motto Ware Coffeepot*

**Coffeepot,** cov., Motto Ware, Scandy patt., "Gude things be scarce, take care of me," Watcombe, 7" h. (ILLUS.) ................... **156**

**Condiment pot,** side handle, Motto Ware, Cottage patt., "Better tae sit still than rise tae fall," Aller Vale, ca. 1902-24, 2 1/4" h. .................................................................. **89**

**Condiment pot,** side-handled, Motto Ware, Cottage patt., "Waste not, Want not," Longpark Torquay England mark, ca. 1930s, 2 1/4" h. .......................................... **65**

**Condiment set:** salt & pepper shakers, cov. mustard pot & center-handled holder; Motto Ware, Cottage patt., mottos on all pieces except the holder, Watcombe, ca. 1920, the set ...................... **167**

**Creamer,** Motto Ware, Cottage patt., "Hasty climbers have sudden falls," Watcombe, 2 1/4" h. .......................................... **45**

**Creamer,** Motto Ware, Cottage patt., "There's a time for all things," Watcombe, 2 1/2" h. ............................................... **39**

**Creamer,** souvenir, Heather patt., "Hastings," white heather on mauve ground, 3 1/4" h. .......................................................... **62**

**Crocus vase,** Motto Ware, Cottage patt., spherical body, "Gather the roses while

ye may" & "Old time is still a flying,"
3" d., 3 3/4" h. .............................................. **95**

*Torquay Cup & Saucer*

**Cup & saucer,** Motto Ware, Cottage patt.,
footed flaring cylindrical cup, inscribed
"Have another cup full," saucer 5 3/8" d.,
cup 3 3/8" d., 3" h. (ILLUS.) ......................... **75**
**Dish,** figural fish, Motto Ware, Colored
Cockerel patt., "A pla(i)ce for ashes,"
Longpark        Torquay, ca.        1904-18,
3 3/4 x 5 3/4" ................................................ **95**
**Dish,** figural fish, Motto Ware, Cottage
patt.,      "A      pla(i)ce      for      ashes,"
Longpark, ca. 1930s, 3 3/4 x 5 1/2" ............... **98**
**Dish,** figural fish, Motto Ware, Sailboat
patt., "Time and tide for no man bide,"
3 1/2 x 5 1/2" ................................................ **72**
**Dish,** figural fish, two-eyed, Motto Ware,
Black Cockerel patt., "A pla(i)ce for
ashes,"        Watcombe, ca.        1920,
3 1/4 x 5 1/4" ................................................ **87**
**Dresser tray,** Motto Ware, Colored Cock-
erel patt., "A place for everything," Longpark Torquay, ca. 1903-09, uncommon,
7 1/2 x 10 3/4" .............................................. **360**
**Dresser tray,** Motto Ware, Scandy patt., "A
place     for     Everything,"     Watcombe
Torquay, ca. 1920s, 7 3/8 x 10 1/2" ............ **234**
**Egg cup,** Motto Ware, Black Cockerel patt.,
"Fresh    today"    Longpark    Tormohun
ware, ca. 1910 .............................................. **67**

*Torquay Footed Egg Cup*

**Egg cup,** footed, Motto Ware, Cottage
patt., "Laid to day," 3 1/4" h., 3 1/2" d.
(ILLUS.) ......................................................... **45**
**Ewer,** cov., Floral patt., white floral spray
on front & reverse on a tan ground, silver
plated cover w/"J.A.R." silversmith's
mark, Watcombe, ca. 1890s, 8 1/2" h. ......... **310**

**Ewer,** Floral patt., fuschia on cream
ground, celeste blue trim, early Watcombe porcelain mark, ca. 1884-1901,
4 1/2" h. ........................................................ **156**

*Scandy Pattern Hatpin Holder*

**Hatpin holder,** footed dished base centered by hourglass-shaped holder, Motto
Ware, Scandy patt., "A present from Arn-
side," Longpark Torquay, ca. 1910-20,
4 5/8" h. (ILLUS.) ........................................... **133**

*Cottage Pattern Hot Water Pot*

**Hot water or coffeepot,** cov., bulbous
ovoid body tapering to a flaring neck
w/rim spout, inset cover w/knob finial,
Motto Ware, Cottage patt., "Never put off
till tomorrow what can be done today -
Newquay," Watcombe, 1925-35 mark,
6" h. (ILLUS.) ................................................ **137**
**Hot water or coffeepot,** cov., Motto Ware,
"Life is mostly froth and bubble...,"
scarce motto, Watcombe, ca. 1925-35
mark, 7 3/4" h. ............................................... **202**
**Hot water pot,** cov., Motto Ware, Colored
Cockerel patt., "Two men look through
prison bars - One sees the mud and the
other the stars," Longpark, ca. 1910-20,
5 1/2" h. ......................................................... **169**
**Hot water pot,** cov., Motto Ware, Scandy
patt., "To err is human, to forgive divine,"
Watcombe Torquay, ca. 1910-27 mark,
6" h. ............................................................... **127**
**Inkwell,** Motto Ware, Shamrock patt., "The
chosen leaf of Bard and Chief," Aller
Vale, ca. 1902-10 mark, 3" h. ....................... **105**
**Jardiniere,** B2 Scroll patt., colored scrolls
on a green ground, H.M. Exeter
Pottery, ca. 1910, 5 1/2" h. ........................... **285**

Jardiniere, faience, Lantern patt., a lantern in branches on blue ground, Barton Pottery mark, ca. 1920s, small, 3 1/2" h. ............ **84**

Jardiniere, Motto Ware, Passion Flower patt., flowers on a blue ground, motto in cream, "For every evil under the sun...," unmarked, Exeter, ca. 1925, 6 1/4" h. .......... **385**

Model of a frying pan, Motto Ware, Black Cockerel patt., "I cum frum Totnes - Waste not, want not," Torquay Pottery Co., ca. 1918-24, 4 1/8" l. plus handle .......... **69**

Mug, child's, Motto Ware, Cottage patt., "Mary had a little lamb," St. Marychurch, 1960s, 3" h. ...................................................... **68**

Mug, child's, Motto Ware, Scandy patt., "Hold me tight and don't be clumsy or you'll break this mug from Romsey," Watcombe, ca. 1902-15, 2 1/4" h. .................. **80**

Mustard pot, cov., Motto Ware, Cottage patt., w/"Lands End" on front & "I improve everything" on back, 2 1/4" d., 2 3/4" h. ....................................................... **55**

Pitcher, 1 3/4" h., miniature, Motto Ware, Cottage patt., "Little Jack Horner - Runswick Bay" (ILLUS. right w/candlestick) ......... **65**

Pitcher, 3 5/8" h., advertising-type, Cottage patt., "The Oldest Chemist Shoppe in England - Knaresborough," Royal Watcombe, ca. 1950 ..................................... **50**

Pitcher, 3 3/4" h., Motto Ware, Cottage patt., "Fresh from the cow," Watcombe, ca. 1930 ..................................... **45**

Pitcher, 4 1/8" h., Motto Ware, Colored Cockerel patt., "Success comes not by wishing but hard work bravely done," Aller Vale, ca. 1891-1901 ............................ **133**

Pitcher, 4 1/8" h., Shakespeare's House patt., faience, rendering of Shakespeare's House w/green sprayed borders, Watcombe, ca. 1910-20 ............................... **96**

*Torquay Motto Ware Pitcher*

Pitcher, 5 1/4" h., 4 1/2" d., Motto Ware, Cottage patt., spherical base tapering slightly to wide cylindrical neck, "Help yourself don't be shy" (ILLUS.) ................... **100**

Pitcher, 5 1/2" h., pierced rim, handle passes through, Motto Ware, Scandy patt., "If it be so so it is you know...," Aller Vale, ca. 1900 ..................................... **185**

Pitcher, 6 1/4" h., artware, Sailboats patt., boats on aqua blue water, Watcombe, ca. 1920s ............................... **123**

Pitcher, 6 1/2" h., Motto Ware, Cottage patt., "Little duties still put off may end in never done," Watcombe, ca. 1930 .............. **142**

*Scandy Pattern Motto Ware Pitcher*

Pitcher, 7 3/4" h., Motto Ware, Scandy patt., "Little duties still put off may end in never done...," Aller Vale, ca. 1891-1910 (ILLUS.) ....................................................... **199**

Plate, 4 1/4" d., miniature doll size, Motto Ware, Scandy patt., "Gude folks are scarce take care of me," colored border, Longpark, ca. 1920 ........................................ **75**

Plate, 4 3/8" d., miniature doll size, Motto Ware, Cottage patt., "A rolling stone gathers no moss," Royal Watcombe, ca. 1950 ............................................................... **65**

Plate, 4 3/8" d., miniature doll size, Motto Ware, Cottage patt., "Good examples are the best sermons," Royal Watcombe, ca. 1950 ..................................... **65**

Plate, 5" d., Motto Ware, Scandy patt., "Do not burden today's strength...," Aller Vale ............................................................... **68**

*Black Cockerel Motto Plate*

Plate, 6" d., Motto Ware, Black Cockerel patt., "Good morning," Aller Vale, 1891-1910 (ILLUS.) ................................................ **125**

Plate, 6 1/4" d., Motto Ware, Cottage patt., "Enough's as good as a feast," Royal Watcombe ......................................................... **60**

Plate, 6 1/2" d., Motto Ware, Sailboat patt., "Gather the roses while ye may...," Watcombe ............................................................. **69**

**Plate,** 7 1/4" d., Motto Ware, Cottage patt., "Be a little deaf and blind, Happiness you'll always find," Watcombe DMW mark, ca. 1918-27 .......................................... **80**

**Plate,** 7 1/4" d., Motto Ware, Scandy patt., "A fellow feeling makes us wondrous kind...," Aller Vale, ca. 1891-1902 mark ....... **120**

**Plate,** 8 1/8" d., Motto Ware, Scandy patt., "As I was going to St. Ives - I met a man with seven wives...," long motto, Watcombe, ca. 1925-35 .............................. **235**

**Plate,** 8 1/2" d., Motto Ware, Cottage patt., "Some hae meat and canna eat...," Scottish prayer motto, Watcombe DMW mark, ca. 1918-27 .......................................... **96**

*Motto Ware Puzzle Jug*

**Puzzle jug,** Motto Ware, Colored Cockerel patt., "May you find that all life's troubles after all are only bubbles," Longpark Tormohun ware, ca. 1910, 4" h. (ILLUS.) .......... **182**

**Puzzle jug,** Motto Ware, Scandy patt., "Within this jug there is good liquor...," Aller Vale, ca. 1910, 4 1/2" h. ....................... **175**

**Salt & pepper shakers,** Motto Ware, Cottage patt., "Waste not, want not" & "A necessity of life," Watcombe, 1920s, 2 3/4" h., pr. ................................................... **55**

*Torquay Scent Bottles*

**Scent bottle,** Devon Violets patt., unmarked Longpark, ca. 1930, 2 1/4" h. (ILLUS. left) ..................................................... **32**

**Scent bottle,** handled, Devon Violets patt., white clay, motto painted on, marked "Made in Great Britain," 1960s, 2 3/4" h. ........ **30**

**Scent bottle,** marked "Genuine Devon Lavender," small silver paper label under name, Watcombe - Made in England mark, ca. 1930 (ILLUS. right) ........................ **62**

**Scent bottle,** Somerset Violets patt., inkwell-shaped, Longpark, ca. 1930, 2"h. ............ **54**

**Scent bottle w/old brass crown stopper,** Devon Violets patt., "Torquay" under green band, Longpark, ca. 1930, 4 1/2" h. (ILLUS. center) ................................ **98**

**Sugar bowl,** cov., Motto Ware, Ivy patt., "Sweeten for yourself," Aller Vale, ca. 1910, 3 1/4" h. ................................................ **62**

**Sugar bowl,** open, round tapering sides, Mottto Ware, Black Cockerel patt., "Be aisy with tha sugar," 3 1/4" d., 1 3/4" h. (ILLUS.) ....................................................... **65**

*Torquay Sugar Bowl*

**Sugar bowl,** open, pedestal base, Motto Ware, Black Cockerel patt., "Be aisy with tha sugar," 5 1/4" d., 4 1/4" h. (ILLUS.) .......... **85**

**Supper dish,** three-part w/handle, Cottage patt., marked "Butter - Cheese - Biscuits," Watcombe Torquay, ca. 1930, 8 x 8 1/2" ....................................................... **165**

**Supper dish,** three-part w/handle, Scandy patt., marked "Jam - Butter - Cream," Watcombe Torquay, ca. 1901-20, 8 x 9" ...... **139**

**Tankard,** Motto Ware, Cottage patt., "I have a good reason for drinking...," Royal Watcombe, ca. 1950, 3 1/2" h. ............. **68**

**Tankard,** Motto Ware, Cottage patt., "To thine own self be true," Dartmouth Pottery, 5" h. ....................................................... **69**

**Tankard,** Motto Ware, Scandy patt., "Every blade of grass...," Aller Vale, ca. 1910, 4" h. ......................................................... **78**

**Teapot,** cov., miniature, Motto Ware, Scandy patt., "Droon yer sorrows in a cup a Tay," Longpark Torquay, ca. 1918-30, 2 3/4" h. (ILLUS. center w/candlestick) ...................................................... **124**

**Teapot,** cov., miniature, nursery rhyme & souvenir, Cottage patt., "Mary had a little lamb..." & "Kents Cavern," Royal Watcombe, 3 3/8" h. ......................................... **153**

*Molded Cottage Teapot*

**Teapot,** cov., Molded Cottage patt., cottage-shaped, inscribed "Old Uncle - Tom Cobley's - Cottage - Widdecombe," Torquay Pottery Co., ca. 1920, 4 7/8" h. (ILLUS.)...................................................... **139**

**Teapot,** cov., Motto Ware, Black Cockerel patt., "Du'ee drink a cup a Tay," Longpark, ca. 1918-30, overall 7 1/2" l., 4 5/8" h....................................................... **124**

*Cottage Pattern Motto Teapot*

**Teapot,** cov., Motto Ware, Cottage patt., "Fair is he that comes but fairer he that brings," Made in England - Watcombe mark, ca. 1930s, overall 7 1/4" l., 4 1/4" h. (ILLUS.)............................................ **89**

**Teapot,** cov., bulbous body, Motto Ware, Cottage patt., "From Torquay" on front & "Du'ee Drink a cup a tay," 4 1/2" d., 3 3/4" h. ...................................................... **110**

**Toast rack,** Motto Ware, Cottage patt., center handle, three tines, "Take a little toast," Watcombe, ca. 1920, 3 1/2" h. .......... **129**

**Trivet,** round, Motto Ware, Cottage patt., "Except the kettle boiling B Filling the tpot spoils the T" & "Mablethorpe," 5 1/2" d. ...................................................... **55**

**Vase,** 1 7/8" h., miniature, Motto Ware, Scandy patt., "Niver say die - Up man and try," Longpark .......................................... **65**

**Vase,** 2" h., miniature, tri-corner pinched top, blue flower on white clay ground, Aller Vale, ca. 1900 ....................................... **80**

**Vase,** 2 1/4" h., miniature, Motto Ware, Scandy patt., "Du'ee think tis yer dooty? Then du et," Longpark, ca. 1910 ................. **109**

**Vase,** 2 3/4" h., Motto Ware, Rose patt., "It's a good horse that never stumbles," ca. 1930...................................... **67**

**Vase,** 3 5/8" h., Motto Ware, Colored Cockerel patt., "We're not the only pebbles on the beach," Longpark Torquay, ca. 1910-24 .................................................. **109**

**Vase,** 4 1/2" h., D1 Scroll patt., colored scrolls on a blue ground, Aller Vale, rare ..... **164**

**Vase,** 4 1/2" h., faience, Tintern Abbey patt., abbey ruins in a landscape, cloud-filled sky, Longpark, ca. 1910....................... **149**

**Vase,** 4 5/8" h., faience, waisted shape w/bulbed top pierced w/holes, Stork patt., white & black stock against green ground w/reeds, Crown Dorset, ca. 1910 (ILLUS.)............................................ **219**

**Vase,** 5 7/8" h., Butterflies patt., spherical body w/four flared necks at top, two butterflies on a streaky mauve ground, Longpark, ca. 1904-18 ............................... **142**

*Stork Pattern Vase*

**Vase,** 7 1/2" h., two-handled, Motto Ware, Scandy patt., "Take fortune as you find her...," H.M. Exeter, ca. 1920 (professional restoration)........................................ **154**

*Longpark Scroll Pattern Vase*

**Vase,** 7 3/4" h., footed tapering cylindrical form, B2 Scroll patt., colored scrolls on a dark green ground, Longpark, ca. 1909 (ILLUS.)......................................................... **143**

**Vase,** 8" h., artware, Wild Rose patt., roses on a black lattice, cream ground, Watcombe Pottery, ca. 1901-20 mark ............... **194**

## UHL POTTERY

*Original production of utilitarian wares began at Evansville, Indiana in the 1850s and consisted mostly of jugs, jars, crocks and pieces for food preparation and preservation. In 1909, production was moved to Huntingburg, Indiana where a more extensive variety of items was eventually produced including many novelty and advertising items that have become highly collectible. Following labor difficulties, the Uhl Pottery closed in 1944.*

*Unless it is marked or stamped, Uhl is difficult to identify except by someone with considerable experience. Marked pieces can have several styles of ink stamps and/or an incised number under glaze on the bottom. These numbers are die-cut and impressed in the glazed bottom. Some original molds were acquired by other potteries. Some production does exist and should not be considered as Uhl. These may have numbers inscribed by hand with a stylus and are usually not glazed on the bottom.*

Many examples have no mark or stamp and may not be bottom-glazed. This is especially true of many of the miniature pieces. If a piece has a 'Meier's Wine' paper label, it was probably made by Uhl.

While many color variations exist, there are about nine basic colors including blue, white, black, rose or pink, yellow, teal, purple, pumpkin and browns/tans. Blue, pink, teal and purple are currently the most sought after colors. Animal planters, vases, liquor/wine containers, pitchers, mugs, banks, kitchenware, bakeware, gardenware and custom-made advertising pieces exist.

Similar pieces by other manufacturers do exist. When placed side by side, a seasoned collector can recognize an authentic example of Uhl Pottery.

*A Variety of Uhl Marks*

**Ashtray,** acorn-shaped, brown, marked "Rustic Tavern" on reverse ........................ **$780**
**Ashtray,** advertising Shell Oil, marked "Dale, Indiana"........................................... **525**
**Ashtray,** figural, dog & fireplug, No. 199, brown ......................................................... **525**
**Ashtray,** marked "American Legion, Post 221, Huntingburg, Indiana" ......................... **140**
**Bank,** figural pig, blue, medium unmarked....... **375**
**Bank,** figural pig, white, large, unmarked ......... **400**
**Bank,** model of a jug, blue, unmarked.............. **185**
**Bean pot,** "Boston Baked Beans," brown & tan, unmarked ............................................... **40**

*Uhl Bottle*

**Bottle,** hand-turned, green ground (ILLUS.)..... **400**
**Bowl,** soup, No. 6, pink ...................................... **40**

*Uhl Buttermilk Feeder & Pitcher*

**Buttermilk feeder/chicken waterer,** acorn marked (ILLUS. left) ................................ **90-100**

*Uhl Canteen*

**Canteen,** footed circular form w/short cylindrical neck, loop handle, blue (ILLUS.) ........ **160**

*Uhl Canteen & Miniature Jugs*

**Canteen,** miniature, jug-shaped, teal, unmarked (ILLUS. bottom row, right) ............. **40**
**Casserole,** handled, No. 200, pink, unmarked ....................................................... **75**
**Casserole,** No. 175, blue, unmarked ................. **50**
**Churn,** white, 3 gal. .......................................... **175**
**Cookie jar,** miniature, brown, unmarked........... **45**
**Cookie jar,** pink............................................... **135**

*Uhl Miniature Cookie Jar*

**Cookie jar,** miniature, globe-shaped, marked "Indiana State Fair 1940," pink ground, 4" h. (ILLUS.) .................................... **625**
**Creamer & sugar bowl,** pink, pr. ....................... **75**

*Various Jars & Jugs*

**Jar,** cov., cylindrical, blue, 6 oz. (ILLUS. bottom) ................................................................ **50**
**Jar,** cov., semi-ovoid body, clamp closure type, blue (ILLUS. center right) add $25.00 for clamp ............................................. **50**
**Jar,** white, acorn mark, 1 gal. ............................. **37**
**Jar,** white, acorn mark, 2 gal. ............................. **42**
**Jar,** white, acorn mark, 5 gal. ............................. **55**
**Jar,** Evansville oval mark, 15 gal. ...................... **225**
**Jar,** cov., white & blue, marked "Flour" ............. **300**
**Jar,** Orange Blossom, No. 118, pink ................. **70**
**Jardiniere,** old ivory, 14 or 16 1/2" h., each ..... **60**
**Jardiniere,** Athenian patt., green, 16 1/2" h. .......................................................... **65**
**Jardiniere,** Roman patt., terra cotta or old ivory, 19" h., each ........................................... **95**
**Jug,** brown & white, 1" h. ..................................... **85**
**Jug,** brown & white, acorn mark, 1 pint ............. **250**
**Jug,** brown & white, acorn mark, 5 gal. ............. **85**
**Jug,** handled bulbous body, red glaze, 1 pt. (ILLUS. middle row, left) ................................... **20**
**Jug,** "1939 Merry Xmas," brown & white ......... **175**
**Jug,** "1942 Merry Christmas," brown & white ...................................................................... **200**
**Jug,** miniature, "Acorn Wares," acorn-shaped (ILLUS. bottom row, center) ........ **30-60**

**Jug,** miniature, baseball-shaped, white, unmarked, paper label (ILLUS. middle row, left) .......................................................... **56**
**Jug,** miniature, bulbous ovoid body, paper label (ILLUS. top row, far right) ................ **30-60**
**Jug,** miniature, football-shaped, brown, unmarked, paper label (ILLUS. middle row, right) .......................................................... **40**
**Jug,** miniature, globe-shaped, purple, unmarked ........................................................ **90**
**Jug,** miniature, "Grecian," blue, unmarked ........ **40**
**Jug,** miniature, Prunella, blue, unmarked (ILLUS. top row, second from right) .............. **60**
**Jug,** miniature, semi-ovoid body, loop shoulder handles, Meier's label (ILLUS. top row, far left) ............................................. **60**
**Jug,** miniature, shouldered, "Grandpa Meiers" label, brown & white, unmarked (ILLUS. middle row, center) .......................... **60**
**Jug,** miniature, square, blue, unmarked, paper label (ILLUS. top row, second from left) ............................................................. **40**
**Jug,** miniature, two-handled, blue, unmarked .......................................................... **55**
**Jug,** miniature, two-handled, "Curacoa" (demijohn), paper label, 2 oz. (ILLUS. bottom row, left) ........................................... **30-60**
**Jug,** "Polar Bear," flat-sided, blue ..................... **325**
**Jug,** refrigerator-type, flat-sided, No. 190, blue ................................................................. **110**
**Jug,** refrigerator-type, globe-shaped, pink ......... **90**
**Jug,** two-handled, Evansville oval mark, 10 gal. .................................................................. **250**
**Jug,** w/advertising, hand-turned, Evansville mark, 3 gal. ...................................................... **275**
**Jugs,** handled, bulbous body, blue glaze, numbered 175, 176, 177 (ILLUS. top row, left & right) .............................................. **20-35**
**Medallion,** relief-molded "Uhl Pottery," brown ............................................................. **225**
**Mixing bowl,** 4" d., blue (one of nine sizes) ....... **80**
**Model of a turtle,** large, unmarked .................. **700**
**Model of lady's slipper,** miniature, blue, pr. ...................................................................... **140**
**Model of lady's slipper,** miniature, white, unmarked pr. .................................................. **80**
**Mug,** barrel-shaped, "Big Boonville Fair 1927," tan & brindle ...................................... **100**
**Mug,** miniature, barrel-shaped, pink ................ **130**
**Pitcher,** cov., squatty body, blue .................... **270**
**Pitcher,** cov., tapering wide cylindrical body, Grape patt., blue, unmarked (ILLUS. right w/buttermilk feeder) ......... **200-250**
**Pitcher,** Grape patt., blue, 3 qt. ....................... **190**
**Pitcher,** barrel-shaped, plum ............................ **45**
**Pitcher,** bulbous body, blue & white sponged, No. 2 size ...................................... **375**
**Pitcher,** bulbous body, Grape patt., No. 181, pink .......................................................... **90**
**Pitcher,** bulbous body, Grape patt., No. 182, pumpkin ................................................... **105**
**Pitcher,** bulbous body, Grape patt., No. 183, purple ...................................................... **195**
**Pitcher,** bulbous body, Grape patt., No. 184, yellow ...................................................... **60**
**Pitcher,** hand-turned, teal ................................ **150**
**Pitcher,** jug-type, "Creme De Coffee," No. 164, pumpkin ................................................... **35**
**Pitcher,** Lincoln profile, blue & white, unmarked, No. 2 size ................................... **275**
**Pitcher,** miniature, pink, unmarked ................... **80**

*Uhl Grape Pattern Pitcher*

**Pitcher,** squatty tapering cylindrical body, Grape patt., blue ground w/white interior (ILLUS.) ........................................................ **160**

*Uhl Barrel-shaped Pitcher Set*

**Pitcher set:** 3 qt. pitcher & six 16 oz. steins; barrel-shaped, blue w/white interior, No. B-3, the set (ILLUS.) ............. **800-1,000**
**Pitcher set:** flagon-type pitcher & six mugs; blue, unmarked, the set ............................... **180**
**Planter,** model of a donkey, white, unmarked ...................................................... **185**
**Planter,** model of an elephant w/wrinkled skin, white, unmarked ................................... **140**
**Plate,** chop, blue ............................................... **80**
**Plate,** hand-turned, blue ..................................... **90**
**Roaster,** blue .................................................... **140**
**Salt & pepper shakers,** pink, unmarked, pr. ...................................................................... **60**

*Polar Bear Sand Jar*

**Sand jar,** wide cylindrical body, Polar Bear patt., old ivory, 12 1/4" d., 14 1/2" h. (ILLUS.) ....................................................... **250**
**Teapot,** cov., No. 131, blue ............................. **135**
**Teapot,** cov., No. 132, yellow ........................... **65**
**Vase,** bud, No. 516, blue .................................. **85**
**Vase,** hand-turned, pink ................................... **75**
**Vase,** No. 114, pink ......................................... **65**
**Vase,** No. 123, blue ......................................... **70**
**Vase,** No. 158, pink ......................................... **90**

## ADVERTISING ITEMS

*Various Uhl Advertising Items*

**Jug,** miniature, brown & white glaze (ILLUS. top row, left) .................................... **125**
**Jug,** miniature, two-handled, yellow glaze (ILLUS. top row, center) .............................. **125**
**Model of a shoe,** baby shoe w/tie, brown glaze (ILLUS. center row, left)...................... **60**
**Mug,** barrel-shaped, yellow glaze (ILLUS. bottom, far left) ............................................... **85**
**Mug,** yellow glaze (ILLUS. top row, right).......... **85**
**Pitcher,** miniature, barrel-shaped w/advertising, red glaze (ILLUS. center row, right) ..................................................... **125-175**
**Pitcher,** tapering cylindrical form, w/advertising for Dillsboro Sanitarium, white glaze, no recorded sale, one other believed to exist, estimated price (ILLUS. bottom, far right)................ **1,800-3,000**

## ART POTTERY VASES

*Various Art Pottery Vases*

**Vase,** cylindrical body w/flaring rim, white glaze (ILLUS. bottom row, left)................. **30-60**
**Vase,** bulbous body w/closed rim, blue glaze (ILLUS. center) ............................... **30-60**
**Vase,** footed bulbous body w/trumpet-form neck, white glaze (ILLUS. top row left)...... **30-60**
**Vase,** footed flattened bulbous body w/flattened flaring neck, yellow glaze (ILLUS. top row, right) ........................................... **30-60**
**Vase,** tall waisted cylindrical body, red glaze (ILLUS. bottom row, right) .............. **30-60**

## CATALOGUE ILLUSTRATIONS

*Uhl Butters*

**Butters,** Kansas City, glazed all-white or
blue inside & outside,1, 1 1/2 & 2 lb.,
each (ILLUS. right) .................................. **20-30**
**Butters,** low, glazed all-white or blue inside
& outside, l to 20 lb., each (ILLUS. left)..... **20-30**
**Churns,** glazed all-white inside & outside, 2
to 6 gal., each ........................................ **85-200**

*Various Uhl Jugs*

**Harvest jug,** 1 gal. w/stoneware handle
intact (ILLUS. top right) ......................... **400-600**
**Ice water jar,** cov., nickled faucet, 3 to 10
gal., each ............................................... **80-125**

*Uhl Water Keg*

**Ice water keg,** cov., blue banded, nickled
faucet, 3 to 10 gal., each (ILLUS. ) ....... **150-250**

*Uhl Pottery Jars*

**Jar,** without bail, glazed all-white inside &
outside, 1/4 to 6 gal., each ...................... **25-50**
**Jar,** 7 gal., extremely rare .............................. **500+**
**Jar,** 8 to 12 gal., each ................................. **50-100**
**Jar,** 15 to 30 gal., each (ILLUS. left).......... **100-250**
**Jar,** 40 to 60 gal., each (ILLUS. right) ....... **250-300**
**Kraut weights,** glazed white, 10" d. to
13 1/2" d., each ....................................... **10-20**

*Various Uhl Pitchers*

**Pitcher,** barrel-shaped, glazed Old Hickory
brown outside, white inside, 3 qt. ............. **40-60**
**Pitcher,** bellied, glazed blue stipple, 1/2 & 1
gal., each (ILLUS. left) .......................... **175-300**
**Pitcher,** Lincoln bust, 5 sizes, each (ILLUS.
right) ....................................................... **175-700**

*Uhl Pitcher Sets*

**Pitcher set:** 2 qt. pitcher & six 12 oz.
steins; Grape patt., glazed Mahogany
outside, white inside, No. G-1, marked, 7
pc. set (ILLUS.) ..................................... **100-125**
**Pitcher set:** 2 qt. pitcher & six 12 oz.
steins; Grape patt., glazed Periwinkle
blue, white inside, No. G-1, marked, 7
pc. set ................................................... **400-500**
**Pitcher set:** 2 qt. squatty pitcher & six 12
oz. steins; Grape patt., glazed Mahogany outside, white inside, No. G-2,
marked, 7 pc. set ................................... **110-135**
**Pitcher set:** 2 qt. squatty pitcher & six 12
oz. steins; Grape patt., glazed Periwinkle blue outside, white inside, No. G-2,
marked, 7 pc. set ................................... **400-500**
**Pitcher set:** 3 qt. pitcher & six 16 oz.
steins; barrel-shaped, glazed Old Hickory brown outside, white inside, No. B-3,
marked, 7 pc. set ........................................ **125**
**Pitcher set:** 3 qt. pitcher & six 16 oz.
steins; Grape patt., glazed Mahogany
outside, white inside, No. G-4, marked, 7
pc. set ................................................... **110-135**
**Pitcher set:** 3 qt. pitcher & six 16 oz.
steins; Grape patt., glazed Periwinkle

blue outside, white inside, No. G-4,
marked, 7 pc. set .................................. **425-525**
**Polar jar,** cov., nickled faucet, blue tint over
white or dark green outside, white inside,
1 to 10 gal., each ................................. **250-600**
**Preserve/mustard jar,** cov., 1/2 to 3 gal.,
each .................................................................. **60**
**Shoulder jugs,** 1/4 to 5 gal., each (ILLUS.
w/Harvest jug) ......................................... **25-75**
**Shoulder jugs,** glazed white outside, dark
inside, 1 gal. (ILLUS. top left w/Harvest
jug) ....................................................... **100-125**
**Sorghum jug,** w/or without faucet hole, 8 &
10 gal., each (ILLUS. bottom right
w/Harvest jug) ....................................... **90-125**
**Squat bailed jug,** 1/2 & 1 gal., each
(ILLUS. bottom left w/Harvest jug) .............. **125**
**Steam table insets,** glazed all-white, for
8 1/2 or 10 1/2" opening, each ................. **40-60**

## MINIATURE ADVERTISING ITEMS

*Various Uhl Miniature Advertising Items*

**Bottle,** miniature, advertising, brown
glaze, ca. 1933 (ILLUS. top row left)..... **400-600**
**Canteen,** miniature, advertising, white
glaze, ca. 1933 (ILLUS. top row,
center).................................................... **400-600**
**Jug,** miniature, advertising, two-handled,
green & brown glaze, ca. 1939 (ILLUS.
center row, right) ................................... **175-225**
**Jug,** miniature, advertising, two-handled,
green & brown glaze (ILLUS. bottom
row, left) ............................................... **225-300**
**Jug,** miniature, advertising, white & brown
glaze, ca. 1933 (ILLUS. top row, right). **400-600**
**Jug,** miniature, advertising, white & brown
glaze, ca. 1939 (ILLUS. center row,
left) ....................................................... **175-225**
**Jug,** miniature, advertising, white & brown
glaze, ca. 1939 (ILLUS. center row,
center) ................................................... **175-225**
**Jug,** miniature, advertising, white & brown
glaze (ILLUS. bottom row, center) ........ **225-300**

# VAN BRIGGLE

*Van Briggle Pottery Mark*

The Van Briggle Pottery was established by
Artus Van Briggle, who formerly worked for Rookwood Pottery, in Colorado Springs, Colorado at the
turn of the century. He died in 1904 but the pottery
was carried on by his widow and others. From 1900
until 1920, the pieces were dated. It remains in production today, specializing in Art Pottery.

*Van Briggle Plate with Poppies*

**Bowl,** 5 1/2" d., 2" h., squatty bulbous body
w/a wide tapering shoulder to the wide
flat mouth, embossed w/holly under a
fine speckled matte green glaze, the
brown clay showing through, ca. 1906,
incised "AA - Van Briggle - Colo Spgs. -
1906" ......................................................... **$880**
**Bowl-vase,** very wide squatty bulbous form
w/the upper sides tapering to a flat
mouth, embossed around the mouth w/a
wide band of mistletoe berries & leaves
down the sides, sheer mottled mauve
glaze, Shape No. 387, dated 1905,
incised mark, 11" d., 5" h.......................... **4,125**
**Bowl-vase,** squatty bulbous body w/shoul-
der tapering sharply to incurved rim,
molded w/triangular leaves under a
matte light green glaze, ca. 1906,
incised "AA - Van Briggle - 1906 - 428 -
3," 4 x 7" ................................................. **2,200**
**Bowl-vase,** wide rounded squatty lower
body below a wide angled & sloping
shoulder to the wide flat mouth, molded
arrowroot leaves around shoulder, turquoise blue matte glaze, ca. 1918,
incised marks, 9 3/4" d., 4 3/4" h. (minor
bubbles in glaze) ......................................... **495**

**Paperweight,** figural, modeled as a horned toad on a thin oval base, the toad in a yellowish amber glaze on a matte green base, unmarked, ca. 1914, 3 1/4 x 4 1/2".... **990**

**Plate,** 8 1/4" d., molded w/a cluster of purple grapes & large leaves against a textured turquoise ground, incised mark, 1907-11 ........................................................ **605**

**Plate,** 8 1/2" d., crisply incised w/poppies & covered in a bright green glaze, incised "AA - Van Briggle - 1902 - III" (ILLUS.) .... **1,540**

**Vase,** 4 x 4", footed bulbous ovoid body w/shoulder tapering to wide short cylindrical neck, embossed w/stylized floral pattern under a matte green & speckled mustard ground, ca. 1915-20, incised "AA - Van Briggle - 20" ............................... **523**

**Vase,** 4 x 4 1/4", wide cylindrical base tapering to rounded shoulder & flat mouth, molded poppies under a fine speckled matte green glaze, the brown clay showing through, ca. 1903, incised "AA - Van Briggle - 1903 - 204 - III" ......... **2,200**

**Vase,** 4 1/4" h., squatty bulbous form, sharply canted sides to flat rim, decorated w/stylized relief-molded flowers & stems, mulberry & blue glaze, incised marks & "U.S.A." & "NP" in rectangle, ca. 1922-26 ........................................................ **523**

**Vase,** 4 1/2 x 5", spherical body w/slightly rolled lip, molded stylized design under a matte green glaze, ca. 1904, incised "AA - Van Briggle - 1904 - V - 148" (restored lines to body) ........................................... **413**

**Vase,** 4 1/2" h., 5 3/4" d., footed compressed spherical body, the wide shoulder tapering to a small cylindrical neck w/molded rim, light robin's-egg blue matte glaze, incised "AA - VAN BRIGGLE - 1905" 1905 ........................................ **358**

**Vase,** 5" h., 3 1/2" d., wide squatty base & tapering cylindrical sides to a small flat mouth, embossed w/swirled yucca leaves up the sides, overall curdled brown glaze, incised mark, Shape No. 162, 1907-11 ........................................... **990**

**Vase,** 5" h., 6" d., footed bulbous body w/wide molded rim, curdled matte bluish green glaze, Shape No. 240C, 1907.......... **330**

**Vase,** 6 1/2" h., slightly flaring cylindrical body w/a bulbed top w/closed mouth, molded around the top w/tulip blossoms, the stems down the sides, ivory w/light green matte glaze, incised marks, ca. 1905 (tight line at top) ................. **358**

**Vase,** 7" h., bottle-form, a thin footring below the bulbous ovoid body tapering sharply to a tall 'stick' neck, fine green & charcoal matte glaze, incised mark, Shape No. 338, ca. 1905 ........................... **275**

**Vase,** 7" h., cylindrical body w/small loop handles & relief-molded design at base, leathery green matte glaze, shape No. 535, incised marks & partially obscured date (grinding chips off base)............ **715**

**Vase,** 7 1/2" h., 3 3/4" d., tall waisted double-gourd form, embossed around the top w/crocus blossoms on tall slender stems w/pointed leaves around the bottom, matte dark green glaze, Shape No. 692, impressed mark, 1907-11 (chip to base, probably in the making) ...................... **770**

*Van Briggle Vase with Papyrus Leaves*

**Vase,** 7 3/4" h., bulbous base tapering to long slender cylindrical neck w/flaring rim, embossed around base w/papyrus leaves under a matte robin's-egg blue glaze, Shape No. 734, 1907-11 (ILLUS.) ..... **770**

**Vase,** 8" h., bulbous w/tapering cylindrical neck & flat rim, embossed w/leaves & covered in a fine mauve glaze w/clay showing through, ca. 1908-11, incised "AA - Van Briggle - Colo. Spgs. - 742" ..... **1,320**

**Vase,** 8" h., cylindrical body w/gently swelled shoulder curving in to a closed-in mouth, matte purple glaze, shape No. 343, 1905 ...................................................... **880**

**Vase,** 9" h., 6 1/4" d., wide gently flaring cylindrical body w/swelled shoulder & closed rim, embossed around the top w/large poppy pods on sinewy stems curving down the sides, overall rich dead matte burgundy & green glaze, incised mark, dated 1902 .................................. **12,100**

**Vase,** 9 1/2" h., trumpet-form, the sides molded w/a horizontal vine w/large & small pointed leaves up & down around the sides, turquoise blue ground w/blue overspray, ca. 1930s.................................. **230**

**Vase,** 10" h., 8" d., wide ovoid body tapering to a cylindrical neck flanked by small loop shoulder handles, molded w/stylized desert flowers & leaves, dark matte green & burgundy glaze, incised mark, dated 1904 ............................................... **2,475**

**Vase,** 10 3/4" h., tall cylindrical body w/low buttress-type handles flanking the flat mouth, molded w/morning glories under a rare matte yellow glaze, ca. 1903, incised "AA Van Briggle - 1903 - 228" (repair to small base chip) ...................... **4,400**

**Vase,** 11" h., footed tall slender cylindrical body gently swelled at the top w/a closed rim, embossed w/leaves atop long vertical stems under a thick, curdled matte green glaze, incised "AA - VAN BRIGGLE - COLO. SPGS." 1907-11 (kiln kiss to shoulder) ............................. **1,320**

**Vase,** 13" h., tapering cylindrical body w/rounded base, closed mouth, embossed w/daffodils under a matte turquoise & blue glaze, ca. 1920s, incised "AA - VAN BRIGGLE - COLO SPGS" ......... **770**

# VERNON KILNS

*Vernon Kilns Mark*

*The story of Vernon Kilns Pottery begins with the purchase by Mr. Faye Bennison of the Poxon China Company (Vernon Potteries) in July 1931. The Poxon family had run the pottery for a number of years in Vernon, California, but with the founding of Vernon Kilns the product lines were greatly expanded.*

*Many innovative dinnerware lines and patterns were introduced during the 1930s, including designs by such noted American artists as Rockwell Kent and Don Blanding. In the early 1940s items were designed to tie in with Walt Disney's animated features "Fantasia" and "Dumbo." Various commemorative plates, including the popular "Bits" series, were also produced over a long period of time. Vernon Kilns was taken over by Metlox Potteries in 1958 and completely ceased production in 1960.*

## 'BITS' SERIES
**Plate,** 8 1/2" d., Bits of Old New England Series, The Whaler ...................................... **$38**
**Plate,** 8 1/2" d., Bits of the Middle West Series, Fourth of July ...................................... **35**
**Plate,** 8 1/2" d., Bits of the Old Southwest Series, San Juan Bautista Mission................ **35**
**Plate,** 8 1/2" d., Bits of the Old Southwest Series, San Juan Capistrano Mission ............ **40**
**Plate,** 8 1/2" d., Bits of the Old West, The Barfly .............................................................. **25**

## CITIES SERIES - 10 1/2" D.
**Plate,** "Los Angeles, California" ......................... **20**

## DINNERWARES
**Bowl,** chowder, tab-handled, Tam O'Shanter patt. .............................................................. **12**
**Bowl,** flower petal-shaped, green, No. 139 ........ **50**
**Bowl,** salad, Organdie patt. ............................. **60**
**Bowl,** fruit, 5 1/2" d., May Flower patt. .................. **8**
**Butter dish,** cov., Tam O'Shanter patt., 1/4 lb. .......................................................................... **28**
**Casserole,** cov., Tam O'Shanter patt................. **48**
**Casserole,** cov., Tickled Pink patt..................... **55**
**Casserole,** cov., Chintz patt., 8" d.................... **140**
**Chicken baker,** cov., Organdie patt.................... **30**
**Coaster,** Homespun patt. .................................. **25**
**Coffeepot,** cov., Tickled Pink patt., 8 cup ......... **60**

**Comport,** footed, Tweed patt. (T-504), 9 1/2" h. ..................................................... **75**

*Coronado Creamer & Sugar Bowl*

**Creamer & open sugar bowl,** Coronado patt., orange (ILLUS.)..................................... **45**
**Cup & saucer,** demitasse, Organdie patt........... **25**

*Scenic Cup & Saucer*

**Cup & saucer,** demitasse, Spanish Courtyard decal patt. (ILLUS.) ................................ **30**

*Frontier Days Pattern Cup & Saucer*

**Cup & saucer,** Frontier Days (Winchester 73) patt. (ILLUS.)............................................ **65**
**Cup & saucer,** Homespun patt. ......................... **15**
**Cup & saucer,** Homespun patt., oversize ........ **155**
**Egg cup,** Homespun patt. .................................. **20**
**Gravy boat,** Chintz patt. .................................... **40**
**Pitcher,** large, Tam O'Shanter patt. ................... **60**
**Pitcher,** water, Organdie patt. ........................... **30**
**Plate,** bread & butter, 6 1/2" d., Homespun patt. ........................................................................ **5**
**Plate,** dinner, 9 3/4" d., Homespun patt............. **18**
**Plate,** 10 1/2" d., Santa Claus decoration.......... **35**
**Plate,** luncheon, May Flower patt. ...................... **12**
**Plate,** chop, 12" d., Chintz patt. ........................ **70**
**Plate,** chop, 12" d., Frontier Days (Winchester 73) patt. ......................................... **120**
**Plate,** chop, 12" d., Monterey patt. .................... **30**

**Plate,** chop, 12 1/2" d., Ultra California patt., (carnation) pink or ice green ................. 45
**Salt & pepper shakers,** Homespun patt., pr. .......................................................... 12
**Salt & pepper shakers,** Organdie patt., pr. ........ 25
**Soup plate w/flanged rim,** Organdie patt., 8" d. .......................................................... 15
**Teapot,** cov., Vernon's 1860 patt. ...................... 75
**Tray,** round, Homespun patt., 12" d. ................ 25
**Trio buffet server,** Country Cousin patt. .......... 50
**Tumbler,** Heavenly Days patt., 14 oz. ................ 16
**Tumbler,** Tickled Pink patt., 14 oz. ................... 18
**Vegetable bowl,** Homespun patt., 9" d. ............ 15
**Vegetable bowl,** open, Tam O'Shanter patt. .......................................................... 15
**Vegetable bowl,** open, divided, Tam O'Shanter patt. .............................................. 28
**Vegetable bowl,** open, oval, divided, Frontier Days (Winchester 73) patt. ...................... 120
**Vegetable bowl,** open, oval, May Flower patt. .......................................................... 20

## DISNEY 'FANTASIA' & OTHER ITEMS
**Bowl,** 10 1/2" d., Sprite, No. 125, blue ............. 260
**Figure of Dumbo** ........................................... 225
**Figure of Hippo,** dancing w/arms out, 5 1/2" h. .......................................................... 450
**Figure of Nubian Centaurette,** No. 24, 7 1/2" h. ...................................................... 1,050
**Figure of Unicorn,** sitting, white, No. 14, 5" h. .......................................................... 600
**Vase,** 7 1/2" h., 12" l., Winged Pegasus patt., a wide flat-sided tapering form w/curved ends & a long rectangular flat mouth, lightly molded w/the winged horse in a landscape, a white ground h.p. in green, brown, yellow & black, glossy glaze, ca. 1941, marked ............................................... 600-1,200
**Vase,** 10 1/2" h., Goddess patt., footed flattened ovoid form w/a low scalloped rim, relief-molded standing figure of a nude female shooting a bow & arrow, blue ................................................... 700-1,200

## DON BLANDING DINNERWARES
**Charger,** Lei Lani patt., 17 1/2" d. .................... 200
**Cup,** Coral Reef patt., maroon ......................... 60

*Hawaiian Flowers Cup & Saucer*

**Cup & saucer,** Hawaiian Flowers patt., maroon (ILLUS.) ............................................. 45
**Cup & saucer,** Lei Lani patt. ............................. 50
**Plate,** 7" d., Lei Lani patt. .................................. 27
**Plate,** dinner, Lei Lani patt. ............................... 45

**Plate,** chop, 12" d., Hawaiian Flowers patt., maroon .......................................................... 132
**Plate,** chop, 14" d., Hawaiian Flowers patt., maroon .......................................................... 150
**Plate,** chop, 14" d., Lei Lani patt., Ultra line ..... 195
**Plate,** chop, 17" d., Lei Lani patt. .................... 200
**Salt & pepper shakers,** Hawaiian Flowers patt., maroon, pr. ......................................... 50
**Sugar bowl,** cov., Lei Lani patt. ........................ 50

## MISCELLANEOUS COMMEMORATIVES
**Plate,** "Badlands, South Dakota" ...................... 18
**Plate,** Mission San Gabriel, multicolored ........... 35
**Plate,** Mission Santa Barbara, multicolored ........ 35

## ROCKWELL KENT DESIGNS
**Bowl,** 9" d., "Our America" series, scene of New York City piers ...................................... 100
**Cup & saucer,** demitasse, Moby Dick patt., blue .......................................................... 75
**Jam jar w/notched cover,** Moby Dick patt., maroon .......................................................... 200
**Mug,** Moby Dick patt., maroon .......................... 80
**Plate,** 9 1/2" d., Moby Dick patt., Ultra shape, blue .................................................... 69
**Plate,** 9 1/2" d., "Our America" series, Ultra shape, blue .................................................... 69
**Plate,** 9 1/2" d., Salamina patt. ........................ 135

*Salamina Plate*

**Plate,** 10 1/2" d., Salamina patt. (ILLUS.) ......... 155
**Plate,** 12" d., Salamina patt. ............................ 275
**Plate,** chop, 12 1/2" d., Salamina patt. ............. 225
**Plate,** chop, 17" d., "Our America" series ........ 300
**Sugar bowl,** cov., Moby Dick patt. ..................... 75
**Teapot,** cov., Moby Dick patt., blue, 6-cup ....... 160

## STATES SERIES - 10 1/2" D.
**Plate,** "New York" ............................................. 15
**Plate,** "North Carolina" ...................................... 15
**Plate,** "Tennessee" ........................................... 20
**Plate,** "Washington - The Evergreen State" ........ 15

# WARWICK

*Numerous collectors have turned their attention to the productions of the Warwick China Manufacturing Company that operated in Wheeling, West Virginia, from 1887 until 1951. Prime interest would seem to lie in items produced before 1914 that were decorated with decal portraits of beautiful women, monks and Indians. Fraternal Order items, as well as floral and fruit decorated items, are also popular with collectors. Donald Hoffmann has prepared the following listing and for more information on his books and video see our Special Contributors section.*

### IOGA

### Warwick Mark

**Mug,** cylindrical, decorated w/the head of an elk & the "BPOE" emblem ...................... **$35**

**Pitcher,** 6 1/2" h., Lemonade shape, brown shaded to brown ground, color floral decoration, No. A-27 ................................... **145**

### Lemonade Shape Pitcher with Lady

**Pitcher,** 9 3/4" h., Lemonade shape, overall pink ground w/color "Aunt Hilda" type bust portrait of a young woman w/dark hair in a bouffant style & holding purple flowers, No. H-1 (ILLUS.) ............................ **300**

**Pitcher,** 10 1/4" h., monk decoration ............... **235**

**Vase,** 4" h., Parisian shape, overall charcoal ground, color nude portrait signed "Carreno," No. C-1 ....................................... **275**

**Vase,** 4 1/2" h., Dainty shape, brown shaded to brown ground, colored floral decoration, No. A-27 ................................... **280**

**Vase,** 6" h., Narcis #3 shape, brown shaded to brown ground, decorated w/a fisherman wearing a yellow slicker, No. A-35 .......................................................... **240**

**Vase,** 6 1/2" h., Clytie shape, overall red ground w/poinsettia decoration, No. E-2 ...... **300**

**Vase,** 6 1/2" h., Clytie shape, tan shaded to brown ground w/beechnut decoration, matte finish, No. M-2 ................................... **320**

**Vase,** 6 1/2" h., Den shape, brown shaded to brown ground, pine cone decoration, No. A-64 ....................................................... **400**

**Vase,** 6 3/4" h., Narcis #2 shape, overall red ground, color portrait of Princess Potaka, No. E-1 ........................................... **260**

**Vase,** 7 1/2" h., Verbenia #2 shape, brown shaded to brown ground, adult portrait of Madame LeBrun, No. A-17 .......................... **250**

**Vase,** 8" h., Carol shape, green shaded to green ground, red rose decoration, No. F-2 ............................................................... **285**

**Vase,** 8" h., Carol shape, overall pink ground decorated w/an "Aunt Hilda" type portrait of a woman wearing a boa, No. H-1 ...................................................................... **315**

**Vase,** 8" h., Chicago shape, brown shaded to brown ground w/red & green floral decoration, No. A-40 ................................... **300**

**Vase,** 8" h., Rose shape, overall red ground w/color portrait of Madame Recamier, No. E-1 ..................................... **230**

**Vase,** 8 1/4" h., Narcis #1 shape, overall white ground w/color bird decoration, No. D-1 ....................................................... **250**

**Vase,** 8 1/4" h., Victoria shape, overall red ground w/red poinsettia decoration, No. E-2 ......................................................... **255**

**Vase,** 9" h., Flower shape, green shaded to green ground, portrait of a young woman w/flowing red hair, No. M-1 .......................... **200**

**Vase,** 9 1/4'" h., brown shaded to brown ground, floral decoration, No. A-23 ............. **250**

**Vase,** 9 1/4" h., Windsor shape, brown shaded to brown ground, acorn decoration, No. A-67 ............................................. **325**

**Vase,** 9 1/2" h., Penn shape, overall green color w/no decoration, matte finish, No. M-6 .......................................................... **270**

**Vase,** 9 1/2" h., Verbenia #1 shape, brown shaded to brown ground, color floral decoration, No. A-6 ................................... **165**

**Vase,** 9 3/4" h., Iris shape, brown shaded to brown ground, nut decoration, No. A-64 ......................................................... **150**

**Vase,** 10" h., Flower shape, brown shaded to brown ground, color floral decoration, No. A-6 ......................................................... **135**

**Vase,** 10" h., Henrietta shape, brown shaded to brown ground, color portrait of a semi-nude young woman, No. A-30 .......... **325**

**Vase,** 10" h., Roberta shape, brown shaded to brown ground, portrait of a monk, No. A-36 ............................................. **290**

**Vase,** 10" h., Royal #2 shape, brown shaded to brown ground, floral decoration, No. A-27 ............................................. **295**

**Vase,** 10" h., Virginia shape, overall pink ground, "Aunt Hilda" type decoration w/portrait of a young woman w/a flower in her hair, No. H-1 ....................................... **300**

**Vase,** 10 1/4" h., Orchid shape, overall red ground, poinsettia decoration, No. E-2 ........ **245**

**Vase,** 10 1/2" h., Bouquet #2 shape, brown shaded to brown ground, portrait of a young woman w/dark hair holding a branch w/white flowers, No. A-17 (ILLUS. top next page) ............................... **245**

**Vase,** 10 1/2" h., Clematis shape, tan shaded to tan ground w/nut decoration, matte finish, No. M-64 ................................. **290**

**Vase,** 10 1/2" h., Magnolia shape, green shaded to green ground, color floral decoration, No. B-30 ................................... **270**

**Vase,** 10 1/2" h., Monroe shape, overall pink ground, "Aunt Hilda" type decoration w/portrait of a young woman wearing a large hat, No. H-1 ................................. **275**

**Vase,** 11" h., Geran shape, overall charcoal ground w/red floral cluster, No. C-6 ........... **250**

*Warwick Bouquet #2 Portrait Vase*

**Vase,** 11" h., Royal #1 shape, brown shaded to brown ground w/colored floral decoration, No. A-40 .................................... **295**

**Vase,** 11 1/2" h., Bouquet #1 shape, brown shaded to brown ground, portrait of young woman wearing a pearl necklace, No. A-17 ..................................................... **265**

**Vase,** 11 1/2" h., Chrysanthemum #3 shape, brown shaded to brown ground, color floral decoration, No. A-6..................... **160**

*Hibiscus Vase with Dogs*

**Vase,** 11 1/2" h., Hibiscus shape, brown shaded to brown ground, large color scene of red & black & white setter dogs hunting, No. A-50 (ILLUS.) ........................... **375**

**Vase,** 11 1/2" h., President shape, tan shaded to tan ground, acorn decoration, matte finish, No. M-4 .................................... **260**

**Vase,** 11 3/4" h., Egyptian shape, brown shaded to brown ground, red floral decoration, No. A-27 (ILLUS. top next column) ......................................................... **325**

**Vase,** 12" h., Flower shape, tan shaded to brown ground, color floral decoration, matte finish, No. M-16 ................................. **150**

**Vase,** 12" h., Queen shape, overall charcoal ground, color floral decoration, No. C-6 .......................................................... **325**

**Vase,** 12" h., tall cylindrical form w/twig handles, colored transfer of a lady holding long-stemmed yellow roses, shaded ground ...................................................... **225**

*Egyptian Shape Vase with Flowers*

**Vase,** 15" h., A Beauty shape, white ground w/red rose (American Beauty) decoration, No. D-2 ................................................ **325**

**Vase,** 15 1/2" h., Chrysanthemum #1 shape, overall red ground w/a Madame LeBrun child portrait, No. E-1 ...................... **225**

## DINNERWARES

**Cup & saucer,** Pattern No. 9572, Silver Poppy decoration ......................................... **10**

**Cup & saucer,** Pattern No. 9903, Grey Blossom decoration...................................... **18**

**Pitcher,** 8" h., buttermilk-type, white ground w/floral decoration of small pink flowers...................................................... **45**

**Pitcher,** 8" h., milk-type, white ground w/floral decoration of blue forget-me-nots ..................................................... **35**

**Plate,** 6 1/2" d., bread & butter, Pattern No. 9437-M, Windsor Maroon decoration ............. **10**

**Plate,** 9" d., Pattern AB-9231 ............................... **8**

**Plate,** 10" d., dinner, Pattern No. 9584, Bird of Paradise decoration w/single bird .............. **10**

**Plate,** 10" d., Pattern No. 2098, Venetian Rose decoration ......................................... **10**

**Vegetable bowl,** cov., Pattern No. 2001 ............ **40**

## COMMERCIAL CHINA

*Warwick "Duckwall's" Mustard Jar*

**Cup,** white w/"Johnny's" logo.............................. **25**

**Cup & saucer,** brown wave decoration, Santone finish ................................................. **45**

**Cup & saucer,** white w/"Duckwall's" logo........... **40**

**Cup & saucer,** white w/Crestwood pattern ........ **25**

**Cup & saucer,** white w/Dakota pattern .............. **20**

**Mustard jar,** cov., white w/"Duckwall's" logo (ILLUS.) ............................................ **28**
**Syrup pitcher,** cov., white w/"Johnny's" logo ................................................................ **40**

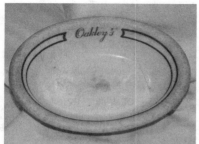

*"Oakley's" Oval Vegetable Dish*

**Vegetable dish,** individual, oval, white w/"Oakley's" logo (ILLUS.) ............................ **18**

# WATT POTTERY

*Founded in 1922, in Crooksville, Ohio, this pottery continued in operation until the factory was destroyed by fire in 1965. Although stoneware crocks and jugs were the first wares produced, by 1935 sturdy kitchen items in yellowware were the mainstay of production. Attractive lines like Kitch-N-Queen (banded) wares and the hand-painted Apple, Cherry and Pennsylvania Dutch (tulip) patterns were popular throughout the country. Today these hand-painted utilitarian wares are "hot" with collectors.*

*A good reference book for collectors is* Watt Pottery, An Identification and Value Guide, *by Sue and Dave Morris (Collector Books, 1933)*

*Watt Pottery Mark*

**Baker,** cov., Cherry patt., No. 53, 7 1/2" d...... **$110**
**Baker,** cov., Apple patt., No. 601, 8" d. ............ **120**
**Baker,** cov., Apple patt., No. 67, 8 1/4" d. ........ **125**
**Baker,** cov., Autumn Foliage patt., No. 110, 8 1/2" d. .................................................................. **75**
**Baker,** cov., Cherry patt., No. 54, 8 1/2" d........ **110**
**Baker,** cov., Open Apple patt., No. 110, 8 1/2" d. ................................................................. **295**
**Baker,** Apple patt., rectangular, No. 85, 9" w. ....................................................................... **1,000**
**Bean cup,** Tear Drop patt., No. 75, 3 1/2" d. 2 1/4" h........................................................... **15**
**Bean pot,** cov., Apple patt., No. 76, 6 1/2" h. ................................................................... **150**
**Bean pot,** cov., Autumn Foliage patt., No. 76, 6 1/2" h. ................................................... **125**
**Bean pot,** cov., bisque, No. 76, 6 1/2" h. ........... **10**

**Bean pot,** cov., Dutch Tulip patt., No. 76, 6 1/2" h. ................................................................... **275**
**Bean pot,** cov., Rooster patt., No. 76, 6 1/2" h. ................................................................... **350**

*Watt Pottery Apple Pattern Bowls*

**Bowl,** 4" d., 1 1/2" d., Apple patt., No. 602 (ILLUS. far left).............................................. **125**
**Bowl,** 4 1/4" d., 2" h., Apple patt., No. 04 ........... **50**
**Bowl,** 4 1/4" d., 2" h., Double Apple patt., No. 04 ...................................................................... **100**
**Bowl,** 5" d., 2" h., Apple patt., No. 603 (ILLUS. center left) ......................................... **100**
**Bowl,** 5 1/4" d., 2 1/2" h., Tear Drop patt., No. 05 ...................................................................... **40**
**Bowl,** 5 1/2" d., 2" h., Reduced Decoration Apple patt., No. 74 ......................................... **30**
**Bowl,** 6" d., 2 1/2" h., Apple patt., No. 604 (ILLUS. center)................................................ **90**
**Bowl,** 6" d., 2 1/2" h. Tulip patt., No. 604 ......... **150**
**Bowl,** 6 1/4" d., 2 1/4" h., Cherry patt., No. 52 ........................................................................... **35**
**Bowl,** 7" d., 3" h., Apple patt., No. 600 (ILLUS. center right)........................................... **50**
**Bowl,** 7" d., 3" h., Tulip patt., No. 600 .............. **125**
**Bowl,** 7 1/4" d., 3" h., Apple patt., No. 07 .......... **50**
**Bowl,** 7 1/4" d., 3" h., Double Apple patt., No. 07 ...................................................................... **70**
**Bowl,** 8" d., 3 1/2" h., Apple patt., No. 601 (ILLUS. far right) ............................................... **60**
**Bowl,** 8" d., 3 1/2" h., Tulip patt., No. 601 ........ **125**
**Bowl,** 8 1/4" d., 3 1/4" h., Starflower patt., No. 54 ...................................................................... **40**
**Bowl,** 8 1/4" d., 3 1/2" h., Apple patt., No. 67 ................................................................... **50**
**Bowl,** 8 1/4" d., 3 1/2" h., Rooster patt., No. 67 ................................................................... **90**
**Bowl,** 9 1/2" d., 4" h., Open Apple patt., No. 73 ................................................................... **250**
**Bowl,** 10" d., 3" h., Autumn Foliage patt., No. 106......................................................................... **85**
**Bowl,** 11" d., 4" h., Starflower patt., No. 55........ **40**
**Bowl,** spaghetti, 13" d., 3 1/2" h., Autumn Foliage patt., No. 39 ..................................... **135**

*Watt Spaghetti Bowl & Casserole*

**Bowl,** spaghetti, 13" d., 3 1/2" h,. Dogwood patt., No. 39 (ILLUS. back)........................... **135**

**Bowl,** spaghetti, 13" d., 3 1/2" h., Dutch Tulip patt., No. 39 ...................................... 400
**Bowl,** spaghetti, 13" d., 3 1/2" h., Open Apple patt., No. 39 ...................................... 800
**Bowl,** spaghetti, 13" d., 3 1/2" h., Rooster patt., No. 39 .............................................. 325
**Bowl,** spaghetti, 13" d., 3 1/2" h., Starflower patt., No. 39 ..................................... 110
**Bowl,** 15" d., 3 1/2" h., Rio Rose patt. ................ 75
**Canister,** cov., Apple patt., No. 82, 5" d. .......... 400
**Canister,** cov., Starflower patt., No. 82, 5" d. ...................................................................... 300
**Canister,** cov., Dutch Tulip patt., No. 81, 6 1/2" d. .................................................................. 400

*Watt Canister, Rio Rose Pattern*

**Canister,** cov., Rio Rose patt., No. 72, 7 1/4" d. (ILLUS.) ........................................... 300
**Canister,** cov., Apple patt., No. 80, 8 1/2" d. .................................................................. 900
**Canister,** cov., Rooster patt., No. 80, 8 1/2" d. .................................................................. 600

*Watt Carafe and Assorted Pitchers*

**Carafe,** cov., Autumn Foliage patt., No. 115, 9 1/2" h. (ILLUS. far left) ...................... 200
**Carafe,** cov., Brown banded, No. 115, 10 1/2" .......................................................... 350

*Apple Pattern Casserole*

**Casserole,** cov., Apple patt., No. 3/19 (ILLUS.) add $75.00 for warmer stand & $50.00 for original box ................................... 350
**Casserole,** cov., Apple patt., No. 18, 5" d. ....... 175
**Casserole,** cov., Dogwood patt., No. 18, 5" d. (ILLUS. front) ....................................... 125
**Casserole,** cov., Silhouette patt., No. 18, 5" d. ....................................................................... 25
**Casserole,** cov., Starflower patt., No. 18, 5" d. ....................................................................... 90

**Casserole,** cov., French handled, Apple patt., No. 18, 5" d. ....................................... 225
**Casserole,** cov., French handled, Rooster patt., No. 18, 5" d. ....................................... 200

*Assorted Watt Autumn Foliage Pattern*

**Chip-n-Dip set,** Autumn Foliage patt., No. 110 & 120 bowls, the set (ILLUS. center) ..... 150
**Chip-n-Dip set,** Double Apple patt., No. 96 &120 bowls, the set .................................... 350
**Churns,** stoneware, Eagle or Acorn patt., various sizes ......................................... **100-150**
**Cookie jar,** cov., Basketweave patt., No. 101, pink w/white lid ................................. 100
**Cookie jar,** cov., "Goodies," No. 76, 6 1/2" h .................................................................. 150
**Cookie jar,** cov., Apple patt., No. 21, 7 1/2" h ................................................................. 400

*Cherry Pattern Cookie Jar*

**Cookie jar,** cov., Cherry patt., No. 21, 7 1/2" h. (ILLUS.) ........................................... 250
**Cookie jar,** cov., Rio Rose patt., No. 21, 7 1/2" h. ................................................................ 150
**Cookie jar,** cov., happy/sad face, wooden lid, No. 34, 8" h .......................................... 150
**Cookie jar,** cov., Starflower patt., No. 503, 8" h. ........................................................... 350
**Cookie jar,** cov., Tulip patt., No. 503, 8" h. ...... 350
**Cookie jar,** cov., Morning Glory patt., cream, No. 95, 10" h. ................................... 600
**Cookie jar,** cov., "Cookie Barrel," wood grain, 10 1/2" h. .............................................. 50

*Watt Pottery Policeman Cookie Jar*

**Cookie jar,** cov., figural, Policeman, 10 1/2" h., rare (ILLUS.) ............................ **1,100**
**Creamer,** Apple (three-leaf) patt., No. 62, 4 1/4" h. ......................................................... **90**
**Creamer,** Apple (two-leaf) patt., No. 62, 4 1/4" h. ......................................................... **150**
**Creamer,** Autumn Foliage patt., No. 62, 4 1/4" h. (ILLUS. left w/Chip-n-Dip set) ........ **250**
**Creamer,** Dutch Tulip patt., No. 62, 4 1/4" h. ......................................................... **275**

*Two-tone Dripped Glaze Creamer & Pitcher*

**Creamer,** green & white drip glaze, No. 62, 4 1/4" h. (ILLUS. left) .................................... **300**
**Creamer,** Morning Glory patt., cream, No. 97, 4 1/4" h. .................................................. **400**

*Assorted Watt Pottery, Starflower Pattern (Five-petal)*

**Creamer,** Starflower patt., five-petal, No. 62, 4 1/4" h. (ILLUS. far right) ...................... **200**

*Assorted Watt Pottery, Starflower Pattern (Four-petal)*

**Creamer,** Starflower patt., four-petal, No. 62, 4 1/4" h. (ILLUS. second from left) ......... **250**
**Creamer,** Tulip patt., No. 62, 4 1/4" h. ............... **225**

*Watt Pottery Crocks*

**Crocks,** stoneware, Eagle or Acorn patt., various sizes (ILLUS. of two) .................... **25-50**
**Cruet set,** cov., Apple patt., 7 1/2" h. ............ **1,500**
**Cruet set,** cov., Autumn Foliage patt., 7 1/2" h. ......................................................... **300**
**Grease jar,** cov., Apple patt., No. 47, 5" h........ **400**
**Grease jar,** cov., Autumn Foliage patt., No. 01, 5" h. ......................................................... **200**
**Grease jar,** cov., Starflower patt., No. 01, 5" h......................................................... **275**
**Ice bucket,** cov., Autumn Foliage patt., No. 59, 7" h......................................................... **200**
**Ice bucket,** cov., Dutch Tulip patt., No. 59, 7" h......................................................... **400**
**Ice tea keg,** cov., brand name, 11" h. ............. **110**
**Ice tea keg,** cov., plain, 11" h. (ILLUS.).............. **60**
**Mixing bowl,** Reduced Decoration Apple patt., Nos. 5, 6, 7, & 9, 5" to 9" d., each ......... **60**
**Mixing bowl,** Morning Glory patt., 5" d. ........... **125**
**Mixing bowls,** nesting-type, Apple patt., Nos. 5, 6, 7, & 9, 5" to 9" d., each .................. **60**
**Mixing bowls,** nesting-type, Apple patt., ribbed, Nos. 5, 6, 7, & 9, 5" to 9" d., each....... **70**

*Autumn Foliage Pattern Mixing Bowls*

**Mixing bowls,** nesting-type, Autumn Foliage patt., Nos. 65, 64, 63, 8 1/2" d., 7 1/2" d., 6 1/2" d., each (ILLUS).................. **95**

*Dutch Tulip Pattern Mixing Bowls*

**Mixing bowls,** nesting-type, Dutch Tulip patt., Nos. 65, 64, 63, 8 1/2" d., 7 1/2" d., 6 1/2" d., each (ILLUS.)............................... **125**
**Mixing bowls,** nesting-type, Morning Glory patt., Nos. 6, 7, 8, & 9, 6" to 9" d., each ......... **80**

*Watt Open Apple Pattern Mixing Bowls*

**Mixing bowls,** nesting-type, Open Apple patt., Nos. 5, 6, 7, & 8, 5" to 8" d., each (ILLUS. of three)........................................... **150**

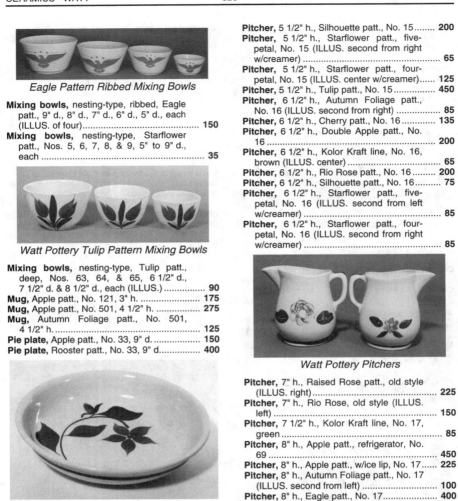

Eagle Pattern Ribbed Mixing Bowls

**Mixing bowls,** nesting-type, ribbed, Eagle patt., 9" d., 8" d., 7" d., 6" d., 5" d., each (ILLUS. of four)............................................ 150
**Mixing bowls,** nesting-type, Starflower patt., Nos. 5, 6, 7, 8, & 9, 5" to 9" d., each ................................................................ 35

Watt Pottery Tulip Pattern Mixing Bowls

**Mixing bowls,** nesting-type, Tulip patt., deep, Nos. 63, 64, & 65, 6 1/2" d., 7 1/2" d. & 8 1/2" d., each (ILLUS.) ................ 90
**Mug,** Apple patt., No. 121, 3" h. ........................ 175
**Mug,** Apple patt., No. 501, 4 1/2" h. .................. 275
**Mug,** Autumn Foliage patt., No. 501, 4 1/2" h. ......................................................... 125
**Pie plate,** Apple patt., No. 33, 9" d. .................. 150
**Pie plate,** Rooster patt., No. 33, 9" d............... 400

Watt Pottery Strawberry Pie Plate

**Pie plate,** Starflower patt., five-petal, No. 33, 9" d. (ILLUS.).......................................... 200
**Pitcher,** 5 1/2" h., Autumn Foliage patt., No. 15 (ILLUS. far right) ................................. 75
**Pitcher,** 5 1/2" h., Cross Hatch patt., No. 15 ................................................................ 250
**Pitcher,** 5 1/2" h., Dutch Tulip patt., No. 15...... 300
**Pitcher,** 5 1/2" h., green & white dripped glaze, No. 15 (ILLUS. right)......................... 200

Kolor Kraft Pitchers

**Pitcher,** 5 1/2" h., Kolor Kraft line, No. 15, yellow (ILLUS. right) ...................................... 60

**Pitcher,** 5 1/2" h., Silhouette patt., No. 15........ 200
**Pitcher,** 5 1/2" h., Starflower patt., five-petal, No. 15 (ILLUS. second from right w/creamer) ................................................... 65
**Pitcher,** 5 1/2" h., Starflower patt., four-petal, No. 15 (ILLUS. center w/creamer)...... 125
**Pitcher,** 5 1/2" h., Tulip patt., No. 15 ................ 450
**Pitcher,** 6 1/2" h., Autumn Foliage patt., No. 16 (ILLUS. second from right) ................. 85
**Pitcher,** 6 1/2" h., Cherry patt., No. 16 ............. 135
**Pitcher,** 6 1/2" h., Double Apple patt., No. 16 ................................................................ 200
**Pitcher,** 6 1/2" h., Kolor Kraft line, No. 16, brown (ILLUS. center) ................................... 65
**Pitcher,** 6 1/2" h., Rio Rose patt., No. 16 ......... 200
**Pitcher,** 6 1/2" h., Silhouette patt., No. 16......... 75
**Pitcher,** 6 1/2" h., Starflower patt., five-petal, No. 16 (ILLUS. second from left w/creamer) ................................................... 85
**Pitcher,** 6 1/2" h., Starflower patt., four-petal, No. 16 (ILLUS. second from right w/creamer) ................................................... 85

Watt Pottery Pitchers

**Pitcher,** 7" h., Raised Rose patt., old style (ILLUS. right)................................................ 225
**Pitcher,** 7" h., Rio Rose, old style (ILLUS. left) .............................................................. 150
**Pitcher,** 7 1/2" h., Kolor Kraft line, No. 17, green ............................................................. 85
**Pitcher,** 8" h., Apple patt., refrigerator, No. 69 ................................................................... 450
**Pitcher,** 8" h., Apple patt., w/ice lip, No. 17...... 225
**Pitcher,** 8" h., Autumn Foliage patt., No. 17 (ILLUS. second from left) ............................. 100
**Pitcher,** 8" h., Eagle patt., No. 17..................... 400
**Pitcher,** 8" h., Morning Glory patt., No. 96 ....... 300
**Pitcher,** 8" h., Rio Rose patt., No. 17 ................ 250
**Pitcher,** 8" h., Starflower patt., four-petal, No. 17 (ILLUS. far right w/creamer) ............. 135
**Pitcher,** 8" h., Starflower patt., refrigerator, No. 69 (ILLUS. far left w/creamer) .............. 500
**Pitcher,** 8" h., Tear Drop patt., four-petal, refrigerator, No. 69 ...................................... 500
**Pitcher,** 8" h w/creamer) ................................... 160
**Plate,** 6 1/2" d., Rio Rose patt. .......................... 20

Watt Moonflower Plate & Platter

**Plate,** 10" d., Moonflower patt. (ILLUS.
right) ............................................................... **60**
**Platter,** 12" d., Cherry patt., No. 49 ......................
**Platter,** 12" d., Rio Rose patt., No. 49 ............... **75**
**Platter,** 15" d., Apple patt., No. 31 .................. **300**
**Platter,** 15" d., Autumn Foliage patt., No.
31 .................................................................. **100**
**Platter,** 15" d., Moonflower patt., No. 31
(ILLUS. left) ................................................... **80**
**Platter,** 15" d., Starflower patt., No. 31 ............ **110**

*Cherry Pattern Popcorn Set*

**Popcorn set,** Cherry patt., in original dis-
play box, the set (ILLUS.) ............................ **500**
**Salt & pepper shakers,** barrel-shaped,
Starflower patt., five-petal, 4" h., the set ...... **200**
**Salt & pepper shakers,** barrel-shaped,
Tear Drop patt., 4" h., the set ....................... **300**
**Salt & pepper shakers,** hourglass-shaped,
Autumn Foliage patt., 4" h., the set
(ILLUS. far right w/Chip-n-Dip set) ............... **160**
**Salt & pepper shakers,** hourglass-shaped,
Rooster patt., 4" h., the set ........................... **375**
**Salt & pepper shakers,** hourglass-shaped,
Starflower patt., six-petal, 4" h., the set ....... **250**
**Salt shaker,** barrel-shaped, Cherry patt.,
4" h. ................................................................. **85**
**Sugar bowl,** cov., Morning Glory patt., No.
98, 4 1/4" h. ................................................... **250**
**Sugar bowl,** cov., Autumn Foliage patt.,
No. 98, 4 1/2" h. (ILLUS. far left w/Chip-
n-Dip set) ....................................................... **275**

*Watt Pottery Teapots*

**Teapot,** cov., Apple patt., No. 505, 5" h.
(ILLUS. left) ............................................... **2,800**
**Teapot,** cov., Apple (three-leaf) patt., No.
112, 6" h. (ILLUS. right) ............................. **1,500**
**Teapot,** cov., Autumn Foliage patt., No.
112, 6" h. .................................................. **1,000**

# WEDGWOOD

*Reference here is to the famous pottery estab-
lished by Josiah Wedgwood in 1759 in England.
Numerous types of wares have been produced
through the years to the present.*

## BASALT

**Bowl,** 5 3/4" d., footed wide rounded form
w/flat rim, applied classical figural relief
designs above an engine-turned band,
impressed mark, late 18th c. ...................... **$403**
**Bust of Cicero,** mounted on a waisted circular socle, impressed title & Wedgwood
and Bentley mark, ca. 1775, 10" h.
(chips to socle rim) ................................... **2,300**
**Bust of Garrick,** miniature, mounted on a
waisted circular socle, impressed mark,
19th c., 3 7/8" h. .......................................... **431**
**Bust of George Washington,** mounted on
a waisted circular socle, impressed title
& mark, 19th c., 19 3/4" h. ........................ **6,038**
**Bust of King George II,** shown wearing a
long wig & parade armor, after a carving
by John Michael Rysbrack, on a raised
square plinth, impressed lower case
marks, ca. 1780, 9" h. ............................... **1,093**
**Bust of Locke,** mounted on a waisted cir-
cular socle, impressed title & mark, late
18th - early 19th c., impressed title &
mark, 9 1/2" h. ............................................. **748**
**Bust of Nelson,** shown wearing his uni-
form w/his empty sleeve draped across
the front, mounted on a waisted circular
socle, impressed mark & inscription
"Pubd. July 22nd 1798 R. Shout Sep.
Holborn," late 18th c., 11" h. (socle rim
chips) ....................................................... **3,450**
**Bust of Newton,** mounted on a waisted cir-
cular socle, impressed mark, 19th c.,
9 1/4" h. ....................................................... **431**

*Rare Basalt Griffin Candlesticks*

**Candlesticks,** figural, model of a large
seated griffin w/a tall candle socket atop
the head, on a rectangular platform
base, traces of later gilding, impressed
mark of Wedgwood and Bentley, ca.
1775, one w/wings restored & small rim
chips on socket & plinth, one w/socket
restored at join & small chips on socket
rim & wings, 12 1/2" h., pr. (ILLUS.) ........ **19,550**
**Coffeepot,** cov., wide baluster form
w/swan's-neck spout, C-form handle &
domed cover w/knob finial, decorated
overall w/large clusters of polychromed
flowers, impressed mark, ca. 1840,
8 3/4" h. ........................................................ **690**
**Cracker jar,** cov., the engine-turned body
below a band of children playing in relief,

silver plate rim, cover & bail handle, impressed mark, late 19th c., 5 1/2" h. ......... **516**

**Creamer,** helmet-form, short pedestal base below the inverted helmet-form body w/a wide arched spout & D-form loop handle, a continuous relief scene of bacchanalian boys at play above an engine-turned band, impressed mark of Wedgwood and Bentley, early 19th c., 4 3/8" h. ............. **518**

**Crocus pot,** figural, the top modeled as a large rounded hedgehog pierced w/holes, in a fitted oblong dished base, impressed marks, 1975, 9 1/2" l. .................. **546**

**Decanter w/stopper,** wide cylindrical form w/an impressed band of Greek key below the rounded shoulder, high C-scroll shoulder handle, the small cylindrical neck & cupped, arched spout in silver w/a matching stopper w/a flattened upright ring handle, impressed mark, late 19th c., 10 1/4" h. .................. **690**

**Ewers,** classical-form w/a large banded ovoid body incised w/stripes below the tall ringed neck w/high arched & scalloped spout & high arched loop handle extending to the shoulder, raised on a square plinth, the body band molded w/laurel leaves w/a bacchus head mask at the base of the handle, impressed lozenge mark, ca. 1775, nicks to edges of base, 9 3/4" h., pr. .................. **7,475**

**Figure of a faun playing flute,** a nude youth standing & leaning against a fur-draped tree trunk, on a rounded rectangular base, impressed title & mark, 19th c., 17 1/4" h. (slight chip restored on instrument) ............................................. **2,645**

**Figure of Voltaire,** standing wearing a long wig, a waistcoat, kneebreeches & a long coat, one arm extended holding a book, after the marble figure by Jean-Claude Rosset, mounted on a free-form circular base, impressed title & mark, 19th c., 10 3/4" h. (footrim chip) ........................... **1,610**

**Figures of Cupid & Psyche,** each seated on a rock-molded circular base, impressed title & marks, late 19th c., 8" h., pr. (Cupid w/slight footrim nicks, Psyche w/large chip on underside of base) ........................................................ **690**

*Wedgwood Basalt Inkstand*

**Inkstand,** a cylindrical flat-topped sander & a cylindrical inkwell w/pierced flat cover w/molded shell, fitted in an oblong two-section center-handled holder, impressed marks, 19th c., 3 3/4" h., the set (ILLUS.)...... **863**

**Lamp bases,** tall classical urn-form w/the sides molded in relief w/oval eagle medallions between foliate festoons terminating at lion mask handles, slender pedestal w/round foot on a square stepped base, 20th c., 21" h., pr. ............. **2,645**

**Medallion,** oval, embossed profile bust portrait of George Washington, set in a brass frame, titled & impressed mark of Wedgwood and Bentley, ca. 1775, 2 1/2 x 3 1/4" (edge flakes) ...................... **1,725**

**Model of a bear,** animal walking on all fours, by Ernest Light, ca. 1915, impressed mark, 2 1/2" h. ............................ **489**

**Mug,** cylindrical w/silver-mounted rim band, sides relief-molded w/classical children representing Spring & Winter, impressed lower case mark, D-form handle, late 18th c., 3 1/2" h. (handle restored)............... **805**

**Orange bowl,** a wide & deep rounded bowl raised on a short wide flaring round pedestal, the exterior of the bowl ornately molded w/scrollwork & basketweave bands & festoons, impressed mark, late 19th c., 8 3/4" d. ..................................... **1,093**

**Pitcher,** 5 1/8" h., Kenlock Ware, slightly tapering cylindrical body w/a D-form ropetwist handle, the sides lightly molded & enameled w/a grotesque beast & long banners, impressed mark, ca. 1900 .................. **316**

**Pitcher,** 5 7/8" h., bottle-form, a footed bulbous ovoid body tapering to a waisted cylindrical neck w/a flaring flattened mouth, arched grapevine handle ending in a bacchus head, the body molded in high-relief w/figure groups representing the Four Seasons, impressed mark, 19th c. ...................................................... **748**

**Pitcher,** 6 1/2" h., jug-type, "Egyptian" patt., club-form, decorated in iron-red, black & white w/a sphinx at either side of a bird in flight, impressed mark, ca. 1854 (rim chip) ...................................................... **690**

**Plant pot & underplate,** acanthus leaf borders on a trellis-molded body, impressed mark, 19th c., 2 7/8" h., 2 pcs. (rim nick)...... **460**

**Plaque,** oval, molded in high-relief w/a scene of two small Bacchanalian boys frolicking w/a large panther, impressed mark, late 18 - early 19th c., 7 1/2 x 10 3/4" ........................................... **2,415**

**Plaques,** oval, each relief-molded, one w/a figure of a dancing nymph, the other w/the figure of a piping faun, impressed marks, early 19th c., 4 5/8 x 6 1/2", pr.......... **863**

**Punch pot,** cov., an engine-turned band below the shoulder, impressed early 19th c. mark, 7 1/2" h. (slight shoulder chips)............................................................. **460**

**Ring,** intaglio-type, oval portrait of the Duke of Gloucester, white gold mounting, impressed mark & numbered 283, Wedgwood and Bentley, intaglio 3/4 x 7/8" .......................................................... **518**

**Stirrup cup,** model of a fox head w/long ears, impressed mark of Wedgwood and Bentley, ca. 1775, restoration to ear, hairline, chip to ear, 4 7/8" h. .................. **2,645**

**Sugar bowl,** cov., cylindrical body tapering in at the bottom, fitted engine-turned domed cover w/rim band & figural sibyl finial, the sides molded w/a scene depicting Domestic Employment, impressed mark, late 18th c., 5" h. ............. **748**

**Teapot,** cov., cylindrical oval form w/straight angled spout & angled C-form handle, domed cover w/figural Sybil finial, enameled w/palmette, leaf, leaf & berry banding, impressed mark, early 19th c., 8" l. (chip on cover)...................... **3,450**

**Teapot,** cov., parapet-shaped, relief-molded design of Domestic Employment above an engine-turned band, figural Sibyl finial on cover, impressed mark, 19th c., 4" h. (slight spout nick) ................... **575**

**Teapot stand,** oval, molded floral & vinework arabesque design, impressed lower case mark, late 18th c., 6 3/8 x 7 3/8" ............................................... **633**

**Vase,** 9 1/4" h., classical urn-form, a square plinth below the short small pedestal supporting the large tall urn-form body w/a wide shoulder centering the waisted neck w/rolled rim, arched loop handles from the rim to the shoulder & ending in bacchus heads, plain body & base, Shape 1, impressed lozenge mark of Wedgwood and Bentley, ca. 1775 (missing cover).................................................. **978**

**Vase,** cov., 9 1/4" h., large egg-form body w/pointed base & domed cover w/radiating acanthus leaves centering a blossom finial, the sides of the body molded w/floral festoons, raised in a ring supported on three goat mask & hoofed legs on a triangular base, impressed mark, 19th c. (chips to petals of finial) ........................... **3,335**

**Vase,** cov., 10 1/2" h., classical urn-form, square plinth w/patterned edges supporting a short flaring engine-turned pedestal below the tall ovoid urn-form body w/a wide shoulder tapering to an engine-turned waisted neck w/flared rim & small domed cover w/knob finial, slender ropetwist loop handles from rim to edge of shoulder ending w/a lion mask, the body w/a relief-molded procession of classical figures, acanthus & laurel leaf borders, impressed mark of Wedgwood and Bentley, ca. 1775 (slight rim flakes on plinth) ..................................................... **3,738**

**Vase,** cov., 10 1/2" h., classical-style, a square plinth supporting a short ribbed & footed pedestal below a rounded base on the wide slightly flaring cylindrical body w/a wide shoulder centering a short ringed & waisted neck w/molded rim & low domed cover w/button finial, high inwardly-curved C-scroll shoulder handles w/leaf-tip terminals, the body w/a narrow lappet band of a wide scenic band of bacchanalian boys at play, impressed lozenge mark of Wedgwood and Bentley, ca. 1775 (replaced cover, rim nicks on shoulder & plinth) ................. **2,300**

# JASPER WARE

**Barber bottle w/stopper,** three-color, classical bottle-form, a low ringed pedestal base supporting a wide bulbous flaring body w/a wide sloping shoulder to the tall cylindrical neck w/a domed cap stopper, dark blue ground w/molded Bacchus heads around the shoulder, lilac ground medallions around the body w/white relief classical figures depicting the Four Seasons & joined by lilac swagged fruiting grapevines, foliate lilac bands around the neck, shoulder & base, impressed mark, mid-19th c., 10" h. (two Bacchus heads restored) .......... **748**

**Basket,** basketweave sides w/molded loop handle, dark blue ground applied w/white relief openwork cells, impressed mark, early 19th c., 4 1/2" h. (slight relief loss)................................................................. **431**

**Book case,** rectangular flattened oak case w/brass hardware, mounted w/seven round light blue jasper medallions w/white relief portraits or classical designs, the case including five leather-bound journals, marked "Howell, James & Co. - Regent Street, London," no visible marks on medallions, ca. 1900, 3 3/8 x 8 1/4", 5" h. .................................... **1,610**

**Bowl,** 5 7/8" d., black ground decorated w/a white relief figural decoration of the Dancing Hours, impressed mark, 20th c. ..... **489**

**Bowl,** 8 1/8" d., footed, the wide low-sided round bowl w/a flat rim raised on a short, wide rounded flaring foot, yellow ground applied w/black relief classical figures in a landscape w/leaf-tips rim & foot bands, impressed mark, 20th c. (stained) ............... **518**

**Box,** cov., round short cylindrical form w/fitted flattened cover, dark blue ground decorated in white slip w/scrolling stems & blossoms on the cover & leaf-tips around the base rim, artist-signed by Harry Barnard, impressed mark, ca. 1900, 2 3/4" d. (shallow rim chip on cover) ........................................................... **633**

**Box,** cov., square w/rounded corners, crimson red ground decorated on the slightly domed top & around the sides w/white relief classical figure groups surrounded by flowering bands & corner scrolls on the base, impressed mark, ca. 1920, 4" w. ......................................................... **1,150**

**Box,** cov., three-color, tall cylindrical form w/flat fitted cover, light blue ground decorated around the sides w/small oval lilac medallions w/tiny white relief figures between heavy white relief fruiting festoons & ribbons, pierced lappet band around the base, the top centered by a white relief classical scene w/white relief border band, impressed mark, late 19th c., 4" d. (restored slight rim chip on cover) ......................................................... **575**

**Box,** cov., wide slightly tapering cylindrical form w/low domed cover, light blue fitted in an ormolu open mount w/floral swags joining the four straight legs w/paw feet, the cover mounted w/ormolu floral swags & an arched branch handle, impressed mark, late 19th c., 4 3/8" d. (rim nick) ...................................................... **460**

**Brooch,** oval, blue ground decorated in white relief w/a classical scene of the marriage of Cupid & Psyche, set in a wide scalloped cut-steel mount, no visible mark, ca. 1800, 2 1/2" l........................... **489**

**Candleholder,** stepped cylindrical form, dark blue ground decorated w/white relief classical figures & foliage designs, impressed mark, mid-19th c., 4" h................ **575**

**Candlesticks,** columnar standard on a wide flaring round foot, deeply cupped candle socket, black ground decorated around the standard w/white relief classical figures & around the foot w/a scrolling foliate band, a thin leaf band under the socket, impressed mark, 19th c., 8" h., pr.................................................... **863**

**Cheese dish,** cov., wide cylindrical domed cover w/flat top centered by a button finial, dark blue ground decorated w/white relief classical figures & trees around the sides & radiating leaves & a foliate band around the finial, the matching dished base w/a flanged flat rim w/white relief foliate band, impressed mark, mid-19th c., 4 3/4" h. .................................................. **345**

*Blue Jasper Ware Clock*

**Clock,** arched pediment w/white relief central winged classical figure flanked by "Tempus Fugit," above the narrow rectangular upright case w/a round dial w/Arabic numerals above two white relief groups of women & children, white relief leaf bands up the sides & scrolls above the dial, on dark blue, impressed mark, ca. 1900, 8" h. (ILLUS.) ...................... **863**

**Coffee cup & saucer,** cylindrical cup, black ground decorated w/white relief classical trophies & medallions between fruiting festoons terminating at rams' heads, mid-19th c., saucer 5 1/4" d. (restored rim chip to saucer)...................................... **690**

**Cracker jar,** cov., cylindrical base supporting a low domed cover w/button finial, black ground decorated w/a wide white relief central band of stylized Egyptian figures & designs above a narrow florette base band, white relief starburst around the finial, impressed factory mark

& mark of retailer W.T. Lamb & Sons, ca. 1911, 5 1/4" h. ......................... **1,093**

*Blue Jasper Cracker Jar*

**Cracker jar,** cov., cylindrical w/wide waisted body, the center molded in relief w/white classical figures on a dark blue ground, upper & lower border bands in light blue, silver plate rim, flat cover w/urn finials & swing bail handle, impressed mark, 19th c., 5" h. (ILLUS.) ....... **288**

**Cracker jar,** cov., low rounded base below the tapering cylindrical sides supporting a low domed cover w/button finial, black ground decorated w/a wide white relief central band of stylized Egyptian figures & designs between narrow florette border bands, white relief starburst around the finial, impressed factory mark & mark of retailer W.T. Lamb & Sons, ca. 1911, 6 1/4" h. (rim nick) ...................................... **1,265**

**Creamer,** jug-form, ovoid body w/wide mouth & rim spout, C-scroll handle, black ground decorated w/heavy fruit festoons between rams' heads, classical & trophy designs, impressed mark, mid-19th c., 2 3/4" h. ............................... **748**

**Cup & saucer** deep rounded cup w/white D-form handle, wide dished saucer, each in black w/white relief classical scrolls & small medallions between thin leaf bands around the cup, radiating leaf band inside saucer, impressed mark, 20th c., saucer 5 1/2" d. ............................. **316**

**Dish,** diamond-shaped shallow form, crimson red ground w/a white relief classical figure in the center & a laurel leaf band around the flanged rim, impressed mark, ca. 1920, 5 3/4" l. ............................. **805**

**Earrings,** almond-shaped medallions in blue decorated w/white relief classical figure, in a narrow cut-steel frame set w/rhinestones, short chain & screw-on clips, impressed marks, 19th c., 1 3/8" l., pr. .................................................... **374**

**Flowerpot,** hanging-type, dark blue ground decorated w/white relief classical figures & foliate designs, unmarked, late 19th c., 6 1/2" h. ......................................... **403**

**Goblet,** commemorative, three-color, Dice Ware, classic chalice form w/a light blue ground decorated w/applied white relief oval portrait medallions of George Washington & Thomas Jefferson separated by leafy festoon & foliate rim & foot bands, green banded trim & quatrefoils, for the 1976 U.S. Bicentennial, No. 59 of 200, impressed mark, 4 3/4" h. .................... **690**

**Jardiniere,** wide footrim below the wide cylindrical body w/a rounded base & flat rim, white relief classical figures of Muses below a band of fruiting grapevine swags suspended from lion masks, narrow border band, on a crimson ground, impressed mark, ca. 1920, 7 1/4" h. (slight surface flake).................... **2,415**

**Jars,** cov., cylindrical on a thin stepped foot, slightly flared rim supporting a low domed cover w/knob finial, dark blue w/applied white relief classical figure groups separated by vertical foliate bands w/beaded band around the rim, similar decorations on the cover, impressed marks, ca. 1900, 3 7/8" h., pr...... **288**

**Pitcher w/hinged pewter cover,** 6 5/8" h., three-color, tapering cylindrical form w/small loop handle w/tab near rim, green ground decorated w/yellow relief trellis bands alternating w/leaf bands between upper & lower leafy bands, impressed mark, 19th c. (light staining in relief) ............................................................ **518**

**Pitcher w/hinged pewter cover,** 8" h., wide baluster-form body tapering to a gently flaring neck w/wide arched spout, C-form handle, dark blue ground w/white relief Portland Vase figural decoration, impressed mark, mid-19th c. ........................ **518**

**Pitchers,** 7 1/2" h., 6 1/4" h., 5 1/4" h., set of slightly tapering cylindrical pieces w/small rim spouts & ropetwist handles, olive green ground w/white relief medallion bust portraits of George Washington within a leaf-tip frame w/a fruiting grapevine border around the rim, impressed marks, ca. 1920, the set (footrim chips) ....... **575**

*Rare Three-color Jasper Planter*

**Planter,** deep oval form w/molded pilasters alternating w/side panels of oval lilac medallions w/white relief classical scenes surrounded by white relief scrolls & leaf swags on a green ground, bold relief white classical figure groups at each end, rounded base band w/thin leaf bands & wide acanthus leaf panels in white, on incurved scroll legs, impressed mark, chip on one foot, under body & rim, late 18th - early 19th c., 17" l. (ILLUS.)...................................................... **8,625**

**Plaque,** rectangular, dark blue ground decorated in white relief w/a classical scene of two chariots & putti in procession,

impressed mark, 19th c., 5 1/4 x 10 1/8" (rim chip) .................................................... **1,380**

**Plaque,** rectangular, black ground decorated w/white relief scene of putti playing blind man's bluff, matted & framed, impressed mark, 19th c., 3 3/8 x 9 1/8" (shallow rim flake) ...................................... **575**

**Plaques,** oval, light blue ground decorated w/white relief classical female figure, impressed marks, 19th c., 5 1/4 x 7 1/4", pr...................................................................... **489**

**Plate,** 8 1/2" d., blue ground decorated in white relief w/a classical figural scene, impressed mark, ca. 1861 ............................ **633**

**Portland Vase,** black ground molded in white relief w/a continuous classical figural scene, half-length figure wearing a Phrygian cap under base, unmarked, late 18th c., 10 1/8" h. (relief loss, surface blister)................................................ **4,600**

**Portland Vase,** 10" h., wide ovoid body tapering to a trumpet neck flanked by arched handles, black ground w/white relief classical figural scene, impressed mark, late 19th c...................................... **2,415**

**Potpourri,** cov., a wide shallow bowl w/a low domed cover pierced w/a large top hole surrounded by smaller holes, raised on a ringed flaring pedestal on a thick square foot, dark blue ground decorated around the bowl w/large white relief arabesque scroll band, gadroon band, vertical stripes & lappet band on pedestal w/urn & scrolls on the foot, quatrefoils on the cover, early 19th c., impressed mark, 6 3/4" h.......................................................... **1,725**

**Scent bottle w/silver cap,** flattened oval form, dark blue ground decorated in white relief w/a classical female figure within an oval framed by a ribbon, leaf & floral wreath, no visible mark, early 19th c., 3 1/4" l. .......................................... **1,035**

**Snuff bottle w/silver cap,** flattened round form, light blue ground decorated in white relief on one side w/a bust portrait of King George IV, on the other side w/Prince of Wales feathers, each framed in floral festoons, unmarked, late 18th c., 2 5/8" l. .......................................... **1,265**

**Spill vases,** a short disk foot supporting a tall slightly tapering cylindrical body, black ground decorated w/white relief foliage above engine-turned white striping, impressed marks, mid-19th c., 4" h., pr. (each w/footrim chips)........................ **1,150**

**Tea set:** cov. teapot, cov. sugar & creamer; solid white ground on wide waisted cylindrical bodies, applied w/foliate relief designs alternating in green & lilac, stained, late 19th - early 20th c., impressed mark, teapot 3 1/2" h., the set (ILLUS. center)........................................ **1,380**

**Tobacco jar,** cov., cylindrical w/a wide flared base rim & a wide molded top ring around the inset flat cover w/button finial, dark blue ground decorated around the sides w/four white relief panels each w/a different large classical figural grouping between vertical scroll & foliate

bands, white relief lappet band around
the base & further white relief decoration
on the rim & cover, impressed mark, ca.
1861, 4 1/2" h. ............................................. **690**

*Gilt-decorated Jasper Ware Vase*

**Vase,** 9 3/4" h., light blue ground decorated
w/ornate h.p. raised gilt large flowers &
leafy stems, impressed mark, 19th c.
(ILLUS.) .................................................... **2,875**
**Vase,** cov., 11 1/2" h., ormolu-mounted, a
deep light green urn-form body decorated w/white relief classical figures
above a pointed leaf band & fitted
around the rim w/a scroll-pierced ormolu
band & classical female mask handles,
the high domed cover w/further white
relief radiating leaves around the ormolu
pine cone finial, all raised on a ringed &
reeded ormolu pedestal on a shaped
square foot, impressed mark (cover
restored) ................................................... **2,415**
**Vase,** cov., 13 1/8" h., a tall square plinth
supporting a classical tall urn-form vase
w/a tall waisted cover w/domed tip &
knob finial, green ground decorated
around the plinth w/a white relief classical figure on each side, the vase body
w/white relief classical figure groups
separated by lattice bands below a
twisted ribbon top band, the cover
w/white relief long lappets, impressed
mark, late 19th c. ....................................... **2,185**
**Vase,** 14 3/4" h., trophy-style, classical urn-
form on a domed round foot, the waisted
neck w/a rolled rim, arched handles from
side of neck to shoulder, dark blue
ground w/white relief classical figures
around the body w/ribbons & trophies
around the neck & foliate borders around
the shoulder & base, impressed
mark, ca. 1900 ........................................... **978**
**Vase,** 5 3/8" h., yellow ground decorated
w/dark blue relief classical figures & foliate & fruiting grapevines, impressed
mark, 19th c. (missing cover) ................... **748**
**Vases** 7 3/4" h., footed bulbous ovoid body
w/a wide shoulder tapering to the flaring
trumpet neck, upright loop handles at
edge of shoulder, dark blue ground decorated w/white relief classical figure
groups alternating w/slender foliate vertical bands, leaf band around the center

of the neck, impressed mark, early 20th
c., pr. ....................................................... **575**

*Large Classical Jasper Vases*

**Vases,** 14" h., classical urn-form, tall ovoid
body tapering to a short waisted neck
w/a wide rolled rim, arched scroll handles from rim to shoulder, raised on a
ringed pedestal on an octagonal plinth,
the body w/a wide band of white relief
figures of the nine Muses w/gadroon &
foliate borders, on a black ground,
impressed marks, early 19th c., restorations to handles of each, also one plinth,
missing covers, pr. (ILLUS.) ..................... **2,415**

*Rare Jasper Dice Ware Wine Cooler*

**Wine cooler,** wide ovoid body w/a wide flat
rim, figural swan head handles w/wings
spread, Dice Ware design w/center panels of a classical "Roman Banquet"
scene in white relief on green, applied
yellow quatrefoils in the dice design,
impressed mark, 19th c., restoration to
handle, lower body & base, 10 1/2" h.
(ILLUS.) .................................................... **4,600**

## QUEEN'S WARE

**Bowl,** 5 1/2" d., footed deep rounded & flaring sides w/rolled rim, h.p. in silver lustre
& puce enamel w/a stylized continuous
landscape scene w/female bathers dis-
robing, artist-signed by Therese Les-
sore, impressed factory mark, ca. 1920 .... **1,150**

*Queen's Ware Breakfast Set*

**Breakfast set:** cov. teapot, cov. sugar bowl, cov. creamer, waste bowl, a cup & saucer & oblong tray; each bulbous piece enamel-decorated w/flowers & insects, tray 16 7/8" l., teapot 4 1/4" h., impressed marks, some restorations, ca 1868, the set (ILLUS.) ............................ **1,035**

**Bust of Penelope,** stylized half-length bust of a Grecian lady, undecorated, modeled by Arnold Machin, printed mark, ca. 1940, 11" h. .................................................. **374**

**Dish,** boat-form w/bearded mask head handles on the oval body fitted w/two circular cups, enamel-decorated w/fruiting grapevine decoration, impressed & printed marks, late 19th c., 13 1/4" l. ............ **316**

**Dish,** oval shell-shape painted on the interior w/colorful cherubs, signed by Emile Lessore, impressed mark, ca. 1860, 13" l. ................................................................ **546**

**Figure of Helen,** standing Grecian lady wearing a long gown, one arm to her side, one arm across her waist, undecorated, modeled by Arnold Machin, printed marks, ca. 1940, 14" h. ................... **748**

**Lobster serving set:** 10" d. bowl & pair of servers; the deep round bowl w/enamel-decorated brown transfer prints of ocean vegetation, supported on three figural lobster feet, silver plate rim band inscribed "Dublin University Athletic Sports 1884 - 440 yd. - Flat Race 2nd Prize Won by L. Kidd - Time 52 4/5 sec.," the servers w/lobster claw handles, impressed marks, ca. 1883, the set..... **489**

**Model of bull,** stylized standing Ferdinand, undecorated, modeled by Arnold Machin, impressed mark, ca. 1940, 12 1/4" l. ...................................................... **288**

**Orange bowl,** cov., low round pedestal foot supporting a wide rounded bowl w/a wide lobe-fluted flaring rim, the high domed cover pierced w/long tapering ovals framed by molded scroll lattice & floral designs, impressed mark, 20th c., 9 1/2" h. .............................................................. **633**

**Plate,** 9 1/4" d., round, the interior painted w/an Aesop's Fable scene of a stork & fox in a tropical landscape, signed by artist Emile Lessore, reverse inscribed "Don't put your nose in another's affairs," impressed mark, ca. 1863 (enamel wear on rim) ......................................................... **173**

**Plate,** 9 7/8" d., polychrome decorated black transfer of a sailing ship centering a floral border, titled "Welvaren 1779" & "D'Maria & Adriana Leendert Steur," lower case mark, ca. 1779 (rim nicks) ......... **805**

**Pot,** cov., kettle-form, three straight tapering angled legs supporting the wide kettle-form body w/slightly flaring cylindrical sides & pointed loop rim handles, a low domed cover w/low arched open handle, decorated by Emile Lessore w/enameled figural landscapes, artist-signed & impressed marks, ca. 1870, 5 1/4" h. (one foot stained) ...................................... **748**

**Sweetmeat baskets,** each w/scalloped rim on a pierced body, impressed mark, early 19th c., 5" h., pr. .............................. **2,415**

**Wash bowl & pitcher,** black transfer-printed designs of Venetian-style subjects, printed marks, ca. 1900, bowl 15 3/4" d., pitcher 11" h., the set (bowl w/light general surface wear on interior) ...... **144**

## MISCELLANEOUS

**Bank,** glazed earthenware, modeled as a cylindrical brick building & inscribed on the footrim "Wedgwood - Etruria 1769 - The Round House," brown glaze, ca. 1969, 4 3/4" h. ............................................... **201**

**Basket & undertray,** creamware, oval basket w/reticulated sides & molded basketweave center on matching undertray, impressed mark, 10" l., 2 pcs. (chip on tray table ring, stains) .................................. **440**

**Bird feeder,** majolica, cylindrical w/large open arched panels around the sides below a narrow angled shoulder & wide flat mouth, overall green glaze, impressed mark, ca. 1870, 2 3/4" h............. **230**

**Bird feeder,** majolica, small barrel-shaped object w/the sides pierced w/large vertical rectangular openings w/arched tops, dark green glaze, impressed mark, ca. 1871, 3 7/8" h. ............................................... **259**

*Wedgwood Art Deco Book Ends*

**Book ends,** earthenware, Art Deco style, each a quarter-round arch w/stepped curved bands above lower fanned ribs, a small stylized figure seated at the top, overall red glaze, designed by Erling Olsen, impressed mark, ca. 1932, 6 5/8" h., pr. (ILLUS.) .............................. **1,840**

**Bottle, cover & underplate,** brown stoneware, impressed marks, ca. 1865, 10 3/4" h., the set (chips on cover).............. **230**

**Bottle, cover & underplate,** the bottle w/a small short pedestal foot supporting a wide sharply tapering conical body banded w/silver plate & ending in a tall ringed cylindrical neck fitted w/a silver plate rim & flat cover w/a figural sphinx finial, the matching underplate w/a silver plate rim, all w/a mottled brown & green glaze, impressed marks, ca. 1875, overall 10 1/4" h., the set (bottle w/slight rim lines & glaze loss) ...................................... **1,035**

**Bowl,** 4 1/2" d., Fairyland Lustre Nizami design, shallow round form, deep green lustre ground exterior & interior, the center w/a Persian scene of a figure in a garden landscape, Pattern Z5494, printed mark, ca. 1920 (very slight interior gilt wear) ............................................. **3,335**

**Bowl,** 5 1/2" d., bone china, a small footring supporting a wide rounded bowl w/upright sides & flat rim, matte black exterior decorated w/gilt lightning overall decoration, the interior w/an enameled Oriental style floral design, printed mark, ca. 1920 ............................................. **633**

**Bowl,** 7 1/8" d., Butterfly Lustre, thin footring below the deep scalloped sides, exterior w/butterflies on a mottled red & green ground, a mottled orange interior w/Oriental gilt dragon, Pattern Z4823, ca. 1920, printed mark .................... **518**

**Bowl,** 8" d., Fairyland Lustre, deep rounded sides, the exterior in coral & brown w/the "Fairy with a Large Hat" scene, pearl interior w/a checker rosette centering a magpie & masks border, Pattern Z5348, ca. 1920, printed mark (interior wear) ........................................... **1,265**

**Bowl,** 8 1/4" d., Daventry Imperial Lustre, a thick footring supporting a wide deep bowl, paneled red ground exterior, a thorn design on the yellow interior ground w/an Oriental landscape in the center, Pattern Z5440, printed mark, ca. 1920 (interior center wear) .......................... **920**

**Bowl,** 11 1/4" d., earthenware, deep footring supporting a wide rounded form w/a flat rim, crimson lustre-decorated, the exterior painted w/bears & foliage, the interior w/a crimson ground & central floral design, designed by William de Morgan, artist-signed by Charles Passenger, impressed factory mark, ca. 1900 (interior glaze wear) .......................................... **920**

**Bread tray,** majolica, rectangular w/curved-out sides, a flat flanged rim band molded w/waves, an argenta ground, the bottom inside molded w/a lattice of strapwork & coral branches, impressed mark, ca. 1880, 12 3/4" l. (surface wear) .................... **546**

**Center bowl,** antique-style, short wide pedestal w/a widely flaring round foot, supporting a deep, wide bell-form bowl w/widely rolled rim, the matte black exterior w/printed floral sprigs, the white interior printed w/colorful flowers & gilt trim, printed mark, ca. 1925, 8 5/8" d. (exterior glaze scratches)................................... **575**

**Charger,** Caneware, large round & slightly dished form h.p. w/a wide outer band of undulating vine w/large serrated leaves in a purple lustre glaze, a large single leaf in the center, attributed to Millicent Taplin, printed mark, ca. 1930, 12 1/2" d...... **374**

**Cheese dish,** cov., majolica, Bird & Fan patt., domed cover & conforming underplate, argenta ground, impressed mark, ca. 1880, 9 5/8" h. (slight staining to bottom rim of cover, base restored) ......... **374**

**Chess figure,** Drabware, a figure of the Queen standing w/long hair looking over her shoulder, wearing a long dress, her arms crossed over her chest, raised socle plinth, impressed mark, early 19th c., 3 7/8" h. .................................................. **489**

*Fine Wedgwood Bone China Clock*

**Clock case,** bone china, D-shaped w/a flat top w/shaped edges overhanging the upright case w/raised pilasters & reeded block feet, a central round dial w/Arabic numerals & a brass bezel, the paneled body decorated overall w/gilt cherubs & flowers & gilt trim on a dark ground, printed mark, late 19th c., top surface worn, 8 3/4" h. (ILLUS.)............................. **1,035**

**Cup,** Fairyland Lustre, Nizami York-type, a central design of deer grazing in a landscape, printed mark, ca. 1920, 3 1/2" d..... **2,530**

*William de Morgan-Designed Dish*

**Dish,** earthenware, deep dished round form, crimson lustre-decorated w/a large bird in the center, pale enamel leaves & oranges in the background, designed by William de Morgan, artist-signed "CP" for Charles Passenger & "W.D.M. Fulham" & impressed factory mark, ca. 1900, slight rim hairline, framed, dish 10 1/4" d. (ILLUS.)...................... **1,955**

**Dish,** majolica, large slightly dished round form, a small central circle w/six radiating bands forming panels w/an argenta ground, each panel molded w/a large colorful chrysanthemum-style flower on a stippled ground, the outer rim band w/a radiating glaze design, impressed mark, ca. 1875, 12 1/4" d. ........................... **460**

**Dresser set:** 12 3/4" l. oval tray, pair 5 3/8" h. candlesticks, 2 1/2" h. ring tray, 2 1/4" h. low covered box, 4" h. tall covered box; bone china, all w/blue transfer-printed decorations w/scrolled foliate designs, the tray w/a central cartouche of Bacchanalian boys, printed marks, ca. 1900, the set ............................................. **518**

**Figure group,** bone china, a ballet group w/a costumed male & female dancer posing, modeled by Kathleen Goodwin, artist-signed, printed & impressed marks, ca. 1932, 7 1/2" h. (chip to his collar) ......................................................... **345**

**Figure group,** Carrara Ware, all-white grouping of "The Finding of Moses" w/the princess & her maid finding baby Moses in his basket, oval base, modeled by William Beattie, impressed artist's name, unmarked by factory, ca. 1860, mounted on a fitted wooden base, 19" h. (footrim chip on back edge & under base) ......................................................... **3,795**

**Figure of a ballerina,** a young girl seated atop a raised plinth, modeled by Kathleen Goodwin, artist-signed, impressed & printed marks, ca. 1931, 9" h. ................. **575**

**Figure of a fisherwoman,** majolica, standing woman modeled leaning over a woven basket & mounted on a circular base, impressed mark, ca. 1872, 10 1/4" h. (one finger restored on each hand, slight edge wear on glaze) ................. **460**

*Wedgwood Carrara Figure of Venus*

**Figure of Venus Victrix,** Carrara Ware, all-white model of the original "Venus de Milo," impressed title & mark, ca. 1880, 20 1/4" h. (ILLUS.).................................... **1,955**

**Fish platter,** majolica, oval w/slightly scalloped rim, a yellow ground molded w/a large salmon atop ferns & leaves, impressed mark, ca. 1880, 25 1/4" l. (light staining)............................................. **5,463**

**Game dish,** cov., majolica, high cylindrical cover w/flat top molded w/dead game & a recumbent rabbit handle, the sides molded w/grapevines & clusters of dead game, mottled dark glaze, impressed mark, ca. 1880, 6 7/8" l. (glaze scratches, no liner)...................................... **805**

**Jardiniere,** majolica, circular form w/overall blue glaze on the molded body w/paneled sides of scrolled flower & urn designs, framed in scrolled strap feet w/foliate relief, printed & impressed marks, ca. 1891, 11" h. ............... **920**

**Jardiniere,** Marsden's Art Ware, footed cylindrical form w/double bands molded at the wide flat rim, paneled sides decorated w/alternating designs of daisy-like flowers & a plain dark glaze, impressed mark, ca. 1890, 7" h. (surface glaze & rim scratches, touch up to enamel flaking near footrim)......................................... **230**

**Jewel stand,** majolica, figural, modeled as a nude child supporting & dragging one end of a flaring fish net-form dish, set on an oval base, impressed mark, ca. 1872, 5" h.......................................................... **1,380**

**Jug w/stopper,** earthenware body of wide ovoid form tapering slightly to a flat bottom, ring shoulder handle, the brown glaze incised & slip-decorated w/a motto within a foliate framed ribbon, motto reads "Who lives a good life is sure to live well," a sterling silver cylindrical neck w/wide arched spout & matching bulbous inverted pear-form silver stopper, impressed mark, artist-signed by Harry Barnard, ca. 1900, 8" h. ............... **575**

**Model of a nuthatch,** bone china, based on an original wood sculpture by Walt Ruch, No. 103 of 500, printed mark, modern, 6 1/4" h............................... **460**

**Mortar & pestle,** Mortarware, flat white mortar & pestle w/tapering hardwood handle, impressed mark on mortar, ca, 1780, 2 3/4" d., 2 pcs. ................................... **978**

**Mug,** earthenware, cylindrical, h.p. w/a stylized tropical bird on a lustrous yellow ground, impressed mark, ca. 1930, 4" h. ..... **144**

**Mussel plate,** majolica, the six-lobed scale-molded dish w/twelve circular fish-molded wells, impressed mark. ca. 1866, 11 1/4" d. (rim chip restored)........... **1,380**

**Pilgrim flask,** long oval foot supporting a large flattened disk-form body w/a tiny top flared neck flanked by tiny loop shoulder handles, moonstone glaze w/raised button border, Norman Wilson design, printed & impressed mark, ca. 1950, 8 3/4" h. ................................... **518**

**Pitcher,** 6 1/4" h., figural jug-form, Rockingham-glazed bust portrait of Elihu Yale, impressed mark, ca. 1933.................. **230**

**Pitcher,** 6 1/4" h., jug-form, porcelain, a wide ovoid lower body below a wide tapering shoulder molded w/wide swirled panels ending in a scalloped rim w/pointed rim spout & angled molded handle, the sides decorated w/bold gilt floral branches on the ivory-glazed ground, printed mark, ca. 1885 (gilt rim wear) .......................................................... **173**

**Pitcher,** 6 1/4" h., majolica, Bird & Fan patt., argenta ground, impressed mark, ca. 1860 ........................................... **345**

**Pitchers,** 8 1/2" h., jug-form, majolica, stepped round low pedestal foot supporting a short wide cylindrical body rounded at the bottom & top, tall cylindrical neck w/a hinged silver plate domed cover & large strap handle, silver plated banding around foot & body, mottled cobalt blue & yellow glaze, impressed marks, ca. 1879, pr. ................... **748**

**Plaque,** earthenware, rectangular, relief-molded w/a long hunt scene w/horses & riders trimmed in colored enamels, impressed mark, ca. 1930, 6 3/8 x 15 1/4" ........................................... **863**

**Plaques,** earthenware, rectangular, embossed bust portraits, one an elderly man w/long beard representing Old Age & a long-haired young maiden representing Youth, brown overall wash, impressed marks, mid-19th c., framed, impressed marks, 7 3/4 x 12 1/2", pr. .......... **633**

**Plate,** 10 1/8" d., lustre-decorated, slightly dished form w/a mother-of-pearl ground decorated w/an Oriental-style ornamented border w/Celtic ornament in the center, Pattern Z4970, printed mark, ca. 1920 (slight gilt rim wear) ........................... **748**

**Plate,** 10 1/4" d., Fairyland Lustre, "Imps on a Bridge" patt., a Roc center reserve, the rim decorated w/a variety of fruits & flowers, the center w/blue water, violet imps on the bridge & coral enamel on the black Roc bird, Pattern W 1050, printed mark, ca. 1920 ........................................ **7,475**

*Rockingham-Glazed Potpourri Jar*

**Potpourri jar,** cov., Rockingham-glaze, bulbous ovoid body tapering to a short neck flanked by upright loop shoulder handles, fitted low-domed cover w/knob finial, overall gilt-decorated w/birds on flowering leafy branches, impressed &

printed marks, ca. 1880, 9 3/4" h. (ILLUS.) ................................................. **1,725**

**Punch bowl,** Celtic Lustre design, a wide low pedestal base supporting a very wide gently flaring bowl, the matte black exterior decorated w/gold Celtic ornaments, a mottled orange & red interior w/armagh center, Pattern Z5265, printed mark, ca. 1920, 10 7/8" d. (exterior surface scratches, interior glaze wear) ............ **805**

*Fine Fairyland Lustre Punch Bowl*

**Punch bowl,** Fairyland Lustre, deep wide rounded bowl on a wide flaring round base, Poplar Tree patt., the exterior decorated w/a black sky behind a tree-filled landscape, the interior w/the Woodland Elves patt. w/a daylight sky, No. Z4968, printed mark, ca. 1920, interior surface wear, 10 3/4" d. (ILLUS.) .......................... **7,475**

**Serving dish,** two-tier, majolica, a pair of large maple-style leaves placed end to end & joined at the center by a rounded strap handle above a raised pair of smaller end to end leaf dishes placed perpendicular to the bottom leaves, impressed mark, ca. 1866, 16 1/4" l. (restored rim chips) ...................................... **489**

**Strawberry set:** a small cov. sugar bowl, small creamer & matching tray; majolica, the oblong tray molded on the interior w/large strawberry leaves & blossoms, two small rounded wells at the end hold the sugar & creamer w/matching designs, impressed mark, ca. 1871, tray 10 1/8" l., creamer 1 3/4" h., sugar 1 7/8" h., the set ...................................... **1,725**

**Tea set:** 4 1/2" h. cov. teapot, 2 1/2" h. cov. creamer, 3 1/4" h. cov. sugar bowl, two cups & saucers; bone china w/red transfer-printed stylized flower & foliage design w/gilt trim, impressed & printed marks, late 19th c., the set (light gilt wear) ............................................................. **489**

**Tea urn,** cov., Rockingham-glazed, a squared base w/scrolled feet & a slender ringed pedestal supporting the deep rounded urn-form lower body flanked by gilt scroll shoulder handles, the wide cylindrical upper body supporting a high domed cover w/button finial, the dark brown ground decorated overall w/gilt floral sprigs & bands of classical designs, metal spigot on the lower body, impressed factory mark & "Beane's Patent Tea Infuser," ca. 1888, 12" h. (restored socle, handle & cover) ................. **316**

**Tile,** majolica, square, molded in low-relief in the center w/a fox head within a small circle surrounded by large scrolled oak leaves framed w/a plain outer band, mottled glaze, impressed mark, 1875, 8" w. (rim nicks)..................................................... **201**

**Vase,** 3 1/2" h., Caneware, New Hispano-Moresque decoration, a footed squatty bulbous form tapering to a short rolled neck, decorated in pink & copper lustre glazes w/a wide band of upright feathered devices below a neck band of small overall loops, impressed mark, ca. 1925...... **489**

**Vase,** 4 1/8" h., Fairyland Lustre, Firbolgs patt., footed baluster-form w/wide short flared neck, shape 2351, a ruby lustre ground, Pattern Z5200, printed mark, ca. 1920 ......................................................... **1,380**

**Vase,** 6 3/4" h., Veronese Ware, wide baluster-form w/a short molded neck, pale red ground decorated w/stylized flowers & trim in silver lustre, impressed mark, ca. 1935 ............................................. **259**

*Wedgwood Lindsay Ware Vases*

**Vase,** 6 7/8" h., Lindsay Ware, bulbous tapering body w/a bulbed neck & flat rim, long angular handles, dark ground decorated overall w/enameled butterflies & leafage, printed mark, ca. 1910 (ILLUS. left) ........................................................... **1,380**

**Vase,** 7 1/4" h., bone china, figural, modeled as a spiky shell supported on a branching coral stem on a round waisted foot, undecorated, printed mark, ca. 1895 ......................................................... **546**

**Vase,** 7 1/4" h., footed banded spherical body w/a short cylindrical neck, straw-glazed body, Keith Murray design, printed mark, ca. 1940 ................................. **431**

**Vase,** 7 1/4" h., white-glazed earthenware, modeled in the Chinese manner & molded w/lion mask & ring handles, impressed mark, ca. 1876........................... **201**

*Lustre-decorated Wedgwood Vases*

**Vase,** 7 5/8" h., earthenware, footed waisted cylindrical body w/a wide short cylindrical neck, white ground decorated w/stylized foliate designs in silver lustre, by Louise Powell, artist-signed, impressed factory mark, ca. 1930 (ILLUS. left) ....................................................... **288**

**Vase,** 8" h., Agate Ware, classical urn-form, a square black basalt plinth supporting the deep urn-form body on a pedestal, the wide shoulder centered by a waisted cylindrical neck w/a wide flattened rim, gilt arched scroll handles from the rim down to the shoulder edge terminating in goat head masks, swirled agate-colored overall glaze, impressed lozenge mark of Wedgwood and Bentley, ca. 1775 (restoration to handle & socle, chips to underside of rim & shoulder, gilt wear) ..................................... **2,875**

**Vase,** 9" h., bulbous base tapering to a large widely flaring trumpet neck, large loop handles from base of neck to bottom of lower body, dark ground enamel-decorated overall w/butterflies & leafage, printed & impressed mark, ca. 1910, restored rim chip, associated hairline (ILLUS. right) ............................................... **1,093**

**Vase,** 9 1/4" h., Marsden's Art Ware, globular form w/a straight-sided neck, paneled body w/slip-decorated flowers & leaves, impressed mark, ca. 1890 ........................... **575**

**Vase,** 9 5/8" h., Marsden's Art Ware, wide ovoid body tapering to a short wide cylindrical neck, slip-decorated flowers & leaves on a buff ground, impressed mark, ca. 1890, slight glaze scratches (ILLUS. right) ............................................... **374**

**Vase,** cov., 10 3/8" h., Porphyry Ware, classical urn-form, square black basalt plinth supporting a short pedestal under the banded cylindrical body w/a wide shoulder centering a short waisted neck w/a small domed cover & knob finial, blue & brown speckled overall glaze w/upright inwardly-scrolled creamware shoulder handles & long cream laurel swags around the sides connecting the handles, impressed lozenge mark of Wedgwood and Bentley, ca. 1775 (hairline & small chips in cover, one handle restored, nicks in shoulder & plinth) .......... **5,175**

**Vase,** cov., 10 3/4" h., White Smear Stoneware, a classical waisted body on a waisted round pedestal & square foot, large bearded mask handles at the sides of the rim, domed cover w/blossom finial, the body & cover applied in blue relief w/a lyre & wreath design centering foliate borders including acanthus leaves & palmettes, unmarked, ca. 1830 ................... **345**

**Vase,** 11" h., large spherical body tapering to a short rolled mouth, grey ground decorated overall w/stylized foliate designs in silver lustre, by Louise Powell, artist-signed, impressed factory marks, ca. 1930 (ILLUS. right) ..................................... **2,070**

*Large Fairyland Lustre Vase*

*Marsden's Art Ware Vases*

**Vase,** 11 1/4" h., Fairyland Lustre, Imps on Bridge patt., a flame lustre sky, coral enamelings & blue Roc birds, Shape No. 3453, No. Z5481, printed mark, ca. 1920, restored hairline in base (ILLUS.) ... **6,900**

**Vase,** 11 1/4" h., stoneware, wide bulbous beehive-shape tapering to a flared club-form spout, brown body w/glazed top band & white spout, impressed potter's monogram for J. Dermer & factory mark, mid-20th c. .................................................. **863**

**Vase,** cov., 22" h., Golconda Ware, large ovoid body w/large upright loop shoulder handles flanking the fitted flat cover w/baluster-form finial, raised on a domed pedestal foot, glazed cane ground w/raised slip leaf & floral overall designs, impressed mark, chip to cover rim, minor slip loss ...................................................... **575**

**Vases,** 5" h., bone china, double-gourd form, the ivory ground decorated w/gilt & enameled flying birds on the lower body & a perched bird on the elongated upper body, printed mark, late 19th c., pr. .............. **316**

**Vases,** 6 1/2" h., bone china, tapering cylindrical form w/flared base & wide rolled rim, yellow-glazed w/bands of enameled colorful Oriental landscapes, No. Z5239, printed mark, ca. 1915, pr. .......................... **431**

**Vases,** cov., 9 1/2" h., Victoria Ware, classical form w/a large ovoid body raised on a slender flared pedestal on a square plinth, the small trumpet neck w/rolled rim supporting a pointed cover w/knob finial, bands of alternating deep teal blue & iron-red grounds decorated w/white relief band of dancing classical ladies or leaf-tips or palmettes, upright scrolled gilt shoulder handles, gilt trim, ca. 1880, pr. (restorations to both covers, one handle on each, one socle, hairline in one socle & one plinth)................................... **1,380**

**Vases,** 14 3/4" h., Marsden's Art Ware, tall ovoid body tapering to a cylindrical neck, slip-decorated floral design on a buff ground, impressed marks, ca. 1885 (ILLUS. of one, left, top next column).......... **805**

# WELLER

*This pottery was made from 1872 to 1945 at a pottery established originally by Samuel A. Weller at Fultonham, Ohio, and moved in 1882 to Zanesville. Numerous lines were produced and listings below are by the pattern or lines.*

*Reference books on Weller include* The Collectors Encyclopedia of Weller Pottery *by Sharon & Bob Huxford (Collector Books, 1979) and* All About Weller *by Ann Gilbert McDonald (Antique Publications, 1989). ALSO SEE* Antique Trader Books Pottery and Porcelain - Ceramics Price Guide, 3rd Edition.

**WELLER**     Weller Pottery

*Weller Marks*

## DICKENSWARE 2ND LINE (Early 1900s)
*Various incised "sgraffito" designs usually with a matte glaze. Quality of the artwork greatly affects price.*

**Vase,** 9 1/2" h., baluster-form body w/closed rim, scene of two Spanish galleons on stormy seas, polychrome glaze, decorated by Carl Weigelt .......... **$1,540**

**Vase,** 10" h., squatty bulbous base tapering to cylindrical body w/slightly flared rim, scene of woman playing golf in polychrome matte glaze on shaded brown & green ground, artist-initialed..................... **1,760**

## GLENDALE (Early to late 1920s)
*Various relief-molded birds in their natural habitats, lifelike coloring.*

**Vase,** 8 1/2" h., ovoid body, decorated w/bridge scene & wrens in a nest, polychrome glazes............................................. **880**

**Wall pocket,** half round bulbous form w/sharply pointed backplate w/hanging hole, two chickadees on a flowering cherry blossom branch, 7 x 7 1/4" ............... **468**

**Wall pocket,** cornucopia-form w/curved tall, arched & scalloped backplate pierced w/a hanging hole, the base molded w/a wren & its young on a flowering cherry blossom branch, unmarked, 6 1/2 x 12 1/2" ............................................. **385**

### HUDSON (1917-34)
*Underglaze slip-painted decoration, "parchment-vellum" transparent glaze.*

**Vase,** 9 1/2" h., footed cylinder w/h.p. blue & white iris w/green leaves, decorated by Mae Timberlake, artist-signed & incised "Weller Pottery" ........................... **1,760**

**Vase,** 15 1/2" h., ovoid body w/wide flaring rim, h.p. large yellow, pink & purple irises on shaded blue ground, decorated by Mae Timberlake, drilled base, artist-signed & stamped "Weller" ....................... **2,310**

### JAP BIRDIMAL (1904)
*Stylized Japanese-inspired figural bird or animal designs on various solid colored grounds.*

**Vase,** 6" h., shouldered ovoid body w/molded rim, decorated in squeezebag w/swimming blue carp on a green ground, unmarked ..................................... **1,100**

**Vase,** 11 3/4" h., ovoid body w/tapering shoulder, short neck w/flaring rim, squeezebag decoration w/geisha playing shamisen under stylized trees, tan, blue & red on brown ground, incised "Weller - Rhead Faience" (couple of shallow scratches to body, two glazed-over glaze flecks to rim, stilt-pull chip to base) ....................................................... **1,045**

### MANHATTAN (Early 1930s-'34)
*Simple modern shapes embossed with stylized leaves or leaves and blossoms and glazed in shades of green or brown.*

**Vase,** 6 1/2" h., footed ovoid body molded around the base w/a band of large rounded leaves, light yellowish green glaze, marked ................................................ **69**

**Vase,** 8 1/8" h., ovoid body tapering slightly to a wide, short flared neck, forked C-scroll handles flank the neck, molded broad leaves, rose mauve glaze w/green highlights, marked .......................................... **55**

### TEAKWOOD (1909)
*Similar to Burnt Wood and Claywood except the colors are reversed in the design. White flowers and dark background. Matte finish. Middle period.*

**Jardiniere,** large wide ovoid body tapering to a thick molded rim, dark charcoal ground decorated around the shoulder w/a wide white relief molded band w/a repeating motif of a bird perched in a swagged branch of fruits & leaves, 13" d. .................................................. **460**

### VELVETONE (Late 1920s)
*Blended colors of green, pink, yellow, brown, green, matte glaze.*

**Candleholders,** pr. ........................................... **143**

# WILLOW WARES

*This pseudo-Chinese pattern has been used by numerous firms throughout the years. The original design is attributed to Thomas Minton about 1780 and Thomas Turner is believed to have first produced the ware during his tenure at the Caughley works. The blue underglaze transfer print pattern has never been out of production since that time. An Oriental landscape incorporating a bridge, pagoda, trees, figures and birds, supposedly tells the story of lovers fleeing a cruel father who wished to prevent their marriage. The gods, having pity on them, changed them into birds enabling them to fly away and seek their happiness together.*

## BLUE

**Ashtray,** figural whale, ca. 1960, Japan ...... **$50-55**
**Ashtray,** unmarked, American ........................... **20**
**Bank,** figural, stacked pigs, ca. 1960, Japan, 7" h. ................................................ **50-55**
**Bone dish,** ca. 1890, unmarked, England:.... **40-50**

*Blue Willow Bone Dish*

**Bone dish,** Buffalo Pottery, 6 1/2" l. (ILLUS.)...................................................... **75-80**
**Bowl,** berry, Allertons, England ..................... **12-15**
**Bowl,** berry, milk glass, Hazel Atlas .................. **15**
**Bowl,** individual, 5 1/4" oval, J. Maddock ........... **20**
**Bowl,** soup, 8" d., Japan ............................... **18-20**
**Bowl,** 6 1/2 x 8 1/4", Ridgways, England ...... **50-55**
**Bowl,** salad, 10" d., Japan............................... **75**
**Butter dish,** cov., Ridgways, England....... **150-175**
**Butter dish,** in wood holder, 6" d. .............. **50-75**
**Butter dish,** cov., 8" d., England...................... **100**
**Butter pat,** Buffalo Pottery ............................... **30**
**Butter pat,** Wood & Sons................................. **25**
**Cake plate,** Green & Co., 8" sq.................... **40-45**
**Cake stand,** child's, Shellware, England, 2 1/2" h........................................................ **75-100**
**Cake stand,** unmarked, England, 10" d. ... **200-225**
**Canister,** cov., round, tin, 5 3/4" h. .............. **20-25**
**Canister set:** cov., "Coffee," "Flour," "Sugar," "Tea," barrel-shaped, ca. 1960s, Japan, the set ................... **350-400**
**Cheese dish,** cov., rectangular, unmarked, England ....................................................... **175**
**Condiment cruet set:** cov. oil & vinegar & mustard cruet, salt & pepper; carousel-type base w/wooden handle, Japan, 7 1/2" h., the set ................................... **200-225**

*Blue Willow Cracker Jar*

**Cracker jar,** cov., silver lid & handle, Minton, England, 5" h. (ILLUS.).................... **200**
**Creamer,** Allerton, England................................ **60**
**Creamer,** individual, Shenango China Co.......... **25**
**Creamer,** John Steventon .................................. **40**

*Blue Willow Figural Cow Creamer*

**Creamer w/original stopper,** figural cow standing on oval base, mouth forms spout & tail forms handle, ca. 1850, unmarked, England, 7" l., 5" h. (ILLUS.)................................................ **700-800**
**Cruets w/original stoppers,** oil & vinegar, Japan, 6" h., the set ...................................... **65**
**Cup & saucer,** "A Present from Towyn," unmarked, England .................................. **55-65**
**Cup & saucer,** Booth .................................. **40-45**
**Cup & saucer,** Buffalo Pottery ..................... **35-45**
**Cup & saucer,** child's, ca. 1900, unmarked, England ........................................ **50**
**Cup & saucer,** demitasse, Copeland, England......................................................... **40**
**Cup & saucer,** "For Auld Lang Syne," W. Adams, England, oversized ................. **100-125**
**Drainer,** butter, ca. 1890, England, 6" sq. .......... **75**
**Egg cup,** Booths, England, 4" h. ................... **45-50**
**Egg cup,** Japan, 4" h...................................... **20-25**
**Egg cup,** Allerton, England, 4 1/2" h. ............. **40-45**
**Ginger jar,** cov., Japan, 5" h. ............................ **30**
**Ginger jar,** cov., Mason's, 9" h...................... **60-75**
**Gravy boat,** Buffalo Pottery .......................... **75-85**

*Blue Willow Gravy Boat*

**Gravy boat,** ca. 1890, unmarked, England, 7" l. (ILLUS.)............................................. **60-65**
**Gravy boat w/attached underplate,** double-spouted, Ridgways, England............... **75-85**
**Hot pot,** electric, Japan, 6" h............................. **75**
**Invalid feeder,** ca. 1860, unmarked, England ............................................... **175-200**
**Knife rest,** ca. 1860, unmarked, England .... **85-95**
**Ladle,** pattern in bowl, floral handle, unmarked, England, 12" l. ................... **185-200**
**Lamp,** w/ceramic shade, Japan, 8" h. ............... **75**
**Lamp,** w/reflector plate, Japan, 8" h............. **85-95**
**Lamp,** Wedgwood, England, 10" h. ........... **200-225**
**Mug,** "Farmer's," Japan, 4" h......................... **15-20**
**Mustache cup & saucer,** Hammersley & Co.......................................................... **150-175**
**Mustard pot,** cov., ca. 1870, unmarked, England, 3" h................................................. **100-125**
**Pastry stand,** three-tiered plates, Royal China Co., Sebring, Ohio, 13" h. ............... **50-60**
**Pepper pot,** ca. 1870, England, 4" h. ....... **100-125**

*Blue Willow Pitcher*

**Pitcher,** 5 1/2" h., Ridgway, England (ILLUS.)...................................................... **85-95**

*Buffalo Pottery Blue Willow Pitcher*

**Pitcher,** cov., 5 1/2" h., Buffalo Pottery (ILLUS.)................................................. **200-225**

*Hancock & Sons Blue Willow Pitcher*

**Pitcher,** 6" h., Royal Corona Ware, S. Hancock & Sons (ILLUS.)............................ **100-125**
**Pitcher,** 6" h., scalloped rim, Allerton, England................................................ **125-150**

*Blue Willow "Chicago Jug"*

**Pitcher,** 7" h., "Chicago Jug," ca. 1907, Buffalo Pottery, 7"h., 3 pt. (ILLUS.)....... **200-225**
**Pitcher,** 8" h., glass, Johnson Bros., England..................................................... **35-40**
**Pitcher w/ice lip,** 10" h., Japan...................... **100**
**Placemat,** cloth, 12 x 16" ............................. **18-20**
**Plate,** bread & butter, Allerton, England ........ **12-15**

*Buffalo Blue Willow Dinner Plate*

**Plate,** dinner, Buffalo Pottery (ILLUS.) .......... **30-35**
**Plate,** dinner, ca. 1870, unmarked, England .. **40-50**
**Plate,** dinner, flow blue, Royal Doulton ......... **75-85**
**Plate,** dinner, Holland ................................... **18-20**
**Plate,** dinner, Japan ..................................... **10-15**
**Plate,** dinner, Mandarin patt., Copeland, England ...................................................... **40-50**
**Plate,** dinner, modern, Royal Wessex .............. **6-8**
**Plate,** dinner, Paden City Pottery ................. **30-35**
**Plate,** dinner, restaurant ware, Jackson ........ **15-20**
**Plate,** dinner, Royal China Co. ...................... **10-15**
**Plate,** dinner, scalloped rim, Allerton, England ...................................................... **30-35**
**Plate,** grill, Allerton, England ........................ **45-50**
**Plate,** luncheon, Wedgwood, England .......... **20-25**
**Plate,** luncheon, Worcester patt. .................. **40-45**
**Plate,** 7 1/2" d., Arklow, Ireland ......................... **20**
**Plate,** 10" d., tin, ca. 1988, Robert Steffy ...... **10-12**
**Plate,** grill, 10" d., Japan................................ **18-20**
**Plate,** 10 1/4" d., paper, Fonda........................ **1-2**
**Plate,** grill, 10 1/2" d., Holland ....................... **18-20**

*Blue Willow Wedgwood Platter*

**Platter,** 9 x 11" l., rectangular, Wedgwood & Co., England (ILLUS.)......................... **100-125**
**Platter,** 8 1/2 x 11 1/2" l., oval, scalloped rim, Buffalo Pottery................................ **100-125**
**Platter,** 9 x 12" l., oval, American ................. **15-18**
**Platter,** 9 x 12" l., oval, Japan ...................... **25-30**
**Platter,** 9 x 12" l., rectangular, Allerton, England ................................................... **150-200**
**Platter,** 11 x 14" l., oval, Johnson Bros., England ..................................................... **85-100**
**Platter,** 11 x 14" l., rectangular, Buffalo Pottery.................................................... **150-200**
**Platter,** 11 x 14" l., rectangular, ca. 1880s, unmarked, England ............................... **150-200**
**Platter,** 15 x 19" l., rectangular, well & tree, ca. 1890, unmarked, England ....... **350-400**
**Pudding mold,** England, 4 1/2" h. ............... **45-55**
**Punch cup,** pedestal foot, ca. 1900, unmarked, England .................................. **50-75**
**Relish dish,** leaf-shaped, ca. 1870, England ................................................. **100-125**

*Blue Willow Salt Box*

**Salt box,** cov., ca. 1960, wooden lid, Japan, 5 x 5" (ILLUS.) ............................ **175-225**
**Salt dip,** master, pedestal base, unmarked, England, 2" h....................................... **100-125**
**Salt dip,** open, silver rim, ca. 1890, unmarked, England, 2" h. .......................... **50-75**
**Salt & pepper shakers,** Japan, pr. .............. **40-45**
**Sauce tureen, ladle & underplate,** cov., ca. 1880s, England...................... **250-275**
**Sauce tureen w/underplate,** cov., pedestal base, ca. 1890, unmarked, England, 6 1/2" h. (ILLUS. top next page)............ **250-275**
**Soup tureen,** cov., ca. 1880, unmarked, England ................................................. **400-450**
**Spoon rest,** Japan ....................................... **40-50**
**Sugar bowl,** cov., Ridgway, England............ **50-75**

*Blue Willow Sauce Tureen w/Underplate*

**Syrup pitcher,** cov., frosted, Hazel Atlas,
6" h. ............................................................ **40-45**
**Tablecloth,** Simtex .................................... **75-85**
**Tea set,** child's, Japan, service for six in
box .................................................... **250-300**
**Tea set,** child's, tin, Ohio Art Co., Bryan,
Ohio, service for four............................ **150-175**
**Tea tile,** ca. 1900, unmarked, England, 6"
sq. ..................................................................... **75**
**Tea tile,** Minton, England, 6" sq. ........................ **75**
**Teapot,** cov., ca. 1890, Royal Doulton ...... **300-350**
**Teapot,** cov., child's, Japan............................ **40-45**
**Teapot,** cov., Homer Laughlin ........................... **100**
**Teapot,** cov., round, Allerton, England...... **250-275**

*Royal Corona Ware Teapot*

**Teapot,** cov., Royal Corona Ware, S. Han-
cock & Sons (ILLUS.)........................... **225-250**
**Teapot,** individual, Moriyama, Japan,
4 1/2" h. ............................................... **75-100**
**Teapot,** cov., Sadler, 4 3/4" h. ....................... **40-45**

*Teapot w/Bamboo Handle*

**Teapot,** cov., bamboo handle, "Semi
China," gold trim, 6" h. (ILLUS.) ............ **250-275**
**Teapot,** cov., enamel, unmarked, 7" h. ............ **100**

*"Yorkshire Relish" Tip Tray*

**Tip tray,** "Yorkshire Relish," England, 4" d.
(ILLUS.)................................................... **50-75**
**Toothbrush holder,** Wedgwood, England,
5 1/4" h. ............................................................ **95**
**Tray,** round, brass, 6" d. .................................... **50**
**Vegetable bowl,** cov., rectangular, Buffalo
Pottery .............................................. **175-200**
**Vegetable bowl,** cov., square, ca. 1900,
England ............................................. **150-175**
**Vegetable bowl,** open, Shenango China,
8" d. ................................................... **30-40**
**Vegetable bowl,** cov., ca. 1930, England,
9" d. ................................................... **125**
**Vegetable bowl,** open, Japan, 9" d. ............. **30-35**
**Wash pitcher & bowl,** ca. 1890,
unmarked, England, the set ................. **500-600**

## OTHER COLORS
**Butter pat,** red, Japan..................................... **20**
**Charger,** brown, Buffalo China, 11" d. .......... **50-60**
**Coffeepot,** cov., ca. 1890, brown,
unmarked, England, 8 3/4" h. ............... **200-225**
**Cup & saucer,** red, ca. 1930, Buffalo China.. **30-35**
**Egg cup,** red, England, 4 1/2" h. ................... **35-40**
**Plate,** 6" d., restaurant ware, brown, Buf-
falo China ......................................................... **15**
**Plate,** 9" d., purple, Britannia Pottery ............ **35-40**
**Plate,** dinner, red, Japan .............................. **15-20**
**Plate,** bread & butter, 6" d., green, Japan ..... **18-20**
**Plate,** 9" d., ca. 1890, brown, John Meir &
Son ................................................... **20-25**
**Plate,** 9" d., Mandarin patt., red, Copeland ... **35-40**
**Plate,** grill, 11 1/4" d., green, Royal Willow
China ................................................. **30-35**
**Platter,** 9 1/4 x 11 1/4", rectangular, red,
Allerton, England.................................. **175-200**
**Platter,** 11 x 19" l., rectangular, green,
John Steventon & Sons........................ **125-150**
**Sugar bowl,** red, Japan ................................ **25-35**
**Teapot,** cov., purple, Britannia Pottery ...... **200-225**
**Vegetable bowl,** cov., round, green, Victo-
ria Porcelain ....................................... **100-125**

## YELLOW-GLAZED EARTHENWARE

*In the past this early English ware was often
referred to as "Canary Lustre," but recently a more
accurate title has come into use.*

Produced in the late 18th and early 19th centuries, pieces featured an overall yellow glaze, often decorated with silver or copper lustre designs or black, brown or red transfer-printed scenes.

Most pieces are not marked and today the scarcity of examples in good condition keeps market prices high.

**Model of a cradle,** decorated w/relief-molded interlocking circle design, 4 5/8" l. (wear) .......................................... **$303**

**Mug,** child's, cylindrical, black transfer-printed decoration of scene titled "Come Up Donkey," second quarter 19th c., 2" h. (minor rim chips, hairline) ..................... **374**

**Mug,** child's, cylindrical, russet transfer-printed design titled "A Rabbit For William," early 19th c., 2 1/2" h. (minor chips)` ........................................................ **633**

**Mug,** cylindrical, black transfer-printed inscription "Super Fine Porter Peace and Roast Beef to the Friends of Liberty," silver lustre trim, early 19th c., 3 1/2" d., 3 1/2" h. (repairs to rim & footring) .............. **431**

*Floral-decorated Yellow-Glazed Pitcher*

**Pitcher,** 6 1/2" h., footed bulbous body decoration w/enameled flowers in red, green, blue & pink lustre on yellow ground, wear & crazing w/hairline in spout (ILLUS.) ...................................... **605**

**Teapot,** cov., bulbous body w/arched neck, inset domed cover, swan's-neck spout & C-form handle, black transfer-printed reserves of three musicians, early 19th c., 5 1/2" h. (restoration to cover finial, minor chips) ................................................. **403**

# YELLOWWARE

Yellowware is a form of utilitarian pottery produced in the United States and England from the early 19th century onward. Its body texture is less dense and vitreous (impervious to water) than stoneware. Most, but not all, yellowware is unmarked and its color varies from deep yellow to pale buff. In the late 19th and early 20th centuries bowls in graduated sizes were widely advertised. Still in production, yellowware is plentiful and still reasonably priced.

**Bank,** figural standing pig, marbleized glaze in brown, green & cream, 6 1/4" l. (wear, glaze flakes) ..................................... **$83**

**Beverage set:** 8" h. pitcher & six 4 3/4" h. mugs; all decorated w/blue stripes at rim & base & impressed "100% Buckeye Pure," the set (slight variation in color & size, one mug w/hairline & pitcher w/small chip) ............................................... **550**

*Yellowware Flask and Toby Bottle*

**Bottle,** figural standing Mr. Toby w/fiddle, crazing w/possible hairline in base, chip on hat brim, 8 1/2" h. (ILLUS. right) ............. **715**

**Bowl,** 7" d., 3 1/2" h., cov., cylindrical, decorated w/blue bands & stripes (crazing & stains) ........................................................ **220**

**Dish,** rectangular, brown & green sponging, 8 1/2" l. (minor wear) ............................ **193**

**Flask,** decorated w/relief-molded morning glories & an eagle, chips, 7 3/8" h. (ILLUS. left) ................................................ **1,210**

**Food molds,** figural rabbit, 9" & 9 1/2" l., pr. (one w/hairline) ....................................... **248**

**Food molds,** round w/spiral design & lady-finger rim, two 4" d., one 6" d., set of 3 ........ **171**

**Mixing bowl,** footed, deep rounded sides w/rim spout, white center band w/blue mocha seaweed decoration, flanked by narrow blue stripes, probably East Liverpool, Ohio, 9 1/4" d., 4 1/2" h. (wear, hairlines in spout & chips) .......................... **468**

**Mixing bowls,** footed, deep rounded sides w/a flared rim, wide white band beneath rim, 12" d., 5 1/2" h. & 16 1/4" d., 7 3/4" h., the set .......................................... **330**

**Mug,** cylindrical w/C-form handle, blue stripes w/white sanded band, 2" h. ............ **182**

**Pitcher,** jug-type, 5" h., strap handle & spout w/strainer, decorated w/blue stripes (flakes) .............................................. **578**

*Yellowware Pitcher*

**Pitcher,** 5 1/4" h., footed bulbous body tapering slightly to wide cylindrical neck w/flared rim, high arched rim spout & C-form ribbed handle w/leaf, light blue & white horizontal stripes around mid-body, faint hairline at base of handle (ILLUS.) ....................................... **358**

**Pitcher,** 5 1/2" h., 5 1/4" h., footed bulbous body tapering slightly to wide cylindrical neck w/flared rim, high arched rim spout

& strap handle, decorated w/white bands
& brown stripes ............................................. **550**

**Pitcher,** jug-type, 6 1/8" h., w/strap handle,decorated w/white bands & black
stripes ........................................................... **688**

**Pitcher,** jug-type, 8 1/2" h., w/ribbed handle, decorated w/white band, repair on
spout ............................................................. **550**

**Pitcher,** 8 7/8" h., footed cylindrical body
w/flared lip, ornate handle, Gothic
design w/relief-molded Mary, John the
Baptist & Jesus, light blue cartouche
label w/registry mark & "Charles Meigh,
Nov 12, 1846, York Minster Jug,"
England ........................................................ **495**

**Soap dish,** round w/drain holes, 5 5/8" d.
(some wear) ................................................. **550**

**Vegetable dish,** open, oval, impressed
mark "Fire Proof," 13 3/8" l. (pinpoint
surface flakes) ............................................. **495**

# CHALKWARE

So-called chalkware available today is actually
made of plaster of Paris, much of it decorated in
color and primarily in the form of busts, figurines
and ornaments. It was produced through most of
the 19th century and the majority of pieces were
originally quite inexpensive when made. Today
even 20th century "carnival" pieces are collectible.

**Deer,** recumbent animal w/head turned &
front leg raised, old worn polychrome
paint, one signed in pencil "Susie D.
Cord," 8 1/2" h., facing pr. (damage &
repair to antlers, one w/hairline) ................. **$935**

*Rare Chalkware Advertising Piece*

**Desk box,** advertising-type, figural, model
of an early racecar atop a rectangular
platform impressed w/"Richfield," on a
dished oval base, ca. 1920s (ILLUS.) .......... **743**

**Dog,** seated Spaniel w/open front legs, on
oblong base, traces of paint, 6 1/8" h.
(worn surface, possible repair to base) .......... **55**

**Dog,** standing stylized poodle on rectangular platform base, crudely modeled
w/original red, black, brown, green & yellow paint, 4 1/2" h. (minor wear, two
open blisters) ................................................ **413**

**Lamb,** recumbent animal on oblong base,
red, blue, yellow & black trim, 4 1/8" l.
(some wear) ................................................. **193**

**Model of a ewe & lamb,** recumbent animals on rectangular base, red, blue &
yellow, 9 1/4" l. (very worn, repairs) ............ **358**

**Model of a parrot,** resting on ball plinth, old
red, black & olive yellow paint, 8 1/4" h.
(some wear) ................................................. **743**

**Model of a rabbit,** sitting, red, yellow &
black, 5 3/8" h. (wear & scratches) .............. **550**

**Model of a rooster,** red, yellow, green &
black, 5 3/4" h. (some color wear, stains
& old repair) ................................................. **715**

**Model of a squirrel,** seated animal holding nut in his paws, on a domed base,
old red & black paint, uneven old brown
varnish (minor wear) .................................... **743**

**Model of compote,** footed, holding fruit,
old red, yellow & orange paint & brown
varnish, 11" h. (some wear & possible
old touch up repair) .................................. **1,100**

# CHARACTER
# COLLECTIBLES

Numerous objects made in the likeness of or
named after comic strip and comic book personalities or characters abounded from the 1920s to the
present. Scores of these are now being eagerly collected and prices still vary widely. Also see LUNCH
BOXES, POP CULTURE COLLECTIBLES, RADIO
& TELEVISION MEMORABILIA, WESTERN
CHARACTER COLLECTIBLES, SPACE AGE
COLLECTIBLES and TOYS.

**Barnacle Bill toy,** windup tin, "Barnacle Bill
Rowboat," cut-out silhouetted sailor
seated rowing a boat, rubber band
mechanism, Emmert-Hammes & Co.,
w/original box & extra oak, 9" l.
(replaced rubber band) .............................. **$121**

**Blondie marionette,** Hazelle's, 15" h. ............ **125**

*Blondie's Jalopy*

**Blondie toy,** windup metal "Blondie's
Jalopy," on front fender of yellow & red
car, showing figure of dog & "Daisy" on
back fender & infant's head & "Cookie"
on door, two heads w/hats on top, Marx,
restored w/good box, 16" l. (ILLUS.) ................. **1,100**

**Bugs Bunny talking alarm clock,** 1974,
clock works, alarm doesn't ............................ **75**

**Captain America car,** package shows
Captain America, Hulk & Spiderman,
No. 2879, Hot Wheels, very good
w/good box ..................................................... **25**

**Demolition Man vehicles,** nine w/display
cube, Hot Wheels, all mint ........................... **40**

**Dick Dastardly racing car w/Mutley,** No.
809, Corgi, very good w/fair box ................... **75**

**Felix the Cat clicker,** ca. 1920s, Germany ........ **85**

**Felix the Cat toy,** windup tin, Felix on a
hand cart, standing pushing & pulling a
front lever on the three-wheeled cart,
cart in orange w/green wheels, Felix in
black & white, attributed to Chein, ca.
1930s, 7" l. ................................................... **690**

**Harold Lloyd toy,** windup tin walker, good,
Marx ............................................................. **300**

**James Bond Aston Martin VB6,** working ejector seat, No. 1001,, Corgi, very good w/fair box......... 60

**James Bond auto set,** five pieces, No. 3082, Corgi, all mint ..... 240

**James Bond Moonraker sets,** each set w/two vehicles, No. E2528, Corgi, very good w/good boxes, two sets......... 85

**Jiggs doll,** jointed wood, painted, wearing original felt shirt & trousers, Schoenhut, ca. 1924, 7" h. ......... 374

**Lady Penelope's Fab 1 auto,** includes her & chauffeur & bag of weapons, No. 100, Dinky, very good w/good box......... 160

**Little King (The) toy,** painted wood action-type, jointed w/elastic spring, marked "Jaymar," w/original box, 3 7/8" h. (spring fatigued) ......... 61

*Little LuLu Tumbler*

**Little LuLu tumbler,** clear glass w/printed design of Little LuLu, Annie/Mops......... 55

**Marvel Super Heroes Limited Edition boxed sets,** each box set w/a reproduction of a comic book cover featuring the hero, the heroes are the X-Men, Spider-man (also includes Daredevil) & Captain America, Corgi, the three ......... 25

**Popeye character cars,** Matchbox, all mint, set of 3......... 125

**Popeye doll,** rubber & cloth, all original, 1958, 20" h. ......... 98

*Popeye Pipe Toss Game*

**Popeye game,** "Popeye Pipe Toss Game," cardboard figure of Popeye w/stand & toss rings, w/original box, copyright 1935 by Kin Features Syndicate, Inc., minor wear to box, game in unused condition (ILLUS.)......... 77

**Popeye & Olive Oyl coin purse** ......... 48

*"Popeye Spinach Eater"*

**Popeye toy,** "Popeye Spinach Eater," ca. 1939, Fisher-Price, No. 488 (ILLUS.)......... 583

**Popeye toy,** windup celluloid & tin, "Popeye Dippy Dumper," Popeye driving old truck, good, Louis Marx, excellent, 9 1/2" l. ......... 700

*Popeye Windup Walker*

**Popeye toy,** windup tin, Popeye walking, blue hat & suit w/red collar, yellow shoes, good, Marx (ILLUS.) ......... 350

**Porky Pig toy,** windup tin, figure of standing Porky holding a small umbrella over his head, colorful, Louis Marx, original colorful box, 8 1/2" h. (minor wear) ......... 508

**Smokey & The Bandit auto set,** two vehicles, No. 1790, Ertl, very good w/very good box ......... 30

**Spider-Man Scenes Machines van,** No. 2842, Hot Wheels, all mint ......... 65

**Superman auto gift set,** five pieces, No. 3080, Corgi, very good w/good box ......... 50

*Superman Krypto Raygun*

**Superman raygun,** Krypto raygun, pressed steel projector pistol, able to flash pictures on wall, embossed design features Superman, Daisy, 7 1/2" x 10" (ILLUS.) ........................................................ **330**

**Superman ring,** silvered metal, cut-corner rectangular top w/a bas-relief picture of Superman flying ........................................... **633**

**Thor van,** No. 2880, Hot Wheels, all mint .......... **55**

**Tom & Jerry auto set,** two vehicles, No. 2507, Corgi, very good w/very good box ........ **30**

# CHILDREN'S BOOKS

*The most collectible children's books today tend to be those printed after the 1850s and, while age is not completely irrelevant, illustrations play a far more important role in determining the values. While first editions are highly esteemed, it is the the beautiful illustrated books that most collectors seek. The following books all in good to fine condition, are listed alphabetically. Also see: COMIC BOOKS and DISNEY COLLECTIBLES*

## CLASSIC CHILDREN'S BOOKS

**Altsheler, Joseph,** "The Sun of Saratoga," New York, 1897, first U.S. edition of his first book ..................................................... **$150**

**Bemelmans, Ludwig,** "Madeline," New York, 1939, first U.S. edition ........................ **175**

**Burgess, Thornton,** "Old Mother West Wind," Boston, 1910, first U.S. edition ......... **100**

**Burnett, Francis Hodgson,** "Little Lord Fauntleroy," New York, 1886, first U.S. edition ................................................... **175**

**Dahl, Roald,** "James and the Giant Peach," New York, 1961, first U.S. edition ............... **500**

**Edwards, Leo,** "Jerry Todd and the Oak Island Treasure," New York, 1925, first U.S. edition ................................................... **50**

**Field, Eugene,** "A Little Book of Western Verse," Chicago, 1889, first U.S. edition ...... **150**

**Gallico, Paul,** "The Snow Goose," New York, 1941, first U.S. edition ........................ **50**

**Hawthorne, Nathaniel,** "Tanglewood Tales, for Girls and Boys," Boston, 1853, first U.S. edition ......................................... **750**

**Irving, Washington,** "The Legend of Sleepy Hollow," New York, 1897, first U.S. edition ................................................... **250**

**Porter, Eleanor H.,** "Pollyanna," Boston, 1913, first U.S. edition .............................. **250**

**Porter, Gene Stratton,** "A Girl of the Limberlost," New York, 1909, first U.S. edition ................................................... **125**

**Sewell, Anna,** "Black Beauty," Boston, 1890, first U.S. edition .............................. **250**

**Sidney, Margaret,** "Five Little Peppers and How They Grew," Boston, 1880, first U.S. edition ................................................... **300**

**Thompson, Kay,** "Eloise," New York, 1955, first U.S. edition .............................. **350**

**Thompson, Ruth Plumly,** "Pirates in Oz," Chicago, 1931, first U.S. edition .................. **325**

**White, E.B.,** "Stuart Little," New York, 1945, first U.S. edition .............................. **200**

**Wiggin, Kate Douglas,** "Rebecca of Sunnybrook Farm," Boston, 1903, first U.S. edition ................................................... **200**

# LITTLE GOLDEN BOOKS

**"Animals Of Farmer Jones (The),"** No. 11, 1942, illustrations by Rudolf Freund, written by Leah Gale, 42 pp. ....................... **40**

*1942 Baby's Book*

**"Baby's Book,"** No. 10, 1942, 1st cover, illustrations & text by Bob Smith, 42 pp. (ILLUS.) ................................................... **75**

**"Big Brown Bear (The),"** No. 89, 1947, illustrations by Gustaf Tenggren, written by Georges Duplaix, 42 pp. ........................ **25**

**"Bugs Bunny And The Indians,"** No. 120, 1951, copyright by Warner Bros. Cartoon, Inc., illustrations by Richard Kelsey, written by Annie North Bedford, 28 pp. ................................................... **14**

*Come Play House*

**"Come Play House,"** No. 44, 1948, illustrations by Eloise Wilkin, written by Edith Oswald, 42 pp. (ILLUS.) ............................... **27**

*Dick Tracy*

**"Dick Tracy,"** No. 497, 1962, copyright by Chicago Tribune-New York Times, illustrations by Hawley Pratt, written by Carl Memling, 24 pp. (ILLUS.) .............................. 22

**"Emerald City Of Oz,"** No. 151, 1952, copyright by Maud Gage Baum, illustrations by Harry McNaught, written by Peter Archer, 28 pp. .............................. 27

**"Fix It, Please,"** No. 32, 1947, illustrations by Eloise Wilkin, written by Lucy Sprague Mitchell, 42 pp. .............................. 27

**"Golden Book Of Fairy Tales (The),"** No. 9, 1942, illustrations by Winfield Hoskins, 42 pp. .............................. 40

**"Good Morning, Good Night,"** No. 61, 1948, illustrations by Eloise Wilkin, written by Jane Werner, 42 pp. .............................. 30

**"Hansel And Gretel,"** No. 17, 1943, illustrations by Erika Weihs, written by Bros. Grimm, 42 pp. .............................. 25

**"Happy Family (The),"** No. 35, 1947, illustrations by Gertrude Elliott, written by Nicole, 42 pp. .............................. 30

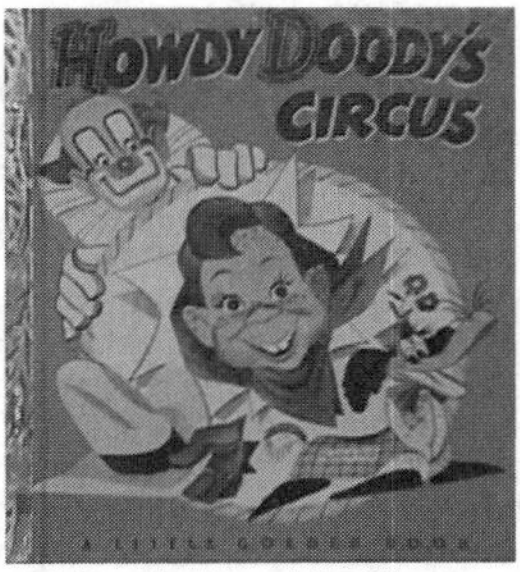


*Howdy Doody's Circus*

**"Howdy Doody's Circus,"** No. 99, 1950, copyright by Robert E. Smith, illustrations by Liz Dauber, written by Don Gormley, 28 pp. (ILLUS.) .............................. 25

**"Huckleberry Hound And His Friends,"** No. 406, 1960, copyright by H-B Enterprises, Inc., illustrations by Ben De Nunez & Bob Totten, written by Pat Cherr, 24 pp. .............................. 18

**"Little Golden ABC (The),"** No. 101, 1951, illustrations by Cornelius De Witt, 28 pp. ......... 8

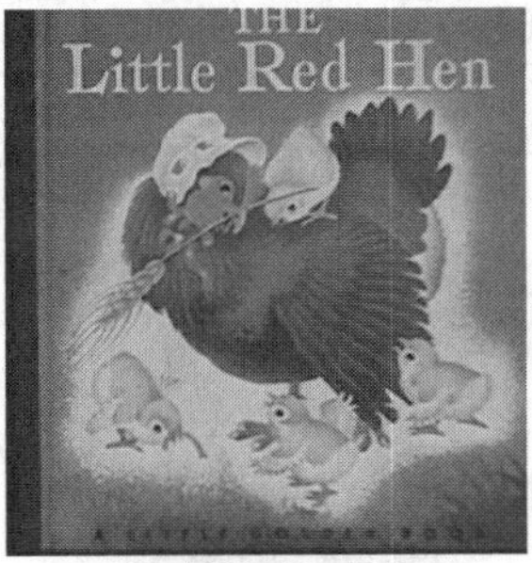


*The Little Red Hen*

**"Little Red Hen (The),"** No. 6, 1942, illustrations by Rudolf Freund, 42 pp. (ILLUS.) .............................. 40

**"Lively Little Rabbit (The),"** No. 15, 1943, illustrations by Gustaf Tenggren, written by Ariane, 42 pp. (ILLUS.) .............................. 25

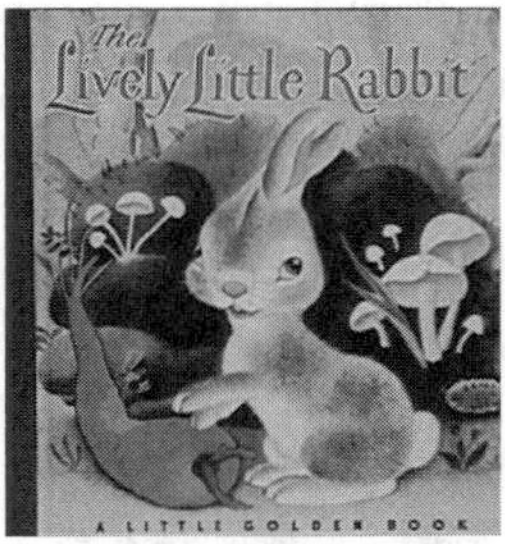


*The Lively Little Rabbit*

**"Mother Goose,"** No. 4, 1942, illustrations by Gertrude Elliott, written by Phyllis Fraser, 42 pp. .............................. 40

**"My Dolly And Me,"** No. 418, 1960, illustrations by Eloise Wilkin, written by Patsy Scarry, 24 pp. .............................. 40

**"New Baby (The),"** No. 41, 1948, 1st cover, illustrations by Eloise Wilkin, written by Ruth & Harold Shane, 42 pp. .............. 30

**"New House In The Forest (The),"** No. 24, 1946, illustrations by Eloise Wilken, written by Lucy Sprague Mitchell, 42 pp. ....... 40

**"Night Before Christmas (The),"** No. 20, 1949, 2nd cover, gilded pictures, illustrations by Corinne Malvern, written by Clement C. Moore, 28 pp. .............................. 14

**"Night Before Christmas (The),"** No. 20, 1949, 3rd cover, illustrations by Corinne Malvern, written by Clement C. Moore, 24 pp. .............................. 6

**"Nurse Nancy,"** No. 154, 1952, Band-Aids pasted to title page, illustrations by Corinne Malvern, written by Kathryn Jackson, 28 pp. .............................. 110

**"Pets For Peter,"** No. 82, 1950, illustrations by Aurelius Battaglia, written by Jane Werner, 28 pp. .............................. 14

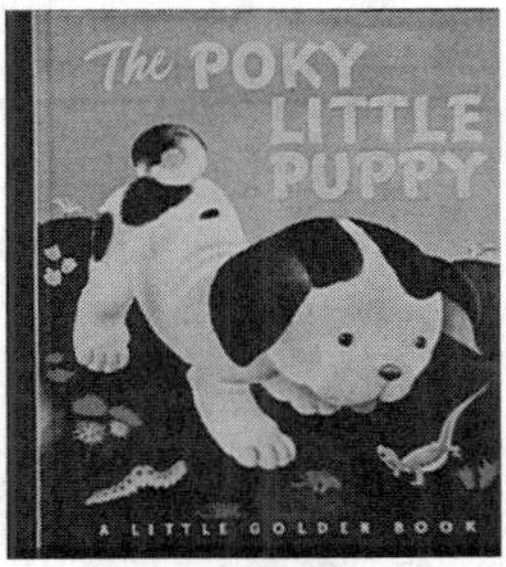


*The Poky Little Puppy, 1942*

**"Poky Little Puppy (The),"** No. 8, 1942, illustrations by Gustaf Tenggren, written by Janet Sebring Lowrey, 42 pp. (ILLUS.) .............................. 40

**"Prayers For Children,"** No. 5, 1942, illustrations by Rachel Taft Dixon, 42 pp. ............ 40

**"Puss In Boots,"** No. 137, 1952, illustrations by J.P. Miller, written by Kathryn Jackson, 28 pp. .............................. 11

**"Tex And His Toys,"** No. 129, 1952, uncut w/tape, illustrations by Corinne Malvern, written by Elsa Ruth Nast, 28 pp. .................. 90

**"This Little Piggy Counting Rhymes,"** No. 12, 1942, illustrations by Roberta Paflin, 42 pp. .................................... **50**

*Three Little Kittens, 1942*

**"Three Little Kittens,"** No. 1, 1942, illustrations by Masha, 42 pp., (ILLUS.) .............. **40**

**"Tootle,"** No. 21, 1945, illustrations by Tibor Gergely, written by Gertrude Crampton, 42 pp. ........................................ **25**

**"Toys,"** No. 22, 1945, illustrations by Masha, written by Edith Oswald, 42 pp. ......... **25**

# YOUTH BOOKS

## HARDY BOYS

**"Clue of the Broken Blade (The),"** No. 21, by Franklin W. Dixon, Carpentieri (pseud.), 1st printing, 44th title printing, ca. 1965, Grosset & Dunlap, ©1942, blue spine pictorial cover w/brown multi-picture endpapers, back cover w/44 Hardy Boys titles, original text (Fn-) ....................... **15**

**"Hidden Harbor Mystery (The),"** No. 14, 1959, by Franklin W. Dixon, Heffelfinger, 1st printing, Grosset & Dunlap, ©1935, beige tweed w/brown multi-picture endpapers, wrap-around dust jacket, front flap w/38 Hardy Boys titles (Fn/Fn) .............. **14**

**"Hooded Hawk Mystery (The),"** No. 34, 1960, by Franklin W. Dixon, Heffelfinger, 1st printing, Grosset & Dunlap, ©1954, beige tweed w/brown multi-picture endpapers, chipping to top of dust jacket spine, wrap-around dust jacket w/39 Hardy Boys titles on front flap (Fn/Fn-) .......... **15**

**"Mystery of the Flying Express (The),"** No. 20, by Franklin W. Dixon, Carpentieri, 1st printing, 44th title printing, ca. 1965, Grosset & Dunlap, ©1941, blue spine pictorial cover w/brown multi-picture endpapers, back cover w/44 Hardy Boys titles, original text (Fn) ......................... **10**

**"Secret of the Caves (The),"** No. 7, by Franklin W. Dixon, Carpentieri, 1st printing, 40th title printing, ca. 1962, Grosset & Dunlap, NY, ©1929, blue spine pictorial cover w/brown multi-picture endpapers, back cover w/40 Hardy Boys titles, interior w/41 titles, original text (Fn) .............. **17**

**"Sinister Signpost (The),"** No. 15, by Franklin W. Dixon, Carpentieri, 1st printing, 44th title printing, ca. 1965, Grosset & Dunlap, ©1936, blue spine pictorial cover w/brown multi-picture endpapers,

back cover w/44 Hardy Boys titles, original text (Fn) .................................................. **15**

# NANCY DREW

*Nancy Drew's The Clue of the Tapping Heels*

**"Clue of the Tapping Heels (The),"** No. 16, 1942, by Carolyn Keene, Farah, 2nd printing, 10th title printing, story by Grosset & Dunlap, ©1939, thick blue cloth w/orange silhouette on front cover & endpapers, good paper w/glossy frontispiece, white spine dust jacket w/19 Nancy Drew titles on front flap, closed tear on dust jacket front cover, VG/VG+ (ILLUS.) ...................................................... **120**

**"Clue of the Tapping Heels (The),"** No. 16, 1961, by Carolyn Keene, Farah, 1st printing, 49th title printing, story by Grosset & Dunlap, ©1939, blue tweed w/multi-picture endpapers, white spine dust jacket w/38 Nancy Drew titles on front flap, closed tear & light chipping to top & bottom of dust jacket spine, spotting on book cover (Fn/VG+) ......................... **25**

**"Mystery at the Moss-Covered Mansion (The),"** No. 18, 1961, by Carolyn Keene, Farah, 2nd printing, 47th title printing, story by Grosset & Dunlap, ©1941, blue tweed w/multi-picture endpapers, white spine dust jacket w/38 Nancy Drew titles on front flap, postage stamp-sized sticker removal area on upper right dust jacket corner (Fn/VG+) .................................. **20**

**"Mystery of the Brass Bound Truck (The),"** No. 17, 1944, by Carolyn Keene, Farah, 1st printing, 11th title printing, story by Grosset & Dunlap, ©1940, blue composition material w/orange silhouette on front cover & endpapers, pulp paper w/wartime message on title page, white spine dust jacket w/21 Nancy Drew titles on front flap (Fn/Fn-) .................. **50**

*Nancy Drew's
The Mystery of the Ivory Charm*

**"Mystery of the Ivory Charm (The),"** No. 13, 1942, by Carolyn Keene, Farah, 2nd printing, 15th title printing, story by Grosset & Dunlap, ©1936, thick blue cloth w/orange silhouette on front cover & endpapers, pulp paper w/glossy frontispiece, white spine dust jacket w/19 Nancy Drew titles on front flap, last thick printing, slight chipping to top & bottom of dust jacket spine Fn-/Fn- (ILLUS.) .......... **180**

**"Mystery of the Ivory Charm (The),"** No. 13, 1960, by Carolyn Keene, Farah, 2nd printing, 48th title printing, story by Grosset & Dunlap, ©1936, blue tweed w/multi-picture endpapers, white spine dust jacket w/37 Nancy Drew titles on front flap, chipping at top & bottom spine of dust jacket & creasing along foredge (VG+/VG) ...................... **20**

**"Mystery of the Lost Dogs,"** Picture Book No. 1, by Carolyn Keene, story by Grosset & Dunlap, ©1977, owner's inscription on front endpapers, 8 1/2 x 11" (Fn) ............. **30**

**"Nancy Drew Secret-Code Activity Book (The),"** by Tony Tallarico & Nancy T. Rockwell, story by Grosset & Dunlap, ©1978, softcover activity book, 8 1/2 x 11" (Fn).............................. **30**

**"Nancy's Mysterious Letter,"** No. 8, 1961, by Carolyn Keene, Farah, 1st printing, 71st title printing, story by Grosset & Dunlap, ©1932, blue tweed w/multi-picture endpapers, wrap-around dust jacket w/38 Nancy Drew titles on front flap (Fn/Fn) ............................ **25**

**"Sign of the Twisted Candles (The),"** No. 9, 1942, by Carolyn Keene, Farah, 2nd printing, 28th title printing, story by Grosset & Dunlap, ©1933, thick blue cloth w/orange silhouette on front cover & endpapers, pulp paper w/glossy frontispiece, white spine dust jacket w/19 Nancy Drew titles on front flap, last thick printing, light chipping to top & bottom dust jacket spine, closed tear on dust jacket (Fn-/VG+)............................ **160**

# CHILDREN'S DISHES
## WHISTLE CUPS

*"Count Down, Blast Off" Whistle Mug*

**"Count Down, Blast Off,"** space mug, rocket ship on handle is whistle, bottom says "Personal Property of (space for child's name)" (ILLUS.)............................ **$25-35**

*Bear "Drink Milk and Whistle" Whistle Cup*

**"Drink Milk and Whistle,"** three small bears play on front while little bear sits on handle, ceramic whistle is separate piece (ILLUS.) ........................................... **35-45**

*New Hampshire Souvenir Whistle Cup*

**"Old Man Of The Mountain, Franconia Notch, NH,"** a souvenir whistle cup, bird tail is the whistle (ILLUS.)......................... **45-55**

*"Sing a Song of Sixpence" Whistle Cup*

**"Sing a Song of Sixpence,"** marked "Genuine Staffordshire Hand Painted Shorter & Son Ltd., England," bird's tail is whistle (ILLUS.) ...................................................... **35-45**

*Florida Souvenir Whistle Cup*

**"Sip N' Whistle Milk Mug For A Little Dear,"** similar to other Sip & Whistle

Mug, but is a Florida souvenir, same poem on the back (ILLUS.) ...................... **45-55**

*"Sip N' Whistle Milk Mug For A Little Dear"*
*Whistle Cup*

**"Sip N' Whistle Milk Mug For A Little Dear,"** whistle cup & straw, bird tail is whistle & stem is straw, poem on back reads "Whistle Whistle On my cup, when I blow, mom fills it up" (ILLUS.) ................. **45-55**

*Train-shaped Whistle Cup*

**Train-shaped cup,** w/whistle handle (ILLUS.) ...................................................... **25-35**

*"Washington, DC" Souvenir Whistle Cup*

**"Washington, DC,"** souvenir whistle cup, bird tail is the whistle (ILLUS.) .................... **45-55**

*Bluebird "Whistle For Milk" Whistle Cup*

**"Whistle For Milk"** two bluebirds face each other on handle, tail is whistle, "Grantcrest Hand Painted - Japan," smaller bird 3" h. (ILLUS.) ......................... **20-30**

*Clown "Whistle For Your Milk" Whistle Cup*

**"Whistle For Your Milk,"** clown w/balloon, Spencer Gifts, 1976 (ILLUS.) .................... **15-25**

*Elephant Head Whistle Cup*

**"Whistle For Your Milk,"** elephant head, trunk is whistle & ears are handles (ILLUS.) ....................................................... **35-40**

*" Whistle For Your Milk" Whistle Cup*

**"Whistle For Your Milk,"** most common whistle cup found, two birds facing away from handle, bird on handle tail is whistle, "Ross Products - Hand Decorated Japan" (ILLUS.) ........................................ **20-25**

*Owl "Whistle For Your Milk" Whistle Cup*

**"Whistle For Your Milk,"** owl w/plastic roly-poly eyes, ceramic whistle is separate piece (ILLUS.) ..................................... **45-55**

# CHILDREN'S FIGURAL TOOTHBRUSH HOLDERS

*Convincing children to brush their teeth is always a challenge. Figural toothbrush holders made this chore a bit easier because the child had something fun and cute to hold their toothbrush and often times toothpaste. Nursery rhyme characters, children and animals were popular themes. Toothbrush holders date back as far as the 1920s or 1930s but most are from the 1940s and 1950s. Whimsical holders are still produced however, the pieces today tend towards cartoon characters and are much larger in size than the older models. The majority of the early toothbrush holders were made in Japan but some were made in Germany and command higher prices.*

*—D. Gillham*

**Animal: Cow,** three holders w/tray (ILLUS. center) .................................................... **$95-125**
**Animal: Pink Elephant,** three holders w/tray (ILLUS. right) ................................. **85-95**

*Animal Toothbrush Holders*

**Animal: Plaid Horse,** three holders w/tray (ILLUS. left) ............................................... **85-95**
**Baker (The),** figural, man wearing white hat, w/red shirt w/blue tie, white pants & white apron, holders by arms, w/front tray (ILLUS. center) ................................. **75-85**
**Blacks,** chef, made in Japan, two holes w/tray (ILLUS. center) ................................. **350**

*Blacks Toothbrush Holders*

**Blacks,** Moore or Swami, Germany, w/two holders (ILLUS. left) ..................................... **200**
**Blacks,** Moore or Swami, sitting, w/two holes in cap (ILLUS. right) .......................... **150**
**Butcher (The),** figural, man wearing red hat, w/blue stripped shirt, red checked pants & white apron, holders by arms, w/front tray (ILLUS. left, top next column) ........................................................ **75-85**

*Butcher, Baker & Candlestick Maker Toothbrush Holders*

**Candlestick Maker (The),** figural, bald man w/glasses wearing blue shirt w/red tie, red & white striped apron & black pants, holders in pockets of apron, w/front tray (ILLUS. right) .......................... **75-85**

*Cartoon Toothbrush Holders*

**Cartoon characters,** Moon Mullins & Kayo, bisque, w/one holder (ILLUS. left) ........ **95**
**Cartoon characters,** Orphan Annie & Sandy, bisque, w/two holders (ILLUS. right) ............................................................... **95**
**Cartoon characters,** Popeye, left arm toothbrush holder & resting spot on pant leg (ILLUS. center) ..................................... **550+**
**Disney Characters,** Mickey & Minnie w/Pluto, bisque, two holders in back (ILLUS. center) ............................................ **250**
**Disney Characters,** pig playing the flute, ceramic, Maws (marked Foreign), w/one holder in back (ILLUS. right) ....................... **150**

*Disney Toothbrush Holders*

**Disney Characters,** Three Pigs, bisque, two holders in back (ILLUS. left) ................. **100**
**Dog,** blue lusterware, w/big nose (ILLUS. right) ............................................................... **55**

*Dog Toothbrush Holders*

Dog, lusterware, multi-color (ILLUS. left) ........... 55
Dog, tan, sitting up, w/holder through
   mouth (ILLUS. center) .................................... 75
German children, Lassie, one holder
   w/tray, 4 1/2" h. (ILLUS. center) ................... 150
German children, Little Boy, one holder
   w/tray, 4 1/2" h. (ILLUS. right) ...................... 150

*German Children Toothbrush Holders*

German children, little girl, one holder
   w/tray, 4 1/2" h. (ILLUS. left) ........................ 150
Nursery rhyme, Old Woman in the Shoe,
   w/tray ...................................................... 75-85
Nursery rhyme, Peter Peter Pumpkin
   Eater, w/tray ............................................. 75-85
Nursery Rhyme Characters, Little Red
   Riding Hood, one holder w/tray (ILLUS.
   center) ..................................................... 85-95
Nursery Rhyme Characters, Old King
   Cole, one holder w/tray (ILLUS. right) ....... 75-85

*Nursery Rhyme Toothbrush Holders*

Nursery Rhyme Characters, Three Bears,
   two holders w/tray (ILLUS. left) ................. 75-85
Soldier, French-looking, w/uniform of blue
   & red, one holder by left arm for brush,
   w/tray in front, 6 1/2" h. (ILLUS. center) ......... 55

*Soldier Toothbrush Holders*

Soldier, man w/red pill box hat, red shirt &
   blue pants, w/holders through arms into
   big brown boots (ILLUS. left) ......................... 55

Soldier, w/red shirt & black pants & hat,
   w/sash across front, holders through
   arms into boots, feet create tray (ILLUS.
   right) ............................................................. 65

# CHRISTMAS COLLECTIBLES

*Today, much excitement ripples through the air whenever anything Christmas comes up for sale, be it at an auction, estate sale, antique show, flea market or on the World Wide Web. For increasing numbers of collectors join the ranks of those who are attempting to recapture the spirit of Christmas past through their collecting. Record prices have been set for Santas, Dresden ornaments, and rare glass figurals, but beginning collectors will find multitudes of items at very inexpensive to moderate prices. Christmas collecting has a wide range of interests and prices. The past few years have seen accelerated prices in the rarer areas, stabilized in the medium to low end items, and even a reduction in price when very common items come up for sale.*

*Even though Christmas has been celebrated for years, its celebration as a national holiday is as recent as 1891 and its unusual appeal as a collectible is, of course, much newer than that. It is in recent years that Americans have become enamored with many different collecting interests in Christmas. Christmas collecting is a vast field and a collector may amass a collection of many different things, but there are certain areas of Christmas that attract more interest than others, such as: feather trees, candy containers, paper ornaments, Dresden paper figures, wax decorations, pressed cotton creations, glass ornaments, early lighting devices, and electric bulbs.*

—Robert Brenner

*An early Christmas postcard*

Candy container, large figure of Santa
   Claus, well detailed & painted papier-
   maché face w/gesso, white fur beard,
   red & blue felt costume w/black papier-
   maché boots, candy container inside the
   body, 19 1/2" h. (boots damaged &
   repaired, belt damaged) ............................ $770

**Feather tree,** green branches w/berries or candle sockets on the tip, turned wood base painted white, early 20th c., 43" h. (wear, damage, several branches droop)..... 165

**Feather tree,** green branches w/red berries, small square block wooden base painted white w/red & green painted garlands, marked "Made in Western Germany," mid-20th c., 15" h. (some wear & damage) ...................... 248

**Figure of Santa Claus on polar bear,** papier-mâché, molded in the round, a startled looking Santa astride a galloping polar bear, white w/red,green & pink trim, ca. 1950s, 9" h. (some wear) ............... 165

**Kugel,** cobalt blue w/brass hanger, 3 1/2" d.............................................. 72

**Kugel,** emerald green w/embossed brass hanger marked "V.G. 1721," 9 1/2" d. .......... 303

**Kugel,** gold w/embossed brass hanger marked "V.G. 1721," 9 1/2" d. .................... 220

**Toy,** musical-type, figure of Santa Claus w/papier-mâché molded head & hat, wire & wood body, carved wood hands & feet, cotton flannel outfit, seated on a paper & wood accordian, late 19th - early 20th c., 9 5/8" h. (fading & wear on outfit) ........................................ 1,035

# ARTIFICIAL & FEATHER TREES

*Green Tree w/Red Berries*

As far back as the last third of the 19th century, artificial trees have been in existence. From what can be determined, feather tree manufacturing was a cottage industry similar to the manufacture of glass tree ornaments. However, it was different in several respects. The parts for the tree—wire, wood, and berries—were factory made & the heavy wire branches were sent to cottages for wrapping. Turkey and goose feathers were the most commonly used feathers, but swan feathers also were used.

Sheared trees, as we know them today, did not exist at that time and feather trees accurately reflected the neutral appearance of live white pines. These trees are a relatively expensive collectors item, they can command prices ranging from $85.00 to $1,200.00 or more, depending on age

and size. It seems to be a rule of thumb that trees are priced about $120.00 to $145.00 per foot.

In addition to feather trees, visca trees made in America and even brush trees from the 1960s are seeing an increase in price. But aluminum trees, which appeal to the younger generation of collectors, are dramatically rising in price. Produced as early as the mid-1950s and into the late 1960s, these trees are snapped up almost as fast as they placed on sale.

**Tree,** green w/red berries, in round white base, 12" (ILLUS.)......................................... 125

**Tree,** green w/candleholders, square white base, 24" ....................................................... 270

**Tree,** white w/red berries, round red base, 24".............................................................. 240

**Tree,** blue w/candleholders, square white base, 46" ....................................................... 480

# CANDY CONTAINERS

*Some of the earliest decorations for the Christmas tree were edibles and the containers that held these "goodies" were often used as decorations for the tree. Many cornucopias and candy containers found today are small and their appearance on the tree seems quite obvious. Candy containers in the shape of Father Christmas command the highest prices and those containers made in Germany easily command over $100.00 each. In fact, the composition and papier-mâché containers are becoming increasingly difficult to find as collectors scramble to add them to collections.*

**Basket,** paper, w/tinsel handle & Santa scrap on front ............................................. 160

**Boot,** papier-mâché, German............................. 40

**Child,** cotton, w/bisque head pushing papier-mâché snow ball ............................... 550

**Cornucopia,** paper, gold foiled cone.................. 85

**Egg,** silk over pressed cardboard..................... 160

**Elf,** composition, sitting on candy container log ...................................................... 325

**Santa,** celluloid head, mesh body .................... 165

**Santa in car,** celluloid head, cardboard car w/wheels ...................................................... 320

*Santa On Bombshell*

**Santa on bombshell,** composition (ILLUS.)........................................................ 850

*Santa on Donkey Candy Box*

**Santa on Donkey,** candy box (ILLUS.) ............ **185**
**Snow ball,** cotton covered w/red cotton
Santa on top, Japan, 4" ............................... **120**

## CHRISTMAS ADVERTISING

*During Victorian times, small lithographed prints known as trade cards were the primary form of written advertisements. These advertising cards were used for products ranging from coffee to farm machinery. Lion Brothers and McLaughins advertised their coffee with some of the most beautiful of cards, many of which used the figure of St. Nicholas as their central theme. Along with the increased use of color in magazines, came numerous new advertisements at Christmas employing Santa Claus and other Christmas-related themes.*

**Biscuit tin,** Kennedy w/Santa .......................... **420**
**Button,** celluloid, Santa w/stocking .................... **95**
**Button,** celluloid, TB, 1936 ................................. **45**
**Calendar top,** blue Santa w/children .............. **120**
**Candy pail,** Santa, early .................................. **425**
**Cigar box,** Santa w/toys inside cover .............. **165**
**Coca-Cola,** standing Santa, ca. 1930s ............ **210**
**Lion Coffee,** Santa w/children chromo ............ **225**
**Snow King,** stand-up Santa w/sleigh .............. **950**
**Soapbox,** Fairbank's ........................................ **600**
**Trade card,** Santa w/sleigh, Snow King
baking powder ................................................ **95**

## CHRISTMAS ORNAMENTS

*Bluebird Clip Ornament*

**Angel,** white, feather, on base, 1950s, 5" .......... **15**
**Bell,** plastic, "Made in Japan", 1950, could
be purchased singly at the local 5 & 10,
a bin item, came in various colors, price
each .................................................................. **3**

**Bluebird clip,** to place on Christmas tree,
white tail feathers made of
fiberglass, ca. 1920s-30s, 4" (ILLUS.) ............ **40**
**Decoration for tree,** paper, Coca-Cola,
1980 ................................................................ **10**
**Decorations,** Shiny Brite, glass, 1950s,
small size, 12 in a box, various single
colors, per box ................................................ **10**
**Grapes,** thin glass, painted green in grape-
shape, 1930s-40s, 2 1/2" ............................... **20**
**Holly ivy,** with hands, face and red cap,
1950s, 3 3/4" ................................................... **8**
**Horn,** small, glass, 1930s, came in other
colors, 2 1/2" ................................................... **15**

*Lantern-type ornaments*

**Lantern-type,** silver w/a second different
color, ca. 1940s, 2 1/2" (ILLUS.) ................... **10**

*Rudolph the Reindeer Ornament*

**Rudolph the Reindeer,** red, made in
Japan, 2 1/2 x 3" (ILLUS.) ................................ **5**
**Star,** 6-pointed, small red ball in the center,
different colors, 1920s-1930s, 4" .................... **15**

## COOKIE MOLDS, CANDY MOLDS, & COOKIE CUTTERS

*Molds and cookie cutters were often fashioned in the shape of Father Christmas. Some of the earliest of molds were created by the gingerbread bakers and lebkuchen creators who were also chandlers (or wax workers). After the mid-1600s, molds were made from carved wood or molded plaster, unlike the earlier molds made of fired, unglazed clay. Candy molds were made of heavy metal and have surprisingly good detail. Even ice cream and cake molds in various Santa shapes have been found. Eppelsheimer and Co. produced pewter ice cream molds in the shape of Father Christmas in the late 1800s.*

*Cookie cutters were at first made at home from tin and these examples of folk art are highly sought after by today's collectors. Many of these were quite large, up to 13" in length. The first ones were* without handles and were awkward to use. Cutters from the 1940s and 1950s are quite interesting as many of them had quite defined shapes. Many of these molds and cutters can make interesting wall displays during the Christmas season

| | |
|---|---|
| **Bell,** candy mold | **60** |
| **Christmas tree,** candy mold | **65** |
| **Santa on Donkey,** candy mold, two-part | **295** |
| **Santas,** candy mold, two rolls of 14 | **140** |

## EARLY LIGHTING DEVICES

Candles were the most popular and widely used method for illuminating the tree. Due to the fact that many fires were caused by tipping candles, balanced weight candleholders were invented. These would keep the candle standing upright, avoiding its tipping over into a branch or another ornament. The earliest and most economical were those with clay or wooden balls at the bottom. Also used as counter-balances were lead figures, heavy glass ornaments, and soft metal ornaments.

Some of the rarest Christmas candleholders include thin, fragile glass lanterns that clip onto the tree. First manufactured just before the turn-of-the-century, they were introduced as being novel alternatives to plain metal candleholders. The counter balance holders many times bring $100.00 or more with the simple clip-ons in the $1.00 to $5.00 range.

*Candleholders*

| | |
|---|---|
| **Candleholder,** counterbalance, tin & lead geometric figure at end, several varieties (ILLUS. of four) | **120** |
| **Candleholder,** counterbalance, w/clay ball at bottom | **20** |
| **Candleholder,** pinch-on, lithographed w/Father Christmas | **185** |
| **Christmas light,** glass, cranberry | **320** |
| **Christmas light,** quilted blue | **75** |
| **Christmas light,** quilted milk glass | **80** |
| **Lantern,** glass, in shape of aviator w/candle insert, clip-on | **685** |
| **Lantern,** metal w/glass panels, six-sided | **95** |
| **Reflector,** tin, American | **5** |

## ELECTRIC LIGHT BULBS

When Christmas trees began to be lit with electricity, a whole new area of collectibles was opened. One type of electric lamp used was the "Festoon Lamp" (sometimes referred to as

"Stringer"), produced around 1895. A Festoon Lamp was a round glass globe with a carbon filament running lengthwise attached to brass connectors on either end with loops for wiring them together in a series.

Around 1908, fancy figural lamps started being imported from Germany, Austria, and Hungary. They were similar to clip-on ornaments and some had an exhaust tip at the top; in the case of many birds, the tip was their beak. The glass had detailed molding, soft shades of paint and expressive faces making them comparable to the early European ornaments.

After World War I, Japan began to manufacture glass figural light bulbs and soon the milk glass figural light was commonplace on American trees. Regardless of whether the lights work or not, they can easily bring more than $30.00, with the European lights being worth over $200.00.

Bubble lights, Italian miniature light sets, and matchless stars continue to set price records. The different types appeal to the younger generation of collectors.

| | |
|---|---|
| **Andy Gump,** milk glass | **90** |
| **Aviator,** milk glass, boy w/airplane | **65** |
| **Ball,** milk glass, red w/stars | **15** |
| **Bird,** brown, early European | **120** |
| **Bubble light,** oil, working | **65** |
| **Bubble light,** shooting stars | **120** |
| **Bulbs,** C-6, Detecto | **5** |
| **Clown head,** milk glass | **35** |
| **Cottage,** milk glass, six-sided | **10** |
| **Dick Tracy,** milk glass | **95** |
| **Dog in basket,** milk basket | **65** |
| **Dresden,** flowers, 3" | **120** |
| **Dresden,** dog, 5" | **225** |
| **Grapes,** milk glass | **15** |
| **Humpty Dumpty,** milk glass, large head | **65** |
| **Jack-O' Lantern,** milk glass | **120** |
| **Lion,** w/tennis racket, milk glass | **50** |
| **Matchless star,** single row points | **45** |
| **Pig,** w/bowtie, milk glass | **85** |
| **Rose,** clear glass, Dresden | **120** |
| **Rose,** clear glass, small, Japan | **10** |

*Various old figural light bulbs*

| | |
|---|---|
| **Santa head,** large, milk glass, 4" (ILLUS.) | **25** |
| **Smitty,** milk glass | **95** |
| **St. Nicholas,** clear glass, early European | **185** |

**Woman in shoe,** milk glass ............................... **65**
**Zeppelin,** milk glass ........................................... **75**
**Boxed set,** Disney Silly Symphony ................. **320**
**Boxed set,** glass, Mother Goose charac-
ters ............................................................ **285**

## GAMES, PUZZLES, & TOYS

Toy collectors cross with Christmas collectors in vying for some very expensive items. With the Victorian fascination with parlor games came the inevitable manufacturing of many Christmas and Santa-related games. These were not manufactured in huge quantities since their use only seemed appropriate during a short period of the year. Wooden puzzles are also of interest to collectors because of the beautiful lithographed images of Father Christmas and later Santa Claus.

Some of the finest old toys available include cast-iron toys made by Hubley, manufactured in the early 1900s. Toys made of pressed tin were made in the Nurnberg area of Germany as early as the late 1700s. Nodders and clockwork Santas were absolutely beautiful and very few of these were saved. Paper lithography enabled the manufacturers to decorate even the most inexpensive toy with color. Especially desirable are the tin German toys such as those made after World War I because many of these survived and are available to collectors today. Those toys depicting Santa riding in mechanical cars, sleighs and airplanes are highly collectible. The tin mechanical toys manufactured in Japan from the 1930s through the 1950s have seen very dramatic price increases.

**Battery-operated,** Santa w/drum, eyes
light up, Japan ............................................. **295**
**Jigsaw puzzle,** lantern, Santa head, Amer-
ican ............................................................ **285**
**Mechanical,** skating Santa, Japan .................. **425**
**Rolly poly,** Santa, Schoenhut, 7" .................... **850**
**Santa on top of house,** 9" .............................. **310**
**Wind-up,** celluloid Santa, Japan ..................... **120**

*Santa with Book Wind-Up Toy*

**Wind-up,** Santa w/book, Japan (ILLUS.) ......... **165**

## GREETING CARDS

Although greeting cards originated as early as 1846 in England, they did not become popular in the United States until the late 1870s. The earliest of these cards were illustrated with flowers, birds, and other such non-Christmas themes. It wasn't until the beginning of the 1920s that Santa was widely used on greeting cards. St. Nick was depicted in every conceivable style of dress and would appear in cars, airplanes, train cars, and engines and even with polar bears. His fine details of color and accessories was interpreted individually by the whims of countless artists. Since his appearance was not standardized, it is fairly simple for a collector to find unusual and interesting cards.

**Fold-out,** airbrush, "Xmas," 1908 ...................... **15**
**Fold-out,** five-layer, nativity scene .................... **110**
**Fold-out,** two-layer, Angels w/nativity ............... **60**

*Father Christmas Greeting Card*

**Fold-out,** two-layer, Father Christmas
(ILLUS.) ...................................................... **125**
**Walt Disney,** Mickey Mouse ............................ **110**

## HALLMARK KEEPSAKE ORNAMENTS (1973-1976)

**Adorable Adornments: Mrs. Santa,** 1975,
No. QX 156-1, handcrafted, by artist
Donna Lee, 3 1/2" h. ...................................... **65**
**Adorable Adornments: Raggedy Andy,**
1975, No. QX 160-1, handcrafted, by art-
ist Donna Lee, 3 1/2" h. ................................. **300**
**Adorable Adornments: Raggedy Ann,**
1975, No. QX 159-1, handcrafted, by art-
ist Donna Lee, 3 1/2" h. ................................. **300**
**Adorable Adornments: Santa,** 1975, No.
QX 155-1, handcrafted, by artist Donna
Lee, 3 1/2" h. ................................................. **65**
**Angel,** 1973, No . XHD 78-5, yarn orna-
ment, gold or white wings, 4 1/2" h. .............. **30**
**Betsey Clark,** 1976, No. QX 210-1, white
satin ball marked "Christmas 1976," 3" d. ........ **50**
**Betsey Clark series,** 1973, No. XHD 110-
2, First Edition, white glass ball, depicts
girl feeding a deer & girl cuddling a lamb,
3 1/4" d. ...................................................... **100**
**Betsey Clark series,** 1974, No. QX 108-1,
second in series, dated "1974," white
glass ball w/orchestra & choir of young-
sters preparing for Christmas celebra-
tion, 3 1/4" d. ................................................ **70**
**Betsey Clark series,** 1975, No. QX 133-1,
third in series, depicts three caroling girls
dressed in pink, blue & yellow calico on

white glass ball, marked "Christmas 1975," 3 1/4" d................................................ **50**

**Boy Caroler,** 1973, No. XHD 83-2, yarn ornament w/blue hat & coat, 4 1/2" h. ............ **25**

**Cardinals,** 1976, No. QX 205-1, marked "Christmas 1976" on white glass ball, 2 5/8" d......................................................... **60**

**Choir Boy,** 1973, No. XHD 80-5, yarn ornament, 4 1/2" h..................................... **25**

**Christmas Is Love,** 1973, No. XHD 106-2, white glass ball, depicts two angels playing mandolins, in shades of green & lavender, 3 1/4" d................................................ **65**

**Elves,** 1973, No. XHD 103-5, white glass ball, depicts elves ice skating, 3 1/4" d.......... **75**

**Green Girl,** 1973, No. XHD 84-5, yarn ornament, green w/red hat & song book, 4 1/2" h......................................................... **28**

**Marty Links,** 1976, No. QX 207-1, marked "Noel 1976" & "Merry Christmas 1976" on white glass balls, set of 2, 2 1/2" d. ........... **55**

**Mr. Snowman,** 1973, No. XHD 76-5, yarn ornament w/blue scarf & black top hat, 4 1/2" h......................................................... **25**

**Mrs. Snowman,** 1973, No. XHD 77-2, yarn ornament w/pink hat & scarf, 4 1/2" h. ........... **25**

**Norman Rockwell,** 1974, No. QX 111-1, white glass ball, depicts Santa wearing apron w/tools & napping in chair as elves work, Santa w/two boys on reverse, 3 1/4" d.......................................... **70**

**Nostalgia Ornaments: Drummer Boy,** 1975, No. QX 130-1, by artist Linda Sickman, reissued 1976, 3 1/4" d................ **165**

**Nostalgia Ornaments: Drummer Boy,** 1976, No. QX 130-1, by artist Linda Sickman, 3 1/4" d. ...................................... **160**

**Nostalgia Ornaments: Joy,** 1975, No. QX 132-1, "Joy" w/baby Jesus in center of "O," by artist Linda Sickman, 3 1/4" d.......... **210**

**Nostalgia Ornaments: Locomotive,** 1976, No. QX 221-1, dated "1976," by artist Linda Sickman, 3 1/4" d...................... **155**

**Nostalgia Ornaments: Peace On Earth,** 1976, No. QX 223-1, dated "1976," by artist Linda Sickman, 3 1/4" d...................... **130**

**Nostalgia Ornaments: Rocking Horse,** 1975, No. QX 128-1, by artist Linda Sickman, reissued 1976, 3 1/4" d. .............. **140**

**Nostalgia Ornaments: Rocking Horse,** 1976, QX 128-1, by artist Linda Sickman, 3 1/4" d............................................... **140**

**Nostalgia Ornaments: Santa & Sleigh,** 1975, No. QX 129-1, by artist Linda Sickman, 3 1/4" d. ...................................... **240**

**Raggedy Ann and Raggedy Andy set:** 1975, No. QX 138-1, front depicts Ann & Andy encircled in green wreath w/"Merry Christmas" on back, second ornament depicts Ann & Andy decorating tree on front w/"Christmas 1975" on back, white glass balls, by artist Linda Sickman, set of 2, 2 1/4" d. .......................................... **55**

**Soldier,** 1973, No. XHD 81-2, yarn ornament, blue w/red hat, boots & bands, 4 1/2" h......................................................... **23**

**Tree Treats: Angel,** 1976, No. QX 176-1, marked "Merry Christmas 1976," 2 3/4-3 5/8" h....................................................... **175**

**Tree Treats: Reindeer,** 1976, No. QX 178-1, marked "Merry Christmas 1976," 2 3/4-3 5/8" h................................................ **100**

**Twirl-Abouts: Angel,** 1976, No. QX 171-1, angel in Christmas tree, marked "Merry Christmas 1976," by artist Linda Sickman, 3 1/2-4" h...................................... **149**

**Twirl-Abouts: Soldier,** 1976, No. QX 173-1, soldier in Guard House, by artist Linda Sickman, dated "1976," 3 1/2-4" h.................. **84**

**Yesteryears: Drummer Boy,** 1976, No. QX 184-1, dated "1976," 2 3/4"-4" h. ........... **140**

**Yesteryears: Partridge,** 1976, No. QX 183-1, dated "1976," 2 3/4"-4" h. .................. **100**

## MISCELLANEOUS

**Beaded spikes,** 1930s-1940s, cardboard silver top, beads colored blue, red, white, green, 6", price each.............................. **6**

**Papier-mâché house,** red w/thin windows, white simulated snow, made in Japan, 1930s, 3" x 4" x 5 1/4"................................. **15**

**Reindeer,** thin Bakelite, stamped "Made in Occupied Japan," 1940s, 2 3/4" x 3"............. **30**

**Santa Claus and Reindeer,** Santa in bright red coat, rough simulated snow on base of figure, Made in Japan, 1920s, 3" l........... **175**

**Santa Claus on sled with eight reindeer,** made in Japan, 1950, 4" ................................. **25**

## POSTCARDS

*Santa and Christmas-related themes have always been incorporated on postcards. The rarest of these include the hold-to-light, silk, mechanical and full-figured European cards. The hold-to-lights are especially of value to collectors because they are composed of multiple layers of cardboard, with the top layer cut-out in strategic places, letting the light shine through. Some cards used pieces of silk fabric to make Santa's clothes and the rarest of these cards are those that use colors other than the traditional red.*

*Father Christmas Carrying Bells & Holly*

**Father Christmas,** dressed in red robe, carrying bells & bag of holly, marked "A Merry Christmas," (ILLUS.) ............................ **15**

*Father Christmas Holding Doll*

**Father Christmas,** dressed in white suit, green glove holding doll dressed in pink, marked "A Merry Christmas," No. 213A, Stecker (ILLUS.)............................................... **14**
**Hold-to-light,** Santa w/child ............................ **240**
**Little girl,** dressed in blue, using umbrella to keep off snow, Winch Publishing, ca. 1911 ..................................................................... **14**
**Mechanical,** Santa w/children ........................... **120**
**Real photo,** Santa w/children ............................ **65**
**Santa Claus on sled waving to two children in house,** "Merry Christmas - Christmas Eve Greetings," 1920 .................... **30**
**Santa Claus on sled with whip,** "Wishing You Every Happiness at Christmas - Tide," (not time), 1928, 3 1/2" x 5 1/2" .......... **30**

*Santa On Skis With Krampus*

**Santa on Skis w/Krampus,** dressed in blue suit, carrying girl w/tree on back, skiing beside Krampus, marked "Gruf vom Krampus," Australia (ILLUS.) ................. **35**
**Santa riding in train** w/children ......................... **35**
**Silk,** Santa leaning over child in chair (ILLUS. w/introduction)................................... **50**
**Silk,** Santa standing w/sack of toys .................... **60**

# PUTZ (NATIVITY) RELATED MATERIALS

**Animals,** composition, assorted, German .......... **25**
**Animals,** wood, assorted, German..................... **45**

*Putz Church and Houses*

**Church,** cardboard, large, Japan (ILLUS. front)................................................................. **35**
**Deer,** celluloid, Japan, 6"..................................... **35**
**Figures,** human, celluloid, Japan ...................... **65**
**House,** cardboard, large, Japan (ILLUS. top right) ......................................................... **25**
**House,** cardboard, medium, Japan (ILLUS. top left) ........................................................... **20**
**Sheep,** composition head, wool body, 4" ........ **120**
**Trees,** brush, small, Japan .................................... **8**
**Trees,** sponge, large, Japan............................... **15**

# SANTA FIGURES

*The most valuable Santa figures are the Victorian papier-mâché items.*

*Papier-mâché (the combination of pulp paper, glue or paste, oil, and rosin) was pressed into two half-molds and once dry, pieces were removed, glued together, and smoothed with sandpaper. They were then sealed with varnish and painted in realistic colors. Many times beards of rabbit fur were glued on for added realism. Originally called Pelze-Nicols, they became known as Belsnickles.*

*Another popular version of the Santa figure used composition. These papier-mâché-type figures were dipped into liquid plaster, which dried in a very thin coat. These figures were realistically painted, paying close attention to the face and hands. They were dressed in authentic clothing and many carried branches or trees made of goose feathers. The candy containers were hidden beneath the flowing cloth skirt. There were numerous other materials also used, including: wood, wax, cotton, plaster, chalk, and metal. All of the earliest European-types command extremely high prices on the market today.*

*Somewhat neglected, even though they are quickly gaining in popularity, are the later cardboard Santas, made from material resembling old eggcartons. These were copies of a more robust Santa, like those seen in Coca-Cola ads. Most had an opening in which candy or small presents could be inserted. They were excellent representations of our jolly American Santa Claus.*

*Belsnickel Santa Figures*

**Belsnickel,** Belsnickel, red, w/feather branch, 7" (ILLUS. center)............................ 400
**Belsnickel,** white, w/feather branch, 11" (ILLUS. right)................................................ 700
**Belsnickel,** blue, w/feather branch, 12" (ILLUS. left)................................................. 785
**Bisque,** miniature, on cardboard........................ 85
**Bisque,** miniature, pulling sleigh ...................... 160

*Standing Celluloid Santa Figures*

**Celluloid,** standing, w/black doll, Japan, 4" (ILLUS. left) ............................................... 160
**Celluloid,** standing, w/pack, Japan, 4" (ILLUS. right)............................................... 140
**Celluloid,** Painted details, Irwin, 12" ............... 290
**Cotton,** w/paper face, 6" .................................. 225
**Japan,** standing, paper, 4" ................................ 55
**Japan,** chenille body over cardboard, composition face, 9"........................................... 420

*Plaster Bank*

**Plaster,** bank, standing, American, 10" (ILLUS.)......................................................... 165
**Plaster,** in chimney, American, 10" ................. 200

# TREE ORNAMENTS

**Kugel,** cobalt blue silvered glass w/brass hanger, 5 3/4" d............................................. 303
**Kugel,** cranberry silvered ball w/brass hanger, 3 1/4" d............................................. 220

## DRESDEN PAPER ORNAMENTS

*Of all the Christmas ornaments, none capture the interest of collectors more than those made primarily from cardboard called "Dresden" ornaments because they originated in or near Dresden, Germany between 1880 and 1910.*

*Three-dimensional Dresdens command the attention of collectors of antique Christmas memorabilia. These heavily embossed cardstock (cardboard) items were part of the Luxus-papier industry in Germany from ca. 1850 to the present. In order to give them the appearance of sheet metal, they were constructed from two or more separately prepared pieces of cardboard and then heavily embossed. The most desirable are made of unusual material, such as the pig with the sacks of money on his back and a four-leaf clover in his mouth. A Dresden in good condition can easily bring over $500.00.*

**Banjo,** three-dimensional, 3" ............................ 160

*Dresden Paper Ornaments*

**Elephant,** three-dimensional, 4" (ILLUS. bottom right) ................................................. 520
**Elf,** holding money bag, three-dimensional, 3"............................................................... 725
**Elk,** brown, three-dimensional, 2" (ILLUS. top center) ................................................. 160
**Face in quarter moon,** three-dimensional (ILLUS. bottom left) ....................................... 525
**Fox,** brown & tan, three-dimensional, 2" .......... 375
**Goat,** black & white, three-dimensional, 2"....... 320
**Heart,** gold, three-dimensional, 3" ...................... 95
**Jockey on horse,** three-dimensional, 3"......... 625
**Lion,** three-dimensional, 2" (ILLUS. top right) ............................................................. 195
**Lobster,** orange, three-dimensional, 4"............ 540
**Monkey on branches,** flat, 4" ........................... 165
**Owl,** tan & black, three-dimensional, 2"............ 410
**Parrot,** gold, three-dimensional (ILLUS. far left) ............................................................... 145
**Pig,** gold, three-dimensional, 2"........................ 620
**Rabbit,** silver, three-dimensional, 3" ............... 300

Santa, gold, three-dimensional, 4" .................. 190
Star, gold, flat, 3" ................................................ 65

## GLASS ORNAMENTS

The first glass ornaments were heavy glass creations that are known to collectors today as Kugels. It is a German term meaning "a round or ball shape." Kugels have become quite popular, especially those of rarer colors including red, amethyst, and cobalt blue. Because of the overuse of the word, many people now call any old, heavy blown-glass ornament a kugel.

Of most interest to collectors in glass ornaments today are the thin glass figural ornaments blown into the shapes of many different objects. From their first early appearance, figural ornaments proved to be exceptionally popular.

Before 1918, the most common glass tree ornaments were the indent, ball-, melon-, and pear-shaped ornaments. Among the outstanding examples of glass ornaments from this period are the unsilvered, Victorian wire-wrapped ornaments produced in profusion before World War I.

The number and variety of glass figurals made from the beginning of production through World War II (1939) have been conservatively estimated to be at least 10,000. Glass ornaments are sometimes worth hundreds of dollars, but only those rarer ones command such prices. Santas, birds, and other common figurals go for much less. Many fine ornaments are once again being manufactured in Europe and collectors should educate themselves in order to know the difference between old and new. Kugels have been reproduced as well. However, some of these newer ornaments are quite desirable, as prices for the original items have risen. Most intriguing is the secondary market for Old World Christmas, Christopher Radko, and Pat Breen as collectors scramble to amass these collectible ornaments.

Al Jolson head, 3 1/4" ................................... 385
Amelia Earhart, 4" ......................................... 245

### Automobile & Los Angeles Zeppelin Glass Ornaments

Automobile, red & silver, 3" (ILLUS. top) .......... 95
Baby, head, glass eyes, 2" (ILLUS. left, top
  next column) ................................................ 165
Baby, w/pacifier, in crib, 2" ............................. 360
Bacchas, head, 2" (ILLUS. right, top next
  column) ....................................................... 420
Bear, 3" ............................................................ 175
Beetle, red & gold, 2" ........................................ 95

### Glass Ornaments of Baby & Bacchas

Bird, game pheasant, 4" ................................... 320
Bird, owl, standing on clip, 4" ........................... 165
Bird, peacock, on clip, fanned spun glass,
  4" .................................................................. 50
Bird, owl, on clip, glass eyes, 5" ....................... 85
Bird, spun glass tail, 5" ...................................... 25
Bird, w/berry in beak, 5" .................................. 165
Boy, whistling, w/hat & scarf, 4" ....................... 95

### Various Glass Ornaments

Carrot, 4" (ILLUS. right center) ...................... 120
Cat, w/fiddle & cap, 3" .................................... 280
Cat in shoe, 4" ................................................ 165
Charlie Chaplin head, 3" ................................. 420
Christ Child head, 3" ....................................... 180
Clown, circus, 4" ............................................... 35
Clown, "My Darling," 4" ..................................... 70
Corn, 4" (ILLUS. right w/carrot) ........................ 85
Devil head, gold, 4" ......................................... 520
Dog, blowing horn, 4" ...................................... 210
Elephant, on ball, 3" ....................................... 320
Elephant, 4" .................................................... 120
Fantasy ornament, bells ................................... 120
Father Christmas, early, 5" .............................. 165
Fish, w/paper fins & tall, 4" ............................. 190
Flower, on clip, venetian dew, 3" .................... 125
Frog, on toadstool, 3" ........................................ 65
Grape cluster, individual grapes, 4" ................. 40
Happy Hooligan, extended legs, 5" ................. 650
Horn, silver w/flowers, 4" ................................. 15
Hot air balloon, angel, 4" (ILLUS. left, top
  next page) ................................................... 160
Hot air balloon, angel, 6" (ILLUS. right, top
  next page) ................................................... 145
Hot air balloon, Santa, 7" (ILLUS. center,
  top next page) ............................................. 320
Indian bust, painted feathers, 4" ..................... 355
Indian head, on clip, 2" ................................... 220
Keystone Cop, extended legs, 5" .................... 650
Kite, chenille string, 3" .................................... 520
Kugel, round, gold, 2" ....................................... 35
Kugel, pear shaped, silver, 3" ......................... 240
Kugel, grape cluster, green, 4" ....................... 300

**Los Angeles zeppelin,** paper label, 4" (ILLUS. bottom, with automobile) ................. **320**
**Mermaid,** red & flesh face, 4" ........................... **400**

*Hot Air Balloons*

**Mrs. Santa Claus,** 4" ......................................... **460**
**Mushroom,** cluster of three on clip, 4" ............... **60**
**Pear,** matte finish, 4" ........................................ **45**
**Pickle,** curved, 4" (ILLUS. left center w/carrot) ........................................................... **130**
**Pine cone,** silver, 4" ............................................ **5**
**Potato,** 4" (ILLUS. left w/carrot) ....................... **175**
**Rabbit,** w/carrot, 4" ............................................ **85**
**Rose,** white w/venetian dew, on clip ................ **110**

*Sailboat Tree Ornaments*

**Sailboat,** angel scrap, 5" (ILLUS. left) .............. **210**
**Sailboat,** Dresden sail, 5" (ILLUS. right) .......... **225**
**Santa,** blue w/tree, 4" ......................................... **45**
**Santa,** in basket, 4" ............................................. **65**
**Santa,** on clip, 4" (ILLUS. right) .......................... **85**

*Santa Ornaments*

**Santa,** red w/tree, 4" (ILLUS. left) ....................... **35**
**Santa,** below ball, 5" (ILLUS. center) ............... **185**
**Snowman,** w/broom, 4" ........................................ **30**

**Songbird,** on clip, 3" ......................................... **10**
**Storks,** mother & baby, on clip, 5" .................... **210**
**Uncle Sam,** full-figure, 3" ................................. **525**
**Walnut,** gold, 2" .................................................. **10**
**Witch,** w/cat & broom, 4" .................................. **620**
**Zeppelin,** wire-wrapped, 5" (ILLUS. right) ........ **310**

*Zeppelins*

**Zeppelin,** wire-wrapped, w/glass gondola, 5" (ILLUS. left) ............................................... **500**

## ITALIAN GLASS ORNAMENTS

*Manufactured in northern Italy following World War II, these free-blown glass figurals are attracting collector interest. The art of blowing glass Christmas ornaments was taught to the Italians by Germans who fled their war-ravaged homeland. These are still being produced today, but the one-of-a-kind 1950s fanciful free-blown glass ornaments are the most desirable. Prices are on the rise every year.*

*Note: Illustrated ornaments Nos. 3 & 7 are not listed but are of similar value.*

**Alpine man,** w/rope, 5" .................................... **125**

*Assorted Italian Glass Ornaments*

**Cat head,** 3" (ILLUS. no. 2) .............................. **60**
**Elf,** seated, 6" (ILLUS. no. 8) ............................. **60**
**Lamp,** 5" (ILLUS. no. 1) ..................................... **55**
**Man in Moon,** 4" (ILLUS. no. 6) ....................... **110**
**Mouse,** playing saxaphone, 6" (ILLUS. no. 5) ....................................................................... **95**
**Robin Hood,** 6" (ILLUS. no. 9) ......................... **120**
**Wizard,** 6" (ILLUS. no. 4) ................................... **85**

## PAPER ORNAMENTS

*Of all the early decorations, perhaps the most revered are the "paper and tinsel" ornaments that hung on almost everyone's Christmas tree. Today, these paper ornaments are known as "scraps," "die-cuts," or "chromos." From the Civil War to the late 1900s, a scrapbook craze swept across America. Almost every woman or child kept a scrapbook.*

By the late 1800s, the Germans with their perfection of the printing process, provided these keepers of memorabilia with a vast array of paper for their scrapbooks. By World War I, the craze for keeping a scrapbook had all but died. The Germans, needing to find a new use for all these scraps, began producing Christmas ornaments and they quickly became fashionable. By the late 1920s, the popularity of papers decreased sharply and paper ornaments were advertised less and less in mail order catalogs. The majority of these ornaments found today date from 1880 to the mid-1920s. Paper ornaments range in price from $15.00 to over $500.00, depending on size and subject material, with Father Christmas ornaments attracting the highest prices.

**Angels,** w/tinsel holder, 3"................................. **25**

*Angels w/Cellophane & Tinsel*

**Angels,** w/cellophane & tinsel, 7" (ILLUS.) ........ **80**
**Miss Liberty,** tinsel & cellophane..................... **115**

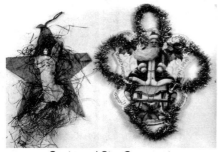

*Santa and Star Ornaments*

**Santa,** full-bodied, riding sled (ILLUS. right)..... **120**
**Santa,** full-bodied, w/tree & toys, 15" w/tin-
sel.............................................................. **180**
**Santa head,** w/tinsel holder, 4" .......................... **20**
**Star w/a scrap angel,** tinsel trim, 6"
(ILLUS. left) .................................................. **45**
**Victorian children,** in car w/Santa, cello-
phane & tinsel trim, 6" .................................. **135**

## PRESSED COTTON ORNAMENTS
The most non-destructible ornaments are those manufactured of pressed cotton (sometimes wrongly called wool). These were primarily manufactured in Breslau. Human figures are probably the most sought-after of cotton ornaments. The end-

less variety of cotton wool people is simply astounding, including clowns, farmers, glass blowers, children, a plant seller, and many others.

Every imaginable animal can also be found— exotic animals such as elephants, tigers, leopards, and giraffes; and common animals such as squirrels, dogs, cats, and rabbits. Most cotton ornaments bring over $180.00 on today's market.

**Angel,** paper face, Dresden wings, 3".............. **225**
**Bell,** blue, 3" ......................................................... **35**
**Cow,** brass bell, 4"............................................. **220**
**Cucumber,** green & yellow, 4" .......................... **95**
**Girl,** bisque head/wool coat, w/lead ice
skates, 4" (ILLUS. left center) ...................... **285**

*Pressed Cotton Ornaments*

**Girl,** paper face, 4" (ILLUS. far left) ................. **200**
**Jockey,** w/horse head, 4"................................. **560**
**Man,** paper crown on head, 4" (ILLUS. cen-
ter right)........................................................ **320**
**Orange,** 3"............................................................ **75**
**Peddler,** cotton fruit in pack, 4" ....................... **325**
**Sailor,** w/cap, 4" ................................................ **400**
**Santa,** school girl, bisque, 4" ............................ **320**
**Victorian lady,** 3" (ILLUS. far right) ................. **220**

## SPUN-GLASS ORNAMENTS
These are actually "glass thread" ornaments consisting of strands of glass manufactured by the glass blowers of Laushau. While white is the most common color found, red, blue, green, and gold were also used. The spun glass is usually combined with paper "scraps" picturing Santas, angels, and people. The larger colored spun-glass ornaments are the most desirable. Spun-glass ornaments are extremely collectible, with prices ranging anywhere from $30.00 to $250.00 depending on desirability and condition.

*Victorian Boy Spun-Glass Ornament*

**Angel,** paper on clip, w/spun glass wings ........ **310**

**Angel,** in circle, 4" ............................................. **70**
**Peacock,** flat, elaborately painted, 5" .............. **190**
**Sailboat,** double sided, in circle, 5" ................... **40**
**Santa,** in circle w/comet tail, 8" ........................ **120**
**Victorian boy,** in circle, 5" (ILLUS.) ................. **55**

## WAX & WAXED ORNAMENTS

*Many photographs of decorated trees from the turn-of-the-century show wax angels and wax children ornaments hanging on the tree. For purposes of easier identification, the angel ornaments must be divided into two categories: "waxed angels" and "wax angels." Waxed angels have a firm core of papier-mâché or composition and had only a very thin coating of wax; wax angels were solid wax. Small, common waxed angels go for between $70.00 and $90.00 while wax angels easily fetch over $300.00. It seems that these angels become more expensive every year and they are becoming as rare as, and as desirable as Dresden ornaments.*

**Angel,** American, ca. 1940s, 4" .......................... **25**

*Waxed Angel Ornaments*

**Angel,** waxed, 4" (ILLUS. left) .......................... **120**
**Angel,** waxed, 5" (ILLUS. right) ....................... **195**
**Angel,** wax, 6" ................................................. **240**
**Angel,** waxed, 6" (ILLUS. middle) .................... **220**
**Bird,** in metal circle, 5" .................................... **280**
**Soldier,** American, ca. 1940s, 4" ....................... **25**

## MISCELLANEOUS CHRISTMAS ITEMS

**Beaded chains,** glass, German, 12" ................. **45**
**Bean bag,** Santa, from "Nightmare Before Christmas" ...................................................... **55**
**Belsnickle,** dressed in red, Germany, 6 1/2" h. ....................................................... **500**
**Book,** "Santa Claus Book of Christmas," DeWolfe Fiske & Co. .................................... **100**
**Catalog,** "Dennison's Christmas Book" ........... **45**
**Christmas tree stand,** cast iron, square w/holly leaves, painted ................................ **145**
**Cloth,** Nast-style Santa Claus in brown printed scene, ca. 1880s ............................. **400**
**Doll,** Santa Claus, musical wind-up, Japan, ca. 1940s .......................................... **85**
**Doll,** Snoopy dressed in Santa outfit, ca. 1970s ............................................................ **80**
**Fence,** cast iron, painted, four-sections ......... **400**
**Fence,** feather w/red berries, 6 pcs. ................ **500**
**Figurine,** bisque, Joe Camel w/Santa hat on ................................................................... **95**
**Figurine,** Santa Claus, celluloid, in car, painted ......................................................... **125**

**Figurine,** Santa Claus, celluloid, w/hand behind back holding doll, 7" h. ..................... **150**
**Figurine,** Santa Claus, molded papier-mâché, dressed in white suit w/red trim, Germany ...................................................... **85**
**Handkerchief,** family decorating tree ............. **325**
**Handkerchief,** Nast Santa ............................... **520**
**Kugel,** figural grape, gold, Germany, 4" h. ....... **150**
**Kugel,** figural grape, green, Germany, 4" h. ..... **175**
**Kugel,** figural grape, purplish blue, Germany, 4" h. ................................................ **200**
**Kugel,** figural grape, silver, Germany, 4" h. ..... **125**
**Mask,** papier-mâché, early 1900s, German ..... **450**
**Mask,** Santa Claus, gauze, lean-faced, early, 12" l. .................................................... **85**
**Match cover,** front cover depicts carolers, candle-shaped matches inside, 3 1/2" .......... **14**

*Santa Claus Name Holder*

**Name holder,** china place card, Santa Claus, ca. 1950s, made in Japan, 2" (ILLUS.) ....................................................... **5**
**Nativity set,** Sunday school fold-out ............... **40**
**Photograph,** shows little boy & girl dressed in nightgowns sitting on front of Christmas tree w/toys, ca. 1910 ............................. **60**
**Russian Santa,** white cotton batting, all-white, 18" h. .................................................. **800**
**Salt & Pepper set,** ceramic, Santa Claus & Mrs. Claus, white rough spaghetti texture to represent fur, ca. 1950s, made in Japan, 5", pr. .................................................. **50**
**Snow Babies figures,** china, sliding down roof, each ....................................................... **310**
**Snow Baby figure,** china, riding polar bear ..... **295**
**Tinsel,** lead, National Tinsel ............................. **20**
**Tinsel,** metallic strand-type, U.S.A., mint in box ............................................................... **18**
**Tray,** tin, oval, depicts full-figure Santa in blue suit w/toys, early tray painted by artist John Moreno in 1997 ......................... **350**
**Tray,** Coca-Cola Santa Claus, 1973, 10 3/4" x 13 1/4" ................................................ **60**
**Tree,** green bristle brush-type, on red base, simulated snow on end of branches, ca. 1940s-1950s, 21" h. ..................................... **35**
**Tree stand,** cast iron, Santa molded on both sides, Germany ................................... **295**
**Tree stand,** lithographed tin, America ............. **65**

# CLOCKS

**Banjo clock,** Federal, the mahogany & gilt gesso case w/a molded brass bezel enclosing a white-painted iron dial w/Roman numerals & an A-frame type weight-driven movement above the rectangular églomisé lower tablet showing Helios framed by spiral moldings & the central body flanked by pierced side brackets, possibly Rhode Island, ca. 1820, overall 34" h. (restoration) ............ **$4,313**

**Grandfather clock,** William Claggett, Newport, Rhode Island, Queen Anne - Chippendale transitional style, cherry, the case w/a flat top w/small corner blocks & pointed ball finials above an arched cornice molding & glazed tombstone door w/engaged columns enclosing the eight-day weight-driven movement & brass dial engraved w/Roman numerals w/strike-silent indicator in the arch flanked by cast dolphin spandrels, an engraved chapter ring seconds hand, calendar aperture below & engraved panel signed "Wm. Claggett Newport" w/cast spandrels, the arch-molded tall rectangular waist door w/a glazed bull's-eye panel on the stepped-out molded base w/ball feet, old refinish, 18th c., 100" h. (restored) ...................................... **9,200**

*Jockey w/Trotter Novelty Clock*

**Novelty,** Ansonia, brass, jockey w/trotter, 30-hour, time only, 6 1/2 x 10 1/2" (ILLUS.) ...................................................... **600**

**Novelty,** Ansonia, cast iron w/black enamel, ship's brass wheel rotates as escapement moves, 15 x 18 3/4" ............. **2,000**

**Novelty,** Ansonia, enameled pot metal, squirrel in tree, 30-hour, time only, 6 x 7".... **400**

*Brass Baby Novelty Clock*

**Novelty,** Ansonia, model of a brass baby holding fan, 30-hour, time only, 5" h. (ILLUS.) .................................................... **375**

**Novelty,** Ansonia, "Novelty 34 or The Advertiser" model, 30-hour, time only, 7" h. ................................................................ **500**

**Novelty,** Lex, rotary metal, tape measure type w/copper fish, time only, ca. 1910, 5" d. ................................................................ **45**

**Shelf or mantel,** "#10," walnut perpetual-calendar w/applied & turned decorations, provisions for date, day & month on lower round tablet, eight-day, time & strike, weight-driven, 36" h. ...................... **3,500**

**Shelf or mantel,** alarm-type, Ansonia "Amazon" model, 5" dial .............................. **150**

**Shelf or mantel,** alarm-type, double bell Snoope, 33 1/2" d. ...................................... **25**

*Alarm-Type Mantel Clock*

**Shelf or mantel,** alarm-type, Toulouse-Lautrec, France, hand moves down when alarm goes off to light a match on clock base & returns to the candle on top, 5 1/2 x 10" (ILLUS.) ............................... **800**

*Ansonia Mantel Clock*

**Shelf or mantel,** Ansonia, "Crystal Palace #1" model, w/two figures under glass dome, mercury pendulum, time & strike, 15 x 19" (ILLUS.) ........................................ **1,500**

**Shelf or mantel,** Ansonia "Juno" model, novelty swing-arm figural clock, bronze-finished metal, gilded pendulum, eight-day time, 4 1/2" dial, 28" h......................... **3,500**

**Shelf or mantel,** Ansonia, "La Charny" model, Royal Bonn porcelain case, porcelain dial, French sash bezel, eight-day, time & strike, 11 x 12"........................... **450**

**Shelf or mantel,** Ansonia, Royal Bonn porcelain case w/open escapement, porcelain dial, eight-day, time & strike, 133 1/2 x 15" ............................................... **800**

*Elephant Mantel Clock*

**Shelf or mantel,** cast iron, model of elephant, France, time only, 4 x 7" (ILLUS.) ....... **75**

**Shelf or mantel,** F. Froeber, cast metal statue of bowman on top of metal clock containing Kroeber's eight-day movement & a patented arrangement so hands can be turned backward without harm, eight-day, time & strike, 15 x 23" ....... **700**

*"Good Luck" Mantel Clock*

**Shelf or mantel,** Lux, Seth Thomas, "Good Luck" metal clock framed by horseshoe, 30-hour time, time only, 7 1/2 x 9" (ILLUS.) .......................................................... **50**

**Shelf or mantel,** Lux, wooden, girl & soldier on blue base, 30-hour, time only, spring driven, 7 x 9" ...................................... **800**

**Shelf or mantel,** metal front, brass case w/angel figure at top, 30-hour, time only, ca. 1902, 8 x 10" .................................... **70**

**Shelf or mantel,** New Haven, bronze & brass, figure of cupid on top, 4 1/2 x 6 1/2" ............................................... **135**

**Shelf or mantel,** New Haven Clock Co., oak perpetual-calendar, w/two parallel dials, inscribed lines, eight-day, time only, 14 x 13" ........................................... **1,800**

**Shelf or mantel,** "Ridgeway" walnut reproduction calendar shelf clock, eight-day, time & strike, 15 1/2 x 27" ........................... **300**

**Shelf or mantel,** Samuel Terry, Plymouth, Connecticut, Federal pillar-and-scroll type, mahogany, scroll-cut cresting joining three brass urn finials above the glazed door enclosing a thirty-hour wooden weight-driven movement & a polychrome & gilt-decorated dial w/Roman numerals, the lower door tablet decorated w/a colorful églomisé landscape, slender free-standing columns at the sides, molded base w/scalloped apron & slender bracket feet, old

refinish, ca. 1825, 32" h. (minor restorations) .......................................................... **4,255**

**Shelf or mantel,** Seth Thomas Clock Co., Thomaston, Connecticut, Federal pillar-and-scroll type, mahogany, scroll-cut cresting joining three brass urn finials above the glazed door enclosing a thirty-hour wooden weight-driven movement & a polychrome & gilt-decorated dial w/Roman numerals, the lower door tablet decorated w/a colorful landscape, slender free-standing columns at the sides, molded base w/scalloped apron & slender bracket feet, old refinish, ca. 1825, 32" h. (minor imperfections) ............ **2,185**

**Shelf or mantel,** Seth Thomas, metal-front, nickel plating over brass, minute hand, time & alarm, 7 x 9" ..................................... **145**

**Shelf or mantel,** Seth Thomas "Prospect #1" model, mahogany, Gothic, time & strike, ca. 1910, 13 1/2" h............................. **190**

**Shelf or mantel,** Seth Thomas "The Whistler" model, gilt-finished metal, eight-day, time, 14" h. ....................................... **500**

**Wag-on-wall clock,** Mercier-Hupel, France, embossed brass, the oval embossed upper case decorated w/ornate scrolls & flowers surrounding a white-enameled round dial w/Roman numerals, a short bar connecting to the very large & long pendulum w/tapering scroll-embossed sides & a large rounded bottom, embossed overall w/ornate scrolling & a small floral bouquet on the upper section & a large bouquet on the lower section, polychrome japanning & gilding, dial labeled "Mercier-Hupel - à Bain de Bretagne," France, 19th c., w/weights & key, overall 55" h......... **770**

**Wall,** Bulova, electric, round, marked w/"Sable's Jewelry" on face, 16" d. .............. **110**

**Wall,** cuckoo-type, Keebler pendulette, molded wood, red & green foliage, 30-hour, time only, spring-driven, 5 x 6 1/2"........ **45**

**Wall,** E. Ingraham Company, walnut-stained simple case, calendar-type w/calendar dates on upper dial, eight-day, time only, 12 x 24" ............................... **525**

*German Cuckoo-Type Wall Clock*

**Wall,** German cuckoo-type, chalet-style, 30-hour, ca. 1950, 9" w. (ILLUS.)................. **225**

**Wall,** New Haven, mahogany, beveled glass, time & bim-bam strike on two rods, ca. 1910, 8 x 24" .................................. **240**

**Wall,** New Haven "Thistle" model, porcelain-cased hanging wall clock w/brass surround & wall chain, 15-day, time only, 10 x 14" ...................................................... **600**

**Wall,** Seikosha, Japan, regulator-type, dark stained, eight-day, time & strike, ca. early 1900s, dial 14" d., 51" h. ..................... **350**

**Wall,** Seth Thomas, model "#60," mahogany, regulator-type, brass pendulum & weight-driven, 18 1/2 x 60"..................................

**Wall,** W. Badger, Ltd., Lowell, English, mahogany, gallery-type, single fusee movement, eight-day, time, 12" d............... **945**

**Wall,** W.L. Gilbert, dark stained, advertising "Saucer's Flavoring Extracts," glass etched & gold leafed coins, eight-day, time only, spring-driven, 40" h.................. **2,000**

**Wall,** Waterbury "Baha" model, gilded ionic case, time & strike, ca. 1900, 13 x 21"........ **350**

**Wall regulator,** E. Howard, Boston, Massachusetts, railroad-type, quarter-sawn oak, a flat crest above a stepped cornice w/bracketed sides & small knob finials above the narrow reeded side frame enclosing an arched-top glazed door opening to the white-painted sheet metal round dial w/Roman numerals above the long pendulum & large round brass bob, flat narrow molded base w/corner drops, ca. 1900, from a railroad dispatcher's office in Indiana, 19" w., 65" h. .. **1,760**

# CLOTHING

*Recent interest in period clothing, uniforms and accessories from the 18th, 19th and through the 20th century compels us to include this category in our compilation. While style and fabric play an important role in the values of older garments of previous centuries, designer dresses of the 1920s and '30s, especially evening gowns, are enhanced by the original label of a noted courtier such as Worth or Adrian. Prices vary widely for these garments which we list by type, with infant's and children's apparel so designated.*

**Coat,** black cashmere, below-the-knee length cocoon style w/wide pointed collar, oversized center front buttons & black satin lining, labeled "I. Magnin" at back neckline, ca. 1950s ........................... **$345**

**Cockatil ensemble,** black brocaded silk, below-the-knee length straight skirt & boxy sleeveless top, boxy jacket w/wide three-quarter length sleeves & wide shawl collar w/one center front button, hand-sewn, Balenciaga, ca. 1950s ............. **575**

**Dress,** gray wool, below-the-knee length w/round neckline, sloped shoulders & elbow-length sleeves, fitted at waist, balloon skirt w/fitted hemline w/center front bow, black taffeta lining, Christian Dior, ca. 1950s (no label) ............................ **316**

**Dress,** "The Trapeze," wool crepe hot pink A-line dress w/sleeveless bodice, band collar, waist cinched w/wide matching belt, pink silk lining in bodice, labeled "Norman Norell, New York" at skirt side seam, numbered tape "15018-501-8 -

The French Shops, Filene's - Boston" at back skirt seam, ca. 1960s........................... **288**

**Evening dress,** black satin floor-length w/net overdress, sleeveless w/V-neck & plunging V-back, bias-cut skirt, overdress w/gathered ruffles trimming neckline & sleeves, eight rows of horizontal ruffles extending from hips to hem, slit from hem to waist at center front, labeled "Milgrim" w/"Mrs. Griffith, 3/2/37, No. 965" written in pen on label, Sally Milgrim, ca. 1937 ........................................ **489**

**Evening dress,** pale aqua & metallic gold, floor-length, fitted bodice w/short sleeves & wide shawl collar, trimed w/black passementerie, attached self-covered belt, full bias-cut skirt w/two side pockets, bodice lined w/pale aqua chiffon, labeled "Elizabeth Arden, New York - Paris" at neckline, late 1940s..................... **173**

**Evening dress,** sheer net w/overall gold sequins in Art Deco inspired pattern, fitted silhouette w/sleeveless bodice, wide V-neck & cape collar at back, hemline mid-calf at front & floor-length at back, late 1920s (previous repair, alterations, additions to hem & sides of bodice) ............. **328**

**Evening gown,** Grecian-style white crepe floor-length w/vertical silver bugle bead stripes, sleeveless wrap bodice w/V-neck & back, heavily beaded faux belt at waist, accordion pleated skirt w/white crepe lining, labeled at skirt seam "Made to Order, Bergdorf Goodman on the Plaza, Mrs. M. Bruck, date 12-3-67, No. 17593," ca. 1967 ........................................ **449**

*Balenciaga Evening Gown*

**Evening gown,** silver floral brocade & lamé, sleeveless fitted bodice w/jewel neckline & low round back, bow at center front waist, full skirt, lined in ivory silk & chiffon, matching boxy jacket w/three-quarter length sleeves & center front self-covered buttons, ivory silk taffeta lining, jacket labeled "Balenciaga, 10 Avenue Georges V, Paris" & "84483"written in pencil on tape attached to back of label, light soil spot at front skirt, late 1950s (ILLUS.) ............................................. **748**

**Evening jacket,** black silk organza, knee-length w/nine rows of large ruffles, round neckline & elbow-length ruffled sleeves, black chiffon lining, labeled "Oscar de la Renta" & "Saks Fifth Avenue" at neckline, early 1960s ......................................... **431**

*Bes Ben Banana & Leaf Hat*

**Hat,** velvet & net close-fitting headpiece adorned w/papier-mâché yellow banana & green leaves w/gold leaf embellishment, labeled "Bes Ben, Made in Chicago," ca. 1940s (ILLUS.) ...................... **546**

**Jumpsuit,** sheer silk printed w/psychedelic pattern in shades of orange & gold on black ground, fitted bodice w/low round neckline, very full bishop sleeves, empire waist, ankle-lenth palazzo pants, bodice lined w/black silk, labeled "Emilio Pucci, Florence - Italy" at back neckline, ca. 1970s ..................................................... **489**

**Paisley shawl,** oblong black cartouche central reserve w/eight scrolled lancets pointing inward from border, the outer design of overall large loops, scrolls & palmettes in shades of red & tan, machine-woven, 19th c., 62 x 140" ............. **275**

*Emilio Pucci Poncho*

**Poncho,** cotton velvet w/printed flower pattern in black, white, red & shades of

green, pink & orange, ruffled collar, center front zipper closure & slit pockets, labeled "Emilio Pucci, Florence - Italy" & "Made Exclusively for Saks Fifth Avenue" at center back, ca. 1970s (ILLUS.) ..... **863**

**Shawl,** paisley, large square black central area surrounded by scrolling floral motifs in red, sky blue, gold, aubergine, & green, borders of similar coloration, Europe, 20th c., (small hole in black area) 10' 6" x 5' 6" ....................................... **288**

## NECKTIES

**1950s,** knitted, labeled "Resilio" ......................... **10**

**1960s,** cotton, day-glo pink, labeled "Designed in Italy by Angelo Correlli" ............ **25**

**Bold Look,** acetate, screen-printed woman w/scotty dog .................................................... **50**

**Bold Look,** fairies & flowers, Countess Mara design .................................................... **40**

*Salvador Dali Designed Tie*

**Bold Look,** guitars w/torsos, Salvador Dali (ILLUS.) ................................................ **300-500**

**Bold Look,** novelty-type, Porky Pig, boy's tie, 1945 ............................................................ **45**

**Bold Look,** seaweed design, Beau Brummel ...................................................................... **35**

**Bold Look,** "Winter Wonderland," Wembley .................................................................... **30**

## COCA-COLA ITEMS

*Coca-Cola promotion has been achieved through the issuance of scores of small objects through the years. These, together with trays, signs and other articles bearing the name of this soft drink, are now sought by many collectors. The major reference in this field is* Petretti's Coca-Cola Collectibles Price Guide, 10th Edition, *by Allan Petretti (Antique Trader Books). An asterisk (\*) indicates a piece which has been reproduced.*

**Advertisement,** cardboard, brightly scene of a couple at masquerade party, man wearing mask, lady holding her mask, wood frame, 19 1/2" w., 28" h. (scratches, denting & soiling) ..................... **$198**

**Bank,** tin, model of bottle dispenser, marked "Drink Coca-Cola - Ice Cold," ca. 1950, 2 1/4 x 4" ............................................. **125**

**Book ends,** figural bottle on flat base, bronze, pr. .................................................. **275**

*Lillian Nordica 1904 Bookmark*

**Bookmark,** 1904, "Drink Coca-Cola 5¢," dark red ground w/Lillian Nordica pictured, wearing white dress trimmed w/large red ribbon & streamers, one hand resting on chair back, pansies & leaves at top & upper sides w/glass in holder in upper center, scrolled edge, 2 x 6" (ILLUS.)............................................ **325**

**Bookmark,** celluloid, two-sided, owl on branch holding book marked "What - Shall -We - Drink" on one page & "Drink -Coca - Cola - 5¢" on the other, reverse w/"Compliments of The Coca-Cola Co. - Atlanta - Philadelphia - New York - Chicago - Boston - Dallas - Los Angeles," 1906, 1 1/2 x 3 1/8" ..................................... **800**

**Bottle,** seltzer, ten-sided, cobalt blue, Bradford, Pennsylvania, 12 1/4" h................ **400**

*Coca-Cola Bottle Carrier*

**Bottle carrier,** cardboard, six-pack size, both sides decorated w/holly, handle w/"Season's Greetings," ca. 1930s, unused, 7 1/4 x 13" (ILLUS.) ........................ **121**

**Bottle topper,** figural classic, 100% intact, 1 5/8 x 7 x 7 1/4" .......................................... **675**

**Button sign,** red lettering on gold, French, 18" d............................................................... **525**

**Button sign,** red w/white lettering, 16" d......... **300**

**Button sign,** shows bottle, 24" d..................... **275**

**Button sign,** shows bottle, convex, 36" d. ....... **225**

**Calendar,** 1908, lady w/dark hair, red dress, long black gloves & feathered red hat, ballet stage in background, matted & framed under glass, 12 1/2 x 19 1/2" ..... **4,200**

*1919 Coca-Cola Calendar*

**Calendar,** 1919, young lady wearing frilly pink dress & hat w/large brim & holding a glass, airfield in background, 12 x 31" (ILLUS.)...................................................... **4,500**

**Calendar,** 1945, young boy in Boy Scout uniform, Boy Scout oath written in background, by Norman Rockwell ...................... **550**

**Cans,** 1996 Coca-Cola 24-pack, each can pictures a reproduction of 1962 Haddon Sundblom scene of Santa playing w/Lionel Santa Fe train set while drinking a Coke, price for each can ........................ **5**

**Chair,** metal, folding-type w/"Drink Coca-Cola" on back, ca. 1960 .............................. **175**

**Cigarette lighters,** figural bottle, pull-apart type w/original box, 2 1/2" h., set of 10 ........ **350**

**Cigarette lighters,** musical, Bluebird model, by Hadson w/original presentation box, works, 2 1/4" h. ............................. **200**

**Clock,** electric, wall-type, metal w/glass face & cover, black outline of bottle in red center w/"Drink Coca-Cola" in white lettering, green border w/Arabic numerals, Pam Clock Co. Brooklyn 1, NY, U.S.A, working, N.O.S., 15" d. ................... **550**

**Clock,** wall-type, electric, square wooden frame, "Drink Coca-Cola in Bottles," 1939, 16 x 16" ........................................... **500**

**Cuff links,** 10k (yellow gold), figural bottle, 3/4" l., pr. ........................................... **50**

**Dispenser,** wooden barrel w/two tin Coca-Cola signs, one Nesbitt's Root Beer sign & one Nesbitt decal, complete, 25 1/2" h...... **650**

*Buddy Lee Doll*

**Doll,** plastic, Buddy Lee dressed in white striped uniform & cap, black visor, bow tie, belt & shoes, emblem on hat & shirt w/"Drink Coca Cola," ca. 1950s, 12" h. (ILLUS.)....................................................... **1,000**

**Door knob,** brass, ca. 1913-1915 .................... **400**

**Fan,** cardboard, fold-out type, front w/bouquet of flowers in vase, reverse w/"Drink Coca-Cola - Delicious and Refreshing," ca. 1950s ................................... **65**

*Coca-Cola Fan*

**Fan,** cardboard, front shows the Sprite boy peeking around bottle w/"Have a Coke" & reverse is marked "Compliments of your local Coca-Cola Bottling Co.," minor discoloration, 9 x 9 1/2 (ILLUS.) .......... **88**

**Fan,** wicker, heart-shaped w/"Drink Coca-Cola in Bottles," ca. 1950s ............................. **65**

*Rare Coca-Cola Fish Festoon*

**Festoon,** end pieces of stamped tin w/wood end logos, six fish are detachable stamped tin, center is stamped tin over wood backing, logo is cut-out wood, canvas straps & rope connectors, ca. 1937, Kay Displays, rare (ILLUS.)............. **3,600**

**Hats,** paper, in original box, lot of 90 ................ **130**

**License plate holder,** metal, w/"Drink Coca-Cola in Bottles," 1940s-1950s (ILLUS.)..................................................... **425**

**Machine,** Model No. 44, restored & working, 58" h. .................................................. **2,300**

**Match holder,** rectangular, celluloid, for stick matches, marked "Drink Coca-Cola in Bottles - Springfield Coca-Cola Bottling Co.," 1930s ........................................... **350**

**Match holder,** Westinghouse vending machine container, can hold twelve packs of matches ...................................... **160**

**Menu board,** die-cut wood w/metal half bottle in original menu insert, Kay Display, early 1940s, all original, 16 1/2 x 34 1/2" ........................................ **1,875**

**Message board,** die-cut tin oval top w/"Drink Coca-Cola - Be refreshed" self-framed w/"Have a Coke!" at bottom, 17 3/4" w., 26" h. (soiling & stains on edges, small hole at bottom, minor scratches & paint chips) ............................ **110**

**Mirror,** pocket-type, die-cut cardboard cat's head, opens to reveal mirror & advertisement, ca. 1920s, Germany, 2 1/2" ......................................................... **600**

*Coca Cola Needle Case*

**Needle case,** cardboard, pictures pretty girl holding glass on front, bottle & filled

glass on table w/flowers in background
on the back, ca. 1924, 2 x 3" (ILLUS.) .......... **88**
**Pencils,** in original sleeves, ca. 1940s, box
of six dozen ................................................ **187**
**Playing cards,** shows bottle being handed
to young woman putting on ice skates,
1956, full deck in original box ........................ **85**

*Coca-Cola Pretzel Dish*

**Pretzel dish,** aluminum, round bowl supported by three bottle-shaped legs, ca.
1930s (ILLUS.) ............................................ **225**
**Radio,** plastic, figural cooler, AM, working,
9 3/4" h. ..................................................... **700**
**Salesman's sample,** counter dispenser
w/three spigots, all plastic w/heavy canvas padded carrying case, ca. 1960s,
12 x 16 1/2" ............................................. **2,500**
**Salt & pepper shakers,** can-shaped,
1970s, pr. ..................................................... **15**

*Salesman of the Month Award*

**Service award,** "Salesman of the Month,"
cast metal, figure of driver standing on
bottle cap, ca. 1930, 6 1/2" h. (ILLUS.) ........ **675**
**Sign,** cardboard, blonde girl emerging from
swimming pool, "Hello Refreshment,"
framed under glass, 1940s,
20 1/4 x 36 1/4" ......................................... **1,800**
**Sign,** cardboard, cut-out, easel back, fea-
tures Loretta Young holding bottle,
marked "Loretta Young - Pause and
Refresh Yourself with Ice Cold Coca-
Cola," Niagara Litho Co., 1932 (ILLUS.
top next column) ........................................ **1,300**
**Sign,** cardboard cut-out, easel back, figure
of Eddie Fisher holding bottle w/"Have a
Coke," 1954, 19" h. ................................... **1,200**

*Coca-Cola Sign w/Loretta Young*

*Coca-Cola 1890s Display Sign*

**Sign,** cardboard cut-out, easel back, young
blonde girl wearing white dress w/blue
ribbon trim at neck, white stockings &
blue slippers, sitting on crate marked "5
cents - Delicious! - Refreshing! - Coca
Cola - at the Soda Fountain," ca. 1890s,
Wolf & Co., Philadelphia, Pennsylvania,
rare 5 1/2 x 8 1/2" (ILLUS.) ...................... **5,000**

*1954 Santa Sign*

**Sign,** cardboard cut-out, stand-up type, Santa holding a bottle & standing next to grandfather clock, bells & bow in foreground w/"Good taste for all - Drink Coca-Cola in Bottles," 1954, 10 1/2 x 19" (ILLUS.)................................... 300

*Coca-Cola Snowman Sign*

**Sign,** cardboard, depicts snowman w/scarf, bottle cap hat & earmuffs on a toboggan w/large bottle, sign in snow reads "Drink Coca Cola" w/"Bring home the Coke" below, gold wood frame, 1957, 16 x 27" (ILLUS.)...................................................... 450

**Sign,** cardboard, girl sitting on floor w/left arm resting on step & holding bottle, talking on telephone w/"I'll bring the Coke," logo in upper corner, ca. 1946, 27 x 56"........................................................ 450

**Sign,** cardboard, girl w/bottle sitting on either side of world globe w/"Drink Coca-Cola - 'Here's to our G.I. Joes'," 1944, 20 x 36"........................................................ 850

**Sign,** cardboard, singer Ricky Nelson, light pink shirt & red cardigan, holding bottle, "Got A Long Thirst? - Get A Long King! - says Ricky Nelson - Coca Cola - Refreshes You Best!" & at the bottom "Tune in the Ozzie & Harriet Show Wednesday Evenings 8:30 P.M.," ca. 1959-60, 14 x 18 1/2" ................................. 600

*1956 Coca-Cola Sign*

**Sign,** cardboard, Western scene of saddle on rail fence near two bottles, mountain in background, "Sign of Good Taste" at top, lithograph by Edwards & Deutsch, Chicago, Illinois, 1956, unused condition, 16 x 27" (ILLUS.)` ................................. 501

**Sign,** cardboard, young woman waving, "Tingling Refreshment," by Niagara Litho, framed under glass, 1931, 23 1/4 x 40 1/4" ....................................... 1,500

**Sign,** die-cut cardboard, easel-backed, Navy "Service Girl," dated 1943, 6 3/8 x 17 1/2" ......................................... 1,000

**Sign,** die-cut porcelain, "Drink Coca-Cola" in white script on light blue background, 5 1/2 x 17 3/4" ............................................. 975

**Sign,** double-sided die-cut porcelain, "Fountain Service," by Tenn Enamel, 1936, 22 3/4 x 25 1/2" ................................. 775

**Sign,** embossed tin lithograph w/"Gas Today," 54" h............................................. 1,600

**Sign,** kick plate, porcelain, five-color, by Tenn Enamel, 1928, 10 x 30".................... 1,000

**Sign,** painted tin, round, bottle in center beneath Coca-Cola," 1934, 45 1/2" d. ......... 700

**Sign,** porcelain, double-sided shield form w/"Fountain Service - Drink Coca-Cola," ca. 1930s, 26" h............................... 2,200

**Sign,** rectangular light-up type w/clock, "Drink Coca-Cola - Please Pay When Served," 20" l................................................. 650

**Sign,** two-sided porcelain, "lollipop" school zone pedestal base w/"Drink Coca-Cola," one side shows silhouette of young girl w/pigtails, running w/books & marked "School - Slow," the reverse w/"Drink Coca-Cola in Bottles," 30" d., 5' h.  ............................................................... 750

**Signs,** "Airplane Hangers," cardboard, lithograph prints of WW II era planes w/original folder, created by William Heaslip, 12 x 14", set of 20 ........................ 730

**Thermometer,** embossed tin lithograph & glass, 16" h............................................... 220

**Tie bar,** silver plate, delivery driver, ca. 1930, 7/8 x 1 3/4" ......................................... 50

*Coca-Cola Toy "Cobot"*

**Toy,** "Cobot," can-shaped w/logo, in original box (ILLUS.) .......................................... **150**
**Toy,** cooler picnic set ........................................ **375**

*1950s GMC Coca-Cola Truck*

**Toy truck,** route delivery type, green & yellow, GMC, ca. 1950s, 5 1/2" ..................... **1,000**

*1932 Coca-Cola Truck*

**Toy truck,** route delivery type, red w/yellow bottle holder in truck bed, marked "Every Bottle Coca-Cola Sterilized," No. 171 Metalcraft w/rubber wheels, 1931 (ILLUS.) ...................................................... **975**

*Coca-Cola 1931 Tray*

**Tray,** 1931, rectangular, smiling young barefoot boy wearing blue shirt, brown trousers, suspenders & straw hat, relaxing under a tree, eating a sandwich & bottle of Coca-Cola, his small black & white dog watching, Norman Rockwell artwork, 10 1/2 x 13 1/4" (ILLUS.) ............ **1,000**
**Tray,** 1936, rectangular, young woman wearing formal white gown w/orchid cor-

sage on left shoulder, holding glass & sitting near low table w/bottles & glass, 10 1/2 x 13 1/4" .......................................... **450**

*1916 Coca-Cola Tip Tray*

**Tray,** tip, 1916, oval, elegantly dressed lady w/large brim hat, decorated wide woodlike rim, lithograph by Passaic Metal Ware Co., New Jersey, 4 1/4 x 6" (ILLUS.) ...................................................... **264**
**Tumbler,** clear glass, flared w/syrup line, ca. 1904 ............................................... **450**
**Watch fob,** engraved brass, 1 1/2" l ................ **110**
**Window display,** cardboard cut-out logshaped planter containing various flower plants, 1924, 11 x 24" ................................... **375**

# COFFEE MEMORABILIA
*Also see ADVERTISING ITEMS, CANS & CONTAINERS and SIGNS & SIGNBOARDS.*

**Advertising sign,** Old Reliable Coffee, tin, flat, painted w/old man smoking cigar w/arm resting on Old Reliable Coffee box, good strong colors & selfframing, ca. 1910, excellent, 6 1/2 x 9" ...... **$350**

*Dwinell-Wright Co. Coffee Box*

**Coffee box,** Dwinell-Wright Co., wooden, rectangular, paper label w/"Most Modern and Complete Coffee Roasting Establishment in the World," w/Boston building, good (ILLUS.) ........................................ **100**

*Coffee Canister*

**Coffee canister,** metal, cylindrical, w/porcelain knob on lid, Germany, ca. 1895, fair, 1 lb. (ILLUS.) .......................................... **55**
**Coffee jar,** Hills Bros., glass, paper label w/Hills man drinking cup of coffee, w/twist-on lid, "Hills Bros. Coffee, The Correct Grind, The Original Vacuum Pack," fair, 1 lb. .............................................. **35**
**Coffee maker,** chrome, round, Art Deco, clear percolator on top w/chrome & black handle attached on sides & running over top, includes stand, LaBelle Silver Co., excellent, 10 x 13" .......................................... **75**
**Coffeepot,** cov., antique graniteware, wire bail handle attached to sides w/round wooden handle & pouring spout at top, fair, 10 1/2 x 12" ........................................... **95**
**Container,** Lady Hellen Coffee, cardboard, round, w/pry top lid, likeness of young woman on front, excellent, 1 lb. .................. **115**
**Cup & saucer,** Maxwell House Coffee, early china, w/advertising by Creek-Neal Coffee Co., w/print of Maxwell House under glaze, probably cafeteria china from Nashville, Tenn. factory, ca. 1920s-1930s, excellent .......................................... **175**

*Hoffmann's Coffee Grinder*

**Grinder,** Hoffmann's Coffee, wood frame on cast-iron base, tin litho front of elderly lady w/cup of coffee, "Hoffmann's old time roasted coffee," John Hoffmann & Sons Co., Milwaukee, w/grinding handle on front, excellent, 13 1/2" h. (ILLUS.) ...... **1,300**
**Match holder,** White House Coffee, tin litho, rectangular, wall hanging-type, showing The White House w/message "The Very Highest Quality", Dwinell-Wright Co., Boston, Chicago, excellent, 5" h. .................................................................. **375**
**Pail,** Campbell Brand Coffee, metal w/wire handles, decorated w/camels in desert, excellent, 4 lbs. ....................................... **75**
**Puzzle,** Folgers Coffee, flat jigsaw-type, Folger's Coffee shape, self framing, all in Folger's Coffee can w/key wind lid, excellent ........................................................ **135**
**Sack,** Gold Bloom Coffee, cloth, w/product information on front, red & blue lettering on white cloth background, excellent, 50 lb. .................................................................... **55**
**Sack,** Gold Bloom Coffee, cloth, w/product information on front, red & blue lettering on white background, excellent, 50 lb. ........... **75**
**Shipping crate,** McLaughlin's Coffee, wooden, rectangular, "McLaughlin's XXXX Coffee" both sides, w/lid, good strong graphics, excellent, 15 x 16 x 24" h. ....................................................... **175**
**Sign,** American Stores Co. Asco Coffee, paper litho, rectangular, w/young lady thoroughbred "Pride of the Plantation" in oval center insert, w/scenes of picking, drying & washing coffee beans in four corners, ca. 1930s, excellent, 11 x 14" ........ **175**

*Hy-Quality Coffee Sign*

**Sign,** Hy-Quality Coffee, cardboard, paper litho die-cut, w/woman in swing drinking cup of coffee, "Try Roth's Hy-Quality Coffee... Delicious to the last sip," excellent, 36 1/2" (ILLUS.) .................................. **1,000**

**Sign,** Lion Coffee, rectangular, double sided, showing redeemable premiums by cutting out heads of lions from 1 pound coffee packages, Woolson Spice Co., Toledo, OH, ca. 1920s, excellent, 11 x 14"...... **250**

**Sign,** Morning Sip Coffee, paper, rectangular, design of product container in left corner, "Drink Morning Sip The Better Coffee," yellow & white lettering on red background, ca. 1920s, Alex Sheppard & Sons, Philadelphia, excellent, 11 1/2 x 21"...... **150**

**Sign,** Old Reliable Coffee, rectangular, trolley car w/old man in spotlight in upper left & steaming cup of coffee in lower right corner, "Welcome as April Showers," excellent, 11 x 21"...... **225**

**Sign,** Red Gate Mocha & Java Coffee, paper litho, rectangular, showing red Oriental gate surrounded by self frame, roasted & packed by Young Bros. Inc., Seattle, Wash., excellent, 10 1/2 x 13 3/4"..... **175**

**Store bin,** Johnson's Log Cabin, tin litho, log cabin shape, good detail of logs complete w/door & window, excellent, 18 x 24 x 28" h. ...... **2,750**

**Store bin,** Lion Coffee, wooden, w/advertising panels inset in center front & lid, lid lifts off to get product, decorated w/lion's head on front & lion pulling chariot on lid, excellent, 32 1/2" h...... **450**

**Store bin,** Scull's Coffee, tin, box shaped w/rounded top, butler serving coffee on lift lid, maid working at coffee grinder on front, great stenciling w/name "Schull's Sterling Coffee" & flowers, excellent, 21 1/2" h...... **925**

**Tin,** Aladdin Coffee, tin litho, round, Aladdin lamp in center of product message, excellent, 1 lb...... **170**

**Tin,** Gold Bloom Coffee, tin litho, round, couple at table enjoying cup of coffee, packed in cans only by M. Livingston & Company, Paducah, KY, steel cut embossed on twist lid, very good, 1 lb. ...... **75**

**Tin,** Golden West Coffee, round w/red paper label, 1905 Lewis & Clark stamp & 1906 Pure Food & Drug Act stamp, coffee produced by Closset & Devers, Portland, Oregon, hard to find item, mint, 1 lb. ...... **45**

**Tin,** Hoffmann's Old Time Coffee, round, w/elderly woman holding steaming cup of coffee, "Hoffmann's Old Time Blended Coffee", mint, 4 1/2" h. ...... **125**

**Tin,** Kellogg's Coffee, tin litho, key wind container, excellent, 1 lb. ...... **30**

**Tin,** King Cole, tin litho, round, w/pry lid, king holding cup of product, excellent, 1 lb. ...... **500**

**Tin,** Red Star, tin metal, rectangular, store counter-type w/twist lid, painted w/"Use the Best, Red Star Choice Roasted Maracibo Coffee New York," ca. 1900s, good (ILLUS. top next column) ...... **425**

**Tin,** Red Wolf, tin litho, pail container w/wire handle, wolf in front center, excellent, 6 lbs...... **200**

*Red Star Tin*

*Sunbeam Coffee Tin*

**Tin,** Sunbeam Coffee, tin, cylindrical, bail w/wire handle, Austin-Nichols & Co., New York, Chicago, good, 5 lb. (ILLUS.) ..... **135**

**Trade card,** Arbuckle's Coffee, cardboard, rectangular, Arizona card litho w/scenes of state map & territories, Indians at camp, Donaldson Bros., New York, mint, 3 x 5"...... **10**

**Tray,** Maxwell House Coffee, metal, oval, painted w/tilted cup of coffee in center, excellent, 12 1/2 x 15"...... **25**

# COMIC BOOKS

*Comic books, especially first or early issues of a series, are avidly collected today. Prices for some of the scarce ones have reached extremely high levels. Prices listed below are for copies in fine to mint condition.*

**Action,** DC Comics, No. 15, Superman in Kidtown, NM...... **$4,200**

**Action,** DC Comics, No. 195, Tiger Woman, NM...... **300**

**Action,** DC Comics, No. 23, NM ...... **6,000**

**Adventure,** DC Comics, No. 244, "The Poorest Family in Smallville," NM ...... **225**

**Adventure,** DC Comics, No. 40, Sandman (first appearance), NM ...... **35,000**

**Adventure,** DC Comics, No. 41, Killer Shark, NM...... **4,000**

**All-American,** DC Comics, No. 2, Ripley's Believe It or Not, NM...... **1,500**

**All-American,** DC Comics, No. 79, Mutt & Jeff, NM...... **550**

**All-American,** DC Comics, No. 98, "End of Sports," NM...... **650**

**All-Star,** DC Comics, No. 1 (Summer 1940-51), Flash, Hawkman, Hourman, Sandman, Spectre, Red White & Blue, NM..... **12,000**

**All-Star,** DC Comics, No. 20, Monster, NM... **1,600**

*Amazing Fantasy*

**Amazing Fantasy,** Marvel Comics, No. 15 (August 1962), VF+ (ILLUS.).................. **13,800**

**Amazing Spider-man,** Marvel Comics, No. 2, NM......................................................... **3,000**

**Amazing Spider-man,** Marvel Comics, No. 3, NM......................................................... **2,000**

**Amazing Spider-man,** Marvel Comics, No. 9, NM........................................................... **900**

**Animal,** Dell Publishing Co., No. 5, Uncle Wiggily, NM.................................................. **325**

**Aquaman,** DC Comics, No. 1 (1st regular series: 1962-78), Quisp, NM ........................ **600**

**Aquaman,** DC Comics, No. 37, Scavenger, NM................................................................. **25**

**Atom,** DC Comics, No. 36, Golden Age Atom, NM............................................................ **65**

**Atom,** DC Comics, No. 8, Doctor Light, NM..... **125**

**Avengers,** Marvel Comics, No. 1 (Sept. 1963), NM ............................................... **2,500**

**Avengers,** Marvel Comics, No. 57, Ultron, NM.................................................................. **70**

**Avengers,** Marvel Comics, No. 9, Wonder Man, NM........................................................ **215**

**Avengers,** Marvel Comics, No. 93, NM ............. **55**

**Batman,** DC Comics, No. 36, Penguin, King Arthur, NM........................................... **900**

**Batman,** DC Comics, No. 4, Joker, NM ........ **6,000**

**Batman,** DC Comics, No. 58, Penguin, NM..... **650**

**Brave & the Bold,** DC Comics, No. 1 (Aug.-Sept. 1955), Viking Prince, Golden Gladiator, Silent Knight, NM..................... **2,800**

**Captain America,** Timely/Atlas, No. 36, Nazis, Hitler, NM ......... **2,000**

**Captain America,** Timely/Atlas, No. 7, Red Skull, NM ...................... **4,500**

**Casper, The Friendly Ghost,** St. John Publishing, No. 4, NM ................................ **350**

**Daredevil,** Lev Gleason Publications, No. 12, The Law, NM...................................... **1,100**

**Daredevil,** Marvel Comics, No. 1 (April 1964), NM ........................................... **2,000**

**Detective,** DC Comics, No. 140, Riddler, NM.................................................................. **4,000**

**Detective,** DC Comics, No. 259, Calendar Man, NM......................................................... **225**

**Detective,** DC Comics, No. 295, Aquaman, NM.................................................................... **125**

**Detective,** DC Comics, No. 38, Robin, The Boy Wonder, NM...................................... **30,000**

**Detective,** DC Comics, No. 95, The Blaze, NM.................................................................... **600**

**Fantastic Four,** Marvel Comics, No. 1 (Nov. 1961), NM...................................... **19,000**

**Flash,** DC Comics, No. 163, Abra-kadabra, NM...................................................................... **65**

**Flash,** DC Comics, No. 18, NM ..................... **1,400**

**Four Color,** Dell Publishing Co., No. 1269 (2nd Series), Rawhide w/Clint Eastwood, NM....................................................... **175**

**Four Color,** Dell Publishing Co., No. 13, Walt Disney's Reluctant Dragon, 1941, NM.................................................................. **1,700**

**Four Color,** Dell Publishing Co., No. 27 (2nd Series), Mickey Mouse & the Seven Colored Terror, NM .................................. **1,000**

**Four Color,** Dell Publishing Co., No. 4, Disney's Donald Duck, NM.......................... **11,000**

**Four Color,** Dell Publishing Co., No. 535 (2nd Series), "I Love Lucy," NM .................. **500**

**Four Color,** Dell Publishing Co., No. 596 (2nd Series), Turok, Son of Stone, NM ........ **600**

**Four Color,** Dell Publishing Co., No. 62 (2nd Series), Donald Duck in Frozen Gold, NM.......................................................... **2,300**

**Green Lantern,** DC Comics, No. 2, Baldy, Tycoon's Legacy, NM.............................. **6,000**

**Green Lantern,** DC Comics, No. 20, Gambler, NM...................................................... **1,000**

**Hawkman,** DC Comics, No. 1 (1st regular series: 1964-68), Chac, NM ........................ **550**

**Hawkman,** DC Comics, No. 14, Chaw, NM........ **75**

**House of Mystery,** DC Comics, No. 12, The Devil's Chessboard, NM ...................... **275**

**House of Mystery,** DC Comics, No. 70, The Man With Nine Lives, NM .................... **100**

**Human Torch,** Marvel Comics, No. 2 (Fall 1940-Aug. 1954), NM.............................. **20,000**

**Human Torch,** Marvel Comics, No. 25, The Masked Monster, NM .................................. **900**

**Incredible Hulk,** Marvel Comics, No. 181, NM.................................................................... **425**

**Incredible Hulk,** Marvel Comics, No. 6, Metal Master, NM........................................ **2,000**

**Justice League of America,** DC Comics, No. 29, NM................................................... **150**

**Justice League of America,** DC Comics, No. 9, NM..................................................... **450**

**Looney Tunes & Merry Melodies,** Dell Publishing Co., No. 3, Bugs Bunny & Porky Pig, NM ........................................... **1,200**

**Marvel Mystery,** Marvel Comics, No. 19, NM.................................................................. **1,800**

**Marvel Mystery,** Marvel Comics, No. 2, NM.................................................................. **21,000**

**Master Comics,** Fawcett Publications, No. 4, Master Man, oversized, NM ................. **1,400**

**Mighty Mouse,** Marvel Comics, No. 2 (1st series), NM.................................................... **450**

*More Fun*

**More Fun,** DC Comics, No. 53, National Periodical Publications, tears to front cover, covers separated from interior paper, fraying & small chips to spine, overall fair condition (ILLUS.) ................... **2,300**
**Pep,** MJL Magazines/Archie Publications, No. 36, 1st Archie, NM ............................. **1,200**
**Sensation,** DC Comics, No. 1 (1942-52), Wonder Woman, Wildcat, NM ................. **22,000**
**Sensation,** DC Comics, No. 35, Sontag Henya in Atlantis, NM.................................... **350**
**Star Spangled,** DC Comics, No. 2, NM ........ **1,400**
**Strange Tales,** Marvel Comics, No. 115, "Dr. Strange," NM........................................ **500**
**Sub-Mariner,** Timely, No. 25, The Blonde Phantom, NM ............................................ **1,000**
**Superman,** DC Comics, No. 3 (1939-86), Superintendent Lyman, NM ...................... **6,500**
**Superman,** DC Comics, No. 53, Superman, NM................................................... **2,000**

# COOKBOOKS

*Cookbook collectors are usually good cooks and will buy important new cookbooks as well as seek out notable older ones. Many early cookbooks were published and given away as advertising premiums for various products used extensively in cooking. While some rare, scarce first edition cookbooks can be very expensive, most collectible cookbooks are reasonably priced.*

*Corn Products Cook Book*

**Advertising,** "Corn Products Cook Book," E. C. Hewitt, Karo Corn Products, NY, w/wraps, illus., 40 pp., very good (ILLUS.).............................................................. **$8**

*"Good Things To Eat" Cookbook*

**Advertising,** "Good Things To Eat," Arm & Hammer, NY, 1932, w/wraps, 33 pp., very good cond. (ILLUS.) ................................. **5**
**Advertising,** "My Favorite Chocolate Chocolate Cakes," NY, 1938, w/wraps, illus., 15 pp., very good cond..................................... **5**

*Ivanhoe Foods Mayonnaise Cookbook*

**Advertising,** "Salad Leaves or Letters to a Daughter in the City," Ivanhoe Foods, Inc. (Mayo), Auburn, NY, w/wraps, illus., 35 pp., very good cond. (ILLUS.) ..................... **6**
**Advertising,** "The Jewett Chafing Dish with a Collection Of Recipes for Chafing-Dish Cookery," J. C. Jewett Mfg. Co., Buffalo, 1892, w/wraps, photo illus., 46 pp., excellent cond. ............................................... **20**
**Advertising,** "The Morrell Menu Maker," J. Morrell & Co., 1950, w/stiff wraps, illus., 331 pp., very good cond.................................. **8**
**Brillat-Savarin, Jean A.,** "The Physiology of Taste," NY, 1948, revised black & gold edition, very good/very good cond. ........ **45**
**Campbell, Mary M.,** "Betty Crocker's Kitchen Gardens," NY, 1971, Illustrated by Tasha Tudor, excellent cond. .................... **18**
**Caron, Emma,** "For the Discriminating Hostess," NY, 1925, privately printed, limited & signed by author, w/boards, very good cond............................................... **25**

**Farmer, Fannie M.,** "Food and Cookery for the Sick and Convalescent," Boston, 1915, revised w/additions, decorated hardcovers, illus., 305 pp. + ads in rear, very good cond. ............................................. **20**

**Fisher, M. F. K.,** "The Art of Eating," NY, 1954, excellent cond. ................................... **40**

**Goldberg, Hymann, (formerly Prudence Penny),** "Our Man in the Kitchen," NY, 1964, illus., 386 pp., w/dust jacket, very good cond. ....................................................... **6**

**Lamberton, Gretchen L.,** "Nita Neighbor's Book of Jelly, Jam, Pickle and Canning Recipes," Minnesota, ca. 1920, w/wraps, 28 pp., good cond. ...................................... **3**

**Leslie, Miss,** "Lady's Receipt-Book, a Useful Companion for Large or Small Families," Carey & Hart, Philadelphia, 1847, rare, good cond. ....................................... **350**

**Manuscript cookbook,** handwritten cookbook belonging to a Julia D. Dixin, dated 1894, w/marbled boards, 56 pp., each recipe is attributed to former recipe owners, good + cond. ........................................ **55**

**Mellish, Katherine,** "Katherine Mellish's Cookery and Domestic Management," NY, 1901, chromo illus., 987 pp., very good cond. .............................................. **325**

**"Modern Priscilla Cook Book,"** (w/original membership certificate entitling advice & assistance from company), Boston, 1925, 352 pp., very good cond. ........ **12**

**Parkins, E. B.,** "Laurel Health Cookery...A Collection of Practical Suggestions and Recipes for the Preparation of Non-Flesh Foods," Massachusetts, 1911, very good cond.............................................. **65**

*"American Cookery" Periodical*

**Periodical,** "American Cookery," Boston, 1939, vol. XLIV, #3, original price 15 cents, (this periodical was formerly the Boston Cooking School Magazine), excellent cond. (ILLUS.).................................... **3**

**Potter, Margaret Yardley,** "At Home on the Range or How to Make Friends With Your Stove," 1947, w/dust jacket, very good cond. ....................................................... **6**

**Princess Pamela,** "Princess Pamela's Soul Food Cookbook," NY, 1969, first edition, paperback, good + cond., (ILLUS. top next column)................................................. **12**

**Ransom, Son & Co. (D),** "Ransom's Family Receipt Book," Buffalo, NY, 1899, w/wraps, 32 pp., includes almanac, good cond. ................................................................. **5**

*"Princess Pamela's Soul Food Cookbook"*

**Rawlings, Marjorie,** "Cross Creek Cookery," NY, 1942, first edition, very good/very good cond..................................... **75**

**Rorer, S. T. (Mrs.),** "Canning and Preserving," Philadelphia, 1887, 32 pp. + ads, very good cond..................................... **30**

**Underhill, Jennie E. (Mrs.),** "Sunshine Cookbook," New London, CT., 1910, w/stiff wraps, 186 pp. + ads., excellent cond. ................................................................. **15**

*Eediotic Etiquette Book*

**Wurdz, Gordon,** "Eediotic Etiquette," NY, 1906, illus., decorative hardcover, 148 pp., good + cond. (ILLUS.) ............................ **15**

# COUNTRY STORE COLLECTIBLES

*The following information is based on assessing some of the dozens of factors that can affect value. Those variables include several broad categories like; market, product, buyer and seller factors. Market factors that affect both buyer and seller are; cost of capital, geography, seasonality, publicity, decorator trends and film and art trends. Condition, rarity, quality and locations are product factors. Some buyer factors include; ability to buy, authority to buy, willingness to buy, experience, knowledge and urgency to fill a collection. Lastly, factors that affect the seller are cost of goods, inventory carry-*

ing costs, cash flow circumstances, ability to replace inventory, knowledge and the "like" factor. This combination of factors, and many others, may result in a wide range of value differences for the same item, but in different factor circumstances than the ones used for the values listed here. For a complete explanation of understanding value, refer to, Mom and Pop Stores: A Country Store Compendium of Merchandising Tools For Display and Value Guide, Publishing, Box 1355, Waterloo, IA 50704-1355.

**Bag sorter,** counter-type, decorated poplar, upright sides w/quarter-round front w/open slots for various bags, the lower sides stenciled in black w/stylized scrolls, leaves & blossoms, old original varnish, red trim, late 19th c., 16" h. (some damage & repair) ............................ **$550**

*Century and "Dakota" Candy Jars*

**Candy jar,** Century, 26" (ILLUS. left) ........ **700-875**
**Candy jar,** "Dakota," cylinder, w/ground stopper, 30" (ILLUS. right).............. **1,600-2,000**

*"Dakota Globe" Candy Jar*

**Candy jar,** "Dakota Globe," w/ground lid, 16" (ILLUS.).......................................... **525-650**
**Candy jar,** six piece, stacking, 20" h. ........ **375-375**

*Cane & Umbrella Case*

**Cane & umbrella case,** oak w/glass on four sides & top, Russell & Sons Co., Ilion, N.Y. c. 1910, 14" x 30", 4" h. (ILLUS.)................................................. **625-700**
**Coffee grinder counter display,** "Elgin National," cast iron, double wheel ......... **400-600**

*"Enterprise" Coffee Grinder Counter Display*

**Coffee grinder counter display,** "Enterprise," cast iron, two-wheel, pat'd. 7-12-98 (ILLUS.).......................................... **400-550**
**Coffee grinder display,** "Enterprise," cast iron, floor model, double wheel, w/brass hopper & eagle, restored................. **1,375-1,800**

*"White Owl" Counter Cigar Cutter*

**Counter cigar cutter,** "White Owl" brand cigars, w/glass front (ILLUS.) ............... **425-650**

*Beech-Nut Counter Display*

**Counter display,** Beech-Nut, tin litho, for mints, fruits & chewing gum, c. 1920, 9 1/2" x 17", 13 1/2" h. (ILLUS.) ............ **750-900**

*Rush Park Seed Counter Display Box*

**Counter display box,** Rush Park Seed Co., "Unrivaled Garden Seed," paper litho inside lid & front of box, c. 1890, 13" x 24", 6 1/2" h. (ILLUS.) .................. **250-325**
**Counter display cabinet,** "Crescent Bread Company," advertising-type, top oak & glass, w/etched glass front panel, 24" h. ............................................................... **600-750**

*Hanford's Counter Display Cabinet*

**Counter display cabinet,** Hanford's, Balsam of Myrrh cabinet, oak w/glass door on front, c. 1890, 9 3/4" x 14 1/2", 24" h. (ILLUS.) ................................................ **450-525**

*"Spencerian Steel Pens" Counter Display Cabinet*

**Counter display cabinet,** "Spencerian Steel Pens," small, oak, 12" x 16", 7" h. (ILLUS.) ................................................ **325-400**

*Arrow Counter Display Case*

**Counter display case,** Arrow, for collars, oak frame w/glass on four sides, reserve transfer lettering on front, three columns of collars, c. 1910, 7" x 19", 26" h. (ILLUS.) ................................................ **775-900**
**Counter display case,** "Wrigley's," for gum, metal w/nickel plating, revolving .. **175-275**
**Counter display case,** "Wrigley's," for gum, tin, five compartments ................. **250-325**

*Colgan's Counter Display Jar*

**Counter display jar,** Colgan's, Taffy Tolu Gum, figural jar top w/lettering on jar, ca. 1910, 5 1/4" x 5", 11" h. (ILLUS.) .......... **325-425**

**Counter showcase,** curved front, nickel trim w/mirrored door, 22" x 30" .............. **273-375**

*Double Steeple Countertop Showcase*

**Countertop showcase,** double steeple, German silver, w/curved glass fronts, original condition, 38 x 74" to top of steeple (ILLUS.) .................................... **4,500-5,000**

*DeLaval Cream Separator Parts Cabinet*

**Cream separator parts cabinet,** DeLaval, oak w/tin litho panel in door "The World's Standard," interior has drawers for parts, early version, ca. 1900, 10 1/2" x 17 1/2", 23 1/2" h. (ILLUS.) .............................. **950-1,150**

*"Borden's" Malted Milk Dispensing Jar*

**Dispensing jar,** "Borden's" malted milk powder, label under glass, embossed lid (ILLUS.) ................................................ **450-600**

*German Display Case*

**Display case,** curved glass, German silver frame, ca. 1900, 21" sq., 12" h. (ILLUS.) ...... **375**

*Robin Hood Shoes Display Figure*

**Display figure,** Robin Hood Shoes, painted plaster, ca. 1920, 15" h. (ILLUS.) ................................................ **375-450**

*Adams Display Tin*

**Display tin,** Adams, spearmint, litho on four sides & top, lift lid, ca. 1920, 4 3/4 x 6 3/4" , 6" h. (ILLUS.) ................. **500-600**

**Dye cabinet,** Diamond Dyes, birch, tin litho front panel shows "Baby," known as the "Presentation" cabinet, Wells & Hope Co., 912-922 Vine St., Philadelphia,

Penn. ca. 1887, VG, 9 1/2" x 16 1/2",
20" h. ............................................. **1,400-1,600**

*Diamond Dyes Dye Cabinet*

**Dye cabinet,** Diamond Dyes, shows "Blue
Washer" woman, paper litho on two
sides, excellent to mint, 8" x 12 5/8",
14" h. (ILLUS.)................................ **1,800-2,400**

*"Peerless" Dye Cabinet*

**Dye cabinet,** "Peerless," roll front,
18" x 32" (ILLUS.) ................................. **375-600**

*Putnam "Fadeless" Dye Cabinet*

**Dye cabinet,** Putnam, "Fadeless," wood
w/multi-colored tin (or paper) panel in
door, shows Colonel Putnam chased by
the redcoats, ca. 1910, 9" x 21", 10" h.
(ILLUS.)................................................. **175-250**

**Hardware cabinet,** octagon, ash & soft
maple, wood pulls, revolves, 72 pie-
shaped drawers, The American Bolt &
Screw Case, Dayton, Ohio, Pat. Apr. 27
'80-May 12 '03, 21 1/2" x 33" .......... **2,000-2,400**

*"San Felice Cigars" Humidor Showcase*

**Humidor showcase,** "San Felice Cigar,"
floor model, for cigars, birch w/cherry
stain, ca. 1920, 24" x 71", 42" h.
(ILLUS.)................................................. **750-900**

*"Eli Lilly Co." Medical Display Cabinet*

**Medical display cabinet,** "Eli Lilly Co.,"
oak, hanging type, double door,
w/engraved company name across top
panel, approximately 7" x 32", 35" h.
(ILLUS.)............................................. **900-1,200**

*Hunt's Pen Cabinet*

**Pen cabinet,** Hunt's, oak, applied gold
lettering, ca. 1920, 15" x 22", 6" h.
(ILLUS.)................................................. **325-400**

*Eisenstadt's Pen Case*

**Pen case,** Eisenstadt's, "Incomparable," floor model, for pens, cherry stained maple w/reverse etched front glass, rare, ca. 1915, 16" x 17", 42" h. (ILLUS.) .... **375-450**

*Potato Chip Display*

**Potato Chip Display,** wood & glass, w/vending display case, approximately 12" sq., 17" h. (ILLUS.) ......................... **200-350**

*Ribbon Cabinet*

**Ribbon cabinet,** oak, 12 tip-out drawers w/glass fronts, six slide-out end racks, three over three, A.N. Russell & Sons,

Ilion, N.Y. USA, ca. 1910, 27" x 28", 38" h. (ILLUS.) .................................... **1300-1600**

*Shot Cabinet*

**Shot cabinet,** ash, rectangular glass windows w/iron lever releases for eight different sizes of shot, ca. 1890, 10" x 25", 12 1/2" h. (ILLUS.) ................................. **700-800**
**Soda fountain syrup bottle,** "Pineapple," label under glass, w/metal top measuring cup ................................................. **150-250**
**Soda fountain syrup bottle,** "Sarsap'lla," label under glass, w/metal top measuring cup ................................................. **150-250**

*J. & P. Coats Spool Cabinet*

**Spool cabinet,** J. P. Coats, 6 drawers, ash, J. P. Co. brass anchor pulls, black lettering on tin inserts, ca. 1890, 18" x 25", 21" h. (ILLUS.) .................................... **900-1,500**

*Kloster Spool Cabinet*

**Spool cabinet,** Kloster, circular, stain poplar wood, ca. 1910, 12" x 14" (ILLUS.) ............................................... **900-1400**
**Spool thread cabinet,** Corticelli Silk, oak, w/eight drawers, good condition, approximately 19" x 23", 30" h. ..................... **875-1,250**

*Steeple-Form Showcase*

**Steeple-form showcase,** oak, w/nickel trim, curved front, Claeks & Tehnbeuten Co., St. Louis, Mo. (ILLUS.) .............. **950-1,400**

**Store bean display counter,** oak, double section, 6 drawers, 24" x 34", 32" h. .. **700-1,000**

*Hills Bros. Coffee Store Figure*

**Store figure,** Hills Bros. Coffee, painted plaster, ca. 1930, 19" h. (ILLUS.).... **1,000-1,300**

**Straw dispenser,** glass, w/metal bottom & lid, dated 1918...................................... **175-300**

**Straw dispenser,** glass w/metal lid, 11 1/2" h. .............................................. **125-250**

*"Clark's Thread" Thread Cabinet*

**Thread cabinet,** "Clark's Thread," oak, w/tambour roll-up side doors, 17" sq., 23" h. (ILLUS.).................................... **975-1,600**

*"J & P Coats" Thread Cabinet*

**Thread cabinet,** "J & P Coats," 2 drawers, tin fronts, for hand & machine, original pulls, 14" x 20", 7" h. (ILLUS.).............. **225-325**

**Thread cabinet,** "J. P. Coats," oak, two drawers ................................................ **175-300**

*Dr. LeSure's Famous Remedies Veterinary Medicine Display Cabinet*

**Veterinary medicine display cabinet,** Dr. LeSure's Famous Remedies, ash, tin litho of horse head in front, ca. 1910, 6 3/4" x 20 1/2", 27" h. (ILLUS.) ...... **3,800-4,500**

*Columbia Veterinary Remedies Cabinet*

**Veterinary remedies cabinet,** Columbia, birch, walnut finish, tin litho in door, The F.C. Sturtevant Co., Hartford, Conn. ca. 1915, 9" x 18", 24" h. (ILLUS.) ........... **950-1,200**

# CURRIER & IVES PRINTS

*This lithographic firm was founded in 1835 by Nathaniel Currier with James M. Ives becoming a partner in 1857. Current events of the day were portrayed in the early days and the prints were hand-colored. Landscapes, vessels, sport and hunting scenes of the West all became popular subjects. The firm was in existence until 1906. All prints listed are hand-colored unless otherwise noted. Numbers at the end of the listings refer to those used in Currier & Ives Prints-An Illustrated Checklist, by Frederick A. Conningham (Crown Publishers).*

*American Farm Scene - Autumn*

**American Farm Scenes - No. 3 (Autumn),** large folio, N. Currier, 1853, framed, 133, spots of foxing (ILLUS.) .................. **$1,495**

**American Winter Sports - Deer Shooting "On the Shattagee,"** large folio, N. Currier, 1855, framed (tears, paper damage & touch-up repairs) ................................... **2,200**

**Battle at Cedar Mountain, Aug. 9th, 1862 (The),** small folio, undated, framed, 381 (margins trimmed w/tears & some damage) ........................................................... **165**

**Battle of Antietam, Md., Sept. 17th, 1862 (The),** small folio, undated, framed, 384 (minor edge damage & 1/4" strip added to top margin) ............................................ **292**

**Battle of Chancellorsville, Va., May 3rd, 1863,** small folio, undated, 395 (stains) ....... **253**

**Battle of Chattanooga, Tenn., Novr. 24th & 25th, 1863 (The),** small folio, undated, framed, 396 (tears & minor stains) .............. **275**

**Battle of Corinth, Miss., Oct. 4th, 1862,** small folio, undated, framed, 401 (stains & tears) ........................................................ **275**

**Battle of Fair Oaks, Va., May 31st, 1862 (The),** large folio, 1862, framed, 403 (minor stains & tear) ............................... **1,045**

**Battle of Fair Oaks, Va., May 31st, 1862 (The),** small folio, 1862, framed, 402 (minor edge damage & stains) .................... **270**

**Battle of Mill Spring, Ky., Jan. 19th, 1862,** small folio, undated, framed, 412 (torn, wear & stains) ................................... **165**

**Battle of Pittsburg, Tenn., April 7th, 1862 (The),** small folio, 1862, framed, 423 (minor stains) ............................................. **281**

**Battle of Pittsburg, Tenn., April 7th, 1862 (The),** small folio, 1862, framed, 423 (minor stains & margin creases) ................. **275**

**Battle of Sharpsburg, Md., Sept. 16th, 1862 (The),** small folio, undated, framed, 429 (minor stains & edge damage) ............. **303**

**Bombardment and Capture of Fredericksburg, Va. Dec. 11th, 1862,** small folio, undated, framed, 592 (stains & edge tears) ........................................................ **165**

**Camping Out "Some of the Right Sort,"** large folio, 1856, framed, 777 (minor toning & staining, possible retouch to some coloring) ..................................................... **2,142**

**Capture of Atlanta, Georgia, Sept. 2nd, 1864,** small folio, undated, framed, 807 (tears & minor stains) ................................. **275**

**Catching a Trout,** large folio, after Arthur Tait, 1854, framed (repaired tears, foxing, toning) ............................................... **1,150**

**Celebrated Trotting Mare Lady Thorn...(The),** large folio, 1866, framed, 918 (staining & toning, margins trimmed)..... **633**

**City of New York - From Jersey City,** small folio, N. Currier, 1849, framed, 1112 (slight toning, staining & creases) ....... **345**

**Dis-United States (The),** small folio, undated, black & white, framed, 1592 (tears, fold line & penciled in date "1861" in title) ............................................................ **248**

**Disputed Heart (A) - Claiming a Foul,** large folio, 1878, 1587, framed (light toning & staining) ........................................... **1,035**

**Draw Poker - Getting 'em Lively,** small folio, 1886, black comical, framed, 1617 (margins trimmed, stains, edge damage)..... **385**

**Fall of Richmond (The),** small folio, 1865, framed, 1823 (margins trimmed, edge damage restored) ........................................ **330**

**Flushing a Woodcock,** small folio, undated, framed, 2071 (margins trimmed, stains, edge damage).................... **385**

**Frontier Lake (The),** small folio, undated, framed, 2153 (minor wear & stains, slightly trimmed) ....................................... **220**

**General Shields at the battle of Winchester, Va., 1862,** small folio, 1862, framed, 2294 (minor stains & margins trimmed) ....... **248**

**Halt by the Wayside (A),** small folio, undated, in old criss-cross frame, 2694 (minor damage & taped repairs) ................. **385**

**Harvesting - the Last Load,** small folio, undated, No. 2750, modern frame (dark water stains in margins) ............................. **220**

**Home in the Wilderness (A),** small folio, 1870, framed, 2861 (minor stains & small hole in center which corresponds to knot hole in backing) ............................. **303**

**Home of Washington (The),** medium folio, undated, framed, 2874 (stains, margins slightly trimmed) ........................................ **275**

**Indian Lake - Sunset,** large folio, 1860, framed, 3091 (margins trimmed, some foxing) ......................................................... **770**

**James K. Polk - Eleventh President of the United States,** small folio, N. Currier, undated, framed, 3161 (stains) ............. **165**

**Lady Woodruff, Miller's Damsel, General Darcy, and Stella,** large folio, 1857, framed, 3399 (few small losses in margins, three tears in upper sheet edges, one extending into image slightly) ............ **1,380**

**Lakeside Home,** medium folio, 1869, framed, 3423 (margins trimmed, professional restoration, vertical stain).................. **275**

**Last Ditch of the Chivalry (The),** medium folio, undated, black & white, framed, 3444 (stains, one covered w/white chalk & some edge damage)................................ **138**

**Life in the Country - Morning,** large folio, 1862, framed, 3506 (toning, staining) .......... **288**

**Life in the Woods - Returning to Camp,** large folio, 1860, framed, 3513 (foxing, minor staining & creases, margins trimmed)................................................. **1,955**

**Life in the Woods - Starting Out,** large folio, 1860, framed, 3514 (staining & toning, margins trimmed) ............................ **1,495**

**Life of a Sportsman (The) - Coming Into Camp,** small folio, 1872, framed, 3524 (margins trimmed, minor edge damage & tear at title )............................................ **660**

*Life of a Sportsman Print*

**Life of a Sportsman (The) - Going Out,** small folio, 1872, framed, margins trimmed, light stains, 3425 (ILLUS.)............. **715**

**Moonlight - The Ruins,** small folio, undated, framed, 4184 (margins trimmed, minor edge damage).................... **160**

**Old Oaken Bucket (The),** small folio, 1872, framed, 4577 (tape repair at bottom, minor stains)............................................... **248**

**Preparing for Market,** large folio, 1856, framed, No. 4870 (toning, staining & soiling, creases, losses to corners) ............... **1,150**

**Presidents of the United States (The),** small folio, N. Currier, 1844, framed, 4892 (stains, some fading & pinpoint hole) ......................................................... **149**

**Race on the Mississippi (A),** small folio, 1870, framed, 5042 (staining, toning, minor abrasions) ........................................ **633**

*Racquet River Currier & Ives Print*

**Racquet River - "Adirondacks,"** small folio, undated, framed, margins trimmed, edge damage & repairs, 5049 (ILLUS.) ....... **330**

**Season of Blossoms (The),** small folio, undated, cross corner frame w/worn finish, 5448 (minor stains, margins trimmed) ....................................................... **248**

**Siege and Capture of Vicksburg, Miss., July 4th, 1863,** small folio, undated, framed, 5507 (margin stains & minor edge tears)...................................................... **319**

**Staten Island and the Narrows,** large folio, 1861, framed, 5715 (toning, staining, scattered foxing)................................ **1,150**

**Storming of Fort Donelson, Tenn., Feb. 15th, 1862,** small folio, 1862, framed, 5823 (minor stains) ..................................... **190**

**Storming of Fort Donelson (The),** small folio, 1862, framed, 5822 (minor wear & stains)...................................................... **248**

**Summer in the Country,** small folio, undated, framed, 5862 (margins trimmed, some edge damage) .................... **248**

**Summer in the Woods,** small folio, undated, framed, 5866 (margin stains & very minor edge damage) ........................... **358**

**Surrender of Cornwallis at Yorktown, Va. 1781,** small folio, N. Currier, 1845, framed, 5904 (minor fading)........................ **275**

**Vigilant and Valkyrie in a 'Thrash to Windward,'** large folio, 1893, framed, 6454 (creasing, staining) ............................. **518**

*"Wooding Up" on the Mississippi*

**"Wooding Up" on the Mississippi,** large folio, 1863, framed, several large repaired tears & losses in margins (ILLUS.)...................................................... **3,450**

# CZECHOSLOVAKIAN COLLECTIBLES

*Czechoslovakia did not exist until the end of World War I in 1918. The country was put together with parts of Austria, Bohemia and Hungary as a reward for the help of the Czechs and the Slovaks in winning the war.*

*In 1993, Czechoslovakia split and became two countries. The Czech Republic and the Slovak Republic.*

*Items are highly collectable because the country was in existence only 75 years.*

*For a more thorough study of the subject, refer to the following books:* Made in Czechoslovakia Books 1 and 2 *by Ruth A. Forsythe;* Czechoslovakian Glass & Collectibles Books I and II *by Dale & Diane Barta and Helen M. Rose;* Czechoslovakian Pottery by Bowers, *Closser & Ellis and* Czechoslovakian Perfume Bottles and Boudoir Accessories *by Jacquelyne Y. Jones North.*

# GLASS

**Basket,** black w/black handle, silver mica flecks, blue lining, 8" h................................. **$350**
**Basket,** red & yellow w/crystal twisted handle, 7" h. ........................................................ **220**
**Beverage set,** amber decanter w/six amber glasses, decanter 9" h., glasses 2 1/2" h., set. ................................................ **250**

*Place Card Holder*

**Place card holder,** blue dancers w/brass footed base, 1 1/2" h. (ILLUS.)...................... **45**
**Place card holder,** clear w/yellow flowers, 2" h. ................................................................ **8**

*Vase with Metal Flower Arranger*

**Vase,** varicolored w/metal flower arranger, 4 1/4" h. (ILLUS.)........................................ **100**
**Vase,** mottled colors w/black edge petal top, 6" h. ........................................................ **110**
**Vase,** opaque white w/rim & floral trim, 6 1/4" h. .......................................................... **65**

*Warrior Vase with Black Handles*

**Vase,** orange w/black handles & painted warriors, 7 1/2" h. (ILLUS.)........................... **175**

*Vase with King Tut Decoration*

**Vase,** pink w/blue luster, King Tut decoration, 7 1/2" h. (ILLUS.)............................... **2,800**

*Glass Fan Vase*

**Vase,** fan-shaped, orange w/yellow overlay, 8" h. (ILLUS.) ........................................ **200**
**Vase,** opaque white w/crsytal rim & handles, 8" h. ....................................................... **85**

*Spiderweb-type Vase*

**Vase,** orange & green spiderweb-type, 8" h. (ILLUS.).............................................. **150**
**Vase,** bud-type, mottled colors, 8 1/4" h. ............ **75**
**Vase,** three-handled, green w/blue handles, Powolny, 8 1/4" h................................. **900**
**Vase,** blue w/black struts, 9" h......................... **125**

## JEWELRY

**Beads,** glass, coral & amber, 30" l. .................... 55
**Beads,** yellow & white faceted, 14" l. ................. 45
**Buckle,** green glass w/gold accents, 3" l. ........... 25
**Earrings,** clip-back, amber & green stones,
1 1/2" l., pr. ................................................ 30
**Earrings,** screw-back, red faceted stones,
1" l., pr. ..................................................... 35
**Pin,** bird-shaped, garnet, gold tone setting,
2" l. ........................................................... 60
**Pin,** bug-shaped, large red stone w/multi-
colored stones, 2" l. ........................................ 45
**Purse,** mutlicolored wood beads, 8" l., 7" h. ....... 55
**Purse,** small black beads w/grey long
beads, round, 6" d. ....................................... 125

## LAMPS

**Lamp,** beaded basket w/glass fruit top,
11" h. ...................................................... 1,200
**Lamp,** beaded tail peacock, brass, onyx
base, 12 1/4" h. .......................................... 1,400
**Lamp,** glass, mushroom dome, painted
windmill scene, 9" h. ...................................... 450
**Lamp,** glass, perfume-type, light blue
w/enameled flowers, 4" h. .............................. 350
**Lamp,** pottery, map of the world, Amphora,
8 1/2" h. ..................................................... 650
**Lamps,** glass, mauve w/band of flowers,
5 1/2" h., pr. ............................................... 125

## PERFUME ITEMS

**Bottle,** brass & green jeweled stopper
w/dangles, 2 1/2" h. ...................................... 150
**Bottle,** clear w/frosted cranes in stopper,
7 1/4" h. ..................................................... 650
**Bottle,** clear w/frosted troubadour in stop-
per, 5 1/2" h. ............................................... 325
**Bottle,** clear w/pink fan stopper, 6" h. ............. 350
**Bottle,** frosted & clear w/opaque black
stopper, 3 1/2" h. ......................................... 125
**Bottle,** frosted & clear, w/red stopper, 5" h. ..... 325
**Bottle,** green w/some frosting, stopper
same, 5" h. .................................................. 175
**Bottle,** heather, heather stopper, rare
color, 5" h. .................................................. 400
**Bottle,** opaque blue, opaque blue stopper,
6 1/2" h. .................................................. 1,800

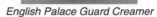

*Jeweled Perfume Bottle*

**Bottle,** purple, purple stopper w/cupids,
jeweled, 5 1/2" h. (ILLUS.) ......................... 2,200

**Bottle,** purple w/purple peacock stopper,
4 1/2" h. ..................................................... 450
**Bottle,** purse-type, topaz w/jewels in brass,
screw-top, 2" h. ............................................ 275
**Bottle,** turquoise, turquoise stopper, rare
color, 7 1/2" h. ............................................. 450
**Mirror,** hand-type, perfume stopper handle,
6 1/2" h. ..................................................... 100
**Powder box,** cov., pink cut glass, 4 1/2" h. ...... 300
**Toilet bottles,** enameled decoration of
people, set of 3, 4 1/2" h., each .................... 250

## POTTERY, PORCELAIN, SEMI-PORCELAIN

**Baby plate,** divided, Humpty-Dumpty
scene, 7 1/4" d. ............................................ 125
**Basket,** majolica, blue panels w/flowers,
Eichwald, 7 1/2" h. ....................................... 185
**Basket,** scarlet flowers & handle, 4 1/2" h. ........ 65
**Basket,** yellow w/band of flowers, 5 1/2" h. ........ 38
**Book ends,** mountaineers, 6 1/4" h., pr. .......... 125
**Bowl,** yellow, flower & fruit, Mrazek,
4 1/2" h. ..................................................... 225
**Box,** cov., cream, sculpted figure of lady's
head on lid, 3 " h. ......................................... 275
**Box,** cov., scarlet, flowers & fruits,
4 1/2" h. l. ................................................... 145
**Cream & sugar,** figural ducks, red, yellow
& blue, 4" h., pr. ........................................... 120
**Creamer,** figural moose, brown & tan,
3 1/2" h. ....................................................... 55
**Creamer,** figural parrot, orange & yellow,
4 1/2" h. ....................................................... 55

*English Palace Guard Creamer*

**Creamer,** figural, scarlet & black, English
palace guard, 4" h. (ILLUS.) .......................... 45

*Fruits & Flowers Cup & Saucer*

**Cup & saucer,** green, flower & fruit decoration, 2 1/2" h. (ILLUS.) .................................. 75

*Dancing Couple Figure Group*

**Figure group,** dancing couple, the woman w/blue & white dress w/gold trim, the man w/greyish blue trousers, white shirt, orange vest & brown hat w/ribbons, 5 1/2" h. (ILLUS.)............................................ **85**
**Kitchen canister set,** cream w/band of roses, 15 pcs. ...................................... **625**
**Mug,** scarlet, silhouette design, 4" h.................. **35**

*Seated Man Pipe Holder*

**Pipe holder,** figural, seated tan & yellow man, 4 1/4" h. (ILLUS.).................................... **50**
**Pitcher,** cream, purple horizontal stripes, airbrushed, 8" h. ........................................... **275**
**Pitcher,** figural ram, yellow, red & black, 8 1/2" h...................................................... **650**
**Pitcher,** floral design w/scarlet handle, 8" h. ............................................................. **145**

*Fruits & Flowers Pitcher*

**Pitcher,** scarlet, fruits & flowers, black handle, 8" h. (ILLUS.)................................... **125**
**Pitcher,** triple-handle, yellow w/scene, 7 1/2" h. ............................................................. **85**

**Planter,** majolica, blue, stripes & floral, Eichwald, 4 1/2" h......................................... **140**
**Teapot,** cov., green florals, stacking-type, 5 1/4" h. ........................................................ **275**
**Teapot,** cov., scarlet, flowers, black handle & spout, 7" h............................................... **295**
**Tobacco jar,** cov., figural fox lid handle, Amphora, 10 1/2" ........................................ **900**

*Coach & Horses Tray*

**Tray,** coach & horses scene, black & greens, 12" l. (ILLUS.).................................... **65**

*Scenic Urn-vase*

**Urn-vase,** bottle-form base, angled handles from shoulder to base of bulbous bowl-shaped upper section w/scalloped & flared rim, decorated w/desert scene w/camels, 5 1/2" h. (ILLUS.).......................... **45**

*Fruits & Flowers Vase*

**Vase,** black, fruits & flowers, 4 1/2" h. (ILLUS.)......................................................... **65**
**Vase,** fan-shaped, blue, white, orange paisley design, 7 1/2" h...................................... **235**
**Vase,** footed, scarlet, fruits & flowers, Mrazek, 8 1/2" h. ............................................ **250**

**Vase,** majolica, yellow & lavender, Eichwald, 8" h........................................................... **145**
**Vase,** orange & blue, slip-decorated, 10" h. ..... **325**
**Vase,** tan w/flowers & leaves, geometric base, Amphora, 10 1/4" h............................. **300**
**Wall pocket,** bird at wishing well, 6 1/4" h. ........ **60**
**Wall pocket,** bird by shell, lustre glaze, 6" h........................................................................ **70**
**Wall pocket,** woodpecker on tree trunk, 6 1/2" h. ............................................................... **70**

# DECOYS

*Decoys have been utilized for years to lure flying water fowl into target range. They have been made of carved and turned wood, papier-mâché, canvas and metal, and some are in the category of outstanding folk art and command high prices.*

**Black Duck Drake,** by Elmer Crowell, East Harwich, Massachusetts, carved wood w/original paint, glass eyes, stamped mark on oval base, 7" h. (minor paint wear, wear to tip of beak)........................... **$460**
**Black Duck Drake,** by Elmer Crowell, East Harwich, Massachusetts, sleeping pose, carved wood w/original paint, glass eyes, stamped mark on oval base, 5 3/4" h. (wear, cracks) ................................ **518**

*Rare Black-bellied Plover Decoy*

**Black-bellied Plover,** by Obediah Verity, carved wood w/original paint, ca. 1860 (ILLUS.)...................................................... **36,300**
**Black-Bellied Plover,** carved wood mounted on a stick on a lead base, original paint, glass eyes, 20th c., 12 1/2" h. (minor paint loss, small chip to beak)........ **2,530**
**Brandt,** carved solid block of wood, two-piece head & neck, old black paint, wire legs, 19 1/2" h. (age crack, head & neck nailed, possibly old replacements) .............. **358**
**Bufflehead Drake,** by Paul Gibson, Havre de Grace, Maryland, carved wood w/original paint, branded "H.F." w/inscription "Made by Paul Gibson, Havre de Grace Ca. 1967, for me and gunned in my rig on the Choptank River, Henry A. Fleckenstein Jr. 3/16/90," 12 1/4" l. (minor wear, shot scars) ........... **330**
**Bufflehead Drake,** carved wood w/fine details & original paint, tack eyes, 16 1/4" l. (paint wear, age cracks)................ **248**
**Canada Goose,** carved & painted wood working model, probably Virginia area, early 20th c., 23" l. (age splits) ................ **11,500**
**Canada Goose,** primitive carved wood w/head in preening position, hollow block w/old paint, 23" l. (cracks in sides)...... **468**

**Coot,** by Charles (Pete) Wilbur, hollow block w/original paint, branded "C.W.," 10 1/4" l. ...................................................... **193**
**Coot,** carved wood w/old working repaint & glass eyes, later inscribed on bottom "Gus Nelow, Oshkosh, Wis. Circa 1920," 13 1/2" l. (crack in neck).............................. **303**

*Rare Obediah Verity Curlew*

**Curlew,** by Obediah Verity, Seaford, New York, carved wood w/old paint, 19th c. (ILLUS.).................................................... **16,500**

*Hand-painted & Carved Fish Decoy*

**Fish,** carved wood, shaded green body w/overall colored speckles & striped fins (ILLUS.).................................................... **55**
**Mallard Drake,** by Henry Perdew, Illinois, carved hollow body w/good old working repaint & tack eyes, lead weight w/cast maker's label, 17" l. .................................... **523**
**Mallard Drake,** hollow-carved wood w/restored paint & glass eyes, Ohio, 19th c., 16 1/2" l. ........................................ **385**

*Ward Brothers Mallards*

**Mallard Drake & Hen,** carved cedar, Ward Brothers, original paint, ca. 1942, pr. (ILLUS.).................................................... **17,325**

*Rare "Shang" Wheeler Mallard Hen*

**Mallard Hen,** by "Shang" Wheeler, Stratford, Connecticut, carved wood w/original paint (ILLUS.) ................................... **44,000**

**Mallard Hen,** Mason's Premier grade, carved wood w/old repaint & glass eyes, hollow block, 16 1/4" l. ................................ **341**

*Fine Ward Brothers Pintails*

**Pintail Drake & Hen,** carved wood w/fine painting, Ward Brothers, pr. (ILLUS.) ...... **12,100**

*Fine Carved Swan Decoy*

**Swan,** swimming position, carved solid pine w/old white paint & metal ring on the bottom, some age cracks & loss on underside, 20th c., 25" l., 19" h. (ILLUS.).. **3,162**

# DISNEY COLLECTIBLES

*Scores of objects ranging from watches to dolls have been created showing Walt Disney's copyrighted animated cartoon characters, and an increasing number of collectors now are seeking these, made primarily by licensed manufacturers.*

*Disney Character Tumblers*

**Blue Fairy (Pinocchio) tumbler,** clear glass w/blue figure, ca. 1940 (ILLUS. right) .............................................................. **$19**

**Davy Crockett play suit,** in original box, appears unused, by Ben Cooper ................... **95**

**Davy Crockett bandana,** yellow w/red & black graphics, 17" sq. ................................. **55**

**Disney characters calendar,** each month w/Disney characters, advertising Morrell Ham, 1942 ..................................................... **235**

**Disney characters coloring book,** "Silly Symphony," Whitman, 1934, 34 pp. ............... **45**

**Disney characters cookie tin,** long, low rectangular metal container w/a colorfully printed lid featuring a landscape scene ful lof Disney characters including the Three Little Pigs, Mickey & Minnie Mouse, Donald Duck, Goofy & Snow White, ca. 1940, 12 x 18" (minor dents & scratches) ..................................................... **125**

**Disney characters dinner set,** china, "Three Little Pigs and Red Riding Hood Set," imported from Bavaria by Schumann Bros., a sub license from George Borgfeldt,1932, the set ................................. **180**

**Disney characters drum,** lithographed tin, illustrates Mickey & Minnie Mouse, Donald Duck, Pluto, etc., Ohio Art Co., (Bryan, Ohio), 6 1/2" ..................................... **305**

**Disney characters entertainment program,** World War II era, illustrations of Mickey, Donald, Minnie & several other characters dressed as soldiers, red, white & blue, mint condition ......................... **125**

**Disney characters iron-on patches,** Bondex, 1946, original package ........................... **60**

**Disney characters jigsaw puzzle,** "Disneyland Christmas," frame-tray type, Whitman, 1956 ............................................... **11**

**Disney characters lunch box,** school bus w/Disney characters, w/thermos bottle, Aladdin Industries............................................ **75**

**Disney characters nodders,** celluloid, Mickey, Donald, Pluto & Goofy, ca. 1950s, 3" h., set of 4 ..................................... **75**

*Disney Character Party Baskets*

**Disney characters party baskets,** molded plastic, each w/the silhouetted figure of a different character on the front & trimmed in color, on original color card, old stock (ILLUS.)............................................ **88**

**Disney characters phonograph record,** "Little Toot," by Capitol Records, 1948 .......... **35**

**Disney characters poster,** "How to catch & cure a cold," advertising Kleenex, 1951 .................................................................. **17**

**Disney characters sand pail,** pictures Donald, Mickey, Pluto & Goofy, Ohio Art Co. ...................................................................... **150**

**Disney characters sand set,** sprinkling can, small bucket, little shovel w/Disney characters plus sand mold & scoop in box, with sand elevator, Ohio Arts, Inc., the set .......................................................... **750**

*Disney Parade Roadster Toy*

**Disney characters toy,** windup tin, "Mechanical Disney Parade Roadster," colorfully lithographed long auto w/plastic figures of various characters in the front & back open seats, Louis Marx, ca. 1950, w/original box (ILLUS.) ...................... **633**

**Disney characters toy,** wind-up tin "Disneyland Roller Coaster," figure-8 roller coaster w/two passenger cards, J. Chein & Co., 1940s, 10" h. .................................... **450**

**Disneyland game,** board-type, "Adventureland," 1956 ............................................. **35**

**Disneyland game,** board-type, "Pirates of the Caribbean" ............................................. **40**

**Disneyland Melody Player,** w/original box, near mint ............................................. **600**

**Disneyland school bag,** red plastic lettering, tan trim, 1960. 13" ................................ **100**

**Disneyland toy,** Express train set, tin, Marx, set, in original box ............................ **500**

**Disneyland toy,** tin jeep w/images of Mickey, Donald, Pluto & Goofy, good, Marx .......................................................... **90**

**Donald Duck baby bottle warmer** ................ **125**

**Donald Duck baby food warming dish,** figural, coral, American Pottery, large ......... **225**

**Donald Duck bank,** composition, w/life preserver, Crown Toy Co., ca. 1938, 6" h. ........................................................... **350**

**Donald Duck book,** "Donald Duck Bringing Up Boys," Whitman Publishing Co., 1948 ................................................................. **40**

**Donald Duck book,** "Donald Duck & His Cat Troubles," 1948 ...................................... **40**

**Donald Duck book,** "Donald Duck & The Mystery of the Double X," Better Little Book ................................................................. **15**

**Donald Duck charm,** sterling silver ................ **145**

**Donald Duck Coffee bank,** tin, "Donald Duck Coffee-Free Sample," short cylindrical can w/coin slot in lid, picture of Donald on the front, fine condition .............. **205**

**Donald Duck toy,** makes quacking noise, very good, Sun Rubber Co............................ **25**

**Donald Duck toy,** on motorcycle, from LIne Mar/WDP, colorful tin litho toy, bright, clean, 3 1/2" long.............................. **220**

**Donald Duck toy,** pull-type, "Donald Duck Choo Choo," Fisher-Price No. 450, 1942..... **125**

**Donald Duck toy,** pull-type, "Donald Duck Xylophone," Fisher-Price, No. 185, 1938 ..... **275**

*Early Donald Duck Tumbler*

**Donald Duck tumbler,** clear glass w/blue printed long-billed Donald Duck, ca. 1930s (ILLUS.) .............................................. **186**

**Donald Duck & Nephews toy,** windup tin, "Marching Soldiers," a fat Donald on two small wheels carrying a rubber rifle over his shoulder & towing in a row his three nephews each w/a rubber rifle & on two small wheels, Line Mar, 1950s, 11 1/2" l. (scratches) ........................................................ **374**

**Donald Duck & nephews tumbler,** colored scene of Donald & his nephews as Boy Scouts, 1942 series .............................. **52**

**Donald Duck & Pluto ceiling globe,** Donald chasing butterflies on one side & Pluto chasing butterflies on the other side, 11" d., mint condition ........................... **400**

**Donald Duck & Pluto toy,** Donald & Pluto in car, Sun Rubber Co., 6 1/2" l.................... **125**

**Dumbo cookie jar w/mouse finial** ................ **180**

**Dumbo salt & pepper shakeres,** Leeds China Co., 4" h., pr. ...................................... **60**

**Dumbo & Pluto cookie jar,** turnabout-type, Leeds China ................................... **150-175**

**Dwarf Doc glass,** dairy, 1938 ........................... **28**

**Dwarf Dopey carpet sweeper,** musical, Fisher Price ...................................................... **225**

**Dwarf Dopey puppet,** hand-type, Gund ........... **40**

**Dwarf Grumpy soap,** Castile, w/original box ................................................................... **38**

**Dwarf Happy figure,** rubber, Seiberling, 5" h................................................................... **85**

**Dwarf Sneezy valentine card,** mechancial, Walt Disney Enterprises, 1938 ................ **37**

**Dwarfs Bashful, Doc, Dopey, Grumpy, Sleepy, Sneezy & Happy figures,** hard rubber, Seiberling, 1938, 5 1/2" h., set of 7 ....................................................................... **600**

**Elmer Elephant tooth brush holder,** twin Elmer Elephants, both w/movable trunks, Borgefelt ......................................... **1,200**

**Fantasia figure,** ceramic, Ostrich bowing, Vernon Kilns, 6" h...................................... **1,100**

**Fantasia figure,** ceramics, Mr. Stork, Vernon Kilns, Incised in the unglazed cavity, plus ink markings, "Disney Copyright 1941 Vernon Kilns U. S. A." ...................... **1,800**

**Ferdinand the Bull coloring book,** 1938......... **25**

**Ferdinand the Bull figure,** ceramic, large, Brayton Laguna............................................. **500**

**Ferdinand the Bull figure,** composition, jointed, signed Walt Disney Enterprises & Ideal ............. 280

**Figaro (Pinocchio's cat) figurine,** porcelain, rolling a ball, Goebel w/full Bee mark ............. 350

**Figaro (Pinocchio's cat) toy,** windup tin, rolls over, good, Marx .................................... 140

**Goofy toy,** windup celluloid, cat on tail, Louis Marx & Co. .................................... 225-250

**Goofy toy,** windup plastic, Goofy being bitten by a chipmunk, very good, Marx ............ 110

**Goofy toy,** windup plastic, Goofy in a convertible automobile, 5" l. .............................. 75

**Huey, Dewey & Louie (Donald Duck's nephews) sweater pins,** in box, set of 3 ..................................................... 140

**Jiminy Cricket (from Pinocchio) wrist watch,** U. S. Time, 1948 ............................ 290

**Joe Carioca pencil sharpener,** Bakelite, 1940s ...................................................... 50

**Johnny Appleseed book,** "Walt Disney's Johnny Appleseed," first edition ..................... 36

**Ludwig Von Drake doll,** plus velveteen, Gund, 18" h. ............................................ 60

**Ludwig Von Drake game,** "Tiddly Winks" ......... 25

**Ludwig Von Drake lunch box,** 1961 ............. 150

**Ludwig Von Drake salt shaker,** ceramic, Walt Disney Productions .......................... 30

**Ludwig Von Drake cookie jar,** cov., pottery, bust portrait of Professor Von Drake, American Bisque, 1961 ................... 250

**Mary Poppins hair dryer,** 1964, original box .................................................... 85

**Mary Poppins lunch box & thermos,** depicting a flying Mary Poppins on both sides of the box, the thermos w/a carousel scene, near mint condition, 1965............ 275

**Mary Poppins pencil case,** vinyl, 1964............. 25

**Mary Poppins spoon,** silver plate, figural handle depicting Mary w/open umbrella, International Silver, 1964, near mint condition................................................ 35

*Mary Poppins Whirling Toy*

**Mary Poppins toy,** windup plastic, figure holding umbrella, whirling action, w/original box, ca. 1964, Marx (ILLUS.) ................. 220

**Mickey Mouse animation drawing of Mickey** 4 x 4 1/2" graphite on paper, from "Alpine Climbers" (1936) ................... 1,500

**Mickey Mouse ashtray,** ceramic, a stylized figure of Micket sits playing a guitar, trimmed in yellow & brown w/black outlines, Holland, 8" h. ................................ 1,600

**Mickey Mouse baby rattle,** light blue plastic, early .......................................... 275

**Mickey Mouse bank,** composition, Mickey w/movable head standing beside chest, Crown Toy Co., 1940, 6 1/4" h. ................... 600

**Mickey Mouse bank,** Mickey w/mandolin seated on drum, pot metal, England, 1930s, 5" h. ........................................ 525

**Mickey Mouse book,** "Book for Coloring," die-cut, shows Mickey skating, 1936 ......... 105

**Mickey Mouse book,** "Mickey Mouse Crusoe," 1938 ..................................... 165

**Mickey Mouse book,** "Mickey Mouse & His Friends," linen, Whitman No. 904, 1936, 12 pp. ......................................... 185

**Mickey Mouse book,** "Mickey Mouse Presents Walt Disney's Nursery Stories from Walt Disney's Silly Symphony," Whitman, 1937, 212 pp. ...................... 125

**Mickey Mouse book,** "Mickey Mouse's Summer Vacation," 1948 ...................... 48

**Mickey Mouse book,** "Mickey & The Golden Touch," 1937, mint w/dust jacket..... 105

**Mickey Mouse book,** "Silly Symphony Babes in the Woods," pop-up type .............. 115

**Mickey Mouse book ends,** cast iron, seated Mickey leaning against a book, John Wright, Inc., Wrightsville, Pennsylvania, 1972, 5" h., pr. ....................... 176

**Mickey Mouse card game,** "Mickey & Beanstalk," complete in original bo, ca. 1940s ......................................... 95

**Mickey Mouse charm,** sterling silver, 3/4" ...... 140

**Mickey Mouse cookie jar,** cov., pottery, figural Mickey wearing chef's outfit & holding a rolling pin, "Flour XXX" on his pocket, marked "Copyright The Walt Disney Co. by HOAN Ltd." ..................... 80

**Mickey Mouse creamer,** china, gold & blue lustre finish ............................... 125

**Mickey Mouse desk,** school master-type w/flip-over blackboard, marked "Falcon Toy" ............................................ 400

**Mickey Mouse figure,** bisque, Mickey holding baseball glove & ball, ca. 1930, 3 1/4" h. ........................................ 195

**Mickey Mouse figure,** bisque, Mickey playing a mandolin, 5" h. ...................... 600

**Mickey Mouse figure,** bisque, Mickey wearing green shorts, hinged arms, the base inscribed "Mickey Mouse" & stamped "Japan," 1930s, 7 1/4" h. .............. 375

**Mickey Mouse figure,** celluloid, cowboy w/jointed arms & legs, 4 1/2" h.................... 350

**Mickey Mouse figure,** jointed wood & compositioin, Fun-E-Flex, painted composition head & wood jointed body w/movable limbs, cloth-covered tail w/wooden knob at end, George Borgfeldt, marked "Mickey Mouse Des. Pat. 82802 by Walt Disney," ca. 1930s, 7" h. (ILLUS. top next page) .............................. 2,860

*Mickey Mouse Fun-E-Flex Figure*

**Mickey Mouse game,** "Pin the Tail on Mickey," includes 16 linen-like tails numbered consecutively & the MIckey target w/his back turned, in colorful box picturing Mickey, Minnie & the Three Pigs, marked "Walt Disney Enterprises," Marx Bros., target 17 1/2 x 22, box 9 1/2 x 10 1/2" (pinkish tinge to upper quarter of target, 2 small splits in box) ......... **350**

**Mickey Mouse game,** "Slugaroo," die-cut cardboard, 6 1/2" h. Mickey batter, 18" of fence, ca. 1950 ......................................... **75**

**Mickey Mouse handkerchiefs,** printed cotton, Days of the Week series, ca. 1930, set of 7 .............................................. **398**

**Mickey Mouse marionette,** composition, dressed in a striped shirt, shorts & shoes, by Madame Alexander, 1938-39, 9 1/2" h. marionette, overall 21" h. ............ **1,250**

**Mickey Mouse pencil box,** rectangular, yellow & red, pictures Mickey w/ Donald Duck (very slight wear at corners) .................. **90**

**Mickey Mouse pillow case,** embroidered, 1932 ..................................................... **180**

**Mickey Mouse planter,** china, lustre ware, Mickey playing saxophone, 1930s, 4" l. ....... **235**

**Mickey Mouse record set,** "Mickey Mouse's Birthday Party," 78 r.p.m. ....... **65**

**Mickey Mouse rocker,** wooden, each side painted w/an early Mickey lying in a pool of water, the sides connected by a seat & play rack, the Mengel Company, ca. 1935, w/a photo of the toy & its original owner, 35" l. (some flaking on one side) ...... **575**

**Mickey Mouse rocker,** wooden, good, Walt Disney Productions ............................. **300**

**Mickey Mouse rug,** pictures Mickey riding a donkey, ca. 1949, 21 x 39" ........................ **165**

**Mickey Mouse sled,** by Allen CO., Philadelphia, PA, 1935-1940, 2 sizes (Sm + L) depicts Mickey on sled w/Minnie, small size ...................................................... **450**

**Mickey Mouse sled,** by Allen CO., Philadelphia, PA, 1935-1940, 2 sizes (Sm + L) Depicts Mickey on Sled w/Minnie, large size ...................................................... **600**

**Mickey Mouse straws,** unopened cardboard boxd w/large color picture of Mickey on the front, "Mickey Mouse Sunshine Straws," some wear & staining on box, ca. 1950s (ILLUS.) .................................. **20**

*Mickey Mouse Straws Package*

**Mickey Mouse toy,** battery-operated, Mickey the drummer, lighted eyes, Line Mar, 1941 ..................................................... **375**

**Mickey Mouse toy,** Mickey on tractor, rubber w/metal axles, black & peach Mickey, red tractor w/white tires, both sides marked "Mickey's Tractor," bottom marked "Sun Rubber Co.," 4 1/2 x 4 1/2" ..... **125**

**Mickey Mouse toy,** SIT-N-GO W-1 Astrocar, Mickey Mouse as driver, windup, Matchbox, all mint ......................................... **210**

*Mickey Mouse & Boy Windup Toy*

**Mickey Mouse toy,** windup celluloid, figure of boy dressed like Pinocchio lifting a jointed plastic figure of Mickey Mouse, early Schuco (ILLUS.) ................................... **880**

**Mickey Mouse toy,** windup tin, "Jazz Drummer," plunger causes a lithographed two-dimensional Mickey to play the drum, by Nifty, Germany, ca. 1931, 6 3/4" h., good (ILLUS. top next page) ...... **2,100**

**Mickey Mouse toy washing machine,** tin, marked Walt Disney Enterprises, Ohio Art Co. .......................................................... **105**

**Mickey Mouse tumbler,** clear glass w/black printed Mickey, ca. 1930s (ILLUS. center next page) ........................... **110**

*Mickey Mouse Jazz Drummer*

*Early Mickey Mouse Tumbler*

**Mickey Mouse wrist watch,** 50th Birthday, Bradley, 1978, mint, w/original box .............. **350**
**Mickey Mouse wrist watch,** "America on Parade," limited edition Bicentennial watch, mint ................................................ **235**
**Mickey Mouse toy,** tin, friction-type, Mickey on motorcycle, very good, Line Mar ................................................................. **175**
**Mickey Mouse toy,** windup tin, "Mickey Musician," standing Mickey playing the xylophone, Line Mar, working, complete w/box, 7" h. (chips to xylophone, box lid torn at corners & top) .................................. **748**
**Mickey Mouse toy,** windup tin, Mickey w/twirling tail, very good, Line Mar .............. **230**
**Mickey Mouse & Donald Duck crayon box,** tin, Transogram, 1946 ........................... **90**
**Mickey Mouse & Donald Duck Sunshine straw holder,** holds 12 flat packages of straws, Walt Disney Productions ................... **45**
**Mickey Mouse & Horace Horsecollar porringer,** silver plate, engraved illustration of Mickey & Horace in the center of the bowl & engraving of Mickey on the handle, International Silver Co., ca. 1930 ..... **360**
**Mickey & Minnie Mouse figure group,** bisque, Mickey & Minnie seated on a

couch w/Pluto at their feet, hand-painted, pie-cut eyes, decal on Mickey reads "Niagara Falls," Japan, 3 3/4" h. ......... **462**
**Mickey & Minnie Mouse figures,** bisque, Mickey playing drum, Minnie playing accordion, 1930s, 3" h., each ...................... **265**

*Mickey & Minnie Acrobats*

**Mickey & Minnie Mouse toy,** windup celluloid & tin acrobats, George Borgfeldt, very good, w/original box, 13" h. (ILLUS.) ......................................................... **691**

*Mickey Mouse Hand Car*

**Mickey & Minnie Mouse toy,** windup tin, Mickey & Minnie Mouse handcar, composition figures on each end of the center handlebar, red car, w/original box, Lionel, 1930s (ILLUS.) ............................. **1,265**
**Mickey Mouse Club cap pistol w/holster,** badge & other accessories, ca. 1965, original package .............................................. **65**
**Mickey Mouse Club Clubhouse,** heavy cardboard, never assembled, 1950s, w/original box, 50" h. .................................... **425**
**Minnie Mouse doll,** cloth, Minnie w/felt ears, wearing polka dot cloth skirt, original Mickey Mouse paper label for the Knickerbocker Toy Company, 1930s, 21" h. (tears around neckline) ................. **1,410**
**Minnie Mouse doll,** plush & felt, Charlotte Clark, late 1940s, 20" h. .............................. **800**
**Minnie Mouse figure,** bisque, w/umbrella, ca. 1930, 3 1/2" h. .................... **150**
**Minnie Mouse figure,** celluloid, jointed arms, wearing a white skirt, red bloomers & blue shoes & hat, Japan, ca. 1930s, 6" h. ............................................... **675**
**Minnie Mouse figure,** jointed wood, "Fun-e-Flex," 5" h. ................................................ **285**

*Ideal Jointed Pinocchio Doll*

*Pinocchio Doll*

**Pinocchio & Figaro planter,** ceramic, standing Pinocchio & Figaro beside a square container, unmarked .......................... **89**

*Pinocchio Windup Tin Walking Toy*

**Pinocchio & Geppetto tray,** serving-type, lithographed tin, Ohio Art, 1939 .................. **105**
**Pluto applique,** iron-on type, Walt Disney Productions, 1946 ........................................ **28**
**Pluto bank,** wooden, sits on haunches, 11" h........................................................... **110**
**Pluto figure,** ceramic, crouching position, Brayton Laguna, unsigned, 1938-40 ........... **200**
**Pluto hand puppet,** Gund, 1950s...................... **65**
**Pluto toy,** windup plastic, Pluto w/twirling tail, good, Walt Disney Productions .............. **55**
**Pluto toy,** windup tin & celluloid, celluloid Pluto performing on a high bar w/"Gym Toy" pennant, Line Mar, in original box, 13" h............................................................. **505**
**Pluto toy,** windup tin, "Musical Pluto," lithographed tin square platform w/crouching figure of Pluto going around in a circle passing through a doghouse & other structure, good condition...................... **440**
**Pluto tumbler,** clear glass w/black Pluto figure, ca. 1936 (ILLUS. left w/Blue Fairy tumbler) ............................................................ **19**
**Pluto wrist watch,** Ingersoll, 1947.................. **225**
**Snow White animated alarm clock,** Bayard, France, 1964, w/box ..................... **525**
**Snow White cookie jar,** Walt Disney Productions, Enesco label ................................. **450**
**Snow White cut-out book,** all characters & dwarfs' house in lustrous color graphics, 1937, 13 x 13"...................................... **150**
**Snow White doll,** dressed in original clothing, Ideal Toy Corp., mint w/original tags, 16" h............................................................. **400**
**Snow White figure,** bisque, 1930s, 2 3/4" h.......................................................... **85**
**Snow White figure,** chalkware, early Carnival-type, 14 1/2" h. (some paint loss) .......... **58**
**Snow White ironing board,** lithographed tin, Ohio Art Co........................................... **150**
**Snow White lamp,** plaster composition, figural, made by La Mode Studios for Walt Disney Enterprises, dated 1938.......... **525**

**Snow White pencil sharpener,** celluloid, Snow White playing mandolin ..................... **135**
**Snow White refrigerator,** lithographed tin, Wolverine ..................................................... **25**
**Snow White & the Seven Dwarfs art stamp set,** 1937, w/box......................... **85-125**
**Snow White & the Seven Dwarfs dolls,** stuffed cloth w/painted composition faces, each dwarf named on his cap, w/original boxes for dwarfs, Ideal, Snow White 15 1/2" h, each dwarf 7" h., set of 8 ................................................................ **2,860**
**Snow White & the Seven Dwarfs figures,** bisque, dwarfs' names on their hats, backs marked "Walt Disney," dwarfs 3 1/2" h., Snow White 4 1/4" h., set of 8....... **725**
**Snow White & the Seven Dwarfs figurines,** porcelain, Goebel Full Bee mark, signed Disney, 1953, the set..................... **1,050**
**Snow White & the Seven Dwarfs lamps,** figural, one depicting Snow White holding the hem of her skirt up, the other Dopey w/his name on the base, one shade pictures Doc & the other shows the seven dwarfs outside their house, "Walt Disney Enterprise" seal on bottom, 1938, pr........................................................ **1,200**
**Snow White & the Seven Dwarfs sheet music,** "Heigh Ho" ....................................... **17**
**Sword in the Stone bracelet charm,** w/images of the owl, castle, etc., on card..... **120**
**Three Caballeros sheet music,** "Three Caballeros," 1943 ....................................... **18**
**Three Little Pigs figure,** bisque, pig playing flute, 1930s, 4 1/2" h............................... **58**
**Three Little Pigs plate,** Salem China.............. **45**
**Three Little Pigs toy top,** lithographed tin, Chein........................................................... **65**
**Three Little Pigs & Big Bad Wolf wall plaques,** figurals in original box marked, "Walt Disney Character Plaq-Ettes," unused, 7 x 15" box, the set ............ **105**
**Thumper (from Bambi) & girlfriend figures,** ceramic, American Pottery Co., L. A., pr...................................................................... **65**
**Thumper (from Bambi) cookie jar,** cov., ceramic................................................................ **165**
**Thumper (from Bambi) figure,** miniature, Hagen-Renaker................................................... **125**
**Thumper (from Bambi) salt & pepper shakers,** ceramic, Leeds China, pr.............. **60**
**Tinkerbell (from Peter Pan) bell,** figural handle, ceramic, sold in Disneyland............ **275**
**20,000 Leagues Under the Sea game,** Jaymar Games, copyright Walt Disney Productions, w/box......................................... **65**
**20,000 Leagues Under the Sea toy,** windup "Nautilus," actual working submarine, w/box....................................... **325-350**
**Walt Disney World map,** "Guide to the Magic Kingdom," in wooden frame, used at Disney World, 32 x 36".......................... **275**
**Winnie the Pooh cookie jar,** cov., Ransburg........................................................... **125**
**Winnie the Pooh toy,** squeeze-type in original package, 1962, 5 1/2" h................... **34**
**Winnie the Pooh toy,** "Tricky Trapeze," 1964, 5 1/2" h. ......................................... **48**

# DOLL FURNITURE & ACCESSORIES

**Carriage,** painted wood chassis in red w/black striping, yellow frame & wheels, black leatherette upholstery & sun shade, mid-19th c., 32" l., 27 1/2" h. (some damage & repainting) ...................... **$288**

**Chest of drawers,** Classical style, grained & painted wood, a rectangular top & backsplash w/two glove drawers above a case w/a single overhanging long drawer above three full drawers flanked by serpentine columns joined by a shaped skirt, wooden pulls, three drawers fitted w/compartments, a pair of lovebirds painted on the glove box top, yellow & pink roses on drawer fronts & case sides, drawers banded w/blue, American 19th c., 8 x 13 1/4", 12 1/2" h. (open pull missing, minor wear & paint loss)............................................................. **690**

**Chest of drawers,** walnut, a rectangular lift-lid fitted w/two ring- and knob-turned uprights flanking an oblong lobed mirror w/arched cut-out finials, the case w/a band of half-round bobbin turning above a pair of small drawers over a long drawer all w/simple turned wood knobs, old finish, ca. 1875-85, 5 1/2 x 10", 16 3/4" h. ......................................... **303**

**Clothing set,** Barbie, "Ballerina," black leotard & tights, silver tutu w/flower accents, white ballet slippers w/ties, pink satin bag w/ties, silver tiara, paper ballet poster, never removed from package (poster discolored, booklet missing)............... **60**

**Clothing set,** "Barbie Best Buy Fashions," #3358, pale pink nightie, matching robe w/fur collar, pale pink open-toed shoes, white plastic pitcher & glass, package dated 1971, never removed from package (backing slightly discolored) ................... **50**

**Clothing set,** Barbie, "Fashion Originals - Peasant Pleasant," No. 3482, orange top w/yarn trim, tan skirt w/orange rickrack, plastic wedgies w/orange plastic leg straps, hanger booklet, package dated 1971, never removed from package (package slightly discolored & scuffed) ......................................................... **65**

**Clothing set,** Barbie, "Get Ups 'N Go," No. 7707, white doctor's jacket w/button accents, blue surgery jacket w/waist tie, matching face mask & cap, plastic stethoscope, head mirror, white square toes, diploma, sketch of a skeleton, never removed from card (backing discolored w/edges & corners worn & creased) ......................................................... **28**

**Clothing set,** Barbie, "Knitting Pretty," royal blue sweater, sleeveless shell & skirt, black open-toed shoes, scissors, wooden bowl w/yarn, "How to Knit" book, booklet & paper label, never removed from box (slight box discoloration & damage) ......................................................... **200**

**Clothing set,** Barbie, "Little Red Riding Hood and the Wolf," No. 880, blue &

white dress, red cape w/neck tie, black corset w/yellow lacings, white knee-hi socks, black vinyl shoes, straw basket w/red & white checked napkin, wax rolls, white & pink cap w/lace trim, red & black cap, wolf head w/felt features (dress & socks discolored, elastic stretched on white & pink cap) .......................................... **135**

**Clothing set,** Barbie, "Sea-Worthy," No. 1872, turquoise dress w/yellow trim, button accents & one vinyl star decal, matching hat w/pompon, yellow ribbon neck tie, turquoise cotton socks w/yellow trim, turquoise tennis shoes, plastic camera, hanger, cellophane w/paper label taped to lower left corner, never removed from carton (booklet missing)........ **270**

**Clothing set,** Francie, "Fashion Originals - Little Knits," No. 3275, pink & white print knit top, hot pink shorts & matching nylon knee socks, white vinyl sandals, white belt, hanger, booklet, package dated 1971, never removed from package (package slightly discolored, faded & scuffed) ......................................................... **55**

**Clothing set,** Francie, "Get-Ups 'N Go," No. 7709, pink & white striped pinafore, matching cap, white bodyshirt w/button accent, white square-toed shoes, blue terry cloth towel, pink plastic soap, blue plastic tray, glass of 'orange' drink w/fizz, plastic hot water bottle, red & blue flower bouquet, yellow blanket w/white satin trim, white pillow, package dated 1973, never removed from package (slight discoloration to backing w/crease & small tear).............................................................. **65**

**Clothing set,** Francie, "Shoppin' Spree," No. 1261, red & white tweed coat w/cotton accents, matching clutch purse w/button closure, pink & white tweed dress, white nylon short gloves, pink soft pumps, hanger booklet, cellophane, never removed from card (plastic covering shoes dented & torn, cardboard dress front flat) ............................................. **70**

**Clothing set,** Ken, "Army and Air Force," No. 797, tan shirt w/decal & button accents, matching pants, tan belt, hat & socks, brown shoes & tie, navy blue hat, belt, tie & shoes, black socks, metal wings, paper pamphlet, paper label, never removed from box (some wear & discoloration to box, blue cap loose inside).............................................................. **80**

**Clothing set,** Ken, "Bold Gold," gold plaid jacket w/button accents, white nylon shirt, gold pants w/attached belt, gold cotton socks, brown shoes, cellophane, never removed from package (booklet missing, writing on lower corner of cardboard backing) ............................................. **40**

**Clothing set,** Ken, "Fraternity Meeting," No. 1408, white cotton shirt w/button closure, brown & white sweater w/button accents, brown pants, booklet, cellophane, never removed from package (small brown stain on shirt bottom) ............... **35**

**Cradle,** painted pine, hooded-type w/rectangular canted dovetailed sides, carved & shaped hood & rockers on molded base, grain-painted, 19th c., 5 1/4 x 10 1/2", 9" h. (small age split, minor paint loss) ............................................ **150**

**Cradle,** painted poplar, rectangular w/gently canted low sides slightly arched at one end, on solid rockers, old worn green paint w/yellow striping & the name "Mollie Allen," 19th c., 10 1/4" l. (some wear) ............................................................. **248**

**Cradle,** walnut, low-sided w/gently arched end boards & canted sides, sides curved down from head to foot, on half-round rockers, old finish, 10 1/4" l. .......................... **193**

**Dollhouse,** Add-A-Room Playhouse, set of five folding cardboard rooms, boxes form foundations, National Paper Box Co., West Springfield, Massachusetts, ca. 1940s, complete set w/boxes, living room is 7 3/4 x 15 1/2", 7" h., other rooms are 7 3/4 x 10 1/2", 7" h. .............................. **250-275**

**Dollhouse,** Adirondack Cabin, lithographed paper over wood, unmarked, two stories, four rooms, open-backed w/one room accessible through former roof, lithographed Native American figure ornaments dormer roof, deer head printed on front gable, exterior lithograph of log pattern, R. Bliss, Pawtucket, Rhode Island, ca. 1904, 10 1/2 x 17 1/2", 17 1/2" h. .................. **2,000-3,000**

**Dollhouse,** Bungalow, painted wood & fiberboard w/pressed cardboard window frames & shutter, off-white exterior, wallpapered interior, one story w/attic, one room side opening, roof lifts for attic access, A. Schoenhut, Philadelphia, Pennsylvania, ca. 1928, 12 x 13", 9" h.. **400-450**

**Dollhouse,** Bungalow, wood & embossed fiberboard, brown exterior w/embossed stone design, one story, one room w/attic space, right side opens & roof lifts up, lithographed interior w/trompe l'oeil windows & "views" of additional rooms through doorways, A. Schoenhut, Philadelphia, Pennsylvania, ca. 1925, 12 1/2 x 14", 11 1/2" h. .......................... **350-500**

**Dollhouse,** Bungalow, wood & embossed fiberboard, gray exterior w/embossed stone design, one story, two rooms w/attic space, both sides open & roof lifts up, interior w/trompe l'oeil windows & "views" of additional rooms through doorways, A. Schoenhut, Philadelphia, Pennsylvania, ca. 1923, 19 x 20", 29 1/2" h. ............................................ **850-1,000**

**Dollhouse,** Colonial, steel, lithographed inside & outside, two stories, five rooms smaller scale appropriate for 1/2" furniture, most common house, printed brown brick on first story & white shingles above, Marx, New York, ca. 1949, 9 x 19 1/2", 15 1/2" h. ............................... **50-65**

**Dollhouse,** Colonial, steel, lithographed inside & outside, two stories w/wing, six rooms, large scale appropriate for 3/4" furniture, metal awnings over windows, printed white brick on first story, red clapboard above, Marx, New York, ca. 1950, 12 x 33 1/2", 18 3/4" h. ................ **100-125**

*Colonial w/Side Porch Dollhouse*

**Dollhouse,** Colonial w/Side Porch, painted wood & fiberboard w/pressed cardboard window frames & shutters, off-white exterior w/red roof embossed in tile pattern, two stories, four rooms, A. Schoenhut, Philadelphia, Pennsylvania, ca. 1932, 15 x 24", 19 1/2" h. (ILLUS.) ............ **1,000-1,200**

**Dollhouse,** Converse two story, two room, w/interior & exterior details printed directly on wood, marked "Converse" on first floor rug, porch across front w/second floor balcony, Morton E. Converse, Massachusetts, ca. 1910, 7 x 10 1/4", 18" h. .................................................. **800-1,000**

**Dollhouse,** Cottage, lithographed US Gypsum hardboard w/plastic windows, one story, one room, Rich, Clinton, Iowa, ca. 1930s, 8 x 19", 13 1/2" h. .......................... **75-95**

**Dollhouse,** Country Estate, No. 2050, printed cardboard, die-cut & slotted for assembly, Art Moderne-style, two stories, three rooms w/awning covered patio, Built-Rite, Warren Paper Products, Lafayette, Indiana, ca. 1942, 12 1/2 x 27", 15" h. ................................. **75-100**

**Dollhouse,** Cozytown Mansion, lithographed steel w/front opening tin two-hinged sections, Tudor-style w/printed half-timbering & door w/rounded tip, six rooms w/metal stairway, Frier Steel, St. Louis, Missouri, ca. 1928, 20 x 26", 22" h. ............................................................ **100**

**Dollhouse,** Garden House, No. 616, lithographed paper over wood, marked "R. Bliss" above porch, two stories, two rooms, open-backed, small house attached to walled garden w/opening gate, pierced metal railing decorates porch & roof edges, R. Bliss, Pawtucket, Rhode Island, ca. 1905, main house 10 x 18", 20 1/2" h., garden house 7 x 11", 14" h., garden base 12 1/2 x 15 1/2" ............................... **1,200-1,500**

**Dollhouse,** Garrison Colonial Home, printed Masonite w/wood frame & metal windows, two stories, six rooms, built-in stairway, kitchen cabinets & fireplace, electrified, unmarked but verified by catalogs, Keystone, Boston, Massachusetts, ca. 1942, 13 x 34 1/2", 20" h. .................................................. **200-250**

**Dollhouse,** Gray two-story, wood & embossed fiberboard, two stories, eight rooms plus attic space, lithographed interior w/trompe l'oeil windows & "views" of additional rooms through doorways, A. Schoenhut, Philadelphia, Pennsylvania, ca. 1923, 25 x 28 1/2", 29 1/2" h. ........................................ **2,500-3,000**

**Dollhouse,** Gutter House, lithographed paper over wood, stone design, on first story w/red clapboard above, hipped roof w/three projecting shed dormers, round turret on left side of first story, bay window on second story, two stories, two rooms, front-opening, unknown manufacturer, USA, ca. 1900, 4 3/4 x 9 3/4", 13" h. ..................................................... **700-800**

*Gutter House Dollhouse*

**Dollhouse,** Gutter House, lithographed paper over wood, stone design on first story w/red clapboard above, hipped roof w/three projecting shed dormers, round turret on left window of first story, bay window on second story, two stories, two rooms, front opening, unknown manufacturer, USA, ca. 1900, 10 x 12 1/2", 18 1/2" h. (ILLUS.) ..... **1,800-2,000**

**Dollhouse,** No. 205, lithographed paper over wood, unmarked, two stories, two rooms, front opening, second floor balcony w/lithographed railing. R. Bliss, Pawtucket, Rhode Island, ca. 1911, 12 x 18", 20" h. ................................ **1,800-2,300**

**Dollhouse,** No. 3035, small wood house w/lithographed exterior paper in clapboard & shingle design, two stories, two rooms w/opening front, roofed porch extends across front of house w/lathe-turned posts, Moritz Gottschalk, Germany, ca. 1900, 8 1/4 x 9", 13 1/2" h. ........................................ **1,200-1,500**

**Dollhouse,** No. 342, lithographed paper over cardboard & wood, unmarked, two stories, two rooms, front opening, lithographed interior w/Victorian wallpaper, draped windows, fireplace, w/mantel clock, potted plants, pictures hanging from cords, R. Bliss, Pawtucket, Rhode Island, ca. 1896, 8 3/4 x 11", 17 1/2" h. ....................................... **1,400-1,600**

*Clapboard Sided Dollhouse*

**Dollhouse,** No. 3582, wood w/lithographed exterior paper depicting clapboard siding, medium size, two story house contains two rooms & features porch which wraps around front side of house, porch w/turned posts & die cut metal railing in circle pattern, front opening, original wallpapers, two chimneys, Moritz Gottschalk, Germany, ca. 1900, 11 x 17 1/2", 21" h. (ILLUS.) ................. **500-600**

**Dollhouse,** Playtime Dollhouse, No. 11, Style No. 4, printed cardboard, die-cut & slotted for assembly, one story, one room, open backed, Built-Rite, Warren Paper Products, Lafayette, Indiana, ca. 1930s, original box, 8 x 11", 8 1/2" h. ........ **60-75**

**Dollhouse,** Red Roof, No. 5472, wood w/pressed cardboard windows, light green exterior, red roof, steeply pitched roof resembles Swiss chalet, one story accessible w/attic, two rooms, left side opens, door in back provides attic access, wrap-around porch, Moritz Gottschalk, Germany, ca. 1920, 12 x 18", 25" h. .............................. **2,000-2,500**

**Dollhouse,** Red Roof, No. 6309, wood w/pressed cardboard windows & porch rail, yellow exterior, red roof, wallpapered interior, two story w/accessible attic, six rooms, working elevator, porch on front & left side, front opens in one section, hinged roof provides access to attic, Moritz Gottschalk, Germany, ca. 1920, 13 1/2 x 21", 24 1/2" h. .......... **2,300-2,800**

*Seaside Residence Dollhouse*

**Dollhouse,** Seaside Residence, No. 574, lithographed paper over wood, marked "R. Bliss" on doors, two stories, three rooms, opens from front & left side, front porch w/lathe-turned posts, attic gable w/lithographed lattice w/squared cut-out, R. Bliss, Pawtucket, Rhode Island, ca. 1901, 10 x 18", 20 1/2" h. (ILLUS.)... **2,500-4,000**

*Whitney S. Reed Dollhouse*

**Dollhouse,** Sled-type base, lithographed paper over wood, two stories, two rooms, front opening, front stoop w/turned posts, opening front door, cut-out windows on second story, Whitney S. Reed, Leominster, Massachusetts, ca. 1898, 5 1/2 x 7", 11 1/2" h. (ILLUS.).......................................... **1,000-1,200**

**Dollhouse,** Tudor, lithographed US Gypsum hardboard w/plastic windows, floors printed, walls plain, two stories, six rooms, open-backed, 1" scale, Rich, Clinton, Iowa, ca. 1948, 15 1/2 x 24", 23" h. ................................................... **175-250**

**Dollhouse,** Tudor-style, printed Masonite w/wood frame & metal windows, two stories, six rooms, printed interior w/built-in stairway, fireplace & two-door closet, Keystone, Boston, Massachusetts, ca. 1947, 12 x 29", 22" h. ........................... **175-250**

*Two-Story Dollhouse*

**Dollhouse,** two-story, wood & embossed fiberboard, gray exterior w/stone design, two stories, two rooms plus attic space, right side opens & roof lifts up, litho-

graphed interior w/trompe l'oeil windows & "views" of additional rooms through doorways, Philadelphia, Pennsylvania, ca. 1923, 11 x 14", 18 1/2" h. (ILLUS.)........................................ **1,200-1,500**

**Jelly cupboard,** pine & buttermilk, a high scrolled crestboard above a rectangular top over two paneled doors w/home-hinges over the scrolled front apron & bracket feet, old dark varnish stain, 19th c., 4 1/2 x 8 1/2", 13 1/4" h. (repair on front feet, one door w/old tin braces)............ **440**

**Secretary,** Biedermeier style, rosewood finish w/gold stenciled trim, four drawers, fall-front, one drawer, mirrored interior, Europe, mid-19th c., 2 5/8 x 4 11/16", 7 1/2" h. ...................................................... **230**

# DOLLS
*Also see: STEIFF TOYS & DOLLS*

*Large A.B.G. Bisque Head Girl*

**A.B.G. (Alt, Beck & Gottschalck) bisque head girl,** marked "689 - M 14," set brown eyes, heavy feathered brows, closed mouth w/accent line between lips, original brown human hair (h.h.) wig, kid body w/bisque lower arms, rivet joints at elbows, gussets at hips & knees, wearing blue dotted Swiss dress w/multicolored lace trim, antique underclothing, lace socks & old shoes, small inherent line on right ear, several repairs to kid legs, kid torn at shoulder plate, 28" (ILLUS.)..................................................... **$925**

**A.B.G. bisque socket head baby,** marked "No. 1 A.B. & G. 1322/30," blue sleep eyes, feather brows, open mouth w/two upper teeth, sparse original brown mohair wig, composition bent-limb baby body, wearing blue knit two-piece outfit, matching cap & booties, 11" (eye rocker repaired, body repainted w/flaking) ............. **250**

**A.M. (Armand Marseille) "googlie" bisque head girl,** marked "Germany

323 - A 11/0 M," blue eyes set & looking to the side, closed smiling mouth w/accent line, original brown mohair wig, five-piece composition toddler body w/painted socks & shoes, wearing original gauze underwear stamped "Germany," replaced taffeta dress & blue felt coat, 7" (unfinished torso, lower arms & legs) .............................................. **800**

**A.M. (Armand Marseille) "googlie" bisque head girl,** marked "Germany - 323 - A 2/0 M," blue sleep eyes looking to side, closed smiling mouth, antique blonde mohair wig, five-piece composition toddler body, wearing faded pink organdy dress, underclothing, socks & shoes, 12" (wear & touch-up on limbs, left foot damaged & glued) ...................... **1,300**

**A.M. "Nobbi Kid" bisque socket head "googlie" girl,** marked "A. 253 M. - Nobbi Kid - Reg. U.S. Pat. Off. - Germany - 11/0," brown sleep side-glancing eyes, single stroke brows, closed smiling mouth, sparse original brown mohair wig, crude five-piece composition body w/unpainted torso, molded & painted socks & black one-strap shoes, wearing original red print dress w/eyelet bodice, original underclothing, red straw hat w/papier-maché cherries, 7" (minimal wear, small flake on right foot) ................... **575**

**A.W. "My Sweetheart" bisque socket head girl,** marked "101 - 6 - A.W. - My Sweetheart - B J & Co.," brown sleep eyes, feathered brows, open mouth w/accented lips & four upper teeth, original brown mohair wig, jointed wood & composition body, wearing possibly original dark red dress trimmed w/lace, original underclothing w/factory chemise & pants, original socks & shoes, 17 1/2" ........ **350**

**Alexander (Madame) "Coco Godey Portrait,"** marked "Alexander 19 (copyright symbol) 66," vinyl head, blue sleep eyes w/real lashes, feathered brows, closed smiling mouth, blonde hair in original set, vinyl body jointed at shoulders & waist, bent right legs, wearing tagged red taffeta dress w/black velvet jacket, black velvet bonnet w/net trim & red roses, original underclothing, stockings, red velvet shoes, 21" (very light shelf dust, light fading on back of dress) ...................... **950**

**Alexander (Madame) "Coco Renoir" vinyl head girl,** marked "Alexander 19 (copyright symbol) 66," amber sleep eyes w/real lashes, closed smiling mouth, original blonde hair in original set, vinyl fashion-type body jointed at shoulders & waist, bent right legs, wearing tagged aqua taffeta dress & matching bonnet, original underclothing, nylon stockings & black velvet shoes, diamond ring on left hand, 21" (ILLUS. top next column) ...................................................... **700**

**Alexander (Madame) "Dionne Quintuplets Toddlers,"** marked "Alexander," composition heads w/painted brown eyes to side, single stroke brows, closed

mouths, molded & painted brown hair, five-piece composition toddler bodies, each wearing original tagged dress in pastel colors, attached panties, matching bonnets, socks & white leatherette center-snap shoes, unplayed-with, 7 1/2", the set (all w/light flaking on back of legs, some w/light crazing) ................... **1,900**

*Madame Alexander Coco Renoir Doll*

**Alexander (Madame) "Dr. Dafoe,"** marked "Madame Alexander - New York" on clothes tag, composition head w/painted blue eyes, closed smiling mouth, original grey mohair wig, five-piece composition body, wearing original tagged two-piece doctor outfit, matching hat, original socks & shoes, unplayed-with in original box, 13" ............................ **1,300**

**Alexander (Madame) "Margaret O'Brien,"** marked "Alexander," composition head w/blue sleep eyes w/real lashes, single stroke brows, closed mouth, original brown mohair wig in looped braids, five-piece composition body, wearing original white organdy blouse w/attached slip, pink jumper, original panties, old replaced socks, original side-snap shoes, straw hat w/flowers, 17" (some overall crazing, wig fragile, moisture damage on feet & ankles) ......................................................... **500**

*Alexander Princess Elizabeth Doll*

**Alexander (Madame) "Princess Elizabeth,"** marked "Princess Elizabeth - Alexander Doll Co.," composition head w/hazel sleep eyes w/real lashes, feathered brows, open mouth w/four upper teeth, original blonde h.h. wig, five-piece composition child body, wearing original tagged pink taffeta dress, original underclothing, original socks & shoes, silver crown, light overall crazing, fine crack under each eye, 22" (ILLUS.) ....................... **600**

*Complete Alexander Sonja Henie Set*

**Alexander (Madame) "Sonja Henie,"** marked "Madame Alexander - Sonja Henie," composition head w/brown sleep eyes & real lashes, single stroke brows, open mouth w/four upper teeth, original blonde mohair wig in original set, five-piece composition body, wearing tagged flowered taffeta skating dress w/attached slip, panties, gold skates, blue ribbon in hair, in original trousseau case w/red ski jacket, blue pants, striped shirt, knit cap, wooden skis, ski poles, pink nightgown, bra & girdle, original dress tag, few fine craze lines, replaced skates, unplayed-with, 14" (ILLUS.) .......... **3,100**

**Alexander (Madame) "Wendy Ann Bride,"** marked "Mme. Alexander," composition head w/blue sleep eyes w/real lashes, single stroke brows, closed mouth, original auburn mohair wig in original set, five-piece composition body, wearing original bride dress & veil, original underclothing, socks & shoes, original bouquet, w/original marked dress tag, 14" ............................................. **375**

*Alexander Wendy Goes on Train Doll*

**Alexander (Madame) "Wendy Goes on Train Journey,"** marked "Alex," hard plastic head w/blue sleep eyes & molded lashes, single stroke brows, closed mouth, original blonde saran wig in original set, hard plastic walker body w/unjointed knees, wearing original sleeveless dress w/pleated skirts, white felt jacket w/star trim, matching tam w/red pompon, original panties & slip, socks & red snap shoes, in original box, remnant of wrist tag, tagged jacket & dress, 8" (ILLUS.) ......................................... **400**

*Allan Doll in Box*

**Allan,** vinyl, painted red hair, beige lips, straight legs, wearing original jacket, blue swim trunks, wrist tag, white cover booklet & cork sandals w/blue straps in cellophane bag, black wire stand, cardboard arm & leg inserts, near mint in box (ILLUS.) ......................................................... **90**

**Allan,** vinyl w/painted red hair, pink lips, straight legs, wearing orange sweatshirt w/necktie, striped swim trunks, green plastic swim fins & plastic face mask w/clear plastic shield, no box, near mint ........ **45**

**Bahr & Proschild bisque socket head baby,** marked "BP (in heart) 585 - G - 5," brown sleep eyes, feathered brows, open mouth w/two upper teeth, old blond mohair wig, bent-limb composition baby body, wearing new white baby dress w/lace trim & embroidered flowers, underclothing, socks & shoes, white lace bonnet, 14" (light wear) ............................... **350**

**Bahr & Proschild bisque socket head baby,** marked "B & P (in X) 0 - 585 - 7 - Germany," blue sleep eyes, feathered brows, open mouth w/accented lips & two upper teeth, synthetic blonde wig, bent-limb composition baby body, wearing old pink baby dress, slip & diaper, 15" (finish, on torso worn & pitted, some repaint, chip off hip socket) ......................... **375**

**Bahr & Proschild bisque socket head girl,** marked "297 dep.," set brown eyes, feathered brows, open mouth w/six upper teeth, pierced ears, old brown mohair wig, jointed wood & composition body, wearing antique red dotted Swiss dress, embroidered pinafore, lace-trimmed bonnet, slip, old red mesh socks & paper shoes, 11 1/2" (tiny flake at lower left eye, light wear on body, right lower arms & upper leg split & glued, right lower leg poorly glued to ball joint) ....... **350**

**Bahr & Proschild bisque socket head girl,** marked "B&P (in X) 0 - 604 - 5," set blue eyes, feathered brows, open-closed mouth w/two upper teeth, pale blonde mohair wig, jointed wood & composition body, wearing ecru wool & net dress, underclothing, old socks & shoes, 16" (eyes set, head not good fit in socket well, body repainted, upper arms don't match, replaced balls at elbows, thighs don't match) .................................................. **500**

*Rare #1 Ponytail Barbie*

**Barbie,** "#1 Ponytail Barbie," blonde hair in original topknot, blue eyeliner, red lips, nostril paint, finger & toe paint, straight legs, wearing black & white striped swimsuit, navy #1 open-toed shoes w/holes, pink pearl earrings, in box marked "T.M.," near mint w/only minor defects (ILLUS.) ....................................... **4,800**

*#2 Ponytail Barbie in Box*

**Barbie,** "#2 Ponytail Barbie," 1960, blonde hair reset into a ponytail, red lips, nostril paint, blue eyeliner, finger & toe paint, straight legs, wearing black & white

striped swimsuit, hoop earrings, pink cover Barbie booklet, black open-toed #1 shoes w/holes & white rimmed glasses w/blue lenses in replaced cello-phane bag, black pedestal stand w/black wire attaching to hole near outside edge, replaced cardboard box liner, near mint in box, bottom of hair flat, body overall white colored, booklet worn & written on, box worn & discolored (ILLUS.) ............... **2,100**

*#3 Ponytail Barbie*

**Barbie,** "#3 Ponytail Barbie," brunette hair w/original topknot, red lips, nostril paint, finger & toe paint, straight legs, wearing black & white striped swimsuit, hoop earrings, #1 black shoes w/holes, white-rimmed glasses w/blue lenses, in box marked "T.M.," w/black wire stand, near mint (ILLUS.) ................................................. **950**

**Barbie,** "American Girl Barbie," 1965, dark blonde hair, tan lips w/touch of peach, finger paint, bendable legs, nude (ends of eyebrows faded, several earring holes in both ears) ................................................. **345**

**Barbie,** "Bubblecut Barbie," 1961, brunette hair, coral lips, nostril paint, finger paint, toe paint, straight legs, wearing red nylon one-piece swimsuit, in box (eyebrows slightly faded, green dot on right ear) .................................................................. **120**

**Barbie,** "Bubblecut Barbie," 1961, white ginger, light pink lips, nostril, face, & toe paint, straight legs, black & white striped swim suit (oily face, torso scratched, edge of neck socket uneven) ...................... **175**

**Barbie,** "Bubblecut Barbie," blonde hair, red lips, nostril paint, oily face, finger & toe paint, straight legs, black & white swimsuit, in box w/black wire stand, cardboard neck & foot inserts, near mint (ILLUS. top next page) ................................. **375**

**Barbie,** "Happy Holidays Barbie," 1988, Special Edition, red gown w/silver accents, No. 1703, never removed from box (upper left box corner creased) ............ **575**

**Barbie,** "Happy Holidays Barbie," 1991, Special Edition, green velvet gown w/sequin accents, No. 1871, never removed from box (scuff on plastic window) ................................................................ **95**

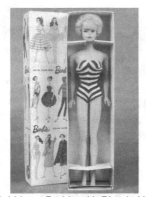

*Bubblecut Barbie with Blonde Hair*

*Fine French Belton Doll*

**Barbie,** "Jeweled Splendor Barbie," first in the F.A. O. Schwarz Signature Collection, No. 14061, box dated 1995, never removed from box ........................................ 125

**Barbie,** "Neptune Fantasy Barbie," Bob Mackie design, Fourth Limited Edition, #4248, 1992, mint in box w/cardboard shipping box, doll removed from box, insert loose, small tear on flap insert ............ 395

**Barbie,** "Theatre Elegance Barbie," 1994, No. 12077, Spiegel Limited Edition, never removed from box ............................... 55

**Barbie,** "Truly Scrumptious," 1969, blonde hair in original set w/pink ribbon bow, pink lips, rooted eyelashes, face & toe paint, straight legs, original outfit including hat w/ribbon, feather & flower accents & tulle tie, pale pink dress w/ribbon & flower sash (light soil on front of tulle overdress, missing shoes) .................... 200

**Barbie,** "Turn 'N Twist Barbie,"1967, blonde hair in original set w/orange hair ribbon, pink lips, cheek blush, rooted eyelashes, finger & toe paint, bendable legs, wearing original two-piece orange swimsuit & net cover up, mint condition, no box ........................................................ 210

**Barbie,** "Turn 'N Twist Barbie," 1967, blonde hair w/blue hair bow & held w/string attached to sides of head, pink lips, cheek blush, rooted eyelashes, bendable legs, wearing two-piece blue & white pak outfit w/hot pink belt & high tongue shoes, also includes Mrs. Beasley doll w/vinyl head, blue & white body & felt hands & feet, Package Date Collection, consignor notes on box "Beautiful Blues Barbie from Gift Set, in pak items. ONLY blue eye-shadow came from gift set," near mint in box (outfit worn, doll soiled) ........................................ 230

**Barbie,** "Twist n' Turn Barbie," dark auburn hair w/orange hair ribbon, pink lips, cheek blush, rooted eyelashes, finger & toe paint, bent legs, wearing two-piece swimsuit w/net cover-up, near mint .............. 225

**Barbie,** "Winter Princess Barbie," limited edition, No. 10655, box dated 1993, never removed from box ............................... 165

**Belton bisque socket head girl,** marked "106 -7," head w/three holes in flat spot on top, blue paperweight eyes, feathered brows, closed mouth w/accented lips & accent line between lips, pierced ears, original brown h.h. wig, jointed wood & composition body w/straight wrists, wooden upper arms & legs, wearing ecru embroidered dress, antique underclothing, socks & shoes, minor flaws & flakes, knee balls reglued, 15 1/2" (ILLUS.) ........................................ 1,400

**Bergmann (C.M.) bisque socket head girl,** marked "C.M. Bergmann - Waltershausen - Germany - 1916 - 3," brown sleep eyes w/real lashes, feathered brows, open mouth w/accented lips & four upper teeth, synthetic wig, jointed wood & composition body, redressed in blue taffeta jacket dress, underclothing, socks & shoes, 19" (slight inherent flaws, body repainted) ................................. 205

**Bergmann (C.M.) bisque socket head girl,** marked "S & H - C.M.B. 8," set brown eyes, molded & feathered brows, open mouth w/accented lips & four upper teeth, pierced ears, synthetic brown wig, jointed wood & composition body, redressed in new ecru lace dress trimmed w/blue riibon, new underclothing, socks & shoes, 20 1/2" (two firing lines at right earring hole, one finger repaired) ............................................... 250

**Bergmann (C.M.) bisque socket head girl,** marked "S & H - C.M.B. 10," brown sleep eyes, molded & feathered brows, open mouth w/accented lips & four upper teeth, pierced ears, original auburn mohair wig, jointed wood & composition body, wearing original factory chemise & pants, original black socks & shoes, 24" ...................................................... 425

**Candi,** "Midnight Blues Candi," No. 96/100, Afro-American doll w/black hair, red lips, royal blue satin dress w/glitter design, shoes, earrings, microphone, pink box w/plastic window signed by Mikelman ............ 18

*Early Covered Wagon China Head*

**China head lady,** covered wagon-style, molded black center-part hair w/ten vertical curls, painted brown eyes, red accent line, closed mouth, kid milliner's model-type body, china lower arms & lower legs w/molded & painted orange boots w/small heel, wearing possibly original white dress, lace-trimmed apron, original underclothing, body patched, kid split & glued at shoulder, 12 1/2" h. (ILLUS.) ......................................................... **575**

**China head lady,** painted brown eyes w/red accent line, single-stroke brows, closed mouth, black Flat Top hair style w/center part & fifteen vertical curls, cloth body w/kid lower arms, wearing antique red dress, antique underclothing, socks & handmade leather shoes, 21" (minor paint flake, light wear, body aged & mended,, arms probably not as old as body) ................................................. **575**

**China head lady w/blonde wig,** solid china dome w/black spot & original blonde mohair wig in curls, painted blue eyes w/red accent line, closed mouth, cloth body w/kid arms w/no hands, stitch-jointed hips & knees, wearing original ecru satin wedding dress, antique underclothing, stockings & tiny kid boots, 12 1/2" ......................................................... **725**

**China head man,** head w/pink tint & painted blue eyes w/red accent line, single-stroke brows, closed mouth, molded & painted dark brown hair w/dark accents, cloth body w/lower china arms, stitch-jointed hip & knees, wearing dark green wool jacket, plaid pants, underclothing, antique socks & shoes, 8 1/2" (tiny pinpoint flaw on bridge of nose) ......................................................... **400**

**Composition rabbit doll,** composition socket head, painted light blue eyes, feathered brows, closed mouth w/accent line between lips, five-piece composition body jointed at shoulders & hips, covered overall w/light rabbit fur & rabbit skin ears, composition hands & feet, 14" (light wear & soil, right toes broken & glued) ......................................................... **160**

**Dressel (Cuno & Otto) bisque socket head girl,** marked "? - Made in Germany - + - 1912.4," brown sleep eyes w/real lashes, feathered brows, open mouth w/accented lips & five upper teeth, original brown mohair wig, jointed wood & composition body, redressed in beige dress trimmed w/flowered lace, new underclothing, socks & shoes, 22" (chips at neck opening of head, repaint on upper torso, hands & left hip joint) .............. **225**

**Dressel (Cuno & Otto) bisque socket head girl,** marked "Germany - (winged COD design) - 1," blue sleep eyes, molded & feathered brows, open mouth w/four upper teeth, original blonde mohair wig in braids, kid body w/bisque lower arms & cloth lower legs, gussets at hips & knees, wearing old white dress w/pink velvet sash, antique underclothing, antique socks & shoes, straw hat, 22 1/2" (some rubs & inherent flaws, repair on left hip) ......................................... **235**

*E.D. French Girl Doll*

**E.D. bisque socket head girl,** marked "E 8 D Depose," bright blue paperweight eyes, feathered brows, open mouth w/accented lips & four upper teeth, pierced ears, antique brown h.h. wig w/long curls, jointed wood & composition body w/straight wrists, redressed in bright blue silk two-piece French-style outfit, antique underclothing, new socks, old shoes, minor inherent flaws, some wear, 20" (ILLUS.) ..................................... **1,150**

**Effanbee composition head "Harmonica Joe,"** marked on shoulder plate, painted blue eyes, single-stroke brows, open mouth w/rubber ring to hold harmonica, molded & painted blond hair, cloth body w/composition arms, jointed at shoulders & hips, rubber ball in torso to force air through harmonica when squeezed, wearing original tagged shirt, labeled overalls, cap w/pin, socks & shoes, rubber ring broken & glued, crack in finish on top of head, 14" (ILLUS. top next page) ..................................................... **400**

**Goodyear Rubber lady doll,** marked "Goodyears Pat. May 6, 1851 - Ext.

1865," rubber shoulder head w/painted blue eyes, single-stroke brows, closed mouth w/accent line between lips, molded & painted blonde hair w/exposed ears, cloth body w/leather lower arms & boots, wearing deep purple taffeta dress w/velvet bodice, antique underclothing, 20" (repaint on forehead, front left shoulder plate & bottom of rear shoulder plate, light flaking & touch-ups, small hole by left fingers, bottom of right foot patched) ....................................................... **425**

*Effanbee "Harmonica Joe" Doll*

**H. & Co. bisque socket head "Viola" girl,** marked "Made in Germany - Viola - H & Co. - 2/0," pale blue sleep eyes, single-stroke brows, open mouth w/four upper teeth, brown h.h. wig, jointed wood & composition body, wearing off-white dress, pants, socks & shoes, 16" (light wear, coloring uneven) ................................ **165**

**Handwerck (Max) bisque socket head girl,** marked "Max Handwerck - Germany - 7 1/2," blue sleep eyes, feathered brows, open mouth w/accented lips & four upper teeth, replaced synthetic blonde wig w/long curls, jointed wood & composition body, redressed in pink flowered dress, new pink underclothing, new socks & shoes, straw bonnet, 24" (some inherent flaws & tiny flakes, normal wear, inside dowel through finish on back) ................................................................ **315**

**Hertel, Schwab & Co. bisque socket head baby,** marked "151 - 12," set blue eyes, feathered brows, open mouth w/accented lips, molded tongue & four upper teeth, lightly molded & brush-stroked hair, composition bent-limb baby body, wearing antique white long baby dress w/embroidered trim, underclothing, 19" (minute flake at neck opening, body repainted & varnished, repair on toes) ............................................................. **400**

**Heubach (Ernst) bisque socket head baby,** marked "Heubach-Koppelsdorf - 300 - 2 - Germany," blue sleep eyes w/real lashes, feathered brows, open mouth w/four upper teeth, brown mohair wig, bent-limb composition baby body,

wearing pink lace-trimmed baby dress, diaper & booties, pink crocheted bonnet, 17" .............................................................. **225**

*Ernst Heubach Toddler Girl*

**Heubach (Ernst) bisque socket head girl,** marked "Heubach - Koppelsdorf 342 - 13/0 - Germany," brown sleep eyes w/real lashes, open mouth w/two upper teeth, original blonde mohair wig, chubby five-piece composition toddler body w/'starfish' hands, wearing original underclothing, embroidered suede jacket & matching bonnet, socks & shoes, antique dress & apron, 10" (ILLUS.) ....................................................... **800**

**Heubach (Gebruder) bisque shoulder head boy,** marked "1 Heubach (in square) 8724 Germany," pink tint head w/blue intaglio eyes, single-stroke brows, closed mouth, molded & painted brown hair, imitation kid body w/bisque lower arms, rivet joints at hips, gussets at knees, cloth lower legs, redressed in dark purple velvet suit, white embroidered shirts, socks & black shoes, 14"......... **425**

**Jumeau (E.) bisque socket head girl,** marked "X. 8," remnants of oval Jumeau label on back of body, brown paperweight eyes, heavy feathered brows, open mouth w/accented lips & six upper teeth, pierced ears, dark brown h.h. wig, jointed wood & composition Jumeau body, wearing pink silk dress w/lace overlay, antique underclothing , socks & pink cloth shoes, 19 1/2" (tiny fleck lower rim of eye, light soil & aging on body, hands repainted) ..................................... **1,700**

**Jumeau (E.) walking, kiss-throwing bisque socket head girl,** marked "8," large blue paperweight eyes, feathered brows, open mouth w/accented lips, six upper teeth, pierced ears, replaced dark brown h.h. wig, jointed wood & composition Jumeau body w/walking mechanism to head, right arm throws kisses, straight legs, wearing pale green flocked nylon dress w/lace trim, new underclothing, socks & shoes, replaced pull string for kissing mechanism, few hand flakes, 22" (ILLUS. top next page) ............................. **1,700**

*Walking - Kiss-throwing Jumeau*

**K\*R bisque head baby,** marked "K\*R - Simon & Halbig 121 - 42," blue sleep eyes, open mouth w/two upper teeth & tongue, blonde mohair wig, composition bent-limb baby body, wearing old white dotted Swiss baby dress & matching bonnet, underclothing & pink booties, 17" (light cheek rub, eyelids repainted) ........ **750**

**K\*R bisque socket head baby,** marked "K\*R - Simon & Halbig - 128 56," blue sleep eyes, feathered brows, open mouth w/two upper teeth, antique h.h. brown wig, composition bent-limb baby body, wearing antique white baby dress, underclothing, old booties, bonnet & wool embroidered cape, 22" (real lashes missing, body repainted, repair to lower right arm & hand) ...................................... **1,000**

*Large Kammer & Reinhardt Girl*

**K\*R bisque socket head girl,** marked "K\*R - Simon & Halbig - Germany - 117n - 55," blue flirty sleep eyes w/tin eyelids & real lashes, feathered brows, open mouth w/four upper teeth, replaced brown h.h. wig, jointed wood & composition body, wearing antique white eyelet dress, maroon velvet jacket, underclothing, new socks & shoes, body cut for non-working crier, finish on body yellowed, 21 1/2" (ILLUS.) ............................. **1,400**

*Large K\*R Girl Doll*

**K\*R bisque socket head girl,** marked "K\*R - Simon & Halbig - 117n - Germany 80," blue flirty sleep eyes w/real lashes, feathered brows, open mouth w/accented lips & four upper teeth, antiqued brown h.h. wig, jointed wood & composition flapper body w/high knee joints & working crier, wearing antique white dress, antique underclothing, socks & replaced shoes, minor flaws & wear, 30" (ILLUS.) .................................... **2,700**

*Kammer & Reinhardt Character Baby*

**K\*R (Kammer & Reinhardt) bisque socket head character baby,** marked "36 K\*R 100," solid dome head w/painted blue eyes, single-stroke brows, open-closed smiling mouth, lightly molded & brush-stroked blond hair, composition bent-limb baby body, wearing antique lace-trimmed christening gown, underclothing, socks & booties, flake at front of neck opening, minor firing imperfections, body repainted, cracks in torso finish, slight finger damage, 14" (ILLUS.) ......................................... **525**

**K (star) R bisque head character boy,** marked "114," 'Hans,' painted intaglio eyes, closed mouth, blond mohair wig, fully jointed composition body, wearing a period blue cotton sailor suit, black broad-brimmed sailor hat, blue romper suit, ca. 1909, 19 1/2" (some paint chipping on limbs, no shoes or socks) ............ **5,175**

*Bent-leg Ken in Box*

**Ken,** vinyl w/painted brunette hair, beige lips, bent legs, wearing blue jacket w/"K," red swim trunks, cork sandals w/red straps, black wire stand, in box, near mint w/some damages to box (ILLUS.) ........ **260**

*King Arthur Ken Doll*

**Ken,** vinyl w/painted brunette hair, beige lips, straight legs, wearing #0773 King Arthur outfit, silver lame hood, jacket & pants, red satin surcoat w/lion emblem, gold belt w/buckle, red plastic spurs, cardboard shield, plastic sword & scabbard, grey plastic helmet, wrist tag, no box, near mint (ILLUS.) ............................... **175**

**Kestner (J.D.) bisque head girl,** marked "4," set brown eyes, closed mouth w/accent line, replaced brown mohair wig, kid body w/cloth upper torso, bisque lower arms, gussets at elbows, hips & knees, wearing a beige plaid antique dress, antique underclothing, replaced socks & shoes, 14 1/2" (very faint forehead hairline, tiny eye flake, general wear & soil) .................................................. **325**

**Kestner (J.D.) bisque head "Hilda" baby,** marked "Q made in Germany 20 J.D.K. 237 ges. gesch. N 1070," blue sleep eyes, open mouth w/accented lips, two upper teeth, spring tongue, original brown mohair wig, bent-limb composition baby body, wearing an antique embroidered baby dress & bonnet, underclothing & knit booties, 25" ............. **2,700**

*Fine Kestner Character Girl*

**Kestner (J.D.) bisque socket head character girl,** marked "189" on head, "Germany 0 1/2" stamped in red on body, brown sleep eyes, closed mouth w/accent line, original brown mohair wig in coiled braids, jointed wood & composition child body, wearing antique two-piece outfit, antique socks, brown sandals, moisture damage on front of torso, shoulder & hip joints, fingers & toes, right thumb missing, 14 1/2" (ILLUS.) ....... **3,700**

*Kestner Mold 143 Girl Doll*

**Kestner (J.D.) bisque socket head girl,** marked "a. made in Germany - 4," blue sleep eyes, feathered brows, open mouth w/two upper teeth, original blonde mohair wig, jointed wood & composition body w/wooden upper legs, wearing antique white lace-trimmed dress, antique underclothing, socks & shoes, lace bonnet, upper arms repainted & possibly replaced, repair to left hip joint, 11 1/2" (ILLUS.) ........................................... **600**

**Kley & Hahn bisque socket head baby,** marked "Germany - K & H (in banner) - 158-2/0," brown sleep eyes, feathered brows, open-closed mouth w/two upper teeth, lightly molded & brush-stroked blond hair, composition bent-limb baby body, wearing old baby dress, under-clothing, booties, 10" (fine hairline at right rear of neck opening, light body wear) .............................................................. 220

**Kley & Hahn bisque socket head baby,** marked "K & H (in banner) Germany 166-9," set blue eyes, closed mouth w/accented lips, molded & painted blond hair, composition bent-limb baby body, wearing old baby romper & knit booties, 16" (tiny flake on black eye liner, minor firing line top of ear, eyes set, wear on fingers & toes) ......................................... 700

*Kley & Hahn Character Baby*

**Kley & Hahn bisque socket head character baby,** marked "Germany - K&H (in banner) 525 -2," blue intaglio eyes, frowning feathered brows, open-closed crying mouth w/accented lips, molded & brush-stroked brown hair, bent-limb composition baby body, wearing white antique-style baby romper w/lace trim, new booties, minor inherent specks & flaw, 11" (ILLUS.) ...................................... 325

**Lenci girl,** pressed felt head, painted side-glancing eyes, single-stroke brows, closed mouth, applied ears, original blonde mohair wig, cloth torso w/felt arms & legs, jointed at shoulders & hips, wearing original white felt shirt w/grey tie, grey shorts, white cotton socks, rust-colored shoes, coat & hat, printed paper tag w/"Bambola - Italia -Lenci, Torino - Made in Italy," 14" (slight fading, few moth holes in clothes) ................................. 525

**Lenci Pan,** pressed felt swivel head, painted side-glancing eyes, molded & painted single-stroke brows, painted upper lashes, open-closed smiling mouth w/eight upper teeth, large pointed applied ears, felt hair w/horns & flowers, felt body jointed at shoulders & hips, legs shaped like animal legs w/hair on hips, wearing original green felt jacket w/Lenci cloth label, white felt diaper

w/blue polka dots, 8" (slight discoloration & soil, few tiny moth holes in jacket) ............ 300

**Lenci Russian peasant man,** pressed felt character face w/painted light blue side-glancing eyes, molded & painted single-stroke brows, open-closed smiling mouth w/four upper teeth, original bright orange mohair wig, cloth body w/felt hands, wearing original felt outfit w/elaborate embroidery, brown felt pants, embroidered felt boots, brown felt hat, wooden vodka jug in right hand, unmarked, 9" (overall light fading & surface soil) ..................................................... 250

*Limoges Bisque Head Boy*

**Limoges bisque socket head boy,** marked "L (anchor) C - 0," set brown eyes, feathered brows, open mouth w/five upper teeth, brown short mohair wig, crude five-piece late French body, wearing original factory chemise under handmade clothing w/feather stitching, watch, velvet spats over shoes, wool beret, finish chipped on hands & fingers, 14" (ILLUS.)............................................... 325

**Mary Hoyer girl,** hard plastic jointed head & body, sleeping blue eyes, light red mohair wig, wearing hand-knit three-piece raspberry snow suit, 1950s, 14" ........ 259

**Midge,** 1963, brunette hair, pink lips w/painted teeth, face & toe paint, straight legs, original pink & red two-piece swim suit (faint pink stain on lower left leg) .......... 200

**Papier-maché head lady,** molded & painted curled hair pulled up, painted features, kid body w/wooden limbs, replaced period-style outfit, ca. 1830s, 9 1/2" (slight paint wear on head)................. 518

**Revalo bisque socket head baby,** marked "Germany - X (in circle) - Revalo - 22-4," blue sleep eyes w/real lashes, feathered brows, open mouth w/two painted upper teeth, replaced short brown wig, bent-limb composition baby body, wearing new lavender print dress & matching bonnet, underclothing, new socks & shoes, 14" (inherent ear chip, unfinished torso, right hand fingers repainted) ............. 235

**S.F.B.J. bisque socket head character boy,** marked "S.F.B.J. - 236 - Paris - 11," dark brown sleep eyes, feathered brows, open-closed laughing mouth w/two upper teeth, replaced dark brown wig, jointed wood & composition heavy toddler body, wearing antique wool sailor suit, white cap, replaced socks & shoes, 23" (old hairline at crown in back, light wear at joints, touch-up on finger) .............. **650**

*Rare S.F.B.J. Character Girl*

**S.F.B.J. (Société Francaise de Frabrication de Bebes & Jouets) bisque head character girl,** marked "S.F.B.J. 252 - Paris - 12," blue sleep eyes w/original lashes, closed pouty mouth, antique h.h. brown wig, jointed S.F.B.J. composition toddler body, wearing old low-waisted dress, underclothing, no socks or shoes, light rubs, minor repair & touch-up on right lower arm, left hand finger repaired, 27" (ILLUS.)............................................. **9,000**

**Schmidt (Franz) bisque socket head baby,** marked "F.S. & Co. - 1272/50 Z Deponiert," blue sleep eyes, feathered brows, pierced nostrils, open mouth w/two upper teeth, lightly molded & brush-stroked hair, composition bent-limb baby body, wearing colorful red, white & blue bold checked dress & matching hat, panties & booties, 19" (tiny flake on right of neck opening, body repainted, two fingers repaired) .................. **625**

**Schoenau & Hoffmeister bisque socket head girl,** marked "3 1/0 S PG (star) H 1909 - 2/0 Germany," blue sleep eyes w/real lashes, open mouth w/four upper teeth, brown h.h. wig, jointed wood & composition body, wearing original blue dress w/embroidery trim, original underclothing, socks & shoes, original paper dress tag reads "I can be dressed and undressed. My Darling I can sleep," unplayed-with, 15" ....................... **300**

**Schoenhut boy toddler,** marked "H.E. Schoenhut - (copyright) - 1913" on head label, wooden socket head w/painted blue eyes, closed mouth, original short brown mohair wig, spring-jointed wooden body w/joints at shoulders, elbows, wrists, hips, knees & ankles, wearing appropriate Schoenhut-style

short romper, underclothing, socks & old shoes, 11" (few light craze lines, brows missing, light soil) ........................................ **300**

**Schoenhut character girl,** all-wood w/blue intaglio eyes, open-closed mouth w/sober expression, blonde mohair wig, wearing original union suit & period cotton dress, early 20th c., 15" .......................... **489**

**Schoenhut character girl,** mark on back, all-wood, molded & painted face w/sober expression, original ash blonde mohair wig, wearing original cotton union suit, on metal stand, early 20th c., 19" (some paint loss on hands & arms)..................... **1,035**

**Schoenhut girl,** marked "Schoenhut Doll - Pat. Jan. 17, '11 U.S.A. & Foreign Countries," wooden socket head w/brown intaglio eyes, closed mouth, carved braids w/blue bow, wooden body jointed at shoulders, elbows, wrists, hips, knees & ankles, wearing blue & white checked gingham dress, white blouse, underclothing, socks & shoes, 16" (slight touch-ups, general body & limb wear, old factory repaint) ........................................ **1,900**

*All-original Shirley Temple Doll*

**Shirley Temple,** marked on back of composition head, hazel flirty eyes w/real lashes, open mouth w/six upper teeth, original mohair wig, five-piece composition child body, wearing tagged dress, original underclothing, socks & shoes, replaced hair ribbon, eyes cloudy w/edge rust, body w/few minor surface cracks & chips, 13" (ILLUS.) ....................... **675**

**Shirley Temple,** marked "20 (backwards) - Shirley Temple - Cop. Ideal N & T Co.," composition head w/hazel sleep eyes w/real lashes, feathered brows, open mouth w/six upper teeth, original blonde mohair wig, five-piece composition child body, wearing original pink pleated organdy dress, original underclothing, old replaced socks, original shoes, tag & original button on dress, 20" (light facial crazing, some lines on body, hair lightly reset) .......................................................... **700**

**Shirley Temple doll,** composition head & jointed composition body, original blonde mohair wig in original set, sleeping hazel eyes, open smiling mouth, wearing original light blue organdy dress w/pink ribbons, original underwear, shoes & socks & dress pin, 1934, 18" (eyes crazed, very minor paint checks on body, dress faded) ................................................................ **633**

**Simon & Halbig bisque head girl,** marked "S & H 1009 - DEP," blue sleep eyes, open mouth w/accented lips & four upper teeth, pierced ears, original brown h.h. wig, kid body w/bisque lower arms, gussets at hips & knees, wearing original handmade lace-trimmed white clothing, 20" (faint hairline on left side of neck, light soil on body & repairs at gussets) ............................................................... **275**

**Simon & Halbig bisque socket head girl,** marked "1078 - Germany - Simon & Halbig - S & H 6," blue sleep eyes w/real lashes, feathered brows, open mouth w/accented lips & four upper teeth, pierced ears, brown h.h. wig, jointed wood & composition body, wearing off-white flowered dress w/matching bonnet, underclothing, new stocking, leatherette shoes, 15 1/2" (very minor wear, lines & repair) .......................................................... **300**

*Large Simon & Halbig Girl Doll*

**Simon & Halbig bisque socket head girl,** marked "SH 1249 Dep - Germany 12," & "Santa" stamped on right hip, blue sleep eyes, feathered brows, open mouth w/accented lips & triangular accent on lower lip w/four upper teeth, pierced ears, brown h.h. wig, jointed wood & composition body, wearing pink eyelet-trimmed dress, matching slip, pants, socks & shoes, small wig pulls, light aging on body, 25" (ILLUS.) ....................... **1,200**

**Simon & Halbig bisque socket head girl,** marked "1339 - S & H - LL&S - 14," brown sleep eyes, molded & feathered brows, open mouth w/accented lips & four upper teeth, pierced ears, original blonde mohair wig w/long curls, heavy

jointed wood & composition body w/wooden upper arms, wearing antique pink silk dress w/net overdress, underclothing, antique socks, old pink leatherette shoes, 29" (needs socket head repaired, right hip ball & left foot repaired, hip touch-up, hands lightly repainted) ................................................. **1,200**

**Skipper,** titian hair w/metal headband & head wrapped w/a clear plastic band, pink lips, straight legs, wearing original red & white one-piece swimsuit, wrist tag, booklet w/red flat shoes & white plastic brush & comb in cellophane bag, gold stand, cardboard box inserts, in box (box & insert w/age discoloration & slight wear) ..................................................................... **145**

**Skipper,** vinyl, blonde hair w/metal headband, pink lips, nostril paint, straight legs, wearing red & white one-piece swimsuit, red flat shoes, in box w/gold wire stand & white cover booklet, near mint (headband discolored, box in good condition) ..................................................... **115**

**Skooter,** vinyl w/brunette hair in original set w/ribbon ties, pink lips, straight legs, wearing #1924 Tea Party yellow dress w/flower decals, yellow flat shoes, no box, near mint ................................................ **65**

**Steffie,** "Walk Lively Steffie," vinyl w/brunette hair, pink lips, cheek blush, rooted eyelashes, bent leg, wearing print nylon jumpsuit, wrist tag, accessories, never removed from box ....................................... **250**

*Steiner Girl with Walking Mechanism*

**Steiner "Premier Pas" bisque head girl,** marked "A-15 Paris," stamped on back of head in red "Le Parisien," deep blue sleep eyes w/real lashes, feathered brows, open smiling mouth w/accented lips & seven upper teeth, pierced ears, brown h.h. wig, jointed composition Steiner body w/key-wind walking mechanism & non-working crier, wearing antique white lace-trimmed dress, slip, socks & antique high-button shoes, tiny firing lines, body repainted, replaced white kid pants, 23 1/2" (ILLUS.) ............... **1,050**

**Walkure bisque socket head girl,** marked "5 1/2 - Walkure - Germany," brown sleep eyes, molded & feathered brows, open mouth w/accented lips & four upper teeth, pierced ears, antique brown h.h. wig, jointed wood & composition body, wearing lovely antique white dress, antique underclothing, replaced socks & shoes, 27" (small flakes at earring holes, tiny flakes at left eye rim, normal body wear)............................................. **425**

**Wax turned-shoulder head boy,** stationary blue glass eyes, closed mouth, cloth body, wax over composition arms & legs w/molded socks & shoes, wearing dove grey wool flannel suit & glengarry, white wool flannel sailor suit & hat w/blue trim, ca. 1870s, 26 1/2" (head wax badly damaged, wig missing, some moth damage on clothes)........................................... **518**

# EPERGNES

*Victorian Cased Glass Epergne*

**Cased glass,** single lily, the footed squatty bulbous bowl w/a wide rolled jack-in-the-pulpit rim, the exterior in white enameled w/orange trumpet flowers on leafy green stems, the interior in deep pink enameled w/reddish flower vines, a tall central trumpet-form jack-in-the-pulpit vase w/similarly decorated white exterior & pink interior, late 19th c., 4 1/8" d., 5 1/2" h. (ILLUS.)....................................... **$175**

**Cased glass,** three-lily, pink & white ruffled bowl w/heavy wire holder decorated w/figural strawberries & leaves winding around the 10" h. lillies, 11" d., 19" h. ......... **350**

*Cranberry Epergne with Two Baskets*

**Cranberry & clear glass,** a tall central tree trunk-form cranberry vase w/clear applied spreading root-form base & applied rigaree around the neck & the rim, a long hook-ended applied clear handle at each side suspending a trumpet flower-form cranberry basket w/an applied clear handle & spiraling applied clear rigaree, attributed to Thomas Webb, late 19th c., 10 1/2" h. (ILLUS.)......... **540**

**Cranberry & clear glass,** three-lily, a ruffled round cranberry dished base w/similarly molded vase-form arms w/three clear twist-turned decorative arms, early 20th c., 23" h. ............................................... **633**

**Cranberry glass,** three-lily, a large upright central lily w/a flared & ruffled top & the sides applied w/spiraling clear rigaree, the smaller angled side lilies also wrapped w/rigaree, a tall slender clear twisted staff-form hook fitted in the front, all fitted into an ornate silver plate holder base, late 19th c., 19 1/2" h.......................... **825**

*Fine Cut Glass & Sheffield Epergne*

**Cut glass & Sheffield plate,** the ornate Sheffield plate stand w/a scroll-footed & trimmed cross-form base supporting a ring-turned section below a large reeded & acanthus leaf-trimmed baluster-form pedestal supporting a wide pierced leafy scroll top basket, the base issuing four long slender scrolling upturned arms each ending in a support ring, a large clear bowl at the top cut w/panels of strawberry diamond & fans alternating w/narrow rounded arches w/diamond point cutting, matching design on the four smaller cut bowls, slight rosing to silver, base repair, some edge wear on bowls, England, early 19th c., 16" h. (ILLUS.)..................................................... **2,530**

**Gilt metal & pink opalescent glass,** three-lily, a round ribbed & ringed tapering pink opalescent glass foot supporting a tall ornate pierced scrolling gilt-metal standard w/two lower sockets issuing large upturned pink opalescent lily-form vases w/widely flaring, rolled & ruffled rims, another upright tall matching trumpet-form vase at the top, probably Europe, late 19th c., 29" (minor base chips).......................................................... **550**

**Silver plate & glass,** single lily, figural cupid holding crystal etched & frosted vase, embossed scenic pedestal w/frol-

icking cupids, Meriden Silver Plate Co.,
late 19th c.......................................................... 175

*Ornate Sterling Silver Epergne*

**Sterling silver,** on an openwork footed
conical foot supporting a central standard w/scrolls, a paneled dome & scalloped, pierced flanges below a standing
classical female at the top below a wide
flaring & ringed bowl w/a rolled leaf-band
rim, the lower standard flanked by two
oval side dishes headed by female
masks, Wood & Hughes, New York,
New York, ca. 1870, 22" h. (ILLUS.) ......... **5,750**
**Yellow glass,** 11-lily, a large pale yellow
trumpet-shaped central vase surrounded
by ten smaller vases on a round ruffled
base, Venice, Italy, early 20th c.,
19 1/2" h. ...................................................... **1,150**

# FARM COLLECTIBLES

*Hay Knife*

**Cant hook,** ice house, red, ice pike w/right
angle hook, Gifford-Wood, ca. 1900s,
5'................................................................ **$30-60**
**Corn knife,** farmer-made, sharpened hoe
on axe handle, ca. 1850s, 24 to 36" l ......... **5-15**
**Corn sheller,** farmer-made from kit, blacksmith nails in wooden construction, ca.
1800-1900, 3' d. ...................................... **50-250**

**Corn sheller,** farmer-made, red paint, hand
operated, ca. 1800-1900, 12 x 18" w/top
& bottom plates ....................................... **50-200**
**Dung hoe,** 4-tang, Ames, ca. 1800s ............. **10-25**
**Hay knife,** diamond, changeable mower
bar teeth, ca. 1850s (ILLUS.) ................... **25-75**

*Orthopedic Horseshoe*

**Horseshoe,** orthopedic, farrier-made, dou-
ble bar lift & front leg support, 1800s
(ILLUS.)................................................. **100-300**
**Horseshoe calks,** Giant Grip, stamped
"G," ca. 1850-1998, in original box, 1/2
to 1", the set (many newer ones now in
use are of no collector value) ..................... **5-25**
**Ox cart,** single axle, corn-blasted, ca.
1750-1850, small .................................. **450-500**
**Plow,** hand style, one-horse, Ames,
unpainted w/slight rust, ca. 1800s........... **50-250**
**Plow,** side hill, hand, one-horse,
unpainted, ca. 1800s.............................. **50-250**
**Ropemaker,** homemade, wooden frame
head & tail, 3-strand, hand-crank style
w/connecting rod, usable, 2' w., 4' h. ...... **75-150**

*Simonds Ice Saw*

**Saw,** ice, farmer's wood case, no rust,
Simonds w/all printing readable, ca.
1850s, 5 1/2' (ILLUS.) ............................ **50-150**
**Saw,** ice, minimal rust, w/original red
wooden case, legible mark of Gifford-
Wood, ca. 1900s, usable condition, 4'....... **25-50**
**Saw,** two-man, wide blade, 5 TPI, for tim-
ber framing, w/original wooden protecting case, ca. 1700-1900, 6' (price will
depend on degree of rust) ..................... **200-500**
**Shaving horse,** wooden w/metal
clamp, ca. 1700-1900, 5' ................................. **75**
**Shovel,** sieve, standard scoop w/numerous
1" holes, short D-handle for clearing ice
channel, ca. 1900s ................................... **25-50**
**Wagon,** work, wide steel wheels, green,
unmarked, 5 x 8'................................... **200-500**
**Wheelbarrow,** child's, wood, light weight
w/wooden wheel, metal shod, removable
sides, usable, ca. 1700-1900 .................. **50-150**
**Windmill weight,** cast iron, cast in the form
of a bob-tail horse, embossed mark no.
"58," late 19th-early 20th c., 17 1/2" w.,
21 1/2" h. (repaint)....................................... **345**
**Windmill weight,** cast iron, cast in the form
of a full-tailed rooster, black paint w/red
comb & wattle, late 19th-early 20th c.,
16 1/2" w., 15 1/2" h. (paint losses).............. **748**
**Windmill weight,** cast iron, cast in the form
of a full-tailed rooster, some white paint,

late 19th-early 20th c., 17" w., 15 1/2" h. (paint loss, corrosion) .................................. **978**

**Windmill weight,** cast iron, cast in the form of a horse standing on a plinth, embossed mark no. "58," traces of white & black paint, late 19th-early 20th c., 17 1/2" w., 18" h. (corrosion, paint losses) .......................................................... **345**

**Windmill weight,** cast iron, cast in the form of a rainbow-tail rooster, traces of red comb & wattle, in a wooden base, late 19th-early 20th c., 17" w., 19" h. ............... **1,380**

**Windmill weight,** cast iron, cast in the form of a red rooster, late 19th-early 20th c., 17" w., 19" h. (repaint)................................. **575**

**Windmill weight,** cast iron, cast in the form of a rooster, red & white paint, late 19th-early 20th c., 17" w., 19" h. (corrosion, repaint) ......................................................... **460**

**Winnower,** fanning mill, red w/complete set of screens, Boston, ca. 1800s ......... **100-300**

# FIRE FIGHTING COLLECTIBLES

**Fire bucket,** painted leather, cylindrical, inscribed "Waltham Fire Club 1824 J. Hastings" in gilt on a dark green ground w/red band & interior, 13" h. (handle missing, paint loss & abrasion) ................. **$460**

**Fire bucket,** painted leather, cylindrical w/black ground inscribed in yellow "B-Stone," red rim band & interior, black strap handle, 19th c., 14 3/4" h. (paint loss & abrasion) .......................................... **978**

*Fire Bucket Marked "Garibaldi"*

**Fire bucket,** painted leather, cylindrical w/leather handle, old decoration of a scrolled banner w/"Garibaldi" in gold, green & black on a red ground, minor wear, 19th c., 13" h. plus handle (ILLUS.)..................................................... **3,080**

**Fire bucket,** painted leather, green tapered bucket w/red rim & swing handle, inscribed "1809" above joined hands & two white banners inscribed "Mutual Fire Society" & "Israel Whiton" surrounded by gilt scrolling foliage, back stamped "C. LINCOLN" twice, 1809, 13 1/4" h. (handle repaired on one side) .......................... **8,050**

**Fire bucket,** painted leather, swelled cylindrical form, black ground decorated in gilt w/inscription "City of Boston Ward No. 11 Fireman No. 3 1826," black interior, early 19th c., 13 1/4" h. (handle missing, paint loss & abrasion) ................. **1,495**

*Early Decorated Fire Buckets*

**Fire buckets,** painted leather w/leather strap handles, each inscribed "Semper Paratus L.T. Jackson" in gilt in a leafy scroll decorated black cartouche on a red ground, black bands & interior, paint wear & abrasions, 19th c., 15 1/2" h., pr. (ILLUS.)..................................................... **7,475**

**Fire extinguisher,** brass & copper, soda & acid-type, "Badgers," 2 1/2 gal. ..................... **35**

*Badger & Empire Extinguisher*

**Fire extinguisher,** brass & copper, soda & acid-type, "Badgers," applied label, pony-size (ILLUS.) ....................................... **100**

**Fire hat,** parade-type, painted leather, green hat painted on front w/a spread-winged eagle clutching a chain in its beak attached to a harp, a laurel branch & cluster of arrows, below a red & gold banner inscribed "HIBERNIA," the back dated "1752," the top inscribed "1" within circle, inside inscribed "S.M.," underside of brim painted red, 19th c., 14 3/8" l., 6 1/4" h. ................................................. **14,950**

**Fire mark,** gilded cast iron, half-round w/a rectangular back w/molded rim enclosing two gilded shaking hands above the raised gilded date "1794," the reverse w/the revised numbers 71, America or Europe, 19th c., 9 1/2 x 10 1/2"................... **518**

**Fire trumpet,** sheet metal, tapered trumpet w/oval mouthpiece, fitted w/two rings for hanging, painted red & gold, 19th c., 16 1/4" l (some dents & imperfections) ........ **977**

**Helmet,** leather lobed hat surmounted by a gilt eagle's head, front applied w/raised lettering "C P & L CO," the brim tooled w/scrolling vine, inside stamped "John Olson Co., 183 Grand St. NY City," 19th c., 14" l., 9 1/8" h. .......................................... **115**

**Lantern,** brass or brass w/nickel plating, "Dietz Fire King," complete & excellent condition ...................................................... **280**

**Lantern,** brass or brass w/nickel plating, "Dietz Queen," hinged wire cage, complete & excellent condition ........................... **800**

**Lantern,** brass or brass w/nickel plating, "Dietz Queen," square shoulder, slideover cage, complete & excellent condition ................................................................... **750**

**Lantern,** steel, "Dietz Fire King," also marked "American LaFrance & Foamite Co.," scarce................................................. **345**

**Lantern,** steel, "Dietz Fire King," coppercovered tank.......................................... **185-210**

**Nozzles for hoses,** brass "standpipe" style, tapering cylinder, hotel & school standpipe types without shut-offs ............. **15-25**

# FIREARMS

*Nineteenth Century Blunderbus*

**Blunderbus,** flintlock model w/walnut stock, short barrel w/flared end, England, ca. 1840 (ILLUS.)........................ **$600**

**Cane gun,** percussion "Days Pat." model, walnut grip, 28" l. round barrel w/worn brown finish, early 19th c., overall 34 1/2" l. (age cracks, chip on the toe)........ **523**

**Derringer,** Moore's Patent #1, .41 caliber, ornate scrollwork on grip, replated barrel w/traces of original signature, 4 7/8" l. ......... **303**

*William Marston Derringer*

**Derringer,** William Marston .32 caliber, three-barrel, brass frame w/rosewood grips, bold signature, spots of pitting, 4" l. barrels, overall 7" l. (ILLUS.) ................. **550**

**Long rifle,** full-stock in curly maple w/engraved patch box & pierced heart on finial, four nickel silver inlays including a star cheek piece, brass hardware w/side plate, old dark finish w/restoration, 36" l. barrel signed "E.M.G.," lock marked "Leman," overall 51" l. ..................... **550**

**Long rifle,** percussion, maple stock w/some figure, Indian head inlay on cheek piece, mellow finish w/brass patchbox & added side plate, signed "L. Coon," probably Levi Coon, Jr., Ithaca, New York, 49" l. (muzzle end shortened)..... **770**

**Long rifle,** percussion-type, old black finish w/pierced & engraved patchbox, silver half-moon & thumbpiece, brass hardware & nose cap replaced, signed "Vanmetre," possibly J.W. Van Metre, Ross County, Ohio, 19th c., overall 54" l. (age cracks)...................................................... **1,375**

*Civil War Era Harper's Ferry Musket*

**Musket,** Harper's Ferry model, .69 caliber, curly walnut stock, Civil War era (ILLUS. of part)...................................................... **1,300**

**Musket,** Maynard percussion conversion, Remington Arms, stock w/old dark patina, local w/legible signature w/"U.S." & "1858," 42" l. barrel w/"P" proof stamp & partial eagle head, sold w/bayonet, overall 57 1/2" l. (missing rear sight & minor age crack behind lock) ...................... **935**

**Musket,** Springfield cadet Model 1851, used by the "Rockingham Grays" of the Stonewall Brigade ...................................... **2,600**

**Musket w/bayonet,** 1853 British Enfield model, three-band-type, w/long-range rear sight, lock marked "Tower 1857," 55 1/8" l. (one band replaced, restoration) ................................................................. **908**

**Pistol,** Acier Fondu double-barrel teat fire model, frame w/well executed engraving & crosshatching, relief-carved grips w/leaf detail & vining, 3 3/8" l. steel barrels, Serial Number 3304, overall 7 3/4" l. ................................................... **303**

**Pistol,** flintlock, walnut stock w/brass hardware & horn nose cap, 8 1/4" l. octagonal to round barrel w/dark surface w/pitting, lock bolts stripped, Europe, 19th c., overall 13 1/2" l................................ **330**

**Pistol,** pepperbox-style, six-shot, scroll engraving on frame, by Allen & Thurber, 4 1/4" l. barrel, overall 8 3/8" l. .................... **440**

**Pistol,** percussion, back-action lock, carved wood grip w/scrollwork & checkering, 7 1/2" l. octagonal barrel in Damascus steel, engraved trigger guard &

cap, signed "H.K. Orte (?) in Coeln," early 19th c., overall 13 3/4" l. (safety broken) .......... 358

**Pistol,** percussion martial-type, converted from flintlock, stock w/good patina & stabilized cracks in wrist, 9" round barrel stamped "U.S.," iron hardware & one barrel band, unsigned, 15" l. (burn mark near lock) .......... 468

**Pistol,** percussion single-shot model, frame engraved "Brayton C.---ard," 2 3/4" screw barrel w/blued finish .......... 138

**Pistol,** protector palm model, Chicago Firearms Co. .......... 375

**Pistol,** Remington 1871 Army rolling block model, clear "CRS" inspector's marks on grip, some case colors remaining on frame, 8" round barrel w/dark brown finish, overall 12 1/4" l. .......... 550

**Pistol,** Sharps four-shot pepper box, .32 cal., Model 4A w/2 1/2" l. barrels, overall good condition w/traces of bluing & bold signature w/patent date, light grey finish on metal .......... 385

**Pistols,** English percussion-type, double-barreled, checkered grips, engraved frames & compartments in grip, signed "Lang," consecutive serial numbers, 19th c., 8 1/2" l., pr. .......... 1,210

**Revolver,** .22 caliber knuckle duster-type, engraved brass frame w/traces of gilding, by J. Reid, cylinder & hammer replated .......... 413

**Revolver,** .31 caliber pocket-model, bold cylinder w/scene of deer & ducks, by Allen & Wheelock, 6" l. (metal carefully cleaned, grips worn) .......... 110

**Revolver,** Colt 1903 pocket model, .32 cal. w/metal box & label .......... 400

**Revolver,** Colt 1917 U.S. Army double action model, .45 cal. .......... 600

*Colt Model 1849 Pocket Revolver*

**Revolver,** Colt Model 1849 pocket-style, .31 caliber, six-shot cylinder w/engraved stagecoach scene, marked "Colt's Patent 12059," back strap engraved "Capt. R.B. Arms CoB. 16th Regt. VT. Vol.," wooden grips (ILLUS.) .......... 6,325

*Cased Colt Model 1849 Revolver*

**Revolver,** Colt Model 1849 revolver, pocket-model, mahogany grips, left side of frame w/Colt name & address, cylinder engraved w/a scene of a stagecoach holdup, 4" l. barrel, in a mahogany case including a "Massachusetts Arms Company" brass powder flask, bronze Colts patent bullet mold, a box of caps & the printed directions, box 5 3/4 x 10", the set (ILLUS.) .......... 9,200

**Rifle,** flintlock, cherry stock w/dark finish & checkerboard wrist, brass hardware engraved buttplate & trigger guard w/pineapple finial, lock marked "T. Ketland & Co.," New England, overall 58 1/2" l. (chips along top edge of barrel channel in one section w/restoration) .......... 1,210

**Rifle,** Marlin-Ballard #2 sporting-type, .32 caliber, walnut butt stock w/some figure, good signature & condition, 28" l. octagonal reblued barrel, later vernier tang sight added, 43 1/4" l. .......... 220

**Rifle,** percussion half-stock, walnut stock w/brass hardware w/a "Golcher" lock, 36" l. barrel, stock varnished, overall 53 1/2" l. (minor age cracks) .......... 330

**Rifle,** percussion half-stock, well-made w/walnut stock w/beaver tail cheek piece, engraved German silver cap w/designs of a squirrel & eagle, 30" l. octagonal barrel w/silver bands & hook breech w/bright finish, overall 48" l. .......... 1,540

**Rifle,** percussion over-and-under style, .45 caliber, walnut stock w/eagle & shield cheek piece, signed "J. Harder & Son, Lock Haven, Pa.," octagonal barrels, .45 caliber on top & smooth bore for shot below, overall 48" l. .......... 935

**Rifle,** revolving percussion underhammer model, .52 caliber six-short cylinder, 32" l. part-round - part octagonal barrel, figured walnut stocks w/Gothic design brass patchbox, attributed to Elijah Jaquith, Brattleboro, Vermont, ca. 1830 (hammer possibly replaced, some corrosion, split in stock behind the cylinder) .......... 6,900

*Early Austrian Wheel Lock Rifle*

**Rifle,** wheel lock model, walnut stock, barrel signed "Joseph Shachner - Innsbruck," w/foliate engraved lock signed "I.G.D.," carved stock, the opposite side inlaid w/brass foliate & bird designs, Austria, 17th c., barrel 34 3/8" l. (ILLUS.).. 2,875

**Rifle,** Winchester 1873, .44 caliber, case colors on buttplate & trigger, 24" l. blued octagonal barrel, overall 43" l. .......... 5,940

**Rifle,** Winchester Model 1873 .......... 1,200

**Rifle,** Winchester Model 1894 .......... 850

# FIREPLACE & HEARTH ITEMS

*Ornate Arts & Crafts Andirons*

**Andirons,** Arts & Crafts style, wrought iron & brass, an obelisk-form upright w/a bulbous four-sided finial above a domed base raised on short legs w/domed feet, a long crossbar w/central shield device, decorated overall w/large hammered brass tacks & ball finials, early 20th c., 31 1/2 x 35", 27" h., pr. (ILLUS.) ............. **$1,955**

**Andirons,** bell metal, Federal style, belted ball-top finial on short tapering shaft on square plinths w/engraved decoration, conforming log stops, spurred legs w/ball-and-claw feet, early 19th c., 18" h., pr. ................................................ **1,610**

**Andirons,** bell-metal & wrought-iron, Federal style, a pointed double ball finial above a large banded sphere on a ring-turned post on a square plinth on arched spurred legs w/claw-and-ball feet, probably New York, ca. 1800, 19 1/2" h., pr. (lacking log stops)` ................................... **1,150**

**Andirons,** brass, Federal style, urn finials above tall columns & square plinths on spurred cabriole legs & ball-and-claw feet, straight stepped iron billet bars, probably Philadelphia, ca. 1780-1810, 26" h., pr. (missing brass billet bar covers) ........................................................... **1,955**

*Early Federal Brass Andirons*

**Andirons,** brass, Federal style, urn-shaped finials above columnar shafts on a square plinth above arched spurred legs w/slipper feet, Philadelphia, late 18th c., 25 1/2" h., pr. (ILLUS.) ............................. **1,380**

*Brass & Iron Knife-blade Andiron*

**Andirons,** brass & iron, knife blade-type, a brass urn finial above a flattened iron shaft swelled at the bottom & resting on the iron log bar & arched slender iron legs w/penny feet, signed "J.C.," attributed to John Clark, American, late 18th c., 18 1/2" h. (ILLUS. of one) ..................... **1,035**

*Grotesque Face Andiron*

**Andirons,** cast iron, figural, a tall heavy upright w/a serrated surface & scrolled ball finials above the front base w/a grotesque lion face flanked by batwings & raised on claw-and-ball feet, original two-tone bronze finish, early 20th c., 21" h., pr. (ILLUS. of one) ........................... **275**

*Duck-shaped Andirons*

**Andirons,** cast iron, figural, modeled as a large duck on straight legs w/webbed feet, heavy curved-down log bar, late 19th c., minor surface rust, 24 1/2" l., 9 3/4" h., pr. (ILLUS.) ................................. **1,380**

**Andirons,** wrought iron & brass, penny feet & arched iron front legs centered by an iron upright w/a brass medallion near the bottom & a brass acorn finial at the top, 19th c., 18" h., pr. (rods w/some heat damage, one rivet polished) ......................... 385

**Andirons,** wrought iron, gooseneck-type, rectanulgar stamp on the arched legs, marked by E.W. Wade, American, 19th c., 17" h., pr. ...................................... 316

**Bellows,** turtle-back style, painted wood, h.p. gold & deep red four-point star in diamond-shaped medallion surrounded by dark gold stylized leaves & blossoms on a creamy yellow ground w/amber trim, long brass nozzle, ca. 1840 (ILLUS. right) ...................................... 180

*Two Early Painted Bellows*

**Bellows,** turtle-back style, painted wood, large h.p. stylized pomegranate design in red w/long green leaves against an amber ground w/black trim, long brass nozzle, 19th c. (ILLUS. left) ........................... 180

**Bellows,** turtle-back style, painted wood & leather, original red paint w/a design of a cornucopia in black, gold & green, brass nozzle, old releathering, 18" l. (wear, touch-up repair) ............................................ 385

**Fireboard,** painted & decorated, diamond & rosette border framing three recessed geometric carved panels centering foliate scrolled designs painted in black, dark green, maroon & yellow, possibly New England, last quarter 19th c., 38 x 39" (minor imperfections) .................... 863

**Fireplace fender,** brass & iron, curved ends & round iron uprights, brass molding, finials & three bun feet, America or England, 19th c., 9 1/4 x 48", overall 9" h. (small losses, imperfections) ............... 288

**Fireplace fender,** brass & wire, a narrow brass upper rail w/square corners & a bowed center section above wire side composed of thin vertical bands, iron base plate, America or England, late 18th - early 19th c., 14 1/2 x 29 3/4", 9 1/2" h. ................................................. 1,495

**Fireplace fender,** brass & wire, the slender curved brass top rail above iron braces & wire bars trimmed w/wire scrolls, American or English, late 18th - early 19th c., 16 1/4 x 39 3/4", 17 3/4" h. (ILLUS.) ....................................................... 1,495

*Early Brass & Wire Fireplace Fender*

**Fireplace fender,** brass & wrought iron, brass frame w/ball-shaped finials & pierced wrought iron resting on paw feet, 42" l., 12" h. (one foot missing) ................... 448

# FISHING COLLECTIBLES

## BOOKS & PAPER ITEMS

**Book,** "The Cascapedia Club," 1920, by F. Gray Griswold, signed by author, Plimpton Press, Norwood, MA, 27 pp. ....... $154

**Catalog,** "Heddon Catalog," 1935, dealer catalog, 28 pp. (light stain on top front cover) ................................................................ 187

**Catalog,** "Pflueger," No. 146, © 1926, 120 pp., tackle ............................................................. 220

**Catalog,** "Pflueger's Tips on Tackle," 1919, 112 pp. (small tear on cover) ...................... 550

**Catalog,** "The Creek Chub Bait Co.," 1942, "Catch More Fish" above man holding stringer of fish, 12 pp. (some creasing) ........ 248

## LURES

**Heddon "Expert,"** four-hook style, slim body w/rimmed brass cups, brass tail cap, aluminum-silver finish w/painted red collar, 1904, possibly repainted, 4 3/8" l. ..... 550

**Heddon "Killer,"** No. 450, marked props, brass cups & two belly weights, aluminum finish, 2 5/8" l. ...................................... 248

**James (W.H.),** spinning fish-shaped squid bait, marked "W.H. James - Pat'd Jan. 27, 1874," 2" l. ................................................ 165

*Charles Lane Wagtail Wobbler Lure*

**Lane (Chas. W.),** fat-bodied wagtail wobbler w/green back & gold scale finish, two long h.p. gill marks, wire leader, metal swinging tail, marked "Chas. W. Lane - Ptd. 3-16-02, Madrid N.Y.," 2 3/4" l. (ILLUS.) .......................................... 220

## REELS

**Abbey & Imbrie,** salmon, "Pat. Jan. 17, 82," German silver & hard rubber, "bullet" handle grasp, double-pillar line guides & elaborate conical shaft, end play adjustment w/knurled locking ring, 1 7/8" w., 4 1/4" d. ...................................... 220

**Haskell (Robert W.),** trout, click-switch type, back engraved "Robert W. Haskell, Naples, Maine, USA - Maker 1994-1," exposed front rim, brass foot & wooden handle, includes original cylindrical wooden case, all handmade, 7/8" w., 3" d. ............................................................ **275**

**Leonard (H.L.),** trout, German silver & bronze, raised pillar, pat. Jan. 12, 1877, 1" w., 2 3/8" d. ........................................ **3,575**

**Mills (Wm.) & Son,** trout, made by Julius Vom Hofe, nickel plating, 1/0 size, 1" w., 2 7/8" d. ......................................................... **330**

**Orvis (C.F.),** trout, click-type, nickel plating, pat. 1874, 3rd model, Manchester, VT, 1/2" w., 2 3/4" d. .................................. **660**

**Shakespears Model No. FE1745** .................... **40**

**Shakespears No. 2080 "Sea Wonder,"** Model FB.......................................................... **100**

**Shakespears "Wonder Wheel,"** No. 1810 ....... **50**

**Silver King No. 250** ......................................... **50**

**Talbot (Wm. H.),** trout, Model No. 100, Serial No. 4319, "Ben Hur," German silver, Abercrombie & Fitch Co., New York, 1" w., 2 1/8" d. ...................................... **4,400**

**Vom Hofe (Edward)** salmon, German silver & hard rubber, marked "Edward Vom Hofe Maker & Patentee, Fulton St. N.Y. Pat'd Sept. 2, 79," "Pat. Jan 23, 83" on rear sliding cover & "J.P." engraved on rim, 6/0 size, 1 7/8" w., 4 1/4" d................. **1,738**

**Vom Hofe (Julius),** trout, pat. Oct. 8, 1889, German silver w/aluminum-raised pillar plates & spool ends, 2/0 size, 1" w., 2 3/8" d. ......................................................... **880**

**Walker (A.L.),** fly, click-type w/six-position drag, Model TR-4, includes original cloth bag, 1" w., 3 1/4" d. .................................... **1,045**

## RODS

**Gillum (H.S.),** fly, "Pinky," No. 1-790, includes original bag & tube, rod professionally & authentically refurbished, 2 pc., 8' 9" l....................................................... **1,100**

**Leonard,** trout, Duracane No. 654-2831, original bag & labeled tube, 2 pc., 6 1/2' l....................................................... **1,430**

**Orvis (C.F.),** trout, fly type, Eggleston's 1882 patent spring reel seat marking & lateral six strip cork handle, butt cap marked "Orvis Co., Maker, Manchester, VT.," German silver parts, original bag & wooden tube, 3 pc., 9' l. .............................. **660**

**Thomas & Thomas,** "Fountainhead" Heritage Limited Edition, No. 9 of 20 rods, 1983, 3 pc., 7 1/2' l. .................................. **3,410**

**Thomas & Thomas,** Sans Noeud Heritage Limited Edition, No. 9 of 20 rods, nodeless construction, original bag & tube, 1981, 2 pc., 7 1/2' l. ................................. **3,300**

## MISCELLANEOUS

**Creel,** marked "Hardy Brothers Ltd. Alnwick" on ivorine tag, whole reed construction w/slant front lid, original peg & twisted loop latch, original hinges, golden brown patina (ILLUS. top next column) ........................................................ **330**

*Whole Reed Creel*

**Creel,** woven wicker, deep tapering sides, flat hinged cover w/leather hasp, canvas shoulder strap, 13 1/2" l. (hasp old replacement, wear, damage) ......................... **99**

*Early Fishing Derby Trophy Flask*

**Flask,** pocket-type, advertising-type, engraved brass w/hinged cap, lower half engraved w/a fish & "4th of July Derby 1925 - Heddon's of Dowagiac" (ILLUS.) ... **1,045**

*Hand-crafted Fly Tying Chest*

**Fly tying chest,** hand-crafted w/cherry case, lift top revealing eleven oak-faced drawers w/small brass pulls, pull-down front & metal reinforced corners, 10 x 13 1/2 x 16" (ILLUS.)............................ **330**

**Minnow bucket,** stenciled "Falls City Splendid Minnow Bucket" in silver lettering, green painted bait pail w/black fish & gold bands, includes lift-out screened inner bucket & perforated lift-up lid (some paint drips on outer surface) ............. **105**

**Painting,** watercolor, by James Prosek, depicts silver trout, bright tones, 10 x 16" image, matted & framed to 18 x 23" ......... **1,100**

**Print,** "Along the Granite Cliff, Moise River Quebec" by Ogden Pleissner, No. 168/350, depicts fly fishermen in canoe on Moise River, published by the Salmon Federation, framed w/a feather wing Atlantic Salmon fly, 16 x 23", matted & gold framed to 26 x 32" ...................... **330**

**Rod case,** rectangular, multi-rod, leather, marked "Lyon & Coulson, Buffalo, N.Y.," felt lined w/leather handle & carrying strap, 2 x 3 1/2 x 41 3/4" .............................. **303**

# FRAKTUR

*Fraktur paintings are decorative birth and marriage certificates of the 18th and 19th centuries and also include family registers and similar documents. Illuminated family documents, birth and baptismal certificates, religious texts and rewards of merit, in a particular style, are known as "fraktur" because of the similarity to the 16th century type-face of that name. Gay watercolor borders, frequently incorporating stylized birds, hand-lettered documents, which were executed by local ministers, school masters or itinerant penman. Most are of Pennsylvania Dutch origin.*

**Birth & baptismal fraktur (Geburts und Taufschein),** printed & handcolored, recording 1798 birth in Montgomery County, printed by Johann Ritter, decorated w/angels, birds & flowers in red, green & pink, framed, 13 1/2" w., 16 5/8" h. (stains & fold line) ........................ **$94**

**Birth & baptismal fraktur (Geburts und Taufschein),** printed & handcolored, rectangular, recording 1816 birth in Lebanon County, printed by "Johann Ritter, Reading," signed & dated "Catharina Nordden 1838," birds, angels & heart illustrations in red, blue, yellow & black, Pennsylvania, framed, 14 3/4" w., 18 3/4" h. (edge wear, damage & stains) ..... **330**

**Birth letter for Elizabeth Ness,** watercolor, pen & ink on paper, ornately decorated inscription framed by scrolls, flowers & berries w/three inscribed hearts, attributed to the Manor Township Artist, 1801, 4 1/4 x 6 1/2" ........................ **1,150**

**Birth letter for Michael Lurich, Burks County,** watercolor, pen & ink on paper, four inscribed hearts trimmed in blue w/orange & green flowers, inscription framed w/orange border in lower portion of painting, attributed to Conrad Trewitz, 1778, 8 x 13" ................................. **2,875**

**Birth record,** pen & ink & watercolor by Martin Brechell, recording 1808 birth in Northampton County, Pennsylvania, shield design flanked by hearts & tulips in red, blue, yellow & black, old curly maple frame, 12" w., 16" h. (stains, tears, damage at fold lines & edges rebacked w/paper) ..................................... **1,100**

**Birth record,** pen & ink & watercolor on laid paper, floral background w/three hearts containing text, records 1782

birth in "Bercks County," (sic), red, yellow, blue, green, purple & black, Pennsylvania, framed, 20 1/2" w., 17 1/2" h. (wear, damage & repair w/one corner poorly restored) ............................................ **385**

**Birth record for Elizabeth Wenger,** pen & ink & watercolor on wove paper, colorful leafy scrolls along the left side & across the top over the ornate German script inscription, in red, black & yellow w/reddish brown ink, dated 1795, Pennsylvania, in early molded frame, 7 1/2 x 10" (minor stains) .............................................. **1,760**

**Birth record for Magdalena Schreiner,** pen & ink & watercolor on laid paper, records 1776 birth of Magdalena Schreiner in Lancaster County, Pennsylvania, floral wreath design in red, yellow & black, old grained wood frame, 12 5/8 x 16 3/4" (stains, damage, repairs, some old touch ups) .................... **1,155**

*Birth Record Fraktur*

**Birth record for Rahel Haas,** pen & ink & watercolor on wove paper, central circle w/text is faded brown & bordered by a wreath of leaves in yellow, orange, green, black & grey, Oley Township, Berks County, Pennsylvania, framed, 10 1/2" w., 12 3/8" h. (ILLUS.) ..................... **715**

**Birth record for Valentine Ritter,** pen & ink & watercolor on laid paper, wide borders of stylized florals flanking a narrow oval reserve at the top above a tall pyramidal reverse, records a birth in 1771 & signed "May the 27th 1788 - gertraut wortten - Valentine Ritter," yellow, brown, black & green, grained frame, 12 x 17" (damage, fold lines, fading) ......... **1,210**

**Book plate,** pen & ink & watercolor on paper, colorful tulips & other flowers in red, black, yellow & blue w/the name "Magdalena Schneiderin 1780," attributed to John Conrad Gilbert, Altalaha, Pennsylvania, mahogany-grained frame, 4 3/4 x 6 1/2" (minor stains, some damage) ............................................................. **880**

**Book plate,** pen & ink & watercolor on wove paper, decorated w/stylized blossomheads above & around a pair of facing birds, tiny blossoms in each corner, in red, yellow, blue & black, modern grained frame, 5 1/2 x 6 1/8" (stains, some paper damage) .................................. **413**

**Book plate,** pen & ink & watercolor on wove paper, large inscription "Jacob Gadon," indicating birth on November 5,

1833, in red, yellow & green, beveled frame, 4 x 6 1/2" (minor stains) .................... **825**

**Book plate,** pen & ink & watercolor, two pages connected at spine, tulip & star design in shades of brown & yellow, second page w/German inscription recording 1821 birth of Maryan Schup, early beveled veneer frame, 6 1/4 x 8 1/2" (damage, stains) ......................................... **330**

**Book plate,** pen & ink & watercolor on wove paper, rectangular, inscribed "Christina Yoder 1828" in red, black & green, new curly maple frame, 3 x 5 1/4" image (stains, edge damage)...................... **413**

**Commemorative,** pen & ink & watercolor on laid paper, a design of two large overlaping circles w/four birds on flowering branches & hearts w/inscription "Lacy Putney born Apl. 5, 1791 - Lydia Putney born apl. 15, 1810," death dates added for 1836 & 1881, very faded blue & yellow, old & probably original frame w/blue paint & wavey glass, attributed to Moses Conner, Jr., New Hampshire, 8 1/4 x 10 1/4" (stains, edge damage, one corner of glass broken) ........................ **495**

*Rare Gift Drawing Fraktur*

**Drawing,** gift-type, pen & ink & watercolor on paper, a scene of two stylized ladies, one seated receiving a flower from another lady standing in front of her, a tall flowering tree on the left, a German inscription across the top & checked & vining narrow border bands, in yellow, red, blue & black, Pennsylvania, dated 1824, framed, 8 x 13" (ILLUS.).................. **8,625**

**Drawing,** pen & ink & watercolor on paper, a design of compass stars, birds, hearts & tulips in brown, black & blue, in old beveled mahogany veneer frame, 8 7/8 x 10 7/8" (colors faded, minor damage & stains, frame veneer damage) ............................................................ **220**

**Drawing,** pen & ink & watercolor on laid paper, stylized floral design in red, yellow, blue & black, bordered by black background paper, framed, 5 1/4" w., 6 3/4" h. (stains, top of flower smeared & some damage from acid ink) ........................ **358**

**Drawing,** pen & ink & watercolor on laid paper, text in large heart w/date "1788" surrounded by stylized floral design w/two birds, red, yellow, green & black, framed, 11 1/2" w., 16" h. (paper is fragile & worn w/tears & small holes) ................ **990**

**Rewards of Merit,** watercolor, pen & ink on paper, stylized tulip standing over inscription, surrounded by thin border, American School, 19th c., framed, 2 x 3 1/2", pr. .......................................... **1,955**

**Verse,** pen & ink & watercolor on laid paper, verse w/"Northumberland County, January 21, 1814," by Martin Brichelle, Pennsylvania, rebacked on paper, framed, 10 1/4" w., 11 1/4" h. (edge tears & slight stains) ...................... **605**

**Vorschrift,** pen & ink & watercolor on laid paper, bold text across the top over alphabets, numbers & signed & dated 1803, yellow, green & black, beveled mahogany veneer frame, 10 3/4 x 12 1/4" (stains, ink blots & wear) ............................................................ **660**

**Vorschrift,** pen & ink & watercolor on wove paper, bold German inscription across top w/English inscription below in the same hand reading "I have gone astray like a lost sheep...1761," red, yellow & black, old beveled frame, 10 3/4 x 15" (fold line, stains, color bleeding w/damage) ............................................................ **385**

**Vorschrift fraktur,** pen & ink & watercolor on laid paper, a bold large heading above a pair of heart & pinwheel designs above the detailed lower inscription, signed "Beymier Jacob Kinig - Lampiter Townschip, Lancaster County, Stadt von Pennsylvania - Fenner den 24 ten, 1833," in red, black, blue & brown, in old beveled grained frame, 15 1/2 x 19 1/2" (damage & stains) ...................................... **825**

**Vorschrift fraktur,** pen & ink on laid paper, red & black ink, German, framed, 8" w., 5 3/4" h. (stains, edge wear & pencil mark) ............................................................ **688**

# FRATERNAL ORDER COLLECTIBLES
*Also see: BARBERIANA*

**F.O.E. (Fraternal Order of Eagles) clock,** electric wall-type, octagonal framed w/green neon light tube around inner rim, Arabic numerials centered by a flying eagle logo above printed initials & wording, 18 1/4" w....................................... **$275**

**G.A.R. (Grand Army of the Republic) walking stick,** carved & painted wood, ebonized shaft relief-carved w/an eagle & shield, a G.A.R. medal, pocket knife, violin, anchor, stars, hearts, etc., late 19th c., 35 1/2" l. ........................................ **805**

**I.O.O.F. (Independent Order of Odd Fellows) secretary,** Victorian country-style, oak, two-piece construction: the upper section w/a rectangular top & deeply molded cornice arched at the center front & carved w/a raised central panel crest w/a flat cornice above the carved Odd Fellow insignia above a single pane glazed cupboard door opening to two shelves over a pair of small narrow drawers, the lower section w/a stepped-out wide slanted writing surface over an apron w/a central small drawer, raised on knob-, ring- and paneled post-turned legs w/knob feet, old worn finish, third quarter 19th c., 24 1/2 x 31 1/4", 81 1/2" h. .................................................. **660**

**I.O.O.F. (Independent Order of Odd Fellows) walking stick,** hickory, cylindrical handle knob above a spiral-carved segment above a section carved in relief w/"I.O.O.F." over four snakes spiraling down the shaft, old natural finish, 34 1/4" l. ................................................ **275**

**Masonic apron,** kid leather, white ground engraved w/the all-seeing eye on the flap & various Masonic symbols below, embellished w/colors & gold, probably New England, 19th c., ca. 1820-40, 15 x 15 1/2", w/a charcoal portrait of George Washington wearing a Masonic apron, 2 pcs. (imperfections) ....................... **805**

*Decorated Masonic Armchair*

**Masonic armchairs,** painted & decorated, the wide flat crestrail decorated w/a gold stenciled Masonic emblem, four simple turned spindles between the turned stiles, S-scroll arms on spindle & canted baluster- and ring-turned arm supports, wide plank seat, ring-, knob- and rod-turned front legs joined by two turned rungs, worn red & black graining w/yellow striping, wear on arms, damage & repair, mid-19th c., 33" h., set of 4 (ILLUS. of one) ........................................... **374**

**Masonic box,** black lacquer, rectangular w/a molded top inlaid w/mother-of-pearl & lacquer Masonic devices, the sides w/floral decoration, Chinese Export, 19th c., 12 1/2 x 16 1/4", 5" h. (top unattached at hinges, lock mechanism missing, minor lacquer loss) ............................... **920**

**Masonic flag bracket,** carved wood, the back constructed w/crossed hatchets, the demi-lune shelf flanked by arrrows w/arched support below centering a Masonic emblem, old mauve paint, late 19th c., 21 x 32 3/4" (ILLUS. top next column) ......................................................... **546**

**Masonic shield,** carved walnut, a shield carved w/a square & compass framing

an arm & gavel, upper end of arm incised "March 6, 1902," 17 1/2 x 19 1/2"..... **230**

*Carved Wood Masonic Flag Bracket*

**Masonic trowel,** sterling silver, diamond-shaped blade engraved w/presentation inscription dated 1923-24 & engraved foliage, long tapering rounded straight ivory handle, 8 1/2" l. ...................................... **66**

# FURNITURE

*Furniture made in the United States during the 18th and 19th centuries is coveted by collectors. American antique furniture has a European background, primarily English, since the influence of the Continent usually found its way to America by way of England. If the style did not originate in England, it came to America by way of England. For this reason, some American furniture styles carry the name of an English monarch or an English designer. However, we must realize that, until recently, little research has been conducted and even less published on the Spanish and French influences in the area of the California missions and New Orleans.*

*After the American revolution, cabinetmakers in the United States shunned the prevailing styles in England and chose to bring the French styles of Napoleon's Empire to the United States and we have the uniquely named "American Empire" style of furniture in a country that never had an emperor.*

*During the Victorian period, quality furniture began to be mass-produced in this country with its rapidly growing population. So much walnut furniture was manufactured, the vast supply of walnut was virtually depleted and it was of necessity that oak furniture became fashionable as the 19th century drew to a close.*

*For our purposes, the general guidelines for dating will be: Pilgrim Century - 1620-85 William & Mary - 1685-1720 Queen Anne - 1720-50 Chippendale - 1750-85 Federal - 1785-1820 Hepplewhite - 1785-1820 Sheraton - 1800-20 American Empire (Classical) - 1815-40 Victorian - 1840-1900 Early Victorian - 1840-50 Gothic Revival - 1840-90 Rococo (Louis XV) - 1845-70 Renaissance - 1860-85 Louis XVI - 1865-75 Eastlake - 1870-95 Jacobean & Turkish Revival - 1870-95 Aesthetic Movement - 1880-1900*

Art Nouveau - 1890-1918 Turn-of-the-Century - 1895-1910 Mission (Arts & Crafts movement) - 1900-15 Art Deco - 1925-40

All furniture included in this listing is American unless otherwise noted.

# BEDROOM SUITES

*Gilbert Rhode Bedroom Chests*

**Art Deco:** tall chest of drawers, a chest of drawers w/mirror, a bed & a nightstand; blonde finished hardwood, the tall chest & chest of drawers w/mirror each w/rectangular tops above stacks of long graudated drawers w/catalin pulls, the round mirror supported on a curved tubular metal angled arm, looped tubular metal legs, the bed w/a curvilinear footboard, round nightstand, signed by designer Gilbert Rhode, manufactured by Herman Miller, Zeeland, Michigan, ca. 1933, tall chest 47" h., the set (ILLUS. of part) ....... **$4,888**

*Heywood Wakefield Bedroom Suite*

**Modern style:** bed, nightstand, tall chest of drawers & chest of drawers w/mirror; all in a wheat finish, the chests w/rectangular tops w/rounded edges over cases fitted w/five or four long graduated drawers w/central low arched long wood pulls, the shorter dresser fitted at the top w/a large rectangular mirror w/rounded top corners, chests on short rounded feet, matching bed & nightstand, attributed to Heywood Wakefield, ca. 1955, tall chest 46 1/2" h., the set (ILLUS. of part)............................................................ **978**

**Victorian Eastlake substyle:** chest of drawers & washstand; walnut & burl walnut, each w/a flat crestrail decorated w/a carved scalloped band flanked by carved corner posts on the tall reeded uprights flanking a large square or rectangular swiveling beveled mirror, the chest w/a reddish brown rectangular marble top above a stack of three long burl-veneered drawers w/pierced brass pulls & a molded apron, the washstand w/a high galleried reddish brown marble splashback on the marble top over a case w/two short burl-veneered drawers beside a paneled, burled door over the molded base, ca. 1880, chest 20 x 44", 76 1/2" h., 2 pcs. ...................................... **1,100**

*Fine Eastlake Bedroom Suite*

**Victorian Eastlake substyle:** double bed, chest of drawers w/mirror & washstand; walnut & burl walnut, the bed w/a high back topped by a pointed arch shell and scroll-carved crest above a burl panel flanked by rondels & turned corner finials above a wide burl panel flanked by side colonettes above a narrow burl band & corner finials above a plain panel, matching lower footboard, the tall chest w/a similar crest above a long rectangular swiveling mirrors above a white marble top over three long drawers, the washstand w/a white marble top w/small shelf above a case w/a long drawer over a pair of doors all trimmed w/burl, ca. 1885, 3 pcs. (ILLUS.) ............................... **6,700**

*Fine Eastlake Bed & Chest of Drawers*

**Victorian Eastlake substyle:** highback double bed & marble top dresser; the bed w/a high crowned crest w/a central rondel & bar crest above a geometrically-pierced crestrail w/a sawtooth-cut lower border overhanging a set-back narrow horizontal frieze band carved w/stylized foliate designs & flanked below for short spindled & scroll-cut galleries above the set-back headboard w/a pair of geometrically-cut square panels flanking a long central burl panel all above lower plain panels, the dresser w/a matching crestrail above a tall rectangular mirror swinging between tall upright & lower candle shelves over floral-carved panels above the rectangular red marble top over a case w/a row of three short drawers over two long drawers all w/angular brass pulls, molded base, ca. 1880, the pr. (ILLUS.) ............... **7,000**

*Fine Classical Tall Poster Bed*

# BEDS

*French Art Deco Palmwood Bed*

**Art Deco bed,** palmwood, the upright thick rectangular headboard joined by low molded siderails continuing into the curved lower footboard on a quarter-round heavy bracket, France, ca. 1930s, veneer losses, 55" w. (ILLUS.) .................. **2,875**

**Chippendale tall-poster bed,** mahogany, the octagonal tapering headposts w/lamb's tongue detail continue to square legs flanking an angled headboard joined to the fluted & stop-fluted footposts w/lamb's tongue detailing above square legs joined by rails fitted for roping, w/accompanying tester frame & bed bolts, old refinish, Rhode Island, 18th c., 55 x 85", 79" h. (imperfections) .... **2,300**

**Classical tall poster bed,** mahogany & mahogany veneer, a high arched headboard w/a cartoche carved at the top flanked by long S-scrolls over a shaped raised panel & a rectangular panel w/cut corners flanked by the tall headposts composed of four clustered round posts above the heavy square legs w/chamfered corners, joined by shaped side & end rails to matching footposts, ca. 1830-40, 108" h. (ILLUS. top next column) .......................................... **4,800**

**Classical tall poster tester bed,** cherry, the four vase- and ring-turned posts continuing to block- and vase-turned legs & joined by a straight testers frame & a scroll-cut headboard, old refinish, New England, ca. 1825, 45 x 70", 90" h. (ILLUS. center next column) .................... **1,955**

*Classical Tall Poster Tester Bed*

*Early Low Poster Rope Bed*

**Country-style low poster bed,** painted, a rounded headboard between square posts w/button finials joined by original hinged side rails to the footposts w/matching finials & joined by a heavy end rail, on ring- and baluster-turned legs w/a pair of fold-down legs where the side rails hinge, original red paint, rails drilled for roping, New England, early 19th c., very minor imperfections, 49 3/4 x 74", 35 1/2" h. (ILLUS.) ................... **805**

**Country-style low poster rope bed,** poplar, heavy ring- and block-turned even head- and footposts w/ring- and ball-turned finials w/a mushroom cap, wide shaped headboard & lower matching footboard, posts joined by heavy round rails w/turned rope knobs, old refinish w/some wear & white stain, original rails, first half 19th c., 55 x 72", 43 1/2" h. ........... **220**

*Early 'Pencil-Post' Tester Bed*

**Country-style 'pencil-post' bed,** birch, four slender octagonal tapering posts continuing to square legs joined by a molded peaked headboard & flat tester frame, side & end rails drilled for roping, probably New England, early 19th c., old surface, 51 x 71", 81" h. (ILLUS.) .............. **2,300**

**Country-style tall poster tester bed,** maple, the vase- and ring-turned reeded footposts joined to the hexagonal tapering headposts w/a simple arched headboard, straight tester frame, old refinish, minor imperfections, probably New England, early 19th c., 46 x 72", 83" h. .... **2,300**

**Federal-Style bed,** carved cherry, the knop finial above a rectangular tester over reeded, ring- and baluster-turned footposts & headposts centering an arched headboard, on square tapering legs w/spade feet, 20th c., 62 1/2 x 87 1/4", 82" h. ......................................................... **1,840**

*George Nelson "Thin Edge" Bed*

**Modern style "Thin Edge" bed,** walnut, the wood frame w/an upright canted caned headboard, resting on a white-painted tubular steel frame & legs, metal tag marked "Herman Miller - George Nelson Design," ca. 1959, 58 x 82 1/4", 33 1/2" h. (ILLUS.)..................................... **8,740**

**Turn-of-the-Century brass bed,** the high headboard w/a straight bar crestrail joined to ring-turned tall cylindrical stiles

w/ball caps & pointed ring-turned finials, the headboard composed of a latticework of ball- and ring-turned vertical & horizontal bars centered by a panel w/a large C-form-formed cartouche, matching lower footboard, on casters, polished, 55 x 72", 67 1/2" h. (one finial missing)..................................................... **1,100**

*Fine Victorian Rococo Tester Bed*

**Victorian Rococo substyle tester bed,** rosewood, the high arched & paneled headboard w/a pierced floral- and scroll-carved arched crest flanked by heavy paneled stiles & slender reeded tapering posts, the low gently arched & paneled footboard flanked by heavy paneled stiles & tall slender reeded posts, wide cornice-form tester frame w/rounded corners, ca. 1850 (ILLUS.) ...................... **13,500**

# BOOKCASES

*English Arts & Crafts Bookcase*

**Art Nouveau bookcase,** carved mahogany, a gently arched top w/outset leaf- and whiplash-carved corners above an arrangement w/a flat long shelf above a stepped shelf unit over a compartmented section over a bottom section w/a square central paneled door flanked by two upright slots on each side, gently tapering sides & curved & molded feet, Diot, France, ca. 1900, 14 x 36 1/2", 79" h. ........................................................ **2,875**

**Arts & Crafts bookcase,** oak & leaded glass, a rectangular top w/molded edges above a frieze band & narrow molding over a pair of tall glazed cupboard doors w/upper panels of geometrically-glazed panels of striated green & colorless glass, opening to four wooden shelves, molded apron w/rounded block front feet on casters, England, late 19th c., wear, 14 1/4 x 40", 58 1/4" h. (ILLUS.) .................. **805**

*Unusual Oak Stacking Bookcase*

**Arts & Crafts bookcase,** stacking-type, oak, five square stacked compartments each w/a geometrically glazed lift-front door resting on a raised molded base & fitted w/a round-fronted top cornice, early 20th c. (ILLUS.) ................................ **2,800**

*Federal Cherry Bookcase on Chest*

**Federal bookcase,** cherry, two-part construction: the upper section w/a rectangular top over a flaring reeded cornice above a pair of 6-pane glazed doors opening to two shelves; the lower stepped-out section w/four long graduated drawers w/replaced clear blown glass pulls & inlaid diamond-form escutcheons, backboards marked "Canfield," short ring- and knob-turned legs, early 19th c., repairs, feet replaced, old finish, top 14 1/2 x 25", 83" h. (ILLUS.) ..... **2,640**

**Federal-Style bookcase,** inlaid mahogany, two-part construction: the upper section w/a serpentine crest & molded edge above a rectangular case w/two glazed doors w/beaded mullions & a conforming banded edge enclosing an interior fitted w/two shelves; the lower section w/a medial shelf & banded edge over beading above a conforming case w/two doors enclosing an interior above beading, on French feet, 20th c., 16 1/2 x 36 1/2", 71 1/2" h. ........................ **1,725**

*L. & J.G. Stickley Mission Bookcase*

**Mission-style (Arts & Crafts movement) bookcase,** oak, a rectangular top w/a low gallery w/double pegged through-tenons above a pair of tall 12-pane glazed cupboard doors opening to shelves, copper plate pulls, double pegged through-tenon base, red Handcraft decal of L. & J.G. Stickley, Model No. 645, ca. 1910, 12 1/2 x 53", 55 1/2" h. (ILLUS.)................................... **6,900**

**Mission-style (Arts & Crafts movement) bookcase,** oak, a rectangular top w/a shaped gallery above a case w/a single tall 6-pane glazed cupboard door opening to shelves, raised on stile legs, branded mark of L. & J.G. Stickley, ca. 1910, 11 x 22", 50" h. (refinished)............. **4,312**

**Mission-style (Arts & Crafts movement) bookcase,** oak, a rectangular top w/three-quarters gallery w/through-tenons above a pair of tall 8-pane glazed doors opening to shelves, flat base w/through-tenons, hammered copper pulls, labeled "The Work of L. & J.G. Stickley," Model No. 643, ca. 1912, 12 1/8 x 36 1/2", 55 1/2" h. (ILLUS. top next page) ................................................. **6,900**

*L. & J.G. Stickley Mission Bookcase*

*Victorian Baroque-Style Bookcase*

**Victorian bookcase,** Baroque-Style, carved ebonized wood, an ornately pierce-carved arched crest w/a pair of half-lion scrolling-tailed beasts flanking & supporting a central shield w/a carved lion above the molded rounded arch cornice above a single tall geometrically-glazed cupboard door w/orange-tinted glass flanked by scroll-carved caryatids on blocks flanking a long dragon-carved drawer, resting on a molded platform supported by two heavy shaped front legs ending in large paw feet, flat rear legs, probably Europe, late 19th c., 17 1/2 x 40 1/2", 99" h. (ILLUS.) .............. **1,210**

**Victorian bookcase,** Renaissance Revival substyle, walnut & burl walnut, breakfront-style, the top w/a band of applied dentil blocks & a stepped-out central section above a pair of very tall single-

pane glazed cupboard doors opening to shelves & flanked by ring- and columnar-turned colonettes flanked by narrow glazed panels & another pair of colonettes beside the two tall stepped-back glazed side panels w/two further colonettes at the front corners, resting on a low rectangular bottom section w/a molded top over a long burl-fronted central drawer flanked by shorter side drawers, molded plinth base, ca. 1880, 96" h. (ILLUS. below) ......................................... **4,675**

*Victorian Breakfront Bookcase*

*Renaissance Revival Bookcase*

**Victorian bookcase,** Renaissance Revival substyle, walnut & burl walnut, the rectangular top w/a narrow molded & flaring cornice above a frieze band w/decorative blocks of burl walnut over a pair of tall glazed doors opening to four adjustable shelves flanked by ring- and post-turned colonettes w/blocked capitals & bases above a molded medial rail above a pair of burl veneered paneled bottom drawers w/replaced glass pulls, molded plinth base, ca. 1880, top 16 x 53 1/4", 64 1/4" h. (ILLUS.)...................................... **1,375**

*Fine Renaissance Revival Bookcase*

**Victorian Renaissance Revival book-case,** walnut & burl walnut, three-door breakfront-style, the tallest central section w/a rectangular top w/rounded front corners over a deep stepped cornice & dentil-carved band over a burl veneer band above a tall glazed cupboard door opening to four shelves flanked by turned & reeded colonettes down the front, the shorter & slightly stepped-back matching side sections with matching cornices & details, burl panels across the conforming base, ca. 1875 (ILLUS.) ... **4,100**

# CABINETS

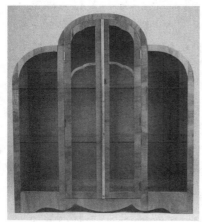

*Small Art Deco China Cabinet*

**China cabinet,** Art Deco style, burl walnut veneer, a stepped & triple-arched top above a conforming case w/a pair of 2-pane tall glazed central doors opening to two long glass shelves flanked by two glazed side panels, on a deep serpentine apron, electrified, ca. 1930s, 11 1/4 x 44 1/2", 50" h. (ILLUS.) ................ **546**

*Harvey Ellis-Designed Cabinet*

**China cabinet,** Mission-style (Arts & Crafts movement), oak, a rectangular top over-hanging a case w/a tall glazed cupboard door w/an arched top rail & a metal plate & ring pull, arched apron, designed by Harvey Ellis, produced by Gustav Stickley, ca. 1904, 15 1/4 x 36", 60" h. (ILLUS.) ...................................................... **8,625**

**China cabinet,** Mission-style (Arts & Crafts movement), oak, a rectangular top w/a top rail & front side stiles flanking a pair of tall glazed doors opening to interior fitted for shelves, glazed side panels, stiles continue to form legs, slightly arched front apron, unmarked, early 20th c., 14 x 45", 59" h. .............................. **575**

**China cabinet,** turn-of-the-century, mahogany veneer, D-form w/a stepped-out center section w/scroll-topped flat pilasters flanking the curved glass door & ending in heavy C-scroll feet, curved glass sides, encloses four wooden shelves w/a rectangular mirror behind the top shelf, on casters, dark finish, ca. 1900, 17 1/4 x 40", 61 1/2" h. (bottom drilled for electric line) .................................. **688**

**China cabinet,** turn-of-the-century, oak, half-round form w/rounded molded side cornices flanking a central serpentine cornice w/scrolled leaf carving & w/carved outset blocks above a conforming case w/a free-standing ring-turned & reeded slender columns separating the curved center door & side panels, conforming base molding on short reeded cabriole legs w/paw feet, ca. 1900 (ILLUS. top next page) ..................... **2,500**

**China cabinet,** turn-of-the-century, oak, the half-round top w/outset front corners above curved glass sides & a curved glass door w/carved lion heads topping the front framework, pair of stylized cabriole legs in the front & simple curved legs at the rear, ca. 1900 (ILLUS. center next page) ................................................. **1,600**

*Finely Finished Oak China Cabinet*

*Ornate Rococo-style China Cabinet*

**China cabinet,** Victorian Golden Oak sub-style, quarter-sawn oak, the tall case w/a rectangular top & stepped cornice w/a thin zipper-carved edge band & cut-out scrolls above a central oval beveled mirror flanked by scroll clusters & above a shelf w/a pierced scroll gallery, each side w/a tall narrow cabinet door w/very large ornately scrolled strapwork hinges above & below a glass pane opening to shelves, the central section w/a pair of smaller tall glazed doors opening to shelves & carved bands above & below, over two long central drawers, the base section w/a beaded medial band above a pair of long drawers w/scroll-carved trim over the low serpentine apron w/a pierced oval scroll-carved panel & scroll-carved feet, old finish, ca. 1900, 14 x 58", 75 1/2" h. .................................... **1,513**

*China Cabinet with Carved Lion Heads*

**China cabinet,** turn-of-the-century, oak, the half-round top w/outset front corners above curved glass sides & a curved glass door flanked by tall columns topper w/carved blocks, conforming base w/short cabriole front legs ending in claw-and-ball feet on casters, ca. 1900 .... **2,000**

**China cabinet,** turn-of-the-century Rococo-style, mahogany, the half-round case w/a high wide arched molded crestrail centered by a high scroll-carved crest above a tall arched glazed cupboard door flanked by curved glass sides all enclosing three glass shelves, conforming base w/scroll-carved apron, on short front cabriole legs w/claw-and-ball feet (ILLUS. top next column) .......................... **9,000**

*Mission Oak Gun Cabinet*

**Gun cabinet,** Mission-style (Arts & Crafts movement), oak, a rectangular top w/a high three-quarters gallery above a tall 2-pane glazed door w/metal pull opening to a rack for rifles above a single drawer at the bottom, arched front apron, original finish & key, brass tag marked "Yeager Gun Cabinet - Allentown Pa - USA.," 14 x 23", 70 1/2" h. (ILLUS.) ..................... **1,650**

*Early Labeled Hoosier Cabinet*

**Kitchen cabinet,** turn-of-the-century Hoosier-style, oak, the superstructure w/a rectangular top above a pair of paneled cupboard doors beside a wide door opening to a bin compartment above a high tambour-front storage area w/metal funnel-form bins flanking a hanging spice rack above a row of storage jars, the lower section w/a rectangular white porcelain-covered metal work surface above a pair of thin pull-out work shelves above a wide rectangular door beside a stack of three graduated drawers, square tapering legs on casters, original paper door inserts, repairs & strips of wood in tambour doors reinstalled, marked "Hoosier," ca. 1900, 22 x 41", 72" h. (ILLUS.)............................................. **825**

**Kitchen cabinet,** turn-of-the-century Hoosier-type, pine, the upper section w/a rectangular top above a pair of glazed cupboard doors beside an arrangement of four small drawers, the bottom one w/a bin bottom, all overhanging a high opening w/curved sides on the stepped-out zinc-covered rectangular work surface above a pair of deep drawers flanking a pair of shorts drawers above a pair of paneled cupboard doors beside w/deep pull-out bin drawer, six short bracketed feet on casters, ca. 1900, 25 1/2 x 41", 65" h. (ILLUS. top next column) ............................................. **600**

*Pine Hoosier-style Kitchen Cabinet*

*Gustav Stickley Music Cabinet*

**Music cabinet,** Mission-style (Arts & Crafts movement), oak, a rectangular top w/a stepped three-quarters gallery above a tall narrow paneled door w/a rectangular plate & ring pull, flat apron, branded mark of Gustav Stickley, Model No. 70w, ca. 1912, 16 x 20", 46" h. (ILLUS.) ... **7,475**

**Side cabinet,** Art Deco, bronze-mounted satinwood marquetry, rectangular top w/serpentine front above a pair of long cupboard doors opening to drawers & flanked by columnar stiles, raised on short cabriole feet & a serpentine apron, the doors w/central vertical bands of stylized marquetry florals, Jules Leleu, France, 1940s, 20 x 45", 58" h. (finish brittle, small losses to veneer).................. **3,162**

*Modern Style Fornasetti Cabinet*

**Side cabinet,** Modern style, transfer-printed decoration, rectangular top w/a black & white printed copy of scrolls & figured designs above a case covered w/a continuous print of a building w/a classical facade, two doors in the case, on tapering brass legs, Piero Fornasetti design, ca. 1950s, 13 3/4 x 27 1/2", 24 3/4" h. (ILLUS.)................................... **5,175**

**Side cabinet,** Victorian Renaissance Revival substyle, marquetry inlaid tulip-wood, mahogany & parcel-gilt, the rectangular top w/outset corners centering an inlaid foliate & scrolling top above parcel-gilt molded edge over a conforming case fitted w/two paneled short drawers above two doors, each w/astragal-shaped insert panel w/inlaid scrolls & diamonds centering a scrolled gilt foliate handle & base flanked by foliate scrolled sides, on a molded base, ca. 1875, 22 x 48", 36" h. ......................................... **2,760**

*Renaissance Revival Side Cabinet*

**Side cabinet,** Victorian Renaissance Revival substyle, walnut, marquetry & parcel-gilt, the angular shaped top w/a removable statuary stand above an incised frieze band over a central cabinet door w/swag-framed & molded panel decorated w/an ornate floral & ribbon marquetry design flanked by reeded pilasters & angled side panels, all on a

molded flaring conforming base w/shaped feet, ca. 1880, minor damage, 22 x 50 1/4", 51 3/4" h. (ILLUS.)........ **3,738**

**Specimen cabinet,** Federal style, mahogany, a rectangular top above a case w/two stacks of nine long narrow cock-beaded drawers fitted w/a locking mechanism & flanked by reeded stiles, on short tapering turned legs w/knob feet, Philadelphia, ca. 1815, 22 x 42 1/2", 38 1/2" h. (shrinkage cracks, top warpage) ................................................... **9,775**

*Victorian Spool Cabinet-Display Case*

**Spool cabinet,** Victorian Eastlake substyle, walnut, a rectangular top wa foliate-carved cornice above a large single-pane cupboard door opening to three display shelves over a slightly stepped-out lower case w/four long line-incised spool drawers w/inset brass pulls, molded flat base, ca. 1890 (ILLUS.).......... **1,000**

*Ornate Louis XV-Style Vitrine Cabinet*

**Vitrine cabinet,** Louis XV-Style, gilt-bronze, kingwood & marquetry, the rectangular top w/rounded & molded edges fitted w/a low pierced brass three-quarters gallery above a floral swag marquetry frieze band above the tall bow-fronted glazed door w/notched top corners above a large rectangular lower panel w/ornate scrolling marquetry designs flanked by corner stiles w/starburst inlay & shaped glazed sides above conforming inlaid lower panels, scrolled ormolu mount on front apron, on slender cabriole legs w/brass mounts at the knees & feet, paper label for Paines Furniture Co., late 19th c., 17 x 28", 61" h. (ILLUS.)...................................................... **2,645**

*Louis XV-Style Inlaid Vitrine*

**Vitrine cabinet,** Louis XV-Style, mahogany veneer, the arched & molded crestrail centered by a large upright scroll-carved crest above a conforming frieze band w/delicate raised molding enclosing herringbone inlay above a pair of tall beveled glass glazed cupboard doors w/scroll carving at the top & opening shelves above a drawer insert, molded sides above a serpentined bottom rail over the conforming apron centered by a scroll-carved cartouche, on demi-cabriole front legs ending in scroll & peg feet, Europe, late 19th c., demountable, top 22 x 55", 99" h. (ILLUS.) ........................... **2,255**

# CHAIRS

**Art Deco armchair,** oak & tubular steel, the low thick upholstered back flanked by heavy plank arms above the deep upholstered seat on a shaped tubular steel framework, grey plaid fabric, France, ca. 1930s (ILLUS. top next column)...................................................... **2,875**

**Art Deco armchairs,** rattan, the rounded upright back frame w/vertical rattan spindles continuing to the wide arched arms

w/rattan spindles continuing to the apron composed of further spindles, gold Naugahyde back & seat cushions, made by Heywood Wakefield, ca. 1935, 30" h., pr. (ILLUS. center this column) ................... **805**

*French Art Deco Armchair*

*Art Deco Rattan Armchairs*

**Art Deco armchairs,** upholstered mahogany, a sloped upholstered backrest flanked by shaped plank arms centering a loose seat cushion raised on reeded round feet, attributed to Dominique, France, ca. 1925, pr. (upholstery distressed) ...................................................... **6,325**

**Art Deco Club chair,** upholstered & ebonized wood, of rectangular outline w/a square upholstered backrest flanked by padded arms centering a loose seat cushion, raised on short block feet, possibly designed by Donald Desky, American, 1930s (upholstery distressed, finish scuffed) ...................................................... **690**

**Art Deco Club chairs,** walnut & leather-upholstered, the high lobed upholstered back continuing to the rounded arms centering a high tight seat raised on short feet on casters, upholstered in pale bluish grey leather upholstery, England, 1930s, pr. (wear at edges) ....................... **1,380**

**Art Nouveau armchair,** fruitwood marquetry w/backsplat inlaid in various woods w/chestnuts & leafage, flanked by twist-carved spindles & molded arms above upholstered seat, raised on twist-carved front legs, Majorelle, France, ca. 1900 (ILLUS. top next page) ............................. **3,450**

**Art Nouveau armchairs,** walnut, a molded serpentine crestrail over an arched upholstered panel above a pierced & foliage- and whiplash-carved back flanked by carved & scrolled open arms on curved arm supports over the over-upholstered seat, simple molded cabriole front legs, Italy, ca. 1900, pr. (ILLUS. of one, center this column)........................ **1,380**

*Art Nouveau Armchair*

*Italian Art Nouveau Armchair*

*Early Thonet Bentwood Side Chairs*

**Bentwood side chairs,** a high tapering bentwood back frame enclosing a wide upper cross rail w/three holes above three slender spindles to a thin lower rail above the caned seat in a bentwood frame forming the front legs joined by a high flat stretcher, a forked downswept bentwood stretcher at each side of the base, Thonet, Austria, late 19th c., paint restoration, 38 1/2" h., pr. (ILLUS.) .............. **575**

*Country Chippendale Side Chair*

**Chippendale country-style side chair,** stained wood, the gently arched crestrail w/short molded ears above a heart- and geometrically-pieced splat above the upholstered slip seat on square legs w/molded outside edges joined by square molded stretchers, old dark stain, Concord, Massachusetts, last quarter 18th c., imperfections, 39" h. (ILLUS.) ......... **805**

*Fine Carved Chippendale Side Chair*

Chippendale side chair, carved mahogany, the shaped crestrail w/carved leafage above a pierced splat flanked by raked stiles on a trapezoidal overupholstered seat, on cabriole front legs w/acanthus leaf & scroll carving & ending in claw-and-ball feet, chamfered canted rear legs, block-, baluster- and ring-turned stretchers, old refinish, some imperfections, attributed to Sewall Short, Newburyport, Massachusetts, 1760-80, 37" h. (ILLUS.).......................................... **3,738**

*Fine Boston Chippendale Side Chair*

Chippendale side chair, carved mahogany, the shaped leaf- and volute-carved crestrail above a pierced strapwork splat & overupholstered seat on acanthus-carved cabriole legs joined by block- and baluster-turned stretchers & ending in claw-and-ball feet, old surface w/dark brown color, Boston, Massachusetts, ca. 1770, 37" h. (ILLUS.)................................. **4,600**

*Fine Chippendale Side Chair*

Chippendale side chairs, carved mahogany, the serpentine crestrail w/a central carved shell w/flanking chip-carved & raking molded ears above the strapwork design pierced splat in scrolls over the trapezoidal upholstered slip seat on molded frame above cabriole front legs w/arris knees & ending in ball-and-claw feet, joined by turned stretchers to the raking square rear legs, old refinish, Boston - Salem, Massachusetts, 1750-1800, imperfections, 37 1/2" h., pr. (ILLUS. of one) ...................................... **27,600**

*Boston Chippendale Side Chair*

Chippendale side chairs, carved mahogany, the serpentine crestrail w/scroll-carved ears above a slender vase-form pierced splat w/carved scrolls flanking floral devices on a molded shoe, trapezoidal slip seat on straight molded frame joining square chamfered legs & molded box stretchers, missing brackets, other minor imperfections, attributed to George Bright, Boston, ca. 1760-90, 36 1/4" h., pr. (ILLUS. of one) .................. **3,450**

*Chippendale Wingchair*

**Chippendale wing armchair,** walnut, the arched upholstered back flanked by slightly flared serpentined upholstered wings above an rolled upholstered arms above the wide cushion seat, square molded legs joined by box stretchers, late 18th c. (ILLUS.) .................................. **3,850**

**Chippendale-Style dining chairs,** walnut, a serpentine crestrail centering a carved shell flanked by scrolled ears above a pierced vasiform splat over a trapezoidal slip seat above a shaped seatrail centering a carved shell, on cabriole legs w/ball-and-claw feet, two armchairs w/downscrolling arms w/hand holds over shaped arm supports, four side chairs, in the Philadelphia manner, 20th c., the set.. **4,025**

**Chippendale-Style side chair,** cherry, double-scrolled crestrail above a solid vasiform splat over a balloon-shaped slip seat above a conforming seatrail w/carved shell, on cabriole legs w/scrolled acanthus-carved knees & returns, ending in ball-and-claw feet, in the Philadelphia manner, 20th c., 41 1/4" h. ..................................................... **920**

**Chippendale-Style side chairs,** mahogany, Gothic-style w/a carved oxyoke crestrail above a pierced Gothic arch & loop-carved splat flanked by outcurved stiles, upholstered slip seat above the shell-carved seatrail, cabriole front legs w/shell-carved knees & ball-and-claw feet, early 20th century w/manufacturer's number "406," 40" h., pr. (seats reupholstered) ......................................................... **605**

*Chippendale-Style Wingchair*

**Chippendale-Style wing-back armchair,** mahogany, the high arched upholstered back flanked by flared wings above the out-scrolled upholstered arms above the cushion seat, cabriole front legs w/shell-carved knees & ending in claw-and-ball feet, squared canted rear legs, old dark finish, early 20th c., 45" h. (ILLUS.).............. **440**

*Classical Children's Side Chairs*

**Classical children's side chairs,** mahogany, a paneled rectangular concave crestrails above a lower horizontal splat joining the raked stiles, upholstered slip seat, on sabre legs, refinished, probably Boston, ca. 1820, 28" h., pr. (ILLUS.) .......... **546**

**Classical country-style side chair,** curly maple, a wide curved & rolled crestrail attached to tapering curved stiles above a lower curved rail over the replaced paper rush seat, front sabre legs joined by a flat stretcher, turned side & back stretchers, ca. 1830, 34 1/4" h. .................... **248**

**Classical side chairs,** carved mahogany, a scrolled tablet crestrail centering two carved cornucopia above shaped molded stiles joined by a lower rail over a trapezoidal caned seat, front sabre legs w/hairy hoof feet, New York City, 1810-15, 32 1/2" h., pr............................. **1,265**

**Country style 'banister-back' side chair,** carved & painted, the scroll-carved & pierced crestrail above four ring- and baluster-turned split banisters flanked by ring-, column- and block-turned stiles w/ball finials over a trapezoidal rush seat, on baluster-, block- and ring-turned legs joined by ring- & bulbous-turned front stretcher & box stretchers, on baluster-turned feet, painted black, New England, mid-18th c., 41 3/4" h. (loss of height) ....................................................... **805**

**Country-style 'banister-back' side chair,** carved maple, the tall back w/baluster- and knob-turned stiles & ball finials above a fan-carved crestrail above four split-balusters continuing to a lower rail w/an arched pendant, the woven splint seat on baluster-, ring- and rod-turned legs joined by two swelled front stretchers & simple turned side & back stretchers, traces of dark green stain, probably New Hampshire, second half 18th c., 44 1/2" h. (reduced in height) ................... **4,600**

**Federal dining chairs,** figured mahogany, gently back-scrolled reeded back stiles joined by a flat crestrail & a lower loop-pierced rail above the overupholstered seat on reeded sabre legs, probably Augusta, Georgia, ca. 1805, 33" h., set of 8 .......................................................... **11,500**

**Federal lolling armchair,** inlaid mahogany, the tall upholstered back w/a gently arched crest, the upholstered seat flanked by open arms w/downswept line-inlaid arm supports, square legs joined by flat stretchers, Massachusetts or New Hampshire, ca. 1790, 46 1/2" h. (repairs).. **1,725**

**Federal side chair,** carved mahogany, shield-shaped back w/a beaded frame w/fan carving on molded stiles & joined to the overupholstered shaped seat, on square tapering molded legs joined by flat stretchers, old refinish, Massachusetts or Rhode Island, ca. 1790, 27 1/4" h. (minor imperfections) ............... **2,645**

**Federal wing-back armchair,** upholstered mahogany, the arched crestrail & rounded upholstered back & wings above rolled upholstered arms over the tight upholstered seat on frontal ring- and baluster-turned legs w/peg feet, square back legs, old refinish, New England, early 19th c., 46" h. (imperfections) ...................................................... **1,725**

**George III-Style dining chairs,** mahogany, ribbon-back style, each w/a back composed of four gently arched & pierced ribbon slats, upholstered seat, square molded legs joined by stretchers, England, late 19th c., 37 1/2" h., set of 8 (restorations) ........................................... **3,738**

*Hitchcock Decorated Side Chair*

**Hitchcock fancy side chairs,** painted & decorated, the turned crestrail above a wide horizontal splat stenciled w/a fox hunting scene flanked by raised stiles w/further stenciled decoration above the rush seat, ring- and knob-turned raked front legs joined by a ring- and knob-turned front stretcher & plain side & back stretchers, gilt & polychrome trim, Hitchcocksville, Connecticut, ca. 1825-30,

imperfections, 33 1/2" h., pr. (ILLUS. of one) .......................................................... **1,150**

**Hunzinger 'patent' platform rocker,** ebonized hardwood, the tall back w/bobbin-turned stiles joined by cross rails supporting a large needlework panel raised above the padded arms on bobbin-turned arm supports & w/cross-braces & curved underarm supports over the needlepoint-upholstered seat, bobbin-turned frame support on the slender platform base, ca. 1880 ............... **1,600**

*Mission Oak Armless Rocker*

**Mission-style (Arts & Crafts movememt) rocking chair without arms,** oak, a flat gently curved crestrail above four slender slats between square stiles, upholstered spring cushion seat, gently arched aprons join square legs on rockers, attributed to L. & J.G. Stickley, ca. 1912, minor wear, 33 3/4" h. (ILLUS.) .......... **374**

**Mission-style (Arts & Crafts movement) armchair,** oak, the tall back w/heavy stiles joined by four wide gently curved slats, flat arms over five slats, upholstered cushion seat, deep flat apron, branded mark of Gustav Stickley, Model No. 324, ca. 1901, 42 3/8" h. .................... **2,185**

**Mission-style (Arts & Crafts movement) dining chairs,** oak, the rectangular back w/stiles & rails enclosing three vertical slats raised above the cushion seat, square tapering legs joined by high flat stretchers, Gustav Stickley Model No. 353, after 1909, 39 1/4" h., set of 6 ........... **2,760**

**Mission-style (Arts & Crafts movement) rocking chair w/arms,** oak, a wide curved crestrail over four narrow & one wide vertical slats flanked by square stiles, flat shaped open arms on front leg supports w/side corbels, spring cushion leather seat, paper label of Harden and Co., early 20th c., some stains & roughness, 37" h. (ILLUS. top next page) ............. **518**

*Harden & Co. Mission Rocker*

*Arne Jacobsen "Ant" Chairs*

**Modern style 'ant' chairs,** molded plywood, the back & seat in a continuous shaped form of walnut-veneered plywood, on three bent & painted tube-steel legs, designed by Arne Jacobsen, manufactured by Fritz Hansen, impressed "FH/Denmark," ca. 1952, 30" h., set of 4 (ILLUS.) ...................................................... **1,150**

*Eames Armchair & Ottoman*

**Modern style armchair & ottoman,** bent & laminated wood & leather, the chair w/a high oblong leather-upholstered & tufted crest panel above an upholstered lower back & wide seat flanked by curved padded arms all within a bent & laminated wood frame swiveling on a five-arm footed base, matching upholstered otto-

man on a four-arm base, designed by Charles & Ray Eames, manufactured by Herman Miller, ca. 1956, some wear & abrasions, chair 32" h., 2 pcs. (ILLUS.)..... **1,265**

*Andre Arbus Armchair*

**Modern style armchairs,** hardwood, the upright rectangular upholstered back flanked by shaped tapering open arms on incurved arm supports above the upholstered seat, on square tapering legs, designed by Andre Arbus, ca. 1945, pr. (ILLUS. of one).......................... **2,070**

*Eames "DCW" Side Chairs*

**Modern style "DCW" side chairs,** walnut plywood, wide curved back panel on curved support over the dished wide curved seat, arched tapering canted legs, designed by Charles Eames, w/paper label, ca. 1950s, 28" h., pr. (ILLUS.)....................................................... **546**

**Modern style music room side chairs,** bentwood, a tall narrow bentwood back frame enclosing an oval upholstered back panel raised above the shaped rectangular upholstered seat, raised on tapering legs set w/spherical brackets in the front, designed by Josef Hoffmann, original label & branded factory mark of J. and J. Kohn, Austria, ca. 1904, pr. (ILLUS. top next page) ................................ **575**

**Modern style "Womb" chair & ottoman,** shell-form, upholstered in grey fabric, on slender chrome legs, designed by Eero Saarinen, made by Knoll International, ca. 1948, 36 1/4" h. ............. **1,036**

*Hoffmann Music Room Side Chairs*

**Nutting-signed Carver armchair,** hardwood, 17th c. style, Model No. 464 .............. **963**

**Nutting-signed Windsor bow-back side chair,** the bowed backrail over eight slender swelled spindles & a pair of brace spindles behind, shaped saddle seat, canted baluster-, ring- and rod-turned legs, original finial, paper label reading "Wallace Nutting," branded "301," early 20th c., 38 1/4" h. ...................... **550**

**Nutting-signed Windsor comb-back armchair,** Pennsylvania-style, Model No. 412 .................................................... **1,045**

**Nutting-signed Windsor continuous-arm armchair,** the rounded crestrail continuing down to slender flattened arms & fitted at the top w/a slender scrolled comb crest on four short spindles, eleven slender swelled spindles in the back & a pair of brace spindles behind, baluster- and ring-turned canted arm supports, shaped saddle seat, canted baluster-, ring- and rod-turned legs joined by a swelled H-stretcher, branded & paper label reading "Wallace Nutting 402," early 20th c., 44 3/4" h. ...................................................... **825**

**Pilgrim Century "Carver" armchair,** turned maple, the baluster- and rod-turned stiles topped w/ball finials w/two turned rails centering three turned spindles, the turned front posts w/ball finials above the rush seat, plain turned box stretchers, old dry finish, dark brown color, Rhode Island, 1670-1700, 39 1/2" h. (feet worn, chips throughout, right arm & right stretcher probably replaced) ................................................ **7,475**

**Pilgrim Century highchair,** turned & painted maple & chestnut, the turned beaker-form back finials on sausage-turned tall rear stiles centering two pointed-arch slats, open arms w/front tall sausage-turned arm supports & legs w/ball finials flanking the plank seat, all joined by box stretchers, New England, probably Rhode Island, 1700-30, 35 3/4" h. (formerly fitted w/a rush seat) ... **4,312**

**Queen Anne corner chair,** carved & figured mahogany, the shaped U-form crest above a shaped scrolled crestrail on three ring-turned supports centering two solid vase-form splats, balloon-form seat on four cabriole legs w/a shell-carved knee on the front leg, ending pad feet, English or Irish, 18th c., 32 1/2" h. .... **4,025**

*Country Queen Anne Armchair*

**Queen Anne country-style armchair,** painted, a double-arched crestrail centered by carved scrolls above the vasiform splat & molded stiles, long shaped & molded open arms ending in scrolled hand grips raised on ring-, knob- and baluster-turned arm supports, woven rush seat, block-, ring- and knob-turned front legs joined by a ball-turned front stretcher, double turned side stretchers to the square canted rear legs, old black repaint, New Hampshire, mid-18th c. (ILLUS.) .................................................... **4,125**

*Country Queen Anne Painted Chair*

**Queen Anne country-style side chair,**
carved & painted, the arched & carved
crestrail above a tall vasiform splat &
molded raked stiles, the rush seat on
block-, baluster- and ring-turned front
legs joined by bulbous turned front &
side stretchers, retains old burnt sienna
& dark brown paint w/yellow pinstriping,
New England, 18th c., 41" h. (ILLUS.) ...... **1,495**

*Massachusetts Queen Anne Chair*

**Queen Anne side chair,** maple, the
spooned crestrail above a vasiform splat
& raked chamfered stiles joined to the
trapezoidal slip seat by a scrolled frame,
on two front cabriole legs ending in pad
feet, raked rear square legs joined by
block-, baluster- and ring-turned stretchers, refinished, imperfections, Massa-
chusetts, 18th c., 40" h. (ILLUS.) .............. **2,070**

**Queen Anne side chair,** maple, the yoked
crestrail above a solid vase-form splat
flanked by molded stiles over a trapezoidal rush seat above a shaped front skirt,
on cabriole front legs ending in padded
disk feet joined by ring- and baluster-
turned front stretcher & side flat stretchers, canted square rear legs, restorations to stretchers, New Hampshire,
1740-60, 42 1/4" h. .................................. **2,070**

**Queen Anne side chair,** walnut, the double arched crestrail w/a central carved
shell above a vasiform splat flanked by
gently canted stiles, an upholstered balloon-shaped seat overupholstered
above the front cabriole legs ending in
padded disk feet & joined by block- and
baluster-turned H-stretchers to the
canted turned rear legs, old surface,
Boston, 1740-65, 40 1/2" h. (imperfec-
tions) ...................................................... **8,050**

**Queen Anne side chairs,** walnut, the serpentine crestrail above a simple vase-
form splat on molded shoes flanked by
gently raked stiles, upholstered slip seat
on cabriole front legs ending in pad feet
on platforms joined to the chamfered
rear legs by cut-out seatrails & block-
and vase-turned stretchers, refinished,

Massachusetts, ca. 1740-60, 38" h., pr.
(minor restoration) ..................................... **8,625**

*Rustic Child's Rocking Chair*

**Rustic style child's rocking armchair,**
the high bent-twig arched back entwined
w/large twig loops flanking a central
board slat above the looped twig arms
above the plank seat w/twig edging on
canted legs w/a twig stretcher above the
wide rockers, New York state, ca. 1900,
old dark natural surface (ILLUS.) ................ **230**

*Early Pressed-back Side Chair*

**Turn-of-the-century 'pressed-back' side
chairs,** oak, the wide crest w/rounded
corners pressed at the sides w/large C-
scrolls flanking a central fanned design
above knob- and rod-turned stiles flanking ten slender baluster-, ring- and rod-
turned spindles, wide shaped plank seat,
ring- and rod-turned front legs joined by
two turned stretchers, plain side & rear
stretchers & legs, some edge damage,
age cracks, one crest incomplete, ca.
1900, set of 6 (ILLUS. of one) ..................... **561**

*Victorian Balloon-back Side Chair*

**Victorian country-style 'ballon-back' side chairs,** painted & decorated, a rounded back rail w/tapering stiles centered by a vase-form splat, shaped plank seat on ring- and rod-turned front legs joined by a turned stretcher, plain turned rear legs & plain turned side & rear stretchers, the crestrail decorated w/a stenciled basket of fruit above the splat stenciled w/an eagle & shield w/"Union," gilt vine stenciled border, stiles, seat & legs w/yellow & salmont striping, Pennsylvania, ca. 1860, some paint wear, 33 1/2" h., pr. (ILLUS.)........................ **460**

**Victorian country-style highchair,** painted & decorated, a wide gently arched crestrail w/upturned ends w/a black ground decorated w/red striping & stenciled fruit & foliage in shades of bronze powder, raised on canted knob- and rod-turned stiles joined by an arched lower rail over three knob- and rod-turned spindles, bentwood seat guards on the round plank seat, raised on tall tapering knob- and rod-turned legs w/knob-turned worn front footrest stretcher & plain turned stretchers at the sides & back, overall black ground w/painted trim, mid-19th c., 35 3/4" h. .......................... **413**

**Victorian Gothic Revival armchair,** carved walnut, the tall back w/a high pointed & pierced crestrail tapering to a point & enclosing an open quatrefoil over a pair of Gothic arch openings between ring- and rod-turned stiles w/ring- and knob-turned pointed finials, a large upholstered oval back medallion rests on a lower rail w/pierced trefoils in the lower corners & pointed drops below, straight square open arms end in large knob grips above baluster- and ring-turned supports flanking the upholstered seat, scalloped seatrail between corners blocks above the knob-, ring- and rod-turned legs w/knob feet on casters, old worn finish, old worn leathered black cloth upholstery, mid-19th c., 52 1/2" h. ...................................................... **413**

**Victorian "patent" platform rocking chair w/arms,** walnut, the high arched back w/a padded headrest above an upholstered oval central medallion between the spiral-turned stiles w/rounded top corners & supported by slender spindles, rounded, curved & spiral-turned open arms above the upholstered seat on spiral-turned supports & spiral-turned stretchers on the platform base, old finish, illegible paper label, attributed to George Hunzinger, ca. 1880s, 41 1/2" h. (ILLUS. below) ................. **660**

*Late Victorian "Patent" Platform Rocker*

**Victorian rocking chair w/arms,** Rococo substyle, Grecian-style w/high balloon back w/walnut thumb-molded frame around the upholstered back, open padded arms above the upholstered spring seat, serpentine veneered seatrail above shaped front legs on long rockers, ca. 1860 ............. **358**

**Victorian Rococo substyle side chair,** mahogany, the open balloon-back w/a rounded & stepped crest carved w/a floral band, the incurved stiles joined by a lower pierced scroll-carved rail above the over-upholstered spring cushion seat, cabriole front legs ending in scroll & peg feet, old finish, newer grey & brown brocade upholstery, ca. 1855, 34 1/2" h. ....................................................... **204**

*Belter "Rosalie" Pattern Side Chairs*

**Victorian Rococo substyle side chairs,**
carved rosewood, an ornate fruit-carved
crest atop the tall tapering balloon back
w/long carved S-scrolls at the sides
above the overupholstered spring seat
on a molded serpentine seat frame,
demi-cabriole front legs on casters,
"Rosalie" patt. by John Henry Belter,
New York City, ca. 1855, pr. (ILLUS.) ....... **2,400**

**Wallace Nutting-signed Windsor "sack-
back" armchair,** hardwood, Model No.
408 ............................................................. **935**

*Wicker Child's Rocking Chair*

**Wicker rocking chair w/arms,** child's, an
arched & rounded tightly woven crestrail
continuing down to form the rounded
arms, the back w/a round medallion
w/delicate weaving (damaged) above
the padded seat, wrapped legs & angled
braces on rockers, ca. 1910 (ILLUS.) .......... **110**

**Windsor "birdcage" rocking armchair,**
the birdcage cresting above seven spindles & turned arms on a shaped seat,
splayed bamboo-turned legs joined by
stretchers on rockers, old refinish, New
England, ca. 1810, 37 1/2" h. ...................... **460**

**Windsor "bowback" side chair,** hardwood, the bowed crestrail over seven
turned tapering spindles on a shaped
saddled seat over bamboo-turned
canted legs joined by a double-swelled
H-stretcher, old dark varnish stain over
white paint, late 18th - early 19th c.,
33 3/4" h. (some variation in spindles) ........ **193**

**Windsor "bowback" side chair,** maple &
ash, the bowed beaded crestrail over
nine tapering bamboo-turned spindles &
an incised saddle seat, bamboo-turned
splayed legs joined by swelled & bamboo-turned H-stretcher, refinished,
branded "S.J. Tuck," Boston, 1790,
38" h. ....................................................... **1,093**

**Windsor "comb-back" armchair,** the serpentine crestrail w/carved rounded ears
above nine spindles over a shaped rail
ending curved arms on baluster- and

ring-turned arm supports & numerous
short spindles, wide D-form shaped
seat, baluster- and ring-turned canted
legs w/ball feet joined by a ball-and-bob-
bin-turned H-stretcher, Pennsylvania,
1770-90, dark finish, 44" h. ...................... **2,070**

**Windsor "comb-back" writing-arm arm-
chair,** the arched comb-back crest on
six tall plain spindles above the shaped
arm rail w/scroll arm terminals & an
oblong writing surface over a thin
drawer, turned spindles under the arm
rail, baluster- and ring-turned canted
arm supports, wide saddle seat over a
deep suspended drawers, on canted
baluster- and ring-turned legs joined by
a swelled H-stretcher, old refinish, attributed to Ebenezer Tracy, Lisbon,
Connecticut, ca. 1770-80, 46" h. (resto-
rations) ...................................................... **5,175**

*Signed Continous Arm Windsor*

**Windsor "continuous arm" brace-back
armchair,** chestnut & maple, the arched
crestrail w/beaded edge continues down
to form arms w/shaped hand holds
above turned spindles & canted baluster-turned arm supports, a shaped saddle seat w/two forked brace spindles to
the top of the back, raised on canted bal-
uster- and ring-turned legs joined by a
swelled H-stretcher, branded "E.B.
Tracy," Lisbon, Connecticut, 1780-1803,
37" h. (ILLUS.) ........................................... **1,093**

**Windsor "continuous-arm" armchair,**
painted, the arched crestrail continuing
to flat arms & hand holds above seven
spindles & baluster- and ring-turned
canted arm supports, shaped saddled
seat on bamboo-turned canted legs
joined by a swelled H-stretcher, old
salmon red paint, attributed to Ebenezer
Tracy, Jr., New London County,
Connecticut, ca. 1800, 35 1/2" h.
(ILLUS. top next page) ............................... **3,105**

*Painted Continuous Arm Windsor*

**Windsor "fan-back" side chair,** painted, the serpentine crestrail over nine spindles flanked by ring- and baluster-turned canted stiles over the shaped saddled seat on canted baluster- and ring-turned legs joined by a swelled H-stretcher, old green paint, Connecticut, 1790-1810, 40" h. (paint wear & loss) .......................... **3,450**

**Windsor "rabbit-ear" side chairs,** painted & decorated, a wide gently curved top crestrail over two thin lower rails over four short turned spindles above the seat all between backswept tapering rabbit-ear stiles, rounded thick plank seat on canted bamboo-turned legs joined by box stretchers, yellow painted ground w/stenciled fruit & leaf designs in green & raw umber w/gilt highlights on the crestrail, dark striping, old repaint, New England, ca. 1830-40, 33 1/2" h., set of 6 (imperfections) ...................................... **3,220**

**Windsor "step-down" side chairs,** shaped stepped crestrail over seven bamboo-turned spindles & raked stiles over the shaped seat, on splayed bamboo-turned legs joined by turned box stretchers, old refinish, later painted decoration, New England, ca. 1810, 33" h., set of 6 (some repairs) ............................. **1,150**

**Windsor-Style "fan-back" armchair,** a long serpentine crest raised on nine slender spindles above a curved medial rail continuing to form out-scrolled flat arms w/scroll handgrips above numerous slender swelled spindles, wide shaped saddle seat & canted baluster- and ring-turned arm supports & pair of back brace spindles to the base of the upper crest, canted baluster-, ring- and tapering rod-turned legs joined by a swelled H-stretcher, original dark finish, early 20th c., labeled "Simonds," 44 3/4" h. ...................................... **330**

**Windsor-Style "fan-back" side chair,** maple, the arched crestrail w/lobed ears

above nine spindles over a shaped plank seat, on ring- and baluster-turned legs joined by a swelled H-stretcher, late 19th - early 20th c., 39 1/4" h. .............................. **575**

# CHESTS & CHESTS OF DRAWERS

**Apothecary chest,** painted poplar, a narrow rectangular top above a case w/twenty-one graduated drawers w/turned wood knobs arranged as two rows of six above a row of five over a row of four all above long narrow hinged panel door at the base, old worn greenish black paint, late 19th c., 9 3/4 x 35", 26 1/4" h. (mismatched knobs, backboards replaced) ...................................... **1,045**

*Art Deco Mahogany Chest of Drawers*

**Art Deco chest of drawers,** mahogany, a rectangular raised-panel mahogany top over a case w/three long canted & zigzag drawers w/square patinated metal pulls, matching sides, the whole supported on tapered angular legs in a lighter shade of mahogany matching the band around the top, scratches, wear, ca. 1935, 20 x 30 1/2", 35 1/2" h. (ILLUS.) .................................... **1,840**

*Chippendale Child's Blanket Chest*

**Blanket chest,** child's, Chippendale country-style, painted pine, six-board construction, a hinged rectangular top w/molded edges above a dovetailed case on a molded base w/scroll-cut bracket feet, original mustard yellow & brown grain paint to resemble exotic wood, probably New England, late 18th c., repairs, 12 x 20 1/2", 14" h. (ILLUS.).... **1,850**

**Blanket chest,** Federal country-style, painted pine, six-board construction, hinged rectangular top w/molded edges opening to a well w/lidded till above the dovetailed case w/metal ring end handles, molded base on shaped bracket feet, early red paint, New York State or Pennsylvania, early 19th c., 21 1/2 x 48", 24 1/2" h. (imperfections)..... **1,093**

**Blanket chest,** pine, six-board construction, rectangular top over a case w/canted front & back, bound in wrought iron w/carrying end handles, old reddish brown paint, Mohawk-Hudson River Valley, New York, late 18th c., 16 x 48", 16" h. ..................................................... **460**

**Blanket chest,** poplar, a rectangular hinged lid w/molded edges opening to a deep well w/lidded till, dovetailed case w/molded base & scroll-cut bracket feet, old dark brown finish, early 19th c., 14 1/2 x 28 3/4", 18 1/2" h. (lid rehinged, till lid repaired)............................................. **660**

**Blanket chest,** country-style, painted & decorated pine, six-board dovetailed construction, the rectangular hinged top w/molded edges opening to a well w/a lidded till, base molding, raised on short, heavy ring- and knob-turned legs, original red vinegar graining on a yellow ground, feet in black, lock w/key, 19th c., 19 3/4 x 43 1/2", 24 1/2" h. ........................... **935**

**Blanket chest,** Chippendale country-style, walnut, a rectangular hinged lid w/molded edges opening to a well w/till, dovetailed case w/original brass butterfly keyhole escutcheon, a mid-molding above a lower row of three drawers each w/butterfly pulls above the molded base on ogee bracket feet, wrought-iron bear-trap lock, mellow finish, Pennsylvania, attributed to Chester County, late 18th - early 19th c., 24 1/4 x 55", 29" h. (slight warp in lid)............................................... **4,950**

**Carpenter's chest,** pine, thick rectangular hinged lid opening to a fitted interior, dovetailed case w/thick top & base molding, rope end handles, refinished, 19th c., 38" l. (edge damage, age cracks)............ **330**

**Chippendale "bowfront" chest of drawers,** mahogany, the rectangular top w/molded edges & bowed front overhanging a conforming case w/four long graduated cockbeaded drawers w/butterfly brasses & keyhole escutcheons, molded base on short cabriole legs w/ball-and-claw feet & scroll-curved brackets, Massachusetts, ca. 1780, 22 x 37 3/4", 34 1/2" h. (brasses replaced, imperfections)........................... **5,463**

*Chippendale Birch Chest of Drawers*

**Chippendale chest of drawers,** birch, rectangular top slightly overhanging a case w/four long graduated cockbeaded drawers w/butterfly pulls & keyhole escutcheons, molded base on tall scroll-cut bracket feet, old refinish, replaced brasses, minor imperfections, Massachusetts, ca. 1770-80, 17 1/4 x 36", 34" h. (ILLUS.)......................................... **6,785**

*Fine Chippendale Chest of Drawers*

**Chippendale chest of drawers,** cherry, a rectangular top w/molded edges & serpentine front above a conforming case w/four long graduated cockbeaded drawers w/butterfly pulls & keyhole escutcheons, molded base on scroll-cut ogee bracket feet, Hartford, Connecticut, ca. 1770-80, 22 1/2 x 34", 32 1/2" h. (ILLUS.).................................. **17,250**

**Chippendale chest of drawers,** cherry, rectangular top w/deep flaring molded cornice above a case w/a pair of short thumb-molded drawers over four long graduated thumb-molded drawers all w/butterfly brasses & keyhole escutcheons, molded base on tall scroll-cut ogee feet, old refinish, probably Rhode Island, ca. 1770-80, 18 1/2 x 36 1/2", 42" h. (replaced brasses, restoration)....... **2,415**

*Mahogany Chippendale Chest*

**Chippendale chest of drawers,** mahogany, the rectangular molded top above a case of four long graduated thumb-molded drawers w/butterfly pulls & keyhole escutcheons on a molded base w/carved claw-and-ball front feet & ogee bracket rear feet, old replaced brasses, refinished, imperfections, possibly Pennsylvania, ca. 1760-80, 21 x 36", 32 1/2" h. (ILLUS.) ...................................... **9,200**

**Chippendale chest-on-chest,** maple, two-part construction: the upper section w/a rectangular top & deep cove molding above a case of five long graduated drawers w/simple bail pulls; lower section w/a mid-molding above a slightly stepped-out case of four long graduated drawers w/simple bail pulls, brass oval keyhole escutcheons, base molding above the apron w/a carved central drop & scroll-carved bracket feet, old pulls, refinished, possibly Massachusetts or New Hampshire, ca. 1760-80, 18 1/2 x 36", 76" h. (minor repairs) ...................... **14,950**

**Chippendale country-style chest of drawers,** maple, rectangular top w/narrow molded cornice above a case of five long graduated thumb-molded drawers, base molding on scroll-cut bracket feet & a central drop pendant, refinished, New England, ca. 1780, 17 x 36 1/2", 41 1/2" h. (replaced bail pulls, repairs) ...................... **1,610**

**Chippendale country-style tall chest of drawers,** cherry, a rectangular top w/a flaring coved cornice above a case of six beaded long graduated drawers w/simple turned wood knobs & brass keyhole escutcheons, molded base on bracket feet, old refinish, possibly Worcester County, Massachusetts, ca. 1790, 17 x 37 1/4", 53 1/4" h. (replaced pulls) .......... **11,500**

**Chippendale tall chest of drawers,** maple, a rectangular top w/a narrow cornice above a case w/a pair of drawers above four long graduated drawers all w/butterfly brasses & keyhole escutcheons, molded base on scroll-cut tall bracket feet, wood w/some curl & old brown finish, late 18th c. ......................... **9,900**

**Chippendale tall chest of drawers,** maple, a rectangular top w/deep molded

coved cornice above a pair of thumb-molded drawers over four long graduated thumb-molded drawers all w/butterfly pulls & keyhole escutcheons, base molding on scroll-cut bracket feet, old refinish, most brasses appear original, probably Massachusetts, ca. 1770-80, 18 x 36 3/4", 44 1/2" h. ............................. **4,025**

**Chippendale-Style chest of drawers,** mahogany, rectangular top w/molded edges above a conforming case fitted w/four long graduated drawers flanked by fluted chamfered corners over a molded base, on ball-and-claw feet w/scroll-carved returns, 20th c., 21 1/2 x 37 1/2", 35" h. ............................. **1,725**

*Chippendale-Style Serpentine Chest*

**Chippendale-Style "serpentine-front" chest of drawers,** mahogany & mahogany veneer, the rectangular molded top w/serpentine front edge above a conforming case w/four long graduated cockbeaded drawers w/oval brass pulls & keyhole escutcheons, molded base on scroll-cut ogee bracket feet, early 20th c. w/some old parts, 21 x 38", 33 1/2" h. (ILLUS.) ...................................... **770**

**Chippendale-Style "serpentine-front" chest of drawers,** mahogany, the rectangular top & serpentine front w/canted corners above a conforming case w/four long graduated cockbeaded drawers flanked by stop-fluted canted corners, on ogee bracket feet, in the Philadelphia manner, 20th c., 34 3/4" h. ........................ **2,070**

**Chippendale-Style tall chest of drawers,** carved mahogany, a rectangular top w/a gadrooned cornice above a case w/a pair of drawers carved w/grotesque masks & scrolls above two stacks of four small, deep leafy scroll-carved drawers w/pierced butterfly pulls flanked by a central stack of four concave-fronted drawers, the top one w/carved scrolls & a fanned design, gadrooned base band on four leaf-carved cabriole legs ending in square pad feet, R.J. Horner Co., late 19th c. (ILLUS. top next page) ................. **1,000**

*Fine Chippedale-Style Tall Chest*

*Classical Stenciled Chest of Drawers*

**Classical chest of drawers w/mirror,** mahogany & stenciled mahogany veneer, a rectangular black-painted & foliate-stenciled mirror frame supported between S-scroll acanthus-carved supports above the stepped-back top w/three small drawers w/stenciled trim above the projecting top over a long convex top drawer w/central fruit cluster stenciling projecting above two long drawers w/star-inlaid wood drawer pulls flanked by free-standing stencil-decorated columns continuing to knob-turned feet, minor imperfections, possibly New York, ca. 1825, 22 1/2 x 36 1/2", 63" h. (ILLUS.)...................................... **2,990**

**Classical country-style chest of drawers,** cherry, rectangular top above a pair of deep beaded drawers above three long graduated beaded drawers, all w/simple turned wood knobs, scalloped apron, ring- and baluster-turned short legs w/knob feet, paneled sides, first half

19th c., 19 1/4 x 40 1/2", 48" h. (minor damage to drawer edges) ............................ **935**

**Classical country-style chest of drawers,** painted & decorated birch & maple, a tall rectangular backboard w/molded edges above the rectangular top over a stepped-out long drawer w/turned wood knobs above three long set-back drawers w/wood knobs flanked by engaged columns raised on baluster- and ring-turned legs w/ball feet, original red paint & faux graining on the drawers simulating mahogany, original pulls, Barre, Vermont area, ca. 1830s, 19 1/4 x 43", 39 1/2" h. .................................................. **2,415**

*Classical Tall Chest of Drawers*

**Classical tall chest of drawers,** tiger stripe maple & cherry, the rectangular top above a case w/a pair of narrow cockbeaded drawers above a long deep drawer w/a walnut-veneered border flanked by sawtooth-carved panels slight projecting above four long graduated cockbeaded drawers flanked by ring- and rod-turned engaged columns continuing to turned feet, simple turned wood pulls, old refinish, minor imperfections, Pennsylvania or Ohio, ca. 1825, 22 x 42 3/4", 56" h. (ILLUS.)..................... **2,760**

*Danish Modern Chest of Drawers*

**Danish Modern chest of drawers,** walnut & cherry, two-part construction: the upper section w/a rectangular top above a pair of flat cupboard doors opening to divided compartments & raised above the lower section; the lower section w/a rectangular top over a stack of four flat long drawers framed by outset turned legs joined by curved cross braces, Scandinavia, ca. 1960, wear, 23 x 44", 48" h. (ILLUS.).............................. **517**

**Federal "bowfront" chest of drawers,** mahogany & bird's-eye maple veneer, the rectangular top w/bowed front & inlaid edge above a comforming case w/four long cockbeaded drawers veneered w/bird's-eye maple surrounded by cross-banded mahogany veneer, scroll-cut apron continuing into tall curved French feet, oval brasses appear original, old refinish, probably New Hampshire, early 19th c., 22 x 39 3/4", 37" h. (minor imperfections) ...................................... **9,775**

*Federal Cherry Chest of Drawers*

**Federal chest of drawers,** cherry, the rectangular top slightly overhanging a case w/four long graduated cockbeaded drawers w/round brass pulls & brass keyhole escutcheons, serpentine apron continuing into tall French feet, old pulls, old finish, southeastern New England, ca. 1800-10, 19 x 36 3/4", 36 1/2" h. (ILLUS.)................................... **4,600**

**Federal chest of drawers,** painted cherry, rectangular top w/ovolo corners above a case of four long cockbeaded graduated drawers w/oval brass pulls & keyhole escutcheons flanked by quarter-engaged baluster- and ring-turned reeded posts continuing to turned legs, old red-painted surface, New England, ca. 1815-20 (replaced brasses, minor imperfections)............................... **3,220**

**Federal chest of drawers,** wavy birch, a rectangular top w/beaded edges slightly overhanging the case w/four long beaded drawers w/simple bail pulls & brass keyhole escutcheons, shaped apron above tall tapering French feet, old refinish w/remnants of red paint, orig-

inal brasses, New Hampshire, early 19th c., 18 x 39 1/2", 38" h. (minor imperfections) ........................................ **1,840**

*Federal Country Chest of Drawers*

**Federal country-style chest of drawers,** cherry, a rectangular top above a pair of very deep drawers w/simple turned wood knobs above three long graduated drawers w/wood knobs, ring- and baluster-turned legs w/knob feet, old dark finish on case & drawer frames, drawer fronts cleaned down to red stain, mid-19th c., top 19 1/2 x 41", 45 1/4" h. (ILLUS.)........................................ **935**

**Federal country-style chest of drawers,** painted & decorated basswood, rectangular top above a case of four long graduated thumb-molded drawers above a curved apron & simple cut-out feet, original painted decoration simulating exotic wood bordered by stringing & cross-banding in shades of tan & light brown, original oval brasses, signed "Henry Davist...Readsboro Feb... 1815 $7.50," Vermont, 19 x 41", 42" h. ....................... **7,475**

**Federal country-style chest of drawers,** painted & decorated pine & poplar, the crestrail across the top cut w/pairs of incurved repeating scrolls flanking a central tab above the rectangular top over a tall case w/a pair of narrow drawers over four long graduated drawers, paneled ends, on short ring- and baluster-turned legs w/knob & peg feet, original overall red graining w/ebonized trim, yellow striping & gold-stenciled flowers, birds & a label on the rail under the top drawers readings "Manufactured by John Sala," end panels in dark blackish brown w/gold stenciled flowers, bird in flowering tree & "G.W. 1852," clear pressed glass drawer pulls, Soap Hollow, Pennsylvania, 20 1/2 x 38 1/2", 46 3/4" h. ................................................. **16,500**

**Federal country-style chest of drawers,** painted pine, rectangular top slightly overhanging the case w/a deep thumb-molded long drawer over three graduated matching drawers all w/pairs of simple turned wood knobs, serpentine apron continuing into simple bracket feet, red & black graining simulating mahogany, New England, early 19th c., 17 1/4 x 39 1/2", 41" h. (replaced pulls, imperfections)............................................. **1,265**

**Federal country-style chest of drawers,** walnut, rectangular top over a case w/four long graduated beaded drawers w/diamond-form inlaid keyhole escutcheons, short ring-turned legs w/knob feet, paneled ends, old worn refinishing, early 19th c., 20 1/2 x 42, 43" h. (some edge damage, replaced pressed glass pulls, one missing)............................................. **715**

**Federal country-style sugar chest,** cherry, a rectangular hinged bin lid above a deep divided interior well, oneboard sides & ends, rod- and ring-turned short legs w/peg feet, mellow refinishing, Southern U.S., first half 19th c., 19 1/2 x 30", 29 1/4" h. (pieced repairs) ... **1,375**

**Federal tall chest of drawers,** inlaid cherry, a rectangular top w/a deep coved cornice w/a dart-inlaid band above a case w/a row of three small drawers above five long graduated cockbeaded drawers w/oval brass pulls & diamondinlaid keyhole escutcheons, inlaid lambrequin corners, herringbone inlaid band across the base, short bracket feet, old refinish, probably Pennsylvania, ca. 1790-1800, 21 x 40 1/2", 60 3/4" h. (replaced brasses, loss of height) ............. **3,450**

*Fine Inlaid Federal Tall Chest*

**Federal tall chest of drawers,** inlaid walnut, rectangular top w/a wide coved cornice above a narrow diamond-inlaid frieze band above a row of three small drawers over five long graduated drawers all w/line-inlaid oval bands, oval brasses & diamond-form inlaid keyhole escutcheons, narrow inlaid banding down front stiles, veneered band around the ‑ base, on tall French feet, soft

rubbed-out finish, Pennsylvania, late 18th - early 19th c., 24 3/4 x 46", 66 1/2" h. (ILLUS.)..................................... **6,325**

*Rare G. Stickley Chest of Drawers*

**Mission-style (Arts & Crafts movement) chest of drawers,** oak, a low crestrail above the rectangular top above a case w/a pair of short drawers over four long drawers, vertical pull plates on drawers form two bands up the front, paneled end w/cut-out feet, branded mark of Gustav Stickley, Model No. 906, ca. 1912, 21 x 41", 48" h. (ILLUS.)............... **13,800**

*Fine Gustav Stickley Tall Chest*

**Mission-style (Arts & Crafts movement) tall chest of drawers,** oak, a low crestboard above the tall case w/slightly bowed side stiles & three pairs of small drawers over three long graduated drawers all w/turned wood knobs, arched apron, designed by Harvey Ellis, red decal mark of Gustav Stickley, Model No. 913, lightly cleaned original finish, slight veneer split, 20 x 36", 51" h. (ILLUS.) .................................................... **7,700**

*Early Painted Mule Chest*

**Mule chest (box chest w/one or more drawers below a storage compartment),** painted pine, a rectangular hinged top opening to a deep well w/two false drawers at the front above two working drawers, all w/simple butterfly pulls & keyhole escutcheons, molded base on bootjack end legs, repainted greyish brown, probably Massachusetts, early 18th c., replaced brasses, 18 x 39 1/2", 37" h. (ILLUS.) .................... **1,150**

**Mule chest (box chest w/one or more drawers below a storage compartment),** painted pine, rectangular hinged top w/molded edges opens to a well above two thumb-molded drawers on a straight front skirt w/side shaping, early hinges, old red paint, New England, late 18th c., 18 1/2 x 43 3/4", 41 1/4" h. (replaced pulls, minor imperfections) ........ **1,840**

*Chinese Chest of Drawers*

**Oriental chest of drawers,** brass-bound mahogany & camphorwood, two-part construction: the upper section w/a rectangular top of a pair of small drawers above a deep long drawer; the lower section w/two long reverse-graduated

drawers, fitted w/brass inset handles & end handles, on small tapering turned feet, refinished, minor imperfections, China, mid-19th c., 19 3/4 x 38 3/4", 34 1/2" h. (ILLUS.) ..................................... **4,025**

*Fine Pilgrim Century Chest of Drawers*

**Pilgrim Century chest of drawers,** painted oak, cedar & yellow pine, joined construction, the rectangular top w/applied molded edges above a case of four long drawers each w/molded fronts & chamfered mitered borders & separated by applied horizontal moldings, the sides w/two recessed vertical molded panels above a single horizontal panel on a base w/applied moldings & four turned ball feet, old red paint, old replaced feet, southeastern New England, ca. 1700, 20 1/2 x 37 3/4", 35" h. (ILLUS.) ..................................... **13,800**

**Pilgrim Century chest over drawer,** pine, a rectangular molded top w/pintle hinges above a single-arch molded base centering a panel w/carved initials "MG" & a single long drawer w/teardrop pulls, on turned ball front feet & square rear feet, pierced brass keyhole oval escutcheons, Massachusetts, early 18th c., apparently original hardware, 18 1/2 x 42", 32 3/4" h. (imperfections) ......................... **4,600**

**Queen Anne chest on frame,** maple, two-part construction: the upper section w/a rectangular top w/a deep stepped cornice above a case of four long graduated thumb-molded drawers w/butterfly brasses & keyhole escutcheons; the lower section w/a mid-molding above a single long narrow drawer over the apron w/two drop pendants flanking a small central carved fan, cabriole legs ending in high pad feet, old refinished surface, Newburyport, 1750-80, 15 1/2 x 36", 56 1/2" h. (replaced brasses, imperfections) ................................ **8,050**

**Queen Anne country-style chest over drawers,** the rectangular hinged molded top opening above a deep well w/a cast front w/a pair of short over one long false drawers above two working long drawers, applied base molding above the scroll-cut arched apron, old refinish, imperfections, probably Connecticut, mid-18th c., 17 1/2 x 35 1/2", 45" h. (ILLUS. below) ........................................ **2,070**

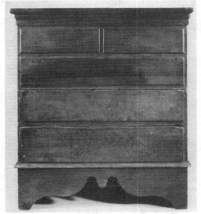

*Queen Anne Chest over Drawers*

**Sheraton country-style chest of drawers,** walnut, rectangular top above a case w/a pair of small beaded drawers above three long graduated beaded drawers, simple turned wood knobs, old varnish finish, baluster- and ring-turned short legs w/knob feet, early 19th c., 20 x 41 1/4", 47" h. ...................................... **770**

*Early Southern Sugar Chest*

**Sugar chest,** cherry, a rectangular hinged lid above a deep dovetailed well divided into three compartments, a long bottom drawer wtwo turned wood knobs, on baluster-, ring- and knob-turned legs w/knob feet, drawer bottom w/scraps of the "Weekly Courier Journal, Louisville" from the 1880s, refinished, age crack in lid, minor edge damage on feet, Southern, 19th c., 19 1/4 x 27 3/4", 40" h. (ILLUS.) ..................................................... **4,675**

*Early Virginia Sugar Chest*

**Sugar chest,** Federal country-style, walnut, a hinged rectangular top opening to a deep well above a single long drawer at the bottom w/simple turned wood pulls, square tapering legs, Shenandoah Valley, Virginia, first half 19th c. (ILLUS.) ....... **2,000**

**Sugar chest on frame,** walnut, the chest w/a rectangular hinged breadboard top opening to a deep well in the dovetailed case, the lower section w/a deep apron w/a single long dovetailed drawer w/two small turned wood knobs, on ring- and baluster-turned legs w/peg feet, refinished, Kentucky, early 19th c., 15 1/2 x 24", 34 1/4" h. (chest missing interior dividers, mid-molding missing, lid reworked) .................................................... **3,245**

*Ornate Tall Rococo Revival Chest*

**Turn-of-the-century tall chest of drawers,** mahogany veneer, Rococo Revival style, two-piece construction: an oblong serpentine-sided beveled mirror in a conforming frame w/a scroll-carved crest swiveling between to S-scroll carved uprights on the rectangular lift-off molded top w/rounded corners above a tall bombé case w/a pair of narrow top drawers w/two pairs of small wood pulls each above four long graduated drawers w/two pairs of small wood knobs each, serpentine scroll-carved apron & cabriole legs ending in scroll & peg feet on casters, ca. 1900 (ILLUS.) ....................... **1,815**

*Fine Late Victorian Tall Chest*

**Turn-of-the-century tall chest of drawers,** mahogany veneer, Rococo-style w/a large cartouche-form beveled mirror in a molded conforming frame w/an ornate scroll-carved crest & tilting between ornate scroll-carved S-form uprights on the rectangular molded top w/serpentine front above a conforming case w/two curved-front small upper drawers flanking a wide curved-front door above three conforming long drawers all w/scroll brass pulls, scroll-carved apron w/central cartouche in front, raised on scroll-carved legs w/paw feet on casters, ca. 1890-1900 (ILLUS.) .......... **1,750**

**Victorian Eastlake substyle chest of drawers,** walnut, a rectangular mirror w/a molded frame & scroll-carved crestrail tilting between plain uprights beside a pair of small handkerchief drawers on the rectangular molded top above the tall case w/a pair of molded drawers beside a small paneled door over three long molded drawers, all drawers w/incised leafy scrolls, molded base on knob & peg feet on casters, paneled sides, ca. 1880 (ILLUS. top next column) ........................................................ **975**

**Victorian Renaissance Revival chest of drawers,** walnut, an inset rectangular white marble top within a molded border w/rounded corners above a case w/two long drawers each w/raised oval band molding enclosing elongated four-point mounts for pulls & small round keyhole

escutcheons, molded plinth base on casters, ca. 1875-80, old finish, 21 1/4 x 45 1/2", 32" h. ............................... **440**

*Tall Eastlake Chest of Drawers*

# CRADLES

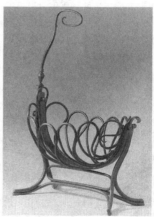

*Bentwood Cradle on Frame*

**Bentwood cradle on frame,** the oblong shell-form bentwood crib suspended within a sinuous bentwood frame surmounted by a shepherd's crook at one end, probably Austria, ca. 1905, wear, 30 x 55", 76" h. (ILLUS.)............................. **1,380**

**Country-style low cradle on rockers,** painted poplar, arched angled head- and footboards w/heart-form cut-out above tapering paneled ends, headboard w/shaped rim brackets on the rounded edge rail over the canted paneled sides, turned knob finials at each corner, beveled into deep scroll-shaped rockers, old worn red paint w/blue sponged panels & white trim, 19th c., 36" l. (rockers restored)...................................................... **413**

# CUPBOARDS

*Exotic Art Deco Corner Cupboard*

**Corner cupboard,** Art Deco, mahogany w/exotic veneers, a central flat rectangular top flanked by squared angled ends above a conforming case w/a central pair of tall cupboard doors w/light panels of triangular veneer centering a small dark rectangular, the side panels w/an arched open top compartment above a tall narrow door w/a tall glazed panel, three interior shelves, raised on simple turned ovoid legs, ca. 1930s, 34 x 71 1/4", 71 1/2" h. (ILLUS.) ............... **2,300**

*Demilune Inlaid Corner Cupboard*

**Corner cupboard,** Baroque Revival style, inlaid mahogany, the high arched & molded top centered by a large oval cartouche above the demilune case w/a dentil molding above a pair of tall cupboard doors w/thin decorative molded panels centered by ribbon bow inlay & an inlaid oval w/flower-filled urn & flanked by blocked pilasters, a heavy

mid-molding above a shorter pair of matching cupboard doors flanked by serpentine heavy pilasters ending in heavy carved paw feet, second half 19th c., Europe., requires some restoration (ILLUS.) ...................................................... **8,800**

*Tall Chippendale Corner Cupboard*

**Corner cupboard,** Chippendale architectural-type, curly maple, one-piece construction, the top w/a broken-scroll pediment w/starburst-carved scroll ends & ball-and-flame-turned finials above a pair of tall arched two-panel cupboard doors w/a short arched panel above a tall rectangular panel above a mid-molding over a pair of paneled cupboard doors, molded base on ogee bracket feet, old refinishing, feet, finials & ends of scrolls replaced, late 18th c., 44 1/2" w., 99 1/2" h. (ILLUS.) ................. **10,450**

*Chippendale Walnut Corner Cupboard*

**Corner cupboard,** Chippendale, walnut, two-piece construction: the upper section w/a broken-scroll molded cornice centered by a block & urn-form finial above an arched molding continuing down to reeded pilasters flanking the arched geometrically-glazed cupboard door opening to three shelves; the lower section w/a mid-molding over a pair of short paneled cupboard doors flanked by reeded pilasters, blocked & scroll-cut base, late 18th c. (ILLUS.) ........................ **6,500**

**Corner cupboard,** Classical country-style, painted & decorated pine & poplar, two-part construction: the upper section w/a stepped & molded flaring cornice above a single large 12-pane glazed door flanked by wood-grained sides imitating mahogany; the lower section w/a mid-molding above a pair of small flush drawers over a pair of paneled doors all flanked by wide side panels & decorated overall w/mahogany wood graining, molded base on bun front feet, Rupp of Yorktown, Pennsylvania, first half 19th c., top 47 1/2" w., overall 86 3/4" h. (replaced hardware, some edge & surface wear) ................................................ **8,800**

*One-piece Cherry Corner Cupboard*

**Corner cupboard,** country-style, cherry & poplar, one-piece construction, the rectangular top w/a wide coved cornice above a pair of two-panel doors w/simple wood knobs above a mid-molding over two single panel cupboard doors, molded base w/deeply scalloped apron & bracket feet, cleaned down to traces of old red, edge damage, repairs, top 44 1/2" w., 76" h. (ILLUS.) ........................ **1,430**

**Corner cupboard,** country-style, cherry, two-piece construction: the upper section w/a flat flared cornice above a pair of tall 6-pane glazed cupboard doors opening to two shelves; the lower section w/a single central drawer above a pair of paneled cupboard doors, flat apron w/simple

cut-out feet, cast-iron thumb latches w/brass knobs, interior w/modern blue paint, refinished, mid-19th c., 48 1/4" w., 82 3/4" h. .................................................. **3,630**

*One-piece Walnut Corner Cupboard*

**Corner cupboard,** country-style, walnut, one-piece construction, the flat top w/a deep stepped & coved cornice above a herringbone-cut band above reeded banding framing a pair of tall two-panel cupboard doors over a mid-molding & a pair of shorter paneled cupboard doors over the shaped apron & bracket feet, refinished, backboards partially patched & renailed, repairs, hinges replaced, found in Kentucky, mid-19th c., top 49 1/2" w., 88 3/4" h. (ILLUS.) .................. **1,980**

*Tall Inlaid Walnut Corner Cupboard*

**Corner cupboard,** Federal country-style corner cupboard, inlaid walnut, one-piece construction, the flat top w/a narrow coved cornice above a pair of tall paneled cupboard doors flanked by leafy vining inlay down the stiles above a central board w/line inlays over a pair of shorter cupboard doors w/string inlay above a low scalloped apron flanked by line inlay, inlaid diamond keyhole escutcheons, refinished, repairs, hinges replaced, door edges restored, backboards renailed, found in Kentucky, early 19th c., top 47" w., 85" h. (ILLUS.) ... **2,090**

*Fine Curly Maple Corner Cupboard*

**Corner cupboard,** Federal country-style, curly maple, two-part construction: the upper section w/a flat top over a coved cornice above a pair of tall 8-pane glazed cupboard doors opening to three shelves; the lower section w/a mid-molding above a pair of paneled cupboard doors w/small knobs, flat apron on shaped bracket feet, old refinishing, replaced hardware, minor edge damage & restoration, early 19th c., 49" w., 83" h. (ILLUS.) ..................................................... **7,920**

*Inlaid Federal Corner Cupboard*

**Corner cupboard,** Federal country-style, inlaid cherry, one-piece construction, the top w/a deep coved cornice above a narrow inlaid band above a pair of tall paneled cupboard doors above a narrow inlaid medial band over a pair of shorter paneled cupboard doors above a narrow inlaid band over the scalloped apron w/a central fan-inlaid drop, simple bracket feet, each door w/inlaid rectangular banding in the panel, early 19th c., feet replaced, repairs, 45 1/4" w., 82 1/4" h. (ILLUS.)...................................................... **3,300**

*Virginia Federal Corner Cupboard*

**Corner cupboard,** Federal country-style, inlaid walnut, the flat top w/a coved cornice above a frieze band w/geometric inlay over a pair of tall 8-pane glazed cupboard doors opening to three shelves above a mid-molding over a pair of cupboard doors w/tombstone-form line inlay, narrow molded base on scroll-cut bracket feet, Shenandoah Valley, Virginia, early 19th c. (ILLUS.) .................. **4,000**

**Corner cupboard,** Federal country-style, pine & poplar, two-piece construction: the upper section w/a cove-molded cornice above a pair of 8-pane glazed doors opening to three shelves; the lower section w/a mid-molding above a pair of small drawers over two paneled cupboard doors, molded base & simple cut-out apron, old yellowish brown grained repaint, first half 19th c., 54" w., 90 1/2" h. ................................................. **2,750**

**Corner cupboard,** Federal country-style, pine, two-part construction: the upper section w/a flat top over a deep stepped flaring cornice above a single wide 16-pane glazed cupboard door opening to three shelves; the lower section projecting above two cupboard doors w/cockbeaded panels, flat base w/applied molding, old refinish, replaced hardware, imperfections, New England, early 19th c., 29 1/2 x 57", 88 3/4" h. (ILLUS. top next page) ................................................. **1,725**

*Federal Country Corner Cupboard*

**Hanging cupboard,** painted & decorated pine, rectangular top above a case w/a single wide board door w/wooden thumb latch, old red & black graining, found in Maine, 19th c., 11 3/4 x 24 3/4", 39" h. (some edge damage, interior shelves replaced) ...................................................... **303**

*Gothic Revival Wall Cupboard*

**Hanging wall cupboard,** Gothic Revival style, walnut, the top composed of three tall pointed pierce-carved flat Gothic spires w/a taller central spire above a narrow arched mirror framed by molding, a pair of small square drawers below over two long drawers, Gothic arch-cut front apron & back panel, old dark finish, replaced clear glass knobs, 19th c., 7 1/4 x 15 3/4", 37 1/4" h. (ILLUS.) .............. **385**

**Hanging wall cupboard,** pine, the rectangular top w/a flaring cornice above a conforming case w/a paneled door opening to a shelved interior, over a molding above a shelf w/shaped sides, red-stained, 19th c., 9 1/4 x 20", 25 1/2" h. (ILLUS. below) ............................ **978**

*Pine Hanging Wall Cupboard*

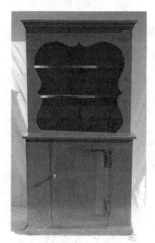

*Nutting Pine Hutch Cupboard*

**Hutch cupboard,** Wallace Nuttting-signed, pine, one-piece construction, the rectangular top w/a wide stepped cornice above a scallop-cut open top enclosing two shaped shelves above the stepped out lower case w/a single flat cupboard door w/HL hinges, Model No. 923 Pine Scrolled Cupboard, early 20th c. (ILLUS.) ...................................................... **4,290**

**Jelly cupboard,** country-style, painted & decorated pine & poplar, the rectangular top w/a three-quarters gallery w/rounded ends above a pair of molded drawers w/large wood knobs overhanging a pair of baluster- and acorn-turned short side drops above a pair of tall paneled doors, scalloped apron & ring- and knob-turned feet, old brownish yellow wood graining w/burl design on drawers & door panels, Pennsylvania, mid-19th c., 24 1/2 x 46 3/4", overall 58 3/4" h. (ILLUS. below) .................. **495**

*Paint-decorated Jelly Cupboard*

**Jelly cupboard,** country-style, poplar, a rectangular top above a case w/two tall doors w/three pierced tin panels decorated w/a large center diamond & circle & smaller corner circles, a long nailed drawer across the bottom, three tin panels in each side, square stile legs, side tins w/embossed label "G.F. Co.," backboards w/old painted inscriptions, refinished, 19th c., 14 1/4 x 40", 50" h. .............. **853**

*Federal Country-style Jelly Cupboard*

**Jelly cupboard,** Federal country-style, cherry, a rectangular top above a pair of cockbeaded drawers w/turned wood knobs over a long rectangular 2-pane glazed cupboard door, paneled ends, molded base on simple short turned legs w/knob feet, Pennsylvania or Ohio, ca. 1830s, refinished, imperfections, 13 1/2 x 28" , 25" h. (ILLUS.) .................. **1,840**

*Grain-painted Federal Jelly Cupboard*

**Jelly cupboard,** Federal country-style, painted & decorated, a rectangular top w/a narrow coved cornice above a case w/a pair of drawers w/oval brasses above a pair of tall paneled cupboard doors, serpentine apron & tall French feet, fine overall reddish brown grain painting imitating mahogany, early 19th c. (ILLUS.) .................................... **7,150**

**Jelly cupboard,** painted pine, low three-quarters gallery on the rectangular top above a case w/a pair of drawers over a single long drawer above a pair of tall paneled cupboard doors, flat apron & simple tapered front stile feet, old repaint w/olive graining on a yellowish ground, 19th c., 16 1/2 x 43", overall 53 1/2" h.(wear, one gallery end repaired) .................................... **1,705**

**Jelly cupboard,** painted pine & poplar, plain rectangular top above a wide tall board & batten door flanked by wide front boards, old yellowish brown graining, 19th c., 15 x 42", 40 1/2" h. .................. **550**

**Jelly cupboard,** walnut, a rectangular top above a pair of long drawers w/white porcelain knobs above a pair of tall double-paneled cupboard doors, the side panels of tin punched w/pots of flowers, on short square stile legs, old worn finish, attributed to Wythe County, Virginia, mid-19th c., 17 1/4 x 50", 47" h. (rust & damage to tin) .......................................... **1,155**

**Linen press,** Chippendale country-style, painted poplar, the rectangular top w/a deep cove-molded cornice above a pair of tall double raised-panel doors w/a short panel above a tall panel & hung w/H-hinges above two long drawers w/butterfly brasses & keyhole escutcheons, molded base on high bracket feet, old red, late 18th - early 19th c., repairs, foot facings & cornice replaced, top 17 x 45 1/2", 73" h. (ILLUS. top next page) .......................................... **4,400**

*Country Chippendale Linen Press*

*Simple Painted Pewter Cupboard*

**Pewter cupboard,** country-style, painted pine, one-piece construction: the flat rectangular top above an open hutch top w/three shelves above a stepped-out top over a case w/a narrow tall one-board door flanked by wide side boards, simple angle-cut feet, red paint, some old reconstruction, 19 x 38 1/4", 71 1/2" h. (ILLUS.)..................................... **2,090**

**Pewter cupboard,** country-style, painted pine, one-piece construction, the flat rectangular top above two wide side boards flanking an open two-shelved compartment, the stepped-out lower section w/a pair of flat board doors flanked by wide side boards, worn old sage green paint over red, shelves somewhat altered, some edge damage & renailing, 19th c., 17 x 49", 73" h. (ILLUS.)..................................... **2,200**

*Early Painted Pewter Cupboard*

**Pewter cupboard,** pine, one-piece construction, the flat rectangular top w/narrow molding across cornice & down the front sides framing the open three-shelf cupboard w/plate rails, the slightly stepped-out lower section w/a pair of paneled cupboard doors, flat base, old nut brown finish, 19th c., 13 1/4 x 41 3/4", 70 1/2" h. (botton rail under doors replaced, feet worn down, repairs, backboards renailed)................... **1,650**

*Fine Cherry & Tin Pie Safe*

**Pie safe,** cherry & punched tin, a rectangular top above a pair of drawers w/simple turned knobs above a pair of large cupboard doors each w/four large rectangular punched tin panels decorated w/a central pinwheel w/fanned leaf devices in each corner, flat base, baluster- and ring-turned legs w/peg feet, old worn brown finish w/traces of oil cloth, two punched tin panels on each end, found in East Tennessee, mid-19th c., 18 3/4 x 53", 49" h. (ILLUS.)..................... **5,225**

*Early Pie Safe with Punched Tin*

**Pie safe,** country-style, hardwoods, the rectangular top w/a low shaped three-quarters gallery above a tall case w/a pair of two three-panel doors w/pierced tin inserts w/scrolling designs above a pair of deep drawers at the bottom, turned & tapering legs w/knob and peg feet, three pierced tins on each side, mid-19th c. (ILLUS.)` ................................ **1,450**

**Pie safe,** painted poplar, rectangular top above a pair of drawers w/small wooden knobs over a pair of tall three-panel doors each tin panel w/a pierced floral design, one-board ends, tall slightly tapering stile legs, old grey repaint, 19th c., 17 x 42 1/2", 57 3/4" h. ........................... **770**

*Poplar & Punched Tin Pie Safe*

**Pie safe,** poplar & punched tin, a flat rectangular top above a pair of tall paneled cupboard doors w/three punched tin panels each decorated w/a large central star in a circle flanked by four small

stars, a long narrow drawer across the bottom, one-board ends, tightly scallop-cut apron, square stile legs, refinished, 19th c., 15 x 40 3/4", 49" h. (ILLUS.)......... **1,375**

**Step-back wall cupboard,** cherry, one-piece construction, the rectangular top w/a narrow flared cornice above a pair of tall double-paneled doors opening to shelves above the slightly projecting lower section w/a pair of paneled shorter doors, flat apron & simple bracket feet, refinished w/traces of old paint, possibly Kentucky, mid-19th c., 13 3/8 x 31 1/8", 81 1/2" h. (some edge damage, filled holes from insect damage, replaced hinges) ...................................................... **1,430**

*Cherry & Poplar Step-back Cupboard*

**Step-back wall cupboard,** country-style, cherry & poplar, two-piece construction: the upper section w/a rectangular top over a simpe coved cornice above a pair of 8-pane glazed cupboard doors opening to three shelves & flanked by wide side boards; the stepped-out lower section w/a pair of tall paneled cupboard doors flanked by wide side boards, flat base, repairs, cut-down w/pie shelf removed, cornice replaced, old finish, mid-19th c., top 15 1/4 x 57", 79 3/4" h. (ILLUS.)...................................................... **1,513**

**Step-back wall cupboard,** country-style, cherry, two-piece construction: the upper section w/a rectangular top w/a coved cornice over a dentil-carved frieze band above a pair of very tall two-panel cupboard doors w/a smaller square panel over a tall rectangular panel above a pair of short drawers w/simple turned wood knobs; the stepped-out lower section w/a pair of paneled cupboard doors over the serpentine apron, refinished, repairs to hinge rails & one upper door w/replaced surface-mounted hinges, replaced pulls, minor edge damage, mid-19th c., top 14 x 45 3/4", 87" h. (ILLUS. top next page) ............................. **1,980**

*Tall Step-back Cherry Wall Cupboard*

*Painted Step-back Wall Cupboard*

**Step-back wall cupboard,** country-style, painted pine, one-piece construction, the rectangular top w/a widely flaring stepped cornice over a frieze band w/molding above a pair of paneled cupboard doors w/molding-trimmed panels & simple wood knobs above the stepped-out lower section over two very small drawers over another pair of matching paneled doors, molded base w/simply cut-out apron, old blue paint over a lighter blue, found in northern Maine, edge wear & damage, 19th c., toop 20 x 62 1/4", 78 1/2" h. (ILLUS.) ....... **6,050**

**Step-back wall cupboard,** country-style, painted poplar, two-piece construction: the upper section w/a flared & stepped cornice above a pair of 3-pane glazed cupboard doors opening to two shelves above an arched piece shelf; the lower stepped-out section w/a pair of flush drawers over a pair of paneled cupboard doors, gently scalloped apron & low bracket feet, old yellowish brown steel comb-graining on a white ground, brass thumb-latch on botton doors, cast-iron latch on upper doors, worn paint, some edge damage, top 13 1/2 x 49", 82 1/2" h. .................................................... **1,045**

**Step-back wall cupboard,** country-style, poplar & walnut, two-part construction: the upper section w/a flaring ogee cornice w/rounded corners above a pair of tall 8-pane glazed cupboard doors opening to three shelves; the stepped-out lower section w/a rectangular top w/molded edges & rounded front corners above an ogee frieze w/a pair of longer drawers flanking a central small drawer all w/simple turned wood knobs above a pair of paneled cupboard doors flanked by rounded front corners, low lightly scalloped apron, refinished, second half 19th c., 19 3/4 x 50 1/2", 81 1/2" h. .............. **825**

**Step-back wall cupboard,** country-style, walnut, one-piece construction, a rectangular top w/a deep coved cornice above a pair of tall 6-pane glazed cupboard doors opening to shelves, the stepped-out lower section w/a pair of paneled cupboard doors, shaped apron w/simple bracket feet, some edge damage, cornice renailed, worn old finish, top 14 3/4 x 46 3/4", 80 1/4" h. ...................... **2,090**

*Tall Walnut Step-back Wall Cupboard*

**Step-back wall cupboard,** country-style, walnut, two-piece construction: the upper section w/a rectangular top w/a simple coved cornice above a pair of tall 8-pane glazed cupboard doors opening to shelves above the open pie shelf w/shaped sides; the lower stepped-out section w/a rectangular top over a row of three drawers above a pair of paneled cupboard doors flanking a narrow central panel, short turned tapering legs w/knob feet, old worn finish, original brass swivel latches on doors, brass knobs replaced, base w/old shipping label "Vandalia RR Co.," mid-19th c., top 13 1/2 x 54", 93 1/4" h. (ILLUS.) ............... **4,400**

*Short Cherry Wall Cupboard*

**Wall cupboard,** country-style, cherry, one-piece construction, a rectangular top above a single 4-pane glazed cupboard door above a raised-panel cupboard door both flanked by wide side boards, old brass hardware & latches, refinished, scalloped apron, 19th c., top 13 1/2 x 32", 54 1/2" h. (ILLUS.) ............... **1,870**

*Walnut One-piece Wall Cupboard*

**Wall cupboard,** country-style, one-piece construction, a flat rectangular top above a band of reeded molding continuing down each side & flanking a tall 12-pane glazed cupboard door above a pair of flat lower cupboard doors, flat base, old dark brown finish over red, hinges replaced, old alterations, 19th c., 47" w., 83" h. (ILLUS.) ........................................... **1,650**

**Wall cupboard,** country-style, painted pine & poplar, one-piece construction, a flat plain top w/no molding above a tall narrow flat one-board door above a shorter flat one-board door w/wide side boards flanking them, cast-iron thumb latches, worn old layers of greenish grey & olive tan paint, 19th c., 14 1/4 x 36 1/2", 74 3/4" h. .................................................. **1,128**

*European Painted Wall Cupboard*

**Wall cupboard,** country-style, painted wood, the rectangular top w/a flat molded cornice above a projecting frieze initials in white "H.S.F. 1833," over two paneled cupboard doors w/applied molded panels & wrought-iron hinges separated by a mid-molding on a low cut-out base, original red paint, probably Northern Europe, 14 3/4 x 34", 69" h. (ILLUS.) .................................................... **3,335**

*Compact Walnut Wall Cupboard*

Wall cupboard, country-style, walnut, one-piece construction, a rectangular top w/a deep flaring ogee cornice above a pair of tall two-panel cupboard doors w/a cast-iron thumb latch above a row of three drawers w/a long central drawer, each w/a cast-iron grip pull over a pair of shorter paneled cupboard doors w/a cast-iron thumb latch, low scalloped apron, second half 19th c., small-sized (ILLUS.)......................................................... **770**

Wall cupboard, Federal country-style, cherry, one-piece construction, the rectangular top w/a flaring stepped cornice over a pair of tall paneled cupboard doors opening to three shelves above a lower shorter pair of cupboard doors, scalloped apron, cut-out feet, old worn soft patina, 19th c., 17 1/2 x 46", 76 3/4" h. .................................................. **2,915**

Wall cupboard, painted pine, one-piece construction, rectangular top w/narrow molding above a case w/a flush long board & batten door above a slightly short matching door w/wooden thumb latch, cleaned down to old red, flat base, 19th c., 16 1/2 x 37", 76 1/4" h. (minor edge damage) ......................................... **1,650**

*Simple Painted Wall Cupboard*

Wall cupboard, painted pine, plain rectangular top above a pair of tall plain doors opening to an interior of numbered shelves, some of which are also labeled, flat base, old light green paint, interior unpainted, New Lebanon, New York area, possibly Shaker, 19th c., some shelves missing, 7 1/2 x 23 3/4", 40 1/2" h. (ILLUS.).................................... **1,610**

# DESKS

Art Deco desk, painted wood & tubular steel, the elevated rectangular wood top above an asymetical arrangement of three short drawers on the right side, supported on a continuous tubular steel frame, attributed to Marcel Breuer, produced by Thonet, Austria, ca. 1930, 30 x 54", 30" h. (ILLUS.) .......................... **2,070**

*Thonet Art Deco Desk*

*"Bonheur du Jour" Desk*

Art Nouveau "bonheur du jour" desk, fruitwood marquetry, central upright case w/fall front opening to an interior fitted w/shelves, pigeonholes, pen tray & glass Waterman inkwell, above a writing plateau w/drawer below, all inlaid w/various woods w/stylized poppies & leafage, the whole raised on tapering legs carved w/poppies, signed in marquetry "Gallé/Nancy," ca. 1900, 21 x 28 1/2 x 46" (ILLUS.)........................................... **5,750**

*Unusual Oak Art Nouveau Desk*

Art Nouveau desk, oak, a rectangular top w/rounded corners above a single apron drawer over a wide arched kneehole w/serpentine sides & line-incised scrolls, each end w/two narrow open shelves, scratches, roughness, ca. 1900, 29 3/4 x 47 1/4", 28 1/2" h. (ILLUS.) ........................ **518**

**Chippendale country-style slant-front desk,** cherry, narrow rectangular top above a wide hinged slant front opening to an interior fitted w/five valanced compartments & drawers above a case w/four long cockbeaded graduated drawers w/replaced round brass knob pulls, molded base on bracket feet, old refinish, probably western Massachusetts, ca. 1780, 18 x 37 1/2", 40" h. (minor imperfections) ..................... **3,105**

**Chippendale slant-front desk,** birch, a narrow rectangular top over a wide hinged slant top opening to a shaped interior of ten compartments & small drawers, the cockbeaded case w/four long graduated drawers on a molded base w/scroll-cut bracket feet, probably Massachusetts, ca. 1780, 21 1/4 x 40", 44 1/4" h. (old refinish, 21 1/4 x 40", 44 1/4" h. (old refinish, imperfections) ...... **1,955**

**Chippendale slant-front desk,** carved mahogany, a narrow rectangular top above a wide hinged slant front lid opening to an interior of central shell-carved concave prospect door opening to two valanced drawers, two compartments & drawer, flanked by three valanced compartments & drawers, flanked by three valanced compartments above blocked drawers & shell-carved drawers above two concave carved drawers, the lower case w/four long graduated thumb-molded drawers w/butterfly pulls, molded base on tall ogee bracket feet, refinished, Townsend-Goddard School, Newport, Rhode Island, late 18th c., 20 1/4 x 38 3/4", 42 1/2" h. (replaced brasses, restoration............................... **18,400**

**Chippendale slant-front desk,** curly maple, a narrow rectangular top above the hinged slant front opening to an interior fitted w/six valanced pigeonholes & five short drawers w/a central fan-carved prospect door, the case w/four long graduated drawers w/butterfly pulls & keyhole escutcheons on a molded base w/central drop pendant & scroll-cut bracket feet, New England, ca. 1780, 18 1/2 x 36", 42" h. (valances of later date, prospect door possibly reworked, repairs to feet) ......................................... **7,475**

**Chippendale slant-front desk,** mahogany, a narrow top above a wide hinged slant lid opening to an interior fitted w/a central concave fan-carved prospect door opening to three concave drawers flanked by baluster-fronted document drawers, three valanced compartments, blocked drawers & a fan-carved drawer above two concave drawers, the case w/four long graduated thumb-molded drawers w/butterfly pulls & small brass keyhole escutcheons, molded base w/scroll-cut bracket feet, old finish, Boston, ca. 1770-80, 19 1/2 x 39 1/2",

42 1/2" h. (brasses replaced, imperfections) ...................................................... **27,600**

*Classical Lady's Desk*

**Classical lady's desk,** carved & veneered mahogany, the rectangular top w/hinged desk box & fitted interior of three drawers above a recessed case of two long drawers w/turned wood knobs flanked by free-standing columns on square plinths continuing to baluster- and ring-turned legs, old refinish, minor imperfections, New England, ca. 1825, 19 1/2 x 36 1/2", 36" h. (ILLUS.)................... **863**

**Country-style school master's desk,** walnut, a low three-quarters gallery around a narrow shelf above the wide hinged slant top w/edge molding opening to a deep well, on rod- and ring-turned legs w/ball and peg feet, old soft finish, 19th c., 26 x 41", 38" h. ....................................... **495**

**Country-style 'stand-up' desk,** pine, rectangular hinged top opening to a well fitted w/eight dovetailed small drawers & six pigeonholes, above three long dovetailed drawers w/simple turned wood knobs, brass keyhole escutcheons, raised on simple turned legs, possibly Shaker, refinished, 19th c., 17 3/4 x 33", 45 1/2" h. (one escutcheon missing, age cracks in ends) ........................................ **2,255**

*Federal Butler's Desk*

**Federal butler's desk,** inlaid mahogany, the rectangular top w/string-inlaid edge above a case w/a deep drawer w/two inlaid ovals set in mitered panels bordered by stringing & opening to an interior of a fold-out writing surface & central prospect door inlaid w/an urn of flowers bordered by stringing, flanked by document drawers w/inlay of simulated pilasters & three small drawers above four valance compartments, the lower case w/three long graduated band inlaid drawer on a serpentine apron & slender French feet, replaced oval brasses, imperfections, 21 x 46", 44" h. (ILLUS.) .... **2,530**

**Federal country-style school master's desk,** walnut & poplar, a low three-quarters gallery around a narrow top shelf above the wide hinged slant lid opening to an interior fitted w/pigeonholes, four dovetailed drawers & a center door, raised on ring- and rod-turned tapering legs w/baluster-turned feet, old red exterior finish, interior w/black painted trim, found in northeast Ohio, first half 19th c., 27 x 29 1/2", 38" h. ...................................... **743**

**Federal "oxbow" slant-front desk,** mahogany & mahogany veneer, a narrow rectangular top above a wide hinged slant front opening to an interior of five drawers & nine valanced compartments, the case w/four long graduated double-serpentine drawers w/oval brasses & keyhole escutcheons, curved apron & flaring French feet, old brasses, old refinish, probably Massachusetts, ca. 1790-1810, 42" w., 44" h. (imperfections) ......................................... **4,600**

**Federal slant-front desk,** cherry, a narrow rectangular top above the wide hinged slant lid opening to an interior fitted w/three small pigeonholes over two narrow drawers on each side of a square center door flanked by letter drawers, the case w/four cock-beaded long graduated drawers, deeply scalloped apron & tall French feet, replaced oval brasses, old mellow refinishing, early 19th c., 19 x 41 1/2", 46" h. (old pieced repairs) .... **3,025**

**Federal slant-front desk,** stained maple, a narrow rectangular top above a wide hinged slant front opening to an interior fitted w/valanced compartments & small beaded drawers over a case w/four long graduated drawers w/oval brasses above the scalloped apron & tall French feet, old dark red stain, original brasses, New England, early 19th c., 20 x 39 1/2", 44" h. ...................................................... **4,313**

**Federal slant-front desk,** wavy birch, a narrow top above a wide hinged slant lid opening to a valanced multi-drawer interior w/pigeonholes over a case w/four long graduated cockbeaded drawers w/simple bail pulls, serpentine apron over simple French feet, old refinish, southern New England, ca. 1780-1800, 19 1/2 x 39 1/4", 43 1/2" h. (replaced brasses, minor imperfections) ................... **2,530**

*Mission Oak Writing Desk*

**Mission-style (Arts & Crafts movement) desk,** oak, a rectangular top w/through corner posts above a narrow central drawer w/turned wood pulls flanked by slatted end book compartments joined by a flat wide medial shelf, unsigned, ca. 1916, 28 x 48", 29" h. (ILLUS.)..................... **805**

*Herman Miller 1950s Desk*

**Modern style desk,** walnut & brass, a demi-lune shaped top above a conforming case w/a three-slot compartment above a stack of two drawers w/round brass pulls & open side compartment to the left of the kneehole, raised on cylindrical brass legs, design attributed to Gilbert Rhode, manufactured by Herman Miller, Zeeland, Michigan, ca. 1950s, minor wear, 24 x 45 1/2", 29 1/4" h. (ILLUS.)..................................................... **1,150**

*Modern Style Desk & Chair*

**Modern style desk & chair,** maple, the desk w/a rectangular top over a central kneehole flanked on each side by a bank of two curved-front drawers w/horizontal wood pulls, raised on turned canted legs, an accompanying side chair w/a wide curved wooden back above an upholstered slip seat on a curved-front seatrail on slender square tapering legs, by Heywood Wakefield, ca. 1950s, desk 22 x 50", 29 1/4" h., 2 pcs. (ILLUS.)............. **403**

**Queen Anne child's slant-front desk,** maple, narrow rectangular top above a wide hinged slant front opening to a compartmented interior above a case w/two long thumb-molded drawers w/butterfly pulls & keyhole escutcheons, molded base & scroll-cut bracket feet, old refinish, New England, ca. 1750, 11 1/2 x 19 1/4", 20" h. (brasses probably replaced, restored) ............................ **2,530**

*Queen Anne Table-top Desk*

**Queen Anne table-top desk,** a narrow rectangular top above a hinged & molded slant-front opening to an interior of valanced compartments above two drawers & a well, the dovetailed shallow case w/pullout trunnels on a molded base w/central shaped pendant & simple bracket feet, refinished, restoration, Pennsylvania, ca. 1740-60, 14 1/4 x 23 1/2", 16 1/2" h. (ILLUS.).................................................... **2,530**

*Ornate Baroque-Style Partner's Desk*

**Victorian Baroque-Style partner's desk,** oak & oak veneer, the long oval top w/molded flaring edges above rounded end sections each w/a pair of drawers centering ornately scroll-carved curved doors centering on each side a long scroll-carved drawer over the kneehole opening, raised on a scroll-carved apron & four heavy animal paw legs on casters, late 19th c. (ILLUS.) .......................... **3,575**

**William & Mary slant-front desk,** maple, a narrow top above a wide hinged slant lid opening to an interior fitted w/valanced pigeonholes & seven short drawers centering a blocked hinged prospect door above a well, the lower case w/a pair of

short drawers w/butterfly pulls & keyhole escutcheons above a pair of long drawers w/similar pulls, molded base raised on large ball feet, probably New York area, 1710-30 (formerly painted white, several valances replaced) .................... **40,250**

*William & Mary Slant-front Desk*

**William & Mary slant-front desk,** walnut veneer, a narrow rectangular top above a wide hinged slant front opening to a valanced interior w/two document drawers w/columns above four drawers w/burl veneer & a well below, a double-arch molded case of two short drawers & two long drawers, the case w/a pair of short drawers above two long drawers each w/butterfly brasses & keyhole escutcheons, molded base on large turned turnip feet, old refinish, replaced brasses, restored, probably Connecticut, early 18th c., 19 1/2 x 34", 40 1/2" h. (ILLUS.).................................................... **5,175**

# DINING ROOM SUITES

**Art Deco:** dining table & eight dining chairs; mahogany & rosewood, the table w/a rectangular canted-corner top w/draw-ends raised on tapering splayed legs ending in brass sabots, two armchairs & six side chairs w/a curved backrest above a leather seat raised on tapering legs, France, ca. 1925, table 42 x 75", 29" h., the set (chair restoration) ........................................................ **8,625**

*Art Deco Dining Suite*

**Art Deco:** dining table & six side chairs; thuya & mahogany, the table w/a rectangular top w/cut corners in veneer over an eight-paneled cone-shaped pedestal on a short waisted band above the flared paneled base, each chair w/an angular arched crestrail above a tapering splat, upholstered seat on slender square tapering legs, faux suede seats in navy blue, Europe, ca. 1938, minor wear, table 49 x 59", 31 1/2" h. (ILLUS.)............. **4,600**

*Art Deco Walnut Dining Room Suite*

**Art Deco:** draw-leaf dining table & eight chairs; walnut & wrought iron, the table w/a rectangular top w/parquetry & raised on four legs inset w/leather panels conjoined by a wood & wrought-iron stretcher, raised on plinths, the chairs w/tall leather-upholsterd back panels & seats on square legs joined by high slender stretchers, ironwork impressed "J. Gallix," France. ca. 1935-40, table open 39 1/4 x 120", 29 1/2" h., the set (ILLUS.)...................................................... **5,750**

**Art Deco:** extension table & four dining chairs; the table in painted wood w/a black rectangular top over a narrow pale green apron on slender tapering square black ends & square open central supports in black & green, the chairs w/a painted black curved crestrail raised on green tubular-metal stiles continuing down & looping to form legs, upholstered seats, designed by Pierre Chareau, France, ca. 1928, w/four table leaves, table 16 1/4 x 58 1/2", 38" h., the set ...... **13,800**

*Art Deco Maple Dinette Set*

**Art Deco:** table & four side chairs; decorated maple, the extension dinette table w/a rectangular top w/cut corners above a reeded apron raised on U-shaped end & central supports w/reeded edges on a trestle-form base w/outswept reeded feet, each chair w/a stepped crest centered by a hand hole above a stencilled American eagle & shield design, shaped seat on square tapering & blocked front legs & slender square back stile legs joined by stretchers, National Chair Co.,

Boston, Massachusetts, ca. 1938, finish wear, table 42" w., chairs 34" h., the set (ILLUS.)........................................................ **345**

*German Art Deco Dining Room Suite*

**Art Deco:** table, two armchairs & four side chairs; exotic wood veneer, the table w/an oval expandable top above a deep apron on four slight incurved square tapering legs, the chairs also of exotic wood w/a lattice-style back & legs matching the table, upholstered seats, Germany, ca. 1930, veneer loss, table, 45 x 55", chairs 34 1/2" h., the set (ILLUS. of part)............................................ **460**

*Fine Classical Revival Dining Suite*

**Classical Revival:** round expandable table, sideboard, wall mirror, eight side chairs & two armchairs; mahogany & mahogany veneer, the table w/a carved edge & deep apron above a central support & four heavy scroll-carved legs on a cross-form plinth, the sideboard w/a high scroll-carved backboard above the rectangular top over an arrangement of drawers & doors, each chair w/a wide shaped crestrail over a wide scalloped splat, scroll-cut front legs w/low H-stretchers, ca. 1900, the set (ILLUS.) ..... **12,075**

**Jacobean Revival:** refractory dining table, six chairs, a court-style cupboard & a sideboard; oak, ornate turned & paneled details w/turned legs, in the 17th c. style, ca. 1920s, the set .......................... **3,410**

*Edward Wormley Dining Room Suite*

**Modern style:** dining table & eight chairs; hardwood, the table w/a long plain rectangular top & apron & square post legs, each chair w/a round-cornered crestrail above square canted rear & front legs w/an upholstered seat cushion, the armchairs w/scrolled open arms, designed by Edward Wormley, labeled by the Dunbar Company, ca. 1950s, table 41 7/8 x 72", 30 1/2" h., the set (ILLUS.)... **4,887**

*William & Mary Revival Dining Suite*

**William & Mary Revival:** dining table, eight chairs & side cabinet; walnut & walnut veneer, the expandable table w/a rectangular top w/rounded corners & molded edges above a scroll-carved border raised on ornate pierced & carved corner legs & squared cross stretchers to the central baluster-turned supports, the high-backed chairs w/pierced & scroll-carved crestrails above the oblong serpentine frame enclosing the upholstered panel above the upholstered slip seat in a serpentine framed w/carved scrolls at front apron & carved cabriole front legs ending in trifid feet, turned rear legs & scrolled & carved flattened H-stretcher, Century Furniture Co., Grand Rapids, Michigan, ca. 1910-30 (ILLUS. of part) ... **12,000**

## DRY SINKS

**Painted pine,** the rectangular well top w/upright board edging above a case w/a pair of narrow flush-mounted single-board doors, old goldenrod repaint, 19th c., 47 3/4" l., 28 1/2" h. (one bottom board loose, feet gone) .............................. **770**

**Painted poplar,** a high board back w/a narrow top shelf above down-curved sides to the rectangular top well beside a small work shelf at one end over a small drawer, the lower case w/a pair of large paneled cupboard doors w/old cast-iron thumb latches w/brass knobs, old green repaint, 19th c., probably old conversion from cupboard, 18 1/4 x 43 1/2", 52" h. (drawer knob replaced, some edge damage) ............................................................. **770**

**Poplar,** hutch-type, a narrow rectangular raised back section w/a row of four drawers above downswept sides flanking the long well w/a rectangular work surface at one end, the lower case w/a stack of three graduated drawers beside a pair of double-paneled cupboard doors

w/cast-iron thumb latches w/porcelain knobs, flat base, short stile feet, old finish, replaced porcelain knobs, found in Ohio, late 19th c., 23 x 73 3/4", 50 1/2" h. (ILLUS. below) ......................... **1,870**

*Large Hutch-style Dry Sink*

**Softwoods,** a long rectangular hinged top opening to a shallow dovetailed well slightly overhanging a case w/a pair of drawers over a pair of simple paneled doors, simple turned wood knobs, flat apron, refinished, late 19th c. ...................... **358**

## GARDEN & LAWN

**Settee,** a serpentine crest cast w/swags & floral clusters above the back composed of latticework arches flanked by scroll-topped arms over scrolled slats, the pierced seat above heavy scroll-cast cabriole front legs, labeled "Mfg. by the Kramer Bros Fdy Co., Dayton, O," 19th c., old white repaint, 43 1/4" l. (break in top rail) ......................................................... **605**

**Settee,** the serpentine ribbon- and flower-cast crestrail above a back composed of repeating rows of rounded arches flanked by downswept arms over scroll supports, openwork seat above a narrow scroll-cast apron & heavy scroll-cast cabriole front legs, old white repaint, second half 19th c., 46" l. .............................. **660**

*Labeled Cast-Iron Garden Settee*

**Settee,** triple-back design, the rectangular back w/a higher central panel topped by a sunburst crest over a band of rings flanked by lower matching crests, each panel w/ornate openwork scroll design flanked by simple scrolled end arms above the pierced criss-cross lattice seat above an apron of pierced rings & scrolled spearpoints, simple bar legs w/end stretchers, painted black, John McLean, New York, second half 19th c., repairs, 17 x 46", 36" h. (ILLUS.) ................. **863**

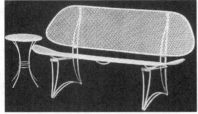

*Fine Rococo Revival Garden Settees*

**Settees,** Rococo Revival style, the serpentine crest cast w/floral swags above a back of delicate openwork arches flanked by stepped scrolled arms on scrolled pierced supports above the ornately pierced seat, floral scroll apron & scroll-cast cabriole legs, old white repaint, New York City or Boston, third quarter 19th c., minor paint wear, 19 5/8 x 45 1/2", 35 3/4" h., pr. (ILLUS.) ... **3,105**

*Modern Style 1950s Garden Suite*

**Suite:** a settee, two side chairs, two round drink tables & a square occasional table; Modern style, iron rod & metal lattice construction, the settee w/a long oblong back w/diamond lattice metal sheeting within a frame raised on curved metal supports above the narrow oblong matching seat w/upturned ends, double-bar curved legs & stretchers, matching chairs & tables w/matching latticework tops & curved metal bar bases, white, ca. 1955, settee 51 1/4" l., 31" h., the set (ILLUS. of part)................................. **805**

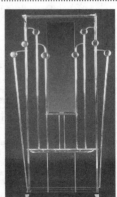

*Victorian Three-Piece Garden Suite*

**Suite:** settee & two armchairs; each back composed of pierced lyre-form & scroll-

ing panels w/a flat crest w/arched & pierced finial, crestrail continuing to scrolled arms above pierced scrolling panels over the pierced lattice seat, leafy scroll apron & simple cabriole legs joined by slender bar stretchers, painted white, late 19th - early 20th c., thet set (ILLUS. in background) .......................................... **1,200**

# HALL RACKS & TREES

**Hall rack,** Arts & Crafts, copper & metal, rectangular patinated lattice strapwork w/eight coat hooks, pierced copper riveted framed on beveled mirror, early 20th c., 48" w., 26 3/4" h. (missing rivet)...... **489**

*Art Deco Hall Tree*

**Hall tree,** Art Deco, black enameled wood, upright rectangular form w/angle-cut top above staggered chrome hooks & a large rectangular tinted mirror w/cut corners above a small projecting drawer, a lower chrome bar rack above the bottom drip tray, on four large ball feet, slight wear, ca. 1930s, 7 3/4 x 33", 76" h. (ILLUS.)....................................................... **489**

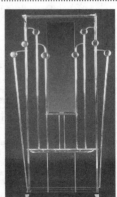

*Art Deco Chromed Aluminum Hall Tree*

**Hall tree,** Art Deco streamline-design, chromed aluminum, the tall rectangular open framework joined by round disk-shaped hat racks & curved brackets to slender uprights supporting at the center a tall narrow rectangular mirror, the outer uprights gently angled out, a narrow loop in the lower section forming an umbrella rack, design attributed to Jean Lucian, France, ca. 1935, 8 x 37 1/2", 70" h. (ILLUS.)...................... **805**

**Hall tree,** Art Deco, wrought iron, rectangular outline w/an upper hat rack above coat hooks & a rectangular mirror flanked by half-round umbrella stands, decorated throughout w/hammering & pierced scrolls, France, ca. 1925, 13 x 37", 71" h. ......................................... **2,875**

*Arts & Crafts Oak Hall Tree*

**Hall tree,** Arts & Crafts, oak, the scalloped crestrail centered by an incised cluster of stylized flowers above incised frieze bands flanked by projecting shaped brackets flanking three turned bars above a backboard fitted w/hooks on the sides flanking two panels centering further rectangular designs of stylized flowers w/a tall rectangular beveled mirror in the center, all above a narrow horizontal panel above a small rectangular central cabinet w/a hinged lid above a tall paneled door w/a floral panel flanked by brass rounded side rails & quarter-round drip trays at the bottom, some wear, early 20th c., 39" w., 80" h. (ILLUS.) ........... **495**

**Hall trees,** Victorian, cast iron, tree-form w/the top cast as openwork leafy tree branches w/coat hooks centered by a small oval mirror, raised on a slender tree trunk-form pedestal w/an oval umbrella ring above the dished oblong base, patent-dated "Nov. 16 '59," second half 19th c., 73" h., pr. (ILLUS. top next column) ........................................ **2,875**

*Fine Victorian Cast-Iron Hall Trees*

# HIGHBOYS & LOWBOYS

## HIGHBOYS

**Chippendale "bonnet-top" highboy,** cherry, two-part construction: the upper section w/a broken-crown crest w/serpentine cove molding centering a shaped finial support above a case w/two shallow drawers flanking a deep fan-carved central drawer over four long graduated thumb-molded drawers; the lower case w/a mid-molding over a long narrow drawer over a row of three deep drawers, the center one w/a carved fan, skirt w/front & side shaping on cabriole legs ending in pad feet, some replaced butterfly brasses, refinished, New England, 18th c., 19 1/2 x 38", 84" h. (repairs, missing finials & pendants) ....... **37,950**

**Chippendale country-style "flat-top" highboy,** cherry, two-part construction: the upper section w/a rectangular top over a deep coved & molded cornice above two pairs of small drawers flanking a small square drawer w/a carved sunburst over a stack of four long graduated dovetailed drawers; the lower section w/a wide mid-molding over a narrow long drawer over two deep drawers flanking a short, narrow central drawer above a deeply scalloped apron w/a fan carving at the center, raised on scroll-carved cabriole legs ending in claw-and-ball feet, small simple brass drawer knobs, old soft finish, 19 x 37 1/4", overall 75" h. (legs possibly old replacements, drawer edge damage & repair, pulls incomplete) ....................................... **4,620**

**Queen Anne "flat-top" highboy,** cherry, two-part construction: the upper section w/a flat rectangular top w/a deep coved cornice above a case of five long graduated drawers; the lower section w/a mid-molding over a case w/a pair of deep drawers flanking a shallow central drawer all above the deep scalloped apron, simple cabriole legs w/raised pad feet, old refinish, old replaced brasses, Massachusetts, ca. 1750, 17 1/2 x 34 1/2", 64" h. (repairs) .................................................. **19,500**

*Fine Curly Maple Queen Anne Highboy*

**Queen Anne "flat-top" highboy,** curly maple, two-part construction: the upper section w/a rectangular top over a deep flaring stepped coved cornice above five long thumb-molded graduated drawers w/butterfly brasses & keyhole escutcheons; the lower section w/a mid-molding over a long narrow drawer above a row of three deep drawers, the center one w/fan carving, shaped apron w/two turned acorn drops, cabriole legs ending in raised pad feet, old mellow finish, New Hampshire, 18th c., minor repair, original brasses, apron drops replaced, top 22 1/2 x 43", 73 1/4" h. (ILLUS.) ............. **55,000**

*William & Mary Reproduction Highboy*

**William & Mary-Style "flat-top" highboy,** curly maple & curply maple veneer, two-part construction: the upper section w/a rectangular top over a stepped flaring cornice over a case of four long graduated drawers w/butterfly brasses & keyhole escutcheons; the lower section w/a stepped mid-molding over a pair of deep drawers flanking shallow drawers above the deeply scalloped apron raised on four tall trumpet-turned front legs joined by flattened scalloped stretchers & raised on ball feet, two matching rear legs joined by flat scalloped side stretchers & a plain rear stretcher, hand-made reproduction, age crack in one end, 20th c., top 19 3/4 x 37", 65 3/4" h. (ILLUS.)..... **5,610**

## LOWBOYS

**Queen Anne-Style lowboy,** walnut, rectangular top w/narrow molded edges over a case w/a long narrow drawer w/three butterfly brasses above a row of three small drawers each w/a butterfly brass, triple-arched apron w/blocked drops, angled cabriole legs ending in pad feet, hand-made reproduction by Bob Pusecker, 20th c., 18 3/4 x 35 1/2", 29 3/4' h........................................................ **385**

# ICE BOXES

*Rare Late Victorian Ice Box*

**Turn-of-the-century,** cabinet-style, oak, the rectangular top w/molded edges above a beaded band flanked by carved lion heads at the top corners above a long rectangular upper mirrored door w/ornate scroll-carved frame & heavy brass hardware above a tall rectangular two-panel door w/ornate scroll carving & heavy brass hardware, spiral-carved front corner rails, egg-and-dart band above the molded base w/carved corner blocks, paneled sides, ca. 1900 (ILLUS.).. **1,750**

*Oak Upright Ice Box*

**Turn-of-the-century,** chest-style, oak, an upright form w/hinged rectangular lid to the ice compartment above a raised panel over a lower paneled cupboard door w/heavy brass hardware, deep molded flat base, ca. 1910-20, 18 x 27", 43" h. (ILLUS.)............................................. **450**

# LOVE SEATS, SOFAS & SETTEES

**Daybed,** Mission-style (Arts & Crafts movement), oak, the upright even ends w/heavy square stiles supporting wide flat upper & lower rails framing six wide slats, wide siderails pinned into end stiles, Gustav Stickley Model No. 220, after 1909, 35 1/2 x 84", 34" h. ................. **3,450**

*Classic Austrian Bentwood Settee*

**Settee,** bentwood, beechwood, the shaped rectangular back composed of sinuous open curves & swirls above the long oval caned seat flanked by curled bentwood arms, on slender turned & gently curved legs joined by a high oval bentwood stretcher, designed by Joseph Hoffmann, fragmentary maker's paper label, Austria, ca. 1905, wear, 45" l. (ILLUS.)..... **3,450**

**Settee,** Classical-Style, mahogany, the bowed crestrail above an upholstered back w/molded outscrolled arm supports over a D-shaped overupholstered seat, on square tapering legs w/casters, 20th c., 35 x 61 1/2", 34 1/2" h. ......................... **1,150**

**Settee,** Federal country-style, hardwood, six-section back, the wide crestrail w/six arched sections across the back above heavy stiles & sets of four slender spindles, divided by four slender open scrolled arms on simple turned supports, S-scrolled long plank seat, six pairs of canted turned tapering legs joined by long slat front & back stretchers, worn & weathered surface w/traces of old red paint, first half 19th c., 109" l. (front foot rest battered, renailed & partially replaced) ...................................................... **880**

*Simple Victorian Rococo Settee*

**Settee,** Victorian Rococo substyle, walnut, the serpentine crestrail w/finger-carving curved down to form closed padded arms & curved arm supports, vertically tufted back, upholstered spring seat, serpentine finger-molded seatrail between demi-cabriole front legs on casters, light blue velvet upholstery, ca. 1860, repairs, 62 1/4" l. (ILLUS.).................. **358**

**Settee,** Windsor "arrow-back" style, a long flat board crestrail above numerous arrow slats between the turned & tapering stiles & S-scroll arms over three turned spindles & a turned & canted arm support, long plank seat raised on four pairs of turned & tapering legs joined by horizontal front arrow stretchers & plain turned side & back stretchers, black repaint, first half 19th c., 78" l. ..................... **495**

**Settee,** Windsor country-style, painted & decorated, double-back form, a long wide crestrail cut-out to form two sections raised on three stiles above lower rails each over six short turned spindles, S-scroll arms over two spindles & a turned canted arm support, long plank seat raised on eight turned & canted legs joined by turned box stretchers, old brown paint w/yellow & blue striping & polychrome floral decoration on the crestrail, Pennsylvania, mid-19th c., overall wear, some surface & edge damage, revarnished, 71" l. (ILLUS. top next page) .......................................................... **1,100**

*Decorated Windsor Settee*

**Settee,** Windsor low-back style, the shaped crestrail continuing to downscrolled knuckled grips above twenty-one turned spindles flanked by ring- and baluster-turned arm supports over a long shaped plank seat, on six ring-, rod- and baluster-turned legs w/tapered ball feet joined by turned & swelled H-stretchers, old green paint, Lancaster County, Pennsylvania, 1770-90, 18 1/2 x 45 1/2", 31" h. .... **2,990**

**Settle,** painted pine, the very tall flat curved back w/a narrow brace between the rounded wing sides continuing down to form sides w/small rounded hand grips, curved plank seat above lower narrow brace, old worn black & grey paint, late 18th - early 19th c., 50 1/2" w., 69" h. (wear, some edge damage) ..................... **4,125**

**Sofa,** Chippendale-Style, mahogany, camel-back design w/a serpentine upholstered crestrail above a canted back over outward scrolling arms above an overupholstered rectangular seat, on Marlborough legs joined by H-stretchers, 20th c., 30 x 90", 38" h. ............................ **2,760**

**Sofa,** Classical, carved mahogany, the serpentine crestrail w/acanthus leaf carving & two rosettes centering a carved shell w/Prince-of-Wales feathers above an upholstered back w/outscrolling arms w/similar Prince-of-Wales feathers & acanthus leaf carving over a rectangular seat w/incised line seatrail, on ring-turned & spiral-carved legs w/casters, ca. 1830-40, 27 x 83", 33" h..... **1,093**

![Late Classical Mahogany Sofa]

*Late Classical Mahogany Sofa*

**Sofa,** Classical, mahogany & mahogany veneer, the serpentine crestrail centered by a pierced scroll-carved crest over the tufted upholstered back flanked by outscrolled arms w/S-scroll carved arm supports above the long upholstered seat on a wide beaded & ogee seatrail joined by scrolled front legs on casters, reupholstered in striped velvet, ca. 1840-50, 84" l. (ILLUS.)................................................ **385**

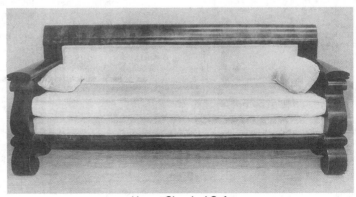

*Heavy Classical Sofa*

**Sofa,** Classical, mahogany veneer, a wide rolled flat veneered crestrail above a low upholstered back flanked by wide gently rounded closed arms w/heavy S-scroll arm supports flanking the upholstered cushion seat, flat rounded seatrail between heavy C-scroll front feet, old finish, reupholstered, some edge wear, ca. 1835-45, 81 3/4" l. (ILLUS. bottom previous page) .............................. **853**

**Sofa,** Federal, inlaid mahogany, the long slightly arched upholstered back continuing to downward sloping upholstered sides & reeded arms on swelled vase- and ring-turned reeded arm supports on bird's-eye maple & string-inlaid panels continuing to ring-turned tapering reeded front legs, canted square rear legs, slighting bowed upholstered front seatrail, old surface, probably Mass. ca. 1810-15, 25 x 78", 37 1/2" h. (imperfections) ...................................................... **8,625**

**Sofa,** Federal-Style, mahogany & satinwood, a long narrow flat crestrail w/satinwood above the upholstered back flanked by downswept arms & upholstered ends, down-curved hand grips above reeded & baluster-turned arm supports flanking the long cushion seat, long flat satinwood seatrail raised on four ring-turned tapering & reeded front legs w/peg feet, old pink satin upholstery, early 20th c., 66" l. (some veneer damage) ...................................................... **1,100**

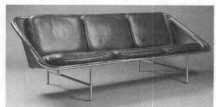

*George Nelson "Sling" Sofa*

**Sofa,** Modern style "Sling" style, leather & chrome, a heavy gauge chrome tube steel framework supporting three leather back & seat cushions. on slender tubular steel legs, designed by George Nelson, manfactured by Herman Miller, ca. 1964, 31 1/2 x 86", 28 7/8" h. (ILLUS.) .............. **4,600**

*Victorian Baroque Revival Sofa*

**Sofa,** Victorian Baroque Revival style, carved mahogany, a wide flat crestrail ornately carved w/leafy scrolls flanking a

central cartouche joining wide scroll-carved stiles above the upholstered back & padded rounded arms over upholstered sides & blocked columnar scroll-carved arm supports flanking the long upholstered seat, a gadroon-carved flat seatrail & heavy block front feet, ca. 1890-1900 (ILLUS.) ................................... **2,500**

*Exceptional Renaissance Revival Sofa*

**Sofa,** Victorian Renaissance Revival substyle, bronze-mounted rosewood & parcel gilt, triple-back style, the high rounded end panels w/tufted upholstery & reeded & carved stiles flank the lower long central section w/tufted upholstery below a central arched crest carved w/leaves & berries above a round medallion carved w/a scene of Leda & the swan, low outswept upholstered arms w/arm supports carved w/full-figural busts of children, long upholstered spring seat w/gently curved seatrail w/gilt line-incised decoration, reeded trumpet-turned front legs, green velvet upholstery, ca. 1875, restoration, 72" l., 36 1/2" h. (ILLUS.) ..................................... **6,900**

*Fine Renaissance Revival Sofa*

**Sofa,** Victorian Renaissance Revival substyle, walnut & burl walnut, triple-back style, the large central panel w/a rounded rectangular upholstered back below the arched crestrail topped w/a carved crown crest centered by the bust of a lady & flanked by square post finials, tapering blocked dividers between the squared upholstered side back panels w/carved bird head stile finials, the back panels raised on burl veneer panels & flanked by curved upholstered arms w/carved lady head arm rests over the long upholstered spring seat, serpentine seatrail w/carved drops, raised on four block- and rod-turned legs w/peg feet, repairs, ca. 1875, 73" l. (ILLUS.) .............. **1,320**

*Fine Renaissance Revival Sofa*

**Sofa,** Victorian Renaissance Revival sub-style, walnut & burl walnut, triple-back design, the central shaped & upholstered back panel topped by an ornate baluster-turned spindle & rondel pierced crest over a burl-trimmed rail curving down to ornately carved & pierced panels joining the outer flaring upholstered back panels w/carved frames above curved padded arms w/carved lady head hand grips over curved supports, long oblong upholstered seat w/an incurved front seatrail w/burl panels, on knob- and ring-turned tapering legs on casters, attributed to John Jelliff, ca. 1875 (ILLUS.).................................................... **1,600**

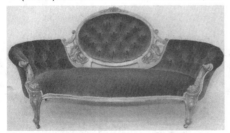

*Victorian 'Medallion-back' Sofa*

**Sofa,** Victorian Rococo substyle 'medallion-back' style, walnut, the back w/a large oval tufted upholstered central back panel w/a leaf-carved crest & raised on wide pierced & scroll-carved panels joining it to the lower upholstered side panels curving around & faced w/scroll-carved arm supports, long upholstered seat on a gently shaped seatrail joined by demi-cabriole front legs on casters, reupholstered in dark blue velvet, ca. 1855-65, 74" l. (ILLUS.)....... **880**

**Tete-a-tete,** Golden Oak style, a pair of wide balloon-form opposing backs tapering to a pierced & leafy scroll-cut section above a shaped rectangular seat, backs joined by a central rail over spindles, curved end arms over turned spindles & arm supports, knob-turned edges joined by knob-turned stretchers, ca. 1900 (ILLUS. top next column) .......................... **1,400**

*Unusual Late Victorian Tete-a-Tete*

**Wagon seat,** child's, ash or chestnut, double-back style, each back section w/two gently arched slats between the three turned, tapering stiles above open rod arms w/turned front supports forming the front end legs, short center leg, woven splint seat, old finish, 19th c., 23 1/4" w., 22 1/2" h. ................................................. **660**

**Wagon seat,** two-part back w/two slightly arched slats in each section between three simple heavy turned stiles, slender shaped open end arms raised on tapering supports continuing to form front legs, central front leg, woven splint seat, simple double rungs at front & sides, refinished, 19th c., 36 1/2" l. (seat old replacement) ................................................. **523**

## MIRRORS

**Chippendale wall mirror,** mahogany, arched & scroll-carved top w/curved corners above a rectangular molded frame enclosing the mirror, delicate scroll-carved projections at each corner & arched scroll-carved bottom panel, labeled "L.C. Lyman, Middletown, Connecticut," 15 1/4 x 24"............................... **4,888**

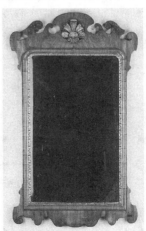

*English Chippendale Wall Mirror*

**Chippendale wall mirror,** walnut & parcel-gilt, the high scroll-carved crest centered by a gilt feathered plume above a molded mirror frame w/rounded top corners, an inlaid gilt-incised liner, a scroll-carved bottom drop panel, England, late 18th c., refinished, imperfection, 24 3/4 x 43 1/4" (ILLUS.) .......................... **2,415**

*Fine Convex Classical Wall Mirror*

**Classical wall mirror,** giltwood & part-ebonized, a round convex mirror plate in a molded round frame set w/spherules, a tall crest carved w/a large spread-winged giltwood eagle on a pile of rocks, a half-round sunburst gilt base drop, possibly American, ca. 1825, repairs, 25" d., 44" h. (ILLUS.) .............................. **5,750**

*Danish Modern Wall Mirror*

**Danish Modern wall mirror,** walnut, a flat crestrail above flaring shaped & molded narrow sides w/a narrow shelf below the tall mirror plate, Denmark, ca. 1955, 17 1/4" w., 24 3/4" h. (ILLUS.) ...................... **201**

**Federal wall mirror,** giltwood, coved & molded crestrail w/stepped-out ends above a conforming frieze over a central panel w/a lozenge pattern flanked by molded engaged pilasters & molded base rail, probably Salem, Massachusetts, ca. 1807-08, 18 1/2 x 34 1/2" (regilding, replaced glass) ........................ **1,725**

**Federal wall mirror,** giltwood & part-ebonized, a round molded frame mounted w/small spheres & a reeded inner band around the convex mirror, surmounted by a carved spread-winged eagle gazing to the right & flanked by scrolls, a gadrooned & ruffled leaf pendant at the bottom, American, ca. 1825, 28 x 42" (repairs to finial & apron) .......................... **2,875**

**Queen Anne wall mirror,** a simple wide arched molded black-painted frame encloses a beveled-edge mirror w/an engraved stylized basket of flowers & vines across the bottom, probably New England, 18th c., 16 x 17 1/2" ...................... **690**

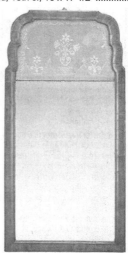

*Etched Queen Anne Mirror*

**Queen Anne wall mirror,** walnut, the shaped crest centering an upper mirror plate etched w/flowers issuing from a vase flanked by birds & smaller vases issuing flowers surmounted by a scrolling foliate border, a lower rectangular beveled mirror w/conforming frame, American or English, 1740-60, 17 x 35 1/4" (ILLUS.) .................................. **3,220**

**Regency girandole mirror,** gilt gesso, the round convex mirror framed in a circular molding w/applied spherules & topped by a carved eagle on a rocky perch flanked by leafage, side candle sconces on leafy brackets, leafy-carved base bracket, probably England, ca. 1810, 20" w., 32 1/2" h. (ILLUS. top next page) ......................................................... **9,200**

*Fine Regency Girandole Mirror*

*Aesthetic Movement Overmantel Mirror*

**Victorian Aesthetic Movement overmantel mirror,** walnut & maple, a wide flat top rail centered by a pointed crest w/fanned finial & flanked by a pair of flat stiles at each end w/carved pointed finials above incised leafy bands, the stiles flanking side panels decorated w/Aesthetic floral designs, wide flat bottom rail, in the manner of Isaac Scott, ca. 1870, 60 1/4" l., 31" h. (ILLUS.) ............................ **748**

# PARLOR SUITES

*Unique Art Deco Upholstered Sofa*

**Art Deco:** sofa & armchair; upholstered black lacquer & Lucite, the sofa w/a long gently rounded vertically-tufted back curving around to end in paneled arm supports consisting of alternating bands of lacquer & Lucite, long gently bowed cushion seat & seatrail, lacquer panel back frame & raised on molded lacquer seatrail, pale grey mohair upholstery, Kem Weber, ca. 1930s, sofa 78" l., the set (ILLUS. of sofa) .................................. **3,450**

*Louis XV-Style Parlor Suite*

**Louis XV-Style:** sofa & two armchairs; giltwood, each w/a serpentine crestrail centered by a foliate-carved cartouche-shaped crest above the Aubusson landscape tapestry-upholstered back flanked by padded open arms on curved arm supports, tapestry upholstered wide seat on serpentine scroll- and cartouche-carved seatrails on demi-cabriole legs, France, late 19th c., sofa 68" l., the set (ILLUS.) ...................................................... **5,750**

*Louis XVI-Style Parlor Suite*

**Louis XVI-Style:** canape, two open-arm armchairs & two chaise-longue; grey-painted, each w/a narrow molded crestrail centered by a ribbon-carved crest above the foliate-carved rectangular back frame around the upholstered back flanked by downswept padded open arms on curved arm supports, wide upholstered spring seat above carved seatrails on knob-turned & tapering reeded legs w/peg feet, ecru silk print upholstery, France, early 20th c., canape 41" l., chairs 36 1/2" h., the set (ILLUS. of part)......................................... **3,450**

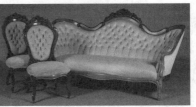

*Fine Belter Parlor Suite*

**Victorian Rococo substyle:** sofa & two side chairs; carved rosewood, the triple-back sofa w/a central crest of finely carved roses & other florals flanked by scroll-carved rails continuing down to form the arms, a molded serpentine seatrail ending in demi-cabriole front legs, matching side chairs w/front casters, John H. Belter, Rosalie without Grapes patt., ca. 1855 (ILLUS.) .............. **7,000**

# SCREENS

*Gallé-signed Inlaid Fire Screen*

**Firescreen,** Art Nouveau, marquetry fruitwood & mahogany, an upright rectangular panel w/a high arched & shaped top, decorated w/an inlaid design of a stalk of blooming irises on a variegated ground, set on a molded cross stretcher joining molded inverted-V end feet, signed in inlay "Gallé," leg repairs, France, ca. 1900, 22 x 33" (ILLUS.) ............................ **2,875**

**Firescreen,** Edgar Brandt, wrought iron raised on strapwork legs, center panel wrought w/hunter holding bow & his prey, reserved against a field of stylized foliage, all within field of looping calligraphic devices, surrounded by a hammered frame, impressed "E. Brandt," 29 1/2" w., 38" h. .................................... **13,225**

*Decorative Lacquered Wood Screen*

**Folding screen,** four-fold, lacquered wood, the four panels depicting on one side a 'trompe l'oeil' decoration of book shelves w/books, pottery & various other objects, the other side depicting musical instruments, in browns, red, yellow, blue & black, designed by Piero Fornasetti, Italy, 1950s, each panel 13 3/4" w., 53 1/4" h. (ILLUS.) .................................... **9,200**

*Painted Leather Folding Screen*

**Folding screen,** four-fold, painted leather, the panels painted as a continuous landscape w/an 18th c. hunting party on horses, early 20th c., minor damage (ILLUS.) .................................... **1,380**

*Unique Art Deco Folding Screen*

**Folding screen,** four-fold, painted wood, Art Deco style, decorated as a continuous scene w/a tall Art Deco lady garbed in a huge fur-trimmed robe following by a small fairy-winged footman in 18th c. attire, all against a stylied wooded landscape, muted colors of green, red & black, signed, ca. 1930, 116" l., 84" h. (ILLUS.) .................................... **1,725**

**Folding screen,** three-fold, Arts & Crafts style, oak, top of each panel w/pyrography decoration depicting poppies & pods, colored in green, yellow & gold, early 20th c., 59 1/4" w., 68" h. (splitting, marring) ...................................... **259**

**Folding screen,** three-fold, Mission style, oak, each tall panel composed of three mortised long boards, side stiles continue down to form short legs, Gustav Stickley, early 20th c. (ILLUS. top next page) ...................................... **22,000**

*Rare Gustav Stickley Folding Screen*

*Art Nouveau Style Screen*

**Folding screen,** three-fold, Art Nouveau style, in the manner of René Lalique, stained leather & wood, each panel well carved & tooled w/flock of gulls & tree branches, beneath pine boughs abundant w/cones, above a field of flowers, stained & heightened w/gilt, all set within wood frame w/plaque stamped "Finnegan, Deansgate, Manchester," ca. 1900, 6'1 x 5' 1/2" (ILLUS.) .............................. **25,300**

# SECRETARIES

**Classical secretary-bookcase,** mahogany & mahogany veneer, two-part construction: the upper section w/a rectangular top & widely projecting flattened cornice over a plain frieze band above a pair of tall geometrically-glazed cupboard doors opening to shelves above a row of three small drawers; the projecting lower section w/a fold-out writing surface which lifts to a well w/two drawers & open compartments, false drawer facade flanked by pull-out supports above a pair of recessed paneled cupboard doors opening to shelves & flanked by S-scroll pilasters raised on heavy leaf- and paw-carved legs, replaced brasses, refinished, restoration, New England, 1825-35, 23 1/4 x 40", 81" h. (ILLUS.) .............. **1,380**

*Tall Classical Secretary-Bookcase*

*Classical Mahogany Secretary*

**Classical secretary-bookcase,** mahogany & mahogany veneer, two-part construction: the upper section w/a rectangular top & deep ogee cornice above a wide frieze band above a pair of tall geometrically-glazed cupboard doors w/Gothic arch top opening to three shelves above a pair of long drawers flanking a small central drawer; the lower section w/a stepped-out fold-out writing surface above a long ogee-front drawer overhanging two long flat drawers flanked by ring- and rod-turned colonettes on blocks above the heavy ring-turned tapering short legs, ca. 1840 (ILLUS.) ...... **3,500**

**Federal secretary-bookcase,** cherry, cherry veneer & poplar, three-part construction: the top section w/a flat molded cornice above a pair of tall cupboard doors w/recessed reeded panels enclosing shelves above a mid-section w/two shorter doors w/recessed reeded panels enclosing compartmented four-drawer interior, the lower projecting base section w/a fold-out writing surface over a case w/a long drawer above a pair of small cupboard doors flanked by narrow bottle drawers & flanked by reeded pilasters, baluster- and ring-turned legs w/knob feet, replaced brasses, old refinish, minor imperfections, New England, ca. 1820, 21 x 39", 80 1/2" h. (ILLUS. below) .......................................... **5,175**

*Unusual Federal Secretary-Bookcase*

*Fine Federal Secretary-Bookcase*

**Federal secretary-bookcase,** inlaid walnut, two-part construction: the upper section w/a rectangular top over a flaring stepped cornice above a pair of tall geometrically-glazed cupboard doors opening to shelves; the lower projecting section w/a rectangular top above a

hinged fall-front writing surface opening to an interior fitted w/seven drawers & pigeonholes, the lower case w/a pair of paneled doors w/circular inlaid bandings above a narrow inlaid band above the scalloped apron & flared French feet, found in Tennessee, attributed to Thomas Hope, minor veneer damage & minor repairs, early 19th c., top 12 1/4 x 43 3/4", 93 3/4" h. (ILLUS.).......... **8,800**

*Fine Federal Walnut Secretary*

**Federal secretary-bookcase,** walnut & walnut veneer, two-part construction: the upper section w/a delicate broken-scroll pediment centered by a block w/urn finial & flanked by corner urn finials above a pair of tall paneled cupboard doors; the lower section w/a wide hinged slant front opening to a compartment w/small drawers over pigeonholes, the case w/four long graduated drawers w/round brass pulls, molded base on cut-out bracket feet, late 18th - early 19th c. (ILLUS.) ..... **20,900**
**Federal-Style secretary-bookcase,** inlaid mahogany, two-part construction: the upper section w/a rectangular top w/cornice above a banded edge above a conforming case w/a line-inlaid frieze over molding above two tambour doors opening to reveal an interior fitted w/four drawers above six valanced pigeonholes centering a prospect door enclosing a valanced pigeonhole over a drawer, all flanked by inlaid pilasters w/Ionic capitals; the lower section w/molding surround above a line-inlaid rectangular hinged top opening to a writing surface over a conforming case fitted wtwo line-inlaid graduated long drawers, on bellflower & line-inlaid square tapering legs, 20th c., 25 x 36", 47 1/4" h. ....................... **1,380**
**George III-Style secretary-bookcase,** mahogany, diminutive size, two-part construction: the upper section w/a broken-arch pediment above a pair of tall narrow geometrically-glazed cupboard

doors opening to shelves; the lower section w/a wide hinged slant front opening to a fitted writing compartment above a case w/a pair of small square drawers flanking a longer center drawer over a pair of drawers above two long drawers at the bottom, all w/butterfly pulls & keyhole escutcheons, molded base on scroll-cut bracket feet, England, late 19th c., 19 1/2 x 27", 81" h. (ILLUS. below)...................................................... **4,313**

*Small George III-Style Secretary*

**Queen Anne secretary-bookcase,** carved & inlaid cherry, two-part construction: the upper section w/a swan's-neck pediment above a pair of raised panel 'tombstone' doors flanked by molded corners & similarly paneled sides opening to three shelves; the lower section w/a mid-molding over a hinged slant front w/a compass star inlay opening to an interior fitted w/eight valanced pigeonholes centering inlaid document drawers & a prospect door opening to three drawers, within an arrangement of five short drawers, the case w/four long graduated drawers w/pierced butterfly pulls & keyhole escutcheons, base molding adorned w/a shaped pendant, on short cabriole legs ending in claw-and-ball feet, Connecticut or New Hampshire, 1750-70, 18 x 36", 92" h. (repair to finial plinth, lacking one valance, one short drawer rebuilt, patches to drawer lips) .... **31,050**

**Victorian Aesthetic Movement secretary,** Modern Gothic-style, walnut, the top w/a flat crestrail over a gallery above two panels over a wide double-panel hinged writing surface w/heavy L-shaped brackets opening to a fitted compartment above a long drawer over a pair of recessed paneled doors w/angled metal brackets over two small drawers at the base, molded botton & blocked side stiles, ca. 1870, 20 1/4 x 36", 63 1/2" h. (ILLUS. top next column) .......................... **2,415**

*Fine Aesthetic Movement Secretary*

**Victorian country-style secretary-bookcase,** cherry, three-part construction: the upper section w/a deep flaring coved cornice above a pair of tall double-paneled doors w/a short panel over a tall panel & opening to an interior fitted w/two rows of pigeonholes w/two dovetailed drawers, the central projecting section w/a hinged slant front opening to an interior fitted w/a row of four drawers over a row of six pigeonholes, the base w/one dovetailed long drawer above the paneled block- and ring-turned legs w/knob feet, attributed to Kentucky, mid-19th c., old finish, 14 3/4 x 41 1/2" top, 85 1/2" h. (replaced brasses, mid-section nailed to base)................................... **4,950**

**Victorian country-style secretary-bookcase,** walnut, two-piece construction: the upper section w/a wide flaring & stepped cornice above a pair of tall single pane glazed cupboard doors w/molded interior edging & rounded top corners opening to three shelves; the lower section w/a wide stepped-out slant-top opening to a fitted interior above a single long drawer w/half-round turned pulls, on ring- and rod-turned legs w/turned feet, old finish, second half 19th c., 19 x 43 1/4", 82 1/4" h. (repaired breaks at hinges)......................................... **990**

**Victorian cylinder-front secretary-bookcase,** Eastlake substyle, walnut & burl walnut, a rectangular top w/flaring cornice above a burled frieze band over a pair of tall glazed cupboard doors opening to shelves above a stepped-out cylinder top w/recessed burl panel opening to a fitted interior above a long drawer above two stepped-back long drawers , flat base, angular brass pulls, ca. 1880 (ILLUS. top next page) ............................. **3,400**

*Victorian Cylinder-Front Secretary*

**Victorian cylinder-front secretary-book-case,** Eastlake substyle, walnut & burl walnut, two-part construction: the upper section w/a high stepped crown crest w/notched edge trim & line-incised diamonds & forked sprigs above a top molding over a pair of tall single-pane glazed cupboard doors trimmed w/forked sprigs & opening to shelves; the lower section w/rectangular back top above the wide cylinder front w/two recessed burl panels opening to an interior fitted w/two drawers & pigeonholes, the lower case w/a stepped-out long line-incised & stylized leafy branch-decorated drawer flanked by sprigged side blocks above two long matching drawers flanked by curved brackets over blocked stiles all w/incised bands, deep molded flat base on casters, ca. 1890, 15 x 40 1/4", 90" h. .................................... **1,870**

*Renaissance Revival Secretary*

**Victorian cylinder-front secretary-book-case,** Renaissance Revival substyle, walnut & burl walnut, the rectangular top w/a carved pediment topped by a leaf-carved crest over a diamond panel & flanked by corner scrolls above a wide frieze band above a pair of tall single-pane glazed cupboard doors opening to three shelves above a burl-paneled cylinder front opening to a fitted interior above a long burl-trimmed drawer above an inset small cupboard door beside two small drawers all flanked by reeded edge molding, flat molded base & paneled ends, ca. 1880 (ILLUS.) .................... **2,200**

*Eastlake Walnut Secretary-Bookcase*

**Victorian secretary-bookcase,** Eastlake "cylinder-front" style, walnut & burl walnut, the rectangular top w/a molded flaring cornice above frieze band over a pair of tall single-pane glazed cupboard doors opening to shelves; the lower section w/a paneled cylinder front opening to an interior w/a pull-out shelf & fitted interior w/two drawers, above a single long burl-veneered drawer projecting over two small burl-veneered drawers w/stamped brass pulls beside a small raised panel burled cupboard door, molded flat base on casters, refinished, ca. 1880, top 14 x 42 1/2", 90 1/4" h. (ILLUS.).................................... **1,705**

**Victorian secretary-bookcase,** Gothic Revival substyle, mahogany & mahogany veneer, two-part construction: the upper section w/a high arched & pierced scroll-carved crestrail w/small turned finials above a plain frieze band over the pair of tall glazed cupboard doors w/quatrefoil & Gothic arch glazing above a pair of thin lower drawers; the lower section w/stepped-out white marble rectangular top above a single long ogee-front drawer above a pair of Gothic arch-paneled cupboard doors flanked by carved pilasters & ending in heavy block feet, ca. 1840 (ILLUS. top next page) ....... **3,000**

*Victorian Gothic Secretary-Bookcase*

*Wooton Standard Grade Secretary*

**Wooton 'Patent' secretary,** walnut & walnut veneer, Standard Grade, a paneled & spindled top gallery above the curved, paneled & hinged double door case opening to an ornately fitted desk interior, on block feet on casters, ca. 1880 (ILLUS.) ..................................................... **12,000**

## SIDEBOARDS

*Fine Art Nouveau Sideboard*

*Golden Oak Secretary-China Cabinet*

**Victorian 'side-by-side' secretary-china cabinet,** Golden Oak substyle, quarter-sawn oak, the superstructure w/a high crestrail w/pointed carved central crest & scroll-carved rounded corners flanking a half-round rail over a scroll-fronted shelf backed by an oblong beveled mirror, the lower case w/a curved glass tall door opening to wooden shelves on the left beside a pair of small glazed doors over the hinged slant front w/applied scroll carving opening to a fitted interior above a stack of three block-fronted drawers w/simple wooden knobs, molded apron on paw-carved front feet on casters, some damage, ca. 1900, 16 x 40", 77 3/4" h. (ILLUS.) ..................................... **1,100**

**Art Nouveau sideboard,** ormolu-mounted inlaid mahogany & rosewood, "Chicorée" patt., the high superstructure w/a gently arched crestrail centered by a stylized carved floral tapering panel, an upright rectangular glass-doored cabinet at each side of a central open shelf w/floral-carved arched apron above an alcove all on the rectangular top w/molded edges, the case w/a pair of small central drawers w/leafy pulls above a pair of tall paneled cupboard doors inlaid w/leafy vines, each front side w/two open shelves fronted by serpentine floral-carved brackets, molded base, Louis Majorelle, France, ca. 1900, 22 x 66", 75" h. (ILLUS.) ......................... **14,375**

*Arts & Crafts Oak Server*

**Arts & Crafts server,** oak, the superstructure w/a peaked crestrail over a narrow shelf w/an arched apron & tapering supports above a long rectangular mirror, a rectangular top above slightly canted sides enclosing a pair of drawers w/metal pulls above a pair of cupboard doors w/an arched & fanned glazed panel over a plain panel above a single long drawer at the bottom, short stile feet, in the style of the Shop of the Crafters, unsigned, some damage, ca. 1915, 19 1/4 x 42", 37 1/2" h. (ILLUS.) .............. **1,265**

*English Arts & Crafts Sideboard*

**Arts & Crafts sideboard,** oak, a long rectangular top w/molded edges above a case w/a short drawer w/drop ring pulls beside a long drawer w/matching pulls over a pair of flat cupboard doors w/heavy long strap hinges & square plate & ring pulls centered by a stack of two deep drawers w/matching pulls, flat base, heavy stiles w/short feet on casters, England, early 20th c., wear, 24 x 73", 37" h. (ILLUS.) ......................... **6,612**

**Classical country-style server,** painted & decorated, a rectangular top above a pair of shallow drawers w/two turned wood knobs each above a deep long

drawer w/turned pulls projecting above a pair of paneled cupboard doors flanked by black-painted turned columns continuing to turned tapering feet, overall red & gold graining simulating mahogany, original paint, most pulls & door hardware changed, Shaftsbury area, Vermont, 1825-40, very minor imperfections, 21 x 46 3/4", 50" h. (ILLUS. below).. **1,840**

*Decorated Country Classical Server*

*Classical Mahogany Server*

**Classical server,** mahogany & mahogany veneer, a rectangular top above a long ogee-molded drawer projecting above a pair of paneled cupboard doors flanked by S-scroll pilasters ending in blocks on C-scroll feet, minor imperfections, Boston, ca. 1825, 18 1/2 x 40", 34" h. (ILLUS.) ...................................................... **1,725**

**Classical server,** mahogany & mahogany veneer, the rectangular top above a case w/a pair of short cockbeaded drawers over a single long cockbeaded drawer w/banded borders flanked by applied Gothic arch panels above the ring-, rod- and spiral-turned legs joined by a medial shelf, all on knob & peg feet on cast brass casters, probably New York, ca. 1825, old refinish, 16 1/4 x 30", 33 1/2" h. (replaced wood pulls, minor imperfections)............................................ **2,070**

*Fine Philadelphia Classical Sideboard*

**Classical sideboard,** carved & veneered mahogany, the rectangular top w/molded cornice above a rectangular mirror in a frame flanked by two colonettes w/Corinthian capitals flanked by acanthus- and fruit-carved scrolling volutes over a rectangular case w/two short drawers, each above two tall doors flanked by similar colonettes & capitals centering two long drawers over gadrooning above two shorter paneled doors over a gadrooned band, on foliate-carved & beaded feet on casters, Philadelphia, ca. 1830-40, 23 x 65 1/2", 58" h. (ILLUS.)......................................... **3,680**

**Federal country-style sideboard,** inlaid walnut & curly maple, rectangular top w/a boldly beaded edge above a case w/a deep bottle drawer at each end flanking two long central drawers, the apron cut w/a band of squared scallops, on eight slender ring- and rod-turned legs w/knob-and-peg feet, a heart inlay at top of one drawer, a second drawer w/replaced inlaid heart & third drawer w/missing heart around keyhole escutcheon, replaced small glass pulls, first quarter 19th c., 21 1/2 x 70 1/2", 43 1/2" h. (wear, edge damage, stains to finish large water stain on top) .................. **5,500**

**Federal sideboard,** inlaid mahogany, rectangular top w/bowed front above a conforming case fitted w/line- and quarter-fan-inlaid long drawers w/banded edge centering an inlaid oval reserve over two doors w/line- and quarter-fan inlay & banded edges, each flanked by a bowed line- and quarter-fan-inlaid short drawer w/banded edges above a similar door & flanked by similar stiles, on square line-inlaid tapering legs w/banded cuffs, New York, 1790-1810, 27 1/4 x 71", 41" h. ....... **2,760**

**Federal sideboard,** inlaid mahogany, the rectangular top w/incurved front end sections & inlaid edges above a conforming case w/a single central drawer flanked by two small end drawers over four cupboard doors & two sectioned bottle drawers, each of these facades outlined in stringing w/ovolo corners, on six square tapering legs w/cuff inlays, replaced oval brasses, refinished, New

England, ca. 1800, 21 x 67 1/2", 41" h. (some restoration) ................................... **11,500**

*Simple Mission-style Sideboard*

**Mission-style (Arts & Crafts movement) sideboard,** oak, a raised plate rail above the rectangular top overhanging a case w/a pair of long narrow drawers over a single long drawer, square copper pulls, gently arched narrow apron, square stile legs joined by mortised end stretchers joined by a medial shelf, light to medium finish, branded mark of the Charles Limbert Co., similar to Model No. 456, refinished, early 20th c., 19 3/4 x 51", 41 1/4" h. (ILLUS.)..................................... **4,025**

**Mission-style (Arts & Crafts movement) sideboard,** oak, the superstructure w/a narrow crestrail above a narrow long shelf w/rounded corners above a long rectangular mirror flanked by small end panels over the D-form long top over a conforming case w/ quarter-round paneled rolling end cupboard doors flanking a pair of shallow drawers over a long deep drawer above a pair of long rectangular plain cupboard doors, square wood knobs, stile legs, ca. 1920s, 23 x 72", 58" h. ............................................ **920**

*Limbert Mission Oak Sideboard*

**Mission-style (Arts & Crafts movement) sideboard,** oak, the superstructure w/a rectangular plate rack over a shelf above a central mirror flanked by slats above the rectangular top, the case w/two graduated drawers flanked by square paneled end cupboard doors above long deep bottom drawers, gently arched apron, square stiles legs joined by three stretchers, branded mark of the Charles Limbert Furniture Co., Model No. 1453 3/4, ca. 1907, 19 x 48", 52" h. (ILLUS.) .................................................. **2,185**

**Victorian server,** Eastlake substyle, walnut & burl walnut, a low flat molded crestrail on the rectangular pink & grey marble top w/molded edges above a case w/a pair of line-incised & burl-veneered drawers w/oblong pierced brass & bail pulls over a pair of cupboard doors w/raised molding around recessed square burl panels over a single long line-incised & burl veneer bottom drawer w/pulls, block-molded & veneered side stiles, molded flat base on casters, ca. 1885,  19 3/4 x 54",  40 1/2" h.  (two rosettes missing at top of stiles, inner edge molding missing on doors) ................. **385**

*Small Golden Oak Server*

**Victorian server,** Golden Oak substyle, quarter-sawn oak, the superstructure w/a flat rectangular top above a pair of small shelves w/spiral-turned column supports flanking a rectangular beveled mirror above the rectangular top w/a serpentine front above a pair of bowed drawers over a single long flat drawer above a pair of paneled & scroll-decorated cupboard doors, scalloped apron, square stile legs on casters, stamped brass bail pulls, ca. 1900, 18 x 40", 61 3/4" h. (ILLUS.) ....................................... **550**

**Victorian server,** Golden Oak substyle, the superstructure w/a rounded slanted crestrail decorated w/an incised sunburst & small lines & crosses between square corner blocks w/turned urn finials above the narrow molded shelf over a panel enclosing three small squared beveled mirrors w/rounded corners above another open shelf w/urn-form corner finials supported on slender ring-, baluster- and knob-turned spindles connected

to the rectangular top backed by a large rectangular beveled mirror, the lower case w/a pair of line-incised small drawers slightly stepped-out over a single long line-incised drawer over two paneled cupboard doors centered by carved, raised sunbursts, line-incised side stiles, molded flat base on casters, ca. 1890, stenciled label on back "From the Shane Furniture Co....Cincinnati, Ohio," 20 1/2 x 44", 78 1/8" h. ...................................... **825**

*Fine Aesthetic Movement Sideboard*

**Victorian sideboard,** Aesthetic Movement substyle, walnut & burl walnut, the superstructure w/a high crowned crest w/a central raised panel w/fan-carved finials over four small leaf-carved panels flanked by line-incised side panels w/fan corner finials above a long narrow shelf supported by front slender turned colonettes & overhanging a large beveled rectangular back mirror flanked by panels w/leaf-carved blocks over the long rectangular marble top over a case w/a row of three burl-paneled drawers over a pair of burl-paneled drawers all projecting above a pair of recessed burl panel doors centered by a carved tall panel of flowers & leaves, carved side rails, molded flat base on casters, ca. 1885 (ILLUS.) .................................................. **2,200**

**Victorian sideboard,** Renaissance Revival substyle, walnut & burl walnut, the superstructure w/a pedimental crest w/burl panels centered by a carved life-like stag head above a pair of small half-round end shelves above a narrow rectangular beveled mirror above a long narrow shelf above a large rectangular beveled mirror, scroll-cut side braces, all above the rectangular top w/ovolo corners over a case w/a pair of long drawers above a pair of raised burl panel lower cupboard doors all flanked by quarter-turned & carved corner pilasters, molded base, ca. 1875 (ILLUS.) .............. **3,900**

*Renaissance Revival Sideboard*

*Ornate Victorian Rococo Sideboard*

**Victorian sideboard,** Rococo substyle, oak & burl oak, the high superstructure w/a very tall arched scrolling pierce-carved crest above an arched crestrail over raised burl panels above an arched mirror w/molded frame flanked by two graduated small open shelves w/brackets & cut-outs on each side above the rectangular white marble top above a case w/a pair of raised panel drawers w/scroll-carved pulls over a pair of cupboard doors w/oval recessed panels centered by relief-carved fruit clusters & w/carved scrolls at each corner, lightly scalloped apron on bracket feet, mirror worn, hardware replaced, ca. 1850-60, 18 1/2 x 54", 96 1/2" h. (ILLUS.) .............. **2,695**

# STANDS

*Gustav Stickley Book Stand*

**Book stand,** Mission-style (Arts & Crafts movement), oak, V-shaped upper shelf w/through-pegged tenons above a flat lower shelf w/through-pegged tenons, solid slides w/D-shaped cut-out at top & low arched base cut-outs, medium brown finish, paper Craftsman label of Gustav Stickley, early 20th c., some wear & staining, 10 x 29 3/4", 30 1/2" h. (ILLUS.)..................................................... **1,840**

**Candlestand,** Chippendale country-style, birch, the square top w/shaped corners tilting on a baluster- and ring-turned pedestal on a tripod base w/cabriole legs ending in carved arris pad feet, probably Massachusetts, refinished, ca. 1780, 17 1/2 x 18", 28" h. .................................... **1,495**

**Candlestand,** Chippendale, mahogany, round dished top on a columnar pedestal w/a ring-turned ball at the bottom above the tripod base w/cabriole legs ending in pad feet on platforms, old finish, probably Pennsylvania, ca. 1760-80, 16" d., 29" h. (imperfections) ................................ **8,050**

*Federal Cherry Candlestand*

**Candlestand,** Federal, cherry, the square top w/ovolo corners on a vase- and ring-turned pedestal on a tripod base w/cabriole legs ending in pad feet w/platforms, probably Connecticut, ca. 1790, minor imperfections, 16 1/2" sq., 28" h. (ILLUS.) ............................................... **1,495**

**Candlestand,** Federal country-style, cherry & tiger stripe maple, a square top w/ovolo corners raised on a vase- and ring-turned pedestal on a tripod base w/spider legs, old refinish, labeled "Jeremiah Gooden Cabinetmaker Milford," New Hampshire, ca. 1800, 16 1/4" w., 28 1/4" h. ....................................... **4,600**

**Candlestand,** Federal country-style, painted hardwood, a rectangular one-board top w/cut corners tilting above a tapering rod-turned pedestal on a tripod base w/spider legs, old black paint, early 19th c., 14 x 19", 29 1/2" h. (old nailed repair at base of pedestal, top slightly warped) ....................................... **715**

**Candlestand,** Federal, inlaid & carved mahogany, the molded octagonal top w/geometric stringing & banded edges tilting above a fluted & leaf-carved urn-turned pedestal on a tripod base w/molded spider legs ending in spade feet, Massachusetts, 1800-15, 18 3/4 x 26 1/2", 30" h. (feet replaced) ............ **1,725**

*Federal Mahogany Candlestand*

**Candlestand,** Federal, mahogany, the wide serpentine top w/pointed squared corners tilting above a baluster- and ring-turned pedestal on a tripod base w/cabriole legs ending in pad feet on platforms, probably Massachusetts, ca. 1800, refinished, minor imperfections, 19 1/2" sq., 25 1/2" h. (ILLUS.) ............ **2,300**

**Candlestand,** Wallace Nutting-signed Windsor-style, Model No. 17 .............. **495**

**Crock stand,** painted hardwood, graduated right angle board shelves forming seven tiers on three notched board supports,

old worn dark red paint, 19th c., 57" w., 41" h. ............................................... **523**

*Rare Mission Oak Drink Stand*

**Drink stand,** Mission-style (Arts & Crafts movement), oak, a round copper-clad top overhanging a conforming apron on four heavy square canted legs joined by wide cross stretchers, L. & J.G. Stickley (ILLUS.) ....................................... **17,680**

**Magazine stand,** bentwood, the two upright sides composed of three entwined bentwood flaring loops joined by curved bentwood panel forming sides & bottom, small ball feet, attributed to Koloman Moser, made by J. & J. Kohn, Vienna, Austria, early 20th c., 18 x 18", 16 1/2" h. ....................................... **2,185**

*Mission-style Magazine Stand*

**Magazine stand,** Mission-style (Arts & Crafts movement), oak, a gently arched crest above four open shelves supported by curved side supports & front stiles, short stile legs, curved aprons, recent finish, unsigned L. & J.G. Stickley, Model No. 45, 12 x 21", 45" h. (ILLUS.) .............. **1,980**

**Magazine stand,** Mission-style (Arts & Crafts movement), oak, rectangular top overhanging a narrow arched apron above three open shelves w/closed sides over the open stile legs joined by base stretchers, original medium brown finish, original Gustav Stickley paper label, Model No. 72, 13 x 21 1/2", 42" h. (minor top stain) ...................................... **2,875**

*Modern Style Nightstand*

**Nightstands,** Modern style, enamel-mounted limed oak, a flat rectangular top above a case w/two deep blocked drawers mounted w/green enameled pulls, raised on short round tapering feet, labeled "Karpen - Guaranteed - Furniture," ca. 1950, finish distressed, 18 x 21", 23 1/2" h., pr. (ILLUS. of one) ....... **805**

*Gallé Inlaid Plant Stand*

**Plant stand,** Art Nouveau, fruitwood marquetry, a small squared top w/molded serpentine edges above narrow arched apron on slender molded & outswept legs joined by a medial shelf on curved & scrolled molded brackets, foliate inlay on

the top & shelf, signed by Gallé, France, ca. 1900 (ILLUS.) ........................ **2,300**

**Sewing stand,** Federal style, mahogany, bird's-eye & tiger maple veneer, the rectangular bird's-eye veneered top outlined w/mahogany veneer & half-round molding above a case w/two bird's-eye maple veneered drawers w/diamond-shaped inlaid bone keyhole escutcheons, on slender ring- and swelled rod-turned tiger maple tapering legs ending in small ball feet, old refinish, Massachu-setts, ca. 1790, 16 3/4 x 20 1/2", 30 1/4" h. (small round brass pulls replaced, minor imperfections) .................................................... **2,990**

**Washstand,** Classical country-style, painted & decorated, the shaped splashboard centering a gilt-stenciled eagle & shield design w/flanking quarter-round shelves above the pierced rectangular top on ring-turned tapering supports continuing to legs & joined by a medial shelf over a drawer decorated w/stenciled fruit, overall beige & burnt sienna painted surface, New England, ca. 1825, 16 x 19", 39" h. (imperfections) ................... **374**

**Washstand,** Classical, painted & decorated, the high scrolled splashboard above a pierced top w/bowfront & square corners on a conforming skirt of two flanking small square drawers, the scroll-cut lower sides joined by a medial shelf over a drawer above baluster- and ring-turned legs w/knob feet, light bluish green background paint w/apple green striped borders, the crest stenciled w/a compote of fruit flanked by long scrolling leaves, the upper & lower apron & drawers in black w/gilt cornucopia & Greek key designs, possibly Vermont, ca. 1825-35, 15 x 18 1/2", 37 1/4" h. .............. **2,300**

*Delicate Federal Washstand*

**Washstand,** Federal, mahogany, a high three-quarters gallery w/small quarter-round corner shelves & shaped sides on the rectangular top w/a pierced hole over narrow serpentine aprons & slender supports above a medial shelf & drawer raised on slender tapering ring- and rod-turned legs w/peg feet, old brass pull, refinished, New England, ca. 1815-25, 16 x 20 1/2", 42" h. (ILLUS.) ..................... **2,070**

**Washstand,** Federal, mahogany & mahogany veneer, a high scroll-cut three-quarters gallery on the rectangular top w/a large round center cut-out framed by four small cut-outs, on columnar turned supports to the medial shelf above a narrow veneered drawer w/original round gilt-brass pulls w/rings, raised on ring-, rod- and knob-turned legs w/knob feet, early 19th c., 15 1/4 x 20", overall 37 1/2" h. (age cracks in top & shelf) .......... **935**

*Federal Mahogany Washstand*

**Washstand,** Federal, mahogany, the square top w/a round molded central opening surrounded by an applied scroll decorative design above the four square supports continuing to beaded edges & square tapering legs joined by a beaded medial shelf over a drawer & lower shaped cross-stretchers w/a central molded platform, old finish, imperfections, possibly Connecticut, ca. 1800, 15 3/4 x 16", 30 1/4" h. (ILLUS.) .................. **690**

**Washstand,** Victorian country-style, painted & decorated poplar, a splashback w/a high arched center above the rectangular top overhanging a cabinet w/a single drawer over a flat cupboard door w/original cast-iron thumb latch w/porcelain knob, overall old brown graining, mid-19th c., 14 1/4 x 24", overall 36 1/2" h. (drawer pull replaced w/thread spool) ............................................. **605**

**Washstand,** Victorian Renaissance Revival substyle, a high white marble backsplash w/a high arched center above rounded corners over two half-round shelves over the rectangular marble top w/molded edges, the walnut case w/a single long paneled drawer w/two leaf- and fruit-carved pulls above a pair of arch-topped paneled doors w/carved central leaf- and fruit-carved clusters, molded base on short bracket feet, ca. 1870 ............................................................. **495**

**Washstand,** Victorian Renaissance Revival substyle, walnut, a high rounded & scroll-cut splashback above the rectangular top w/rounded front corners above a case w/a single long drawer w/raised oval molding & two carved fruit & leaf pulls over a pair of cupboard doors w/arched panels, paneled sides, wide molded base on casters, side pull-out narrow shelf on top right side, 17 x 31", overall 31 1/4" h. .......................... **523**

**Washstand,** Victorian Renaissance Revival substyle, walnut & burl walnut, a tall white marble backsplash w/a pointed crest & rounded corners over two small half-round shelves above the rectangular white marble top w/molded edges, the case w/a long upper drawer w/two shaped rectangular raised burl panels w/pear-shaped drops flanking a large carved keyhole escutcheon & flanked by chamfered corners w/raised burl panels, a mid-molding over a pair of raised panel cupboard doors flanked by beveled front corners w/scrolled blocking, lower molding above the deep conforming flat apron on porcelain casters, ca. 1875, 15 1/2 x 29 1/4", overall 41" h. (crack in top & damage to one shelf) ......................... **550**

*Victorian Marble Top Washstand*

**Washstand,** Victorian Renaissance Revival substyle, walnut & burl walnut, the white marble top w/a high arched backsplash w/two small shelves above the rectangular top over a case w/a deep long drawer w/geometric raised burl panels & hinged metal pulls projecting above two matching long lower drawers, molded side stiles, base molding over flat apron flanked by blocked feet, some missing pulls, small edge chips on marble, ca. 1880, 17 1/2 x 31 5/8", over-all 38 3/4" h. (ILLUS.) ................................... **495**

**Federal country-style one-drawer stand,** cherry, a rectangular one-board top slightly overhanging an apron w/a single drawer w/a turned wood knob, raised on ring-, ball- and tapering rod-turned legs ending in ball feet, good old finish, early 19th c., 17 1/2 x 19 3/4", 28" h. ................... **440**

**Federal country-style one-drawer stand,** cherry, rectangular top overhanging an apron w/a single drawer w/two small turned wood knobs, square tapering legs, old finish, early 19th c., 17 1/4 x 20 1/2", 29" h. (top reworked) ......... **550**

**Federal country-style one-drawer stand,** painted & decorated cherry & poplar, the nearly square top overhanging an apron w/a single drawer, raised on slightly tapering turned legs w/ring-turned segments at the top & knobbed ankles on the peg feet, later yellow paint w/orangish red striped graining, first half 19th c., 22 1/4 x 22 1/2", 31 1/4" h. (wear, pull & drawer lock missing) ................................. **1,100**

**Federal country-style one-drawer stand,** painted & decorated poplar, a rectangular top overhanging an apron w/a single drawer raised on tapering ring- and knob-turned legs w/peg feet, original red graining w/yellow striping & gold stenciled detail around porcelain knob, drawer bottom w/inscription "Barbara Kaufman Yoder, married to Daniel Yoder," attributed to J. Stahl, Soap Hollow, Pennsylvania, mid-19th c., 20 3/4 x 22", 29 1/2" h. (filled age crack in top, some wear) .................................... **4,070**

Pennsylvania, ca. 1830, 21 1/2" sq., 28 1/2" h. (ILLUS.) .................................... **1,955**

**Federal country-style two-drawer stand,** curly maple, square top overhanging an apron w/two narrow drawers w/pairs of small round brass replaced pulls, on ring- and rod-turned slender legs w/knob-and-peg feet, old mellow refinishing, early 19th c., 18 3/4" sq., 29" h. (top reattached, some plugged holes, one drawer bottom partially replaced) ....... **1,183**

**Federal one-drawer stand,** cherry, a rectangular two-board top above a narrow apron w/one dovetailed drawer w/old round brass pull, on tall slender tapering square legs, old varnish finish, early 19th c., 16 3/4 x 19 1/4", 27" h. ........................... **770**

**Federal one-drawer stand,** fruitwood, square top w/inset ovolo corners above a conforming apron w/a long drawer, on turned & reeded tapering legs w/ball feet, 19th c., 18 1/4" sq., 27" h. ................. **1,035**

**Federal one-drawer stand,** mahogany & birch, a nearly square top in mahogany above a figured birch apron drawer raised on slender square tapering legs, old refinish, New England, ca. 1790-1800, 17 x 17 1/2", 27 3/4" h. (minor imperfections) ............................................. **2,875**

**Federal one-drawer stand,** mahogany & cherry, a rectangular top w/serpentine edges & canted corners widely overhanging an apron w/a single narrow drawer w/a round brass pull, raised on tall slender square tapering legs, refinished, probably Massachusetts, ca. 1800, 15 x 20 1/4", 28 1/2" h. (minor imperfections) ............................................. **2,070**

*Painted Federal One-drawer Stand*

**Federal country-style one-drawer stand,x** painted poplar & pine, a square top overhanging a a deep apron w/a single drawer raised on ring-, knob- and rod-turned slightly canted legs w/ball feet, painted red & black,

*Federal Tiger Stripe Maple Stand*

**Federal one-drawer stand,** tiger stripe maple, square top w/ovolo corners overhanging the apron w/a single drawer w/a tiny replaced brass knob, on square tapering legs, old refinish, very minor imperfections, New England, ca. 1800-10, 19 1/2 x 19 3/4", 28" h. (ILLUS.) .......... **4,313**

**Federal two-drawer stand,** pine, rectangular one-board top overhanging a case w/two drawers w/turned wood knobs, on tall slender square tapering legs, refinished w/good color, 19th c., 16 1/2 x 20",. 28 5/8" h. .............................. 330

**Federal work stand,** mahogany & mahogany veneer, rectangular top above two narrow cockbeaded graduated drawers w/simple turned wood knobs, straight cockbeaded skirt raised on long ring- and baluster-turned tapering legs w/ball feet, old refinish, New England, ca. 1820, 15 1/2 x 18", 28 1/4" h. (minor imperfections).......................................... 2,070

*Gustav Stickley One-Drawer Stand*

**Mission-style (Arts & Crafts movement) one-drawer stand,** oak, a square top above a single narrow drawer w/turned wood pulls raised on tall square legs joined by a medial shelf, branded mark of Gustav Stickley, ca. 1912, 16" sq., 28 1/2" h. (ILLUS.).................................... 90,576

# STOOLS

**Classical footstool,** mahogany & mahogany veneer, a rectangular deep upholstered concave top on a conforming frame & Grecian cross legs joined by a vase- and ring-turned cross stretcher, probably New York, ca. 1830-35, 14 1/2 x 19", 17" h. ..................................... 748

*Fine Classical Footstool*

**Classical footstool,** mahogany & mahogany veneer, the rectangular concave over-upholstered top on a conforming veneered framed on forked scrolled supports & legs terminating in applied bosses & joined by a baluster- and ring-turned stretcher, old refinish, probably Boston, ca. 1835, 17 x 25", 16" h. (ILLUS.)...................................................... 1,380

**Country-style stool,** burl wood, oval top on four turned legs w/double bands, old finish, late 19th c., 10 x 18", 6 3/4" h. (very minor imperfections)........................... 288

**Footstool,** country-style, painted pine, rectangular board top once upholstered above long cut-out sides forming legs, old olive grey paint, 19th c., 7 x 17 1/2", 5" h. (wear, some damage) ......................... 220

**Footstool,** inlaid pine, a rectangular top w/deep aprons inlaid w/a band of stars, stylized leaves, wreath & stars, old worn varnish finish, late 19th - early 20th c., 8 x 16".................................................. 165

*Ornate Italian Carved Stool*

**Italian Renaissance-Style stool,** carved walnut, the lower back w/a central carved shell flanked by scroll-carved braces above the upholstered adjustable round seat w/carved bead border, over a round platform supported by a realistically-carved three-quarters figure of a nearly nude putto supporting the seat & standing among rocks on the stepped & molded round base w/flattened disk feet, 19th c. (ILLUS.) ......................................... 1,000

**Queen Anne footstool,** carved mahogany, the rectangular slip seat above a conforming frame, on cabriole legs w/shell-carved knees & stocking trifid feet, 18th c., 21" l., 16 1/2" h. ..................................... 1,725

**William & Mary joint stool,** maple, the rectangular molded top overhanging an apron w/splayed block-, vase- and ring-turned legs on knob feet, joined by flat box stretchers, old refinish, probably Massachusetts, early 18th c., minor imperfections, 16 x 24", 23" h. (ILLUS. top next page) ......................... 8,050

*Early William & Mary Joint Stool*

## TABLES

*Leleu Art Deco Center Table*

**Art Deco center table,** mahogany, a rounded top above a heavy squared cross-form pedestal on four cross-form downswept feet, designed by Jules Leleu, France, ca. 1925, 40" d., 29" h. (ILLUS.) ..................................................... **8,050**

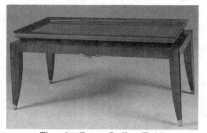

*Fine Art Deco Coffee Table*

**Art Deco coffee table,** ormolu-mounted mahogany, a rectangular dished top w/beaded edge raised on an inset frieze above the rectangular frame w/thin ormolu angular mounts at the center apron & raised on tapering curved squared legs ending in brass feet, Jules Leleu, France, ca. 1935, 18 x 30", 15" h. (ILLUS.) ..................................................... **7,475**

**Art Deco console table,** Macassar ebony, rectangular top w/rounded front corners above downswept side supports & a central reeded flat post on a serpentine, stepped plinth, France, ca. 1925, 16 x 42 1/2", 30" h. (finish uneven) .......... **2,300**

*Paul Kiss Art Deco Console Table*

**Art Deco console table,** wrought iron & marble, a half-round top w/flat & angled front edges above a narrow dentil-carved apron raised on wide central S-scroll upright brackets w/a central dentil band, set on a small stepped rectangular foot w/dentil-carved band, antiqued patina, designed by Paul Kiss, ca. 1925, 9 3/4 x 24 1/2", 34" h. (ILLUS.) ................. **4,140**

**Art Deco dining table,** rosewood, the rectangular top w/two draw-leaf extensions above downswept supports on a flaring plinth, France, ca. 1925, 36 x 61", 30" h. (missing leaves, uneven finish) ................. **1,955**

**Art Nouveau side table,** fruitwood marquetry, two-tier, a shaped & molded rectangular top w/rounded corners w/foliage marquetry above a conforming lower open shelf, all joined by slender molded shaped legs, signed by Gallé, ca. 1900, 14 x 25", 30" h. (veneer lifting, refinished) ....................................................... **1,955**

*Arts & Crafts Round Dining Table*

**Arts & Crafts dining table,** oak, an expandable round top above a conforming apron, supported on a square tapering pedestal pierce-carved w/stylized fleur-de-lis cut-outs, raised on a curve-sided platform base w/curved corbels on casters, late 19th - early 20th c., minor stains & scratches, 48" d., 30 3/4" h. (ILLUS.)....................................................... **805**

**Chippendale dining table,** carved walnut, a rectangular top flanked by a pair of deep drop leaves, scroll-cut apron above four cabriole legs ending in claw-and-ball feet, refinished, Massachusetts, ca. 1780, open 47 x 47 1/2", 28" h. (imperfections)..................................................... **2,070**

**Chippendale dining table,** mahogany, a rectangular top flanked by wide drop leaves, scalloped end skirts joining four molded straight legs, old refinish, New England ca. 1780, open 47 x 47 1/4", 27 3/4" h. (minor imperfections) ............... **1,150**

*Chippendale Games Table*

**Chippendale games table,** mahogany & mahogany veneer, folding turret-top style w/deep rounded corners & scalloped aprons w/fan-carved drops, raised on cabriole legs w/shell-carved knees & ending in paw feet (ILLUS.)....................... **3,750**

*Chippendale Tilt-top Tea Table*

**Chippendale tea table,** carved mahogany, a round dished top tilting on a columnar pedestal w/a spiral-carved urn & knob at the base above the tripod base w/cabriole legs ending in pad feet on platforms, old refinish, imperfections, England or America, ca. 1780, 27" d., 21" h. (ILLUS.)......................................... **1,380**

*English Chippendale Tea Table*

**Chippendale tea table,** carved mahogany, a round top supported on a dovetailed mahogany box open at both ends rotating above a baluster-form pedestal carved w/diamonds enclosing scratch-carved details on a tripod base w/cabriole legs carved at the knees w/acanthus leaves & ending in ball-and-claw feet, old surface, repairs, England, late 18th c., 32 1/4" d., 29" h. (ILLUS.)..................... **2,415**

*Fine Classical Card Table*

**Classical card table,** carved mahogany & mahogany veneer, the rectangular folding top above a conforming frieze w/beaded edge on a tapering pedestal carved around the lower half w/bold acanthus leaves & basket of fruit on a shaped concave platform w/acanthus leaf-carved paw feet on casters, Philadelphia area, ca. 1825, refinished, 18 1/2 x 38", 30 1/4" h. (ILLUS.)................ **4,888**

**Classical country-style breakfast table,** painted & decorated, a rectangular top flanked by deep rectangular drop leaves w/rounded corners above a straight apron raised on a heavy square pedestal above a shaped platform on ball feet w/casters, old red & brown graining simulates mahogany, original surface, minor imperfections, Maine, 1830-40, open, 41 1/2 x 42", 28" h. (ILLUS. below) ............. **690**

*Maine Classical Breakfast Table*

**Classical country-style card table,** grain-painted, a fold-over rectangular top on a tapering square support & concave platform on turned feet on casters, painted reddish brown to resemble mahogany, New England, ca. 1825-30, 17 x 34", 29 3/4" h. (imperfections) ............................ **316**

**Classical country-style dressing table,** bird's-eye & tiger stripe maple, a narrow rectangular top supporting a pair of tall S-scroll uprights flanking a tall rectangular beveled mirror frame, above a pair of narrow drawers w/large round brass pulls over the stepped-out rectangular top above a single long drawer w/matching pulls, raised on block-form legs w/ring- and knob-turned tops & tapering turned feet, replaced pulls, refinished, imperfections, Vermont, 1835-45, 19 x 36 3/4", overall 58" h. ....................... **1,093**

**Classical dining table,** carved & veneered mahogany, a rectangular overhanging top flanked by deep rounded leaves over a straight beaded apron w/a small drawer at each end, raised on two lyre-form supports centering a carved fan w/applied brass rosettes on molded arched & outswept molded legs ending in cast-brass hairy paw feet, ring-turned & beaded square medial stretchers, old refinish, probably New England, ca. 1820, open 50 x 51 1/2", 28 3/4" h. ........... **2,990**

**Classical dressing table,** mahogany & mahogany veneer, the top fitted w/tall S-scroll brass-mounted supports flanking a rectangular tilting mirror frame, a narrow rectangular top above a pair of drawers w/oval pulls above a stepped-out rectangular top above an apron w/a single long drawer w/oval pulls, raised on ring- and rod-turned legs ending in peg feet, restoration, New England, 1825-35, 19 1/4 x 36 1/2", overall 63 1/2" h. (ILLUS. top next column) .......................... **2,645**

**Classical side table,** mahogany, rectangular molded top w/a scrolled gallery above two short drawers & a base of two vase- and ring-turned front legs & two rear square tapering legs, old refinish, possibly New England, first quarter 19th c.,

19 1/2 x 44", 35 1/2" h. (minor imperfections) ............................................................ **748**

*Classical Dressing Table with Mirror*

*Classical Sofa Table*

**Classical sofa table,** carved mahogany & mahogany veneer, the long rectangular top flanked by wide drop leaves w/reeded edges above a long ogee-molded frame w/two short drawers, raised on shaped end supports w/Ionic capitals & applied banded panels on molded plinths & outswept square tapering legs ending in brass hairy paw feet joined by a square molded tapering stretcher, old refinish, some imperfections, probably New York, ca. 1820-25, 19 1/2 x 41", 30" h. (ILLUS.)...................... **2,990**

**Classical work table,** mahogany & mahogany veneer, the rectangular top inlaid w/sections centering a circular panel w/ovolo corners above quarter-engaged ring-turned posts ending in acorn pendants flanking the two graduated drawers on a vase- and ring-turned spiral-carved pedestal on a rectangular platform w/outset corners above outward flaring beaded legs & applied brass rosettes & ending in brass casters, old round brass pulls, refinished, imperfections, possibly New York, ca. 1815-25, 14 x 20", 29 1/2" (ILLUS. top next page)... **1,265**

*Classical Mahogany Work Table*

**Country-style work table,** maple, a long rectangular overhanging top w/thumb-molded edges above an apron w/a single long drawer w/two small turned wood knobs raised on baluster- and ring-turned supports on blocks w/knob feet joined by square box stretchers, old refinish, New England, ca. 1740, 19 x 40", 29" h. (replaced pulls, very minor imperfections)................................... **6,900**

**Country-style work table,** painted pine, a rectangular overhanging top w/a single drop leaf along one side, straight apron joining four square tapering splayed legs, old red paint, New England, early 19th c., open 28 1/2 x 30", 28 1/2" h. ........ **1,150**

**Country-style work table,** turned walnut, heavy rectangular top w/molded edges overhanging a deep apron w/a single long drawer w/molded lip, on four baluster- and ring-turned legs joined by ring-, block- and baluster-turned H-stretcher, on squat turned ball feet, apprears to retain original decorated iron bail drawer pull, Pennsylvania, mid- to late 18th c., 25 1/2 x 45 1/4", 27 1/2" h. ........................ **6,900**

**Danish Modern coffee table,** walnut, long narrow rectangular top w/rounded corners raised on four tapering cylindrical legs, signed w/metal tag "Illums Boli-ghus," Copenhagen, Denmark, ca. 1950, 19 3/4 x 60", 16" h. ............................. **201**

*Danish Modern Dining Table*

**Danish Modern dining table,** walnut, a wide rectangular top flanked by wide half-round drop leaves, raised on four plain turned & slightly tapering legs, w/one leaf insert, designed by Hans Wegner, Denmark, ca. 1950 (ILLUS.).......... **863**

**Early American tavern table,** painted wood, long rectangular two-board top widely overhanging a deep apron w/a single deep drawer w/wooden knob, raised on baluster- and ring-turned supports on tall block feet joined by box stretchers, old red paint, New England, mid-18th c. (replaced drawer pull, some height loss) .................. **3,105**

**Federal card table,** carved & figured mahogany, the hinged serpentine-fronted top w/edge reeding & outset corners above a conforming apron w/a molded edge flanked by leaf-carved & punchwork-decorated dies on ring-turned reeded tapering legs ending in brass cups & casters, Salem area, Massachusetts, ca. 1815, open 34 3/4 x 35", 29 1/2" h. ............................ **2,875**

*Fine Federal Mahogany Card Table*

**Federal card table,** carved mahogany & mahogany veneer, the hinged fold-over top w/serpentine edges & ovolo corners above a conforming apron, the rounded corners carved w/acanthus leaves above turned, reeded & leaf-carved legs ending in turned peg feet on casters, attributed to Salem, Massachusetts, early 19th c. (ILLUS.) ............................... **1,800**

**Federal card table,** inlaid mahogany, a fold-ing half-round serpentine top w/elliptic front & cross-banded edge above a con-forming apron w/an inlaid oval panel bor-dered by geometric band within a mitered rectangle, the cross-banded skirt joining four square double-tapering legs w/string-ing & inlaid cuffs, old finish, Massa-chusetts, ca. 1790-1800, 17 x 36 1/4", 28 7/8" h. (some imperfections) ............... **6,325**

**Federal card table,** inlaid mahogany, the hinged top w/elliptical front & square cor-ners & crossbanded edge above a con-forming apron w/a central inlaid oval panel flanked by shaped panels defined by stringing joining four square tapering legs, the dies w/contrasting panels above banding, a leaf device & stringing, old refinish, probably Rhode Island, ca. 1800, 17 1/2 x 34 3/4", 28 3/8" h. (restoration) ......... **2,800**

*Federal Inlaid Mahogany Card Table*

**Federal card tables,** inlaid mahogany, the half-round hinged top w/flattened slightly projecting front section above a conforming apron w/a long oval inlaid reserve at the front flanked by line-inlaid blocks, raised on four square tapering slender legs, early 19th c., pr. (ILLUS. of one) ......... **12,100**

**Federal country-style card table,** inlaid cherry, rectangular hinged top above a deep plain apron, on tall square tapering legs, stringed inlay on legs & apron defined in rectangles & bands, stringing on both sides of top forming an oval on each surface, old finish, early 19th c., open 35 x 36", 29 1/4" h. ......... **2,860**

**Federal country-style dressing table,** painted pine, a long flat-topped splashboard w/scroll-cut ends above the wide D-form top overhanging an apron w/a single long dovetailed drawer w/two replaced brass pulls, on slender square tapering legs, old red repaint, early 19th c., 14 x 28", overall 33" h. (top renailed) ......... **660**

**Federal country-style tavern table,** painted pine & maple, a long rectangular top w/breadboard ends overhanging a deep apron joining four square tapering legs, old red paint on base, New England, ca. 1790-1810, 28 x 46", 28" h. (imperfections) ......... **2,530**

**Federal country-style work table,** cherry & walnut, scrubbed one-board rectangular top widely overhanging a deep apron, on square tapered legs w/corner bead, old worn finish, first half 19th c., 26 x 41 3/4", 28 1/4" h. (minor edge wear, age cracks, minor top warp) ......... **825**

**Federal country-style work table,** poplar, wide rectangular three-board top widely overhanging the deep apron w/mortised & pinned square tapering legs, refinished, 19th c., 37 x 71", 30" h. (stains on top, repairs to legs, apron braced) ......... **495**

*Federal Country-style Work Table*

**Federal country-style work table,** tiger stripe & bird's-eye maple, a rectangular top flanked by rounded wide drop leaves above a deep apron w/two drawers w/small brass knobs, on ring-, baluster- and rod-turned legs ending in knob feet, replaced brasses, refinished, probably New York, ca. 1825, 17 x 24", 28" h. (ILLUS.) ......... **805**

**Federal country-style work table,** walnut, wide rectangular two-board removable top widely overhanging the deep apron w/two drawers, one longer than the other, raised on well done ring-, rod- and knob-turned legs w/peg feet, old mellow refinishing, Pennsylvania, 19th c., 33 x 50 1/2", 30" h. (age crack in top) ......... **1,705**

*Phyfe-style Federal Dining Table*

**Federal dining table,** carved & veneered mahogany, two-pedestal form, the oblong reeded top w/reeded corners opening to accept one leaf, raised on two urn-form pedestals above a tripod base w/outswept acanthus-carved legs ending in brass paw caps & casters, in the manner of Duncan Phyfe or one of his contemporaries, repairs to some legs, open 45 x 84", 29" h. (ILLUS.) ......... **2,875**

**Federal games table,** inlaid cherry, the rectangular string-inlaid top w/ovolu corners, the apron w/a central long drawer w/round brass pull flanked by oval inlaid dies atop six square tapering legs, appears to have original brass, New

York or Connecticut, ca. 1800, closed
17 x 34 1/4", 29 3/4" h. ........................... **4,887**

**Federal library table,** carved & figured
mahogany, the rectangular top flanked
by trefoil hinged leaves above a paneled
apron w/turned corner drop finials on
four leaf- and baluster-turned columnar
supports above a block raised on downswept acanthus-carved legs ending in
brass paw caps & casters, in the manner
of Duncan Phyfe, New York, ca. 1815,
open 39 x 51", 28 1/4" h. (repairs to two
legs) ......................................................... **2,875**

*Inlaid Cherry Pembroke Table*

**Federal Pembroke table,** inlaid cherry,
rectangular top w/rounded ends flanked
by half-round drop leaves w/incised
beaded edges above a conforming skirt
w/an end drawer, the lower edge inlaid
w/contrasting stringing, on four square
tapering legs w/icicle inlay, stringing &
banded cuffs, original drawer handle, old
refinish, minor imperfections, probably
Rhode Island, ca. 1800, 32 3/4 x
36 3/4", 27 3/4" h. (ILLUS.) ...................... **7,475**

**Federal Pembroke table,** inlaid mahogany, a rectangular top flanked by ellipti-
cally edged leaves w/square corners &
stringing above a crossbanded apron of
working & faux birch-veneered end
drawers, bordered by stringing joining
four square tapering legs inlaid w/wavy
birch panels in the dies above stringing
& inlaid legs, New York, ca. 1790-1800,
20 1/2 x 30 1/2", 28 1/2" h. (refinishing,
some sun fading)..................................... **2,300**

**Federal tea table,** inlaid mahogany, a rectangular top w/cut corners bordered
w/inlaid geometric stringing & cross-
banding tilting on a vase- and ring-
turned post on a tripod base w/spider
legs inlaid w/geometric banding, old
refinish, probably Massachusetts,
16 1/4 x 23 1/4", 29" h. (imperfections) ..... **2,990**

**Federal-Style card table,** inlaid mahogany, a rectangular hinged top w/rounded
inset corners above a conforming apron
w/line-inlaid reserves, the center w/an
inlaid shell, flanked by two inlaid urns
over a banded edge, on square tapering

legs w/bellflower & line inlay & banded
cuffs headed by inlaid rosettes, 20th c.,
open 34 x 36", 29" h. ................................. **460**

**"Harvest" table,** country-style, pine, a
large rectangular two-board 'pumpkin
pine' top raised on a quilt frame base
w/braced upright end legs on cross-form
feet w/curved toes, worn old red, 19th c.,
38 3/4 x 78", 28 3/4" h. (leg repairs) ........... **688**

**Hutch (or chair) table,** cherry, round three-
board scrubbed top on scalloped braces
tilting above a nearly square hinged seat
lid w/a deep scalloped apron, on wide
board legs w/scalloped edges on
shaped shoe feet, underside of top in old
black paint, late 18th - early 19th c.,
43 x 45 1/2", 28 1/2" h. (some edge
damage to feet, repair at hinge of seat,
age cracks on seat lid) ............................. **9,350**

**Hutch (or chair) table,** painted maple &
pine, wide square breadboard top widely
overhanging & tilting above four square
chamfered tapering posts joined by two
horizontal rails & continuing to form
square legs joined by a medial square
seat & box stretchers, old red paint, New
England, late 18th c., 44 1/2 x 46 3/4",
27 1/2" h. (loss of height) ......................... **5,175**

**Hutch (or chair) table,** painted pine, the
oblong scrubbed top tilts above the base
on shoe feet, lift seat over deep box
compartment, old red paint, New
England, 18th c., 42 1/2 x 43 1/4",
26 1/2" h. (top squared at the ends,
other minor imperfections) ....................... **1,380**

**Hutch (or chair) table,** pine, long rectangular top hinged on two sides w/demi-
lune tops & cut-out feet joined w/a
medial shelf w/exposed tenons, old surface, possibly Pennsylvania, early 19th
c., 35 3/4 x 55", 29 3/4" h. ......................... **1,380**

**Hutch (or chair) table,** pine & maple,
round top overhanging & tilting above a
seat between square leg stiles & box
stretchers, old refinish, New England,
early 19th, 44" d., 29" h. ............................. **805**

*Louis XV-Style French Console Table*

**Louis XV-Style console table,** giltwood,
the half-round marble top w/serpentine
molded edges above a deep pierced
trellis-carved apron centered by a foliate-carved cartouche, raised on shell-,
berry- and foliate-carved incurved
scrolled legs joined by a floral-carved X-

form stretcher centered by a shell, stamped four times "Sormani," by Paul Sormani, Paris, France, late 19th c., 55" w., 37" h. (ILLUS.)................................ **8,625**

**Mission-style (Arts & Crafts movement) library table,** oak, rectangular top above an apron w/a row of three drawers w/metal plates & looped pulls, square stile legs joined by a cross stretcher w/wide upright splat & a medial wide shelf, red decal & paper label of Gustav Stickley, Model No. 659, ca. 1909, 31 3/4 x 53 7/8", 29 3/4" h. ...................... **7,475**

*Fine Gustav Stickley Library Table*

**Mission-style (Arts & Crafts movement) library table,** oak, the round leather-covered top trimmed w/large brass edge tacks overhanging the canted & arched apron joining the heavy canted rectangular legs w/through-tenon cross stretchers, Gustav Stickley Model No. 636, early 20th c. (ILLUS.) ...................... **24,750**

**Mission-style (Arts & Crafts movement) tea table,** oak, square top on four square post legs joined by a single lower shelf, paper label of L. & J.G. Stickley, Model No. 587, 1902-16, 15 7/8 x 16", 27" h. ............................................................. **460**

*Fine Modern Style Coffee Table*

**Modern style coffee table,** maple, glass & brass, the long tapering oval plate glass top raised on a widely flaring V-shaped maple three-part support w/a pair of forked legs at the front & tiny brackets at the back, an oval plate glass medial shelf, designed by Carlo Mollino, manufactured by Singer and Company, New York, glass shelves acid-etched "Secuisit," ca. 1952, 24 1/2 x 50 1/2", 16" h. (ILLUS.)......................................... **19,550**

**Modern style coffee table,** patinated bronze, the round top cast in low-relief w/Chinese figures in a landscape, raised on round-section legs headed by brackets & ending in casters, signed by Philip La Verne, 1950s, 45" d., 17" h. (ILLUS. below)......................................................... **2,070**

*Modern Style Bronze Coffee Table*

*Modern Style Trestle Dining Table*

**Modern style dining table,** golden birch, draw-leaf trestle-style, the rectangular top incised w/a grid flanked by the ends sliding open to accept a leaf at each end, raised on X-form trestle supports joined by a wide stretcher, design attributed to T. H. Robsjohn-Gibbings, ca. 1950s, 40 x 60", 30" h. (ILLUS.)............................ **1,380**

**Modern style dining table,** rectangular top w/grey laminate resting on a black frame, designed by Charles & Ray Eames, made by Herman Miller, ca. 1952, 34 x 54", 29" h. ................................... **862**

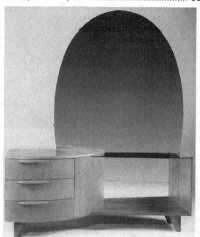

*Haywood Wakefield Dressing Table*

**Modern style dressing table,** mahogany, a high pointed arch mirror above a tapering rectangular top on conforming open compartment at one end w/a quarter-round rank of three drawers w/long wooden pulls at the opposite end, on tapering bracket feet, champagne finish, mark of Haywood Wakefield, Model No. M586, ca. 1955, 19 1/4 x 50", 62 3/4" h. (ILLUS.) ........................................................ **345**

*Queen Anne Country Tea Table*

**Queen Anne country-style tea table,** maple & pine, the rectangular breadboard top widely overhanging a valanced apron w/a single long drawer, raised on four cabriole legs ending in pad feet, old refinish, top of different origin, other imperfections, New England, 18th c., 26 x 38 1/4", 27" h. (ILLUS.) ......... **2,875**

**Queen Anne dining table,** mahogany, a narrow rectangular top flanked by two wide rectangular drop leaves above a scalloped apron & four cabriole legs w/arris knees continuing to pad feet, old refinish, New England, late 18th c., 46 x 47", 27 3/8" h. (imperfections) .......... **2,760**

**Queen Anne dining table,** mahogany, a rectangular top w/gently rounded ends flanked by wide half-round drop leaves above the straight apron on turned cabriole legs ending in small high pad feet, Rhode Island, 1790s, opened 34 1/2 x 48 1/2", 28" h. (refinished, repaired) .................................................... **2,070**

**Queen Anne dining table,** painted maple, a rectangular top w/rounded ends flanked by D-form hinged drop leaves over the deep straight skirt on ring- and baluster-turned legs w/turned tab feet, scrubbed top, original surface, faint greyish green paint, original but rough condition, Rhode Island, late 18th c., 14 1/2 x 42", 26 3/4" h. ............................. **5,463**

**Queen Anne dressing table,** walnut, the thumb-molded rectangular top w/shaped front corners overhanging a case w/one long drawer over a row of three deep drawers, the central one w/a lunette, flat arched apron w/drop pendants, on cabriole legs ending in high pad feet, replaced brasses, old refinish, repairs, Boston, 1730-50, 21 x 34 1/2", 30 1/2" h. (ILLUS. top next column) ........................ **10,350**

*Boston Queen Anne Dressing Table*

**Queen Anne tea table,** cherry, round dished top tilting & turning on a birdcage mechanism over a ring- and baluster-turned pedestal above a tripod base w/cabriole legs ending in slipper feet, Connecticut River Valley, 1760-90, 23 1/2" d., 28 1/2" h. ................................. **2,530**

**Queen Anne tea table,** maple, oval overhanging top on a deep apron w/corner blocks continuing into turned tapering legs ending in pad feet, old refinish, 26 x 32 1/2", 25 3/4" h. (minor imperfections) ... **3,220**

**Queen Anne tea table,** maple, oval top overhanging the valanced apron raised on four block-turned tapering round legs ending in raised pad feet, old refinish, New England, late 18th c., 26 1/2 x 32 3/4", 27 1/2" (minor imperfections) ...................................................... **5,463**

**Queen Anne-Style dressing table,** mahogany, rectangular top w/molded edges above a conforming case fitted w/one thumb-molded long drawer over three thumb-molded short drawers, above a shaped skirt, on tapering cylindrical legs w/shaped knee returns & padded disk feet, early 20th c., 18 1/2 x 29 1/2", 28" h. ............................................. **1,380**

*Queen Anne-Style Dressing Table*

**Queen Anne-Style dressing table,** painted & decorated, the shaped splash-board above a rectangular top w/black detailing over a conforming case fitted w/one thumb-molded long drawer over three thumb-molded short drawers over a scalloped apron, on cabriole legs ending in padded disk feet, yellow paint w/graining, 19th & 20th centuries, 22 1/2 x 40 1/2", 41 3/4" h. (ILLUS.) ......... **1,840**

*Queen Anne-Style Side Table*

**Queen Anne-Style side table,** walnut, a round tan marble top w/a long pierced brass gallery raised on a reeded turned & tapering pedestal on a tripod base w/simple cabriole legs ending in pad feet on casters, ca. 1920, 24" d., 25" h. (ILLUS.) ........................................................ **300**

*Fine Regency Sofa Table*

**Regency sofa table,** rosewood, a rectangular top w/rounded corners & rounded edges slightly overhanging a conforming apron w/a beaded lower edge, raised on ring-, knob & baluster-turned & reeded end legs on blocked cross bars on bun feet, England, early 19th c. (ILLUS.) ......... **4,000**

**"Sawbuck" table,** painted pine, wide rectangular four-board top on heavy braces raised on crossed end legs joined by slender crossed brace stretchers, old green repaint, square & wire nail construction, some old added braces, 19th c., 40 1/2 x 60 1/4", 29" h. ............................ **330**

*Early Stained Tavern Table*

**Tavern table,** country-style, stained pine & maple, the long rectangular top w/breadboard ends overhanging an apron w/a long single drawer & simple wood knob, raised on baluster-, ring- and block-turned legs joined by a block-, ring & sausage-turned H-stretcher, on turned tapering feet, old surface, alterations, probably Mid-Atlantic States, 18th c., dark stain, 23 1/2 x 37", 26 1/4" h. (ILLUS.) .................................................... **2,875**

*Fine English Baroque Revival Table*

**Victorian Baroque Revival library table,** carved walnut, a long rectangular top w/molded edges above a deep apron carved w/scrolled gadrooning raised on heavy shell- and fruit-carved tapering supports on shoe feet ending w/carved recumbent lions, the ends joined by a carved trestle stretcher w/baluster-turned spindles, England, late 19th c. (ILLUS.) .................................................... **3,000**

**Victorian parlor center table,** Eastlake substyle, walnut & burl walnut, a rectangular purplish grey marble top w/rounded corners above a reeded conforming apron w/scalloped trim & central drop panels w/burl veneer trim, raised on a four-part base w/angled, molded & burl-paneled sections joined to a turned central column, on casters, ca. 1885, 20 1/4 x 30", 30" h. ...................................... **385**

**Victorian parlor center table,** Renaissance Revival substyle, rosewood, a round white marble top w/molded edge above a conforming apron carved w/scrolls flanking raised cartouches, raised on serpentine inwardly tapering supports resting upon heavy outswept S-scroll legs joined at a central turned post & resting upon a flattened carved cross stretcher resting on bun feet, ca. 1860 (ILLUS. below) ................................. **1,400**

*Round Renaissance Revival Table*

*Fine "Turtle-top" Parlor Table*

**Victorian parlor center table,** Renaissance Revival substyle, rosewood, oblong white marble "turtle-top" above a conforming panel-carved serpentine apron raised on four S-scroll-carved legs joined by double S-scroll-carved cross stretchers joined in the center by a post w/a large urn-carved finial, ca. 1850-60 (ILLUS.) ..................................................... **3,000**

**Victorian parlor center table,** Renaissance Revival substyle, walnut, a rectangular white marble top w/notched & rounded corners above a conforming molded & flaring apron w/angular line-incised central drops, raised on a four-part base w/molded S-scroll supports continuing to outswept molded legs & joined to a central block topped by a columnar ring-turned post, refinished, ca. 1870, 22 1/2 x 33", 28" h. (hairline in one corner of marble) ................ **660**

*Ornate Renaissance Revival Table*

**Victorian parlor center table,** Renaissance Revival substyle, walnut, burl walnut, marquetry, part-ebonized & gilt-incised, the rectangular top w/wide rounded ends ornately inlaid w/marquetry swag & scroll designs & a central trophy panel, on a conforming apron w/raised burl & gilt-incised panels & drops, raised on scrolled end supports flanking a block-, urn- and knob-turned central column on flat stretchers w/shoe feet, joined by a ring-turned & reeded cross-stretcher w/central knob & turned finial, all w/gilt-incised decoration, third quarter 19th c., 26 x 45", 28 1/2" h. (ILLUS.) ..................................................... **3,738**

**Victorian parlor center table,** Rococo substyle, carved rosewood, the shaped "turtle-top" inset w/conforming white marble, the shaped apron w/carved floral clusters at the center of each side, molded edging & pointed long drops at each corners, raised on a four-part base w/scroll-carved & molded flaring legs joined to a central paneled post w/drop finial, each leg w/carved acanthus leaf trim, on casters, ca. 1855, 25 x 43", 30" h. (age cracks, repair, old metal brace holding legs) ..................................... **1,760**

**Victorian parlor center table,** Rococo substyle, walnut, a white marble "turtle-top" above a conforming apron carved w/border scrolls & w/turned drops at each corner, raise on four flattened S-scroll supports tapering to a central short post w/urn-turned finial & raised on four outswept S-scroll legs on casters, ca. 1855 ....................................................... **1,800**

*Victorian Marble Top Parlor Table*

**Victorian parlor table,** Renaissance Revival substyle, walnut, an oval white marble top w/molded edge above a conforming molded apron w/thin scroll-carved drops, raised on four molded S-scroll supports centered by a ring- and knob-turned posts & raised on four molded outscrolled legs, ca. 1870, 24 x 32", 27 1/2" h. (ILLUS.) ......................... **450**

**Victorian Renaissance Revival substyle card tables,** carved & grain-painted, each w/a D-shaped hinged top w/tongue

& groove molded edge above a conforming frame fitted w/one drawer & a cartouche w/C-scrolls flanked by volutes over
ring- and vasiform-turned paneled base
enclosed by C-scrolled supports w/foli-
ate carving above a tripartite base surmounted        by        a        line-incised
embellishment, on casters, ca. 1870,
open 35 1/2 x 36", 30 1/2" h., pr............... **2,070**
**Wallace Nutting-signed Pembroke table,**
mahogany, rectangular top flanked by
drop leaves, Model No. 628b .................... **1,485**

*Early William & Mary Dining Table*

**William & Mary dining table,** maple, gate-
leg type, a rectangular top w/rounded
ends flanked by wide rounded drop
leaves forming an oval top above an
apron on six block-, ring- and baluster-
turned legs joined by block-, ring- and
baluster-turned      stretchers,      flattened
knob feet, refinished, imperfections,
Massachusetts, early 18th c., open
41 1/2 x 52 1/4", 22" h. (ILLUS.) ............... **9,775**
**William & Mary tavern table,** a long rectangular top widely overhanging a deep
apron w/a single long drawer, raised on
rod- and block-turned legs joined by box
stretchers & on small turned feet, old finish, southeastern New England, 18th c.,
28 x 41 3/4", 27 1/2" h. (minor imperfec-
tions) ...................................................... **2,990**

*William & Mary Tavern Table*

**William & Mary tavern table,** the rectangular top widely overhanging a flat apron
w/a single long thumb-molded drawer
joining four block-, baluster- and ring-
turned legs continuing to turned feet
joined by box stretchers, old refinish,
some imperfections, New England, 18th
c., 26 x 37 1/2", 26 1/2" h. (ILLUS.)........... **2,070**

# WARDROBES & ARMOIRES

*Louis XV-Style Veneered Armoire*

**Armoire,** Louis XV-Style, mahogany
veneer, the arched & molded crestrail
centered by a carved flute & shell crest
above a raised veneered frieze panel
above the pair of tall mirrored doors
w/narrow serpentine molded top & bottom rails & decorated w/herringbone
veneering, above a pair of veneered bottom drawers w/raised panels over the
serpentine apron w/a scroll-carved central cartouche, raised on short scroll-
carved front cabriole legs, demountable,
Europe, late 19th c., 24 x 60", 94 1/2" h.
(ILLUS.)...................................................... **1,870**

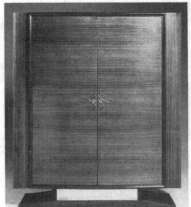

*French Art Deco Armoire*

**Art Deco armoire,** mahogany & bird's-eye
maple, the shaped rectangular top
above a pair of wide doors set w/copper
looping handles & opening to an interior
w/mirror, shelves & drawers, all raised
on a shaped, stepped plinth, in the man-

ner of Dominique, France, ca. 1935, 19 x 62", 78" h. (ILLUS.) ........................... **2,875**

*Early Pennsylvania Kas*

**Kas,** (American version of the Netherlands Kast or wardrobe), butternut, poplar & cherry, made to disassemble, the rectangular top w/a deep stepped & coved cornice above a wide frieze band w/thin molding above a pair of tall three-panel doors w/two large square raised-panel segments centered by a rectangular chamfered panel, a narrow molding above the wide base band & coved molded flat base, old soft finish, one side of interior w/wooden garment hooks on swivel arms, other side w/shelves, modern metal latches added, Pennsylvania, late 18th - early 19th c., top 25 x 75 1/2", 83" h. (ILLUS.)........................................... **2,035**

*French Provincial Carved Armoire*

**Louis XV Provincial-Style armoire,** hardwood w/walnut finish, the arched & molded cornice above a frieze band carved w/a fruit basket flanked by leafy vines above the cupboard door w/a beveled mirror flanked by pairs of raised panels & floral-carved reserves above the serpentine apron w/a central low-relief carved urn & leafy scrolls, on short scroll-carved front legs, demountable, Europe, late 19th - early 20th c., top 20 x 60", 90" h. (ILLUS.)........................... **1,980**

# WHATNOTS & ETAGERES

*Ornate Renaissance Revival Etagere*

**Etagere,** Victorian Renaissance Revival substyle, carved rosewood, the arched & molded crestrail w/an ornate pierce-carved crest centered by an arched crest over an oval floral-carved panel above the arched scroll-carved frieze panel over an arched tall mirror plate w/outset corners above a narrow shaped shelf & bracket above an similar smaller lower mirror, flanked by scroll-carved sides w/four quarter-round graduated shelves alternating w/rounded rectangular veneer panels & cut-outs, the bottom sides w/ornate pierce-carved panels flanking a pair of slender turned spindles on a white marble rectangular shelf w/serpentine front above a conforming drawer w/scroll-carved pull, serpentine scalloped apron on short turned legs, ca. 1875 (ILLUS.)........................................... **3,105**

**Etagere,** Victorian Rococo substyle, walnut, an arched & pierced scroll-cut crest above an open shelf above five graduated open shelves supported between scroll-cut sides & each backed by scroll-cut trim, a central two-panel fold-down writing surface opening to a fitted interior, ca. 1850-60 (ILLUS. top next page) ........................................................ **2,300**

*Unusual Victorian Etagere*

# GAMES & GAME BOARDS

*Also see: CHARACTER COLLECTIBLES, DIS-NEY ITEMS and RADIO & TELEVISION COL-LECTIBLES.*

**Baseball Game,** board-type, spinner & nine wooden pieces, original box w/player in period uniform, McLoughlin... **$1,150**

**Checkerboard,** painted pine, a central rectangle painted w/old red & black squares within raised side & edge molding forming compartments, outer edge molding, 19th c., 18 3/4 x 26 3/4" (edge damage) ........................................ **44**

**Game board,** folding-type, painted & deco-rated wood, pine dovetailed & glued fold-ing box w/smoke-decorated & painted exterior in black & white checkerboard, interior painted w/a black, red & yellow backgammon board, trimmed w/abstract floral designs, 19th c., closed 7 1/2 x 15 3/4", 3" h. (old repairs, some paint loss, dirt) .......................................... **863**

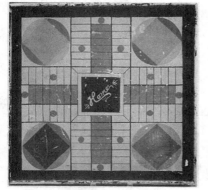

*Decorated Two-sided Game Board*

**Game board,** painted & decorated wood, board w/molded edge painted green, brown, black, red & yellow on one side, black & red checkerboard on the other, late 19th - early 20th c., paint wear, minor losses to edge, 18 1/2 x 18 3/4" (ILLUS.) ...................................... **1,495**

**Game board,** painted wood, nearly square, painted in pink, light blue & orange on a creamy white ground outlined in black, early 20th c., 20 1/2 x 21" (cracks, minor paint wear) .................................... **920**

**Game board,** painted wood, square, one side painted in black & red w/a checker-board, the reverse w/a geometric pattern within a circle, both on a dark green ground, 19th c., 14" w. (some edge wear) ......................................... **7,475**

**"Games of John Gilpin - Rainbow Back-gammon - Bewildered Travelers,"** board-type, w/book-form boards, instruc-tion booklet, spinner, various pieces & folding wooden case, McLoughlin Bros., ca. 1900 (worn) ................................... **115**

*"Major League Indoor Base Ball" Game*

**"Major League Indoor Base Ball,"** board-type, the oak case w/color-printed front w/photographs of league players includ-ing H. Wagner & Ty Cobb, the interior w/a colored field, spinner & instructions, fifteen of sixteen team line-up cards, eighteen of twenty wood players, six score pegs & one of two play pegs, Phil-adelphia Game Manufacturing Co., con-siderable wear especially to field, early 20th c. (ILLUS.) ....................................... **1,725**

**"Mansion of Happiness (The),"** board-type, color lithographed figures & Ives label, dated 1864, the set ........................... **259**

**"Picture Lotto,"** chromolithographed cards & colored & numbered disks, w/a set of chromolithographed paper on wood alphabet-nursery rhyme blocks, a group of alphabet-picture cards & a set of faces, McLoughlin Bros., 1888, the set ........ **316**

**"Siege of Manila,"** board-type, playing board on bottom of box, w/spinner, drawer w/four metal ships, dice, cup & shells, w/a book "The Life Story of The Hero of Manila for Our Boys and Girls," Parker Bros., ca. 1898, the set (missing lid) ................................................................. **288**

# GLASS

## AGATA

*Agata was patented by Joseph Locke of the New England Glass Company in 1887. The application of mineral stain left a mottled effect on the surface of the article. It was applied chiefly to the Wild Rose (Peach Blow) line but sometimes was applied as a border on a pale opaque green. In production for a short time, it is scarce. Items listed below are of the Wild Rose line unless otherwise noted.*

*Also see Antique Trader Books American & European Decorative & Art Glass Price Guide, 2nd Edition.*

**Cruet w/original stopper,** Green Opaque, spherical body tapering to a slender neck w/tricorner rim, applied green handle & facet-cut green stopper .................. **$1,650**
**Finger bowls & underplates,** deep round upright ruffled bowls & matching ruffled underplates, fine mottling, set of 6 ........... **7,920**
**Pitcher,** 5 1/4" h., milk, bulbous ovoid body w/a short squared neck, applied handle ....... **935**
**Toothpick holder,** cylindrical w/square rim, good mottling ............................................... **1,100**
**Toothpick holder,** Green Opaque, bulbous body tapering gently to a slightly flared rim .............................................................. **990**
**Toothpick holder,** ovoid body tapering to a short cylindrical neck ................................ **1,760**
**Vase,** 8 1/4" h., bottle-form, ovoid body tapering to a tall slender 'stick' neck, good mottling on the lower half .................... **798**

## AMBERINA

*Amberina was developed in the late 1880s by the New England Glass Company and a pressed version was made by Hobbs, Brockunier & Company (under license from the former). A similar ware, called Rose Amber, was made by the Mt. Washington Glass Works. Amberina-Rose Amber shades from amber to deep red or fuchsia and cut and plated (lined with creamy white) examples were also made. The Libbey Glass Company briefly revived blown Amberina, using modern shapes, in 1917.*

*Amberina Mark*

**Basket,** swirled body w/applied amber ropetwist handle & applied amber feet, finely enameled w/florals, 11" h.................. **$440**
**Bowl,** 5" d., 4" h., squatty bulbous form tapering to a wide triangular rim, attributed to Mt. Washington .............................. **165**
**Celery vase,** tall slightly waisted cylindrical body w/a squared lightly scalloped rim, Diamond Quilted patt. ................................. **220**

**Condiment set:** cylindrical salt & pepper shakers w/silver plate lids & an ovoid mustard jar w/silver plate lid all fitted in a silver plate frame w/central handle; each container in the Raindrop patt., frame marked by the Pairpoint Mfg. Co., the set ......................................................... **2,200**
**Cruet w/original facet-cut amber stopper,** Plated Amberina, spherical body w/a tall slender neck & a tricorner rim, applied amber handle................................ **5,225**
**Cruet w/original stopper,** squatty bulbous body tapering to a tall slender neck w/tricorner rim, Inverted Thumbprint patt., applied amber handle & facet-cut amber stopper, 6" h. .............................................. **220**
**Finger bowl,** round optic ribbed design w/ruffled rim, New England Glass Co. ......... **165**
**Lemonade set:** 10" h. pitcher & six 4" h. tumblers; pitcher w/cylindrical melon-lobed body over a reverse diamond-quilted design, the angled shoulder centered by a tall square neck, clear applied handle, matching tumblers, the set ............ **385**
**Mug,** barrel-shaped, swirled optic-ribbed pattern w/applied amber handle, 3" d., 3 3/4" h. ............................................. **55**
**Pickle castor,** cylindrical Amberina insert in the Coin Spot patt., ornate silver plate holder ....................................................... **523**
**Pitcher,** 5" h., bulbous body w/a squared rim & applied amber handle, Inverted Thumbprint patt. ...................................... **220**
**Pitcher,** 5" h., tankard-type w/paneled design.......................................................... **275**
**Pitcher,** 6 5/8" h., tankard-type, slightly tapering ten-paneled cylindrical body, applied reeded amber handle ..................... **316**
**Pitcher,** 7" h., tankard-type, slightly tapering cylindrical Diamond Quilted patt., applied amber handle.................................. **431**

*Inverted Thumbprint Amberina Pitcher*

**Pitcher,** 8 1/2" h., 6 1/2" d., nearly spherical body w/a tall tri-lobed neck, Inverted Thumbprint patt., applied amber handle (ILLUS.).......................................................... **250**
**Toothpick holder,** cylindrical w/rounded bottom raised on a short pedestal foot, Inverted Thumbprint patt. ............................ **193**
**Toothpick holder,** cylindrical w/square rim, Diamond Quilted patt. .................................. **143**
**Toothpick holder,** cylindrical w/tricorner rim, Diamond Quilts patt.............................. **330**

**Toothpick holder,** ovoid body tapering to
  short flared neck, Diamond Quilted patt........ **165**
**Toothpick holder,** pressed Daisy & Button
  patt., cylindrical sides w/rounded bottom
  raised on three small peg feet ...................... **275**
**Toothpick holder,** squatty bulbous base
  below the tapering cylindrical sides,
  Plated Amberina..................................... **11,000**
**Tumbler,** optic rib design, fuchsia to amber....... **55**
**Tumbler,** cylindrical, Plated Amberina,
  4" h. ...................................................... **1,650**
**Tumblers,** Diamond Quilted patt., set of 6 ....... **264**

*Amberina Vase with Applied Decor*

**Vase,** 8 1/2" h., 3" d., tall slender cylindrical
  form w/twisted optic design, applied
  amber serpent twists around base, on
  applied amber leaf feet (ILLUS.) .................. **175**
**Vase,** 13 1/2" h., 5 1/2" d., blown optic
  glass w/applied foot, attributed to Libbey.. **1,350**

# ANIMALS

*Americans evidently like to collect glass animals.
For the past sixty years, American glass manufacturers have turned out a wide variety of animals to
please the buying public. Some were produced for
long periods and some were later reproduced by
other companies, while others were made for only a
short period of time and are rare. We have not
included late productions in our listings and have
attempted to date the productions where possible.
Evelyn Zemel's book,* American Glass Animals A to
Z, *will be helpful to the novice collector. Another
helpful book is* Glass Animals of the Depression
Era *by Lee Garmon and Dick Spencer (Collector
Books, 1993).*

**Barnyard Rooster,** black, Dalzell/Viking
  Glass Co. reissue of Paden City Glass
  Co., 8 3/4" h. ............................................ **$550**
**Bird,** light blue, Paden City Glass Co., 5" h...... **165**
**Elephant w/long trunk extended,** clear,
  (Mama), Heisey Glass Co., 1944-55,
  6 1/2" l., 4" h. ........................................... **425**
**Elephant w/trunk raised,** clear, (Baby),
  Heisey Glass Co., 1944-53, 5" l.,
  4 1/2" h....................................................... **225**
**Fighting Rooster,** clear, Heisey Glass Co.,
  1940-46, 7 1/2" h.......................................... **145**
**Fish book end,** clear, A.H. Heisey & Co.,
  1942-52, 6 1/2" h. ....................................... **145**

*Heisey Giraffe*

**Giraffe,** clear, A.H. Heisey & Co., 1942-52,
  3" l., 10 3/4" h. (ILLUS.)............................... **275**
**Goose,** wings down, clear, A.H. Heisey &
  Co., 1947-55, 4 1/2" l., 4 1/2" h. (small
  bubble in neck)............................................. **375**
**Goose,** wings half up, clear w/Carleton
  roses decoration, A.H. Heisey & Co.,
  1947-55, 5 1/2" l., 5" h.................................... **95**
**Goose,** wings half up, clear, A.H. Heisey &
  Co., 1947-55, 5 1/2" l., 5" h. ........................ **110**

*Heisey Balking Colt*

**Horse,** Colt, balking, clear, A.H. Heisey &
  Co., 1941-45, 3 1/2" h. (ILLUS.).................. **220**
**Horse Head book ends,** A. H. Heisey Co.,
  1937-55, clear, 6 7/8" h., pr......................... **275**
**Horse, Head Up,** clear, New Martinsville
  Glass Co., 8" h. ........................................... **85**
**Mama Bear,** clear, No. 488, New Martins-
  ville Glass Co., 6" l., 4" h. ........................... **145**
**Papa Bear,** clear, No. 489, New Martins-
  ville Glass Co., 6 1/2" l., 4" h....................... **165**
**Plug Horse,** clear, A. H. Heisey & Co.,
  clear, 1941-46, 4" l., 4" h. ........................... **125**
**Police Dog (German Shepherd),** clear,
  No. 733, New Martinsville Glass Co.,
  5" h. ......................................................... **55**
**Ringneck Pheasant,** clear, Heisey Glass
  Co., 1942-53, 12" l., 5" h. ........................... **145**
**Rooster (Chanticleer),** pale blue, Paden
  City Glass Co., 9 1/2" h. .............................. **175**
**Rooster Head Stopper,** clear, A.H. Heisey
  & Co., 4 1/2" h. ............................................ **45**

**Rooster with Crooked Tail,** clear, No. 668, New Martinsville Glass Co., 8" h. ........... 60
**Small Cat,** black satin, No. 9446, Tiffin Glass Company............................................. 250
**Sparrow,** clear, A.H. Heisey & Co., 1942-45, 4" l., 2 1/4" h. .......................................... 100
**Squirrel,** clear, No. 674, New Martinsville Glass Co., 4 1/2" h. (no base) ........................ 45
**Tiger, Head Up,** clear, New Martinsville Glass Co., 6 1/2" h. ...................................... 150
**Wolfhound,** black, No. 716, Dalzell/Viking Glass Co. reissue of New Martinsville Glass Co., 7" h. ............................................ 450

# ART GLASS BASKETS

*Popular novelties in the late Victorian era, these ornate baskets of glass were usually hand-crafted of free-blown or mold-blown glass. They were made in a wide spectrum of colors and shapes. Pieces were highlighted with tall applied handles and often applied feet; however, fancier ones might also carry additional appliqued trim.*

*Shaded & Enameled Glass Basket*

**Cased,** footed spherical form w/wide mouth crimped down on two sides, the exterior in shaded brown to yellow enamel w/white & pink daisies, gold leaves, branches & scrolled border, applied twisted clear handle, 5 1/2 x 7 1/4", 8" h. (ILLUS.).................................................... **$225**
**Cased pale blue,** the squatty lobed bowl w/an upright crimped & ruffled rim w/applied clear edging, white interior, applied clear angled thorn handle, 6 1/2" w. ....................................................... 110

*Sapphire Blue Art Glass Basket*

**Sapphire blue,** squatty bulbous optic ribbed body tapering to a flared rim, clear applied petal feet, petal rim band & high twisted handle, 5" d., 9" h. (ILLUS.)...... 175
**Spangled,** butterscotch exterior w/gold mica flecks, ruffled rim w/applied clear edging & handle, white lining, 8 1/4" h. .......... 77

*Large Spangled Glass Basket*

**Spangled,** round w/wide rolled & crimped rim, the back edge pulled up into a point, interior in blue, white & gold spatter w/silver mica flecks, clear applied edging & tall pointed reeded handle, white exterior, 8" d., 11 1/2" h. (ILLUS.) ...................... 275
**Spatter,** deep upright ribbed & fluted bowl w/spatter exterior in maroon, blue, gold & blue, white interior, applied clear twisted thorn handle, 6" d., 7" h. .................. 165

*Egg-shaped Amber Spatter Basket*

**Spatter,** tall ovoid egg-shaped body in amber w/a Diamond Quilted patt., white spatter throughout, crimped rim, applied twisted amber handle, 6" h. (ILLUS.) .... **200-225**

# BACCARAT

*Baccarat glass has been made by Cristalleries de Baccarat, France, since 1765. The firm has produced various glassware of excellent quality as well as paperweights. Baccarat's Rose Teinte is often referred to as Baccarat's Amberina.*

**Cologne bottle w/stopper,** cylindrical w/short cylindrical neck w/flared rim, dark blue Swirl patt., matching Swirl ball stopper, 2 1/4" d., 5 3/4" h........................... **$85**

*"Rose Teinte" Cologne Bottle*

**Cologne bottle w/stopper,** "Rose Teinte," cylindrical shouldered form w/short cylindrical neck & flared rim, Pinwheel patt. w/matching ball stopper, 2 1/2" d., 6 1/4" h. (ILLUS.)............................................. **85**

*Baccarat Cruet with Paper Label*

**Cruet w/stopper,** spherical body w/a slender cylindrical neck w/pinched spout, sapphire blue w/applied clear handle, clear facet-cut stopper, the sides enameled w/flowering branches, a disc & reserve in gold, yellow & white, original paper label, 4 1/2" d., 8 1/2" h. (ILLUS.) ...... **225**

**Decanter w/stopper,** "Rose Teinte," spherical body molded w/plain swirled bands alternating w/square hob bands, tall paneled & ringed neck w/a flared rim, matching original knob stopper, 5" d., 10 1/4" h. (ILLUS. top next column) ............. **225**

**Vase,** 12" h., tall waisted cylindrical form, clear frosted & textured ground enameled in lavender, rust & white w/a large iris & gilded foliage, base marked "Les Vaporisateurs Paris Baccarat," ca. 1900 (wear to gilded rim) ...................................... **345**

*"Rose Teinte" Baccarat Decanter*

# BLOWN THREE MOLD

*This type of glass was entirely or partially blown in a mold and was popular from about 1820 to 1840. The object was formed and the decoration impressed upon it by blowing the glass into a metal mold, usually of three—but sometimes more—sections hinged together. Mold-blown glass actually dates back to ancient times. Recent research reveals that certain geometric patterns were reproduced in the 1920s; some new pieces, usually sold through museum gift shops, are still available. Collectors are urged to read all recent information available. Reference numbers are from George L. and Helen McKearin's book,* American Glass.

*Pieces are clear unless otherwise noted.*

*Barrel-Shaped Decanter with Stopper*

**Creamer,** geometric, ovoid body tapering to a wide flared neck w/pinched spout, applied strap handle w/end curl, 3 1/4" h. (GIII-26) ...................................................... **$550**

**Creamer,** miniature, geometric, applied handle, 2 7/8" h., GII-18 (chip at handle tip) ................................................................. **110**

**Decanter w/hollow blown stopper,** geometric, molded in relief w/"Rum" on the front, 8 1/4" h., GIII-2 (minor stain) ............... **303**

**Decanter w/plain flat teardrop stopper,** geometric, cylindrical ribbed sides below the tapering ringed neck w/flared lip, overall 6 3/4" h., GI-15 (minor stains) ........... **220**

**Decanter w/wheel stopper,** geometric, barrel-shaped body w/tapering shoulder to a short neck w/pinched spout, polished pontil, slightly frosted interior, probably Keene, New Hampshire, 8 3/4" h., GII-7 (ILLUS.) ................................ **204**

**Model of a top hat,** geometric, cylindrical sides w/wide rolled rim, probably Boston & Sandwich Glass Co., 1825-40, 2 1/2" h. (GIII-8) ............................................. **143**

**Model of a top hat,** geometric, tapering cylindrical sides w/narrow flared & folded rim, probably Boston & Sandwich Glass Co., cobalt blue, 2" h. (GII-18) ...................... **715**

**Model of a top hat,** miniature, geometric, tapering cylindrical sides w/deeply rolled rim, Boston & Sandwich Glass Co., 1 3/4" h. (GII-16) ............................................. **330**

**Pan,** geometric, wide shallow round dish w/folded rim, pontiled, slightly weak impression, 8 1/2" d., 1 1/2" h. (GIII-15) ....... **550**

*Quality Blown Three Mold Pitcher*

**Pitcher,** geometric, bulbous ovoid body tapering to a flaring neck w/pinched spout, applied strap handle w/end curl, pontil, 6 3/4" h., GIII-5 (ILLUS.) .................... **935**

**Salt dip,** cylindrical sides w/deeply rolled rim, fifteen-diamond base w/pontil, probably Boston & Sandwich Glass Co., cobalt blue, ca. 1825-40, 2 1/4" d., 2" h. (GII-21) ............................................................ **2,750**

**Salt dip,** geometric, wide tulip-form bowl w/rolled rim on a short applied pedestal foot, 2 3/8" h., GII-21 (pinpoint lip flakes) ..... **165**

**Tumbler,** geometric, cylindrical w/diamond point band, 3 1/4" h. (GII-18) ...................... **171**

**Tumbler,** geometric, slightly tapering cylindrical form, 5 3/4" h., GII-18 .......................... **259**

# BOHEMIAN

*Numerous types of glass were made in the once-independent country of Bohemia and fine colored, cut and engraved glass was turned out. Flashed and other inexpensive wares also were made; many of these, including amber- and ruby-*
*shaded glass, were exported to the United States during the 19th and 20th centuries. One favorite pattern in the late 19th and early 20th centuries was Deer & Castle. Another was Deer and Pine Tree.*

**Chalice,** barrel-shaped bowl raised on a tall facet-cut & ringed stem on a scallop-cut round foot, clear w/amber flashing, the bowl intricately engraved w/a herd of deer on a forested bluff, late 19th c., 11" h. (minor nicks to facets) ..................... **$748**

*Fine Bohemian Covered Chalice*

**Chalice,** cov., tall bell-form bowl raised on a tapering panel-cut knopped stem & octagonal foot, clear flashed in deep ruby red & engraved around the bowl w/a scene of a stag & deer in the woods, silver plate chased foliate cover w/tall knopped finial, a grape leaf silver plate band around the foot, ca. 1860, wear, 9 3/4" h. (ILLUS.) .......................................... **748**

**Console set:** 12" d. footed bowl & pair 12" h. candlesticks; each amber-colored & etched w/foliate & landscape designs, late 19th - early 20th c., the set ................... **230**

**Goblet,** blue overlay cut to clear, etched w/titled scenes & dated "1857," flower-form foot, third quarter 19th c., 5 7/8" h. ....... **288**

**Goblet,** double overlay, pink cut to clear w/white interior, 19th c., 5 3/4" h. ................ **115**

**Jewelry casket,** cov., rectangular, clear molded & cut block design w/green overlay in each block, 5 1/2" l., 4" h. ................... **182**

**Lamps,** cut-overlay, baluster-form body of ruby overlaid in white & cut w/trellis & oval panels, decorated w/red, orange, blue & green enameled flowers, raised on a chased silvered metal base, ca. 1925, overall 35" h., pr. (replaced lamp fittings) ......................................................... **403**

**Vase,** 9 1/2" h., squatty bulbous base below tall tapering slender body w/flared lip, ambergris decorated w/a zig-zag textured bluish green iridescent surface highlighted w/white streaks, early 20th c. ...... **173**

# BURMESE

*Burmese is a single-layer glass that shades from pink to pale yellow. It was patented by Frederick S. Shirley and made by the Mt. Washington Glass Co. A license to produce the glass in England was granted to Thomas Webb & Sons, which called its articles Queen's Burmese. Gundersen Burmese was made briefly about the middle of this century, and the Pairpoint Crystal Company is making limited quantities at the present time.*

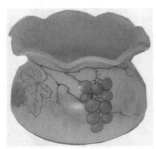

*Decorated Miniature Burmese Vase*

**Bowl,** 7" d., 4 1/2" h., footed squatty bulbous body tapering to a widely flared four-lobed ruffled & crimped turned-down rim, decorated w/enameled stylized flowers, satin finish, attributed to Mt. Washington ............................................... **$880**

**Condiment set:** pair of cylindrical ribbed salt & pepper shakers w/original metal tops & a squatty bulbous ribbed cruet tapering to a slender neck & arched spout w/original ribbed pointed stopper, all in a Pairpoint silver plate frame w/a shaker flanking the central cruet, overhead fixed arched handle & tab feet, the set .......................................................... **1,595**

**Dish,** short cylindrical body w/a widely flaring four-lobed & crimped rim, 5" d. ............... **165**

**Oil bottle w/stopper,** cylindrical ribbed body, attributed to Mt. Washington ............. **440**

**Pitcher,** 4" h., miniature, slender waisted tankard-form, decorated w/enameled & painted flowers on the sides & pink trim bands on the rim & handle, satin finish ..... **1,760**

**Pitcher,** 5 1/4" h., bulbous body tapering to a ruffled top, Mt. Washington ....................... **550**

**Plate,** 8" d., glossy finish ................................. **138**

**Rose bowl,** spherical w/eight-crimp rim, 3 1/2" d., 3" h. .............................................. **138**

**Toothpick holder,** cylindrical w/folded over tricorner rim, lightly ribbed & enameled w/white & yellow daisies & green stems, Mt. Washington ........................................... **550**

**Toothpick holder,** cylindrical w/tricorner rim, Diamond Quilted patt., satin ground decorated w/enameled strawflowers ............ **550**

**Toothpick holder,** short cylindrical form w/incurved tricorner rim, the body enameled in color w/a spray of berries, Mt. Washington ........................................... **935**

**Toothpick holder,** tall cylindrical form w/squared rim, Mt. Washington .................... **220**

**Tumbler,** lemonade-type, tall slightly tapering cylindrical form w/a small applied loop handle at the base, 4 7/8" h. (broken interior blister) ..................................... **138**

**Vase,** 2 3/4" h., spherical body w/a short hexagonal neck, enameled w/floral clusters, satin finish ......................................... **413**

**Vase,** 2 3/4" h., 3 1/2" d., miniature, squatty bulbous body tapering to a widely flared ruffled rim, enameled w/yellow & green leaves & clusters of orange & pink berries satin finish, Thomas Webb & Son (ILLUS.). ....................................................... **435**

**Vase,** 3 5/8" h., bulbous base tapering to cylindrical vertically ribbed sides w/a tricorner rim ......................................................... **330**

**Vase,** 4 1/8" h., small baluster-form, enameled in color w/bittersweet berries & leaves ............................................................. **275**

**Vase,** 5" h., bulbous ovoid body w/a short cylindrical neck, finely enameled w/clusters of daisies ...................................... **715**

**Vase,** 6" h., footed ovoid lower body w/four pinched indentations below the tall slender neck, satin finish .................................. **193**

**Vase,** 7" h., classical urn-form w/high arched angled handles from rim to shoulder, short pedestal base, attributed to Mt. Washington, No. 153 ................. **770**

**Vase,** 7 1/2" h., footed bulbous body w/four pinched indentations, tapering to a tall slender cylindrical neck, enameled in greens, browns & pink w/leafy flower branches, satin finish ................................. **743**

**Vase,** 10" h., bottle-form, bulbous ovoid base tapering to a tall slender cylindrical neck, the sides enameled w/a large delicate pale yellow chrysanthemum on a green leafy stem....................................... **1,100**

**Vase,** 10 1/8" h., lily-form, round foot & tricorner rim, satin finish ................................. **303**

**Vase,** 10 1/4" h., rounded conical body tapering to a tall 'stick' neck, sparsely decorated w/h.p. trailing roses in white, pink, grey, yellow, brown & green, raised white dot border outlined in black & gilt line around rim, attributed to Mt. Washington, late 19th c. ...................................... **575**

**Vase,** 11" h., bulbous base w/tall 'stick' neck, molded ribbing from top to base w/uneven dots in design............................... **264**

**Vase,** 14 1/2" h., a tall trumpet-form glossy vase set in a foliate-pierced cylindrical brass mount w/a raised round foot (repair to mount)......................................... **345**

# CAMBRIDGE

**NEAR CUT**

TUSCAN

*Cambridge Marks*

*The Cambridge Glass Company was founded in Ohio in 1901. Numerous pieces are now sought, especially those designed by Arthur J. Bennett, including Crown Tuscan. Other productions included crystal animals, "Black Amethyst," "blanc opaque," and other types of colored glass. The firm was finally closed in 1954. It should not be confused with the New England Glass Co., Cambridge, Massachusetts.*

**Ashtray,** Caprice patt., Crystal, 4".................... $10
**Ashtray/match holder,** Caprice patt., Moonlight...................... 12
**Basket,** Janice patt., ruby w/clear handle ........ 195
**Bonbon,** Caprice patt., Crystal, 6" .................... 20
**Bowl,** 5" sq., jelly, two-handled, Caprice patt., No. 151, Crystal .......................... 15
**Bowl,** 7 1/2" d., footed, Azurite.......................... 40
**Bowl,** 9" d., four-footed, Caprice patt., Moonlight...................... 125
**Bowl,** 10" d., shallow, four-footed, Caprice patt., Crystal .......................... 45
**Bowl,** 11" d., etched Rose Point patt., four-footed, No. 3400/45, Crystal ...................... 150
**Bowl,** 11" d., etched Rose Point patt., No. 3400/48, Crystal.............................. 135
**Bowl,** 12" d., etched Chantilly patt., Martha line blank, four-footed, Crystal .................... 275
**Bowl,** 12" d., pressed Caprice patt., Decagon line, pink .............................. 68
**Bowl,** 12" l., etched Wildflower patt., oblong, fancy edge, No. 3900/160, Crystal .......................... 125
**Bowl,** salad, 13 1/2" d., Caprice patt., No. 82, Moonlight.............................. 325
**Bowl,** etched Diane patt., four-footed, square, Crystal .......................... 75
**Bowl,** etched Diane patt., Tally-Ho line, Crystal .......................... 155
**Butter dish,** cov., etched Diane patt., Crystal .......................... 195
**Candlestick,** Caprice patt., three-light, Crystal, 6" h.......................... 40
**Candlestick,** etched Rose Point patt., two-light, keyhole stem, gold-encrusted, No. 3400/647, Crystal, 6" h.................. 95
**Candlestick,** etched Wildflower patt., two-light, No. 647, Crystal .................... 55
**Candlesticks,** etched Rose Point patt., two-light, keyhole stem, gold-encrusted, No. 3400/647, Crystal, 6" h., pr. .................. 150
**Candlesticks,** etched Wildflower patt., two-light, fleur-de-lis stem, No. 3400/647, gold-encrusted Crystal, 6" h., pr.................. 125
**Candlesticks,** Caprice patt., No. 67, Moonlight, 2 1/2" h., pr. .............................. 55
**Candlesticks,** Caprice patt., three-light, Crystal, 6" h., pr.............................. 80
**Candlesticks,** Caprice patt., No. 69, Moonlight, 7" h., pr. .......................... 160
**Candy dish,** cov., three-footed, Caprice patt., Crystal .......................... 45
**Candy dish,** cov., etched Diane patt., Crystal .......................... 130
**Claret,** pressed Caprice patt., Moonlight, Alpine etching.............................. 165
**Cocktail,** blown Caprice patt., No. 301, Moonlight, 3 oz. .......................... 45
**Cocktail,** etched Portia patt., No. 3121, Crystal, 3 oz. .............................. 122
**Cocktail,** Statuesque (No. 3011) line, Amethyst bowl, clear Nude Lady stem, 4 1/2 oz., 6 1/2" h. .......................... 110

**Cocktail,** etched Rose Point patt., Crystal, 3 oz., 6" h. .............................. 30
**Cocktail icer,** etched Diane patt., Crystal ......... 78
**Cocktail & icer,** etched Rose Point patt., No. 968, Crystal, 2 pcs.................... 110
**Cocktail shaker,** etched Rose Point patt., No. 3400/175, Crystal .................... 200
**Cocktail shaker,** etched Rose Point patt., No. 98, Crystal .......................... 210
**Compote,** open, 7" d., low, footed, Caprice patt., Crystal .......................... 24
**Compote,** open, 8" d., Mt. Vernon line, Crystal.......................... 25
**Compote,** open, Statuesque line, Cobalt, clear Nude Lady stem .................... 425
**Console bowl,** etched Apple Blossom patt., rolled edge, Gold Krystol, 12 1/2" d. .......................... 125
**Cordial,** Caprice patt., Moonlight.................... 130
**Cordial,** etched Rose Point patt., No. 3121, Crystal, 1 oz. .......................... 110
**Cordial,** Line No. 3500, Carmen ...................... 90
**Cordial,** Mt. Vernon line, footed, Crystal, 1 oz. .......................... 22
**Crown Tuscan candy dish,** cov., three-part .......................... 95
**Crown Tuscan cocktail,** topaz bowl w/Nude Lady stem, 6 1/2" h. .................... 150

*Crown Tuscan Plate*

**Crown Tuscan plate,** 7" d. (ILLUS.) .................. 45
**Crown Tuscan plate,** torte, 14" d. .................. 125
**Cruet w/original stopper,** etched Rose Point patt., No. 3900/100, Crystal, 6 oz. ...... 145
**Cruet w/original stopper & metal holder,** No. 3400 line, oil, Emerald .................... 40
**Cup,** Caprice patt., No. 17, Crystal.................... 14
**Cup & saucer,** demitasse, No. 3400 line, Crystal .......................... 15
**Cup & saucer,** Mt. Vernon line, Crystal ........... 14
**Decanter w/stopper,** etched Rose Point patt., No. 1372, cut neck & stopper, Crystal .......................... 1,950
**Goblet,** Mt. Vernon line, Crystal, 12 oz. ............ 12
**Goblet,** Statuesque line, table-size, Carmen bowl, clear Nude Lady stem, 9 1/2" h. .......................... 275
**Goblet,** water, pressed Caprice patt., No. 300, Crystal, 9 oz. .......................... 16
**Goblet,** Mt. Vernon line, Crystal, 10 oz. ............ 15

**Goblet,** etched Diane patt., Regency line, Crystal .......................................................... 65
**Honey jar,** etched Rose Point patt., No. 3500/139, Crystal ...................................... 500
**Martini pitcher,** etched Diane patt., Crystal, 60 oz. .......................................... 1,995
**Model of a swan,** Crown Tuscan, 6" h. .......... 150
**Pitcher,** etched Elaine patt., jug-form, Crystal ....................................................... 295
**Pitcher,** Caprice patt., Moonlight, 32 oz. .......... 375
**Pitcher,** Caprice patt., ball-shaped, Moonlight, 80 oz. ........................................... 360
**Pitcher,** etched Diane patt., ball-shaped, Crystal ....................................................... 295
**Plate,** 6 1/2" d., etched Portia patt., bread & butter, Crystal ...................................... 9
**Plate,** 7" d., Caprice patt., Crystal ...................... 15
**Plate,** 8" d., Caprice patt., Crown Tuscan .......... 35
**Plate,** 8" d., Caprice patt., Crystal ...................... 14
**Plate,** 8" d., No. 739 line, Mandarin Gold .......... 11
**Plate,** 9" d., Caprice patt., Crystal (slight wear) .......................................................... 20
**Plate,** 10" d., two-handled, etched Martha patt., Crystal .......................................... 19
**Plate,** 10 1/2" d.dinner, etched Portia patt., Crystal ....................................................... 70
**Plate,** 11" d., three-footed, Caprice patt., Crystal ....................................................... 26
**Plate,** 14" d., three-footed, Caprice patt., Crystal ....................................................... 38
**Plate,** cabaret, Caprice patt., Moonlight ............ 55
**Relish dish,** etched Diane patt., two-part, Crystal, 6" l. .......................................... 27
**Relish dish,** divided, Caprice patt., 6" l. .............. 25
**Relish dish,** No. 3400 line, three-part, Emerald, 7" l. .......................................... 28
**Relish dish,** etched Rose Point patt., No. 3400/1093, two-part, Crystal .......................... 85
**Relish dish,** etched Elaine patt., No. 3500/67, Crystal, 6 pcs. ........................... 250
**Relish dish,** etched Rose Point patt., five-part, Crystal ...................................... 375
**Salt dip,** No. 3400 line, Amethyst........................ 15
**Salt & pepper shakers,** etched Elaine patt., Crystal, pr. (one glass lid) ..................... 40
**Salt shaker w/original chrome top,** No. 3400 line, Cobalt (dark blue) ...................... 30
**Salt shaker w/original top,** etched Apple Blossom patt., Moonlight.............................. 130
**Saucer,** Caprice patt., No. 17, Crystal.................... 3
**Sherbet,** Mt. Vernon line, Crystal, 6 1/2 oz. ....... 10
**Sherbet,** etched Elaine patt., Crystal, No. 3035 ................................................................ 18
**Sherbet,** Rose Point etching, No. 3500, Crystal, tall ...................................................... 24
**Sugar bowl,** individual, Caprice patt., Crystal ....................................................... 12
**Sugar bowl,** Caprice patt., Crystal, No. 38, medium ........................................................ 11
**Sugar bowl,** Caprice patt., Crystal, No. 41, large ............................................................. 13
**Tray,** oval, Caprice patt., Crystal, 9" l. ................. 22
**Tray,** for individual creamer & sugar bowl, Caprice patt., Crystal...................................... 18
**Tray,** wafer, etched Cleo patt., green .............. 365
**Tumbler,** etched Apple Blossom patt., footed, No. 3135, Crystal, 12 oz.................... 22
**Tumbler,** etched Portia patt., footed, No. 3077, Crystal, 12 oz. ...................................... 25

**Tumbler,** pressed Caprice patt., footed, No. 180, Moonlight, 5 oz. ............................... 55
**Tumbler,** pressed Caprice patt., footed, No. 300, Moonlight, 5 oz. ............................... 40
**Tumbler,** pressed Caprice patt., footed, No. 310, Moonlight, 5 oz. ............................... 85
**Tumbler,** pressed Caprice patt., footed, No. 10, Moonlight, 10 oz. ............................... 50
**Tumbler,** pressed Caprice patt., footed, No. 300, Moonlight, 10 oz. ............................. 40
**Tumbler,** pressed Caprice patt., flat, No. 184, Moonlight, 12 oz. ................................. 55
**Tumbler,** pressed Caprice patt., footed, No. 184, pink, 12 oz. ..................................... 50
**Tumbler,** pressed Caprice patt., footed, No. 300, Moonlight, 12 oz. ............................. 40
**Tumbler,** ice tea, pressed Caprice patt., flat, Moonlight.............................................. 115
**Tumbler,** ice tea, Caprice patt., No. 310, 5 1/4" h. ................................................... 115
**Tumbler,** Square Line, No. 3797, Crystal........... 13
**Vase,** 6" h., etched Apple Blossom patt., No. 1308, green .......................................... 600
**Vase,** 8" h., flip, etched Rose Point patt., No. 3500/139, Crystal .............................. 125
**Vase,** 8 1/2" h., ball-shaped, pressed Caprice patt., three ring, Moonlight ............ 450
**Vase,** bud, Statuesque line, Amber, clear Nude Lady stem ......................................... 775
**Vegetable bowl,** cov., etched Cleo patt., Amber, 9" ...................................................... 190

# CARNIVAL

*Earlier called Taffeta glass, the Carnival glass now being collected was introduced early in this century. Its producers gave it an iridescence that attempted to imitate that of some Tiffany glass. Collectors will find available books by leading authorities Donald E. Moore, Sherman Hand, Marion T. Hartung, Rose M. Presznick, and Bill Edwards.*

*For a more extensive listing of Carnival Glass, please refer to Antique Trader Books'* American Pressed Glass & Bottles Price Guide, 2nd Edition.

## ACORN (Fenton)
**Bowl,** 6" d., vaseline...................................... $113
**Bowl,** 7" d., amber, ruffled......................... 105-115
**Bowl,** 7" d., aqua .............................................. 84
**Bowl,** 7" d., blue ......................................... 65-70
**Bowl,** 7" d., marigold ...................................... 49
**Bowl,** 7" d., red................................................ 615
**Bowl,** 7" d.,red, ice cream shape ................... 300
**Bowl,** 7" d., sapphire blue, ice cream shape .............................................................. 400
**Bowl,** 7" d., vaseline, ruffled............................. 105
**Bowl,** 7 1/2" d., blue .......................................... 48
**Bowl,** 7 1/2" d., blue, ruffled ............................ 105
**Bowl,** 7 1/2" d., marigold .................................. 43
**Bowl,** 7 1/2" d., purple ...................................... 140
**Bowl,** 8" d., amber ......................................... 165
**Bowl,** 8" to 9" d., blue ...................................... 55
**Bowl,** 8" to 9" d., marigold ............................... 42
**Bowl,** 8" to 9" d., purple, ribbon candy rim ...................................................... 110-115
**Bowl,** 8" to 9" d., red, ruffled .......................... 683
**Bowl,** ice cream shape, aqua................... 165-175
**Bowl,** ice cream shape, blue .............................. 48
**Bowl,** ice cream shape, green ......................... 105

Bowl, ice cream shape, vaseline...................... 195
Bowl, red, deep ............................................... 428
Bowl, red, flat ................................................. 950
Bowl, ruffled, aqua opalescent......................... 130
Bowl, ruffled, sapphire blue.............................. 675
Bowl, white...................................................... 185

## APPLE BLOSSOMS
Bowl, 5" d., marigold ......................................... 40
Bowl, 6" d., marigold ......................................... 22
Bowl, 7" d., marigold, collared base................... 34
Bowl, 7" d., purple, collared base...................... 78
Bowl, 7" d., marigold, ribbon candy rim......... 30-45
Bowl, 9" d., peach opalescent, three-in-one
  edge ............................................................ 130
Rose bowl, marigold ......................................... 65
Tumbler, blue, enameled ................................... 85
Water set: pitcher & 1 tumbler; blue, enam-
  eled, 2 pcs..................................................... 300

## AUSTRALIAN
Bowl, 9" to 10" d., Emu, purple ........................ 600
Bowl, 9" to 10" d., Kangaroo, black ame-
  thyst............................................................. 650

*Australian Kangaroo Bowl*

Bowl, 9" to 10" d., Kangaroo, purple
  (ILLUS.)................................................ 250-275
Bowl, 9" to 10" d., Kingfisher, purple......... 150-200
Bowl, 9" to 10" d., Kiwi, marigold, ruffled .. 240-250
Bowl, 9" to 10" d., Kookaburra, purple ............. 188
Bowl, 9" to 10" d., Magpie, marigold ............... 185
Bowl, 9" to 10" d., Swan, marigold................... 138
Bowl, 9" to 10" d., Swan, purple................ 140-150
Bowl, 9" to 10" d., Thunderbird, marigold........ 215
Bowl, 11" d., Kookaburra, marigold, ice
  cream shape ......................................... 185-200
Compote, Butterflies & Waratah, marigold ...... 200
Sauce dish, Kangaroo, purple ........................... 57
Sauce dish, Magpie, purple ............................. 300

## CAPTIVE ROSE
Bonbon, blue, two-handled, 7 1/2" d............. 80-90
Bonbon, green, two-handled, 7 1/2" d. ............. 75
Bowl, 8" d., blue, three-in-one edge................. 108
Bowl, 8" d., purple, three-in-one edge.............. 106
Bowl, 8" to 9" d., blue .................................... 102
Bowl, 8" to 9" d., green ..................................... 75
Bowl, 8" to 9" d., marigold............................ 90-95
Bowl, 8" to 9" d., purple.................................... 65
Bowl, 8" to 9" d., blue, candy ribbon edge ......... 75
Bowl, 8" to 9" d., green, candy ribbon edge..... 122
Bowl, 8" to 9" d., marigold, candy ribbon
  edge .............................................................. 60

*Captive Rose Bowl*

Bowl, 8" to 9" d., purple, candy ribbon edge
  (ILLUS.)........................................................ 121
Compote, blue ................................................... 75
Compote, green ................................................. 58
Compote, ice blue ..................................... 125-150
Compote, marigold.......................................... 70-80
Compote, purple .............................................. 100
Compote, purple, candy ribbon edge ............... 130
Compote, white ............................................... 149
Plate, 7" d., blue ............................................. 250
Plate, 7" d., purple .......................................... 250
Plate, 9" d., blue ..................................... 475-525
Plate, 9" d., green............................................ 400
Plate, 9" d., marigold ...................................... 400
Plate, 9" d., purple .................................. 525-575

## DIAMOND POINT COLUMNS
Vase, ice blue ................................................. 450
Vase, ice green................................................ 475
Vase, 6" h., marigold ......................................... 60
Vase, 7" h., green ..................................... 130-135
Vase, 7" h., marigold ......................................... 40
Vase, 7" h., purple ............................................ 80
Vase, 7 1/2" h., white....................................... 165
Vase, 8" h., blue w/electric iridescence ............ 325

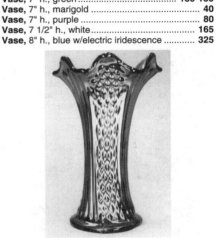

*Diamond Point Columns Vase*

Vase, 8" h., green (ILLUS.)................................. 43
Vase, 9" h., green .............................................. 90
Vase, 9" h., purple ............................................ 65
Vase, 9 1/2" h., purple ..................................... 185
Vase, 10" h., blue opalescent ......................... 900
Vase, 10" h., green ........................................... 73
Vase, 10" h., marigold ....................................... 51
Vase, 10" h., purple .......................................... 85
Vase, 10" h., sapphire blue.............................. 800
Vase, 11" h., blue .............................................. 70
Vase, 11" h., green ............................................ 65

Vase, 11" h., marigold ................................... 45-50
Vase, 11" h., purple ............................................ 120
Vase, 11" h., white .............................................. 190
Vase, 12" h., marigold ........................................ 28
Vase, 12" h., purple ............................................ 75
Vase, 13" h., green ............................................. 78
Vase, 13" h., purple ............................................ 50
Vase, 16" h., blue .............................................. 275
Vase, 16" h., ribbon candy rim, white .............. 325
Vase, teal ............................................................ 320

## DRAGON & LOTUS (Fenton)

Bowl, 7" to 9" d., blue, three-footed ................... 65
Bowl, 7" to 9" d., green, three-footed .......... 90-95
Bowl, 7" to 9" d., lime green opalescent,
three-footed ...................................................... 550
Bowl, 7" to 9" d., marigold, three-footed ............ 55
Bowl, 7" to 9" d., purple, three-footed ............... 70
Bowl, 8" to 9" d., amber, collared base ..... 200-225
Bowl, 8" to 9" d., blue, collared base .......... 95-125
Bowl, 8" to 9" d., green, collared base ............... 82
Bowl, 8" to 9" d., lime green opalescent,
collared base ........................................ 500-550
Bowl, 8" to 9" d., marigold, collared base.... 85-100
Bowl, 8" to 9" d., moonstone, collared base.. 1,100
Bowl, 8" to 9" d., peach opalescent, col-
lared base ...................................................... 500
Bowl, 8" to 9" d., purple, collared base ..... 160-165
Bowl, 8" to 9" d., red ...................................... 1,485
Bowl, 9" d., amber, ice cream shape, col-
lared base ...................................................... 166
Bowl, 9" d., amber opalescent. ice cream
shape, collared base ...................................... 300
Bowl, 9" d., aqua opalescent, ice cream
shape, collared base ................................... 2,400
Bowl, 9" d., blue, ice cream shape, collared
base ................................................................. 85
Bowl, 9" d., green, three-in-one edge .............. 185
Bowl, 9" d., marigold ......................................... 95
Bowl, 9" d., marigold, ice cream shape,
collared base ............................................. 60-65
Bowl, 9" d., marigold, scalloped ...................... 185
Bowl, 9" d., moonstone w/peach marigold
overlay, ice cream shape, collared base... 1,375
Bowl, 9" d., purple, ice cream shape, col-
lared base ...................................................... 199

*Dragon & Lotus Ice Cream Bowl*

Bowl, 9" d., red, ice cream shape, collared
base (ILLUS.) ............................................. 2,553
Bowl, 9" d., Reverse Amberina, ice cream
shape, collared base ................................. 1,125

Bowl, amber, ruffled, Bearded Berry exte-
rior ................................................................. 195
Bowl, blue, ruffled ............................................ 143
Bowl, green, ruffled, spatula-footed ................ 200
Bowl, ice cream shape, red ............................. 800
Bowl, lavender, ruffled ..................................... 195
Bowl, lavender, three-in-one edge .................. 295
Bowl, marigold opalescent, ruffled .................. 675
Bowl, marigold, ruffled ..................................... 150
Bowl, marigold w/vaseline base ............... 200-225
Bowl, moonstone ........................................... 1,700
Bowl, peach opalescent, low, ruffled, three-
in-one edge ................................................... 293
Bowl, peach opalescent, ruffled, flat ............... 375
Bowl, peach opalescent, ruffled, spatula-
footed ............................................................ 350
Bowl, purple, ice cream shape, spade-
footed ............................................................ 105
Bowl, purple, ruffled .......................................... 65
Bowl, red, ruffled ........................................... 1,900
Bowl, smoky ..................................................... 425
Bowl, vaseline .................................................. 200
Bowl, violet opalescent, three-in-one edge ..... 800
Nut bowl, blue, spatula-footed ........................ 205
Nut bowl, marigold, spatula-footed ................. 225
Plate, 9" d., blue ........................................... 1,975
Plate, blue, collared base .............................. 1,750
Plate, blue, edge turned up ............................. 250
Plate, marigold, collared base, ruffled .......... 2,200
Plate, marigold, spatula-footed ....................... 638
Plate, 9" d., marigold .................................... 2,600

## FENTON'S FLOWERS ROSE BOWL - SEE ORANGE TREE PATTERN

## FRUITS & FLOWERS (Northwood)

Bonbon, aqua opalescent, stemmed, two-
handled ......................................................... 550
Bonbon, blue, stemmed, two-handled ............. 200
Bonbon, blue, stippled ..................................... 550
Bonbon, blue w/electric iridescence,
stemmed, two-handled .................................. 208
Bonbon, green, stemmed, two-handled ........... 105
Bonbon, green, stippled ................................... 650
Bonbon, ice blue opalescent, stemmed,
two-handled ................................................... 875
Bonbon, ice blue, stemmed, two-handle ....... 750
Bonbon, ice green, stemmed, two-handled ..... 750
Bonbon, lavender, stemmed, two-handled ...... 800

*Fruits & Flowers Bonbon*

Bonbon, marigold, stemmed, two-handled
(ILLUS.) .......................................................... 95
Bonbon, marigold, stippled .............................. 200
Bonbon, purple, stemmed, two-handled .......... 135
Bonbon, sapphire blue, two-handled ............ 1,100

Bonbon, teal ............................................... **3,000**
Bonbon, white, stemmed, two-handled .... **300-350**
Bowl, 6" d., green, ruffled................................ **55-65**
Bowl, 6" d., purple, ruffled.................................... **40**
Bowl, 7" d., blue w/electric iridescence ..... **275-300**
Bowl, 7" d., green, ruffled, Basketweave
  exterior .......................................................... **105**
Bowl, 7" d., green, stippled ............................. **325**
Bowl, 7" d., ice green, ruffled .......................... **350**
Bowl, 7" d., purple............................................. **60**
Bowl, 9 1/2" d., green, ruffled, Bas-
  ketweave exterior .......................................... **70**
Bowl, 9 1/2" d., marigold, ruffled, Bas-
  ketweave exterior .......................................... **75**
Bowl, 10" d., ice green, ruffled ........................ **475**
Bowl, 10" d., purple, ruffled ............................ **250**
Bowl, master berry, 10" d., green............. **100-125**
Bowl, master berry, 10" d., ice green ............... **450**
Bowl, master berry, 10" d., marigold ................. **75**
Bowl, marigold, ruffled, stippled ........................ **50**
Plate, 7" d., blue ............................................. **320**
Plate, 7" d., marigold ...................................... **178**
Plate, 7" d., purple........................................... **170**
Plate, 7 1/2" d., purple, handgrip ..................... **175**
Plate, 9 1/2" d., marigold ................................. **250**
Sauce dish, marigold ......................................... **30**
Sauce dish, purple........................................ **30-35**

## GOOD LUCK (Northwood)

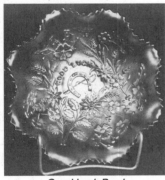

*Good Luck Bowl*

Bowl, 8" d., blue, ruffled (ILLUS.)..................... **312**
Bowl, 8" d., blue, ruffled, stippled..................... **375**
Bowl, 8" d., blue w/electric iridescence, ruf-
  fled ................................................................ **410**
Bowl, 8" d., green, ruffled................................. **250**
Bowl, 8" d., green, ruffled, Basketweave
  exterior .......................................................... **275**
Bowl, 8" d., lavender, ruffled ........................... **350**
Bowl, 8" d., marigold, ruffled ........................... **152**
Bowl, 8" d., marigold, ruffled, Basketweave
  exterior .......................................................... **255**
Bowl, 8" d., marigold, ruffled, stippled.............. **190**
Bowl, 8" d., purple, ruffled ............................... **265**
Bowl, 8" d., purple, ruffled, Basketweave
  exterior .......................................................... **280**
Bowl, 8" to 9" d., aqua opalescent, piecrust
  rim .............................................................. **2,900**
Bowl, 8" to 9" d., blue, piecrust rim .......... **425-450**
Bowl, 8" to 9" d., blue w/electric irides-
  cence, piecrust rim ....................................... **585**
Bowl, 8" to 9" d., green, piecrust rim................ **365**
Bowl, 8" to 9" d., marigold, piecrust rim .... **275-325**

Bowl, 8" to 9" d.,marigold, piecrust rim,
  Basketweave exterior........................... **250-300**
Bowl, 8" to 9" d., marigold, piecrust rim,
  stippled..................................................... **325-375**
Bowl, 8" to 9" d., purple, piecrust rim .............. **275**
Bowl, 8" to 9" d., teal blue, piecrust rim......... **2,750**
Bowl, 8" to 9" d., aqua opalescent, ruffled .... **1,025**
Bowl, 8" to 9" d., blue, ruffled.......................... **475**
Bowl, 8" to 9" d., green, ruffled........................ **650**
Bowl, 8" to 9" d., ice blue, ruffled .................. **3,800**
Bowl, 8" to 9" d., lavender, ruffled ................... **225**
Bowl, 8" to 9" d., marigold, ruffled ................... **170**
Bowl, 8" to 9" d., marigold, ruffled,
  stippled..................................................... **425-450**
Bowl, 8" to 9" d., teal blue, ruffled ................ **1,350**
Bowl, 9" d., aqua opalescent, ruffled,
  ribbed exterior ........................................... **2,425**
Bowl, blue w/electric iridescence, piecrust
  rim, stippled, ribbed exterior........................ **642**
Bowl, emerald green, piecrust rim................. **1,500**
Bowl, ice blue, piecrust rim ........................... **5,000**
Bowl, ice green, ruffled .................................. **4,500**
Bowl, marigold iridescence, stippled ............... **380**
Bowl, pastel marigold, piecrust rim, stip-
  pled ............................................................... **410**
Bowl, purple, piecrust rim, ribbed exterior........ **337**
Bowl, purple, ruffled, Basketweave exterior..... **378**
Plate, 9" d., green............................................ **1,650**
Plate, 9" d., green, Basketweave exterior ........ **650**
Plate, 9" d., marigold ...................................... **375**
Plate, 9" d., marigold, stippled...................... **2,000**
Plate, 9" d., purple.......................................... **500**
Plate, 9" d., purple, Basketweave exterior. **600-650**
Plate, 9" d., purple, stippled............................ **700**

## GRAPE & CABLE (Northwood)

Banana boat, banded rim, stippled, aqua........ **575**
Banana boat, blue ..................................... **425-500**
Banana boat, blue, banded rim,
  stippled ........................................... **1,000-1,200**
Banana boat, green, banded rim, stippled **550-600**
Banana boat, green, stippled................... **300-325**
Banana boat, marigold............................. **150-200**
Banana boat, purple ....................................... **335**
Bonbon, two-handled, blue............................... **100**
Bonbon, two-handled, green...................... **75-100**
Bonbon, two-handled, marigold ......................... **75**
Bonbon, two-handled, purple..................... **75-100**
Bonbon, two-handled, white .................... **500-550**
Bowl, 5" d., green.............................................. **60**
Bowl, 5" d., marigold ......................................... **30**
Bowl, 5" d., purple............................................. **60**
Bowl, 6 1/2" d., Amberina (Fenton) ................. **650**
Bowl, 6 1/2" d., marigold ................................... **38**
Bowl, 7" d., ice cream shape, marigold
  (Fenton)........................................................... **35**
Bowl, 7" d., ice cream shape, purple (Fen-
  ton)................................................................... **55**
Bowl, 7" d., ice cream shape, vaseline
  (Fenton)........................................................... **45**
Bowl, 7" d., ruffled, green (Fenton) ................... **58**
Bowl, 7" d., ruffled, red...................................... **800**
Bowl, 7" d., spatula-footed, green (Fenton) ....... **85**
Bowl, 7 1/2" d., ball-footed, blue (Fenton)... **75-100**
Bowl, 7 1/2" d., ball-footed, marigold (Fen-
  ton)................................................................... **55**
Bowl, 7 1/2" d., ball-footed, purple (Fenton)....... **89**
Bowl, 7 1/2" d., ball-footed, red (Fenton) ......... **575**
Bowl, 7 1/2" d., ruffled, green............................. **85**
Bowl, 7 1/2" d., ruffled, red...................... **800-825**

Bowl, 7 1/2" d., ruffled, vaseline,..................... 100
Bowl, 8" d., ice cream shape, footed, blue
(Fenton)............................................................. 60-65
Bowl, 8" to 9" d., ball-footed, green (Fenton)..................................................................... 76
Bowl, 8" to 9" d., ball-footed, pastel marigold (Fenton)..................................................... 55
Bowl, 8" to 9" d., piecrust rim, aqua opalescent (Northwood)....................................... 3,450
Bowl, 8" to 9" d., piecrust rim, blue,
stippled......................................................... 375-425
Bowl, 8" to 9" d., piecrust rim, green......... 100-110
Bowl, 8" to 9" d., piecrust rim, ice blue.......... 1,300
Bowl, 8" to 9" d., piecrust rim, marigold ............. 85
Bowl, 8" to 9" d., piecrust rim, purple ........ 135-150
Bowl, 8" to 9" d., spatula-footed, blue
(Northwood) ......................................................... 250
Bowl, 8" to 9" d., spatula-footed, green
(Northwood) ........................................................... 90
Bowl, 8" to 9" d., spatula-footed, marigold
(Northwood) ........................................................... 65
Bowl, 8 1/2" d., scalloped, marigold.................... 85
Bowl, 8 1/2" d., scalloped, purple (Northwood) .................................................................. 95
Bowl, berry, 9" d., clambroth ............................. 88
Bowl, berry, 9" d., green................................... 188
Bowl, berry, 9" d., ice green ............................. 838
Bowl, berry, 9" d., marigold .............................. 135
Bowl, berry, 9" d., purple .................................... 80
Bowl, orange, 10 1/2" d., blue, footed.............. 475
Bowl, orange, 10 1/2" d., green, footed........... 325
Bowl, orange, 10 1/2" d., ice green, footed... 1,050
Bowl, orange, 10 1/2" d., marigold, footed .... 188
Bowl, orange, 10 1/2" d., marigold, footed,
stippled............................................................. 400
Bowl, orange, 10 1/2" d., purple, footed.......... 450
Bowl, orange, 10 1/2" d., white, footed .......... 1,538
Bowl, 11" d., ice cream shape, blue.............. 1,200
Bowl, 11" d., ice cream shape, green ............. 600
Bowl, 11" d., ice cream shape, ice blue ........ 2,425
Bowl, 11" d., ice cream shape, ice green ...... 1,350
Bowl, 11" d., ice cream shape, marigold......... 400
Bowl, 11" d., ice cream shape, purple...... 350-400
Bowl, 11" d., ice cream shape, white .............. 375
Bowl, 11" d., ruffled, green............................... 195
Bowl, fruit, blue ................................................ 438
Bowl, fruit, green .............................................. 488
Bowl, fruit, purple ............................................. 750
Bowl, ruffled, marigold (Fenton) ......................... 45
Breakfast set: individual size creamer &
sugar bowl; green, pr. ..................................... 172
Breakfast set: individual size creamer &
sugar bowl; marigold, pr.................................. 140
Breakfast set: individual size creamer &
sugar bowl; purple, pr..................................... 188
Butter dish, cov., amber .................................. 115
Butter dish, cov., blue ..................................... 350
Butter dish, cov., green ............................... 200-250
Butter dish, cov., ice blue................................ 350
Butter dish, cov., marigold ......................... 125-150
Butter dish, cov., purple (ILLUS.).............. 150-225
Candle lamp, green ....................................... 1,000
Candle lamp, marigold.................................. 1,100
Candle lamp, purple ......................................... 850
Candle lamp shade, green .............................. 575
Candle lamp shade, marigold ......................... 750
Candlestick, green ........................................... 135
Candlestick, marigold......................................... 75
Candlestick, purple........................................... 115

*Grape & Cable Butter Dish*

Candlesticks, green, pr. ................................... 223
Candlesticks, purple, pr. ................................. 300
Centerpiece bowl, marigold .................... 250-300
Centerpiece bowl, purple ....................... 375-425
Compote, cov., purple, large................... 550-600
Compote, cov., purple, small .......................... 375
Compote, open, green, large ............... 925-1,100
Compote, open, marigold, large..................... 425
Compote, open, purple, large ........................ 475
Compote, open, purple, small ................. 275-300
Cracker jar, cov., marigold...................... 400-425
Cracker jar, cov., purple ......................... 375-425
Creamer, green ............................................... 125
Creamer, marigold ...................................... 75-80
Creamer, purple ................................................ 86
Creamer, green, individual size.................. 75-80
Creamer, marigold, individual size ................... 65
Creamer, purple, individual size.................. 75-85
Cup & saucer, purple............................... 250-300
Cuspidor, purple ............................... 3,000-4,000
Decanter w/stopper, whiskey, marigold ......... 175
Dresser set, purple, 7 pcs............................. 1,500
Dresser tray, green........................... 250-275
Dresser tray, ice blue ................................. 1,500
Dresser tray, marigold ..................................... 200
Fernery, purple........................................ 725-775
Hat shape, green ............................................... 75
Hat shape, marigold .......................................... 55
Hat shape, purple ........................................ 50-60
Hatpin holder, marigold........................... 300-375
Hatpin holder, purple ...................................... 225
Humidor, cov., marigold........................... 300-375
Humidor, cov., purple .............................. 550-600
Nappy, green, single handle ............................. 80
Nappy, marigold, single handle.................... 50-60
Pitcher, tankard, 9 3/4" h., green ................. 1,500
Pitcher, water, 8 1/4" h., green ....................... 475
Pitcher, water, 8 1/4" h., marigold................... 275
Pitcher, water, 8 1/4" h., purple .............. 185-275
Pitcher, tankard, 9 3/4" h., ice green............. 8,000
Pitcher, smoky .................................................. 800
Plate, 9" d., Basketweave exterior, green ........ 350
Plate, 9" d., Basketweave exterior, marigold ................................................... 130-140
Plate, 9" d., Basketweave exterior, purple. 175-200
Plate, 9" d., blue, spatula-footed .............. 145-150
Plate, 9" d., blue, stippled............................ 1,200
Plate, 9" d., clambroth ............................... 165
Plate, 9" d., green............................................ 400
Plate, 9" d., green, spatula-footed ................... 200
Plate, 9" d., ice green, spatula-footed ....... 850-875
Plate, 9" d., marigold, spatula-footed ........ 100-115

Plate, 9" d., purple, spatula-footed .................. 135
Plate, 9" d., stippled, green ............................. 725
Plate, 9" d., stippled, marigold ........................ 700
Plate, 9" d., stippled, purple ........................... 450
Plate, 9" d., stippled, sapphire blue ..... 3,300-3,500
Powder jar, cov., green ................................... 335
Powder jar, cov., marigold .............................. 175
Powder jar, cov., purple ................................. 155
Punch bowl & base, horehound, 11" d., 2
  pcs. .............................................................. 2,450
Punch bowl & base, purple, 14" d., 2 pcs. ...... 575
Punch bowl & base, marigold, 17" d., 2
  pcs. .............................................................. 1,000
Punch cup, marigold ........................................ 28
Punch cup, purple .......................................... 25-30
Punch set: 11" bowl, base & 6 cups; pur-
  ple, 8 pcs. .................................................... 575
Punch set: 14" bowl, base & 6 cups; pur-
  ple, 8 pcs. .................................................... 1,375

*Grape & Cable Punch Set*

Punch set: 14" bowl, base & 6 cups; white,
  8 pcs. (ILLUS.) ............................................. 5,500
Punch set, master: 17" bowl, base & 6
  cups; purple, 8 pcs. ..................................... 3,200
Punch set, master: 17" bowl, base & 8
  cups; marigold, 10 pcs. ............................... 2,450
Punch set, master: 17" bowl, base & 12
  cups; marigold, 14 pcs. ............................... 3,100
Sauce dish, green ........................................... 25
Sauce dish, marigold ...................................... 45
Sauce dish, purple ......................................... 25-30
Sherbet or individual ice cream dish,
  marigold ....................................................... 30
Sherbet or individual ice cream dish,
  purple ........................................................... 55-65
Sherbet or individual ice cream dish,
  white ............................................................. 160-170
Spooner green ................................................ 100
Spooner marigold ........................................... 68
Spooner purple ............................................... 85
Sugar bowl, cov., marigold ............................. 85
Sugar bowl, cov., purple ................................. 145-175
Sugar bowl, individual size, purple ................. 60-70
Sweetmeat jar, cov., purple ............................ 300
Table set: cov. sugar bowl, creamer, cov.
  butter dish & spooner; green, 4 pcs. ............ 450
Tumbler, green ............................................... 55-65
Tumbler, ice green .......................................... 375-400
Tumbler, marigold ........................................... 50-75
Tumbler, purple ............................................... 35
Water set: pitcher & 8 tumblers; purple, 9
  pcs. .............................................................. 600-625
Whiskey set: whiskey decanter w/stopper
  & 6 shot glasses; marigold, 7 pcs. ............. 1,100
Whiskey shot glass, marigold ................... 125-150

## GRAPE DELIGHT
Nut bowl, six-footed, blue .......................... 100-125

Nut bowl, six-footed, ice blue ............................. 60
Nut bowl, six-footed, ice green ......................... 88

*Grape Delight Nut Bowl*

Nut bowl, six-footed, purple (ILLUS.) .......... 80-100
Nut bowl, six-footed, white ............................. 70-90
Rose bowl, six-footed, amber ........................... 70
Rose bowl, six-footed, blue ............................. 120
Rose bowl, six-footed, marigold ........................ 60
Rose bowl, six-footed, purple .................... 95-100
Rose bowl, six-footed, white ................... 100-120

## HATTIE (Imperial)
Bowl, 7 1/4" d., blue ......................................... 60
Bowl, 8" to 9" d., green .................................... 69
Bowl, 8" to 9" d., marigold ............................... 48
Bowl, 8" to 9" d., purple ................................... 90

*Hattie Bowl*

Bowl, 8" to 9" d., smoky (ILLUS.) ................. 75-85
Plate, 10" d., green .......................................... 400
Plate, chop, 10 1/2" d., amber ...................... 3,250
Plate, chop, green ........................................... 675
Plate, chop, marigold ...................................... 538
Plate, chop, purple ....................................... 2,188

## HOLLY SPRIG - SEE HOLLY WHIRL PATTERN

## HOLLY WHIRL OR HOLLY SPRIG (Millersburg, Fenton & Dugan)
Bowl, 6" w., green, tricornered ......................... 85
Bowl, 6" w., marigold, tricornered ................... 295
Bowl, 6" w., purple, tricornered ....................... 125

Bowl, 7" d., green .............................................. 60
Bowl, 7" d., marigold ........................................ 55
Bowl, 7" d., purple, ruffled ............................ 60-70
Bowl, 7" w., tricornered, marigold .................... 180
Bowl, 7 1/2" w., tricornered, purple ................... 98
Bowl, 8" d., ice cream shape, marigold,
  variant ..................................................... 125-150
Bowl, 8" d., ice cream shape, purple ............... 325
Bowl, 8" to 9" d., green ..................................... 80
Bowl, 8" to 9" d., marigold ............................ 75-80
Bowl, 8" w., tricornered, green .......................... 97
Bowl, 10" d., ruffled, marigold ........................... 55
Bowl, 10" d., ruffled, purple (Millersburg) .. 150-200
Bowl, ruffled, green (Millersburg) ..................... 250
Card tray, two-handled, green ...................... 50-85
Card tray, two-handled, marigold ............... 75-100
Nappy, single handle, peach opalescent,
  (Dugan) ......................................................... 65
Nappy, single handle, purple (Dugan) ......... 75-100
Nappy, tricornered, green (Dugan) .................... 98
Nappy, tricornered, marigold (Millersburg) ......... 95
Nappy, tricornered, purple (Dugan) ........... 100-125
Nappy, tricornered, purple (Millersburg) .... 175-200
Nappy, two-handled, green (Dugan) ................. 85
Nut dish, two-handled, green ................... 100-125
Nut dish, two-handled, marigold ....................... 66
Nut dish, two-handled, purple ........................... 84
Rose bowl, blue ....................................... 275-300
Sauce dish, green, 6 1/2" d.
  (Millersburg) ......................................... 100-125
Sauceboat, peach opalescent (Dugan) ........... 135

**LOVING CUP (Fenton) - SEE ORANGE TREE**

**MILLERSBURG PEACOCK - SEE PEA-COCK & URN PATTERN**

**ORANGE TREE (Fenton)**
Berry set: master bowl & 6 sauce dishes;
  blue, 7 pcs. .......................................... 300-375
Bowl, 8" to 9" d., blue ............................... 90-100
Bowl, 8" to 9" d., green ........................... 225-275
Bowl, 8" to 9" d., marigold ......................... 55-60
Bowl, 8" to 9" d., purple .................................. 195
Bowl, 8" to 9" d., white ............................ 100-125
Bowl, 10" d., three-footed, blue ................ 250-325
Bowl, 10" d., three-footed, green .................... 235

*Large Orange Tree Bowl*

Bowl, 10" d., three-footed, marigold
  (ILLUS.) ...................................................... 175
Bowl, 10" d., three-footed, purple .................... 325
Bowl, 10" d., three-footed, white ..................... 200
Bowl, ice cream shape, blue ........................... 100

Bowl, ice cream shape, blue, w/trunk cen-
  ter ............................................................. 230
Bowl, ice cream shape, green ......................... 300
Bowl, ice cream shape, marigold ...................... 85
Bowl, ice cream shape, purple .................. 250-300
Bowl, ice cream shape, red ......................... 2,100
Bowl, ice cream shape, white .......................... 125
Bowl, milk white w/marigold overlay.... 1,150-1,250
Bowl, peach opalescent ............................... 1,900
Bowl, ruffled, amber ................................. 275-300
Bowl, three-in-one edge, marigold ............... 85-90
Breakfast set: individual size creamer &
  cov. sugar bowl; marigold, pr. ..................... 195
Breakfast set: individual size creamer &
  cov. sugar bowl; purple, pr. ........................ 239
Breakfast set: individual size creamer &
  cov. sugar bowl; white, pr. ..................... 150-200
Butter dish, cov., blue .................................... 375
Butter dish, cov., marigold ............................. 350
Centerpiece bowl, footed, purple, 12" d.,
  4" h. .................................................. 1,000-1,500
Compote, 5" d., blue ........................................ 50
Compote, 5" d., green ...................................... 85
Compote, 5" d., marigold ............................. 35-45
Creamer, footed, blue ...................................... 80
Creamer, footed, marigold ............................... 47
Creamer, footed, purple .................................... 50
Creamer, footed, white .............................. 125-175
Creamer & sugar bowl, blue, footed, pr. ......... 100
Dish, blue, ice cream, footed ........................... 38
Dish, marigold, ice cream, footed ................ 30-40
Goblet, aqua ................................................... 110
Goblet, blue ..................................................... 55
Hatpin holder, blue .................................. 300-350
Hatpin holder, marigold ............................ 300-325
Loving cup, aqua opalescent .................... 15,000
Loving cup, blue .............................................. 225
Loving cup, green ...................................... 400-475
Loving cup, marigold ....................................... 325
Loving cup, purple ........................................... 400
Loving cup, white ............................................ 150
Mug, amber ...................................................... 89
Mug, Amberina ............................................... 385
Mug, blue ..................................................... 65-75
Mug, green ............................................... 875-900
Mug, lavender ................................................. 180
Mug, lime green .............................................. 500
Mug, marigold ............................................. 35-45
Mug, red .......................................................... 500
Mug, vaseline ......................................... 100-150
Mug, white ...................................................... 948
Pitcher, water, blue ......................................... 325
Pitcher, water, marigold .................................. 275
Plate, 9" d., flat, blue ..................................... 400
Plate, 9" d., flat, clambroth ...................... 300-350
Plate, 9" d., flat, green ................................ 3,000
Plate, 9" d., flat, marigold ....................... 250-350
Plate, 9" d., flat, pastel marigold .............. 175-200
Plate, 9" d., flat, purple .................................. 600
Plate, 9" d., flat, teal blue .................... 1,000-1,500
Plate, 9" d., flat, white .................................... 180
Plate, 9 1/2" d., trunk center, Beaded Berry
  exterior, clambroth ....................................... 250
Plate, 9" d., flat, Beaded Berry exterior,
  blue ............................................................. 550
Plate, 9" d., trunk center, white ...................... 275
Plate, 9" d., Blackberry exterior, "Souvenir
  of Hershey," blue .......................................... 335
Powder jar, cov., blue ............................... 150-175

Powder jar, cov., green............................ 400-500
Powder jar, cov., marigold ......................... 75-100
Punch bowl & base, blue, 2 pcs. ............. 275-300
Punch bowl & base, marigold, 2 pcs. ...... 185-195
Punch bowl & base, white, 2 pcs. ................... 595
Punch cup, blue............................................... 32
Punch cup, white ............................................. 50
Punch cups, marigold, set of 6 ................. 125-150
Punch set: bowl, base & 6 cups; marigold,
    8 pcs.......................................................... 330
Punch set: bowl, base & 6 cups; white, 8
    pcs.............................................................. 900
Punch set: bowl, base & 10 cups; blue, 12
    pcs.............................................................. 650
Rose bowl, blue ............................................... 85
Rose bowl, clambroth ...................................... 90
Rose bowl, green...................................... 100-125
Rose bowl, purple .................................... 100-125
Rose bowl, white ...................................... 200-225
Sauce dish, footed, white ......................... 100-125
Shaving mug, blue ........................................... 50
Shaving mug, green ....................................... 875
Shaving mug, marigold ..................................... 50
Shaving mug, marigold, large ................. 100-125
Shaving mug, olive green................................ 975
Shaving mug, purple...................................... 195
Shaving mug, red...................................... 600-650
Spooner, blue ............................................. 60-70
Spooner, marigold ........................................... 50
Sugar bowl, cov., blue ..................................... 60
Sugar bowl, cov., marigold .............................. 98
Sugar bowl, cov., white .................................. 100
Tumbler, blue ................................................... 60
Tumbler, marigold............................................ 40
Tumbler, white ............................................... 100
Wine, marigold ................................................ 25

# ORIENTAL POPPY (Northwood)

*Oriental Poppy Water Set*

Pitcher, tankard, marigold............................... 265
Pitcher, water, green.................................... 1,250
Pitcher, water, marigold ........................... 415-425
Pitcher, water, purple ............................... 750-850
Pitcher, water, white .......................... 1,500-2,000
Tumbler, ice green......................................... 275
Tumbler, marigold............................................ 35

Tumbler, purple.......................................... 50-60
Tumbler, white ......................................... 155-165
Water set: pitcher & 4 tumblers, white, 5
    pcs.......................................................... 2,000
Water set: pitcher & 5 tumblers, marigold,
    6 pcs.................................................... 500-600
Water set: pitcher & 6 tumblers, green, 7
    pcs................................................. 1,800-2,500
Water set: pitcher & 6 tumblers, purple, 7
    pcs. (ILLUS.) ........................................ 1,225

# PEACOCK & URN (Millersburg, Fenton & Northwood)

Berry set: master bowl & 6 sauce dishes;
    marigold, 7 pcs. (Northwood) ..................... 700
Bowl, ruffled, Bearded Berry exterior, mari-
    gold .......................................................... 198
Bowl, three-in-one edge, green........................ 375
Bowl, 5" d., ice cream shape, blue, stippled..... 125
Bowl, 5 1/2" d., ruffled, blue (Millersburg) ..... 1,700
Bowl, 6" d., ice cream, blue w/electric iri-
    descence.................................................... 375
Bowl, 6" d., ice cream shape, green (Mill-
    ersburg)...................................................... 263
Bowl, 6" d., ice cream shape, purple (Mill-
    ersburg)...................................................... 250
Bowl, 6" d., ice cream shape, purple satin ....... 130
Bowl, 7" d., ruffled, green (Millersburg)........... 250
Bowl, 7" d., ruffled, marigold (Millersburg) ....... 395
Bowl, 7" d., ruffled, purple (Millersburg) .......... 350
Bowl, 7 1/2" d., "shotgun," ruffled, green.......... 550
Bowl, 8" d., ice cream shape, green (Fen-
    ton) ..................................................... 250-300
Bowl, 8" d., ice cream shape, marigold
    (Fenton)................................................ 100-125
Bowl, 8" to 9" d., blue (Fenton) ...................... 250
Bowl, 8" to 9" d., green (Fenton) ...................... 300
Bowl, 8" to 9" d., green (Millersburg)................ 375
Bowl, 8" to 9" d., marigold (Fenton) .......... 140-160
Bowl, 8" to 9" d., purple (Fenton) .................... 155
Bowl, 8" to 9" d., white (Fenton)................ 225-250
Bowl, 8 3/4" d., ice cream shape, purple
    (Millersburg) ........................................... 1,000
Bowl, 9" d., ice cream shape, blue (Fenton)..... 250
Bowl, 9" d., ice cream shape, marigold
    (Fenton)...................................................... 185
Bowl, 9" d., ruffled, blue (Fenton)..................... 135
Bowl, 9" d., ruffled, purple (Fenton) .......... 275-300
Bowl, 9" d., ruffled, white.................................. 235
Bowl, 9 1/2" d., berry, purple (Millersburg) 550-600
Bowl, 10" d., ice cream shape, aqua opal-
    escent (Northwood)................................. 25,000
Bowl, 10" d, ice cream shape, blue (North-
    wood) .................................................... 1,000
Bowl, 10" d., ice cream shape, blue, stip-
    pled (Northwood)...................................... 1,000
Bowl, 10" d., ice cream shape, cobalt blue,
    stippled (Northwood) ............................... 1,100
Bowl, 10" d., ice cream shape, green
    (Northwood) ........................................... 1,500
Bowl, 10" d., ice cream shape, honey
    amber, stippled (Northwood).................... 1,400
Bowl, 10" d., ice cream shape, ice green
    (Northwood) .................................... 1,000-1,100
Bowl, 10" d., ice cream shape, marigold
    (Millersburg) ........................................ 375-425
Bowl, 10" d., ice cream shape, marigold
    (Northwood) ............................................... 305
Bowl, 10" d., ice cream shape, marigold,
    stippled (Northwood) .................................. 700

**Bowl,** 10" d., ice cream shape, pastel marigold (Northwood)................................... **550-600**
**Bowl,** 10" d., ice cream shape, purple (Millersburg)...................................................... **1,100**
**Bowl,** 10" d., ice cream shape, purple Northwood ............................................... **600**
**Bowl,** 10" d., ruffled, marigold ......................... **145**
**Bowl,** 10" d., ruffled, purple ....................... **350-400**
**Bowl,** 10" d., three-in-one edge, purple (Millersburg) ....................................... **650-700**
**Bowl,** 10 1/2" d., ruffled, purple (Millersburg)................................................ **300**
**Compote,** 5 1/2" d., 5" h., aqua (Fenton) ......... **165**
**Compote,** 5 1/2" d., 5" h., blue (Fenton) ... **125-150**
**Compote,** 5 1/2" d., 5" h., green (Fenton)........ **230**
**Compote,** 5 1/2" d., 5" h., marigold (Fenton) ...................................................... **50-60**
**Compote,** 5 1/2" d., 5" h., white (Fenton)........ **245**
**Compote,** marigold (Millersburg Giant)......... **1,700**
**Compote,** purple (Millersburg Giant)............. **2,000**
**Goblet,** marigold (Fenton) ................................ **65**
**Ice cream dish,** blue w/electric iridescence..... **180**
**Ice cream set:** large bowl & 4 small dishes; purple, 5 pcs.............................................. **350**
**Plate,** 6 1/2" d., green (Millersburg).............. **1,500**

*Peacock & Urn Plate*

**Plate,** 6 1/2" d., marigold, Millersburg (ILLUS.)................................................. **1,000**
**Plate,** 6 1/2" d., purple (Millersburg) .... **1,000-1,200**
**Plate,** 9" d., blue (Fenton)................................ **400**
**Plate,** 9" d., marigold (Fenton)........................ **375**
**Plate,** 9" d., white (Fenton) ....................... **400-500**
**Plate,** chop, 11" d., marigold (Millersburg) .... **2,200**
**Plate,** chop, 11" d., purple, (Northwood) ...... **1,400**
**Sauce dish,** blue (Millersburg) ............ **1,000-1,200**
**Sauce dish,** blue, stippled (Northwood).... **150-160**
**Sauce dish,** lavender (Millersburg) ................. **100**
**Sauce dish,** marigold (Northwood) .................. **85**
**Whimsey sauce dish,** purple, 5 1/4" d. ..... **275-300**

## SINGING BIRDS (Northwood)
**Bowl,** master berry, marigold ........................... **75**
**Bowl,** master berry, purple ............................... **90**
**Butter dish,** cov., marigold ............................. **295**
**Butter dish,** cov., purple ................................. **400**
**Creamer,** green ............................................... **150**
**Creamer,** marigold ..................................... **65-75**
**Creamer,** purple ....................................... **125-150**
**Mug,** aqua opalescent .................................. **1,150**
**Mug,** blue................................................... **175-200**

**Mug,** blue, stippled ....................................... **675**
**Mug,** blue w/electric iridescence............... **200-250**
**Mug,** green, stippled................................. **400-450**
**Mug,** ice blue ........................................... **700-750**
**Mug,** lavender............................................ **250-300**
**Mug,** marigold ........................................... **65-75**
**Mug,** marigold, stippled ........................... **140-150**
**Mug,** purple .............................................. **100-125**
**Mug,** purple, w/advertising, "Amazon Hotel".......................................... **175-200**
**Mug,** Renniger blue, stippled....................... **1,500**
**Mug,** white ................................................ **600-625**
**Pitcher,** green ................................................. **625**
**Pitcher,** marigold ............................................ **350**
**Pitcher,** purple........................................... **450-500**
**Sauce dish,** blue w/electric iridescence.... **200-250**
**Sauce dish,** green ....................................... **30-45**
**Sauce dish,** marigold ...................................... **55**
**Sauce dish,** purple.......................................... **45**
**Spooner,** green .............................................. **150**
**Spooner,** purple ........................................ **100-125**
**Sugar bowl,** cov., marigold ........................ **90-110**
**Table set:** cov. sugar bowl, creamer & spooner; marigold, 3 pcs. ........................... **225**
**Table set,** purple, 4 pcs.................................. **750**
**Tumbler,** purple........................................... **55-65**
**Tumblers,** marigold, set of 6 ........................... **300**

## STAG & HOLLY (Fenton)
**Bowl,** 7" d., spatula-footed, blue .............. **200-275**
**Bowl,** 8" d., footed, ice cream shape, blue....... **184**
**Bowl,** 8" d., footed, ice cream shape, green..... **200**
**Bowl,** 8" d., footed, ice cream shape, marigold ...................................................... **100-125**
**Bowl,** 8" d., footed, ice cream shape, purple ...................................................... **250-275**
**Bowl,** 8" to 9" d., footed, ice cream shape, lavender ...................................................... **185**
**Bowl,** 8" to 9" d., spatula-footed, green........... **228**
**Bowl,** 8" to 9" d., spatula-footed, marigold ....... **105**
**Bowl,** 8" to 9" d., spatula-footed, purple.... **175-200**
**Bowl,** 10" to 11" d., three-footed, blue............. **450**
**Bowl,** 10" to 11" d., three-footed, green........ **1,050**
**Bowl,** 10" to 11" d., three-footed, marigold ........................................................... **150-200**

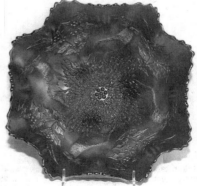

*Stag & Holly Bowl*

**Bowl,** 10" to 11" d., three-footed, purple (ILLUS.)...................................................... **425**
**Bowl,** 10" to 11" d., three-footed, vaseline **300-400**

**Bowl,** 10 3/4" d., footed, ice cream shape,
   marigold ............................................... 150
**Bowl,** 11" d., flat, amber ................................. 750
**Bowl,** 11" d., ruffled, blue ............................... 250
**Bowl,** 12" d., ice cream shape, blue .......... 300-325
**Bowl,** 12" d., ice cream shape, green ............. 900
**Bowl,** 12" d., ice cream shape, marigold... 125-150
**Bowl,** spatula-footed, red ............................. 1,750
**Plate,** 9" d., spatula-footed, marigold ........ 800-825
**Plate,** chop, 12" d., three-footed,
   marigold .......................................... 700-800
**Plate,** chop, 13" d., three-footed, marigold.... 1,400
**Rose bowl,** blue, large .............................. 1,665
**Rose bowl,** marigold, large ............................ 150
**Rose bowl,** marigold, giant ..................... 375-400

### STORK & RUSHES (Dugan or Diamond Glass Works)
**Basket,** marigold, handled ......................... 125-150
**Bowl,** marigold, master berry or fruit ................. 55
**Butter dish,** cov., marigold ............................ 135
**Creamer,** marigold ........................................ 72
**Hat shape,** blue ............................................ 40
**Hat shape,** marigold ...................................... 25
**Mug,** blue .................................................. 750
**Mug,** marigold .......................................... 30-35
**Pitcher,** water, marigold ................................ 375
**Punch bowl & base,** marigold, 2 pcs. ............. 225
**Punch cup,** blue ........................................... 35
**Punch cup,** marigold ..................................... 17
**Punch cup,** purple ..................................... 20-35
**Punch set:** bowl, base & 6 cups; marigold,
   8 pcs.............................................. 300-325
**Sauce dish,** marigold .................................... 38
**Spooner,** marigold ........................................ 80
**Spooner,** purple ........................................... 90
**Tumbler,** blue ........................................... 50-60
**Tumbler,** marigold ..................................... 30-35
**Vase,** marigold ......................................... 30-35
**Water set:** pitcher & 1 tumbler; blue,
   2 pcs.............................................. 450-500
**Water set:** pitcher & 4 tumblers; marigold,
   5 pcs.................................................. 513

### STRAWBERRY (Millersburg)
**Bowl,** 6" d., ruffled, purple ............................. 135
**Bowl,** 8" to 9" d., green, three-in-one edge ...... 300
**Bowl,** 8" to 9" d., marigold ............................ 260
**Bowl,** 8" to 9" d., vaseline ......................... 1,375
**Bowl,** 9 1/2" w., square, green ...................... 600
**Bowl,** 10" w., tricornered, green ..................... 410
**Compote,** green ........................................... 300
**Compote,** marigold ....................................... 375

### TEN MUMS (Fenton)

*Ten Mums Pitcher*

**Bowl,** footed, three-in-one edge, green ..... 500-575
**Bowl,** 8" to 9" d., ribbon candy rim, blue ... 140-250
**Bowl,** 8" to 9" d., ribbon candy rim,
   green ........................................... 325-350
**Bowl,** 8" to 9" d., ribbon candy rim,
   purple ........................................... 200-250
**Bowl,** 10" d., green, ribbon candy rim ............. 185
**Bowl,** 10" d., marigold, ruffled ........................ 200
**Bowl,** 10" d., purple, ribbon candy rim ...... 250-300
**Bowl,** 10" d., purple, ruffled ..................... 250-300
**Pitcher,** water, blue (ILLUS.)....................... 1,650
**Pitcher,** water, marigold ........................ 750-1,000
**Pitcher,** water, white ................................ 1,200
**Tumbler,** blue ............................................. 75
**Tumbler,** marigold ........................................ 65
**Water set:** pitcher & 1 tumbler; marigold, 2
   pcs............................................. 1,000-1,200
**Water set:** pitcher & 5 tumblers; blue, 6
   pcs................................................ 1,263
**Water set:** pitcher & 6 tumblers; marigold,
   7 pcs........................................... 1,200-1,500

### THREE FRUITS (Northwood)
**Bowl,** 5" d., marigold ..................................... 30
**Bowl,** 6" d., marigold ..................................... 30
**Bowl,** 7" d., dome-footed, Basketweave &
   Grapevine exterior, purple............................ 150
**Bowl,** 8" d., dome footed ............................. 115
**Bowl,** 8" d., dome-footed, Basketweave &
   Grapevine exterior, white ...................... 250-275
**Bowl,** 8" d., ruffled, green.............................. 95
**Bowl,** 8" d., ruffled, marigold ...................... 75-100
**Bowl,** 8" d., ruffled, purple ............................ 100
**Bowl,** 8 1/2" d., collared base, Bas-
   ketweave & Grapevine exterior, green........... 90
**Bowl,** 8 1/2" d., dome-footed, Basketweave & ... 170-190
**Bowl,** 8 1/2" d., dome-footed, ruffled, Bas-
   ketweave & Grapevine exterior,
   marigold ......................................... 95-125
**Bowl,** 8 1/2" d., piecrust rim, green ................. 155
**Bowl,** 8 1/2" d., piecrust rim, marigold.......... 65-75
**Bowl,** 8 1/2" d., piecrust rim, purple .................. 68
**Bowl,** 8 1/2" d., piecrust rim, purple, Bas-
   ketweave exterior ................................... 105
**Bowl,** 8 1/2" d., ruffled, blue .......................... 95
**Bowl,** 9" d., dome-footed, Basketweave &
   Grapevine exterior, green ............................ 135
**Bowl,** 9" d., dome-footed, Basketweave &
   Grapevine exterior, purple ........................... 145
**Bowl,** 9" d., piecrust rim, green, stippled,
   ribbed exterior ................................ 725-750
**Bowl,** 9" d., piecrust rim, smoky ..................... 500
**Bowl,** 9" d., purple ............................... 100-125
**Bowl,** 9" d., ruffled, blue .............................. 175
**Bowl,** 9" d., ruffled, green ............................ 190
**Bowl,** 9" d., ruffled, marigold ......................... 110
**Bowl,** 9" d., spatula-footed, aqua opales-
   cent ............................................. 600-725
**Bowl,** 9" d., spatula-footed, emerald green ...... 425
**Bowl,** 9" d., spatula-footed, ice
   green ........................................ 1,045-1,075
**Bowl,** 9" d., spatula-footed, marigold ................ 95
**Bowl,** 9" d., spatula-footed, marigold,
   Meander exterior ...................................... 145
**Bowl,** 9" d., spatula-footed, purple ............ 200-225
**Bowl,** 9" d., stippled, marigold.................. 100-125
**Bowl,** 9" d., stippled, purple........................... 275
**Bowl,** 9" d., stippled, white .............................. 487
**Bowl,** ruffled, stippled, green............................ 300

**Bowl,** aqua opalescent, collared
base ................................................ **1,100-1,200**
**Bowl,** aqua opalescent, ruffled, spatula-
footed w/Meander exterior ........................ **1,150**
**Bowl,** blue, stippled, footed ............................. **450**
**Bowl,** ice blue, ruffled, stippled, footed .. **800-1,000**
**Bowl,** ice green, dome-footed, ruffled, Vin-
tage exterior ................................................. **300**
**Bowl,** marigold, stippled, piecrust rim ............. **205**
**Bowl,** marigold, stippled, ruffled, ribbed
exterior ................................................. **165-175**
**Bowl,** purple, spatula-footed, stippled ............. **175**
**Bowl,** white, dome-footed, Basketweave &
Meander exterior ......................................... **325**
**Plate,** 9" d., blue .............................................. **825**
**Plate,** 9" d., blue, stippled, ribbed exterior..... **1,300**
**Plate,** 9" d., green............................................. **255**
**Plate,** 9" d., marigold ................................. **150-200**
**Plate,** 9" d., purple, stippled, ribbed exterior..... **650**

*Three Fruits Plate*

**Plate,** 9" d., stippled, aqua opalescent
(ILLUS.)................................................... **2,900**
**Plate,** 9" d., stippled, aqua opalescent,
w/ribbed exterior............................... **3,650-4,000**
**Plate,** 9" d., stippled, blue w/electric irides-
cence........................................................ **1,013**
**Plate,** 9" d., stippled, honey amber,
w/ribbed exterior........................................ **2,400**
**Plate,** 9" d., stippled, lavender............. **1,250-1,400**
**Plate,** 9" d., stippled, marigold ........................ **225**
**Plate,** 9" d., stippled, pastel marigold .............. **750**
**Plate,** 9 1/2" w., 12-sided, blue (Fenton) ... **250-300**
**Plate,** 9 1/2" w., 12-sided, green (Fenton). **250-300**
**Plate,** 9 1/2" w., 12-sided, marigold (Fen-
ton) ............................................................. **145**
**Plate,** 9 1/2" w., 12-sided, purple (Fenton)....... **165**
**Plate,** plain back, stretch "electric" finish,
purple .................................................. **350-400**

## TIGER LILY (Imperial)

*Tiger Lily Tumbler*

**Pitcher,** water, green ............................... **200-250**
**Pitcher,** water, marigold ........................... **100-125**
**Tumbler,** aqua................................................ **165-175**
**Tumbler,** blue.................................................... **250**
**Tumbler,** green.................................................. **55-65**
**Tumbler,** marigold............................................ **30-40**
**Tumbler,** purple (ILLUS.) ......................... **140-150**
**Tumblers,** green, set of 6............................... **350**
**Water set:** pitcher & 2 tumblers; green, 3
pcs............................................................. **390**
**Water set:** pitcher & 6 tumblers; marigold,
7 pcs.......................................................... **394**

## VINTAGE OR VINTAGE GRAPE

*Vintage Epergne*

**Bowl,** 6" d., blue (Fenton).................................. **40**
**Bowl,** 6" d., green (Fenton) ............................... **38**
**Bowl,** 6" d., purple (Fenton) .......................... **25-35**
**Bowl,** 6" d., vaseline, ruffled........................... **120**
**Bowl,** 6 1/2" d., ice cream shape, green ........... **43**
**Bowl,** 7" d., fluted, blue ................................... **42**
**Bowl,** 7" d., fluted, green (Fenton) ................... **33**
**Bowl,** 7" d., ruffled, vaseline....................... **115-125**
**Bowl,** 7 1/2" d., ice cream shape, blue ............. **55**
**Bowl,** 8" d., ribbon candy rim, blue.............. **95-100**
**Bowl,** 8" d., ribbon candy rim, blue, Wide
Panel exterior ............................................... **55**
**Bowl,** 8" to 9" d., aqua opalescent ...... **1,000-1,200**
**Bowl,** 8" to 9" d., blue, footed (Fenton) ......... **40-45**
**Bowl,** 8" to 9" d., blue, ruffled ........................... **70**
**Bowl,** 8" to 9" d., green (Fenton) ...................... **49**
**Bowl,** 8" to 9" d., marigold (Fenton) .................. **35**
**Bowl,** 8" to 9" d., purple, footed (Fenton) ........... **38**
**Bowl,** 8" to 9" d., purple, ruffled, footed ....... **40-45**
**Bowl,** 8" to 9" d., red, ruffled .............. **2,800-3,000**
**Bowl,** 9" d., purple ............................................ **100**
**Bowl,** 9 1/2" d., green...................................... **85**
**Bowl,** 9 1/2" d., marigold, ruffled, dome-
footed .......................................................... **70**
**Bowl,** 10" d., Hobnail exterior, green (Mill-
ersburg)................................................... **1,175**
**Bowl,** 10" d., ice cream shape, blue................ **200**
**Bowl,** 10" d., ice cream shape, red (Fen-
ton) ..................................................... **2,500-3,500**
**Bowl,** 10" d., ice cream shape, vaseline
(Fenton)...................................................... **225**
**Bowl,** 10" d., ruffled, green............................... **65**
**Bowl,** 10" d., ruffled, purple ............................. **50**
**Bowl,** 10" d., ruffled, vaseline w/marigold
overlay......................................................... **110**
**Bowl,** 11" d., ice cream shape, marigold.......... **200**
**Bowl,** three-in-one edge, red........................ **4,500**
**Compote,** 7" d., blue (Fenton)........................... **90**
**Compote,** 7" d., green, fluted (Fenton) ............. **75**
**Compote,** 7" d., marigold (Fenton)..................... **68**

**Compote,** 7" d., purple (Fenton) ........................ 75
**Epergne,** blue (Fenton) .................................... 165
**Epergne,** green (Fenton)................................. 150
**Epergne,** green, large .............................. 225-250
**Epergne,** purple, small (ILLUS.)........................ 95
**Fernery,** footed, blue (Fenton) .................... 75-100
**Plate,** 7" d., green (Fenton) ...................... 225-250
**Plate,** 7" d., marigold (Fenton)......................... 150
**Powder jar,** cov., marigold ............................. 85
**Sauce dish,** blue ........................................... 30
**Sauce dish,** marigold (Fenton) ........................ 20

## WAFFLE BLOCK
**Basket w/tall handle,** marigold, 10" h. ............. 46
**Basket w/tall handle,** teal, 10" h. ................... 120
**Bowl,** 7 1/2" sq., marigold ................................ 36
**Pitcher,** water, marigold ................................ 103
**Sugar bowl,** clambroth.................................... 30
**Tumbler,** marigold........................................... 215

## WATER LILY (Fenton)
**Bowl,** 5" d., aqua............................................. 95
**Bowl,** 5" d., blue ............................................. 70
**Bowl,** 6" d., aqua........................................... 145
**Bowl,** 6" d., blue ............................................. 83
**Bowl,** 9" d., footed, marigold ............................ 75
**Bowl,** 10" d., footed, marigold ......................... 100

## WISHBONE (Northwood)
**Bowl,** 8" to 9" d., footed, green ....................... 375
**Bowl,** 8" to 9" d., footed, marigold............. 125-150
**Bowl,** 10" d., footed, blue ............................... 600
**Bowl,** 10" d., footed, ruffled, purple ................. 165
**Bowl,** 10" d., footed, ruffled, stippled, purple ...................................................................... 850
**Bowl,** footed, ruffled, marigold ........................ 200
**Epergne,** green .............................................. 988
**Epergne,** marigold.................................... 500-525
**Epergne,** purple .............................................. 750
**Pitcher,** water, purple...................................... 900

*Wishbone Plate*

**Plate,** 8 1/2" d., footed, purple (ILLUS.)............. 325
**Plate,** chop, 11" d., green ............................. 3,000
**Plate,** chop, 11" d., marigold ........................ 1,200
**Plate,** chop, 11" d., purple ............................ 1,523
**Plate,** footed, marigold ................................ 1,375
**Tumbler,** green .............................................. 180
**Tumbler,** marigold...................................... 95-100
**Tumbler,** purple........................................ 135-145

## WREATHED CHERRY (Dugan)
**Berry set:** master bowl & 4 sauce dishes; marigold, 5 pcs................................................. 230
**Berry set:** master bowl & 4 sauce dishes; purple, 5 pcs.................................................. 315
**Berry set:** master bowl & 4 sauce dishes; white, 5 pcs. ............................................. 400-450
**Bowl,** berry, 9 x 12" oval, blue.......................... 290
**Bowl,** berry, 9 x 12" oval, marigold.................... 90
**Bowl,** berry, 9 x 12" oval, pastel marigold........ 150
**Bowl,** berry, 9 x 12" oval, peach opalescent............................................. 200-250
**Bowl,** berry, 9 x 12" oval, purple ..................... 175
**Bowl,** berry, 9 x 12" oval, white ................. 250-300
**Butter dish,** cov., purple .......................... 175-225
**Creamer,** marigold .......................................... 55
**Pitcher,** water, white w/gold cherries ........ 700-750
**Sauce dish,** 5" to 6" l., oval, marigold ............... 32
**Sauce dish,** 5" to 6" l., oval, purple ................... 35
**Sauce dish,** 5" to 6" l., oval, white................. 50-60
**Spooner,** marigold .......................................... 55
**Spooner,** white............................................... 95
**Tumbler,** marigold....................................... 45-50
**Tumbler,** purple......................................... 60-70

# CONSOLIDATED

*The Consolidated Lamp and Glass Company of Coraopolis, Pennsylvania was founded in 1894 and for a number of years was noted for its lighting wares but also produced popular lines of pressed and blown tablewares. Highly collectible glass patterns of this early era include the Cone, Cosmos, Florette and Guttate lines.*

*Lamps and shades continued to be good sellers but in 1926 a new "art" line of molded decorative wares was introduced. This "Martelé" line was developed as a direct imitation of the fine glasswares being produced by René Lalique of France and many Consolidated patterns resembled their French counterparts. Other popular lines produced during the 1920s and 1930s were "Dancing Nymph," the delightfully Art Deco "Ruba Rombic," introduced in 1928, and the "Catalonian" line, imitating 17th century Spanish glass, which debuted in 1927.*

*Although the factory closed in 1933, it was reopened under new management in 1936 and prospered through the 1940s. It finally closed in 1967. Collectors should note that many later Consolidated patterns closely resemble wares of other competing firms, especially the Phoenix Glass Company. Careful study is needed to determine the maker of pieces from the 1920-40 era.*

*A book which will be of help to collectors is Phoenix & Consolidated Art Glass, 1926-1980, by Jack D. Wilson (Antique Publications, 1989).*

*Consolidated Martelé Label*

# CONE

*Cone Pattern Caster Set*

**Caster set,** four Cone patt. shakers w/original metal lids, in green, light blue, darker blue & pink, fitted in a silver plate holder w/rings centered by a figural donkey below an upright loop handle, on a square footed base, 4 1/2" w., 7" h. (ILLUS.) ...................................................... **$325**

# COSMOS
**Pitcher,** water, h.p. molded flowers on white ground.................................................. **220**

# FLORETTE
**Pitcher,** 6 3/4" h., bulbous w/applied clear handle, cast pink satin` ................................ **144**

# GUTTATE
**Syrup pitcher w/original lid,** pink cased, glossy finish, applied clear handle, tall.. **250-275**

# LATER LINES
**Vase,** 6 1/2" h., Chickadee patt., wide flattened ovoid form w/rectangular mouth, stained red birds on ruby leafy branches against a clear ground................................. **110**

*Rare Ruba Rombic Pattern Vase*

**Vase,** 6 1/2" h., Ruba Rombic patt., angular tapering cylindrical form, silvery grey, minor nicks (ILLUS.)...................................... **633**
**Vase,** 10" h., Love Bird patt., bulbous ovoid body w/a small short rolled neck, pairs of salmon-colored birds on a creamy white ground ......................................................... **238**

# CORALENE

*Coralene is a method of decorating glass, usually satin glass, with the use of beaded-type decoration customarily applied to the glass with the use of enamels, which were melted. Coralene decoration has been faked with the use of glue.*

**Tumbler,** shaded rose red satin ground decorated w/overall yellow "seaweed" coralene beading, white lining.................. **$248**
**Vase,** 4 1/4" h., bulbous ovoid body w/a wide short cylindrical neck, red shaded to white mother-of-pearl Diamond Quilted patt., decorated overall w/yellow "seaweed" coralene beading, 19th c. .......... **330**
**Vase,** 5 1/2" h., ovoid body w/short cylindrical flaring neck, rainbow satin ground shading from blue to white to pink decorated w/yellow coralene beaded panels filled w/small beaded flowerheads, 19th c. ...................................................................... **138**
**Vase,** 6 5/8" h., footed spherical lower body w/a slender waist below the swelled cupped neck, shaded blue mother-of-pearl satin Diamond Quilted patt., decorated overall w/pink "seaweed" coralene beading, frosted clear applied snake around the central neck, 19th c. .................. **385**
**Vase,** 7" h., double gourd-form w/cylindrical upper neck, shaded pink to white satin ground decorated w/yellow "seaweed" coralene beading.......................................... **715**

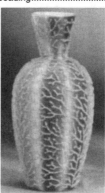

*Colorful Coralene Vase*

**Vase,** 8" h., slender ovoid body tapering to a small trumpet neck, opal white ground decorated w/enameled vertical stripes in yellow, pink, green & blue, decorated overall w/yellow "seaweed" coralene beading, worn gilt rim, minor beading loss (ILLUS.) .............................................. **144**
**Vases,** 7 1/4" h., swelled cylindrical melon-lobed body tapering to a short trumpet

neck, rainbow satin ground in pink, green, blue, yellow & white decorated w/yellow "seaweed" coralene beading, 19th c., pr. .................................................. **275**

## CRANBERRY

*Gold was added to glass batches to give this glass its color on reheating. It has been made by numerous glasshouses for years and is currently being reproduced. Both blown and molded articles were produced. A less expensive type of cranberry was made with the substitution of copper for gold.*

*Decorated Cranberry Bottle*

**Bottle w/stopper,** ovoid body tapering to a slender cylindrical neck w/a flared rim, enameled w/white dots & gold bands, clear facet-cut stopper w/white dots, 2 1/2" d., 8 1/2" h. (ILLUS.) ....................... **$165**
**Bottle w/stopper,** wide slightly tapering cylindrical shouldered body tapering to a tall cylindrical neck w/flared rim, the exterior w/an overall craquelle finish, worn gold trim bands, clear facet-cut stopper, 4" d., 9 3/4" h. .............................. **145**
**Bowl,** 4 1/2" d., decorated w/heavy gold enameling & multicolored florals in pinks, blues, yellow, greens & pink opalescent, several applied jewels, gold feet...... **248**
**Cordial set,** decanter w/stopper, four cordials & a square tray, late 19th c., the set..... **330**
**Cruet w/original stopper,** an oval medallion encircling the body w/gold stain, surrounded by enameled decoration, applied clear handle .................................... **138**
**Decanter w/stopper,** an applied clear ribbed foot supporting a tall slender ovoid optic ribbed cranberry body w/a knobbed tall cylindrical neck w/a tricorner rim, appled clear pinched handle, large clear ball stopper, 3" d., 12 1/2" h. ..... **175**
**Pitcher,** 6 1/8" h., 4 1/2" d., bulbous spherical body tapering to a wide cylindrical neck w/a pinched spout, rippled optic design, applied clear angled handle (ILLUS. top next column) ............................ **110**
**Pitcher,** 11 1/4" h., 5 1/2" d., tall tapering ovoid tankard-form w/tricormer rim, ice

bladder at the back, overall frosted ice finish on the exterior, applied clear handle .............................................................. **195**

*Bulbous Cranberry Pitcher*

**Vases,** 16" h., 7" d., tall slender waisted form w/central raised ring, optic ribbed design, enameled w/large soft yellow flowers & small white flowers & green leaves, pr. ...................................................... **450**

## CUP PLATES

*Produced in numerous patterns beginning over 170 years ago, these little plates were designed to hold a cup while the tea or coffee was allowed to cool in a saucer. Cup plates were also made of ceramics. Where numbers are listed below, they refer to numbers assigned to these plates in the book, American Glass Cup Plates, by Ruth Webb Lee and James H. Rose. Plates are of clear glass unless otherwise noted. A number of cup plates have been reproduced. Also see CUP PLATES under Ceramics.*

**L & R 10,** round, small finely ribbed rim & ray center, 3 3/8" d. (ends of five rays tipped) .......................................................... **$40**
**L & R 15,** round, ringed center surrounded w/ribbed rays, zigzag border w/smooth edge, 3 7/16" d. (small rim flake).................... **45**
**L & R 36,** round w/large scallops around rim, 3 1/4" d. ............................................... **90**
**L & R 36,** round w/large scallops around rim, opal opaque, 3 1/4" d. ........................... **350**
**L & R 38,** round w/large scallops around rim w/a blossomhead in each scallop, plain center, opal, 3 1/4" d. (two tiny spalls ) ........................................................... **340**
**L & R 77,** round, smooth rim, leafy vine border enclosing a ring of spiral legs around a central wheel ............................................. **176**
**L & R 80,** round, smooth rim, leafy rope border enclosing a leafy rope band & central cluster of hearts, 3 3/4" d. (areas of cloudiness) ........................................................ **60**
**L & R 81,** round, smooth rim, leafy sprig border enclosing a leafy rope band & central cluster of hearts, rope table ring, opal w/lavender overtones, 3 3/4" d. (tiny flake on rope edge) ........................... **900**
**L & R 109,** octagonal w/incurved edges, a central cluster of four pineapple-like devices enclosed in a geometric border

band, opal, 3 7/16" w. (edge flakes, roughness) ..................................................... **320**

**L & R 145b,** round, checkerboard center design w/a small cross & stippling in each square, leaf band border, tiny scallops around rim, 2 3/4" d. (one scallop chipped, others w/slight tipping) .................. **525**

**L & R 324,** round, central starburst forming four panels each w/a starburst, rayed rim band, finely scalloped rim, amethyst (light mold roughness) .................................... **132**

**L & R 500,** round, Sunburst center, finely scalloped rim, light blue (light mold roughnes) ....................................................... **231**

**L & R 612-A,** octagonal w/finely scalloped rim, central design of a sidehwheeler within shield & scroll border, silver nitrate inner rim, probably Pittsburgh area, ca. 1830s (two scallops missing, five tipped) ..... **770**

## CUT

*Cut glass most eagerly sought by collectors is American glass produced during the so-called "Brilliant Period" from 1880 to about 1915. Pieces listed below are by type of article in alphabetical order.*

*Hawkes, Hoare, Libbey and Straus Marks*

## BOWLS

*Squared Cut Glass Bowl*

**Hawkes-signed,** cut w/four large hobstars separated by large pointed panels w/smaller hobstars & a strawberry diamond panel forming a rim point, crosscutting forms triangles in the design surrounding a large hobstar in the bottom, 10" d., 3 1/4" h. (small rim flakes) ............. **$413**

**Hoare-signed,** cut w/three large sunbursts alternating w/cane-cut panels surrounded by deep cross cuts, notched rim, 8 1/4" d., 3 1/2" h. (edge flakes) ............ **220**

**Hoare-signed,** shallow round form, cut overall w/small detailed hobstars

w/some forming a large cross across the center, 9" d., 2 1/4" h. .................................. **330**

**Hobstars & cane cutting,** squared shape w/deeply notched & lobed rim, pointed fan cuts at each corner, 10 1/2" w. (ILLUS.) ......................................................... **485**

*Sylph Pattern Bowl*

**Monroe's Sylph patt.,** oblong w/flared zipper-cut sides above a large central hobstar surrounded by eight smaller hobstars, 7 1/2 x 10 1/2", 3 1/4" h. (ILLUS.) ......................................................... **375**

## DECANTERS

*Rare Ruby Cut to Clear Decanter*

**Clark-signed,** ruby cut to clear, tapering conical body cut w/alternating clear & ruby graduated rings, ringed neck w/spout, matching ringed knob stopper, applied notch-cut handle, 5 1/2" d., 8" h. (ILLUS.) ..................................................... **1,650**

*Decanter with Rounded Body*

**Cross-cut diamonds & fans,** flattened round body w/a panel-cut shoulder & slender zipper-cut neck, facet-cut applied handle, facet-cut ball stopper, 4 x 6", 9 1/2" h. (ILLUS.) .............................. **320**

*Hobstar-cut Decanter*

**Hobstars,** tapering conical body cut w/a wide band of hobstars around the bottom below the panel-cut shoulder & neck, notch-cut applied handle & facet-cut stopper, 10" h. (ILLUS.) .......................... **425**

## LAMPS

*Elaborate Dorflinger Lamp*

**Boudoir lamp,** Dorflinger-signed, tall slender inverted trumpet-form base cut w/fans along the base, strawberry diamonds & panels below the connector to the bulbous strawberry diamond-cut font w/metal collar, burner & open-topped ovoid strawberry diamond-cut shade (ILLUS.) .................................................. **4,650**

**Table lamp,** by Everett Stage, the large pointed domical shade cut w/alternating wide bands of panels & strawberry diamonds, fitted on a matching baluster-form standard w/cupped top & a wide

domed foot, electrified, 20" h. (ILLUS. below) ....................................................... **3,950**

*Fine Early Cut Electric Lamp*

## MISCELLANEOUS

*Sinclaire-engraved Clock*

**Clock,** table model, Sinclaire-engraved, Gothic arch-form case w/rectangular base, the round dial surrounded by finely engraved leafy floral vines & scrolls, a floral vine around the base, 8" h. (ILLUS.) .................................................... **1,250**

*Large Bishop's Hat-form Compote*

**Compote,** bishop's hat-form, the bowl cut w/large hobstars & triangles, the widely rolled rim cut w/fans, hobstars & strawberry diamond-cut panels, star-cut foot, large, 12" d., 8 3/4" h. (ILLUS.) ................ **2,450**

*Dorflinger-attributed Cut Compote*

**Compote,** ruby-cut-to-clear, wide shallow bowl cut w/a band of petals enclosing crosshatching, panel-cut stem on star-cut foot, attributed to Dorflinger, 8 1/4" d., 4 1/4" h. (ILLUS.) ......................... **510**

*Sterling-rimmed Loving Cup*

**Loving cup,** wide swelled cylindrical body tapering to an applied sterling silver rim w/a raised grapevine design, the sides cut w/deep panels & zipper bands, applied notch-cut handles, 3 3/4" h. (ILLUS.) ...................................................... **395**

## PITCHERS

**Pedestal-based,** Hoare-signed, the very tall slender cylindrical body cut w/long panels of zipper cutting framed by diamond plaid panels below the high arched panel-cut spout, long notch-cut applied handle, paneled pedestal base w/star-cut bottom (ILLUS.) ....................... **3,250**

*Tankard Pitcher with Tiffany Silver Rim*

**Tankard,** flared base below tall cylindrical sides, cut w/bands of large hobstars in zippered diamonds & fans around the base & top w/zipper-cut bands in the center, applied Tiffany sterling silver rim w/raised band of shells & scrolls, 5 1/2" d., 12 1/4" h. (ILLUS.) .................... **1,235**

## PUNCH BOWLS, CUPS & SETS

*Hawkes' Brazilian Pattern Punch Bowl*

**Punch bowl,** Hawkes' Brazilian patt., a central hobstar framed by ornate fan, crossed-block & crosshatched panels framed by a fan-cut rim, 12 1/2" d., 6 1/2" h. (ILLUS.)...................................... **1,575**

**Punch or egg nog bowl,** the bowl cut w/large hobstars alternating w/fans & cane cutting, the flaring base w/a facet-cut rim above a design matching the bowl, 10" d. ................................................. **795**

**Punch set:** bowl, base & eight cups; Egginton's Arabian patt., curved cut bands intersecting large clusters of hobstars on the bowl & base, cups 3" d., 3 1/4" h.,

*Fine Pedestaled Hoare-signed Pitcher*

bowl 14 1/2" d., 12" h., the set (ILLUS. of
bowl, below) ............................................. **11,750**

*Egginton's Arabian Pattern Punch Bowl*

## TRAYS

*Libbey's Wedgemere Celery Tray*

**Celery,** Libbey's Wedgemere patt., pointed
oblong form cut w/central radiating zipper-cut bands framing strawberry diamond panels & graduated hobstars w/a
large hobstar at each end, 11 1/2" l.
(ILLUS.)...................................................... **1,050**

*Hawkes' Centauri Serving Tray*

**Serving,** Hawkes' Centauri patt., a large
central cut star framed by small hobstars
& comet-cut panels w/an outer border of
large hobstars in pointed panels, 12" d.
(ILLUS.)...................................................... **1,295**

## VASES

*Hawkes' Queens Pattern Vase*

**Hawkes' Queens patt.,** tall slender trumpet-form w/a four-lobed notched rim, diamond-form panels of graduated hobstars
down the sides, notch-cut stem on star-
cut foot, 12" h. (ILLUS.)............................ **1,250**

*Wide Trumpet-form Vase*

**Trumpet-form,** widely flaring bowl cut
w/varied designs of graduated hobstars
& fan cutting, paneled pedestal & star-
cut foot, 8" d., 9" h. (ILLUS.)........................ **565**
**Ungers Brothers' Hobart patt.,** tall
waisted cylindrical form, detailed cutting
w/stripes of small hobstars alternating
w/zipper cutting, large hobstars in diamonds around the base & fan-cut rim,
12" h. ......................................................... **650**
**Urn-form,** the baluster-form body on a
tapering pedestal & thick disk foot, the
finely reeded neck below a widely flared
cupped rim, the rim & body cut overall
w/hobstars divided by arched deep
grooves separated by diamond point

cutting, panel-cut stem & star-cut foot, rim chips, 16" h (ILLUS. below)............... **1,725**

*Large Ornate Cut Glass Vase*

## DAUM NANCY

*This fine glass, much of it cameo, was made by Auguste and Antonin Daum, who founded a factory in 1875 in Nancy, France. Most of their cameo and enameled glass was made from the 1890s into the early 20th century.*

*Daum Nancy Marks*

**Bowl,** 7 3/4" d., 3" h., rounded incurved low sides w/a pinched rim, mottled white, pink, purple & yellow etched & intricately enameled w/Coreopsis daisies in shades of yellow w/green foliage, signed in enamel on the side, ca. 1910 (interior burst bubble) .......................................... **$2,070**

*Enameled Daum Nancy Bowl*

**Bowl,** 8" w., the quatrefoil body in grey tinted w/apple green, cut & enameled in green, brown & black w/a spring land-

scape, signed in enamel, ca. 1910 (ILLUS.) .......................................... **1,380**

**Cameo bowl,** 3 7/8" h., cushion foot below the squatty bulbous body w/a four-lobed rim, cream mottled w/yellow & overlaid in dark green, wheel-carved w/a design of berried leafy branches, signed, ca. 1900 .. **4,600**

**Cameo lamp,** pointed mushroom-shaped shade w/flaring ruffled rim raised on wrought-iron fittings above the slender baluster-form matching base w/domed flaring foot, pale yellow overlaid w/dark aubergine & cameo cut w/a continuous sunset landscape w/leafy trees by water, signed, ca. 1900, 17 1/8" h...................... **11,500**

**Cameo vase,** 7 1/4" h., tall square form, clear cased to a yellow interior & cameo-etched & engraved as wild roses, gold enamel highlights & borders, base signed in gold enamel .................................. **805**

**Cameo vase,** 8 1/4" h., bulbous baluster-form w/flared short neck & cushion foot, mottled grey & purple rising to yellow, layered in vitrified colors of red, purple & green & etched w/grapes on the vine, highlighted by an applied glass snail & etched signature in the polished pontil (ground spot at loss of second snail) ........ **2,875**

**Cameo vase,** 9" h., Martelé-type, elongated bell-form w/a slender & bulbed neck, pink overlaid in grass green, carved & etched w/a flowering thistle on a martelé ground, base signed, ca. 1900 .. **1,610**

**Cameo vase,** 11 1/8" h., gently swelled squared form on four small peg feet, pulled into points at the top corners, mottled blues & greens overlaid in dark blackish blue & cameo cut w/a continuous landscape of leafy trees by water, signed, ca. 1900 ...................................... **4,887**

**Center bowl,** Ice patt., heavy walled crystal square form, molded decoration of ice formations at base, inscribed on base, 3 3/8" h. ...................................................... **173**

**Vase,** 4 1/4" h., bulbous ovoid body w/thick D-form handles flanking the rim, light green & pale red etched & enameled w/a Japanese-style scene of herons & water plants & gilded trailing vines, mounted w/finely cast & chased silver mounts w/roses & foliage around the rim & raised round foot, French hallmarks for 925 fine, etched & gilt signature, ca. 1894 .......................................................... **3,105**

**Vase,** 7" h., deeply waisted cylindrical body, frosted grey ground etched & enameled w/a winter landscape in shades of black, white & grey, a leafless birch tree & blackbirds in the foreground, signed, ca. 1900...................................... **5,462**

**Vase,** 10 1/4" h., bell-form bowl on a short pedestal & square foot, deep emerald green cut w/a row of upright rectangles, signed, ca. 1925 (ILLUS. top next page)... **3,162**

**Vase,** 15 1/4" h., a cushion foot below a bulbed stem supporting the tall slender swelled body w/a small molded mouth, mottled yellow rising to white, etched & intricately enameled in naturalistic

greens & yellows w/iris, signed among
the leaves, ca. 1900 .................................. **3,738**

*Daum Nancy Acid-etched Vase*

**Wine glasses,** ovoid bowl on a slender
stem on a disk foot, opalescent & frosted
sea green, etched & enameled w/violets
in pale rose & green, gilded rims, base
inscribed & enameled "Daum Nancy
Rube 62 B2 Haussmann Paris," pr. (light
wear) ......................................................... **2,185**

# DEPRESSION

*The phrase "Depression Glass" is used by collectors to denote a specific kind of transparent glass produced primarily as tablewares, in crystal, amber, blue, green, pink, milky-white, etc., during the late 1920s and 1930s when this country was in the midst of a financial depression. Made to sell inexpensively, it was turned out by such producers as Jeannette, Hocking, Westmoreland, Indiana and other glass companies. We compile prices on all the major Depression Glass patterns. Collectors should consult Depression Glass references for information on those patterns and pieces which have been reproduced.*

*For a more extensive listing of Depression Glass, please refer to Antique Trader Books American Pressed Glass & Bottles Price Guide, 2nd Edition.*

## ADAM, Jeanette Glass Co., 1932-34 (Process-etched)

*Adam Candlestick*

**Bowl,** 5 3/4" sq., cereal, pink........................... **$56**

**Bowl,** 7 3/4" sq., dessert, green ......................... 26
**Bowl,** 7 3/4" sq., nappy, pink............................. 29
**Bowl,** cov., 9" sq., green ................................... 85
**Bowl,** cov., 9" sq., pink ..................................... 72
**Bowl,** 10" oval, vegetable, green ...................... 32
**Bowl,** 10" oval, vegetable, pink ......................... 33
**Butter dish,** cov., green ................................... 351
**Butter dish,** cov., pink...................................... 105
**Cake plate,** footed, green, 10" sq...................... 30
**Cake plate,** footed, pink, 10" sq. ...................... 29
**Candlestick,** green, 4" h. ................................... 42
**Candlestick,** pink, 4" h...................................... 51
**Candlesticks,** pink, 4" h., pr. (ILLUS. of
    one) ................................................................ 92
**Coaster,** clear, 3 1/4" sq.................................... 17
**Coaster,** green, 3 1/4" sq. ................................. 22
**Creamer,** green .................................................. 23
**Creamer,** pink .................................................... 22
**Cup,** green.......................................................... 23
**Cup,** pink ............................................................ 30
**Cup & saucer,** green ......................................... 31
**Pitcher,** 8" h., 32 oz., cone-shaped, clear ......... 35
**Pitcher,** 8" h., 32 oz., cone-shaped, green ........ 43
**Pitcher,** 8" h., 32 oz., cone-shaped, pink .......... 40
**Pitcher,** 32 oz., round base, pink ...................... 53
**Plate,** 6" sq., sherbet, green .............................. 9
**Plate,** 6" sq., sherbet, pink................................. 9
**Plate,** 7 3/4" sq., salad, green ........................... 17
**Plate,** 7 3/4" sq., salad, pink ............................. 16
**Plate,** 9" sq., dinner, green ................................ 30
**Plate,** 9" sq., dinner, pink.................................. 36
**Plate,** 9" sq., grill, green ................................... 23
**Plate,** 9" sq., grill, pink..................................... 28
**Plate,** salad, round, pink ................................... 60
**Plate,** salad, round, yellow .............................. 110
**Platter,** 11 3/4" l., green ................................... 34
**Platter,** 11 3/4" l., pink..................................... 33
**Relish dish,** two-part, green, 8" sq. ................... 25
**Salt & pepper shakers,** footed, green,
    4" h., pr. ......................................................... 99
**Salt & pepper shakers,** footed, pink, 4" h.,
    pr. ................................................................... 86
**Saucer,** green, 6" sq........................................... 6
**Saucer,** pink, 6" sq. ............................................ 8
**Sherbet,** green, 3" h. ......................................... 36
**Sherbet,** pink, 3" h............................................ 31
**Sugar bowl,** cov., pink ...................................... 48
**Tumbler,** cone-shaped, green, 4 1/2" h., 7
    oz. .................................................................. 30
**Tumbler,** cone-shaped, pink, 4 1/2" h., 7
    oz. .................................................................. 36
**Tumbler,** iced tea, green, 5 1/2" h., 9 oz............ 56
**Tumbler,** iced tea, pink 5 1/2" h., 9 oz. ............. 77
**Vase,** 7 1/2" h., green ........................................ 87

## AMERICAN SWEETHEART, MacBeth - Evans Glass Co., 1930-38 (Process-etched)

**Bowl,** 3 3/4" d., berry, pink ................................. 85
**Bowl,** 4 1/2" d., cream soup, Monax ............... 125
**Bowl,** 4 1/2" d., cream soup, pink...................... 89
**Bowl,** 6" d., cereal, Monax ................................ 18
**Bowl,** 6" d., cereal, pink.................................... 18
**Bowl,** 9" d., berry, Monax ................................. 65
**Bowl,** 9" d., berry, pink ..................................... 61
**Bowl,** 9 1/2" d., soup w/flanged rim, Monax ....... 91
**Bowl,** 9 1/2" d., soup w/flanged rim, pink .......... 75
**Bowl,** 11" oval vegetable, Monax ...................... 91
**Bowl,** 11" oval vegetable, pink .......................... 76
**Console bowl,** blue, 18" d. ........................... 1,688

Console bowl, Monax, 18" d. .......................... 574
Console bowl, ruby red, 18" d. ................... 1,863
Creamer, footed, Monax ................................... 15
Creamer, footed, pink......................................... 15
Creamer, footed, ruby red .............................. 106
Cup, Monax ......................................................... 10
Cup, pink ............................................................. 20
Cup, ruby red....................................................... 90
Cup & saucer, blue.......................................... 151
Cup & saucer, Monax ........................................ 13
Cup & saucer, pink............................................ 22
Cup & saucer, ruby red ................................... 121
Lamp shade, Monax ........................................ 703
Pitcher, 7 1/2" h., 60 oz., jug-type, pink .......... 933
Pitcher, 8" h., 80 oz., pink.............................. 749
Plate, 6" d., bread & butter, Monax ..................... 7
Plate, 6" d., bread & butter, pink.......................... 7
Plate, 8" d., salad, blue.................................... 130
Plate, 8" d., salad, Monax.................................. 10
Plate, 8" d., salad, pink...................................... 13
Plate, 8" d., salad, ruby red ............................ 102
Plate, 9" d., luncheon, Monax ........................... 14
Plate, 9 3/4" d., dinner, Monax .......................... 29
Plate, 9 3/4" d., dinner, pink .............................. 39
Plate, 10 1/4" d., dinner, Monax ........................ 30
Plate, 11" d., chop, Monax ................................ 21
Plate, 12" d., salver, blue................................ 235
Plate, 12" d., salver, Monax.............................. 25

*American Sweetheart Salver*

Plate, 12" d., salver, pink (ILLUS.) ..................... 23
Plate, 15 1/2" d., w/center handle, Monax........ 235
Plate, 15 1/2" d., w/center handle, ruby red ..... 396
Platter, 13" oval, Monax .................................... 71
Platter, 13" oval, pink ........................................ 61
Salt & pepper shakers, footed, Monax, pr. ..... 458
Salt & pepper shakers, footed, pink, pr. ......... 563
Saucer, blue........................................................ 31
Saucer, Monax ...................................................... 4
Saucer, pink .......................................................... 5
Saucer, ruby red................................................. 25
Sherbet, footed, pink, 3 3/4" h........................... 25
Sherbet, footed, Monax, 4 1/4" h. ..................... 22
Sherbet, footed, pink, 4 1/4" h. ......................... 20
Sugar bowl, cov., Monax (only) ...................... 445
Sugar bowl, open, Monax..................................... 9
Sugar bowl, open, pink...................................... 15
Sugar bowl, open, ruby red (ILLUS.
w/creamer) ..................................................... 120
Tidbit server, three-tier, Monax ...................... 324
Tidbit server, two-tier, Monax.......................... 89
Tidbit server, two-tier, pink.............................. 56

Tidbit server, two-tier, ruby red ...................... 322
Tumbler, pink, 3 1/2" h., 5 oz. ......................... 103
Tumbler, pink, 4 1/4" h., 9 oz. ........................... 90
Tumbler, pink, 4 3/4" h., 10 oz. ....................... 171

## CAMEO OR BALLERINA OR DANCING GIRL, Hocking Glass Co., 1930-34 (Process-etched)

Bowl, 4 1/4" d., sauce, clear............................... 5
Bowl, 4 3/4" d., cream soup, green ................. 190
Bowl, 5 1/2" d., cereal, clear ............................... 6
Bowl, 5 1/2" d., cereal, green ............................ 38
Bowl, 5 1/2" d., cereal, yellow ........................... 37
Bowl, 7 1/4" d., salad, green ............................. 59
Bowl, 8 1/4" d., large berry, green..................... 39
Bowl, 9" d., soup w/flange rim, green................ 87
Bowl, 10" oval vegetable, green....................... 33
Bowl, 10" oval vegetable, yellow....................... 44
Butter dish, cov., green .................................. 265
Cake plate, three-footed, green, 10" d. ............. 26
Candlesticks, green, 4" h., pr. ........................ 123

*Cameo Candy Jar*

Candy jar, cov., green, 4" h. (ILLUS.) ............. 100
Candy jar, cov., yellow, 4" h............................. 98
Candy jar, cov., green, 6 1/2" h. ..................... 215
Compote, mayonnaise, 5" d., 4" h., cone-
shaped, green ................................................. 37
Console bowl, three-footed, green, 11" d......... 86
Console bowl, three-footed, pink, 11" d. .......... 65
Console bowl, three-footed, yellow, 11" d........ 95
Cookie jar, cov., green.................................... 60
Creamer, green, 3 1/4" h.................................. 22
Creamer, yellow, 3 1/4" h................................. 22
Creamer, green, 4 1/4" h.................................. 28
Cup, clear ............................................................ 5
Cup, green......................................................... 15
Cup, yellow........................................................... 8
Cup & saucer, green ......................................... 23
Cup & saucer, yellow......................................... 11
Decanter w/stopper, green, 10" h. ................. 200
Goblet, wine, green, 4" h. ................................. 81
Goblet, water, green, 6" h. ................................ 67
Goblet, water, pink, 6" h................................... 164
Ice bowl, tab handles, green, 5 1/2" d.,
3 1/2" h................................................................ 223
Jam jar, cov., closed handles, green, 2" ......... 196
Juice set: pitcher & four 3 oz. footed tum-
blers; green, 5 pcs........................................ 200
Pitcher, syrup or milk, 5 3/4" h., 20 oz.,
green ............................................................. 207
Pitcher, juice, 6" h., 36 oz., green ................... 56
Pitcher, water, 8 1/2" h., 56 oz., jug-type,
green ............................................................... 65
Plate, 6" d., sherbet (or ringless saucer),
clear ................................................................. 2

**Plate,** 6" d., sherbet (or ringless saucer), green ............................................................ 7
**Plate,** 6" d., sherbet (or ringless saucer), yellow ........................................................... 3
**Plate,** 8" d., luncheon, green .............................. 13
**Plate,** 8" d., luncheon, yellow ............................ 10
**Plate,** 8 1/2" sq., green .................................... 46
**Plate,** 8 1/2" sq., yellow .................................. 310
**Plate,** 9 1/2" d., dinner, green ........................... 22
**Plate,** 9 1/2" d., dinner, yellow .......................... 9
**Plate,** 10" d., sandwich, green .......................... 20
**Plate,** 10" d., sandwich, pink ............................ 61
**Plate,** 10 1/2" d., dinner, rimmed, green........... 111
**Plate,** 10 1/2" d., grill, green ............................ 13
**Plate,** 10 1/2" d., grill, yellow ............................ 8
**Plate,** 10 1/2" d., grill, closed handles, green .................................................................. 77
**Plate,** 10 1/2" d., grill, closed handles, yellow ................................................................. 7
**Platter,** 12", closed handles, green .................... 27
**Platter,** 12", closed handles, yellow .................. 41
**Relish,** footed, three-part, green, 7 1/2" ............. 38
**Salt & pepper shakers,** green, pr. ..................... 73
**Salt & pepper shakers,** pink, pr. ................. 1,325
**Sherbet,** green, 3 1/8" h. ................................... 17
**Sherbet,** pink, 3 1/8" h. ..................................... 83
**Sherbet,** yellow, 3 1/8" h. .................................. 41
**Sherbet,** thin, high stem, green, 4 7/8" h............. 38
**Sherbet,** thin, high stem, yellow, 4 7/8" h. .......... 42
**Sugar bowl,** open, green, 3 1/4" h. .................... 21
**Sugar bowl,** open, yellow, 3 1/4" h. ................... 18
**Sugar bowl,** open, green, 4 1/4" h. .................... 28
**Tumbler,** juice, green, 3 3/4" h., 5 oz. ................ 33
**Tumbler,** water, clear, 4" h., 9 oz. ..................... 10
**Tumbler,** water, green, 4" h., 9 oz..................... 31
**Tumbler,** water, pink, 4" h., 9 oz. ...................... 95
**Tumbler,** footed, yellow, 5" h., 9 oz. .................. 16
**Tumbler,** green, 4 3/4" h., 10 oz. ....................... 28
**Tumbler,** green, 5" h., 11 oz. ............................ 35
**Tumbler,** yellow, 5" h., 11 oz............................ 58
**Tumbler,** green, 5 1/4" h., 15 oz. ....................... 74
**Vase,** 5 3/4" h., green...................................... 275
**Vase,** 8" h., green ............................................. 42
**Water set:** pitcher & 6 tumblers; green, 7 pcs....................................................................... 250

## COLONIAL OR KNIFE & FORK (Press-mold)

*Colonial Butter Dish*

**Bowl,** 3 3/4" d., berry, pink ................................. 53
**Bowl,** 4 1/2" d., berry, green.............................. 18
**Bowl,** 4 1/2" d., berry, pink ................................ 15
**Bowl,** 4 1/2" d., cream soup, green .................... 71
**Bowl,** 5 1/2" d., cereal, clear ............................. 33
**Bowl,** 7" d., soup, green ..................................... 69

**Bowl,** 7" d., soup, pink........................................ 72
**Bowl,** 9" d., green ............................................... 34
**Bowl,** 9" d., pink ................................................. 35
**Butter dish,** cov., clear (ILLUS.) ....................... 44
**Butter dish,** cov., pink........................................ 700
**Celery or spooner,** clear .................................. 75
**Creamer or milk pitcher,** clear, 5" h., 16 oz. .................................................................... 22
**Cup & saucer,** pink ............................................ 18
**Goblet,** cordial, green, 3 3/4" h., 1 oz. ................ 31
**Goblet,** wine, clear, 4 1/2" h., 2 1/2 oz. ............. 15
**Goblet,** wine, green, 4 1/2" h., 2 1/2 oz. ............ 26
**Goblet,** cocktail, green, 4" h., 3 oz. .................... 27
**Goblet,** claret, green, 5 1/4" h., 4 oz. ................. 25
**Goblet,** water, clear, 5 3/4" h., 8 1/2 oz. ............ 21
**Goblet,** water, green, 5 3/4" h., 8 1/2 oz. .......... 33
**Pitcher,** ice lip or plain, 7" h., 54 oz., clear......... 33
**Pitcher,** ice lip or plain, 7" h., 54 oz., green ...... 54
**Pitcher,** ice lip or plain, 7" h., 54 oz., pink .......... 56
**Plate,** 6" d., sherbet, clear ................................. 4
**Plate,** 6" d., sherbet, green ................................ 8
**Plate,** 6" d., sherbet, pink .................................. 7
**Plate,** 10" d., dinner, green ................................ 63
**Plate,** 10" d., dinner, pink ................................. 62
**Plate,** 10" d., grill, clear.................................... 19
**Plate,** 10" d., grill, green .................................. 25
**Plate,** 10" d., grill, pink .................................... 26
**Platter,** 12" oval, clear ...................................... 14
**Platter,** 12" oval, green .................................... 26
**Platter,** 12" oval, pink ...................................... 33
**Salt & pepper shakers,** clear, pr. ...................... 72
**Salt & pepper shakers,** green, pr...................... 145
**Sherbet,** clear, 3 3/8" h. ...................................... 7
**Sherbet,** green, 3 3/8" h. .................................. 15
**Sherbet,** pink, 3 3/8" h ..................................... 11
**Sugar bowl,** cov., clear .................................... 23
**Sugar bowl,** cov., green ................................... 26
**Sugar bowl,** cov., pink ...................................... 60
**Tumbler,** whiskey, clear, 2 1/2" h., 1 1/2 oz. .................................................................. 12
**Tumbler,** whiskey, green, 2 1/2" h., 1 1/2 oz. .................................................................. 16
**Tumbler,** whiskey, pink, 2 1/2" h., 1 1/2 oz. ....... 14
**Tumbler,** footed, pink, 3 1/4" h., 3 oz. ................ 17
**Tumbler,** juice, green, 3" h., 5 oz. ...................... 24
**Tumbler,** juice, pink, 3" h., 5 oz......................... 20
**Tumbler,** footed, green, 4" h., 5 oz. ................... 43
**Tumbler,** footed, pink, 4" h., 5 oz. ..................... 31
**Tumbler,** water, clear, 4" h., 9 oz. ..................... 14
**Tumbler,** water, green, 4" h., 9 oz...................... 21
**Tumbler,** water, pink, 4" h., 9 oz. ...................... 21

## DIANA, Federal Glass Co., 1937-41 (Press-mold)

*Diana Salad Bowl*

Bowl, 5" d., cereal, amber ................................... 11
Bowl, 5" d., cereal, pink................................... 10
Bowl, 5 1/2" d., cream soup, amber .................. 16
Bowl, 5 1/2" d., cream soup, clear ...................... 7
Bowl, 5 1/2" d., cream soup, pink..................... 32
Bowl, 9" d., salad, pink (ILLUS.) ....................... 19
Candy jar, cov., round, clear.............................. 19
Candy jar, cov., round, pink ............................. 45
Coaster, amber, 3 1/2" d................................... 11
Coaster, clear, 3 1/2" d. ..................................... 3
Coaster, pink, 3 1/2" d........................................ 7
Console bowl, pink, 11" d.................................. 40
Creamer, oval, amber .......................................... 9
Plate, 9 1/2" d., dinner, amber............................ 9
Plate, 9 1/2" d., dinner, clear ............................. 6
Plate, 9 1/2" d., dinner, pink ............................ 16
Platter, 12" oval, amber .................................... 13
Salt & pepper shakers, amber, pr.................. 101
Salt & pepper shakers, clear, pr. ..................... 21
Salt & pepper shakers, pink, pr. ...................... 82
Sherbet, amber .................................................. 10
Sherbet, pink .................................................... 15
Sugar bowl, open, oval, amber........................... 9
Sugar bowl, open, oval, clear ............................. 4
Sugar bowl, open, oval, pink ............................ 14
Tumbler, amber, 4 1/8" h., 9 oz. ....................... 26
Tumbler, clear, 4 1/8" h., 9 oz............................ 26
Tumbler, pink, 4 1/8" h., 9 oz. .......................... 53

## (OLD) FLORENTINE OR POPPY NO. 1, Hazel Atlas Glass Co., 1932-35 (Process-etched)

Ashtray, clear, 5 1/2" ....................................... 18
Ashtray, green, 5 1/2"........................................ 21
Ashtray, pink, 5 1/2"........................................... 27
Ashtray, yellow, 5 1/2" ...................................... 28
Bowl, 5" d., berry, clear .................................... 11
Bowl, 5" d., berry, cobalt blue .......................... 27
Bowl, 5" d., berry, green .................................... 11
Bowl, 5" d., berry, pink ..................................... 19
Bowl, 5" d., berry, yellow .................................. 13
Bowl, 6" d., cereal, clear .................................. 20
Bowl, 6" d., cereal, pink.................................... 20
Bowl, 6" d., cereal, yellow ................................ 38
Bowl, 8 1/2" d., clear ........................................ 22
Bowl, 8 1/2" d., green........................................ 36
Bowl, 8 1/2" d., pink .......................................... 36
Bowl, 9 1/2" oval, cov., vegetable, clear ........... 47
Bowl, 9 1/2" oval, cov., vegetable, pink............. 54
Bowl, 9 1/2" oval, cov., vegetable, yellow ......... 85
Butter dish, cov., clear ................................... 134

*(Old) Florentine Butter Dish*

Butter dish, cov., green (ILLUS.)..................... 138
Butter dish, cov., yellow ................................. 169
Coaster-ashtray, clear, 3 3/4" d. ...................... 14
Coaster-ashtray, green, 3 3/4" d. ..................... 20

Coaster-ashtray, pink, 3 3/4" d......................... 32
Coaster-ashtray, yellow, 3 3/4" d. ................... 26
Creamer, plain rim, clear.................................... 7
Creamer, plain rim, green ................................. 13
Creamer, plain rim, pink .................................. 18
Creamer, ruffled rim, cobalt blue ...................... 71
Cup, clear............................................................ 8
Cup, green........................................................... 9
Cup, pink ............................................................ 9
Cup, yellow ....................................................... 10
Nut dish, handled, ruffled rim, clear................. 25
Nut dish, handled, ruffled rim, cobalt blue ........ 72
Nut dish, handled, ruffled rim, green................. 24
Nut dish, handled, ruffled rim, pink .................. 20
Pitcher, 6 1/2" h., 36 oz., footed, clear............. 42
Pitcher, 6 1/2" h., 36 oz., footed, green ............ 41
Pitcher, 6 1/2" h., 36 oz., footed, pink .............. 45
Pitcher, 6 1/2" h., 36 oz., footed, yellow............ 37
Pitcher, 7 1/2" h., 48 oz., clear......................... 66
Pitcher, 7 1/2" h., 48 oz., green ....................... 77
Pitcher, 7 1/2" h., 48 oz., pink ........................ 135
Plate, 6" d., sherbet, clear ................................. 5
Plate, 6" d., sherbet, green ................................ 6
Plate, 6" d., sherbet, pink .................................. 7
Plate, 8 1/2" d., salad, clear............................... 8
Plate, 8 1/2" d., salad, green ............................ 10
Plate, 8 1/2" d., salad, pink .............................. 12
Plate, 8 1/2" d., salad, yellow ........................... 14
Plate, 10" d., dinner, clear ................................ 14
Plate, 10" d., dinner, green ............................... 17
Plate, 10" d., dinner, pink ................................. 30
Plate, 10" d., grill, clear.................................... 11
Platter, 11 1/2" oval, yellow .............................. 26
Salt & pepper shakers, footed, clear, pr. ......... 39
Salt & pepper shakers, footed, green, pr.......... 36
Salt & pepper shakers, footed, pink, pr. .......... 57
Salt & pepper shakers, footed, yellow, pr........ 57
Saucer, clear ...................................................... 4
Saucer, green...................................................... 3
Saucer, pink ........................................................ 5
Sherbet, footed, clear, 3 oz. ............................. 10
Sherbet, footed, green, 3 oz. ............................ 11
Sherbet, footed, pink, 3 oz. .............................. 12
Sherbet, footed, yellow, 3 oz. ........................... 11
Sugar bowl, cov., green..................................... 27
Sugar bowl, cov., pink ...................................... 45
Sugar bowl, open, clear...................................... 9
Sugar bowl, open, green ..................................... 9
Sugar bowl, open, pink ..................................... 14
Sugar bowl, open, ruffled rim, cobalt blue ........ 48
Sugar bowl, open, ruffled rim, green ................ 30
Sugar bowl, open, ruffled rim, pink .................. 38
Tumbler, juice, footed, green, 3 3/4" h., 5
    oz. ............................................................... 16
Tumbler, juice, footed, yellow, 3 3/4" h., 5
    oz. ............................................................... 20
Tumbler, ribbed, clear, 4" h., 9 oz..................... 14
Tumbler, water, footed, green, 4 3/4" h., 10
    oz. ............................................................... 24
Tumbler, water, footed, pink, 4 3/4" h., 10
    oz. ............................................................... 25
Tumbler, water, footed, yellow, 4 3/4" h.,
    10 oz. .......................................................... 23

## IRIS OR IRIS & HERRINGBONE, Jeannette Glass Co., 1928-32 (Press-mold)

Bowl, 4 1/2" d., berry, beaded rim, amber
    iridescent.................................................... 11
Bowl, 4 1/2" d., berry, beaded rim, clear............ 50
Bowl, 5" d., cereal, clear ................................. 158

Bowl, 5" d., sauce, ruffled rim, amber iridescent .......................................................... 26
Bowl, 5" d., sauce, ruffled rim, clear ..................... 8
Bowl, 7 1/2" d., soup, amber iridescent ............. 70
Bowl, 7 1/2" d., soup, clear ............................. 172
Bowl, 8" d., berry, beaded rim, amber iridescent .......................................................... 24
Bowl, 8" d., berry, beaded rim, clear ............... 112
Bowl, 9 1/2" d., salad, amber iridescent ............ 16
Bowl, 9 1/2" d., salad, clear .............................. 15
Bowl, 11 1/2" d., fruit, ruffled rim, amber iridescent .......................................................... 19
Bowl, 11" d., fruit, straight rim, amber ................ 72
Bowl, 11 1/2" d., fruit, ruffled rim, clear ............. 14
Butter dish, cov., amber iridescent .................... 49
Butter dish, cov., clear ...................................... 50
Candlesticks, two-branch, amber iridescent, pr. ........................................................ 44
Candlesticks, two-branch, clear, pr. .................. 43
Candy jar, cov., clear ...................................... 190
Coaster, clear ................................................. 119
Creamer, footed, amber, iridescent .................. 12
Creamer, footed, clear ...................................... 12
Cup, demitasse, clear........................................ 39
Cup, clear ......................................................... 15
Cup & saucer, amber iridescent ........................ 24
Cup & saucer, clear........................................... 29
Goblet, wine, amber iridescent, 4" h., 3 oz. ....... 30
Goblet, wine, clear, 4 1/4" h., 3 oz. ................... 17
Goblet, clear, 5 1/2" h., 4 oz. ............................ 29
Goblet, clear, 5 1/2" h., 8 oz............................. 28
Lamp shade, blue .............................................. 88
Lamp shade, clear ............................................. 93
Lamp shade, pink .............................................. 77
Pitcher, 9 1/2" h., footed, amber iridescent ........ 46
Pitcher, 9 1/2" h., footed, clear.......................... 40
Plate, 5 1/2" d., sherbet, amber iridescent ......... 15
Plate, 5 1/2" d., sherbet, clear .......................... 16
Plate, 8" d., luncheon, clear............................. 138
Plate, 9" d., dinner, amber iridescent ................ 46
Plate, 9" d., dinner, clear .................................. 57
Plate, 11 3/4" d., sandwich, amber iridescent .......................................................... 34
Plate, 11 3/4" d., sandwich, clear ...................... 42
Saucer, demitasse, clear.................................. 140
Saucer, amber iridescent .................................. 11
Saucer, clear .................................................... 11
Sherbet, footed, amber iridescent, 2 1/2" h........ 18
Sherbet, footed, clear, 2 1/2" h. ........................ 29
Sherbet, footed, clear, 4" h. .............................. 27
Sugar bowl, cov., footed, amber iridescent ....... 27
Sugar bowl, cov., footed, clear .......................... 26
Sugar bowl, open, footed, amber iridescent .......................................................... 10
Sugar bowl, open, footed, clear......................... 12
Tumbler, clear, 4" h. ........................................ 158
Tumbler, footed, amber iridescent, 6" h. ............ 23
Tumbler, footed, clear, 6" h............................... 19
Tumbler, footed, clear, 6 1/2" h ........................ 37
Vase, 9" h., amber iridescent............................. 25
Vase, 9" h., clear .............................................. 26

## LACE EDGE OR OPEN LACE, Hocking Glass Co., 1935-38 (Press-mold)

Bowl, 6 1/2" d., cereal, pink (ILLUS. top next column)................................................... 25
Bowl, 7 3/4" d., salad or butter dish bottom, pink .............................................................. 26
Bowl, 9 1/2" d., plain or ribbed, pink (ILLUS. w/cereal bowl) .................................... 30

Butter dish or bonbon, cov., pink..................... 69

*Lace Edge Bowls*

Candy jar, cov., ribbed, pink, 4" h. .................... 55
Compote, cov., 7" d., footed, pink...................... 60
Compote, open, 7" d., footed, pink .................... 27
Console bowl, three-footed, pink, 10 1/2" d. ...................................................... 200
Cookie jar, cov., pink, 5" h. ............................... 74
Creamer, pink.................................................... 23
Cup, pink .......................................................... 25
Cup & saucer, pink ........................................... 38
Flower bowl w/crystal block, pink...................... 34
Plate, 7 1/4" d., salad, pink................................ 23
Plate, 8 1/4" d., luncheon, pink.......................... 26
Plate, 10 1/2" d., dinner, pink ............................ 36
Plate, 10 1/2" d., grill, pink ............................... 26
Plate, 13" d., solid lace, pink ............................ 47
Platter, 12 3/4" oval, pink .................................. 40
Platter, 12 3/4" oval, five-part, pink ................... 40
Relish dish, three-part, deep, pink, 7 1/2" d. ...................................................... 67
Relish plate, three-part, pink, 10 1/2" d. ............ 25
Relish plate, four-part, solid lace, pink, 13" d.............................................................. 68
Sherbet, footed, clear........................................ 10
Sherbet, footed, pink ...................................... 115
Sugar bowl, open, pink...................................... 21
Tumbler, pink, 4 1/2" h., 9 oz. ........................... 23
Tumbler, footed, pink, 5" h., 10 1/2 oz. .............. 76

## MADRID, Federal Glass Co., 1932-39 (Process-etched)

Ashtray, amber, 6" sq. ..................................... 264
Ashtray, green, 6" sq. ...................................... 195
Bowl, 4 3/4" d., cream soup, amber ................... 16
Bowl, 5" d., sauce, amber .................................... 6
Bowl, 5" d., sauce, blue ..................................... 35
Bowl, 5" d., sauce, green ................................... 10
Bowl, 7" d., soup, amber .................................... 16
Bowl, 7" d., soup, green ..................................... 18
Bowl, 8" d., salad, amber ................................... 14
Bowl, 8" d., salad, green .................................... 16
Bowl, 9 3/8" d., large berry, amber..................... 22
Bowl, 9 3/8" d., large berry, pink ....................... 24
Bowl, 9 1/2" d., salad, deep, amber ................... 32
Bowl, 10" oval vegetable, amber........................ 21
Bowl, 10" oval vegetable, green......................... 21
Butter dish, cov., amber .................................... 76
Cake plate, amber, 11 1/4" d. ............................ 15
Cake plate, pink, 11 1/4" d. ............................... 14
Candlesticks, amber, 2 1/4" h., pr. .................... 21
Candlesticks, pink, 2 1/4" h., pr......................... 25
Console bowl, flared, amber, 11" d. ................... 15

Console bowl, flared, iridescent, 11" d. ............. 16
Console bowl, flared, pink, 11" d. ..................... 17

*Madrid Cookie Jar*

Cookie jar, cov., amber (ILLUS.) ...................... 47
Cookie jar, cov., pink ...................................... 37
Creamer, amber ................................................. 8
Creamer, green ............................................... 11
Cup, amber ......................................................... 6
Cup, blue .......................................................... 18
Cup, clear ........................................................... 5
Cup, green ........................................................ 10
Cup, pink ............................................................. 8
Cup & saucer, amber ......................................... 9
Cup & saucer, green ........................................ 15
Cup & saucer, pink .......................................... 15
Gelatin mold, amber, 2 1/8" h. ......................... 14
Hot dish coaster, amber, 5" d. ......................... 40
Jam dish, amber, 7" d. ...................................... 25
Jam dish, green, 7" d. ....................................... 25
Lazy susan, walnut base w/seven clear hot
     dish coasters ............................................. 871
Pitcher, juice, 5 1/2" h., 36 oz. amber .............. 40
Pitcher, 8" h., 60 oz., square, amber ................ 47
Pitcher, 8" h., 60 oz., square, blue ................. 167
Pitcher, 8" h., 60 oz., square, green ............... 145
Pitcher, 8 1/2" h., 80 oz., jug-type, amber ........ 64
Pitcher w/ice lip, 8 1/2" h., 80 oz., amber ........ 63
Plate, 6" d., sherbet, amber ............................... 4
Plate, 6" d., sherbet, blue ................................ 12
Plate, 6" d., sherbet, clear ................................. 4
Plate, 6" d., sherbet, green ................................ 7
Plate, 6" d., sherbet, pink .................................. 4
Plate, 7 1/2" d., salad, amber .......................... 10
Plate, 7 1/2" d., salad, green ............................. 9
Plate, 7 1/2" d., salad, pink ............................... 9
Plate, 8 7/8" d., luncheon, amber ...................... 8
Plate, 8 7/8" d., luncheon, blue ....................... 18
Plate, 8 7/8" d., luncheon, clear ........................ 6
Plate, 8 7/8" d., luncheon, green ..................... 11
Plate, 10 1/2" d., dinner, clear ......................... 21
Plate, 10 1/2" d., grill, amber ............................. 9
Plate, 10 1/2" d., grill, green ............................ 19
Platter, 11 1/2" oval, amber ............................. 17
Platter, 11 1/2" oval, blue ................................ 29
Platter, 11 1/2" oval, green .............................. 19
Relish plate, amber, 10 1/2" d. ......................... 15
Salt & pepper shakers, amber, 3 1/2" h.,
     flat, pr. ....................................................... 47
Salt & pepper shakers, green, 3 1/2" h.,
     flat, pr. ....................................................... 63

Salt & pepper shakers, footed, amber,
     3 1/2" h., pr. .............................................. 150
Saucer, amber ................................................... 4
Saucer, blue .................................................... 11
Saucer, green .................................................... 5
Saucer, pink ...................................................... 7
Sherbet, amber .................................................. 7
Sherbet, blue ................................................... 15
Sherbet, clear .................................................... 7
Sherbet, green ................................................. 12
Sugar bowl, cov., amber .................................. 52
Sugar bowl, cov., clear .................................... 33
Sugar bowl, cov., green ................................... 58
Sugar bowl, open, amber ................................... 8
Sugar bowl, open, blue .................................... 19
Tumbler, juice, amber, 3 7/8" h., 5 oz. ............. 14
Tumbler, footed, amber, 4" h., 5 oz. ................ 27
Tumbler, footed, green, 4" h., 5 oz. ................. 38
Tumbler, amber, 4 1/2" h., 9 oz. ...................... 15
Tumbler, clear, 4 1/2" h., 9 oz. ........................ 10
Tumbler, green, 4 1/2" h., 9 oz. ....................... 25
Tumbler, pink, 4 1/2" h., 9 oz. ......................... 22
Tumbler, footed, amber, 5 1/4" h., 10 oz. ......... 30
Tumbler, amber, 5 1/2" h., 12 oz. ..................... 24
Tumbler, clear, 5 1/2" h., 12 oz. ....................... 18
Tumbler, green, 5 1/2" h., 12 oz. ...................... 33

## OYSTER & PEARL, Anchor Hocking Glass Corp., 1938-40 (Press-mold)

Bowl, 5 1/4" heart-shaped, w/handle, pink ......... 14
Bowl, 5 1/4" heart-shaped, w/handle, white
     w/pink ........................................................... 9
Bowl, 5 1/2" d., w/handle, clear ......................... 9
Bowl, 5 1/2" d., w/handle, ruby ....................... 13
Bowl, 6 1/2" d., handled, pink .......................... 14
Bowl, 6 1/2" d., handled, ruby ......................... 23
Bowl, 10 1/2" d., fruit, clear ............................ 20
Bowl, 10 1/2" d., fruit, pink ............................. 31
Bowl, 10 1/2" d., fruit, ruby ............................. 55
Bowl, 10 1/2" d., fruit, white w/green ................ 14
Bowl, 10 1/2" d., fruit, white w/pink ................. 14
Candleholders, pink, 3 1/2" h., pr. .................... 31
Candleholders, ruby, 3 1/2" h., pr. ................... 54
Candleholders, white w/green, 3 1/2" h.,
     pr. .............................................................. 14
Plate, 13 1/2" d., sandwich, pink ...................... 33
Plate, 13 1/2" d., sandwich, ruby ..................... 49
Relish, divided, pink, 10 1/4" oval .................... 12

## QUEEN MARY OR VERTICAL RIBBED, Hocking Glass Co., 1936-49 (Press-mold)

Ashtray, clear, 3 1/2" d. ..................................... 5
Ashtray, ruby, 3 1/2" d. ...................................... 8
Bowl, 4" d., nappy, clear .................................... 4
Bowl, 4" d., nappy, pink ..................................... 7
Bowl, 4" d., nappy, single handle, clear ............. 4
Bowl, 4" d., nappy, single handle, pink .............. 5
Bowl, 5" d., berry, clear ..................................... 7
Bowl, 5 1/2" d., two-handled, pink .................... 15
Bowl, 6" d., cereal, clear .................................... 7
Bowl, 6" d., cereal, pink ................................... 29
Bowl, 7" d., nappy, clear .................................... 8
Bowl, 7" d., nappy, pink ................................... 12
Bowl, 8 3/4" d., large berry, clear ...................... 9
Butter (or jam) dish, cov., clear ....................... 25
Butter (or jam) dish, cov., pink ....................... 160
Candlesticks, two-light, clear, 4 1/2" h., pr. ....... 16
Candy dish, cov., pink ...................................... 60
Cigarette jar, clear, 2 x 3" oval .......................... 6
Coaster, clear, 3 1/2" d. ..................................... 3

Coaster, pink, 3 1/2" d........................................... 4
Coaster-ashtray, clear, 4 1/4" sq...................... 4
Coaster-ashtray, pink, 4 1/4" sq........................ 9
Compote, 5 3/4" d., clear ................................... 7
Creamer, oval, clear............................................ 5
Creamer, oval, pink ........................................... 12
Cup & saucer, clear............................................ 8

*Queen Mary Cup & Saucer*

Cup & saucer, pink (ILLUS.)............................. 18
Plate, 6" d., sherbet, clear ................................. 4
Plate, 6" d., sherbet, pink ................................... 6
Plate, 8 1/2" d., salad, clear............................... 7
Plate, 9 3/4" d., dinner, clear ........................... 14
Plate, 9 3/4" d., dinner, pink ............................ 62
Plate, 12" d., sandwich, clear .......................... 12
Plate, 12" d., sandwich, pink ........................... 28
Plate, 14" d., serving, clear.............................. 11
Relish, three-part, clear, 12" d ......................... 11
Relish, four-part, clear, 14" d. ........................... 9
Salt & pepper shakers, clear, pr. ...................... 21
Sherbet, footed, clear......................................... 5
Sherbet, footed, pink ........................................ 10
Sugar bowl, open, oval, clear ............................ 5
Sugar bowl, open, oval, pink ............................ 10
Tumbler, juice, pink, 3 1/2" h., 5 oz................... 16
Tumbler, water, clear, 4" h., 9 oz. ...................... 7
Tumbler, water, pink, 4" h., 9 oz. ...................... 17
Tumbler, footed, clear, 5" h., 10 oz. ................. 29
Tumbler, footed, pink, 5" h., 10 oz. .................. 72

## ROYAL LACE, Hazel Atlas Glass Co., 1934-41 (Process-etched)

Bowl, 4 3/4" d., cream soup, blue ..................... 46
Bowl, 4 3/4" d., cream soup, clear .................... 17
Bowl, 4 3/4" d., cream soup, green ................... 34
Bowl, 4 3/4" d., cream soup, pink...................... 34
Bowl, 5" d., berry, clear .................................... 18
Bowl, 5" d., berry, pink ..................................... 47
Bowl, 10" d., berry, blue ................................... 87
Bowl, 10" d., berry, green.................................. 34
Bowl, 10" d., three-footed, ruffled edge, clear ................................................................ 47
Bowl, 10" d., three-footed, ruffled edge, pink.................................................................. 88
Bowl, 10" d., three-footed, straight edge, blue.................................................................. 92
Bowl, 10" d., three-footed, straight edge, green................................................................ 58
Bowl, 10" d., three-footed, straight edge, pink.................................................................. 72
Bowl, 11" oval vegetable, blue.......................... 72
Bowl, 11" oval vegetable, clear ......................... 21

Bowl, 11" oval vegetable, pink .......................... 43
Butter dish, cov., clear....................................... 75
Butter dish, cov., green .................................... 287
Butter dish, cov., pink....................................... 200
Candlesticks, rolled edge, pink, pr. ................. 114
Candlesticks, ruffled edge, blue, pr................. 291
Candlesticks, straight edge, blue, pr. ............. 143
Candlesticks, straight edge, clear, pr. .............. 32
Cookie jar, cov., blue ....................................... 436
Cookie jar, cov., clear ........................................ 41

*Royal Lace Cookie Jar*

Cookie jar, cov., green (ILLUS.) ...................... 117
Cookie jar, cov., pink ......................................... 70
Creamer, footed, blue ........................................ 61
Creamer, footed, clear ....................................... 14
Creamer, footed, green ...................................... 30
Cup, blue ........................................................... 36
Cup, clear............................................................ 9
Cup, green.......................................................... 21
Cup, pink............................................................ 22
Cup & saucer, blue ............................................ 53
Cup & saucer, clear ........................................... 14
Cup & saucer, green .......................................... 33
Cup & saucer, pink ............................................ 30
Pitcher, 48 oz., straight sides, blue ................. 200
Pitcher, 48 oz., straight sides, clear ................. 39
Pitcher, 48 oz., straight sides, green ............... 120
Pitcher, 48 oz., straight sides, pink ................... 92
Pitcher, 8" h., 68 oz., w/ice lip, clear ................ 58
Pitcher, 8" h., 68 oz., w/ice lip, pink ................ 124
Pitcher, 8 1/2" h., 96 oz., w/ice lip, clear........... 58
Pitcher, 8 1/2" h., 96 oz., w/ice lip, green......... 153
Plate, 6" d., sherbet, blue ................................. 14
Plate, 6" d., sherbet, clear .................................. 8
Plate, 6" d., sherbet, green ................................ 14
Plate, 6" d., sherbet, pink .................................. 10
Plate, 8 1/2" d., luncheon, green ....................... 21
Plate, 8 1/2" d., luncheon, pink.......................... 23
Plate, 9 7/8" d., dinner, blue ............................. 54
Plate, 9 7/8" d., dinner, clear ............................ 21
Plate, 9 7/8" d., dinner, green ........................... 36
Plate, 9 7/8" d., dinner, pink ............................. 33
Plate, 9 7/8" d., grill, blue ................................. 27
Plate, 9 7/8" d., grill, clear.................................. 9
Plate, 9 7/8" d., grill, green ............................... 29
Plate, 9 7/8" d., grill, pink ................................. 21
Platter, 13" oval, blue........................................ 70
Platter, 13" oval, clear....................................... 15
Platter, 13" oval, green...................................... 43
Platter, 13" oval, pink........................................ 46
Salt & pepper shakers, blue, pr. ...................... 338
Salt & pepper shakers, clear, pr. ...................... 42

Salt & pepper shakers, green, pr.................... 162
Salt & pepper shakers, pink, pr. ..................... 99
Sherbet, footed, blue.................................. 51
Sherbet, footed, clear................................. 17
Sherbet, footed, green ............................... 29
Sherbet, footed, pink................................. 23
Sherbet in metal holder, blue ...................... 40
Sherbet in metal holder, clear ....................... 6
Sugar bowl, cov., blue ............................... 215
Sugar bowl, cov., clear................................ 28
Sugar bowl, cov., green............................... 85
Sugar bowl, cov., pink ................................ 74
Sugar bowl, open, blue................................ 25
Sugar bowl, open, clear................................. 9
Sugar bowl, open, green............................... 25
Sugar bowl, open, pink................................. 19
Tumbler, blue, 3 1/2" h., 5 oz........................ 65
Tumbler, green, 3 1/2" h., 5 oz. ..................... 32
Tumbler, pink, 3 1/2" h., 5 oz. ...................... 29
Tumbler, blue, 4 1/8" h., 9 oz........................ 52
Tumbler, clear, 4 1/8" h., 9 oz....................... 16
Tumbler, green, 4 1/8" h., 9 oz. ..................... 39
Tumbler, pink, 4 1/8" h., 9 oz. ...................... 31
Tumbler, clear, 4 7/8" h., 10 oz. .................... 27
Tumbler, clear, 5 3/8" h., 12 oz..................... 33
Tumbler, clear, 5 3/8" h., 12 oz..................... 59

## SIERRA OR PINWHEEL, Jeannette Glass Co., 1931-33 (Press-mold)
Bowl, 5 1/2" d., cereal, green ....................... 18
Bowl, 5 1/2" d., cereal, pink......................... 16
Bowl, 8 1/2" d., berry, green......................... 32
Bowl, 8 1/2" d., berry, pink.......................... 36
Bowl, 9 1/4" oval vegetable, pink ................... 78
Butter dish, cov., green.............................. 90
Butter dish, cov., pink............................... 52
Creamer, green ....................................... 24
Creamer, pink......................................... 20
Cup & saucer, green ................................. 23
Cup & saucer, pink ................................... 20
Pitcher, 6 1/2" h., 32 oz., green ..................... 168
Pitcher, 6 1/2" h., 32 oz., pink ...................... 113
Plate, 9" d., dinner, green............................ 21
Plate, 9" d., dinner, pink ............................ 21
Platter, 11" oval, green............................... 51
Platter, 11" oval, pink................................ 45
Salt & pepper shakers, green, pr..................... 38
Salt & pepper shakers, pink, pr. ..................... 43
Serving tray, two-handled, green .................... 19
Tumbler, footed, green, 4 1/2" h., 9 oz. ............ 83

## SWIRL OR PETAL SWIRL, Jeannette Glass Co., 1937-38 (Press-mold)
Bowl, 5 1/4" d., cereal, Delphite ..................... 14
Bowl, 5 1/4" d., cereal, pink.......................... 11
Bowl, 5 1/4" d., cereal, ultramarine .................. 17
Bowl, 9" d., salad, Delphite .......................... 30
Bowl, 9" d., salad, pink .............................. 21
Bowl, 9" d., salad, ultramarine ....................... 30
Bowl, 10" d., fruit, closed handles, footed,
  ultramarine ........................................ 34
Bowl, 9" d., rimmed, pink ............................ 18
Butter dish, cov., pink................................ 237
Butter dish, cov., ultramarine ........................ 318
Candleholders, double, ultramarine, pr. ............. 53
Candy dish, cov., pink ............................... 120
Candy dish, cov., ultramarine......................... 173
Candy dish, open, three-footed, pink,
  5 1/2" d. ........................................... 14

Candy dish, open, three-footed, ultrama-
  rine, 5 1/2" d. ..................................... 20
Coaster, pink, 3 1/4" d., 1" h. ........................ 12
Coaster, ultramarine, 3 1/4" d., 1" h. ................ 13
Console bowl, footed, ultramarine,
  10 1/2" d. .......................................... 33
Creamer, Delphite .................................... 11
Creamer, pink.......................................... 9
Creamer, ultramarine ................................. 16
Cup, ultramarine...................................... 15

*Swirl Delphite Cup & Saucer*

Cup & saucer, Delphite (ILLUS.) ...................... 16
Cup & saucer, ultramarine............................ 20
Plate, 6 1/2" d., sherbet, Delphite .................... 8
Plate, 6 1/2" d., sherbet, pink......................... 5
Plate, 6 1/2" d., sherbet, ultramarine ................. 7
Plate, 7 1/4" d., ultramarine .......................... 14
Plate, 8" d., salad, ultramarine ....................... 19
Plate, 9 1/4" d., dinner, Delphite ..................... 16
Plate, 9 1/4" d., dinner, pink ......................... 16
Plate, 9 1/4" d., dinner, ultramarine .................. 21
Plate, 12 1/2" d., sandwich, pink ..................... 17
Plate, 12 1/2" d., sandwich, ultramarine ............. 30
Platter, 12" oval, Delphite............................. 35
Salt & pepper shakers, ultramarine, pr. ............. 48
Sherbet, pink.......................................... 15
Sherbet, ultramarine ................................. 24
Soup bowl w/lug handles, ultramarine ............. 52
Sugar bowl, open, pink................................ 10
Sugar bowl, open, ultramarine....................... 15
Tumbler, footed, ultramarine, 9 oz. .................. 45
Tumbler, ultramarine, 4" h., 9 oz...................... 38
Tumbler, ultramarine, 5 1/8" h., 13 oz. ............. 153
Vase, 6 1/2" h., pink................................... 17
Vase, 8 1/2" h., ultramarine .......................... 28

## TEA ROOM, Indiana Glass Co., 1926-31 (Press-mold)
Banana split dish, flat, green, 7 1/2"................. 99
Banana split dish, footed, green, 7 1/2"............. 78
Bowl, 8 3/4" d., salad, green ........................ 150
Bowl, 8 3/4" d., salad, pink .......................... 130
Bowl, 9 1/2" oval vegetable, green.................... 69
Bowl, 9 1/2" oval vegetable, pink .................... 76
Candlesticks, green, pr. .............................. 66
Candlesticks, pink, pr. ............................... 64
Celery or pickle dish, green, 8 1/2" .................. 35
Celery or pickle dish, pink, 8 1/2".................... 35
Creamer, pink, 3 1/4" h................................ 26
Creamer, footed, green, 4 1/2" h. .................... 20
Creamer, footed, pink, 4 1/2" h. ..................... 20
Creamer & open sugar bowl on center-
  handled tray, pink .................................. 93
Creamer & open sugar bowl on rectan-
  gular tray, green.................................... 90
Creamer & open sugar bowl on rectan-
  gular tray, pink .................................... 60

Cup, green......................................................... 59
Finger bowl, green ......................................... 115
Finger bowl, pink .............................................. 90
Goblet, green, 9 oz. ........................................ 78
Goblet, pink, 9 oz. ........................................... 70
Ice bucket, green.............................................. 85
Ice bucket, pink................................................ 67
Lamp, electric, green, 9" ................................. 152
Lamp, electric, pink, 9" ................................... 127
Mustard, cov., pink.......................................... 210
Parfait, pink.................................................... 135
Pitcher, 64 oz., green...................................... 140
Pitcher, 64 oz., pink ....................................... 175
Plate, 8 1/4" d., luncheon, green ...................... 32
Plate, 8 1/4" d., luncheon, pink.......................... 31
Plate, 10 1/2" d., two-handled, green ................ 50
Plate, sandwich, w/center handle, green.......... 203
Plate, sandwich, w/center handle, pink ............ 155
Relish, divided, green ...................................... 25
Salt & pepper shakers, green, pr...................... 70
Salt & pepper shakers, pink, pr........................ 63
Saucer, green.................................................. 25
Sherbet, low, flared edge, green....................... 30
Sherbet, low, flared edge, pink......................... 26
Sherbet, low footed, green................................ 30
Sherbet, low footed, pink ................................. 26
Sugar bowl, cov., green, 3" h. ......................... 100
Sugar bowl, cov., pink, 3" h. ........................... 130
Sugar bowl, open, footed, green, 4 1/2" h. ........ 22
Sugar bowl, open, footed, pink, 4 1/2" h. .......... 17
Sugar bowl, open, rectangular, green .............. 23
Sundae, footed, ruffled, green.......................... 115
Tray, rectangular, for creamer & sugar
    bowl, green.................................................. 48
Tray, rectangular, for creamer & sugar
    bowl, pink ................................................... 59
Tray w/center handle, for creamer & sugar
    bowl, green.................................................. 225
Tray w/center handle, for creamer & sugar
    bowl, pink ................................................... 225
Tumbler, footed, green, 6 oz............................. 42
Tumbler, footed, pink, 6 oz. ............................. 32
Tumbler, green, 4 3/16" h., 8 oz. ...................... 105
Tumbler, footed, green, 5 1/4" h., 8 oz. ............. 35
Tumbler, footed, pink, 5 1/4" h., 8 oz. ............... 32

*Tea Room Tumbler*

Tumbler, footed, pink, 11 oz. (ILLUS.)............... 51
Tumbler, footed, green, 12 oz............................ 70
Vase, 6 1/2" h., ruffled rim, green ..................... 110
Vase, 6 1/2" h., ruffled rim, pink........................ 113
Vase, 11" h., straight, green ............................. 151

## WINDSOR DIAMOND OR WINDSOR, Jeannette Glass Co., 1936-46 (Press-mold)

Ashtray, Delphite, 5 3/4" d. ............................... 48
Ashtray, green, 5 3/4" d. ................................... 45
Ashtray, pink, 5 3/4" d. ..................................... 41
Bowl, 4 3/4" d., berry, clear ................................ 6
Bowl, 4 3/4" d., berry, green.............................. 11
Bowl, 4 3/4" d., berry, pink................................ 11
Bowl, 5" d., cream soup, green ......................... 29
Bowl, 5" d., cream soup, pink............................ 21
Bowl, 5" d., pointed edge, clear .......................... 7
Bowl, 5" d., pointed edge, pink.......................... 25
Bowl, 5 1/8" or 5 3/8" d., cereal, clear................. 7
Bowl, 5 1/8" or 5 3/8" d., cereal, green.............. 25
Bowl, 5 1/8" or 5 3/8" d., cereal, pink ............... 24
Bowl, 7" d., three-footed, clear ........................... 7
Bowl, 7" d., three-footed, pink .......................... 33
Bowl, 8" d., pointed edge, clear ........................ 13
Bowl, 8" d., pointed edge, pink.......................... 65
Bowl, 8" d., two-handled, clear ........................... 6
Bowl, 8" d., two-handled, green ........................ 21
Bowl, 8" d., two-handled, pink........................... 19
Bowl, 8 1/2" d., berry, clear .............................. 11
Bowl, 8 1/2" d., berry, pink ............................... 23
Bowl, 9 1/2" oval vegetable, clear ....................... 9
Bowl, 9 1/2" oval vegetable, green..................... 32
Bowl, 9 1/2" oval vegetable, pink ...................... 25
Bowl, 10 1/2" d., pointed edge, clear ................ 25
Bowl, 10 1/2" d., pointed edge, pink.................. 154
Bowl, 10 1/2" d., salad, clear............................ 19
Bowl, 7 x 11 3/4" boat shape, clear ................... 20
Bowl, 7 x 11 3/4" boat shape, green .................. 37
Bowl, 7 x 11 3/4" boat shape, pink..................... 35
Bowl, 12 1/2" d., fruit, clear .............................. 28
Bowl, 12 1/2" d., fruit, pink ............................... 128
Butter dish, cov., clear ..................................... 27

*Windsor Butter Dish*

Butter dish, cov., pink (ILLUS.) ......................... 54
Cake plate, footed, clear, 10 3/4" d.................... 8
Cake plate, footed, pink, 10 3/4" d. ................... 22
Candlesticks, clear, 3" h., pr. ........................... 24
Candlesticks, pink, 3" h., pr.............................. 95
Coaster, green, 3 1/4" d. .................................. 16
Coaster, pink, 3 1/4" d...................................... 13
Creamer, flat, clear........................................... 5
Creamer, flat, green ......................................... 17
Creamer, flat, pink ........................................... 12
Creamer, footed, clear ....................................... 7
Cup & saucer, clear........................................... 7
Cup & saucer, green ........................................ 21
Cup & saucer, pink ........................................... 17
Pitcher, 4 1/2" h., 16 oz., clear.......................... 23
Pitcher, 6 3/4" h., 52 oz., clear.......................... 12
Pitcher, 6 3/4" h., 52 oz., green ........................ 69
Pitcher, 6 3/4" h., 52 oz., pink........................... 31

Plate, 6" d., sherbet, clear ........................................ 3
Plate, 6" d., sherbet, green.................................. 7
Plate, 6" d., sherbet, pink .................................. 5
Plate, 7" d., salad, green ................................... 25
Plate, 7" d., salad, pink.................................... 20
Plate, 9" d., dinner, clear ................................... 7
Plate, 9" d., dinner, green................................. 25
Plate, 9" d., dinner, pink ................................... 26
Plate, 10 1/4", sandwich, handled, clear ............. 9
Plate, 10 1/4", sandwich, handled, green............. 24
Plate, 10 1/4", sandwich, handled, pink ............. 18
Plate, 13 5/8" d., chop, clear ............................ 10
Plate, 13 5/8" d., chop, green............................ 41
Plate, 13 5/8" d., chop, pink.............................. 45
Platter, 11 1/2" oval, clear.................................. 8
Platter, 11 1/2" oval, green................................. 22
Platter, 11 1/2" oval, pink .................................. 23
Powder jar, cov., clear ....................................... 14
Relish, divided, pink, 11 1/2"............................ 276
Salt & pepper shakers, green, pr..................... 52
Salt & pepper shakers, pink, pr....................... 37
Sherbet, footed, clear.......................................... 5
Sherbet, footed, green ....................................... 15
Sherbet, footed, pink .......................................... 13
Sugar bowl, cov., flat, green............................. 33
Sugar bowl, cov., flat, pink............................... 33
Tray, pink, 4" sq., w/handles ............................. 10
Tray, pink, 4" sq., without handles..................... 61
Tray, green, 4 1/8 x 9", w/handles ..................... 15
Tray, pink, 4 1/8 x 9", w/handles ...................... 17
Tray, clear, 8 1/2 x 9 3/4", w/handles .................. 5
Tray, clear, 8 1/2 x 9 3/4", without handles ........ 13
Tray, pink, 8 1/2 x 9 3/4", w/handles ................. 23
Tray, pink, 8 1/2 x 9 3/4", without handles........ 138
Tumbler, clear, 3 1/4" h., 5 oz. ......................... 10
Tumbler, green, 3 1/4" h., 5 oz. ........................ 33
Tumbler, pink, 3 1/4" h., 5 oz. .......................... 25
Tumbler, clear, 4" h., 9 oz................................. 6
Tumbler, green, 4" h., 9 oz. .............................. 35
Tumbler, pink, 4" h., 9 oz. ................................ 21
Tumbler, clear, 5" h., 12 oz............................... 9
Tumbler, green, 5" h., 12 oz. ............................ 47
Tumbler, pink, 5" h., 12 oz. .............................. 34
Tumbler, footed, clear, 4" h., 9 oz....................... 7
Tumbler, footed, clear, 5" h., 11 oz..................... 9
Tumbler, footed, clear, 7 1/4" h......................... 17

# DUNCAN & MILLER

*Canterbury Rose Bowl*

Duncan & Miller Glass Company, a successor firm to George A. Duncan & Sons Company, produced a wide range of pressed wares and novelty pieces during the late 19th century and into the early 20th century. During the Depression era and after, they continued making a wide variety of more modern patterns, including mold-blown types and also introduced a number of etched and engraved patterns. Many colors, including opalescent hues, were produced during this era and especially popular today are the graceful swan dishes they produced in the Pall Mall and Sylvan patterns.

The numbers after the pattern name indicate the original factory pattern number. The Duncan factory was closed in 1955. Also see ANIMALS and PATTERN GLASS in the Glass section.

Almond dish, Early American Sandwich
   patt., clear ..................................................... $12
Basket, handled, etched First Love patt.,
   10" oval ........................................................ 175
Basket, Early American Sandwich patt.,
   clear, 12" ...................................................... 100
Bowl, 8" d., Spiral Flutes patt., clear ................. 18
Bowl, 9" d., tab-handled, Caribbean patt.,
   clear .............................................................. 35
Bowl, 11 1/2" d., fluted, Early American
   Sandwich patt................................................ 50
Bowl, 10" d., flared, etched First Love patt.,
   clear .............................................................. 50
Bowl, bouillon, Spiral Flutes patt., pink ............. 15
Bowl, Canterbury patt., oval, clear .................... 35
Butter dish, w/metal cover, Teardrop patt.,
   (No. 301), clear, 1 lb. .................................... 20
Cake salver, pedestal foot, Early American
   Sandwich patt., clear, 13" d., 5" h. ................. 80
Candlesticks, two-light, Canterbury patt.,
   clear, 6" h., pr. .............................................. 50
Claret, Canterbury patt., clear, 5" h................... 20
Cocktail, Early American Sandwich patt.,
   clear, 3 oz...................................................... 13
Cocktail shaker, etched First Love patt.,
   clear, 16 oz.................................................... 135
Creamer, Teardrop patt., ( No. 301), clear.......... 5
Cup, Canterbury patt., clear .............................. 10
Cup, Puritan patt., footed, clear......................... 7
Cup & saucer, Early American Sandwich
   patt., clear ..................................................... 10
Deviled egg plate, Early American Sand-
   wich patt., clear ............................................. 63
Goblet, Caribbean patt., clear, 3 oz., 4" h. ......... 25
Goblet, Teardrop patt., clear, 4 oz., 5" h. ........... 12
Goblet, water, Canterbury patt., clear,
   7 1/4" h. ......................................................... 17
Goblet, etched First Love patt., clear,
   6 3/4" h............................................................ 28
Model of a swan, Pall Mall patt. (No.
   30 1/2), clear, 7" l. ......................................... 15
Nut bowl, Early American Sandwich patt.,
   clear .............................................................. 11
Pitcher w/ice lip, 8" h., Early American
   Sandwich patt., clear, 80 oz. ......................... 120
Plate, 7" d., Spiral Flutes patt., pink ................... 4
Plate, dessert, 7" d., Early American Sand-
   wich patt., clear ............................................. 5
Plate, 7 1/2" d., Canterbury patt., (No. 115),
   clear .............................................................. 10
Plate, salad, 7 1/2" sq., etched First Love
   patt., clear ..................................................... 20
Plate, salad, 8" d., Early American Sand-
   wich patt., clear ............................................. 10
Plate, salad, 8" d., Early American Sand-
   wich patt., green............................................. 10

**Plate,** torte, 14" d., Teardrop patt. (No. 301), clear ...................................................... 22

**Plate,** 16" d., Early American Sandwich patt., clear .................................................... 105

**Plateau for cheese plate,** Teardrop patt., (No. 301), clear ........................................... 15

**Relish dish,** Canterbury patt., three-part, handled, clear, 9" d. ...................................... 18

**Relish dish,** Caribbean patt., five-part, clear ........................................................... 40

**Relish dish,** Teardrop patt., (No. 301), two-part, round, clear .............................................. 8

**Rose bowl,** Canterbury patt., Jasmine, yellow opalescent (ILLUS.) .......................... 90-110

**Salt dip,** Early American Sandwich patt., clear ................................................................ 8

**Saucer,** Early American Sandwich patt., clear ................................................................ 4

**Sherbet,** Early American Sandwich patt., green ............................................................. 10

**Tumbler,** juice, Early American Sandwich patt., clear, 5 oz. ............................................ 10

**Tumbler,** juice, Canterbury patt., clear, 4 1/4" h. .......................................................... 8

**Vase,** 4" h., Canterbury patt. (No. 115), clear ............................................................... 17

**Vase,** 5" h., Canterbury patt., amber ................. 25

**Vase,** 6" h., Canterbury patt. (No. 115), clear ............................................................... 25

**Vase/flower arranger,** 7" h., Canterbury patt. (No. 115), clear ...................................... 40

**Wine,** Caribbean patt., clear, 3 oz. ..................... 15

# DURAND

*Durand Lamp Base*

*Fine decorative glass similar to that made by Tiffany and other outstanding glasshouses of its day was made by the Vineland Flint Glass Works Co. in Vineland, New Jersey, first headed by Victor Durand, Sr., and subsequently by his son Victor Durand, Jr., in the 1920s.*

**Ginger jar,** cov., wide ovoid shouldered body w/a domed cover fitted w/an amber button finial, the body & cover w/an over-

all golden iridescent King Tut design on a dark ground, mounted as a lamp on a round bronze base raised on eight paw-form feet, overall 11 1/2" h. ..................... **$2,035**

**Lamp base,** bulbous squatty base below a tall slender trumpet-form neck, decorated overall w/green & iridescent King Tut swirled design, fitted on a silvered metal round foot & w/an electric socket cap fitting, shape No. 1730, glass 6 1/2" h. (ILLUS.)..................................... **690**

**Vase,** 4" h., overall gold iridescence, Shape No. 1710, signed in script.............................. **330**

**Vase,** 5" h., 4" d., squatty bulbous body, overall gold iridescence, signed "Durand #20172-5"..................................................... **385**

**Vase,** 7" h., ovoid ringed 'beehive' form, overall dark iridescent blue, signed & numbered ................................................... **1,320**

**Vase,** 7 1/2" h., simple ovoid body w/a short wide flaring neck, grey & yellow w/peach iridescence & green trailing vines w/heart-shaped leaves, signed "DURAND - 1812 - 7" w/a "V," 1920s .......... **977**

**Vase,** 7 3/4" h., Cluthra, wide ovoid body tapering to a wide flared neck, colorless w/trapped bubbles & mottled blue & green rising to the yellow neck, obscured silver Durand signature on the polished pontil, ca. 1926............................................. **633**

**Vase,** 9" h., cut-overlay, large ovoid body w/a small, short cylindrical neck, deep ruby cut to clear w/a design of large punties & crossed petals, panel-cut around the base ............................................................... **2,475**

**Vase,** 9 1/2" h., slender baluster-form w/short trumpet neck, iridescent dark cobalt blue abundantly decorated w/silver heart & vine iridescent design, silvery blue interior iridescence, polished pontil signed "Durand 1707," ca. 1925 ...... **1,955**

**Vase,** 10" h., tall slender waisted form w/a swelled top w/closed mouth tapering to a gently flaring base, overall pale green & gold King Tut design, Shape No. 1717 ..... **1,540**

**Vase,** 10" h., tall waisted form w/swelled top & closed rim, white King Tut design on a gold iridescent ground, signed in script............................................................. **935**

*Large & Smaller Durand Vases*

**Vase,** 12 1/4" h., cushion base below the widely flaring trumpet-form body w/an angled shoulder to the wide trumpet neck, grey w/orange, yellow & silver iridescence, signed "DURAND - 20139-12," ca. 1920s (ILLUS.) ............................... **977**

**Vase,** 14" h., tall slender trumpet-form, the sides decorated w/a tall pulled feather design on the creamy ground, on a purplish amber applied round foot, model No. 1724 ...................... **935**

## FOSTORIA

*Fostoria Glass company, founded in 1887, produced numerous types of fine glassware over the years. Their factory in Moundsville, West Virginia closed in 1986.*

*Fostoria Mark*

**Appetizer or ice cream set:** 10 1/2" oblong tray w/six individual 1 3/4" h. inserts, American patt., amber, the set ................ **$1,100**

**Ashtray,** individual, Century patt., clear, 2 3/4" ......................... **12**

**Bonbon,** three-footed, American patt., clear, 7" d. ................................... **15**

**Bonbon,** three-footed, Colony patt., clear, 7" d. ................................... **12**

**Bowl,** almond, 2 1/4" d., footed, Colony patt., clear ........................... **17**

**Bowl,** 4 1/2" d., three-handled, American patt., clear ...................... **45**

**Bowl,** 8 1/2" d., three-handled, American patt., clear ...................... **300**

**Bowl,** salad, 9 3/4" d., Colony patt., clear ......... **40**

**Bowl,** 10 1/2" d., high-footed, Colony patt., clear ...................................... **112**

**Bowl,** fruit, 10 1/2" d., three-footed, American patt., clear.............................. **40**

**Bowl,** 11" tri-cornered, three footed, American patt., clear.............................. **40**

**Bowl,** fruit, low, 14" d., Colony patt., clear......... **70**

**Butter dish,** cov., oblong, American patt., clear, 1/4 lb., 3 1/4 x 7 1/2", 2 1/8" h. ............ **14**

**Cake plate,** handled, Colony patt., clear, 10" d. ........................................... **22**

**Cake plate,** three-footed, American patt., clear, 12" d. ...................................... **25**

**Cake salver,** Colony patt., clear, 12" d.............. **75**

**Candlestick,** Romance etching, clear, 5 1/2" h. ...................................... **38**

**Candlestick,** two-light, American patt., clear, 4 3/8" h. ................................... **35**

**Candlestick,** two-light, Chintz etching .............. **38**

**Candlestick,** three-light, Romance etching, clear ...................................... **55**

**Candlesticks,** Chintz etching, clear, 4" h., pr. .......................................... **50**

**Candlesticks,** Navarre patt., clear, No. 2496, 4" h., pr............................ **45**

**Candlesticks,** cone-footed, American patt., clear, 15 points, small, pr. ........................... **400**

**Candlesticks,** cone-footed, American patt., clear, 16 points, large, pr............................. **300**

**Candlesticks,** two-light, Romance etching, No. 6023, clear, pr........................... **38**

**Candy dish,** three-part, Chintz etching, clear ...................................... **165**

**Centerpiece,** American patt., clear, shallow, 17" ....................................... **550**

**Chamber candles,** American patt., clear, pr........................................... **95**

**Champagne,** Romance etching, clear, 7" h. .......................................... **18**

**Champagne,** Chintz etching, clear..................... **20**

**Cheese compote,** American patt., clear ........... **24**

**Cheese & cracker dish,** Chintz etching, clear ...................................... **70**

**Claret,** American Lady patt., clear, 3 1/2 oz., 4 5/8" h. ................................... **18**

**Cocktail,** footed, American patt., clear, 3 oz. .......................................... **12**

**Cocktail,** American Lady patt., clear, 3 1/2 oz., 4" h. ...................................... **14**

**Cocktail,** Holly cutting, clear, 3 1/2 oz., 5 1/4" h. ..................................... **12**

**Cocktail,** Romance etching, clear, 3 1/2 oz....... **18**

**Compote,** jelly, cov., Colony patt., clear............. **35**

**Console set:** bowl & pr. of double candlesticks; Chintz etching, clear........................... **125**

**Cracker jar,** cov., American patt., clear........... **800**

**Creamer,** American patt., clear, medium.............. **9**

**Creamer,** American patt., hexagonal foot, clear ...................................... **800**

**Creamer,** Chintz etching, clear......................... **20**

**Creamer,** American patt., clear, 4 1/4" h., 9 1/2 oz. ..................................... **12**

**Creamer,** individual, Century patt., clear, 4 oz. ............................................ **9**

**Creamer,** individual, Colony patt., clear, 3 1/4" h., 4 oz. ................................. **6**

**Creamer & cov. sugar bowl,** American patt., clear, large, pr. ............................. **45**

**Creamer, open sugar bowl & tray,** individual, American patt., clear, the set................... **38**

**Creamer & sugar bowl,** Coronet patt., clear, pr. ......................................... **12**

**Crushed fruit jar,** cov., American patt., clear, 10" h. (chip on lid)............................ **1,600**

**Cup,** footed, Colony patt., clear, 6 oz. ................. **7**

**Cup,** American patt., clear, 7 oz. ......................... **8**

**Cup,** Century patt., clear ................................... **17**

**Cup & saucer,** American patt., flared, clear....... **12**

**Cup & saucer,** Colony patt., clear....................... **8**

**Cup & saucer,** Fairfax patt., orchid .................. **14**

**Dresser bowl,** oblong, American patt., clear, 1 3/4 x 5" ................................ **600**

**Glove box,** cov., American patt., clear (some stretch marks) ........................ **600**

**Goblet,** American patt., clear, 5 1/2" h., 9 oz. .......................................... **13**

**Goblet,** Chintz etching, water, clear, 9 oz. ......... **32**

**Goblet,** Colony patt., water, clear, 5 1/8" h., 9 oz. .................................. **14**

**Goblet,** Jamestown patt., water, blue, 9 oz., 4 1/4" h. .................................. **20**

**Goblet,** Romance etching, water, clear, 9 oz. .......................................... **28**

**Goblet,** American Lady patt., clear, 10 oz., 6 1/8" h. ..................................... **18**

Goblet, American Lady patt., cobalt blue, 10 oz., 6 1/8" h. ............................................. 85

Goblet, Holly cutting, clear, 10 oz, 8 3/8" h. ........ 18

Hair receiver, cov., American patt., clear, 3" sq. ......................................................... 700

Honey jar, cover & spoon, American patt., clear ....................................................... 500

Jewel box, cov., American patt., clear, 2 1/4 x 5 1/4", 2" h. .................................... 400

Mayonnaise bowl, divided, American patt., clear, 3 1/4" d., 6 1/4" h. ............................. 15

Mayonnaise bowl, Century patt., clear............ 18

Mayonnaise bowl, Colony patt., clear .............. 15

Mayonnaise bowl & liner, Colony patt., clear .............................................................. 25

Mayonnaise bowl w/underplate, Colony patt., clear, 2 pcs. ........................................ 35

Mustard jar, cov., American patt., clear ............. 30

Mustard jar, cover & spoon, round, American patt., clear (inkwell) ............................ 1,200

Nappy, American patt., flared, green, 4 1/2"..... 150

Nappy, handled, American patt., clear, 4 1/2" d. .................................................... 10

Nappy, tri-cornered, handled, American patt., clear, 5" ...................................... 10

Novelty, model of a top hat, American patt., clear, 2 1/2" h. ................................. 25

Olive dish, American patt., clear, 6" l............... 12

Oyster cocktail, American Lady patt., clear, 4 oz., 3 1/2" h. .............................. 14

Oyster cocktail, Colony patt., clear, 3 3/8" h., 4 oz. ............................................ 12

Party plate, Century patt., clear, 8" ................. 24

Pickle dish, American patt., clear, 8" l. .............. 13

Pickle dish, Century patt., clear, 8 3/4" ............. 15

Pickle jar, cov., American patt., clear, 6" h. ..... 500

Pitcher, milk, Century patt., clear ..................... 60

Pitcher w/ice lip, 8 1/2" h., Colony patt., clear, 3 pt. ........................................... 260

Plate, bread & butter, 6" d., American patt., clear ...................................................... 8

Plate, salad, 7" d., Baroque patt., clear ................ 4

Plate, 7 1/2" d., Chintz etching, clear ................ 18

Plate, 7 1/2" d., Navarre patt., clear .................. 18

Plate, 9" d., Colony patt., clear ........................ 18

Plate, torte, 13" d., Colony patt., clear................ 28

Plate, torte, 13 1/2" oval, American patt., clear ...................................................... 45

Plate, torte, 14" d., American patt., clear............ 55

Plate, torte, 14" d., Century patt., clear .............. 30

Plate, torte, 14" d., Holly cutting, clear .............. 38

Plate, torte, 15" d., Colony patt., clear................ 60

Plate, salad, American Lady patt., cobalt blue ....................................................... 15

Plate, sandwich, center handle, Colony patt., clear ............................................... 35

Pomade or rouge box, cov., American patt., clear, 2" sq. ...................................... 395

Puff box, cov., American patt., clear, 1 1/2" d. ................................................. 700

Puff box, cov., American patt., clear, 2 1/2" d. .................................................. 700

Puff box, cov., American patt., clear, 3" sq...... 200

Puff box, cov., American patt., clear, 4 1/2" sq. ..................................................... 1,400

Punch cup, American patt., clear ........................ 8

Relish dish, two-part, Colony patt., clear, 7 1/4" ................................................... 16

Relish dish, four-part, rectangular, American patt., clear, 9" l........................................ 38

Relish dish, three-part, American patt., clear, 9 1/2" l. ....................................... 40

Relish dish, boat-shaped, handled, divided, American patt., clear, 12" l. ............... 20

Rose bowl, American patt., clear, 5" d.............. 35

*Baroque Rose Bowl*

Rose bowl, Baroque patt., blue (ILLUS.) ... **75-100**

Rose bowl Colony patt., footed, clear ............. 125

Salt & pepper shakers Century patt., clear, pr. ........................................................ 20

Salt & pepper shakers, Coronet patt., footed, clear, pr. ...................................... 15

Salver, Century patt., clear, 12 1/4" .................. 36

Sauce boat & underplate, American patt., clear, 2 pcs. ......................................... 55

Sherbet, American patt., footed, handled, clear, 4 1/2 oz. ...................................... 140

Sherbet, American patt., low, flared, clear, 5 oz., 3 1/4" h. .......................................... 9

Sherbet, American Lady patt., clear, 5 1/2 oz., 4 1/8" h. ............................................ 14

Sherbet, American Lady patt., cobalt blue, 5 1/2 oz., 4 1/8" h. .................................. 45

Sherbet, Century patt., clear, 5 1/2 oz., 4 1/4" h. ............................................... 13

Sherbet, Navarre patt., clear, 6 oz. ................... 24

Sherbet, Jamestown patt., blue, 6 1/2 oz., 4 1/4" h. ...................................................... 17

Shrimp bowl, American patt., clear, 12 1/4" ....................................................... 395

Spice box, cov., American patt., clear ............. 900

Straw jar, cov., American patt., clear ............... 323

Sugar bowl, cov., American patt., clear, 5 1/4" h. ................................................. 60

Sugar bowl, individual, Baroque patt., Topaz ....................................................... 16

Sugar bowl, individual, Colony patt., clear.......... 6

Sugar bowl, individual, Century patt., clear, 3 3/8" h. .......................................... 9

Sugar bowl, American patt., clear, medium........ 9

Sugar bowl, American patt., hexagonal foot, clear ......................................... 800

Sugar bowl, Chintz etching, clear .................... 20

Sugar shaker, American patt., clear, tall.......... 295

Tray, muffin, handled, Colony patt., clear, 8 3/8" ................................................. 45

Tray, snack, Colony patt., clear, 10 1/2"............ 40

Trifle bowl, American patt., deep, clear............ 395

Tumbler, juice, footed, American Lady patt., clear, 5 oz., 4 1/8" h. ............................ 14

Tumbler, juice, footed, Jamestown patt., smoke, 5 oz., 4 3/4" h.................................. 10

**Tumbler,** juice, footed, American Lady patt., cobalt blue, 5 oz., 4 1/8" h. .................... 65

**Tumbler,** footed, American patt., clear, 9 oz., 4 3/8" h. ......................................................... 12

**Tumbler** water, Coin patt., ruby, 9 oz., 4 1/4" h. .......................................................... 105

**Tumbler,** water, Jamestown patt., amber, 9 oz., 4 1/4" h. ..................................................... 6

**Tumbler,** ice tea, footed, Colony patt., clear, 12 oz., 4 7/8" h. ..................................... 26

**Tumbler,** ice tea, footed, Holly cutting, clear, 12 oz., 6" h. ..................................... 14

**Vase,** sweet pea, 4 1/2" h., American patt., clear .............................................................. 75

**Vase,** 6" h., American patt., aqua ..................... 150

**Vase,** 6" h., American patt., peach .................. 150

**Vase,** 6" h., handled, Coronet patt., clear .......... 45

**Vase,** bud, 6" d., Colony patt., clear ................. 12

**Vase,** 7" h., footed, cupped, Colony patt., clear .............................................................. 45

**Vase,** 7 1/2" h., handled, Century patt., clear .............................................................. 75

**Water bottle,** American patt., clear, 9 1/4" h., 44 oz. ............................................. 800

**Wine,** American Lady patt., clear, 2 1/2 oz. ........ 28

**Wine,** American patt., clear, 2 1/2 oz., 4 3/8" h. .......................................................... 12

**Wine,** Romance etching, clear, 3 oz. ................. 35

**Wine,** Jamestown patt., amber, 4 oz., 4 5/16" h. .......................................................... 8

**Wine,** Jamestown patt., green, 4 5/16" h., 4 oz. .................................................................... 20

**Wine,** Chintz etching, clear .............................. 39

# GALLÉ

*Gallé glass was made in Nancy, France, by Emile Gallé, a founder of the Nancy School and a leader in the Art Nouveau movement in France. Much of his glass, both enameled and cameo, is decorated with naturalistic motifs. The finest pieces were made in the last two decades of the 19th century and the opening years of the 20th.*

*Pieces marked with a star preceding the name were made between 1904, the year of Gallé's death, and 1914.*

*Gallé Marks*

**Cameo flower bowl,** pale pink footed bowl w/four pulled points, overlaid in light yellowish green & amber & etched w/clusters of blossoms on leafy branches, signed w/a star & signature among the leaves, ca. 1904, 7 3/4" d., 4 1/4" h. (several bubble bursts, wear to interior) ..... **$690**

**Cameo vase,** 4 3/4" h., swelled & gently flaring cylindrical body w/a narrow angled shoulder below the short, wide rolled neck, pinkish lavender layered in pastel cornflower blue, etched w/blossoms w/subtle shading, signed at side ....... 690

**Cameo vase,** 6 1/8" h., wide cylindrical body w/flared rim, grey shaded to pink at interior base & layered in leaf green, etched as a branch w/suspended blossoms, cameo signed w/a star above the stepped base, ca. 1904 ............................ 460

**Cameo vase,** 8" h., bulbous base w/a tall slender neck, grey w/pink streaks, layered in periwinkle & green, acid-etched w/a stalk of stylized flowers, signed near base .............................................................. 863

**Cameo vase,** 10" h., baluster-form, yellow cased in deep rose & maroon & cameo-carved around the body w/large branches of wild roses, signed ................. **4,235**

*Gallé Vase with Apples*

**Cameo vase,** 11 5/8" h., ovoid body w/a wide flat mouth, grey infused w/yellow, overlaid w/lime green & deep amber & molded in medium- and low-relief w/branches laden w/ripening apples, signed in cameo (ILLUS.) ......................... **9,775**

**Cameo vase,** 11 5/8" h., simple ovoid body tapering to a short neck w/a flattened rim, shaded light to dark golden yellow overlaid w/deep rose & maroon & cut w/branches of fuchsia dropping from the rim, signed, ca. 1925 .............................. **8,625**

**Cameo vase,** 13" h., footed tall slender ovoid body tapering to a flattened flared cylindrical neck, amber & frosted clear layered in light green & olive green & etched as leafy Japanese maple branches, signed near base ....................... 920

**Cameo vase,** 13" h., wide thin cushion foot below the tall slightly tapering cylindrical body in grey & yellow overlaid in purple & etched w/a blossoming clematis vine, signed ............................................................ 978

**Cameo vase,** 13 1/4" h., a low cushion foot below the tall waisted cylindrical body, clear w/pink streaks layered in light green & etched w/a vine & delicate hanging blossom, signed on the side .......... 575

**Cameo vase,** 14 1/2" h., wide squatty bulbous body w/angled low shoulder tapering sharply up to the short flared & flattened neck, mottled golden yellow & orange overlaid in dark reddish orange & maroon & cameo cut around the sides w/large swirled calla lily blossoms & leafage, signed, ca. 1925 ............................ **74,000**

*Two Tall Gallé Cameo Vases*

**Cameo vase,** 15 1/2" h., elongated & flared neck on an ovoid body, pale transparent smoky amber layered in opaque pink & etched w/hanging vines of wisteria over clouds, signed among the clouds, large polished pontil (ILLUS. right) .................... **1,380**
**Cameo vase,** 15 5/8" h., tall footed ovoid form w/the shoulder tapering to a short cylindrical neck, golden yellow overlaid in dark green, cameo cut w/dark green leafy branches w/mold-blown pale blue plums, signed, ca. 1900 ........................... **6,900**
**Cameo vase,** 19 7/8" h., footed slender ovoid body tapering to a flat trumpet neck, yellow overlaid w/maroon & cameo cut w/trumpet vine & blossoms pendent from the upper rim, signed, ca. 1900 ........................................................ **11,500**
**Cameo vase,** 20 1/8" h., tall ovoid body w/angled shoulder centered by a short widely flaring trumpet neck, mottled golden yellow & orange overlaid w/blue & dark greenish brown, cameo cut w/upright clusters of blue trumpet-form blossoms on leafy branches, signed, ca. 1900 ........................................................ **10,925**
**Cameo vase,** 23 1/2" h., cylindrical w/swollen base, grey & rose layered in chartreuse & leaf greens, etched w/leafy branches & suspended chains of florettes, cameo-signed w/a star, ca. 1904 (ILLUS. left) .............................................. **2,070**
**Cameo vase,** 24 3/4" h., tall baluster-form body w/short trumpet neck, mottled golden yellow overlaid in dark green & blue, cameo cut w/large pendent clusters of blue wisteria & leafy branches, signed, ca. 1900 ..................................... **28,750**
**Cameo vase,** 29" h., tall slender baluster-form w/wide cushion foot & short flattened flaring neck, cream & tan overlaid w/pale green & light brown & cameo cut

overall w/large leafy hydrangea-type flowers, signed, ca. 1900 ......................... **6,325**
**Tazza,** a trefoil dish in amber applied & enameled w/pink & green thistles, the underside acid-etched w/leaves, on a pedestal silver foot chased w/thistles, signed in enamel "Cristallerie - d'Emile Gallé - à Nancy," ca. 1900, 5 1/8" d. ......... **1,380**
**Vase,** 8 1/2" h., barrel-form in transparent topaz etched & enameled as grains of barley in naturalistic colors, signed near base, ca. 1890 (some enamel wear) ........... **863**

# HEISEY

*Numerous types of fine glass were made by A.H. Heisey & Co., Newark, Ohio, from 1895. The company's trademark, an H enclosed within a diamond, has become known to most glass collectors. The company's name and molds were acquired by Imperial Glass Co., Bellaire, Ohio, in 1958, and some pieces have been reissued. The glass listed below consists of miscellaneous pieces and types. Also see ANIMALS and PATTERN GLASS under "glass."*

*Heisey Diamond "H" Mark*

**Ashtray,** Mahabar patt., clear, 3" sq. .............. **$12**
**Basket,** Lariat patt., footed, clear, 10" ............. **225**
**Bowl,** 6" d., Empress patt., Sahara .................... **35**
**Bowl,** 8" d., Rococo patt., clear ......................... **85**
**Bowl,** gardenia, 9" d., Queen Ann patt., Orchid etching, clear ................................... **60**
**Butter dish,** cov., square, Orchid etching, clear ............................................................ **235**
**Butter dish,** cov., Rose etching, clear, cabachon, 1/4 lb. ........................................ **375**
**Candleholder,** Queen Ann patt., No. 1509, dolphin-footed, clear ................................... **45**
**Candlesticks,** Pluto patt., No. 114, Moongleam, 3 1/2" h., pr. .............................. **60**
**Candlesticks** two-light, Lariat patt., clear, pr. ...................................................................... **70**
**Candlesticks** two-light, Lariat patt. w/Moonglo cutting clear, pr. .......................... **80**
**Candlesticks,** three-light, Rose etching, clear, pr. .......................................................... **300**
**Candy dish,** cov., Lariat patt., caramel ............. **75**
**Candy dish,** cov., Rose etching, clear, tall, seahorse stem ............................................... **250**
**Candy dish,** Orchid etching, clear, tall w/seahorse stem ......................................... **250**
**Candy dish,** cov., Plantation patt., clear, 5" h. .............................................................. **195**
**Celery tray,** Empress patt., Sahara .................... **35**
**Champagne,** saucer-type, Carcassone patt., clear stem w/Sahara bowl, 6 oz. .......... **35**
**Champagne,** saucer-type, Old Dominion patt., Empress etching, clear stem w/Marigold bowl .............................................. **20**

**Cigarette holder,** square, footed, Orchid etching, clear..................................................... 99
**Coaster,** Lariat patt., clear ................................. 12
**Cocktail,** American Lady patt., cobalt blue, 3 1/2 oz., 4" h.......................................................... 75
**Cocktail,** Carcassone patt., clear stem w/Sahara bowl, 3 oz........................................ 35
**Cocktail,** Lariat patt. w/Moonglo cutting, clear ................................................................. 25
**Cocktail,** saucer-type, Old Dominion patt., Empress etching, clear stem w/Marigold bowl ................................................................... 20
**Cocktail icer w/insert,** Orchid etching, clear .............................................................. 275
**Compote,** 6" h., Waverly patt., Orchid etching, clear................................................... 50
**Compote,** 7" h., oval, Rose etching, clear........ 165
**Compote,** Orchid etching, low, footed, clear .............................................................. 50
**Cordial,** Chintz patt., No. 3389, clear, 1 oz. ..... 120
**Cornucopia-vase,** Warwick patt., cobalt blue, signed, 5 1/2" h........................................ 125
**Creamer,** Empress patt., dolphin-footed, Sahara................................................................ 40
**Creamer,** Empress patt., pink .......................... 50
**Creamer,** Ridgeleigh patt., clear ...................... 30
**Creamer,** individual size, Ridgeleigh patt., clear ................................................................. 20
**Creamer & sugar bowl,** individual, Empress patt., oval, Sahara, pr.................... 70
**Cruet,** Lariat patt., oil, clear, 6 oz. ..................... 75
**Cruet w/stopper,** Orchid etching, footed, 3 oz. ...................................................................... 200
**Cruet w/stopper,** Rose etching, clear.............. 225
**Cup,** Old Sandwich patt., pink ........................... 60
**Cup,** Waverly patt., clear ..................................... 12
**Cup & saucer,** Waverly patt., clear.................... 20
**Decanter w/sterling stopper,** sherry, Orchid etching, clear ...................................... 270
**Decanter w/stopper,** sherry, oval, Orchid etching, clear................................................... 360
**Goblet,** Empress patt., Sahara, 9 oz. ............... 65
**Goblet,** blown, Lariat patt., clear, 10 oz. ......... 22
**Goblet,** water, Lariat patt. w/Moonglo cutting, clear, 10 oz.......................................... 27
**Goblet,** water, Orchid etching, clear, tall, 10 oz. ................................................................. 50
**Goblet,** Carcassone patt., clear stem w/Sahara bowl, 11 oz.................................... 50
**Goblet,** Carcassone patt., clear stem w/Sahara bowl, 11 oz., short....................... 45
**Goblet,** Victorian patt., two-ball stem, clear ....... 26
**Goblets,** water, Victorian patt., clear, 9 oz., set of 8 .......................................................... 110
**Mustard jar, cover & spoon,** Empress patt., Sahara............................................... 90
**Nut dish,** Empress patt., footed, Sahara............ 30
**Parfait,** Yeoman patt., clear ................................. 9
**Pitcher,** Rose etching, clear, 76 oz. ............... 660
**Pitcher,** Orchid etching, clear........................... 535
**Plate,** 7" d., Empress patt., Sahara ................... 15
**Plate,** 7" d., Empress patt., Tangerine............. 165
**Plate,** 7" d., two-handled, Crystolite patt., clear ................................................................. 20
**Plate,** salad, 7" d., Crystolite patt., clear............ 15
**Plate,** 7 1/2" d., Empress patt., Alexandrite........ 90
**Plate,** 8" sq.., Empress patt., Sahara ................. 22
**Plate,** torte, 14" d., Waverly patt., Rose etching, clear .................................................. 79

**Plate,** dinner, Lariat patt., clear ....................... 115
**Plate,** dinner, Rose etching, clear .................. 395
**Plate,** Orchid etching, center-handled, clear..... 135
**Platter,** dinner, Orchid etching, clear............... 235
**Punch cup,** Lariat patt., clear .............................. 6
**Punch set:** 14" d. punch bowl, 21" d. underplate, six punch cups & ladle; Lariat patt., clear, 9 pcs. .................................... 190
**Relish dish,** Plantation patt., four-part, clear, 8" l. .................................................... 70
**Relish dish,** Crystolite patt., three-part, clear, 9 1/2" ................................................... 29
**Relish dish,** Rose etching, three-part, oval, clear, 11" l. ............................................ 80
**Relish dish,** Lariat patt., three-part, clear, 12"........................................................... 28
**Salt & pepper shakers,** Orchid etching, clear, pr. ............................................................ 85
**Sherbet,** blown Lariat patt., clear, 5 oz.............. 14
**Sherbet,** Carcassone patt., clear stem w/Sahara bowl, 6 oz..................................... 40
**Sherbet,** Lariat patt. w/Moonglo cutting, clear ................................................................. 20
**Sherbet** Old Dominion patt., Empress etching, clear stem w/Marigold bowl, low.............. 18
**Sherbet,** Victorian patt., two-ball stem, clear ................................................................. 15
**Sugar bowl,** Empress patt., dolphin-footed, Sahara................................................................ 40
**Sugar bowl,** Lariat patt., clear............................ 20
**Tumbler,** Arch patt., cobalt blue ...................... 100
**Tumbler,** Duquesne patt., Tangerine, 5 1/4" h. ...................................................... 155
**Tumbler,** juice, Carcassone patt., clear stem w/Sahara bowl, 5 oz. ............................ 40
**Tumbler,** juice, Provincial patt., footed, clear, 5 oz....................................................... 11
**Tumbler,** Provincial patt., footed, clear, 8 oz. ...................................................................... 15
**Tumbler,** Greek Key patt., flat, clear, 10 oz........ 99
**Tumbler,** ice tea, Twentieth Century patt., Dawn ............................................................. 60
**Tumbler,** ice tea, Lariat patt., Moonglo cutting, footed, clear, 12 oz............................ 32
**Vase,** 4" h., Ivy etching, No. 4224, clear........... 275
**Vase,** 7" h., Lariat patt., footed, clear ................ 45
**Vase,** 7" h., Warwick patt., Sahara .................... 95
**Violet vase,** Orchid etching, clear, 4" h. ........... 145
**Wine,** pressed Lariat patt., clear, 3 1/2 oz. ......... 20

# IMPERIAL

*Imperial Marks*

*Imperial Glass Company, Bellaire, Ohio was organized in 1901 and was in continuous production, except for very brief periods, until its closing in June 1984. It had been a major producer of Carnival Glass earlier in this century and also produced*

other types of glass, including an art glass line
called "Free Hand Ware" during the 1920s and its
"Jewels" about 1916. The company acquired a
number of molds of other earlier factories, including
the Cambridge and A.H. Heisey Companies, and
reissued numerous items through the years. Also
see CARNIVAL GLASS under Glass.

## CANDLEWICK

**Ashtray,** No. 400/118, clear ............................ **$12**
**Baked apple dish,** No. 400/53X, clear,
6 1/2" ....................................................................... 25
**Bowl,** 5", heart-shaped, No. 400/49H, clear..... **175**
**Bowl,** 6" d., clear, No. 400/3F ............................ 12
**Bowl,** 10" d., fruit, footed, No. 400/103C,
clear ....................................................................... 229
**Bowl,** 9-10", heart-shaped, No. 400/73H,
clear ....................................................................... 55
**Butter dish,** cov., No. 400/276, clear............... 140
**Cake plate,** No. 400/160, clear w/swirl cen-
ter, 72 candle holes in rim, 13-14" d ........... 390
**Candleholders,** No. 400/81, 3 1/2" h.,
clear ....................................................................... 112
**Candleholders,** No. 400/207, 4 1/2" h.,
clear, pr. .............................................................. 260
**Candy box,** cov., three-part, No. 400/110,
clear, 7" d. ........................................................... 172
**Cheese & cracker set,** No. 400/88, clear,
10" d., 2 pc. ......................................................... 65
**Compote,** No. 400/220, clear, 5" h.................... 145

*Imperial Compote Rose Decoration*

**Compote,** 10" h., crimped, three-bead
stem, No. 400/103F, clear w/h.p. pink
roses & blue ribbons (ILLUS.) .............. **260-400**
**Cordial,** No. 3400, clear, 1 oz. ........................... 48
**Creamer & sugar bowl,** individual, No.
400/122, clear, pr. .......................................... 21
**Cruet w/original stopper,** No. 400/119,
clear ..................................................................... 25
**Cup & saucer,** demitasse, No. 400/77AD,
clear ..................................................................... 30
**Goblet,** No. 400/190, water, clear, 10 oz. .......... 25
**Icer & liner,** No. 400/53, clear.......................... 135
**Mayonnaise set:** divided bowl & under-
plate; No. 400/84, clear, 2 pcs. ..................... 80
**Plate,** luncheon, 9" d., No. 400/7D, clear ........... 15
**Punch set:** 13" d. punch bowl, 17" d.
cupped-edge underplate, 12 cups &
ladle; No. 400/20, clear, 15 pcs.................... 260
**Relish dish,** two-part, No. 400/234, clear,
7" sq. ...................................................................... 140
**Relish tray,** three-part, No. 400/213, han-
dled, clear, 10" l................................................ 74

**Salt dip,** No. 400/61, clear, 2" ........................... 12
**Salt shaker w/chrome top,** No. 400/96,
clear ..................................................................... 8
**Seafood cocktail,** No. 400/190, clear,
3 1/2-4 oz. .......................................................... 89
**Tray,** No. 400/72C, two-handled, crimped,
clear, 10" ............................................................. 30
**Tumbler,** water, No. 400/19, clear, 10 oz. .......... 15
**Vegetable bowl,** No. 400/69B, clear w/cut-
ting, 8 1/2" d. ...................................................... 55
**Wine,** No. 3400, clear, 4 oz. ............................... 16

## CAPE COD

**Bar bottle,** clear ................................................. 150
**Basket,** No. 160/73/0, clear............................... 350
**Bowl,** 11" oval, divided, No. 160/125, clear....... 95
**Center bowl,** No. 160/75L, ruffled edge,
clear ..................................................................... 65
**Coaster,** No. 160/78, clear .................................. 10
**Cruet w/original stopper,** No. 160/119,
amber, 4 oz. ........................................................ 45
**Decanter w/original stopper,** No.
160/163, clear, 30 oz. ...................................... 75
**Decanters w/original stoppers,** square-
shaped, clear, in chrome rack w/lock, the
set ........................................................................ 225
**Goblet,** water, No. 1602, Verde green, 9
oz. .......................................................................... 8
**Mug,** clear, 12 oz................................................... 50
**Pitcher w/ice lip,** No. 160/19, clear, 40 oz. ....... 85
**Salt & pepper mill,** amber, pr. ........................... 55
**Salt & pepper shakers w/original tops,**
Verde green, pr. ................................................ 40
**Whiskey set w/metal rack,** No. 160/260,
clear bottles w/raised letters "Bourbon,"
"Rye" & "Scotch," the set ........................... 650

# MISCELLANEOUS PATTERNS & LINES

## FREE HAND WARE

**Candlestick,** slender baluster-form stem
w/cushion foot in clear w/white heart &
vine decoration, a tall cylindrical iridescent dark blue socket, original paper
label, 10" h. ..................................................... 440
**Vase,** 8 1/2" h., cylindrical, iridescent green
heart & vine design on a white ground,
marigold lining w/some wear....................... 385
**Vase,** 10" h., tall slender form, iridescent
orange exterior w/deep orange throat .......... 193

## MOLLY

*Molly Rose Bowl w/Silver Deposit*

**Rose bowl,** black w/silver deposit floral decoration, 5" h. (ILLUS.) .......................... **40-50**

# LACY

*Lacy Glass is a general term developed by collectors many years ago to cover the earliest type of pressed glass produced in this country. "Lacy" refers to the fact that most of these early patterns consisted of scrolls and geometric designs against a finely stippled background which gives the glass the look of fine lace. Formerly this glass was often referred to as "Sandwich" for the Boston & Sandwich Glass Company of Sandwich, Massachusetts which produced a great deal of this ware. Today, however, collectors realize that many other factories on the East Coast and in the Pittsburgh, Pennsylvania and Wheeling, West Virginia areas also made lacy glass from the 1820s into the 1840s. All pieces listed are clear unless otherwise noted. Numbers after salt dips refer to listings in Pressed Glass Salt Dishes of the Lacy Period, 1825-1850, by Logan W. and Dorothy B. Neal. Also see CUP PLATES and SANDWICH GLASS.*

**Bowl,** toy-size, footed oval form w/scalloped rim & lacy sides, very light aqua, 3/4" h. (two small chips on base) ..... **$165**

**Compote,** open, 5 3/4" d., 3 3/4" h., Roman Rosette patt., wide shallow flared bowl joined by a wafer to the unrecorded ribbed pedestal base (few chips, mold roughness) .......................................... **198**

*Large Roman Rosette Lacy Compote*

**Compote,** open, 6 1/4" d., 10 1/2" h., Roman Rosette patt., deep widely flaring bowl attached w/a wafer to the short stem & round patterned base, one inch line & several small rim chips (ILLUS.) ........ **825**

**Creamer,** toy-size, footed ovoid body w/flared rim & integral handle, lacy scroll design, light fiery opalescent, 1 3/4" h. (mold roughness, base chips) ..................... **385**

**Creamer,** toy-size, footed ovoid body w/flared rim & integral handle, lacy scroll design, rare smokey amethyst, 1 3/4" h. (crack next to handle, chip w/short crack on base) ............................................................. **495**

**Dish,** toy-size, shallow oval form w/scrolled lacy border design, clear, 3" l. (light mold roughness) ..................................................... **66**

**Lamp,** miniature, blown spherical font on an appied knopped stem on an inverted lacy cup plate foot, 4" h. (chips on base) ..... **385**

**Salt dip,** footed round & flared bowl w/a design of panels w/fine diamond point below a bull's-eye each separated by a

thin rim, purplish blue, PR-1b (mold roughness, slight rim underfill) .................... **248**

*Rare Lafayet Boat Salt Dip*

**Salt dip,** model of a sidewheeler, "Lafayet" on side of wheel, silvery opaque light blue, BT-8 (ILLUS.) ..................................... **2,750**

**Salt dip,** rectangular w/corner posts & tiny knob feet, the sides w/embossed baskets of fruit, medium green, JY2b, 3" l. (rim chips) ................................................... **193**

**Salt dip,** rectangular w/scrolled ends & flat rectangular base, the sides w/branched sprigs below a rim band of roundels, clear (OG-1) ................................................... **523**

**Salt dip,** sleigh-form, inwardly scrolled ends & outscrolled legs, scrolled rim & scroll designs on the sides, cobalt blue, CN-1A (chip on one corner) ........................ **413**

**Tea plate,** octagonal, beaded outer border, inner border of leafy scrolls around a central scene of a tall-masted sailing ship above "Union," 6 5/8" w. (small rim chips) ................................................................ **963**

**Tea plate,** octagonal, shells & scrolls around central oval reserve showing a sidewheel steamboat & "Pittsburgh," 6 1/2" w. (edge chips) ................................. **880**

*Midwestern Lacy Tea Plate*

**Tea plate,** round w/finely scalloped rim, border of bull's-eyes & shells around a band of roundels & a central pinwheel, probably Midwestern, blue, ca. 1830-45, light mold roundness, 5 7/8" d. (ILLUS.) ...... **220**

# LALIQUE

*Fine glass, which includes numerous extraordinary molded articles, has been made by the glasshouse established by René Lalique early in this century in France. The firm was carried on by his son, Marc, until his death in 1977 and is now headed by Marc's daughter, Marie-Claude. All Lal-*

*ique glass is marked, usually on, or near, the bottom with either an engraved or molded signature. Unless otherwise noted, we list only those pieces marked "R. Lalique" produced before the death of René Lalique in 1945.*

# R. LALIQUE

### FRANCE

$R\ LALIQUE$

### FRANCE

*R. Lalique France N°3152*

### Lalique Marks

**Ashtray,** "Dindon," circular dish centering a molded turkey, smoky brown, inscribed "R. Lalique - France - No. 287," ca. 1925, 3" h. .................................................. **$690**

**Bowl,** 12" d., "Montigny," wide shallow round form, the exterior molded in medium-relief w/four serrated-edge leaves, raised on a ring of pyramidal feet centering a flowerhead, smoky brown, molded "R. Lalique - France," introduced in 1928, molded mark.................................. **575**

**Clock,** table model, an upright rounded flat colorless sheet etched w/two classical maidens wrapping a wreath of flowers around the central round clock dial, raised in a flaring rectangular metal base w/gilt leafy scroll design & raised on small knob feet, the base lighted, ca. 1926, 13 1/2" l., 13 1/2" h. (slight wear & abrasions to base)..................................... **6,900**

**Clock,** table model, "Deux Figurines," grey cast in reverse w/two robed females amid flowers flanking the round clock dial, inset into a rectangular raised metal base w/internal light source, molded "R. Lalique," introduced in 1926, 14 1/2" h.... **20,700**

*L'Air du Temps Display Bottle*

**Display bottle w/stopper,** "L'Air du Temps," ovoid spiral-ribbed clear bottle supporting a stopper w/a pair of large fly-

ing doves in frosted clear w/polished highlights, model created in 1947, overall 12 1/4" h. (ILLUS.) .................................... **403**

**Hood ornament,** a slender press-molded ovoid disk in clear w/a frosted intaglio picture of a running greyhound, signed "R. Lalique France," ca. 1928, 7 3/4" l....... **1,725**

**Hood ornament,** "Longchamps," frosted clear model in full-relief of a horse head, molded "R. Lalique," introduced in 1929, 5" h. (polished chip on one ear) ................ **2,530**

**Luminaire,** "Gros Poisson," grey glass full-relief model of a fresh water fish, resting on a cast bronze round base pierce-cast w/seaweed, glass molded "R. Lalique," base inscribed "R.Lalique," introduced in 1922, 17" w., overall 15 1/8" h.................. **6,900**

**Luminaire,** "Groupe de six moineaux," rectangular nickled-metal light box base supporting a clear frosted row of small birds in various positions, introduced in 1933, acid-stamped "R. Lalique - France," 11 3/4" l., 2 pcs. ........................ **10,925**

**Platter,** 14 1/2" d., "Pivoines," round & slightly dished grey form molded w/a large swirled branch of stylized rounded peony-like blossoms & slender leaves all enameled in dark blue, signed in intaglio "R. Lalique," introduced in 1920 (minor rim chip) ........................................................ **9,200**

**Serving set:** ten 7 3/4" d. plates & an 11" d. tray; Black Alga, each in black satin polished crystal w/molded aquatic plant designs, bases signed "Lalique France," designed by Marc Lalique, ca. 1950, the set ................................................ **633**

**Vase,** 7 1/8" h., "Danaides," footed swelled cylindrical form, opalescent, molded in low-relief w/a band of stylized maidens emptying vessels of water, signed "R. Lalique - France - No. 972," introduced in 1926 ...................................................... **3,737**

**Vase,** 8 1/2" h., "Domremy," tapering ovoid opalescent body molded in relief w/thistles, inscribed "R. Lalique - France," introduced in 1926.................................... **1,495**

**Vase,** 9 1/2" h., "Aras," footed widely swelled squatty bulbous form w/a small short tapering neck at the top, rich wintergreen molded overall w/large exotic birds perched on entwined berried vines, original white patina, inscribed "R. Lalique France No. 919," introduced in 1924 ...................................................... **11,500**

**Vases,** 16" h., "Palestre," flat-bottomed ovoid body w/a short, wide flared rim, molded around the sides w/standing & walking nude males in various poses, frosted clear, unsigned, drilled for use as lamps, introduced in 1928, pr.................. **17,250**

# LOETZ

*Iridescent glass, some of it somewhat resembling that of Tiffany and other contemporary glasshouses, was produced by the Bohemian firm of J. Loetz Witwe of Klostermule and is referred to as Loetz. Some cameo pieces were also made. Not all pieces are marked.*

*Loetz Mark*

*Rare Loetz Cameo Vase*

**Cameo vase,** 10 1/4" h., swelled cylindrical form w/lightly flared rim, yellow overlaid in grey & etched w/vertical bands w/panels of stylized leafy vines above diamond & dot designs, designed by Josef Hoffmann, Model 8127, ca. 1912, unsigned (ILLUS.)................................................... **$9,200**

**Vase,** 4 3/4" h., "Lava," ovoid body, cobalt blue, the surface of bubbled decoration w/bluish green iridescence, polished pontil (rim imperfection)............................... **518**

**Vase,** 5" h., pinched ovoid form in amber decorated w/pulled iridescent gold threads in a scalloped drapery design, highlighted w/opalescent blue lustre, polished pontil, ca. 1900 (slight wear to iridescence)...................................................... **575**

**Vase,** 5 1/2" h., simple ovoid form w/a short neck & widely flaring flattened rim, pale pink decorated w/pulled & swirled silver iridescent threads & oval dots over gold oil spot lustre surface, polished pontil, ca. 1900......................................... **1,495**

**Vase,** 6" h., waisted cylindrical upper body on a tapered rounded base, grey shaded w/peach & w/cobalt blue trailings & amber oil spot decoration, overlaid w/engraved silver overlay flowers & whiplash vines, ca. 1900......................... **2,587**

**Vase,** 6 1/2" d., squatty domed form w/the sides deeply pinched in & twisted below a pulled & flaring rim w/three large lobes, overall swirled silvery blue iridescent design, signed......................................... **1,950**

**Vase,** 6 3/4" h., ovoid body w/slightly everted lip, amber w/pink iridescent trailings & heart-form leaves, unsigned, ca. 1900 ......................................................... **1,610**

# MARY GREGORY

*Glass enameled in white with silhouette-type figures, primarily of children, is now termed "Mary Gergory" and was attributed to the Boston and Sandwich Glass Company. However, recent research has proven conclusively that this was not decorated by Mary Gregory, nor was it made at the Sandwich plant. Miss Gregory was employed by Boston and Sandwich Glass Company as a decorator; however, records show her assignment was the painting of naturalistic landscape scenes on larger items such as lamps and shades, but never the charming children for which her name has become synonymous. Further, in the inspection of fragments from the factory site, no paintings of children were found.*

*It is now known that all wares collectors call "Mary Gregory" originated in Bohemia beginning in the late 19th century and were extensively exported to England and the United States well into this century.*

*For further information, see* The Glass Industry in Sandwich, Volume #4, *by Raymond E. Barlow and Joan E. Kaiser, and the book,* Mary Gregory Glassware, 1880-1900, *by R. & D. Truitt.*

**Cologne bottle w/stopper,** footed optic ribbed ovoid body w/a ringed short cylindrical neck w/flared rim, amber w/white enameled figure of a young lady in a garden, clear bubbled stopper, 3" d., 8" h. ..... **$175**

*Mary Gregory Decanter with Girl*

**Decanter w/stopper,** slightly flaring cylindrical optic ribbed body w/a wide tapering shoulder centering a tall cylindrical neck w/flared rim, sapphire blue w/a white enameled figure of a young girl walking in a garden, 3 1/2" d., 8 1/2" h. (ILLUS.)...................................................... **195**

**Jewel box w/hinged cover,** round squatty bulbous optic ribbed form, amber w/white enameled figure on the cover of a

boy walking & holding up a bird,
3 1/2" d., 3 1/4" h. (ILLUS. below) ............... **225**

*Mary Gregory Jewel Box*

*Black Amethyst Mary Gregory Vase*

**Vase,** 7" h., 3 1/2" d., footed squatty bulbous tapering base w/wide shoulder
centered by a knob at the base of a tall
slender trumpet neck, black amethyst
w/white enameled girl in a garden
(ILLUS.) ...................................................... **135**

**Vases,** 10 3/4" h., tall waisted cylindrical
form w/a wide ringed shoulder below the
slightly flaring short neck, applied clear
rigaree down each side, dark green
w/white enameled figure of a youth on
one & a maiden on the other, each
w/colored enamel faces, pr. (pinpoint
flakes) ........................................................ **358**

# MILK GLASS

*Opaque white glass, or "opal," has been called
"milk-white glass" perhaps to distinguish it from
transparent or "clear-white glass." Resembling fine
white porcelain, it was viewed as an inexpensive
substitute. Opacity is obtained by adding bone ash
or oxide of tin to clear molten glass. By the addition
of various coloring agents, the opaque mixture can
be turned into blue milk glass, or pink, yellow,
green, caramel, even black milk glass. Collectors of
milk glass now accept not only the white variety but
virtually any opaque colors and color mixtures,
including slag or marbled glass. It has been made
in numerous forms and shapes in this country and
abroad from about the first quarter of the 19th century. It is still being produced, and there are many
reproductions of earlier pieces. Pieces are all-white
unless otherwise noted. Also see HISTORICAL,
PATTERN GLASS and WESTMORELAND.*

**Animal covered dish,** Crouching Rabbit,
Portieux, 7" l. ................................................. **$275**

**Animal covered dish,** Dog on Steamer
Rug w/floral base, blue, Vallerysthal,
excellent, 5" h. ............................................... **130**

**Animal covered dish,** Dog on Steamer
Rug w/floral base, opaque yellow, Val-
lerysthal, round paper label "P.V.
France," excellent, 5" h. ............................... **260**

**Animal covered dish,** Dog, Pomeranian
on diamond & stippled base, fair paint,
Sandwich Glass Co., excellent, 4 3/4" l. ....... **450**

**Animal covered dish,** Dolphin with fish fin-
ial, Kemple, excellent, 7 1/2" l. ...................... **65**

**Animal covered dish,** Dominecker Duck
w/wavy base, glass eyes, fired-on paint,
Challinor, Taylor & Co., 8" l. (top rim chip
under tail, tiny open bubble on base) .......... **310**

**Animal covered dish,** Duck, Atterbury,
very good, 11" l. ............................................ **200**

**Animal covered dish,** Duck, blue & white
slag, L. G. Wright, Atterbury type, good,
6" l. .............................................................. **50**

**Animal covered dish,** Duck on Basket,
caramel slag satin, original factory
sticker Jan. 1946 manufacturing date,
Imperial, excellent ....................................... **50**

**Animal covered dish,** Duck on Rush
Base, very good, 5 1/2" l. .............................. **60**

**Animal covered dish,** Duck Swimming,
blue, Vallerysthal, 5" l. (mite bite on
edge) ............................................................ **80**

**Animal covered dish,** Duck Swimming,
traces of paint, Vallerysthal, 5 3/4" l.
(crack on top edge of base) ......................... **270**

**Animal covered dish,** Elephant w/rider,
blue, signed "Vallerystahl," 7" l. (broken
bubble on ear) .............................................. **600**

**Animal covered dish,** Fish, blue, some
original paint, signed "Vallerysthal," 7" l.
(small ship inside nose of fish) .................... **450**

**Animal covered dish,** Hen on Basketweave base, blue body w/white head,
Westmoreland Specialty Company
excellent, 5 1/2" l. .......................................... **35**

**Animal covered dish,** Hen on Basketweave base, blue, Vallerysthal, excel-
lent, 6" l. ....................................................... **140**

**Animal covered dish,** Hen on Basketweave base, signed "Vallerysthal,"
good, 7 1/2" l. ............................................ **200-250**

**Animal covered dish,** Hen on Flared Basketweave Base, orange slag, Kanawha,
excellent, 7 1/4" h. ......................................... **100**

**Animal covered dish,** Hen on lacy base,
blue, Atterbury, excellent, 7" l. ..................... **210**

**Animal covered dish,** Hen on lacy base,
blue marble top, white base, red eyes,
Atterbury, excellent, 7 1/2" l. ........................ **310**

**Animal covered dish,** Hen on Ribbed Base, red eyes, Atterbury, excellent, 7 1/4" l. .......................................... 160

**Animal covered dish,** Hen on rush base, excellent, 5 1/2" l. ............................................ 40

**Animal covered dish,** Hen on Scalloped Basket base, blue, Vallerysthal, top excellent, 5" l. (small flake on base rim) ......... 60

*Horse on Split-Ribbed Base Dish*

**Animal covered dish,** Horse on split-ribbed base, 1989 convention commemorative, Summit Art Glass Co., excellent, 5 1/2" l. (ILLUS.).......................................... 160

**Animal covered dish,** Hummingbird, ca. 1930s, Consolidated, excellent, 7" .............. 200

*Lamb on Split-Ribbed Base Dish*

**Animal covered dish,** Lamb on split-ribbed base, 1991 convention commemorative, Boyd's Crystal Art Glass Co., excellent, 5 1/2" l. (ILLUS.)............................ 70

**Animal covered dish,** Lion on Lacy Base, caramel slag, Imperial, excellent, 8 1/2" l. ........................................................ 160

**Animal covered dish,** Lion on split-ribbed base, McKee, top signed, mint, 5 1/2" l. (base not McKee) ....................................... 240

**Animal covered dish,** Lion, Ribbed Lion on lacy-edged base, patent-dated, Atterbury, very good, 7 1/4" l. .............................. 145

**Animal covered dish,** Love Birds, Westmoreland, marked entwined "WG" in base, good, 5 x 6" ........................................ 40

**Animal covered dish,** Mother Eagle, Challinor, Taylor, near perfect, 7" l. .............. 650

**Animal covered dish,** Peep Emerging from Egg on Basket, top sits down on flange, not on top, traces of paint, very good, 3 1/2" h. ...................................... 260

**Animal covered dish,** Peep on Basket, Gillinder, much paint, excellent, 3 1/2" h. ...... 170

**Animal covered dish,** Pig on split-ribbed base, McKee, 5 1/2" l. (chip on tail) ........... **4,100**

**Animal covered dish,** Quail on Scroll Base, excellent, 6 1/2" l. ................................ 65

**Animal covered dish,** Rabbit, green slag, 1988 convention commemorative, Summit, excellent, 5 1/2" l. ...................... 400

**Animal covered dish,** Rabbit, Lop-eared, some paint, signed "Vallerysthal," excellent, 6 1/2" l. ......................................... 725

**Animal covered dish,** Rabbit on Diamond Basket with Eggs, blue, Westmoreland Specialty Co. drilled eyes, very good, 7 1/2" l. ........................................................ 60

**Animal covered dish,** Rabbit on split-ribbed base, green w/white head, green base, excellent, 5 1/2" l. ........................... 300

**Animal covered dish,** Rabbits Cuddling, green, maker unknown, 6 1/4" l., 5 1/4" h. (lid repaired) ...................... **1,750**

**Animal covered dish,** Rooster, base & top w/stippled interior, Kemple, "K" in circle on bottom, most of paint on comb, 7 1/4" l. (slight roughness base & top rims) ........................................................ 70

**Animal covered dish,** Rooster on Basketweave Base, Challinor, Taylor, 7 1/2" l. ........................................................ 90

**Animal covered dish,** Rooster Standing, blue, signed "Portieux," 9" h. (two no-show flea bites on top) ............................... 100

**Animal covered dish,** Snail on Strawberry, Vallerysthal, 5" h. (chip on inside flange of top) ....................................................... 90

**Animal covered dish,** Snapping Turtle, excellent, 9 3/4" l. ...................................... 350

**Animal covered dish,** Squirrel, McKee, excellent, 5 1/2" l. (probably not old base) ............................................................ 225

**Animal covered dish,** Squirrel on fancy base, Vallerysthal, excellent, 5" l. .............. 90

**Animal covered dish,** Steer's Head, old eyes, Challinor Taylor, 7 7/8" l. (small chips inside bottom rim) ...................... **5,500**

**Animal covered dish,** Swan on Water, basketweave bottom, moulded eye, Challinor, Taylor, mismatch ?, 7" l. (small chips & roughness top & bottom rims) ........................................................ 160

**Animal covered dish,** Swan, open neck, signed in raised letters inside base, Vallerysthal, 5 1/2" l. (minor roughness top & bottom edges) ....................................... 80

**Animal covered dish,** Swan, purple slag, L.G. Wright, good, 5 1/2" l. ........................... 80

**Animal covered dish,** Swan with Raised Wing, flat place for glass eyes, Atterbury, excellent, 10 1/4" l. .............................. 170

**Animal covered dish,** Turkey, entwined "IG" on base, Imperial, ca. 1952-60 (ILLUS. top next page) ................................ 60

**Animal covered dish,** Turkey Standing, L.E. Smith ?, excellent, 7 1/8" h. ................... 90

**Animal covered dish,** Turtle with Snail, Portieux, excellent, 8" l. ................................ 475

*Imperial Turkey Covered Dish*

**Ashtray,** figural clown, excellent, some paint, maker unknown, 3 3/4 x 6 1/4" .......... 105

**Banana boat,** open lace top w/basket base, blue, Atterbury, excellent, 11" w. ........ 130

**Basket,** cov., w/metal tray insert to hold three perfume bottles, clear top w/embossed painted flowers, excellent, good paint, 4 1/4" d., the set (few small rust spots on tray) ....................................... 70

**Bonbon container,** La Tsarine, figural bust of Alexandra of Russia w/"LA Tsarine" & "Bonbons - John Tavernier" embossed above metal base closure, 13" h. (rusty metal closure)............................................. 200

**Bone dish,** Sardines & Salmon w/embossed inside bottom, Flaccus, excellent, 6 1/2" l., 2 pcs. ............................. 70

**Book ends,** Fighting Cock, Kemple Glass, very good, 8 1/4" h., pr. .................................. 90

**Bottle,** Baby Emerging from Egg, ground neck w/cork, black paint on baby, gold paint in cracks of shells, half of crescent-shaped label - "Rose," 2 1/2" h.................... 204

**Bottle,** Eagle patt., plastic silver lid, good, 5 3/4" h. ......................................................... 25

**Bottle,** Spanish Lady, red shawl, tambourine under arm, good, 12 1/4" h.................... 120

**Bottle,** Spanish Parrot, 8" h. (slight age lines)............................................................... 75

**Bottle w/original stopper,** Pinch Bottle, yellow, very good, rare, 9 1/2" h.................... 55

**Bottles,** Billiken, shaker caps, base impressed "The God Of Things As They Ought To Be" & "Billiken," one w/label marked "Black Pepper Union Spice Co. Chicago, Ill.," 4 1/8" h., pr. .......................... 130

**Bowl,** cov., 6 1/2" d., Rib & Scroll patt., four-footed, Vallerysthal, excellent ................ 45

**Butter dish,** cov., Cow, top & bottom signed "Vallerysthal," some paint, 7" l. (few cooling lines) ...................................... 450

**Butter dish,** cov., Dolphin & Shell, blue, Vallerysthal, excellent, 5" d. .......................... 80

**Cake salver,** Open Hand, 6 1/4" h. (nick on top edge) ................................................... 70

**Candlestick,** Sirene, Portieux, mint, 9 1/2" h. ............................................................ 250

**Candlesticks,** dolphin-footed, snake wrapped around column, blue, Portieux, excellent, 9 3/4" h., pr.................................... 206

**Candy container,** model of opera glasses, 2 7/8" h. .................................................. 150

**Candy container,** model of trunk, domed, very good ........................................................ 70

**Candy container,** Oaken Bucket, good brown paint, tin closure, small........................ 60

**Candy container,** Oaken Bucket, good green paint, tin closure, large ........................ 60

**Candy container,** Trumpet, closure, good paint ....................................................... 140

**Celery vase,** fluted, Challinor Taylor, blue, good, 8 1/4" h. ............................................. 85

**Celery vase,** 9" h., The Hunt ("Trophee,") blue, Portieux, excellent ............................... 175

**Christmas bulb,** Boy with Hat, "Little Chubby Man," good paint, excellent, 3 3/4" h. ........................................................ 35

**Cigarette box,** cov., Turtle, Thousand Eye patt., Westmoreland, excellent, 7 1/2" l........ 100

**Compote,** 6 1/4" h., open, square, Portieux, excellent............................................. 20

**Compote,** open, 6 7/8" h., Chimeres design, blue, Portieux, excellent ................... 70

*Atterbury Lacy Edge Compote*

**Compote,** open, 10" h., lacy-edge, ribbed base, Atterbury, excellent (ILLUS.) ................ 65

**Compote,** open, basin top w/dolphin base, excellent, Westmoreland? ............................ 195

**Condiment or salt set:** carousel-type w/removable revolving tray of three cups supported by a center column w/blunt, knob-like top; swirl design, Portieux, 6 1/2" h., 2 pcs. ........................................... 90

**Covered dish,** Boy with Dog (Puppy Love), divided inside, excellent, 4 1/4" .................... 410

**Covered dish,** Cinderella's Coach, L.E. Smith, excellent, 6 3/4" l. .............................. 210

**Covered dish,** Fainting Couch, good paint, very good, 5" l. ........................................... 220

**Covered dish,** heart-shaped w/"Love Laughs at Locks," good paint, excellent, 4 1/2" w. ......................................................... 50

**Covered dish,** Little Red Schoolhouse, all original labels, excellent brown paint, Westmoreland Specialty Co., excellent, 3 3/4" h. ...................................................... 150

**Covered dish,** Log Cabin, excellent brown paint, all original labels, Westmoreland Specialty Company, excellent, 4" h. ............. 130

**Covered dish,** Moses in Bulrushes, excellent, 5 1/2" l. .............................................. 250

**Covered dish,** Pineapple, blue, Vallerysthal, excellent, 7 1/2" h. ................................... 25

**Covered dish,** Robed Santa Claus on Sleigh, some gold, Dobson & Co., very good, 8" l. (ILLUS. top next page) .............. 300

**Covered dish,** Stagecoach, Fostoria, 7" l (small nick on running board) ...................... 200

*Robed Santa Claus on Sleigh Dish*

**Covered dish,** Trunk with Straps, France, 5 1/2" l. (small chip on base) .......................... 30

**Creamer,** Louis XV patt., blue, excellent, 4 1/2" h. ...................................................... 20

**Cuspidor,** lady's, fluted, blue, excellent, 8" d. ............................................................. 140

**Figure,** American Indian Chief, no paint shows "C or G" on back of right leg, excellent, 6 1/2" h. ..................................... 150

**Figure,** Dewey bust, Gillinder ?, good, 5" h. ..... 130

**Flask,** Klondike, "Woodley House" label, closure, excellent .......................................... 70

**Flask,** "Night Cap," imprinted w/face of man wearing night cap, metal closure, good paint, excellent, 4" h. ..................................... 80

**Flowerpot,** Neptune patt., Portieux, excellent, 6" h. .................................................... 200

**Fruit jar,** Owl, threaded metal closure w/embossed eagle on insert, original eyes, excellent, 6 1/4" h., 1 pt. ..................... 140

*Westmoreland Covered Gravy Boat*

**Gravy boat,** cov., figural dolphin lid, Westmoreland, excellent, 7 1/4" l. (ILLUS.) ............ 50

**Holy water font,** crucifix form, frosted, 6 1/2" h. (small chip on center under top rim) ...................................................................... 55

**Jardiniere,** Mermaid patt., blue, Portieux, 6 1/2" w., 12" l., 5" h. ................................... 375

**Lamp,** Chubby Dog, Consolidated, excellent & excellent paint, new wiring, 6 1/2" h. ................................................................ 350

**Lamp,** Skull, battery lit type, good, 3" to 5" h. ........................................................................ 40

**Lamp globe,** "Fels Point," ovoid, vase-form w/embossed sailboat, very good, 16 1/2" h. .................................................................. 100

**Marmalade jar,** Monkey patt., smooth top & rays on bottom, good paint, excellent, Duncan, 4 3/4" h. ............................................ 303

**Match holder,** figural Indian Head, Challinor, Taylor, 4 3/4" h. ..................................... 75

**Match holder,** model of an Easter basket w/chicken head on one side, & rabbit on reverse, gold & yellow paint, excellent, McKee, 4 1/4" l. ......................................... 65

**Match holder,** model of pickle, green paint, excellent ......................................................... 35

**Match holder,** Old Man with Basket, blue, Portieux, excellent, 4" h. ............................... 190

**Match holder,** pierced for hanging, figural butterfly, Alpha, good, 4 1/8" w., 3 1/2" h. ........................................................ 50

**Match holder,** pierced for hanging, Jolly Jester, 4 1/4" h. ........................................... 90

**Match holder,** pierced for hanging, figural cluster of grapes, Challinor, Taylor, good, 4 1/4" h. ......................................... 100

**Model of car,** Model T Convertible, 4" l. (age cracks inside bottom) ........................... 105

**Model of egg,** Easter Egg with Emerging Chick, flat base, Gillinder, good paint, excellent, 2 1/2" l. ...................................... 45

**Model of egg,** Easter Egg with Emerging Chick, flat base, Gillinder, good paint, excellent, 3 1/4" l. ...................................... 55

**Model of egg,** Ugly Chick Emerging from Egg, excellent, 5" l. ..................................... 260

**Model of egg,** w/recessed portrait panel, gold paint, 4 1/4" l. (rim chip) ..................... 70

**Model of rolling pin,** blown, small amount of paint, ca. 1860s, England ........................ 50

**Mug,** Bird & Wheat, Atterbury, Eastlake, excellent, some paint, 2 1/4" h. ..................... 40

**Mug,** Bleeding Heart patt., U.S. Glass, 3 1/4" h. (small chip on bottom edge, not visible from side view) ................................... 50

**Mug,** Cupids in Arches patt., good, 3 3/8" h. ......................................................... 25

**Mug,** Elephant handle, panels w/relief-molded nursery characters, signed "IG," Imperial, excellent, 3" h. ............................... 40

**Mug,** Grumpy Old Man & Woman, double-faced, opalescent, 2" h. (minor interior roughness) ..................................................... 90

**Mustard jar,** cov., hexagonal, Dutch scene decoration, Westmoreland, some paint, 4 1/4" h. (age marks) ................................... 45

**Mustard jar,** cov., square, Oriental design, gold & blue paint, Westmoreland Specialty Company, 3 1/2" h. ............................... 35

**Paperweight,** Queen Victoria Bust, black, Thomas Kidd & Co., 3 1/2" l. (small flake on left side of headdress) ........................... 850

**Paperweight,** St Bernard Dog, signed "Valerysthal," excellent paint, 5 1/2" l. (line across bottom, small flake underside) ......... 300

**Paperweight,** Turtle, PL mark by front leg, 5" l. (two stress lines on bottom rim) ............ 40

**Pin,** oval black glass cameo w/profile of woman smelling flowers, gold wire wrap around edge, excellent, 1 1/4" ....................... 50

**Pitcher,** 7" h., bulbous body w/wide cylindrical neck, pinched spout & large C-form handle, embossed decoration of three little birds perched on branches on each side w/leaf decoration around neck, traces of paint (age marks) ................. 100

**Pitcher,** 8" h., figural owl, white eyes not original, Challinor, Taylor, near perfect ........ 150

**Plaque,** "Easter," Horseshoe with Rabbit, embossed rabbit, basket, chick, signed "P.L. Co." on back, fair paint, excellent, 6 1/4" l. ......................................................... 70

**Plate,** 7 1/2" d., Maid of the Mist, boat & waterways on bottom, two flags on top, no paint, very good ........................................... 75

**Plate,** 7 1/2" d., Owl Lovers, excellent ............... 35

**Plate,** 7 1/2" d., Sunken Rabbit w/"Easter Greetings," excellent ....................................... 55

**Plate,** 7 1/2" d., U.S. Battleship Maine, variant, Gothic border, white w/color decal (minor age cracks on border & minor flea bites on back rim) .......................................... 55

**Plate,** 9 1/4" d., Lincoln on Backward C border, L. E. Smith, excellent ......................... 40

**Plate,** Columbus, center bust of Columbus w/"1492 - 1892" on shoulders, club & shell border, mounted in footed silver plate holder w/handles, very good, good paint, 9 3/4" d. ........................................... 55

**Platter,** 11 1/2" oval, Rock of Ages, white & clear, dated, excellent ................................. 105

**Pomade jar,** cov., Black Face, face forms lid, 2 7/8" h. (roughness around inside of base, several age cracks around rim) .......... 155

**Punch set:** 4 5/8" d. punch bowl & six 1 5/8" d. cups; Little Red Riding Hood patt., Nursery Rhyme series, decorated w/scenes from the fairy tale, 7 pcs. (flake on edge of two cups) .................................... 130

**Salt dip,** master, open, double, Fighting Roosters, marked "SV" on base, 6 1/4 l. (stress mark on base & rim) ......................... 130

**Salt dip,** model of sleigh w/eagle head between front runners, old gold paint on rim, 4 3/4" l. (mold roughness & glass overruns on runners, tiny peck on upper rim) ................................................................. 80

**Salt dip,** open, master, Flying Fish, blue & yellow paint, excellent, 4 1/2" l. .................... 180

**Salt dip,** open, master, Swan, Gillinder, excellent, 5 1/2" l. (no chariot) ....................... 55

**Salt & pepper shaker (dredge) w/original top,** Twin, figural stein, dispenses salt from one side & pepper from the other, Atterbury, 3 3/8" h. (1/8" chip to base rim) ................................................................. 75

**Shaker w/original top,** Hen & Rabbit, egg-shaped, M. T. Thomas, patent applied for 1900, excellent, 3" h. .................... 25

**Shaving mug,** Centennial patt., decorated w/helmeted head of Viking, base marked "Patent Shaving Mug July 16," Brooks & McGrady, 3 1/4" h. (mold mark, small crack on side) ................................................. 85

**Smoking set,** match holder & tray, some gold, 5 1/2" l., 2 pcs. (small chip under edge of tray) .................................................. 20

**Spooner,** Strawberry patt., Bryce Brothers, good, 6" h. .............................................. 40

**Sugar bowl,** cov., figural pear, blue, gold painted leaves & stem, Vallerysthal, 5 1/2" h. ......................................................... 370

**Sugar bowl,** cov., Renaissance patt., blue, Portieux, 6 1/2" d. (mold marks inside bowl, two shades of blue) ............................... 50

**Table set,** The Family, figural heads, Little Boy creamer, excellent, Little Girl spooner, very good, Mother cov. sugar, very good, Father cov. butter, the set (sugar cover (hat) missing, butter w/tiny nicks) ............................................................. 1,500

**Tray,** fish-shaped, excellent, Sweden, 10 1/2" l. .................................................... 50

**Tray,** Indian Chief's Head, lightly etched "Youghiocheny Opalescent Glass," Youghiocheny, excellent, 7 1/4" l. ................. 75

**Tray,** Old Man Smoking Pipe, excellent, 7 1/2" l. ...................................................... 65

**Trinket box,** cov., Three Kittens patt., great paint, Westmoreland, 2 1/2" sq. (chip underside lid) ............................................. 60

**Trivets/ashtrays,** marked w/entwined "IG," Imperial, good, in original box, 5 1/2" h., set of 4 ......................................................... 28

**Vase,** 9 1/4" h., Three Figures with Satyr, Portieux, very good ....................................... 80

**Water set:** pitcher & six tumblers; Floral Band patt., reddish floral trim, 7 pcs. (one tumbler w/tiny nick) ............................... 90

# MT. WASHINGTON

*A wide diversity of glass was made by the Mt. Washington Glass Company of New Bedford, Massachusetts, between 1869 and 1900. It was succeeded in 1900 by the Pairpoint Corporation. Miscellaneous types are listed below.*

**Bowl,** 8 1/2" d., squatty melon-lobed body w/applied silver plate collar, the white body decorated w/bouqets of pink roses & blue forget-me-nots .............................. **$165**

**Cameo bowl,** 9" w., rounded body w/crimped & ruffled rim, white overlaid in blue & cameo cut w/grotesque figures & scrolling vines .............................................. 495

*Mt. Washington Cracker Jar*

**Cracker jar,** cov., barrel-shaped, shaded pink & creamy white ground decorated w/delicate flowering branches, silver plate rim w/crimped edge, domed cover & arched bail swing handle, silver w/Pairpoint logo, slight wear to silver plate, 7" h. (ILLUS.) ..................................... 345

**Cracker jar,** cov., squatty bulbous melon-lobed body in creamy white enameled w/florals, silver plate rim, cover & bail handle, silver marked "Mt. Washington #4415," 7" h. ................................................ **330**

**Salt & pepper shakers w/original metal lids,** Fig mold, enameled daisy & forget-me-not decoration, pr. ................................. **193**

**Salt & pepper shakers w/original metal lids,** molded acorn shape, h.p. floral decoration, pr. ............................................. **138**

**Sugar shaker w/original metal lid,** egg-shaped, creamy satin ground enameled w/a slender branch of dainty yellow blossoms ...................................................................... **165**

## MULLER FRERES

*The Muller Brothers made acid-etched cameo and other fine glass at Luneville, France, starting in 1910 and until the outbreak of World War II in Europe.*

*Muller Freres Mark*

**Cameo vase,** 8 1/4" h., fluogravure-style, footed ovoid body tapering to a short neck w/swelled ring below the flat upright rim, dark orange over white overlaid w/pale lavender, blackish green & white & cut & enameled w/a continuous landscape w/birch trees in the foreground, signed, ca. 1900 .......................... **$4,887**

**Cameo vase,** 17" h., ovoid body tapering to a small neck w/flared rim, grey cased over brilliant orange & encased by deep brown, cut w/four ovoid reserves enclosing stylized flowerheads, signed in cameo, ca. 1925 ........................................... **805**

**Cameo vase,** 17" h., wide gently flaring cylindrical body w/an angled shoulder to the low wide flat neck, dark orange shaded to pale yellow mottled w/pale green & overlaid in deep orangish red & brown, cameo cut w/large roses on long leafy stems, signed, ca. 1925 ................... **7,475**

*Muller Freres Table Lamp*

**Lamp,** table model, molded & frosted grey subtly shaded w/pale amber, the globular base molded in medium-relief w/spread-winged swans & bands of berried foliage, mounted w/a silvered wrought-iron three-arm mount supporting a domed shade molded in medium-relief w/a star-form flower on a field of overlapping petals, the shaped rim w/sunbursts alternating w/stylized flowerheads, molded mark on shade, chips, ca. 1935, 15" h. (ILLUS.) ................ **2,300**

## NAILSEA

*Nailsea was another glassmaking center in England where a variety of wares similar to those from Bristol, England were produced between 1788 and 1873. Today most collectors think of Nailsea primarily as a glass featuring swirls and loopings, usually white, on a clear or colored ground. This style of glass decoration, however, was not restricted to Nailsea and was produced in many other glasshouses, including some in America.*

*Fine Nailsea Bottle*

**Bottle,** no stopper, cylindrical w/wide angled shoulder to a short cylindrical neck w/a flattened rim, clear w/white & light pink looping, pontiled base, probably made for a cork closure, 19th c., 6 1/4" h. (ILLUS.) ...................................... **$385**

**Flask,** flattened ovoid form w/pointed base & short cylindrical neck, clear w/pulled white & pink looping, 8 3/4" l. ...................... **220**

*Colorful Nailsea Flask*

**Flask,** flattened ovoid form w/pointed base & short ringed cylindrical neck, heavily looped bands of red, white & blue, light wear, 8 1/2" h. (ILLUS.) .................................. 303

**Flask,** long flattened ovoid form w/narrow flat base & short cylindrical neck, clear w/tightly pulled white & pink looping, 7 3/4" l. .......................................... 193

**Rolling pin,** cylindrical w/knob ends, clear w/blue & red spattering on a white ground, tooled ends, one w/a pontil, other w/a cork, light overall wear, 15" l. ........ 275

**Rolling pin,** cylindrical w/long tapering handles, clear w/red, white & blue loopings, tooled ends, light wear, 14" l. ............... 193

**Rolling pin,** cylindrical w/short knob handles, clear w/deep blue & white loopings, tooled ends, one w/polished pontil, other w/cork, overall wear, 14 1/2" l. ..................... 204

## NEW MARTINSVILLE

*The New Martinsville Glass Mfg. Co. opened in New Martinsville, West Virginia in 1901 and during its first period of production came out with a number of colored opaque pressed glass patterns. They also developed an art glass line they named "Muranese," which collectors refer to as "New Martinsville Peach Blow." The factory burned in 1907 but reopened later that year and began focusing on production of various clear pressed glass patterns, many of which were then decorated with gold or ruby staining or enameled decoration. After going through receivership in 1937, the factory again changed the focus of its production to more contemporary glass lines and figural animals. The firm was purchased in 1944 by The Viking Glass Company (later Dalzell-Viking).*

**Bonbon,** Janice patt., clear .............................. $20
**Book end,** "Nautilus," clear, 6" h........................ 22
**Bowl,** 11" oval, Janice patt., No. 4551-2SJ, two swan handles, red .............................. 225
**Celery dish,** Janice patt., No. 4521-1SJ, oval, swan handle, red, 11" l. ...................... 125
**Celery dish,** Janice patt., No. 4521-2SJ, oval, two swan handles, red, 11" l. ............... 225
**Cruet w/original stopper,** Prelude patt., clear ................................................................. 50
**Cup & saucer,** Janice patt., blue ...................... 22
**Mayonnaise dish,** Janice patt., clear, 6" .......... 18
**Plate,** 8" d., Janice patt., blue............................ 12
**Platter,** Janice patt., blue ................................. 50
**Relish dish,** Radiance patt., No. 42, two-part w/metal handle, red (light wear on handle) ......................................................... 38
**Sherbet,** Janice patt., blue ................................ 18
**Tumbler,** Janice patt., footed, blue ................... 20
**Vase,** Janice patt., cupped rim, red .................. 165
**Vase,** Janice patt., flared, black........................ 150
**Vase,** 3 1/2" h., Janice patt., blue ...................... 25

## PADEN CITY

*The Paden City Glass Manufacturing Company began operations in Paden City, West Virginia in 1916, primarily as a supplier of blanks to other companies. All wares were hand-made, that is, either hand-pressed or mold-blown. The early products were not particularly noteworthy but by the early*

*1930s the quality had improved considerably. The firm continued to turn out high quality glassware in a variety of beautiful colors until financial difficulties nessitated its closing in 1951. Over the years the firm produced, in addition to tablewares, items for hotel and restaurant use, light shades, shaving mugs, perfume bottles and lamps.*

**Bowl,** two-handled, Orchid etching, red ......... $250
**Bowl,** 9" d., footed, Peacock & Rose etching, pink........................................................ 175
**Bowl,** 11" d., footed, Ardith etching, Mrs. "B" line No. 411, yellow ......................... 55
**Bowl,** 11" d., rolled edge, Cupid etching, pink............................................................... 400
**Cake plate,** Cupid etching, footed, pink (scratches) ..................................................... 175
**Cake plate,** footed, Peacock & Rose etching, pink............................................................. 155
**Cake salver,** Regina etching, No. 555 line, clear .............................................................. 125
**Candy dish,** cov., square, Ardith etching, green ............................................................. 150
**Cheese plate,** etched Lela Bird patt., green........ 64
**Compote,** Cupid etching, pink.......................... 325
**Compote,** 6 1/2" h., Black Forest etching, pink............................................................... 100
**Console bowl,** rolled edge, Peacock & Rose etching, green, 14" d.......................... 180
**Cup,** Ardith etching, yellow ................................ 35
**Cup,** Futura etching, No. 836 line, cobalt blue ...................................................................... 9
**Cup & saucer,** Crow's Foot (No. 412) line, red ...................................................................... 15
**Cup & saucer,** Cupid etching, pink ................... 165
**Cup & saucer,** Nora Bird etching, pink ............ 210
**Gravy boat,** Ardith etching, green ...................... 80
**Ice tub,** Black Forest etching, pink .................. 155
**Ice tub,** Cupid etching, green ............................ 325
**Ice tub,** Cupid etching, pink.............................. 325
**Ice tub,** green ...................................................... 55
**Ice tub,** Peacock & Wildrose etching, green..... 215
**Mayonnaise dish & ladle,** Nora Bird etching, green, 2 pcs. ......................................... 120
**Mayonnaise dish, liner & ladle,** Orchid etching, yellow, 3 pcs. .................................. 160
**Mayonnaise dish & underplate,** Cupid etching, green ............................................... 230
**Plate,** two-handled, Ardith etching, pink ........... 125
**Plate,** 10" sq., Orchid etching, red..................... 85
**Plate,** 11" d., Gazebo etching, clear .................. 50
**Punch set:** punch bowl & seven punch cups; No. 555 line, clear, the set................... 75
**Server,** center-handled, Black Forest etching, green ................................................... 80
**Server,** swan-necked center handle, Gazebo etching, Line 1504, clear, 10" l. ..... 100
**Tray,** center-handled, No. 1504 line, clear ........ 35
**Tray,** Cupid etching, oval, pink .......................... 380
**Tray,** center-handled, etched Lela Bird patt., pink, 10 1/2" l. ...................................... 125
**Tumbler,** Crow's Foot (No. 412) line, flat, blue ................................................................. 100
**Tumbler,** Regina patt. (No. 210), clear, 5 oz. ...................................................................... 3
**Vase,** elliptical, Peacock & Rose etching, green ............................................................. 375
**Vase,** 10" h., etched Lela Bird patt., black........ 165
**Vase,** 10" h., Peacock & Rose etching, black............................................................... 325

**Water set:** pitcher & six tumblers; Ardith etching, green, 7 pcs.................................... **575**

## PATE DE VERRE

*Pate de Verre, or "paste of glass," was molded by very few artisans. In the pate de verre technique, powdered glass is mixed with a liquid to make a paste which is then placed in a mold and baked at a high temperature. These articles have a finely-pitted or matte finish and are easily distinguished from blown glass. Duplicate pieces are possible with this technique.*

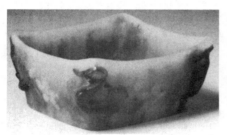

*Pate De Verre Marks*

*A.Walter Bowl with Salamanders*

**Bowl,** 4" w., square form w/slightly flared sides, grey mottled w/pink, the sides molded w/yellow flowers flanked by green leaves & the corners w/spotted brown salamanders, signed in intaglio "AWalter - Nancy" (ILLUS.) ..................... **$3,450**

**Box,** cov., low round shape, mottled pale yellow ground, the flattened cover centered by an orangish red molded grotesque mask framed by a ring of black & yellow leaf forms enclosed in a scalloped black ring w/small yellow stars between each scallop, the sides w/matching scalloped band, leaves & stars, cover molded "G. Argy-Rousseau," base molded "France," ca. 1923, 5 3/4" d., 3 3/8" h. ..................................................... **8,625**

**Model of a chick,** modeled standing on a naturalistic base w/head cocked slightly to one side, in cobalt blue shaded w/green in the grass at its feet, inscribed "A. Walter - Nancy," ca. 1930, 4 1/8" h. .... **1,725**

**Pen tray,** figural, the edge molded w/an amber beetle on a blue ground, signed by Walter - Nancy, 9 1/2" l......................... **3,300**

**Vase,** 6 3/4" h., tapering cylindrical form w/flaring lip & small foot, grey shaded w/amber & purple, molded w/flutes & vetruvian scrolls, impressed "Décorchemont," France, ca. 1925 .......... **1,955**

## PATTERN

*Though it has never been ascertained whether glass was first pressed in the United States or abroad, the development of the glass pressing machine revolutionized the glass industry in the United States and this country receives the credit for improving the method to make this process feasible. The first wares pressed were probably small flat plates of the type now referred to as "lacy," the intricacy of the design concealing flaws.*

*In 1827, both the New England Glass Co., Cambridge, Mass. and Bakewell & Co., Pittsburgh, took out patents for pressing glass furniture knobs and soon other pieces followed. This early pressed glass contained red lead which made it clear and resonant when tapped (flint.) Made primarily in clear, it is rarer in blue, amethyst, olive green and yellow.*

*By the 1840s, early simple patterns such as Ashburton, Argus and Excelsior appeared. Ribbed Bellflower seems to have been one of the earliest patterns to have had complete sets. By the 1860s, a wide range of patterns was available.*

*In 1864, William Leighton of Hobbs, Brockunier & Co., Wheeling, West Virginia, developed a formula for "soda lime" glass which did not require the expensive red lead for clarity. Although "soda lime" glass did not have the brilliance of the earlier flint glass, the formula came into widespread use because glass could be produced cheaply.*

*An asterisk (\*) indicates a piece which has been reproduced.*

*For an expanded listing of Pattern Glass, see Antique Trader Books American Pressed Glass & Bottles Price Guide, 2nd Editon.*

### ALASKA (Lion's Leg)
**Banana boat,** blue opalescent ............... **$200-250**
**Banana boat,** emerald green ................... **165-185**
**Butter dish,** cov., blue opalescent ........... **350-375**
**Butter dish,** cov., clear opalescent ................. **102**
**Card tray,** blue opalescent ................................. **29**
**Celery tray,** blue opalescent w/enameled florals.......................................................... **250**

*Alaska Creamer*

**Creamer,** canary opalescent (ILLUS.)............... **85**
**Creamer & cov. sugar bowl,** blue, pr. ........... **110**
**Cruet w/original stopper,** blue opalescent w/enameled florals ...................................... **300**
**Pitcher,** water, blue opalescent................ **300-350**

**Pitcher,** water, clear opalescent w/enam-
eled florals & gold trim.................................. 125
**Salt & pepper shakers w/original tops,**
emerald green, pr........................................... 95
**Sauce dish,** blue opalescent w/enameled
florals.............................................................. 65
**Sauce dish,** white opalescent............................ 58
**Spooner,** blue opalescent.................................. 70
**Spooner,** canary opalescent.............................. 63
**Sugar bowl,** cov., blue opalescent................... 188
**Sugar bowl,** cov., canary opalescent.............. 273
**Tumbler,** blue opalescent w/enameled flo-
rals .............................................................. 150
**Tumbler,** canary opalescent ........................ 75-85
**Water set:** pitcher & 6 tumblers; canary
opalescent, 7 pcs. ................................. 775-800

## BANDED BUCKLE
**Bowl,** open, flat, smooth rim............................. 30
**Butter dish,** cov. ............................................... 85
**Compote,** cov., 6" d., low standard.................... 50
**Cordial** ............................................................. 50
**Creamer,** footed, applied handle........................ 85
**Egg cup** ............................................................ 50
**Goblet** .............................................................. 45
**Jam jar,** cov...................................................... 75
**Pickle dish,** oval, deep bowl ............................. 30
**Pitcher,** water, 1/2 gal. ..................................... 45
**Salt,** individual .................................................. 20
**Salt,** master ..................................................... 30
**Spooner** ........................................................... 36
**Sugar bowl,** cov. .............................................. 85
**Syrup pitcher w/original top,** applied hol-
low handle.................................................... 190
**Tumbler,** bar ............................................... 55-60
**Wine** ................................................................ 40

## BARBERRY
**Bowl,** cov., 8" d. ................................................ 45
**Butter dish,** cov., pattern on base rim .............. 93
**Cake stand,** 11" d. .......................................... 125
**Celery vase** ...................................................... 40
**Compote,** cov., 8" d., high stand, shell fin-
ial................................................................. 99
**Creamer** ........................................................... 45
**Egg cup** ........................................................... 30

*Barberry Goblet*

**Goblet** (ILLUS.) .................................................. 25
**Pitcher,** milk ..................................................... 75
**Pitcher,** water, 9 1/2" h., applied handle ......... 125
**Plate,** 6" d., amber ........................................... 38
**Salt dip,** master size ......................................... 25
**Sauce dish,** flat or footed.................................. 25
**Spooner,** footed ............................................... 32

**Sugar bowl,** cov., shell finial ............................. 46
**Sugar bowl,** open ............................................. 28
**Syrup jug w/original top** ................................. 125
**Tumbler,** footed................................................. 32
**Wine** ................................................................ 34

## BEADED GRAPE (California)
**Bowl,** 5 1/2" sq., green...................................... 22
**Bowl,** 6 1/2" sq., green ...................................... 21
**Bowl,** 7 1/2" sq., green...................................... 32

*Beaded Grape Bowl*

**Bowl,** 8" sq., clear (ILLUS.) ............................... 24
**Bowl,** 6 1/4 x 8 1/2" rectangle, green ................ 28
**Butter dish,** cov., square, clear.......................... 55
**Butter dish,** cov., square, green ........................ 75
**Cake stand,** green, 9" sq., 6" h. ....................... 145
**Celery tray,** clear .............................................. 28
**Celery tray,** green ............................................. 35
**\*Compote,** cov., 8 1/2" sq., high stand,
clear ........................................................... 125
**Compote,** open, jelly, 4" sq., green .................... 75
**Compote,** open, 8 1/2" sq., high stand,
clear ............................................................. 60
**Compote,** open, 8 1/2" sq., high stand,
green ............................................................ 85
**Cordial** ............................................................. 40
**Creamer,** clear .................................................. 60
**Creamer,** green ................................................. 90
**Cruet w/original stopper,** clear......................... 70
**Cruet w/original stopper,** green .................... 100
**Egg cup** ........................................................... 30
**\*Goblet,** clear ................................................... 35
**\*Goblet,** green .................................................. 50
**Pitcher,** milk, green ......................................... 150
**Pitcher,** water, square, green........................... 125
**Pitcher,** water, tankard, clear ............................ 60
**Pitcher,** water, tankard, green w/gold ............. 135
**Platter,** 7 1/4 x 10 1/4", clear............................ 55
**Platter,** 7 1/4 x 10 1/4", green .......................... 85
**Salt & pepper shakers w/original tops,**
green, pr....................................................... 75
**\*Sauce dish,** clear............................................. 10
**\*Sauce dish,** green ........................................... 20
**Sauce dish,** handled, clear ............................... 20
**Sauce dish,** handled, green .............................. 30
**Spooner,** clear .................................................. 40
**Sugar bowl,** cov., green.................................... 60
**Toothpick holder,** clear.................................... 30
**Toothpick holder,** green w/gold trim ................ 70
**\*Tumbler,** clear ................................................ 28
**\*Tumbler,** green ............................................... 45

*Wine, clear ......................................................... 35
*Wine, green ........................................................ 66

## BIRD & STRAWBERRY (Bluebird)
Bowl, 7 1/2" d., footed, clear ............................. 62
Bowl, 7 1/2" d., footed, w/color ........................... 70
Bowl, 9" d., flat, clear ....................................... 55
Bowl, 9" d., flat, w/color .................................... 75
Bowl, 10" d., flat, clear ................................. 60-70
Butter dish, cov., clear ................................... 165
Butter dish, cov., w/color ......................... 200-225
Cake stand, 9" to 9 1/2" d. ............................... 98
*Celery tray, 10" l. ...................................... 50-60
Celery vase, pedestal base, 7 1/2" h. ............... 65
Compote, cov., jelly, 4 1/2" d., 7 1/2" h.,
   clear ........................................................... 165
Compote, cov., jelly, 4 1/2" d., 7 1/2" h.,
   w/color ...................................................... 250
Compote, cov., 6" d., low stand, clear .............. 85
Compote, cov., 6" d., low stand, w/color ......... 125
Creamer, clear .......................................... 60-70
Creamer, w/color ........................................... 115
Dish, heart-shaped .......................................... 65
Goblet, flared bowl, w/color .......................... 725
Pitcher, water, clear .............................. 300-350
Pitcher, water, w/color ........................... 450-500
Punch cup ..................................................... 25
Spooner, clear ................................................ 60
Spooner, w/color ..................................... 100-125
Sugar bowl, cov., clear ................................... 65

*Bird & Strawberry Tumbler*

Tumbler, clear (ILLUS.) ..................................... 43
Tumbler, w/color ............................................. 95
Wine .......................................................... 55-65

## BRYCE - See Ribbon Candy Pattern

## BUTTON ARCHES
Banana dish, green ........................................... 35

*Button Arches Souvenir Bowl*

Bowl, 8" d., ruby-stained, souvenir
   (ILLUS.) ...................................................... 60
Butter dish, cov., clear ................................... 52
*Butter dish, cov., ruby-stained ....................... 95
Celery vase, ruby-stained, souvenir ............ 75-85
Compote, open, jelly, 4 1/2" h., ruby-
   stained ....................................................... 40
*Creamer, ruby-stained ................................... 38
Creamer, ruby-stained, souvenir, 3 1/2" h. ........ 30
Cruet w/original stopper, ruby-stained.... 180-185
*Goblet, ruby-stained ..................................... 50
Mug, child's, ruby-stained, souvenir .................. 23
Mug, clear .................................................... 25
Mug, ruby-stained ...................................... 30-35
Pitcher, water, tankard, 12" h., ruby-
   stained ...................................................... 145
Pitcher, water, tankard, ruby-stained, sou-
   venir of Pan American Exposition ............... 150
Punch cup, clear ............................................. 9
Punch cup, ruby-stained ................................. 19
Salt dip ....................................................... 19
Salt & pepper shakers w/original tops,
   clear, small, pr. ........................................... 35
Salt shaker w/original top, ruby-stained .......... 27
Sauce dish, clear ........................................... 17
Sauce dish., ruby-stained ................................ 30
Spooner, ruby-stained w/clear band ................. 63
Sugar bowl, cov., clear ................................... 45
*Sugar bowl, cov., ruby-stained ....................... 85
Syrup pitcher w/original top, clear ................. 133
Syrup pitcher w/original top, ruby-stained ..... 175
Toothpick holder, clear ................................... 15
Toothpick holder, ruby-stained ........................ 28
Tumbler, clear ............................................... 16
Tumbler, ruby-stained ..................................... 47
Whiskey shot glass, ruby-stained .................... 47
Wine, clear ................................................... 31
Wine, ruby-stained ......................................... 38

## CANADIAN

*Canadian Goblet*

Bowl, 6" d., handled ........................................ 28
Bowl, berry, 7" d., 4 1/2" h., footed ................... 69
Bowl, 8" d., handled ....................................... 45
Bowl, 9 1/2" d. .............................................. 55
Bread plate, handled, 10" d. ......................... 40-50
Butter dish, cov. ............................................ 63
Cake stand, 9 3/4" d., 5" h. ......................... 35-50
Celery vase ................................................... 70
Compote, cov., 6" d., 9" h. ............................. 124

Compote, cov., 7" d., low stand ........................ 133
Compote, cov., 7" d., 11" h. .............................. 113
Compote, cov., 8" d., low stand ......................... 92
Compote, cov., 8" d., 11" h. .............................. 150
Compote, open, 6" d., footed ............................. 40
Compote, open, 7" d., 6" h. ................................ 35
Compote, open, 8" d., 5" h. ................................ 48
Cordial ............................................................... 37
Creamer ............................................................. 67
Goblet (ILLUS.) .................................................. 71
Honey dish, flat, 3 1/2" d. .................................. 15
Marmalade jar, cov. .......................................... 210
Pitcher, milk, 8" h. ............................................. 113
Pitcher, water .................................................... 95
Plate, 6" d., handled .......................................... 32
Plate, 7" d., handled .......................................... 45
Plate, 8" d., handled .......................................... 44
Plate, 8 1/2" d., handled .................................... 35
Plate, 9" d. ........................................................ 36
Sauce dish, flat or footed, each ........................ 19
Spooner .............................................................. 45
Sugar bowl, cov. ................................................ 70
Sugar bowl, open ............................................... 21
Wine .................................................................. 40

## CATHEDRAL
Bowl, 6" d., clear ............................................... 16
Bowl, 7" d., clear ............................................... 20
Bowl, berry, 8" d., amber ................................... 48
Bowl, berry, 8" d., blue ...................................... 40
Bowl, berry, 8" d., canary .................................. 28
Cake stand, amber ............................................ 55
Cake stand, canary ........................................... 60
Cake stand, clear, 10" d., 4 1/2" h. ................... 38
Compote, cov., 8" d., high stand, blue ............. 185
Compote, open, 7 1/2" d., high stand, ame-
thyst, fluted rim.............................................. 145

*Cathedral Compote*

Compote, open, 10 1/2" d., 8" h., clear,
shaped rim (ILLUS.) ...................................... 55
Compote, open, 10 1/2" d., 8" h., ruby-
stained............................................................ 125
Creamer, clear ................................................... 35
Creamer, ruby-stained ....................................... 50
Cruet w/original stopper, amber ...................... 118
Goblet, amber ................................................... 39
Goblet, canary................................................... 42
Goblet, clear ..................................................... 26
Goblet, ruby-stained.......................................... 65
Lamp, kerosene-type, blue font, amber
base, 12 3/4" h. ............................................. 310
Pitcher, water, clear ......................................... 125
Pitcher, water, ruby-stained .............................. 178
Relish, fish-shaped, clear .................................. 32
Relish, fish-shaped, ruby-stained....................... 55
Salt dip, canoe-shaped, blue ............................. 33

Salt dip, master size, amber .............................. 25
Sauce dish, flat or footed, blue .......................... 25
Sauce dish, flat or footed, ruby-stained ............. 22
Spooner, amber ................................................. 43
Spooner, clear ................................................... 28
Spooner, ruby-stained ....................................... 40
Sugar bowl, cov., clear ...................................... 45
Sugar bowl, cov., ruby-stained .......................... 70
Sugar bowl, open, clear ..................................... 23
Sugar bowl, open, ruby-stained.......................... 29
Tumbler, amber ................................................. 31
Tumbler, ruby-stained........................................ 43
Wine, amber ...................................................... 50
Wine, canary ..................................................... 65
Wine, clear ........................................................ 28
Wine, ruby-stained ............................................ 45

## COMPACT - See Snail Pattern

## DAHLIA
Banana bowl, 12 1/2", green .................... 125-160
Bread platter, 8 x 12"........................................ 40
Butter dish, cov., canary.................................... 65
Butter dish, cov., clear....................................... 54
Cake stand, canary, 9 1/2" d............................. 75
Cake stand, clear, 9 1/2" d. ......................... 30-35
Cake stand, amber, 10" d................................... 75
Cake stand, clear, 10" d..................................... 25
Champagne, amber ............................................ 75
Champagne, clear .............................................. 35
Compote, cov., 7" d., high stand, clear ............. 85
Cordial, clear..................................................... 40
Creamer, amber ................................................ 55
Creamer, clear .................................................. 25
Cruet w/original stopper, clear........................... 45
Egg cup, clear ................................................... 25
Egg cup, double ........................................... 45-50
Goblet, blue....................................................... 60
Goblet, clear...................................................... 35
Mug, amber ....................................................... 45
Mug, blue........................................................... 60
Mug, child's, blue............................................... 45
Mug, child's, clear.............................................. 30
Pickle dish, amber............................................. 40
Pickle dish, shell handles .................................. 55
Pitcher, milk, clear, applied handle ................... 51
Pitcher, water, amber......................................... 105
Pitcher, water, clear........................................... 45
Plate, 7" d., amber............................................. 43
Plate, 7" d., clear............................................... 18
Plate, 9" d., amber, w/handles ........................... 25
Plate, 9" d., blue, w/handles .............................. 50
Plate, 9" d., clear, w/handles ............................. 18
Relish, amber, 5 x 9 1/2".................................... 20
Sauce dish, amber, flat....................................... 22
Sauce dish, canary, flat...................................... 35
Spooner, amber ................................................. 48
Spooner, apple green ........................................ 65
Spooner, canary ................................................ 55
Spooner, clear ................................................... 35
Sugar bowl, cov., clear ................................. 45-55
Wine, amber ...................................................... 70
Wine, clear ........................................................ 45

## DAISY & BUTTON
Banana boat, blue ............................................. 110
Basket, silver plate handle, 6" h. ....................... 125
Boot, high-top, ruby-stained buttons ................. 125
Bowl, 8" w., clear, tricornered ........................... 45
Bowl, 9" sq., Amberina....................................... 183

**Bowl,** 10 x 11" oval, 7 3/4" h., canary, flared ............................................................. 95
**Bowl,** fruit, rectangular, ornate silver plate frame .......................................................... 250
**Butter chip,** square, Amberina .................. 75
**\*Butter dish,** cov., model of Victorian stove, green ................................................ 215
**Butter dish,** cov., scalloped base, clear ........... 65
**Canoe,** amber, 8" l. ..................................... 115
**Castor set,** 3-bottle,amber, clear & blue, in clear glass frame ...................................... 120
**Celery tray,** flat, boat-shaped, 14" l., canary ...................................................... 125
**Celery vase,** triangular, amber ........................... 65
**Cheese dish,** cov., canary .............................. 165
**\*Cruet w/original stopper,** amber .................. 100
**Cup & saucer,** blue ...................................... 65

*Daisy & Button Finger Bowl*

**Finger bowl,** blue, 4 3/8" d., 2 7/8" h. (ILLUS.) ................................................... 32
**Goblet,** ruby-stained rim & buttons .................. 50
**Hat shape,** clear, 8 x 8", 6" h. .......................... 60
**Humidor,** cov., amber ..................................... 185
**Inkwell,** amber ............................................... 145
**Inkwell w/original insert,** cat seated on cover .................................................................. 210
**Match holder,** wall-hanging scuff, clear ............. 65
**\*Pickle castor,** sapphire blue insert, w/silver plate frame & tongs ................................ 238
**Pitcher,** water, canary, bulbous, applied handle, scalloped top .................................. 135
**Pitcher,** water, ruby-stained buttons, bulbous, applied handle ..................................... 325
**Powder jar,** cov., amber 3 3/4" d., 2" h. .............. 30
**Relish,** "Sitz bathtub," amber ......................... 125
**\*Salt & pepper shakers w/original tops,** blue, pr. ............................................................ 48
**Sauce dish,** amber, rectangular .......................... 36
**Sauce dish,** clear, cloverleaf-shaped ................. 24
**Slipper,** ruby-stained buttons .............................. 80
**Sugar bowl,** cov., barrel-shaped, blue ............... 50
**Syrup pitcher w/original pewter top,** blue ........................................................................ 175
**Toothpick holder,** coal hod form, amber ........... 35
**Toothpick holder,** three-footed, Amberina ...... 275
**Tray,** water, amber, 11" d. ................................. 90
**Tumbler,** water, amber ....................................... 26
**Tumbler,** water, canary, pattern half way up .................................................................... 30
**Waste bowl,** clear ............................................ 30
**Whimsey,** "canoe," wall hanging-type, ruby-stained buttons, 11" l. ......................... 110
**Whimsey,** "umbrella," original metal handle, canary .................................................... 425

## DELAWARE (Four Petal Flower)
**Banana boat,** amethyst w/gold, 11 3/4" l. ... **75-125**
**Banana boat,** green w/gold, 11 3/4" l. ................ 70

**Berry set:** boat-shaped master bowl & 4 boat-shaped sauce dishes; clear w/rose flowers & gold, 5 pcs. ........................... **150-200**
**Berry set:** round master bowl & six sauce dishes; green w/gold, 7 pcs. ...................... 175
**Bowl,** 8" d., clear ............................................ 50
**Bowl,** 8" d., green w/gold ........................... **40-50**
**Bowl,** 8" d., rose w/gold .................................... 50
**Bowl,** 9" d., rose w/gold, scalloped rim ............ 75
**Bride's basket,** boat-shaped open bowl, rose w/gold, in silver plate frame, 11 1/2" oval ............................................................... 395
**Bride's basket,** boat-shaped open bowl, green w/gold, miniature .............................. 175
**Butter dish,** cov., clear ............................. **95-110**
**\*Butter dish,** cov., green w/gold ...................... 113
**Butter dish,** cov., rose w/gold ......................... 145
**Claret jug,** green w/gold ................................. 150
**Compote,** 9 1/2" d., 6 1/2" h., green, pewter base ...................................................... **85-110**
**Creamer,** clear w/gold ...................................... 45
**\*Creamer,** green w/gold .................................... 54
**Creamer,** individual size, clear w/gold ............... 25
**Creamer & cov. sugar bowl,** green w/gold, pr. ................................................... 132
**Cruet w/original stopper,** clear ..................... 100
**Cruet w/original stopper,** green w/gold .......... 310
**Cruet w/original stopper,** rose w/gold ........... 460
**Custard cup,** green w/gold ................................ 35
**Custard cup,** rose w/gold ................................. 42
**Pin tray,** rose w/gold ................................... **75-85**
**Pitcher,** tankard, green w/gold ....................... 150
**Pitcher,** water, clear w/gold ......................... **50-75**
**Pomade jar w/jeweled cover,** rose w/gold ...... 335
**Salt & pepper shakers w/original tops,** green w/gold, pr. ...................................... 495
**Sauce dish,** boat-shaped, green w/gold ........... 20

*Delaware Boat-shaped Sauce Dish*

**Sauce dish,** boat-shaped, rose w/gold (ILLUS.) ............................................................ 38
**Sauce dish,** round, green w/gold ...................... 23
**Spooner,** clear w/gold ...................................... 50
**Spooner,** green .............................................. 35
**Spooner,** green w/gold ..................................... 75
**Spooner,** rose w/gold (ILLUS.) .......................... 57
**Sugar bowl,** cov., clear .................................... 63
**\*Sugar bowl,** cov., green w/gold ....................... 78
**Sugar bowl,** cov., rose w/gold .......................... 90
**Sugar bowl,** open, clear ................................... 34
**Sugar bowl,** open, green w/gold ........................ 45
**Sugar bowl,** open, rose w/gold ......................... 40
**Sugar bowl,** individual size, green .................... 55
**Sugar bowl,** individual size, green w/gold .......... 30
**Sugar bowl,** individual size, rose w/gold ........... 95

**Table set:** cov. butter dish, cov. sugar bowl
& spooner; rose w/gold, 3 pcs. .............. **300-350**
**Toothpick holder,** clear ..................................... **38**
**Toothpick holder,** clear w/rose-stained flo-
rals & gold ...................................................... **145**
**Toothpick holder,** green w/gold ...................... **100**
**Toothpick holder,** rose w/gold ......................... **120**
**Tumbler,** clear ..................................................... **12**
**Tumbler,** clear w/gold .......................................... **40**
**Tumbler,** green w/gold ......................................... **35**
**Tumbler,** rose w/gold ........................................... **53**
**Water set:** water pitcher & 3 tumblers; rose
w/gold, 4 pcs. ................................................ **295**

## DOUBLE LOOP - See Ribbon Candy Pattern

## EGG IN SAND
**Bread tray,** clear, handled ........................... **30-35**
**Butter dish,** cov. ................................................. **48**
**Creamer,** clear ................................................... **32**

*Egg in Sand Goblet*

**Goblet,** clear (ILLUS.) ........................................ **29**
**Pitcher,** water, amber .......................................... **70**
**Pitcher,** water, blue .............................................. **98**
**Pitcher,** water, clear ............................................. **38**
**Sauce dish** ......................................................... **12**
**Spooner,** blue .................................................... **60**
**Spooner,** clear .................................................... **35**
**Sugar bowl,** cov., blue .................................. **85-95**
**Tray,** water, flat .................................................... **45**
**Tumbler,** amber .................................................. **35**
**Tumbler,** blue ..................................................... **65**
**Tumbler,** clear .................................................... **30**
**Water set,** pitcher & four goblets, amber, 5
pcs. ................................................................. **250**
**Water set,** pitcher & four goblets, blue, 5
pcs. ................................................................. **350**
**Water set,** pitcher, tray & five goblets,
clear, 7 pcs. .............................................. **225-240**

## EGYPTIAN
**Berry set,** master bowl & 5 sauce dishes, 6
pcs. ................................................................. **150**
**Bowl,** 8 1/2" d. ...................................................... **65**
**Bread platter,** Cleopatra center, 9 x 12" .......... **50**
***Bread platter,** Salt Lake Temple
center ....................................................... **220-225**
**Butter dish,** cov. ................................................. **73**
**Compote,** cov., 6" d., 6" h., sphinx base ... **100-125**

**Compote,** cov., 7" d., high stand, sphinx
base ............................................................... **195**
**Compote,** cov., 8" d., high stand, sphinx
base ............................................................... **262**
**Creamer** .............................................................. **55**
**Goblet** ................................................................. **45**
**Honey dish** ......................................................... **20**
**Pickle dish** ......................................................... **20**
**Pitcher,** water ..................................................... **275**
**Plate,** 10" d. ........................................................ **65**
**Plate,** 12" d., handled .......................................... **80**
**Relish,** 5 1/2 x 8 1/2" ........................................... **27**
**Sauce dish,** flat ................................................... **21**

*Egyptian Spooner*

**Spooner** (ILLUS.) ........................................... **35-45**
**Sugar bowl,** cov. ................................................ **68**
**Sugar bowl,** open .............................................. **32**
**Table set,** 4 pcs. ......................................... **250-275**

## EYEWINKER

*Eyewinker Salt Shaker*

**Banana stand** .................................................. **115**
**Berry set,** master bowl & five sauce
dishes, 6 pcs. .......................................... **125-135**
**Bowl,** master berry or fruit, 9" d., 4 1/2" h. ......... **70**
**Bowl,** cov., 9" d. ................................................. **85**
***Butter dish,** cov. .......................................... **80-85**
**Cake stand,** 9 1/2" d. ....................................... **200**
**Celery vase,** 6 1/2" h. ......................................... **55**
**Compote,** cov., 6" d., high stand ....................... **50**
**Compote,** open, 4" d., 5" h., scalloped rim .... **30-35**
**Compote,** open, 5 1/2" d., high stand ............... **60**
**Compote,** open, 6 1/2" sq., high stand .............. **70**
**Compote,** open, 8 1/2" d., high stand ............... **75**
**Compote,** open, 9 1/2" d., high stand ....... **125-150**
**Compote,** open, 10" d., high stand .......... **140-160**
**Cracker jar,** cov. ............................................. **125**

Creamer ........................................................ 45
Cruet w/original stopper ............................. 110
Doughnut stand ......................................... 75-85
*Goblet ........................................................ 40
*Honey dish, cov. ......................................... 90
Lamp, kerosene-type, w/original burner,
    9 1/2" h. ............................................... 180
Pitcher, milk ................................................ 70
*Pitcher, water ............................................. 80
Plate, 10" sq., 2" h., turned-up sides .................. 65
Salt & pepper shakers w/original tops,
    pr. (ILLUS. of one)........................................ 43
Sauce dish, square............................................ 12
Spooner ...................................................... 45-50
*Sugar bowl, cov. .......................................... 52
Tumbler ........................................................ 28

## FINECUT & BLOCK

*Finecut & Block Pitcher*

Bowl, fruit, 9" d., blue, collared base................. 40
Bowl, round, handled, pink blocks .................... 50
Cake stand ..................................................... 35
Celery tray, blue, 11" l. ..................................... 65
Celery tray, clear, 11" l. ..................................... 28
Celery tray, clear w/amber blocks, 11" l. .......... 85
Champagne, amber .......................................... 70
Champagne, clear w/blue blocks....................... 68
Compote, open, jelly, clear w/amber blocks.. 55-65
Compote, open, jelly, clear w/pink blocks..... 65-75
Compote, open, 10" d., 9" h., amber ........... 40-45
*Creamer, clear................................................ 34
Creamer, clear w/amber blocks ........................ 63
Creamer, clear w/blue blocks............................ 53
Creamer, clear w/pink blocks............................ 70
Creamer, clear w/yellow blocks......................... 77
Egg cup, single, clear ...................................... 28
Egg cup, single, clear w/blue blocks................. 55
Egg cup, single, clear w/pink blocks ................. 55
Egg cup, double............................................... 29
*Goblet, amber ................................................ 65
*Goblet, clear ............................................. 25-30
Goblet, clear w/amber blocks............................ 80
Goblet, clear w/blue blocks .............................. 70
Goblet, clear w/pink blocks .............................. 62
Goblet, clear w/yellow blocks............................ 52
Goblet, large, clear........................................... 25
Goblet, large, clear w/blue blocks ................. 35-40
Goblet, large, clear w/pink blocks ..................... 80
Ice cream tray, clear w/amber blocks............... 85
Lamp, kerosene-type, w/ring handle,
    amber.................................................... 125-130
Marmalade jar, blue.................................. 100-125

Nappy, footed, 4" d............................................ 35-40
Pitcher, water, amber (ILLUS.) .......................... 85
Pitcher, water, clear.......................................... 43
Pitcher, water, clear w/amber blocks .............. 125
Pitcher, water, clear w/blue blocks.................. 125
Pitcher, water, clear w/pink blocks.................. 195
Relish, clear w/amber blocks, handled,
    7 1/2" ................................................... 55
Relish, clear w/blue blocks, handled, 7 1/2"....... 50
Sauce dish, amber............................................ 16
Sauce dish, blue .............................................. 15
Sauce dish, clear ............................................... 9
Sauce dish, clear w/amber blocks ..................... 13
Sauce dish, clear w/blue blocks......................... 23
Spooner, clear ................................................. 40
Spooner, clear w/amber blocks.......................... 45
Spooner, clear w/blue blocks............................. 55
Spooner, clear w/pink blocks ............................ 48
*Sugar bowl, cov., clear.................................... 35
Sugar bowl, open, clear w/blue blocks ............. 35
Tray, clear w/blue blocks, corset-shaped,
    12 1/2 x 14 1/2" ...................................... 75
Tray, water, clear w/amber blocks, round........... 85
Tumbler, amber ............................................... 23
Tumbler, blue .................................................. 30
Tumbler, clear.................................................. 18
Tumbler, clear w/blue blocks ............................ 40
Waste bowl, amber........................................... 55
*Wine, amber ................................................... 47
*Wine, blue ................................................ 65-70
*Wine, clear..................................................... 35
Wine, clear w/amber blocks............................... 48
Wine, clear w/blue blocks ................................. 45
Wine, clear w/pink blocks ........................... 50-55

## FROSTED LION (Rampant Lion)

*Frosted Lion Goblet*

Bread tray, oval, lion handles, frosted or
    non-frosted, 10" l. ...................................... 110
Bread tray, amber, rope edge, closed han-
    dles, 10 1/2" d. ............................................ 85
Bread tray, canary, rope edge, closed han-
    dles, 10 1/2" d. ...................................... 150-200
Butter dish, cov., collared base, rampant
    lion finial ............................................. 165-170
Cheese dish, cov., rampant lion finial............. 625
Cologne bottle w/stopper ................. 1,000-1,200
Compote, cov., 5" d., 8 1/2" h. ........................ 175
Compote, cov., 5 1/2 x 8 3/4" oval, 8 1/4" h.,
    rampant lion finial ................................. 170-180
*Compote, cov., 6 3/4" oval, 7" h., collared
    base, rampant lion finial ........................ 150-175

**Compote,** cov., 8" d., high stand, overall floral etching ................................................. **545**
**Compote,** open, 7" oval, 7 1/2" h. .................... **140**
**Compote,** open, 8" d. ...................................... **175**
**Creamer** ................................................... **85-95**
**Creamer** child's, clear & frosted ................. **90-110**
**Cup & saucer,** child's, clear frosted or blue opaque ........................................................ **80-225**
***Egg cup** ......................................................... **83**
***Goblet** (ILLUS.)............................................... **135**
**Inkwell** .................................................... **750-900**
**Marmalade jar,** cov., lion's head finial ............. **155**
**Paperweight,** embossed "Gillinder & Sons, Centennial" ................................................... **238**
***Pitcher,** water ......................................... **550-750**
**Relish** ............................................................ **50**
***Sauce dish,** 4" & 6" d. ............................... **20-25**
***Spooner** ....................................................... **100**
**Spooner,** child's, clear & frosted ............... **110-125**
**Sugar bowl,** cov., crouched lion finial ....... **100-125**
**Syrup pitcher w/original dated top** .............. **463**
**Wine,** 4 1/8" h. ......................................... **75-100**

## GALLOWAY (Mirror)
**Bowl,** 9 1/2" d., flat .................................... **25-30**
**Butter dish,** cov., clear ............................... **65-70**
**Butter dish,** cov., rose-stained ................. **140-150**
**Celery vase,** clear .......................................... **30**
**Celery vase,** rose-stained ................................ **75**
**Compote,** open, 10" d., 8" h., scalloped rim....... **75**
**Cracker jar,** cov. .......................................... **175**
**Creamer,** clear .......................................... **20-25**
**Creamer,** rose-stained ..................................... **75**
**Cruet w/stopper** ....................................... **55-60**
**Mint dish,** footed ...................................... **30-35**
**Nappy,** handled, gold rim, 5" d. ......................... **30**
**Nappy,** handled, tricornered, 5 3/4" w. .......... **30-35**
**Pickle castor w/silver plate lid,** no frame.... **75-85**
**Relish,** 8 1/4" l. .............................................. **17**
**Salt & pepper shakers w/original tops,** gold trim, 3" h., pr. .......................................... **48**
**Spooner,** clear .............................................. **23**
**Spooner,** rose-stained ..................................... **80**
**Sugar bowl,** cov., clear ................................... **85**
**Syrup pitcher w/metal spring top,** clear .......... **73**
**Tray,** flat, 8" d. ............................................ **195**
**Tumbler,** clear............................................... **30**
**Waste bowl** ................................................... **38**
**Wine,** clear .............................................. **40-45**

## GEORGIA - See Peacock Feather Pattern

## GOOD LUCK - See Horseshoe Pattern

## GOTHIC

*Gothic Egg Cup*

**Bowl,** master berry or fruit, flat ........................ **120**
**Butter dish,** cov. ...................................... **100-125**
**Castor bottle** ........................................... **10-15**
**Castor set,** mustard, cruet & shaker & original wire holder .............................................. **165**
**Castor set,** five-bottle, w/pewter frame ....... **95-110**
**Dish,** 5 1/4 x 7" oblong ..................................... **25**
**Egg cup,** 3 1/2" h. (ILLUS.) ....................... **55-65**
**Plate** (rare) ............................................ **125-135**
**Sugar bowl,** cov. ........................................... **105**
**Sugar bowl,** open ..................................... **35-40**
**Tumbler** ...................................................... **110**
**Wine,** 3 3/4" h. .......................................... **100-125**

## GREEK KEY (Heisey's Greek Key)
**Bowl,** 8 1/2" d. ............................................. **65**
**Butter dish,** cov. .......................................... **125**
**Celery tray,** 9" l. ............................................ **38**
**Champagne** ............................................ **90-100**
**Compote,** open, jelly, 5" d., low stand............... **28**
**Compote,** open, 6" d., 7" h............................... **19**
**Creamer** ....................................................... **35**
**Creamer & open sugar bowl,** pr. ..................... **56**
**Creamer & sugar bowl,** individual size, pr. ..... **125**
**Goblet** ......................................................... **70**
**Humidor,** cov. .............................................. **285**
**Ice tub,** hotel size .......................................... **135**
**Ice tub,** small................................................. **95**
**Lamp,** kerosene-type, large .......................... **85-95**
**Lamp,** kerosene-type, miniature...................... **100**
**Nappy,** handled ............................................. **30**
**Nut dish,** individual size .................................. **22**
**Pickle dish,** 8" l. ............................................ **25**
**Pitcher,** pt. .................................................. **125**
**Pitcher,** tankard, clear, 1 1/2 qt....................... **225**
**Pitcher,** tankard, ruby-stained, 1 1/12 qt......... **115**
**Plate,** 5 1/2" d. .............................................. **25**
**Plate,** 6 3/4" d. .............................................. **30**
**Plate,** 9" d. ................................................... **30**
**Punch bowl & pedestal base,** 2 pcs............. **250**
**Punch cup** ..................................................... **15**
**Punch set,** bowl, base & 12 cups, 14 pcs........ **430**
**Relish,** 9" l. ................................................... **30**
**Salt dip,** master size ....................................... **20**
**Sauce dish** ................................................... **10**
**Sherbet** ....................................................... **23**
**Soda fountain (straw-holder) jar** .................. **128**
**Spooner** ....................................................... **75**
**Sugar bowl,** open ..................................... **25-30**
**Toothpick holder** ......................................... **400**
**Tumbler** ....................................................... **75**
**Vase,** 6 1/2" h., footed ................................. **65-70**
**Wine** ........................................................ **75-85**

## HALLEY'S COMET

*Halley's Comet Wine*

Celery vase .......................................................... 42
Goblet ............................................................. 40-45
Jar, cov., three-footed ...................................... 49
Pitcher, water, tankard, engraved.................... 135
Pitcher, water, tankard, plain ....................... 60-65
Relish, 4 1/2 x 7" ............................................... 15
Spooner ......................................................... 30-40
Tumbler ......................................................... 50-75
Wine (ILLUS.)..................................................... 65

## HORSESHOE (Good Luck or Prayer Rug)
Bowl, cov., 5 x 8" oval, flat, triple horse-
shoe finial .................................................... 310
*Bread tray, single horseshoe handles......... 45-55
Bread tray, double horseshoe handles.............. 95
Butter dish, cov. ....................................... 150-200

*Horseshoe Cake Stand*

Cake stand, 9" d., 6 1/2" h. (ILLUS.)............. 80-90
Cake stand, 10" d. .......................................... 85-95
Celery vase clear ........................................... 65-85
Compote, cov., 12" d. ............................... 110-120
Compote, cov., 8" d., low stand .................... 65-85
Creamer ........................................................ 40-45
Doughnut stand, 7" d. ................................... 75-80
Goblet, knob stem ......................................... 60-65
Goblet, plain stem ......................................... 35-45
Marmalade jar, cov. ................................... 175-200
Relish, 5 x 7" ................................................. 15-20
Salt dip, individual size ................................. 30-35
Salt dip, master size, horseshoe shape........ 75-85

*Horseshoe Spooner*

Spooner (ILLUS.)............................................ 35-40
Sugar bowl, cov............................................. 80-90
Table set, 4 pcs.............................................. 345

## KING'S CROWN (Also see Ruby Thumbprint)
Banana stand ................................................. 195
Butter dish, cov. .............................................. 65
Cake stand, 10" d. ........................................... 85
Castor set, salt & pepper shakers, oil bot-
tle w/stopper & cov. mustard jar in origi-
nal frame, 4 pcs............................................ 325
Compote, cov., 6" d., 6" h. ............................... 85
Compote, cov., 11" d. ..................................... 145
Compote, open, jelly ........................................ 38
Creamer, clear ................................................ 48
*Cup & saucer ................................................. 55
Goblet, clear .................................................... 25
Honey dish ...................................................... 50
*Lamp, kerosene-type, stem base, 10" h. ........ 195

*King's Crown Mustard Jar*

Mustard jar, cov. (ILLUS.).............................. 40-50
Nappy, 7 1/2" d................................................. 32
Pitcher, tankard, 13" h., engraved .................. 225
Salt & pepper shakers w/original tops,
pr. .............................................................. 65-70
Sauce dish, boat-shaped.................................. 21
Wine, clear ...................................................... 21

## LION, FROSTED - See Frosted Lion

## LION - See Frosted Lion Pattern (Gillinder)

## MAINE (Stippled Flower Panels)
Bowl, master berry, 8 1/2" d., clear .................. 40
Butter dish, cov. .............................................. 68
Cake stand, 8 1/2" d., green ............................. 65
Compote, cov., green, small ............................. 65

*Maine Jelly Compote*

Compote, open, jelly, 4 3/4" d. (ILLUS.) ............ 24
Creamer ................................................................. 28
Cruet w/original stopper ................................. 60
Mug ....................................................................... 55
Pitcher, milk ................................................. 65-70
Platter, oval .......................................................... 38
Salt & pepper shakers, w/original tops,
   pr. .................................................................. 80-85
Sauce dish ........................................................... 13
Spooner ................................................................ 32
Syrup pitcher w/original top, clear ................. 70
Toothpick holder, clear ................................... 385
Wine, clear ..................................................... 40-45

## MASCOTTE
Apothecary jar, cov. ........................................... 65
Butter dish, cov., engraved ............................. 85
Butter dish, cov., plain ...................................... 38
Cake basket w/handle ....................................... 76
Cake stand, 12" d. ............................................ 155
Cheese dish, cov. ............................................... 65
Compote, cov., 8" d., 12" h. .......................... 85-90

*Mascotte Creamer*

Creamer, clear (ILLUS.) ..................................... 45
Goblet, plain ........................................................ 30
Jar, cov., pyramid, flat base, three jars-
   high, bottom of jar sections embossed
   "Patented May 20, 1873" (minor rough-
   ness inside rim of lid, sold w/two extra
   lids, one w/flakes inside rim, one
   w/roughness to finial) ............................... 1,000
Marmalade jar, cov., 4 1/2" d., 8" h., clear.... 25-30
Pitcher, water ................................................. 75-80
Salt dip, individual size .................................... 25
Salt & pepper shakers w/original tops,
   pr. .................................................................. 55-60
Salt shaker w/original top ......................... 30-35
Sauce dish, flat or footed, each ....................... 10
Spooner, clear, plain .......................................... 22
Sugar bowl, cov., plain ...................................... 39
Tray, water, clear, plain ...................................... 59
Tumbler, clear, plain ........................................... 25
Wine, clear, plain ................................................ 26

## MINERVA
Bread tray, 13" l. ................................................. 75
Butter dish, cov. ................................................. 80
Cake stand, 8" d. ...................................... 100-110
Compote, cov., 7" d., 10 3/4" h. ...................... 145
Creamer ................................................................ 70
Marmalade jar, cov. ......................................... 150
Pitcher, water ............................................ 100-110

Plate, 9" d., handled, plain center....................... 56
Platter, 13" oval................................................... 60
Sauce dish, flat, 5" d........................................... 20
Spooner ................................................................ 40
Sugar bowl, cov. ............................................ 90-95
Table set, creamer, cov. butter dish &
   spooner, 3 pcs................................................ 195
Waste bowl, 6" d.................................................. 55
Wine ..................................................................... 50

## MIRROR - See Galloway Pattern

## NEW HAMPSHIRE (Bent Buckle)
Creamer, individual, 3 1/4" h., clear ................... 35
Cruet w/original stopper, clear....................... 60
Cruet w/original stopper, rose-stained........... 250
Goblet, clear........................................................ 21
Goblet, rose-stained...................................... 60-65
Mug, medium size, clear..................................... 23
Mug, large size, rose-stained ............................. 60
Olive dish, diamond-shaped, 6 5/8" w.,
   rose-stained .................................................... 20
Pitcher, water, tankard, clear, 1/2 gal. ............. 150
Salt shaker w/original top, small &
   tapered w/fluted neck, clear ........................... 50
Sauce dish, round, rose-stained, 4" d............... 14
Sugar bowl, cov., breakfast size, clear.............. 14
Sugar bowl, cov., breakfast size, rose-
   stained.............................................................. 17
Sugar bowl, open, individual, double-han-
   dled, rose-stained............................................ 21
Tumbler, water, clear ..................................... 20-25
Vase, 6" h., thick stem, rose-stained ................. 25
Wine, flared bowl, clear ...................................... 19
Wine, flared bowl, rose-stained ......................... 55
Wine, straight-sided, rose-stained..................... 45

## OAKEN BUCKET (Wooden Pail)
Butter dish, cov., blue ....................................... 85
Butter dish, cov., canary.................................. 110
Butter dish, cov., clear....................................... 65
Creamer, blue ..................................................... 65
Creamer, canary ........................................... 65-75
Pitcher, water, blue .................................... 100-120
Pitcher, water, canary ....................................... 120
Pitcher, water, clear ............................................ 80
Spooner, blue ................................................ 45-55
Spooner, canary ................................................. 48
Spooner, clear ..................................................... 35
Sugar bowl, cov., blue ....................................... 48
Sugar bowl, cov., canary ................................. 105
Sugar bowl, cov., clear ...................................... 45
Table set, blue, 4 pcs. ...................................... 250

## PEACOCK FEATHER (Georgia)

*Peacock Feather Compote*

Bonbon dish, footed .......................................... 23
Bowl, 8" d. ....................................................... 30
Bread plate .................................................. 30-35
Butter dish, cov. ............................................... 40
Cake stand, 8 1/2" d., 5" h. .......................... 35-40
Celery tray, 11 3/4" l. ....................................... 35
Compote, open, 8" d., high stand (ILLUS.) ........ 43
Creamer .......................................................... 24
Creamer & cov. sugar bowl, pr. ..................... 100
Cruet w/original stopper ................................. 70
Goblet ............................................................. 25
Lamp, kerosene-type, low hand-type
    w/handle, 5 1/4" h., blue......................... 160-165
Lamp, kerosene-type, low hand-type
    w/handle, 5 1/2" h., clear........................... 85-90
Lamp, kerosene-type, table model w/han-
    dle, 9" h., blue ...................................... 250-275
Lamp, kerosene-type, table model, 10" h.,
    amber...................................................... 225-250
Mug ............................................................ 35-40
Pitcher, water.................................................... 55
Salt & pepper shakers w/original tops,
    pr.................................................................. 85
Sauce dish ....................................................... 13
Spooner ...................................................... 30-35
Sugar bowl, cov. ............................................... 37
Table set, creamer, cov. sugar bowl & cov.
    butter dish, 3 pcs........................................ 125
Tumbler ............................................................ 35
Water set, pitcher & six tumblers, 7 pcs.... 250-275

## PYGMY - See Torpedo Pattern

## RAMPANT LION - See Frosted Lion

## RIBBON CANDY (Bryce or Double Loop)
Bowl, cov., 6 1/4" d., footed ............................... 35
Butter dish, cov., flat .................................... 35-40
Butter dish, cov., footed ............................... 55-60
Cake stand, 8" to 10 1/2" d. .............................. 80
Compote, cov., 7" d. .......................................... 90

*Ribbon Candy Creamer*

Creamer (ILLUS.)............................................... 35
Cruet w/faceted stopper ................................ 225
Doughnut stand .............................................. 150
Goblet .............................................................. 78
Pitcher, milk ................................................ 30-35
Spooner ........................................................... 40
Sugar bowl, cov. ............................................... 45
Table set, 4 pcs........................................ 125-150
Wine .................................................................. 95

## SNAIL (Compact)

*Snail Banana Stand*

Banana stand, 10" d., 7" h. (ILLUS.) ............... 275
Bowl, berry, 8" d., 4" h.................................... 34
Bowl, cov., vegetable, 5 1/2 x 8" ..................... 125
Bowl, 9" d., 2" h.......................................... 40-50
Butter dish, cov., clear.................................... 102
Cake stand, 10" d. ......................................... 120
Compote, cov., 7" d., 11 1/2" h. ...................... 155
Cracker jar, cov., 8" d., 9" h. ........................... 295
Creamer, clear ................................................. 58
Cruet w/original stopper, clear...................... 145
Goblet ............................................................ 125
Pitcher, milk, bulbous, applied handle,
    large ...................................................... 195-215
Rose bowl, large ......................................... 65-75
Spooner, clear .................................................. 45
Spooner, ruby-stained ...................................... 85
Sugar bowl, cov., clear, plain .......................... 69
Sugar bowl, cov., ruby-stained .................. 135-145
Syrup jug w/original brass top .............. 145-165
Table set, 4 pcs.............................................. 275
Tumbler, clear............................................. 55-65
Vase, 12 1/2" h., scalloped rim ......................... 80

## TORPEDO (Pygmy)

*Torpedo Syrup Jug*

Bowl, cov., master berry..................................... 80
Bowl, 7" d., clear, flat ....................................... 24
Bowl, 8" d., clear ............................................. 33
Bowl, 8" d., ruby-stained .................................. 75
Butter dish, cov. ............................................. 110
Compote, open, 8" d., high stand, flared
    rim ............................................................ 110
Creamer, collared base..................................... 55
Cup & saucer ............................................. 60-65

Goblet, clear.................................................. 45-55
Lamp, kerosene, hand-type w/finger grip,
    w/burner & chimney ............................. 125-150
Marmalade jar, cov. ......................................... 55
Pickle castor, silver plate cover & tongs ......... 250
Pitcher, milk, 8 1/2" h., clear ............................. 85
Pitcher, milk, 8 1/2" h., ruby-stained ............... 120
Salt & pepper shakers w/original tops,
    pr. ................................................................ 90-95
Sauce dish ...................................................... 16
Spooner ....................................................... 35-40
Sugar bowl, cov. ............................................... 95
Syrup jug w/original top, clear (ILLUS.).. 100-125
Syrup jug w/original top, ruby-stained .......... 250
Tumbler, clear, plain ..................................... 35-40
Waste bowl ................................................... 65-70
Wine, clear ....................................................... 85
Wine, ruby-stained ........................................ 103

### WESTWARD HO
Bread platter ................................................. 115
*Butter dish, cov. ...................................... 175-200
*Celery vase ................................................. 138
Compote, cov., 5" d., high stand.............. 100-110
Compote, cov., 6" d., high stand................... 325
*Compote, cov., 6" d., low stand..................... 120
*Compote, cov., 4 x 6 3/4" oval, low stand ...... 150
Compote, cov., 5 x 7 3/4" oval, high
    stand ...................................................... 200-225
Compote, cov., 8" d., high stand.................... 295

*Westward Ho Compote*

Compote, cov., 8" d., low stand (ILLUS.)......... 495
Compote, cov., 5 1/2 x 8" oval, high stand ...... 473
Compote, cov., 8" d., 14" h. ........................... 350
Compote, cov., 6 1/2 x 10" oval, low
    stand ...................................................... 225-250
Compote, open, 5" d. ...................................... 150
Compote, open, 7" d., high stand ............. 135-145
Compote, open, 7" d., low stand.................... 175
Compote, open, 8" d. ..................................... 125
Compote, open, 9" oval, high stand................ 100
*Creamer ........................................................ 175
*Goblet ........................................................ 80-85
Marmalade jar, cov. ........................................ 258
Mug, child's, clear, 2 1/2" h. ........................... 225
Pickle dish, oval .............................................. 65
Pitcher, milk, 8" h. .......................................... 598
Pitcher, water.......................................... 375-425
Platter, 9 x 13"............................................... 175
Relish, deer handles ....................................... 100

Sauce dish, footed ........................................... 43
Spooner ......................................................... 160
*Sugar bowl, cov. ..................................... 125-150
Sugar bowl, open ............................................. 55
Wines, set of 6 ............................................... 350

### WINDFLOWER
Butter dish, cov. .............................................. 45
Celery vase ...................................................... 40
Compote, cov., 8" d. ........................................ 85
Compote, cov., 8 1/2" d., low stand ............. 75-80
Compote, open, 8" d......................................... 30
Creamer ...................................................... 25-30
Egg cup ........................................................... 35
Goblet ............................................................. 45
Pitcher, water .................................................. 65
Salt dip, master size ........................................ 20
Sauce dish ....................................................... 13
Spooner ........................................................... 34
Sugar bowl, cov................................................ 39
Tumbler, water.................................................. 40
Wine ................................................................ 40

### WOODEN PAIL - See Oaken Bucket Pattern

# PEACH BLOW

*Several types of glass lumped together by col-lectors as Peach Blow were produced by half a dozen glasshouses. Hobbs, Brockunier & Co., Wheeling, West Virginia, made Peach Blow as a plated ware that shaded from red at the top to yel-low at the bottom and is referred to as Wheeling Peach Blow. Mt. Washington Glass Works pro-duced an homogeneous Peach Blow shading from a rose color at the top to pale blue in the lower por-tion. The New England Glass Works' Peach Blow, called Wild Rose, shaded from rose at the top to white. Gunderson-Pairpoint Co. also reproduced some of the Mt. Washington Peach Blow in the early 1950s and some glass of a somewhat similar type was made by Steuben Glass Works, Thomas Webb & Sons and Stevens & Williams of England. New England Peach Blow is one-layered glass and the English is two-layered.*

*Another single layered shaded art glass was produced early in this century by the New Martins-ville Glass Mfg. Co. Originally called "Muranese," collectors today refer to it as "New Martinsville Peach Blow."*

### GUNDERSON - PAIRPOINT
Bowl, 9" d., satin finish .................................. $330
Compote, 7 1/2" h., bowl w/a softly flared
    rim raised on a swirled stem ....................... 275
Vase, 4" h., wide rounded bottom below
    angled shoulder w/sides tapering to a
    quatreform neck, applied white reeded
    handles, ca. 1940........................................ 460

### NEW ENGLAND
Toothpick holder, cylindrical w/gently flar-
    ing squared rim .......................................... 413
Toothpick holder, cylindrical w/tricorner
    rim .............................................................. 413

### WEBB
Vase. 10 1/2" h., stick-form, applied gold
    prunts in a floral decoration, unusual
    applied green base & green lining................ 523

## WHEELING

*Wheeling Peach Blow Cruet*

**Cruet w/original facet-cut amber ball stopper,** bulbous ovoid body tapering to a short neck w/high arched spout, dark reddish amber applied reeded handle, 7" h. (ILLUS.)............................................. 1,200
**Pitcher,** 4 1/4" h., wide ovoid body w/a flared quatreform neck, applied amber handle, late 19th c. ...................................... 495
**Pitcher,** 5 1/4" h., wide ovoid body w/a flared quatreform neck, applied amber handle, late 19th c. (interior bubbles, some staining) ............................................. 374

*Wheeling Peach Blow Drape Pitcher*

**Pitcher,** 6 1/2" h., footed squatty bulbous body tapering to a flaring quatrefoil neck, mold-blown Drape patt., applied amber reeded handle (ILLUS.)............................... 460
**Toothpick holder,** footring below a bulbed base ring below the cylindrical sides......... 1,265
**Tumbler,** cylindrical, glossy finish, 3 3/4" h. ..... 259
**Vase,** 8 1/2" h., a thin footring below the elongated teardrop-form body tapering to a tall 'stick' neck, glossy finish................. 633

## PILLAR-MOLDED

*This heavily ribbed glassware was produced by blowing glass into full-sized ribbed molds and then finishing it by hand. The technique evolved from earlier "pattern moulding" used on glass since ancient times but in pillar-molded glass the ribs are very heavy and prominent. Most examples found in this country were produced in the Pittsburgh, Pennsylvania area from around 1850 to 1870, but similar English-made wares made before and after this period are also available. Most American items were made from clear flint glass and colored examples or pieces with colored strands in the ribs are*

*rare and highly prized. Some collectors refer to this as "steamboat" glass believing that it was made to be used on American riverboats, but most likely it was used anywhere that a sturdy, relatively inexpensive glassware was needed, such as taverns and hotels.*

**Bar bottle,** eight-rib, tapering conical form w/a double applied collar below the small cylindrical neck fitted w/a pewter jigger cap, clear, 10" h. (small lip chips)..... **$220**

*Pillar-Molded Swirled Celery Vase*

**Celery vase,** eight-rib, tall inverted bell-form bowl w/ribs swirled to the right in the upper half, on an applied knop stem & heavy disc foot, probably Pittsburgh, 9" h. (ILLUS.).............................................. 385
**Celery vase,** eight-rib, tall tulip-form bowl w/a widely flaring flat rim, knobbed pedestal on a thick applied disk foot, clear, ca.1860, 9 7/8" h. .............................. 187
**Compote,** 3 7/8" h., eight-rib, a deep rounded bowl w/folded rim & very heavy ribs on a short wafer stem & thin disk foot, cobalt blue, 19th c. ........................... 1,265
**Compote,** 4 3/8" h., eight-rib, wide squatty bulbous bowl w/heavy ribs & widely flared rim w/a band of cut punties, on a short applied stem & foot, ground pontil, emerald green, attributed to Pittsburgh, mid-19th c. ................................................. 1,100
**Creamer,** eight-rib, bulbous body tapering to a wide arched spout, applied strap handle, bottom ground flat, 5 5/8" h. (minor wear) ............................................... 275

*Pillar-Molded Syrup Pitcher*

**Syrup pitcher w/hinged metal lid,** eight-rib, sharply tapering conical form w/ringed neck fitted w/a pewter collar w/arched spout & hinged lid w/scroll finial, applied long strap handle w/end curl, clear, wear & residue under base, 11" h. (ILLUS.) ........................................ **495**

# SANDWICH

*Numerous types of glass were produced at The Boston & Sandwich Glass Works in Sandwich, Massachusetts, on Cape Cod, from 1826 to 1888. Those listed here represent a sampling. Also see PATTERN GLASS and LACY in the "Glass" section.*

*All pieces are pressed glass unless otherwise noted. Numbers after salt dips refer to listings in Pressed Glass Salt Dishes of the Lacy Period, 1825-1850, by Logan W. and Dorothy B. Neal.*

**Candlestick,** Acanthus Leaf patt., paneled waisted stem & matching flared socket on a domed paneled base, all w/leaf designs, medium translucent opaque blue, 9 1/2" h. (minor imperfections) ....... **$3,300**

**Candlestick,** figural dolphin stem w/petal socket, on a stepped square base, canary, 9 3/4" h. (small chip on one petal, some light mold roughness) .............. **660**

**Candlesticks,** flaring hexagonal base below the ringed stem supporting a heavy paneled tulip-form socket, deep golden amber, 7" h., pr. (one w/mold roughness & tiny base corner chip, other w/two large chips) ........................................ **605**

**Christmas salt & pepper shakers,** barrel-shaped w/patented metal lid w/pointed finial, amethyst, 2 5/8" h., pr. ...................... **303**

*Amber Christmas Salt & Peppers*

**Christmas salt & pepper shakers,** barrel-shaped w/patented metal lid w/pointed finial, golden amber, 2 5/8" h., pr. (ILLUS.) ........................................ **154**

**Christmas salt & pepper shakers,** barrel-shaped w/patented metal lid w/pointed finial, rare emerald green, 2 5/8" h., pr. .... **1,320**

**Compote,** cov., Loop patt., pagoda-form cover w/knob finial, paneled base joined to flaring bowl w/a wafer, round foot, clear, 9 1/2" h. (some molded roughness) ........................................ **275**

*Fine Sandwich Cut-Overlay Lamp*

**Lamp,** kerosene table model, cut-overall, the inverted pear-shaped font in cranberry cut to white cut to clear w/bands of stars, quatrefoils & elongated oval, punties & pointed ovals, fitted w/a brass collar, reeded brass stem on a square stepped marble base w/brass trim, mid-19th c., minor imperfections, 11 1/2" h. (ILLUS.) ........................................ **3,738**

**Lamp,** kerosene table model, cut-overlay, inverted pear-shaped font in light emerald green cut to clear w/stars, quatrefoil, elongated ovals, punties & pointed ovals, fitted w/a brass collar & reeded standard on a square stepped marble base, mid-19th c., 12 3/4" h. (minor imperfections) ........................................ **1,150**

**Lamp,** kerosene table model, cut-overlay, the inverted pear-shaped cobalt blue to clear 'Washington cut' design font fitted w/a brass collar & connector on an opalescent white columnar standard & square base w/gilt trim, mid-19th c., 13 3/4" h. (mold imperfections, gilt wear) ..... **748**

**Lamps w/hurricane shades,** the clam-broth pressed three-dolphin figural base w/hexagonal rim mounted w/a round embossed brass collar holding the tall clear cylindrical shade w/flared rim, 18" h., pr. (one w/interior crack around heads of dolphins, other w/longer crack around two heads & down the base) ......... **2,200**

**Scent bottle w/original pointed stopper,** Elongated Loop patt., lime green, polished pontil, 7" h. ........................................ **750**

**Scent bottle w/original stopper,** Star & Punty patt., canary yellow ........................... **550**

**Vase,** 7 1/4" h., Pressed Leaf patt., tall slender flared leaf-design bowl w/pointed scallops on rim, short paneled stem on flaring scalloped foot, canary ......... **825**

**Vase,** 9 7/8" h., tulip-form paneled bowl on a flaring octagonal pedestal foot, dark amethyst, mid-19th c. (minute base chips, rim roughness) ................................ **1,035**

**Vase,** 10" h., tulip-form, the tall flaring octagonal bowl w/scrolled rim raised on a flaring octagonal pedestal base, amethyst (minor foot flakes) ............................ **1,760**

## SATIN

*Satin glass was a popular decorative glass developed in the late 19th century. Most pieces were composed of two layers of glass with the exterior layer usually in a shaded pastel color. The name derives from the soft matte finish, caused by exposure to acid fumes, which gave the surface a "satiny" feel. Mother-of-pearl satin glass was a specialized variety wherein air trapped between the layers of glass provided subtle surface patterns such as Herringbone and Diamond Quilted. A majority of satin glass was produced in England, Bohemia and America, but collectors should be aware that reproductions have been produced for many years.*

**Bowl,** 3" d., ruffled rim, shaded pink mother-of-pearl Diamond Quilted patt. ........ **$110**

**Bowl,** 5" d., 4" h., squatty round form tapering slightly to a wide triangular rim, lightly ribbed pink, attributed to Mt. Washington ............................................... **1,210**

**Bowl,** 9 1/2" oval, shaded apricot mother-of-pearl Diamond Quilted patt., heavily enameled w/pears & stems w/gold trim ....... **495**

**Cruet w/original stopper,** shaded blue mother-of-pearl Raindrop patt., applied frosted reeded handle & stopper .................. **385**

**Cruet w/original stopper,** spherical body tapering to a short neck w/flaring tricorner rim, yellow mother-of-pearl Herringbone patt., applied frosted clear handle, frosted clear ball stopper, white lining, 5 3/4" h. ......................................................... **330**

**Ewer,** bulbous body tapering to a neck w/a ruffled top, shaded pink mother-of-pearl Diamond Quilted patt., applied pink thorn handle, 7" h. ....................................... **220**

*Decorated Pink Satin Jam Dish*

**Jam dish in holder,** squatty bulbous bowl w/wide flat mouth in shaded pink decorated in enamels around the sides w/a black bird on a branch, black berries & green leaves, in a footed silver plate holder w/swing bail handle, overall 4 1/2" d., 6" h. (ILLUS.) ............................... **245**

**Pitcher,** water, folded ruffled rim, shaded apricot mother-of-pearl Diamond Quilted patt., late 19th c. ........................................... **550**

*Blue Satin Mother-of-Pearl Vase*

**Vase,** 5" h., 4 1/2" d., nearly spherical body w/a short neck & high crimped & ruffled rim, shaded blue mother-of-pearl Diamond Quilted patt., applied frosted clear edging, white interior (ILLUS.) ...................... **225**

**Vase,** 5 3/4" h., ovoid body tapering to a short neck w/a widely flaring crimped rim w/two sides pulled up, shaded blue mother-of-pearl Herringbone patt., enameled w/large stylized orange & red blossoms on brown branches, signed by Webb ................................................................. **330**

**Vase,** 5 3/4" h., ovoid body tapering to a three-ringed lower neck tapering to a widely flaring tricorner rim, Rainbow mother-of-pearl Diamond Quilted patt. ......... **413**

**Vase,** 9 1/2" h., slender ovoid form tapering to a small neck & wide crimped rim & three large pulled petals rolled back to touch the shoulder, alternating stripes of lavender & pale pink, mother-of-pearl Honeycomb patt. .......................................... **330**

**Vase,** 10" h., double gourd-form, shaded peach mother-of-pearl Diamond Quilted patt. ................................................................. **165**

**Vase,** 10 3/4" h., footed slender ovoid body w/a four-lobed crimped rim, shaded pink mother-of-pearl Diamond Quilted patt., ornately decorated w/enameled wildflowers in white, green & yellow w/large leafy stems, gilt trim, applied frosted clear rim band, polished pontil .................... **201**

## SCHNEIDER

*This ware is made in France at Cristallerie Schneider, established in 1913 near Paris by Ernest and Charles Schneider. Some pieces of cameo were marked "Le Verre Francais" (which see) and others were signed "Charder."*

**Aquarium,** jade in brown, white & yellow w/hints of lavender, signed, 6 1/2" h. ......... **$468**

**Bowl,** 12" d., squatty bulbous form w/wide flared rim, red mottled w/purple & white, blown into a wrought-iron frame w/panels of scroll designs between top & base bands, apparently unsigned, ca. 1925 ...... **1,380**

**Bowl,** 12" d., 3 1/2" h., a wide flat bottom w/low rounded sides w/a wide flat rim, yellow shading to orangish red w/streaks of maroon, cased in clear, base inscribed "Schneider France - Ovington New York" ...................................................... **374**

**Lamp,** table model, elongated baluster form on a wide spreading base, amethyst & blue w/deep purple or amethyst at the dropped footed base w/delicate random tangerine highlights, cased in clear subtly graduating into two-toned pale blue & a dense blue flame design, signed, adjustable, 18 3/4" h.................. **1,100**

**Tazza,** a wide shallow round flat-sided bowl in white w/a mottled amethyst & blue rim, raised on a slender double-bulbed amethyst stem & disk foot, foot signed, ca. 1920, 7 5/8" h............................. **863**

**Vase,** 3 5/8" h., miniature, "Aux Grappes de Raisins," ovoid body in clear cased in speckled yellow w/"marqueterie -sur-verre" decoration of stems around the neck & three clusters of red grapes, each centered by a black spot, engraved highlights, signed, ca. 1925 (rim polished down)................................................ **575**

**Vase,** 4" h., bulbous ovoid body tapering to a small flared neck, jade red ground w/four small dark blue cabochons applied around the shoulder, signed........... **880**

**Vase,** 7" h., a thick cushion foot & short slender pedestal supporting a wide ovoid body tapering sharply to a rolled rim, mottled pink, red & yellow ground w/heavy dark purple mottling around the upper half, signed...................................... **1,045**

**Vase,** 8 1/2" h., baluster-form w/ringed stem on cushion foot supporting a wide ovoid body w/a widely flaring neck, grey shaded mottled pale yellow & amethyst applied w/a medial band of black martelé glass w/yellow blossoms w/orange centers, signed in gilt enamel "Schneider - France," ca. 1925 ...................................... **7,475**

**Vase,** 9" h., ovoid tapering body w/folded lip, shaded purple on a circular dark purple foot, acid-etched w/stylized interlaced ropes, signed, ca. 1925 ...................... **402**

**Vase,** 11" h., triple gourd-form, white & purple mottled decorated w/dark purple vertical dashes & yellow dots, acid-etched "Schneider - France - Ovington," ca. 1925 (ILLUS. top next column) ................... **920**

**Vase,** 11" h., trumpet-form, jade in brilliant tomato red w/dark purple inclusions............. **550**

**Vase,** 11 1/4" h., tapering ovoid body in clear shading to purple w/acid-etched & molded fluting on a deep purple circular foot, acid-etched mark, ca. 1925 ............ **575**

**Vase,** 12" h., footed slightly flaring cylindrical form w/rounded base & shoulder w/a short widely flaring neck, swirled pink, red, white & clear enhanced w/Cluthra-like bubbles, etched "Schneider" on foot & "France" on base ...................................... **978**

*Schneider Mottled Glass Vase*

**Vase,** 13" h., elongated baluster-form w/cushion foot, swirled orange rising from deep aubergine, signed "Schneider - France" on base, polished pontil, ca. 1925 ......................................................... **403**

**Vase,** 14" h., thick cushion foot supporting a flaring tall swelled body w/a closed rim flanked by small loop shoulder handles, mottled & veiled form in rose pink, yellow & orange above pinkish red & brick red, amethyst handles, footed signed "Schneider" ............................................... **1,265**

**Vase,** 17" h., bulbous body tapering to a small mouth, burnt orange w/a mixture of darker veining throughout, signed................ **440**

# SMITH BROTHERS

*Originally established as a decorating department of the Mt. Washington Glass Company in the 1870s, the firm later was an independent business in New Bedford, Massachusetts. Beautifully decorated opal white glass was their hallmark but they also did glass cutting. Some examples carry their lion-in-the-shield mark.*

*Smith Brothers Mark*

**Cracker jar,** cov., swelled cylindrical body, light yellow ground enameled w/large white & yellow daisies and sprigs of brown fern, fitted silver plate cover w/knob handle marked "Smith Bros.," 4 3/8" h......................................................... **$215**

**Sweetmeet jar,** cov., squatty bulbous melon-lobed form, creamy white enameled w/white & green lilies, resilvered Pairpoint rim w/flared spearpoint band, domed cover & swing bail handle, signed.................................................................. **825**

*Decorated Smith Brothers Vase*

**Vase,** 5" h., footed bulbous body deeply pinched-in on three sides, small short flared neck, creamy white satin ground enameled around the sides w/leaves & gingko tree branches in green, brown & rust w/gilt trim highlighted w/white dots, trademark on base (ILLUS.)` ........................ **173**

**Vase,** 8 1/2" h., large ovoid melon-lobed body w/a squatty bulbed neck molded w/a repeating design of foliate, the body h.p. w/chrysanthemum blooms & leaves in shades of yellow, pink, brown & green on a cream ground, gold enamel trim, late 19th c. (wear to gold, mold imperfection in neck) ........................... **460**

## STEUBEN

*Most of the Steuben glass listed below was made at the Steuben Glass Works, now a division of Corning Glass, between 1903 and about 1933. The factory was organized by T.G. Hawkes, noted glass designer, Frederick Carder, and others. Mr. Carder devised many types of glass and revived many old techniques.*

*Steuben Marks*

### ACID CUT-BACK
**Lamp base,** baluster-form shouldered base w/an etched Alabaster surface overlaid in gold Aurene & acid-cut in the Newport patt., mounted in a two-socket gilt-metal fitting w/fleur-de-lis finial, wear to gilt, overall 30 1/2" h. (ILLUS. top next column) ........................................................ **$3,450**

**Vase,** 10" h., simple ovoid form w/a short cylindrical neck, Alabaster overlaid in Jade Green & cut w/a continuous scene of large birds perched in blossoming branches, shape No. 3219 ........................... **825**

**Vase,** 12" h., bulbous ovoid lower body w/an angled shoulder tapering to a tall cylindrical neck, Oriental-style w/a dark green sculptured ground overlaid in black & cut w/grapevines w/grape clusters, pointed lappets around the rim, signed ....................................................... **3,300**

*Steuben Acid Cut-back Lamp Base*

### AURENE
**Atomizer w/original metal fittings,** tall slender form, overall blue iridescence, signed "Aurene #5612," 7" h. ...................... **880**

*Gold Aurene Small Bowl*

**Bowl,** 4 3/4" d., 2 1/2" h., deep rounded sides w/flattened flaring rim, overall gold iridescence, ca. 1910 (ILLUS.) .................. **550**

**Bowl,** 10" d., slightly rounded tapering sides & an inverted lip, overall iridescent blue, w/original paper label & signed "AURENE 2637," ca. 1904 .......................... **920**

**Bowl,** 12" d., footed shallow form w/deep blue iridescent center & stretched rim, signed "Steuben Aurene #2586" ................. **413**

**Goblet,** bell-form bowl raised on a slender stem w/a twist at the upper end, round disk foot, overall gold iridescence, shape No. 2361 ....................................................... **385**

**Goblet,** tall bell-form bowl on slender twisted stem & disk foot, overall gold iridescence, Shape No. 4231, 6 1/2" h. .......... **330**

**Goblets,** tall bell-form bowls on slender twisted stems on a flattened disk foot, overall deep gold iridescence w/blue highlights, signed "Aurene" & numbered, 7" h., set of 6 ........................................... **2,530**

**Perfume atomizer,** tapered cylindrical form in amber w/strong gold iridescence, disk foot & stepped rim w/chased metal mount, shape No. 61361, ca, 1925, 7 1/4" h. (wear to metal finish)..................... 489

**Perfume bottle w/stopper,** tapering cylindrical form w/rounded base, small flared neck & pointed mushroom stopper. overall blue iridescence, signed, shape No. 2835, 3 1/4" h............................................. 715

**Perfume bottle w/stopper,** tapering paneled body w/a small trumpet neck holding a floral molded stopper, strong blue iridescence w/green & purple highlights on the blue ground, pontil signed "Aurene 2758," ca. 1920, 4 1/4"h. (light surface scratches)....................................... 863

**Potpourri jar,** cov., fine bright gold iridescent surface on oval body, conforming cover w/three drilled fragrance holes & applied finial, shape No. 2812, 5 3/4" h........ 633

**Sherbets & underplates,** rounded bowl on a short stem, matching round plates, overall deep gold iridescence, signed & numbered, pr................................................. 550

**Vase,** 4" h., short waisted cylindrical body w/a widely flaring six-ruffled rim, overall gold iridescence on amber, stretched at rim, shape No. 723 ..................................... 316

**Vase,** 4 3/4" h., baluster-form w/short neck & wide flattened rim, gold iridescent ground decorated around the shoulder w/green pulled loops, shape No. 209, signed........................................................ 1,035

**Vase,** 5" h., footed blossom-form w/a squatty bulbous base below the widely flaring tall trumpet neck, overall blue iridescence, signed ..................................... 715

**Vase,** 5" h., ovoid body w/slightly everted lip & a cushion foot, grey w/amber, pink & blue iridescence, inscribed "Aurene," ca. 1920 ..................................... 345

**Vase,** 5" h., 5 1/2" d., classical form, overall gold iridescence, signed............................ 440

**Vase,** 5 1/2" h., ten-ribbed flared body w/extraordinary smooth & lustrous blue iridescent color, base inscribed "Steuben," shape No. 913 (shade).............. 546

**Vase,** 7 3/4" h., stick-type, slender cylindrical body on a disk foot, overall blue iridescence, signed "Aurene" ........................ 259

*Peacock Feather Aurene Vase*

**Vase,** 8" h., slightly waisted cylindrical form w/flaring neck, delicate blue peacock feathers pulled through a gold iridescent ground, signed "Aurene 261" (ILLUS.) ...... **4,313**

**Vase,** 8 1/4" h., angular six-sided rim on flared brightly iridized oval raised on disk foot inscribed "Steuben Aurene 6241" on base, shape No. 6241 ................................. **690**

**Vase,** 8 1/2" h., double-gourd form, a bulbous base w/four deep 'dimples' tapering to a tall very slender swelled 'stick' neck, gold ground w/pale green loops from the top, gold, purple & green iridescent highlights, signed "Aurene #203B - F. Carder"................................................. **1,430**

**Vase,** 8 1/2" h., stick-form, tall slender cylindrical body on a round disk foot, overall blue iridescence, signed "Aurene #2556"......................................................... **440**

## BRISTOL YELLOW
**Center bowl,** low ruffled rim enhanced by mirror black threads on the exterior, fleur-de-lis mark, 16" d., 4 1/2" h. ................ **403**

**Decanter w/stopper,** gourd-form w/wide squatty bottom section connected by slender stem & four hollow buttresses to the matching upper section all w/swirled optic ribbing, the short small ruffled neck w/a solid teardrop stopper, 19" h................. **575**

**Serving plate,** round dished form w/wide flanged rim, radiating optic ribbing, Shape No. 3579, ca. 1925, 14 1/4" d., 2" h. (wear, scratches) ................................. **201**

## CALCITE
**Bowl,** 10" d., wide low form w/flattened inverted rim, Calcite exterior & gold Aurene interior, ca. 1920 (light interior wear) ............................................................. **259**

## CLUTHRA
**Vase,** 9 3/4" h., bubbled white & green body w/a clear base ................................... **468**

## CYPRIAN

*Cyprian Candelabrum*

**Candelabrum,** aquamarine tinted verre de soie w/Celeste blue accent rims on three-arm candleholder (2959), w/central pink, green, & blue decorative floral finial supported on brass connector, original conforming VDS candlecups, shape No. 7382 variant, 19" h., one finial flower petal chipped (ILLUS.) .................... **1,840**

## GROTESQUE

**Vase,** 9 1/4" h., upright floriform ruffled & ribbed bowl in amethyst shading to colorless, raised on an applied colorless disk foot, Steuben mark on the polished pontil, Shape No. 7090, ca. 1930 (light scratch) ........................................ **518**

## IVRENE

**Bowl,** 9 1/2" d., 4 3/4" h., footed wide squatty bulbous form w/four double-ribbed side panels curving up to the gently ruffled closed rim, Shape No. 7337, unmarked ............................................. **431**

**Bowl-vase,** applied domed ribbed foot supporting the widely fanned ribbed bowl, Shape No. 7307, ca. 1930, 6 1/2" h. ........... **431**

**Candleholders,** Grotesque line, iridescent white holders w/oval ribbed & folded bobeche cups, each inscribed on base "Steuben," Shape No. 7564, 4" l., 3 1/4" h. (one ruffle rough, as made) ........... **431**

**Candlestick,** floriform, a round disk foot supports two ribbed stems, one taller than the other, each supporting a petal-form drip pan centered by a tall cylindrical candle socket, Shape No. 7317, 10 1/2" h. ............................................... **546**

**Centerbowl,** Grotesque line, four-rib oval of lustrous opaque white w/manipulated undulating rim, Shape No. 7449, 12" l., 7" h. (base evened, minor chips) .................. **345**

**Urns,** classical form w/square stepped pedestal foot below the bulbous body w/tall upright curved loop handles & a tall wide trumpet neck, Shape No. 7468, 12" h., pr. ............................................... **2,070**

**Vase,** 10" w., 8" h., twelve-ribbed white iridescent flared body w/six-ruffle top, base inscribed "Steuben," Shape No. 723 ............................................... **345**

## JADE

**Vase,** 7 1/4" h., bulbous ovoid form w/closed rim & small cushion foot, Green Jade w/spiral ribbing, signed ...................... **575**

**Vase,** 8" h., fan-shaped, Green Jade fanned top on an Alabaster knopped stem & disk foot ............................. **330**

**Vase,** 10 1/2" h., footed bulbous ovoid body w/flared neck, applied alabaster "M" handles, ca. 1929, Green Jade, polished pontil (light scratch) ................................. **1,093**

## MATSU NOKE

**Lemonade mug,** optic ribbed colorless goblet-form w/Pomona Green Cintra rim, handle & three fan-shaped decorations, Shape No. 3329, 6" h. ................................ **230**

## MILLEFIORE

**Vase,** 5" h., style J baluster-form gold Aurene internally decorated w/green hearts & vines interspersed w/clusters of white 'blossoms,' fine 'platinum' gold iridescence overall, Shape No. 573 (ILLUS. top next column) .......................... **2,760**

*Millefiore Vase*

## MOSS AGATE

**Lamp base,** a slender classic urn-form glass pedestal in swirled purple, blue & red Moss Agate mounted in a gilt-metal cupped base on a short pedestal & flaring ringed foot w/relief acanthus leaf design, metal fittings at the top w/a purple jewel at the top, needs rewiring, Shape No. 8023, ca. 1930, glass 10 1/4" h. .................................................. **2,415**

**Lamp base,** tall slender baluster-form glass shaft of swirled purple, red & blue, mounted in gilt-metal base lamp fittings w/an acanthus leaf socket above a short ringed pedestal & disk foot w/a band of acanthus leaf decoration, further electric fittings at the top w/a purple glass jewel finial, Shape No. 8023, glass 10" h. .......... **2,645**

**Vase,** 6" h., gently swelled cylindrical form w/rounded shoulder centering a wide low flared neck, mottled green internally decorated by multicolored swirling powders in red, blue, white, brown, black & occasional metallic clusters, recessed polished pontil, possibly the work of Frederick Carder ............................................. **633**

## POMONA GREEN

**Bowl,** 10 1/2" d., 6" h., a deep flaring six-panel Pomona Green bowl w/a swirled optic rib design raised on a short flaring ribbed Topaz funnel foot, Shape No. 6241 ............................................. **230**

**Vase,** 5 1/4" h., a four-pillared base, the body decorated w/airtrap designs, five top openings ............................................. **303**

**Vase,** 8" h., a disk foot below a knopped stem supporting a slender trumpet-form bowl w/a twisted rib design & a deeply pinched-in trefoil rim, Shape No. 6441 ......... **230**

**Vase,** 9" h., shaded ribbed body, white lining, signed ............................................. **303**

## ROSALINE

**Vase,** 8 1/2" h., stick-form, tall slender cylindrical body on a round disk foot, pink body on an Alabaster disk foot, unsigned ............................................. **275**

## SELENIUM RED

**Centerpiece bowl,** wide shallow round form w/incurved rim, shape No. 3196, autographed "F. Carder - Steuben," 14" d., 6" h. (some use scratches) .............. **403**

## SILVERINA

**Candleholders,** a flaring domed base in mica-flecked light amethyst w/a controlled bubble design attached to a dark amethyst disk wafer to the cylindrical tall candle socket w/a flattened & widely flaring socket rim which matches the base, Shape No. 6637, 5" h., pr. ........................... **863**

## SPANISH GREEN

**Pitcher,** 9" h., a raised disk foot below a short knopped stem supporting a bulbous ovoid optic ribbed body tapering to a short flared neck w/pinched spout, applied angled shoulder handle, Shape No. 6665, marked on base, ca. 1925 .......... **460**

## THREADED

**Bowl,** 4 1/2" d., 3" h., footed low clear form w/black threading, signed............................ **110**
**Powder box,** cov., round, diamond quilted clear body w/black threading, signed, 6 1/2" d. ........................................................ **440**

## TOPAZ

**Candlestick,** Shape No. 6384, 5 1/2" h. .......... **105**
**Compote,** 8 1/2" d., 8 1/4" h., open w/wide flat shallow bowl w/rib-molded design & low incurved rim in amber Topaz raised on a slender knopped Pomona Green stem on a double-cupped flaring ribbed Topaz foot, Shape No. 6044 ......................... **431**
**Vase,** 13" h., mounted, flared trumpet-form vessel w/rounded base inserted into black metal leaf design holder, Shape No. 7201 variant........................................... **173**

## VERRE DE SOIE

**Perfume bottle w/stopper,** squatty melon-lobed body tapering to a small flared neck, fitted w/a Celeste Blue flame-form stopper, Shape No. 1455, ca. 1915, 4 1/2" h. ........................................................ **403**

## WISTERIA

**Candlesticks,** round disk foot & swelled stem supporting a cylindrical candle socket w/wide flattened rim, dichroic leaded glass, engraved Pillar patt., reverse-engraved dots on base, marked, Shape No. 7093, ca 1927, 8 1/4" h., pr. ..... **1,035**
**Finger bowls & underplates,** footed flaring bell-form bowl engraved in the Pillar patt., reverse-engraved dots on bowl base, w/matching underplates, dichroic leaded glass, marked, Shape No. 1679, ca. 1927, underplate 7 1/4" d., bowl 4 3/4" d., 2 3/4" h., three bowls & four underplates, the set ............................ **748**
**Goblets,** bell-shaped bowls on tapering rounded stems & round feet, in a dichroic leaded glass, the bowl engraved w/the Pillar patt., reverse-engraved dots on the foot, Shape No. 7182, ca. 1927, 9" h., set of 4 ............................................. **1,150**

## MISCELLANEOUS WARES

**Center bowl,** crystal, broad conical form w/a deep well applied w/four swirled leaf forms, base engraved "Steuben," 10 3/4" d., 7" h. ............................................... **316**
**Center bowl,** crystal, shallow bowl supported by a hemisphere base on four scroll feet, polished pontil, signed, John Dreves design, created in 1942, signed, 10 1/2" d., 4" h............................................ **288**
**Goblet,** toasting-type, bowl held aloft on a spiral-twist stem, designed by Golda Fishbein in 1958, base inscribed "Steuben," Shape No. 8202, 17 1/2" h. (light interior stain)....................................... **259**
**Model of a wild dove,** crystal, stylized bird w/turned head, designed by Bernard Wolff, Shape No. 8426, base inscribed "Steuben BXW," 9 1/4" l., 4 3/4" h. ............... **316**
**Model of fox,** seated w/tail wrapped, inscribed "Steuben" on base, Shape No. 8260, designed by Lloyd Atkins, ca. 1971, 8 3/4" h............................................. **1,265**
**Models of geese,** gander & preening goose, Shape No. 8519, designed by Lloyd Atkins, 5 1/4" h., pr. ........................... **345**
**Trillium bowl,** crystal, tri-cornered bowl supported by a pinched trillium-shaped base, designed by Donald Pollard, designed in 1958, signed, 10" d., 5" h.......... **316**
**Vase,** 12 1/2" h., 9 1/4" d., Mansion Vase, colorless crystal, large urn-form w/large flaring bell-form bowl flanked by large upright applied "M" handles, raised on a knop over a flaring square stepped base, designed by Frederick Carder in 1934, Shape No. 7389 (nick in base) .................. **1,035**

# TIFFANY

*This glassware, covering a wide diversity of types, was produced in glasshouses operated by Louis Comfort Tiffany, America's outstanding glass designer of the Art Nouveau period, from the last quarter of the 19th century until the early 1930s. Tiffany revived early techniques and devised many new ones.*

*Various Tiffany Marks*

**Bowl,** 4 1/2" d., 2 1/2" h., wide rounded body tapering slightly to a wide flat rim, decorated w/small pulled prunts around the lower body, overall peacock blue iridescence, signed ....................................... **$743**

**Bowl,** 5" d., 1 1/4" h., flared rim on a small round bowl w/optic-ribbed opalescence shading to aqua blue, stretched iridescence at the interior rim, polished pontil, base signed "1777 LCT Favrile".................. **575**

**Bowl,** 6" d., ten-ribbed deep form w/a white opalescent exterior & deep cobalt blue interior rim, base signed "L.C. Tiffany Inc. Favrile" ........................................ **978**

**Bowl,** 6" d., 2" h., ruffled rim on ten-ribbed body, overall blue iridescence, inscribed "L.C.T. Favrile" ..................................... **690**

**Bowl,** 7 1/4" d., 2" h., footed, shallow widely flaring sides w/a flattened rim, green pastel body shading to an optic ribbed opalescent & clear rice grain design, signed "L.C.T. Favrile #1855" ......... **495**

**Bowl-vase,** paperweight-type, wide squatty bulbous form w/the wide shoulder centered by a short wide cylindrical neck, colorless internally decorated w/white millefiori flowers among trailing green hearts & pale aubergine vines, base signed "L.C. Tiffany Favrile V149," 4" h. ... **3,450**

**Candleholders,** a clear disk foot & tapering stem supporting a milky white opalescent socket shaded to stretched deep pink on the wide flattened rim, signed "L.C. Tiffany - #1927," 4" h., pr.................. **1,650**

*Tiffany Iridescent Candlestick*

**Candlesticks,** spirally ribbed base in amber w/flared foot & cupped rim, mounted w/a white candle w/green pulled leaf decoration & surmounted by a gilt-metal shade support, signed "L.C.T.," 14 1/2" h., pr. (ILLUS. of one) ..... **2,070**

**Compote,** open, 5 1/4 x 7", 3 1/4" h., a ribbed oval bowl in pale yellow w/applied stem & disk foot, subtle stretch iridescence at rim, polished pontil, signed "LCT Favrile 18930" ................................... **690**

**Compote,** open, 5 1/2" d., a shallow wide optic ribbed bowl w/flattened rim on a knop stem & small round foot, the bowl in frosted clear w/a blue & white rim,

clear knop & foot, signed "L.C. T. Favrile #1871".......................................................... **440**

**Cordial,** tall bell-shaped bowl on a tall slender stem & round foot, gold w/gold iridescent highlights, signed "LCT Favrile," 5 1/2" h. ................................................... **275**

**Cordial set:** decanter w/stopper & five cordials; "Royal" patt., the 9 1/2" h. decanter w/a wide round cushion-form body centered by a tall slender neck w/flared rim & fitted w/a hollow mushroom stopper, the cordials w/bell-form bowls raised on slender tapering twisted stems on disk feet, each in amber w/overall gold iridescence, decanter signed "L.C. Tiffany - Favrile 601," cordials w/initials, the set ............................. **4,025**

*Tiffany Decanter for Cordial Set*

**Cordial set:** decanter w/stopper & ten cordials; the globular decanter w/a tapering base & a tall slender neck w/flared rim, decorated around the shoulder w/twisted points in the glass, fitted w/a bulbous matching stopper, the cordials w/a bell-form bowl on a baluster-form stem & round foot, each in amber w/orange, pink & blue iridescence, each signed "L.C.T. - Favrile," cordials 3 7/8" h., decanter 10 3/4" h., the set (ILLUS. of decanter) ................................................. **4,600**

**Dish,** round w/ten molded ribs & a scalloped rim, overall gold iridescence, polished pontil, signed on base "L.C.T. Favrile," 4 1/2" d. ...................................... **518**

**Finger bowls & underplates,** round ruffled bowls w/prunt decoration, matching ruffled underplates, overall bluish gold iridescence, marked, set of 6 ...................... **3,465**

**Goblet,** tapering ovoid bowl w/a slightly everted lip, on a slender baluster-form stem & round foot, amber w/silvery pink iridescence, signed "L.C.T. - Favrile - L.C.T. 1267," 9 1/4" h. ............................... **1,035**

**Goblets,** wide cylindrical bowl w/rounded bottom, raised on a slender stem w/disk foot, each engraved around the rim w/a band of grape clusters & leaves, amber w/gold iridescence, signed "L.C.T. Favrile," 6 1/8" h., set of 8 .......................... **7,187**

**Roundel,** round disk w/indented center, a large central blossom-form w/pulled & swirled white & gold threading within a pale gold stretched border band, overall light iridescence, experimental, signed "X2294" & w/original Tiffany Glass and Decorating Company paper label, early 20th c., 14" d. ........................................... **2,875**

**Salt dip,** broad shouldered round form w/eight pulled prunts, blue w/strong blue iridescence, signed "L.C. T. Favrile X620," 2 1/8" d. ............................................ **805**

**Salt dip,** bulbous squatty form w/heavy ribs & applied small prunts, tan to green overall iridescence, signed "LCT 02647"... **1,375**

**Salt dip,** rounded bottom below the upturned shallow ribbed, crimped sides, overall gold iridescence, signed "L.C.T.," 2 1/2" d., 1" h. ......................................... **165**

**Salt dip,** squatty bulbous form w/incurved crimped rim, molded ribbing, overall bluish gold iridescence, signed "L.C.T.," 2 1/2" d., 1 1/8" h. ....................................... **176**

**Salt dips,** raised & flared rims on faintly ribbed bodies, deep blue overall iridescence, each base signed "L.C.T. Favrile X355," 1 1/2" h., pr. (nicks).......................... **748**

**Salt dips,** ruffled rim on shallow bowl of amber w/overall gold iridescence, signed "L.C.T.," 3" d., pr......................................... **489**

**Tumblers,** waisted cylindrical form w/applied threading around the middle, iridescent amber, all signed "L.C.T.," three numbered "5359" & three w/a "W" & number, ca. 1905, 4" h., set of 6 ............ **1,265**

**Vase,** rose bowl-shaped, spherical w/small closed mouth, green ground w/overall random swirls in reds, golds, rust & purple, signed................................................. **5,500**

**Vase,** 2 2/3" h., miniature, bulbous form w/a band of prunts & dimples, gold iridescence at the top w/caramel around the center, signed "LC Tiffany - #659"......... **385**

**Vase,** 3 3/4" h., bulbous ovoid ten-ribbed body tapering to a short flared & scalloped rim, cobalt blue w/overall iridescent blue lustre, signed "L.C. Tiffany - Favrile - 1103-7725K," ca. 1915 (some surface scratches)..................................... **863**

**Vase,** 5" h., simple ovoid form w/widely flaring neck, eight-ribbed body in ambergris cased to transparent peacock blue exterior, the interior w/gold Favrile lustre, ribs in downward pulled silver dots, base signed "L.C. Tiffany - Favrile R812" (ILLUS. top next column) ........................ **2,875**

**Vase,** 5 1/2" h., floriform, a bulbous body in cobalt blue w/a wide flared & ruffled rim, stretch iridescence at the rim, strong blue lustre, short stem & applied disk foot, signed "L.C. Tiffany - Favrile 9041E".................................................... **978**

**Vase,** 5 1/2" h., ovoid body tapering to a small thick molded mouth, millefiori-type in amber iridescent w/green heart-shaped leaves on trailing vines & small

white cane flowers w/red & yellow centers, signed "L. C. Tiffany W8517 Favrile," ca. 1905 ..................................... **1,840**

*Tiffany Internal Lustre Vase*

**Vase,** 6 3/4" h., bud-type, footed waisted ovoid body tapering to a tall slender waisted neck w/cupped rim, opalescent w/pink & gold iridescent trailings, signed "L.C.T. - 010626"...................................... **1,725**

**Vase,** 7 1/8" h., "Tel el Amarna," flared base tapering to a widely flaring trumpet body w/a rounded shoulder centered by a domed neck w/small mouth, body in iridescent reddish bronze, the neck w/gold iridescent ground decorated w/interlaced green & gold zigzag bands, signed "L.C. Tiffany - Favrile 8699G," ca. 1912............. **4,600**

**Vase,** 7 1/4" h., paperweight-type, a broad ovoid body tapering to a short cylindrical neck, pale aqua decorated internally w/yellow, red & black millefiori flowers among trailing heart leaves & vines of deep green w/ochre swirls, base signed "L.C. Tiffany - Favrile 3527 P," also w/paper label, ca. 1920 ............................. **6,900**

**Vase,** 8" h., waisted cylindrical lower body below a wide compressed bulbous upper body w/a band of dimples below the low rolled rim, grey w/overall silvery blue & gold iridescence, "L.C. Tiffany Inc. Favrile 38-763," early 1900s................. **575**

**Vase,** 9" h., a tall ten-ribbed tapering ovoid body w/a slightly flared scalloped rim, raised on a slender knobbed stem & ribbed slightly domed foot, blue w/strong blue iridescence, signed "L.C. Tiffany - Favrile - 1524-3333 P," ca. 1920.............. **2,415**

**Vase,** 9" h., disk foot below squatty bulbous base tapering to a tall ribbed cylindrical neck w/a flaring flattened rim, gold iridescence w/bluish purple highlights, signed "LC Tiffany Favrile #1834"............... **880**

**Vase,** 10" h., slender trumpet-form w/a disk button pedestal on a flattened round foot, deep blue w/golden blue iridescence, signed "7244J L.C. Tiffany - Favrile" ......................................................... **977**

**Vase,** 18 7/8" h., jack-in-the-pulpit form, wide ruffled rim turned up in the back & down in the front, raised on a very slender stem on a round cushion foot, overall gold iridescence, signed "L.C. Tiffany - Favrile 732C," ca. 1908............................ **16,100**

**Vase,** 20 1/4" h., double-bulbed form w/an elongated neck of ambergris decorated w/blue iridescent pulled feathers rising to red & gold lustre at the top base, signed "L.C.T. E550" & w/a paper label, ca. 1895 (rust-colored blemish to neck iridescence, inclusions in neck) ................... **2,760**

**Vases,** 20" h., conical base tapering sharply to a tall slender 'stick' neck, iridescent greenish blue band of upright pointed leaves around the base, overall iridescent gold necks, signed "L.C. Tiffany - Favrile," numbered "8929J" & "8934J," ca. 1915, pr. ............................... **3,737**

**Wines,** deep stepped, flaring & gently ruffled bowl on a slender stem & round domed foot, pastel blue w/wide white opalescent bands, some signed, some w/paper label, set of 10 ........................... **3,450**

## TIFFIN

*A wide variety of fine glasswares were produced by the Tiffin Glass Company of Tiffin, Ohio. Beginning as a part of the large U.S. Glass Company early in this century, the Tiffin factory continued making a wide range of wares until its final closing in 1984. One popular line is now called "Black Satin" and included various vases with raised floral designs. Many other acid-etched and hand-cut patterns were also produced over the years and are very collectible today. The three "Tiffin Glassmasters" books by Fred Bickenheuser, are the standard references for Tiffin collectors.*

**Candlesticks,** etched Cadena patt., No. 5831, yellow, pr. .......................................... **$115**

**Candlesticks,** model of a cat, Black Satin, No. 69, pr. ........................................................ **275**

**Candlesticks,** two-light, etched Cherokee Rose patt., No. 5902, clear, pr. ................... **127**

**Candy dish,** cov., pedestal foot, Gazebo etching, blue................................................ **145**

**Champagne,** cut Charlton patt., clear ............... **22**

**Champagne,** etched Cherokee Rose patt., No. 17403, clear ....................................... **20**

**Champagne,** etched Cherokee Rose patt., No. 17399 stem, clear, 4 oz. ........................ **31**

**Champagne,** Classic (platinum) patt., clear....... **25**

**Champagne,** cut Mystic patt., clear ................... **26**

**Champagne,** etched Persian Pheasant patt., No. 17358, clear.................................... **24**

**Claret,** etched Cherokee Rose patt., No. 17399, clear ............................................. **50**

**Claret,** etched June Night patt., clear, 6 1/4" h. ................................................... **40**

**Claret,** gold-encrusted Minton patt., clear .......... **20**

**Claret,** etched Persian Pheasant patt., No. 17358, clear ....................................... **39**

**Cocktail,** etched Cherokee Rose patt., No. 17399, clear, 3 1/2 oz. ............................. **18**

**Cocktail,** etched Cherokee Rose patt., No. 17403, clear, 3 1/2 oz. ................................. **25**

**Cocktail,** etched Flanders patt., No. 15024, yellow, 4 3/4" h. ...................................... **31**

**Cocktail,** etched Fuchsia patt., No. 15083, clear, 4 1/4" h. ........................................ **19**

**Cocktail,** cut Lausanne patt., clear ................... **17**

**Compote,** stemmed, etched Flanders patt., pink................................................. **750**

**Console bowl,** flared, etched Byzantine patt., clear, 12 5/8" ...................................... **135**

**Cordial,** etched Fuchsia patt., clear, 1 oz.......... **80**

**Cordial,** etched Fuchsia patt., No. 15083, clear ....................................................... **43**

**Cordial,** etched June Night patt., clear, 5 1/4" h. ................................................... **48**

**Cordial,** etched Rambling Rose patt., clear....... **28**

**Cordial,** etched Rose patt., No. 17474, clear ....................................................... **25**

**Cup & saucer,** etched Flanders patt., clear, pr. ......................................................... **45**

**Flower arranger,** Twilight cutting, free-form, clear (manufacturing flaw).................. **60**

**Goblet,** sherry, etched Cherokee Rose patt.No. 17399, clear...................................... **40**

**Goblet,** water, etched Cherokee Rose, No. 17399, clear, 9 oz. ..................................... **32**

**Goblet,** sherry, etched June Night patt., clear ....................................................... **39**

**Parfait,** etched June Night patt., clear, 6 5/8" h. ................................................... **60**

**Pitcher,** footed, etched Flanders patt., pink, 64 oz. ...................................................... **495**

**Plate,** 8" d., etched Flanders patt., pink ............ **22**

**Plate,** 8" d., etched June Night patt., clear ......... **11**

**Tray,** center-handled, etched Flanders patt., pink...................................................... **430**

**Tumbler,** footed, etched Classic patt., clear, 2 1/2 oz., 2 3/4" h. ............................. **40**

**Tumbler,** ice tea, etched June Night patt., clear, 6 5/8" h. ......................................... **34**

**Tumbler,** juice, footed, etched June Night patt., No. 17403, clear .................................. **26**

**Vase,** 6 1/2" h., bud, etched Fuchsia patt., clear ....................................................... **30**

**Vase,** 8 1/2" h., Twilight cutting, blue.................. **65**

**Vase,** bud, 11" h., etched Fuchsia patt., No. 15082, clear .......................................... **100**

**Wine,** Classic (platinum) patt., clear, 4 15/16" h. ................................................... **32**

## VENETIAN

*Venetian glass has been made for six centuries on the island of Murano, where it continues to be produced. The skilled glass artisans developed numerous techniques, subsequently imitated elsewhere.*

**Bowl,** 10 3/4" l., "filigrano," footed deep rounded elongated leaf-form in clear internally decorated w/alternating pink, blue & white filigrano threading, unsigned Fratelli Toso.............................. **$373**

*Large Venetian Glass Bowl*

**Bowl,** 14" l., the oblong bowl composed of caramel-colored tiles of glass delineated in black, designed by Ercole Barovier, inscribed "barovier & toso - murano," ca. 1956 (ILLUS.)........................ **1,265**

**Bowl-vases,** flat base w/rounded flaring cut & curled sides, cased w/coarse pink powder application, enhanced by gold foil on the exterior, 20th c., 4" h., pr. .......... **345**

**Decanter w/stopper,** tall cylindrical form tapering to the rim, colorless w/pink latticino striped design on the body & the hollow ball-shaped stopper, mid-20th c., 18 1/2" h....................... **173**

**Figure,** drum major, clear stylized standing figure w/blue applied hat, epaulets, buttons & tooled leaf, on blue-trimmed disk foot, unsigned, attributed to Barovier Seguso Ferro, ca. 1930s, 8 3/4" h. .............. **517**

**Figures,** jazz musicians, each seated w/the body in blue powders cased in clear "bullicante" glass, applied heads, hands & feet in clear w/foil inclusions, one holding banjo, the other an accordion, unsigned Barovier & Toso, ca. 1930, 6 1/2" h., pr. ........................................... **2,875**

*Venetian Lamp with Encased Figure*

**Lamps,** figural, each a freeform crystal upright slender block w/trapped bubble highlights encasing a figure of a stylized man or woman in black & white period costume w/gold foil trim, supported by an applied dome base, metal lamp fittings, mid-20th c., glass 18 1/2" h., pr. (ILLUS.)..................... **978**

**Model of a bird,** free-blown elongated "J-form" stylized bird in bluish green w/millefiore eyes & three bands of murines around the body in blue & red, designed by Alessandro Pianon, ca, 1961, label reads "Vistosi," 12 1/4" h. ....... **1,840**

**Model of a bird,** swan-like bird w/a clear applied long comb on head & pointed beak on a blue head & curved long neck shading to a red body w/raised ribbed

wings, on a clear ribbed pedestal, paper label w/"Made in Italy - Murano," 11" h.......... **72**

**Model of a bird,** blown egg-shaped body w/applied head & beak & high arched tail, twisted purple & white ribbons between layers of gold leaf, ca. 1950s, 6" l. ............... **69**

**Model of a bird,** whimsical creature blown as a brilliant red sphere w/applied "murrhine" eyes & tiny point for beak, raised on clear knobs w/wire legs & feet, designed by Alessandro Pianon, unsigned but w/paper label "MADE IN ITALY - MURANO," ca. 1961, 9" h. .......... **2,185**

**Model of a bull,** free-blown in orange & clear, signed "Seguso," 14" l. ...................... **805**

**Model of a dove,** large stylized bird in white latticino & pink twisted filigrano, applied clear beak & feet, original paper label w/"G.F. Murano made in Italy," ca. 1950s, 7" h. ...................... **173**

**Model of a pigeon,** "a trina," footed deep rounded body w/upright head & long forked tail, upright pointed wings, clear internally decorated w/white, black & copper-colored aventurine trailings, the figure molded w/ribs, applied beak & crest, designed by Dino Martens, unsigned Aureliano Toso, ca. 1954, 5 1/2" h. ...................... **747**

**Model of a polar bear,** "scavo," highly stylized model of a bear w/arched back & pointed snout, grey w/roughened & spotted textured surface, designed by Alfredo Barbini, ca. 1952, unsigned, 10 1/2" l., 5 3/4" h. ...................... **862**

**Model of a rooster,** "mezza filigrana," blown deep U-form body w/the head held high & a long arched & fluted tail, the body & tail in clear internally decorated w/spiraling canes in white, red & copper colored inclusions, the crest, beak & base in clear w/gold foil inclusions, designed by Dino Martens, unsigned Aureliano Toso, ca. 1954, 9 3/4" h. ...................... **460**

**Model of a swan,** "a trina," round-footed deep rounded body w/a long curved neck & pointed tail, raised wings at the sides, clear internally decorated w/white canes & trails of copper-colored aventurine, applied black glass beak & eyes, designed by Dino Martens, unsigned, Aureliano Toso, ca. 1954 ...................... **575**

**Sculpture,** in amber yellow & green, disk molded w/the surrealistic image of a face, designed by Max Ernst Elfo III, for Fucina degli Angeli Venezia, inscribed "Elfo 3/di Max Ernst 159/300," mounted on plexiglass, ca. 1966, 1 1/2" thick, 6 1/4" d. ...................... **1,265**

**Vase,** 4 3/4" h., handkerchief-type, folded upright ruffled form composed of opaque light blue, transparent blue, gold & clear in vertical stripes, paper foil label w/"Murano Glass Made in Italy," mid-20th c. ...................... **230**

**Vase,** 4 3/4" h., "scavo," wide squatty bulbous body tapering to a small short

flared neck, pale orange w/a roughly textured surface, designed by Gino Cene-
dese, unsigned, ca. 1952 ......................... **1,035**
**Vase,** 5" h., Amberina coloration, original
paper label "Murano - Seguso," 1950s........... **78**
**Vase,** 6 1/4" h., "zanfirico," footed slender
ovoid body tapering to a small molded
mouth, body w/vertical bands of "zanfirico" canes in orange & white latticino &
blue & clear cane strips, applied clear
foot & rim w/gold foil inclusions,
unsigned Aureliano Toso, ca. 1940s............ **373**

## VICTORIAN COLORED GLASS

*There are, of course, many types of colored
glassware of the Victorian era and we cover a great
variety of these in our various glass categories.
However, there are some pieces of pressed, mold-
blown and free-blown Victorian colored glass which
don't fit well into other specific listings, so we have
chosen to include a selection of them here.*

**Bowl,** 5 1/4" d., 3 1/4" h., deep cylindrical
sides w/a widely ruffled rim, sapphire
blue enameled around the sides w/color-
ful flowers & leaves in orange, blue,
white, green & pink...................................... **$110**
**Box w/hinged lid,** squatty bulbous round
body in lime green decorated w/white
enameled scrolls, the low domed matching cover decorated w/gold foliage &
white scrolls, 6 1/4" d., 3 1/2" h. ................... **195**
**Cruet w/stopper,** optic ribbed ovoid body
tapering to a tall cylindrical neck
w/pinched spout, sapphire blue decorated around the shoulder w/yellow &
white daisy-like blossoms & white stems
& leaves, applied amber handle & amber
teardrop stopper, 3" d., 8" h. ...................... **165**
**Cruet w/stopper** pressed Tree of Life patt.,
blue opaque ..................................................... **80**

*Decorated Liqueur Set*

**Liqueuer set:** 9 1/2" h. decanter, four
matching cups & a round tray w/flared
rim; all in greenish amber, the decanter

w/a footed bottle-form optic ribbed body
w/a tricorner rim & applied amber handle
& teardrop stopper, matching optic
ribbed cups w/applied handles, decanter
& cups enameled w/stylied blossoms &
leaf sprigs, tray 8 1/2" d., decanter
9 1/2" h., the set (ILLUS.)............................ **225**
**Syrup pitcher w/original metal lid,**
Inverted Coin Spot patt., swirled base,
blue, Central Glass Co. ............................... **138**

*Ornate Fanned Vase*

**Vase,** 11 1/4" h., 7 1/2" w., cylindrical sapphire blue body w/a widely flattened &
fanned top, heavily enameled w/a gold
banner trimmed w/pink & yellow flowers
& sprays on the front & a small spray on
the back, applied clear ruffled rim band
& tall applied clear feet (ILLUS.) ................. **245**
**Whimsey,** figural shoe thimble, blue ............... **148**

## WAVE CREST

*Now much sought after, Wave Crest was pro-
duced by the C.F. Monroe Co., Meriden, Connecticut, in the late 19th and early 20th centuries from
opaque white glass blown into molds.*

*It was then hand-decorated in enamels and
metal trim was often added. Boudoir accessories
such as jewel boxes, hair receivers, etc., were predominant.*

### WAVE CREST WARE
*Wave Crest Mark*

**Bowl,** 5 1/2" d., dresser-type, scroll-molded
design w/floral decoration on a dark blue
ground, marked .......................................... **$138**
**Box w/hinged lid & metal feet,** decorated
w/pink blossoms on blue ground, key
lock, 5" sq., 6" h............................................ **743**
**Cigar box w/hinged lid,** Egg Crate mold,
the front panel marked "Cigars," the
other sides & top decorated w/delicate
rose strawflowers & stems, separate lid
compartment for sponge, unmarked,
6 1/2" w. ....................................................... **770**

*Wave Crest Cracker Jar*

**Cracker jar,** cov., barrel-shaped w/a cream ground decorated w/soft pink, blue & yellow flowers & green leaves on brown branches, unmarked, replated silver plate rim, cover & bail handle, 5 1/4" d., 8 1/4" h. (ILLUS.) .......................................... **295**

**Cracker jar w/hinged lid,** Puffy mold w/overall decoration of large sprays of blue flowers & leaves, 9 1/2" h. .................... **245**

**Dish,** round w/applied brass collar, decorated w/pansies, signed, 5 1/2" d. ............... **110**

**Dresser box w/hinged lid,** Helmschied Swirl mold, decorated w/a wide central pale blue band decorated w/white daisies & green leafy stems, outlined in delicate gilt scrolls on a white ground, unlined, unmarked, 7 1/4" d. ....................... **403**

**Dresser box w/hinged lid,** round squatty cover w/ornate wide border of molded scrolls enclosing a cluster of flowers against a pink blush ground, the low matching base in opaque white, signed, 7 1/2" d. ....................................................... **523**

**Dresser box w/hinged lid,** squared shape w/heavy rib in each corner & rounded edges, scroll-bordered cartouches on cover & each side, decorated w/flowers in each cartouche, marked, 5" w. (key missing) .......................................................... **358**

**Dresser box w/hinged lid,** Petticoat mold top decorated w/h.p. florals, Baroque Shell base, hinged gilt-metal rims, trademark on the base, 3" h. ................................ **316**

**Ewer,** ovoid egg-shaped body decorated w/large pink wild rose blossoms & green leafy stems, an attached ormolu neck & handle, the spiral-twist neck topped by a high wide spout, the scrolled handle topped w/a winged putto head, signed, 6 1/2" h. ....................................................... **990**

**Handkerchief box w/hinged lid,** rectangular low domed cover w/rounded corners & sides molded w/a border of scrolls centering a wild rose decoration, the matching low rounded base raised on an

ormolu frame w/scrolled legs, signed, 6 x 9 1/2" .................................................. **1,155**

**Jardiniere,** large bulbous form w/a transfer decoration of large blue flowers, 10" d., 7 3/4" h. ....................................................... **275**

# WESTMORELAND

*Westmoreland Specialty Company was founded in East Liverpool, Ohio in 1889 and relocated in 1890 to Grapeville, Pennsylvania where it remained until its closing in 1985.*

*During its early years Westmoreland specialized in glass food containers and novelties but by the turn of the century they had a large line of milk white items and clear tableware patterns. In 1925 the company name was shortened to The Westmoreland Glass Company and it was during that decade that more colored glasswares entered their line-up. When Victorian-style milk glass again became popular in the 1940s and 1950s, Westmoreland produced extensive amounts in several patterns which closely resemble late 19th century wares. These and their figural animal dishes in milk white and colors are widely collected today but buyers should not confuse them for the antique originals. Watch for Westmoreland's "WG" mark on some pieces. A majority of our listings are products from the 1940s through the 1970s. Earlier pieces will be indicated.*

*Westmoreland Marks*

**Ashtray,** Beaded Grape patt., milk white ......... **$10**

**Ashtray,** square, Paneled Grape patt., milk white, large ..................................................... **19**

**Basket,** Paneled Grape patt., footed, scalloped, milk white, 10 1/2" ............................. **90**

**Bowl,** cov., 4" sq., Beaded Grape patt., milk white ................................................... **30**

**Bowl,** cov., 5" sq., footed w/flared rim, Beaded Grape patt., milk white ..................... **20**

**Bowl,** 8 1/2" d., lipped rim, Paneled Grape patt., milk white .......................................... **90**

**Bowl,** 9" d., footed, lipped, Paneled Grape patt., milk white .......................................... **88**

**Cake salver,** skirted square, footed, Beaded Grape patt., milk white, 11" d. ........... **67**

**Cake stand,** Beaded Grape patt., footed, milk white, 9 1/2" sq. ..................................... **70**

**Candlesticks,** Beaded Grape patt., milk white, 4" sq., pr. ............................................ **16**

**Candlesticks,** Paneled Grape patt., milk white, 4" pr. ................................................. **21**

**Celery vase,** Paneled Grape patt., milk white .......................................................... **35**

**Celery vase,** footed, Paneled Grape patt., milk white, 6" h. .......................................... **39**

**Cigarette box,** cov., Beaded Grape patt., milk glass, 4 x 6" ............................................. **25**

**Compote,** cov., 7" h., footed, Paneled Grape patt., milk white .................................. 33
**Cordial,** footed, Waterford patt., No. 5, clear w/ruby stain, 1 oz. .............................. 49
**Cruets w/original stopper,** Paneled Grape patt., milk white, pr. ......................................... 38
**Cup,** Paneled Grape patt., milk white .................. 8
**Flowerpot,** Paneled Grape patt., milk white, 4 1/4" h.............................................. 30
**Gravy boat & liner,** Paneled Grape patt., milk white ................................................. 40
**Jardiniere,** Paneled Grape patt., milk white, 5" h.................................................. 18
**Jardiniere,** Paneled Grape patt., milk white, 6 1/2" h.............................................. 20
**Nappy,** round, Paneled Grape patt., milk white, 4 1/2" d. ............................................. 9
**Nappy,** round, handled, Paneled Grape patt., milk white, 5" d. ........................... 14
**Pickle dish,** Paneled Grape patt., oval, milk white, 8" l. ............................................. 13
**Pitcher,** milk, Paneled Grape patt., milk white, small ................................................. 18
**Vase,** 14" h., Paneled Grape patt., milk white.............................................. 55
**Vase,** 11 1/2" h., bell-rimmed, footed, Paneled Grape patt., milk white .......................... 45

# GOLDILOCKS & THE THREE BEARS COLLECTIBLES

*The story of The Three Bears is probably the most loved children's story of all time. It has been printed in almost every language, and done in pantomime & play form. The story has been celebrated in musical versions, children's games, books & toys. It is as new & exciting to today's children as it was when it was written in 1831. Goldilocks did not appear until the 1880s.*

**Advertisement,** Morton Salt, featuring Goldilocks & The Three Bears, 1955 .......... **$22**
**Art print,** The Three Bears............................ **22-30**

*Mechanical Bank, 1950-1960*

**Bank,** mechanical, lithographed, three bears fishing, Japan, made from 1950 to 1960 (ILLUS.)............................................. **200**
**Blanket,** 1960s .............................................. **10-12**
**Book,** Big Golden Book, 1948.................... **12-20**
**Book,** Blue Ribbon pop-up, oversized, illustrated by C. Carey Cloud & Harold B. Lentz, 1934 .................................................. **125**

**Book,** by Bertha Moore, Triplets Series, 1938-48 ...................................................... **15**
**Book,** by Margaret Hillert, easy to read version, 1963 ............................................... **5**
**Book,** by Reilly & Britton, Children's Red Books Series, two stories in each small book, The Three Bears were paired w/Cinderella, 1915, hardback......................... **45**

*Hurst Cut-out & Paste Book*

**Book,** cut-out & paste book, Hurst & Co., 1916 (ILLUS.)................................................. **60**
**Book,** Eight Fairy Tales, edited by Watty Piper, Platt & Munk Co., 1950........................ **25**
**Book,** Golden Shape Book, 1976...................... **2-7**
**Book,** illustrated by C.R. Stone, large format linen-like book, Whitman, 1933 ......... **40-50**
**Book,** illustrated by Frances Brundage, early 1900s............................................... **40-55**

*1900 Warne & Co. Book*

**Book,** illustrated by Leslie Brooke, Warne & Co., ca. 1900 (ILLUS.) ........................... **50-75**
**Book,** illustrated by Lilian Obligado, Merrigold Press, 1980 .............................................. **5**

*1888 McLoughlin Version*

**Book,** illustrated by R. Andre, McLoughlin
Brothers, 1888 (ILLUS.) .................................. **75**
**Book,** Linen Series, oversize, Saalfield,
1919 ...................................................................... **35**
**Book,** Little Golden Book, 1965 ...................... **3-6**
**Book,** Little Golden Book, illustrated by
Feodor Rojankovsky, 1st edition, first
cover only had one printing, 1948 .................. **60**

*1948 Little Golden Book*

**Book,** Little Golden Book, illustrated by
Feodor Rojankovsky, 2nd cover, 1948
(ILLUS.)...................................................................... **10**
**Book,** mini pop-up, Price Stern Sloan, no
date .............................................................................. **3-6**
**Book,** paper cover, standard size, Platt &
Munk Co., 1930s ............................................. **35**
**Book,** paper, oversized, Whitman, 1941 ........... **12**
**Book,** Platt & Munk 3000 Series, linen-like
paper w/12 pages, color illustrations, ca.
1930s ...................................................................... **35**
**Book,** Platt & Munk 3000 Series, smooth
paper w/12 pages, color illustrations, ca.
1930s ...................................................................... **10**
**Book,** pop-up, Czechoslovakia, 1971 ........... **10-15**

*1972 School Primer*

**Book,** primer, The Three Bears on the
cover & also the first story, 1972
(ILLUS.)...................................................................... **5-10**
**Book,** Read and Hear Golden Book,
record/book combination............................. **5-8**
**Book,** Square Golden Book, 1967 .................. **4-10**

**Book,** Stampkraft Series, oversize/oblong,
w/colored illustrations on stamps to
paste on story pages..................................... **45**
**Book,** Story Parade, illustrated by Milo
Winter, Merrill, 1940...................................... **15**
**Book,** Tell-a-Tale edition, 1952 ........................ **5-7**
**Book,** Tell-a-Tale edition, 1955 ........................ **7-8**
**Book,** Tell-a-Tale edition, first cover, 1945........ **15**
**Book,** Tell-a-Tale edition, second cover,
1945 ...................................................................... **10**
**Book,** The Three Bears & Other Stories,
illustrated by George Trimmer, Merrill,
1951 ...................................................................... **8-10**
**Book,** Tip Top Elf Book, illustrated by Clare
McKinley, 1951.................................................. **12-15**
**Book,** Tip Top Elf Book, illustrated by Eliza-
beth Webbe, 1959 ......................................... **3-5**
**Book,** Wee Books for Wee Folks Series,
Platt & Munk Co., 1930s-40s ...................... **15**
**Card game,** Milton Bradley, ca. 1920............ **50-55**
**Cereal premium,** Kelloggs, early 1960s ........... **20**
**Charm,** sterling silver, 3D .................................. **12**
**Coloring book,** 1948 ....................................... **10-12**
**Cookie cutters,** Goldilocks & The Three
Bears...................................................................... **12**
**Cookie jar,** ........................................................... **75**
**Doll,** topsy-turvy type, cloth, ca. 1960s.............. **25**
**Embroidered picture,** framed, early 1900s.. **25-40**
**Figures,** bisque, small, Japanese, the set......... **35**
**Figures,** The Three Bears Family,
w/removable clothes, shown in the FAO
Schwarz Catalog of 1932, the set ............... **150**
**Game,** Cadaco-Ellis, 1954.................................. **30**
**Game,** Little Goldenlocks & The Three
Bears, McLoughlin Bros., 1892 .................... **250**
**Instructor Magazine,** w/TheThree Bears
cover, 1920s...................................................... **15**
**Nesting set,** Russian .......................................... **15**
**Paper dolls,** The Three Bears in great big
cut-outs, #2142, Saalfield........................... **60-75**
**Pillow case,** vintage............................................ **10**
**Play book,** folding panorama type, 1890s ......... **75**
**Postcard,** early 1900s........................................ **10**

*1980s Reproduction Block Puzzle*

**Puzzle,** block type, early 1980s reproduc-
tion (ILLUS.) ....................................................... **12**
**Puzzle,** lithographed, original box, 1925 ........... **50**
**Puzzle,** tray type, Japan ..................................... **18**
**Record,** Columbia, 1947 ...................................... **8**
**Sand bucket,** w/shovel, Chein .......................... **30**
**Tea set,** china, miniature, 1980s ....................... **15**
**Tea set,** tin, no markings ............................... **35-50**
**Theater,** cardboard, Goldilocks, 1915 ........... **60-75**
**Toy suitcase,** child's .......................................... **20**

# GRANITEWARE

This is a name given to metal (customarily iron) kitchenware covered with an enamel coating. Featured at the 1876 Philadelphia Centennial Exposition, it became quite popular for it was lightweight, attractive, and easy to clean. Although it was made in huge quantities and is still produced, it has caught the attention of a younger generation of collectors and prices have steadily risen over the past few years. There continues to be a constant demand for the wide variety of these utilitarian articles turned out earlier in this century and rare forms now command high prices.

## BLUE & WHITE SWIRL

*Blue & White Swirl Cream Can*

**Cream can,** cov., 5" d., 9" h. (ILLUS.) ............ **$275**
**Double boiler,** cov., 3 pc.s, 6 1/2" d.,
    8 1/2" h. ....................................................... **225**

*Blue & White Swirl Railroad Mug*

**Mug,** railroad advertisement, "C.G.W.Ry." (Chicago and Great Western Railroad), 2 3/4" d., 2 3/4" h. (ILLUS.) .......................... **350**
**Mug,** straight-sided Columbian Ware, one of a set of 4, 4" d., 2 3/4" h., each .............. **125**

## BLUE DIAMOND WARE (IRIS BLUE & WHITE SWIRL)

*Blue Diamond Coffee Biggin*

**Coffee biggin,** cov., three-piece, 3 1/2" d., 7 1/2" h. (ILLUS.) ..................................... **1,000**

*Blue Diamond Sugar Bowl*

**Sugar bowl,** cov., 3 1/2" d., 6 1/4" h. (ILLUS.) ....................................................... **500**
**Vegetable dish,** oval, 9 1/2" l., 7 1/2" w. ......... **200**

## BROWN & WHITE SWIRL

*Brown & White Swirl Coffee Biggin*

**Coffee biggin,** tin biggin & cover, 3 1/2" d.,
 7 1/2" h. (ILLUS.)........................................ **1,000**

*Brown & White Swirl Pitcher*

**Pitcher,** 5" d., 7 1/2" h. (ILLUS.)........................ **500**
**Spoon,** 9 3/4" l. .................................................. **150**

## CHRYSOLITE & WHITE SWIRL (DARK GREEN & WHITE SWIRL)

**Coaster,** 3/4" h, 3 1/2" d. ................................. **300**

*Chrysolite Cream Can*

**Cream can,** w/tin cover, 4 1/2" d., 7" h.
 (ILLUS.)........................................................ **700**
**Mug,** miner's, tankard, 4 1/4" d., 5" h. ............. **200**

*Chrysolite Pitcher*

**Pitcher,** tankard, 7" d., 12" h. (ILLUS.)............. **600**

*Chrysolite Skillet*

**Skillet,** 1 3/4" h., 10 1/4" d. (ILLUS.) ............... **300**

## COBALT BLUE & WHITE SWIRL

*Cobalt Blue Swirl Candlestick*

**Candlestick,** 5" d., 2 1/2" h. (ILLUS.)............... **950**

*Cobalt Blue Swirl Dinner Bucket*

**Dinner bucket,** cov., three-piece, 7 1/4" d.,
 10 1/4" h. (ILLUS.).................................... **1,000**
**Measurer,** 2 3/4" d., 3 1/2" h. .......................... **600**
**Measurer,** 3 1/2" d., 4 1/2" h. .......................... **550**
**Measurer,** 4" d., 6 1/2" h. ............................... **500**
**Measurer,** 5" d., 8 1/4" h. ............................... **500**

*Cobalt Blue Swirl Sugar Bowls*

**Sugar bowl,**    open,   footed,   4 1/2" d.,
 2 3/4" h. (ILLUS.)........................................... **400**

**Sugar bowl,** cov., 4 1/2" d., 5 3/4" h. (ILLUS.) ........................................ **950**

## EMERALD WARE
## (GREEN & WHITE SWIRL)

*Emerald Ware Plate*

**Plate,** dinner, 9" d. (ILLUS.) ............................. **225**

*Emerald Ware Syrup or Molasses Pitcher*

**Syrup or molasses pitcher,** cov., 3 1/2" d., 6 1/4" h. (ILLUS.) ....................... **1,000**

## GRAY (MOTTLED)

*Canning Jar*

**Canning jar,** 3 1/2" d., 4 1/2" h. (ILLUS.) ........ **400**

*Octagonal Ansonia Clock*

**Clock,** octagonal, Ansonia, works, one of a kind, 9" d. (ILLUS.) ............................ **Priceless**
**Teapot,** cov., 3 1/2" d., 5" d. (ILLUS.) ............... **200**

*Gray Graniteware Teapots*

**Teapot,** cov., straight spout, 3 1/2" d., 5" h. (ILLUS.) ...................................................... **200**

## CHILDREN'S ITEMS,
## MINIATURES & SALESMAN'S
## SAMPLES

*Saleman's Sample Chamber Pot*

**Chamber pot,** salesman's sample, blue & white swirl, 2 1/2" d., 1 3/4" h. (ILLUS.) ........ **500**

*Child's Feeding Dish*

**Dish,** child's feeding, solid blue w/girl & Teddy bear, 1 1/4" h., 7 1/2" d. (ILLUS.) ........ **85**

*Miniature Percolator Funnel*

**Funnel,** percolator, miniature, solid blue, white interior, 2 1/4" d., 3 3/4" h. (ILLUS.) ...................................................... **200**
**Gravy boat,** miniature, solid blue, white interior, 1 1/2" h., 3 1/2" l. ............................ **200**

*Saleman's Sample Gravy Kettle*

**Kettle,** saleman's sample, gravy, w/tin cover, 2 3/4" d., 3" h. (ILLUS.) ..................... **500**

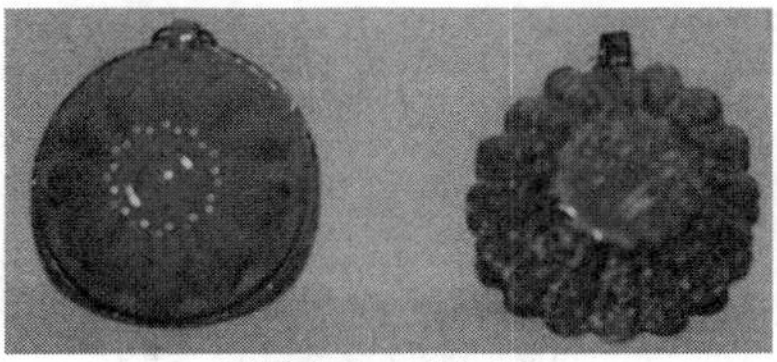

*Miniature Molds*

**Mold,** miniature, fluted, blue w/white specks, 2 1/4" d. (ILLUS. right) ................... **150**
**Mold,** miniature, Turk's head, solid blue, w/white interior, 2 1/4" d. (ILLUS. left) ......... **225**
**Pitcher & bowl set,** salesman's sample, gray, bowl 1 1/4" h., 4 1/4" d., pitcher 2 1/4" d., 2 3/4" h. ....................................... **500**

*Miniature Tea Set*

**Tea set:** miniature, cov. teapot, four cups, four saucers, creamer & cov. sugar bowl; white w/blue design, teapot 3 1/4" d., 5 1/4" h., the set (ILLUS.)............. **450**

# MISCELLANEOUS GRANITEWARE & RELATED ITEMS

*Cookbook*

**Cookbook,** "Granite Ware," dated 1883, 3 1/2" x 5" (ILLUS.)....................................... **200**
**Paperweight,** stove advertising, gray enamel on cast iron, 2 1/2" d., 3 1/2" h. ...... **200**
**Sign,** advertising, "Nesco Enameled Ware," wooden, light blue w/cobalt blue lettering, 34" l., 8 1/2" h. ..................................... **350**

# HARDWARE

*Egpytian Revival Door knocker*

**Bin pulls,** iron, eyebrow form w/reticulated decoration, 1 1/2 x 3", set........................... **$130**
**Coat hooks,** one w/lion's head, other in form of deer antlers, 4 1/2" l., ea. .................. **75**
**Display board,** bronze, hardware store, oval knob & rosette on wood base, 4" sq........ **25**
**Display board,** hardware store, door latch w/built-in stand, Sargent, 5 x 15".................... **15**
**Door handle,** "bluebird", owl, urn, sunflowers, fern & chevrons, marked "Nashua" on reverse, 2 1/2 x 15" (sunflower on thumb latch is heavily worn) ......................... **750**

**Door handles,** French-type, bronze w/curled ends, set of 4, ca. 1920s, 4 1/2" l., each ................................................. 40

**Door handles,** nickel plated, S-form w/curled ends, group of 5, 4 1/2" l., each ....... 25

**Door knob,** copper clad Roman warrior, cast lead covered w/copper, R&E, ca. 1875, 2 1/2" ................................................. 400

**Door knob,** Flying Crane, sharp details & good color, marked on reverse, R&E, 2 1/4" ....................................................... 750

**Door knocker,** Egyptian revival, large scale w/fine bronze patina, European origin, 19th c., 4 x 8" (ILLUS.) ................. 200

**Door plates,** passage-type, each w/figural motif such as stork & sunflower, 2 x 4", each .............................................................. 60

**Doorbell,** cast iron, "T" lever, neo-grec style, ca. 1875, 1 1/2 x 4" ............................... 45

**Doorbell button,** bronze, Colonial revival-style, late 1880s, 2 1/2 x 9 1/2" .................... 100

*Double Doorbell Button*

**Doorbell button,** double-type, neoclassical style w/anthemions, beading, & egg & dart decoration, 2 x 7" (ILLUS.) ...................... 60

**Doorbell knob,** glass, brass shank, tapered spindle w/original threaded back plate, ca. 1860s, 1 1/5" d. ............................... 35

**Doorbell knobs,** cast bronze, miniature, one by Russell & Erwin, other by Mallory Wheeler, 2" d., pr. ......................................... 90

**Doorbell lever,** bronze, knob end, Corbin, ca. 1880, 1 1/2 x 4" .......................... 220

*Coiled Rope Entry Doorknob*

**Doorknob,** bronze, entry-type, "Coiled Rope," Art Deco styling, 2 1/2" (ILLUS.) ....... 100

*Bronze Entry Doorknob*

**Doorknob,** bronze, entry-type, Crow Wing County Courthouse from Minnesota, some wear, 2 1/2" (ILLUS.) ........................... 325

**Doorknob,** cast bronze, entry-type, on slender, footed shank, 2 1/2" ....................... 225

**Doorknob,** entry-type, Canova patt., solid bronze w/banded edge, Penn Hardware, 2 1/2" d. ................................................... 60

**Doorknob,** entry-type, Dragonfly, European origin, slotted shank, 2 1/2" (some wear) .............................................................. 275

**Doorknob,** entry-type, finely cast details including Greek key border, Branford, 5" d. ........................................................... 55

**Doorknob,** entry-type, w/acanthus leaves, high relief & two part construction ................. 15

**Doorknob,** entry-type, w/initials CB, 2 1/2" d. (some bad drilling around screw hole & shank) ..................................... 35

*Lime Green Glass Entry Knob*

**Doorknob,** glass, entry-type, lime green, cut & polished to a point, w/large chip on base & sawn off spindle (ILLUS.) ................. 150

**Doorknob,** "Judgment", passage size, excellent condition, 2 1/4" ............................ 700

**Doorknob,** mercury glass w/nickel-plated shank, "Dewdrop," Nashua Lock Company, ca. 1865, 2 1/2" ........................... 325

**Doorknob,** millifiore paperweight-type, Bohemian, shank still attached, ca. 1890, 2 1/4" d. ............................................. 450

**Doorknob,** passage-type, Aesthetic style, knurled banding around edge, 2 1/4" d. ......... 15

**Doorknob,** passage-type, beautiful knurling, incised banding around recessed edge, trademark scalloped edge pattern, P.F. Corbin, 2 1/4" d. ...................................... 55

**Doorknob,** passage-type, bronze, Serilly patt., fleur-de-lis center w/heavily cast concentric borders, Corbin, 2 1/4" d. ............ 120

**Doorknob,** passage-type, calligraphic Blatz beer logo w/beaded edge, 2 1/4" ......... 85

*Cherub & Eagle Passage Doorknob*

**Doorknob,** passage-type, cherub & eagle, Branford Lock Works, ca. 1880, 2 1/4" (ILLUS.) ......................................................... 100

**Doorknob,** passage-type, decorated, recessed edge w/interesting starburst pattern on top, Corbin, 2 1/4" ........................ **40**

**Doorknob,** passage-type, decorated w/strong details on both top & reverse, 2 1/4" d. ...................................................... **20**

**Doorknob,** passage-type, Floral, from Japanese Collection, R&E, ca. 1880, 2 1/4" ...... **350**

**Doorknob,** passage-type, from building in New York, Knickerbocker Village, stylized "KV", 2 1/4" ........................................ **80**

**Doorknob,** passage-type, hand w/lightning bolts, from an electrical worker's Union Hall, 2 1/4" ................................................ **75**

**Doorknob,** passage-type, hummingbird, R&E, ca. 1880, 2 1/4" .................................. **170**

**Doorknob,** passage-type, oval, heavy beaded edge & flat back, beautiful patina ....... **55**

**Doorknob,** passage-type, pavilion top w/five pointed star & all Renaissance decoration, Mallory Wheeler, dated 1874 on shank & w/original rosette ...................... **70**

**Doorknob,** passage-type, thin profile, banded edge & decoration on reverse side, 2 1/4" d. ............................................ **45**

**Doorknob,** passage-type, Turk's Head, ca. 1980s, from building in Providence, RI, 2 1/4" ...................................................... **300**

**Doorknob,** passage-type, w/address "1930," 2 1/4" ......................................... **40**

**Doorknob,** passage-type, w/George Washington, American flag under the bust, 2 1/2" (some wear & dents) ................ **275**

**Doorknob,** passage-type, w/initials ALB, nice weight & fancy calligraphy, 2 1/4" d. (few minor rim nicks) ...................................... **45**

**Doorknob,** passage-type, w/knurling, Mallory Wheeler, ca. 1885, 2 1/2" d. .................... **45**

*R&E Passage Doorknob*

**Doorknob,** passage-type, w/triangular back plate, plate w/old finish w/traces of gilding & very crisp, R&E, knob once polished & shows some wear, knob 2 1/4" d., plate 4 1/2" (ILLUS.) .................... **110**

**Doorknob,** pressed amber glass on brass shank & attached rosette, large, European origin, 2 3/4" ...................................... **150**

**Doorknob,** "Three Feather Indian" passage-type, from Midwestern hotel, 2 1/4" ..... **110**

**Doorknob,** w/plate, from Cook County Courthouse in Chicago, interesting laurel leaf borders & marked "Yale" on back, plate 3 x 10" ................................................ **75**

**Doorknobs,** acrylic, red, orange & clear plastic, ca. 1950s, 2 1/4" ea. ........................ **110**

**Doorknobs,** controlled bubble style on brass shank, probably Pairpoint Glass Co., 2 1/2" d. ................................................ **80**

**Doorknobs,** dark amber glass on brass shanks, pressed designs & polished tops, 2 1/2" d., pr. ...................................... **300**

**Doorknobs,** passage-type, bright green glass on brass shank, fluted sides, ca. 1920, 2 1/4" ...................................................... **100**

**Doorknobs,** passage-type, powder blue glass on nickel-plated shank, fluted sides, ca. 1920, 2 1/4" .................................. **100**

**Doorknobs,** passage-type, vaseline yellow/green glass on brass shank, fluted sides, ca. 1910, 2 1/4" .................................. **150**

**Doorplate,** complete w/keyhole cover, Corbin, 6 1/2" (excellent condition) ................ **65**

**Doorplate,** decorated w/pharaoh heads, scimitar, quarter moon & star motifs, from a Shriner's Temple, 3 x 20" .................. **180**

**Doorplate,** figural, one of the "Big 3", w/chalice, stork & powerful, fanciful bird forms, R&E, 3x10" (missing keyhole cover) .......................................................... **210**

**Entry plate & knob,** double keyhole-type, Damascene pattern, R&E, ca. 1880, plate 2 x 8" ...................................................... **65**

*Keyhole Escutcheons*

**Escutcheons,** keyhole, MCCC/R&E, from original 1870 collection, both are missing swing cover, 3 1/2" l. (ILLUS.), pr. .................. **80**

**Escutcheons,** open keyhole-type, 1870s, 2 1/5", each ....................................................... **35**

*Norwalk Hinge*

**Hinge,** trademark hoofed urn motif, Norwalk, 3 1/2" square (ILLUS.) .......................... **85**

**Hinges,** cast iron, marked "Mallory Wheeler", 3 1/2" sq., pr. .................................. **30**

**Hinges,** shutter-type, Aesthetic-style, marked "Nashua", 2" & 2 3/4", two pair ........ **150**

**Keyhole escutcheons,** covered, ca. 1870s, one by R&E, other by Corbin, 3" ....... **45**

**Mortise lock,** entry-type, Sargent's Ekado pattern, including strike plate, lock in working order, 3 1/2 x 7" ............................. **130**

**Pocket door pull,** nice urn & flower design on finger plate & strong Mallory Wheeler mark on reverse, 2 x 5" .................................. **80**

**Pocket door pulls,** cast brass, w/neoclassical decoration, marked "Chicago", 2 x 10", pr. ...................................................... **65**

**Pocket door pulls,** cast bronze, w/diaper decoration, dated 1884 on reverse, 2 1/4 x 5 3/4", pr. ...................................... **45**

**Sash lifts & locks,** cast brass w/incised decoration, for railroad car window, includes jamb stops, lock 1 x 2" ..................... **30**

*Ornate Sash Locks*

**Sash locks,** highly ornate & complete w/keeper, ca. 1870s, 2 1/2 x 2 1/2", set of three (ILLUS.).......................................... **160**

**Set of hardware,** pocket door hardware including four plates & two interlocking mortise locks, Hopkins & Dickenson, ca. 1880, plates 2 x 4 3/4", the set.................... **100**

**Set of hardware,** Sargent Ekado pattern including entry plate, entry & passage doorknobs, in "sunken center" variant, plate 2 1/2 x 10" (plate missing the ferrule) ............................................................. **275**

# HATPINS & HATPIN HOLDERS

## HATPIN HOLDERS

*Northwood Hatpin Holder*

**Carnival Glass,** Grape & Cable patt., ice blue, signed Northwood, 6 3/4" h. (ILLUS.)......................................... **$1,800-2,000**

**Celluloid,** cone-shaped, handpainted violets on each side, top w/9 holes, center of top w/pincushion for scarf pins or stickpins ................................................. **185-210**

**Custard glass,** Grape & Cable patt., Northwood, nutmeg stain, 6 1/2" h. (ILLUS. top next column).................................... **750-900**

*Custard Glass Hatpin Holder*

*Bohemian Hatpin Holder*

**Cut overlay glass,** cobalt blue to light ruby, brass cap features a floral fence border w/brass screen for holding hatpins, Bohemian (ILLUS.)................................. **450-725**

*Czechoslovakian Hatpin Holder*

**Czechoslovakian porcelain,** decoration of peacock w/moriage trim on feathers, top w/nine holes, solid bottom, 5" h. (ILLUS.)................................................... **140-165**

*R.S. Germany Hatpin Holder*

**R.S. Germany porcelain,** bullet-shaped w/wild rose decoration, combined w/cobalt blue & brilliant gold trim, 4 1/2" h. (ILLUS.)................................... **165-189**

*R.S. Germany Hatpin Holder*

**R.S. Germany porcelain,** white lily decoration combined w/gold at the top, 17 holes in top, solid bottom (ILLUS.) ........ **140-165**

*Rosenthal Hatpin Holder*

**Rosenthal porcelain,** dark blue ground w/very heavy silver overlay bands & leaf springs, large top center hole surrounded by twelve small holes, solid bottom, 3 3/4" h. (ILLUS.)........................... **375-400**
**Royal Bayreuth porcelain,** figural lamplighter,top w/16 holes, solid bottom, blue mark, 4 1/2" h. (ILLUS. top next column) ................................. **850-900**

*Royal Bayreuth Hatpin Holder*

*Royal Bayreuth Hatpin Holder*

**Royal Bayreuth porcelain,** "Rose Tapestry," pink, yellow & white roses, reticulated base, blue mark, 4 1/2" h. (ILLUS.)................................................. **400-650**

*Schafer & Vater Hatpin Holder*

**Schafer & Vater jasper ware,** dark green ground w/white relief Kewpie decoration, signed "Rose O'Neil," top w/8 holes, solid bottom, two sizes, children's 3 3/4" & adult's 4 1/4" h. (ILLUS.)................... **475-850**

# HATPINS

**Copper w/silver overlay,** poppy blossom form head enclosing relief bust portrait of Art Nouveau lady w/flowing hair, head 1 1/2" w., shaft 8 1/2" l. (ILLUS. top next page ) ..................................................... **130-165**
**Cut glass,** red cut blossom, reverse-painted in shaded red, in flower-shaped

brass fitting, head 1 1/8" d., shaft 8" l. (ILLUS. center this page) ...................... **165-180**

*Copper w/Silver Overlay Hatpin*

*Cut Glass Hatpin*

*Ivory Bee Hatpin*

**Ivory,** head carved as a bee sitting on twig, inlaid yellow eyes, wings carved w/veining, head 1 1/2" l., shaft 7" l. (ILLUS.) ... **250-325**

*Ivory Dragonfly Hatpin*

**Ivory,** head carved as a dragonfly sitting on twig, inlaid yellow eyes, body possibly shortened, head 1 1/2" w., shaft 7" l. (ILLUS.) ................................................ **250-325**

*Ivory Elephant Hatpin*

**Ivory,** head carved as elephant on ball, head 1 1/2" w., shaft 9" l. (ILLUS.) ........ **390-550**

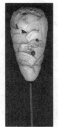

*Ivory Walrus Hatpin*

**Ivory,** head carved as walrus w/ivory tusks at the top of head, two more walrus' swim in kelp, shown as head is turned, head 1 1/2", shaft 11" (ILLUS.).............. **250-325**

*Molded Glass Hatpin*

**Molded glass,** green upright oblong form head w/colored flowers in the center & roses on the side, w/1/2" dangle on chain at side, head 1 1/2" l. (ILLUS.)..... **140-160**

*Art Deco Style Hatpin*

**Porcelain & brass,** Art Deco style, oval plaque w/bust portrait of young lady set in ornate oval frame, shaft 10" l. (ILLUS.)................................................. **135-155**

*Rhinestone Hatpin*

**Rhinestone,** large round head set w/77 red & 25 white rhinestones, plus five rectangular cut stones, head 2" d., shaft 10" l. (ILLUS.) ............................................... **132-160**

*Rhinestone-Trimmed Hatpin*

**Rhinestone-trimmed,** half-length color portrait of lovely lady in raised enamel, surrounded by band of large blue rhinestones, head 1 3/4", shaft 8 1/2" l. (ILLUS.) ............................................... **200-230**

*Silver Hatpin*

**Silver,** round ring enclosing pierced design of winged dragon w/fine detail, cut garnet eye, dragon w/white rhinestone in mouth, head 1 3/4" d., shaft 11" l. (ILLUS.) ............................................... **135-210**

*Sterling Silver Head Hatpin*

**Sterling silver head,** blue art glass ring w/copper flecks, center of intricate silver foliage set w/cut marcasites, marked "935 Made in Austria", head 1 1/2", shaft 11 1/4" (ILLUS.) ................................... **189-200**

# HEINTZ ART METAL SHOP WARES

*Otto Heintz (Buffalo, N.Y., 1877-1918) changed the name of his Art Crafts Shop to Heintz Art Metal Shop in 1906 as he shifted his focus from copper to machine-formed bronze bodies and from colored enamels to sterling silver overlays as decoration. A patent for the solderless application of the overlays was awarded in 1912 and the diamond mark enclosing the conjoined letters "HAMS" came into use. A series of sophisticated chemical patinas and plated finishes was developed for a line of vases, bowls and book ends. Otto died suddenly in 1918, but the company struggled through the Depression until the end came on Feb. 11, 1930. Values are a function of form, rarity, overlay and originality of patina.*

**Book ends,** No. 7115, brown patina, silver overlay, sea gulls in flight, 5 x 5 3/4", pr. ..... **$375**

*Heintz Art Metal Book Ends*

**Book ends,** No. 7201, French grey patina, parrot in ring w/pot of flowers, 1/4" raised bronze border, 4 1/2 x 5 1/2", pr. (ILLUS.) .......................................................... **435**

*Heintz Art Metal Bowl*

**Bowl,** No. 1852, polished liner, (double weight), brown patina, silver overlay of leaves (ILLUS.) ............................................ **450**
**Bowl,** No. 3706, green patina, silver pine needles overlay, 9" d., 2" h. ........................ **450**

*Heintz Art Metal Candlesticks*

**Candlesticks,** No. 3119, brown patina, half-inch diameter shaft, w/Arts & Crafts overlay, 4 1/2" diameter base 10 1/4" tall, pr. (ILLUS.) ............................................ **600**
**Chamberstick,** No. 3079, brown patina, floral overlay, hourglass shape w/handle, 5" d. base, 4" h. ..................................... **410**
**Cigar ashtray,** No. 2648, brown patina, landscape overlay on rim, two cigar rests, 6" d. .................................................. **225**

*Heintz Art Metal Cigar Ashtray*

**Cigar ashtray,** No. 2652, green patina, silver overlay design of two dogs fighting, on arm supporting single cigar rest, missing glass insert, 4 1/4" d. (ILLUS.) ........ **135**

*Heintz Art Metal Cigarette Box*

**Cigarette box,** cov., No. 4050, acid-etched silver finish, Moorish overlay on lid, 4 ball feet, 3 1/2 x 3 1/2", 21/2" h. (ILLUS.)..... **350**

**Cigarette box,** cov., No. 4099, cedar lined, w/domed hinged lid, green patina, w/overlay of butterflies taking nectar, 3 1/2 x 5 1/2," 2" h. ..................................... **425**

**Desk lamp,** a 7" d. bell-shaped shade w/a silver-overlay linear band trim, raised on a flaring pedestal base w/a silver shield inlay, old cleaning of patina, felt on base, 12" h. ................................................................. **495**

**Desk set,** No. 1103, brown patina, seven pieces w/stamp box, blotter corners & pad, freesia overlay, the set ........................ **500**

**Desk set,** No. 1199, brown patina, 6 pieces, Venetian Gondolier scenic overlay, the set ..................................................... **450**

**Humidor,** cov., rectanglar w/chamfered molded base, the flat hinged cover decorated w/three silver-overlay medallions reticulated w/Canadian geese in flight over a lake, cedar-lined, marked, 4 1/4 x 7 1/2", 3 1/2" h. ................................. **303**

*Heintz Art Metal Humidor*

**Humidor,** cov., No. 2609, wide slightly tapering cylindrical body w/a low domed cover w/an angular handle, brown patina, the body w/sterling silver overlay of a fox hunting scene, impressed mark, 6" d., 6 3/4" h. (ILLUS.) ............................... **725**

*Heintz Art Three Graces Lamp*

**Lamp,** acid-etched silver finish, conical shade, w/spearpoint cut-outs over lining, bulbous base w/overlay front & rear of Three Graces, 9" shade, 13" h. (ILLUS.)... **3,000**

*Heintz Art Bell Helmet Lamp*

**Lamp,** table model, solid bell-shaped "helmet" shade supported on harp arms, silver overlay of leaves & vines on base & shade, brown patina, 9" d. shade, 15" h. (ILLUS.)...................................................... **2,900**

**Picture frame,** brown patina, Art Nouveau overlay, oval opening, easel back, 6 x 9" overall.............................................................. **900**

**Vase,** No. 3651, flared rim & base, brown patina, California pepper overlay, 4" h. ........ **290**

**Vase,** No. 3670, trumpet form on squat, brown patina, daffodil overlay, 4" d. base, 6 1/2" h. .............................................. **410**

**Vase,** No. 3681, corset-form, brown patina, coneflower overlay, 12" h. ............................ **700**

**Vase,** No. 3710, bullet shape, brown patina, chrysanthemum overlay, 10" h. ........ **500**

**Vase,** No. 3736, cylinder w/flared foot, brown patina, stylized floral overlay, 2" d., 9" h............................................................ **545**

**Vase,** No. 3804, cylinder w/rolled out rim, expanded base, brown patina, holly overlay, 5" h. ................................................... **250**

**Vase,** cylindrical w/a flared rim, tall silver-overlay stems of primroses over the green patinated ground, inscribed "Mayview Farms Trophy," early 20th c., marked, 2 3/4" d., 6" h. (patina wear, small rim dents)............................................. **248**

**Vase,** cylindrical form w/corseted ring below the wide cupped rim, green patinated ground w/silver-overlay cluster of daffodils & leaves, marked, 4" d., 10" h. ...... **770**

## ICART PRINTS

*The works of Louis Icart, the successful French artist whose working years spanned the Art Nouveau and Art Deco movements, first became popular in the United States shortly after World War I. His limited edition etchings were much in vogue during those years when the fashion trends were established in Paris. These prints were later relegated to the closet shelves and basements but they have now re-entered the art market and are avidly sought by collectors. Listed by their American titles, those appearing below have been sold within the past eighteen months. All prints are framed unless otherwise noted.*

*"A Versailles" Oil Painting*

**A Versailles,** oil on canvas, titled on reverse, monogrammed "LI/Paris," dated XII-23, 13 x 16 1/8" (ILLUS.) ................. **$14,950**

**Coursing II,** 1929, 15 x 25", full sheet........... **2,185**

**Gust of Wind,** 1925, 17 5/8 x 21 1/8" ........... **1,725**

**Intimacy, The Green Screen,** 1928, matted & framed, 15 x 17 3/4"......................... **1,150**

**Lady of the Camelias,** 1927, matted & framed, 17 1/2 x 22 3/4" ............................. **1,265**

**Masks (The),** 1926, matted & framed, 14 1/2 x 18 1/2" oval................................. **1,380**

**Mealtime,** 1927, matted & framed, 13 x 17 1/2" oval...................................... **1,380**

**Poem (The),** 1928, matted & framed, 18 x 21 1/2" .............................................. **1,840**

**Scared,** 1920, 11 x 14 7/8"............................. **1,495**

**Speed,** 1927, 14 3/4 x 24 7/8" ........................ **2,300**

**Spilled Milk,** 1925, framed, 16 1/4 x 20 3/4" ........................................ **1,380**

*Venus in the Waves Icart Print*

**Venus in the Waves,** 1931, framed, 16 x 19" (ILLUS.)...................................... **2,185**

**Winsome,** 1935, 15 1/4 x 17 ......................... **1,265**

## INDIAN ARTIFACTS & JEWELRY

**Basket,** cov., Athabaskan, hand-woven, round cylindrical form w/flat hinged cover, block & diamond geometric design in light & dark fiber, 6 3/4" d., 3 3/8" h. (several missing stitches)............. **$358**

**Basket,** cov., Tinglit, basketry, finely woven small size w/shaman's hat design on body in dyed beargrass & fern front design on cover, possibly Haida, 3" d., 2 1/8" h. (minor wear)................................. **605**

**Basket** cov., Wakeshan, basketry, small cylindrical form w/fitted cover, Nootka twined type w/knob top & polychrome design including a whale, bird, canoe & animal.............................................................. **303**

**Basket,** cov., Washo, basketry, oblong, finely woven Great Basin one-rod coil type, identification mark on the rim & a zig-zag design in red hue around the body & on the flat cover, 3 1/2 x 7 1/2", 3" h. (ILLUS. left w/bowl)............................... **715**

**Basket,** Woodland, woven splint, rectangular w/low upright sides & bentwood loop end rim handles, painted & potato print designs in red, yellow & blue, 10 x 16", 4 3/4" h. ........................................................ **605**

**Bowl,** Cahuilla, basketry, wide squatty bulbous form w/wide mouth, woven in variegated juncus body w/a black repeating design of stylized cactus or birds, Southern California Mission-type, good age, 9" d., 4" h. ..................................................... **633**

**Bowl,** Pima, basketry, wide deep ovoid form finely woven w/checker diamond design & overcast rim stitching in dark martynia, willow weft w/fine sheen, 7" d., 5" h. (few missing stitches)............................ **825**

**Bowl,** Pima, basketry, wide squatty bulbous form finely woven w/a geometric maze design around the body in martynia & willoa, 5 3/8" d., 4 1/8" h. (very minor wear, few lost stitches)...................... **468**

**Bowl,** Pomo, basketry, gift-type, wide squatty rounded form of coiled sedge w/shell disks sewn around the rim, remnant of feathers on the surface, 3" d., 1 3/4" h. ...................................................... **275**

**Bowl,** San Ildefonso Pueblo, pottery, bulbous form tapering on the upper half to a wide flat mouth, blackware w/highly polished zigzag band, signed by "Blue Corn, San Ildefonso Pueblo," 3" d., 2 1/2" h. (minor wear)................................. **248**

**Bowl,** Whilkut, basketry, deep rounded form w/half-twist & full-twist overlay in simple design of maidenhair fern, red alder-dyed woodwardia & beargrass, Northern California, 5" d., 3 1/2" h. (rim stitches loose in one spot)............................ **275**

**Jar,** Hopi, pottery, wide squatty cushionform body centered on top by a short tapering small neck, decorated around the body w/curvilinear & geometric designs in soft orange, umber & ochre on an smoked orangish buff slip ground, signed w/the insignia of Frogwoman, J. Navasie, 6 1/2" d., 6" h. (wear, scratches, slip loss)................................... **330**

**Jar,** Santo Domingo Pueblo, pottery, bulbous ovoid form w/flat wide mouth, large scale foliate design w/red ochre flowers & black leaves on a creamy buff slip ground, 7" d., 7 3/8" h. (wear on bottom, minor overall wear)..................................... **275**

**Mittens,** Algonquin, Iroquois, beaded moosehide, black velvet cuffs w/polychrome floral beading in mainly green, bluish green & gold w/cut metallic bands, edged w/red tape, ca. 1880, 14 1/2" l., pr. (minor wear, small repair)...................... **825**

**Mocassins,** Western Sioux, fully beaded body w/white Bohemian bead background, blue bands & white-heart red accents, late 19th c., 9" l., pr. (heel tabs broken off, one cuff stiff w/split)................... **578**

**Necklace,** Navaho, squash blossom-type, twelve blossoms set w/turqoise on double strands of silver beads, naja w/three carinated silver supports w/seven turquoise & one center turquoise, turquoise w/soft green patinated aging to blue stones................................................................. **523**

**Necklace,** Santo Domingo heishi-type, set of turquoise, shell & coral jacla drops on strand of turquoise nuggets & shell heishi, strung on a cord, 20 1/2" l................. **330**

**Pouch,** Iroquois of Niagara Falls area, pictorial beaded-type, high beaded pictorial panel work, two sides w/red velvet w/a polychrome flag & bird, the other two sides w/worn blue silk & the date "1923," cover w/fine folky spider design, beaded handle & white beaded selvage w/beaded drops, 3 1/2 x 5", 4 1/4" h. ........... **110**

**Rug,** Navaho, Crystal area, stepped grey diamonds w/dark brown borders on a carded light brown & natural background w/banded border, 46 x 51"........................... **605**

**Rug,** Navaho, fine Two Grey Hills type, central diamond & radiating interlocked terraces w/a graphic stylized feather border, white & black on a grey ground, attached paper label & "Certificate of Authenticity" for weaver Jenny Etsitty, Tohatchi, New Mexico, 54 x 88"............... **1,100**

**Rug,** Navaho, Ganado area, connected stepped terraced triangles in double-dye red & natural, outlined in dark brown on a carded tan ground, 1920s, 51 x 76" (edge wear, few warp breaks, stains, both ends folded over & sewn)................. **1,100**

**Rug,** Navaho, Klagetoh area, outlined central grey design surrounded by diamond stepped elements in black, carded grey & double-dye red on a natural ground w/black & red border, 36 x 59 1/2" (stains, small area of edge wear) ................. **440**

**Rug,** Navaho, Crystal area, natural handcarded wool w/linear connected diamonds in grey, white & black flanked by serrated bands in tan & black, stepped terrace border in tans & black, corner tassels, 35 x 62" (light stains)...................... **468**

**Rug,** Navaho, Klagetoch or Ganado area, central design in white, black & double dye red w/stepped diamonds & a border of connected blocks outlined in white, black border & carded grey ground, finely hand-carded & spun wool, 42 x 62" (edge wear, minor color bleeding) ................................................................. **440**

**Rug,** Navaho, Ganado area, design of three expanding serrated diamonds in nautral, black, browns & double dye red, ca. 1920-30, 43 x 66" (warp break, light stains, minor color bleeding)................. **440**

**Rug,** Navaho, Crystal area, unusual diamond design in natural, red, dark brown & faded vegetal tan, 33 1/2 x 67" (edge wear, stains, breaks) ................................... **330**

*Large Navaho Rug*

**Rug,** Navaho, Western Reservation Tees Nos Pas area, rectangular w/connected & outlined serrate diamonds in red, dark brown w/centered hourglass & cruciform star designs, serrate mountain border in natural wool w/outer border in carded browns w/red zig-zag line, dark brown border, ca. 1925-30, edge wear, some stains, soiling & holes, 44 x 76" (ILLUS.)......................................................... **715**

**Rug,** Navaho, probably Crystal Trading, carded soft brownish tan wool ground w/diamond & triangle design in dark brown, natural & red, ca. 1915-25, 54 x 79" (edge wear, few warp breaks, minor color bleeding).................................. **715**

**Tray,** Northern California Hupa, woven basketry, flattened round ceremonial meal-type, banded geometric & lightning design, 13 3/4" d., 3" h. (minor wear, rim damage)...................................................... **165**

**Tray,** Piaute, Navaho basketry wedding-type, wide shallow coiled form w/bands of serrated rings in colors, ca. 1920, finely woven, 14 3/8" d. (some soiling & damage)...................................................... **468**

**Tray,** Pima, basketry, wide round shallow form w/expanded maze pattern & central start in dark martynia w/willow, good age, 9 7/8" d., 2 3/4" h. (few missing stitches)..................................................... **385**

**Tray,** Yavapai, basketry, coil construction w/expanding star design in dark martynia & willoa, 7 3/8" d. (one missing stitch)........................................................ **880**

**Trinket box,** cov., Wakashan, basketry, oblong, finely woven Nootka form w/whale boat & bird, fitted cover, small stain, rim split, 5" l., 3" h. (ILLUS. center w/bowl) ........................................................ **660**

# JEWELRY

## AMERICAN PAINTED PORCELAIN

*American painted porcelain jewelry comprises a unique category. While the metallic settings and porcelain medallions were inexpensive, the painted decoration was a work of fine art. The finished piece possessed greater intrinsic value than costume jewelry of the same period because it was a one-of-a-kind creation, but one that was not as expensive as real gold and sterling silver settings and precious and semi-precious jewels. Note that signatures are rare, backstamps lacking.*

*Belt Buckle Brooch with Violets*

**Bar pin,** decorated w/pink roses & greenery, brass-plated bezel, ca. 1880s, 7/16 x 1 1/2" .............................................. **$30**

**Bar pin,** decorated w/pink roses on a pale green ground, burnished gold tips & brass-plated bezel, ca. 1900-1915, 2 5/8" w. ................................................... **50**

**Belt buckle brooch,** oval, decorated w/deep purple violets on a gradating yellow to dark green background, brass-plated bezel, ca. 1900-17, 1 3/4 x 2 1/8" (ILLUS.)........................................................... **100**

**Belt buckle brooch,** oval, decorated w/yellow roses, burnished gold rim & brass-plated bezel, 1 7/8 x 2 3/8"........................... **115**

*Belt Buckle Brooch with Pink Roses*

**Belt buckle brooch,** oval, decorated w/pink roses, burnished gold scrolls at top & burnished gold edge, brass-plated bezel, ca. 1900-17, 1 7/8 x 2 5/8" (ILLUS.)........................................................... **90**

**Brooch,** decorated w/a conventional-style trillium w/raised paste & burnished gold pistols & burnished gold background, brass-plated bezel, ca. 1910-15, 1 9/16" d........ **35**

**Brooch,** decorated w/violets on a light yellow brown ground w/raised paste scrolled border covered w/burnished gold & burnished gold rims, gold-plated bezel, ca. 1890-1920, 1 1/2" d. ...................... **45**

**Brooch,** horseshoe shape, decorated w/pink & ruby roses on a green & yellow ground, white enamel highlights & burnished gold tips, ca. 1880s - 1915, 1 1/4 x 1 1/2" ................................................. **65**

*Brooch with Forget-me-nots*

**Brooch,** lozenge shape, decorated w/forget-me-nots on a pink & pale yellow ground w/white enamel highlights & burnished gold rim, brass-plated bezel, ca. 1890-1920, 7/8 x 1 5/8" (ILLUS.)..................... **35**

**Brooch,** oval, decorated w/a tropical Florida scene, burnished gold border & brass-plated bezel, ca. 1920s, 1 1/2 x 2" ....... **60**

*Brooch with Pansy Decoration*

**Brooch,** oval, decorated w/purple pansies on a pale yellow & violet background w/white enamel highlights & raised paste scrolled border covered w/burnished gold, brass-plated bezel, ca. 1880-1915, 1 1/2 x 2" (ILLUS.) ........................... **75**

**Brooch,** oval, decorated w/a conventional-style Colonial dame in light blue & yellow w/opal lustre background & burnished gold rim, brass-plated bezel, ca. 1915-25, 1 5/8 x 2 1/8" .......................... **55**

**Brooch/pendant,** heart shape, decorated w/daisies on a light shading to dark blue ground, gold-plated bezel, ca. 1900-20, 1 13/16 x 2" .................................. **50**

**Cuff pin,** rectangular, decorated w/a purple iris outlined & bordered in burnished gold, brass-plated bezel, ca. 1900-15, 1/4 x 1 1/6" ............................. **15**

**Flapper pin,** oval, decorated w/bust of stylized red-haired flapper on a pastel polychrome ground, burnished gold rim & brass-plated bezel, ca. 1924-28, 1 5/8 x 2 1/8" .......................... **75**

**Handy pin,** decorated w/forget-me-nots w/white enamel highlights & rounded burnished gold tips, ca. 1890-1915, 1 1/2" w. .................................. **35**

**Handy pin,** crescent shape, asymmetrically decorated w/a purple pansy on an ivory ground, burnished gold tip & brass-plated bezel, ca. 1880-1915, 2" w. ......... **35**

**Pendant,** decorated w/a purple pansy w/white enamel center accents & burnished gold border, gold-plated bezel, ca. 1880s-1914, 1" d. ......................... **50**

**Scarf pin,** decorated w/violets, brass-plated bezel & shank, ca. 1880-1920, medallion 1 1/4" d., shank 3" l. ..................... **45**

**Shirt waist button,** decorated w/a central design of pink roses w/outer pale blue band, inner & outer raised paste scrolled borders covered w/burnished gold, ca. 1890s, 1" d. .................................. **35**

*Shirt Waist Buttons with Three Color Roses*

**Shirt waist buttons,** decorated w/white, pink & ruby roses on a polychrome background w/raised paste scrolled border covered w/burnished gold, ca. 1890-1910, 3/4" d., pr. (ILLUS.) ............................. **70**

**Shirt waist buttons,** decorated w/violets on an ivory ground w/white enamel highlights & burnished gold rims, signed "E," ca. 1890-1920, 1 1/16" d. ...................... **60**

**Shirt waist set:** oval brooch & pr. of oval cuff links; decorated w/blue forget-me-nots on an ivory background w/white enamel highlights, brass-plated mounts, ca. 1900-10, brooch w/burnished gold free-form border & rim, 1 3/8 x 1 3/4", cuff links w/burnished gold rims, 13/16 x 1 1/16", the set .............. **250**

*Watch Chatelaine*

**Watch chatelaine,** oval, decorated w/a woman wearing a rose-colored bodice, light shading to dark warm green ground, set in gold-plated rim w/twisted gold edge, ca. 1880s, 1 1/8 x 1 3/8" (ILLUS.) ....................................... **115**

# ANTIQUE (1800-1920)

**Bar pin,** gold (14k yellow) w/lobed terminals & wiretwist accents (discoloration to one side) ...................................... **230**

*Victorian Gold Bar Pin*

**Bar pin,** gold (15k yellow), navette-shaped, centered w/an octagonal-cut peridot, flanked on either side by foliate devices set w/half-pearls & two rubies, hallmarked "G," Victorian, w/fitted box (ILLUS.) ...................................... **1,035**

**Bar pin,** gold, Art Nouveau-style, centered by a disc depicting a female bust in relief, 18k yellow gold, marked "RL" (minor dents to back) .................. **288**

**Bracelet,** enamel & pearl, centered by a baroque pearl surrounded by engraved bi-color 18k gold leaves & hinged curved sections w/green enamel stripes, French import mark, adjustable from 6 1/2 to 7 1/4" l. (repair to tongue of clasp) ............ **1,840**

**Bracelet,** gold (14k yellow), slide-type, mesh, the quatrefoil slide w/seed pearl accents, black enamel tracery & fox-tail tassels, Victorian ........................................ **748**

*Victorian Gold & Enamel Bracelet*

**Bracelet,** gold & enamel, the hinged rect-angular plaques inlaid w/champleve enamel in white, navy & rust, 18k yellow gold mount, Victorian, 7 3/4" l. (ILLUS.) ....... **805**

**Bracelet,** gold & mixed metal, Damascene-style, hinged design cuff centered by a circular plaque depicting a horse & rider in relief flanked by six-pointed stars w/foliate & beaded accents ...................... **1,150**

**Brooch,** gold (14k yellow), circular design w/ram's head centered by a spherical pendant, Victorian Revival (minor dents) ..... **575**

**Brooch,** gold & crystal, reverse intaglio cir-cular form depicting a bird in flight within an 18k yellow gold frame accented by four gold cubes, Victorian (minor solder evident) ....................................................... **690**

*Antique Bullfight Brooch*

**Brooch,** gold & enamel, a three-dimen-sional scene depicting a bullfighter & a bull in polychrome enamel, rose-cut dia-mond accents, 18k yellow gold mount, signed "Duval," minor wear to enamel, French hallmarks (ILLUS.) .......................... **978**

*Miniature Portrait Brooch*

**Brooch,** gold, miniature portrait-type, the circular plaque depicting Marie Anto-

inette, surrounded by 18k yellow gold feather motif frame accented by pearl & rose diamond flowers, French hallmark (ILLUS.) ...................................................... **690**

**Brooch,** gold, modeled as a violin w/bi-color 18k gold body & white gold strings, verso engraved in French (some scratches) ............................................... **1,380**

**Brooch,** gold, pietra dura, two birds nesting on a floral branch, 10k yellow gold frame w/gold bead & floret decoration, Victo-rian ....................................................... **748**

**Brooch,** pearl, coral & enamel, the domed oval center pavé-set w/seed pearls & coral, framed w/light blue opaque enamel inset w/coral & pearls, 18k yel-low gold mount, locket compartment on reverse, in original fitted box, signed "James Muirhead & Sons, Glasgow," Victorian (minor chips to enamel)................ **690**

**Brooch,** silver metal, Art Nouveau-style, raised lady's head w/flowing hair, 2 x 2 1/4" ...................................................... **65**

**Brooch,** silver-gilt, plique-a-jour enamel, peridot & pearl, Art Nouveau-style, the foliate motif centered by a collet-set fac-eted oval peridot, peridot accents, baroque pearl drop, silver-gilt mount (crazing to one plique panel) ...................... **230**

**Brooch,** sterling silver, Arts & Crafts style, scrolled openwork design of a calla lily blossom & leaves, stamped sterling mark, early 20th c., 1 1/2 x 2 3/4"................ **288**

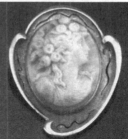

*Coral Cameo Brooch/Pendant*

**Cameo brooch/pendant,** carved coral, Art Nouveau-style, depicting a woman in profile within a 14k yellow gold whiplash frame, hallmark (ILLUS.) .............................. **748**

*Edwardian Cameo Brooch/Pendant*

**Cameo brooch/pendant,** carved shell, depicting "Three Graces" within narrow gold frame, Edwardian, 2 1/4" l. (ILLUS.) ..... **325**

**Cameo necklace,** carved jasper, the festoon design featuring four oval cameos w/14k yellow gold frames, completed by an 18k yellow gold trace link chain, the clasp labeled "Amitie," boxed .................... **1,380**

**Chain,** silver & enamel, Arts & Crafts-style, the double-sided flowerhead links inlaid w/enamel in green & white alternating w/black & white, w/elongated pear-shaped terminals in black, sky blue & yellowish green enamel, hallmark for Bernard Cuzner, for Liberty & Co., 57" l. (overall pitting to enamel, probably from original firing) .......................................... **1,840**

**Chatelaine,** gold & gemstones, hand-chased & engraved in a foliate design w/a pair of lions, enameled shields & a crown w/gemstone accents, tri-color 18k gold, European hallmark, "no. 356," (pendant attachments missing) ................. **1,150**

**Cloak fasteners,** gold & sapphire, Art Nouveau-style, coiled snakes set w/two bezel-set oval sapphires, connected by a removable curb link chain, 14k yellow gold .......................................................... **1,725**

**Cloak pin,** ruby & diamond, modeled as a sword, the hilt set w/old mine-cut diamonds, ruby accents, pearl terminals, 14k yellow gold mount, 6" l. ........................... **748**

**Cross pendant,** gold, floral chased & engraved 10k yellow gold cross w/seed pearl & black enamel accent, suspended from a shield-shaped clasp w/black enamel tracery, 14k woven gold chain, 20" l. ...... **575**

**Cuff links,** gold, Art Nouveau-style, each depicting a different female bust representing the four seasons, accented by different color gemstones, in a box marked "J. E. Caldwell, Philadelphia," pr...... **748**

**Earpendants,** gold & turquoise, Etruscan Revival-style, the round tops set w/buff-top turquoise, accented w/black enamel, suspending tapering gold pendants, 18k yellow gold, 2 3/4" l., pr. ........................... **2,300**

*Diamond Lavaliere Pendant*

**Lavaliere,** platinum & diamond, rounded crescent shape w/filigree & foliate diamond accents, centered by a collet-set old European-cut diamond & suspending a row of collet-set old European-cut diamond drops, platinum paperclip-link chain, 15 1/2" l. (ILLUS.) ........................... **1,840**

**Locket,** gold (14k yellow), decorated w/an applied cross design in black enamel & rose-cut diamonds (repair to back) ............. **316**

**Locket,** ruby & diamond, oval w/three vertical rows bead-set w/eight round rubies & ten old mine-cut diamonds, 18k yellow gold mount, engraved edge "no. 2911" ..... **1,380**

**Lockets,** gold, two heart lockets, each centered by an old mine-cut diamond in a star motif setting, verso engraved, gold bead chain, pr. ................................................. **403**

**Necklace,** amethyst & pearl, designed w/clusters of prong-set round amethysts suspending a fringe of five seed pearl-set chains terminating in amethyst briolettes, 14k yellow gold trace link chain, ca. 1900, 16" l. .................................. **805**

*Edwardian Festoon Necklace*

**Necklace,** pearl & garnet, festoon-type, the floral center highlighted by seed pearls & bezel-set garnet & glass doublets, 10k gold mount, Edwardian, 15 1/2" l. (ILLUS.) ..................................................... **403**

**Pendant,** micromosaic, depicting a beetle within an oval frame w/scroll & wiretwist accents, gilt mount & 23" l. trace link chain, later clasp, Victorian ......................... **345**

**Pendant,** photographic, oval, ambrotype portrait of a young man, gold frame w/initials, 1 1/2" l. ...................................... **110**

**Pillbox pendant,** gold (18k yellow), Art Nouveau-style, covered round hinged box w/repoussé foliate motif overall ............. **633**

*Pearl & Diamond Clover Pin/Pendant*

**Pin/pendant,** pearl & diamond, modeled in a clover form, the four leaves & stem pavé-set w/seed pearls, centered by an old European-cut diamond, 14k yellow gold mount, retractable bail, Edwardian (ILLUS.)...................................................... **403**

**Ring,** citrine, man's, Art Nouveau-style w/center buff-top rectangular citrine, naturalistic 14k yellow gold mount, hallmark..... **748**

**Ring,** gold & tourmaline, centered by a prong-set rectangular mixed-cut green tourmaline in an abstract 18k yellow gold mount, signed "Georg Jensen, no. 313".... **1,610**

**Ring,** sapphire & diamond, pave bead-set w/seven old mine-cut diamonds edged w/channel-set sapphaires, platinum-topped 18k yellow gold mount................... **1,150**

## SETS

**Brooch & earrings,** enamel & gold, brooch modeled as a pansy w/shaded purple enamel petals, centered by a prong-set old mine-cut diamond, 14k yellow gold mount, matching earrings w/screwbacks, hallmark for A.J. Hedges & Co., the set (tiny chip to brooch & one earring) .......................................................... **1,380**

*Victorian Gold Grapevine Suite*

**Brooch & earrings,** gold (14k yellow), a grapevine design brooch w/gold répoussé leaves accented w/seed pearls, matching earrings, Victorian, repairs (ILLUS. of part) .................. **546**

**Necklace & ear clips,** gold (14k yellow), a mesh necklace w/central buckle & foxtail fringe, black enamel tracery, matching pair of ear clips, the set (enamel loss) ........ **920**

**Necklace & earrings,** onyx, the necklace w/shaped onyx links surmounted by seed pearl decoration suspending an oval pendant w/reverse hair locket, similar earrings, Victorian, the set (chips to glass, later findings) ..................................... **978**

**Necklace/brooch & earpendants,** coral, a carved rose bouquet necklace w/bar links, detachable matching round brooch, both w/silver gilt findings, together w/matching earpendants w/modern 14k ball findings, Victorian, the set (repairs to necklace)........................ **748**

# COSTUME JEWELRY

*Twentieth century costume jewelry was made of inexpensive materials and was created to accessorize designer's clothing collections. It wasn't meant to last longer than the ensembles it accessorized and designers could create freely, incorporating the very latest fads and art designs into their costume jewelry. Originally referred to as "craftsman's jewelry," it became known as "costume jewelry" in the 1930s. Today collectors value costume jewelry for it's art, design, and craftsmanship and representative of another time. It is these factors which determine it's price, rather than the value of the materials. Costume jewelry was affordable in it's time and continues to be so for today's collector.*

**Bracelet,** Bakelite, bangle-type, moss green carved leaves design, 3/4" w. ....... **95-110**

**Bracelet,** brass, hinged bangle-type, applied carved black Bakelite sides w/smooth circle design in front, 1 1/8" w. ................................................. **165-185**

**Bracelet,** charm, gold-washed sterling, chain links w/fifteen assorted charms ... **150-185**

**Bracelet,** charm, music box-type, chain links, figure of cat, plays "Beyond the Sea" ............................................................ **90-125**

**Bracelet,** gold-filled, Retro design, links w/three cabochon set topaz colored stones, hallmarked, signed "Double" ..... **95-120**

**Bracelet,** gold-plated, chains, single crown charm w/"jade" beads, red rhinestones, signed "Vendome" ...................................... **50**

**Bracelet,** gold-plated, hinged bangle-type, applied oak leaves & acorns, signed "Freirich,"3/8" w. ..................................... **50-75**

**Bracelet,** gold-plated, hinged bangle-type, diagonal stripe design, large blue, red & purple cabochon rhinestone ends, signed "Ciner" ......................................... **55-75**

**Bracelet,** gold-plated, hinged bangle-type, large rhinestone ends interchangeable w/large pearl & black enamel designs, mint in box, signed "Joan Rivers" .......... **95-125**

**Bracelet,** gold-plated, hinged bangle-type, ornate front w/center 1" shell cameo, signed "Florenza" ................................... **55-75**

**Bracelet,** Lucite, bangle-type, clear w/applied black domes, 2" w. ................... **50-70**

**Bracelet,** Lucite, hinged bangle-type, clear w/interior metallic blue glitter, 2" w. overlap in front ................................................. **45-65**

**Bracelet,** matte gold-plated hinged cuff-style, grape-color marquise rhinestones leaves, signed "Monet," 1 1/2" w. ............... **150**

**Bracelet,** sterling, link-style, each link a handmade flower & leaf design, signed "Cini," ca. 1943, 1 1/8" w. ............................ **395**

*Bracelet of Flowers and Leaves*

**Bracelet,** sterling, links of flower & leaves motif, signed "G. Cini," 1" w. (ILLUS.) .. **250-275**

**Bracelet watch,** silver, cuff-style, gold ribbed, Alice Caviness, 1" w. ..................... **65-85**

**Chain w/locket,** gold-plated, 2 1/2" d. lion's head w/ring in mouth, signed "Judith Leiber," 18" l. .......................................... **75-90**

**Chain w/locket,** sterling silver, Art Deco octagon shape w/stripes 18" l. .................. **75-85**

**Chatelaine pin,** pink gold-plated curved sword w/purple rhinestone trim, connected by double chain to clear rhinestone trimmed black enamel scabbard, can be worn as single pin w/sword inserted into scabbard, ca. 1943 .............. **75-90**

*Butterfly and Clown Chatelaine Pins*

**Chatelaine pin,** pink gold-plated, two butterflies w/center floral design of a pearl surrounded w/multicolored rhinestones, connected by double chain, ca. 1945 (ILLUS. top) ............................................ **75-90**

**Chatelaine pin,** white metal, two figural clowns w/red rhinestone eyes, connected by double chain (ILLUS. bottom) ... **70-85**

**Chatelaine pin,** white metal, two figural does, connected by double chain .............. **50-65**

**Clip,** Bakelite, Art Deco, red carved triangle, 2 1/4" ................................................ **45-65**

**Clip,** Bakelite, black, carved three-dimensional leaves ................................................ **45**

**Clip,** enamel, fur-type, black Teddy bear w/large pearl belly, rhinestone trim ........... **65-80**

**Clip,** gold-plated, fur-type, Retro ribbon motif w/eight large soft red tapered unfoiled open-set stones, 2 3/4" .................... **75**

*Gem-set Clips*

**Clip,** gold-plated, fur-type, Retro style, tapering flat metal design w/coiled clip below large emerald cut topaz color stone, 2" (ILLUS. right) ............................. **50-65**

**Clip,** rhinestone flower w/turquoise bead trim, unusual design, 2" ................................... **30**

**Clip,** sterling silver set w/marcasite, ornate openwork leaves in coil design w/center cabochon-set faux aquamarine, 1 3/4" (ILLUS. left) ............................................. **75-100**

**Clips,** glass & enamel, large red glass spheres w/red enameled ribbon style coils & clear rhinestone accents, signed "Coro Duette".............................. **85-110**

**Clips,** gold-plated, sweater-type, leaf motif connected w/chain, pearls in center ......... **20-25**

**Clips,** rhinestone, Art Deco bow motif, larger emerald, triangle rhinestone accents, 1" h., pr. ......................................... **35**

**Clips,** sterling, sweater-type, circles connected w/chain links w/original flannel storage case, signed "Tiffany & Co." ....... **95-125**

**Earrings,** enamel on sterling, fan motif, blue, green, black enamel, Siam, 1 1/4" h., pr. ...................................... **35**

**Earrings,** fresh water pearl ball drops, clip-ons, 1" l., pr. ............................................. **25-35**

**Earrings,** glass, button style, red art glass, screw-ons, 3/4" d., pr. ............................. **20-25**

**Earrings,** glass, button style, white, raised scalloped arc design, screw-ons, 3/4" d.... **15-20**

**Earrings,** gold-plated, shell motif, clip/screw-ons, signed "Napier," pr. ........... **30-45**

**Earrings,** goldtone, wide textured hoop style, clip-ons, signed "Avon," 3/4" w., pr. ...................................................... **35**

**Earrings,** large pearl ball drops below three baguette rhinestone links, screw-ons, 2" l., pr. .................................................... **30-45**

**Earrings,** pearl teardrops, screw-ons, 1 1/8" l., pr. ............................................ **25-35**

**Earrings,** plastic, Christmas tree motif, screw-ons ................................................... **10-15**

**Earrings,** rhinestone, Art Deco, clear rhinestones in white metal geometric design drops, screw-ons, 2 1/2" l., pr. ................... **75-95**

*Fish-shaped Earrings*

**Earrings,** silver tone fish drops, six flexible linked segments, clip-ons, signed "DKNY" Donna Karen, New York, 4" l., pr. (ILLUS.) ............................................... **65-85**

**Earrings,** silver tone, fish motif, entire body made movable by individual links, clip-ons, signed "DKNY (Donna Karen)," 4" l., pr. ........................................................ **55**

**Earrings,** silver tone shrimp motif in hoop style, clips, 3/4", pr. ........................................ **30**

**Earrings,** sterling marcasite set, bows, arc motif, clip-ons, 1 3/4" l., pr............................ **75**

**Earrings,** sterling silver, concave triangles, clip-ons, Mexico, pr. .................................. **25-35**

**Earrings,** textured gold finish, hinged hoop-style, on original card, 7/8" d., pr...... **20-30**

**Hatpin,** antiqued goldtone, figural butterfly in profile, 9" l........................................... **95-115**

**Hatpin,** antiqued goldtone, figural cat's face w/amber rhinestone eyes, 9" l. ........ **95-115**

**Hatpin,** clear rhinestone, round top, 12 3/4" l. .................................................. **95-110**

**Hatpin,** English sterling, figural cat, hallmarked, 10" l. .............................................. **175**

**Hatpin,** figure of smiling man wearing derby hat, worn paint, 6 3/4" l................. **95-120**

**Hatpin,** rhinestone, large purple stone in clear rhinestone frame, 8 1/2" l. ............... **75-85**

**Hatpin,** silver-plated, Art Nouveau woman w/long flowing hair reading book, 8" l..... **85-100**

**Hatpin,** white metal, pavé rhinestone-set flying bird, 2" w., 10 1/2" l. ............................ **75**

**Lapel pendant watch,** 800 standard silver set w/marcasite, marcasite-set bow pin w/center swiveling drop to hold watch which can detach & be added to 30" marcasite accented chain, 17 jewel, w/original cylindrical box, signed "Bucherer" ............................................ **350-400**

**Lapel watch,** chrome, clip-style, French, black enamel, back of watch marked "Deposé," front signed "Riviera" .................... **75**

**Lapel watch,** chrome, clip-style, watch on one side, black enamel w/initial on reverse, signed "Riviera" ....................... **125-150**

**Lapel watch,** clear rhinestones in white metal frame suspended by four large rhinestone links attached to looped rhinestone-set bar pin, signed "Fidelity" ............................................... **100-125**

*Collectible Lapel Watch*

**Lapel watch,** enameled cherries motif, hanging from brown bar pin, larger cherry contains watch by Clifford (ILLUS.) ...................................................... **125**

**Lapel watch,** gold (12k yellow) on sterling silver, Retro style geometric rectangular watch on open rectangle suspended from bar pin, watch signed "Solex"........ **150-200**

**Lapel watch,** gold-filled (12k yellow), floral spray w/watch set as a flower, signed "CA" pierced by an arrow (Carl-Art), 2 3/8" h. (ILLUS. top next column) ................................................ **150-200**

**Lapel watch,** rolled gold, 10k, scallop framed watch hanging by two bars from bow-motif bar pin............................................ **65**

*Floral Design Lapel Watch*

**Lapel watch,** rolled gold (10k yellow), scalloped metalwork around watch suspended from Retro style bar pin, signed "Helbros" ............................................. **125-150**

**Lapel watch,** sterling marcasite set, flower spray w/watch as a flower, watch is signed "Merit," 2 3/4" h. ............................... **155**

**Lapel watch,** sterling silver floral spray set w/marcasite, watch is set as a flower, signed "Merit," 3" h. .............................. **195-250**

**Necklace,** antiqued gold, ethnic style openwork, three large circles on double swag design chains w/suspended drops, ca. 1935, 14" l. ................................................. **50-65**

**Necklace,** beads, Aurora Borealis clear, faceted, graduated, 22" l., adjusts up to 25" l. ..................................................... **50-65**

*Collar Style Glass Bead Necklace*

**Necklace,** beads, coral glass, collar style, hanging from gold-plated swag design chains, ca. 1955, 15" l. (ILLUS.) ............. **100-150**

**Necklace,** beads, garnet, small, 31".................. **55**

**Necklace,** beads, glass, Art Deco style, large red teardrop-shape beads & oval faceted beads alternating w/small red & black beads, 33" l. ................................... **85-100**

**Necklace,** beads, green glass, ca. 1925, 32" l. w/5" tassel drop.................................. **125**

**Necklace,** beads, long & round maroon glass beads, geometric shapes w/matching plastic center w/silver leaves design, signed "Czechosla" 16" l. ............. **65-80**

**Necklace,** beads, rope of shaded blue & green art glass beads, round, cylindrical, oval & irregular shaped beads, 52" l. ........ **50-75**

**Necklace,** blue rhinestone pendant w/flower on long chain, signed "Miriam Haskell" .......................................................... **65**

**Necklace,** cloisonné enamel on green enameled links, pendant-style w/watch, 4" drop attached to Art Deco watch, ca. 1930 ...................... **125-150**

**Necklace,** enameled collar-style, enameled links in red, forest green, signed "Lanvin Paris" ............................................... **60**

**Necklace,** gold chain alternating w/pearls & art glass beads, six-part tassel drop, signed "Liz Claiborne," 34" l w/4" l. drop .. **40-55**

**Necklace,** gold chain w/large black center circle, signed "Trifari," 16" l. ...................... **30-45**

**Necklace,** gold-plated, bib-style composed of multiple chains w/ornate 6 1/2" pendant w/pink, fuchsia & moss green rhinestones, pink & blue art glass stones, pearl teardrop clusters on drop & bib portion, signed "Florenza" .................... **125-175**

**Necklace,** gold-plated chain alternating w/long clear art glass beads, glass perfume bottle pendant set in gold frame w/attached gold stopper, signed "YSL," Yves St. Laurent, 26" l. .............................. **65-85**

**Necklace,** gold-plated, four graduated chains, center three have Victorian style ornate pendants w/mesh fringes, ca. 1965, longest chain 40" .......................... **75-95**

**Necklace,** gold-plated large heart on large chunky gold-plated chain, signed "Erwin Pearl," heart 2" l., 32" l. .................................. **65**

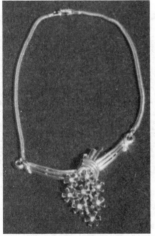

*Corocraft Flower Spray Necklace*

**Necklace,** gold-plated, red baguette rhinestone-set flower spray motif, green baguette stems on snake chains, short, signed "Corocraft" (ILLUS.) .......................... **125**

**Necklace,** light gold-plated, pendant-type, spinning ballerina inside circle, 24" l. ........ **25-45**

**Necklace,** pearls, choker-style, double strand small & medium baroque pearls, very ornate gold openwork center of seed pearl flowers, marquise emerald rhinestones, tiny blue, clear & maroon rhinestones, signed "Denbé," 12" l, adjusts 2 3/4" longer.................................. **85-110**

**Necklace,** rhinestones set in sterling, single strand w/18 hanging pear-shaped rhinestone drops, signed "Coro Sterling," 13 3/4" l. .................................................... **85-125**

**Necklace,** rhinestones set in white metal, Art Deco style center w/three marquise rhinestones, signed "Coro," 14" l. .............. **40-65**

**Necklace,** sterling, pendant-style, ornate openwork heart, 24" l. ............................... **65-85**

*Egyptian Motif Pendant & Chain*

**Necklace,** sterling, pendant-type, double chain w/Egyptian profile motif on textured background, 24" l. (ILLUS.).......... **100-150**

**Pin,** Bakelite, bar-style, carnelian color, outer edge trimmed w/gold-plated chain, 1 x 3" ......................................................... **70-85**

**Pin,** enamel, bird on branch, long tail, red glass "jelly belly" center, rhinestone trim, signed "Art," 3 1/4" h. ............................ **120-150**

**Pin,** enamel, Chinese style white lion, rhinestone trim, signed "Pauline Rader," 2 x 2 3/4" .................................................... **60-75**

**Pin,** gold on sterling, butterfly set w/faux cabochon moonstones & rubies, pavé rhinestone trim on body & wing tips, signed "Trifari," 2 1/4"............................ **220-250**

**Pin,** gold on sterling, curved Retro style flowers, pavé aqua rhinestone centers, pavé clear rhinestone trim, signed "Pennino," 2 1/4 x 2 3/4" ............................... **350-395**

**Pin,** gold on sterling, floral spray, three royal blue marquise stones in center, signed "Coro," 3 1/4" h. ............................ **70-90**

**Pin,** gold on sterling, flower w/very large emerald-cut red glass stone w/coiled leaves at sides, ca. 1940s, signed "Jolle," 2 3/4 x 3 3/4" ............................ **100-125**

*Flower Spray Pins*

**Pin,** gold on sterling Retro flower spray, two large red unfoiled open set stones in flowers, 3" (ILLUS. left) ................. **125**

**Pin,** gold on sterling, Retro spray flower, leaves, unfoiled open set pink & light blue stones, old Boucher mark, 2 1/4" ....... **250**

**Pin,** gold on sterling, small stars on top surrounding a center faux blue sapphire, clear rhinestone trim, signed "Nettie Rosenstein," 1 3/4" .............................. **100-145**

**Pin,** gold on sterling, two large Retro-style flowers, large turquoise rhinestone pavé set centers, clear rhinestone trim, signed "Pennino," 2 7/8 x 2 3/8" (ILLUS. right) ....... **395**

**Pin,** gold-plated, basket w/three-dimensional pavé-set rhinestones, puppy leaning over edge, 1 1/4" h. ............................. **40-55**

**Pin,** gold-plated figural chick, textured finish, amber rhinestone eye, signed "Trifari," 1 3/4" h. ...................................... **60-75**

**Pin,** gold-plated, figural lion head, large amber stone in mouth, mane made of chains, unsigned, designer quality, 3" ....... **75-95**

**Pin,** gold-plated, woman wearing 1940s hat & suit carrying flower set w/purple rhinestone, signed "Coro," 2 1/2" ..................... **65-85**

**Pin,** rhinestone, cat motif, entire body, head & ears completely covered w/hand-set amber Aurora Borealis rhinestones, signed "Warner," 1 3/4" h. ............................. **35**

**Pin,** rhinestone, Christmas tree w/clear baguette "candles" & trimmed w/red & green rhinestones, signed "Hollycraft," 2" h. ......................................................... **75-90**

**Pin,** rhinestone, figural cat w/ball, pavé-set w/lavender & red rhinestones, Alice Caviness, 1 3/4" .............................................. **35-45**

**Pin,** rhinestone, flower all clear pavé-set w/large teardrop-shaped faux green emerald center, 2 1/4" .............................. **40-55**

**Pin,** rhinestone & gold tone, cat motif, large red cabochon stones in body & head, clear rhinestone teardrop ears, baguette & round stone trim, signed "Trifari," 1 3/4" ......................................................... **35**

**Pin,** rhinestone, head of cat motif, pavé hand-set pink stones, pink pear-shape rhinestone ears, red marquise eyes, red round nose, signed "Weiss," 1 1/4" .............. **25**

**Pin,** rhinestone, multicolored, large triangular, emerald-shaped, pear-shaped, marquise & round stones, designer quality, 2 1/2" ......................................................... **75-100**

*Figural Panther and Tiger Pins*

**Pin,** sterling, Art Deco style figural black enamel panther, 1 3/4" (ILLUS. left) ........ **75-100**

**Pin,** sterling, cat, 14k gold nose, sapphire eyes, original case & box, signed "Tiffany & Co.," 1 3/4" ................................. **125-150**

**Pin,** sterling, marcasite & enamel tiger on top of large black onyx circle, 2 x 2" (ILLUS. right) ......................................... **100-145**

**Pin,** sterling, marcasite set, exotic bird w/bluish green glass body, Alice Caviness, 2 3/4" h. (unsigned, originally had a tag) ...................................................... **100-145**

**Pin,** sterling, three-dimensional cat w/movable face, signed "Beau," 2" .......................... **35**

**Pin,** white metal, three musical instruments, two hands, word "JAMMIN" suspended in individual letters, 3 x 3 1/2" ...... **65-75**

**Pin/pendant,** sterling, handmade abstract design w/polished grey shell center, signed "A. Idan." 2 1/4" .......................... **100-125**

## SETS

**Necklace & bracelet,** gold-plated swirled Retro style openwork links, signed "Monet Jewelers," bracelet 7" l, necklace 16" l., the set ............................................. **65-90**

**Necklace & earrings:** glass "jade" inside openwork gold, rhinestone pendant, green bead trim, matching clip earrings, signed "Kramer," necklace 24", the set .......... **85**

**Necklace & earrings,** rhinestone, bib style w/large multicolored stones in oval center, earrings match oval center, clip-ons, 2", necklace 16" l., the set (unsigned, designer quality) ...................................... **85-115**

**Necklace & fur clip,** gold-plated, 14" snake chain necklace w/diamond-shaped center set w/emerald green diamond-shaped rhinestones, raised gold centerpiece leading to chain, matching 2 3/4" clip, signed "Trifari," the set ......... **150-165**

*Gold & Enamel Turtle Set*

**Necklace & pins,** enamel on gold, 3" l. white figural turtle on 17" chain, matching scatter pins 1 1/2" l., signed "Miriam Haskell," the set (ILLUS.) ..................... **295-365**

**Pin & earrings,** brushed gold, sunflower centered w/large open-set topaz glass stone, matching clip-on earrings, 1" d., pin 3" d., the set (unsigned, designer quality) ...................................................... **75-95**

**Pin & fur clips,** pink gold on sterling silver, flying birds motif w/rhinestone trim on body & wings, signed "Sterling Coro-Craft," pin 2", clips, 1 1/2", the set ......... **275-300**

## MODERN (1920-1960s)

*Ruby & Diamond Bar Pin*

**Bar pin,** ruby & diamond, yellow gold & silver scrolled openwork design altgernately set w/five rubies & four round diamonds (ILLUS.) ...................................... **920**

**Bracelet,** garnet, bangle-type, hinged design set w/three rows of faceted garnets, gilt-metal mount .................................. **288**

**Bracelet,** gold & aquamarine, 14k white gold oval links alternating w/prong-set faceted cushion-cut aquamarines, 8" l. ........ **575**

**Bracelet,** gold, ruby & sapphire, alternating oval & rectangular 14k yellow gold plaques set w/square-cut rubies & faceted oval sapphires, gold bead accents, stamped "BH" ............................................ **345**

*Gold Bracelet/Ring*

**Bracelet/ring,** gold & gemstone, eight hinged engraved circular links that convert from a bracelet to a ring, the clasp forming the top of the ring w/two interchangeable gemstones, one a blue zircon, the other a citrine, French hallmarks (ILLUS.) ......................................................... **805**

*Gold Owl Brooch*

**Brooch,** gold (18k yellow), designed as an owl on a branch, detailed & textured feathers, green stone eyes, Italy (ILLUS.) ...................................................... **345**

**Brooch,** gold & coral, designed as an 18k yellow gold branch w/four coral acorns (solder evident) ............................................ **805**

*Gold & Diamond Floral Brooch*

**Brooch,** gold & diamond, floral circle design, prong set w/seven round brilliant-cut diamonds, 14k yellow gold mount, hallmark (ILLUS.) ............................. **978**

**Brooch,** gold "Figure 8," bicolor 14k gold concentric loops centered by rose gold bars, hallmarked for Lester ......................... **374**

*Flowerpot Brooch*

**Brooch,** gold, pearl & ruby, designed as a baroque pearl planter surmounted by spiky 18k yellow gold leaves, accented w/four prong-set round rubies (ILLUS.) ........ **920**

*Silver Kingfisher Brooch*

**Brooch,** sterling silver, rectangular frame decorated as a Kingfisher perched on a leafy branch, impressed "M" with a circle "Sterling Denmark 390," 1 3/4" d. (ILLUS.) ................................................................ **460**

**Cameo ring,** hardstone, finely carved profile of a classical warrior surrounded by graduated collet-set diamonds, 18k yellow gold mount ............................................ **460**

**Choker,** pearl, four strands of pink button-shaped pearls spaced by gold bars & clasp ........................................................... **748**

**Cuff links,** gold (14k yellow), "Tragedy/Comedy," oval design depicting a frowning head & a smiling head on either side, pr. ...................................................... **1,035**

**Cuff links,** gold (18k yellow), hollow circle centered by a bar, oblong monogrammed T-bar, signed "Georg Jensen, no. 1091," pr. ............................................... **690**

**Cuff links,** mother-of-pearl & enamel, the circular disc centrally set w/a cabochon blue stone, edged in cobalt blue enamel, mounted in 14k yellow gold, hallmark for Krementz, pr. ................................................. **345**

**Cuff links,** sterling silver, domed rectangular form w/cut-out fish motif & copper eye accent, signed "Ed Wiener," pr. ............. **345**

**Earrings,** moonstone & ruby, center set w/a prong-set round moonstone, surrounded by round rubies, 14k yellow gold mount, pr. ............................................. **633**

**Locket,** gold (18k yellow), rectangular w/applied monogram, Austria.................... **1,150**

**Pin,** diamond & enamel, fish w/pierced body decorated w/blue-green enamel scales & yellow-orange fins, diamond-set mouth, ruby eye, 18k yellow gold mount, hallmark (minor enamel loss) ........... **633**

**Pin,** enamel, butterfly design, the silver-topped wings set w/pearls, opals, colored gemstones & diamond accents, bordered by orange guilloche enamel, 19k yellow gold mount, Portuguese hallmarks ........................................................ **633**

**Pin,** gold & pearl, "Golden Mink," designed as a textured 14k yellow gold mink w/sapphire eye accents, surmounting three baroque pearls, signed "Rotter" ......... **259**

**Pin,** gold & pearl, mistletoe design w/pearl berries, brushed 18k yellow gold leaves & branches, numbered & signed "Buccellati" .................................................... **863**

**Pin,** gold & silver, sterling silver eagle surmounting a shield atop two crossed anchors in 14k yellow gold, signed "Tiffany & Co." .................................................. **460**

*Amethyst Heart-shaped Pin*

**Pin/pendant,** amethyst & diamond, heart-shaped amethyst surrounded by twenty prong-set round diamonds, 14k yellow gold mount (ILLUS.) ..................................... **862**

*Diamond & Sapphire Pin/Pendent*

**Pin/pendant,** diamond & sapphire, center set round diamond w/rose-cut diamonds in the circular white gold openwork design & framed by twelve round sapphires (ILLUS.) ......................................... **1,840**

**Ring,** gold & elephant hair, woven design of alternating elephant hair & 18k yellow gold, marked "France," size 5 1/2 ............... **288**

**Ring,** gold, ruby & sapphire, domed 18k yellow gold coiled wire design surmounted by prong-set ruby & sapphire

flowerheads, bordered by bead-set diamonds set in platinum ................................... **748**

**Ring,** opal & diamond, center oval opal cabochon surrounded by eighteen round diamonds, 14k yellow gold mount ............. **1,035**

## SETS

*Citrine & Diamond Brooch & Earrings*

**Brooch & earrings,** citrine & diamond, the brooch designed as a four-leaf clover w/heart-shaped citrine leaves centered by a circular-cut diamond w/a bead-set diamond stem, 14k yellow gold mount, matching earrings (ILLUS. of part) ............... **546**

**Brooch & earrings,** gold (18k yellow), orchid design in textured gold w/seed pearl accent, w/matching earrings, the set ................................................................ **316**

**Earrings & pendant,** aquamarine, prong-set emerald-cut aquamarine earrings & similar pendant suspended from a 20" l. 14k white gold box-link chain, 14k white gold mounts, the set ..................................... **403**

*Opal & Diamond Necklace*

**Necklace & earrings,** opal & diamond, the necklace centered by an opal suspended within a blue enamel engraved plaque w/diamond accents, further suspending a similar drop, the fine 10k yellow gold chain w/old mine-cut diamond floral links spaced by opal-set plaques, together w/silver-topped gold mount earrings, the set (ILLUS. of necklace) .......... **2,300**

# JUKE BOXES

**AMI Continental,** 1961, 200-selection, unrestored, working.................................. **$1,600**

**AMI Model D40,** 1951, 40-selection, unrestored, working.......................................... **400**

*AMI Model E120*

**AMI Model E120,** 1953, 120-selection, working, unrestored (ILLUS.) ...................... **900**

*Rock-Ola Standard*

**Rock-Ola Luxury Light-up Standard,** 1939, 20-selection, unrestored, working (ILLUS.)....................................................... **100**

**Rock-Ola Model 433,** 1966, 160-selection, unrestored, working..................................... **500**

**Rock-Ola Regular,** 1936, 12-selection, unrestored, working..................................... **500**

**Seeburg Model 100R,** 1954, 100-selection, unrestored, working........................... **1,400**

**Seeburg Model 147,** 1947, 20-selection, unrestored, working..................................... **800**

**Seeburg Model 222,** 1959, 160-selection, unrestored, working................................. **1,500**

**Seeburg Model LPC480,** 1964, 160-selection, unrestored, working............................. **600**

**Wurlitzer Model 1100,** 1947-1949, 24-selection, unrestored, working ................. **3,500**

**Wurlitzer Model 1800,** 1955, 104-selection, unrestored, working.......................... **2,000**

**Wurlitzer Model 1900,** 1955-1956, 104-selection, unrestored, working ................. **1,700**

*Wurlitzer Model 61 Juke Box*

**Wurlitzer Model 61,** table model, burl wood, metal & red & white plastic (ILLUS.)..................................................... **1,750**

# KITCHENWARES

## COFFEE MILLS

*Coffee mills, commonly called grinders, are perfectly collectible for many people. They are appealing to the eye and are frequently coveted by interior decorators and today's coffee-consuming homeowners. Compact, intricate, unique, ornate, and rooted in early Americana, coffee mills are intriguing to everyone and are rich and colorful.*

*Coffee milling devices have been available for hundreds of years. The Greeks and Romans used rotating millstones for grinding coffee and grain. Turkish coffee mills with their familiar cylindrical brass shells appeared in the 15th century, and perhaps a century or two later came the earliest spice and coffee mills in Europe. Primitive mills were handmade in this country by blacksmiths and carpenters in the late 1700s and the first half of the 19th century. These were followed by a host of commercially-produced mills which included wood-backed side mills and numerous kinds of box mills, many with machined dovetails or fingerjoints. Characterized by the birth of upright cast-iron coffee mills, so beautiful with their magnificent colors and fly wheels, the period of coffee mill proliferation began around 1870. The next 50 years saw a staggering number of large and small manufacturers struggling to corner the popular home market for box and canister-type coffee mills. After that, the advent of electricity and other major advances in coffee grinding and packaging technology hastened the decline in popularity of small coffee mills.*

*Value-added features to look for when purchasing old coffee grinders include:*

*•good working order and no missing, broken, or obviously replaced parts*

*• original paint*

• attractive identifying markings, label or brass emblem

• uncommon mill, rarely seen, or appealing unique characteristics

• high quality restoration, if not original.

—Mike White

## BOX MILLS

*Arcade Mfg. Co. IXL Coffee Mill*

**Box mill,** tall wood box w/iron top, cover & handle, w/side crank, top embossed "Arcade Mfg. Co. IXL" (ILLUS.) .................. **$400**

*Kenrick & Sons Coffee Mill*

**Box mill,** tapered iron box, English mill w/porcelainized hopper, marked "Kenrick & Sons Patent Coffee Mill" (ILLUS.) ...... **150**

*Logan & Strobridge Coffee Mill*

**Box mill,** wood box w/embossed covered hopper, marked "Logan & Strobridge Pat' Coffee Mill," some damage to box (ILLUS.) .......................................................... **80**

*Sun No. 1085 Challen Fast Grinder Coffee Mill*

**Box mill,** wood box w/handle on top, sunken tin hopper, label reads "Sun No. 1085 Challenge Fast Grinder" (ILLUS.) ....... **140**

*Arcade Coffee Mill*

**Box mill,** wood box w/raised iron hopper & tin dust cover, straight handle, Arcade, unmarked (ILLUS.) ....................................... **150**

*Austrian Coffee Mill*

**Box mill,** tapered wood box w/brass hopper, Austrian, 3 1/2 x 3 1/2" top (ILLUS.) ..... **180**

*PeDe Dienes Mokka Coffee Mill*

**Box mill,** wood box w/tin dome & sliding cover, label marked "PeDe Dienes Mokka," 4 x 4" top (ILLUS.) ........................... **60**

*T & C Clark Co. Coffee Mill*

**Box mill,** tapered cast-iron box w/brass hopper, marked "T. & C. Clark Co.," England, 4 1/2 x 4 1/2" top (ILLUS.)............. **250**

*Grand Union Tea Co. Coffee Mill*

**Box mill,** all iron box w/original paint, raised hopper cover reads "Grand Union Tea Co.," 5 x 5" base (ILLUS.) ..................... **750**

*Peugot Freres Coffee Mill*

**Box mill,** wood box w/wood hopper & pivoting wood cover, Peugot Freres, 51/2 x 51/2" top (ILLUS.)............................. **160**

*Parker's National No. 30 Coffee Mill*

**Box mill,** iron top, handle & covered hopper, "Parker's National No. 30," 6 x 6" top (ILLUS.) ................................................ **160**

*Parker's Eagle No. 314 Coffee Mill*

**Box mill,** tin hopper & red label reads "Parker's Eagle No. 314," 6 x 6" top (ILLUS.) ........................................................... **90**

*Arcade No. 367 Coffee Mill*

**Box mill,** wood box, tin hopper w/partial cover, well-marked "Arcade No. 367," 6 1/2 x 6 1/2" top (ILLUS.)............................ **120**

*PS&W No. 350 Coffee Mill*

**Box mill,** wood box, raised hopper w/pivoting cover, PS&W No. 350 (unmarked), 7 x 7" top (ILLUS.).......................................... **250**

## PRIMITIVE COFFEE MILLS

*G. Selsor Coffee Mill*

**Box mill,** w/pewter hopper, signed "G. Selsor #2" on crank, 7 x 7" top (ILLUS.)............. **170**

*Iron Coffee Mill*

**Iron mill,** post-mounted blacksmith's-type, 5" open hopper (ILLUS.) ............................... **350**

## SIDE MILLS

*Parker Union Coffee Mill*

**Side mill,** iron, double grinding gear, Parker Union, unmarked (ILLUS.)................ **130**

*Kenrick & Sons Coffee Mill*

**Side mill,** w/sliding cover, "Kenrick & Sons (1815) Patent Coffee Mill" (ILLUS.).............. **150**

*Wilson's Coffee Mill*

**Side mill,** w/wood back, "Increase Wilson's Best Quality No. 3" (ILLUS.)......................... **100**

*L&S Brighton Coffee Mill*

**Side mill,** w/wood block, marked "L&S Brighton" (ILLUS.) .......................................... **90**

## UPRIGHT MILLS

*1898 Enterprise Coffee Mill*

**Upright mill,** cast iron, covered hopper & double wheels, original red paint & decals, 1898 patent date, wheels embossed "Enterprise Mfg. Co, Philadelphia, U.S.A." (ILLUS.) .............................. **1,000**

*Elma Upright Coffee Mill*

**Upright mill,** cast iron, single-wheel mill w/wooden drawer & covered tin hopper, on wooden base, Elma, unmarked (ILLUS.)........................................................ **150**

*1887 Coles Coffee Mill*

**Upright mill,** cast iron, spread-winged eagle atop brass hopper, tin catcher, double wheels, original paint & decals, 1887 patent date, wheels embossed "Coles Mfg. Co., Phila. Pa.," model No. 8, eagle replaced (ILLUS.) ........................ **1,200**

*LF&C Universal No. 11 Coffee Mill*

**Upright mill,** cast-iron w/covered hopper, green w/gold trim, marked "LF&C Universal No. 11" (ILLUS.) ................................ **320**

*Cha's Parker Co. Coffee Mill*

**Upright mill,** cast-iron w/tin drawer, sliding cover on hopper, double wheels, original red, blue & gold paint, 9" wheel embossed "The Cha's Parker Co., Meriden, Conn. U.S.A.," model No. 200 (ILLUS.)..................................................... **1,200**

**Upright mill,** counter-type, cast iron, two-wheel, cast-iron drawer at bottom on a wooden base, worn original black paint w/red & gold trim & decals, marked "Land" 12" h................................................. **660**

*Enterprise No. 4 Upright Coffee Mill*

**Upright mill,** cast iron, spread-winged eagle perched atop brass hopper, w/double 11" wheels repainted red, blue & gold, replaced drawer, Enterprise No. 4 (ILLUS.)..................................................... **600**

*Peugot Freres 2A Coffee Mill*

**Upright mill,** cast iron, w/wooden drawer & tin covered hopper, painted green w/gold trim, 13" wheel w/gears, embossed "Peugot Freres 2A, Brevetes S.G.D.G." (ILLUS.) ....................................... **450**

*Parnall & Sons Coffee Mill*

**Upright mill,** cast ircn, decorative scrolls, w/brass hopper, crank & single wheel, black w/gold trim, 15" wheel embossed "Parnall & Sons, Bristol (England)" (ILLUS.)..................................................... **1,000**

## WALL CANISTER MILLS

*"Golden Rule Blend" Coffee Mill*

**Wall canister mill,** bronzed cast-iron canister w/glass window & cup, embossed canister reads "Golden Rule Blend Coffee The Finest Blend In The World, The Citizens Wholesale Supply Co., Columbus Ohio.," 18" h. (ILLUS.) ........................... **450**

*PeDe Wall Canister Coffee Mill*

**Wall canister mill,** ceramic canister w/glass cup, marked "PeDe" (ILLUS.).......... **130**

*"Kaffee" Leinbrock Ideal DRGM Coffee Mill*

**Wall canister mill,** ceramic canister w/glass cup & wood backing board, cannister marked "KAFFEE," Leinbrock Ideal DRGM (ILLUS.) ................................... **220**

*Universal 0012 Coffee Mill*

**Wall canister mill,** steel canister w/steel cup, green label reads "Universal 0012 Coffee Mill Pat. Feb. 14, 1905, Landers, Frary & Clark, New Britain, Conn. U.S.A.," 13" h. (ILLUS.) ............................... **160**

*Bronson-Walton Holland Beauty Coffee Mill*

**Wall canister mill,** tin lithographed canister, pictures a young girl wearing white

dress, yellow apron & bonnet, Bronson-Walton Holland Beauty, 13" h. including cup (ILLUS.) .................................................. **350**

*Wilmont-Castle Coffee Mill*

**Wall canister mill,** steel canister w/glass cup, embossed "Pat 1891," Wilmont-Castle, 15" including glass cup (ILLUS.) ...... **280**

*Enterprise No. 100 Coffee Mill*

**Wall canister mill,** glass canister & cup, embossed "Enterprise No. 100," 16" h. (ILLUS.) ........................................................ **180**

*Arcade Crystal No. 3 Coffee Mill*

**Wall canister mill,** glass canister & cup, marked jar, Arcade Crystal No. 3, 18" h. (ILLUS.) ........................................................ **350**

## MISCELLANEOUS

*"Little Tot" Arcade Coffee Mill*

**Box mill,** child's, gold painted hopper & crank, labeled "Little Tot," Arcade 21/2 x 21/2" top (ILLUS.)................................. **90**

*Child's Coffee Mill*

**Box mill,** child's, painted tin, w/brass hopper, 3 x 3" top (ILLUS.).................................... **70**

*Clamp-on Coffee Mill*

**Clamp-on mill,** open hopper, original red paint w/label, LF&C No. 01 (ILLUS.) ............ **120**

*Holwick Electric Coffee Mill*

**Electric mill,** aluminum hopper & tin catch can, red w/gold trim, Holwick 1/4 horsepower, 27" h. (ILLUS.).................................. **180**

*Brass Turkish Coffee Mill*

**Turkish mill,** brass, engraved cylindrical casing w/folding crank (ILLUS.) .................... **50**

*Arcade Miniature Coffee Mill*

**Upright mill,** miniature, cast-iron w/double wheels, red w/gold trim, embossed "ARCADE," 4" h. (ILLUS.) ............................ **150**

# EGG BEATERS

*A & J USA Ecko Egg Beater*

Eggbeaters are pure Americana! No other invention (although apple parers come close) represent America at its best from the mid-19th century to the 1930s or '40s. Eggbeaters tell the unbeatable story of America—the story of demand for a product, competition, success, retreat, failure, faith, and revival.

The mechanical (rotary) eggbeater is an American invention, and ranks up there with motherhood and apple pie, or at least up there where it counts—in the kitchen. American ingenuity produced more than 1,000 patents related to beating eggs, most before the 20th century.

To put it in perspective, try to imagine 1,000 plus ways to beat an egg. Here's a clue, and it's all due to Yankee tinkering: There are rotary cranks, archimedes (up and down) models, hand-helds, squeeze power, and rope and water power—and others. If you ever wanted a different way to beat an egg it was (and is) available.

Today, eggbeaters are a very popular Americana kitchen collectible—a piece of America still available to the collector, although he/she may have to scramble to find the rare ones.

But, beaters are out there, from the mainstay A & J to the cast-iron Dover to the rarer Express and Monroe. There is always an intriguing mix, ranging in price from less than under $10.00 to the hundreds of dollars.

—Don Thornton

*Items are listed alphabetically by manufacturer*

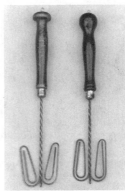

*A & J Egg Beaters*

**A & J,** archimedes "up & down" style, marked "A & J Pat'd Oct. 15 07 Other Pats Pending," 12 1/2" (ILLUS. left) ............... **35**

**A & J,** Ecko, wood handle, rotary w/apron marked "A&J USA Ecko," on a two-cup measuring cup marked "A&J" (ILLUS.) .......... **35**

**A & J,** metal, rotary crank, marked "A&J Pat. Oct. 9, 1923 Made in U.S.A.," 8 1/4" to 10" ............. **10**

**A & J,** archimedes "up & down" style, marked "Patd Oct. 15 07 Other Pat Pend'g," 9 1/4" (ILLUS. right) ......................... **35**

**Androck,** Bakelite handle, metal rotary, marked "Androck," 11" (ILLUS.) ..................... **30**

**Androck,** metal rotary, wood handle, marked "Androck," 11" (ILLUS.) ..................... **15**

**Androck,** plastic handle, rotary, marked "Another Androck Product," 12 1/2" (ILLUS.) .......................................................... **15**

**Aurelius Bros.,** wood handle, rotary marked "Ideal Mille Lacs Mfg. by Aurelius," 10 3/4" h. (ILLUS. right) ...................... **400**

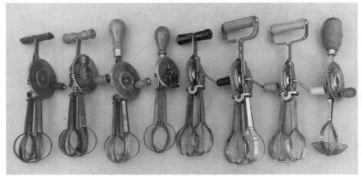

*Various Androck Rotary Crank Beaters*

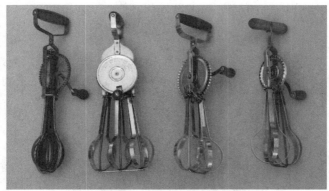

*Aurelius Bros. Egg Beaters*

**Aurelius Bros.,** wood handle, rotary, rare triple dasher, rotary marked "Master Egg Beater Mfd. By Aurelius Bros., Braham, Minn. Pat. Appld. For," 11 1/2" h. (ILLUS. left center) ...................................... **450**

**Aurelius Bros.,** wood handle, rotary w/double gearing, marked "Aurelius Bros., Braham, Minn. Pat. Nov. 9, 1926," 11 1/2" h. (ILLUS. left)................................... **45**

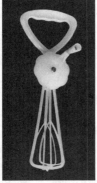

*Blisscraft of Hollywood Egg Beater*

**Blisscraft of Hollywood,** plastic, rotary, marked "Blisscraft of Hollywood Pat. USA Pend.," scarce, 12" h. (ILLUS.) .............. **75**

*Cylcone Egg Beaters*

**Cyclone,** cast iron, rotary marked "Cyclone Pat. 6-25 and 7-16 1901," 11 1/2" h. (ILLUS. center two) ........................................ **75**

**Cyclone,** cast iron, rotary marked "Cyclone Pat 6-25-1901 Reissue 8-26-1902," 13 1/2" h. (ILLUS. far left & right) .................. **90**

**Dover,** cast iron, rotary tumbler model (smaller dashers to fit in glass or tumbler), marked "Dover Egg Beater Pat'd Made in Boston U.S.A.," 9" ........................... **95**

**Dover,** cast iron, nickel-plated, D-handle, rotary marked "Genuine Dover, Dover Stamping Co.," 11 1/4" h. .............................. **50**

**Dover,** cast iron, rotary marked "Dover Egg Beater Patd May 6th 1873 Apr 3d 1888 Nov. 24th 1891 Made in Boston U.S.A. Dover Egg Beater Co.," 11 1/4" h.................. **50**

**Dover,** cast iron, rotary marked "Dover Egg Beater Pat. May 31 1870," 12 1/2" h. ........... **175**

**Dream Cream,** rotary turbine marked "The Dream Cream Trade Mark Whip Manufactured by A.D. Foyer & Company Chicago," 10" h. ................................................ **30**

*Express Egg Beater w/Fly Swatter*

**Express,** cast iron, rotary w/fly swatter dasher, marked "Pat. Oct. 25, 1887" only, rare, 11 1/2" h. (ILLUS.).................... **1,250**

**F. Ashley,** archemides, "up & down" style, marked "F. Ashley Patent Appl For," 15"... **1,000**

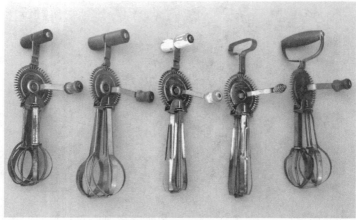

*Various Ladd Ball Bearing Beaters*

**Hand-held,** plastic handle, marked "Patent
No. 2906510" ................................................. **5**
**Hand-held,** all-wire, unmarked, 13" h................ **35**

*Holt-Lyon Side-Handle Egg Beaters*

**Holt-Lyon,** cast iron, side-handle, marked
"H-L Co.," 8 1/2" h. (ILLUS. right)................. **300**
**Holt-Lyon,** cast iron, side-handle, marked
"Holt's Egg Beater & Cream Whip Pat.
Aug. 22-'98 Apr. 3-00," 8 1/2" h. (ILLUS.
left) ............................................................ **275**
**Holt-Lyon,** cast-iron propeller, marked
"Lyon Egg Beater Albany N.Y. Pat. Sep
7 '97," 10" h. (ILLUS. top next column) ........ **150**
**Jaquette Bros.,** scissors-type, cast iron,
marked "Jaquette Bros No. 1," 7 1/2" l..... **1,100**
**Jaquette Bros.,** scissors-type, cast iron,
marked "Jaquette Bros No. 2," 8 3/4" l. ........ **750**
**Ladd,** metal rotary, marked "No. 0 Ladd
Beater Pat'd July 7, 1908 Feb. 2 1915
United Royalties Corp.," 9 3/4" h.
(ILLUS.)........................................................ **15**
**Ladd,** wood handle, metal rotary, marked
"No. 00 Ladd beater Patd Oct. 18, 1921
United Royalties Corp.," 11" l. (ILLUS.).......... **12**
**Ladd,** metal rotary, marked "No. 1 Ladd
Beater July 7, 1908, Oct, 1921,"
11 1/2" h. (ILLUS.)......................................... **15**

*Holt-Lyon Egg Beater*

**Ladd,** tumbler model, metal rotary, marked
"No. 5 Ladd Ball Bearing Beater Oct. 18
1921," 11 1/2" h. (ILLUS.) .............................. **35**
**Ladd,** beater held in two-part apron marked
"Ladd No. 2," embossed on pedestal jar
"Ladd Mixer No. 2," 13 1/2" h. (ILLUS.),........ **325**

*Monroe Rotary Egg Beater*

**Monroe,** cast-iron rotary, shelf mount, marked "EP Monroe patented April 19 1859," 10 1/2" h. (ILLUS.) ......................... **1,500**

**P-D-&-Co.,** cast-iron rotary w/spring dasher bottom w/the word "E - A - S- Y" cut-out on spokes of main gear wheel & marked "Pat Sept. 28 26," 9 3/4" h. .......................... **900**

**S & S Hutchinson,** cast-iron rotary (w/Hutchinson cut-out in wheel) marked "Hutchinson New York Pat. apld For," glass apron on bowl embossed "130 Worth St. New York J. Hutchinson S&S Trade Mark," 9 1/2" h. ................................. **950**

*S & S Hutchinson Rotary Egg Beater*

**S & S Hutchinson,** heavy tin rotary marked "S&S Hutchinson No. 2 New York Pat. Sept. 2, 1913," w/heavy tin apron on ribbed glass jar embossed "National Indicator Co. No. 2 S&S Trade Mark Long Island City," 9 1/2" h. (ILLUS.)............. **600**

*Taplin Rotary Egg Beater*

**Taplin,** cast-iron rotary, marked "The Taplin Mfg. Co. New Britian Conn, U.S.A Light Running Pat. Nov. 24 '08," 12 1/2" h. (ILLUS.)........................................ **45**

# EGG TIMERS

*A little glass tube filled with sand and attached to a figural base measuring between 3" and 5" in* height was once a commonplace kitchen item. *Many beautiful timers were produced in Germany in the 1920s and later Japan, reaching their heyday in the 1940s. These small egg timers were commonly made in a variety of shapes in bisque, china, chalkware, cast iron, tin, brass, wood or plastic. Although egg timers were originally used to time a 3-minute egg, some were also used to limit the length of a telephone call as a cost saving measure.*

*Goebel Baker Egg Timer*

**Baker,** ceramic, Goebel (ILLUS.) ....................... **90**

*Black Baby Egg Timer*

**Black baby,** ceramic, sitting w/left arm holding timer (ILLUS.) ..................................... **95**

**Black chef,** ceramic, sitting w/arm up holding timer, variety of sizes, Germany............. **100**

**Black chef,** ceramic, standing w/large fish, timer in fish's mouth, Japan, 4 3/4" h. ......... **145**

*Black Chef w/Frying Pan Egg Timer*

**Black chef with frying pan,** composition, Japan (ILLUS.) .............................................. **125**

*Bo-Peep Egg Timer*

**Bo-Peep,** ceramic, Japan, "Bo-Peep" on base (ILLUS.) ............................................... **125**
**Boy,** ceramic, skiing, Germany, 3" h. ................. **75**
**Cat,** ceramic, standing by base of grandfather clock, Germany, 4 1/2" h. ......................... **75**
**Chef,** composition, w/cake, Germany ................. **95**
**Chef,** ceramic, winking, white clothes, timer built in back, turns upside down to tip sand, 4" h. ......................................................... **60**
**Chick with cap,** ceramic, Josef Originals ......... **55**
**Chicken,** on nest, green plastic, England, 2 1/2" h. .............................................................. **25**
**Chimney sweep,** ceramic, Goebel, Germany ..................................................................... **95**
**Chimney sweep,** ceramic, carrying ladder, Germany, 3 1/4" h. ......................................... **85**

*Clockman Planter*

**Clock,** ceramic, clock face, w/man's plaid suit & tie below, w/planter in back, Japan (ILLUS.) .......................................................... **65**

*Clown Egg Timer*

**Clown,** ceramic, Germany (ILLUS.) ................. **100**
**Clown on phone,** ceramic, standing, full-figured, Japan ................................................. **75**
**Colonial lady with bonnet,** ceramic, variety of dresses & colors, Germany, 3 3/4" h., each ................................................. **85**
**Dog,** ceramic, black poodle, sitting, Germany ..................................................................... **95**

*Lustreware Dog*

**Dog,** white w/brown ears & tail, lustreware, Japan (ILLUS.) ................................................. **75**
**Dutch girl & boy,** ceramic, Goebel, Germany ..................................................................... **125**
**Dutch girl w/flowers,** chalkware, walking, unmarked, 4 1/2" h. ......................................... **75**
**Elephant,** ceramic, sitting w/trunk up, white, Germany ............................................... **85**
**Elf by well,** ceramic, Manorware, England......... **45**

*English Bobby Egg Timer*

**English Bobby,** ceramic, Germany (ILLUS.)......................................................... **125**
**Friar Tuck,** ceramic, single, Goebel, Germany, 4" h. ...................................................... **75**
**Golliwog,** bisque, England ............................... **200**
**House with clock face,** ceramic, yellow & gold, Japan...................................................... **65**
**Huckleberry Finn,** ceramic, sitting in front of post, Japan ......................................... **95-125**
**Lighthouse,** ceramic, blue, cream & orange lustreware, Germany, 4 1/2" h. .......... **95**
**Little boy,** ceramic, standing wearing black shorts & shoes & large red bow tie, Germany (ILLUS. top next page) ........................ **95**
**Little girl on phone,** ceramic, sitting w/legs outstretched, pink dress, Germany .................. **5**

*Little Boy Egg Timer*

**Little girl with chick on her toes,** ceramic, Goebel, Germany ........................................ 100
**Mammy,** tin, w/lithographed picture of her cooking, w/potholder hooks, unmarked, 7 3/4" h. ...................................................... 145

*Mother Rabbit Egg Timer*

**Mother rabbit,** ceramic, holding carrot w/basket, Japan (ILLUS.) ............................... 60

*Mrs. Claus Egg Timer*

**Mrs. Claus,** ceramic, in yellow dress w/green collar, cuffs & hem, w/red bag full of gifts & black bag w/timer (ILLUS.) ........ 65
**Newspaper boy,** ceramic, Japan, 3 1/4" h. ......... 65
**Owl,** ceramic, Goebel (ILLUS. top next column) ........................................................... 100
**Parlor maid with cat,** ceramic, Japan ............... 65
**Penguin,** chalkware, England, 3 3/4" h. ............. 75
**Rabbit with floppy ears,** ceramic, standing, tan, Germany........................................ 100
**Rabbits,** double, ceramic, various color combinations, Goebel, Germany, 4" ............ 100

*Goebel Owl Egg Timer*

**Rooster,** cut-out painted wood w/sequins .......... 35
**Sailboat with sailor,** ceramic, lustreware, Germany ...................................................... 100
**Sailor,** ceramic, blue, Germany.......................... 85
**Scotsman with bagpipes,** plastic, England, 4 1/2" h............................................ 65

*Sea Gull Egg Timer*

**Sea gull,** ceramic, timer in beak, Germany (ILLUS.)....................................................... 100
**Telephone,** ceramic, black, Japan ..................... 40
**Vegetable person,** ceramic, Japan.................... 95
**Veggie man or woman,** bisque, Japan, 4 1/2" h., each ................................................ 75
**Welsh woman,** ceramic, Germany, 4 1/2" h. ......................................................... 85

*Windmill w/Pigs Egg Timer*

**Windmill,** ceramic, w/pigs on base, Japan (ILLUS.)....................................................... 100
**Windmill,** ceramic, w/dog or pigs on base, Japan, 3 3/4" h., each .................................. 100

## KITCHEN UTENSILS

*Apple Corer - Segmentor*

**Apple corer - segmentor,** cast iron & steel, a circle w/12 segmentors, cores & segments when apple is pushed through it, marked "Apple Cutter, Rollman Mfg. Co., Mr. Joy," 4 1/2" d. (ILLUS.) ..................... 35

**Apple parer,** cast iron, clamp-on type, a turntable w/push-off, marked "D.H. Whittemore," known as the "Union" ................... 250

**Apple parer,** cast iron, commerical-size, marked "The Dandy" ................................... 400

**Apple parer,** cast iron, turn-table-type, occasionally galvanized, marked "Granite State," 13" h............................................ 250

**Apple parer,** wooden, table mount-style w/attached paring arm, slides onto board, occasionally w/a paper label ........... 185

**Bake board,** tin, curved bottom to hold rolling pin, approximately 19" w., 22" h. .......... 350

**Baking pan,** tin, square, advertises "Snowking Baking Powder," 7 1/2" w. ............. 25

**Beater crock,** stoneware w/blue band decoration, rounded botton inside, marked "Beat It To Gettle & Rusie, Groceries & Hardware, Green Mountain, Iowa," 5" d., 4 1/2" h. ........................................................ 150

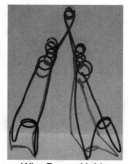

*Wire Broom Holder*

**Broom holder,** wire, ca. 1890 (ILLUS.) ............. 65
**Bundt pan,** tin, hand-made, 10" d. ................... 18
**Butter mold,** wood, carved cow design on plunger ....................................................... 285
**Can opener,** cast iron & steel, marked "World's Best, Pittsburgh, PA"......................... 45

*Can Opener*

**Can opener,** cast iron, three-way, punctures & opens can, no markings (ILLUS.)....... 85
**Can opener,** steel w/wooden handle, marked "Sure Cut," patent-dated "7-19-94" ..................................................................... 15
**Cherry pitter,** cast iron, clamp-on style, push action pits two cherries at one time, marked "New Standard Cherry Stoner, Duplex No. 35 Mt. Joy PA U.S.A." ................. 85

*Spring-action Cherry Pitter*

**Cherry pitter,** tin, spring-action, pits eight cherries at once, marked "Marshall Mfg. Co. Cherry Pitter, Omaha, Neb. Pat. Jan. 4 1916" (ILLUS.).................................... 250

**Coffee grinder,** cast iron, counter-top model, double-wheel model, on square base, embossed "Enterprise Mfg. Co., Philadelphia," wooden drawer labeled "No. 5," late 19th c., worn red & black paint w/decals, 17" h. (porcelain drawer knob chipped)............................................... 605

**Coffee grinder,** wooden, lap type w/drawer, pewter hopper & cast-iron crank handle, marked "Adams" ................... 175

**Coffee roaster,** cast iron, hinged "cannon ball" shape sits in a three-legged rim, wire bail handle, marked "Wood's Patent, Roys and Wilcox Co., Harrington's Import, Berlin Ct. Pat'd 5 17 1859," two sizes .......................................... 585

*Davidson's Coffee Roaster*

**Coffee roaster,** cast iron w/tin lid, marked "Davidson's," patent dated July 13, 1886 (ILLUS.)..............................................................

**Collander,** tin, round, footed w/two handles, nice star design pierced on sides .......... 75

*Rooster Cookie Cutter*

**Cookie or cake cutter,** rooster, heavy plated tin w/back; cutter edge 3/4" deep, handmade (ILLUS.) ........................................ **95**

*Reindeer Cookie Cutter*

**Cookie or cake cutter,** tin, hand-made design of a reindeer, tin cut closely to edge of design, no handle, 5 x 6" (ILLUS.) ..................................................... **125**

**Cookie or cake cutter,** tin, hand-made in the shape of a hand, medium weight w/back & top handle, 4 1/4" l. ...................... **110**

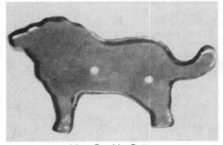

*Lion Cookie Cutter*

**Cookie or cake cutter,** tin, light-weight stylized design of a lion, manufactured, also found as a rabbit, doll-like girl, etc., on a rectangular background, handled, each (ILLUS.) ............................................... **15**

**Cookie or cake cutter,** tin heart, bulbous, short, squatty design, hand-made w/back cut close to design, 3" h. x 3 1/2" w. ............................................... **45**

**Dish protector,** wire screen dome, edge banded in tin, wooden knob on top, used as food protector from insects, 7" d. ............... **45**

**Dough scraper,** brass & tin, tubular tin handle, stamped "P.D." for Peter Derr ........ **550**

**Egg beater,** cast iron, "D-O-V-E-R" spelled out on the rotary wheel ................................ **225**

*Cast-iron & Glass Egg Beater*

**Egg beater,** cast-iron mechanism on a footed glass bowl base, marked "S &S Hutchson, New York, Pat. Appl. For" (ILLUS.) ....................................................... **375**

**Egg beater,** cast-iron top, wires, glass jar w/measurements, marked on bottom of jar "Silvers - Brooklyn" w/bridge outline as trade-mark .............................................. **275**

**Egg beater,** metal, "Up-To-Date" egg/cream whip works on the Archimedian up & down action, patented April 10, 1906 ...................................................... **275**

**Egg beater,** tin, child's, marked "Beats Anything in a Cup or Bowl," blue & white wooden handle, 7 1/2" l. ................................. **30**

**Egg beater,** wall mount-type, wire looped beater w/original wall bracket, marked "Licensed To Be Sold Only According To Established Price List of Maker, Keystone, Pat. Dec. 5,85" on each of rotary wheel ............................................................ **475**

**Egg beater,** metal, "Holt's Egg Beater & Cream Whip, Pat. Aug. 22, 99, Apr. 3, 00 USA" marked on wheel, 11" ........................... **45**

*Wire Egg Carrier*

**Egg carrier,** wire, round w/loops of wire forming bottom below six rings to hold egss, looped wire center handle, ca. 1890 (ILLUS.) ............................................... **125**

**Egg lifter,** wire, two concave wire shapes at end of squeeze-action wire handle ............ **35**
**Egg separator,** tin, circular w/edge slots, stamped "Rumford Egg Separator" ................ **65**

*Early Wooden Flour Sifter*

**Flour sifter,** wooden, elevated frame w/revolving brush inside, stamped "W. Foyes Flour Sifter, Patented Sept 12, 1865" (ILLUS.).............................................. **325**
**Flour sifter/scoop,** tin & wire mesh, half round scoop w/removable screwed-on long handle, marked "Pillsbury's Flour Universal Scoop with Flour Attachment" ...... **110**
**Fruit & lard press,** cast iron, "Griswold No. 3" ......................................................... **275**
**Grater,** tin, central pivot displays several grating surfaces or circular base, heavy wire handle...................................................... **15**
**Grater,** tin, punched half-cylinder on wire frame w/black wooden handle, 11" h. ............ **20**
**Griddle,** cast iron, "Griswold No. 108"............... **32**
**Griddle greaser,** wire, separates on one end to hold wrapped cloth used to grease griddles, called "The Fairy," patent-dated December 29, 1903 .................. **35**

*Sectional Pancake Griddle*

**Griddle - pancake iron,** cast iron, divided into three or more round areas each w/a lift-lid, marked "Pat. Jan 25 1881, S Mfg. Co., New York" (ILLUS.) .............................. **175**
**Jar opener,** cast iron, wrench-style, marked "C.A. Powell, Cleve'd. O"................... **24**
**Jar opener,** steel, two sections rotate on a pivot to loosen jar lid, patent-dated "1 7 08"..................................................................... **25**
**Knife & fork carrier,** walnut, rectangular dovetailed case, divided into two sections by a raised & shaped divider used as a handle................................................. **175**
**Lemon squeezer,** wood & tin, two folded tin pieces fit into a nicely shaped handle

w/center groove to catch juice, sometimes one tin section is serrated, scarce, 6 1/4" l. ...................................................... **150**
**Lemon squeezer,** wooden, footed base for table-top use, hinged lever action ............... **175**

*Handi-hands Lifter*

**Lifter,** handi-hands-style, wire, two hinged hand-like sections used to lift items from kettles, etc. (ILLUS.)..................................... **55**
**Lunch pail,** tin, w/insert & cup on top, oval ...... **110**

*Tin Collapsable Lunch Pail*

**Lunch pail,** tin & wire, collapsible-type, four sections, marked "Pat. Feb. 26 1884" (ILLUS.)....................................................... **85**
**Measuring cup,** tin, one-cup w/measuring lines, marked "Rumford"................................ **30**
**Measuring spoons,** metal, advertising Swans Down Cake Flour, graduated set of 4 ................................................................. **25**
**Nutmeg grater,** cast iron & tin, wire handle connected to a circular tin dish w/cast-iron nutmeg grater holder, marked on the back "Pat'd Mar 9 1886" ........................ **300**
**Nutmeg grater,** tin, elongated rectangle w/sliding box above grater, marked "The Boye"................................................................ **110**
**Nutmeg grater,** tin, small grater attached to colorful box marked "Stickney & Poors," six whole nutmegs ............................ **65**
**Nutmeg grater,** tin & wood, a top composed of three tin strips forming a triangle w/the bottom strip pierced as the grater, a strap handle mounted on one of the angled sides & this triangle mounted to swing on slender wire supports attached to a lower metal cylinder w/sliding wooden plug for feeding in the nut-

meg, traces of blue japanning, 19th c.,
5 1/2" l. ........................................................ **523**

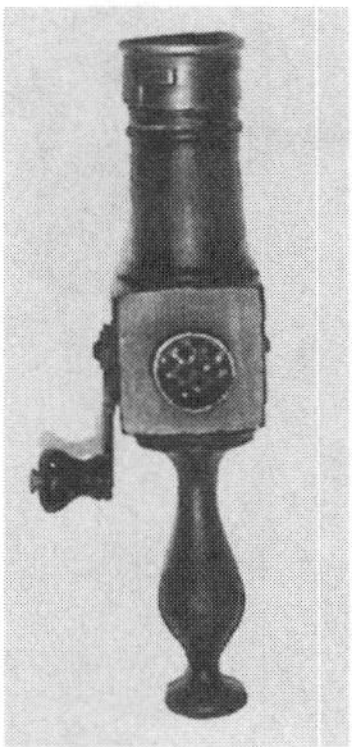

*"Champion" Nutmeg Grater*

**Nutmeg grater,** wooden, nicely turned
base handle below squared grater box
w/side crank handle & cylindrical top fitted w/a brass cap marked "Patent Apr 2
1867," paper label reads "Champion
Grater Co. Boston" (ILLUS.)......................... **475**
**Nutmeg grater,** tin mechanical cylinder
body measures 4 3/4" long w/wire handle protruding from one end, small 1 3/4"
cylinder w/screw cap extends perpendicular to long cylinder about 1/2" from
end w/handle, referred to as "stovepipe
grater" sometimes marked "The Snyder" ..... **400**
**Pastry blender,** wires w/wooden handle,
marked "Androx, Pat. Jan 12 29" ..................... **8**

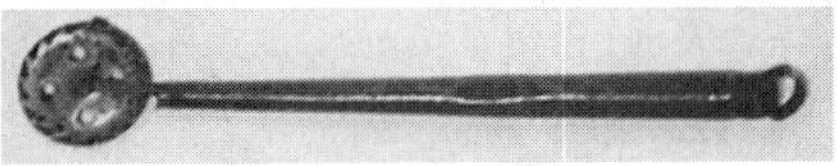

*Brass & Tin Pie Crimper*

**Pie crimper,** brass & tin, a brass serrated
wheel w/a long slender cylindrical tin
handle w/end loop, 6 1/2" l. (ILLUS.).............. **85**
**Pie crimper,** wood, tin & steel, green han-
dle w/tin crimped wheel................................... **12**
**Pie lifter,** cast iron & heavy wire, two
prongs w/center cast-iron slide, patent-
dated "Jan 30 83" ......................................... **55**

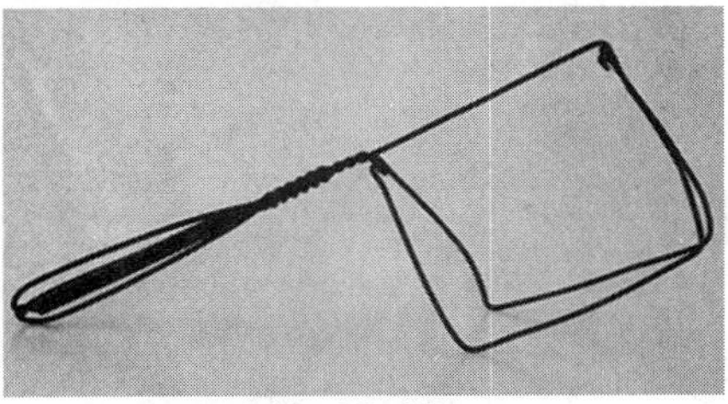

*Wire Pie Lifter*

**Pie lifter,** wire handle w/wood insert, two
hinged wings on opposite end which act
to grab pan (ILLUS.)........................................ **95**

*Wassell Pie Pan*

**Pie pan,** tin, advertising, marked "Baked By
Wassel," apple design in center (ILLUS.)....... **30**
**Pie pan,** tin & wire, a tin rim w/wire screen
for bottom, tiny feet, sits under a pie pan
to allow for cooling ......................................... **18**
**Pie pan,** tin, impressed "Crusty Pie" w/sun
rays extending from center, 9 1/2" d. ............. **15**

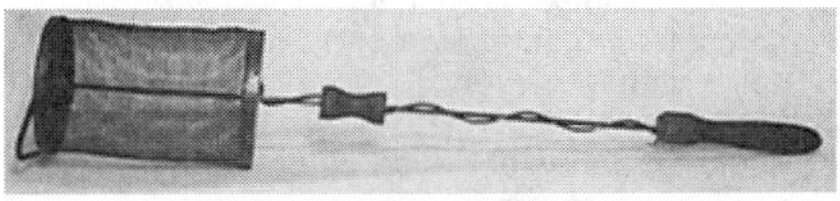

*Wire & Tin Popcorn Popper*

**Popcorn popper,** tin & wire mesh, archi-
median-style, round wire cylindrical cage
w/a long wire handle & turned wood handle, marked "Pat. Apr 16 1897," rare
(ILLUS.)......................................................... **375**
**Popcorn popper,** wire, rectangular cage
w/lift lid, wooden handle, common ................. **20**
**Pot & pan scraper,** tin, triangular
w/inverted thumbprint in center, advertis-
ing for various products, each ........................ **85**
**Pot scraper,** wire, a series of attached wire
rings form a pocket to hold soap,
unusual w/the pocket ..................................... **65**

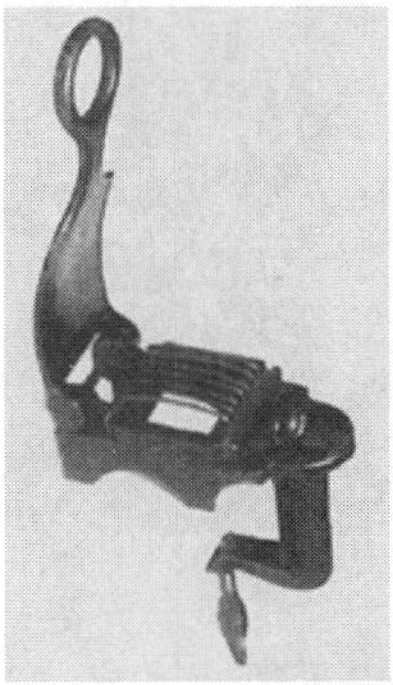

*Clamp-on Raisin Seeder*

**Raisin seeder,** cast iron, clamp-on style, a
frame w/seven wires below a hinged
cast-iron top, clamp below, marked "Pat.
June 9, 1881" (ILLUS.)................................. **500**
**Raisin seeder,** cast iron, clamp-on style
w/long gooseneck, marked "The Crown
Pat. Applied For," 6" h. .................................. **85**

**Rolling pin,** wooden, barrel roller w/T-frame handle ............................................. **200**

*Corrugated Wooden Rolling Pin*

**Rolling pin,** wooden, corrugated barrel & wooden handles, 11 1/4" l. (ILLUS.) .............. **35**

**Rolling pin,** turned curly maple, 18" l. ............ **116**

**Scale,** brass & cast iron, spring balance-type, marked "PS&W Co.," 7" ........................ **23**

**Scale scoop,** tin, footed, center pierced for use on home scales ....................................... **20**

**Sink brush,** tin & wire, scoop on one end, other end w/brush ........................................... **45**

**Skillet,** cast iron, "Griswold No 4" ..................... **26**

**Spatula,** tin, heart design in blade, stamped "Rumford - The Wholesome Baking Powder"...................................... **28**

**Spice box,** cov., wooden, round box rimmed top & bottom w/tin, contains eight individual tin-banded wood spice containers each stamped w/different spice name, 9 1/4" d.................................. **350**

**Spice set,** wood, a circular box & cover opening to reveal seven spice containers, cover stamped "Spices," check to see that all the spice containers are different, the set .............................................. **350**

**Spoon,** metal w/screen center, wooden handle ............................................................. **35**

**Strainer,** tin, perforated bottom, wooden handle & hanger ring..................................... **25**

**Toaster,** wire w/wooden handle, bread placed between two decorative wires held together w/a sliding ring, simple circular design.................................................... **30**

**Toaster,** wire & wood, two long wires culminating in circular designs extending from end of wood handle, complete w/a tension-producing sliding ring ........................ **45**

*Wire Trivet*

**Trivet,** wire, rounded starburst design of stamped wire w/double-loop ends & triangles, used as a coffeepot or teapot stand (ILLUS.) .............................................. **45**

**Whisk,** tin & wire, spiral wire under a flat circular disk , the whole attached to a wooden handle, made in England, 9 1/2" l. ........................................................... **75**

# MISCELLANEOUS GLASSWARE

*"Artbeck" Baster*

**Baster,** "Artbeck," PYREX glass tube, w/original container (ILLUS.) ..................... **10-12**

*Fire King Tulip Bowl*

**Bowl,** footed, Tulip patt., came in different colors, by Fire King (ILLUS.) ....................... **9-10**

**Cake pan,** crystal, "Flamex," from Sears, Roebuck & Co., maker unknown............... **10-12**

**Canister & lid,** "Blue Circle" patt., Cereal, manufactured by the Hocking Glass Company, unusual, scarce........................ **30-40**

**Canister & lid,** "Blue Circle" patt., Flour, manufactured by the Hocking Glass Co.... **25-30**

**Canister & lid,** "Blue Circle" patt., Sugar, manufactured by the Hocking Glass Co.... **20-25**

*SILEX "Dripolator" Coffeepot*

**Coffeepot (Drip),** cov., SILEX "2 Cup Dripolator," sapphire, complete with hard-to-find insert, 3 pc. set, attributed to Anchor Hocking because of sapphire color, but no documentation (ILLUS.) ....... **40-45**

*Cobalt "Chevron" Creamer*

**Creamer,** "Chevron" patt., cobalt, rectangular top, 3 " h. (ILLUS.)................................ **12-15**

*Child's Creamer & Sugar*

**Creamer & sugar,** child's, ivory, "Laurel" patt., by McKee Glass Co. (ILLUS.) .......... **35-45**

*"Tom & Jerry" Cups*

**Cups,** Jadeite, marked "Tom & Jerry," made by McKee Glass Co. (ILLUS.) ......... **35-45**

*Fire King "Flared" Custard Cup*

**Custard cup,** sapphire blue FIre King by Anchor Hocking, w/Philbe "flared" design, w/original label (ILLUS.) ................... **5-7**

*Pyrex Custard Cups w/Original Box*

**Custard cups,** crystal, PYREX, in original box, set of 6 (ILLUS.) ................................ **10-15**

*Demitasse Cup & Saucer*

**Demitasse cup & saucer,** Jadeite Jane Ray, Fire King by Anchor Hocking (ILLUS.)...................................................... **65-90**

*Jadeite Dessert Set*

**Dessert set,** Jadeite, Fire King Leaf & Blossom, manufactured 1951-1952 by Anchor Hocking, leaf plates 8 1/2" d. & blossom bowls 4 3/4" d. (ILLUS.) .............. **30-35**

*FLAMEX Covered Loaf Pan*

**Loaf pan,** cov., FLAMEX patt., w/original labels, from Sears, Roebuck & Co., unknown maker (ILLUS.) .......................... **18-20**

**Loaf pan,** crystal, "Glasbake" by McKee Glass Co., red-painted handles, 5 x 9"........ **8-10**

**Measuring cup,** Jadeite, Jeannette Glass Company, stacking-type, 1 cup size only .. **30-40**

**Measuring cup,** Jadeite, Jeannette Glass Company, stacking-type, 1/2 cup size only.......................... **30-35**

**Measuring cup,** Jadeite, Jeannette Glass Company, stacking-type, 1/3 cup size only.......................... **20-24**

**Measuring cup,** Jadeite, Jeannette Glass Company, stacking-type, 1/4 cup size only.......................... **20-25**

**Measuring cup set,** Jadeite, Jeannette Glass Company, stacking cups: 1/4 cup, 1/3 cup, 1/2 cup & 1 cup, in original box, full set.......................... **350-500**

**Mixer,** electric, Sunbeam Mixmaster, beige w/Jadeite mixing bowls & juicer bowl, ca. 1930s .......................... **60-80**

*Sunbeam Mixmaster*

**Mixer,** electric, Sunbeam Mixmaster, Chicago Flexible Shaft Co., cream colored metal body, folding handle on stand, pink, yellow or blue, w/matching bowls, ca. 1960s (ILLUS.) .......................... **40-80**

*Butter Churn for Mixmaster*

**Mixer accessory,** butter churn for Sunbeam Mixmaster (ILLUS.) .......................... **50-70**

**Mug,** sapphire blue w/Philbe design, Fire King by Anchor Hocking.......................... **35-40**

**Pepper shaker,** Roman Arches patt., black, by McKee Glass Co., (part of a 4 piece range set ), "short," 3 1/2" .............. **30-35**

*Sapphire Philbe Pie Plate*

**Pie Plate,** sapphire blue, Fire King by Anchor Hocking, w/Philbe design, 9 5/8" (ILLUS.).......................... **12-15**

**Pitcher,** milk, "Beads & Bars" patt., Fire King by Anchor Hocking, Jadeite .......... **175-250**

*Jadeite Plain Milk Pitcher*

**Pitcher,** milk, Jadeite, plain, Fire King by Anchor Hocking (ILLUS.) .......................... **65-80**

**Pitcher,** tilted spout, ball-shape, Royal Ruby patt., by Anchor Hocking, 20 oz. ..... **35-40**

*Royal Ruby Swirl Pitcher*

**Pitcher,** tilted spout, ball-shape, Royal Ruby Swirl patt., by Anchor Hocking, 80 oz. (ILLUS.) .............................................. **40-45**

**Range set:** salt & pepper shakers & grease or drippings jar; Jadeite, w/"Tulip" lids, Fire King by Anchor Hocking, shakers 4 1/4" h ............................. **100-110**

*Pepper Shaker from 5-pc. Range Set*

**Range set,** five-part set made by Hazel Atlas Glass Company in the 1920s, shakers w/"High Hat" tops 4 1/2" h., shakers each (ILLUS. of pepper shaker only) ........................................................ **25-30**

*Criss Cross Refrigerator Jar w/Lid*

**Refrigerator jar,** cov., crystal, Criss Cross patt., by Hazel Atlas, 4 x 4" (ILLUS.) ......... **18-20**

*"Gay Fad" Refrigerator Jar*

**Refrigerator jar,** "Gay Fad" Peaches & Grapes hand-painted patt., Fire King by Anchor Hocking, bought by Gay Fad Studios of Lancaster, Ohio & hand-painted for resale, late 1950s & 1960s (ILLUS.) ..................................................... **12-15**

*PYREX "Bluebelle" Refrigerator Jar*

**Refrigerator jar,** PYREX "Bluebelle," in Canadian blue, w/blue lid, not a fired on color, but blue glass, scarce, 3 1/2 x 4 3/4" (ILLUS.) ............................... **40-45**

*Jadeite Philbe Refrigerator Boxes*

**Refrigerator jars,** Jadeite, w/Philbe design, Fire King by Anchor Hocking, sapphire lid for largest jar in photograph, if all Jadeite w/Philbe, the set (ILLUS.) ................................................. **150-180**

**Refrigerator jars,** Jadeite, w/Philbe design, Fire King by Anchor Hocking, small jars, 4 x 4", each (ILLUS.) ..................... **40**

*Ivory Shaving Mug*

**Shaving mug,** ivory, by Fire King, rare (ILLUS.) ................................................... **12-15**

**Skillet,** Jadeite, single spout, not for stove top use, Fire King by Anchor Hocking, 6 1/4" d. at top, not counting the spout or handle ................................................... **80-100**

*Azurite Swirl Sugar Bowl*

**Sugar bowl,** Azurite Swirl patt., by Fire King, missing lid (ILLUS.) .................................. **5**

*Cobalt "Chevron" Open Sugar Bowl*

**Sugar bowl,** open, cobalt "Chevron," 4" h. (ILLUS.) ...................................................... **12-15**

*Moderntone Child's Teapot*

**Teapot,** child's, Moderntone patt., by Hazel Atlas, lid missing (ILLUS.) ......................... **18-20**

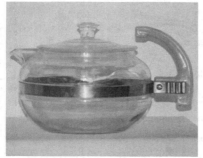

*PYREX Teapot w/Blue Handle*

**Teapot,** cov., crystal, PYREX, w/upturned blue glass handle (ILLUS.) ....................... **20-25**

*Crystal Criss Cross Water Bottle*

**Water bottle,** crystal, Criss Cross patt. by Hazel Atlas, one-quart capacity (ILLUS.) .. **23-25**

*Anchor Hocking Water Bottle w/Lid*

**Water bottle w/original lid,** crystal, bulbous shape, Anchor Hocking (ILLUS.) ........ **8-10**

# NAPKIN DOLLS

*Napkin Doll w/Expressive Eyes*

*These lovely ladies never fail to be the talk of the table. Until about two years ago they were a relatively obscure collectible and those lucky enough to have gotten in on the ground floor will be amazed at their increasing value and desirability. Although most commercially made napkin dolls probably date to the 1950s, they were apparently a popular project in ceramic craft classes from the 1930s through the 1980s.*

**Bisque,** figure of woman, pink & blue dress w/bell sleeves & ruffled skirt w/gold trim, golden hair, yellow hat & expressively painted eyes, ink-marked "Japan," 9" h. (ILLUS.) .................................................... **80-95**

*"Christine" Napkin Doll*

**Ceramic,** "Christine," blue figure of woman w/purple rose trim, blonde hair & pointing foot, slits in rear only, Jamar-Mallory Studios, 9" h. (ILLUS.) ........................... **125-150**

*Woman with Fruit Basket Napkin Doll*

**Ceramic,** figure of a woman in pink carrying a ceramic basket of fruit w/toothpick holes, 10 1/2" h. (ILLUS.) ...................... **100-135**

**Ceramic,** figure of angel, pink & white, Japan, paper label, 5 3/8" h. ..................... **75-95**

**Ceramic,** figure of bartender holding tray w/indentation for a candle, black & white & red, sticker marked "Gold Viking/Handmade in Japan," 8 3/4" h. (ILLUS. top next column) ........................ **90-115**

**Ceramic,** figure of bartender, matching salt & pepper shakers, black & white & red, sticker marked "Gold Viking/Handmade

in Japan," 3 1/4" h., pr. (ILLUS. w/napkin holder) ...................................................... **25-35**

*Bartender Napkin Holder w/Shakers*

*Girl with Flowers Napkin Doll*

**Ceramic,** figure of girl holding flowers, marked "Copyright Byron Molds," 8 1/2" h. (ILLUS.) ...................................... **65-75**

*Figural Santa Napkin Doll*

**Ceramic,** figure of Santa, 1950s-look, slits in rear only, toothpick holes in hat, 6" h. (ILLUS.) ...................................................... **75-90**

*Spanish Dancer Napkin Doll*

**Ceramic,** figure of Spanish dancer, blue & white dress, holding tambourine, marked "#460 California Originals USA", 13" h. (ILLUS.) ................................................ **110-135**
**Ceramic,** figure of Spanish dancer holding tambourine, blue & white dress, marked "#460 California Originals USA," 8 3/4" h. ........................................................... **95**
**Ceramic,** figure of Spanish dancer holding tambourine, blue & white dress, marked "#460 California Originals USA," 15" h. ........ **165**

*Napkin Doll w/Blue Hat & Blue Bowl*

**Ceramic,** figure of woman, blonde, wearing dress w/pink & maroon flowers & green leaves, holding blue bowl & wearing blue hat, marked "Helen Lewis," 9 1/2" h. (ILLUS.) ................................................ **135-175**
**Ceramic,** figure of woman holding a green toothpick tray, in yellow dress w/painted flowers on bottom of skirt, made in Japan, 9 3/4" h. ......................................... **75-95**
**Ceramic,** figure of woman in green dress, holding poodle & wearing a hat that masks candleholder, jewel decorated, marked "Kreiss & Co.", 10 1/4" h. (ILLUS. top next column) ..................... **100-125**
**Ceramic,** figure of woman, in white w/pink trim, hands clasped behind back, dark brown face, 12" h. .................................... **55-65**

*Napkin Doll Holding Poodle*

**Ceramic,** figure of woman, pink & yellow Colonial dress w/bell sleeves & ruffles w/gold trim, red hair, large hat & expressively painted eyes, ink marked "Japan", 9 1/2" ......................................................... **75-95**

*Sunbonnet Miss Napkin Doll*

**Ceramic,** Sunbonnet Miss, w/flowers on yellow dress, marked "Holt Howard 1958," 5" h. (ILLUS.) .............................. **95-130**
**Ceramic & metal,** baker or chef, half figure, w/wire bottom, holding tray of rolls w/holes for toothpicks in one hand, towel over other arm, marked "2026", 9" h. ... **110-165**
**Ceramic & metal half-doll,** figure of Santa, holding a gift & a stocking w/holes for toothpicks, wire bottom, 7" h. ................ **150-175**

*"Suzette" Napkin Doll*

**Ceramic & plastic,** "Suzette," half figure of Colonial style woman clasping hands, w/plastic base, ca. 1957, 10" (ILLUS.) .. **125-150**

**Chalkware,** figure of woman w/beige lace skirt & fitted jacket, candleholder in hat, 13" h. .................................................... **100-135**

*Art Deco Napkin Doll*

**Metal,** figure of Art Deco woman, silhouette, black w/gold trim, marked "E Kosta DBGM 1744970", 8 7/8" h. (ILLUS.) ...... **135-155**

*Pottery Napkin Doll*

**Pottery,** figure of woman, red & blue dress w/yellow apron & yellow scarf on head, holding toothpick tray overhead, California pottery style, 12 1/2" h. (ILLUS.) ..... **135-175**

*Napkin Doll from Finland*

**Wood,** figure of woman in yellow, wearing small picture hat, Finland, ca. 1949, 10 1/2" h. (ILLUS.) .................................... **35-50**

**Wood** half-figure of woman, multicolored w/lace cap, marked "Patent No. 11381," bases marked w/Swedish province, ca. 1949, 10 1/2" h. ....................................... **25-35**

*Wooden Musical Napkin Doll*

**Wood,** half-figure of woman, red & white, wearing a lace cap, marked "Patent No. 11381," musical base marked w/Swedish province, ca. 1949, 11 1/2" h. Add $35-45 for box & instructions (ILLUS.) ...... **40-50**

**Wood,** red half-figure of chef, 12 1/2" h. ....... **60-75**

## PIE BIRDS

*A pie bird can be described as a small, hollow device usually between 3-1/2" to 6" long, glazed inside and vented from the top. Its function is to raise the crust of a pie to allow steam to escape, thus preventing juices from bubbling over onto the oven floor while providing a flaky, dry crust. Originally, in the 1880s, pie birds were funnel-shaped vents used by the English for their meat pies. Not until the turn of the century did figurals appear, first in the form of birds, followed by elephants, chefs, etc. By the 1930s, many shapes were found in America. Today the market is flooded with many reproductions and newly created pie birds, usually in many whimsical shapes and subjects. It is best to purchase from knowledgeable dealers and fellow collectors.*

**Advertising,** "Kirkbrights China Stores Stockton on Tees," ceramic, white, England ......................................................... **75**

**Advertising,** "Lightning Pie Funnel England," ceramic, white, England.......... **75-120**

*Paulden's Advertising Pie Bird*

**Advertising,** "Paulden's Crockery Depart-
ment Stretford Road," ceramic, white,
England (ILLUS.)........................................... 70
**Advertising,** "Roe's Patent Rosebud,"
ceramic, England, 1910-30 ...................... 55-65
**Advertising,** "Rowland's Hygienic Patent,"
ceramic, England, 1910-30 ...................... 55-65
**Advertising,** "Sequel...Porcelain," ceramic,
white, England................................................ 50
**Advertising,** "The Gourmet Crust Holder &
Vent, Challis' Patent," ceramic, white,
England ...................................................... 100
**Advertising,** "The Grimmage Purfection
Pie Funnel," ceramic, England, 1910-30... 55-65
**Baby chicks,** ceramic, black w/gold beaks
& feet, for child's pie, each ....................... 40-50

*Jackie Sammond Pie Bird & Owl*

**Bird,** black, ceramic, 3" h., by Jackie Sam-
mond, early 1970s (ILLUS. right) ................ 150
**Bird,** black on white base, yellow feet &
beak, Nutbrown, England.............................. 50
**Bird,** black, perched on log, England ................ 95
**Bird,** ceramic, black, England ....................... 20-30
**Bird,** ceramic, brown & lavender trim, puff-
chested, ca. 1940s ............................... 175-200
**Bird,** ceramic, Camark Pottery, Camden,
Ark., ca. 1950s-60s, 6 1/2" h. .................. 95-115

*Ceramic Bird Pie Bird*

**Bird,** ceramic LaPere, Zanesville, Ohio, ca.
1930s-60s, hard to find (ILLUS.) ........... 100-150
**Bird,** ceramic, "Midwinter," black, England... 50-60
**Bird,** ceramic, Rowe Pottery, two-piece
w/detachable base, 1993 ......................... 15-20

*Sunglow Pie Bird*

**Bird,** ceramic, Sunglow, England (ILLUS.)......... 95

*Half-doll Style Pie Bird*

**Bird,** ceramics, half-doll style, blue & yellow
on conical base, USA (ILLUS.) ................... 125
**Bird,** pottery, "Scipio Creek Pottery, Hanni-
bal, MO" ......................................................... 25

*Bird on Nest Pie Bird*

**Bird on nest w/babies,** ceramic, Artisian
Galleries, Fort Dodge, IA (ILLUS.) .............. 500
**Birds,** ceramic, Pearl China, various col-
ors, USA, each ...................................... 100-125
**Black chef,** ceramic, full-figured, green
smock, "Pie-Aire," USA .............................. 185
**Black chef,** ceramic, resembles "Pie-Aire" 125-150
**Blackbird,** ceramic, black, 5 x 2 1/2" ............. 80-95

*Blackbird for Child's Pie*

**Blackbird,** ceramic, for child's pie, 2 3/4"
(ILLUS.)................................................... **35-50**
**Blackbird,** ceramic, Jackie Sammond,
USA. ca. 1970s, 3" h. ........................... **125-150**

*Very Large Black Pie Bird*

**Blackbird,** ceramic, very large, 2 1/2"
w x 5" h., English (ILLUS.) ........................... **125**

*Black Bird w/Black Glaze*

**Blackbird,** ceramic, w/black glaze, ca.
1930s-40s, English (ILLUS.) ........................... **95**
**Blackbird,** ceramic, w/yellow trim on brown
base ............................................................... **85**

*Wide-Mouth Blackbird*

**Blackbird,** ceramic, wide-mouth, yellow
beak, fat, English (ILLUS.) ........................... **175**
**Blackbird,** clay w/black & yellow glaze, ca.
1960s-70s ................................................. **65-75**
**Blackbird,** red clay w/black glaze, ca.
1930s-40s ................................................. **75-85**
**Bluebird,** ceramic, Japan, post 1960 ........... **20-30**
**Chef,** "Benny the Baker," w/tools & box,
Cardinal China, New Jersey, USA .............. **125**
**Chef,** ceramic, "A Lorrie Design, Japan,"
Joseph Originals, 1980s.......................... **75-95**

*"Benny the Baker" Pie Bird*

**Chef,** ceramic, "Benny the Baker," w/tools
& box, Cardinal China Co., USA
(ILLUS.)....................................................... **175**
**Chef,** ceramic, half-figure, all-white,
England ......................................................... **90**

*"Pie-Aire" Chefs*

**Chef,** ceramic, "Pie-Aire," solid color, green, red or yellow, each (ILLUS.) ............. 100
**Chef,** ceramic, "Servex Oven China, Bohemia, Guaranteed Heatproof, RD 17494 Aus., RD 4098 N.Z.," Australia, 4 5/8" h. .................................. **195-250**
**Chef,** ceramic, white, England ...................... **80-90**

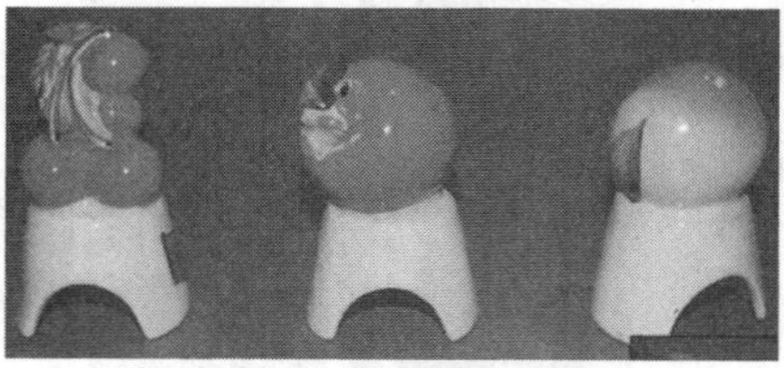

*Cherry, Apple & Peach Pie Birds*

**Cherry, apple & peach,** ceramic, ca. 1950s, in original box, set of three (ILLUS.) ................................................. **500-600**

*Chick w/Dust Cap*

**Chick,** ceramic, w/dust cap, Josef Originals (ILLUS.) ........................................................... **95**
**Chick,** ceramic, yellow w/pink lips, Josef Originals ....................................................... **55**
**Chicken,** ceramic, "A Lorrie Design, Japan," Josef Originals, 1980s .................. **75-95**
**Donald Duck,** ceramic, USA, rare ................. **900+**
**Donald Duck,** ceramic, Walt Disney marked on one side & Donald Duck on the other, rare ............................................. **500**

*Dopey Pie Bird*

**Dopey,** ceramic, Disney (ILLUS.) ..................... **500**
**Dragon,** ceramic, Creiciau Pottery, Wales, U.K. ............................................................. **110**

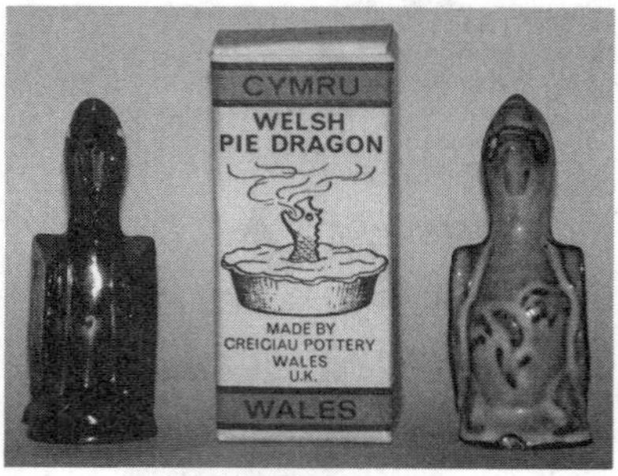

*Welsh Pie Dragons*

**Dragon,** ceramic, Creiciau Pottery, Wales, United Kingdom (ILLUS.) ............................ **150**
**Duck,** ceramic, brown, England ....................... **125**

*Brown English Duck Pie Bird*

**Duck,** ceramic, brown w/white & yellow beak, black trim, white base, England (ILLUS.) ..................................................... **125**
**Duck,** ceramic, pink, blue or yellow, full-bodied, USA, each ...................................... **70**
**Duck,** ceramic, pink, yellow or blue, USA ...... **55-75**
**Duck,** ceramic, white, England ......................... **100**
**Duck,** ceramic, yellow beak, white w/black detail, England .......................................... **100**

*Duck Head Pie Bird*

**Duck head,** ceramic, pink, England (ILLUS.)...................................................... **125**
**Dutch girl,** ceramic, doubles as pie vent, measuring spoon holder, and/or receptacles for scouring pads & soap, rare....... **125-150**
**Elephant,** ceramic, grey & pink w/swirled pink base, Cardinal China Co., USA ........... **250**

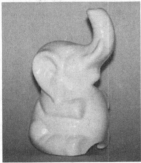

*Elephant Pie Bird*

**Elephant,** ceramic, white, ca. 1930s (ILLUS.)...................................................... **200**

*Granny Pie Baker*

**Granny,** ceramic, "Pie Baker," figure of a lady holding a bowl by Josef Originals (ILLUS.)........................................................ **95**

*Luzianne Mammy Pie Baker*

**Luzianne Mammy,** ceramic, black woman dressed in yellow shirt & green skirt, carrying a red tray w/coffee service, white turban on head (ILLUS.)............................ **150+**

*Multi-purpose Mammy*

**Mammy,** ceramic, doubles as pie vent, measuring spoon holder, and/or receptables for scouring pads & soap (ILLUS.) .. **85-100**

*Mammy In Yellow*

**Mammy,** ceramic, in yellow (ILLUS.)................ **150**
**Mammy,** ceramic, outstretched arms, USA........ **95**
**Old Woman,** ceramic, "A Lorrie Design, Japan," Joseph Originals, 1980s............... **75-95**

*Josef Originals Owl*

**Owl,** ceramic, "A Lorrie Design, Japan,"
Josef Originals, 1980s (ILLUS.) ................... **300**
**Owl,** ceramic, Jackie Sammond, USA. ca.
1970s (ILLUS. left with black bird) .............. **150**

*"Patrick" Pie Bird*

**"Patrick,"** ceramic, by California Cleminson, many color variations, USA, each
(ILLUS.) .......................................................... **60**

*Peasant Woman Pie Baker*

**Peasant woman,** ceramic, brown glaze,
1960s-70s (ILLUS.) ....................................... **95**
**"Pie Boy,"** ceramic, by Squire Pottery of
California, USA............................................. **250**

*"Pie Chef" Pie Bird*

**"Pie Chef,"** ceramic, by Josef Originals,
ceramic (ILLUS.) ............................................ **95**
**"Pie-Chic,"** ceramic, given as premium in
Pillsbury Flour, USA ...................................... **55**
**Rooster,** ceramic, Marion Drake .................. **65-85**
**Rooster,** ceramic, multicolored, Clemin-
son, USA......................................................... **50**
**Rooster,** ceramic, Shawnee & Morton Pot-
teries, unmarked, pastel painted .................. **200**

*Pearl China Rooster Pie Bird*

**Rooster,** ceramic, white w/tan trim, Pearl
China, USA (ILLUS.) .................................... **175**

*Songbird*

**Songbird,** ceramic, beige, blue & pink variations, USA, each (ILLUS.) ........................... **50**

*LaPere Songbird*

**Songbird,** ceramic, black w/gold beak, feet
& trim, LaPere, Ohio, USA (ILLUS.)............. **150**

*Sunglow Pie Bird*

**Sunglow bird,** ceramic, orange, ca. 1950s
(ILLUS.).................................................. **90-110**

*"The Bleriot Pie Divider" Pie Bird*

**Unusual pie vent,** ceramic, "The Bleriot
Pie Divider," white, 1910-20 (ILLUS.)........... **200**
**Yankee pie bird,** ceramic, Millford, New
Hampshire, ca. 1960s .............................. **40-50**
**Yellow chick,** ceramic, Josef Originals,
w/pink lips, ca. 1970s .............................. **60-75**

## REAMERS

*Figural Clown Reamer w/Matching Cups*

Once a staple in the American household during
the 1920s-40s, manual juice reamers have again
gained popularity as a hot commodity in todays collectible market. Although some wooden reamers
date to the mid-1800s, the majority found today
were produced during the reamers heyday. They
range from American-made Depression glass and
pottery to exquisitely painted ceramics and
uniquely shaped figurals from far off places like

Japan, France, Germany and Czechoslovakia.
Lovely silver plate and sterling examples that once
graced elegant Victorian tables now command
hefty prices. Even the early electric and Deco
chrome models of the 1950s have found a collectible niche.

**Ceramic,** cream pitcher, two-piece, w/blue
& green garden gate & multi-colored
flowers, marked "Universal Cambridge,
Ovenproof Made in USA," 9" h............. **175-195**
**Ceramic,** figure of clown, green & white
body w/yellow & orange trim, marked
"Hand Painted Made in Japan," 8 3/4"
(ILLUS. center)...................................... **175-200**
**Ceramic,** figure of clown, green & white
cups w/yellow & orange trim to match
reamer, marked "Hand Painted Made in
Japan," 3 1/8", each (ILLUS. w/reamer).... **10-25**

*Figural Clown Reamer*

**Ceramic,** figure of clown, pink & white,
w/yellow, green & white cone, 4 1/2" h.
(ILLUS.)...................................................... **65-85**
**Ceramic,** figure of clown, two-piece,
maroon & white, w/maroon & green
cone, marked "Made in Japan," 5 1/2" h. **75-100**

*Figural Monkey Reamer*

**Ceramic,** figure of cross-legged monkey,
brown & tan w/white top, marked "Ger-
many," 4 1/4" h. (ILLUS.)....................... **200-245**
**Ceramic,** figure of dog, marked "Made in
Japan," 4 3/4" h. ................................... **350-400**
**Ceramic,** figure of man's head w/blue lus-
tre top, two-piece, 4" h. (ILLUS. top next
page) ...................................................... **150-185**
**Ceramic,** figure of Toby face, w/brown hair,
green shirt, light green bow tie, blue hat
& white cone, marked "Japan," 4 1/4" h.
(ILLUS. center next page) ..................... **250-300**
**Ceramic,** figure of white elephant, stand-
ing, back covered w/multicolored blanket, w/sticker that says "Souvenir of
Montreal," 6" h. (ILLUS. next page)....... **150-195**

*Man's Head Reamer*

*Toby Face Reamer*

*Standing Elephant Reamer*

*Portuguese Elephant Reamer*

**Ceramic,** figure of white elephant w/pink tint, marked "Mideramica Made in Portugal," 4" d. (ILLUS.) ................................... **25-35**

*Jiffy Juicer Reamer*

**Ceramic,** Jiffy Juicer, pink, marked "US Pat. 2130,755, Sept. 20, 1938," 5 1/4" h. (ILLUS.) ........................................................ **75-90**

*Figural Fish Reamer*

**Ceramic,** model of fish, yellow, 5 1/2" d. (ILLUS.) ........................................................ **50-75**

*House w/Windmill Reamer*

**Ceramic,** model of house w/windmill, beige w/multi-colored trim & yellow cone, marked "Martutomoware, Handpainted Japan," 4 1/2" h. (ILLUS.) ...................... **125-175**

*Two-Handled Reamer*

**Ceramic,** two-handled, two-piece yellow w/two dogs under a red umbrella, w/yellow, green, red & white cone, marked "75/476 Made in Japan," 4 1/4" h. (ILLUS.) ........................................................ **65-85**

**Ceramic & metal,** white bowl on green base, Presto Juicer National Electric Appliance Corp. Bridgeport, Conn., 7 5/8" h. (ILLUS. top next page) .............. **85-125**

**Ceramic & wood,** blue & white cone w/wood handle, 10 1/8" l. (ILLUS. center next page) ........... **150-175**

**Glass,** black, embossed "Sunkist," marked "Pat. No. 18764 Made in USA," McKee Glass Co., 6" d. ................................... **750-900**

**Glass,** crystal, 6 3/4" d. ............................... **35-45**

**Glass,** French ivory, McKee Glass Co., 6" d. ........................................................ **50-75**

*Presto Juicer*

*Wood-handled Reamer*

**Glass,** green saucer-type w/ridges & tab handle, Anchor Hocking Glass Co., 5 3/8" d. .................................................. **20-25**

*Two Piece Reamer*

**Glass,** green, two-piece, two-cup measure, 5 1/8" h. (ILLUS.)...................................... **50-65**

*Hazel Atlas Glass Reamer*

**Glass,** pink, Hazel Atlas Glass Co., 5 5/8" d. (ILLUS.)...................................... **50-65**

*Sauceboat-Shaped Reamer*

**Glass,** pink, sauceboat-shaped, 3 1/4" d. (ILLUS.)................................................. **100-125**
**Glass,** pink, two-piece, four cup measure w/etched flowers on one side & four-cup measure on the other, Paden City Party Line Measuring set, 8 3/4" h. ................ **150-175**
**Glass,** ruby red, two-piece, w/bulbous bottom, Fenton Art Glass Co., 6 3/8" h. ........................................... **1,300-1,500**
**Glass & metal,** hinged black metal w/clear glass insert, marked "Williams," 7 3/4" l. ... **50-75**
**Metal,** hand-held, marked "Lemon Squeezer," 6 3/4" l..................................... **8-10**
**Metal,** sauceboat-shaped, gold plate outside, silver plate inside, Lyn-Silversmith, 4" d. ......................................................... **95-125**
**Metal,** tilt model, w/clamp-on base, marked "Seald Sweet Juice Extractor," 13" h.......... **60-75**

*Dur-X Fruit Juice Extractor & Corer*

**Plastic,** Dur-X Fruit Juice Extractor & Corer, w/original box, marked "Kwiki-P1 Juicer Pat. Pend.," 2 3/4" h. (ILLUS.) ........ **10-15**
**Plastic,** green w/two different size cones, 7 1/2" l. ......................................................... **6-10**

*Cocktail Shaker/Reamer*

**Silver plate,** cocktail shaker, w/black & red enamel stripes, reamer on top, marked "Germany," 5" h. (ILLUS.) ...................... **95-125**

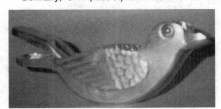

*Figural Bird Reamer*

**Silver plate,** model of bird, Muss Bach,
4 1/2" l. (ILLUS.)...................................... **20-25**
**Silver plate & wood,** England, 7 3/4" h. ... **175-200**
**Wood,** hand-held, hinged back w/small
hole strainer, 12" l. ................................. **35-50**

## SALT & PEPPER SHAKERS

## FIGURAL

### NOVELTY FIGURAL PAIRS
**Black angel head,** stacking-type, Ross-
ware, 3 1/4" h. .............................................. **60**
**Black chef w/blue suit,** stacking-type,
5 1/2" h. ...................................................... **125**

*Miniature Bowling Pin & Ball*

**Bowling pin & ball,** miniature, 1 1/2" h.
(ILLUS.)............................................................ **28**
**Boxer dogs w/bandages,** 4" h. ...................... **19**
**Children w/kitten praying beside bed,**
condiment, 3 1/2" h. ...................................... **43**
**Chili peppers,** Fitz and Floyd, 2" h. ................... **24**
**Donkeys wearing vests,** heads back, 3" h........ **17**
**Dressed dogs w/rhinestone eyes,** Lefton,
3 1/2" h............................................................. **17**
**Dressed pigs on base,** one-piece, C.
Miller, Regal China, 4" h................................. **28**
**Dutch boy & girl,** Ceramic Arts Studio,
3" h. ............................................................... **21**
**Fisherman lying in boat,** Elbe Art, 3" h. .......... **14**
**Fishing creel & string of fish,** miniature,
1" h. ............................................................... **33**
**Fox & goose,** Ceramic Arts Studio, 3" h. ......... **163**

*Golliwog Driving Car Shaker*

**Golliwog driving car,** England, 4" h.
(ILLUS.)............................................................ **95**
**Goofy on cannon,** 6 1/2" h. .............................. **19**
**Graduate cats,** 3" h........................................ **17**
**Heart w/keyhole & gold key,** 3 1/2" h. ............. **17**
**Hitchhiker & brown bag,** 3 1/2" h. .................... **19**
**Kitchen witch & cauldron,** Fitz and Floyd,
3 1/2" h............................................................ **43**

*Las Vegas Showgirl with Dice*

**Las Vegas showgirl w/dice,** England,
5" h. (ILLUS.).................................................. **75**
**Mom & baby kangaroo nodder,** 4" h. .............. **68**
**Moose,** natural-looking, 4" h.............................. **33**
**Native eating watermelon,** 3 1/2" h. ................. **70**
**Native mom holding baby,** 4 3/4" h. .................. **48**

*Mini Perfume Atomizer & Powder Dish*

**Perfume atomizer & powder dish,** minia-
ture, 1 1/2" h. (ILLUS.) ................................... **33**
**Pheasant nodder in common white
base,** 3 1/4" h................................................. **33**
**Seagram's Seven 7s,** 3" h.............................. **17**

*Shakespeare Busts*

**Shakespeare busts,** 3 1/2" h. (ILLUS.) ............. **23**
**Snowman salt w/cane pepper under
arm,** 4" h. ...................................................... **24**

## STRING HOLDERS

*String Holders were standard equipment for
general stores, bakeries and homes before the use
of paper bags, tape and staples became prevalent.
Decorative string holders, mostly chalkware, first
became popular during the late 1930s and 1940s.
They were mass-produced and sold in five-and-
dime stores like Woolworth's and Kresge's.
Ceramic string holders became available in the late
1940s through the 1950s. It is much more difficult to
find a chalkware string holder in excellent condition,
while the sturdier ceramics maintain a higher quality over time.*

**Apple,** ceramic, handmade, 1947 ................. **35-55**
**Apple w/berries,** chalkware, common .......... **15-35**
**Apple w/face** ceramic, PY................................ **135**

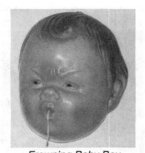

*Frowning Baby Boy*

**Baby boy,** chalkware, frowning (ILLUS.) .. **225-275**

*Banana String Holder*

**Bananas,** chalkware, ca. 1980s-present (ILLUS.)....................................................... **25-50**

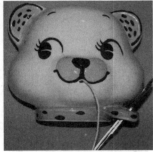

*Bear w/Scissors In Collar*

**Bear,** w/scissors in collar, ceramic, Japan (ILLUS.) ............................................... **75**

*Betty Boop String Holder*

**Betty Boop,** chalkware, original (ILLUS.) ........ **250**

*"String Swallow" Bird String Holder*

**Bird,** ceramic, in birdhouse, "String Swallow" (ILLUS.) .................................................. **75**
**Bird & birdhouse,** wood & metal ................. **45-55**

*Bird In Birdcage*

**Bird in birdcage,** chalkware (ILLUS.) .............. **150**
**Bird in birdhouse,** chalkware, bird is peeking out of birdhouse....................................... **175**
**Bird on birdhouse,** chalkware, cardboard, "Early Bird," bobs up & down when string is pulled, handmade .................................. **45-55**
**Bird on branch,** ceramic, Royal Copley ........... **85**
**Bird on branch,** wooden, w/birdhouse ......... **25-45**
**Bird on nest,** ceramic, countertop-type, Josef Originals .......................................... **75-95**
**Black butler,** ceramic, Japan, difficult to find ............................................................... **350**

*Bonzo Face String Holder*

**Bonzo face,** ceramic, marked "Japan," rare (ILLUS.) ................................................ **500**

*Boxer String Holder*

**Boxer dog,** ceramic (ILLUS.) ...................... **95-135**

*Boy w/Tilted Cap*

**Boy,** w/tilted cap, chalkware (ILLUS.) .............. **150**

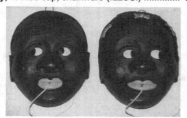

*Man & Woman String Holder*

**Brother Jacob and Sister Isabel,** chalkware, newer vintage, each (ILLUS.) .......... **55-60**
**Bulldog,** chalkware, w/studded collar, ca.
1933 .................................................... **125-175**

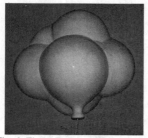

*Fitz & Floyd Balloon String Holder*

**Bunch of balloons,** ceramic, Fitz & Floyd
(ILLUS.) .......................................................... **95**

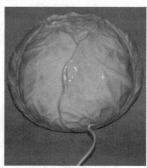

*Cabbage String Holder*

**Cabbage,** ceramic, Japan (ILLUS.) .................. **100**
**Campbell Soup boy,** chalkware, face only.... **500+**

*Black Cat w/Gold Bow*

**Cat,** ceramic, black w/gold bow, handmade
(ILLUS.) .......................................................... **75**
**Cat,** ceramic, climbing a ball of string .......... **95-125**
**Cat,** ceramic, full-bodied w/flowers & scis-
sors ......................................................... **25-45**
**Cat,** ceramic, full-figured on top of ball of
string ....................................................... **55-85**
**Cat,** ceramic, "Holt Howard," 1958 ............... **35-55**

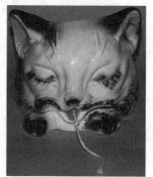

*"Knitter's Pal" String Holder*

**Cat,** ceramic, "Knitter's Pal" (ILLUS.) ................. **75**
**Cat,** ceramic, w/matching wall pocket............ **55-75**

*Cat w/Plaid Collar*

**Cat,** ceramic, w/plaid collar, space for scissors, Japan (ILLUS.) ...................................... **75**
**Cat,** ceramic, w/scissors in collar, "Babbacombe Pottery, England" ........................... **25-50**
**Cat,** ceramic, white face w/pink & black polka dot collar ............................................... **50**
**Cat,** chalkware, grinning, on a ball of string, Miller Studio, 1952 ..................................... **65-85**
**Cat,** chalkware, on ball of string, Miller Studio, 1948 .................................................. **45-65**
**Cat,** chalkware, w/bow holding ball of string.. **45-75**
**Chef,** ceramic, "Gift Ideas Creation, Phila., Pa.," w/scissors in head ............................ **35-65**

*Chef w/Rosy Cheeks*

**Chef,** ceramic, w/rosy cheeks, marked "Japan" (ILLUS.) ......................................... **50-75**
**Chef,** chalkware, baby face w/chef's hat ......... **200**

*Chef String Holder*

**Chef,** chalkware, "By Bello, 1949," chubby-faced, rare (ILLUS.) ...................................... **450**
**Chef,** chalkware, "Little Chef," Miller Studio ..... **150**
**Chef,** chalkware, Rice Crispy ........................... **145**

*Chef w/Bushy Eyebrows*

**Chef,** chalkware, unsuual version of chef w/bushy eyebrows (ILLUS.) ......................... **150**

*Chef w/Large Hat*

**Chef,** chalkware, w/large hat facing left (ILLUS.) ...................................................... **150**
**Cherries,** chalkware, a bunch ......................... **175**
**Chicken,** ceramic, "Quimper of France," found in several patterns, still in production ........................................................ **65-85**
**Chicken,** ceramic, unmarked ....................... **40-50**
**Chipmunk,** ceramic ...................................... **35-45**
**Collie,** ceramic, "Royal Trico," Japan ........ **125-175**

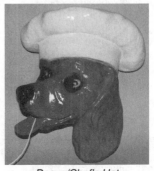

*Dog w/Chef's Hat*

**Dog,** w/chef's hat, chalkware, "Conovers Original" (ILLUS.) ......................................... **200**

**Dog,** wood, "Sandy Twine Holder," body is ball of string................................................. **45-65**
**Dog w/black eye,** ceramic ........................ **125-175**

*Dog w/Black Eye*

**Dog w/black eye,** ceramic, w/scissor holder in collar, right eye only circled in black, England (ILLUS.) ................................. **95**
**Dove,** ceramic, Japan ......................................... **65**
**Dutch Girl,** chalkware, face only, common ....... **60**
**Dutch girl,** chalkware, w/large hat ................ **65-95**
**Elephant,** ceramic, "Hoffritz, England" .......... **65-85**

*Elephant String Holder*

**Elephant,** ceramic, marked "Babbacombe Pottery, England," scissors as glasses (ILLUS.)..............................................................

*French Chef String Holder*

**French chef,** chalkware, w/scarf around neck, (ILLUS.) ............................................. **185**
**Funnel,** w/thistle or cat & ball, ceramic .......... **110**
**German Shepherd,** ceramic, "Royal Trico, Japan" .................................................... **125-175**
**Gourd,** chalkware........................................... **150**
**Grapes,** chalkware, a bunch ........................... **150**

**Green bird,** ceramic, "Arthur Wood, England," also found in blue & brown ....... **35-45**
**Green pepper,** ceramic.................................... **95**
**Green pepper,** ceramic, Lego sticker............ **50-75**
**Humpty Dumpty,** ceramic, sitting on wall....... **125**
**Indian with headdress,** chalkware.................. **300**
**Iron w/flowers,** ceramic .................................. **75**
**"Kitchen String,"** ceramic, by Burleigh Ironstone, Staffordshire, England, w/scissors in top ......................................... **75**
**Ladybug,** chalkware ............................... **225-275**
**Latchstring house,** ceramic, California Cleminsons ................................................. **150**
**Little Red Riding Hood,** chalkware, head wearing hood................................................. **250**

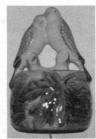

*Lovebirds String Holder*

**Lovebirds,** ceramic, Morton Pottery (ILLUS.)......................................................... **78**
**Maid,** ceramic, Sarsaparilla, 1984 ..................... **85**
**Mammy,** ceramic, Japan, full-figured, plaid & polka dot dress .................................. **125-175**

*Mammy Holding Flowers*

**Mammy,** chalkware, full-figured, holding flowers, marked "MAPCO" (ILLUS.)............. **295**
**Mammy,** chalkware, head only, "Ty-Me" ......... **250**

*"Genuine Rockalite" Mammy*

**Mammy,** chalkware, head only, w/polka-dot bandana, marked "Genuine Rockalite," made in Canada (ILLUS.) ............................ 350
**Mammy,** cloth-faced, "Simone," includes card that reads "I'm smiling Jane, so glad I came to tie your things, with nice white strings," rare................................ 150-195

*Coconut Mammy*

**Mammy,** coconut, w/red and blue floral scarf (ILLUS.) ................................................ 35
**Mammy face,** felt, w/plastic rolling eyes ....... 50-75

*Gigolo Man String Holder*

**Man,** chalkware, marked across collar, "Just a Gigolo" (ILLUS.) ............................... 150
**Mexican man,** chalkware, head only, common ................................................................. 60
**Mexican man,** chalkware, w/ornate hat ...... 85-100
**Monkey,** chalkware, sitting on ball of string, found in various colors ......................... 225-275
**Mouse,** ceramic, countertop-type, Josef Originals sticker......................................... 55-75
**Mouse,** ceramic, England............................ 85-100
**Oriental man,** ceramic, w/coolie hat, Abingdon..................................................... 400
**Owl,** Babbacombe Pottery, England ............. 45-65
**Owl,** ceramic, Josef Originals sticker ............ 35-55

*Pancho Villa String Holder*

**Pancho Villa,** chalkware (ILLUS.) ................... 275
**Parlor maid,** ceramic, early 1980s, marked "Sarsasparilla" ................................. 95
**Parrot,** chalkware, brightly colored............ 125-175
**Peach,** ceramic................................................. 85
**Pear,** chalkware................................................ 55
**Peasant woman,** ceramic, full-figured, knitting sock, sticker reads "Wayne of Hollywood" ................................................... 175

*Porter String Holder*

**Porter,** clay, without teeth, marked "Fredericksburg Art Pottery, U.S.A." (ILLUS.).......... 295
**Rooster,** porcelain, head only, Royal Bayreuth.................................................... 500
**Scottie,** ceramic, "Royal Trico, Japan"...... 125-175

*White Scottie*

**Scottie,** chalkware, white w/studded color (ILLUS.).................................................. 125-175
**Shaggy dog,** ceramic, full-figured, w/scissors as glasses, marked "Babbacombe Pottery, England" .......................................... 50
**Snail,** ceramic............................................... 45-65
**Soldier Face,** chalkware, w/hat......................... 75

*Sunfish String Holder*

**Susie Sunfish,** chalkware, Miller Studio,
1948 (ILLUS.)....................................... **225-275**
**Teapot,** ceramic, Japan, w/parakeet ......... **85-125**
**Teddy Bear,** ceramic, brown, marked
"Babbacombe Pottery, England," hole
for scissors in bow at neck ........................... **50**
**Thatched-Roof Cottage,** ceramic ................ **45-75**
**Tom cat,** ceramic, "Takahashi, San Fran-
cisco," Japan ............................................. **55-75**
**Tomato,** chalkware............................................. **55**

*Tomato Chef String Holder*

**Tomato chef,** ceramic "Japan" eyes closed
(ILLUS.)................................................. **125-150**

*Westie String Holder*

**Westie,** chalkware (ILLUS.).............................. **200**
**Willy the worm,** chalkware, worm is on the
front of an apple, Miller Studio, 1948 ........ **45-75**
**Witch in pumpkin,** ceramic, winking ............... **150**

*Young Girl String Holder*

**Young black girl,** ceramic, w/surprised
look, Japan (ILLUS.) ............................. **250-295**

# TEAPOTS - FIGURAL

*Figural teapots were first made by the Chinese
as a natural expression of their interest & pleasure
in nature & natural beauty. The first ones were
probably made in the early 1500s, although the
actual date is uncertain. Bird or dragon spouts &
crabstock or serpent handles were not uncommon
in the early ceramic ware sent from China to
Europe and later to England.*

*When English potters started to create new tea-
pots & tried to make porcelains, they let their imagination run free from the beginning. First fruits &
vegetables, then bears & dogs, & by the mid-nine-
teenth century Victorian whimsy had given rise to
teapots shaped like people & objects. The one constant was that it must make & pour tea.*

*By the late twentieth century the British Tea
Council held competitions for innovative teapot
designs with nothing being off-limits for the
designer. The ensuing output was sometimes a little startling, but always fun.*

**Aesthetic,** ceramic, male on one side,
female on reverse, burgundy hat, dark
blonde hair, moss green shirt, Worcester, bottom marked "Fearful conse-
quences through the laws of natural
selection," unmarked, 6 1/2 x 7"............ **600-750**

*Airplane Teapot*

**Airplane,** ceramic, green, Carltonware,
6 1/2 x 8" (ILLUS.)................................. **245-300**
**Aladdin,** ceramic, blue, from Disney movie,
very limited production & sales, marked
"Disney and Co.," & "Schmid," music box
in bottom, 5 x 7 3/4" ............................. **295-350**
**Androcles lion,** ceramic, tawny yellow &
brown, Albert Kessler marked AK Tai-
wan, 7 1/2 x 8"......................................... **15-25**
**Backhoe machine w/driver,** ceramic, yel-
low, Carltonware, 7 x 9" (reproductions
being made w/different markings) ......... **225-310**
**Banko elephant w/mahout on top,**
ceramic, brown w/polychrome & gold
trim, no markings, Japan, 5 x 7".............. **80-150**
**Bellhop,** ceramic, grey, black & gold trim,
color & shading variations depending on
year of production, impressed "Swine-
side," 10 1/2 x 10 1/2" .......................... **250-400**
**Bunnykins rabbit,** ceramic, shaded brown
w/green leaves, Royal Doulton,
5 x 8" ............................................... **2,400-3,000**

*Cat on Radiator Teapot*

**Cat on radiator,** ceramic, black cat, grey radiator, white print towel under cat, Swineside Ceramics, England, 5 x 7" (ILLUS.) ................................. **75-100**

**Cauliflower,** ceramic, green & white, early Wedgwood, 6 x 8" .......................... **3,200-8,000**

*Cottage Teapot*

**Cottage,** ceramic, light brown & foliage colors, marked "Price Kensington," wreath mark, 5 1/2 x 6" (ILLUS.) ........................ **50-125**

**Cottage,** ceramic, oval, brown brick, dark grey thatch, two children, marked "Tony Wood Studios," 5 x 8" ............................... **45-70**

**Crime writer's desk,** ceramic, glossy brown w/black typewriter, platinum trim, Cardew Design, England, 7 x 7 3/4" ..... **175-200**

**Crinoline lady,** ceramic, solid color dress, either pink, blue, yellow or lavender, blonde hair, Sadler, made in England, 6 x 7 1/2" ............................................. **120-195**

**Crinoline lady,** ceramic, solid color dress, either pink, blue, yellow or lavender, blonde hair, Sadler, made in Czechoslovakia, 6 x 7 1/2" ..................................... **85-130**

**Crinoline lady,** ceramic, solid color dress, either pink, blue, yellow or lavender, blonde hair, Sadler, made in Japan, 6 x 7 1/2" ................................................. **45-80**

*Delivery Van Teapot*

**Delivery van,** ceramic, driver is handle, spare tire is lid knob, light blue body,

marked "Roy Simpson for J. Luber," impressed mark No. 11, 7 1/2 x 8 1/2" (ILLUS.) ................................................... **85-115**

**Dessert tea cart,** ceramic, brown w/desserts & plates, Richard Bailey for Tony Carter, 7 1/4 x 8" ................................... **130-200**

**Donald Duck,** ceramic, polychrome blue hat & yellow bill, head only, embossed "W. Disney" w/sticker "The Good Company," 9 1/2 x 10" ................................. **275-350**

**Donald Duck w/original configuration,** polychrome early production, small head, entire body including feet, Wade Heath, 5 x 6" .................................... **2,400-3,000**

**Dutch girl w/pitcher & basket of flowers,** ceramic, mottled grey dress w/azure trim, striped water pitcher, Germany & Czechoslovakia, 1930s, 6 x 8 1/2" .......... **90-135**

**Hardware merchant market wagon,** "T. Potts & Sons," polychrome, w/pots, pans & shovel, Tony Wood, Staffordshire, 6 x 8" ......................................................... **45-85**

**Humpty Dumpty on wall,** ceramic, lime green or yellow, solid colors, Lingard, England, impressed mark, 8 x 10 1/2" .... **95-200**

**Joseph Chamberlain, M.D.,** ceramic, green jacket, yellow waistcoat, monocle in eye, Foley, 5 x 7" ........................ **2,200-2,400**

*Kitchen Tap Teapot*

**Kitchen tap-faucet handle,** ceramic, white w/narrow green stripe on bottom of overlid, Carltonware, England, 4 x 8 1/2" (ILLUS.) ................................................. **160-180**

**Little Red Riding Hood,** ceramic, white & red, poppy & gold trim, Hull, marked "USA," 8 x 8 3/4" ................................... **275-370**

*Mad Hatter Teapot*

**Mad Hatter,** ceramic, black hat, burgundy clothing, head only, marked "Tony Wood, England" 5 x 8" (ILLUS.) .............. **80-150**

**Margaret Thatcher,** ceramic, white glaze, marked "Hall made in U.S.A.," 8 x 11" .. **125-195**
**Moose w/squirrel on shoulder,** beaver on back, ceramic, brown w/green on base, Clay Art, 8 x 11" .................................... **125-155**

*Motorcycle Teapot*

**Motorcycle w/male & female riders,** ceramic, black w/platinum overshine, Parrington Designs, Barnstable, Kent, England, 8 1/2 x 11" (ILLUS.)................ **175-250**
**Mr. Punch of Punch & Judy,** ceramic, yellow & green striped, string of sausages around his neck, marked "Tony Wood Staffordshire England," 6 x 10" .............. **90-105**
**Old woman in a shoe,** ceramic, yellow & lime green, impressed "Lingard, Made in England," 6 1/2 x 8".............................. **125-200**

*Parlor Maid Teapot*

**Parlor maid,** ceramic, black & white, white mob hat sits on busty black dress, one in a series w/no head, Carltonware, 5 x 6 1/4" (ILLUS.)................................ **195-200**
**Queen Victoria,** ceramic, red dress, polychrome trim, Fitz & Floyd, 7 x 8" ............ **90-100**

*Rabbit Teapot*

**Rabbit,** ceramic, brown & black, marked "Germany," Erphila, 7 1/2 x 8" (ILLUS.) .. **85-135**

*Ronald Reagan Teapot*

**Ronald Reagan,** ceramic, white glaze, marked "Hall made in U.S.A.," 7 x 11" (ILLUS.)................................................ **125-195**
**Sadiron w/cat on handle watching mouse on lid,** ceramic, majolica blue w/brown & polychrome trim, Minton, England, 7 x 8" .............................. **1,750-2,325**
**Sairy Gamp,** polychrome, Beswick version, green cap w/black trim, Beswick, England, 5 1/2 x 8" .............................. **125-175**
**Sam Weller,** ceramic, green hat, brown hair, Royal Doulton, 6 x 8".................... **120-175**
**Snowman,** ceramic, white w/top hat, yellow broom, Fritz & Floyd, 8 x 10".................. **90-100**
**St. Basil's Cathedral,** ceramic, white w/gold & jewel colors, Fitz & Floyd, 9 1/2 x 11" ................................................ **80-110**
**T44 airplane,** ceramic, white w/red & blue markings, Clive Hall design has Vandor paper sticker, 4 x 5 1/2".......................... **90-145**
**Tea table w/tea set atop,** ceramic, special commission from English Tea Council, white w/small blue pattern, signed on bottom by artist "J. Morton," 7 x 8" ........ **125-200**
**Tent w/children peeping at flap entrynursery ware,** polychrome, green tent, Shelley #726181, 6 x 9" .................. **2,250-2,700**

*The Waiter Teapot*

**The waiter,** ceramic, black suit, brown hair, Roy Simpson for J. Luber, 8 1/2 x 9 1/2" (ILLUS.)................................................ **110-135**
**Three-legged isle of man,** ceramic, early 1800s version, blue jacket, sailor hat, white breeches, unmarked, 6 x 7 1/2" .. **600-750**

*Toby Dog Teapot*

**Toby dog,** ceramic, black & white w/yellow muff on neck, marked "Tony Wood Studios," 5 x 8 1/2" (ILLUS.) ............................ **40-85**

*Tom the Piper's Son Teapot*

**Tom the Piper's son,** ceramic, yellow, azure & burgundy, impressed "Tom, the piper's son," Shawnee USA, 6 x 7 1/2" (ILLUS.) .................................................... **70-110**

**Victorian fireman,** ceramic, black helmet & red uniform or yellow helmet w/blue uniform, Sari, 6 x 8 1/2" ................................. **80-115**

**William,** ceramic, Toby-type figure w/both legs in air, colors vary, waistcoat & coat always different colors, black hat, Tony Wood, Staffordshire, 6 x 8" ........................ **45-85**

## TOASTERS

**A.J. Lindemann & Hoverson,** Model 205, automatic type, open door at top to insert two slices of bread & lower doors close, timer is set & when done lower doors open & toast drops down on base plate on each side, bottom doors may also be opened manually by use of lift lever on one end of toaster, L&H Electrics, Milwaukee, WI, 1930s ........................ **250**

**A. Mecky Co.,** The Ledig, Model 500, single, sides somewhat like opposing automobile headlight reflectors w/heating elements, basket slides between holding bread, accessories include sandwich holder & butter melter, Philadelphia, PA, early 1920s ...................................... **1,000-1,500**

**All-Rite Co.,** porcelain, Hostess sandwich-type, single or double size, variety of solid colors, two-tone colors, floral patterns & solid polished aluminum, Rushville, IN, 1920s, singles (ILLUS. top next column) ............................................... **400-2,025**

*Hostess Sandwich Toaster*

**All-Rite Co.,** porcelain, Hostess sandwich-type, single or double size, variety of solid colors, two-tone colors, floral patterns & solid polished aluminum, Rushville, IN, 1920s, doubles, up to ................. **3,800**

*Pincher Style Toaster*

**American Electric Heating Co.,** steel & mica panels, Model No. 5825G, pincher-style, unique plate heating element similar to that found in irons, resistance ribbon wire between layers, variety of late & early models w/different handles on doors, patented in 1914 by makers of American Beauty irons (ILLUS.) ............. **80-250**

*Dropper Type Toaster*

**Beardsley & Wolcott,** nickel-plated, dropper-type, single size, insert bread in slot at top, when complete a timer releases one side to swing out allowing toast to drop down for retrieval, embossed detail on front & back, Waterbury, CT, 1930s (ILLUS.) .................................................. **150-250**

**Chicago Electric Mfg. Co.,** Handyhot, metal base, painted black, Type AEUB, Deco style w/one curved top edge, modern cutout design in doors, originally considered low-end piece, now rare to find in excellent condition & is highly desirable, mid-1930s (ILLUS. top next page ) .................................................. **350-650**

*Handyhot Art Deco Toaster*

*Toast Oven Toaster*

**Coleman,** chromium plate finish, Model No. 2, toast oven-type, double size, Bakelite handles, embossed side designs, removable crumb tray, toasts on both sides at once & shuts off automatically when done, to retrieve grasp handles on end & pull out drawer-type cages (ILLUS.)............................................ **443-1,323**

**D.C. Hughes,** Elektro Toaster, pincher w/black enameled metal base adorned w/gold striping, flip down toast rack on top, unable to find literature on this piece, but have been told it was made by the U.S. Navy, Chicago, IL........................ **3,000**

*Swirled Finish Aluminum Toaster*

**Dalton,** aluminum frame, machine swirled finish, handle swings out to turn bread from side to side, coil heating element encased in glass tubing, very rare (ILLUS.)......................................... **2,000-3,000**

**Delta Manufacturing Corp. or Pennsylvania Aircraft Works, Inc.,** anodized aluminum, brilliant red or blue, pop-down type, more common models are either polished aluminum or chrome plated, models w/sandwich racks are higher

priced & most rare is solid light pink anodized color, some engraved w/concentric design on both sides, carrying handles on ends are engraved w/Penn-Air or Delta, earlier Penn-Air aluminum were made of scrap WWII aircraft aluminum , Philadelphia, PA , 1930s-40s ..... **100-610**

*The "Ramp" Toaster*

**Dominion Electrical Mfg. Co.,** known as the "Ramp," single slice size, drop bread in slot at top & when finished the timer released latch on door at end & toast slides out on the "ramp," Minneapolis, MN, a must for serious or advanced collectors (ILLUS.) .................................. **700-1,500**

*"El Tosto" Toaster*

**Edison Electrical Appliance. Co., Inc.,** Model 214T2 (also known as Hotpoint Model 114T5), "El Tosto," evolution of one of earliest electric toasters by Pacific Electric Heating Co., New York, Chicago, Ontario, CA, early 1900s (ILLUS.)........ **75**

**Electroweld Mfg.,** swinger w/doors sliding side to side, waffle pattern cutout doors, also version w/Gibson Girl shaped top plate & variety of handle styles, 1922-25, Lynn, MA ............................................... **100-150**

*First Family Toaster*

**Estate Stove Co.,** first family size toaster that cooks 4 slices at once, swing the knob away from heating elements & all four carriers swing around to toast other side, several variations produced during the 1920s w/slight changes, Hamilton, OH, also manufactured under Quality Brand by Great Northern Manufacturing Co., Chicago, IL (ILLUS.) ..................... **150-450**

*Star Electric Toaster*

**Fitzgerald Mfg. Co.,** Star Electric Toaster, Model 75000, swinger style, also referred to as "Star-Rite" toaster selling originally for $5, top mounted, pilgrim hat shaped turning knobs of non-heating composition allows doors to swing out & away from heating element, Torrington, CT, 1925-1930 (ILLUS.)....................... **100-250**

**General ElecHewlitt Elec. & Mfg. Co.,** Hotpoint Cat. No. 159T25, nickel plated turner w/cut-out doors, laced open coil heating element, fiber feet & black painted metal handles, made to accommodate large slices of bread, Bridgeport, CT, Ontario, CA, late 1920s .......................... **40**

*Flat Bed Toaster*

**Hewlitt Elec. & Mfg. Co.,** chrome plated, black wood knob on top to lift lid up & back, on/off switch in front, flat bed toaster, elegant design detail, Arlington, MA (ILLUS.) ........................................ **100-200**

**Kenmore,** for Sears Roebuck Co., Model No. 344-6332, chrome plated automatic pop-up type, green, yellow, red or brown Bakelite feet & handles, some also marked "Manufactured by Arvin Norblitt-Sparks Industries for Sears Roebuck Co.," 1940s ........................................... **75-250**

**Landers, Frary & Clark,** heart-shaped, considered to be the most beautiful toaster, Model E9411 unadorned version, Model #9410 has embossed design on base, designed & patented by George E. Curtiss in May 1929, New Britain, CT, short lived due to the Depression, but remains a must for every collection (ILLUS. ) .................. **350-1,200**

*Heart-Shaped Toaster*

**Manhattan Electrical Supply Co.,** The Mesco, nickel or silver plated, white, cream or black base, Model Nos. 575, 576, 577, among top ten toasters of all time, unique accordian type door hinge allows bread basket to pull away from heating element for adjustable, easy & safe operation, heavy ceramic base, New York, NY, 1914-15, very well made ................................................. **500-4,000**

**Manning Bowman & Co.,** Article 1228, MB Means Best label, referred to as a Tip-and-Turn toaster, open coil element laced up & down over ceramic spools, covered by a 1925 M&B patent, serial numbers on Manning Bowman pieces are guides to their date of manufacture, Meridian, CT, 1927-1931 ............................... **45**

*Commander Toaster*

**Mattatuck Mfg., Co.,** Commander Model 101, variation of theme of Edicraft, insert bread in side cages & turn timer/starter knob to desired setting, when done sides slowly begin to open allowing removal of toast, very rare, Waterbury, CT, 1930s (ILLUS.)........................................... **4,000-5,000**

**Merit Made, Inc.,** 2/3 round-shaped Model A w/red jewel light in center, exceptionally rare, Model Z without design, w/rising sun design or w/concentric design in painted, polished, or chrome finish is more common, 1940s, Buffalo, NY ....... **150-200**

*Toast-Rite Toasters*

**Pan Electric Co.,** Toast-Rite, percher type, solid porcelain double fired body, unusual shape, several variations & patterns, Cleveland, OH, late 1920s, each (ILLUS.)............................................. **500-8,500**

*Crown Electric Toaster*

**Paragon Electric Co.,** Crown Electric Toaster, nickel plated, rudimentary percher type, base is folded thin metal, legs & upper toast rack are folded wire, two slender horizontally mounted mica elements, wood block electrical fitting on side, looks homemade but literature confirms that it was a production model, retailing at $2.25, Chicago, IL, pre-1920, note screw-in plug, only known one to exist - beyond rare (ILLUS.) ............ **2,000-5,000**

**Pelouze Manufacturing Co.,** nickel plated, vertical percher type, curved legs, top mounted toast rack w/"X" cut-out pattern, side carrying handles, Chicago, IL, early 1900s........................................ **250-1,500**

*Excelsior Electric Toaster*

**Perfection Electric Products Company,** Excelsior electric toaster, one turn of knob at top operates both large racks turning them simultaneously to brown other side, coiled heating element alternates between close & wide spaces which was said to give a more even distribution of heat, originally sold for $7.50, New Washington, OH, late 1920s, very scarce & expensive (ILLUS.).............. **400-1,500**

**Permway Electric Mfg. Co.,** Thoro-Bread Electric Toasters/SuperLectric Products (Clear Vision) Models No. 66 (2 slice) and No. 55 (1 slice), Nichrome element, nickel plated, black rubberoid handles, fibre feet, tilting bread holder w/bone buttons, automatic self-centering device (claimed to be an exclusive SuperLectric feature), heat retained by asbestos insulation, St. Louis, MO, 1927-28 .............. **100-250**

**Radiron Corp.,** "Rosebud" Model 25-1, nice plump shaped automatic pop-up type, w/engraved Rosebud filled w/red color, black Bakelite handles & feet, Miamisburg, OH .................................... **300-500**

**Riverside Mfg. Co.,** Ypsilanti Junior Toaster, Model 1002, polished aluminum, turner type, black texture finish w/painted metal base, Bakelite door pulls, vertically laced open coil heating element, Ypsilanti, MI, 1930s ......................... **75**

**Robeson Rochester Corp.,** Royal Rochester, Model 13260, chrome plated, turner type, w/black Bakelite handles & feet, attractive flame pattern cutout in doors, Rochester, NY, 1930s ................. **75-125**

**Robeson Rochester Corp.,** The Aristocrat, Model 13370, chrome plated, turner type, w/black Bakelite knobs, chain link cutout & embossed design in doors, manually set signal control lever, signal bells alert you when one side of toast is dome, Rochester, NY, 1930s ................. **75-150**

**Samson United Corp.,** Model 5147N, chrome plated body w/brown Bakelite handles, dials, knobs & base, long single slot allows two pieces of bread to be inserted in tandem, bread is lowered by turning large center dial & toast may be manually released by use of toast release button on lower right, 1950s, Rochester, NY................................................. **55**

**Samson United Corp.,** Tri-matic Model 194, triple size, chrome plated body w/engraved vertical striped design, shuts off automatically when toast is done, toast removed manually, one model uses release button while another utilizes timing arm to release toast, 1930s, Rochester, NY...................................... **200-225**

**Simplex Electric Co.,** Model T-211, very sturdy & heavy polished metal body (came either nickel plated, silver plated or copper finished) in center of which is upright heating element set on black enameled base, each side has a door which swings outward & downward, opening sufficiently to permit placing or removing bread without burning fingers, wire toast rack on top, when finished rack slides back into frame out of sight, removable doors permit crumbs to be cleaned from base, Boston, MA ............ **100-600**

**Son-Chief Electrics Inc.,** Model 680, sometimes referred to as Magic Maid, chrome no-frills flopper with black hard plastic handles, variety of simple door styles & black painted/chrome combinations all under same model number, most common toaster found, 1930s, Winsted, CT, .................................................. **20**

*"Edicraft" Automatic Toaster*

**Thomas A. Edison, Inc.,** "Edicraft" automatic toaster, originally known as the Automaticrat of the Breakfast Table, now referred to as a "clamshell" because of manner that door opens automatically & simultaneously when toast is done, streamlined piece, Orange, NJ, late 1920s to early 1930s (ILLUS.) .......... **400-2,400**

*Three-Sided Toaster*

**Union Metalworks Corp.,** solid chrome plated doors & top, manufactured for Great Northern Products Co., most unusual piece because it is three-sided, black painted metal frame & plastic handles, Unionville, CT, very rare & highly sought by collectors (ILLUS.) ................... **2,000**

# LAUNDRY ROOM ITEMS

## CLOTHES SPRINKLER BOTTLES

*Plastic Bottle*

**Bottle,** plastic, pink, marked "Laundry Sprinkler" (ILLUS.) ...................................... **$15**
**Bottle-shaped,** plastic, red & yellow ................ **15**

*Green Sprinkler Bottle*

**Bulb-shaped,** rubber, green, marked "Made in USA" (ILLUS.) ................................ **75**

*Sunruco Clothes Sprinkler*

**Bulb-shaped,** rubber, red, w/original box marked "Sunruco Clothes Sprinkler, No Drip" (ILLUS.) ................................................ **45**

*Clear Glass Shaker Bulb*

**Bulb-shaped shaker,** clear glass, w/original label (ILLUS.) ......................................... **85**

*Green Glass Shaker Bulb*

**Bulb-shaped shaker,** green glass w/metal cap (ILLUS.) ................................................ **125**

*Black Cat Sprinkler Bottle*

**Cat,** ceramic, black Siamese w/green eyes, handmade (ILLUS.) ...................................... **350**

**Cat,** ceramic, Siamese, tan ............................ 175

*Siamese Cat*

**Cat,** ceramic, Siamese, tan w/black face &
paws (ILLUS.) ............................................ 200
**Cat,** ceramic, w/marble eyes, American
Bisque, each ............................................. 300

*White Cat Sprinkler Bottle*

**Cat,** ceramic, white w/red rhinestone eyes,
gold trim (ILLUS.) ....................................... 225
**Chinese Man,** ceramic, marked "104" on
bottom, handmade, all colors ........................ 75

*Chinese Man Sprinkle Plenty*

**Chinese man,** ceramic, marked "Sprinkle
Plenty" & "104," handmade, orange and
peach, metal top (ILLUS.) ............................ 75
**Chinese man,** ceramic, Sprinkle Plenty,
white, green, & brown, holding iron ............ 200
**Chinese man,** ceramic, Sprinkle Plenty,
yellow & green, Cardinal China Co. .............. 30
**Chinese man,** ceramic, w/removeable
head ........................................................... 300
**Chinese man,** ceramic, white w/aqua &
black trim, Cleminsons .................................. 40
**Chinese man,** ceramic, white w/aqua &
black trim, w/original shirt tag hanging
around neck, Cleminsons ............................. 95

*Chinese Man Holding Towel*

**Chinese man,** ceramic, white w/green col-
lar, holding towel (ILLUS.) .......................... 300
**Clothespin,** ceramic, w/smilely face .............. 200

*Clothespin Sprinkler Bottle*

**Clothespin,** ceramic, yellow and white,
w/unusual face, metal cap (ILLUS.) ............ 275

*Frigadaire Sprinkler Bottle*

**Cone-shaped,** plastic, grey w/red & yellow rings & green cap, "Frigadaire" give-away (ILLUS.) ................................................ **65**
**Dearie is Weary,** ceramic, Enesco ................. **325**
**Dutch Boy,** ceramic, green & white ................ **200**
**Dutch Girl,** ceramic, handmade ...................... **175**
**Dutch Girl,** ceramic, wetter-downer ................ **200**
**Dutch girl,** plastic, white w/red trim .................... **45**
**Elephant,** ceramic, pink & grey, trunk up, Cardinal China Co. ......................................... **75**

*American Bisque Elephant*

**Elephant,** ceramic, trunk is used for handle, American Bisque (ILLUS.) ...................... **600**

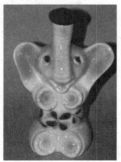

*Elephant w/Clover*

**Elephant,** ceramic, white w/pink w/clover on tummy (ILLUS.) ...................................... **125**

*Emperor Sprinkler Bottle*

**Emperor,** ceramic, "Sprinkle Plenty," blue w/yellow face & black hat, metal cap (ILLUS.) ...................................................... **150**
**Emperor,** ceramic, variety of colors & designs, Holland Mold, handmade, each ..... **150**

*Fireman Sprinkler Bottle*

**Fireman,** ceramic, California Cleminsons, rare (ILLUS.) ............................................. **1,000**
**Iron-shaped,** ceramic, blue Delft design .......... **150**
**Iron-shaped,** ceramic, farm couple ................. **225**

*Iron-Shaped Aquarena Springs Bottle*

**Iron-shaped,** ceramic, souvenir of Aquarena Springs, San Marcos, Texas (ILLUS.) ...................................................... **275**

*Iron-Shaped Florida Souvenir*

**Iron-shaped,** ceramic, souvenir of Florida, w/pink flamingo, marked "A touch of

sun, a drop of rain, helps your clothes
feel fresh again" (ILLUS.) ............................. **300**

*Iron-Shaped Wonder Cave Souvenir*

**Iron-shaped,** ceramic, souvenir of Wonder
Cave (ILLUS.) ............................................. **375**

*Iron-Shaped w/Housewife*

**Iron-shaped** ceramic, w/housewife ironing, housewife dressed in red skirt
w/green blouse (ILLUS.) ............................... **65**
**Iron-shaped,** ceramic, white w/embossed
rooster ........................................................ **150**

*Iron-Shaped w/Green Ivy*

**Iron-shaped,** ceramic, white w/green ivy
decorations, black cap (ILLUS.) ..................... **70**
**Mammy,** ceramic ............................................. **350**

*Mammy Sprinkler Bottle*

**Mammy,** ceramic, handmade, blue & yel-
low, marked "Emma" (ILLUS.) ...................... **250**
**Mary Poppins,** ceramic, Cleminsons of
California ...................................................... **300**

*Merry Maids*

**Merry Maid,** plastic, in a variety of colors,
each (ILLUS.) ................................................ **35**
**"Mr. Sprinkle,"** plastic, red & white striped ........ **25**
**Myrtle,** ceramic, Pfaltzgraff ............................... **325**
**Poodle,** ceramic, grey, pink, or white .............. **275**

*Prayer Lady Sprinkler Bottle*

**Prayer Lady,** ceramic, by Enesco, head removes to fill w/water (ILLUS.) .................. **750**
**Rooster,** ceramic, red, white & green .............. **150**
**Vase,** plastic, white w/rose on front & rose sprinkler top.................................................... **35**
**Watering can,** ceramic, white w/pink & green dots .................................................... **225**

# IRONS

**Advertising iron,** tailor iron, Tailors Trimmings, John L. Bobo & Co., 3 7/8" l. ............ **400**

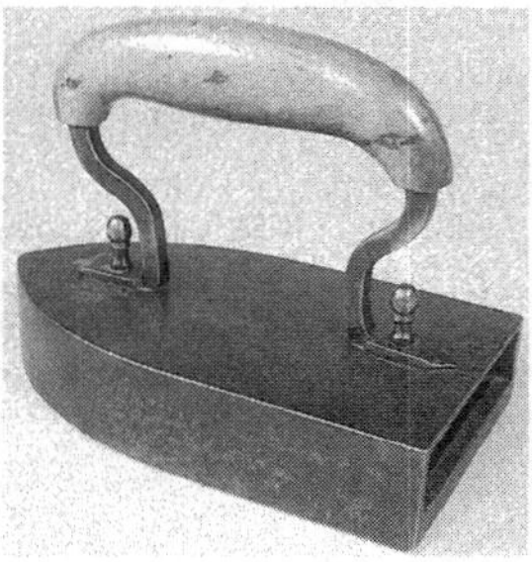

*Alsace-Lorraine Box Iron*

**Box iron,** drop-in, Alsace-Lorraine, France, 18th c. (ILLUS.) ........................................... **400**
**Box iron,** lift-top, Bless & Drake, "Salamander," U.S.A. ........................................... **450**

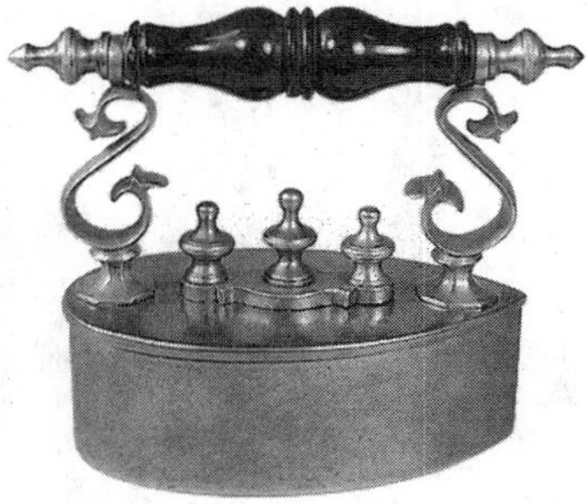

*Scottish Box Iron*

**Box iron,** Scottish, arrowhead "S" uprights (ILLUS.)..................................................... **2,600**
**Box iron,** swivel gate, goffering pin on gate, leather gate, German ......................... **900**

*Box Iron w/Porcelain Handle*

**Box iron,** swivel gate, porcelain handle decorated w/pink flowers, w/slug (ILLUS.)...................................................... **800**
**Charcoal iron,** "Acme Carbon Iron," U.S.A...... **100**
**Charcoal iron,** revolving chimney, Japan ........ **200**
**Charcoal iron,** split chimney, Portugal............. **325**

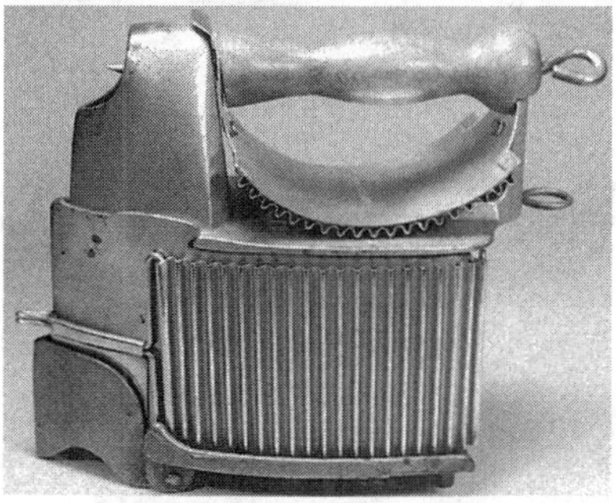

*Pease Combination Charcoal Iron*

**Combination iron,** charcoal, Pease, w/trivet (ILLUS.) ......................................... **800**

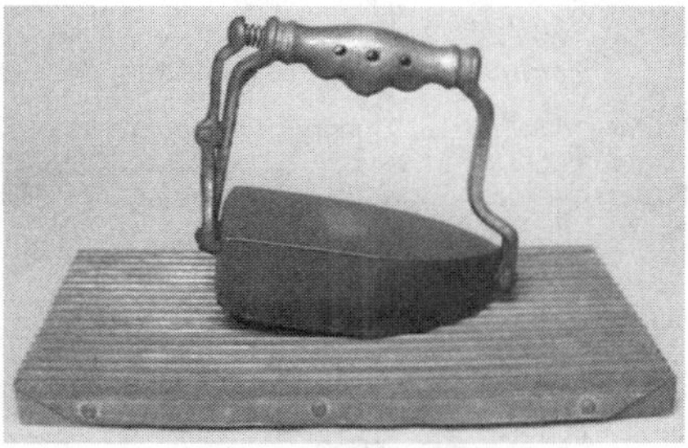

*"Hewitt" Combination Iron*

**Combination iron,** sadiron/fluter, "Hewitt," w/original fluter bed (ILLUS.)..................... **1,200**

*"Little Giant" Combination Iron*

**Combination iron,** sadiron/flutter, "Little Giant," w/fluter bed (ILLUS.) ..................... **1,000**
**Combination reversible iron,** "Majestic," w/fluter bed & slug.................................... **2,000**
**Detachable handle iron,** Harper set: sleeve base, two double-point bases, one handle ................................................. **275**
**Electric iron,** A. C. Williams, double-point side connection .............................................. **90**

*"Silver Streak" Iron*

**Electric iron,** Art Deco style, "Silver Streak," Saunders, green (ILLUS.)............ **2,000**

*Fluter with Separate Stand*

**Fluter,** hand-type, "Sundry," w/separate stand (ILLUS.) ............................................ **250**
**Fluter,** machine, Eagle, 5 1/2" rollers ............... **175**

*Knox & Corrister Fluter*

**Fluter,** machine, Knox & Corrister, patented 1866 (ILLUS.).................................. **2,200**

*"Osborne" Fluter*

**Fluter,** machine, "Osborne," w/wheel tension adjustment (ILLUS.).............................. **700**

*"Sun Flame" Fuel Iron*

**Fuel iron,** petroleum, "Sun Flame," maroon porcelain body, Model 6966 (ILLUS.)........... **200**

*Gas Comfort Iron*

**Gas iron,** Comfort "I Want U," w/trivet (ILLUS.)...................................................... **150**

*Three-barrel Goffering Iron*

**Goffering iron,** three-barrel, brass, center barrel on standard, two barrels at right angles (ILLUS.) ........................................ **4,000**

*Two-barrel Goffering Iron*

**Goffering iron,** two-barrel, brass tripod (ILLUS.) ..................................................... **1,700**

*"Baerricks" Advertising Iron*

**Little advertising iron,** commemorative, "Baerricks—53," 2 3/8", tri-bump grip (ILLUS.) ........................................................... **50**

*Little "Pet" Iron*

**Little detachable handle iron,** "Pet," 3 3/4" l. (ILLUS.) ........................................... **750**

*Little French Iron*

**Little French Iron,** woman ironing on face, 4" l. (ILLUS.) ................................................ **290**

*"Dover Faker" Little Iron*

**Little iron w/wood grip,** "Dover Faker," all-metal, mimicking wood grip, 3 3/4" l. (ILLUS.) .......................................................... **75**

*Little Swan Iron*

**Little swan iron,** original paint, w/trivet, 2 3/8" l. (ILLUS.) .......................................... **250**

*Mangle Board*

**Mangle board,** carved horse handle, dated "1793" (ILLUS.) ......................................... **2,500**

*"Gem" Polisher*

**Polisher box,** marked "Gem," w/slug (ILLUS.) ....................................................... **900**

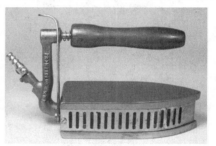

*"Prometheus" Reversible Iron*

**Reversible iron,** gas, "Prometheus" (ILLUS.) ..................................................... **1,000**

*"Pluto" Sleeve Iron*

**Sleeve iron,** electric, "Pluto," made by Consolidated Elec. Appliance Co. Ltd., Pat'd May 7, 07 (ILLUS.) ...................................... **350**

*Tailor Iron*

**Tailor iron,** marked "Crows eating corn," J. L. Haven & Co. (ILLUS.) ........................... **1,500**

# LIGHTING DEVICES

## HANDEL LAMPS

*The Handel Company of Meriden, Connecticut (1885-1936) began as a glass and lamp shade decorating company. Following World War I they became a major producer of decorative lamps which have become very collectible today.*

*Handel Boudoir Lamp with Landscape*

**Boudoir lamp,** a small pyramidal green slag glass shade in a brass frame, raised on a squared gilt brass base w/a stepped flaring foot, shade & base signed, worn gilding, early 20th c., 16 1/4" h. ...................................................... **$880**

**Boudoir lamp,** small domical hexagonal reverse-painted shade w/a slightly scalloped base rim, decorated w/a tropical sunset scene w/palm trees & reflections in water in shades of green, blue, orange & yellow, signed "Handel 6313 W.R.," on a slender copper base w/molded braiding above a quatrefoil foot, cloth label under base, ca. 1916, 14 1/2" h. (rim chips on shade) ........................................ **2,587**

**Boudoir lamp,** 6 3/4" d., conical reverse-painted shade decorated w/a landscape in shades of green, brown & blue, signed "Handel 6363" w/an "R" within a diamond, on a vase-form patinated copper base w/a round foot & applied Handel label, repaired rim chip on shade, ca. 1910, overall 13 3/4" h. (ILLUS.) ............... **4,312**

**Boudoir lamp,** 7 3/8" d. tapering hexagonal shade w/flattened bottom rim reverse-painted w/an overall leafy jungle scene w/green & yellow leaves & pink berries & a blue parrot, signed "Handel.7010.AG," raised on a fluted columnar base w/a scroll-pierced round foot, molded Handel mark, ca. 1910, overall 13" h. ......................................................... **3,450**

*Handel Harbor Scene Boudoir Lamp*

**Boudoir lamp,** 8" d. domical ribbed textured reverse-painted shade, decorated w/a watercolor palette featuring a harbor scene w/sailing vessels, brown tones against blue water & sky at sunset, signed "6356 Handel Co.," raised on a single-socket slender reeded cylindrical standard on a round patinated metal base, impressed "Handel," wear to patina, ca. 1916, 14 1/2" h. (ILLUS.) ......... **2,300**

**Desk lamp,** a bell-form hexagonal shade w/flat rim band composed of a pierced metal overlay in a tropical palm tree design over panels of sunset-colored slag glass, the lower curvilinear border over green & white slag glass, raised on a scroll-trimmed tall C-form arm above the circular bronze base, shade marked, early 20th c., 14 1/2" h. (cracked shade border segments) ..................................... **2,300**

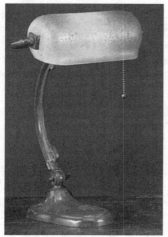

*Handel Desk Lamp*

**Desk lamp,** long cylindrical open-bottomed shade in acid-etched Mosserine glass, supported on a long bronze bracket raised on a tall curved upright arm above the scalloped oblong base, shade & base marked, shade 10 1/2" l., overall 15 1/2" h. (ILLUS.) ......................... **1,540**

*Water Lily Handel Table Lamp*

**Table lamp,** bronze & leaded glass, the floriform piece composed of three water lily-form blossoms w/the petals in white & striated green slag glass above two bronze buds & the bronze stemmed base rising from the center of lily pad leaves, raised Handel mark, one loose petal, early 20th c., 10 1/4" h. (ILLUS.) ..... **3,220**

**Table lamp,** 16" d. reverse-painted shade w/a domed central section flaring widely to deep cylindrical sides, decorated w/large mums in yellow, reddish orange & a touch of green, the exterior textured & frosted, raised on a slender squared & ribbed base, shade signed "Handel #5698R," overall 24" h............................... **5,225**

*Handel Lamp with Scenic Shade*

**Table lamp,** 17 1/4" d. domical reverse-painted shade w/chipped ice exterior, painted on the interior w/a continuous band of trees silhouetted against a shaded pink sky & pools of blue water, w/blossoming foliage & vines in tones of yellow, orange, black & blue, raised on a bronze base w/a slender central column flanked by three slender scroll supports all resting on a round disk foot, shade signed "Handel 7202 - PAL," wear to base patina, one shade pull missing, early 20th c., 24" h. (ILLUS.) .................... **6,325**

*Rare Handel Table Lamp*

**Table lamp,** 18" d. domical reverse-painted shade decorated w/a colorful jungle scene in greens, golds, oranges & yellows centered by a pair of large red, blue, green & yellow parrots, raised on a dark bronze shouldered cylindrical base w/an etched shoulder band, 23 1/2" h. (ILLUS.).................................................. **20,000**

*Handel 'Treasure Island' Lamp*

**Table lamp,** 18" d. domical reverse-painted shade decorated w/a Treasure Island design w/sailing ship & tropical isle in naturalistic colors, raised on a dark cast bronze slender waisted standard w/thick round foot (ILLUS.).................................. **10,000**

*Handel Lamp with Banded Shade*

**Table lamp,** 18" d. domical reverse-painted shade w/a chipped ice exterior, the interior decorated w/a wide border of repeating flowers, birds & scrolls in shades of brownish green, blue, pink & yellow on a mottled amber ground, raised on a bronze base w/three flattened scroll supports resting on a stepped round base, impressed "Handel Lamps" on top shade rim, felted base w/"Handel Lamps"

woven cloth label, base patination loss, early 20th c., 24 1/2" h. (ILLUS.)............... **4,888**

*Choice Handel Peacock Lamp*

**Table lamp,** 18" d. domical shade in dark mottled brown painted on the exterior w/an elaborate design of a colorful peacock perched among flowering branches w/golden yellow & blue blossoms & green leaves, early 20th c., 23 1/2" h. (ILLUS.).................................................. **31,000**

# PAIRPOINT LAMPS

*Pairpoint "Puffy" Rose Bouquet Lamp*

**Boudoir lamp,** 14" d. "Puffy" reverse-painted open-topped shade in the Rose Bouquet patt., decorated w/blossoms in creamy white & pink w/green leaves on a dark green ground, raised on a socket ring support, gilt patinated metal base w/baluster-shaped standard ending in a domed circular base w/raised lily pad &

blossom design on floriform feet, base w/impressed Pairpoint mark & "3037," minor shade rim chip, overall 21" h. (ILLUS.) ..................................................... **4,025**

**Boudoir lamp,** 6 3/4" d. "Puffy" reverse-painted Rose shade w/four rose blossoms painted in pink & yellow on a green ground, raised on a silvered cast metal tree trunk base marked "Pairpoint - B3079" & Paintpoint diamond trademark, ca. 1910, overall 11" h. (two shade support arms missing) ................... **5,175**

*Pairpoint Boudoir Lamp and Shade*

**Boudoir lamp,** 7 1/2" d. bell-form reverse-painted shade decorated w/a landscape of sheep grazing in a field in shades of purple, green & brown, the cast gilt-metal base in the form of a tree trunk, base molded "Pairpoint - B3079" w/Pairpoint trademark, ca. 1910, overall 14 1/4" h. (ILLUS.) ................................... **1,725**

*Pairpoint Candle Lamps*

**Candle lamps,** tall swelled cylindrical shade w/flared rim, chipped ice exterior painted w/a landscape of leafy birch trees on an interior-painted yellow ground, metal mounts for fitting into the turned mahogany candlestick base w/a domed round foot & slender baluster-turned standard below the tulip-form socket, early 20th c., stress cracks in one shade & metal base of shade, overall 21 1/2" h., pr. (ILLUS.) ............................ **805**

*Rare "Puffy" Pairpoint Apple Tree Lamp*

**Table lamp,** 15" d. "Puffy" domical Apple Blossom shade, reverse-painted on the large apples in golden yellow & orange w/light green leaves against a dark green ground w/brown branches & flying bees, raised on a patinated metal tree trunk base, shade stamped in gilt "The Pairpoint Co., Posted July 9, 1906," base w/impressed Pairpoint trademark & "3091," ca. 1907, overall 23" h. (ILLUS.) ..................................................... **40,250**

**Table lamp,** 12" d. "Puffy" reverse-painted Poppy shade raised on silvered metal shade ring over a silver metal base w/a central cylindrical ring-pierced column flanked by three slender reeded & curved ring supports all issuing from the domed round base w/a molded grape-vine border band ..................................... **31,350**

**Table lamp,** 17" w. hexagonal reverse-painted 'Directoire' open-topped shade, painted in shades of pale orange, pink, green, blue & brown w/a classical monument in a lakeside landscape between paneled border bands, raised on a gilt-metal & glass Louis XVI-style base w/three electric candle sockets on upscrolled arms attached to a central column above a large clear controlled-bubble glass ball above the octagonal black foot, ca, 1910, overall 26 3/4" h. (ILLUS. right) ............................................. **7,475**

*Two Pairpoint Table Lamps*

**Table lamp,** 17" w., tapering open-topped nine-sided reverse-painted shade decorated w/a gold Baroque-style scrolling floral vine design on a green ground between dotted borders, raised on a gilt-metal, glass & marble Louis XVI style base w/three electric candle sockets on arms above a twisted clear glass column above the round metal & marble round foot, ca. 1910, overall 26" h. (ILLUS. left).. **1,495**

*Pairpoint Lamp with Floral Shade*

**Table lamp,** 22" d. reverse-painted 'Lansdowne' shade decorated w/a colorful band of large blossoms in yellow, pink, blue & orange, dark border bands, raised on a silvered metal base w/a slender central column enclosed by three slender S-scroll columns raised on a band marble round foot, base marked, 22" h. (ILLUS.)............................................. **4,600**

# TIFFANY LAMPS

**Desk lamp,** a mushroom-shaped Favrile glass shade in amber & yellow shading to orange opalescence raised on a shade ring & light socket on a repaired cylindrical stem resting on a domed opalescent & amber iridescent swirled glass foot w/metal liner, metal impressed "Tiffany Studios - New York - TGDCo. - 28N - 27071," overall 11 1/2" h. (ILLUS. below)...................................................... **1,725**

*Small Tiffany Desk Lamp*

**Desk lamp,** counter-balance style, a 7 3/4" d. deep domical gold & green damascene shade mounted on a bronze base w/high arched arm pivoting w/a large round counter-balance ball above the slender waisted standard on a domed disk foot, shade & base signed, 16" h. ................................................ **6,038**

*Two-shade Tiffany Desk Lamp*

**Desk lamp,** patinated bronze base w/oval scalloped foot surmounted by a twisted central stem w/a bud finial flanked by two upcurved arms w/bulbous urn-form electric sockets, reddish green patina, fitted w/two tulip-form ribbed amber iridescent shades signed "L.C.T. - Favrile," the base signed "Tiffany Studios - New York - 1230," one shade w/chips on fitting rim, shades 5" h., overall 9 1/4" h. (ILLUS.)...................................................... **2,875**

**Floor lamp,** a 10" d. domical damascene swirled green & gold banded shade suspended from a long S-scroll counter-balance arm above the tall slender knopped bronze pedestal w/a rounded paneled foot, shade signed "5 - L.C.T. - Favrile," base impressed "Tiffany Studios - New York - 677," 56" h. .................................. **12,650**

*Tiffany Favrile Hall Fixture*

**Hall fixture,** a bronze fixture w/a tight cast coil design above a plain cap supporting a bulbous teardrop-shaped shade in greenish yellow Favrile glass w/a golden amber pulled feather design, shade signed "D 1745," mount depatinated, shade 9" d., overall 52" h. (ILLUS.) .......... **6,900**

*Two-arm Tiffany Student Lamp*

**Student lamp,** the brownish green patinated bronze lamp w/a thick round foot centered by a tall slender standard topped by a ring-looped finial flanked by two downcurved arms suspending 10" d. damascene green & gold iridescent banded domical shades, shades signed "L.C.T.," base impressed "Tiffany Studios - New York - 28600" w/Tiffany Glass and Decorating Company mark, 26" h. (ILLUS.) ......................................... **13,800**

*Tiffany Acorn Lamp with Urn-form Base*

**Table lamp,** "Acorn," a 16" d. domical leaded glass shade w/a design of radiating orangish amber tiles divided by a wide band of stylized acorns in shades of mottled blue, amber & white, raised on a dark bronze urn-form base raised on four curved supports on a squared foot w/rounded corners, 22 3/4"h. (ILLUS.) .................................................. **15,000**

*Tiffany Apple Blossom Table Lamp*

**Table lamp,** "Apple Blossom," 16" d. domical open-topped leaded glass shade composed of creamy white segments forming the blossoms on metal branches w/dark & light green mottled leaves against lighter mottled green ground, rubbed dark brown bronze base w/a reeded & ringlet-trimmed slender standard above the thick domed base w/scale design raised on four curved feet, shade marked "Tiffany Studios -

New York," base impressed "Tiffany Studios - New York - 26878," 21" h. (ILLUS.) .................................................... **19,550**

**Table lamp,** "Lily," three-light, the patinated bronze cushion-form base w/petals, lobes & scrolling foliage issuing four upright arched stems, three terminating in foliate mounts w/opalescent striped pale green glass lily-form shades each signed "L.C.T.," base signed "Tiffany Studios - New York - 320," 8 1/2" h. .......... **4,887**

**Table lamp,** "Linenfold," 16" d. ten tapering sides w/panels of linenfold design glass w/narrow border bands at the top & base, on a gilt-bronze base w/a slender stem above a round foot w/molded rim & tab feet, 24" h. ........................................... **8,625**

**Table lamp,** "Linenfold," the 18 1/2" d. wide conical shade composed of stripes of green Linenfold glass between metal bands running from a top arched & pierced gilt-bronze crown to a wider matching border band, raised on a gilt-bronze slender paneled standard w/a round paneled disk foot, shade impressed "Tiffany Studios - New York - 1923," base impressed "Tiffany Studios - New York - 533," 22 1/2" h. ...................... **9,775**

*Rare Tiffany Nasturtium Lamp*

**Table lamp,** "Nasturtium," 23" d. domical leaded glass shade w/a curved apron, intricately leaded in the design of trailing nasturtium blossoms in red, yellow & orange among foliage in mottled & striated greens, two border rows of bluish green rectangular panels signed w/metal tags, impressed "Tiffany Studios - New York - 1506," supported on a six-socket bronze reeded standard w/an encircling leaf border on the cushion-form footed base, base signed "Tiffany Studios - New York - 5378," few cracked segments, 31 1/2" h. (ILLUS.) ....................... **63,000**

**Table lamp,** "Peony Border," 24" d. domical leaded glass shade w/radiating golden tiles above the wide border band of mottled red peony blossoms & mottled green leaves, domed pieced bronze cap & raised on a slender bronze tree trunk base w/greenish brown patina, shade marked "Tiffany Studios - New York - 1574," base impressed "Tiffany Studios - New York - 553," 39 1/2" h. ..................... **90,500**

**Table lamp,** "Pine Needle," a domical shade in patinated bronze in the pine needle filigree design backed by green striated slag glass, raised on a patinated bronze baluster-form base w/round foot cast overall in low-relief w/pine needles, shade impressed "Tiffany Studios - New York," early 20th c., 21" h. ......................... **6,325**

*Tiffany Swirling Leaf Table Lamp*

**Table lamp,** "Swirling Leaf," an 18" d. open-topped domical leaded glass shade composed of radiating small blocks of amber glass w/a shoulder band of mottled green & amber swirling leaves above the wide drop apron composed of amber blocks, shade marked "Tiffany Studios - New York - 1470," on a slender gilt-bronze standard w/an overlapping pointed leaf design continuing to a widely flaring round foot, base impressed "Tiffany Studios - New York - 1651," 21 3/4" h. (ILLUS.) ...................... **14,375**

**Table lamp,** "Tulip," 16" d. domical open-topped leaded glass shade composed of dark golden yellow tulip blossoms & mottled green leaves & stems against a dark blue ground, raised on a slender waisted bronze standard over a domed round base on four ball feet, brownish green patina, shade marked "Tiffany Studios - New York," base impressed "Tiffany Studios - New York - 9954," 22" h. .............. **87,750**

**Table lamp,** "Tulip," a 14" d. domical leaded glass shade w/a capped open top, the shade composed of yellow & orangish yellow segments forming tulip blossoms w/dark green leaves & striated lighter blue background segments, raised on a slender dark brown patinated standard w/spaced raised ribs tapering to a round ribbed disk foot on small knob feet, shade marked "Tiffany Studios - New York," base impressed "Tiffany Studios - New York - 431," 21 1/4" h. .......... **27,600**

**"Turtleback tile" table lamp,** the 18" d. domical leaded glass shade w/an open capped top composed of radiating graduated bands of mottled dark & lighter green tiles w/a wide medial band composed of iridescent greenish turtleback tiles, raised on a slender dark blackish brown patinated bronze ribbed standard continuing to the deep leaf-incised cushion base raised on four small curved feet, shade marked "Tiffany Studios - New York - 1432," base impressed "Tiffany Studios - New York - 383," 24" h. .... **24,150**

**"Turtleback tile" table lamp,** the ovoid shade of triangular section, inset w/two domed amber iridescent turtleback tiles & applied w/bosses & wire decoration, pivoting on two curved upright supports continuing to a leaf-cast circular patinated bronze base w/inset amber iridescent glass cabochons, on five ball feet, impressed "Tiffany Studios - New York - 408 - 9948," drilled for wiring, 14 1/2" h. .. **6,325**

*Tiffany Turtleback Tile Sconces*

**Wall sconces,** "Turtleback tile," each shade composed of three greenish iridized turtleback tiles resting on a square white marble platform above a glass & metal support arm, pr. (ILLUS.).............. **23,100**

# LAMPS, MISCELLANEOUS

## ALADDIN© MANTLE LAMPS

*Aladdin Hanging Lamp*

The Mantle Lamp Company of America, creator of the world famous Aladdin Lamp, was founded in

Chicago in 1908. Like several of its competitors, the Aladdin coupled the round wick technology with a mantle to produce a bright incandescent light comparable to the illumination provided by a 60 to 75 watt bulb. Through aggressive national advertising and an intensive dealer network, the Aladdin Lamp quickly overcame its competitors to become the standard lighting fixture in the rural American home.

From the company's origin until 1926, Aladdin Lamps were produced in table, hanging, and wall bracket styles made mostly of brass and finished in either satin brass or nickel plate. With the purchase of an Indiana glass plant in the mid-1920s, the Mantle Lamp Company began to make their own glass shades and chimneys, in addition to the manufacture of glass lamp bases. Glass shades, both plain and decorated with reverse painting, were made in a variety of styles. Later, colorful parchment shades were produced in a myriad of colors and with decorations ranging from large, gaudy flowers in the early 1930s to delicate florals and intricate geometrics, sometimes with flocking, from the mid-1930s through the post-war years.

Aladdin kerosene lamps are probably best known for the colorful glass bases made from the late 1920s to the early 1950s. The earliest glass lamps were vase lamps that consisted of a glass vase finished in different colors that had a drop-in brass kerosene font. Later, seventeen different glass patterns were produced and most patterns were offered in a variety of different glass colors. Crystal glass lamp bases commonly came in clear, green, or amber colors, but for a few years crystal bases were produced in ruby red and cobalt blue. The latter two colors are especially prized by collectors. A translucent to opaque glass called moonstone was produced during the 1930s and was available in white, green, rose, and for one pattern in the late 1930s, yellow. A few styles had white moonstone fonts attached to a black stem and foot. Other lamps had a moonstone font mounted on a metallic base.

An ivory to white glass called Alacite is unique to the Aladdin Lamp. The late 1930s glass formula contained uranium oxide, and the ivory to marble-like appearance sometimes leads to its confusion with the Crown Tuscan glass of Cambridge. With the commencement of the Manhattan Project, this compound was placed on the restricted list and, as a consequence, the glass formula was changed. Early Alacite lamp bases will glow under a black-light, whereas later ones will not. The later Alacite lamps also tend toward a white color rather than ivory.

Aladdin kerosene lamps are still being made today. The Mantle Lamp Company left Chicago in 1948 and was absorbed into Aladdin Industries, Inc. In April, 1999, the Aladdin Mantle Lamp Company was formed in Clarksville, TN. The new limited partnership produces kerosene lighting for domestic and foreign markets and supplies/accessories for older lamps. Aladdin kerosene lamps and their related accessories have been avidly collected over the last thirty years. As a consequence, prices have risen steadily even for the common lamps. Expectedly, condition of the lamp or shade is a very *important consideration in determination of value. Glass damage, electrification, or missing parts can seriously depreciate value. By comparison, lamps in mint, unused condition and in the original carton fetch premium prices.*

*—Thomas W. Small*

**Hanging lamp,** decorated w/hand painted roses on ball shade, Model No. 6 (ILLUS.)........................................... **4,000-4,500**

*Aladdin Student Lamp*

**Student lamp,** original w/functional tank, unelectrified, Model No. 4 (ILLUS.)... **7,000-8,000**

*Aladdin Table Lamp, Model No. 8*

**Table lamp,** brass finish, No. 8 flame spreader & No. 401 shade, Model No. 8 (ILLUS.)................................................ **425-475**
**Table lamp,** nickel finish, No. 10 flame spreader, Model No. 10....................... **400-450**
**Table lamp,** nickel plated, No. 6 flame spreader, Model No. 6........................... **80-100**
**Table lamp,** nickel plated w/embossed foot, 1/2 qt. font, Model No. 1 (ILLUS. top next column).................................... **600-700**
**Vase lamp,** blue variegated, gold foot edge, three feet, 10 1/4"....................... **600-650**
**Vase lamp,** green w/dark green foot edge, model No. 12, six feet, 10 1/4" h. .......... **200-250**
**Vase lamp,** variegated green, gold foot edge, three feet, 101/4".......................... **300-350**

*Aladdin Table Lamp, Model No. 1*

*Aladdin Vase Lamp*

**Vase lamp,** variegated peach, gold foot edge, three feet, 10 1/4" (ILLUS.) ......... **275-325**

*The following pattern glass names are from J.W. Courter reference books on Aladdin Lamps*

**Table lamp,** Beehive patt., clear, Model B **100-125**
**Table lamp,** Beehive patt., green or amber crystal.................................................... **125-175**
**Table lamp,** Cathedral patt., green or amber crystal........................................ **150-200**
**Table lamp,** Cathedral patt., rose moon-stone ..................................................... **400-450**
**Table lamp,** Cathedral patt., white moon-stone ..................................................... **350-400**
**Table lamp,** Corinthian patt., amber or green crystal.......................................... **100-125**
**Table lamp,** Corinthian patt., clear.............. **80-100**
**Table lamp,** Corinthian patt., white moon-stone font w/green, rose or black foot ... **250-300**
**Table lamp,** Diamond Quilted patt., green moonstone .......................................... **250-300**
**Table lamp,** Lincoln Drape patt., short, amber or ruby crystal w/metal collar at font top ................................................. **100-125**
**Table lamp,** Lincoln Drape patt., short, ruby crystal, raised glass collar at font top ..................................................... **900-1,000**
**Table lamp,** Lincoln Drape patt., tall, cobalt blue, foot top w/circular ring ............ **1,600-1,800**

**Table lamp,** Lincoln Drape patt., tall, cobalt blue, scalloped ring on foot top ....... **1,900-2,100**

**Table lamp,** Lincoln Drape patt., tall, ruby crystal, lower value for light ruby, higher for dark ............................................. **850-1,100**

**Table lamp,** Lincoln Drape patt., tall, slightly tapered stem, Alacite ............... **125-175**

*Aladdin Table Lamp, Orientale Pattern*

**Table lamp,** Orientale patt., ivory, green, or bronze enamel, metallic finish (ILLUS.) ............................................... **125-150**

**Table lamp,** Queen patt., green, white, or rose moonstone on metallic foot .......... **250-350**

**Table lamp,** Simplicity patt., Alacite, green or white enamel .................................... **150-175**

**Table lamp,** Simplicity patt., rose enamel ................................................. **175-200**

**Table lamp,** Solitaire patt., white moonstone ............................................. **2,800-3,500**

**Table lamp,** Venetian patt., clear, fused stem-foot/bowl, Model A ...................... **350-400**

**Table lamp,** Venetian patt., clear, green or peach enamel ........................................ **125-150**

**Table lamp,** Venetian patt., white enamel ................................................. **100-125**

**Table lamp,** Vertique patt., green moonstone ................................................. **450-500**

**Table lamp,** Vertique patt., yellow moonstone ................................................. **600-650**

**Table lamp,** Victoria patt., ceramic w/floral decoration & gold bands ........................... **600-650**

**Table lamp,** Washington Drape patt., clear crystal, plain stem, w/or without oil fill ... **75-100**

**Table lamp,** Washington Drape patt., clear, green, or amber w/open, thick round stem ................................................... **100-150**

**Table lamp,** Washington Drape patt., green or amber crystal, plain stem ........ **100-150**

## MISCELLANEOUS

*Aladdin Lamp Chimneys*

**Chimneys,** boxed, each (ILLUS.) ................ **25-100**

**Mantles,** boxed, each (ILLUS. center) ............. **5-15**

*Aladdin Mantles*

**Mantles,** boxed, each (ILLUS. left) ............. **75-125**

**Mantles,** boxed, each (ILLUS. right) ............. **40-60**

*Aladdin Matchholder*

**Matchholder,** copper w/accessories & instruction booklet (ILLUS.) ................... **100-150**

**Others,** each (ILLUS.) ................................. **25-40**

**Shades,** floral, No. 601F roses ................. **600-700**

**Shades,** green cased, No. 202 artichoke, No. 204 eight panel, each ................. **800-1,000**

**Shades,** plain, No. 201, No. 301, No. 401, No. 501 (for Model No. 11), No. 601, each ..................................................... **100-125**

**Shades,** plain, opal No. 205 w/fire polished bottom rim ........................................... **400-500**

**Shades,** reverse painted, No. 601 Log Cabin, No. 616 Gristmill, No. 620 Windmill, each ............................................... **300-350**

**Shades,** reverse painted, No. 616F poppies, No. 620F roses, each ................ **800-1,000**

**Shades,** Whip-O-Lite parchment, floral, geometric, or scenic, 14", each ............. **150-200**

*Aladdin Wicks*

**Wicks,** boxed, mounted, each (ILLUS. left stack) ...................................................... **30-40**

**Wicks,** boxed, No. 11 & No. 12, each (ILLUS. right center & right) ...................... **10-20**

**Wicks,** boxed, No. 6, mounted, each (ILLUS. left center) .................................... **20-25**

## KEROSENE & RELATED LIGHTING

*Kerosene lamps were used from about 1860 until replaced by electric lighting when it became available. In cities and towns this was generally from about the turn-of-the-century until 1920. Rural electrification occurred in the 1930s or later.*

*Today, kerosene lamps are sought after for their appearance and function. Some owners light them occasionally, while a few enjoy them every night. Certainly experimenting with the lamps can add another dimension to collecting. Try placing lamps strategically—not just to illuminate a room but to create dramatic shadows.*

*If a hanging lamp is the only source of illumination in a room, patterns of light and shadow and perhaps colors will be splayed out on the ceilings and walls. The flickering of an open flame will create shadows in motion which can give a favorite piece of folk art or furnishings, such as a clock or collectible, a different nighttime look. Natural wood finishes which can look flat under incandescent light will glow with a warm sheen to create the mood of a century ago. Most examples shown here are ones that would have been relatively inexpensive when they were made and are compatible with country furnishings. There was tremendous competition and production in the kerosene lamp business. This led to the creation of an astounding variety of lamps and accessories. Because electric lighting was not perfect, kerosene lamps were preserved for emergencies. Thus Americans are blessed with a good supply and an appreciation that will ensure a continuing demand.*

*—Catherine Thuro-Gripton*

*Note: Lamps do not include burner & chimney, unless otherwise noted.*

### PRE-KEROSENE LAMPS

*Various Pre-Kerosene Lamps*

**Hand lamp,** pressed waffle design, flared font w/applied handle, burning fluid burner, ca. 1850 (ILLUS. right) .................... **250**

**Table lamp,** free-blown squatty bulbous font above a flared columnar standard, w/whale oil burner, ca. 1850 (ILLUS. left) ...................................................... **225-250**

**Table lamp,** pressed Star-and-Punty patt., slightly flared font w/smooth domed top, w/burning fluid burner, ca. 1850 (ILLUS. center) ................................................. **300-325**

## KEROSENE & RELATED LIGHTING

### KEROSENE LAMPS

**Hand lamp,** blue opalescent pressed glass, Sheldon Swirl patt., footed ......... **550-650**

**Hand lamp,** blue pressed glass, Whirlpool patt., footed .......................................... **250-300**

**Hand lamp,** clear pressed glass, Bullseye patt. ...................................................... **125-150**

*Polka Dot Pattern Kerosene Hand Lamp*

**Hand lamp,** clear pressed glass, Polka Dot patt., ovoid font decorated w/opalescent cranberry or ruby dots, applied handle, all above circular domed base, kerosene burner & baluster-shaped chimney w/slightly scalloped rim (ILLUS.) .. **1,550 and up**

**Hand lamp,** clear pressed glass, Quartered Block patt., one-piece, kerosene burner & "pie crust" chimney, ca. 1880s (ILLUS. left) ...................................................... **125-150**

*Various Quartered Block Table Lamps*

**Hand lamp,** clear pressed glass, Quartered Block patt., w/handle, flat bottom, kerosene burner & "pie crust" chimney, ca. 1880s (ILLUS. center) .......................... **150-200**

**Hand lamp,** clear glass, Ribbed patt., globular font w/applied handle, ca. 1850s-1870s (ILLUS. right front) ..................... **125-150**

*Ribbed Pattern Kerosene
Hand & Table Lamps*

**Hand lamp,** clear pressed glass, Ribbed patt., bulbous globular font tapering into flared foot, ca. 1850s-1870s (ILLUS. center front) ............................................ **75-100**

**Hand lamp,** clear pressed glass, Ribbed patt., squatty bulbous font, applied handle, ca.1850s-1870s (ILLUS. left front) ..................................................... **75-100**

*Atterbury & Co. Kerosene Hand Lamp*

**Hand lamp,** clear pressed glass, squatty ovoid font w/ribbed center ring, tapering to domed foot w/applied handle, patented, marked, Atterbury & Co., ca. late 1860s-1870s (ILLUS.) ............................ **75-100**

*Adams & Co. Kerosene Hand Lamp*

**Hand lamp,** milk glass, flared foot below angular font w/handle & wide lip below clear glass top, Collin's burner & milk glass Sun chimney tapering at top,

Adams & Company, rare complete (ILLUS.) ........................................... **1,200-1,500**

*Kerosene Lamps*

**Hand lamp,** tin & glass, painted tin w/handle & removable glass font, w/Columbia burner & cylindrical glass chimney combination, font & holder marked "Bradley's Security Factory Lamp" (ILLUS. left) ..... **250-300**

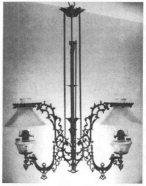

*Adjustable Hanging Kerosene Lamp*

**Hanging lamp,** adjustable, cast iron & glass, elaborately cut-out cast-iron arms holding two lamps, etched glass fonts decorated w/star- and cross-like designs, glass chimneys & glass shades, original finish & shades, ca. 1860s-1880s (ILLUS.) .................... **1,500-2,000**

**Mechanical lamp,** Wanzer Mechanical lamp, metal base w/forced draft for operation even without a shade, shown w/a 5" d. opalescent Hobnail shade (ILLUS. far right), lamp base only ...................... **550-650**

**Mechanical lamp,** Wanzer Mechanical lamp, metal base w/forced draft for operation even without a shade, shown w/a 5" d. opalescent Hobnail shade (ILLUS. far right w/hand lamp), shade only .. **100 and up**

**Parlor lamp,** milk glass, squatty ovoid shade tapering to slightly flaring rim above squatty pear-shaped bottom, both decorated w/raised & painted flowers, ca. 1880s-1890s (ILLUS. top next page) ....................................... **325 and up**

*Kerosene Parlor Lamp*

*Parlor Vase Lamp*

**Parlor vase lamp,** globular white glass shade w/hand-painted roses w/cylindrical glass chimney, above baluster-shaped vase w/scroll-cut lip & scrolled handles, all on elaborately scroll-cut footed base (ILLUS.) .................................... **375**

*Student Lamp*

**Student lamp,** brass & glass, cylindrical chimney w/milk glass shade, original finish & parts, kerosene burner, ca. 1879 (ILLUS.) ................................................ **600-700**

**Student lamp,** brass & glass, Manhattan Brass Co., original nickel-plate base & cased green glass shade (ILLUS. center back) ............................................... **450 and up**

*Blown Glass Table Lamp*

**Table lamp,** clear blown glass, globular font, brass standard on square marble base, or chimney, the appropriate chimneys & burners (as shown here) could easily double or triple the value, ca. 1860s (ILLUS. w/chimney & burner), lamp w/burner & chimney, each............ **225-275**

**Table lamp,** clear blown glass, globular font, brass standard on square marble base, or chimney, the appropriate chimneys & burners (as shown here) could easily double or triple the value, ca. 1860s (ILLUS. w/chimney & burner), burners & chimney only.................. **150 and up**

*Bullseye & Fleur-de-Lis Table Lamp*

**Table lamp,** clear pressed glass, Bullseye & Fleur-de-lis patt., font tapering to baluster-shaped standard, late 1860s (ILLUS.) ................................................ **150-200**

**Table lamp,** clear pressed glass, Chadwick patt., w/milk glass base ........................ **175-200**

**Table lamp,** clear pressed glass, Corn patt., ovoid font tapering to ridge at top w/bulging below burner, glass standard & base, marked w/patent date of 1873, La Belle Glass Company, Bridgeport, Ohio (ILLUS. top next page) ................ **175-225**

**Table lamp,** clear pressed glass, Corn-in-Shield patt., Oval Band patt. base........ **175 -225**

*Corn Table Lamp*

*Daisy & Button Table Lamp*

**Table lamp,** clear pressed glass, Daisy and Button patt., glass font w/domed top & angled bottom above paneled standard & base, ca. 1890s (ILLUS.) ................... **100-125**

*Eyewinker Table Lamp*

**Table lamp,** clear pressed glass, Eyewinker patt., cylindrical font above baluster-shaped standard & base, Dalzell, Gilmore & Leighton Company (ILLUS.) ............... **125-150**

*Gaiety Table Lamp*

**Table lamp,** clear pressed glass, Gaiety patt., angular ribbed font decorated w/opalescent feathered design, cylindrical glass standard on circular base, kerosene burner & baluster-shaped chimney w/scalloped rim (ILLUS.) ......... **425-500**
**Table lamp,** clear pressed glass, McKee Tulip patt. ...................................... **300 and up**
**Table lamp,** clear pressed glass, Moon and Crescents patt., w/brass stem & marble base ...................................................... **300-350**

*Ewing Patent Table Lamp*

**Table lamp,** clear pressed glass, ovoid font above Ewing patent drip catcher above clear glass baluster-shaped standard, ca. 1870s (ILLUS.) ............... **200-250**
**Table lamp,** clear glass, Quartered Block patt., w/handle, footed, kerosene burner & "pie crust" chimney, ca. 1880s (ILLUS. right) ..................................................... **150-200**
**Table lamp,** clear pressed glass, Ribbed patt., globular font, columnar standard w/flared ribbed base, ca. 1850s-1870s (ILLUS. back left) .................................. **125-150**
**Table lamp,** clear pressed glass, Ribbed patt., inverted pear-shaped font, on baluster-shaped standard, ca. 1850s-1870s (ILLUS. back right) ............................... **125-150**
**Table lamp,** clear pressed glass, Riverside Wild Rose patt. ...................................... **250-300**

*Sawtooth Table Lamp*

**Table lamp,** clear pressed glass, Sawtooth patt., globular font w/diamond-like pattern on lower half, tapering brass connector, slightly flared columnar milk glass standard & base, includes burner & tall, thin cylindrical chimney (ILLUS.) ................................................ **300-350**

*Snowflake Pattern Table Lamp*

**Table lamp,** clear & cranberry opalescent pressed glass, Snowflake patt., squatty ovoid font in opalescent cranberry, above ribbed clear standard, Hobbs (ILLUS.) ................................................ **650-750**

*Veronica Table Lamp*

**Table lamp,** clear pressed glass (on inside of lamp), Veronica patt., ovoid font tapering to brass standard on a marble base, Hobbs Brockunier & Company, ca. mid-1860s - mid-1870s (ILLUS.) ................. **150-200**

*Cut-overlay Table Lamp*

**Table lamp,** cut-overlay, inverted pear font in white cut to green, tapering brass connector, tapering to slightly flared columnar green alabaster standard & base, (ILLUS.) ....................................... **1,800 and up**

*Figural Table Lamp*

**Table lamp,** figural, angular etched clear glass font w/star- and cross-like designs, above spelter fisherwoman holding spear w/a basket full of fish at her feet, all on tiered square base, Bradley & Hubbard Mfg., ca. 1888 (ILLUS.) .......... **250-300**
**Table lamp,** figural, clear frosted glass font w/Greek Key design above spelter bust of Empress Eugenie (wife of Napoleon III), ca. 1870s (ILLUS. top next page) ... **175-225**
**Table lamp,** figural, clear pressed glass font & spelter figure of Mary & her Lamb .................................................. **125-225**
**Table lamp,** green pressed glass, Vera patt. ...................................................... **175-225**
**Table lamp,** marigold Carnival pressed glass, Zipper Loop patt. ........................ **750-850**
**Table lamp,** Ripley Wedding Lamp, blue & clear pressed glass, two matching blue fonts flanking toothpick holder, above white glass base........................... **1,800 and up**

*Figural Table Lamp*

## OTHER MISCELLANEOUS LAMPS

*Modern Vandermark Art Glass Lamp*

**Art glass table lamp,** 9" d. high mushroom-shaped shade w/flared rim, in iridescent light blue glass w/iridescent orange & green pulled-feather design, raised on a single-socket three-arm spider support on a vasiform glass base ending in a ruffled foot & decoration matching the shade, shade signed near rim "Vandermark DM - SS 1980," Doug Merit for Vandermark, 22 3/4" h. (ILLUS.)...................... **403**

**Arts & Crafts table lamp,** a conical hammered copper-framed shade fitted w/wide mica panels raised on a four-arm support above a Japanese mixed-metal double gourd-form spittoon base decorated w/engraved lotus & resting on a round footed carved wood foot, unsigned shade by Dirk Van Erp, ca. 1915, overall 15" h. ................... **1,380**

**Arts & Crafts table lamp,** oak & glass, the wide square oak-framed shade w/four pyramidal panels topped by a low flat gallery pierced w/holes above amber slag glass panels & oak frames above

the flat drop apron w/pierced holes over slag glass, raised on a swelled tapering four-sided quarter-sawn oak pedestal w/metal loop handles near the top of each side, set on a square stepped oak foot, original finish, early 20th c., minor glued repair, shade 18 3/4" w., overall 23" h. ...................... **1,430**

*Fine Cut-Overlay Astral Lamp*

**Astral table lamp,** cut-overlay glass & gilt brass, a clear frosted wheel-cut & acid-etched tulip-form shade w/Gothic arches & roundels resting on a font ring suspending long triangular prisms above the cut-overlay standard in red cut to white w/gilt & polychrome foliate & scroll designs, on a scrolling gilt-brass base, attributed to the Boston & Sandwich Glass Co., mid-19th c., electrified, one prism missing, gilt wear, minor shade chips, 33" h. (ILLUS.) ............................... **3,450**

*Unusual Austrian Cat Lamp*

**Austrian table lamp,** figural, a patinated cast bronze base modeled as a stretching cat w/inset glass eyes, the curved tail suspending a bell-form metal shade w/ruffed edges & chased w/four cat faces w/inset green & black glass eyes below a red glass border, signed "TO fecit - mod. Eichberg," reddish brown patina, late 19th - early 20th c., overall 15 1/2" h. (ILLUS.)...................................... **3,737**

**Banquet lamp,** kerosene-type, Louis XVI-style, gilt-bronze & marble, the bulbous dark marble font set in an bronze openwork laurel leaf band fitted w/three large rams' head masks at the top of three tall slender curved supports centered by a slender standard & raised on a tripartitie marble base w/metal bun feet, the tall kerosene burner fitted w/an open-topped ball shade acid-etched overall w/delicate florals & a frosted glass chimney, electrified, Europe, late 19th c., 24" h. ................ **2,070**

**Betty lamp on stand,** tin, a round saucer base centered by a slender cylindrical stem supporting the deep pointed oblong tin font w/rim spout & strap handle from top to the center of the stem, Portsmouth, New Hampshire, 19th c., worn layers of silver paint, 6" h. ................... **165**

*Fine Bigelow & Kennard Floor Lamp*

**Bigelow & Kennard floor lamp,** 24" d. domical leaded glass shade composed of panels of scale pattern crinkled amber glass divided by tapering panels of dark brown, light brown & amber bands & petals w/a scalloped bottom rim composed of brown & mottled tan segments, on a tall bronze slender standard above a wide disk foot w/a lappet border band & a brown patina, ca. 1915, 59" h. (ILLUS.).................................................. **32,200**

*Bradley and Hubbard Boudoir Lamp*

**Bradley and Hubbard boudoir lamp,** 10 1/2" sq. domical shade w/bent-panels of striated green slag glass framed in a dark patinated metal riveted strapwork frame, raised on a single-socket standard w/similar bowed strap over the round domed foot, raised mark on base, early 20th c., overall 18 1/2" h. (ILLUS.) ... **1,035**

*Early Bradley and Hubbard Lamp*

**Bradley and Hubbard kerosene table lamp,** 10" d. domical open-topped milk glass shade h.p. w/delicate roses, violets & forget-me-nots, w/a three-arm spider support over silvered-metal baluster-form reservoir & circular domed base w/gadrooned border, raised "B & H" on reservoir screw cap, late 19th c., 20 1/4" h. (ILLUS.)........................................ **863**

*Bradley and Hubbard Table Lamp*

**Bradley and Hubbard table lamp,** 17 1/4" d. wide domed bent-panel slag glass shade w/green & amber shade & ribbed panels, mounted in a radiating bronze-patinated metal framework w/leafy floral band around the flattened rim, raised on a two-socket tapering & paneled patinated metal standard w/flared base & raised lappet petal design, early 20th c., minor patination wear, 21 1/2" h. (ILLUS.).............................. **978**

*Quality Duffner and Kimberly Lamp*

**Duffner and Kimberly table lamp,** a 20" d. domical leaded glass shade composed of oblong panels w/golden yellow diamond lattice design framed by brown & amber geometric band & scrolled bands w/large palmettes spaced around the shaped rim, raised on a slender reeded bronze standard continuing into the swirl- and leaf-cast undulating round foot, unsigned, ca. 1910, 24 1/2" h. (ILLUS.).................................................... **7,475**

*Hand-Painted Fenton Table Lamp*

**Fenton table lamp,** Victorian-style, the wide domed shaded Burmese shade tapering to a cylindrical open top w/ruffled rim, decorated w/a mountainous landscape, w/a pierced brass shade ring above the electric fittings above the squatty bulbous glass font w/matching decoration, raised on a knopped brass stem above a round base w/four scroll-cast feet, w/glass chimney, signed "Fenton Art Glass Co. Williamstown, W.VA - October 1974 - Hand Painted by Connie Ash 2520," overall 19 1/2" h. (ILLUS.).......... **518**

*Unusual Austrian Figural Floor Lamp*

**Floor lamp,** figural, jeweled & pierced cold-painted metal, the wide scroll-pierced umbrella-form shade set w/large cabochon jewels above the beaded fringe border, raised on a tall slender urn-form metal standard w/an overall delicate pierced scrolling design & fitted on an octagonal table base in engraved metal set on each side w/rectangular panels of diamond-shaped glass segments, a large cold-painted metal figure of a Middle Eastern woman seated on the edge of the table, raised on a platform base w/arched aprons, Vienna, Austria, late 19th - early 20th c., overall 55" h. (ILLUS.)..................................................... **6,900**

*Rare Fulper Pottery Table Lamp*

**Fulper Pottery table lamp,** 13 1/2" d. domical pottery shade w/a streaked yellow & dark brown glaze & inset w/geometric green & ivory leaded glass pieces, raised on a tall pottery base w/wide round base in a fine Cat's Eye flambé glaze, rectangular ink mark, two very short hairlines, tiny chip on shade, overall 16" h. (ILLUS.).................................... **11,000**

**Gone-with-the-Wind table lamp,** a frosted clear glass ball shade ornately embossed overall w/leafy scrolls & roses, joined by the burner fitting & gilt brass flared & scalloped shoulder collar to the bulbous ovoid matching glass base raised on a scroll-pierced squared metal foot, electrified, ca. 1900, 23 1/2" h. ..................................................... **275**

*Rare Grueby & Tiffany Table Lamp*

**Grueby Pottery table lamp,** the wide baluster-form Grueby Pottery base molded w/large upright leaves & a band of arched rim handles w/an overall green glaze, the metal collar & fittings supporting a domical Tiffany Glass "turtleback" tile shade (ILLUS.) ............................... **286,000**

**Jefferson table lamp,** wide domical reverse-painted shade in textured grey glass decorated w/a continuous verdant lakeside landscape in shades of green, brown, blue & white, raised on a gilt-metal slender lobed baluster-form base w/fluted round foot, shade & base signed, ca. 1910, overall 22" h. ................. **2,300**

*Cranberry Glass Bracket Lamp*

**Kerosene bracket lamps,** a squatty bulbous cranberry glass font decorated w/scrolling gilt designs & fitted w/a brass collar, burner & clear chimney, supported on a ornate scrolling brass swing arm attached to a cast brass scrolling wall bracket mount, pr. (ILLUS. of one)........ **495**

**Kerosene hanging parlor lamp,** a domed frosted pink 14" d. open-topped shade w/a brass crown & set in a pierced brass shade ring suspended by four chains from a metal cross below the pierced & scalloped ceiling cap, a squatty clear pattern glass font set in a brass cup support suspended between ornately scrolling brass arms joined to the shade ring & fitted w/colored glass 'jewels,' clear & colored prisms incomplete, ca. 1890s, 28 1/2" h. (ILLUS.)...................................... **715**

**Kerosene hanging parlor lamp,** a wide open-topped domical blue satin glass shade w/a diamond lattice design fitted w/a pierced brass flared crown & resting in a pierced brass shade ring suspended from four chains & hung w/facet-cut prisms, two pierced leafy scroll brass brackets set w/large round red jewels suspend the burner & brass collar on the compressed spherical matching blue satin glass font w/a brass drop ring, ca. 1890s (ILLUS. top next page) ................... **4,480**

**Kerosene parlor hanging lamp,** a domed, open-topped cranberry Hobnail patt. glass shade fitted in a pierced brass ring frame hung w/faceted prisms & fitted w/a brass crown, hung from forked brass chains joined to an upper brass ring, fitted w/a simple bulbous brass font marked "Rayo" & flanked by long thin brass S-scrolls, finger ring at bottom of font, late 19th c., electrified, 14" d., 33" h. ........................................................ **825**

*Rare Victorian Parlor Hanging Lamp*

**Kerosene table lamp,** clear pressed flint pattern glass, Bellflower patt., the bulbous font in ribbed single vine Bellflower patt. tapering to a glass connector to a flaring paneled glass pedestal base w/round scalloped rim, ca. 1860, 7 1/4" h. (flakes on base) ........................... **220**

**Kerosene table lamp,** pressed glass, the spherical blue font w/a raised berry design, a brass connector to the clambroth glass pressed pedestal squared base w/rounded corners, ca. 1870, 9" h. ...... **275**

**Kerosene table lamp,** Ripley marriage lamp, a pair of blue opaque fonts flanking a cup-form match holder & supported on a forked harp above a turned brass connector above the milk glass pedestal & domed squared base, marked "D.C. Ripley & Co. - Pat. Pending," late 19th c., 11 3/8" h. (chips, in-the-making defects in base)......................................... **660**

**Lard lamp,** painted tin & cast iron, trunnion type, the tin lozenge-shaped font w/two wick tubes suspended from a cast-iron foliate frame & base, gilt, green & red decoration on a yellow ground, brass stamped label "S.N. & H.C. Ufford 117 court St. Boston Kinnear Patent Feb. 4, 1851," Boston, mid-19th c., 9 x 12" (minor paint loss)......................................... **489**

**Moe Bridge table lamp,** 15" d. deep domical reverse-painted shade decorated w/a lakeside landscape w/trees in naturalistic colors, signed on the rim, raised on a bronze base w/a swelled cylindrical standard above the round undulated foot incised w/a large clover leaf design, marked on the base, shade w/interior rim chip, early 20th c., overall 20 1/2" h.` ........ **2,300**

*Tower-shaped Glass Night Light*

**Night light,** pressed blue opaque glass, modeled as a cylindrical block tower w/arched opening at one side below the conical fishscale-design roof w/vent holes & a metal vent cap, marked on base "Deposé - Pantin," w/numbers, France, early 20th c., 3 1/2" d., 7 1/2" h. (ILLUS.)....................................................... **195**

**Pittsburgh table lamp,** 17 1/2" d. high domed reverse-painted shade in chartreuse painted w/russet & large maple leaves around the sides, raised on a gilt-metal baluster-form lobed base w/a flaring round lobed foot w/red & black enamel highlights, ca. 1915, overall 25" h. ...................................................... **2,875**

*Pittsburgh Reverse-painted Lamp*

**Pittsburgh table lamp,** half-round oblong reverse-painted shade decorated w/a riverside landscape in naturalistic tones, supported by a gilt-bronze high curved adjustable arm above the paneled & floral-cast oblong foot, marked on the turn switch, light wear to gilt, 14" h. (ILLUS.)....... **690**

*Decorative Quezel Desk Lamp*

**Quezal desk lamp,** a 10 1/2" d. domical shade w/small top opening in opal glass lined w/bright gold iridescence & on the exterior w/a glossy surface w/five broad gold pulled feather designs, signed inside the top rim, mounted on a three arm spider on an elegant black bronze slender standard w/the round foot composed of overlapping leaf designs, minor nicks to top shade rim, 19" h. (ILLUS.)...... **1,725**

*Fine Seuss Leaded Glass Table Lamp*

**Seuss table lamp,** 18" d. conical leaded glass shade w/a flat rim band, composed of radiated panels of caramel & soft green colored glass, the dropped apron w/square & triangular red jewels & tile-shaped segments within oblong segments, raised on a slender cylindrical

bronze standard w/three sockets on a flattened wide round foot w/an etched wave pattern, early 20th c., minor patina ware, missing shade cap, overall 21 1/2" h. (ILLUS.).................................... **2,990**

*Lamp with Bent Slag Glass Shade*

**Slag glass table lamp,** 16 1/2" d. domical open-topped shade composed of six bent panels of striated caramel & white slag glass mounted in a gilt- and enamel floral-decorated framework w/lattice border, raised on a slender tall waisted gilt-metal standard w/ribbing & raised mistletoe design on a round matching foot w/light blue enameled highlights, early 20th c., gilt wear, 21" h. (ILLUS.) ................. **431**

*Bent-panel Slag Glass Table Lamp*

**Slag glass table lamp,** an 18 1/2" d. domical shade composed of six tapering bent panels of mottled blue, green, purple, white & caramel slag glass within a bronze-finished metal frame w/foliate decorated bands, raised on a matching tapering cylindrical glass & metal base w/leaf-tip molded base ring, early 20th c., 22" h. (ILLUS.) ........................................ **805**

*Steuben Desk Lamp*

**Steuben desk lamp,** patinated bronze base w/verdigris finish, the oval domed foot supporting a scrolled upright harp suspending a bell-form gold Aurene glass shade, chip to shade top rim, early 20th c., overall 15 1/4" h. (ILLUS.) ............ **1,495**

*Fine Steuben Floor Lamp*

**Steuben floor lamp,** a domical Steuben brown Aurene glass shade w/gold iridescent rim band w/brown stripe suspended from a patinated metal harp above the tall slender standard, early 20th c., 58" h. (ILLUS. of top) ............................... **4,000**

**Student lamp,** kerosene-type, brass cylindrical font connected to a curved arm w/a single burner & ring supporting a pyramidal milk glass shade, adjusting on a slender rod standard w/a ring loop at

the top & centered on a low domed round foot, late 19th c., electrified, 20 1/4" h. (needs rewiring, chip on base rim of shade) ................................................ **248**

*Fine Leaded Glass Suess Lamp*

**Suess table lamp,** 24 1/4" d. wide parasol-shaped leaded glass shade composed of branching striated pink & yellow apple blossoms descending from the top rim on a green ground, raised on a slender bronze three-socket standard w/a wide round disk base etched w/a wave border, Chicago, ca. 1906, spotting on base, 23 1/2" h. (ILLUS.) .......................... **9,775**

*Unusual Wedgwood Jasper Lamp*

**Wedgwood Jasper Ware table lamp,** the classical urn-form light blue jasper ware base decorated w/white relief classical figures & mounted w/a brass foot, connector ring, collar & scroll handles, the top brass cap supporting a clear half-round glass font fitted w/a kerosene burner & spider supporting a domical open-topped milk glass shade & clear glass chimney, England, ca. 1871, impressed mark, vase base 17 1/2" h. (ILLUS.) ........................................................ **920**

# OTHER LIGHTING DEVICES

## CHANDELIERS

**Art Deco,** wrought iron & molded glass, the inverted wide conical pale pink glass shade molded w/a border of roses centering a star, suspended from four candlearms connected at the center to three iron bars applied w/stylized circle & tassel decoration, France, ca. 1925, 48" h..... **1,265**

*Unusual Astral Lamp Chandelier*

**Astral lamp chandelier,** tin, brass & glass, the squatty wide tapering conical tin & brass flat-bottomed font issuing four upright scrolled hanging hooks, the top fitted w/an Astral burner & fitted w/an old tulip-form frosted & engraved glass shade w/ruffled top, the font w/traces of original gilding & paint, stenciled label "Patented Jan 6, 1875," repairs, 5 1/2" h. plus shade (ILLUS.) ...................................... **523**

*Daum Nancy Chandelier*

**Daum Nancy-signed,** Art Deco style, the metal standard w/three flaring pale amber glass cups above the spreading circular frosted shade, shade signed "Daum Nancy France," ca. 1930s, 24" d., 18" h. (ILLUS.) .............................. **1,265**

**Lalique glass,** "Bandes de Roses," wide & deep bowl-form in frosted grey, molded w/four narrow graduated bands of stylized rose blossoms in blocks alternating w/wide plain bands, introduced in 1924, original brown patina, molded name, 20 1/2" d. ................................................. **28,750**

*Louis XV-Style Chandelier*

**Louis XV-Style,** gilded brass & porcelain, eight-light, the central standard composed of a rolled brass cap above a conical brass cap on a squatty spherical porcelain ball w/dark blue bands flanking a wide band transfer-printed in color w/flowers & figures in 18th c. dress, joined w/a brass connector to an tapering ovoid long porcelain section w/matching decoration & flanked by scrolled handles, all above the bottom brass & porcelain base drop issuing eight leaf-cast S-scroll candlearms ending in cupped electric candle-style sockets, early 20th c., 28" h. (ILLUS.) ................ **990**

*Louis XVI Gilt-Bronze Chandelier*

**Louis XVI,** gilt-bronze, twelve-light, the leaf-tip-cast central standard supporting foliate-scrolled candle branches, the upper section fitted w/a gilt-bronze & marble urn within a tri-form cage hung w/tasseled drapery, France, 18th c., 56" h., overall 86" h. (ILLUS.) ................ **18,400**

**Pewter,** six-light, the central baluster- and knob-turned standard suspending a large round ball w/acorn drop finial, the top of the ball issuing six long S-scroll arms ending in candle sockets w/drip trays, Europe, probably 19th c., 24" d. (several arms sagging from metal fatigue) ......................................................... **550**

*Metal Chandelier with Quezel Shades*

**Quezel glass & metal,** six-light, Arts & Crafts style, a large brown patinated metal central disk w/curled inward rim panels suspended from straight brackets connected to a central hooked hanger, the disk suspending six brackets w/leaf-form sockets each fitted w/a ribbed golden iridescent tulip-form signed Quezel glass shade, 19" w.,  overall 37" h. (ILLUS.)..................................... **9,487**

*Venetian Art Glass Chandelier*

**Venetian art glass,** the trumpet & baluster-shaped shaft w/thirty-two branching floral & leaf glass armatures in white, yellow, transparent green & clear, one branch missing, minor loss to glass, Italy, mid-20th c., 29" h. (ILLUS.) ................ **863**

# LANTERNS

*Two Old Candle Lanterns*

**Candle lantern,** punched tin Paul Revere-type, cylindrical w/curved hinged door & conical top w/vent holes & a ring strap handle, pierced overall w/a star & diamond design & the punched inscription "P.O. More, Bellfontaine,O.," rusted finish, 13 1/4" h. plus handle (ILLUS. right)...... **633**

*Paul Revere-type Tin Lantern*

**Candle lantern,** punched-tin Paul Revere-style, cylindrical w/a pierced design of circles & quarter arcs, a hinged door on the side, a tall conical cap w/pierced design & vent holes, large strap ring handle at top, 19th c. (ILLUS.) .................... **110**
**Candle lantern,** tin & glass, upright square dark tin framework w/four glass sides, one forming a hinged door w/cross-form wire guard, flat top w/cylindrical capped vent cover w/shaped wire swing bail handle, old glass, some soldered repair, 13 1/2" h. plus handle (ILLUS. left) ............. **358**
**Candle lantern,** wood & glass, the upright hard- and softwood square frame w/four panes of reputtied glass, one side a hinged door, top vent hole & wire bail handle, traces of red, 14" h. (age cracks & worm holes) ............................................. **193**
**Hall lantern,** gilt-bronze, four-light, Lous XV-Style, a rounded cylindrical gilt-bronze frame enclosing three clear glass curved panels, the frame decorated w/a top foliate-scrolled band & hung w/floral

festoons topped by four tall arched & leaf-scrolled supports, a pierced metal gallery band around the bottom, France, 19th c., 34" h. (ILLUS. below) .................. **8,625**

*Louis XV-Style Hall Lantern*

**Skater's lantern,** tin & glass, a ringed & domed tin font base w/side handle & ring support for the clear pressed glass tapering shade w/a domed pierced cap & swing wire bail handle, 7" h. ...................... **83**

*Brass Whale Oil Lantern*

**Whale oil,** brass, a squared metal font base below the upright square framework enclosing four beveled clear glass panels, one forming a hinged door, a domed metal top w/mushroom-form vent cap, wire bail handle w/turned wood grip, fiited w/unusual whale oil burner, damage & splits to vent cap, 9 1/4" h. plus handle (ILLUS.) ........................................... **110**

# SHADES

*Handel Leaded Glass Shade*

**Handel-signed,** 22 1/2" d. domical leaded glass shade composed of caramel & white striated glass tiles & a border of pale pink & pale green stylized flowers, ca. 1910 (ILLUS.) ......................... **1,150**

*Fine Leaded Glass Shade*

**Leaded glass,** wide parasol-shaped open-topped shade w/dropped apron & undulating rim, composed of a background of cascading mosaic segments in shades of pale mauve, pink & dichronic glass, interspersed w/rose blossoms, rose blossom & bud border executed in striated reds & pinks, some w/green & orange undertones, green border segments, w/metal mounts, needs rewiring, some cracked segments, early 20th c., 22" d. (ILLUS.) .......................................... **1,725**

*Leaded Shade with Ornate Border*

**Leaded glass,** wide domical shade composed of a radiating pattern of light turquoise blue slag glass above a wide intricately leaded drop apron of turquoise blue & amber fleur-de-lis & foliate designs on a deep maroon & navy blue striated ground, attributed to Duffner and Kimberly, early 20th c., few cracked segments, 22 1/2" d. (ILLUS.) ......................... **9,775**

**Pairpoint,** candle lamp-type, flared shape w/chipped ice finish, exterior enamel-decorated w/leafy birch trees over an interior painted yellow ground, metal mounts, early 20th c., 9" h., pr. (stress cracks to one mount).................................... **403**

**Quezal-signed,** swelled long blossom-form w/flaring scalloped rim, gold & green pulled feather decoration on an iridescent gold ground, white interior ................... **138**

**Quezal-signed,** trumpet-form, gold iridescent ground w/pulled feather design outlined in green, pr. ......................................... **440**

**Quezal-signed,** tall trumpet-form w/flattened flaring & scalloped rim, applied random gold threading over iridescent gold & green heart leaf design, gold iridescent interior, 5 1/2" ., pr. ......................... **550**

**Quezal-signed,** ribbed w/flared rims, golden iridescence, pr., 6" h......................... **660**

**Quezal-signed,** trumpet-form, gold pulled feather design & green outlined in white, 6 1/4" h.......................................................... **165**

*Rare Steuben Brown Aurene Shade*

**Steuben-signed,** bell-shaped w/flattened drop rim, the main exterior body in brown Aurene w/random gold iridescent looping, the rim in creamy white Aurene w/random gold looping & leaf-like designs, 5 1/2" h. (ILLUS.) ...................... **1,000**

**Steuben-signed,** ribbed trumpet-form, overall gold Aurene iridescence, 5 1/2" h., pr.................................................... **440**

*Rare Green Aurene Steuben Shades*

**Steuben-signed,** waisted tulip-shaped w/stepped shoulder, dark green Aurene body w/a silver & amber iridescent flared base band trimmed w/green & white zig-zag bands, 5 1/2" h., pr. (ILLUS.).............. **3,000**

*Steuben Globe Shade*

**Steuben-signed,** globe-type, a bulbous ovoid form w/pointed tip, white Aurene ground decorated w/gold iridescent random loopings & heart-shaped leaves, 6 1/2" h. (ILLUS.)......................................... **500**

*Tiffany Crocus Pattern Shade*

**Tiffany,** "Crocus," 16" d. domical open-topped leaded glass shade composed of large pendent crocus blossoms in orangish amber & green against a striated dark green ground, amber tile border, unsigned (ILLUS.) ..................................... **10,350**

**Tiffany-signed,** high domed open-topped ten-ribbed form w/a white exterior decorated overall w/green swirls highlighted w/trailing gold iridescent ribbons, white interior, rim signed "L.C.T. Favrile," 7" d. (rim chips, wear on iridescence) .............. **3,738**

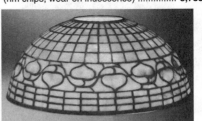

*Tiffany Acorn Pattern Shade*

**Tiffany-signed,** 14" d. domical open-topped leaded glass Acorn patt., composed of radiating tile segments & a center band of acorn-shaped segments in mottled shades of pale green, grey, dark green & amber, rim impressed "Tiffany Studios - New York - 1420 - 21," some cracked segments, early 20th c. (ILLUS.)...................................................... **5,463**

**Tiffany-signed,** "Crimson Bouquet," 28" d. wide cone-shaped leaded glass shade designed as a bouquet of radiant red, pink & creamy white unfolding buds &

full-blown blossoms w/mottled yellowish orange centers, the leaves in striated greens, some w/pink, grey & blue undertones, the background color (some in confetti glass) include grey, blue, violet & green, the border segments in rippled mossy green, beaded bronze edge at top & bottom, three bronze hooks at top, metal tag impressed "Tiffany Studios - New York" (some cracked segments) ..... **71,800**

# LIPSTICK HOLDER LADIES

*Collecting items for the woman's vanity has gained much popularity in recent times. There has always been a need to organize all her paraphernalia, whether it be jewelry, perfume, hair accessories or makeup. Everyone knows that the right color lipstick is essential to the outfit one wears. Where do we keep all these different shades of lipstick? In the 1940s through the 1960s the lipstick "lady" seemed to be the answer. What a cute way to have your lipsticks right at hand. These adorable ladies, usually made from some type of ceramic material, seem to have gotten the job done well. Keeping them within reach at your dressing table kept them readily available.*

*Lipstick ladies are not easy to find. Because of their fragile nature, many were relegated to the trash can after use or damage.*

*Girl w/Blue Bonnet*

**Bust of a girl,** blonde hair & blue bonnet, on one side of an upright base, w/a round center indentation & two holders to one side (ILLUS.) ..................................... **$45**

*Lady in Pink Lipstick Holder*

**Bust of a girl,** long blonde hair topped w/a cluster of red flowers, large eyes, on a pink flower-trimmed round base w/lipstick holes, Josef Originals (ILLUS.) .............. **75**

*Two Girls Lipstick Holder*

**Figure group,** two girls standing back to back, one wearing a pink party dress, the other blue jeans, stump-form brown holders (ILLUS.) ............................................. **95**

*Angel Lipstick Holder*

**Figure of angel,** seated atop a round lobed & footed pink box, gold hair & trim, Josef Originals (ILLUS.) ........................................... **75**

*Geisha Girl Lipstick Holder*

**Figure of Geisha girl,** standing wearing a long blue robe, on an oblong, scalloped base w/a large round framed mirror at her side, gold trim on base (ILLUS.) .............. **50**

*Girl Holding Flowers*

**Figure of girl,** standing holding bouquet of colored flowers, wearing flaring white dress w/gold trim w/lipstick holes & a white bonnet (ILLUS.) .................................... **55**

*Girl w/Green Dress*

**Figure of girl,** standing, wearing a long-sleeved & widely flaring green skirt w/applied roses on bodice (ILLUS.) ............... **40**

*Lady Curtseying Lipstick Holder*

**Figure of lady,** curtseying, wearing a widely flaring all-white dress & hat, holder holes at the back (ILLUS.).................... **45**

*Lady w/Real Lace Gown*

**Figure of lady,** seated beside round mirror w/holders in front, wearing a real lace gown & holding lipstick, base & mirror frame in yellow w/gold trim (ILLUS.) ............. **45**

*Lady w/Apron Lipstick Holder*

**Figure of lady,** standing holding apron open, long pink dress w/white apron trimmed w/blue & green sprigs forming holders (ILLUS.) ............................................. **50**

*Lady in 18th Century Style Gown*

**Figure of lady,** standing holding edge of her 18th c. style pink gown, gold trim (ILLUS.)......................................................... **65**

*Lady Holding Pink Blossom*

**Figure of lady,** standing holding pink blossom, wearing a long blue & green dress w/pink flower trim, a green-trimmed rectangular mirror behind her (ILLUS.) ................ **50**

# MAGAZINES

The most sought after elements in many of the old magazines (especially pre-1930 issues) are the ILLUSTRATOR/or Artists who designed magazine covers, advertisements and story illustrations for numerous periodicals. These are especially apparent in the pre-photographic period which was from about 1895 to the mid-1930s in general. Also most issues which featured movie stars, personalities, sports and specialty articles are in great demand by collectors who have interest in a particular person or subject matter.

The most valuable issues are those with multiple value, such as a cover by an important illustrator, auto or other advertising, articles & story illustrations. Most often older issues are parted by dealers for their overall sale content. The magazine values given here are for those sold to the individual who usually only buys 1 or 2 at a time, or just those issues in their area of collecting interest. Dealers pay much, much less because they buy in quantity and expect large discounts for doing so. The prices given here are for clean, undamaged and complete magazines.

Below are the top selling American illustrators. Values in general are given here for various magazine illustrations.

MP = Maxfield Parrish (1895-1936) $12.00 to 200.00
RA = Rolf Armstrong (1914-1932) 8.00 to 100.00
E = Erté (1916-1936 12.00 to 125.00
GP = Petty (1932-1955) 7.00 to 90.00
NR = Norman Rockwell (1914-1975) 1.00 to 500.00
HF = Harrison Fisher (1890-1935) 7.00 to 70.00
RO = Rose O'Neill (1896-1935) 4.00 to 150.00
VA = Vargas (1920-1974) 4.00 to 175.00
JCL = J.C. Leyendecker (1896-1954) 4.00 to 100.00

FXL = F.X. Leyendecker (1896-1924) 3.00 to 90.00
JWS = Jessie Wilcox Smith (1900-1934) 4.00 to 50.00
CP = Coles Phillips (1907-1927) 3.00 to 50.00
GENERAL CIRCULATION MAGAZINES General issues, high and low value range: Ar = Articles; C=Covers; I=Illustrations; A=Advertising; COW=Cream of Wheat ad.

Where there are three columns of values ON ONE LINE: the 1st is the value of the average issue, with nothing on cover or within that can be sold to a collector; second column shows values at the lowest level of saleable items; far right column maximum value. V1, first editions always bring a premium value for most publications.

**American Legion,** February 1927, HC Christy cover ................................................. **$25**
**American Magazine (The),** April 1919, NM San-Tox ad......................................................... **5**
**Ballou's Pictorial,** April 3, 1858, Africa ............. **18**
**Baseball Digest,** July 1987, Witt........................ **7**
**Bluebook,** October 1967, U.S. Marines .............. **7**
**Cavalier,** September 1973, Jimmy The Greek ............................................................... **8**
**Collier's,** October 1920, Jemina ad ................ **10**
**Cosmopolitan,** March 1933, NM Portrait Illus........................................................................ **7**
**Country Gentleman,** July 26, 1919, H. Cady B&W........................................................... **7**
**Dude,** July 1973, Vaughn Bode........................ **10**
**Family Circle,** November 1952, General ............ **3**
**Family Circle,** September 1962, Fashions ......... **1**
**Fate Magazine,** 1940s-1970s Ar ................. **1; 7**
**Frauds & Rackets,** November 1955, Peyote ......................................................................... **11**
**Gaze,** June 1961, Diane Weber ........................ **10**
**Good Housekeeping,** April 1929, NM Bab-O ad ........................................................................ **4**
**Good Housekeeping,** February 1929, Fangel frig. ad ..................................................... **11**
**Heavy Metal,** 1970s-1980s (I) ....................... **4; 10**
**Hippies,** 1960s, Ar Photos ........................... **15; 20**
**Holiday,** March, 1946......................................... **20**
**Islander (The),** 1960s Ar, Photos................... **5; 7**
**Ladies' Home Journal,** August 1908, Henry Hutt B&W................................................ **7**
**Ladies' Home Journal,** December 1917, NM Soap ad ....................................................... **11**
**Ladies' Home Journal,** January 1960, Pat Boone................................................................... **5**
**Ladies' Home Journal,** June 1895, Stephens cover .................................................. **12**
**Liberty,** September 1940, Daltons Ar.................. **7**
**Life (New),** December 1981, Brooke Shields ................................................................. **3**
**Life (New),** June 1989, A Bra .............................. **2**
**Life (New),** June 20, 1949, High School.............. **9**
**Life (New),** March 1984, Daryl Hannah ............... **3**
**Life (New),** October 1986, Coke Smoker ............ **2**
**Life (New),** September 28, 1959, Ducks .............. **7**
**Mans Adventure,** 1960s Ar............................. **7; 10**
**McCalls,** December 1977, NR Story Illus............. **6**
**McCalls,** October, 1984, Sally Field.................... **1**
**Modern Screen,** February 1975, Barbra Streisand ............................................................... **6**
**Modern Screen,** September 1983, Marilyn Monroe ................................................................. **8**
**Motion Picture,** October 1977, Bissett C ............ **7**

# MARBLES

*Blue Base Guinea Marble*

**Blue base Guinea,** colorful spots & streaks
cover most of the transparent cobalt blue
ground, single cut-line, 5/8" d. (ILLUS.) ..... **$440**
**Cane-dipped,** latticinio swirl in red, white &
blue w/yellow core, Germany, ca. 1880,
2 3/8" d............................................... **175-200**
**China,** bright orange & blue painted flower
w/green leaves on one side, a blue spiral
on the other, glaze white ceramic, 3/4" d.
(three small in-the-making rough spots)....... **358**
**China,** finely decorated w/a set of three
bright blue lines & a set of three bright
green lines running perpendicular to
each other, a dramatic dark orange triple
leaf spray in each quadrant, early period,
touch of overall soiling, 3/4" d. (ILLUS.
top next column)........................................... **605**
**Clear base Guinea,** colorful spots &
streaks run from one cut-line to the other
on a clear base, 11/16" d. ............................. **468**
**Divided core,** cane-dipped swirl in red,
white & blue, ca. 1870-80, 1 1/2" d. ...... **100-110**

*Rare Early Painted China Marble*

*Divided Ribbon Core Swirl Marble*

**Divided ribbon core swirl,** fat core of four
colorful core ribbons surrounded by four
outer sets of thin yellow & white
lines, 7/8" d. (ILLUS.) ..................................... **83**
**Egg-yolk oxblood,** band of oxblood edged
w/yellow on one side, swirls on a translucent white base, 3/4" d. (touch of surface
wear, tiny nick) ................................................ **88**
**Flame,** thin orange lines form dramatic
flame designs on a pastel blue opaque
ground, 5/8" d.............................................. **286**
**Latticinio core swirl,** slim white latticinio
core surrounded by four outer bands,
each made of bright red, yellow & green,
9/16" d. ........................................................ **30**
**Latticinio core swirl,** white latticinio core
surrounded by four outer bands, three
transparent red & three white, ground
pontil, 9/16" d. .............................................. **24**

*Latticinio Core Swirl Marble*

**Lattincinio core swirl,** white latticinio core
surrounded by six outer bands, three
purple & white & three pink &
white, 7/8" d. (ILLUS.) ................................... **52**
**Limeade oxblood,** two very thin lines of
oxblood run from cut-line to cut-line on a
yellow & green Limeade ground, 3/4" d. ...... **148**

**Multicolor corkscrew,** wide band of four different shades of yellow to orange corkscrewing w/two shades of blue & a hint of lavender, 5/8" d. ............................... **110**

**Navarre horizontal swirl,** white swirls within a dark amber matrix forming a horizontal swirling design around the marble, symmetrical spiral opposite the pontil, late 19th c., 11/16" d. (touch of wear, one tiny subsurface moon) ................. **220**

*Rare Nude Solid Core Swirl Marble*

**Nude solid core swirl,** unusual type w/very fat yellow core w/eight color stripes, four red & four green, one green w/a thin line of red, core expands almost to the surface, early, faceted ground pontil, 9/16" d. (ILLUS.) ................................. **440**

**Onion skin,** lobed w/lutz design, America, 1993, 1 5/8" d. ......................................... **50-60**

**Red slag,** white swirls within a bright cherry red matrix, dramatic patterns around the sides, some blended orange, 11/16" d. .......... **33**

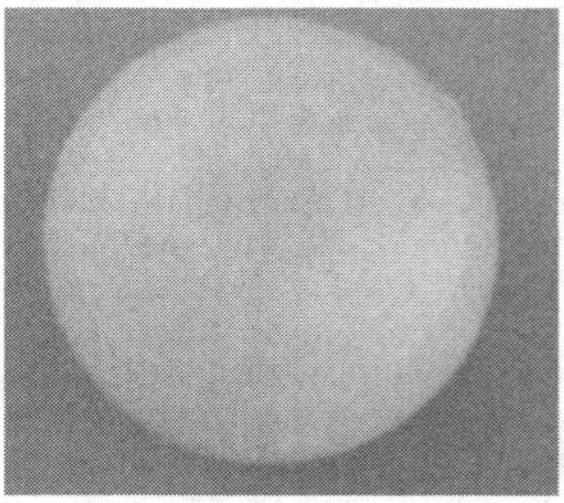

*Rare Semi-Opaque Yellow Marble*

**Semi-opaque,** semi-opaque yellow vaseline, hand-made, large & rare, 1 7/8" d. (ILLUS.) ...................................................... **998**

*Early Latticinio Marble*

**Solid core,** tri-level latticinio swirl caneclipped, Germany, ca. 1880-90, 2 1/6" d. (ILLUS.) ................................................ **250-275**

**Solid core swirl,** core of bright red & blue stripes w/four outer bands of decoration, two yellow & two of thin white line, 9/16" d. ...................................................... **286**

*Solid Core Swirl Marble*

**Solid core swirl,** English-type, blue core w/white bands, outer layer w/three orange bands alternating w/three yellow bands, 1 5/16" d. (ILLUS.) ........................... **683**

**Sparkler,** rainbow palate of colors run from pole to pole nearly filing the clear matrix, great color, 5/8" d. ...................................... **143**

*Early Stone Marble*

**Stone,** solid white, ancient, 1 3/4" d. (ILLUS.) ......................................................... **15**

**Striped opaque,** bright orange lines & bands swirl from one cut-line to the other producing a dramatic pattern, 9/16" d. ........... **50**

**Striped opaque,** bright orange stripes run from one cut-line to the other on a green opaque ground, 9/16" d. .............................. **209**

**Sulphide,** bear on hind legs, 2 1/4" d. (several surface spalls) ...................................... **275**

*Early Sulphide*

**Sulphide,** bear walking, Germany, early 20th c., 1 1/2" d. (ILLUS.) ............................. **100**

**Sulphide,** Billy goat, 1 1/2" d. (light surface spalls) ......................................................... **110**

**Sulphide,** cow, 1 1/4" d. (surface spalls) .......... **110**

**Sulphide,** poodle on hind legs, 1 1/8" d. (figure slightly off-center, spalls) .................. **110**
**Sulphide,** rabbit, running, 1 1/2" d. (figure slightly off-center, surface spalls) ................. **110**

# MELMAC DINNERWARE

*Melamine is the actual plastic used by dinnerware manufacturers since its discovery in the late 1930s. Melmac is a trade name used by American Cyanimid Corporation for Melamine they produced. Melmac has become a generic name used in the collectibles field for all Melamine dinnerwares. Full sets of Melmac dinnerware were first available to the American household in 1947. From that year until the mid-1950s, Melmac was available in rich and trendy colors, was styled by "designers" and quite sturdy. By 1955, decals were created, pastel colors dominated and pieces became thinner and less expensive. By the mid-60s, Melmac had become ubiquitous and synonymous with cheap. Vintage Melmac has seen a surge of popularity as a collectible in the last few years. Most desirable are the older solid-colored sets and pieces, followed by 1950s high-style pieces in pink and turquoise. Patterned Melmac pieces are just beginning to catch collectors' attention. Like china and glass, condition is a major factor for Melmac collectors.*

*The above introduction and following price listings were submitted by Michael Goldberg of Portland, Oregon. This selection provides an overall sampling of many popular and hard to find lines of melmac dinnerware.*

*Boonton Belle Line*

**Bowl,** cereal, Boonton Belle, Boonton Molding Co., Boonton, NJ, pink (ILLUS.) ....... **$5**
**Bowl,** cov., serving, Boonton, Boonton Molding Co., Boonton, NJ, pink ..................... **25**
**Bowl,** serving, Residential, Russel Wright, Northern Industrial Chemical Co., divided, yellow ............................................. **20**
**Bowl,** soup, Florence by Prolon, Prophylactic Brush Co., Florence, MA, Chinese red .................................................................. **8**
**Bowl,** soup, Lifetime Ware, tab-handled, brick red ......................................................... **6**
**Butter dish,** cov., Watertown Lifetime Ware, Watertown Manufacturing, Watertown, CT, turquoise (ILLUS. top next column) ................................................................. **15**
**Creamer,** Spaulding Ware, Spaulding Industries Inc., American Plastics Corp., Chicago, IL, red ................................................ **4**

*Lifetime Ware Line*

**Creamer,** Talk of the Town, burgundy ................. **6**
**Cup & saucer,** Brookpark, Joan Luntz Modern Design, International Molded Products, Cleveland, OH, black ...................... **8**
**Cup & saucer,** Fostoria, Fostoria Glass Co., Moundsville, WV, Blue Meadow patt. .......................................................................... **10**
**Gravy boat & undertray,** Oneida Premiere, harvest gold ........................................... **6**
**Pitcher,** water, LifetimeTranslucent, light blue ...................................................................... **25**
**Plate,** bread & butter, Branchell Color-Flyte, coppertone ............................................. **3**

*Florence Pattern by Prolon*

**Plate,** dinner, Florence patt. by Prolon, Prophylactic Brush Co., Florence, MA, lacquer red (ILLUS.) ............................................. **8**

*Melmac Decal Patterns*

**Platter,** Brookpark, Fantasy patt., Joan Luntz Modern Design, International Molded Products, Cleveland, OH (ILLUS. center) ............................................... **10**
**Platter,** Brookpark, oval, International Molded Products, Cleveland, OH, white w/stylized leaf patt. .......................................... **8**

# METALS

## BRASS

**Door knocker,** cast, urn & acorn form w/original fastenings, America or England, late 19th - early 20th c., 4 1/4 x 7 3/4" ............................................. **$115**
**Ewers,** a wide round stepped base below a very slender stem supporting a slender tapering ovoid body engraved around

the middle w/a palmette band w/an applied mask mount at the front, a very tall slender ringed neck ending in a high upright curved spout, a long slender arched & scrolled handle from the top rim to the shoulder, late 19th c., 16 3/4" h., pr. (one handle loose) ................ **248**

*Rare English Brass Honor Box*

**Honor box,** cov., deep rectangular sides, raised on four tiny bun feet, the top w/a T-shaped coin slot & flip-up cover, top w/engraved design & inscription "A sixpence put into the till, when the lid opens you may fill, when you have fill'd with out delay, shut down the lid or a shilling pay - William Shanlike," England, 18th c., w/key, 5 3/4" l. (ILLUS.)............................ **4,620**

**Kettle,** spun, cylindrical w/wrought-iron bail handle, marked "The American Brass Kettle," 13 3/4" h. (minor splits) .................... **165**

**Kettle,** spun, marked "Hayden's Patent," wrought-iron swing bail handle, 19th c., 24 1/2" d., 18" h............................................ **193**

**Urns,** Art Deco style, flattened baluster form w/a flared base & wide flared neck, designed by Josef Hoffmann, marked "Wiener Werkstatte - Made in Austria," ca. 1925, 6 1/4" h., pr. (small unobtrusive dents to rim corners).............. **1,380**

**Wall sconce,** a cast fixture w/scrolled arms, candle cup & drip dish fitted into a stepped circular bracket, 19th c., 11 3/8" l. ........................................................ **374**

# BRONZE

**Candelabra,** gilt-decorated, five-light, Empire-Style, modeled as a winged classical female figure on a floral-cast columnar pedestal, supporting above her head a floral corona topped by swan-form candlearms, Europe, late 19th c., 26 1/2" h., pr. ............................... **3,737**

**Jardiniere,** Louis XVI-Style, gilt-decorated, tall cylindrical form, the body w/a continuous cast bacchanal scene, the base band w/a Greek key border & fitted w/satyr masks & hung w/fruiting swags, raised on a shaped central pedestal & four tall slender C-scroll supports on the cross-form base, the wide ringed rim case w/delicate leaf bands & large acanthus leaf mounts & side mounts for ring handles, signed "F. Barbedienne,"

France, late 19th c., overall 33" h. (ILLUS. below) ........................................ **20,700**

*Fine French Bronze Jardiniere*

*Aquamarine Luminiere*

**Luminiere,** aquamarine, silvered, gilt & cold-painted bronze, three fish, seaweed & shells on green onyx base, Marcel-André Bouraine, French, 21" l. (ILLUS.).. **23,000**

*Art Deco Bronze Tea Cart*

**Tea cart,** Art Deco style, a two-tier rectangular frame w/four corner uprights & legs on casters, the top ends w/a wide scroll-arched frame enclosing gilded loop & diamond scrolls, greenish patina on frame, designed by Edgar Brandt, ca. 1930, glass shelves missing, 18 x 29", 32" h. (ILLUS.)............................................ **4,600**

**Twine holder,** Bookmark patt., hexagonal form w/hinged lid, gilded w/a reddish patina in the lower recesses of the decoration, impressed "Tiffany Studios New York 905," early 20th c., 3" h. (minor spotting) .................................................. **1,035**

*French Classical Bronze Urn*

**Urns,** Classical Revival style, tall bullet-form body w/waisted flaring neck & upright scrolled shoulder handles, raised on three animal legs headed by cherub masks, the body cast w/a scene of Pegasus & Bellerophon, on a tripartite marble base, France, early 20th c., 18" h., pr. (ILLUS. of one) ........................ **2,185**

**Urns,** cov., Louis XVI-Style, gilt-decorated, tall slender ovoid body raised on a short ringed & flaring round pedestal on a square back w/blocked corners, the lower body cast w/an upright band of leafy bullrushes, leafy vine bands running up the sides & forming handles & continuing around the tapered neck w/flared rim supporting the domed leaf-cast cover, France, late 19th c., overall 18" h., pr. .................................................... **2,875**

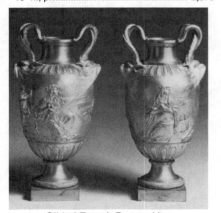

*Gilded French Bronze Urns*

**Urns,** gilt-decorated, tall ovoid body raised on a short flaring round pedestal & square plinth, tapering to a short waisted neck flanked by arched entwined loop handles ending in a carp's mask, the body w/lappet bands around the shoulder & base & cast around the middle w/a wide continuous classical figural band, signed "F. Barbedienne, Paris," France, late 19th c., 16" h., pr. (ILLUS.) ................ **2,875**

**Wall sconce,** gilt-decorated, four-light, the backplate cast w/a central shield fitted w/a winged male term issuing four foliate-scrolled candle branches, Europe, ca. 1900, electrified, 38" h. .......... **2,875**

## COPPER

**Bowl,** hand-hammered, Arts & Crafts style, tall flaring lobed bowl w/a scalloped rim, on a small flared round base, impressed "Marie Zimmerman Maker" on base, ca. 1912, 9 3/4" d., 7 1/4" h. (polished) ........... **1,495**

*Arts & Crafts Copper Box*

**Box,** cov., Arts & Crafts style, hand-hammered, a rectangular slightly domed cover widely overhanging the rectangular box, signed "H. Dixon - San Francisco - 1920" (ILLUS.) ................................. **900**

**Can with spout,** cylindrical w/integral spout up the side ending in a short angled pouring spout, a low domed half-cover at the top below the arched strap side-to-side handle, a small strap handle at the top back edge, hand-made, found in Zoar, Ohio, 17" h. (some soldered repair) ............................................................ **193**

**Candlestick,** Arts & Crafts style, a slender flaring three-sided standard w/a bulbed bottom & a large bulbed top below the triangular rimmed drip tray & cylindrical candle socket, each side enameled w/a red stylized blossom on a long green leafy stem, raised on a wide disk foot, unmarked Art Crafts Shop, early 20th c., 12" h. ............................................................ **330**

**Candlestick,** Arts & Crafts style, hand-hammered, a round low domed foot w/a riveted square slender shaft supporting a dished drip tray & short cylindrical socket w/a wide flat rim, stamped mark of Handel, No. 5277, early 20th c., 9 1/2" h. (some lightening of patina)............ **303**

**Candlesticks,** Arts & Crafts style, hand-hammered, Princess-style, a rectangular low pyramidal foot supporting two slender square standards below the dished drip rim below the cylindrical socket, impressed mark of Karl Kipp, early 20th c., pr. ........................................................... **550**

**Candy kettle,** hand-hammered, wrought-iron bail handle, 31" d., 17" h. ...................... **358**

**Charger,** Arts & Crafts style, wide round dished center w/a raised edge & a wide flattened rim embossed w/oblong & pod-shaped organic shapes, fine original dark patina, impressed mark of Benedict Studios, early 20th c., 20" d. ..................... **2,750**

**Cigarette box,** cov., Arts & Crafts style, hand-hammered, rectangular w/corner buttresses continuing down to form short feet, fitted peaked cover, old cleaned finish, die-stamped mark of Carl Sorensen, early 20th c., 4 x 6", 2" h. ............................ **385**

*Jarvie Copper Dresser Tray*

**Dresser tray,** Arts & Crafts style, hand-hammered, long rectangular form w/a dished center, the wide flat rim embossed w/an intertwined linear design at the ends, patina cleaned, incised Jarvie mark, early 20th c., 6 x 12" (ILLUS.)..................................................... **2,860**

**Jardiniere,** Arts & Crafts style, hand-hammered, narrow footring below the large spherical body w/a wide rolled flat rim, fine original patina, rare form, open box mark of Dirk Van Erp, early 20th c., 9 1/2" d., 7 1/2" h. (minor dent, wear) ....... **4,400**

**Kettle,** cylindrical w/wrought-iron rim band & bail handle, old patina, early, 18" d., 16 1/2" h. ..................................................... **165**

**Kettle,** dovetailed cylindrical form w/wrought-iron bail handle, 19th c., 20" d, 14" h. ..................................................... **193**

**Pan,** cylindrical dovetailed construction w/long flat cast steel rim handle w/hanging hole, mark of Henry Trottman, Philadelphia, 19th c., 8" d. plus handle, 5 1/2" h. ..................................................... **110**

**Pitcher,** Arts & Crafts style, hand-hammered, tall slender conical form w/wide arched rim spout w/a brass band trim, high arched & banded strap handle down the back, Stickley Brothers mark & No. 133, early 20th c., 5 1/2" d., 9" h. .......... **330**

**Serving spoon,** Arts & Crafts style, hand-hammered, a flat tapering long handle ending in a deep round bowl pierced w/stylized scrolled & curved designs, stamped mark "Handicraft Guild - Minneapolis," early 20th c., 8" l. (some cleaning to patina) ............................................. **770**

**Teakettle,** cov., a wide swelled cyindrical lower body w/a curved tapering upper half w/a short cylindrical neck fitted w/a disk cover w/finial, scrolled arched overhead swing handle, long slender angled spout, handle stamped "Thompson 10," early, 12 1/2" h. (old repairs) ........................ **165**

**Teakettle,** cov., bulbous flat-bottomed form w/curved spout & upright swing handle w/brass cover knob, impressed on handle "G. Tryon," Pennsylvania, 19th c., 11 1/2" h. (dents, wear) ................................ **690**

**Teakettle,** cov., bulbous wide form w/curved spout & upright swing handle, cover w/brass finial knob, handle impressed "H. Dehuff," Pennsylvania, 19th c., 12 1/2" h. (dents, wear) .................. **805**

**Teakettle,** cov., wide swelled cylindrical dovetailed body w/a wide rounded shoulder centering a mouth w/a low domed cover, arched swing strap handle stamped "J. Grimes - Pittsburgh," angled spout, 7" h. (battered, repaired) ................... **385**

**Teakettle,** cov., wide swelled cylindrical dovetailed body w/a wide slightly rounded shoulder centering the low domed cover & high looped swing strap handle, angled spout, handle marked "J. Sheriff, Pittsburgh," ca. 1837, 7" h. plus handle (battered, damage, small holes in cover) ......................................................... **385**

**Tray,** Arts & Crafts style, hand-hammered, slightly dished long oval form w/simple loop end handles, fine new dark patina, stamped mark of Gustav Stickley, 11 x 23"....................................................... **770**

**Tray,** hand-hammered, Arts & Crafts style, elongated oval w/rolled rim & two riveted handles, original patina, impressed Gustav Stickley mark, ca. 1912, 11 1/4 x 23 1/4" (scratches, spotting).......... **575**

**Vase,** Arts & Crafts style, hand-hammered, a thin wide footring below the wide squatty bulbous body tapering sharply to a flat mouth, rare red patina w/some verdigris & some wartiness near base, open box mark of Dirk Van Erp, early 20th c., 5 3/4" d., 5" h. .......................................... **1,540**

*Dirk Van Erp Copper Vase*

**Vase,** Arts & Crafts style, hand-hammered, tall corseted shape w/a wide base, fine original dark patina, closed box mark of Dirk Van Erp, early 20th c., 7" d., 9 1/2" h. (ILLUS.) ..................................... **1,870**

**Vase,** Arts & Crafts style, hand-hammered, a footring supporting a wide half-round lower body w/a wide angled shoulder tapering to a tall cylindrical neck, original medium patina, die-stamped mark of Jauchen's Olde Copper Shop, early 20th c., 5" d., 10 1/2" h. ..................................... **1,210**

**Vase,** Arts & Crafts style, hand-hammered, a wide flared footring below the squatty bulbous lower body tapering sharply to a trumpet-form neck w/a thin raised ring at the base of the neck, original dark patina, Stickley Brothers & marked No. 2, early 20th c., 6" d., 11 3/4" h. ................... **990**

*Rare L. & J.G. Stickley Copper Vase*

**Vase,** Arts & Crafts style, hand-hammered, urn-form w/a round disk foot below the urn-form body w/a very tall waisted neck w/flared rim, long slender S-scroll handles issuing from the bottom & ending at the rim, impressed mark of L. & J.G. Stickley, No. F15, early 20th c., 10" d., 18" h. (ILLUS.) ......................... **4,400**

# IRON

**Doormat,** sheet iron, rows of shaped hearts connected by a wire rod running through the shoulders & lower point of each heart, America, late 19th - early 20th c., 22 x 35 1/2" ..................................... **259**

**Models of eagles,** cast, modeled spread-winged & perched on a rock w/a menacing expression, w/orange & gilt paint, 20th c., 31" w., pr. ....................................... **747**

**Models of eagles,** cast, spread-winged bird decorated w/gilt, on a stepped rectangular base, 19th c., 5 3/4" h., pr. (minor gilt wear) ......................................... **173**

**Ornament,** cast, model of a high-topped Victorian lady's button-up shoe raised on a rectangular waisted plinth, old worn red & yellow repaint, 19th c., 8 1/4" h. .......... **193**

**Oven peel,** hand-wrought, a wide flat blade squared & flared at the end & rounded at the top, bolted to a long narrow flat handle w/loop end & decorated w/brass inlays & engraved initials, a heart & "1827," 21 5/8" l. ......................................... **110**

**Picture frame,** cast, oval form w/the wide border cast w/openwork pendent blossoms & leafy vines, a spread-winged eagle crest, oval center opening w/mir-

ror, old gold repaint, 19th c., 11 1/4" w., 15 1/2" h. ................................................... **220**

**Pipe tongs,** hand-wrought, 18th c., 19 1/2" l. ................................................... **1,150**

**Rush light holder,** hand-wrought, an arched tripod base w/penny feet supporting a twisted standard w/downswept twisted arm ending in rush holder, 7 1/4" h. ......................................... **385**

*Early Skewer Holder & Skewers*

**Skewer holder & skewers,** hand-wrought, the holder w/a flat round top w/pierced hanging hole above a slender stem to a swelled flat oval section above the forked pair of outscrolled holding hooks, w/eleven old skewers, found in New Hampshire, overall 15 1/2" l. (ILLUS.) ....... **1,045**

**Teakettle,** cov., individual-size, cast, bulbous body raised on three short peg feet, long angled spout, short wide neck w/fitted low domed cover & brass finial, wire bail handle, 4 5/8" h. (handle probably old replacement) ..................................... **358**

**Umbrella stand,** cast, figural, a standing figure of an English sailor in uniform holding out two open round loops for umbrellas, raised on a half-round small platform above a tapering platform composed of cast crossed anchors, oars & coil of rope, half-round pointed base rim around drip pan, late 19th c., 28" h. ............. **825**

**Utensil rack,** hand-wrought, a flat cross bar fitted w/five hooks, the two end hooks continue up to form the arched & stepped to joined to the center hook by a twisted central thin bar flanked by pairs of scrolls, the other two hooks topped by scrolled fleur-de-lis ornaments, early, 16" l. ............................................. **495**

# PEWTER

**Basin,** round w/deep upright sides, touch of Samuel Hamlin, Hartford, Connecticut & Providence, Rhode Island, 1767-1801, 5 3/4" d., 2" h. (wear, repair) ....................... **523**

**Basin,** round deep sides w/molded rim, faint eagle touch, possibly Gersham Jones, Providence, Rhode Island, 1774-1809, 7 3/4" d. .................... **275**

**Basin,** round w/flanged rim, touch mark of Samuel Hamlin, Hartford & Middletown, Connecticut, 1767-73, 7 3/4" d. .................. **193**

*Basin by Nathaniel Austin*

**Basin,** deep wide rounded sides w/narrow flattened rim, eagle touch of Nathaniel Austin, Charlestown, Massachusetts, 1763-1800, wear & dents, 8" d. (ILLUS.) ..... **550**

**Basin,** deep wide rounded sides w/narrow flattened rim, partial eagle touch of Thomas Danforth Boardman et al, Hartford, Connecticut, 1805-50, 8" d. (minor wear)..... **385**

**Basin,** round deep sides w/molded rim, touch marks of Townsend & Compton, England, late 18th - early 19th c., 9 1/8" d. (wear, pitting) ..................... **165**

**Basin,** wide w/rounded sides & narrow flattened rim, touch mark of Compton, Fenchurch Street, London, England, dark patina, 14" d., 3 1/2" h. ..................... **424**

**Bowl,** wide shallow rounded form w/wide flanged rim, eagle touch of Ashbil Griswold, Meriden, Connecticut, 1802-42, wear & knife scratches, 11" d. (ILLUS. back w/mug) ..................... **468**

**Candlestick,** domed foot below tall flaring & ringed cylindrical standard below the corseted candle socket w/flattened rim, touch of Henry Hopper, New York City, 1842-47, 9 1/2".......................... **237**

**Candlesticks,** wide round low domed foot below the ringed & flared cylindrical shaft below the tall corseted socket w/fitted bobeche, touch mark of Henry Hopper, New York, 1842-47, 10" h., pr. ............. **660**

**Candlesticks,** low domed foot below the tall ringed & flaring cylindrical shaft supporting the corseted socket w/rolled rim, reeded bands around foot, top of shaft & on the rim, unmarked, 19th c., 10 1/4" h., pr. ................. **248**

**Charger,** round w/flanged rim, "London" touch marks, England, 10 7/8" d. (polished, scratches) .......................... **303**

**Charger,** round dished center w/wide flanged rim, "Love" touch, late 18th c., 12" d. (wear, pitting, scratches)................... **440**

**Charger,** round dished form w/wide gently upcurved reeded rim w/stamped initials, crown & rose touch marks, Europe, 12 1/4" d. (wear)......................... **193**

**Charger,** round w/wide flanged rim, engraved coat-of-arms on the rim, marked "Nicholson" & partial eagle touch "Robert...," England, 13 1/2" d..................... **303**

**Charger,** round w/wide flanged & reeded rim, English crowned rose touch mark, 14 1/4" d. (some wear) ................................ **220**

*Very Large European Pewter Charger*

**Charger,** very wide round dished center w/a very wide flanged rim w/beaded edge, Europe, wear, pitting & small repair, 24" d. (ILLUS.) .............................. **2,750**

**Chocolate set:** cov. pot, six small cylindrical tumblers & a tray; Art Nouveau style, the tall pot in the form of a stylized duck w/slender handle down the back, on a slightly dished oval tray, marked "Kayserzinn," Germany, early 20th c., pot 8" h., the set ................................................. **275**

**Cookie board,** cast, rectangular divided into twelve segments representing varied topics including berries, birds, flowers, animals & people, wooden backing, 4 1/2 x 7 1/2" .............................................. **165**

**Cookie board,** cast, rectangular w/twelve square segments each w/a different scene representing a human occupation, wooden back, 4 3/4 x 8" (attachment damage to top corners) .............................. **193**

**Creamer,** short pedestal base below the wide baluster-form body w/a peaked center band, ornate C-scroll handle & wide integral rim spout, touch mark of Boardman & Hart, New York, 1828-53, 6 1/2" h. (dents, handle crooked) ................ **110**

**Flagon,** tall cylindrical form decorated w/stylized wheat stalks & hops in low-relief, impressed Kayserzinn mark & "4289," Germany, early 20th c., 15 7/8" h. .......................................................... **201**

**Lamp,** low domed round foot tapering to a slender stem supporting the acorn-form font w/old whale oil burner, touch mark of Eben Smith, Beverly, Massachusetts, 1814-1856, 5 5/8" h. (corroded) ................... **193**

**Lamp,** round dished foot supporting a slender turned shaft supporting the inverted acorn-form font w/camphene burners, mark of Capen & Molineux, New York City, 1848-54, polished, 7 5/8" h. ................. **303**

**Measures,** cylindrical w/molded base & rim, a long angled side handle, France, late 19th - early 20th c., 1 3/4" to 7" h., graduated set of 7 ...................................... **121**

**Mug,** tapering cylindrical form w/flared base & ring around lower body, cast C-scroll handle, indistinct interior touch, American (wear & dents)............................. **578**

*Group of American Pewter Pieces*

**Mug,** tapering cylindrical form w/flared base & ring around lower body, cast C-scroll handle, eagle touch of Thomas Danforth Boardman et al, Hartford, Connecticut, 1805-42, somewhat battered, handle resoldered, small split in base, 4 1/2" h. (ILLUS. front left)........................... **935**

**Pitcher,** water, wide baluster-form body w/a rim spout & simple C-scroll handle, faint touch of Rufus Dunham, Westbrook, Maine, 1837-60, 6 1/2" h. (small handle split, repairs)................................... **220**

**Pitcher,** water, wide baluster-form body w/angled & pointed handle & wide integral rim spout, touch mark of Freeman Porter, Westbrook, Maine, 1835-60, 7" h. (wear, dents)...................................... **303**

**Pitcher,** water, bulbous baluster-form body w/wide rim spout & cast C-scroll handle, medial band, touch mark of Sellew & Co., Cincinnati, Ohio, 1832-60, 9" h. (dented ring below belly rib) ........................ **358**

**Plate,** flanged rim, eagle touch of Samuel Kilbourn, Baltimore, Maryland, 1814-39, 7 3/4" d. (minor wear)................................. **220**

**Plate,** flanged rim, eagle touch of Samuel Kilbourn, Baltimore, Maryland, 1814-39, 7 3/4" d. (wear, scratches) .......................... **358**

**Plate,** flanged rim, eagle touch of Thomas Badger, Boston, Massachusetts, 1787-1815, 7 3/4" d. (minor wear, scratches) ....... **385**

**Plate,** round w/flanged rim, "Love" touch, late 18th c., 7 7/8" d. (minor wear) .............. **303**

**Plate,** flanged rim, double touches of Blak(e)lee Barn(e)s, Philadelphia, Pennsylvania, 1812-17, 8" d............................... **275**

**Plate,** round w/wide flanged rim, eagle touch of Robert Palethorp, Jr., Philadelphia, 1817-21, 8 3/8" d. (minor wear) ............ **440**

**Plate,** flanged rim, touch mark of Nathaniel Austin, Charlestown, Massachusetts, 1763-1807, 8 1/2" d..................................... **248**

**Plate,** flanged rim, touch of David Melville, Newport, Rhode Island, 1776-93, 8 1/2" d. ........................................................ **160**

**Plate,** dished center & wide flanged rim, lion touch mark of Thomas D. Boardman, 1830 on, 9 1/2" d. (pitted)................... **385**

**Plate,** round w/flanged rim, eagle touch of Boardman & Co., New York, 1825-27, 10 3/4" d. (wear, corrosion, scratches)......... **275**

**Plate,** deeply dished w/wide flanged rim, touch mark of Parks Boyd, Philadelphia, 1795-1819, 11" d. (wear, scratches) ........... **550**

**Plate,** flanged rim, touch mark of Joseph Danforth, Middletown, Connecticut, 1780-88, 12" d.............................................. **358**

*B. Barns Pewter Plates*

**Plates,** dished w/wide flanged rim, eagle touch mark of Blak(e)slee Barn(e)s, Philadelphia, 1812-17, some battering, wear & scratches, 7 7/8" d., set of 6 (ILLUS. of part).......................................................... **1,870**

**Porringer,** round w/scroll-pierced tab handle, touch mark of Thomas D. & Sherman Boardman, Hartford, Connecticut, 1810-30, 4 1/2" d...................................... **297**

**Porringer,** cast crown handle, marked "IC," attributed to the Boston area, 4 3/4" d......... **193**

**Porringer,** round w/plain rounded tab handle w/hanging hold, scratch-engraved date "1848" on back of handle, 5 1/4" d. (wear) ............................................................ **110**

**Porringer,** round bowl w/pierced Old English style handle, unmarked American, 19th c., bowl 5 1/2" d. .......................... **193**

**Porringer,** round w/cast crown handle, marked "S.G." on handle, New England, 5 1/2" d. ...................................................... **303**

**Sugar bowl,** cov., thick pedestal base supported w/wide squatty bulbous lower body w/a wide flared upper body, double C-scroll cast handles, inset domed & pointed cover w/incomplete wafer, attributed to Robert Palethorpe, Jr., Philadelphia, 1817-22, 8 1/8" h. (somewhat battered, handles resoldered) ..................... **220**

**Syrup jug,** cov., flared base on tall cylindrical body w/wide flared rim, hinged pointed cover w/button finial, double C-scroll cast handle, integral rim spout, unmarked American, mid-19th c., 6 1/8" h. ............................................................... **193**

**Tankard,** cov., cylindrical ringed body w/a wide flaring ringed foot, cupped rim w/spout, flat hinged cover w/forked thumbrest, strap handle, top dated "1605," stamped "Zanon...Antoine," Switzerland, 8 1/4" h. (ILLUS. top next page) .......................................................... **748**

*Early Swiss Pewter Tankard*

*Rare American Pewter Tankard*

**Tankard,** cov., slightly tapering body w/banded base & rim, hinged domed cover w/molded thumbrest & overhanging rim, case S-scroll handle, Peter Young, Albany, New York, ca. 1795, 4 3/4" d., 7" h. (ILLUS.) ........................... **16,100**

**Tankard,** cov., slightly tapering cylindrical body w/flaring foot & lower body ring, stepped & domed hinged cover wthumbpiece, cast C-scroll handle, faint interior touch w/"WC," possibly William Charlesley, England, 7" h. ....................................... **550**

**Teapot,** cov., individual-size, footed small bulbous body tapering to a tall waisted neck w/pointed cover w/button finial, long swan's-neck spout & wooden C-scroll handle, mark of Atkin Brothers, Sheffield, England, 19th c., 6 1/4" h. ............ **138**

**Teapot,** cov., low tapering foot below the squatty bulbous body tapering to a flared neck w/hinged domed cover, swan's-neck spout & angled scrolled handle, touch mark of George Richardson, Cranston, Rhode Island, 1830-45, 7 1/4" h. ......... **248**

**Teapot,** cov., footed spherical body w/a flaring neck & hinged domed cover, swan's-neck spout, metal C-scroll handle w/worn black paint, George Richardson, Cranston, Rhode Island, 1830-45, 7 1/2" h. (wear, dent in handle) ................... **193**

**Teapot,** cov., cylindrical w/flared base & rim, hinged domed cover w/button finial, swan's-neck spout & ornate S-scroll handle in black, touch mark of Morey & Ober, Boston, Massachusetts, 1852-55, 8" h. ............................................................. **303**

**Teapot,** cov., pedestal base below squatty rounded central body flanked by flattened bands below the tall waisted neck & pointed domed cover, simple swan's-neck spout & ornate C-scroll handle in black, marked "Hall, Boardman & Co. - Best Britannia Metal," Philadelphia, 1846-48, 8 1/8" h. ........................................ **248**

**Teapot,** cov., tall footed inverted pear-shaped baluster-form w/flaring rim & inset hinged cover w/blossom finial, swan's neck spout & angled C-scroll handle, Roswell Gleason, Dorchester, Massachusetts, 1822-71, 10 1/2" h. (ILLUS. front right w/mug) ........................... **220**

**Teapot,** cov., flared foot below a bulbous lower body w/a stepped band below the very tall waisted neck w/cupped & flared rim, stepped & domed hinged cover w/button finial, swan's-neck spout & ornate C-scroll handle, eagle touch probably of Luther Boardman, South Reading, Massachusetts, 1836-42, 10 3/4" h. ...................................... **468**

**Teapot,** cov., tall footed pear-shaped body w/hinged domed cover w/cast floral finial, ribbed swan's-neck spout & long C-scroll handle, attributed to Homan & Co., ca. 1850s, 11" h. .................................. **110**

**Teapot,** cov., tall baluster-form body w/hinged domed cover w/finial, swan's-neck spout & ornate C-scroll handle, unmarked American, ca. 1850, 11 3/4" h. (minor repairs, finial probably replaced) ..................................................... **193**

**Tumblers,** footed cylindrical form w/slightly flared rim & a thin raised band around the upper half, maker's mark "W.R. Loftus - 146 Oxford St.," pub name "The Cricketeers," England, 1/2 pt., set of 6 ......... **523**

# SHEFFIELD PLATE

*Early Sheffield Plate Hot Water Urn*

**Cup,** two-handled, the tall cylindrical body w/a rounded bottom & slightly flared rim, decorated w/a chased & engraved armorial within a large cartouche & partially fluted base, hollow C-form handles, low domed foot, weighted, early 19th c., 6 3/4" h. (solder repairs) .............................. 345

**Dish-cross,** a deep round fuel well at the center of four flat sliding cross arms each fitted at the top w/a scrolled & shell-tipped dish support & raised on a matching foot, early 19th c., some wear, 12 1/2" l. ........................................................ 517

**Hot water urn,** cov., the large ovoid body decorated w/wide sawtooth reeded bands around the top & bottom, tapering to a gadrooned neck back & tapering domed cover w/figural pineapple finial, outscrolled loop shoulder handles & shaped spigot w/a leaf-capped turned wood handle, raised on a gadroon banded & reeded tall pedestal w/a shaped square base w/a pierced zigzag design apron & raised on four scroll legs w/shell feet, the body w/a large engraved central monogram, interior fitted w/a liner, few splits, some wear, late 18th - early 19th c., overall 19 1/2" h. (ILLUS.)...................................................... 1,380

**Tea urn,** cov., shaped ovoid form, mounted w/scroll handles & a reeded spigot, the domed cover w/an orb-form finial, early 19th c., 21 1/2" h. ...................................... 1,495

*Sheffield Classical Style Tea Urn*

**Tea urn,** cov., wide classical urn-form w/a tapering curved shoulder supporting the domed cover w/urn finial, lion mask & ring shoulder handles, engraved band of leafy scrolls around the shoulder, a shaped spigot near the bottom of the body above the tapering pedestal on a square plinth w/ball feet, early 19th c. (ILLUS.)...................................................... 1,400

**Wine coolers,** campana-form, a knopped stem supporting the urn-form body w/foliate-capped handles & rim, fitted w/a liner & collar, engraved w/a crest, early 19th c., 12" h., pr. .............................. 2,530

# SILVER

## AMERICAN (STERLING & COIN)

**Bank,** figural, a model of smiling egg-shaped Humpty Dumpty seated atop a rectangular high brick wall-form base w/a coin slot on top, 3 3/4" h. ...................... 287

**Basket,** a wide shallow round bowl w/reeded rim raised on a wide low round flaring base, swing bail handle, the interior acid-etched w/festoons & foliate sprays on a trelliswork ground, Tiffany & Co., New York, early 20th c., 9" d. .............. 632

**Basket,** deep flaring sides w/two sides turned up & joined by a swing bail reeded handle, the sides pierced overall w/scrolls, the shaped rim w/a border, engraved w/a monogram, Black, Starr & Frost, ca. 1900, 13 7/8" l. .......................... 1,380

**Beaker,** coin, cylindrical w/top & base molded rims, engraved, Anthony Rasch, Philadelphia, 1807, 3" d., 3" h. (minor dents) ............................................................. 489

**Bowl,** a rounded eight-lobed bowl w/a wide upward flaring eight-scalloped rim pierced w/a decorative border band & engraved designs, anniversary presentation dated "1896-1921," Towle Silversmiths, Newburyport, Massachusetts, 13" d., 3" h. .............................................. 220

**Bowl,** ovoid w/reticulated sides, on four scroll & flowerhead feet, the body w/guilloche & scroll piercing, the shaped edge w/applied shells, scrolls & husk drops, scroll handles, monogrammed, Black, Starr & Frost, New York, late 19th c., 12 3/4" l., 5" h. .......................................... 1,725

**Bowl,** small dished round center w/widely flanged & gently upturned rim, hand-hammered w/lightly chased & enameled inside w/a band of turquoise & white grapevine & a matching central patera, by Mary C. Knight, Boston, Massachusetts, 1906, 4 1/2" d. ................................ 4,025

**Bowl,** shaped border pierced w/shells & scrolls, the rim applied w/scrolls, the base engraved w/a monogram & dated 1905, on four scroll feet, gilt interior, Gorham Mfg. Co., Providence, Rhode Island, 13" l.................................................. 862

**Centerpiece,** Art Nouveau style, a fluted hexagonal form resting on the wide everted rim pierced & engraved w/flowers & scrolls, the rim applied w/cast whiplash scrolls, marked by Mauser Mfg. Co., New York City, ca. 1900, 16" d......... 2,587

**Cigar box,** cov., low rectangular form w/ cedar lining & humidor fitting, the cover w/applied monogram "FHR," marked on the base by the Kalo Shop, Chicago, Illinois, early 20th c., 13 1/4" l. ...................... 1,725

**Coffeepot,** cov., Art Nouveau style, of tall slender double-gourd form w/a wide squatty bulbous base raised on a short pedestal w/wide undulating foot, a small domed cap, long slender vine-entwined swan's-neck spout, large scrolled openwork blossom & leaf handle, the body chased & applied w/irises on a ground lightly finished w/tendrils & matting, marked, Reed & Barton, Taunton, Massachusetts, ca. 1905, 11 3/8" h. ........ **3,450**

*Dominick & Haff Sterling Compote*

**Compote,** La Salle patt., deep round fluted & flaring bowl w/a wide rolled rim decorated w/a pierced border band, knopped stem & paneled domed foot w/pierced border band, monogrammed, Dominick & Haff, ca. 1930, 10" d., 7 1/2" h. (ILLUS.) ...................... **400**

**Creamer,** coin, Classical fluted helmet-form, on a slender pedestal w/round base on a square foot, the sides engraved w/tasseled drapery below a band of running leaves & roundels, slender loop handles, foot engraved w/leaft-ips at the angles & a circle of husks on the raised center, the front of the body engraved w/a contemporary monogram "JR," the foot engraved "J.R. Sept 2, 1891 - J.R. Nov 3, 1798," the base weight later, Paul Revere, Jr., Boston, ca. 1798, unmarked, 7 1/8" h. ..... **17,250**

**Creamer,** coin, ovoid form w/an applied rim, molded base & strap handle, engraved on the bottom, Joseph Foster, 1760-1839, 4 3/4" h. (minor dents) .............. **489**

**Cup,** coin, short round foot supporting a tall bell-form body, slender S-scroll handle, engraved cartouch w/"John Laurens Babbidge from N.B. July 1, 1853," w/hallmarks on bottom & "Pure Silver Coin," 3 5/8" h. ...................... **220**

**Dish,** cov., coin, footed, bowl ornamented w/applied gadrooning at the rim & applied strawberry handles, a strawberry finial attached to lid, bowl engraved "CPJ," marked by Eoff & Shepherd, New York City, & Ball, Black & Co., New York, 6" d., 6 1/4" h. (very minor dent) ................. **431**

**Dish,** cov., coin., wide rounded base raised on four scroll & shell feet, topped w/a flattened scalloped rim supporting a high stepped domed cover w/twisted & pointed finial, the base decorated

w/repoussé flowers & scrolls w/a matching design on the cover centered by a scrolled cartouche w/engraved mottoed crest & initials, Ball, Tompkins & Black, New York, New York, 1839-50, 5 1/2" h. (ILLUS. below) .............................................. **489**

*Fine Coin Silver Covered Dish*

**Flask,** ovoid form w/broad shoulders, engraved w/a monogram, Black, Starr & Frost, early 20th c., 8" h. .............................. **345**

**Ladle,** Arts & Crafts style, hammered surface w/notched handle & entwined raised "KP" monogram, impressed "Sterling Kalo 8597" on handle, Kalo Shop, Chicago, early 20th c., 8 1/8" l. ................... **259**

**Loving cup,** scallop-molded round domed foot & short pedestal supporting a high ovoid lobed body w/a ruffled flattened rim, molded large scrolls around the lower body & under the rim, w/three angled stag horn handles mounted around the sides, Gorham Mfg. Co., Providence, Rhode Island, early 20th c., 7 3/4" h. ...................................................... **862**

**Pitcher,** coin, jug-form, stepped round foot w/low stem, ewer-form body chased & embossed w/florals & foliage, plain central roundel, serpentine handle topped by a flat leaf, Gorham Mfg. Co., Providence, Rhode Island, third quarter 19th c., 7 5/8" h. .................................................. **431**

**Pitcher,** Colonial Revival-style, domed foot, baluster-form body w/scroll handle topped w/a flat leaf, spout w/horizontal reeding, Chicago Silver Co., early 20th c., 8 3/4" h. ..................................................... **690**

**Pitcher,** octagonal baluster-form w/repousse & chased decoration, applied scroll handle, moldings, shell & scroll feet, a coat-of-arms engraved below spout, marked by William I. Teney, New York City, ca. 1840, 11 1/4" h. ................................................. **1,150**

**Pitcher,** squat baluster-form on stepped domed foot, stamped w/a wide band of flat leaves around the lower section, scroll handle, scrolled rim, monogrammed, Dominick & Haff, retailed by Bailey, Banks & Biddle, early 20th c., 8 1/4" h. ....................................................... **633**

**Pitcher,** water, Classical-style, plain wide ovoid body w/a wide short cylindrical neck & high arched spout all w/molded borders, a capped double-scrolled handle, engraved w/a Gothic initial "B," marked by Hayden & Gregg, Charleston, South Carolina, ca. 1840, 8 1/4" h. ........... **2,587**

**Pitcher,** water, baluster-form, chased overall w/scrolling blossoms on a stippled ground, centering an engraved monogram, A.E. Warner, Baltimore, 1874-89, 10" h. ........................................................ **2,587**

*Kalo Shop Sterling Silver Pitcher*

**Pitcher,** Arts & Crafts style, tapering ovoid body w/lobed ribs flanking a large central panel w/an applied monogram "B," short neck w/a wide arched spout & simple hollow C-form handle from the rim to the shoulder, stamped mark "Sterling - Hand Wrought - The Kalo Shop - Chicago - USA - 5 Pints," early 20th c., 8" d., 10 1/2" h. (ILLUS.).................................... **2,860**

**Pitcher,** water, urn-form, engraved w/a monogram, mounted w/a leaf-capped scroll handle, Tiffany & Co., New York, ca. 1900, 12" h. ............................... **1,610**

*Ornate Kirk & Son Water Pitcher*

**Pitcher,** water, wide ovoid form w/rounded shoulder to a wide short neck w/arched spout over a grotesque mask, high arched scrolled & beaded S-scroll handle, on a short pedestal w/domed foot, decorated overall w/repoussé & chased flowers, foliage & a band of scrolling

grapevine on a matte ground, marked by S. Kirk & Son, Baltimore, ca. 1885, 13 1/4" h. (ILLUS.).................................... **6,037**

**Porringer,** coin, round deep bowl w/bombé sides & domed center, pierced keyhole handle, marked three times w/maker's mark, Elias Pelletreau, Southampton, New York, ca. 1760, 5 3/4" d..................... **5,175**

**Porringer,** coin, round w/pierced scrolling tab rim handle, Zachariah Brigden, Boston, Massachusetts, 1734-87, partial mark, 5 1/2" d. (repair) ............................... **633**

**Porringer,** shallow round bowl w/a scroll-pierced pointed rim tab handle, monogrammed, handle marked by Samuel Casey, South Kingsdon, Rhode Island, 1724-73, 5" d. (repairs) ........................... **1,045**

**Punch ladle,** coin, deep round bowl, long slender tapering handle w/rounded handle tip engraved w/a monogram, Joseph & Nathaniel Richardson, Philadelphia, 1785-91, 14 1/4" l. (dents in bowl)............... **633**

**Salt dips,** figural, a deep rounded urn-form bowl w/a wide rolled rim raised upon the tails of three upright dolphins resting on a tripartite platform & three paw feet, S. Kirk & Son, 1830-46, 3 1/2" h., pr............. **1,035**

**Spoon,** Arts & Crafts style, elongated tapering hand-hammered handle w/rounded end, wide pointed bowl, marked "Sterling Kalo H201," ca. 1910, 13 3/4" l. ...................................................... **316**

**Stationery stand,** the rectangular base mounted w/four graduated shaped rectangular dividers w/beaded rims, the front & rear dividers chased w/a pair of putti holding a wreath, w/beaded rims, engraved w/a monogram, on four scroll feet, Shiebler Co., ca. 1900, 8 3/4" l......... **1,955**

**Sugar bowl,** cov., coin, squat baluster-form on a stepped round foot, wide band of engine-turning, one plain & one monogrammed cartouche, two serpentine handles, domed cover w/flower-form finial, Gorham Mfg. Co., Providence, Rhode Island, mid-19th c., 8" h. ................... **173**

**Tablespoons,** coin, oval pointed bowls & long down-turned handles monogrammed "TSG" & numbered 1-6, mark of Seril Dodge, Providence, Rhode Island, ca. 1759-1802, 8 3/4" l., set of 6 (small tear in one bowl, minor dents) .......... **690**

**Tankard,** cov., coin, tapered cylindrical form, the molded base band w/reeded top, stepped domed cover w/flaming urn finial, scroll thumbpiece, the handle applied w/a baluster & engraved w/"WEN" & dated 1774, convex oval shield terminal marked in center of base "R (pellet) FAIRCHILD" in a rectangle, Robert Fairchild, Connecticut, ca. 1770, 9 3/8" h. ................................................... **21,850**

**Tazze,** a shallow wide rounded dished top w/the shaped border applied w/shells & scrolls alternating w/paterae suspending bellflowers, the center engraved w/a monogram, raised on a slender tapering standard & pierced flaring round foot, Tiffany & Co., New York, early 20th c., 8 3/4" d., pr............................................... **1,840**

**Tazze,** a wide shallow bowl w/the wide scalloped rim pierced w/scrolls & rose branches, raised on a short pedestal base w/the rim & flaring round foot cast & pierced w/further scrolls & rose branches, Bailey, Banks & Biddle, Philadelphia, ca. 1890, marked, 11 1/2" d., pr............................................ **2,587**

*American Classical Tea Set*

**Tea & coffee service:** cov. coffeepot, cov. teapot, cov. sugar bowl, cream & waste bowl; coin, Classical style, each piece w/a gadrooned finial above a deep curved & decorated upright rim band over the rectangular lobed body on a pedestal above a stepped oval base on four ball feet, the die-stamped band on the shoulder of rural scenery, a single narrow band of anthemion leaves on the finial & at the upper & lower rims, William B. Heyer, New York City, first quarter 19th c., minor dents, coffeepot 11" h., the set (ILLUS.)........................................ **3,565**

**Tea & coffee service:** cov. teapot, cov. coffeepot, handled cov. sugar bowl, creamer & waste bowl; each of ovoid urn-form, angled handles, applied w/an oval monogrammed cartouche amid scrolling foliage, w/ovolo & stylized banded rims, Wallace Silversmiths, early 20th c., coffeepot 10 1/2" h., the set......... **1,955**

**Tea & coffee service:** cov. teapot, cov. coffeepot, kettle on lampstand, creamer, two-handled cov. sugar bowl, waste bowl & two-handled rectangular tray; Lord Robert patt., each piece of rectangular bombé form, the gadrooned rims w/foliate-capped shells at intervals, on four ball feet, engraved w/a monogram, International Silver Co., 20th c., tray 28" l., coffeepot 13 1/2" h., the set........... **5,462**

**Tea service:** cov. teapot, cov. hot water urn on stand, creamer, sugar bowl missing cover, waste bowl; all ovoid form on a domed stepped foot, beaded detailing, cover w/swan finial, the urn w/presentation inscription on one side, urn stand on four heavy paw feet w/scrolls & anthemion, monogrammed, Shreve, Stanwood & Co., 1860s, hot water urn 16" h., the set (burner missing) ........................... **2,185**

**Tea set:** cov. teapot, cov. sugar bowl & helmet-form creamer; Medallion patt., the tapering ovoid bodies each applied w/a profile medallion & anthemion engrav-

ing, sugar w/ring handles, teapot & creamer w/angled handles, covers w/helmet-form finials, monogrammed, Ball, Black & Co., third quarter 19th c., teapot 6" h., the set (ILLUS. below) ......... **2,185**

*Medallion Pattern Tea Set*

**Tea set:** cov. teapot, creamer, cov. sugar bowl & waste bowl; coin, footed tall pear-shaped bodies on the teapot, sugar & creamer, all pieces embossed & chased w/bands of scrolling ivy on a matted ground w/strapwork cartouches, beaded borders & urn finials, Albert Cole, New York, New York, ca. 1850-55, teapot 11 3/8" h., the set ..................................... **3,450**

**Tray,** oval, the border engraved w/classical revival band & floral swags, Frank M. Whiting & Co., early 20th c., 15 5/8 x 22"..... **863**

**Tray,** rectangular, the wide border & two handles applied w/urns of fruit alternating w/scrolling foliage, the center engraved w/a foliate monogram, Whiting Mfg. Company, ca. 1900, 33" l. ................. **5,175**

**Tray,** square w/rounded corners, the center engraved w/a border of rocaille decoration, the wide everted border applied w/foliage & scrolls, on three leaf-capped round feet, Tiffany & Co., New York, late 19th c., 11" w............................................. **1,725**

**Vase,** trumpet foot w/engraved band of lines & circles, tapered baluster-form body w/engraved laurel wreaths on each side, one w/a monogram, everted rim w/engraved band similar to foot, J.E. Caldwell & Co., late 19th - early 20th c., 15 3/4" h. ..................................................... **748**

*Gorham Martelé Presentation Vase*

**Vase,** Martelé, three-handled presentation-type, a low serpentine flared & footed base below the wide swelled cylindrical lower body below the wide bulbous tapering upper half w/a tricorner rolled rim, large C-scroll handles from the shoulder to the lower base, worked w/ornate scrolling vines & grape leaves & clusters, engraved presentation & dated "1921," Britannia Standard, Gorham Manufacturing Co., Providence, Rhode Island, 9" h. (ILLUS.) .................... **9,200**

**Vase,** two-handled, cylindrical, the shoulder flat-chased w/Persian style foliage on a stippled ground & suspended w/tassels & fringe, the narrow cylindrical neck mounted w/two arched & openwork foliate handles, Gorham Mfg. Co., Providence, Rhode Island, late 19th c., 9 1/2" h. ...................................... **1,725**

**Vase,** slightly flaring cylindrical form, chased & engraved at the shoulder w/shells & scrolling folilage, engraved w/a monogram, on a conforming circular foot, Tiffany & Co., New York, New York, early 20th c., 14" h. ................................. **1,840**

**Vegetable dish,** open, oval w/beaded border, Tiffany & Co., New York, ca. 1907-38, 10" l. ....................................... **201**

## ENGLISH & OTHERS

**Basket,** almond-shaped bowl w/a flanged upcurved rim w/reticulated band, on a recticulated footring, center arched swing handle, Peter & Ann Bateman, London, England, 1791-92, 14 3/4" l. (repair) ...................................... **3,190**

**Basket,** oval boat-shaped w/wide flanged rim w/gadrooned rim & cast shells at ends, raised on a low oblong platform on ball feet, central swing handle, untraced maker, New Castle, England, 1812-13, 12 3/4" l. ....................................... **1,100**

**Basket,** oval w/deep rounded flaring delicately reticulated sides raised on an upright oval reticulated ring foot, pierced central swing handle, engraved coat-of-arms in bottom, Edward Aldridge (?), London, England, 1764-65, 15 1/2" l. ........ **4,180**

**Basket,** oval w/high lattice-pierced & galleried sides, pierced swing strap handle, Turin, Italy, 18th c., 7" l. ............................ **1,150**

**Basket,** square form w/each corner pierced & chased w/festoons & urns, the round center chased w/cherubs in a landscape, w/a foliate garland around the rim, Germany, ca. 1900, 14 1/2" l. ............... **805**

**Bowl,** wide rounded body raised on a flared & pierced footring, the exterior w/a raised chrysanthemum decoration, scalloped rim w/molded edge, Chinese Export, Sing Fat maker, Canton, China, early 20th c., 6" d., 3" h. ............................... **345**

**Box,** cov., wide bulbous ovoid body raised on low scroll-pierced feet, fitted w/a low domed cover, overall Rococo repoussé & cast designs including an engraved coat-of-arms & a Chinese man, John Langford & John Sebille, London, England, 1764-65, 5 1/4" h. ....................... **2,255**

**Caster,** footed bulbous inverted pear-shaped lower body below a cylindrical neck fittted w/a tall domed & decoratively

pierced cap, the body engraved w/a griffin, Samuel Wood, London, 1745-56, 7 3/4" h. (dents) ........................................... **770**

**Caster,** footed squatty bulbous inverted pear-shaped body w/a repoussé gadrooned design below a tapering cylindrical ringed neck engraved w/a "G," a fitted high domed ornately pierced cap w/a pointed finial, William Grundy, London, England, 1749-50, 9" h. (repair) .. **1,045**

**Center bowl,** round w/lobed lower half, raised on a lobed round base, James Deakins & Sons, Sheffield, England, 1895-96, 10" d. ........................................... **518**

**Centerpiece bowl,** oval, the deep oval base applied w/scrolling vines & clusters below a lobed band, the deep bowl w/a flared rim & four pendent rings w/applied clusters around the rim, Georg Jensen Silversmithy, Copenhagen, Denmark, 1933-44, marked & numbered "296A," 14 3/8" l. .................................................. **17,250**

*Edwardian English Coffee Server*

**Coffee server,** cov., plain tapering cylindrical body w/closed rim spout, the cover w/a turned ivory finial, ivory C-form handle, maker's mark "SG," London, England, 1910-11, some dents, 8" h. (ILLUS.) ....................................... **863**

*Early English Siver Coffee Urn*

**Coffee urn,** cov., the tall urn-form ribbed body w/a wide rim band w/a ribbed swag band around a wreath-form spigot hole, animal mask & ring side handles, tapering leaf-engraved shoulder to a flat rim fitted w/a domed leaf- and berry-engraved cover w/engraved pointed finial, raised on a waisted pedestal w/a gadroon band at the bottom & raised on a square plinth w/bun feet, London, England hallmarks, 1804-05 (ILLUS.) ...... **3,025**

**Coffeepot,** cov., low wide ringed foot on the tall tapering cylindrical body w/a hinged domed cover & turned pointed finial, scroll-trimmed swan's-neck spout, S-scroll wooden handle, engraved amorial design w/a dog & "Perseverance," maker's mark incomplete, London, England, 1744-45, 9 1/2" h......................... **2,640**

**Coffeepot,** cov., presentation-type, pear-shaped body on four scroll & shell feet, the body chased & embossed w/flat leaves around the lower portion & the serpentine spout, reeded & leaf handle w/ivory heat stops, the cover w/a flower-form finial, engraved inscription dated 1853, Chinese Export, by Khecheong, 10 3/4" h. .................................................... **3,105**

**Coffeepot,** cov., tall pyriform body cast w/leafy scrolls continuing to a scrolled spout & wooden handle, w/a domed cover, raised on a circular foot, George III period, Francis Crump, London, England, 1769-70, 11 3/4" h...................... **1,093**

*Ornate German Glass-lined Compote*

**Compotes,** the raised oval flat-topped base stamped w/a band of scrolls & shells supporting four legs composed of putto herm flanked by husk swags supporting the deep rounded reticulated bowl w/a design of winged putti, scrolls, swags & foliate baskets, a monogrammed cartouche on two sides, clear glass liner, Germany, .800 fine, late 19th c., 7 3/8" l., 6" h., pr. (ILLUS. of one) ........ **1,840**

**Creamer,** bulbous base tapering to flared scalloped rim w/long pointed spout, raised on three hoof feet, ornate double C-scroll handle, the body w/Rococo repoussé floral decoration, John Harvey, London, England, 1750-51, 3 7/8" h............. **385**

**Dish cross,** adjustable w/shell-form tips on ends of cross-bars & raised on shell-form feet, a round burner in the center, William Plummer, London, England, 1767-68, 10 3/4" l. .................................... **2,200**

**Ewer,** Renaissance-Style, the snail-form body w/flared spout & scrolled handle, raised on a repoussé oval foot, Austria, late 19th c., 11 1/2" h. ............................ **1,610**

**Fish server,** long flat blade curved & pointed along one side, pierced herringbone design, w/a Fiddle Thread & Shell patt. handle, Paul Storr, London, England, 1820-21, 11 3/4" l.......................... **825**

**Fish server,** pointed oval silver blade w/scrolled edges & pierced interior surface, tapering rounded straight green horn handle, back engraved "Amicus - 1794," Samuel Godbehere, London, England, 1793-94, 11 3/8" l. (crack in horn handle) ................................................ **303**

**Gravy boat,** deep boat-shaped bowl w/forked loop side handles w/grape cluster terminals, raised on a ribbed pedestal on attached oval undertray, Georg Jensen Silversmithy, Copenhagen, Denmark, Grape patt., No. 14, ca. 1930-32, 6 3/4" l., 4 1/2" h.................................... **3,737**

*George III Period Hot Water Kettle*

**Hot water kettle,** cov., large bulbous ovoid body surmounted by a tall spire-form cover w/swelled top knop below a flame finial, looped shoulder handles w/large leaf terminals, a leaf-scrolled spigot w/arched T-form ivory handle, a waisted pedestal raised on a square w/a gadrooned border band above a pierced latticework apron & raised on four claw-and-ball feet, George III period, England, 18th c., overall 21" h. (ILLUS.) .................. **2,300**

**Hot water kettle on lampstand,** the kettle w/an inverted pyriform body engraved w/scrolling floral leafage, continuing to a raffia-covered swing handle, raised on conforming stand w/leafage-cast cabriole legs w/aprons of openwork flowers &

centering a fixed lamp, ending in shell feet, George II period, William Cripps, London, England, 1748-49, overall 14 1/4" h., 2 pcs. ........................................ **1,610**

**Hot water pitcher,** cov., footed tall slender baluster-form body w/a domed hinged cover w/urn finial, pointed rim spout w/beaded decoration down the front, the lower half of the body w/repoussé swirled floral bands alternating w/ribbed bands, C-scroll wooden handle, Fuller White, London, England, 1747-48, 7 7/8" h. ...................................................... **1,650**

*Elaborate English Kettle on Stand*

**Kettle on stand,** wide tapering ovoid body w/a high arched scroll handle & swan's-neck spout, decorated overall w/ornate repoussé scrolls & floral clusters surrounding a central cartouche, raised on a domed pierced scrolling base w/high scrolled legs ending in scrolled feet all centering a fuel burner, melon-form finial on cover, Edward, John & William Barnard, London, England, 1838-39, overall 16 1/4" h., 2 pcs. (ILLUS.) .................... **2,415**

**Mug,** footed gently flaring cylindrical body w/heavy ornate cast C-scroll handle, body w/chased floral design w/a monogram, E.J. & E.W. Barnard, London, England, 1839-40, 3 5/8" h. .......................... **468**

**Mug,** footed ovoid body tapering gently to a flat rim, ornate double C-scroll handle, the body decorated w/Rococo repoussé florals & a monogram, John Swift, London, England, 1754-55, 4 3/4" h. (minor dents & repair) .............................................. **660**

**Mug,** footed slightly ovoid body tapering to a flared rim, ornate double C-scroll handle, the body w/Rococo floral repoussé decoration, John Langlands, New Castle, England, 1759-60, 4" h. (restorations) ......................................................... **358**

**Neff (figural ship-form table centerpiece),** realistically modeled as an early galleon under full sail w/sailors manning cannons & climbing rope, the removable deck opening to a plain hull, on four openwork wheels, Holland, w/English import marks for London, 1928, repairs, few losses, 14 1/2" h. (ILLUS. below) ....... **2,875**

*Elaborate Dutch Neff*

**Pitcher,** cov., footed baluster-form body on a domed foot w/vertical reeding, the body w/repoussé design of foliage, birds & putti around the lower section, the neck w/a band of fluting, short rim spout w/a putto, beaded serpentine handle, the domed cover w/vertical reeding, repoussé & vegetal finial, engraved name on base, .833 fine, Holland, late 19th c., 5 1/2" h. ......................................... **259**

*Ornate Indian Silver Punch Bowl*

**Punch bowl,** deep wide bowl on a stepped & domed foot, the body of the bowl w/a detailed continuous East Indian tiger hunting scene w/a band of flat leaves around the bottom, the base w/another band w/hunting scenes above a narrow leafy band, w/silver removable liner, India, late 19th - early 20th c., 12 5/8" d., 10 1/2" h. (ILLUS.) ..................................... **4,025**

**Punch bowl,** the sides chased w/a wide band of shells alternating w/acanthus above a fluted lower body, on a conforming foot, Barnard, London, England, 1840, 10 1/4" d. ........................................ **1,610**

**Punch ladle,** deep round shell-form body, long tapering handle w/rounded end engraved w/a lion's head, Thomas Chawner, London, England, 1772-73, 13 1/2" l. ......................................... **550**

**Salver,** footed, round w/scrolled rim w/shells, cast feet, the top finely engraved in the center w/a coat-of-arms for "Edison," John Hutson, London, England, 1787-88, 18 1/2" d..................... **2,420**

**Sauce pan,** slightly tapering cylindrical bowl on a ringed slightly flared foot, wide rolled rim, cylindrical angled side handle w/a turned wood grip, William Fleming, London, England, 1716-17, bowl 3 5/8" d., handle 4 1/4" l. ........................... **1,155**

**Sauceboat,** deep oblong boat-form w/high arched spout, arched C-scroll handle, raised on three small double-scroll legs, beaded rim, Daniel Smith & Robert Sharp, London, England, 1770-71, 8 1/2" l. (minor dents) .................................. **880**

**Stuffing spoon,** oblong bowl & long tapering handle w/rounded end w/a bright-cut oval, Hester Bateman, London, England, 1788-89, 12 3/8" l. ........................................ **468**

**Sugar bowl,** cov., low-footed wide rounded body w/cylindrical sides & low domed cover, Rococo repoussé floral decoration, John Gibbons, London, England, 1722-23, 4" d., 3" h. .................................... **715**

**Sugar shaker,** spreading cylindrical form, London, England, ca. 1910, 5 1/2" h. ........... **201**

**Sweetmeat dishes,** on a shaped rectangular slab base cast as water, the shell-form dish drawn by sea creatures, the reins held by two putti flanking a central standing putto on the stern poised as Neptune holding a trident-form fork, Odiot, Paris, late 19th - early 20th c., 5 1/2" l., 5" h., pr..................................... **2,070**

**Tablespoon,** oblong pointed bowl, long Fiddle Thread w/Shell patt. handle, Edinburgh, Scotland, 1829-30, 12" l ................... **138**

**Tankard,** cov., ringed tapering cylindrical body w/a hinged flattened domed cover w/scrolled thumbrest, tapering S-scroll handle, Anthony Nelme, London, England, 1705-06, 8 1/2" h. (repairs) ........ **4,840**

**Tankard,** cov., stepped foot below the tapering cylindrical body w/bulbous lower section, engraved w/a central plain roundel flanked by geometrics & foliage sprays w/perching birds, geometric banding above & below, shaped ear handle, cover w/thumbpiece & flattened urn finial, Russia, maker's mark "A.C.," 1894, 7 7/8" h. .............................................. **863**

**Taper sticks,** a squared domed & stepped foot supporting a slender double-knop standard below the slender ring-turned cylindrical candle socket, James Gould, London, England, 1723-24, 4 1/2" h., pr. .. **3,960**

**Tea caddy,** cov., oval cylindrical form w/low domed cover w/turned wood finial, decorated w/bright-cut florals w/swags & a lion head in a crown, possibly Samuel

Woods, London, England, 1784-85, 5 1/4" h...................................................... **1,815**

**Teapot,** cov., a bulbous ovoid body raised on a slender short pedestal & round foot, a short rolled neck w/a hinged domed cover w/pointed finial, the body ornately embossed w/flowers, fruits & rococo foliage framing a central oval reserve w/the monogram "C," scroll-decorated swan's-neck spout & decorative angled handle, mark of Walker and Hall, Sheffield, England, 1889-90, 9 1/4" h....................... **1,045**

**Teapot,** cov., footed bulbous inverted pear-shaped body w/hinged dome cover w/berry finial, swan's-neck spout w/figural hawk head tip, arched & scrolling handle, the body w/Rococo repoussé scroll decoration, Samuel Courtauld, London, England, 1759-60, 6 3/8" h. (repair).................................................... **3,410**

**Teapot,** cov., wide squatty bulbous body raised on four scrolled tab feet, the shoulder tapering to a flattened flanged neck w/hinged stepped, domed cover w/blossom finial, tapering swan's-neck spout, slender C-scroll handle, overall cast & repoussé floral decoration, maker's mark "GH," London, England, 1787-88, 6 3/8" h................................... **1,045**

**Toast rack,** small oblong dished tray on four small peg feet, arched toast loops around the top w/a central loop-topped handle, made to disassemble, unknown maker "B.D.," London, England, 1782-83, 5 3/4" l. .............................................. **1,045**

**Tray,** oval, cast feet & open handles, the center engraved w/flowers & foliage w/a coat-of-arms, George Smith & Thomas Hayter, London, England, 1800-01, 25" l. ......................................................... **4,510**

*Fine Georgian Silver Tray*

**Tray,** wide oblong form w/gadrooned border w/large cast shell devices at outer corners & smaller shells at the center sides, arched scroll- and shell-cast end handles, engraved in the center w/a large armorial crest, George III period, Thomas Robins, London, England, 1814-15, 30" l. (ILLUS.)............................ **9,200**

**Vegetable dish,** cov., elongated octagonal form w/molded rim & conforming flat-topped domed cover w/removable reeded scroll loop center handle, engraved on the side of the cover w/an armorial, George IV period, Robert Garrard, London, England, 1822-23, 12 1/2" l. .................................... **2,875**

**Vegetable dish, cover & lampstand,** the circular dish w/straight gadrooned rim & hinged bail handles on a lampstand w/three fluted cabriole legs ending in acanthus scrolls, mark of William Stroud, London, England, 1813, 11 3/4" h. ............ **2,185**

**Wash pitcher & bowl,** tapering cylindrical tankard pitcher w/high arched spout & C-form hollow handle, footed wide rounded bowl w/flared rim, both w/overall hand-hammered finish, G. Keller, Paris, France, ca. 1890, bowl 10" d., pitcher 13" h., pr. ....................................... **4,600**

# SILVER PLATE (HOLLOWWARE)

*English Silver Plate Candlesticks*

**Candlesticks,** squared scalloped wide foot below the tall ringed & baluster-turned standard & tall ringed & corseted socket w/a flattened rim, marked "Sheffield - E.P.N.S. - Made in England," early 20th c., 12 1/4" h., set of 4 (ILLUS. of part) ....... **1,375**

**Chafing dish, cover & stand,** the cartouche-form dish w/gadrooned borders, raised on a stand w/cabriole legs, George III-Style, England, early 20th c., 16" l., the set .............................................. **258**

**Meat dome,** oval high domed shape w/top loop handle, monogrammed "R," 18" l. ........ **172**

**Pitcher & bowl set,** Art Nouveau style, the baluster-form pitcher w/a tall neck & upright pointed spout, a looped high whiplash handle & spreading round foot, chased w/two female profile busts, tulips & whiplash designs, the bowl w/a wide flaring rim chased w/tulips & whiplash leaves, both impressed "Anezin Hnos & Cia," Europe, early 20th c., bowl 18" d., pitcher 18 1/2" h. ....................................... **287**

**Sweatmeat basket,** flaring reticulated body w/long narrow ovals decorated w/hat-form bosses w/ribbon & basket trim, twisted rope bands around the base & reeded rim, arched swing bail handle, cobalt blue glass liner, probably Europe, late 19th - early 20th c., resilvered, 6 1/2" d., 7 1/8" h. (ILLUS. top next column) ....................................... **175**

*Decorative Basket with Glass Liner*

*American Silver Plate Syrup Pitcher*

**Syrup pitcher,** cov., footed bulbous ovoid body decorated w/large repoussé blossoms & leaves & tapering to a plain flared neck w/ruffled rim & hinged flower-embossed cover w/knob finial, angled handle, Wilcox Silver Plating Co., late 19th c., 4" d., 4 1/2" h. (ILLUS.) ..................... **95**

**Tea & coffee service:** cov. teapot, cov. coffeepot, creamer, cov. sugar bowl & tray; Art Deco style, each of faceted globular form w/angular handles, the tray w/ten curved sides & rounded handles, designed by Maurice Dufrene, Christofle, France, ca. 1925, tray 10" l., the set ...................................................... **2,300**

**Tea set:** cov. teapot, cov. sugar bowl, creamer & spooner; each w/a tall bulbous body tapering to a flared & cupped rim, each raised on four tall outswept animal leg feet, ornate angular handles, the body w/a band of decorative engraving, pointed cover w/handled urn-form finials, marked "Quadruple Plate - Wilcox Silver Co.," ca. 1875-80, teapot 12" h., the set (plating worn) ....................... **138**

**Tray,** oval, the wide dished border band cast w/a continuous scene of village people & landscapes, the oval interior engraved w/a rusticated design, International Silver Co., late 19th c., 13" l. .............. **230**

**Tray,** rectangular, mirrored interior, chamfered corners & a pierced gallery, on four
pierced scroll feet, early 20th c., 24" l. ......... **977**

**Vase,** Art Nouveau style, a bottle-form vessel w/an ornately molded naturalistic
decoration including waves in the background w/molded carp & aquatic flowers
& two full-figure mermaids wrapped
around the neck & base, a lobster, snail
& more flowers, France, ca. 1900, 23" h.
(some losses).......................................... **1,725**

## STERLING SILVER (FLATWARE)

### ACORN (Georg Jensen)

| | |
|---|---:|
| **Baby spoon,** curved handle............................ | 108 |
| **Berry spoon,** pierced..................................... | 710 |
| **Bonbon spoon** ................................................. | 95 |
| **Bouillon spoon** ............................................... | 65 |
| **Butter fork** ...................................................... | 50 |
| **Butter spreader** ............................................. | 75 |
| **Cake fork** ........................................................ | 65 |
| **Cake knife** ...................................................... | 95 |
| **Canape server,** short..................................... | 238 |
| **Cheese knife** .................................................. | 100 |
| **Cheese plane** .................................................. | 175 |
| **Cheese scoop** ................................................. | 225 |
| **Cheese server** ................................................ | 58 |
| **Cheese slicer** ................................................. | 68 |
| **Cheese snag** ................................................... | 55 |
| **Cherry fork** ..................................................... | 50 |
| **Citrus spoon** .................................................. | 83 |
| **Cocktail fork** .................................................. | 60 |
| **Cocktail picks,** set of 6.................................. | 240 |
| **Coffee spoon** .................................................. | 29 |
| **Cold meat fork,** 6 5/8" ................................... | 100 |
| **Cream ladle,** 5 1/2" l. ..................................... | 130 |
| **Cream soup spoon** ......................................... | 85 |
| **Demitasse spoon** ........................................... | 36 |
| **Dessert spoon** ................................................ | 85 |
| **Dinner fork,** 7 3/4" ......................................... | 103 |
| **Dinner knife,** 9 7/8" ........................................ | 112 |

*Acorn Dinner Service*

**Dinner service:** 8 each dinner knives, dinner forks, luncheon knives, 7 each salad
forks & dessert spoons, 4 butter spread-
ers, 5 coffee spoons, 10 teaspoons, 2-
pc. salad set, 1 serving spoon & 1
cheese plane, 61 pcs. (ILLUS. of part)...... **4,600**

| | |
|---|---:|
| **Fish knife** ........................................................ | 115 |
| **Fish server,** pierced, 10 1/2"........................... | 750 |
| **Fish serving fork** ............................................ | 90 |
| **Food pusher** ................................................... | 100 |
| **Fruit knife** (dinky)........................................... | 55 |
| **Fruit spoon** ..................................................... | 70 |
| **Gravy ladle** ..................................................... | 275 |
| **Hors d'oeuvre fork,** 3 3/4" l............................ | 40 |
| **Ice cream fork** ................................................ | 93 |
| **Iced teaspoon** ................................................. | 88 |
| **Lemon fork** ...................................................... | 75 |
| **Luncheon fork,** 6 5/8"...................................... | 40 |
| **Luncheon knife** ............................................... | 53 |
| **Meat fork,** hollow handle, 2-tine..................... | 63 |
| **Mixing spoon** .................................................. | 250 |
| **Oyster fork** ...................................................... | 85 |
| **Pastry fork** ...................................................... | 65 |
| **Pickle fork** ...................................................... | 96 |
| **Pie server** ....................................................... | 292 |
| **Pie server,** engraved blade............................ | 550 |
| **Salad fork,** 4-tine ............................................ | 103 |
| **Salad serving set** ........................................... | 567 |
| **Salad set,** hollow-handle, 8" l........................ | 145 |
| **Salad spoon,** 8 7/8" ........................................ | 325 |
| **Salt spoon,** individual size ............................. | 35 |
| **Sardine fork** .................................................... | 125 |
| **Sauce ladle** ..................................................... | 213 |
| **Seafood fork** ................................................... | 55 |
| **Serving fork** .................................................... | 275 |
| **Serving spoon** ................................................ | 125 |
| **Soup spoon,** oval bowl .................................... | 85 |
| **Strawberry spoon,** pierced, 8 7/8" .................. | 496 |
| **Sugar spoon** ................................................... | 95 |
| **Sugar tongs** .................................................... | 125 |
| **Tablespoon,** 7 1/2" .......................................... | 130 |
| **Tea caddy spoon** ............................................ | 225 |
| **Teaspoon** ........................................................ | 70 |
| **Tomato server,** 6"............................................ | 323 |

### AMERICAN BEAUTY (George W. Shiebler)

| | |
|---|---:|
| **Asparagus tongs,** individual........................... | 428 |
| **Baked potato fork** .......................................... | 29 |
| **Berry spoon** .................................................... | 215 |
| **Bonbon spoon** ................................................. | 183 |
| **Bouillon spoon** ............................................... | 26 |
| **Butter spreader** ............................................. | 31 |
| **Cheese server,** large ...................................... | 150 |
| **Cocktail fork** .................................................. | 32 |
| **Cold meat fork** ............................................... | 88 |
| **Cream ladle** ..................................................... | 125 |
| **Demitasse spoon** ........................................... | 15 |
| **Dessert spoon** ................................................ | 50 |
| **Dinner fork** ..................................................... | 55 |
| **Ice cream fork** ................................................ | 45 |
| **Lettuce fork** .................................................... | 90 |
| **Luncheon fork** ................................................ | 30 |
| **Luncheon knife** ............................................... | 29 |
| **Meat fork** ........................................................ | 150 |
| **Salad fork** ....................................................... | 61 |
| **Salad set** ........................................................ | 400 |
| **Sardine fork** .................................................... | 68 |
| **Sauce ladle** ..................................................... | 73 |
| **Serving spoon** ................................................ | 49 |
| **Serving spoon,** pierced .................................. | 57 |
| **Sherbet spoon,** 5 3/8" ..................................... | 40 |
| **Soup spoon** ..................................................... | 40 |
| **Strawberry fork** .............................................. | 55 |
| **Sugar tongs** .................................................... | 95 |
| **Tablespoon** ..................................................... | 50 |
| **Teaspoon** ........................................................ | 25 |

Tomato server ............................................... 110
Youth fork ..................................................... 55

## CARNATION (R. Wallace & Sons)
Baked potato serving fork ......................... 29
Berry spoon, 7 1/4" ................................... 118
Butter serving knife, flat handle ...................... 40
Luncheon fork .............................................. 15
Luncheon knife 11 1/2" l. .............................. 25
Pie/cake server ............................................ 26
Salad fork ..................................................... 43
Strawberry fork ............................................ 28
Tongs ............................................................ 40

## EMPIRE (Whiting Mfg. Co.)
Beef fork ...................................................... 38
Berry spoon ................................................ 110
Cracker scoop ............................................ 225
Cream ladle .................................................. 75
Dinner knife ................................................. 42
Gravy ladle ................................................... 80
Ice spoon ................................................... 225
Lettuce fork .................................................. 95
Pickle fork .................................................... 28
Pie server .................................................... 28
Preserve spoon .......................................... 143
Sardine tongs .............................................. 75
Seafood fork ................................................ 13
Sugar shell ................................................... 35
Sugar sifter .................................................. 75
Tablespoon .................................................. 48
Teaspoon ..................................................... 14

## HERALDIC (Whiting Mfg. Co.)
Berry spoon ................................................ 245
Bonbon server, scalloped edge ...................... 55
Butter, individual .......................................... 24
Butter serving knife, master .......................... 41
Cake knife .................................................... 47
Cheese scoop ............................................. 175
Cold meat fork ............................................ 135
Crumber, 12 3/4" ......................................... 250
Demitasse spoon .......................................... 18
Fish serving set, 2 pcs. .............................. 195
Gravy ladle ................................................. 135
Luncheon knife ............................................ 55
Mustard ladle ............................................... 80
Pickle fork, 2-tine ......................................... 12
Pie server .................................................. 245
Punch ladle ................................................ 350
Salad serving set, 12 1/4" l. ...................... 458
Sardine tongs ............................................. 295
Sauce ladle ................................................ 375
Soup spoon, oval bowl .................................. 34
Sugar spoon ................................................. 43
Tablespoon .................................................. 62
Tablespoon, pierced bowl ............................. 71

## KINGS (Dominick & Haff)
Berry spoon ................................................ 110
Bouillon ladle .............................................. 225
Bouillon spoon ............................................. 25
Breakfast knife, 8 1/4" l. .............................. 55
Butter knife, master ...................................... 59
Butter serving knife ...................................... 70
Butter spreader, flat handle .......................... 20
Cherry fork .................................................... 35
Citrus spoon ............................................... 150
Cocktail fork ................................................. 28
Cream soup spoon ........................................ 27

Demitasse spoon ........................................... 18
Dessert spoon .............................................. 45
Dinner fork ................................................... 60
Dinner knife ................................................. 48
Egg spoon .................................................... 30
Escargot fork ................................................ 15
Fish fork ....................................................... 45
Fish knife ..................................................... 53
Fruit knife .................................................... 43
Fruit spoon ................................................... 40
Grapefruit spoon .......................................... 45
Gravy ladle ................................................. 100
Gumbo spoon ............................................... 42
Luncheon fork .............................................. 42
Luncheon knife ............................................ 38
Oyster ladle ............................................... 225
Platter spoon .............................................. 225
Salad fork ..................................................... 42
Salad serving set ........................................ 205
Sugar tongs .................................................. 40
Tablespoon .................................................. 68
Tablespoon, pierced bowl ............................. 62
Teaspoon ..................................................... 19

## MARIE ANTOINETTE (Dominick & Haff)
Asparagus fork ........................................... 195
Berry spoon ................................................ 110
Butter spreader, flat handle .......................... 25
Cold meat fork, 7 1/4" l. ................................ 55
Cucumber server .......................................... 45
Dinner fork ................................................... 24
Fruit spoons, gold-washed bowl, ball top
   twist, set of 8 .......................................... 175
Gravy ladle ................................................... 50
Salad fork ..................................................... 24
Salad serving fork ...................................... 175
Sardine fork ................................................. 55
Soup ladle .................................................. 275
Steak carving set, 2 pcs. .............................. 39
Sugar spoon ................................................. 35

## POPPY (Gorham Mfg. Co.)
Beef fork ...................................................... 44
Beef fork, large ............................................ 95
Berry fork ..................................................... 44
Berry spoon .................................................. 93
Bouillon spoon ............................................. 33
Butter spreader ............................................ 16
Cake slice .................................................. 210
Carving set, steak ......................................... 50
Chipped beef server ...................................... 65
Citrus spoon ................................................ 30
Cocktail fork ................................................. 19
Coffee spoon ................................................ 10
Cold meat fork .............................................. 85
Cream ladle .................................................. 30
Cream soup spoon ........................................ 30
Demitasse spoon .......................................... 19
Dessert spoon .............................................. 24
Dinner fork ................................................... 31
Dinner knife ................................................. 38
Fish fork ....................................................... 48
Grapefruit spoon .......................................... 27
Gravy ladle ................................................... 20
Ice cream spoon ........................................... 33
Lettuce fork .................................................. 70
Luncheon fork .............................................. 26
Luncheon knife, blunt .................................... 25
Mustard ladle ............................................... 65
Nut spoon .................................................... 30

| | |
|---|---|
| Olive fork | 48 |
| Oyster fork | 120 |
| Pastry fork | 36 |
| Salad fork | 39 |
| Salad set | 175 |
| Serving fork | 42 |
| Soup spoon, oval bowl | 32 |
| Strawberry fork | 30 |
| Sugar spoon | 34 |
| Tablespoon | 58 |
| Teaspoon | 20 |

### WINSLOW (Samuel Kirk & Son)

| | |
|---|---|
| Cocktail fork | 16 |
| Cream soup spoon | 29 |
| Demitasse spoon | 12 |
| Gravy ladle | 41 |
| Iced tea spoon | 22 |
| Luncheon fork | 32 |
| Luncheon knife | 30 |
| Salad fork | 28 |
| Tablespoon | 52 |
| Teaspoon | 17 |

# TIN & TOLE

**Box w/hinged cover,** tole, cylindrical w/fitted flat cover w/center ring handle, original dark brownish black japanned ground decorated near the rim w/a white band w/colored blossoms above the dark ground w/further florals in red, white, yellow, green & black, first half 19th c. 7" d., 6 1/2" h. .......................... **743**

**Bread tray,** tole, rectangular w/widely flaring sides & rounded ends, the interior w/original dark brown japanning w/floral decoration at the ends in red, yellow & green, 19th c., 8 x 14 1/4" (wear, flaking)..... **440**

**Bread tray,** tole, red, green & yellow floral decoration w/yellow swag border & red edge on black ground, 19th c., 8 1/4 x 12 1/2" (minor paint loss).................. **345**

**Candle mold,** r twelve-tube, round flanged top w/an apparent compartment w/stuck tin lid, round flanged small base, 19th c., 13 3/4" h. ............................................... **1,100**

**Candle mold,** tin, twelve-tube, rectangular flanged top w/side strap handle, arched base support, 19th c., 11 1/2" h. .................. **303**

*Early Tin Candle Sconces*

**Candle sconces,** tin, the tall ribbed backplate w/rounded & crimped top w/hanging hole, half-round base compartment w/candle socket, minor corrosion, vestiges of black paint, 19th c., 3" w., 13 1/2" h., pr. (ILLUS.) .................................. **633**

*Early Tole Canister*

**Canister,** cov., tole, cylindrical w/hinged flat cover w/wire loop handle, red japanned ground, decorated around the top & cover w/red cherries & green leaves on a white band, yellow stylized leaves & swag borders, leaf decoration on top of cover, minor scratches, 19th c., 6 1/2" d., 6" h. (ILLUS.) ............................... **403**

**Canister,** tole, cylindrical w/ring handle, decorated w/red cherries, green leaves on a white border, red flowers, yellow stylized leaves, starburst on the handle, black ground, 19th c., 8 1/2" d., 8 1/2" h. (minor paint loss)........................................ **288**

*Early Pierced Tin Cheese Sieve*

**Cheese sieve,** tin, deep cylindrical form w/a ring of holes around the top above three continuous bands of tiny holes around the body, vertical loop strap rim handles, raised on three ring feet, 4 1/2" d., 4 1/4" h. (ILLUS.) ......................... **110**

**Cheese strainer,** tin, heart-shaped w/a punched design, on three small legs, 19th c. ......................................................... **220**

**Coffeepot,** cov., tin, a flared foot below a flared cylindrical lower body & a tall tapering cylindrical upper body w/ringed bands up the sides, lower domed small cover w/replaced opalescent glass knob, long angled spout, large strap handle w/grip at shoulder, 19th c., 11" h. (ILLUS. top next page) ................................. **330**

*Tall Tin Coffeepot*

**Coffeepot,** cov., tin, a round disk foot below the lower flaring wide cyindrical body divided w/a medial band from the wide tapering upper half body, domed fitted cover w/pewter knob, wide integral spout & arched strap handle, 19th c., 9 1/2" h. ...................... **248**

**Coffeepot,** cov., tole, lighthouse-form, floral decoration w/bands of stylized leaves at the top & bottom, low domed cover w/brass finial, 19th c., 10" h. (minor paint loss)............................................... **748**

*Fine Tole Coffeepot & Deed Box*

**Coffeepot,** cov., tole, tall tapering cylindrical body w/flared foot, the domed cover w/a small finial, angled long spout, C-form handle w/hand grip, original black ground decorated w/yellow birds, red pomegranates & yellow stylized leaves, lid unattached, minor paint loss, repair to final, 19th c., 10 1/2" h. (ILLUS. left) ......... **1,093**

**Coffeepot,** cov., tole, tapering cylindrical form w/goose-neck spout, domed hinged cover & strap handle, red & yellow flowers & stylized leaves on a black ground, 19th c., 10 1/2" h. (paint loss)....................... **489**

**Colander,** tin, deep heart-shaped sides w/bands of pierced holes, raised on three small pointed tab feet, 19th c., 4 1/2" w. ...................................... **231**

**Deed box,** cov., tole, deep rectangular side w/hinged domed cover w/ring bail handle, old yellow ground w/green striping & polychrome bowl of front on the front, 6 x 9 1/2", 6 1/2" h. (wear, alligatoring) ..... **1,045**

*Early Tole Mug & Deed Box*

**Deed box,** cov., tole, deep rectangular side w/hinged flat cover w/ring bail handle, worn original brown japanning w/white band & stylized floral bands in red, green, black & yellow, w/hasp, good color, 19th c., 8 1/8" h. (ILLUS. right) .......... **605**

**Deed box,** cov., tole, deep rectangular sides w/hinged domed cover w/wire loop handle, old red japanned ground decorated w/red, yellow & green fuit & foliage & yellow stylized leaf borders, 19th c., minor scratches 5 1/8 x 9 1/2", 6 1/2" h. (ILLUS. right w/coffeepot) ........................ **5,463**

**Deed box,** cov., tole, rectangular w/domed, hinged top w/wire bail loop handle, original yellow painted ground, the front stenciled w/a bowl of fruit & foliage, green stripe around the lid, early 19th c., 9 1/2" l. (wear, front decoration very crazed) ......................................................... **495**

**Deed box,** cov., tole, rectangular w/hinged domed top w/brass bail handle, original brown japanning decorated w/swags, striping & other designs in red, blue, white & yellow, 12" l. (wear, some alligatoring) ......................................................... **880**

*Unusual Silver-gilt Tin Rooster*

**Model of a rooster,** tin w/silver gilt, ornate stylized bird w/scalloped comb & wattle, separate wing feathers & ornate arching tail feather, on slender legs perched on a carved wood rockwork base, Europe, probably 19th c., gilt wear, minor losses, 24 1/2" l., 29" h. (ILLUS.)........................... **1,035**

**Model of a top hat,** tin, 10th anniversary memento, complete w/narrow hat band, 19th c., 6 1/2" h. ..................................... **1,320**

**Mug,** tole, large cylindrical form w/wide strap handle, original stylized floral decoration in red, yellow & brown w/a very worn brown japanned ground, 19th c., 5 3/4" h. (ILLUS. right, top next page).......... **385**

*Early Tole Mug & Sugar Bowl*

**Mug,** tole, tall cylindrical form w/strap handle, original dark brown japanning w/a white rim band w/floral decoration in red, green & yellow, good color, 19th c., some wear, 4 1/2" h. (ILLUS. w/deed box) ............................................................. 660

**Spice box,** cov., tin, ectangular w/hinged top, the sides punched w/designs of long spearpoint leaves issuing from a small pot, ring handle on front of cover & raised on small ring feet, opening to four-part interior w/a center compartment for a grater, 8" l..................................... 110

**Sugar bowl,** cov., tole, flared foot below slightly flaring cylindrical body w/fitted low domed cover w/scrolled tab finial, original stylized floral decoration in red, yellow & brown on a very worn brown japanned ground, 19th c., 5 3/4" h. (ILLUS. left) .................................................. 385

**Tinder box,** cov., tin, low cylindrical form divided at the center, a small ring handle at the bottom half, a cylindrical candle socket centered on the flat cover, interior w/flint, steel & damper, 19th c., 4 1/2" h. (rush damage on damper).......................... 358

**Tinder box,** cov., tin, low cylindrical wide form w/ring handle on the base & the fitted flat cover centered by a cylindrical candle socket, 19th c., 3 1/4" h. (interior w/flint but no steel, damper missing) ............ 110

*Ornate European Tole Urn*

**Urns,** tole, Classical style, the tall body raised on a slender pedestal w/a flared round foot, fitted w/a tall slender pointed cover w/acorn finial, high wide arched loop side handles, decorated w/floral sprays & birds w/scalloped floral & repeating gilt leaf borders, weighted base, paint loss, one lower handle detached, probably France, 19th c., pr. (ILLUS. of one)............................................. 575

# MILITARIA & WARTIME MEMORABILIA

*Since the early 19th century, every war that America has fought has been commemorated with a variety of war-related memorabilia often in the form of propaganda items produced during the conflict or as memorial pieces made after the war ended. These materials are today quite collectible and increasingly important for the historic insights they provide. Most common are items dating from World War I and II.*

## CIVIL WAR

**Ambrotype,** ninth-plate, half-length portrait of a Confederate solider, seated wearing a battle shirt w/red trim, cased, 2 3/8 x 2 7/8" (small background spots) ..... **$385**

**Book,** "Regulations of the Army of Confederate States," by J.W. Randolph, Richmond, 1863, hardcover, penciled inscription "Arthur Huger, Dec, 1863 - Savannah" (minor stains) ........................... 550

*Iron Civil War Canon Tube*

**Canon tube,** cast iron, marked "C.A. & Co. Boston," 68" l. (ILLUS.) .......................... **15,680**

*Scarce Confederate Civil War Canteen*

**Canteen,** Confederate, flattened disk-form, cherry w/fine patina, iron staves & strap holders, one side carved "R.B: SL," the other "E.B. & FAP," turned spout w/carved plug, some age cracks in spout, 7 3/8" d., 2 3/8" h. (ILLUS.)............. **1,980**

**Drum,** cylindrical frame w/painted spread-winged eagle w/body paint flaking but head showing, rim bands in red w/early repair, head stenciled "D.C. Connely Stewarts Run, PA," inside marked "Edward Baack, N.Y.," sold w/copy of soldier's war record (ILLUS. right)............... **798**

*Civil War Snare Drum*

**Drum,** snare-type, cylindrical, decorated w/thirteen gold painted stars in an arch above "Hubert O. Moore 36th Regt. Mass. Vols.," beneath the peephole where fourteen battles & engagements of the regiment are listed, interior w/paper label "Massachusetts Drum Manufactory John C. Haynes & Co., 38 Court St., Boston Wholesale & Retail Dealers in Sheet Music Musical Instruments & Musical Merchandise," woven carrying strap, repaint, replaced rope, head missing (ILLUS.)............................. **4,370**

**Epaulets,** embroidered cloth w/gilded finish & buttons marked "G & cie. Paris," by Schuyler, Hartley & Graham, cased in tin box w/worn japanning, 6 1/4 x 7 1/2 x 9 1/4', pr. ...................................................... **165**

*Group of Rare Civil War Items*

**Hat,** Hardee-style, w/metal bugle insignia on the front w/a "I" & "2," along w/a brass eagle & shield plate, signed "U.S. Army extra manufacture," several repairs, 6 x 13 1/2" (ILLUS. top left) ...................... **1,540**

**Hat insignia,** embroidered cloth, Infantry officer's, rectangular w/tufted area w/a silver "18" in the crook of the horn, fine quality gold embroidery, 2 x 3 3/8" ............. **138**

**Kepi,** Artillery model, red wool w/white piping & a black band around base, w/eagle "A" buttons, marked "Bent & Bush - Bos-

ton," moth damage, lining separating (ILLUS. front left)......................................... **605**

**Lap desk,** traveling-type, mahogany, rectangular w/lift top, carved name on bottom "Maj. A.B. Parkell, 4 Iowa," w/copies of book discussing Parkell's action in a battle (reglued age crack in top).................. **248**

*Rare Civil War Mortar*

**Mortar,** cast iron, dome-shaped, marked "U.S. C.A. & Co. Boston," dated 1855, 1500 pounds, 30" h. (ILLUS.).................. **45,932**

**Pipe,** carved burl, the bowl carved as the head of a Civil War solider wearing a kepi, well-executed, found in Ohio (couple of age cracks)........................................ **550**

**Pipe,** presentation-type, carved burl, carved in relief w/an American eagle & "Union - From W. Keech, Capt. Co. B. - 61st Regt. NY S.V. To E.M. H. - Oxford, N.Y.," carved around top of bowl in relief "Camp Mars, Va. - Feb. 21, 1863," fine brown patina (stem missing) .................... **1,045**

*Civil War Projectile Tube*

**Projectile tube,** iron, engraved "Gettysburg," 7 1/2" l. (ILLUS.) ................................. **952**

**Regimental roster,** painted paper, decorated in bright colors & inscribed "Co. B., 160th Regt. N.IY. vols.," in shadowbox frame, 21 1/2 x 26 1/2" (short tear, stains at top)................................................. **138**

**Sabre,** cavalry officer, brass wrapped grip & brass hilt in metal scabbard w/drag & carrying ring, Schnipzler & Kirschbower, ca. 1840.............................. **1,008**

**Surgeon's kit,** cased set containing twenty tools including tourniquet, pliers, trepanning tool, three saws, nine scalpels & knives, silk thread, needles, probes, etc., all but a few w/checkered ebony handles & some w/W.F. Ford & Caswell Hazard company marks, fitted in rosewood veneer case w/brass oval engraved "J.R. Roberts, M.D.," case 6 x 13 3/8", 4" h., the set (seventeen pieces missing, minor chips to case, some wire inlay missing on case) ........................................ 2,090

**Surgeon's kit,** pocket-type, contains eight tools including scissors, tweezers, three scalpels, pick w/bone handle & a probe, by J. Teufel, Philadelphia, mahogany case, 2 7/8 x 7 1/4", 1 1/2" h., the set .......... 385

**Sword,** Ames 1850 Infantry officer's model, etched & engraved black w/a Chicopee, Massachusetts address, cast hilt w/openwork, leather scabbard w/brass bands & drag, engraved "Lt. Geo. Trembley, 174th N.Y. S.I.," 30 1/4" blade, overall 36 1/4" l. ........................................ 1,980

*Civil War Era Sword & Scabbard*

**Sword & scabbard,** U.S. Model 1850 (ILLUS.) ................................................ 1,870

**Tintype,** quarter-plate, full-length portrait of a cavalryman standing against a camp backdrop & wearing gauntlets, cased, 3 5/8 x 4 5/8" (minor plate bends) ................ 380

**Tintype,** quarter-plate, full-length portrait of a standing infantryman, wearing uniform & holding musket, w/cartridge box, cased, 3 5/8 x 4 5/8" .................................. 440

**Tintype,** sixth-plate, full-length portrait of a standing Union officer, wearing a uniform & Hardee hat, a holster & his sword drawn from scabbard, rich image w/gilding, thermoplastic case w/scene of a man & woman w/palm trees, 3 1/4 x 3 3/4" (edge chips on case) ............... 523

**Tintype,** sixth-plate, half-length portrait of a Union infantryman, seated wearing a kepi & U.S. oval beltplate, holding a small frame revolver, identified as Geo. S. Marsh, Ohio Vol. Inf., cased, 3 1/8 x 3 5/8" ............................................. 468

**Tintype,** sixth-plate, three-quarters length standing portrait of a young infantryman, wearing a kepi & w/a musket, cartridge box & cap box, gilt buttons, patriotic case, 3 1/8 x 3 5/8" (minor emulsion spots) ............................................. 303

**Uniform insignia,** brass, model of a castle, for Corps of Engineers, fine condition, 1 1/2 x 1 3/4" ............................................. 220

**Uniform insignia,** brass, officer's crossed cannon, most gilding remaining, 2 1/2" l. ....... 55

**Uniform insignia,** embroidered cloth, Infantry officer's, rectangular w/heavy gold thread w/sequins around bell & mouthpiece, backing in an oval (moth holes in backing) ........................................ 110

*Civil War Uniform Set*

**Uniform set,** long jacket w/double rows of buttons, leather belt & buckle & shoulder strap, short jacket w/brass buttons & presentation sword & scabbard, from a Civil War Major from Iowa, the group (ILLUS.) .................................................... 11,200

# MINIATURES (REPLICAS)

**Andirons,** brass & iron, ball-topped uprights, late 19th c., 6" h., pr. ................ $1,093

*Miniature Bed Warmer*

**Bed warmer,** brass & wood, the round brass pan w/hinged lid w/lightly embossed floral design, detailed ring- and baluster-turned wooden handle, 10" l. (ILLUS.) ............................................. 429

**Blanket chest,** painted & decorated pine, rectangular hinged top w/molded edges opening to a well, molded base over a scalloped apron & bracket feet, reddish brown graining over a yellow ground w/red showing through, Pennsylvania, early 19th c., 15 1/2" l. (ILLUS. top next page) ......................................................... 5,610

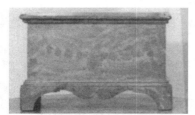

*Fine Decorated Blanket Chest*

**Blanket chest,** painted pine, six-board construction, a rectangular hinged top w/wire hook closure opening to the well, nailed sides w/molded base, raised on four short square legs, old bluish grey paint, 6 1/2" l. ............................................. 220

**Blanket chest,** painted pine, six-board construction, the lift-off molded edge top on arched end boards, original blue paint, American, early 19th c., 5 x 14", 6 3/4" h. (loss to leg, till & one end molding missing) ............................................. 1,610

**Box,** cov., wallpaper-covered poplar, rectangular w/domed top & tin hasp, traces of leather hinges, predominately red, blue & white wallpaper glued to light green which forms edging, American, 19th c., 3 x 4 1/4", 2 3/4" h. (minor staining, hinges missing) ................................... 633

**Bucksaw,** wood & steel, long turned end handles joined by a central cross brace & string across the top w/a thin metal serrated blade at the bottom, dated "1859," 8 1/2" l. ............................................. 138

**Candle mold,** tin, eight-tube w/rectangular flared rim & foot, loop handle at side of top rim, 4 1/2" h. ...................................... 1,375

**Chest of drawers,** Classical style, figured mahogany veneer, the top w/a row of three small set-back nailed drawers above the case w/a projecting long ogee-fronted drawer over three long set-back drawers w/simple turned wood knobs flanked by half-round turned columns, scrolled feet, 19th c., 7 1/4 x 14 7/8", 14" h. (some veneer damage) ..................................................... 605

*Federal Cherry Miniature Tall Chest*

**Chest of drawers,** Federal tall-type, inlaid cherry, rectangular top above four long graduated dovetailed drawers w/tiny round brass replaced knobs, scrolled apron & French feet, minor edge damage, early 19th c., 8 1/4 x 15", 19 1/4" h. (ILLUS.) ..................................................... **3,960**

*Federal-Style Bowfront Chest*

**Chest of drawers,** Federal-Style bowfront-type, inlaid mahogany veneer, the rectangular top w/molded edges & bowed front overhanging a conforming case w/a pair of small drawers over three long drawers w/tiny metal ring pulls, serpentine apron, old but not period, 8 1/4 x 14 1/2", 14" h. (ILLUS.).................... **440**

*Early Miniature Stoneware Churn*

**Churn,** stoneware, tall swelled cylindrical form w/eared shoulder handles, fitted cover w/disk handle, brushed cobalt blue sprig, chips, hairlines, filled-in base chip, 19th c., 6 1/4" h. (ILLUS.) .......................... **1,210**

**Highboy,** Queen Anne-Style, walnut, two-part construction: the upper section w/a rectangular top w/molded edges above a case w/a pair of small drawers over three long drawers w/simple wooden knobs; the lower section w/mid-molding of a pair of small drawers, scalloped apron & cabriole legs, wire nail construction, old finish, late 19th - early 20th c., 17 1/2" h. (damage, repairs)........................ **495**

**Pitcher,** stoneware, ovoid body tapering to cylindrical neck w/pinched rim spout, applied strap handle, cobalt blue brushed flowers & blue highlights in incised areas, incised "Clara Hirdman 1877," incised bottom inscription "Compliments W.D.," attributed to Walter Donaghho, 3 18" h. .......................................... **1,485**

**Plough,** wrought-iron & wood, an early style horse-drawn plough w/two upright curved handles at the back & wood & iron shaft, 19th c., on a modern stand, 16 1/2" l. ...................................................... **385**

**Sugar bucket,** cov., stave-constructed, slightly tapering cylindrical form w/two wooden bands around the body, fitted flat cover w/band rim, copper tacks, bentwood swing handle, cleaned down to traces of red, 19th c., 4 1/2" d., 5 1/2" h. plus handle..................................... **440**

**Wall box,** pine, trapezoidal w/shaped backboard & wire loop hanger, early 19th c., 2 1/4 x 5", 6" h. (crack in backboard) ........ **1,495**

# MOVIE MEMORABILIA
*Also see: AUTOGRAPHS and PAPER DOLLS*

## COSTUMES

*"Terminator" Leather Jacket*

**Arnold Schwarzenegger,** "The Terminator," 1984, black leather biker's jacket w/zippered closure & belt at waist, four pockets, laced details at sides, labeled inside "An original by Bates California," extensive intentional distressing, w/letter of provenance, 2 pcs. (ILLUS.) ............. **$16,100**

**Christopher Reeve,** "Superman IV: The Quest For Peace," 1987, the four-piece outfit comprising a long-sleeved leotard of blue & red stretch jersey, the front decorated w/the red & yellow Superman logo, belt loop at top of red trunks (belt missing), four snap closures on shoulders for cape attachment, "Bermans & Nathans" label w/typed details, a pair of blue stretch nylon pants w/matching label, a cape of scarlet wool w/padded shoulders, & a pair of red leather knee-length boots w/zip fastening, the group (ILLUS.).................................................. **25,875**

*"Superman IV" Superman Suit*

*Lana Turner Dress from "Diane"*

**Lana Turner,** "Diane," 1956, a black satin dress w/silver thread & bead ornamentation centering ornate metal plaques w/'silver' tipped tassels on bodice, layered underskirts, label marked "Lana Turner #9 1675 - 4399," some wear, three plaqus missing, one damaged (ILLUS.)......................................................... **862**

*Leslie Howard Confederate Jacket*

**Leslie Howard,** "Gone With The Wind," 1939, deliberately distressed Confederate jacket made for Howard as Ashley Wilkes, faded grey jacket w/yellow collard & shaped insets at sleeves, w/tattered yellow braiding above cuffs, large blue patch on right sleeves, several simulated stitched repairs, the closure w/mismatched buttons, Selznick Int. Pictures label inside, marked "20-108-M-33" (ILLUS.)............................................ **18,400**

**Space suit,** a white helmet featuring a decal w/glowing sun motif surrounded by the words "United States Astronauts Agency Clavius Base," the suit of silver form-hugging material, adorned w/four stripes at shoulder & a patch on left arm similar to one on helmet, zippered closure on back, w/separate ridge-molded support unit w/front & back panels connected by straps, also seal clamp gloves & grey leather boots w/rubber soles, w/three packing crates marked "M.G.M.," from "2001: A Space Odessey," 1968, the set.................................... **3,450**

**Tom Cruise,** "Rain Man," 1988, the silvery grey wool pants w/black & white line detail, label in waistband inscribed in black "Tom Cruise W30 L31," a blue cotton short sleeve polo shirt labeled "Carroll and Company, Beverly Hills" w/costume tag pinned to sleeve & typed inscription "Tom Cruise "Rain Man" United Artists 1988," along w/movie still, the set ...................................................... **3,737**

*"Forrest Gump"Army Outfit*

**Tom Hanks,** "Forrest Gump," 1994, army outfit comprising an olive cotton combat coat w/sewn "Gump" tag on right chest, "U.S. Army" tag on right chest, label inside, a pair of olive cotton combat trousers similarly labeled & a pair of olive cotton boxer shorts & an olive soft brimmed hat (ILLUS. of part).................... **4,600**

**Vivian Leigh,** "Gone With The Wind," 1939, dress worn during her escape from Atlanta scene & her return to Tara, orchid percale consisting of a bodice w/two-tier ruffled sleeves, lace at collar & sleeves & black button front closure, w/matching skirt & cotton petticoat, three labels in skirt, together w/still showing

Leigh holding a prop costume sign, lace probably replaced, some small signs of wear, some stitched repairs (ILLUS. below)...................................................... **90,500**

*Famous "Gone With The Wind" Dress*

## LOBBY CARDS

**"Flying Down to Rio,"** RKO, 1933, title card, color images of stars in the film & various scenes on a black ground, 11 x 14"................................................ **3,162**

**"Key Largo,"** Warner, 1948, tall insert type w/several photo images of the various stars against a black, red & white ground, unfolded, 14 x 36" (ILLUS.).......... **3,450**

**"Shall We Dance,"** RKO, 1937, complete set of eight color cards, each 11 x 14", the set ...................................................... **2,587**

**"Stagecoach,"** Walter Wanger, 1939, title card, variation w/heads of Claire Trevor & John Wayne on the left, title & credits on the right above a stagecoach scene, 11 x 14"......................................................... **575**

**"Tarzan and His Mate,"** MGM, 1934, insert card, color photos of the stars at the bottom overprinted w/the title, credits & sketches of racing wild animals in the upper half ................................................ **4,312**

**"The Big Sleep,"** Warner, 1946, tall insert card w/two large sets of portraits of Bogart & Bacall in color against red & white ground w/red, white & black lettering, unfolded, 14 x 36" .................................... **1,150**

**"The Roaring Twenties,"** Warner, 1939, window card, color portraits of James Cagney & Priscilla Lane on the lower right, credits & titles on the left & bottom, 14 x 22" .................................................. **1,495**

**"Top Hat,"** RKO, 1935, window card, colorful scene of Fred Astaire & Ginger Rogers dancing at the top against a black ground, titles & credits above & below them, 14 x 35" (ILLUS. top next page) ...... **2,070**

*Original "Top Hat" Lobby Window Card*

## POSTERS

**"2001: A Space Odyssey,"** 3-D type featuring a small space craft departing a double wheel space station w/partial cloudy Earth & deep space background, 1968, 23 x 33" (some scratches to plastic surface)................................................ **1,265**

*Large "An American in Paris" Poster*

**"An American in Paris,"** MGM, 1951, large color image of Gene Kelly & Leslie Caron dancing in the center w/a smaller portrait of Kelly to the right above sketches of Paris, red, blue, yellow & black type on white ground, linen-backed, six-sheet, 81" sq. (ILLUS.)........... **4,312**

**"Angels with Dirty Faces,"** Warner, 1938, color w/portraits of James Cagney & Pat O'Brien on the right, titles & small sketched figures in the lower left, linen-backed, one-sheet, 27 x 41" ........ **7,475**

**"Dial M for Murder,"** Warner, 1954, top section w/scene of man leaning over an outstretched woman w/her arm out & a phone off the hook, titles below, linen-backed, three-sheet, 41 x 81" (ILLUS. top next column)...................................... **2,875**

*"Dial M for Murder" Movie Poster*

*"Forbidden Planet" Movie Poster*

**"Forbidden Planet,"** MGM, 1956, bold color central image of Robby the Robot carrying a fainting woman, bizarre planet background scene, large yellow title across the top, linen-backed, one-sheet, 27 x 41" (ILLUS.)...................................... **5,462**

**"Invaders From Mars,"** Edward L. Alperson, 1953, bold color images of the stars & various creatures w/the title slashed across the middle, linen-backed, one-sheet, 27 x 41" (ILLUS. top next page) ..... **2,587**

*"Invaders From Mars" Movie Poster*

*"It's A Wonderful Life" Colorful Poster*

**"It's A Wonderful Life,"** Liberty, 1946, large color image of James Stewart lifting Donna Reed in the upper half, titles & credits in blue, red & black below, linen-backed, one-sheet, 27 x 41" (ILLUS.) ................................................. **7,475**

**"Lawrence of Arabia,"** Columbia, 1962, large central bust of the shadowy face of Lawrence w/color sketches of the other characters around him, title & orange sky background at top, art by Howard A. Terpning, linen-backed, one-sheet, 27 x 41" ................................................. **8,050**

**"Miracle on 34th Street,"** 20th Century-Fox, colorful images of the stars w/credits & titles above & below all on a dark yellow ground, linen-backed, six-sheet, 81" sq. ................................................. **2,070**

**"My Darling Clementine,"** 20th Century-Fox, 1946, large images of the stars fill

the upper half w/the title & credits in the lower half, art by Sergio Gargiulo, linen-backed, one-sheet, 27 x 41" ..................... **2,875**

**"Notorious!,"** Selznick, 1946, large color bust portraits of Cary Grant & Ingrid Bergman in upper left inside an outlined key, colored background w/yellow, white & black lettering & a small color portrait of Claude Rains in the lower left, linen-backed, six-sheet, 81" sq. ......................... **3,737**

**"Rear Window,"** Paramount, 1954, dark side of building w/Stewart & Kelly looking out a window, linen-backed, style B half-sheet, 22 x 28" ................................... **1,380**

*Original "Swing Time" Poster*

**"Swing Time,"** RKO, 1936, large color image of Astaire & Rogers dancing in the lower half, credits & titles in large red, blue & yellow lettering above them, paper-backed, one-sheet, 27 x 41" (ILLUS.) ..................................................... **5,750**

**"Taxi Driver,"** Columbia, 1976, black & white w/scene of Robert DeNiro walking down the street, signed by DeNiro, Jodi Foster, Martin Scorsese & Paul Schrader, paper-backed, one-sheet, 27 x 41" ................................................. **3,737**

**"The Outlaw,"** Howard Hughes, 1946, dramatic color sketch of Jane Russell being dragged through a doorway by a cowboy, bold white lettering on a black ground, yellow banner across the top, linen-backed, one-sheet, 27 x 41"............. **1,725**

**"The Treasure of the Sierra Madre,"** Warner, 1948, large sketches of the heads of the stars across the bottom, title & credits in upper half, red, black, white & blue, linen-backed, one-sheet, 27 x 41" ..................................................... **3,162**

**"To Catch a Thief,"** Paramount, 1955, artwork featuring heads of Cary Grant & Grace Kelly ready to kiss w/shadowy figure & lighted doorway to the right, title below in black, dark blue & white, linen-backed, six-sheet, 81" sq. ......................... **2,875**

**"Vertigo,"** Paramount, 1958, orange, white & black w/man in spinning bull's-eye on left, narrow photo of James Stewart & Kim Novak on right, linen-backed, style A half-sheet, 22 x 28".............................. **1,840**

*"Virginia City" Movie Poster*

**"Virginia City,"** Warner, 1940, color bust portraits of Errol Flynn & Miriam Hopkins across the center, names at the top & title in the lower left, red, yellow, white, black & blue, linen-backed, one-sheet, 27 x 41" (ILLUS.)...................................... **1,955**

## MISCELLANEOUS

**Agreement,** signed by Marilyn Monroe, four-page typescript "Stipulation of Settlement" between Monroe & Irving L. Stein, dated February 19, 1959................. **3,450**

**Certificate of nomination,** Rock Hudson's Academy of Motion Picture Arts and Sciences Certificate of Nomination Award for Best Actor for his role in Giant, December 31, 1956, mounted on a black wooden plaque together w/an auction catalog of the Estate of Rock Hudson, 2 pcs.......................................................... **3,165**

**Contract,** performance type, signed by Judy Garland, three-page document from Bing Crosby Enterprises for the star to record a radio show to be broadcast in early 1951, signed on last page in black ink, dated January 9, 1951, together w/framed photo of Garland in 'The Wizard of Oz,' overall 23 x 27 1/2"..................... **805**

**Contract,** United Artists document signed by Charlie Chaplin, Douglas Fairbanks & Mary Pickford, the two-page typescript document concerning the division of revenue for 1926, dated December 3, 1925 .. **3,450**

**Letter,** written by Charlie Chaplin in black ink on Golden-Park Apartments, Los Angeles, California letterhead, addressed to a man & his son thanking them for their interest in his work, includes a signed early publicity postcard of Chaplin signed "Sincerely Charlie Chaplin," dated January 5, 1915, the group......................................................... **805**

**Movie prop,** officer's swept-hilt rapier from "Charge of the Light Brigade," used by Errol Flynn, the sword featuring steel & shagreen-wrapped grip w/shaped guard formed by pierced scrolling foliate design, w/scabbard having two strap loops, w/three movie stills & framed plaque, 1936, the group ........................... **4,600**

*"Stargate" Throne of Ra*

**Movie prop,** Throne of Ra the Sun God, from "Stargate," the technodeco throne of wood & composite materials of majestic proportions & form, sphinx wing armrests w/front legs incised w/hieroglyphic characters, painted to simulate bronze, together w/the roy foot rest, w/letter of authenticity & movie still, 1994, 36" w., 46" h. (ILLUS. front) .................................. **4,887**

**Movie prop,** throne room pedestals, from Ra's throne, from "Stargate," a pair of rectangular form columns featuring raised panels incised w/hieroglyphic style characters, used in several key scenes, w/letter of authenticity, 1994, 34 x 36", 46" h., the set (ILLUS. back with throne) .............................................. **1,725**

**Smoking ensemble,** custom-made personal set made for Clark Cable, a maroon silk tivoli pattern brocade jacket w/black silk lapels & waist tie, breast pocket embroidered "CG" within diamond design, together w/black silk pants w/tasseled tie at waist, jacket & pants w/labels for "A. Sulka & Company," breast pocket w/small label "2/7/52" & "45739" (silk grayed at collar, discoloration on edge of one sleeve, pants w/some small holes)................................. **3,335**

# MUSIC BOXES

*Fine Mira Floor Model Disc Music Box*

**Mira disc music box,** floor model, mahogany French-style cabinet w/applied decorations of musical instruments & garlands, the bowfront w/fretwood banding obover a two-door base enclosing a fitted storage compartment, applied filigree brass handles, working, w/one disc, water spot w/raised veneer on top, 23 1/2 x 28 1/2", 41 1/2" h. (ILLUS.) ....... **$6,600**

*Fine Oak Cylinder Music Box*

**Orpheus Swiss cylinder music box,** carved oak case w/interior of lid labeled "Ideal Sublime Harmonie - Orpheus - Switzerland," glass cover over cylinder, the front w/a rectangular scroll-carved panel over a molded & stepped apron w/a pull-out storage drawer, patent dates of 1885-1890, w/three 11" l. cylinders, case 20 1/2" l. (ILLUS.) .................... **5,225**

**Orpheus Swiss cylinder music box,** oak case w/interior of the lid labeled "Ideal Sublime Harmonie - Orpheus - Switzerland," glass cover on cylinder works, patents of 1885-1890, scrolled cast-metal corner ornaments on the front w/a central bar ornament above the molded & stepped base w/a central pull-out stor-

age drawer, w/two 11" l. cylinders, works play but need adjustments, case 30 1/2" l. (ILLUS. below) .......................... **2,750**

*Swiss Orpheus Cylinder Music Box*

*Regina Mahogany Floor Model*

**Regina disc music box,** floor model, the mahogany music box case w/beaded band trim & opening to a double-comb mechanism for 15 1/2" d. discs, side crank handle, raised on a upright mahogany base w/a rectangular top w/molded apron raised on four short baluster-turned supports above the lower cabinet w/a pair of paneled doors above the molded base w/block feet, late 19th c. (ILLUS.) ................................................ **8,500**

**Regina disc music box,** upright floor model, oak cabinet w/a scroll-crested galleried top w/small spindles on a molded flaring cornice above a medial band above reeded pilasters flanking the square scroll-trimmed window showing the disc above a pair of tall panels over a mid-molding & a lower case w/two panels & a wide flared molded base, some wear & slight damage to case, ca. 1900, 15 1/2 x 22", 79" h. (ILLUS. top next page) ........................................................ **6,000**

*Regina Upright Floor Model*

**Swiss cylinder music box,** inlaid & ebonized mahogany, rectangular hinged lid opens to show label reading "Bells in Sight," a glass cover over the cylinder mechanism w/three bells, the center of the lid & front inlaid w/musical trophies, eight-tune 6" l. cylinder, 17 3/4" l .............. **1,320**

*Fine Inlaid Swiss Cylinder Music Box*

**Swiss cylinder music box,** inlaid rosewood case, a narrow rectangular top compartment w/beveled & inlaid corners & floral inlaid long reserves on the front & pull-out drawer, resting on the rectangular lower case w/beveled corners & an inlaid lift top, w/six cylinders, ca. 1890, case 27" l., 12" h. (ILLUS.) ........................ **4,500**

# MUSICAL INSTRUMENTS

**Fife,** rosewood w/plated metal ends, stamped "Geo. Cloos Crosby," 19th c., 16 7/8" l. ................................................... **$165**

**Glass harmonica,** Classical style, mahogany & mahogany veneer case, rectangular w/hinged top & rounded front corners, the interior holding rounded open painted glass vessels identified by stenciled letters & musical notations, music produced by adding water to these, raised on ring-, knob- & spiral-turned tapering legs on casters, some case imperfections, probably New England, 1830s, 23 1/4 x 41", 34" h. (ILLUS. below) ....................................................... **2,300**

![Classical Glass Harmonica]

*Classical Glass Harmonica*

**Grand piano,** Arts & Crafts style, oak & hammered bronze, the angular case in thick quarter-sawn lumber w/hinged front opening to a keyboard section painted olive green w/the words "clear noted as a brook, soft noted like the bees, last noted as the shivering wind forlorn through the forest trees," signed "G. Rossetti," the case set w/elaborate hammered & filed bronze strap hardware, raised on four tapering square legs on casters, keyboard signed in gold paint "John Broadwood & Son - London," designed by M.H. Baillie Scott, England, ca. 1895, 62 1/2 x 80", 35 1/2" h. .............................................. **16,100**

*Early Elbow-type Melodian*

**Melodian,** lap elbow model, rosewood & tiger stripe maple, grain-painted wood & fabric-lined case w/iron hardware, five octaves, ivory keys w/centered articulated scale, D.B. Bartlett, Concord, New Hampshire, mid-19th c., minor imperfections, w/case, 14 x 28 3/4", 7" h. (ILLUS.) ....................................................... **863**

*Early Portable French Melodian*

**Melodian,** portable, wood & cast iron, the narrow rectangular hardwood case w/narrow keyboard at the top w/a fold-over lid, supported on a cast-iron reeded pedestal w/scrolls on the tripod base w/cloth-covered pedal, France, 19th c. (ILLUS.).................................................... **3,500**

*Thomas Gibson Piano Forte*

**Piano forte,** Classical style, carved, veneered & stenciled mahogany, the rectangular case w/cross-banded rosewood veneer in outline w/gilt fruit & flower stenciling on the case front above the leaf-carved & reeded tapering legs on casters, old surface, labeled "Patent Thomas Gibson 61 Barclay's New York," ca. 1830, minor imperfections, 27 7/8 x 67 1/2", 34 1/2" h. (ILLUS.) ......... **1,380**

# NAUTICAL ITEMS

*The romantic lure of the sea, and of ships in general, has opened up a new area of collector interest. Nautical gear, especially items made of brass or with brass trim, is sought out for its decorative appeal. Virtually all items that can be associated with older ships, along with items used or made by sailors, are now considered collectible, for technological advances have rendered them obsolete. Listed below are but a few of the numerous nautical items sold in recent months.*

**Model of a warship,** the U.S.S. Constitution, wood, metal, cloth, string, etc., three masts fully rigged, good detail w/two sailors on deck, original paint, 25 1/2" l. (minor damage to sails & rigging) ....................................... **$578**

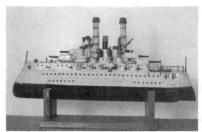

*Model of U.S.S. Pennsylvania*

**Model of Battleship "U.S.S. Pennsylvania,"** metal over wood hull, well detailed upper deck w/pierced wire cylindrical chimneys, painted white, black & red, built by Claude Ham, Scandia, New York, ca. 1890s (ILLUS.)........................... **3,575**

*Model of the Schooner "Traviata"*

**Model of the Schooner "Traviata,"** plumb stern planked model yacht w/original rigging, a lifeboat, captain's gig & sailing kayak, above a lead keel on a stand monogrammed "CA" & w/a brass plate engraved "R. Lincoln Lippitt," ca. 1875, 10 1/2" l., 74" h. (ILLUS.)................ **9,775**

**Model of the U.S. Frigate "Constitution,"** copper-clad hull, fully-rigged, in a glass case w/rectangular wooden base w/incised metal plaque reading "U.S. Frigate Constitution Built in Boston Mass. 1797...," 1/8 inch scale, 20th c.,14 1/2 x 43", 30" h. (crack in glass case) ....................................................... **1,380**

*Ebony, Brass & Ivory Sextant*

**Sextant,** ebony w/brass & ivory trim, signed "J. Good, High St. Hull," damage to ivory, 13" l. (ILLUS.) .................................. **440**

**Ship's lantern,** copper & glass, fitted w/a Fresnel lens, embossed labels "Seahorse G.B. Trademark 35413 - Anchor," 20th c., 9 1/2" d., 13" h. ............................. **316**

# NUTCRACKERS

*Bird Nutcracker*

*Bird Nutcracker*

**Bird,** wood, tail lever, nut cracks in mouth, 10" h. (ILLUS.) ...................................... **175-225**

**Boxers,** wood, screw-type, hand carved figures on top, 8" h. .............................. **200-225**

**Cat,** brass, figure w/bow tie, very shiny ....... **50-125**

*Cat Nutcracker*

**Cat,** wood, lever opens mouth, nut cracks in back, 9" h. (ILLUS.) ........................... **150-200**

*Dinosaur Nutcracker*

**Dinosaur,** brass, tail lifts nut to mouth, 16" l. (ILLUS.) ...................................... **200-300**

*Dog Nutcracker*

**Dog,** carved wood, levers open & nut cracks in back, found in different dog breeds & animal species, 9" l. (ILLUS.) ................................................. **150-175**

Tracking down nutcrackers for a collection can become a real treasure hunt. While no formal inventor has ever been assigned to the nutcracker, we do know that in an early inventory of the contents of the Louvre in Paris (1420) a gilded silver nutcracker is listed. Furthermore, King Henry VIII gave Anne Boelyn a gift of a nutcracker. The first nutcrackers were probably nothing more than two large stones; the nut placed on the bottom stone was hit with a heavier rock. Nutcrackers, in fact, are as versatile as people themselves. They come in all shapes, colors, sizes, weights and types. There are three basic types of nutcrackers. The first is the screw type. A nut is placed in a hollowed out interior and a wooden screw is turned into it. The pressure of the end of the screw against the nut will break or crack the nut open. The second type has a handle that serves as a lever and pivots at one end. Some of this type have been reinforced with metal and are not uncommon. And finally, there is the sort which works on indirect pincer action. Two levers are pivoted off center with the short end jaws closing as a result of pressure on the long ends of the levers. Many of this kind are animals that crack the nuts in their mouth.

There are many nutcrackers that employ both direct and indirect methods. Nutcrackers can be as small as two inches or as tall as a six foot man. Nutcrackers are made of wood, metal, porcelain, glass or ivory and are one-of-a-kind specimens.

Painted nutcrackers in the form of people often have folklore elements featuring the brightly colored costumes of a region; most being from Germany. The most popular makers are Christian Steinbach and Christian Ulbricht. Each year there are new editions and new series.

**Barrel,** wood, screw-type, 2" w., 4" l. .............. **$5-10**

**Bird,** nickel plated cast iron, bird w/big bill (ILLUS.) .................................................. **75-125**

**Bird,** wood, screw-type, 7" l. ....................... **100-125**

**Dog,** cast iron, nut cracks in mouth, several
varieties ...................................................... **45-85**

*Elephant Nutcracker*

**Elephant,** cast iron, painted, often painted
red, 9" l. (ILLUS.) ................................... **325-350**

*Elephant Nutcracker*

**Elephant,** wood, two levers open & nut
cracks in back of head, 9" l. (ILLUS.) .... **150-200**
**Fish,** wood, Greek, 1" deep, 8" l .................... **50-75**
**Giant nut,** aluminum, Taiwan ....................... **10-20**

*Half Moon Nutcracker*

**Half moon,** brass, mouth opens to crack
nut (ILLUS.) ........................................... **200-250**
**Kissing couple,** brass, East India .............. **75-100**
**Legs,** brass, 7" l., pr. ..................................... **65-85**
**Legs,** chrome, 7" l., pr. ................................. **35-45**
**Legs,** wood, 7" l., pr. ..................................... **35-50**
**Miller,** aluminum, patent no. 3966810, 7" h... **20-30**
**Parrot,** cast iron, 10" l ................................. **75-100**

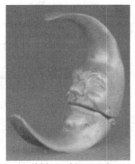

*Sailor Nutcracker*

**Sailor,** wood, screw-type, marked "made in
Taiwan" (ILLUS.) ......................................... **7-15**
**Squirrel,** brass, marked "made in Taiwan,"
reproduction ............................................. **10-15**
**Squirrel,** cast iron, base patent dated "May
28, 1878, Patent No. 204,255" ............. **700-800**
**Squirrel,** wood, screw-type, 7" l. ............... **100-125**

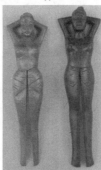

*Woman Nutcracker*

**Woman,** wooden, Filipino woman, x-rated
(ILLUS.) ..................................................... **25-35**

# OFFICE EQUIPMENT

*By the late 19th century business offices around
the country were becoming increasingly mecha-
nized as inventions such as the typewriter, adding
machine, mimeograph and dictaphone became
more widely available. Miracles of efficiency when
introduced, in today's computerized offices these
machines would be cumbersome and archaic.
Although difficult to display and store, many of
these relics are becoming increasingly collectible
today.*

## TYPEWRITERS

**Bennett,** smaller than a shoebox, black or
silver, 1910 ................................................. **$100**
**Blickensderfer,** electric, rare, ca. 1915 ........ **5,000**

*Blickensderfer Typewriter*

**Blickensderfer,** Model No. 7, three-row
keyboard, wheel mechanism, open
frame on oak platform base (ILLUS.) ............. **60**
**Boston,** ca. 1890, rare, index machine ......... **1,500**
**Chicago Typewriter,** No. 3, 1900, small
machine ....................................................... **300**
**Corona,** 1912, No. 3 .......................................... **50**

*Crandell Typewriter*

**Crandell,** two-row curved keyboard, type sleeve, black metal case w/gilt scroll trim (ILLUS.)...................................................... **1,000**
**Emerson,** Model No. 3, 1907 ........................... **200**
**Ford,** cast aluminum, 1897, made in New York, very rare........................................... **1,500**

*"Ford" Typewriter*

**"Ford,"** three-row, thrust action, ornate scroll-pierced silvered metal case (ILLUS.)..................................................... **1,000**

*Hall Typewriter*

**Hall,** 1882, several models, vary w/where they were manufactured (ILLUS.) ......... **400-600**

*Hammond Typewriter*

**Hammond,** 1890, lovely durable machine (ILLUS.) later models up to ...................... **1,000**
**Hammond,** 1890, lovely durable machines...... **150**
**Harris Visible,** 1911, very ordinary looking, rare............................................................. **75**
**Keyboard machine,** 1901, common............... **100**
**Lambert,** cast iron, very attractive index machine, decorative, 1903 .................... **600-700**
**Mignon,** index machine, 1904 & made up until WWII............................................ **100-500**
**Model No. 1,** or colored machines up to ......... **500**

*Odell Typewriter*

**Odell,** small cast iron index machine, Model No. 4, 1890s, very unusual looking, most common, early models have Indian motif on case (ILLUS.)................ **300-700**
**Oliver,** ca. 1900, several examples................. **100**
**'Olivetti Lettera 22,'** turquoise enameled casing w/original carrying case, 1950s, 12 x 14", 4" h............................................... **385**
**Pittsburgh Visible,** made outside of Pittsburgh, ca. 1890s ........................... **100-600**
**Remington,** No. 2, 1879, (blind writer)...... **400-450**
**Remington,** No. 5, ca. 1886, fairly common, first Remington machine that allowed typist to see what was being typed ............................................... **150-200**
**Royal,** Grand, rare, 1910................................. **800**
**Sholes Visible,** 1901, rare ...................... **500-600**
**Smith Premiere,** Model No. 1, decorative ironwork on sides, 1890 ............................. **200**
**Standard Folding Typewriter Co.,** aluminum, 1915 ................................................... **150**

*Sun Index Typewriter*

**Sun,** index machine, 1890, very desirable (ILLUS.)................................................... **1,000**

*"The Chicago" Typewriter*

**"The Chicago,"** three-row keyboard, type sleeve, unnumbered model, patent dates 1889, 1891 & 1892 (ILLUS.).............. **125**

*"The Fox" Typewriter*

**"The Fox,"** four-row keyboard, up-strike mechanism, black metal case (ILLUS.).......... **75**
**Williams,** 1895, curved keyboard..................... **500**

*Williams Typewriter*

**Williams,** 1895, straight keyboard (ILLUS.) ..... **200**

# PAPER COLLECTIBLES

*Also see: BLACK AMERICANA, CHARACTER COLLECTIBLES, FIRE FIGHTING COLLECTIBLES, FRATERNAL ORDER ITEMS, MAGAZINES, MUCHA ARTWORK, PAPER DOLLS, POLITICAL ITEMS, POP CULTURE COLLECTIBLES, RADIOS, RADIO & TELEVISION MEMORABILIA, ROYCROFT ITEMS, SIGNS & SIGNBOARDS, SPACE AGE COLLECTIBLES, STEAMSHIP COLLECTIBLES, TOBACCIANA, WESTERN CHARACTER COLLECTIBLES, and WORLD'S FAIR COLLECTIBLES.*

**Billhead,** printed paper, billhead/waybill of a Cincinnati merchant for goods shipped on March 14, 1825 to Louisville, Kentucky, nice vignette of early steamboat at the top, 7 1/2 x 9 1/2" (folds, water stains)...................................................... **$121**

**Broadside,** printed paper, "A Day of Reckoning, at hand!," an anti-War of 1812 document printed in upstate New York urging voters to elect anti-war candidates, discusses all the financial troubles caused in New York & New England because of the war effort, dated April 1813, 9 1/2 x 13" (folded, small holes, worn edges, foxing & soil) ................ **198**

*Clara Barton-autographed Broadside*

**Broadside,** printed paper, announcing a lecture by Clara Barton, "American Hall, Thomaston -Wednesday Eve'ng, May 29, 1867 - Lecture by Miss Clara Barton!...," autographed in pencil in lower right "Yours, Clara Barton" & also "Dorence Atwater," foxing, some soil, 6 x 9 1/4" (ILLUS.)..................................... **1,041**

**Broadside,** printed paper, "Miracle Magnetic Mineral Mud Bath!," promotes mud pool near Attica, Indiana w/descriptions of ills cured or treated & testimonials, ca. 1892, 18 x 24" (folds, some edge tears, browning) ....................................................... **51**

*Victorian Calligraphic Drawing*

**Calligraphic drawing,** pen & ink on paper, a dramatic scene of a large lion leaping across water towards a bank w/a large-blossomed flower & grasses, signed at the center bottom "A.E. Degler penman," late 19th c., framed, 22 x 28" (ILLUS.)...... **1,380**

**Catalog,** printed fold-out paper, Buckeye Bell Foundry, Cincinnati, Ohio, illustrated w/sketches of various types of bells w/listings, tentatively dated to 1864, 8 pp., 3 1/4 x 5 1/2"........................................... **47**

**Cut-work picture,** a scene of a church, trees, birds, rabbit & picket fence in brown, green, yellow, blue & marbleized paper on a white ground, old black molded frame, 19th c., 11 3/4 x 14 1/4" ....... **330**

*Rare Paper Cut-work Picture*

**Cut-work picture,** a scissorwork picture of intricate work cut paper featuring ornate vines & rosettes enclosing an American eagle w/flag & serpent both picked-out in watercolor w/pencil detail, the word "Victory" across the top, the whole mounted on a black ground, ca. 1860-70, 7 3/4 x 12 1/4" (ILLUS.) ............................ **7,475**

**Deed,** handwritten on laid paper, pen & ink, for a parcel of land in Rochester, New York, dated 1721, framed, 16 x 19" (rebacked w/damage, wax seal damaged) ...................................................... **110**

**Deed,** printed form w/handwritten inscriptions, for land near Bucyrus, Ohio, secretary-signed for President Andrew Jackson, 1835, framed, 14 x 20" (insect damage at fold line)....................................... **83**

*Revolutionary Era Fractional Dollar*

**Fractional currency,** printed "One Third of a Dollar, According to a Resolution of Congress passed at Philadelphia - February 17, 1776 - B," w/vignette of a sundial w/"Fugio - Mind Your Business," serial number written at the top & bold red signature at the bottom, uncirculated (ILLUS.)........................................................ **748**

*Early Printed Lottery Ticket*

**Lottery ticket,** long rectangular form, from the Providence, Rhode Island Episcopal Church, dated November 1797, bold red serial number w/light signature in lower right, about uncirculated (ILLUS.) ................ **218**

**Menu,** printed card stock, cover printed w/a large split-open orange, for a banquet of the Lithographic Apprentices & Pressfeeders in New York City, August 1903, string-bound, 4 pp., 4 1/2 x 6 1/2" (slight soil & wear, pencil marks) ............................. **11**

**Newspaper,** "Columbian Centinel," July 12, 1826, Boston, Massachusetts, news story reporting the death on July 4th of Thomas Jefferson, also the replies from various Revolutionary leaders to participate in the 50th Anniversary celebration in New York City, black-bordered, 4 pp., 15 1/2 x 21 3/4" ............................................. **213**

*"Machine Gun Kelly" Newspaper Story*

**Newspaper,** "Jackson Daily News," September 27, 1933, Mississippi, large front page photo & article on the capture of "Machine Gun" Kelly in Memphis, Tennessee, more photos inside, 6 pp., light overall toning, 17 x 22" (ILLUS.) .................. **173**

**Newspaper,** "The Daily Express," March 9, 1861, Petersburg, Virginia, prints full text of the "Virginia Ordinance of Secession," also unfavorable reactions of several Southern states to Lincoln's inauguration, 2 pp., 16 x 23 1/4" ............................. **207**

**Newspapers,** "The Woman's Journal," 1879, early suffrage newspaper edited by Lucy Stone & Julia Ward Howe, 32 issues from the year, all folded & disbound w/old library sticker, the group .......... **193**

**Pin-prick picture,** white paper w/pricked design of a floral wreath & central medallion w/two small birds cut-out w/opening for portrait, 19th c., narrow old frame, 13 1/2 x 16" (minor stains) .......... **275**

**Plot map,** pen & ink on paper, for land near Chillicothe, Ohio, black, yellow & pale blue ink, dated 1817, old gilt molded frame, 13 1/2 x 17 1/2" (fold lines, stains)........................................................... **220**

**Poster,** card stock, advertising a serial newspaper column memoir by Eleanor Roosevelt, "The woman who knew him best shows you the real FDR! -'This I Remember...'," bust photo of Mrs. Roosevelt on the left side, 8 1/2 x 13 1/2" (slight ding in lower corner) ............................................................ **61**

*Early Communist Campaign Poster*

**Poster,** "Vote Communist.....," red on white w/a dramatic design of a muscular worker holding the hammer & sickle over his head, for 1924 presidential campaign of Wm. Z. Foster, 13 1/2 x 22" (ILLUS.) .... **1,265**

**Press ticket,** "Buffalo Bill's Wild West," brown & pink partly-printed for two reserved seats for an editor in exchange for press coverage, reverse w/the image of a buffalo's head & an Indian wearing a headdress, dated 1908, 3 x 8 1/4" .............. **316**

**Print,** lithographed, white ground w/three oval medallions w/bust photos of Elizabeth Cady Stanton, Carrie Chapman Catt & an engraved portrait of Lucretia Mott, late 19th c., unused............................. **48**

**Reward of merit,** pen & ink, crayon & watercolor on lined paper, a pair of facing birds in blue inside an orange rounded arch above four bands of meandering foliage in blue & green, signed "Sparrow - Presented to Miss Mary Riley For Good - Conduct in School - L. Williams, teacher, 27 Octr. 1844," beveled mahogany veneer frame, 7 1/2 x 10" (stains) ...................... **1,265**

**Steamboat pass,** printed paper, for the paddle-wheeler "Massachusetts," shows early boat w/"Boston & Salem" on the side, printed "Admit the Bearer," blank space for treasurer to sign, unused, early 19th c., 4 x 5"........................................ **67**

**Stock certificate,** "The Des Moines Cattle Company," w/vignette of herd of cattle, company based in Buffalo, Wyoming Territory, dated November 7, 1885, 7 1/4 x 10 1/4" (original folds, small spot & stain) ......................................... **145**

**Union membership card,** "Order Railway Telegraphers," pink card stock, signed by member from Marietta, Ohio, dated 1890, 2 1/2 x 4 1/2" (slight foxing)................. **15**

# PAPERWEIGHTS

**Ayotte (Rick) Paradisia Butterfly weight,** bouquet of pale pink, yellow & white roses w/dark green leafy stems, signed "Rick Ayotte LE - 35 '98," 1998, 3 3/4" d. .... **$690**

**Baccarat "Amber Flashed" weight,** interior engraved w/a stag in the forest on an amber-flashed ground, 3" d. ......................... **385**

*Baccarat Butterfly Garland Weight*

**Baccarat "Butterfly Garland" weight,** the insect w/flattened millefiori wings, marbled in shades of orange, green, blue, yellow, purple & red, attached to an eggplant-purple body, w/a black head & antennae & turquoise eyes, floating over a star-cut ground inside a garland of emerald green, ruby & white cog/stardust canes alternating w/salmon, white & emerald green cog/star canes, 2 3/4" d. (ILLUS.)........................................ **7,150**

**Baccarat "Close Packed Millefiori" weight,** containing complex six-pointed star canes, stardust canes, shamrock canes, whorls, arrow canes, trefoil canes, quatrefoil canes, fortress canes, cog canes & bull's-eye canes in cobalt blue, pink, ruby, turquoise, salmon, leaf green, emerald green, yellow, lavender & white, 2 5/8" d. ............................................ **935**

**Baccarat "Double Overlay Interlaced Trefoil Garland Millefiori" weight,** w/a trefoil of emerald green, cobalt blue, ruby & white arrow/six-pointed star canes interlocked w/a garland of white & lime green stardust/bull's-eye canes, around a central arrow/fortress cane encircled by a garland of salmon & white cog/star canes, pink over white double overlay cut w/a top facet & two rows of side facets, 3 1/8" d. ............................... **7,700**

**Baccarat "Spaced Millefiori" weight,** cluster of colorful canes including seven silhouettes, a "B 1848" cane & a few swirls all on an upset muslin ground, 2 1/2" d. (few very minute nicks) .............. **1,760**

**Baccarat "Stardust Carpet Ground" weight,** including a six-pointed star, arrow, whorl, cog, shamrock & trefoil canes, in coral, orange, yellow, plum, cadmium green, cobalt blue, ruby & turquoise, in a sea of red & white stardust canes, various silhouette canes including rare primrose portrait cane & signature date cane "B 1848," 3 1/8" d. ........... **11,000**

**Baccarat "Wallflower Garland" weight,** containing five white petals outlined in ruby, around a red, white & blue cog/six-pointed star cane center, on a stalk w/emerald green leaves, nestled on a white upset muslin ground inside a garland of cobalt blue, emerald green, white & ruby arrow/six-point star canes, 2 7/8" d. ..................... **1,100**

**Bohemian "Scattered Millefiori" weight,** w/star, cross, cog & bull's-eye canes, in pink, royal blue, ruby, turquoise & white, on a white lace ground decorated w/pieces of colored filigree, 2 3/4" d. ......... **2,200**

**Clichy "Chequer" weight,** w/a pink & green rose & a purple & white rose amid large complex pastry mold, cog, six-pointed star & bull's-eye canes in pink, cadmium green, cherry, Naples yellow, lilac, black, thalo blue, turquoise & cobalt blue, divided by cables of white filigree, 3 1/4" d. ..................... **3,300**

**Clichy "Garland" weight,** a pink central rose cane w/blue millefiori circlet & pink garlands, 2 3/8" d. ..................... **770**

**Clichy "Rose Bud" weight,** containing a large millefiori rose cupped in emerald green sepals, on a stalk w/emerald & sea green leaves, over a swirling white latticinio ground, 3" d. ..................... **9,900**

**Clichy "Scattered Millefiori" weight,** scattered canes on a turquoise ground, 2 3/4" d. ..................... **1,320**

**Clichy "Spaced Millefiori Colorground" weight,** a central pink & green rose & a pink rose amid complex pastry mold, cog, stardust, bull's-eye, star, edelweiss & moss canes, in ruby, opaque pink, cadmium green, royal blue, Naples yellow & white, on an opaque cobalt blue colorground, 3" d. ..................... **6,600**

**Clichy "Spaced Millefiori" weight,** multi-colored spaced millefiori canes on a turquoise ground, 2 3/8" d. ..................... **1,870**

*Clichy Swirl Weight*

**Clichy "Swirl" weight,** alternating cobalt blue & white pinwheels radiating from a large central pink & green rose cane, 2 9/16" d. (ILLUS.)..................... **7,150**

**Clichy "Three-color Swirl" weight,** w/alternating cobalt blue, teal green &

white pinwheels radiating from a large central cadmium green, white & ruby pastry mold cane, 3 1/8" d. ..................... **1,430**

*New England Apple Weight*

**New England Glass Co. "Apple" weight,** the blown three-dimensional yellow fruit w/a rose peach blush on a round clear cookie base, w/a yellow stem & a green glass stamp on the blossom end, base 3" d. (ILLUS.)..................... **1,045**

**New England Glass Co. "Crown" weight,** two-color ribbons in ruby, royal blue, yellow, emerald green & white interspersed w/white latticinio filigree spokes emanating from a mint green, white & ruby complex cog cane, 2 9/16"..................... **1,650**

**New England Glass Co. "Fruit Bouquet" weight,** a formal arrangement containing five blushing pears & four ruby cherries nestled in a bed of green leaves on a white double-swirl latticinio basket, the blossom end of each fruit decorated w/green glass, 2 1/2" d. ..................... **605**

*Rare New England Bouquet Weight*

**New England Glass Co. "Magnum Floral Sheaf Upright Bouquet" weight,** a dimensional portrayal containing a blue double clematis w/a blue & pink millefiori center & a yellow double clematis w/a white millefiori center crowning a bouquet w/variegated green leaves & clematis blossoms in amethyst, yellow, white & pink, a large ruby bud peeks from beneath green leaves on one side of arrangement, on a white double-swirl latticinio ground, 3 7/8" d. (ILLUS.) ............. **10,450**

**New England Glass Co. "Pear" weight,** the blown three-dimensional fruit w/a peach-colored blush on a round clear cookie base, a pink & yellow stem & a green glass stamp on the blossom end, 3" d. .............. **1,320**

**New England Glass Co. "Poinsettia" weight,** the flower w/a double tier of pointed petals around a swirled matched center grows on a stalk w/a realistic furled ruby bud & spring green leaves, on a white double-swirl latticinio ground, 2 11/16" d. .............. **1,045**

**Rosenfeld (Ken) "Apples & Blossom" weight,** a spray of three red apples w/pink blossoms & two buds on clear, "R" signature cane, 1989, 2 3/4" d. .............. **352**

**St. Louis "Carpet Ground" weight,** a patterned arrangement containing five complex florets composed of lime green, white, Persian blue & pink, crimped cog/irregular leaf/quatrefoil canes, around a central floret w/powder blue, ruby, white & lime green cog & six-pointed star canes in a sea of pale pink & white crimped cog canes, 2 7/8" d. ........ **9,350**

**St. Louis "Miniature Pansy" weight,** the flower w/two amethyst upper petals & three brown-striped amber lower petals outlined in cobalt blue around a yellow matched center, on a curved stalk w/emerald green leaves, on a white double-swirl latticinio ground, 1 13/16" d....... **1,100**

**St. Louis "Nosegay Garland" weight,** four complex cane blossoms including complex cog & star canes in Persian blue, sulphur yellow, salmon & white, inside a tiara of spring green leaves, on a white lace ground inside a garland of chartreuse, powder blue & white cog/star canes alternating w/Persian blue, white & salmon star canes, 2 3/16" d. .............. **1,210**

**St. Louis "Pompon" weight,** pompon on a red swirl latticinio ground, signature & 1975 date cane, 2 3/4" d. .............. **440**

**St. Louis "Pompon" weight,** the pink flower w/segmented C-shaped petals around an unusual millefiori center containing tiny ruby figure eight-shaped canes, on a stalk w/a ruby bud & variegated spring green leaves over a white double-swirl latticinio ground, 3 3/16" d..... **4,125**

**St. Louis "Three-color Crown" weight,** containing ruby & cadmium green twists, alternating w/white latticinio spokes & ruby & cobalt blue twists, emanating from a central Persian blue, ruby & white cog/star cane, 2 13/16" d. .............. **6,600**

**St. Louis "Turnip" weight,** the five vegetables in pink, amethyst, amber & white w/emerald green tops in a central radiating arrangement in a white double-swirled latticinio funnel basket, 2 9/16" d. (ILLUS. top next column) .............. **1,320**

**St. Louis "Upright Bouquet" weight,** a white clematis w/a complex cog cane center tops a gathering of four lampwork blossoms in salmon, yellow, cobalt blue

& white, on a bed of light green leaves w/a three-dimensional stem that extends down to a star-cut ground, inside a blue & white lace filigree torsade, six side facets, 2 3/4" d. .............. **2,475**

*St. Louis Turnip Weight*

**Trabucco (Victor) "Rose" weight,** a Chinese red rose w/four buds & green leaves, signed cane, 1987, 3" d. .............. **413**

**Val Saint Lambert "Pansy" weight,** the flower w/two amethyst upper petals & three yellow-striped amethyst lower petals around a yellow center bloom on a stalk w/green & grey leaves, over an opaque black ground, the arrangement encircled by a pink & white spiral torsade, 3 1/2" d. .............. **990**

# PERFUME, SCENT & COLOGNE BOTTLES

*Decorative accessories from milady's boudoir have always been highly collectible and in recent years there has been an especially strong surge of interest in perfume bottles. Our listings also include related containers such as pocket bottles and vials, tabletop containers & atomizers. Most readily available are examples from the 19th through the mid-20th century, but earlier examples do surface occasionally. The myriad varieties have now been documented in several recent reference books which should further popularize this collecting specialty.*

*English Cameo Glass Long Perfume*

**Amber glass,** blown-molded squatty paneled lower body w/arches in each panel, tapering paneled neck w/flared rim & a tall lily-form stopper, retains 80% of original gold decoration, attributed to Baccarat, France, 6" h. .............. **$413**

**Cameo glass,** extraordinary large size full-bodied figural fish bottle of red glass overlaid in white, cameo carved in intricate realistic detail overall & mounted w/hallmarked two-part hinged rim & 'tail' cover enclosing original glass stopper, underside inscribed "Rd 15711," original satin fitted box & letter authenticating the registry #15711 to Thomas Webb & Sons in Oct. 1884 for fish design, 11" l. .. **25,300**

**Cameo glass,** long slender tapering conical form, dark blue overlaid in white & cut w/a long stem of wild rose blossoms & buds, sterling silver neck ring & cap, England, late 19th c., 8 1/2" l. (ILLUS.) ..... **2,016**

**Cameo glass,** teardrop-shaped green oval decorated by white snowdrop blossoms & buds, hallmarked silver rim & hinged cover w/glass interior, 4" l. ........................ **1,380**

*Decorated Cranberry Perfume Bottle*

**Cranberry glass,** squatty bulbous ribbed body decorated w/bands of colored enameled flowers & gold stripes, brass neck & chain w/hinged domed cap engraved w/a six-point star, possibly American, 1890s, 1 3/4" h. (ILLUS.) ............. **225**

**Cut overlay glass,** cylindrical body w/rounded shoulder to a short panel-cut neck w/flattened rim, large cut knob stopper, ruby cut to clear in an octagonal button & diamond design, star-cut base, possibly Boston & Sandwich Glass Co., mid-19th c., 6 1/4" h. (few tiny nicks) .......... **495**

**Glass,** cologne, clear baluster-form body w/millefiori paperweight-style base & stopper, France, 6 1/2" h. ........................... **201**

**Glass & sterling silver,** perfume, the silver stopper w/pink guilloche enameling above a bell-form glass body etched w/vines, Bailey, Banks & Biddle, 7 1/2" h. ...................................................... **431**

**Green glass,** blown-molded w/a sharply waisted body surrounded by oval loops below the paneled neck w/flared rim, tall knob stopper topped by a petal-form cupped finial, retains 80% of the original gold decoratoin, possibly Boston & Sandwich Glass Co., mid-19th c., 5 1/2" h. ...................................................... **1,100**

**Iridescent,** whimsey-type, attributed to Carder Steuben 'lunchbox' production lightly striated green Aurene-type glass w/gold heart & vine shoulder decoration iridized overall, polished base fitted w/ribbed leaf-flame stopper w/dauber, base 3 1/4" d., 5 1/4" h. .............................. **633**

**Light amethyst glass,** bulbous tapering body w/tall neck w/flared rim, plain mushroom stopper, Hobnail patt., polished pontil, probably American, 5 3/4" h. ...................................................... **385**

*English Satin Glass Perfume Bottle*

**Mother-of-pearl satin glass,** spherical body in heat-reactive dark amber shaded to green Spiral patt., English hallmarked silver small neck & chased silver cap, ca. 1890, 4 3/4" h. (ILLUS.) ......... **633**

**Opaque white glass,** hexagonal body w/raised diamond point panels w/pointed ends, short ringed neck w/original teardrop knobby stopper, New England Glass Co., ca. 1869-75, 4 1/2" h. ................... **99**

**Steuben glass,** Green Jade, a short squatty bulbous melon-lobed form tapering to a short neck w/an Alabaster stopper, shape No. 1455, 4 3/4" h. ..................... **660**

**Steuben glass,** Verre de soie, tall slender footed cylindrical form w/a Celeste Blue flame stopper, shape No. 1988, 8" h. ........... **440**

**Tiffany glass,** footed bulbous base w/a wide shoulder to a tall slender waisted neck w/button-top stopper, overall blue iridescence, 6" h. ........................................... **990**

# PHONOGRAPHS

## EDISON CYLINDER PHONOGRAPHS

**Amberola 1A,** inside horn w/wood grill, table model ............................................... **$3,000**

**Amberola 30,** w/internal horn, 4-minute reproducer, oak table-top case, w/metal grill ................................................................. **400**

**Amberola 50,** w/internal horn, 4-minute reproducer, mahogany table-top case, ca. 1905 ............................................. **495**

*Edison Concert Phonograph*

**Concert,** w/large all-brass horn & floor stand, plays huge 5" cylinder records (ILLUS.) ..................................................... **2,750**
**Fireside,** without horn ...................................... **490**
**Fireside A,** w/black metal cygnet horn ......... **1,200**

*Fireside & Columbia Phonographs*

**Fireside B,** w/maroon Fireside, two-piece 19" l. horn (ILLUS. right)............................... **970**

*Black & Maroon Gem Phonographs*

**Gem,** black cylinder player, w/24" black metal horn (ILLUS. left) ................................ **675**
**Gem,** maroon metal case w/cylindrical movement, w/24" maroon metal morning glory horn, ca. 1895 (ILLUS. right) ............ **1,500**
**Home,** w/banner decal & large black "witches hat" horn......................................... **875**
**Home,** w/cygnet question mark shaped black horn................................................. **1,185**
**Home,** w/Edison "signature" decal & large black "witches hat" horn .............................. **850**
**Home,** w/large colored horn w/flowers painted inside ............................................. **1,100**
**Home,** without horn ......................................... **480**
**Opera,** w/large wood horn, ca. 1912 (ILLUS. top next column) .......................... **5,700**

*Edison Opera Phonograph*

*Edison Standard w/Blue Flowered Horn*

**Standard,** w/large blue colored horn, w/flowers painted inside (ILLUS.)................. **900**
**Standard,** w/large cygnet black metal horn ..... **910**
**Standard,** w/large "witches hat" black metal horn..................................................... **585**
**Standard Model A,** table model, without horn, ca. 1901-5 .......................................... **400**
**Standard Model C,** w/original 14" black & brass bell horn, ca. 1908-9.......................... **520**
**Standard Model C,** w/reproduction 14" black & brass bell horn, ca. 1908-9.............. **435**
**Triumph,** large colored horn, w/flowers painted inside .............................................. **975**
**Triumph,** table model, without horn ................. **775**
**Triumph,** w/10-panel cygnet black metal horn ............................................................ **1,200**
**Triumph,** w/large "witches hat" black metal horn ............................................................ **890**

*Edison Triumph w/Oak Cygnet Horn*

**Triumph,** w/oak cygnet horn, wooden bell & metal elbow (ILLUS.) ............................ **3,000**

## EDISON DIAMOND DISK PHONOGRAPHS

**Model A-100,** open bottom, plays Edison thick 78 records............................................ **400**
**Model B-80,** table model, inside horn, plays Edison thick records.................................... **465**
**Model C-150,** plain style floor model................ **390**
**Model C-19,** inside horn, plays Edison thick 78" records, slot storage ............................ **420**
**Model C-250,** inside horn, plays Edison thick 78" records, drawers for record storage ................................................................ **510**
**Model H-19,** floor model.................................. **400**
**Model S-19,** floor model .................................. **400**

## VICTOR DISC PHONOGRAPHS

**Victor D,** fancy case D, w/large black & brass bell horn............................................. **3,200**
**Victor D,** plain case D, w/large black & brass bell horn............................................. **1,500**
**Victor E (Monarch Jr.),** table model w/oak case, disc player, pre-dog logo tag, medium size black metal & brass bell horn, ca. 1910 ......................................... **1,450**
**Victor IV,** w/large black & brass bell-metal horn .................................................................. **1,400**
**Victor IV,** w/large nickel horn ........................ **1,750**

*Victor IV Phonograph*

**Victor IV,** w/smooth mahogany wood horn (ILLUS.)...................................................... **3,700**
**Victor I (Vic. I or V-I),** table model, 78 record player, w/large black & brass bell-metal horn ................................................. **1,200**

*Victor II Humpback w/Oak Horn*

**Victor II,** "humpback," has corner columns, back is raised where bracket attaches, w/smooth oak horn (ILLUS.) .................... **1,300**
**Victor II,** table model, w/large black & brass bell-metal horn ................................. **1,250**
**Victor III,** table model, 78 record player, w/large black & brass bell-metal horn ...... **1,310**

*Victor III w/Oak "Spear Tip" Horn*

**Victor III,** w/large oak "spear tip" horn (ILLUS.).................................................... **3,000**

*Victor "M" Monarch w/Rigid Arm*

**Victor M (Monarch),** front mount or rear mount w/medium size black & brass bell-metal horn, rigid arm (ILLUS.).................. **1,500**

*Victor "P" Premium Phonograph*

**Victor P (Premium),** w/black & brass horn, actually given away as a premium (ILLUS.)................................................... **1,275**

*Victor "R" Royal Phonograph*

**Victor R (Royal),** w/medium black & brass
bell horn (ILLUS.) ...................................... **1,400**
**Victor V,** w/large black & brass bell-metal
horn .......................................................... **1,600**

*Victor V Phonograph*

**Victor V,** w/large oak wood "spear tip" horn
(ILLUS.)...................................................... **3,900**
**Victor VI,** w/large black & brass bell-metal
horn.......................................................... **4,100**

*Victor VI w/Large Wood Horn*

**Victor VI,** w/large mahogany "spear tip"
horn (ILLUS.)............................................. **6,000**

# VICTOR VICTROLAS

**VV-50,** portable wood case, inside horn,
table model.................................................... **275**
**VV-IV,** inside horn table model, no
lid, ca.1902-20 ............................................. **280**
**VV-IX,** inside horn, mahogany table model,
slightly larger than the VIII, ca. 1911-25....... **325**
**VV-VI,** inside horn table model, no lid,
slightly larger than the VV-IV ...................... **290**
**VV-VIII,** inside horn table model, w/lid ............. **325**
**VV-X,** floor model, mahogany cabinet, ca.
1910-21 ...................................................... **390**
**VV-X,** table model.............................................. **325**
**VV-XI,** floor model............................................. **390**
**VV-XI,** table model............................................. **325**
**VV-XVIII,** fancy floor model w/bowed sides ... **2,600**

# OTHER MODELS

**Beatles,** small portable electric phono-
graph made in 60s ..................................... **1,750**
**Bing Pigmyphone,** 6" x 6" colorful tin
case, wind-up toy, made in Germany.......... **265**
**Brunswick,** floor model, simple case.............. **245**
**Busy Bee,** small cylinder phonograph, only
plays Busy Bee odd size cylinders.............. **520**
**Busy Bee Grand,** plays 78 flat records,
w/square "lug" by center hole, front
mount ........................................................ **650**
**Cameraphone,** small camera shaped pho-
nograph that actually plays 78s................... **245**
**Columbia BI Sterling,** 78 player w/large
nickel plated horn (ILLUS. left)................ **1,200**
**Columbia Eagle,** small cylinder phono-
graph, usually has very small horn.............. **510**
**Columbia Favorite,** table model, two doors
in front that exposed wood wall, inside
horn ............................................................ **395**
**Columbia Grafanola,** floor model, inside
horn 78 player, louver door ......................... **325**
**Columbia Grafanola,** table top model,
inside horn 78 player, louver front............... **280**
**Columbia Graphophone Model AB,** plays
both standard & 5" cylinders...................... **1,650**
**Columbia Graphophone Model AT,** cylin-
der phonograph, w/brass horn ..................... **620**
**Columbia Graphophone Model BKT,** rear
mount horn, cylinder player w/tone arm .... **1,395**
**Columbia Q,** small cylinder player, w/out-
side horn .................................................... **500**
**Harmony,** table top, inside horn model, 78
player ......................................................... **190**
**Harmony,** table top, outside horn, front
mount ......................................................... **600**
**Harmony,** table top, outside horn, rear
mount ......................................................... **600**
**Kalamazoo Duplex,** has two large horns,
fancy label................................................. **4,500**
**Madame Hendren,** talking doll, wind-up
phonograph ................................................ **650**
**Pathé,** cylinder player w/horn ....................... **1,030**
**Pathé,** simple floor model w/fancy grill,
inside horn .................................................. **340**
**Silvertone,** inside horn, floor model, sold
by Sears Roebuck....................................... **350**
**Silvertone,** inside horn, table model, sold
by Sears Roebuck....................................... **285**
**Sonora,** upright simple cabinet........................ **325**
**Sonora,** upright w/curved sides, fancy .......... **1,200**

**Fake reproduction,** usually has large shiny brass horn, plays 78s, has the look of a rear-mount Victor phonograph, usually has a decal of the dog & phonograph .......................................... **100-200**

## PHOTOGRAPHIC ITEMS

**Ambrotype,** eighth-plate, half-length portrait of a Confederate soldier seated & holding a Remington-type revolver, in old thermoplastic case, 2 1/2 x 3" (minor spots in background, edge chips on case) .......................................................... **$660**

**Ambrotype,** ninth-plate, half-length portrait of a Confederate Lieutenant, seated wearing shoulder strap w/insignias & button w/gilding, ornate thermoplastic case marked "Peck," 2 1/2 x 3" ................... **550**

**Ambrotype,** quarter-plate, half-length portrait of Confederate soldier, seated wearing belt w/bayonet scabbard & holding a musket, cased, 3 1/4 x 4 3/4" (spots in background, an area of emulsion wear)................................................. **550**

**Ambrotype,** sixth-plate, half-length portrait of a seated Civil War officer holding a sword, ornate thermoplastic case signed "Peck," 3 1/4 x 3 3/4" (halo around image, edge hairlines in case) ................ **193**

**Ambrotype,** sixth-plate, half-length portrait of Confederate soldier seated wearing a double-breasted coast w/gilt buttons, in restored hinged case, mat signed "Lanneau, Artist," 3 1/8 x 3 5/8".......................... **275**

**Camera,** Agfa Box 54, red Agfa on front, good condition .......................................... **35**

**Camera,** Anniversary Speed Graphic press camera, 4x5, good working condition.......... **200**

**Camera,** Anscoflex II, reflex grey & silver color, fair condition ...................................... **12**

*Argus C3*

**Camera,** Argus C3, 35 mm, very common, ca. 1939-66, fair condition (ILLUS.)............................................... **15**

**Camera,** Asahi Pentax S, 35 mm, w/f1.8 55 mm preset lens, ca. 1957-65, fair condition .......................................................... **100**

**Camera,** Bell & Howell Foton, 35 mm, Amotal f2.2 50 mm lens, w/case, fair condition........................................... **700**

**Camera,** Canon AE-1, 35 mm, w/FD 50 mm f1.8 lens, very popular SLR, fair condition................................................ **150**

**Camera,** Canon Pelix, 35 mm SLR, body only, ca. 1965-66, good condition .............. **175**

**Camera,** Hasselblad 500C, medium format roll film w/back, finder & f2.8 80 mm Planar lens, ca. 1957-71, good working condition............................................ **1,500-2,000**

**Camera,** Kodak Autographic Kodak 3A, folding, ca. 1914-34, fair condition ............... **20**

**Camera,** Kodak Baby Brownie camera, w/New York World's Fair on faceplate, good condition.......................................... **250**

*Kodak Medalist*

**Camera,** Kodak Medalist 1, Ektar 3.5 100 mm lens, 620 film, ca. 1941-48, good condition (ILLUS.) ...................................... **200**

**Camera,** Kodak No. 2 Brownie, box camera, black body, ca. 1901-33, fair condition ...................................................... **10**

**Camera,** Kodak Signet 30, ca. 1957-59, fair condition............................................... **25**

**Camera,** Kodak Tourist, ca. 1948-51, good condition................................................ **15-30**

**Camera,** Leica IIIc, without lens, w/serial number below #400,000, made in wartime Germany, ca. 1940-46, fine condition ................................................... **300-450**

**Camera,** Leica IIIg, chrome, ca. 1956-60, mint condition.............................. **1,000-1,500**

**Camera,** Mamiya/Sekor Auto XTL, 35 mm SLR, f1.8 55 mm lens, 1971, fair condition ....................................................... **100-150**

**Camera,** Minolta SR-7, 35 mm SLR, f.14 58 mm lens, 1964, good condition .............. **100**

**Camera,** Minolta Super A, 35 mm SLR, f2.8 50 mm lens, 1957, good condition ................ **55**

**Camera,** Minox II, subminiature "spy camera", made in Germany, ca. 1949-51, good condition....................................... **400-600**

**Camera,** Nikor S2 (rangefinder), chrome, 35 mm, Nikor 50 mm f1.4 lens, fair condition .................................................... **700**

**Camera,** Pacemaker Crown Graphic press camera, 4x5, good condition ...................... **250**

**Camera,** Petri 35, f3.5 Orikkor lens, 1954, good condition.............................................. **75**

**Camera,** Rolleicord II, ca. 1936-50, good condition............................................ **100-150**

**Camera,** Rolleiflex 4x4, original, known as "Baby Rollei," ca. 1931-38, excellent condition................................................... **350**

**Camera,** Rolleiflex Automat 1939, ca. 1939-49, good condition........................ **150-225**

**Carte-de-visite,** Civil War camp scene w/infrantrymen in front of tents, a haversack reads "71 - N.Y.," glued-down to later mat, molded period gilded frame w/repaint, 4 3/4 x 6 1/2"................................ **193**

**Tintype,** quarter plate, half-length portrait of a seated young man w/one hand on his coat lapel, in Civil War era thermoplastic case in dark brown, embossed on the front w/an American eagle w/shield & flags & "The Union and Constitution," image hand-tinted ........................................ **220**

**Tintype,** quarter-plate, full-length portrait of a standing Civil War cavalryman, in uniform w/a saber & wearing a forage cap, in patriotic thermoplastic case w/eagle & stand of flags, labeled "Littlefield, Parsons & Co.," 3 15/16 x 4 7/8" (edge chips on case) ............................................ **413**

**Tintype,** quarter-plate, three-quarters length portrait of Civil War Infantry officer identified as Lt. Jesse Horton, wearing gloves, epaulets & holding a Hardee hat, paint-decorated case w/mother-of-pearl inlay, 4 x 4 7/8" (rust under liner) ................. **330**

**Tintype,** sixth-plate, full-length shot of three standing Civil War Naval officers in uniform, scrollwork thermoplastic case w/leaves & star design, 3 1/4 x 3 3/4" (small edge chips on case) .......................... **330**

*Cased Civil War Tintype*

**Tintype,** sixth-plate, half-length portrait of a Civil War Union sergeant, wearing uniform w/bold stripes & "I" & "12" on collar, thermoplastic case marked "Littlefield, Parsons & Co.," two corners of case chipped, 3 1/4 x 3 3/4" (ILLUS.) ................... **248**

**Tintype,** sixth-plate, half-length portrait of a Civil War Union solider, seated w/a backdrop of a colored flag, 3 1/8 x 3 5/8" ..... **220**

**Tintype,** sixth-plate, half-length portrait of Civil War soldier, seated wearing a kepi & holding a telescope, cased, 2 3/8 x 2 7/8" .............................................. **248**

# PLANT WATERERS

*Ceramic plant waterers were designed in a variety of shapes, ranging from obvious forms like watering cans to animals (such as birds, cats, owls & frogs), flowers, people & an assortment of whimsical creations. While size may vary, the majority usually range from 4" to 6". The top has a hole that is filled with water (typically a seven day supply) which seeps through the pointy porous stem into the planter or flowerpot. This ingenuous invention allowed the homeowner to leave town without fear that their plants would die of thirst.*

*Plant waterers continue to be made today in both ceramic & terra cotta. However, except for a few of newer vintage that are worth noting, most of these listed are from the 1950s-60s.*

*Josef Originals Bird Plant Waterer*

**Ceramic,** bird, perched on bird bath edge, marked on sticker "Josef Originals," 4" h. (ILLUS.) ................................................... **$22-30**

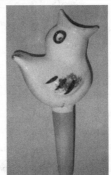

*"Weekend Willie" Plant Waterer*

**Ceramic,** bird, "Weekend Willie," by Holt Howard, ca. 1952, 6" h. (ILLUS.) ............. **18-25**

**Ceramic,** bird, white w/yellow beak, 4 1/8" h. ...................................................... **6-10**

**Ceramic,** bird, yellow, perched on nest, 6 1/2" h. ................................................... **20-25**

**Ceramic,** cat, black, 4 3/4" h. .......................... **8-15**

*Enesco Chick Plant Waterer*

**Ceramic,** chick, yellow, marked "Enesco" on sticker, 5 3/4" h. (ILLUS.) ..................... **18-22**

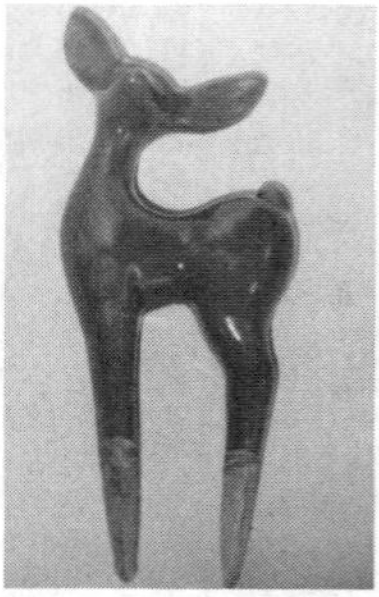

*Deer Plant Waterer*

**Ceramic,** deer, green, w/two "legs," 5 3/4" h. (ILLUS.) ..................................... **15-20**

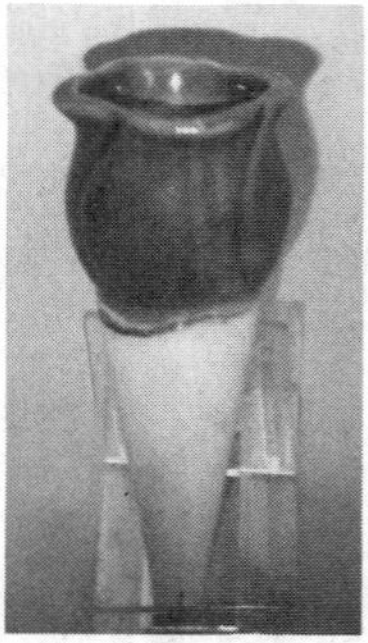

*Tulip Plant Waterer*

**Ceramic,** flower, tulip, light burgundy, 4 1/2" h. (ILLUS.) ..................................... **22-28**
**Ceramic,** frog, green, in sitting position, 6 1/8" h. ...................................................... **6-10**
**Ceramic,** frog, green, w/detachable head, 6" h. ......................................................... **40-50**
**Ceramic,** frog, perched on bird bath edge, marked "Korea" on sticker, 4 1/2" ............. **18-25**
**Ceramic,** frog, white, w/yellow flowers & green dots, 4 1/8" h. .................................. **6-10**
**Ceramic,** girl, in blue bonnet, holding watering can, by Josef Originals, 6" h. ...... **45-60**
**Ceramic,** mushroom, double, light brown, 4 1/2" ......................................................... **8-12**

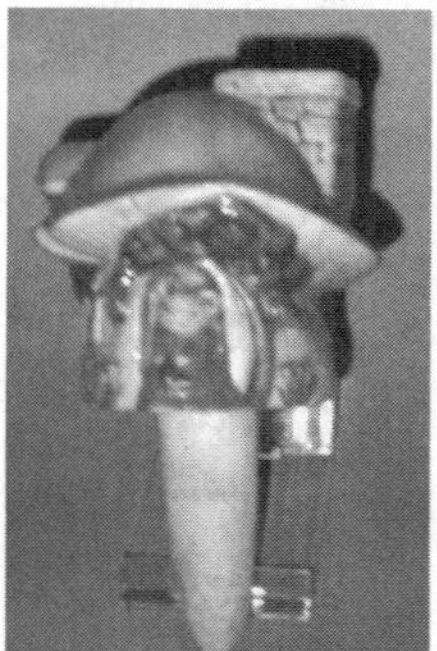

*Mushroom House Plant Waterer*

**Ceramic,** mushroom house, w/mouse inside, ca. 1985, 4 3/4" h. (ILLUS.) ........... **10-15**
**Ceramic,** owl, golden brown, w/white rimmed eyes, 4" h. (ILLUS. left) ............... **10-15**

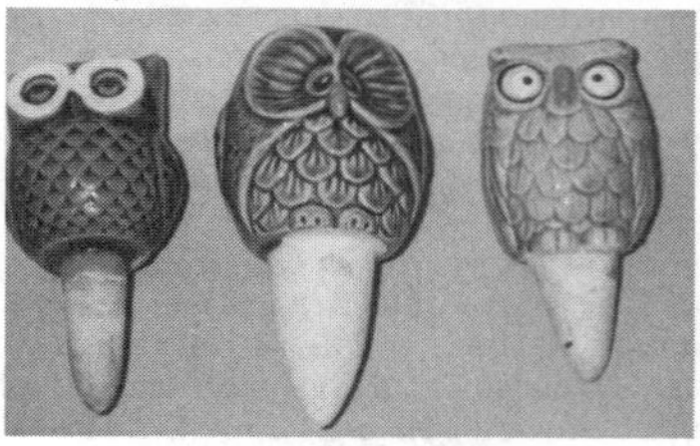

*Owl Plant Waterers*

**Ceramic,** owl, round, blue, 4" h. (ILLUS. center) ......................................................... **10-15**
**Ceramic,** owl, tan w/bulging white eyes, 3 3/8" h. (ILLUS. right) ............................... **10-15**
**Ceramic,** panther, pink, holding watering can, marked "UA," ca. 1982, 4" h. ............. **40-60**

*Pelican Plant Waterer*

**Ceramic,** pelican, blue, 6" h. (ILLUS.) ........... **14-20**
**Ceramic,** pelican, pink & black, marked "Hand Painted NASCO," 6" h. ................... **18-25**
**Ceramic,** pump, water, black, 5" h. ............... **15-25**

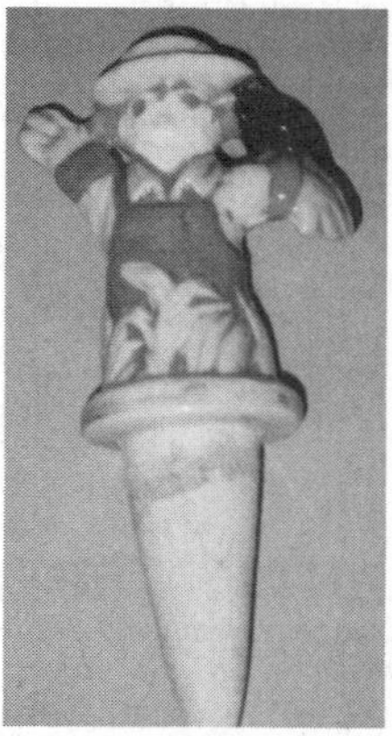

*Scarecrow Plant Waterer*

**Ceramic,** scarecrow, w/crow on extended arm, 6" h. (ILLUS.) ................................... **15-22**
**Ceramic,** snail, brown, 4 1/2" h. .................... **8-12**
**Ceramic,** swan, white w/green wings, 3 5/8" h. (ILLUS. top next column) ............. **6-10**
**Ceramic,** turtle, green, 4" h. ........................... **8-12**
**Ceramic,** watering can, overall dark green glaze, marked "Water" on front, 4 3/8" h. (ILLUS. left, center next column) ................. **8-15**

*Swan Plant Waterer*

*Watering Cans Plant Waterers*

**Ceramic,** watering can, white w/multi-col-
ored flowers, marked "Water" on front,
4 3/8" h. (ILLUS. right)................................. **8-15**
**Ceramic,** watering can, white w/pink flow-
ers & blue trim, 4" h. (ILLUS. center) .......... **8-12**

*Woman In Robes Plant Waterer*

**Ceramic,** woman in robes, green, spike
marked "© INARCO, Cleve.-Ohio, E-189
2," 6" h. (ILLUS.) ...................................... **20-25**

*Blue Worm Plant Waterer*

**Ceramic,** worm, blue, w/removable head,
6 1/8" h. (ILLUS.)...................................... **15-22**

# PLAYING CARDS

*The following prices are a composite of recent
sales and auctions for the more "findable" playing
card decks. Decks listed are complete with original
boxes and no serious defects. Condition is excellent showing only light wear. For decks in better or
worse condition, substantial adjustments may be
necessary. Mint decks may be 25-75% higher,
rough decks 25-75% lower. Missing jokers or original boxes may reduce value 25% or more. The
more rare the deck, the less important condition is
to the value, and even a missing card or two for an
important deck will not deter a collector. Collectors
would like to find all their decks in mint condition,
but we have to be realistic when it comes to rare
material. The mint-condition mid-1880s rare deck
may command a price in the thousands. On the
other hand, age alone does not determine rarity or
value to a collector. Decks from the turn of the century, which are standard and not rare or highly collectible, may be worth very little.*

*The following listings indicate the deck name,
manufacturer, date, type of deck or design, and the
number of cards and joker. "EC" means "extra
card.*

*Reference material recommended:Encyclope-
dia of American Playing Cards, Hochman, 6 vols.,
soft-cover, 1976-1982. The Bible for American deck
collectors.Playing Cards of the Fournier Museum,
Vol. 1, Fournier, Vitoria, Spain, 1982. Valuable for
identifying foreign decks. Cary Collection of Playing
Cards, 4 vols., Keller, Yale University Library, New
Haven, 1981. Excellent, expensive set for identifying worldwide cards.*

*Scott Specialized Catalog of U.S. Stamps, Scott
Publ. Co., Sidney, OH. Reference for U.S. revenue
playing card stamps.*

*Playing card collector clubs:52 Plus Joker, The
American Antique Deck Collector's Club, Rhonda
Hawes, Sec./Treas., 204 Gorham Ave., Hamden,
CT 06514. www.52plusjoker.org. Write or call for
information. Club was founded in 1985 and has 500
members worldwide. It furnishes a quarterly publication and member directory, and offers several
auctions yearly, conventions and free appraisals for
members.*

*International Playing Card Society; Mike
Tregear, 34 Guest Rd., Prestwich, Manchester,
M25 3DL, England. Founded in 1972 and international in scope, this club is heavily into research
and learned articles about playing cards.*

**American Airlines DH-4,** USPC, 1972, standard, 52+JJ (ILLUS.) .............................. **$7**

**Anma,** Anma Co., 1941, military caricature courts, 52+Chief (ILLUS.) ............................... **50**

**Bijou #1,** USPC, ca. 1930, plaid back w/coat of arms, includes extra cards, 11 & 12 for game of 500, 60+J ............................ **75**

**Blue Spade,** Hanzel, 1925, non-revoke deck w/blue spades, yellow diamonds & green clubs, unique courts, 52+J ................ **120**

**Buster Brown,** USPC, 1906, miniature, advertising, cartoons on each card based on comic characters, 52+J ............... **100**

**Cabinet,** Russell & Morgan Ptg. Co., 1890, 52+J (ILLUS.) .............................................. **300**

**California,** Rieder, 1911, souvenir photos each card, 52+J (ILLUS.) ............................... **50**

**Cheer-up,** Stancraft, 1960, hospital cartoons, common, 52+JJ (ILLUS.) ...................... **5**

**Congress,** USPC Co., 1947, narrow, Minnehaha, 52+J (ILLUS.) ................................... **20**

**Double Action,** Double Action Co., 1935, unusual, 52+J (ILLUS.) ................................. **25**

**Excelsior,** Dougherty Co., 1860, square corners, no indices, 52 (ILLUS.) ................... **300**

**Flickers,** Creative, 1974, photos of movie stars, 52+JJ (ILLUS.) ...................................... **15**

**Florida E. Coast,** Interstate, 1920, photos, common, 52+J (ILLUS.) ................................. **25**

**Four Seasons,** Piatnik, Austria, 1900, 32 complete (ILLUS.) ......................................... **40**

**Grand Imperial Sec.,** USPC, 1900, wine advertising, 52+J+EC, (ILLUS.) .................. **100**
**Hunt & Sons,** England, 1830, no indices, one-way courts, square cornered, 52 complete, no box.......................................... **160**

**Inca,** Brown & Bigelow, 1948, original designs, 52+JJ (ILLUS.)................................. **25**

**Kem,** Kem Co., 1950, narrow, leaves on back, 52+JJ X2 double (ILLUS.) ..................... **6**
**Mlle. Le Normand Fortune Telling,** United Novelty, early 1900s, miniature, fortunes on each card w/miniature playing cards, 36+booklet complete ..................................... **35**
**Murphy Varnish,** Dougherty, 1883, unique advertising/transformation deck, drawing each card, one of most sought-after decks, 52+J ............................................. **3,200**

**Nation's Capital,** USPC, 1922, photos each card, 52+J+EC (ILLUS.) ....................... **40**

**Ocean To Ocean,** Goodall, Canada, photos each card, 52+JJ (ILLUS.)....................... **50**

**Petty,** unknown maker, 1960, narrow, pinup, girl w/bugle, 52+J (ILLUS.)....................... **20**

**Pittsburgh,** USPC, 1905, souvenir photos
each card, 52+J (ILLUS.) ............................ **100**
**Rhode Island,** USPC, 1910, photos of the
state on each card, 52+J+EC ..................... **100**

**Rockwell Int'l.,** 1980, original advertising &
aerospace interest, 52+JJ (ILLUS.)................ **40**

**Stage #65X,** USPC, 1908, photos stage
stars, 52+J (ILLUS.) .................................... **135**

# POLITICAL
# & CAMPAIGN ITEMS

## CAMPAIGN

*Bromo Seltzer Republication Promo*

**Advertising card,** 1908 campaign, rectangular card printed w/four oval portraits of the leading Republican presidential contenders before the convention, the names "Taft - Hughes - Fairbanks - Cannon" under each photo, above them "Who?," printed below the photos "National Republican Convention - Chicago, June 16th-19th, 1908 - The Unanimous choice of The People" above a blank rectangular box w/the caption "For People's Choice Hold Lighted Match Two Inches Under The Blank Space,"when done the blank reads "Bromo Seltzer Cures Headaches," unused, light tan paper (ILLUS.) ............... **$121**

*Rare William J. Bryan 1900 Banner*

**Banner,** 1900 campaign, multi-colored cloth, William Jennings Bryan, large bust portrait of the Democratic candidate, marked in lower corner "20th Cent. Studio, Coshocton, O.," minor wrinkles, rare, 24 x 35" (ILLUS.) ................................. **633**
**Banner,** 1912 campaign, Theodore Roosevelt & Hiram Johnson, Progressive Party, rust color printed on muslin depicting a bullmoose flanked by portraits of Roosevelt & Johnson, 36 x 60" (minor staining) ........................................... **633**

*1960 Nixon Campaign Button*

**Button,** 1960 campaign, oval plastic, "Our Nation Needs Nixon" over image of Nixon's face & an outline of the United States (ILLUS.)................................................ **20**

*Benjamin Harrison Campaign Photo*

**Cabinet photo,** 1892 campaign, Benjamin Harrison, an exterior photo of "The Cumberland Campaign Ball" rolled from Cumberland, Maryland to Harrison's home in Indianapolis where it is shown w/a large group of supporters beside it, edge of mount also marked "President Harrison's Residence, Indianapolis" & "Cumberland (MD.) Workman Print," small crinkle in photo (ILLUS.) .................... **266**

**Card,** 1916 campaign, Woodrow Wilson, light brown printed in black w/lengthy inscription with questions to voters, at bottom "Then Vote for - Wilson," 3 1/2 x 5 1/2" (slight browning)....................... **24**

*Grant & Colfax Carte de Visite*

**Carte de visite,** 1868 campaign, Ulysses S. Grant & Schuyler Colfax, dual bust images based on engravings, "Grant & Colfax" at the bottom, creamy mount, light foxing (ILLUS.)....................................... **75**

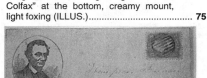

*Lincoln-Illustrated 1860 Envelope*

**Envelope,** 1860 election, stamped envelope w/a printed bust portrait of a beardless Abraham Lincoln within an oval over his facsimile signature, canceled three cent stamp & postmark "Gradiner, Me. - Sep. 27," slightly soiled (ILLUS.) ................. **213**

**Pamphlet,** 1920 election, "National Platform of the Socialist Party - 1920," lengthy printed text, 4 pp., 6 x 9" (fragile, slight edge tears)...................................... **40**

**Pin,** photo-type, "Wendell Wilkie," 1 1/4" d. ........ **95**

**Poster,** 1972 campaign, George McGovern, a design with a stack of three stylized flying white doves w/green laurel leaves in their beaks & wording in each "Time For Growth - Time For Care - Time For Peace," above the name "McGovern" in red, artist-signed, from McGovern for President Committee, Washington, D.C., 14 x 22" ........................... **53**

*1868 Grant Campaign Ribbon*

**Ribbon,** 1868 campaign, Ulysses S. Grant, woven multi-colored silk w/"General Grant - Our - Next President" at the top above an American eagle over a stars & stripes design enclosing an oval bust portrait of Grant, made in Basel, Switzerland, small slit at top, slight toning, 1 1/4 x 3 3/4" (ILLUS.).................................. **345**

Ribbon, 1884 campaign, James G. Blaine & John Logan, gold letters on green silk, "Blaine & Logan - 1884 - Irish-American Independents," 2 1/4 x 6" very good .............. **61**

Sheet music, 1868 campaign, Ulysses S. Grant & Schuyler Colfax, "Grant and Colfax - Our Nation's Choice," oval engraved bust portraits of the candidates below a spread-winged American eagle, by Paulina & Seibert, published by Lyon & Healy, Chicago, ink stamp mark of Pittsburgh merchant, owner's name written at top, disbound, 4 pp., 10 1/4 x 13 1/4" (slight soiling) .................... **156**

*Grant & Colfax 1868 Sheet Music*

Sheet music, 1868 campaign, Ulysses S. Grant & Schuyler Colfax, "Grant and Colfax - Campaign March," oval reserves w/engraved bust portraits of the candidates below a spread-winged American eagle, by G. W. Lovejoy, published by Oliver Ditson & Co., Boston, copyright by Lyon & Healy, Chicago, name stamp of Pittsburgh merchant, owner's name at the top, disbound, 6 pp., very slight soiling, 10 1/4 x 13 1/4" (ILLUS.)...................................................... **168**

*James G. Blaine Sheet Music*

Sheet music, 1884 campaign, "Blaine's Triumphal March," large engraved bust portrait of Republican candidate James G. Blaine, by Gus B. Brigham, published by National Music Co., Chicago, 6 pp., slight browning, some minor wear (ILLUS.)........................................................ **55**

Tintype in frame, 1872 campaign, tintype of Democratic candidate Horace Greeley in a homemade oval starburst frame w/central hole for picture, rare, very slight dings to upper corners, card frame 2 1/2 x 4" (ILLUS. next column) .................. **484**

*Rare Horace Greeley Tintype*

*Taft-Sherman 1908 Tip Tray*

Tip tray, 1908 campaign, William Taft & James Sherman, lithographed tin, round w/flanged rim, multi-colored w/blue & gold prominent, around the rim "Grand Old Party - 1856 to 1908," center w/a view of the White House above large oval portraits of Taft & Sherman, border also lists names of all Republican presidential candidates since Fremont in 1856, 4" d. (ILLUS.).................................... **117**

# NON-CAMPAIGN

*1932 Washington Anniversary Banner*

Banner, woven cloth, Washington 200th Anniversary, reads "200th Anniversary - 1732-1832 - George Washington," a large central color image of Washington, gold lettering, gold fringe along the bottom on wooden hanging rod w/golden end caps, 34" sq. (ILLUS.) .......................... **374**

Chromolithograph, "President Garfield and Cabinet," showing a grouping of standing men in an interior, also w/advertising for "Warner's Safe Pills," includes two old business cards, print in walnut shadowbox frame, late 19th c., 9 1/4 x 25 1/4" .............................................. **275**

Eglomisé bust silhouette of George Washington, shown facing right & wearing his military uniform, marked "Washington 1791," the black portrait against a white ground in a molded oval black frame w/small hanging ring at the top, late 18th - early 19th c., 4 3/4 x 6"............... **770**

**Handkerchief,** printed silk, "Presidential Victims of Assassins," printed in red, black, blue, yellow & green w/a bust portrait of President McKinley at the top center flanked by American flags, wreaths & leafy branches above scrolled banners flanking bust portraits of James Garfield & Abraham Lincoln, ca. 1901, framed, 16 x 16 1/2" (wear, holes) ................ **55**

*Lincoln 1865 Inaugural Ball Invitation*

**Inaugural ball invitation,** Abraham Lincoln & Andrew Johnson, a large printed invitation w/"National Inauguration Ball - March 4th, 1865" above portraits of Lincoln & Johnson above "The honor of ____ Company is requested" above the long list of managers, all flanked by perched American eagle atop tall ribbon-entwined columns, printed along bottom edge "Designed & Drawn by Bruff" & "Engraved by Dempsey & O'Toole," chip missing at lower right corner," 7 1/2 x 10 1/2" (ILLUS.)............................ **2,760**

**Inaugural ball program,** 1881, printed "Inauguration Ball" above an American eagle over the oval portraits of James Garfield & Chester Arthur," w/flags & scenes of the U.S. Captiol & White House at the bottom above date "March 4th, 1881," multicolored cover, 16 pp., 4 1/2 x 6" (soil, light water stains, center fold mostly split) ............................................. **55**

**Lithograph,** oval bust portrait of James K. Polk, printed by Nathanial Currier, an American eagle & crossed flags above star-trimmed oval border around the portrait, shield & flags Rfpbelow above his name, 1840s, 8 3/4 x 12" (crease, small tear at top).................................................. **265**

**Lithograph,** printed in black & white & hand-tinted, bust portrait of William Henry Harrison, by Kellogg &

Comstock, ca. 1840, early beveled wood frame w/original red graining, overall 12 1/4 x 16 1/4" (dark stains, damage) ........ **110**

*Cast Iron Medallion of Washington*

**Medallion,** cast iron, oval, raised bust profile portrait of George Washington, in a contemporary wood frame, 21 1/2 x 26 1/2" (ILLUS.) ....................................................... **595**

*Rare Franklin Roosevelt Silk Portrait*

**Memorial picture,** woven silk, bust portrait of Franklin D. Roosevelt done in shades of grey, black ribbon across upper left corner, below the portrait printed "The Great President" above his dates, woven in Belgian silk, matted & framed, portrait 11 x 13" (ILLUS.)......................................... **345**

**Memorial ribbon,** Andrew Jackson, 1845, blue on cream silk w/half-length portrait of Jackson & wording "In Memory of Departed Worth - Gen. Andrew Jackson. Born: Mar. 15, 1767. Died: June 8, 1845, in his 79th year. His fair renown shall never fade away. - Nor shall the Mention of his name decay. - Though to the Dust his mortal part we give, His Fame in Triumph o'er the Grave shall live," 3 x 7 3/4" (four tiny pin holes at top)............. **220**

**Mourning card,** for Abraham Lincoln, enamel-glazed card, printed by a Salem newspaper, reads "President Lincoln - DIED - At 22 minutes past 7 o'clock THIS MORNING," in lower corner "Salem, April 15th, 1865," black border, 3 x 4 1/4" (ILLUS. top next page) ................ **431**

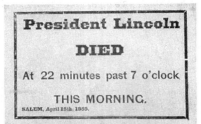

*President Lincoln Mourning Card*

**Poster,** memorial-type, William McKinley, printed in olive & black, an elaborate design on black w/a dove & banner above framed bust photograph of assassinated President McKinley above an elaborate monument-style base w/long memorial inscription, published in 1901 by the Home Art Company of Chicago, 16 x 20" (folds along left edge, some margin tears) .............................................. **138**

*Memorial Print of James A. Garfield*

**Print,** memorial-type, James A. Garfield, an uncolored print w/a large central oval portrait of assassinated President Garfield w/a border of small portraits of all the Presidents before him including his successor, Chester Arthur, memorial inscriptions printed at the bottom in small letters, laid on canvas backing, some minor fraying & edge chipping, 21 1/4 x 27 1/2" (ILLUS.) ............................. **293**

**Print,** "Star of the North or The Comet of 1861," shows the head of Abraham Lincoln forming a comet w/a striped body against a dark background of stars & a crescent moon, by Samuel C. Upham, Philadelphia (slightly soiled) ........................... **65**

**Ribbon,** memorial-type, 1832 George Washington Centennial silk memorial, printed black on rose-colored silk, a top block printed "Centennial Celebration" above an American eagle & shield over a banner w/"Washington" above a round wreath enclosing a bust of Washington, 2 x 9" ............................................................. **460**

*Lincoln Memorial Sheet Music*

**Sheet music,** "The Nation in Tears - In Memoriam - A Dirge In Memory of the Nation's Chief," black & white lithographed bust portrait of Abraham Lincoln on the front, six disbound pages, lyrics by R.C., music by Konrad Treuer, published by Wm. Jennings Demorest, New York, New York, inside illustrated w/Lincoln funeral scenes, 1865, 10 1/4 x 13 1/4" (ILLUS.) ............................. **138**

*Lincoln Service Soup Plate*

**Soup plate,** porcelain, from the Lincoln Presidential service, the gilt Alhambras style & Solferino-colored border centers a spread-winged American eagle atop a shield w/banner "E Pluribus Unum," retailer's mark on the base for J.W. Boteler & Bro., Washington, ca. 1877 or 1884, restoration to two hairlines, very minor chips & minor gilt wear, 9 1/2" d. (ILLUS.) ...................................................... **805**

**Wax silhouette portraits,** cast bust portraits of George & Martha Washington, mounted against a dark background in narrow giltwood shadowbox frames, each 4 3/4 x 5 7/8", facing pr ...................... **715**

# POP CULTURE COLLECTIBLES

*The collecting of pop culture memorabilia is not a new phenomenon; fans have been collecting music-related items since the emergence of rock* and roll in the 1950s. But it was not until the 'coming of age' of the post-war generation that the collecting of popular culture memorabilia became a recognized movement. The most sought-after items are from the 1960s, when music, art, and society were at their most experimental. This time period is dominated by artists such as The Beatles, The Rolling Stones and Bob Dylan, to name a few. From the 1950s, Elvis Presley is the most popular. Below we offer a cross-section of popular culture collectibles ranging from the 1950s to the present day.

**Award,** American Music Award presented to Gloria Estefan & Miami Sound Machine for 'Favorite Duo or Group Pop/Rock,' 1989, 14 1/4" h...................... **$3,737**

*The Eagles Grammy Award*

**Award,** Grammy award presented to The Eagles for "Lyin' Eyes," for 'Best Pop Performance By A Duo Or Group With Vocal - 1975,' 6 1/2" h. (ILLUS.)............... **6,325**

**Beatles dress,** white cotton, sleeveless, knee-length w/horizontal yellow thin & wide stripes & printed w/various Beatles-related images in blue & black including words & music of their songs, the Beatles' faces & signatures, ca. 1960s............... **460**

**Beatles tie tack set,** on card, Nems, ca. 1964 ............................................................. **35**

*Madonna Bustier*

**Bustier,** worn by Madonna, front zip closure w/lace detail, labeled "Lady Marlene," in custom made lucite case w/two color snapshots of Madonna wearing it on the Johnny Carson Show, ca. mid-1980s, 5 1/4 x 18 1/4" (ILLUS.)................. **2,875**

**Electric guitar,** Aria Pro II model autographed by Pink Floyd, red finish, twenty-one fret fingerboard w/dot inlays, three pickups, selector switch, three rotary controls & white pickguard, signed on the body in black felt pen by Roger Waters, Rick Wright & Nick Mason, w/additional printed inscription "Pink Floyd" by Mason & on one pickguard in blue felt pen by Dave Gilmour, accompanied by photo of Waters posing w/the guitar after signing ..................................... **2,875**

**Gold disc,** 'in house' type, for the single "Thank You Girl" by The Beatles, presented to David R. Stern, accompanied by a letter on the provenance from Bruce Spizer w/an autographed copy of his book 'Beatles Records on Vee-Jay,' 12 1/2 x 15 1/2", the group........................ **4,600**

*Elvis "Jailhouse Rock" Movie Jacket*

**Jacket,** worn by Elvis Presley in the movie "Jailhouse Rock," blue denim, metal button fastening on front, white tag on left breast w/inmate number stenciled in black felt pen "G239," green MGM label inside inscribed in blue ink "Elvis Presley 1719 #3," accompanied by five black & white photos of Elvis wearing the shirt & a video copy of the movie, the group (ILLUS.).................................................. **13,800**

*Janis Joplin-autographed Magazine*

**Magazine,** "Rolling Stone," cover photo of Janis Joplin & signed by her on the front in black ballpoint pen, dated March 15, 1969, accompanied by a certificate of authenticity (ILLUS.).................................. **1,840**

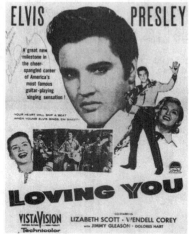

*Elvis-signed Movie Handbill*

**Movie handbill,** for "Loving You," autographed by Elvis Presley, featureing several images of Elvis w/his name across the top & title & credits across the bottom, signed in blue ink "Ann yours, Elvis Presley," matted, 9 x 11 1/4" (ILLUS.).................................................... **1,725**

THE BEATLES

*Beatles-signed Publicity Photo*

**Photograph,** autographed publicity shot of The Beatles, signed on front in blue ink by all four members of the group, matted, 1963, 8 x 10" (ILLUS.)........................ **5,175**

**Poem,** "Players," handwritten partial poem by Jim Morrison, comprising eight lines in blue biro on a piece of yellow paper, matted w/a color photo of The Doors, overall 14 x 16"......................................... **5,175**

**Poster,** "Jefferson Airplane - Berkeley Strike Benefit," pop art design by West Wilson featuring a wide band of twisted & distorted humans w/distorted lettering above & below, for a February 1967 concert, also included Quicksilver, Country

Joe & Fish & Loading Zone at Fillmore West, 13 1/2 x 23"......................................... **88**

*1968 Multi-band Concert Poster*

**Poster,** mini-size, "Steppenwolf - Creedence - Butterfield - 10 Years After," a Lee Conklin design w/"Fillmore" across the top above a long oval filled w/an abstract design of distorted human figures & the names of the bands, reverse has entire Fillmore summer series schedule, 1968, unused, tape pulls at corners, 4 1/2 x 7" (ILLUS.) .............. **72**

**Poster,** mini-size, "The Turtles," band name in large letters across the top above a design of band members as turtles, location & date of concert at the bottom, 1966, unused, 5 x 7" (staple holes at top center, tape pulls on back) .................. **11**

**Poster,** mini-sized, "Jefferson Airplane - Great Society," modernistic distorted balloon design w/bands of lettering including name of band & dates of the concert, 1966, unused, 5 x 7"....................... **11**

**Record,** the single "Burning Of The Midnight Lamp" autographed by The Jimi Hendrix Experience on the front of the sleeve in blue ink, Jimi & Noel adding "Love...," matted, overall 14 x 18 1/2" ....... **3,162**

*Elvis-signed Record Album Cover*

**Record album cover,** "Elvis - "Fun in Acapulco,"" signed by Elvis Presley, some wear (ILLUS.) ..................................... **225**

*Elvis Presley 1965 Movie Shirt*

**Shirt,** worn by Elvis Presley in the movie "Paradise, Hawaiian Style," sky blue linen w/two panels on front decorated w/a blue & white printed floral pattern, accompanied by two movie stills showing Elvis wearing the shirt & a letter on the provenance, 1965 (ILLUS.) .............. **10,350**

*Janis Joplin Leather Shoulder Bag*

**Shoulder bag,** owned by Janis Joplin, brown leather w/carrying strap/drawstring, accompanied by photo of Joplin holding the bag & a letter on the provenance, 17" h. (ILLUS.) .............................. **5,175**

**Song lyrics,** handwritten for the song 'Help On The Way' by The Grateful Dead, fourteen lines in red felt pen on the reverse of a printed "Session Data Sheet," matted w/a black & white machine-print photograph of the group, lyric sheet 8 1/4 x 10 1/2" ......................... **2,875**

**Vest,** black faux fur w/intricate multicolored beaded trim & black fringe, worn by Jimi Hendrix at Memorial Auditorium, Dallas, 20th April, 1969, accompaned by two color photocopy photos of Hendrix wearing a similar vest & a letter on the provenance (ILLUS. top next column) ................ **6,325**

*Jimi Hendrix Vest*

# POSTERS

*Also see: ADVERTISING ITEMS, MOVIE MEMORABILIA, DISNEY COLLECTIBLES, WESTERN AMERICANA, SPORTS MEMORABILIA, WESTERN CHARACTER COLLECTIBLES & POP CULTURE.*

*Anti-Viet Nam War Poster*

**Anti-war,** "Moratorium Days - Nov. 13,14,15 - Washington D.C. - Help Free America From Our Tragic Involvement in Viet Nam," bold lettering across the top & down the sides w/a central image of white doves flying above a Federal building, locally designed & produced by Antioch Bookplate Co., Yellow Springs, Ohio, slight sprinkle of blue on white, creases at bottom, 1969, 16 1/2 x 22" (ILLUS.) ...................................................... **$165**

**Circus,** "Ringling Bros. and Barnum & Bailey Circus," blue & red on white, bold lettering & a large image of a clown's head, ca. 1950s, 28 x 40" (folds, tiny tear in bottom edge) ..................................... **253**

**Magician,** "Lippincoot The Magician," red lettering on white, reads "Coming Here Soon! Lippincott The Magician - Big Fun and Mystery Show - the Main Who Makes Himself Disappear," probably 1920s, vertical fold, 21 x 28" .......................... **46**

*Carter The Great Spiritualist Poster*

**Spiritualist,** "Carter The Great," large color design w/title at the top above a dramatic scene of Carter surrounded by witches, demons, skeletons, etc., ca. 1920s, 77 x 104 3/4" (ILLUS.) ...................... **575**

**Student protest,** "International Student Strike - April 26, 1968 - Bring The Troops Home Now! - End Racial Oppression - Stop the Draft - Student Mobilization Committee to End the War in Vietnam," w/large photo images of student protests, red, white & blue w/black & white photos, 17 1/2 x 22 1/2" ....... **91**

*Viet Nam War Protest Poster*

**Student protest,** "War Is Hell! Ask The Man Who Fought One... Demonstrate to End the War - April 27, 1968 - Bring Our Men Home From Vietnam Now!," black & white w/photo of Vietnam soldiers cradling a wounded comrade, from the Student Mobilizaition Committee to End the War in Viet Nam, folded, 17 x 22" (ILLUS.) ......................................... **259**

*Christy World War I Poster*

**World War I,** "Americans All! - Victory Liberty Loan," a colorful Howard Chandler Christy image of a lightly clad maiden standing in front of a large American flag & pointing to a monument engraved w/the names of various nationalities, ca. 1918, 26 x 39" (ILLUS.).............................. **400**

*Dramatic World War I Poster*

**World War I,** "And They Thought We Couldn't Fight - Victory Liberty Loan," artwork by Clyde Forsythe showing a U.S. doughboy standing in a battle field, his rifle over one shoulder & two German helmets in the other hand, some tape repair on back, framed, 21 x 31" (ILLUS.) ....................................... **207**

**World War I,** "Clear The Way! - Buy Bonds - Fourth Liberty Loan," a red, white & blue image of Miss Liberty & a large American flag cheering on a group of sailors firing a ship's cannon, by Howard Chandler Christy, 19 x 29" (ILLUS. top next page ) ................................... **275**

*Christy Battle Scene Poster*

**World War I,** French, "Credit Lyonnais - Souscrivez Av 4e Emprunt National," bold color design of a barechested French soldier holding a large flag up w/one arm & ready to thrust his sword into a large German eagle, linen-backed, 31 3/4 x 47" (minor paper loss) .................... **230**

**World War I,** French, "On les aura! (We've got them) - 2e Emprunt de La Defense Nationale - Souscrivez," large color image of a charging French soldier carrying a rifle, linen-backed, 31 x 44 1/2" ........ **150**

*Merchant Marine World War II Poster*

**World War II,** "Let's Finish the Job! - Urgent - Experienced Seamen Needed!...," large bust image of a Merchant Marine at the helm, printed on a bright yellow ground, 20 x 28" (ILLUS.)........ **288**

**World War II,** "They Did Their Part - the five Sullivan brothers 'missing in action' off the Solomons," w/a group photograph of the brothers who were all killed while serving abroad the same ship,

because of this tragedy the Navy changed its policy & didn't allow family members to serve on the same vessel, tape remnants at corners, small piece missing from top center at fold, w/original envelope, 22 x 28" (ILLUS. below)......... **127**

*World War II Sullivan Brothers Poster*

# PURSES & BAGS

*Hermé's Alligator Kelly Bag*

**Alligator,** chestnut brown Kelly bag w/lock & key, detachable shoulder strap, brown leather lining, "Hermé's, Paris, Made in France" stamped in gold under flap, "Hermé's - Paris" stamped on hardware, ca. 1970s, 5 x 9 1/2 x 12 1/2" (ILLUS.) .............................................. **$9,200**

**Alligator,** rectangular, taupe shoulder bag w/front flap, circular goldtone clasp & alligator shoulder strap, taupe leather lining, stamped "Hermés Paris, Made in France" on lining, ca. 1970s, 2 x 7 x 10" ... **1,150**

**Beaded,** barrel form champagne pink velvet embroidered w/metallic goldtone yarns, rhinestones & gold seed beads in overall vine pattern, short top handle & champagne satin lining w/one interior pocket, lining stamped "Nettie Rosenstein," ca. 1950s, some rhinestone loss below flap closure, 4 x 4 1/2 x 8 1/4" (ILLUS. top next page) ..... **173**

*Embroidered Beaded Evening Bag*

**Beaded,** cut steel foliate pattern in red, gold & silver, goldtone frame w/rhinestone clasp, short beaded handle, red satin lining, labeled "Langlois & Jargeais, 4 Rue Vaucanson, Paris" on interior, 1 x 6 x 8" ....................................... **460**

**Beaded,** tiny cut steel beads forming 18th century inspired pastoral scene w/young couple, filigree frame at top & 2" beaded fringe at bottom, iridescent green silk lining w/pocket & mirror, 8 x 13 1/2" ............... **575**

**Canvaswork,** multicolored floral needlepoint & goldtone filigree frame inset w/simulated onyx & pearls, short chainline handle, champagne silk lining, early 20th c., 1/2 x 5 x 6 1/2" .................................... **69**

**Chain-link,** goldtone & silvertone chain shoulder bag w/metallic gold leather interior & coordinating silver leather change purse, labeled "Made in Italy, Lewis Imports," ca. 1950s, 6 x 9" .................. **58**

**Crocodile,** black, box bag w/short handle, flap closure, black leather three-compartment interior, four inner pockets, stamped "Nettie Rosenstein - Made in Florence, Italy" on interior, ca. 1950s, 4 1/2 x 9 x 9 1/2" ......................................... **920**

*"The Lilly" Box Bag*

**Fabric,** "The Lilly," hard-sided box bag covered w/patchwork of multicolored Pulitzer fabrics, goldtone frame, top closure & clear plastic handle, hot pink felt lining w/mirror & labeled "The Lilly, Lilly Pulitzer, Inc.," ca. 1960s, 4 x 5 x 8" (ILLUS.) ...................................................... **489**

**Fur,** rectangular, brown, black, white & grey patchwork design w/taupe leather frame & handles, four compartments w/goldtone

closures & numerous inner pockets, "Judith Leiber" stamp on interior goldtone plate, ca. 1970s, 4 x 9 1/2 x 11 1/4" .............. **489**

**Leather,** circular olive green kid leather w/large round enameled Limoges plaque, sterling silver setting w/bright blue enamel & central scene depicting Cupid & young woman, ruched leather border, grey moiré & ivory kid interior, enamel frame stamped "sterling," lining stamped "Made in Austria," ca. 1900, 1 1/2 x 6" ...................................................... **374**

*Multicolored Lucite Handbag*

**Lucite,** rectangular form w/rounded ends, olive green, red & metallic gold, square top flap, goldtone hardware & top handle, mirrored inner top & black interior, stamped "Myles Originals of Miami" on interior, ca. 1950s, 3 3/4 x 5 x 7 1/2" (ILLUS.) ...................................................... **431**

**Satin,** black rectangular petal-form design, three compartments, rhinestone clasp & rhinestone "vines" handle attachments, black satin lining w/three interior pockets, stamped "Gucci" on lining, ca. 1940s, 3 x 7 x 9 1/2" .................................... **374**

*Nantucket Straw Bags*

**Straw,** woven basket bag w/bamboo handle & silver metal hardware, large center front closure w/heart motif & fish-shaped clasp, Nantucket, ca. 1940s, 6 x 7 1/2 x 10" (ILLUS. right) .............................................. **58**

**Straw,** woven basket bag w/top lid, wooden handle, leather & bone toggle closure, scrimshaw embellishment on top of lid depicts jockey on horse vaulting fence, Nantucket, ca. 1970s, 6 3/4 x 7 x 8" (ILLUS. left) ................................................ **460**

**Wool crepe,** black, drawstring pouch w/gold metallic embroidery & dangling faux jade teardrops, green satin lining, Japanese-inspired, ca. 1920s, 7 x 12" ........ **115**

# RADIOS & ACCESSORIES

*The first radio broadcast occurred in 1920. It started a rush by the public to purchase a radio. Programming increased and thousands of companies began to manufacture radios of various sorts and sizes. There was a radio for each price range. Over the years the majority of manufacturers disappeared due to intense competition.*

*The Golden Age of Radio stretched from the 1930s into the mid 1950s. In fact many of the first television shows were radio shows that made the move to the new medium.*

*"Introducing You To Radio" Book*

**Book,** "Introducing You to Radio by National Radio Institute," Washington, D.C., series of instructional books for course in radio w/some information on early television, 1937, price each (ILLUS.) ........................................ **$15**

**Coil,** ignition, from Model T Ford automobile, employed from 1908-1927, one of the first sending devices, could send about 10-15 miles ........................................ **75**

*Atwater Kent Table Cathedral Style*

**Radio,** Atwater Kent, wooden table model, Cathedral styling, early 1930s, also known as "midget" or "Depression" models, price depends on the company, several variations of style found (ILLUS.) ........................................ **150 and up**

**Radio,** "Charlie McCarthy (The)," by Majestic, table model, white Bakelite, w/Charlie McCarthy figure on front of radio, 1930s ........................................ **950**

*Crosley Table Model Radio*

**Radio,** Crosley Model 123, table model, plastic, late 1940s-early 50's, light green w/two large dials for control & two large dials above, one containing clock, the second for station control, 4 x 6 1/2 x 8" (ILLUS.) ........................................ **250**

**Radio,** Emerson, clock-radio, 1950s, various models w/wake-up control ........................................ **20**

*FADA Radio w/Aerial Inside*

**Radio,** FADA 7, wooden case w/gold dials for tuning & volume, w/fold out aerial inside, manufactured by Frank Angelo D'Andrea Co., operated 1920-1932, 25 x 13 1/2 x 11" (ILLUS.) ........................................ **500**

*General Electric Floor Model Radio*

**Radio,** General Electric, floor model, last radio manufactured in Canada prior to the start of World War II, 1939, 30 x 15 x 41" (ILLUS.) .................................. **175**

*Marconi 6 Tube Radio*

**Radio,** Marconi 6 tube, table model, 1930s, three bands, w/large fabric speaker on side, 22 x 10 x 13" (ILLUS.) ......................... **200**

*Northern Electric Table Radio*

**Radio,** Northern Electric, table model, one-band, black w/two dials, Art Deco scroll-work, 1940s, 10 x 6 x 6 1/2" (ILLUS.)............. **75**

**Radio,** Oceana Japanese, portable, plastic, various colors, early 1960s ........................... **75**

*Pfanstiehl Model 7 Radio*

**Radio,** Pfanstiehl Model 7, "Listening to a Pfanstiehl is like being there yourself," wooden case, w/wooden cutouts over speaker area, manufactured in Highland Park, Ill., 36 x 16 x 15" (ILLUS.) ................ **1,200**

*Stromberg Carlson Floor Model 180*

**Radio,** Stromberg Carlson Model 180, floor model w/cabinet doors & accoustical sound system, 1936 (ILLUS.) ........................ **300**

*Victor Talking Machine Model 143*

**Radio,** Victor Talking Machine Model #143, table model w/illuminiated dial, four bands & four controls, 1930s, 13 x 16 x 20" (ILLUS.) ................................... **150**

**Radio advertising,** RCA ads, from various magazines in the 1920s, full page featuring the Radiola Superheterodyne, could bring in signals from 3,000 miles away ........ **300**

*Atwater Kent Radio & Phonograph*

**Radio & phonograph,** Atwater Kent floor model, wooden case w/elaborate scrolling, phonograph hidden by wood sliding doors (ILLUS.) ............................................. **500**

*Hammond Radio Receiver*

**Radio receiver,** "The Hammond 1923," of Guelph, Ontario, large, black wooden case (ILLUS.) ............................................. **200**

*Speakers for Various Radios*

**Speakers,** some manufactured by Music Master, various sizes, name usually appears on speaker or inside the horn, price varies due to size & condition (ILLUS.).............................................. **50 and up**

# RADIO & TELEVISION MEMORABILIA

*Not long after the dawning of the radio age in the 1920s, new programs were being aired for the entertainment of the national listening audience. Many of these programs issued premiums and advertising promotional pieces which are highly collectible today.*

*With the arrival of the TV age in the late 1940s, the tradition of promotional items continued and in addition to advertising materials, many toys and novelty items have been produced which tie-in to popular shows.*

*Below we list alphabetically a wide range of items relating to classic radio and television. Some of the characters originated in the comics or on the radio and then found new and wider exposure through television. We include them here because they are best known to today's collectors because of television exposure.*

*Addams Family Oil Painting Set*

**Addams Family paint set,** numbered oil painting set featuring Morticia Addams, in original box, 11 x 14" (ILLUS.)...... **$800-1,200**
**Alice costume accessories,** sailor cap & slippers worn by character "Mel," played by actor Vic Taybeck, 3 pcs. (ILLUS. top next column).......................................... **200-400**

*Alice Costume Accessories*

**Amos & Andy toy,** "Fresh-Air Taxi," windup tin, ca. 1930s, Marx, good, 8" l. ....... **700**
**Andy (Amos & Andy) toy,** windup tin walker, good, Marx...................................... **500**
**Batman (TV) Corgi auto gift set,** five-piece, No. 3080, very good w/good box, the set .................................................................. **280**
**Batman (TV) Corgi batboat on trailer,** includes two figures, No. 1003, excellent w/very good box ............................................. **90**
**Batman (TV) Corgi batmobile & batboat,** No. 2519, good w/good box, the set ................................................................... **50**
**Ben Casey charm bracelet,** w/card, ca. 1962 ................................................................. **45**

*Clarabell Clown Delivery Wagon*

**Clarabell Clown (Howdy Doody) toy,** friction action tin delivery wagon, very good w/good box, very rare, Line Mar (ILLUS.).................................................. **10,500**
**Daktari Corgi auto set,** three vehicles, No. 14, all mint.................................................... **530**

*Flintstone Flivver*

**Flintstones toy,** Flintstone Flivver, friction-action, ca. 1962, Marx, 6 3/4" l. (ILLUS.) ..... **413**
**Fred Flintstone (The Flintstones) toy,** battery-operated, Fred on Dino, w/original box, Marx (ILLUS. top next page) ......... **497**

*Fred Flintstone on Dino*

*Honey West Phonograph Album*

**Honey West phonograph album,** long-play album marked "Original Music From The Soundtrack - Honey West - starring Anne Francis - co-starring John Ericson," cover shows the star holding a gun in one hand & in the other a leash attached to a large reclining cat (ILLUS.) ................................................ **100-200**

**Howdy Doody bank,** Metlox ........................... **595**

**Howdy Doody lamp** ....................................... **575**

**Howdy Doody scarf** ...................................... **145**

*"I Love Lucy" Store Display Sign*

**I Love Lucy sign,** story display w/a large heart marked "Take a Flooring Tip from the 'I Love Lucy' home" above Lucy & Ricky depicted holding a copy of a book titled "Floor Planning for Your 'I Love Lucy' Home," sign marked "published by Sloane Delaware Superior Floor Products" (ILLUS.) ........................................ **400-700**

*Bill Cosby's Emmy Nomination Plaque*

**I Spy plaque,** Emmy nomination of Bill Cosby for his performance in the television series during 1965-1966 (ILLUS.) .............................................. **250 - 500**

*Jerry Mahoney Figural Lamp*

**Jerry Mahoney (Paul Wihchell & Jerry Machoney Show) lamp base,** seated figure of the puppet from The Paul Winchell & Jerry Mahoney Show, legs crossed at knee, hands folded over the knee, wearing sport jacket & polka dot bowtie (ILLUS.) ..................................... **450-750**

**Monkee-Mobile,** enameled metal, battery-operated musical friction-type, red w/colorful plastic half-figures of each Monkee mounted in seats, w/original box, ca. 1967, Japan (ILLUS. top next page) ..... **500-700**

*Monkee-Mobile*

**Monkeemobile,** w/four Monkees, No. 1004, Corgi Junior, very good w/good box ............................................................ **120**

**Mr. Magoo toy,** battery-operated, "Official Mr. Magoo Car," tinplate & plastic in yellow & green, w/eccentric rear wheel action, front steering, bouncing Mr. Magoo, removable top, Hubley, ca. 1960s, 9" l. (some scratching) ...................... **115**

**Orphan Annie Club manual & badge,** 1937 Secret Society manual w/Sunburst brass decorder badge, 1 3/4 x 2" .................. **83**

**Orphan Annie decoder badge,** "Mysto-Matic," plated brass, ca. 1939, 1 3/4" d. ........ **55**

**Orphan Annie mug,** Beetleware plastic cold Ovaltine shake-up mug, green w/figures of Orphan Annie & Sandy, red top, ca. 1940, 2 3/4 x 4 3/4" .......................... **55**

**Orphan Annie pinback button,** celluloid, shows Annie & "Orphan Annie Loves - Red Cross Macaroni" around border, white, red & black, Parisan Novelty Co., Chicago, Illinois, 1 1/4" d. (minor surface scratches) ...................................................... **55**

*Patty Duke Doll*

**Patty Duke doll,** wearing stripped pants & sweater, w/telephone & autographed photo, in original box, ca. 1965, Horsman, 12" h. (ILLUS.) .............................. **300-400**

**Petticoat Junction poster,** store display marked "Tyco's Petticoat Junction Official HO Scale Electric Train Set - Loco-

motive with Operating Headlight - An Authentic 1890 Train Complete with Track and Ready-To-Run," showing the train in the center w/figures from the television show in background (ILLUS. below) ...................................... **100-200**

*Petticoat Junction Poster*

**Scooby Doo & friends Corgi auto set,** five-piece auto set includes figures of Fred Flintstone, Barney Rubble, Wilma Flintstone, Scooby Doo & Yogi Bear, No. 3108, mint w/mint box, the set ...................... **95**

**Starsky & Hutch Corgi auto sets,** each set w/two vehicles, No. E2528, very good w/good boxes, two sets ........................ **85**

*Streets of San Francisco Prop Badge*

**Streets of San Francisco prop,** metal seven point star-shaped badge mounted in frame under autographed photograph of the stars, Karl Malden & Michael Douglas (ILLUS.) ......................................... **750-900**

**The Avengers Corgi auto gift set,** two vehicles & two figures, No. GS40, very good ............................................................. **210**

**The Honeymooners' bus,** pressed steel w/wood wheels, red, white & blue w/flesh-tone faces of Honeymooner characters depicted at windows, Jackie Gleason in front window as driver, marked over windshield "Awa-a-y We Go Bus" w/"POW!" on license plate & side marked "Honeymooners' Special - Jackie Gleason Bus" Wolverine Toys, ca. 1955, 4 1/2 x 4 1/2, 14" (ILLUS. top next page) .................... **400-600**

*The Honeymooners' Bus*

**The Man From U.N.C.L.E. Corgi auto,** includes two figures, No. 1003, w/very good box, excellent ...................................... 160

**The Munsters doll,** plastic, Herman Munster in sealed original box, ca. 1964, mint, Remco ............................................. **1,980**

*Munster Dolls*

**The Munsters doll,** plastic, Lily Munster in sealed original box, ca. 1964, mint, Remco (ILLUS. left).................................. **2,090**

**The Munsters doll (TV),** plastic, Grandpa Munster in sealed box, 1964, mint, Remco (ILLUS. right) ............................... **1,760**

**The Simpsons auto sets,** Hot Wheels, three pieces, all mint, 3 sets........................... 45

# RAILROADIANA

**Bell,** brass w/yoke, "Illinois Central Railroad," from steam locomotive, yoke marked "ICRR" ...................................... **$1,750**

**Calendar,** 1937, "Chesapeake & Ohio Railroad," scene of infant waking & stretching, toy bunny near foot, black kitten tucked in bed, four pages, each w/three months, complete w/original mailing tube, 13 1/2 x 16 1/2" ..................................... 66

**Cap badge,** "Missouri, Kansas & Texas Railway," metal, brakeman............................ 60

**Cap badge,** "Missouri Pacific Railroad," metal, porter .......................................... 110

**Cap badge,** "St. Louis & San Francisco Railway" (Frisco Lines), metal, brakeman ................................................................ 70

**Carte de visite photo,** Pittsburgh Railroad group shot of a work gang, ten men standing beside tracks holding shovels & picks, by B. Dabbs, Pittsburgh (soiling, top stain) ....................................... 124

**Conductor's lantern,** nickel-plated kerosene font w/a clear etched shade w/a foliate wreath centering "G.A. Pierce," marked by Adams & Westlake & patent-dated "64," 10 1/2" h................................... 460

**Engine builder's plate,** brass, round, "The Baldwin Locomotive Works Philadelphia USA #56912," 9 1/2" d. ............................. **675**

**Engine builder's plate,** brass, oval, "Beyer, Peacock & Co. Makers & Owners, Manchester, 1869," 7 x 15" ........... **700**

**Engine builder's plate,** brass, round, "Baldwin Locomotive Works Philadelphia USA 556," 17" d................................. **950**

**Engine builder's plate,** brass, round, "Built at Mt. Clare L-2b 10-26," 8" d. ................. **1,525**

**Glass,** juice, "Union Pacific Railroad"................ 12

**Hat,** brakeman, "Missouri, Kansas & Texas Railway" ............................................. 120

**Key,** switch-type, "St. Louis & San Francisco Railway" .................................... 60

**Key,** switch-type, "St. Louis & San Francisco Railway" .................................... 65

**Key,** switch-type, "Texas & Pacific Railroad" ................................................... 35

**Lantern,** "Boston & Albany Railroad," tall globe-type, red unmarked globe ................... 90

**Lantern,** "Canadian Pacific Railroad," short globe-type, clear globe w/raised lettering, wooden handle .................................... 50

**Lantern,** "Chesapeake & Ohio Railway," short globe-type, clear etched globe ............. 60

**Lantern,** "Chicago & Eastern Illinois Railroad," short globe-type, clear etched globe also w/"Safety First" ......................... 60

**Lantern,** "Chicago & Western Indiana Railroad," short globe-type, unmarked red globe ................................................... 65

**Lantern,** "Cleveland, Cincinnati, Chicago & St. Louis Railway," tall globe-type, clear globe w/raised wording "Safety First" ........... 80

**Lantern,** "Colorado Midland," tall globe-type, clear unmarked globe ....................... 400

**Lantern,** "Denver & Rio Grande Railroad," short globe-type, red etched globe ............. 105

**Lantern,** "Denver & Rio Grande Railroad," tall globe-type, clear globe w/raised wording "Safety First" .................................... 130

**Lantern,** "Erie Railroad," tall globe-type, clear globe w/raised lettering ....................... 90

**Lantern,** "Gulf, Colorado & Santa Fe Railway," tall globe, bell-bottom style, clear globe w/raised wording "Santa Fe" ............. 210

**Lantern,** "Gulf, Mobile & Ohio Railroad," tall globe-type, "Dietz" barn style, unmarked cobalt blue globe ................................. 170

**Lantern,** "Illinois Central Railroad," tall globe-type, clear globe w/raised lettering ..... 135

**Lantern,** "Missouri Pacific Railroad," tall globe, bell-bottom brass top type, clear globe w/raised lettering .......................... 625

**Lantern,** "Missouri Pacific Railroad," tall globe-type, red globe w/raised lettering ...... 160

**Lantern,** "Nashville, Chattanooga & St. Louis Railway," short globe-type, red etched globe ................................................ 75

**Lantern,** "Pere Marquette Railroad," short globe-type, unmarked red globe ................. 50

Lantern, "Pittsburgh & Lake Erie Railroad," short globe-type, globe etched "Omaha" ....... 55

Lantern, presentation-type, all-brass, bell bottom style, unmarked tall clear globe, M.M. Buck & Co. ........................................ 325

Lantern, presentation-type, all-brass, tall clear globe, frame & globe marked "Pullman," Adams & Westlake Co. ..................... 450

Lantern, presentation-type, chrome-plated, bell bottom style, green & clear tall globe etched w/initials & wreath, M.M. Buck & Co. ............................................................... 950

Lantern, "Richmond, Fredericksburg & Potomac Railroad," short globe-type, clear etched globe ......................................... 80

Lantern, "Rock Island Lines," tall globe-type, clear globe w/raised lettering .............. 100

Lantern, "Seaboard Air Line Railway," short globe-type, etched red globe ............. 100

Lantern, "St. Louis & South Western Railway," tall globe-type, clear globe w/raised wording "Cotton Belt Route" ......... 400

Lantern, "Texas & Pacific Railway," tall globe-type, clear etched globe .................... 200

Plate, "Denver & Rio Grande Western Railroad," dinner, china, "Blue Adam" patt. ......... 50

Plate, "New York Central Railroad," bread & butter, china, "Dewitt Clinton" patt. ........... 23

Plate, "Northern Pacific Railroad," bread & butter, china, "Monad" patt. .......................... 33

Plate, "Pennsylvania Railroad," grapefruit, china, "Mt. Laurel" patt. ................................. 45

Platter, "Pennsylvania Railroad," service, china, oval, "Liberty" patt. ............................. 25

Platter, "Union Pacific Railroad," china, oval, "Challenger" patt. .................................... 18

Platter, "Union Pacific Railroad," china, small oval, "Harriman Blue" patt. ................... 33

Platter, "Union Pacific Railroad," china, oval, "Harriman Blue patt.," 7 1/4 x 11" ......... 70

Print, "Pennsylvania Railroad," multicolor print, signed Grif Teller, 1933, framed, 20 x 26 1/2" (some staining, minor crease) ...................................................... 171

Service plate, "Denver & Rio Grande Western Railroad," china, "Prospector" patt. ................................................................. 30

Service plate, "New York Central Railroad," china, "Mercury" patt. ......................... 50

Service plate, "New York Central Railroad," china, "Mohawk" patt. ......................... 50

Service plate, "Union Pacific Railroad," china, "Desert Flower" patt. ......................... 60

Service plate, "Union Pacific Railroad," china, "Winged Streamliner" patt. ................... 50

Serving dish, cov., "Missouri Pacific Railroad," silver plate, by International Silver ..... 140

Soup bowl, "Union Pacific Railroad," china, "Harriman Blue" patt. ................................... 20

Step stool, "Panama Limited," metal ............... 225

Torch can, "Missouri Pacific Railroad," metal ................................................................ 23

Torch can, "St. Louis & San Francisco Railway," metal, early type ............................ 60

# RECIPE BOOKLETS

Recipe booklets originally appeared at the end of the 1800s as tags on early appliances, or as give-aways from companies to entice sales. They flourished throughout the 20th century as technology altered the American kitchen and the foods that people ate. Hundreds of recipe booklets and pamphlets are available for the collector. Favorites among the numerous categories are radio or celebrity tie-ins, appliance recipe & instruction booklets, wartime booklets, colorful illustrations and covers designed by famous early 20th century artists like Maxfield Parrish. Pre-30s booklets were beautifully illustrated with watercolor and painted images. By the 1930s, tasteful photographs and whimsical illustrations filled the booklets. The 1950s through the 1980s produced tons of booklets that are still being offered today by many companies. Most recipe booklets are still modestly priced and often informative.

*Brer Rabbit's Molasses Recipes*

101 Refrigerator Helps, Frigidare Division, General Motors, 1944, 34 pp ........................ **$6**

340 Recipes for the New Waring Blendor, Waring Products Corp., 1947, 64 pp......... **8**

A Cook's Tour With Minute Tapioca, Minute Tapioca Co., 1931, 48 pp .................. **10**

Around the World Cook Book, Kalamazoo Stove & Furnace Co., 1951, 50 pp ........... **5**

Aunt Jenny's Favorite Recipes, Lever Brothers, Spry shortening recipes, radio tie-in, 1940s, 50 pp...................................... **12**

Brer Rabbit's New Book of Molasses Recipes, Penick & Ford, Ltd., 1936, 50 pp (ILLUS.)...................................................... **8**

*Sucaryl Recipes*

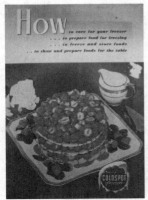

**Calorie Saving Recipes With Sucaryl,** Abbott Industries, 1950, 32 pp (ILLUS.) .......... 6

*Coldspot Freezers*

**Coldspot Freezers,** Sears, Roebuck, & Co., "How to" manual, 1950, 38 pp (ILLUS.) .......... 6

**Cook Master Heat Control,** Landers of Arkansas, 1957, 24 pp .......... 4

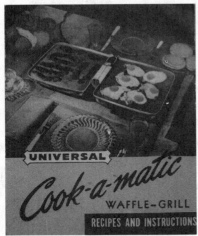

*Universal's Waffle-Grill*

**Cook-a-matic Waffle-Grill,** Universal, 1948, 24 pp (ILLUS.) .......... 6

**Country Inn Cookware, A Wealth of Wonderful Recipes** West Bend Co., shows complete cookware lines, 1969, 37 pp (ILLUS. top next column) .......... 5

**Cutco Cook Book (World's Finest Cutlery!),** Wear-Ever Aluminum Co., photos of complete line, 1961, 130 pp .......... 4

**Electric Cookery,** Montgomery Wards, 1948, 50 pp .......... 6

**Electric Cooking With Your Kenmore Range,** Sears & Roebuck, 1956, 34 pp .......... 5

**Electric Mix Treasures, Dormeyer Mealmaker,** Dormeyer Corp., 1949, 36 pp .......... 8

**Frozen Food Cook Book,** Amana Refrigeration Inc., 1953, 66 pp .......... 6

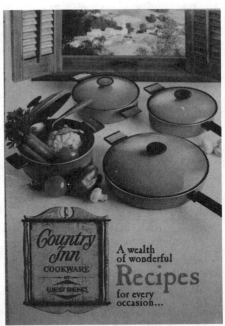

*Westbend's Country Inn Cookware*

**GE Automatic Skillet,** General Electric, late 1950s, 36 pp .......... 3

**Grid-O-Matic Automatic Table Cooker,** Dominion Electric Corp., brochure type, 1936 .......... 10

**Hershey's Recipes,** Hershey Chocolate, 1940, 32 pp .......... 12

*Sunbeam Mixmaster*

**How to Get the Most Out of Your Sunbeam Mixmaster,** Sunbeam Corp., 1948, 44 pp (ILLUS.) .......... 8

**Instructions and Tested Recipes, Food Mixer & Mixguide,** Hamilton Beach, ca. 1948, 52 pp .......... 5

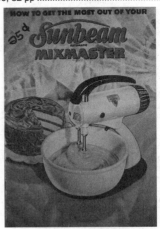

**Kenmore Automatic Grill-Waffler,** Sears, Roebuck & Co., 1950s, 22 pp .......................... 3

**Kitchen Tested Recipes, Sunbeam Mixmaster,** Sunbeam Corp., ca. 1950, 50 pp ............................................................ 6

**Lamb Time for Young Americans,** National Lamb Council, pamphlet-style, 1960 ............................................................ 2

**Namco Crab,** National Mercantile Co., 1927, 14 pp ............................................ 12

**New Exciting! Casual Cooking,** Reynolds Metals Co., 1954, 16 pp ......................... 6

**New Recipes for Good Eating,** Proctor & Gamble, Crisco recipes, 1949, 113 pp............ 5

**Once Upon a Table,** General Foods, Bird's Eye recipes, 1971, 31 pp ................................ 3

**Pressure Sauce Pan,** General Electric, early 1950s, 12 pp.......................................... 3

**Presto Cooker Recipe Book,** National Pressure Cooker Co., 1947, 130 pp ................ 4

**Presto Vertical Broiler,** National Presto Industries, Inc., 1960s, 22 pp .......................... 3

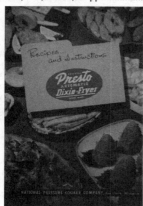

*Presto Dixie-Fryer*

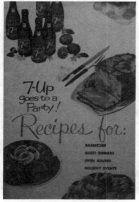

**Recipes and Instruction, Presto Dixie-Fryer,** National Pressure Cooker Co., 1950, 42 pp (ILLUS.)........................................ 4

**Recipes and Instructions, Ovenette,** West Bend Aluminum Co., 1940s, 16 pp ......... 2

*Recipes for 7-Up*

**Recipes for 7-Up,** The 7-Up Co., 1961, 14 pp (ILLUS.)........................................................ 3

*Revere's Guide to Better Cooking*

**Revere's Guide to Better Cooking,** Revere Copper and Brass Inc., 1941, 32 pp (ILLUS.)........................................................ 8

**Roto-Broil '400' King Size,** Roto-Broil Corp. of America, late 1950s, 16 pp................. 5

*Shefford Cheese Recipes*

**Shefford Cheese Recipes,** Shefford Cheese Co., brochure type, 1950s (ILLUS.)............................................................ 10

**Tasty Recipes, Oster Mixers,** John Oster Mfg. Co., 1946, 34 pp........................................ 5

**Teflon Coated Automatic Electric Skillet,** Westbend Corp., brochure type, ca. 1964 ............................................................ 3

**The Complete Jello Recipe Book,** G F Corp., 1929, 48 pp ........................................... 10

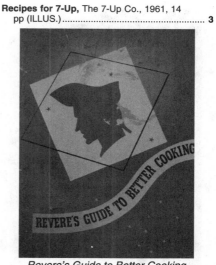

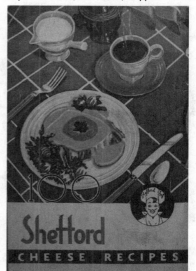

*Miracle Maid Cook-Ware*

*Westinghouse Econo Cooker*

*Betty Crocker's "Your Share"*

# RIBBON DOLLS

In the days when young girls and ladies were often judged by their handiwork, ribbon dolls were a popular art form. Sometimes also referred to as ribbon ladies or ribbon pictures, from the 1930s-50s the components were often available in kit form, complete with paper doll, ribbon supplies, instructions, frame & glass. Others were made from a simple pattern sold for ten cents, while faces & bodies were homemade.

Although the majority of subjects were women, occasionally a male example will surface, often as part of a set. Women dressed in hooped skirts & carrying bouquets, baskets of flowers or parasols, brides & similar colonial-looking figures are the most often found today. While most were mounted on plain black backings some examples include exquisitely decorated backgrounds or unusual poses, including smoking a cigarette or cutting flowers in a garden. Occasionally, the artist signed & dated her work, or inscribed the back as a gift.

*Little Girl Ribbon Doll*

**Girl,** in blue ribbon dress & black ribbon sash, holding basket of multi-colored flowers, 4 1/8" h. (ILLUS.) ..................... **$95-125**

*Little Girl w/Real Hair Ribbon Doll*

**Girl,** w/real brown hair, in lace dress & bonnet, decorated w/ribbon flowers, back marked "Made by Hilda Peterson, Feb. 18, 1931," 6 1/2" h. (ILLUS.) ..................... **45-60**

**Girl,** wearing a lace sunbonnet, in a green ribbon dress, trimmed in lace, holding a coordinating nosegay, 6" h. ....................... **35-55**

*Lady In Yellow Ribbon Doll*

**Lady,** blonde, bobbed-haired, w/elongated neck, long-lashed eyes cast downward, wearing yellow velvet dress trimmed in lace & ribbon, holding ribbon & lace bouquet (ILLUS.) ......................................... **100-135**

*Lady In Green Ribbon Doll*

**Lady,** made completely of green ribbon, trimmed in pink ruffled ribbon & decorated w/needlepoint designs & flowers, holding matching bouquet, 7 1/2" h. (ILLUS.) .................................................... **45-65**

*Lady on Tip-Toe Ribbon Doll*

**Lady,** on tip-toe, w/pink satin ribbon dress, holding a closed parasol, 5 1/2" h. (ILLUS.) .................................................... **60-85**

*Red-haired Lady Ribbon Doll*

**Lady,** red-haired, in peach satin ribbon dress, trimmed in yellow-tipped lace, black sash w/ribbon roses on large-brimmed hat, holding coordinating lace-

encircled ribbon rose bouquet, 6 1/4" h.
(ILLUS.) ...................................................... **65-85**

*Colonial Man Ribbon Doll*

**Man,** Colonial, in green ribbon pantaloons
& dark pink waistcoat, w/ruffled ribbon
cuffs & collar, companion to Colonial
woman, 8 1/2" h. (ILLUS.) ........................ **50-65**

*Colonial Man & Woman Ribbon Busts*

**Set:** Colonial man & woman busts: man in
top hat w/lace cuffs & cravat; blonde
woman in bonnet w/lace-trimmed bodice
& black sash, 4 3/4" h. (ILLUS.) .............. **85-100**

*Little Boy & Girl Ribbon Doll Set*

**Set:** Little girl & boy: girl in red ribbon dress
& hat w/lace & multicolored ribbon flower
trim, green bow at neck, 3 1/2" h.; boy in
grey trousers & mauve shirt w/lace color,

holding multicolored ribbon flower bouquet w/ribbon streamers, 3 1/2" h.
(ILLUS.) ...................................................... **95-125**
**Woman,** blonde, in black ribbon dress
w/white ribbon petticoat, flaring skirt to
reveal legs, 9 1/4" h. ................................. **75-100**
**Woman,** bride, dressed in off-white ribbon
gown & veil, holding bouquet w/ribbon
streamers, 7 1/2" h. ................................... **55-75**

*Colonial Woman At Spinning Wheel*

**Woman,** Colonial, blonde, wearing a dark
& light pink ribbon ruffled dress, sitting in
a chair & working on a spinning wheel,
8 1/4" h. (ILLUS.) ...................................... **75-85**
**Woman,** "Colonial Dame," white haired, in
pink ribbon dress w/lace trim, holding a
red feather, Bucilla, ca. 1930s-40s,
8 3/4" h. ...................................................... **75-95**
**Woman,** Colonial, in dark pink ribbon dress
& hat w/green ribbon sash & trim, holding multicolor ribbon bouquet, compan-
ion to Colonial man, 8 1/2" h. (ILLUS.) ...... **50-65**

*Colonial Woman Ribbon Doll*

*Colonial Woman Ribbon Doll*

**Woman,** Colonial, w/transparent pink shell-like dress trimmed in marcasite beads & ribbon flowers, no hair, 9" h. (ILLUS.) .................................................... **30-40**

*Woman In Pink Ribbon Doll*

**Woman,** in salmon-pink satin dress, w/black lace cuffs, holding matching open parasol, w/large ribbon & lace bouquet, background decorated w/painted & ribbon flowers (ILLUS.) .......................... **100-135**
**Woman,** w/black hair, in black & white ribbon dress, w/ruffled cuffs & neck band, wearing black hat, blue feather in hat & hand, 7 1/2" h. (ILLUS. top next column) .. **55-65**

*Black-haired Woman Ribbon Doll*

# ROYCROFT ITEMS

*Roycroft Copper Chandelier*

Elbert Hubbard, eccentric entrepreneur of the late 19th century, founded Roycroft Shops and established a craft community in East Aurora, New York in 1895. Individuals were trained in the trades of bookbinding, leather tooling and printing. Craft-style furniture in the manner of Gustav Stickley and known as "Aurora Colonial" furniture was produced. A copper workshop, begun in 1908, turned out numerous items. All of these, along with those pieces of Buffalo Pottery china which were produced exclusively for use at the Roycroft Inn and carry the Roycroft symbol, constitute a special category associated with the Arts and Crafts movement.

**Ashtray,** brass-washed hand-hammered copper, arm-top style, a small shallow rounded cup attached to one end of a suede strip w/tooled, weighted leather ends, original patina, marked, 14 3/4" l. (some suede wear) ..................................... **$220**

**Ashtray,** table model, hand-hammered copper, a wide low cylindrical form w/flared bottom edge & a flattened rim fitted w/four cigarette holders around the wide dished interior centered by a upright forked scroll handle, normal cleaning to original patina, marked, 9 1/2" d. .................................. **990**

**Book ends,** hand-hammered copper, flat rounded sides w/a small crimp at the center top, the sides embossed in the center w/an owl's head, riveted bases, original patina, marked, 5 x 5 1/2", pr. .......... **275**

**Book ends,** hand-hammered copper, large stamped poppy blossom on the rounded side, mint original patina, marked, 5 1/2 x 5", pr. ................................. **990**

**Book ends,** hand-hammered copper & leather, the half-round upright centered by a round leather medallion w/an embossed stylized owl, original patina, marked, 4 x 4 1/2", pr. (some leather shrinkage in one medallion) ........................ **330**

**Book ends,** hand-hammered copper, upright rectangular sides embossed w/a medallion of a four-leaf clover & incised edge bands, on a verdigris-patinated squares, fine original dark patina, marked, 4 1/4 x 5", pr. (one w/loose rivet) ................................................. **440**

**Bookstand,** Arts & Crafts style, oak, "Little Journeys" type, a rectangular top above two-slat uprights joined by two keyed through-tenon lower shelves raised on arched shoe feet, overcoated original finish, brass tag mark, 14 x 26", 26" h. .......... **715**

**Box,** cov., mahogany, "Goodie Box," rectangular footed form w/strap hardware & riveted corner brackets, carved "Mildred Hopper," carved mark, 12 1/2 x 24", 10 1/2" h. (some wear & scratches to original finish) ............................................. **990**

**Candelabrum,** hand-hammered copper, a wide thin disc foot centered by a twisted slender shaft w/long C-scroll brackets supporting the long narrow crossbar w/curled-up ends & fitted w/a row of six candlecups, some wear to patina, marked, 13 1/2" w., 13 1/2" h. ...................... **550**

**Candlesticks,** hand-hammered copper, a wide disc foot centered by a tall slender cylindrical shaft w/a cylindrical candle socket w/wide rolled rim, original dark patina, marked, 9 3/4" h., pr. ........................ **825**

**Candlesticks,** hand-hammered copper, a wide disc foot centered by a tall slender shaft w/a twist near the base, tulip-form socket w/a wide flattened rim, fine original dark patina, marked, 4 3/4" d., 12 1/4" h., pr. ............................................. **1,100**

**Candle sconces,** wall-type, hand-hammered copper, tall backplate w/curved-down top, embossed w/an oblong arrowhead design, angled small platform at the base supports the cylindrical candle socket, fine original patina, marked, 2 1/2" w., 9" h., pr. (minor wear to bottom of one) ................................................. **550**

**Candlesticks,** hand-hammered copper, a wide thin disc foot centered by a low tulip-form socket w/widely rolled rim, mint original patina, marked, 4" d., 2" h., pr. ................................................................. **303**

**Chandelier,** Arts & Crafts style, hand-hammered copper, an inverted conical dome w/a wide riveted upper rim band suspended by three heavy chains to the domed ceiling plate, excellent original finish, possibly from the Grove Park Inn, unmarked, 17 1/2" d., 8" h. (ILLUS.) ........... **550**

**Chest of drawers,** child's, Mission-style (Arts & Crafts movement), oak, a rectangular-framed mirror above the top swiveling between square uprights, a rectangular top slightly overhanging a case of three long drawers w/small plate & ring pulls, designed for Hubbard's granddaughter, 1912, mint original condition, carved orb & cross mark on top drawer, complete w/letter of provenance from Ms. Hubbard, 11 x 26", 34" h. (several small shallow nail holes on top of front right corner) ..................................... **14,300**

**Console set:** shallow console bowl & a pair of candlesticks; brass-washed hand-hammered copper, the footed bowl w/a wide shallow top flanked by wide angled loop handles, the candlesticks w/a round lightly scalloped stepped disc foot w/a tall slender shaft & bell-form socket w/rolled rim, original patina, marked, bowl 9" d., the set ......................................... **605**

**Frame,** Arts & Crafts style, oak, a large rectangular form w/wide flat board sides, holding Elbert Hubbard's "The Adman's Philosophy" signed by Hubbard, matted, ca. 1915, 24 x 33 1/2" .................... **660**

**Humidor,** cov., hand-hammered copper, cylindrical w/slightly flared base, fitted cover w/large button finial, the sides embossed w/a trefoil design, fine original dark patina, marked, 4 1/4" d., 5 1/2" h. ....... **935**

**Inkstand,** hand-hammered copper, a long narrow rectangular tray w/a dished rectangular central section flanked at each end by square clear glass inkwells w/square metal caps, fine original patina, marked, 2 1/2 x 15" .......................... **660**

**Lamp base,** copper, hand-hammered, circular base w/slender cylindrical standard segmented w/stepped rings & disks, double socket, twisted copper finial, dark patina, stamped mark, 19 1/4" h. ................. **748**

**Letter opener,** hand-hammered copper, shaped like a saber w/a slight arched handle, fine original patina, marked, 10" l. ................................................................. **88**

**Plate,** hand-hammered copper, round dished form w/a wide flat flanged rim embossed w/three trefoils against heavy gauge verdigris panels, marked, 10" d. (some pitting) ............................................. **330**

**Poker chip rack,** hand-hammered copper, a flared pedestal foot supporting a deep cylindrical cover w/a flattened top centered by a pointed finial, complete w/original chips, mint original dark patina, marked, 4 3/4" d., 6 1/2" h. .............. **660**

**Side chair,** Mission-style (Arts & Crafts movement), oak, a tall back w/slightly curved square stiles flanking rails joined by a tacked-on original hard leather panel raised above the seat w/matching leather, deep apron, square legs joined by box stretchers, from the Roycroft Inn, excellent original finish, inventory mark only, 41" h. (small tears to seat & back panel) ......................................................... **1,430**

*Fine Roycroft Sideboard*

**Sideboard,** Arts & Crafts style, oak, the backboard raised & enclosing a mirror between flat stiles w/rounded tops above the rectangular top overhanging a case w/a stack of three central drawers flanked by leaded glass doors over a long single drawer across the bottom, raised on squared knob feet, the carved orb & cross mark on the bottom drawer, mint original finish, crack in one glass pane, 25 x 60", 55" h. (ILLUS.) .............. **28,600**

**Tray,** hand-hammered copper, long oval dished form w/slightly upturned edges, angled end loop handles, embossed w/a stylized flower on a verdigris panel, slight patina wear, marked, 22" l. ................. **550**

**Vase,** brass-washed hand-hammered copper, simple cylindrical form w/a polychrome patina w/diamond quatrefoils around the top & thin-banded panels around the sides, wear to patina, marked, 2 1/2" d., 7" h. (ILLUS. left, top next page) ................................................ **1,540**

**Vase,** hand-hammered copper, 'Egyptian Flower Holder" type, tall slender cylindrical body w/four nickel-silver squares spaced around the top & four full-length rounded buttress handles, made for the Monterey Mission of California, excellent original patina, stamped w/the Mission's own orb & cross mark, 4 1/2" d., 7" h. ....... **6,600**

**Vase,** brass-washed hand-hammered copper, tall cylindrical form, polychrome patina w/a band of diamond quatrefoils around the rim each suspending a thin line w/a diamond tip, excellent original

patina, marked, 3" d., 10" h. (ILLUS. right, below) ............................................. **2,640**

*Two Roycroft Copper Vases*

**Vase,** hand-hammered copper, a tall cylindrical form w/a ring at the bottom above the wide flaring foot, old cleaned finish, marked, 6" d., 10 1/2" h. ............................ **2,860**

**Vase,** hand-hammered copper, 'American Beauty' type, footed wide squatty base w/a wide shoulder tapering to a tall, ringed cylindrical neck w/flared rim, medium size, excellent new patina, marked, 6" d., 12" h. ................................ **3,080**

**Wastepaper basket,** Arts & Crafts style, oak, heavy square tapering framework w/each side enclosing six flat slats, original ebonized finish, marked, 14" sq. ......... **2,310**

# RUGS - HOOKED & OTHER

## HOOKED

*Cat & Kitten Hooked Rug*

**Cat & kitten,** a half-oval form w/a seated black cat & kitten in the central reserve framed by a wide vining floral border, worked in shades of black, brown, blue, red & yellow, mounted, wear, fading, late 19th - early 20th c., 24 x 29" (ILLUS.) ........ **$546**

**Cats & ball of yarn,** three cats in white & grey playing w/a ball of yarn against a magenta ground w/blue & white narrow edge stripes, cats named on border

"Skeeks," "Shasta" & "Minnie," mounted on a stretcher, 21 x 33 1/2" (wear, minor damage & color bleeding) ............................ **468**

**Dog reclining,** rectangular, small brown spaniel-like dog reclining on the ground between flowering leafy plants, wide brown fern leaf-like border, 39 x 66" (minor repairs, losses).................................. **690**

**Dogs,** rectangular, two black dogs on a hit-or-miss ground, mounted on a black frame, 33 x 63 1/2" (fading, minor repair)..... **748**

**Eagle & laurel branches,** rectangular, a spread-winged American eagle clutching arrows in brown & white against a blue ground w/white stars & within a shaped oblong reserve w/a wide yellow frame w/red & green laurel leaves & flowers, dark brown outer ground, 38 x 51" (soiling, stains, some overall & edge wear) ........ **303**

*Large Muriel Bordon Hooked Rug*

**Floral & geometric blocks,** room-sized, blocks of colored floral bouquets alternating w/dark square w/a light cross design, dark border, made by Muriel Bordon, minor damage (ILLUS.) ............... **3,410**

*Very Early Large Hooked Rug*

**Flowerpot & vines,** a scrolling leafy vine border surrounding a reserve w/a large stylized potted plant, worked in sage, olive, ecru, red & grey, yarn & cloth on a homespun ground, backed, scattered repairs, fading, minor splits, very minor losses, New England, first half 19th c., 48 x 49" (ILLUS.)...................................... **2,070**

**Geometric design,** rectangular w/a center design of triangles & wide ribbons bordered by a circular & oval pattern,

worked in shades of brown, blue, & grey on a black field, 27 x 43" (some wear) ........ **495**

**Geometric medallion,** the central medallion surrounded by large triangular corner blocks w/a wide border enclosing leafy scrolls, in olive green, blue, red & white, 59" sq. (some wear & damage) ......... **935**

**Heron with butterfly,** Waldoboro-type, rectangular scene of a heron w/butterfly standing amid cattails & water lilies, foliate border, late 19th - early 20th c., 27 1/2 x 52 1/2" (fading, minor split, repairs) ......................................................... **288**

**Horse,** standing animal in central rectangular scene framed by inscription "Feb. 12 - 1920 - Bess" & curve leaf-like designs in corners, wide double band border of leaf-like designs, navy blue & grey border, tan horse, pink letters & numbers & multicolored ground, 26 1/2 x 32" (overall edge wear, binding frayed) ..................... **715**

*Hooked Rug with Horses*

**Horses,** rectangular w/a large central oval reserve enclosing a large & small horse, large stylized floral sprigs at each corner, worked in shades of red, mustard, beige, black & grey mounted on a stretcher, early 20th c., 18 x 35 1/2" (ILLUS.) ..................................................... **1,035**

*Leaves & Scrolls Large Rug*

**Leaves & scrolls,** room-sized, the striated & scrolling leaf border centers a field of repeating geometric leaf clusters alternating w/clusters of oak-like leaves, worked in red, brown, celery, sage & burnt umber, backed, areas of wear, very minor loss, late 19th - early 20th c., 61" sq. (ILLUS.)........................................ **2,530**

*Noah's Ark Hooked Rug*

**Noah's Ark,** a long rectangular form w/a large scene of various pairs of animals coming off the ark from the left while Noah & his wife sit on the right edge before a large rainbow, woven titled at the bottom "Glad They Were To Be Ashore," worked in shades of blue, brown, green, red, purple, yellow & grey on a multicolored ground, minor wear & staining, 20th c., 30 x 54" (ILLUS.)............ **1,380**

**Sailing ship at sea,** a seascape worked in navy blue, red, blue & rust on a striated taupe & cream ground, navy border, 29 x 38 3/4" (minor fading losses)................ **173**

*Ship, Eagle & Fire Wagon Rug*

**Ship, eagle & fire wagon,** rectangular w/a left oval reserve enclosing a large sailing ship & a right reserve enclosing an early hook & ladder fire wagon, the center w/a large spread-winged eagle & a ground of scattered stars, worked in gold, red, slate blue, black & brown fabrics, late 19th - early 20th c., 34 x 56" (ILLUS.)....... **1,092**

**Squirrel & tree,** oversized orange squirrel reaching up to eat an acorn from a small leafy oak tree, in green, blue, brown, red & grey w/red & black border stripes, 27 1/2 x 39 1/2" (overall wear) .................... **935**

**Winter landscape,** rectangular, detailed snowy scene w/oxen pulling a wagon & a horse & figures in the foreground, a rail fence & horse w/trees in the middle ground & hills & trees in the distance, shades of brown, blue, black, red & green on an off-white ground w/dark narrow border band, 30 x 46" (wear, some fading) .......................................................... **715**

## OTHER

**Knitted,** geometric design composed of square in 'light and shadow,' expanding diamond pattern in shades of brown, green, rose & tan, late 19th - early 20th c., framed, 30 x 53" (minor losses).............. **460**

**Penny rug,** felt & wool, rectangular ground w/appliqued stars & three-leaf clovers overall, in reds, yellow, green, blue & grey on a goldenrod cotton ground, 19 x 36" (some color loss)............................ **248**

**Penny rug,** hexagonal w/a repeating applied penny patch design, scalloped border worked in shades of blue, red, black, brown & olive wool, America, late 19th c., mounted, 37 x 25" .......................... **316**

**Penny rug,** oblong, composed of multicolored mostly wool circles embroidered in bands into a tan twill ground, initialed "P.P.," late 19th - early 20th c., 23 x 43" (wear, dark stain on one edge) .................... **330**

# SALESMAN'S SAMPLES

*The traveling salesman or "drummer" has all but disappeared from the American scene. In the latter part of the 19th century and up to the late 1930s, they traveled the country calling on potential customers to show them small replicas of their products. Today these small versions of kitchenwares, farm equipment and even bathtubs, are of interest to collectors and are common in a wide price range.*

*Barber Chair Salesman's Sample*

**Barber chair,** porcelainized metal & leather, fancy filigree trim, Koken model, early 20th c., 15" h. (ILLUS.) ................ **$48,875**

*Griswold Sample Dutch Oven/Griddle*

**Dutch oven, cover & griddle,** cast iron, "Griswold Tite Top," wire bail handle, very good condition, early 20th c., griddle 7" d., the set (ILLUS.)................................ **77**

**Egg carrier & tray,** wood, cardboard & wire, a rectangular wooden frame w/slatted bottom & thin wire bail handle, marked "Star Egg Carrier and Tray," w/one dozen wooden ball "eggs" & advertising pamplet, late 19th - early 20th c., 3 1/2 x 4 1/2" (damage to one bottom slat) .................................................. **512**

*Horton's Horse Rake & Seed Sower*

**Horse rake & seed sower,** wood & metal, hickory frame w/red cast-iron spoked wheels, copper raking & lifting arms, brass tooth-wheels, seat & control lever, detachable seed sower w/trough & adjustable seed size gauge, Horton's "Improved Horse Rake & Seed Sower," ca. 1868, together w/printed product material in wood box, axle length 12 1/2", the set (ILLUS.) ................ **1,265**

**Porch light,** figural black jockey on pedestal, fine original paint, overall 12" h. ............. **878**

*Griswold Sample Teakettle*

**Teakettle,** cov., cast iron, Griswold, colonial design w/wire bail handle, very good condition, 6" l. (ILLUS.) ................................ **121**

*Griswold Waffle Iron Sample*

**Waffle iron,** cast iron, hinged iron on griddle base, Griswold, early 20th c., very good condition, 8" l. (ILLUS.) ........................... **8**

# SCALES

**Balance scales,** analytical-type, small brass pans suspended from a pierced metal cross-arm on a central standard, on a rectangular mahogany base, marked "Central Scientific Co.," late 19th - early 20th c., 17 1/2" h. ............................ **$182**

**Balance-type,** torsion model w/glass casing & plated finish, 9 x 20 1/2", 9 1/2" h. (one pan replaced) ..................................... **165**

**Sidewalk scales,** cast metal, Art Deco style w/framed top mirror in red enamel, one-cent coin slot for birth month, readout in pounds, on a white enameled body w/chrome decoration, foot plate w/marking of American Scale Manufacturing Co., Washington, D.C., ca. 1938, overall 61" h. (needs calibration) ................. **460**

**Sidewalk scales,** Fair Weight Golf Scale, penny action, Colonial Novelty Co., one of eleven made in 1920, 92" h ................. **25,875**

*Rare Rosenfeld Reliance Scale*

**Sidewalk scales,** Rosenfeld Reliance, cast iron, penny action, one of four known (ILLUS.) .................................................. **10,925**

**Sidewalk scales,** talking scale, five-cent action, w/phonograph record ready to speak your weight ..................................... **15,525**

**Sidewalk scales,** W.T. Avery cast iron one cent action, classical Greek Temple design, bold red, black & gold paint, all original & working w/original keys & locks, Birmingham, England ...................... **5,750**

**Steelyard scale,** steel & brass, a slender brass arm w/flattened end suspending a ring, ring & hook & weight, stamped "Wm. B. Preston - Boston," 18 1/4" l. ............. **94**

# SCIENTIFIC INSTRUMENTS

**Alidade,** cased, lacquered finish, original leather-covered case w/loose buckle, signed "W. & L.E. Gurley, Troy, N.Y.," 19th c., 11" l. (minor spots on finish) ......... **$440**

**Barometer,** self-recording pocket model, interior stamped "Brevette," cased, stained on label inside cover, 5 1/2 x 7 1/8", 2 1/8" h. ................................. **193**

*Victorian English Barometer*

**Barometer,** stick-type, oak-cased, the molded tall case w/white painted rectangular top dial above the throat thermometer w/beveled glass & base w/raised panel & molded bracket, marked "Pinkham and Smith," England, late 19th c., 40 1/2" h. (ILLUS.)............................... **1,035**

**Barometer,** stick-type, tall slender columnar mahogany case w/turned detail & original finish, gold stenciled label "Woodruff's Patent - June 5, 1860,"" silver face plate w/engraved label "S.A. Sperry, Ann Arbor," original tube, 41" h. ... **2,145**

**Drafting kit,** pocket-type, contains six tools plus two brass tips, includes a brass protractor, wooden rule, engraved ivory scale, brass & steel compass, etc., sharkskin-covered case, 2 1/2 x 7", 1 1/4" h., the set ......................................... **220**

**Microscope,** brass, small size w/two brass sections w/a mirror, includes four fittings w/different magnifications, three slides included w/botanical specimens & early handwritten note w/details about the slides, 19th c., 3 x 7 3/4", 2 1/8" h., cased set...................... **165**

**Microscope,** lacquered metal, a revolving three-power turret w/two additional lenses & extra eye piece, serial number 21662, Bausch & Lomb, cherry case w/raised panel door w/a drawer, 14 1/4" h....................................... **385**

**Microscope,** small brass & cast-iron model, w/two lenses, marked "Universal Household Microscope - James Queen, Phila.," w/walnut case, 7 1/4" h. ................. **248**

**Octant,** ebony, ivory inlaid signature panel, scale w/brass trim, signed "Riggs & Bro. - Philadelphia," 19th c., 10 7/8" l. ................. **550**

**Surveyor's compass,** 5" d. engraved face, tripod, plumb bob, small magnifying glass, ivory scale & cherry case, compass signed "Wm. Davenport - Phila.,"

case stenciled "A.C. Farrington" in gold & white, 19th c., 14" l................................. **1,155**

**Surveyor's compass,** cased, 6" d. compass w/engraved face, walnut case w/fine lithographed label showing an eagle, ship & maker's signature "Richard Patten - New York," w/ivory tripod, 19th c. (minor age cracks in lid, brass cover w/resoldered rim) ......................................... **990**

*Early Surveying Instrument*

**Surveyor's instrument,** wood & brass, a rectangular board w/a detailed incised graduated arc above a glass-enclosed level-type instrument, signed & dated "Made by C. Elliott in New-London 1766," missing stand, 4 7/8 x 10 1/4", 1 3/4" h. (ILLUS.)...................................... **3,738**

**Surveyor's transit,** brass, the silver dial labeled "Herm Pfister, Maker, Cincinnati," complete w/a mahogany case w/paper label "Wm. H. Pfister, successor to Herm Pfister," w/tripod & transit, Ohio, 12" h. transit ............................................. **1,320**

# SCOTTISH TARTANWARE

*Small wooden snuff & trinket boxes, hand-decorated with pen & ink scenes or portraits, were made in Scotland in the early 19th century and are the forerunner to Mauchline wares. Named after the Scottish village of Mauchline where numerous small sycamore boxes & souvenirs of excellent quality were produced, its production was not limited to that particular town. The "tartan" wares, first produced about 1820, originally were hand painted with the famed tartan plaids. A less expensive method that allowed for transfer printing directly to the wood was introduced later & by the late 19th century transfer-printed tartan paper or scenes were glued to the wood & varnished over. This latter type of ware, primarily with plaid decoration, is what the collector will most frequently encounter today. The Mauchline firm of W. & A. Smith, & their descendants, turned out enormous quantities of the ware until their boxworks was destroyed by fire in 1933.*

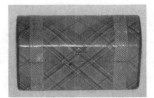

*Tartanware Dome-shaped Box*

**Box,** dome-shaped rectangular form (ILLUS.) ..................................................... **$125**

*Box For Playing Cards*

**Box,** rectangular, for holding playing cards, scene of cards on cover (ILLUS.) ................. **150**

*Tartanware Calling Card Case*

**Calling card case,** picture of Robert Burns on the front (ILLUS.) ..................................... **150**

*Egg Cup w/Original Cloth Cozy*

**Egg cup & original cloth cozy** (ILLUS.) ......... **275**

*Tartanware Egg Timer*

**Egg timer,** original glass timer (ILLUS.) ........... **150**

*Game Score Board*

**Game score board,** rows of numbers w/small holes for pegs (ILLUS.) ................... **125**

*Tartanware Glasses Case*

**Glasses case,** oblong w/hinged end opening (ILLUS.) ................................................ **350**

**Ink dip pen,** tartan-handled (ILLUS. w/inkstand) ............................................................. **125**

*Inkwell & Ink Dip Pen*

**Inkstand,** horseshoe-shaped w/jockey hat form lid for inkwell, opening for tartan-handle pen, rare, inkstand only (ILLUS.) ...... **850**

*Tartanware Inkwell*

**Inkwell,** clear, domed glass well w/Tartanware lid (ILLUS.) ......................................... **150**

*Tartanware Napkin Ring*

**Napkin ring,** (ILLUS)......................................... **50**

*Heart-shaped Pincushion*

**Pincushion,** heart-shaped w/cloth cushion around the sides (ILLUS.) ........................... **125**

*Tartanware Pincushion w/Box*

**Pincushion,** on lid of square box (ILLUS.)....... **150**

*Tartanware Round Stamp Box*

**Stamp box,** low round form w/stamp on lid (ILLUS.)...................................................... **200**

*Tape Measure, Pincushion & Waxer*

**Tape measure-pincushion-thread waxer,** upright cylindrical form w/pincushion on top, tape measure in center and waxer around bottom, ca. 1820 (ILLUS.)............... **800**

*Egg-shaped Thimble Holder*

**Thimble holder,** egg-shaped, can be opened at center (ILLUS.)........................... **200**

*Tartanware Thread Holder*

**Thread holder,** round box w/tiny holes for thread around the base, real photo on lid (ILLUS.)...................................................... **225**

# SCOUTING ITEMS

*Scout rules and regulations, handbooks and accouterments have changed with the times. Early items associated with the Scouting movements are now being collected. A sampling follows.*

## BOY SCOUT MEMORABILIA

*The Boy Scouts were founded by military hero Lord Baden-Powell in Great Britain at the turn of the century. The scouts have many of the same characteristics as a military unit.*

*In 1909 American businessman William Boyce became lost in the fog of London. He was helped by a young boy and when he offered a reward, the boy replied, "No, thank you, sir. I am a scout, I can't take anything for helping." He was so impressed that he formed the Boy Scouts of America when he returned from England.*

*Boy Scout material and souvenirs contain thousands of items. From books, to badges and uniforms and, of course, material connected to the various Jamborees, including the world gatherings. Many collectors just specialize in one area due to the vast amount of material.*

*Also see BANKS, MECHANICAL & STILL, GAMES & GAME BOARDS and POSTCARDS.*

**Book,** "Adventuring for Senior Scouts," published by Boy Scouts of America, 1939 edition .................................................. **$20**

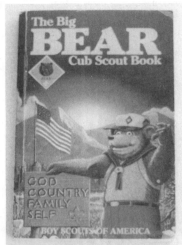

*"Big Bear Cub Scout Book"*

**Book,** "Big Bear Cub Scout Book (The)," 1984, published by Boy Scouts of America (ILLUS.) ..................................................... **5**

**Book,** Boy Scout Handbook, 1910 edition, first printed in 1910, includes a wealth of information every Boy Scout needs, updated periodically to keep pace w/a changing world ............................................. **650**

**Book,** Boy Scout Song Book 1913, includes songs to be sung at meetings & by the campfire .............................................. **50**

*Canadian Scout Handbook*

**Book,** Canadian Scout Handbook, 1990 issue (ILLUS.) ................................................ **2**

*Handbook for Patrol Leaders*

**Book,** Handbook for Patrol Leaders, published by Boy Scouts of America, 1959 edition (ILLUS.) ............................................. **25**

*"Lassie & The Cub Scout"*

**Book,** "Lassie & The Cub Scout," a Whitman book, published by Whitman Publishing of Western Publishing Co., Racine, Wisc., 1966 (ILLUS.) ........................ **15**

*"The Way To The Stars" Book*

**Book,** "The Way To The Stars," 1966, cover illustration of a satellite circling above the earth, full of experiments & projects to do (ILLUS.) ................................... **15**

**Boy Scout merit badges,** from the 1920s, price each ........................................................ **20**

**Boy Scout pocket knife,** model 1004, manufactured by New York Knife Co. of Walden, N. Y., w/four blades & bone stag handle, handle inscribed w/Boy Scout motto, "Be prepared," 3 3/4" l. ........... **250**

*Boy Scout Compass*

**Compass,** silver, clear, pocket-style, w/ring at top for attaching to belt, 1950s, 1 3/4" (ILLUS.).......................................................... **15**

*Boys' Life Magazine April, 1963*

**Magazine,** "Boys' Life," April, 1963, w/Yogi Berra of the New York Yankees on cover (ILLUS.).......................................................... **40**

*Boys' Life Magazine Ad for Coca-Cola*

**Magazine advertisement,** from back page of Boys' Life, for Coca-Cola, featuring Boy Scout merit badges & Coke soda cap, March 1964 (ILLUS.) ............................. **25**
**Neckerchief,** silk, from 1950 National Jamboree.......................................................... **80**
**Patch,** from National Jamboree, 1950............... **25**

*"The Pathfinder"*

**Photo,** "The Pathfinder," laminated, 1930s, shows Boy Scout w/Jesus in background, 8 1/2 x 5" (ILLUS.)............................. **50**
**Signal set,** "Official Boy Scout Twin Signal Set," for international Morse Code, w/original damaged box & instructions, the set .......................................................... **23**

*1975 Ghana Stamp*

**Stamp,** issued by Ghana, 1975, for 14th World Scout Jamboree in Norway (ILLUS.).......................................................... **2**

*40th Anniversary of B.S.A. Stamp*

**Stamp,** United States 3¢, honoring the 40th Anniversary of the Boy Scouts of America, mint, uncancelled (ILLUS.) ........................ **3**

*Boy Scout Tie Tac*

**Tie tac,** w/Scout symbol, on gold chain, 1950s (ILLUS.) ............................................. **25**

# BROWNIE

*Brownies is the Girl Scout program for girls 7 to 10. It was an experimental program in the 1920s and was established in the 1930s. There was a major change in the Brownie program in 1938 with the elimination of many terms and features originally borrowed from the English Girl Guides. Since WWII the Brownie program has become very large and all the memorabilia from that period has become quite easy to find. Thus, the emphasis here has been on the earlier, more challenging things.*

*In trying to collect some of the discontinued items from before 1938 it is important to distinguish between the USA Girl Scout version and the English and Canadian Girl Guide version. For pins, at least, the Girl Guides generally had the maker's name and a Registry number on the back while the Girl Scouts had nothing but a makers initial. In cloth patches it is more difficult to be sure which is which. It helps if the source of such items is available.*

*Doll information and pictures were supplied by Sydney Ann Sutton, Lakeland, FL.*

*Achievement Award*

**Achievement award,** golden bar, brown felt, rectangular gold embroidery on brown patch, before 1938, golden bar (ILLUS.) ........................................................ **$8**

**Achievement award,** golden hand, brown felt, rectangular gold embroidery on patch, before 1938, .................................... **100**

**Doll,** stuffed cloth, Georgene, w/brown cotton Brownie uniform, self belt, Peter Pan collar, two pockets & a brown pointed elf hat, painted cloth face, simulated shoes, yellow yarn hair, 1936-37, 14" ..................... **550**

*Effanbee Brownie Doll*

**Doll,** soft vinyl, Effanbee, w/light brown uniform, brown plastic belt, brown felt beanie, orange ribbon tie, socks, shoes & panties, white skin, "Fluffy," 1964-74, mint in box, 8" h. (ILLUS.) .............................. **75**

**Doll,** soft vinyl, Effanbee, w/light brown uniform, brown plastic belt, brown felt beanie, orange ribbon tie, socks, shoes & panties, black skin, 1968-72, 8" h. ........... **150**

**Doll,** soft vinyl, long straight blonde hair, w/light brown jumper & print blouse, brown panties, plastic belt, brown felt beanie, orange ribbon tie, brown socks, black shoes, 1874-83, 11 1/2" h. .................. **125**

**Doll,** soft cloth body, vinyl head, Georgene, w/braided blonde pigtails w/red ribbons, wearing replica tan Brownie uniform w/self belt, brown felt hat, white socks, brown shoes, 1949-56, 13 1/2" h. ............... **200**

*Georgene Doll*

**Doll,** stuffed cloth, Georgene, w/brown cotton Brownie uniform, self belt, pointed collar, one breast pocket, brown felt beanie w/white felt Brownie figure on front, painted cloth face, simulated shoes, red yarn hair, 1938-44, 14" h. (ILLUS.) ........................................................ **450**

**Doll,** composition body, vinyl head, Effanbee, white skin, brunette, brown felt beanie, plastic belt, brown socks & shoes, marked "Patsy Ann/C 1959" at neck, 1959-63, 15" h. .................................. **300**

*Emblem w/Mythical Figure*

**Emblem,** brown felt, square, embroidered patch w/mythical figure, identifies members of a group within a troop, eight dif-

ferent designs, before 1938, each
(ILLUS.)...................................................... **125**

**Equipment catalog,** sent to every registered Brownie, 1941-62, 10-20 pp.................. **15**

**Handbook,** for Brownie Girl Scouts, orange
soft cover, first printing of 1963 ed., 224
pp., excellent condition.................................... **6**

**Handkerchief,** thin cotton, printed in 5 colors on white cotton lawn, design is
Brownie washing clothes & hanging
them out to dry, three other designs in
the set of four, 1949, 8 1/2 x 9 1/2", each....... **20**

**Leader's insignia,** brass, tiny elf figure
w/fine chain attached, leader pin, chain
connected to Girl Scout trefoil pin, 1939-
65 ................................................................... **20**

*Leader's Insignia*

**Leader's insignia,** enameled brass,
orange, for Brown Owl (troop leader),
head of owl, 1927-38 (ILLUS.) ..................... **350**

**Leader's insignia,** enameled brass,
orange, for Tawny Owl (asst. leader), full
body of owl, 1927-38.................................... **500**

**Leader's insignia,** round cut-edge embroidered patch showing owl's head, 1929-
38 ................................................................. **140**

**Literature,** hard cover, "Brownie Scout
Handbook," first printing, 1951, 95 pp.,
excellent condition......................................... **15**

**Literature,** hard cover, "The Brownies,"
Scribners, 1st ed., 1946, adapted from "
Brownie and Other Stories" by Juliana
Horatia Ewing (orig. pub. 1885), story of
the source of the Brownie name & pro-
gram ............................................................... **20**

**Literature,** soft cover, "Brown Book for
Brown Owls," summary of suggestions
for leaders, by Edith Balliner Price, 2nd
ed., 1926, good condition, 91 pp................... **75**

**Literature,** soft cover, "Leader's Guide to
the Brownie Scout Program," 1939, 229
pp. ................................................................. **25**

*Membership Card*

**Membership card,** tan stock, printed in
dark brown ink, front has silhouette
drawing showing an owl, rabbits, mushroom & Brownie being lead by an elf,
space for name in front, 1926-32
(ILLUS.)......................................................... **40**

*Bridge to Juniors Patch*

**Patch,** Bridge to Juniors, green twill w/tan
letters, half-circle arch, surrounds the
three Brownie B segments, yellow, red &
blue, one for each Brownie participation,
1977-86, the set (ILLUS.)............................... **6**

*Fly-up Wings Patch*

**Patch,** Fly-up Wings, black or brown felt,
feathered wings, red, green or white,
1926-38, each (ILLUS.)................................ **175**

**Patch,** Fly-up Wings, dark green felt, feathered wings, yellow on dark green, 1938-
present .............................................................. **1**

**Patch,** Fly-up Wings, grey-green fabric,
feathered wings, brown on Girl Scout
fabric, 1931-38 ............................................ **200**

*Brownie Daisy*

**Pendant,** brass, 5-petaled flower, one for
each year, hung from Brownie pin, commonly called Brownie Daisy, 1939-56
(ILLUS.)............................................................ **5**

*First Issue Brass Pin*

**Pin,** brass, first issue, figure of elf, some have horizontal bar across middle to support pin, others the pin is soldered to the arms, before 1938, each (ILLUS.).......... **125**

*Pin w/Trefoil Outline*

**Pin,** brass or steel, trefoil outline, not reticulated around figure, 1943-44 (ILLUS.)............ **40**

**Pin,** brass, reticulated w/elf figure inside trefoil-shaped outline, 1939-present................. **1**

*Brass Pin*

**Pin,** brass, round outline reticulated w/elf inside circle (ILLUS.) .................................. **150**

*Postcard w/Brownie Promise*

**Postcard,** dark brown on tan, shows Brownie promise, law & motto, by E.B. Price, w/running girl , Girl Scout logo on the address side, 1930-38 (ILLUS.) ............... **20**

**Ring,** gold-filled, oval red glass insert w/Brownie figure on both sides, 1950-74, adjustable............................................... **20**

**Ring,** sterling, oval face, raised Brownie figure, adjustable, 1963-74 ............................... **10**

**Ring,** sterling, oval face, raised Brownie figure, non-adjustable, 1932-42, size 2-7........... **30**

**Ring,** sterling, rectangular face, raised Brownie figure, adjustable, 1949-62............... **15**

**Uniform,** brown cotton, slip-over washable raglan dress laced at the neck w/two breast pockets, Peter Pan collar, bloomers, pointed hat, leather belt, official label at the neck, 1927-36, size 8-12..... **400**

**Uniform,** brown cotton, slip-over washable raglan dress w/zipper neck, two patch pockets & Peter Pan collar, French panties, pointed hat, self belt, official label at neck, 1936-41, sizes 8-12 ............................ **250**

**Uniform,** chambray or gingham, shirtwaist dress w/four gored circular skirt & side-seam zipper, embroidered Brownie on breast pocket, brown felt beanie cap w/tan Brownie elf, tan cotton socks w/trefoil on brown cuff, 1941-56, sizes 8-12 ...................................................................... **50**

**Uniform make-up set,** chambray, large envelope w/2 1/2 yds. of 36" chambray, Advance pattern, buttons, thread & embroidery floss, ca. 1950, sizes 6-12........... **50**

# SCRIMSHAW

*Scrimshaw is a folk art by-product of the 19th century American whaling industry. Intricately carved and engraved pieces of whalebone, whale's teeth and walrus tusks were produced by whalers during their spare time at sea. In recent years numerous fine grade hard plastic reproductions have appeared on the market so the novice collector must use caution to distinguish these from the rare originals.*

**Corset busk,** engraved whalebone, scalloped end, decorated w/whaling vignettes enclosed by vine borders, flanked w/wreaths, 19th c., 13 1/8" l. (some warping) .......................................... **$518**

**Corset busk,** whale bone, long narrow flat strip w/double arch at the top, engraved down the front w/a compass, stars, tree, flags, hot air ballon, etc., 19th c., 11 1/4" l. ...................................................... **468**

**Corset busk,** whalebone, long narrow thin strip of bone decorated w/engraved sunburst, eagle w/shield, fan & other linear & geometric designs, 19th c., 11 3/4" l. (crack) ............................................................ **431**

**Corset busk,** whalebone, long slender flat busk engraved w/a neoclassical urn w/willow tree, "Love," a ship under sail, coconut tree & lighthouse, polychrome highlights, 19th c., 14 1/8" l. (faded, slightly warped, minor crack)....................... **230**

*Engraved Corset Busk*

**Corset busk,** whalebone, obverse engraved w/a whaling scene w/whale boat in pursuit flanked by hearts bearing portraits of sweethearts, the reverse w/vignettes of cityscape & country scene flanked by hearts, one bearing an anchor, the other w/the inscription "On

Board Brig Bruce," 19th c., 13 5/16" l.
(ILLUS.)..................................................... **2,530**

**Jagging wheel,** carved whale ivory, carved
in the form of a scrolling serpent w/the
body & eyes inlaid w/contrasting wood,
the end fitted w/a fluted wheel, probably
American, mid-19th c., 6 1/4" l. ................. **1,380**

**Jagging wheel,** carved whale ivory & pan-
bone, a baluster-turned & incised pan-
bone handle w/ring tip continuing to two
fluted jagging wheels on opposing short
arms centered by a three-tined fork tip,
probably American, mid-19th c., 8" l. ........ **1,380**

**Model of a baby cradle,** miniature, whale
bone, the canted sides joined by square
corner posts w/turned finials, each side
w/a scalloped top rail over an openwork
row of short turned spindles above the
solid sides w/incised designs, inset rock-
ers, good detail, 5" l. (minor crack).............. **523**

**Pie crimper,** whale ivory, rare three-
wheeled crimper w/squared & baluster
handle sprouting bird's heads w/fas-
tened pair of crimpers & pricking wheel,
handle base incised w/rose blossom &
bud stamp, mid 19th c., 8 1/4" l................. **5,175**

**Sailor's fid,** whale bone, long slender
pointed cylindrical form, old worn sur-
face, 11" l. .................................................. **193**

**Swift,** whalebone, expanding frame composed of narrow strips of bone decorated w/silk ribbon bows on a circular
wooden stand w/heart-shaped mother-
of-pearl inlay, together w/a fitted pine
case, American, 19th c., swift expanded
18 3/4" d.,  18 3/4" h.,  case  22 1/2" h.
(mother-of-pearl loss)............................... **2,645**

**Swift,** whalebone & ivory, double swift,
scribed staves, turned & scribed cup,
shaft & clamp, inlaid w/coin silver plaque
& rings, 19th c., 16" l. (minor losses &
damage)................................................... **1,840**

*Finely Engraved Walrus Tusk*

**Walrus tusk,** engraved w/various vignettes
including two eagles, a lady, an Indian &
a vulture, age cracks, 19th c., 18 7/8" l.
(ILLUS.)..................................................... **1,840**

**Whale's teeth,** decorated w/three quarter
view of Victorian ladies in elegant dress,
19th c., 3 3/4" l., pr. (age cracks) ............... **489**

*Scrimshaw Whale's Teeth*

**Whale's teeth,** each decorated w/incised
full-length figure of elegantly attired Victorian ladies, 19th c., 6" l., pr. (ILLUS.) ..... **2,875**

**Whale's tooth,** decorated w/an engraved
ship, a woman resting on an anchor
holding a flag & two potted plants, 19th
c., 4 3/8" h. (chips, minor cracks)................. **690**

**Whale's tooth,** engraved w/a portrait of
Captain Charles M. Scammon, initials
"PVD" beneath inscription "Nov 1857
Brig Boston & Schooner Marin Baja Cali-
fornia," reverse decorated w/a map of
"Scammons Lagoon," 19th c., 6" h.
(minor wear) .................................................. **403**

**Whale's tooth,** engraved w/a spiraling
design of various ships under sail & a
whaling scene, late 19th - early 20th c.,
6 1/4" l. (stained, minor cracks)................. **1,093**

**Whale's tooth,** engraved w/an elegant lady
& a seated nude woman, initials "OM,"
late 19th c., 5 1/8" l. (minor crack, very
minor chips)..................................................... **863**

**Whale's tooth,** obverse decorated w/eagle
in oval reserve, reverse w/seated Liberty
figure, inside curve, a compass rose &
initials "TN" outside curve, w/anchor &
rope, ocean waves & geometric border,
on carved hexagonal mahogany wooden
base inset w/four round ivory inlays, 20th
c., 5 1/2" h. .................................................. **1,495**

**Whale's tooth,** obverse depicting a sailor
holding an American flag, reverse
depicting a lady wearing a red dress &
necklace, holding a rose in one hand & a
handkerchief in the other hand, 19th c.,
4 1/2" l. (age crack) ...................................... **633**

**Whale's tooth,** polychrome decorated, an
American eagle & shield above a circular
reserve depicting a vessel under full sail,
heightened w/red, blue & yellow colors,
5 1/2" l. (age cracks) .................................. **1,150**

**Whale's tooth,** polychrome decorated,
obverse lettered w/"U.S." above an
eagle & an American flag, vine & floral
border, reverse w/an American ship,
both sides, heightened w/red color, 19th
c., 4 3/4" l. (age cracks)............................. **2,300**

**Whale's tooth,** decorated w/a reserve of a
whaling scene flanked by various whaling implements, rope border, early 20th
c., 9 1/4" l. (cracks).................................... **2,760**

# SEWING ADJUNCTS

*With sewing tools and accessories so popular,
collectors in the United States, Canada and
England actively search for these small antiques.
The wide variety available gives buyers a good
selection from which to choose - and allows for
plenty of different price ranges too. Be cautious of
reproductions - Victorian and Georgian styled sterling thimbles and needlecases marked "Thailand"
are found frequently and new pewter thimble holders are sometimes sold as old. A good reference
book on sewing tools and accessories is Gay Ann
Rogers' An Illustrated History of Needlework Tools,
which can be found in many bookstores. All items
listed below are in good condition, minor wear and
with no missing parts.*

**Pincushion,** figural, model of a stylized crouching cat on a thick square pillow, the cat in beige velvet on an orange velvet pillow, glass eyes, red neck ribbon w/bell, two small spools of thread in front of the cat atop the pillow, 4 1/2" h. ............. **$220**

**Sewing box,** cov., painted wood, rectangular, the attached lid w/molded edging, decorated w/a landscape scene w/two large buildings, trees in the background, contains a small group of lace fragments, painted in red & black, mid-19th c., 6 1/2 x 9 1/4", 2 3/4" h. (minor wear).... **5,175**

**Sewing box,** hard & softwood, stacking-type, composed of four graduated overlapping drawers in conforming framework, all w/porcelain pulls, replaced cloth pincushion on top, one drawer marked "18.R.13, Marlboro," 11 x 11 3/4", 15" h. ( one drawer old replacement, minor edge damage) ............. **660**

**Sewing box,** painted bentwood, round w/a flat top centered by a small ring-turned pedestal w/a cloth pincushion top, molded base band, old yellow repaint w/a stenciled design on the side w/a beaded rectangle around stylized blossoms in red, green & black, 19th c., 5 1/2" d., 5 1/2" h. (replaced pincushion cloth) ......... **605**

**Tape measure,** figural, model of a seated cat, white flannel w/black paint trim, red neck ribbon & glass eyes, mouth opens when head pushed, 5 1/2" h. (squeak silent).......... **385**

# THIMBLES

**9ct Gold silver-lined "Dorcas,"** the plain border stamped, "C.H., 9ct Gold Dorcas Silver Lined," English, Charles Horner, ca. 1910 ......................................... **704**

**9ct Gold steel-lined "Dorcas,"** the plain border stamped, "9ct gold steel lined, C.H., Dorcas," English, Charles Horner, ca. 1910, in fitted case .................... **407**

**Blush ivory porcelain,** the sides painted w/a bird on a foliate branch, a foliate spray on the reserve, Worcester, late 19th c. ................................................. **407**

**Bronze,** indentations running down to a border decorated w/script within reeded borders, Hispano-Moresque, ca. 13th c. ...... **555**

**Bronze,** with plain top, the indentations running down the sides to meet a ribbed rim, Turko-Slavic, ca. 16th c........................ **241**

**Gold,** border w/applied flowers, trailing foliage, a bird in flight & a shaped cartouche engraved w/initials, all on a matted ground, Simons Bros., late 19th c. .............. **481**

**Gold,** cast in the form of the Liberty Bell, the wide border bearing the legend, "Proclaim Liberty in the land to the Inhabitants. By Order of the Assembly of Pennsy. in Phila. 1752," probably Simons Bros., late 19th c. ............................ **241**

**Gold,** indented all over, English, probably late 18th c. ............................................. **2,407**

**Gold,** the body enameled overall w/birds, foliage & flowers in shades of red, blue, green & white, w/blue enameled rim, Indian (Jaipur Region), probably early 19th c. ................................................. **241**

**Gold,** the body w/an applied contrasting color frieze of rising foliage, reeding above & below, French, late 18th c. ............. **482**

**Gold,** the body w/an applied two-color gold floral & foliate frieze on a matted ground, the border w/engraved initials, French, late 18th c. ............................................. **481**

**Gold,** the body w/applied foliate frieze, reeding above & below, French, late 18th c. ............................................. **889**

**Gold,** the body w/applied three-colored gold flowers & foliage & a shield-shaped cartouche w/engraved initials, set w/a stone top, English, late 18th - early 19th c. ............................................. **407**

**Gold,** the border case w/a scroll design within heavy floral & foliate borders, w/waffle-type indentations, probably South American, mid 19th c. ...................... **315**

**Gold,** the border chased w/flowers & foliage & the phrase "Forget Me Not," probably English, ca. 1840 ................................ **241**

**Gold,** the border chased w/the legend, "World's Columbian Exposition, 1492-1892" supporting a shaped vacant scrollwork cartouche, above a cast shell rim, Simons Bros., late 19th c. ........................ **1,759**

**Gold,** the border diagonally fluted & w/vacant shaped cartouche, each flute w/applied alternate split pearls & turquoises, Ketcham & McDougall, American, late 19th c. .................................... **778**

**Gold,** the border w/a chased view, in relief, of Buckingham Palace, the Coronation coach & Westminster Abbey & the legend, "G.M. 1911," the body w/applied crown, made to commemorate the coronation of George V, Goldsmiths & Silversmiths Co., in fitted case .......................... **741**

**Gold,** the border w/an applied chain link, some links w/inset turquoise, on a matted ground, English, late 19th c. ................ **1,018**

**Gold,** the border w/an applied raised floral & foliate frieze, reeding above & below, English, late 19th c. ................................. **926**

**Gold,** the border w/an applied row of turquoise, English, late 19th c. ........................ **296**

*Blue Enameled Thimble*

**Gold,** the border w/applied arches highlighted in blue enamel, the underside of each arch set w/a diamond, English, late 19th c. (ILLUS.) ............................................. **443**

**Gold,** the border w/applied cherubs holding garlands of flowers & supporting a foliate cartouche engraved w/an initial, Simons Bros., early 20th c. (ILLUS. top next column) ......... **229**

*Cherub Designed Thimble*

*Flowers & Foliage Designed Thimble*

**Gold,** the border w/applied contrasting color gold flowers & foliage & a vacant shaped cartouche, all on a matted ground above a cast floral & foliate rim, French, late 19th c. (ILLUS.) ...................... **444**

*Foliage Designed Thimble*

**Gold,** the border w/applied contrasting colored gold foliage & a vacant shaped cartouche on a matted ground, English, late 19th c. (ILLUS.) ............................................ **592**

**Gold,** the border w/applied contrasting gold flowers & foliage on a matted ground, the side w/applied vacant shield-shaped cartouche, French, late 19th c...................... **407**

*Scrollwork Designed Thimble*

**Gold,** the border w/applied engraved scrollwork decoration interspersed w/turquoise & a vacant shield-shaped cartouche, all on a matted ground, w/waved rim & conforming border above, English, late 19th c. (ILLUS.)............ **229**

**Gold,** the border w/applied flowers & foliage on a matted ground, probably English, late 19th c...................................... **889**

**Gold,** the border w/applied foliate frieze, French, late 18th c. ...................................... **352**

**Gold,** the border w/applied roses, thistles & foliage on a matted ground above a cast foliate border, English, late 19th c. ............... **214**

**Gold,** the border w/applied two-color gold flowers & foliage on a matted ground, Simons Bros., late 19th c. ............................ **129**

**Gold,** the border w/applied two-color gold flowers & foliage on a raised matted ground, the body w/applied vacant shield-shaped cartouche, French, late 19th c. ......................................................... **315**

*Foliage & Flowerhead Designed Thimble*

**Gold,** the border w/applied two-color gold foliage & flowerheads, each flowerhead set w/an emerald, on matted ground & w/vacant shaped cartouche, above an engraved rim, English, mid-19th c. (ILLUS.)............................................................ **555**

**Gold,** the border w/applied two-color gold foliage set w/turquoise, French, late 19th c. (some deficient turquoise) ........................ **333**

**Gold,** the border w/applied wire-work scrollwork interspersed w/stars set w/alternate split pearls & turquoise, w/moonstone top, probably English, late 19th c. ......................................................... **741**

*Geometric Designed Thimble*

**Gold,** the border w/heavily cut friezes highlighted w/blue enameled geometric designs, English, late 19th c. (ILLUS.) ......... **407**

*Dropped Rim Thimble*

**Parcel-gilt "Dropped Rim,"** the border featuring holly leaves & berries surrounding a ruby set cartouche, Ketcham & McDougall, early 20th c. (ILLUS.)............. **129**

*Squat Form Porcelain Thimble*

**Porcelain,** of squat form, the border decorated w/flowers & foliage above a faintly visible gilt rim, American Belleek, late 19th c. (ILLUS.) ........................................... **241**

*Porcelain Thimble*

**Porcelain,** the border decorated w/roses & foliage above a wide gilt rim, American Belleek, late 19th c. (ILLUS.) .................... **1,111**
**Porcelain,** the border decorated w/roses & foliage on a white ground below a pale green body, above a gilt rim, American Belleek, late 19th c. ..................................... **370**

*American Belleek Porcelain Thimble*

**Porcelain,** the border painted w/roses, forget-me-nots & foliage above a gilt rim, American Belleek, late 19th c. (ILLUS.) ....... **926**
**Silver,** made to commemorate the Coronation of Queen Victoria, the rim engraved, "Heaven Protect Our Sovereign Lady," the body engraved w/a crown & the legend, "Queen Victoria Born May 24th 1819, Ascended the Throne June 20th 1837, Crowned June 28th 1838," English, ca. 1838......................................... **407**

*Commemorative Thimble*

**Silver,** made to commemorate the wedding of Princess Alexandra to the Prince of Wales, the border chased w/their bust portraits & the legend, "Princess Alexandra Born 1st Dec 1844, Prince of Wales Born 9th Nov 1841," English, ca. 1862 (ILLUS.)....................................................... **888**
**Silver,** the body decorated w/two two-color floral & foliate friezes separated by a plain band, French, late 18th - early 19th c. ......................................................... **463**
**Silver,** the border chased in relief w/a depiction of the Cromwell Road International Exhibition building & stamped w/the diamond registration mark, the rim engraved, "International Exhibition 1862," English, mid-19th c. .......................... **648**
**Silver,** the border chased in relief w/a view of the Crystal Palace & the legend, "Exhibition of all Nations 1851" above a faceted rim, English, mid-19th c. .................. **555**

**Silver,** the border chased w/a view of the Crystal Palace, the rim engraved, "Great Exhibition Hyde Park 1851," English, mid-19th c. .................................................... **259**
**Silver,** the border enameled w/three concentric rings in red, white & blue, English, Charles Homer, Chester, 1936....... **241**

*"A Stitch For The Red White & Blue" Thimble*

**Silver,** the border enameled w/three concentric rings in red, white & blue above the phrase, "A Stitch For The Red White and Blue" in blue enamel, English, Chester, 1914 (ILLUS.)...................................... **1,573**

*Indian Thimble*

**Silver,** the sides chased w/flowerheads & scrolled foliage, w/scalloped rim, Indian, late 19th c. (ILLUS.) ..................................... **407**

*Russian Thimble*

**Silver,** the wide border decorated w/cloisonné enameled flowers & foliage below a blue dot border, Russian, St. Petersburg, 1908-17 (ILLUS.) ............................... **315**
**Silver "Golden Spike,"** made to commemorate the St. Louis World's Fair 1904, the border depicting a train, wagons & a hunting scene, America, Simons Bros., early 20th c.................................................. **352**

*"Salem Witch" Thimble*

**Silver "Salem Witch,"** the border chased w/a cat, a witch, a new moon, witchpins & the legend, "Salem 1692," either side of a vacant shaped cartouche, American, Webster Co., late 19th c. (ILLUS.) ....... **518**

*"Salem Witch" Thimble*

**Silver "Salem Witch,"** the border chased w/a cat, a witch, a new moon, witchpins & the legend, "Salem 1692," either side of a rectangular cartouche w/engraved initials, American, Ketchum & McDougall, late 19th c. (ILLUS.)............................ **1,296**

*Norwegian Thimble*

**Silver-gilt,** the body w/applied enameled flowers & foliage in shades of pink & green, w/moonstones top, the apex engraved w/a Registration Number 1904, Norwegian, ca. 1900 (ILLUS.)............ **518**

**Silver-gilt,** the border decorated w/applied cloisonné enameled flowerheads & foliage above a white dot border, Russian, St. Petersburg, 1908-17 .............................. **444**

*Cloisonné Thimble*

**Silver-gilt,** the border decorated w/applied cloisonné enameled scrollwork, a white dot frieze above, blue below, Russian, St. Petersburg, 1908-17 (ILLUS.)................ **370**

**Silver-gilt,** the border w/applied cloisonné enameled flowerheads & stylized foliage, Russian, probably ca. 1910.................. **333**

**Silver-gilt,** the border w/shaded cloisonné enameled flowers & scrollwork above an arched frieze, Russian, St. Petersburg, 1908-17 ...................................................... **592**

**Silver-topped Piercy's patent tortoiseshell,** the body w/applied silver tip & a gold rim & the Royal Coat of Arms supported by a scroll engraved w/the legend, "Piercy's Patent," English, ca. 1825 ............................................................ **343**

# SHAKER ITEMS

*The Shakers, a religious sect founded by Ann Lee, first settled in this country at Watervliet, New York, near Albany, in 1774. By 1880 there were nine settlements in America. Workmanship in Shaker crafts is an extension of their religious beliefs and features plain and simple designs reflecting a chaste elegance that is now much in demand though relatively few early items are common.*

*Mt. Lebanon Cupboard-Chest*

**Bed,** maple & pine, the four block-turned legs joined by shaped head- and footboards & straight sides, old refinish, probably New England, first half 19th c., 29 x 64", 30 1/4" h...................................... **$690**

**Blanket box,** cov., cherry, rectangular molded hinged top above a dovetailed case w/two short drawers w/incised beading & turned pulls, canted feet, painted white over earlier surface, possibly Mt. Lebanon, New York, ca. 1840, 17 1/4 x 43 1/2", 25 1/2" h. ........................ **1,380**

**Bonnet,** lady's, finely woven two-tone poplar splint, floral-printed cloth ribbon, paper lining stenciled "7" (wear, minor damage) ........................................................ **193**

**Broom,** cobweb-type, fanned straw end w/a long slender wooden handle, Union Village, Ohio, late 19th c., 94" l. (wear, stitching incomplete) ..................................... **138**

**Bucket,** stave constructed w/two metal bands, wide slightly tapering sides in old grey paint, wire bail handle w/diamond side attachments & a turned wood hand grip, 13 3/4" d., 12" h.................................... **165**

**Bucket,** butternut, rectangular box-form w/canted sides & an iron bail handle attached w/hammered copper pins, 19th c., 10 7/8 x 11 1/2", 6 7/8" h. ..................... **1,150**

**Cheese ladder,** hickory, two long side rails joined by two horizontal flat rails, each pair of rails joined by an arched slat, old patina, worn white paint, 25" l. .................... **578**

**Chip carrier,** pine, rectangular dovetailed deep box w/added tin corner braces, high center bentwood handle w/copper rivets, Mount Lebanon, New York, old worn finish, 12 1/4 x 18 1/2", 7" h. (wear, edge damage) ............................................. **330**

**Cloak hanger,** pine & poplar, serpentine coat hanger-form w/long flat central stick, attributed to Harvard, Massachusetts, 36 1/2" l. ............................................. **193**

**Clock shelf,** walnut, a tall rectangular backboard w/a narrow shelf at the lower end above a single drawer framed by shaped side brackets, drawer w/a label from a Shaker medicine crate, old refinish, Union Village, Ohio, 16" w., 42" h. ......... **963**

**Cradle,** stained butternut & poplar, high rounded end boards & deep slightly canted sides w/low inset rockers, old worn red finish, 36" l. .................................. **440**

**Cupboard over chest of drawers,** cherry, built-in type. rectangular top w/no cornice above wide rails surrounding the single raised panel cupboard doors w/a tiny wood knob opening to a single shelf above a mid-molding over a case of four long thumb-molded drawers w/small turned wood knobs, refinished, sides replaced, Mt. Lebanon, New York, ca. 1830, 15 1/2 x 30 3/4", 77" h. (ILLUS.) ..... **6,900**

*Early Shaker Trustee's Desk*

**Desk,** trustee's, cherry, the shaped gallery above a lift-top opening to a tombstone compartment interior on a base w/a single drawer & straight apron joining four turned tapering legs, old refinish, imperfections, ca. 1830, 20 1/4 x 30 3/4", 50 3/4" h. (ILLUS.) .................................... **2,875**

**Dining chair,** the low back w/two notch-ended slats above the replaced woven splint seat, simple turned legs tapering at the bottom joined by double front & side rungs & a single rear rung, refinished, Union Village, Ohio, 28" h. ................. **825**

**Dust pan,** wooden, turned maple handle, 19th c., 16 1/2" l. ......................................... **460**

**Egg carrier,** bird's-eye maple, a square box-form w/flat lid w/wire fasteners w/wooden spring clip & small bail handle, old patina, Enfield, New Hampshire, 13" sq., 11" h. ............................................ **1,375**

**Lap desk,** pine, poplar & walnut, a sloped hinged lid w/breadboard ends opening to a well, a small pull-out end drawer, old worn patina, Hancock, Massachusetts, 12 1/2 x 17 1/2", 4 1/2" h. .............................. **935**

**Pegboard,** painted pine & hardwood, long narrow board w/beaded edges & mounted w/six oversized turned pegs probably for holding horse tack, old worn & soiled yellow paint, 101" l. .......................... **770**

**Pie lifter,** wrought steel & wood, a slender steel U-form fork w/iron bar inserted into the simple turned wood handle, 13 1/4" l. ....... **94**

**Rocker without arms,** maple & birch, three arched slats joining turned stiles top the tape seat, on turned legs joined by stretchers, old refinish, probably Enfield, New Hampshire, ca. 1840, 41" h. .................. **805**

**Rocking chair w/arms,** the tall back stiles w/pointed turned finials joined by three gently arched slats above the flat shaped arms w/mushroom handholds over baluster-turned arm supports, replaced green, beige & black woven tape seat, simple turned legs w/inset rockers, single box stretchers, old refinishing, size No. 0, Mount Lebanon, New York, 23" h. (repaired split in one rocker) ..... **770**

*Early Shaker Rocking Chair*

**Rocking chair w/arms,** the tall back w/four arched slats joining turned stiles w/ovoid finials & above scrolled arms on turned tapering supports continuing to turned legs on rockers joined by turned stretchers, old refinish, probably Canterbury, New Hampshire, ca. 1850, 43" h. (ILLUS.) .................................................... **7,475**

**Rocking chair w/arms,** the tall back w/three slender gently arched slats between turned stiles w/pointed finials, flat shaped arms w/mushroom handholds above baluster-turned supports, old worn woven tape seat in faded green & yellow, simple turned legs w/inset rockers, old dark brown finish w/gold stenciled label "Shaker's Trademark - Mt. Lebanon, N.Y. No. 1," 29" h. (repair to one foot at rocker) .................................... **633**

**Rocking chair w/arms,** the tall turned back stiles w/turned pointed finials flank the woven tape back panel above flat shaped arms w/mushroom handgrips over baluster-turned arm supports, replaced woven tape seat in brownish red & white, simple turned legs w/double front & side rungs & single rear rung, impressed "#7" on top slat, refinished, 41 1/4" h. ...................................................... **413**

**Rocking chair without arms,** child's, tall back w/three gently arched slats between the simple turned stiles w/pointed finials, replaced paper rush seat on the simple turned legs w/double stretchers in the front & sides, worn original dark brown finish, stenciled label on bottom slat "Shaker's Trade Mark - Mt. Lebanon, N.Y.," No. 1 model, late 19th - early 20th c., 28 3/4" h. ............................... **798**

**Rocking chair without arms,** tall back w/four gently arched slats, a shawl bar across the top joining the stiles, later upholstered seat, simple turned legs & stretchers, top slat impressed "7," Mt. Lebanon, New York, 42" h. .......................... **413**

**Rocking chair without arms,** tall turned back stiles w/pointed turned finials flanking the replaced red & black woven tape back panel raised above the replaced woven tape seat, simple turned legs w/inset rockers & double front & side stretchers & a single rear stretcher, original dark finish w/revarnishing, stenciled label "Shaker's Trade Mark - Mt. Lebanon, N.Y. No. 3," 34" h. (repaired split in one rocker) ..................................................... **413**

**Rocking chair without arms,** turned wood, tall back above a seat, seat & back w/several layers of later upholstery over old tape, Mt. Lebanon, New York, late 19th c., 35 3/4" h. ................................... **230**

**Rug,** woven rag, rectangular, multicolored stripes, brown buggy robe binding w/some Shaker tape repair, 33 x 53" (sewn repair) ................................................. **138**

**Scarf,** sister's, woven homespun in a tiny tan, blue & white plaid center & woven border pattern, one corner initials "A.P.," 29 x 30" (wear, edge damage, some soiling) ....................................................... **303**

**Seed box,** cov., pine, shallow rectangular form w/original finish & paper label reading "Shaker's Genuine Garden Seeds, Mount Lebanon, NY," late 19th c., 11 1/2 x 23 1/2", 3 1/4" h. (inside lid label missing) ............................................. **770**

**Sewing basket,** cov., oval bentwood, three finger-lappets, bentwood swing handle, lined in red satin, old refinish, possibly Mt. Lebanon, New York, early 20th c., 8 1/2 x 12", 4 1/4" h. (replaced ribbons, minor staining) .............................................. **460**

**Sewing box,** tiered-type, cherry, maple & walnut w/old natural patina, the rectangular top tier w/a turned wood knob w/pincushion opening to hold spools of thread w/holes along the sides, the wider lower tier w/a drawer, on small turned legs, 19th c., 6 3/4" h. (edge damage, top lid w/repaired splits) ............................. **303**

**Sewing rocker without arms,** tall back w/three gently arched slats, simple stiles w/turned pointed finials, replaced woven tape seat, stenciled label on bottom slat "Shakers - Mt. Lebanon, N.Y. - No. 3," original dark finish, 34" h. ..................... **358**

**Side chair,** hardwood, the tall back w/three rounded slats between the simple turned stiles w/oval knob finials, new woven tape mauve, grey & beige seat, simple turned legs joined by double front & side rungs & a single back rung, refinished w/good soft finish, Mount Lebanon, New York, 19th c., 40 1/2" h. ................................. **523**

**Side chair,** maple, the tall back w/three slats each w/a convex shape on the top & bottom edges between the turned stiles w/oval finials, replaced tape seat, simple turned legs w/double turned stretchers at the front & sides, refinished w/remnants of yellow paint, Canterbury, New Hampshire, ca. 1850, 40 1/2" h. (minor surface imperfections) ...................... **748**

*Early Shaker Seed Sorting Stand*

**Sorting stand,** walnut, seed sorting-type, nearly square top w/raised molded edges w/small front opening over deep pegged apron on simple block- and rod-turned legs joined by square stretchers, old surface, one stretcher missing, probably Union Village, Ohio, ca. 1840-60, 20 3/4 x 21", 30 1/2" h. (ILLUS.)............... **1,093**

**Storage box,** cov., bentwood, oval, double finger lappet construction w/copper tacks on the base & a single lappet on the fitted cover, shiny varnish finish, late 19th c., 12" l. ............................................... **413**

**Storage box,** cov., oval bentwood, three finger lappets in base & one in the cover w/tack construction, old deep blue paint, Sabbathday Lake, Maine, 9" l. .................. **2,365**

**Storage box,** cov., oval bentwood, three finger lappets in the base & one in the cover w/copper & steel tacks, added red stain & original worn black stencil label "Sabbathday Lake Shakers," 10 1/2" l. (minor age cracks) ..................................... **495**

**Storage box,** cov., painted pine, rectangular top w/thin molded edges opening to a well partially lined w/Shaker blue paper, the exterior w/original green paint, dovetailed case w/a flat bottom, top branded "S.T. Bradford," Enfield, New Hampshire, 11 3/4 x 19 3/4", 10 1/2" h. (repaired nail breakouts on cover, some paint touch-up, repair & edge damage to hinge rail of top) ................................ **715**

**Storage box,** cov., round bentwood w/three finger lappets on the base & one on the cover, steel tacks, old brown finish, Mount Lebanon, New York, 9 7/8" d., 4 1/8" h. (minor edge damage, small lid repairs) ......................... **358**

**Tool chest,** cherry, flat rectangular top on a dovetailed case w/nine shallow graduated dovetailed drawers each w/a single turned wood knob, refinished, Union Village, Ohio, 8 1/4 x 15", 24" h. (cleaned, drawer interiors varnished, back replaced) ....................................... **1,100**

**Yarn swift,** table model, painted maple & birch, translucent yellow wash, extendible, probably Hancock, Massachusetts, ca. 1850-60, 29" d. open, 24 1/4" h. (very minor imperfections) ......................... **403**

## SHEET MUSIC

**"Angel God Sent From Heaven (The),"** WWI, by Sgt. Frant Ventra (G+) .................. **$20**

**"Blue Jay Rag,"** 1907, by Frand Wooster (VG+ to EX-) ................................................ **38**

**"Calla Lily Rag,"** 1907, by Logan Thame (VG+) ...................................................... **40**

*Chocolate Creams*

**"Chocolate Creams,"** 1909 by Warren Camp, VG+ (ILLUS.) ..................................... **55**

**"From Valley Forge To France,"** WWI (VG-) .................................................................. **9**

**"Gems From The Governor's Son,"** 1901, by Geo. M. Cohan (VG) ................................. **30**

*Glory of Jamestown*

**"Glory Of Jamestown,"** 1907, by James W. Casey (ILLUS.) ....................................... **147**

**"I Wish I Was Back To My Livery Barn,"** 1905, by S. Jones & Pringle (VG+) ................ **20**

**"I'm Just An Old Jay From The U.S.A.,"** WWI, words by Edmoran & Vincent Bryan, music by Harry Von Tilzer (EX-) ......... **25**

**"I'm So Glad My Mamma Don't Know Where I'm At,"** 1918, by Willie Toosweet (VG-) .............................................. **20**

**"On Broadway In Dahomey, Bye and Bye,"** 1902, by Alex Rogers & Al Johns (VG-) .............................................................. **27**

**"Please Tell Me Why,"** by Fat Waller ............... **28**

**"Polar Bear Rag,"** 1910, by George Howard (VG) ............................................... **60**

**"Pride Of The Regiment,"** 1910, by Mitchell W. Meyers ........................................... **30**

**"Princess Rag,"** by James Scott .................... **105**

**"Red Cross Roll Call (The),"** 1919, by Beyerstedt (G-) ........................................... **50**

*School Life*

**"School Life,"** 1912, by Chris L. Johnson (ILLUS.) ........................................................ **22**

**"Steamin' Down The Old Ohio,"** 1920, composed by Raymond Stillwell (VG-) ........... **10**

**"Stewin' De Rice,"** 1918, by Perry Bradford ................................................................. **40**

**"Teach You To Rock,"** from movie "Rock Around the Clock," song by Freddie Bell & Pep Lattanzi (NM) ..................................... **13**

**"When The Tennessean Leaves For Tennessee,"** 1940, words & music by Josephine C. McCormack (VG) ............................ **17**

## SIGNS & SIGNBOARDS

*Also see: ADVERTISING ITEMS, BREWERIANA, COCA-COLA COLLECTIBLES, DRUGSTORE & PHARMACY ITEMS and TOBACCIANA.*

*White Rock Sign*

**Bathtubs,** "United States Mfg. Co. Sanitary Bathtubs," paper lithograph depicting woman sitting in tub, framed under glass, 23 1/2" h. (creases & repairs) ......... **$600**

**Beer,** "Chief Osh-Kosh." die-cut tin flange showing Native American Indian in top hat & tuxedo, 13 1/2 x 18" ........................... **975**

**Beverage,** "Silver Springs Beverages," tin, self-framed, 11 x 35" (some damage) ............ **55**

**Beverage,** "White Rock Sparkling Beverages," embossed tin depicting young woman crouching on large rock near water, ca. 1950s, shallow dent, heavy scratch on raised border, light wear, 33 x 57" (ILLUS.) ........................................... **550**

**Bread,** "American Bread," tin lithograph w/image of child, self-framed, 17" h. (slight scratches) ...................................... **425**

**Bread,** "Sunbeam Bread," embossed tin, self-framed w/large image of Miss Sunbeam, dated 4/62, 11 3/4 x 29 3/4" .............. **375**

**Bulk oil,** "Gargoyle/Mobiloil," porcelain, "GW" for gears, 8 3/4 x 10 3/4" ................. **1,100**

**Bus,** "Greyhound Lines," porcelain, double-sided, 20 1/4 x 36" ................................... **725**

**Bus depot,** "National Trailways System," porcelain, double-sided, by Burdick Enamel, 18 1/4 x 22" ..................................... **500**

**Bus depot sign,** "Greyhound Bus Line," porcelain, double-sided showing bus, 30" h. ....................................................... **2,300**

*Bit-O-Honey Sign*

**Candy,** "Bit-O-Honey," embossed tin, left side of sign w/green plant, the product package & several almonds w/"Bit-O-Honey Candy with roasted almonds," 9 x 20" (ILLUS.) ........................................... **220**

*Life Savers Sign*

**Candy,** "Life Savers," porcelain, black w/red arrow & package of candy in white & yellow, marked "Real Life Savers - 'Always good taste,'" ca. 1920s-30s, some touchup & repair, clear coated, 27 x 60" (ILLUS.) ...................................... **1,100**

**Cigars,** "Diamond Bell," tin lithograph w/"Organized Labor ask for 'Diamond Bell' & 'Full Jewel' 5¢ Cigars - Made by Your Own Craft - A.K. Walch, Phila PA," red & white, 7 3/4 x 13 3/4" (minor scratches & fade) ...................................... **176**

*Old Dutch Cleanser Sign*

**Cleanser,** "Old Dutch," tin over cardboard, figure of Dutch girl on left w/"For Healthful Cleanliness There's nothing like Old Dutch," ca. 1930s-40s, light paper marking from original paper, corner nicks, shallow dent, 9 x 18" (ILLUS.) ...................... **935**

**Cleanser,** "Sunbrite," porcelain, curved corner mount w/sun & cloud graphics, 15 x 17 3/4" ............................................. **525**

**Cocoa,** "Walter Baker & Co.," tin lithograph shows Colonial woman serving cup of cocoa, framed, 13 x 19" ........................... **1,450**

*Old Reliable Coffee Sign*

**Coffee,** "Old Reliable Coffee," tin, shows man in coat & hat w/product package nearby, marked "Always Good - Old Reliable Coffee," ca. 1920s-30s, 6 1/2 x 9 1/2" (ILLUS.) ...................................................... **660**

**Credit card,** "Gulf," porcelain, double-sided, 30" d. ................................................. **400**

**Dairy,** "Driggs Dairy Farms," reverse glass painted milk bottle on black on left w/"Driggs Dairy Farms Certified Quality Milk - Cream" in red letters on tan, original metal frame for easel mount or wall hang, by Micro Products, High Point, North Carolina, 8 x 16" ................................. **385**

*Shamrock Dairy Sign*

**Dairy,** "Shamrock Dairy," porcelain, depicts leprechaun surrounded by shamrocks, marked "Shamrock Dairy - Guernsey - America's Table Milk," ca. 1940s-50s, light wear, marks, chips & nicks, 22 x 56" (ILLUS.) .................................... **1,100**

**Dog food,** "Friskies," tin flange sign w/"For Your Dog," 17 1/2 x 17 3/4" .......................... **520**

**Dye,** "Diamond Dyes," tin lithograph over cardboard w/"A Busy Day in Dollville," 17" l. ........................................................ **2,900**

**Farm implements,** "John Deere," porcelain, by Veribrite Sign, Chicago, Illinois, 24 x 72" ................................................. **4,500**

**Farm lubricant,** "Texaco," porcelain, single-sided, dated "10-8-48," 22 x 30" ............. **500**

**Farm machinery,** "Adriance Buckeye Harvesting Machinery," paper lithograph shows young woman gathering grain surrounded by four images of various horse-drawn harvesting machines, matted & framed, image 26" h. (creases & minor stains) ............................................... **475**

**Farm supplies,** "Big Dutchman Automatic Feeders," porcelain, 24 x 35" ...................... **360**

**Fertilizer,** "Griffith and Boyd," paper lithograph showing woman playing solitaire, under glass in oak frame, image 21 1/2" h. ................................................. **625**

**Fertilizer,** "Swift's Red Steer Brand," die-cut porcelain, 20 x 30" ............................. **1,200**

**Flour,** "Pied Piper Flour" (Aunt Jemima Mills), porcelain, curved corner-style, by Burdick of Beaver Falls, Pennsylvania, 18 x 22", rare ............................................ **1,500**

**Four,** "Gold Medal Flour," painted wood in wooden frame, 66" l. (stains & scratches) .................................................... **450**

*Piggly Wiggly Sign*

**Grocery store,** "Piggly Wiggly," porcelain, round blue sign w/yellow head of pig wearing butcher's hat marked "Piggly Wiggly," ca. 1940s, 42" d. (ILLUS.) ........... **1,045**

**Gum,** "Wrigley's," porcelain, shows both Spearmint & Doublemint packages, 36" l. ...................................................... **1,900**

*Nestle Sign*

**Hair care,** "Nestle Permanent Waving," die-cut & dimensional display sign, shaded tan w/gold highlights, woman's head at top w/"Nestle Permanent Waving - Licensed Nestle Shop," original paper tag on back, by Kay Display Signs, rests on wooden feet, easily detached for moving, slight fading & wear to gold, light soiling, 15 x 18" (ILLUS.) .................. **1,265**

**Heating oil,** "Standard," die-cut porcelain, 15 3/4 x 20" (probably used on delivery trucks) ................................................... **525**

*Gollam's Ice Cream Sign*

**Ice cream,** "Gollam's," two-sided, heavy metal, depicts small boy holding very large ice cream cone, marked "We Serve Gollam's Lebanon Ice Cream," ca. 1941, minor dents at edge, scratches & paint chips, slightly ambered (ILLUS.) ......... **550**

**Ice cream,** "Storock's Ice Cream," reverse painting on glass depicts stork, wood frame, 21 1/2" l. .......................................... **325**

*Niagara Fire Insurance Sign*

**Insurance,** "Niagara Fire Insurance," porcelain, fired-on ink scene of the falls, marked "Safety Fund Policies - Niagara Fire Insurance Company - New York," ca. 1910-15, 11 x 21" (ILLUS.) ..... **2,970**

**Lubricant,** "Texaco Marine Lubricants," porcelain, dated "10/2/59," 15 x 30", rare.. **2,600**

**Milk,** "Arden Milk," die-cut porcelain, double-sided w/scene of boy & large creamer bottle, 28 x 33" ............................... **575**

*Kerr-View's Milk Sign*

**Milk,** "Kerr-View's Milk," two-sided die-cut porcelain, bottle-shaped sign marked "From Our Own Herd - Use Kerr-View's Raw & Pasteurized Milk and All Other Dairy Products," ca. 1920s-30s, minor edge chips & nicks, 19 x 48" (ILLUS.) ...... **1,760**

**Motor oil,** "Ace High," porcelain, double-sided, 17 1/4 x 23 1/4", very rare ............. **3,400**

**Motor oil,** "Mother Pen," porcelain, double-sided, by Reliance Adv. Co., Chicago, Illinois, 13 x 20" .......................................... **750**

**Motor oil,** "Texaco 'New' Motor Oil," heavy tin, double-sided, dated "2-37," 11 1/4 x 21 1/2" ............................................ **450**

**Motor oil,** "Wolf's Head Oil," embossed tin, self-framed, 13 3/4 x 19 3/4" ........................ **400**

**Nuts,** "Tom's Nuts/Snacks," embossed tin, self-framed, dated 9/58, 19 1/2 x 28" .......... **355**

**Overalls,** "Duckhead Overalls" (O'Bryan Brothers), porcelain, by Ing-Rick, 12 x 16" ....................................................... **325**

*Lee Union Overalls Sign*

**Overalls,** "Lee," embossed tin, workman in overalls in lower left corner, logo at right

& "Lee - Union-Alls -Overalls - Whizits - Union Made," ca. 1930s-40s, minor bends, edge wear, chips & nicks & light scratches, 13 x 27" (ILLUS.) ........................ **413**

**Paint,** "Sherwin Williams," die-cut embossed porcelain w/"Cover the Earth," 19 1/4 x 34 1/2" ................................ **550**

*Gillette Razor Blades Sign*

**Razor blades,** "Gillette," two-sided die-cut porcelain flange sign, relief-molded safety razor depicted next to box of blades & marked "Gillette," trademark appears in French in small print, made in Europe, possibly Canadian in origin, ca. 1920-30, light edge wear, chips & cracks, 19 x 22" (ILLUS.) .......................... **3,080**

*Remington UMC Poster*

**Rifles,** "Remington - UMC," poster, colorful scene of two men w/rifles on mountaintop, clouds in background, marked "Remington - UMC - Firearms - Ammunition" by H. G. Edwards, lithograph by American Litho Co., NY, minor wrinkles, 18 x 26" (ILLUS.)...................................... **1,870**

**Seeds,** "Aggeler & Mussler," porcelain w/"Plant Seeds in Confidence," 20 x 30" ...... **575**

**Shoes,** "Paul Bunyan Loggers," cardboard easel-back countertop type, showing the logger w/an axe & his bull Babe & marked "Hand Made - Union Made - Bone Dry Shoe Mfg. Co.," 12 3/4 x 21 1/2" ......................................... **121**

**Shoes,** "Peters Weatherbird Shoes," double-sided, painted wood sidewalk sign, 43 1/2" h. ...................................................... **1,500**

**Shoes,** "Red Goose Shoes," die-cut cardboard stand-up type, three dimensional, 23" l. ......................................................... **2,000**

**Soap,** "Ivory Soap," paper lithograph titled "A Busy Day" by Maude Humphrey, artist-signed, gesso frame, 10" w., 22 1/2" h. ........ **259**

**Soap,** "Lifebuoy Soap," cardboard, trolley-type w/scene of teacher & pupils, "Teachers and Mothers know that LIFE-BUOY Health Soap Protects Health," wood frame, 12 1/4 x 22 1/4" ............... **132**

**Soft drink,** "Barq's," tin, embossed bottle & "It's Good" & "Barq's," by Donaldson Art Sign Co., 11 3/4 x 29 3/4" ........................... **220**

**Soft drink,** "Canada Dry Beverages," porcelain kick plate, 10 x 30" ............................... **50**

**Soft drink,** "Canada Dry," embossed lithographed tin palm press, 3 x 9" ..................... **110**

**Soft drink,** "Crescent Cola," embossed tin lithograph w/image of woman ..................... **230**

**Soft drink,** "Dr. Pepper," cardboard, winter scene w/woman & dog & "Smart List," 20 1/2 x 33" ............................................... **250**

*Gold-en Cola Sign*

**Soft drink,** "Gold-en Cola," tin flange sign showing cup & saucer marked "Gold-en Girl Cola - Sun-drop - Refreshing as a Cup of Coffee," ca. 1940s-50s, 15 x 21" (ILLUS.)................................................. **358**

**Soft drink,** "Grapette Soda," oval, embossed tin, 28 x 47 1/2"........................... **210**

**Soft drink,** "Hire's Ginger Ale," embossed tin tacker sign w/"None So Good," 9 3/4 x 13 3/4" (some minor damage) ........ **135**

**Soft drink,** "Mit-Che Cola," embossed tin, 15 1/2 x 23 1/2" (some wear & rust).............. **85**

**Soft drink,** "Nehi," string-hung cardboard, features young woman, 15 1/4 x 23", very rare (some damage w/repair) .............. **210**

**Soft drink,** "Nesbitt's Orange," porcelain, 3/8" reverse lip at edges, 10 x 19" ...................................................... **305**

**Soft drink,** "Orange Crush," embossed tin, self-framed baseball scoreboard, dated 10/39, by Scioto Signs, 18 x 54" (some nicks & creases ........................................... **600**

**Soft drink,** "Pennsylvania Dutch 'Birch Beer,'" string-hung celluloid, shows Amish man drinking, "Ju-C Orange of America" at bottom left, copyright 1955, 9 1/4 x 14 3/4" ....................................... **30**

**Soft drink,** "Rock Creek Ginger Ale," convex tin lithograph, 12" h. ............................. **160**

**Soft drink,** "Squeeze," die-cut heavy cardboard, easel-back type, shows father & son fishing in a boat, 19" h. ...................... **175**

**Soft drink,** "Squirt," double-sided masonite w/"Open" & "Closed" 1955, 12 x 16"...... **170**

**Soft drink,** "Squirt," embossed tin, dated 1958, 9 1/2 x 27 1/2" .............................. **135**

**Soft drink,** "Vernor's Ginger Ale," convex tin lithograph, 29 1/2" l................................ **200**

**Soft drink,** "Ward's Orange Crush," embossed tin tacker, rare, 14 1/2 x 27 1/2" ...................................... **425**

**Soft drink,** "Whistle," embossed tin tacker sign w/"Thirsty - 5 cents," dated 1939, 3 x 12 3/8" ......................................... **150**

**Soft drink,** "Whistle," heavy paper sign w/"Giant Family Size," 15 x 35" ..................... **30**

**Spark plugs,** "Champion Spark Plugs," embossed tin w/spark plug at center, 14 1/4 x 30" ...................................... **400**

**Store sign,** "Hub Clothing," metal figure of black boy holding sign, 53" h................... **2,100**

**Store sign,** "Hudson's Soap," porcelain, clock-style w/"We Close At........Today," 10 1/2 x 18" ...................................... **725**

**Store sign,** "Red Owl," porcelain, double-sided, shows large red owl, 56" h............. **1,700**

**Store sign,** "World Soap," porcelain flange sign w/"Groceries, Teas & Coffees" by Ing-Rich, ca. teens, 12 x 18" ................... **1,100**

**Stoves,** "Enterprise Stove," tin, flange, double-sided, flat surface, 18" l. (minor flaking) ................................................ **350**

**Tavern sign,** painted pine, plank construction w/border molding & an inner rectangular panel w/molded frame, the back painted "Royalton House - 1845," the front w/a spread-winged American eagle w/banner in its beak in the central panel w/"1845" above & "J.M. Currier" below, signed "S. Dodge, painter, Enfield, NH," black ground w/white lettering & dark red & white eagle, suspended on wrought-iron hinges, 34 1/4 x 42 1/2" .................... **9,755**

**Tea,** "Horniman's Pure Tea," porcelain, by Patent Enamel Co., Ltd, 24 x 30" ............... **800**

**Telephone,** telephone pay station w/independent shield logo, porcelain flange sign, 8 x 18"................................................ **400**

**Toothpaste,** "Euthymol Toothpaste," paper lithograph w/young woman, framed under glass, 37 1/4" h. ............................ **1,000**

**Underwear,** "Wright's Union Suits," tin lithograph in wood frame, two pieces attach at center, depicts man standing in union suit, 72" h. (some flaking & stains) .. **1,050**

**Watch,** "Hamilton Watch," tin lithograph over cardboard, raised center image, 19" h. .................................................. **1,200**

**Whiskey,** "Buffalo Club Rye Whiskey," tin lithograph w/buffalo in oak frame, by Chas. W. Shonk Co. Litho, Chicago, Illinois, 29 x 38"................................................ **900**

**Whiskey,** "Paul Jones Rye," tin lithograph, shows old man pouring a drink, self-framed, 28 1/2" h. .................................... **1,400**

**Whiskey,** "Westminister Rye," tin lithograph of early motoring scene w/intregral frame, 25 x 38" ................................. **2,300**

# SILHOUETTES

*These cut-out paper portraits in profile were named after Etienne de Silhouette, Louis XV's unpopular minister of finance and an amateur profile cutter. As originally applied, the term was synonymous with cheapness, or anything reduced to its simplest state. These substitutes for the more expensive oil painting or miniatures were popular from about 1770 until 1850 when daguerreotype images replaced the vogue. Silhouettes may be either hollow-cut, with the head cut away leaving the white paper frame for mounting against a dark background, or the profile itself may be cut from black paper and pasted to a light background.*

*Mother & Children Silhouette*

**Bust portraits of gentleman & lady,** he wearing a high collared shirt w/cravat & high-collared jacket, she w/her hair pulled up & held in the back w/a comb, wearing a balloon-sleeved dress w/a wide lacy collar, each w/watercolor highlights, in embossed brass over wood frames, 1840s, overall  4 3/8 x 5 1/8", facing pair................................................ **$1,035**

**Bust portraits of man & wife,** cut-out, he facing right wearing a high-collared shirt & coat, she facing left w/her hair pulled up in back & held w/a comb, wearing a white collar Empire-style dress, ink details, each in a rectangular beveled rosewood-veneered frame, ca. 1830, frames 5 1/2 x 6 5/8", pr. .............................. **578**

**Bust portraits of man & wife,** cut-out, the lady facing right & wearing a high lace cap, high-collared lace-trimmed Empire gown, the man facing left wearing a top hat, high-collared jacket & shirt w/cravat & vest, both w/ink washed details & mounted under an ink-stenciled mat w/two oval openings w/starburst trim & scattered small starbursts & a pair of

small blue hearts below "We Are One," in a narrow wooden rectangular frame w/stenciled bronze powder designs on black, ca. 1830, frame 6 x 9" .................... **3,630**

**Family group,** a mother standing on the right & facing left while holding a baby, a young girl standing on the left facing right & holding a flower, simple ink wash ground, ogee frame,  10 1/2 x 12 5/8" (ILLUS.) ....................................................... **385**

**Family group,** four full-length cut figures, a standing man on the far left facing right & wearing a high-collared dress coat & leaning on a cane, to his right a seated lady in a chair, her hair dressed in a chignon, wearing a balloon-sleeved dress w/one arm over the chair back, next a standing young boy facing left & holding a bow & arrows, on the far right an older lady wearing a mob cap seated in a chair facing left, the adults each holding white reading material, greyish tan background w/simple ink wash detail, signed "Aug. Edouart fecit 1847," old back w/inscription listing members of the Wm. Matthews family, bird's-eye veneer ogee frame, 16 x 22 1/4" (glue stains) .............. **1,430**

**Figure of a man,** a standing stocky older gentleman facing right, wearing a frock coat & top hat & leaning on a cane, black & white lithographed landscape background, signed "M. Socke fecit 1844," framed, 8 5/8 x 12 1/2" ................................ **550**

**Full-length figure of a lady holding a flower,** cut-out & laid down on lithographed background, printed signature, artist identified on reverse as Augustin Edouart, 1825, early 19th c., framed, 7 1/4 x 9 1/2" ................................................. **518**

*Edouart Silhouette of Naval Officer*

**Full-length portrait of a Naval officer,** standing facing right w/a high-collared shirt & a long-tailed jacket, labeled below image "U.S. Navy Boston 1st March 1842 on John Adams Sloop of War," Lt.

Edward M. Yard, attributed to Auguste Edouart, unsigned, toning, staining, framed, 5 1/4 x 11 3/4" (ILLUS.)................... **748**

**Half-length portrait of a young man,** shown facing right, his long hair curled under above his high collar & wide lapels, wearing a cravat, gilt detail to his hair & costume, applied white collar, ca. 1850, in a rectangular beveled bird's-eye maple frame w/gilt liner, 5 1/4 x 6 5/8" ......... **550**

**Half-length portrait of a young woman,** hollow-cut w/black cloth backing, her head cut-out facing right, her hair pulled up to the back & held by a high comb, a black lithographed balloon-sleeved dress w/blue water-color details, old molded gilt frame, ca. 1830-40, 4 1/8 x 5 1/8" ............................................... **550**

**Three-quarters length portraits of sisters,** hollow-cut & backed w/black cloth, each young woman seated in a chair facing right & holding a book in her lap, their hair pulled up in back & held w/a large comb, each wearing a wide white collar on their long-sleeved dress, water-color details of the chair, books & collars in blue, red, black & yellow, wide flat rectangular mahogany veneer frames, ca. 1830-40, 6 x 7 3/4", pr. (minor stains, cloth w/tears) ..................... **1,870**

# SODA FOUNTAIN COLLECTIBLES

*The neighborhood ice cream parlor and drugstore fountain are pretty much a thing of the past as fast-food chains have sprung up across the country. Memories of the slower-paced lifestyle represented by the rapidly disappearing local soda fountain have spurred the interest of many collectors today. Anything relating to the soda fountains of old and the delicious concoctions they dispensed are much sought-after.*

**Bottle topper,** "Fowler's Cherry Smash," die-cut cardboard, shows boy in Colonial outfit & tricorn hat, 7 1/4 x 11 1/2" ................ **$30**

**Clock,** "Borden's," electric wall-type, metal body w/glass face & cover, center w/flower petals surrounding decal of Elsie, "Borden's - Milk & Cream Sold Here" in red lettering around edge, black hands & 3, 6, 9 & 12 marked on face, working, 20 1/2" d. (soiling & scratches, part of decal missing, overall yellowing)....... **171**

**Cone dispenser,** glass & metal w/cone holder, 14" h. ................................................... **525**

**Dispenser,** "Dixie-Flip," ceramic w/pump, painted on one side, 14" h. (pump not original, scratches & wear)........................ **7,200**

**Glasses,** "Orange Crush," syrup line, etched detail, 4 7/8" h., set of 6.................... **650**

**Malt powder dispenser,** Hamilton Beach Model No. 20D40182B, porcelain base w/metal frame around cylindrical acrylic top, Pat. No. 1.965.741, 18 1/2" h. ............. **396**

**Mug,** "Hires," glass, boy on front & "Hires" on back, 4" h. ............................................. **270**

**Sign,** "Carnation Ice Cream," on-sided die-cut porcelain, ice cream sundae in footed dish, red, white & green, 22" w., 23" h. (scratches, chips to mounting holes, soiling) ............................................. **605**

*Dairy Maid Ice Cream Sign*

**Sign,** "Dairy Maid Ice Cream," embossed tin w/wood frame, depicts young child sitting & holding ice cream cone w/"You're sure - It's pure," soiling, edge wear & minor scratches, 26" w., 35" h. (ILLUS.)....................................................... **770**

*French Bauer Ice Cream Sign*

**Sign,** "French Bauer Ice Cream," electric, figural milk glass cone mounted in wooden base, wear, ca. 1930s-40s, 17" h. (ILLUS.)......................................... **2,420**

*Hires Sign*

**Sign,** "Hires," celluloid, bust portrait of young woman w/short brown curly hair, green dress, marked "Drink Hires" (ILLUS.) ........................................................ **770**

*Hood's Ice Cream Sign*

**Sign,** "Hood's Ice Cream," two-sided circular, flange type, painted metal w/trademark cow in center, red border w/white lettering, some surface paint missing, rust & waterstain on flange, 19" d. (ILLUS.) ..................................................... **1,320**

*Western Candy Co. Sign*

**Sign,** "Western Candy Co. Denver, CO.," embossed die-cut depicts bright & colorful portrait of beautiful lady w/flowers in her long wavy hair, 10 1/2 x 12" (ILLUS.)..... **303**

*Dr. Pepper Dispenser*

**Soda dispenser,** "Dr. Pepper," plastic, tombstone-style, two spigots, light green, logo in center, ca. 1960s, wear & pitting, surface scratches, interior soiling, small crack on side below tag (ILLUS.) ........ **386**

**Soda dispenser,** "Fowler's Cherry Smash," ceramic w/pump, printed on both sides, 15" h. (some scratches & wear) ................ **1,400**

**Soda dispenser,** "Fowler's Root Beer," ceramic w/pump, painted on both sides, 14" h. (some scratches & wear) ................ **1,900**

**Soda dispenser,** "Hires," ceramic w/pump, 13" h. ..................................................... **550**

**Stools,** porcelain counter stools w/revolving wooden seats & brass foot rests, 29" h., set of 4 ........................................... **550**

**Syrup dispenser,** "Cherry Smash," ceramic w/original marked pump, cherries & leaves on branch in center, ca. 1920 (surface marks, base chips) ................ **880**

*Cherry Smash Syrup Dispenser*

**Syrup dispenser,** "Fowler's Cherry Smash," cranberry red glass, original nickel chrome fixtures, names on both sides, bowl 7 1/2 x 9", overall 17" l. (ILLUS.) ........................................................ **633**

*Haines-CeBrook Ice Cream Tray*

Tray, "Haines-CeBrook Ice Cream," lithographed tin, young woman wearing black dress w/large white collar, large red beret-type hat, eating a dish of ice cream w/"Haines-CeBrook Ice Cream - 'The Better Kind'," Parker Brawner, Washington, D.C., minor scrapes & blemishes, 10 1/2 x 15 1/4" (ILLUS.)............ **182**

# SPACE AGE COLLECTIBLES

*Although fiction novels about space exploration have been around since the 19th century, and such space fantasies as "Flash Gordon" and "Buck Rogers" were popular in the 1930s, the modern Space Age started after World War II. There have been dozens of space science fiction movies and television shows produced since the early 1950s when Russia and the United States were locked in the "Space Race." Our listings include items which were produced to tie-in to all the movies, TV shows and works of fiction released since the early 1950s. These listings are arranged alphabetically by the name of the character, show or movie.*

*Also see: CHARACTER COLLECTIBLES, TOYS and LUNCH BOXES.*

## SPACE EXPLORATION MEMORABILIA

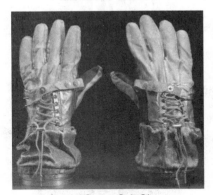

*Gemini Space Suit Gloves*

Coin, 1961 D. Roosevelt dime w/sterling silver bezel which can be linked to sterling silver disk engraved "Liberty Bell 7 - 21 July 1961," carried in Gus Grissom's spacesuit during second U.S. manned space flight, together w/typed letter signed by Mrs. Betty Grissom ............... **$4,600**
Flag, silk United States flag mounted on personal letterhead & inscribed "Flown on Apollo 7 Wally Schirra," flag 4 x 6," text typed & signed by Schirra .................. **4,025**
Flashlight, brass, flown on Apollo 7, 6" l., together w/typed letter signed by Schirra.. **2,760**
Flight suit, flame retardant material w/multiple zippered pockets & label from Land Manufacturing Company, Wichita Kansas, issued to Gordon Cooper in 1964

for general flying & spacecraft testing, w/typed letter signed by Cooper............... **1,725**
Gloves, aluminized coated high temperature nylon, used w/Gemini space suit, made by Goodrich & adapted for use w/the David Clark Company's G2C space suits, pr. (ILLUS.).......................... **18,400**
Headset, used by Neil Armstrong for purposes of communication, 1967, signed by Armstrong, Pacific Plantronics, together w/plastic carrying case................ **4,830**

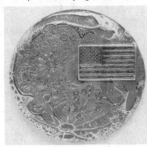

*Apollo XII Lapel Pin*

Lapel pin, metal, circular w/shape of moon & United States flag near center, reverse reads "Flown to the Moon by an Intrepid crew, Apollo XII, November 1969," w/Navy wings & names of the crew & manuscript card by Conrad, 3/4" d. (ILLUS.)...................................................... **9,775**

*NASA Apollo 11 Portrait*

Portrait, Apollo 11 crew in spacesuits, color, signed by Neil Armstrong, Mike Collins & Buzz Aldrin, NASA (ILLUS.)..... **11,500**
Watch, Mercury recovery wristwatch issued to Gordon Cooper while on the carrier USS Kearsarge, the day of splashdown after Faith 7 flight May 16, 1963, Timex, w/typed letter signed by Cooper ...................................................... **1,150**

## SPACE FANTASY ITEMS

"Chewbacca" (Star Wars) bank, figural, ceramic, Sigma, ca. 1982, 10 1/2" h. (ILLUS. top next column) ........................... **$95**
Dolls, "Snoopy" astronauts, one inscribed & signed by Tom Stafford on back of helmet w/"'Snoopy' LM-4 Call Sign, Tom

Stafford, Apollo X Cdr, May 69" & the second w/"'Snoopy' LM-4, Gene Cernan, Apollo X LMP," Determined Productions, 1969, 10" h., set of two (ILLUS. center, this column)............................................... **2,530**

*Star Wars "Chewbacca" Bank*

*"Snoopy" Astronaut Dolls*

**Jet Patrol lunch box & thermos,** metal, 1957, Aladdin ............................................... **201**

*Lost in Space Lunch Box & Thermos*

**Lost in Space lunch box & thermos,** metal, dome-type, 1967-68, King See-ley Thermos (ILLUS.) ........................... **450-650**

**Lost in Space official robot,** plastic, silver, w/stop & go action, w/original box, Ahi, 10 1/2" h. (ILLUS. top next page)................. **201**

**Space Patrol "Space-O-Phone,"** w/origi-nal string attached, Ralston premium, 1950s ............................................................ **85**

**The Jetsons (TV) lunch box w/thermos,** metal, dome top, 1963, Aladdin .................. **978**

**Tom Corbett, Space Cadet lunch box w/thermos,** metal, 1954, Aladdin ............... **431**

*Official Lost in Space Robot*

**Tom Corbett space gun,** windup tin, Marx, good w/good box........................................... **500**
**Tom Corbett space ship,** windup tin, Marx, good ..................................................... **550**

# SPICE CABINETS & BOXES

**Box,** cov., round bentwood, low cylindrical wide form w/the interior holding eight individual canisters, original varnish w/black stenciled labels, including "Spices" on the cover, & trim, impressed patent dates & stenciled label "S.C. Bowman...Iowa," 9" d. ............................... **$468**

**Box,** cov., round shallow bentwood base w/fitted flat cover stenciled in the center "Spices," base & cover w/tin edging, holds eight small matching bentwood canisters w/stenciled labels on the cov-ers, old varnish, 19th c., 9 1/2" d., the set..... **275**

**Box,** hanging-type, cherry, an arched crest w/hanging hole above a rectangular dovetailed case enclosing three small dovetailed drawers w/divided interiors, old worn finish, 5 3/4 x 9 1/4", 13" h. (some edge damage) ............................... **1,320**

**Box,** painted bentwood, round w/single lap-pet on the base & single lappet on the fit-ted flat cover, old green repaint, 19th c., 6" d. ...................................................................... **303**

**Cabinet,** hanging-type, ash, a narrow crestboard w/flat top & incurved edges pierced w/two hanging holes above a small rectangular top on the case enclosing eight small drawers w/inset turned wood knobs, natural finish & black stenciled labels, wire nail construc-tion, 5 1/4 x 10 3/4", 15 1/2" h. ..................... **413**

**Cabinet,** hanging-type, birch, a square case w/wire nail construction & plywood back holding six small drawers, rounded tabs at each back corner, old varnish fin-ish, 12 3/4" sq. (minor damage to back cut-outs) ....................................................... **248**

**Cabinet,** hanging-type, hardwood, a low galleried crestboard w/hanging holes & curved ends above a narrow long rect-angular top on the case enclosing two rows of four small square drawers each,

small turned wood knobs, traces of stenciled labels, refinished, 4 3/4 x 18",
8 3/4" h. ........................................................ **495**

*Three-tier Spice Cabinet*

**Cabinet,** painted pine, a three-tiered form
w/overhanging molded edges & a
shaped backboard & round wood pulls,
painted red, 19th c., minor wear,
6 1/2 x 15 1/2", 12 3/4" h. (ILLUS.) .......... **1,840**

**Cabinet,** poplar & walnut, a rectangular thin
top above a case w/two stacks of three
small nailed drawers above a single long
bottom drawer, old finish, two small
brass button pulls missing, 19th c.,
7 x 15 1/2", 14 3/4" h. ................................... **385**

*Hanging Spice Cabinet*

**Cabinet,** wall-type, bird's-eye maple &
mahogany, a rectangular flat top
w/molded cornice above a tall dovetailed
case w/a pair of small drawers over a tall
narrow paneled central door flanked on
each side by four small square drawers
above another pair of drawers at the bottom, flat base, porcelain knobs, wire nail
construction, refinished, 5 x 15 1/4",
18 5/8" h. (ILLUS.) ........................................ **468**

*Fine Pennsylvania Spice Cabinet*

**Cabinet,** walnut, the rectangular top w/a
cove-molded cornice above a raised
arched panel hinged door w/H-hinges &
a brass keyhole escutcheon opening to
an interior of eleven small drawers
w/brass pulls, on a molded base, old
surface, Pennsylvania, 1780-1800,
minor imperfections, 11 x 15 1/2",
18 1/4" h. (ILLUS.) ................................. **14,950**

**Canister,** toleware, a low cylindrical container holding five smaller canisters & a
nutmeg grate, exterior w/brown paint,
late 19th c., the set ......................................... **66**

# SPORTS MEMORABILIA
*Also see BASEBALL MEMORABILIA*

## BASKETBALL

**Banner,** 1971 Utah Stars ABA Champions
banner, red, white & blue basketball logo
at the top above red lettering on white
ground, wooden rod for hanging,
18 x 30" ...................................................... **$285**

**Basketball,** 1973-74 New York Knicks
team-signed ball, Spalding Official
model, signed by fifteen team members ...... **766**

*Larry Bird 1991 Signed Jersey*

**Jersey,** 1991 Larry Bird game-worn model,
green mesh w/white lettering & number

33, sweat-stained at collar & sleeves, signed by Bird on the rear number (ILLUS.) .................... **3,058**

**Ring,** 1980 Los Angeles Lakers Championship model, awarded to Jim Chones, Balfour, 14k gold w/central diamond ......... **5,604**

## BOXING

**Advertisement,** color-printed cardboard Coca-Cola ad featuring a half-length photo of Sugar Ray Robinson, bright pink background, 1952, slight stains, tape damage on back, framed, 12 x 15" (ILLUS. below) ......................................... **1,495**

*Sugar Ray Robinson Coca-Cola Ad*

**Belt,** Willie Pep 1938 Championship model, gilt-metal buckle w/two boxers in action below blue enamel "Conn. Amateur Championship," red, white & blue cloth band mounted w/two one-inch pins on either side of buckle, buckle 1 3/4 x 2 1/2" (somewhat worn & age faded) ...................................................... **2,690**

**Photograph,** Gene Tunney-signed, full-length pose w/Tunney standing w/hands on hips, inscribed "To Al Wilson with best wishes Gene Tunney Dec 12-26," black & white, 11 x 14" .............................. **348**

**Photograph,** Sonny Liston-signed, black & white promotional photo w/Liston in fighting stance, facsimile inscription w/his real autograph below, near mint, 3 1/2 x 6" ................................................. **1,190**

**Postcard,** black & white glossy photo card of Sugar Ray Robinson, printed description at the bottom, autographed by Robinson, 1950s (ILLUS. top next column) ........ **268**

*Sugar Ray Robinson Postcard*

**Poster,** newspaper advertising-type, yellow cardboard w/black lettering & photos of boxers' heads in upper corners, reads "First! Pictures and Story - Sharkey - Carnera - Fight Result - Daily Record," framed, for 1933 Jack Sharkey vs Primo Carnera, 12 x 18" ..................................... **1,113**

## FOOTBALL

*1958 Colts Signed Football*

**Football,** 1958 Baltimore Colts World Championship team-signed, Wilson model stamped "Baltimore Colts - 17 Giants World's Champions 23 Colts '58," covered w/forty-six signatures (ILLUS.) .... **2,406**

*1920s Leather Football Helmet*

**Football helmet,** 1920s, leather, fleece lining, elastic hinges & chin strap, marked "Wilson" & "72," some sweat stain on liner (ILLUS.) ................................................. **633**

**Jersey,** Ken Stabler game-worn type, black mesh w/white lettering, collar tag reads "Medalist Sand-Knit 46," 1970s ................. **1,390**

Postcard, real photo-type, shows "Green Bay 'Packers' Football Team 1925," produced by Stillere Company of Green Bay, unused, near mint ................................. 447

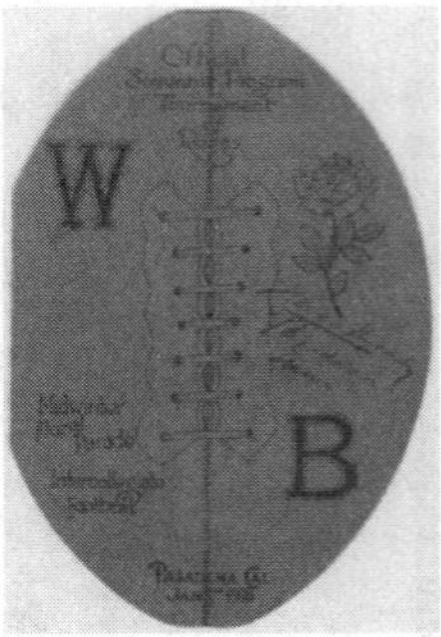

*1916 Rose Bowl Program*

Program, 1916 Rose Bowl program, booklet shaped like a football printed "Official Souvenir Program - Tournament of Roses - Midwinter Floral Parade - Intercollegiate Football - Pasadena, Cal. - Jan. 1st, 1916," twenty-seventh annual event w/Brown against Washington State, some writing on cover (ILLUS.) ...... 3,260

Program, New York Jets vs Kansas City Chiefs, September 18, 1965, first professional game & touchdown for Joe Namath, cover in white w/green & gold printing & cartoon-style design of two football players ........................................... 348

Ring, 1975 Pittsburgh Steelers Super Bowl Championship model, salesman's sample in 10k w/twin diamonds, Super Bowl X, from Balfour ........................................ 2,021

Ticket stub, 1942 Rose Bowl game, moved to Durham, North Carolina from Pasadena because of fears of Japanese attack, yellow ground w/image of Duke Stadium, green & red lettering ..................... 759

Ticket stub, college game, white printed in dark blue & red w/"Football Homecoming - Saturday November 21 at 2:30 P.M. - Illinois - Ohio - Ohio Stadium - 1925 - $2.50," final game ticket for Red Grange (rounded corners) ........................... 348

Whiskey flask & case, 1958 Baltimore Colts, clear glass flask in original faux-leather case resembling an elongated change purse, printed on front w/a helmeted horse leaping over a goal post between words "Baltimore Colts," then written just below "The Big Game" .............. 201

# GOLF CLUBS

## WOODEN SHAFTED

Aitken (Alex), iron, smooth face, shaft stamp .......................................................... 100

Aitken (Alex), putter, short hosel & blade w/deep face (B) ........................................... 400

Anderson (James), mashie, short head w/deep face blade, smooth face, heavy hosel, ca. 1890 ........................................... 350

Anderson (James), niblick, small head, smooth face, ca. 1885 ................................... 800

B. G. I. Company, driver, No. 71, Dunn model, splice head ...................................... 250

B. G. I. Company, driving cleek, No. 103, Carruthers-type hosel .................................. 175

B. G. I. Company, putting cleek, No. 120, deep face ..................................................... 150

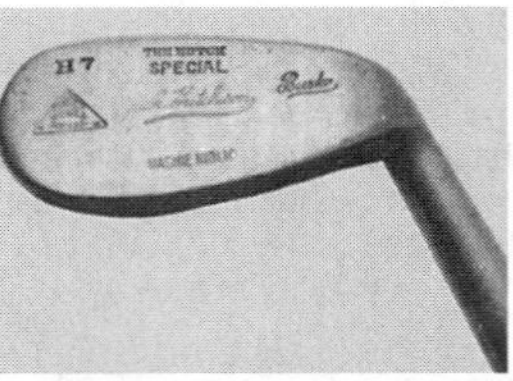

*Burke Golf Company Mashie Niblick*

Burke Golf Company, mashie niblick, Hutchison Autograph Series, No. H7, monel, offset head, slot face, D (ILLUS.)..... 150

Burke Golf Company, wood cleek, Grand Prize series, No. 45, bulls-eye face insert ............................................................ 200

Carrick (F. & A.), mashie, short blade, wide toe, marked for J.H. Hutchison, ca. 1890 ............................................................ 500

Carrick (F. & A.), iron, 4 3/4" hosel, straight line name stamp, ca. 1875 .......................... 800

Dunn (Wm. Jr.), brassie, splice head w/bulger face ............................................... 400

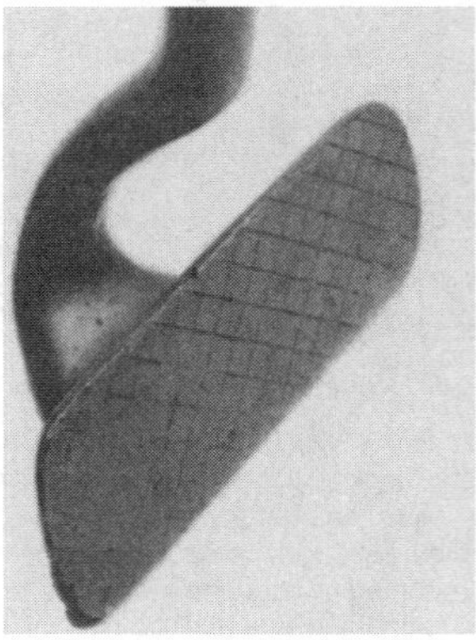

*Fitzjohn Putter*

Fitzjohn (Ed), putter, center shaft attached to back of blade, inverted question mark shape, U (ILLUS.) .................................... 3,500

*Forgan & Son Driving Iron*

Forgan & Son (Robert), driving iron, dot face, crown cleek mark, 20th c. (ILLUS.) ....... 50

**Forgan & Son (Robert),** putter, Whee model, combination wood & metal shaft, 20th c. ........................................................ **600**

*Forgan & Son Spoon*

**Forgan & Son (Robert),** spoon, Prince of Wales plume mark, ca. 1890s, L (ILLUS.).......................................... **1,000-2,500**

**Gibson & Company (William),** brassie, bulldog shape.............................................. **125**

**Gibson & Company (William),** niblick, Skoogee model, concave face .................... **450**

**Gibson & Company (William),** putter, all square model, square hosel, offset blade..... **175**

**Gibson & Company (William),** putter, Brown Vardon style, gun metal head .......... **275**

**Gibson & Company (William),** putter, Princeps model, top edge weighted ............. **300**

**Kempshall Manufacturing Company,** driver, wood head w/pyralin marked & dated face insert (U)................................. **400**

**Kroydon Golf Company,** spade mashie U 5, Short Stop model, brick patt. face (D) ...... **350**

**Lee Company (Harry C.),** baffy, Schenectady-shaped head w/17-degree lofted face................................................ **2,500**

**MacGregor,** brassie, short splice head, shamrock in circle cleek mark ..................... **175**

**MacGregor,** driver, model 125 short bull-dog head, face insert............................... **125**

**MacGregor,** driver, model 326, dread-nought, large head .................................... **100**

**MacGregor,** niblick, smooth face, very thick head & hosel, shamrock in circle ........ **300**

**MacGregor,** putter, model 20-J, swan's-neck model, gun metal blade ..................... **250**

**MacGregor,** putter, model 486, Down-It, wood mallet head, brass face ..................... **250**

**MacGregor,** putter, model 70, gun metal dominie style, round back ........................... **225**

**MacGregor,** woods, Chieftain model, matched set of 3....................................... **1,250**

**McEwan & Son,** driver, guttie ball period, short head, leather face insert, ca. 1895 (S) ..................................................... **750-1,000**

**McEwan & Son,** putter, feather ball period, slightly hooked face, ca. 1840 (L)............................................. **10,000-15,000**

**Morris (Tom),** cleek, guttie ball period, smooth face, Stewart pipe cleek mark, oval stamp............................................... **300**

**Nicoll, George,** putter, swan's-neck model, before 1898................................................. **350**

**Park & Son (William),** putter, Willie Sr., long head (L) ................................... **2,000-5,000**

**Ross (Donald),** cleek, smooth face, Dor-noch stamp................................................ **300**

**Sayers (Bernard),** brassie, Domey model, rounded sole, stripe top.............................. **125**

**Spalding & Brothers Company (A.G.),** driver, Gold Medal series, Model 7, real ivory inserts, two screws ............................. **400**

**Spalding & Brothers Company (A.G.),** driver, Morristown series, splice head.......... **175**

**Spalding & Brothers Company (A.G.),** driving niblic, "The Spalding" series, large oval head, smooth face .................... **2,750**

**Spalding & Brothers Company (A.G.),** lofting mashie, "The Spalding" series, center shafted, round head (U) ................. **3,000**

**Spalding & Brothers Company (A.G.),** putter, doubleline 'baseball' mark, long slender splice head (L) ............................. **1,500**

**Standard Golf Company,** brassie, BS1 model, semi-long nose ................................. **350**

# STATUARY - BRONZE, MARBLE & OTHER

*Bronzes and other statuary are increasingly pop-ular with today's collectors. Particularly appealing are works by "Les Animaliers," the 19th-century French school of sculptors who turned to animals for their subject matter. These, together with figures in the Art Deco and Art Nouveau taste, are common in a wide price range.*

## BRONZE

*Barye Senegal Elephant Bronze*

**Barye, Antoine-Louis,** Senegal elephant, running animal w/trunk down, greenish brown patina, signed "F. Barbedienne" & stamped "FB," base w/incised numbers "676/44," late 19th c., 5 1/2" h. (ILLUS.).................................................. **$10,925**

**Berman,** figure of a Middle Eastern girl, dancing w/swirling movable skirt open-ing to reveal her nude body, marble base, signed "Namgreb" w/foundry seal, 10" h. ......................................................... **2,875**

**Chiparus, Demetre,** Figure of Lazzarone, the little boy standing & playing an accordian & singing, wearing wrinkled knickers & jacket, a scarf, a hat & boots, brown & gold patina, signed "D. Chiparus," on a round onyx base, 9 1/2" h. (ILLUS. top next page) .............. **2,875**

*Bronze Figure of Lazzarone*

**Chiparus, Demetre H.,** "Dourga," standing on tiptoes w/arms outstretched, gilt-bronzed, inscribed "D. Chiparus," Romanian, 24 3/4" h.............................. **29,900**

**Fritz, M. Hermann,** Europa and The Bull, the nude female seated astride the bull, he bending down for a drink of water, golden brown patina, signed "M. Hermann Fritz," on a rectangular thick marble base, ca. 1920, 15 1/2" l. (ILLUS. below)...................................................... **2,415**

*Europa and The Bull Figure Group*

**Lorenzl (Joseph),** figure of a dancer, the female figure standing on one foot, arms outstretched & face uplifted, stands on a tall eight-sided pillar over stepped

square green onyx base, figure signed "Lorenzl," Austria, ca. 1925, chips to base edge, patina wear, 27" h. (ILLUS. below) ......................................... **3,105**

*Lorenzl Figure of a Dancer*

**Madrassi, Luca,** figure group of a young peasant couple, titled "Courtship," base inscribed "L. Madrassi," dark brown patina, on marble & bronze footed base, 29" h. ....................................................... **4,025**

**Simard, Marie-Louise,** Trojan horse, patinated bronze, inscribed "Simard," French, ca. 1920s, 20 1/2" h. ................. **12,650**

*Bronze of a Walking Lion*

**Vidal, Louis,** lion walking, on a thick narrow rectangular base, greenish brown patina, signed & dated 1874, 27" l., 14 1/2" h. (ILLUS.)..................................... **2,415**

*Vienna Bronze of a Dove*

**Vienna bronze,** model of a dove, cold-painted in shades of grey & brown, stamped for Bergman, ca. 1920, 8" l. (ILLUS.) ....................................................... **920**

**Villanis, Edouard,** bust of a woman, titled
"Seule," signed & w/impressed foundry
mark, 22 1/2" h. .......................................... **2,300**

# MARBLE

*Fine Marble Bust of a Maiden*

**Bust of a young woman,** the pious looking
maiden wearing a dress w/an elaborate
bodice & a large cross, her hair parted &
in a braid, fine detail, on a marble socle,
Italy, late 19th c., bust 26" h. (ILLUS.)....... **7,475**

*Marble Figure of Girl & Bank*

**Frilli, A.,** figure of a young girl standing &
depositing a coin in a bank, 19th c.
(ILLUS.)...................................................... **7,150**

*Lorenzo de Medici Marble Statue*

**Lorenzo de Medici,** seated figure in classical armor, after Michelangelo, 22" h.
(ILLUS.)...................................................... **690**
**Russo, G.,** bust of a veiled maiden, one
arm clutching the veil around her face &
close to her neck, signed "G. Russo,
Roma," Italy, late 19th - early 20th c.,
w/associated Italian black marble spi-
raled pedestal, overall 76" h., 2 pcs. ......... **5,750**

*St. Francis & the Christ Child*

**St. Francis & the Christ Child,** the standing saint holding a blossom in one hand
& the Christ Child in his other arm, on a
three-part base, late 19th - early 20th c.,
figure 55 1/2" h. (ILLUS.)........................... **4,600**

*Marble Figure of Venus*

**Venus,** three-quarters length figure partially
draped, looking down to the side, after

the antique, square base, 19th c., 25" h.
(ILLUS.)..................................................... **1,150**

# OTHER

**Ivory,** bust of a woman, her hair drawn up
& set w/leaves, raised on an onyx ped-
estal, Europe, 19th c., 11" l. ......................... **863**

*Terra Cotta Satyr Grouping*

**Terra cotta,** figure group of a satyr w/a
grape-filled tambourine & two young
satyrs, after Clodion, 17" h. (ILLUS.)......... **2,185**

# STEIFF TOYS & DOLLS

*From a felt pincushion in the shape of an ele-
phant, a world-famous toy company emerged. Margarete Steiff (1847-1909), a polio victim as a child
and confined to a wheelchair, planned a career as a
seamstress and opened a shop in the family home.
However, her plans were dramatically changed
when she made the first stuffed elephant in 1880.
By 1886 she was producing stuffed felt monkeys,
donkeys, horses and other animal forms. In 1893
an agent sold her toys at the Leipzig Fair. This ven-
ture was so successful that a catalog was printed
and a salesman hired. Magarete's nephews and
nieces became involved in the business, assisting
in its management and the design of new items.*

*Through the years, the Steiff Company has pro-
duced a varied line including felt and plush animals.
Teddy Bears, gnomes, elves, felt dolls with celluloid
heads, Kewpie dolls and even radiator caps with
animals or dolls attached as decoration. Descendants of the original family members continue to be
active in the management of the company still
adhering to Margarete's motto "For our children, the
best is just good enough."*

**Cat,** crouching pose w/front paws in a cylindrical pink muff, beige velvet w/black
paint trim, faded red neck ribbon, button
in ear, 7" l. (wear, tail sewn back) .............. **$550**
**Cat on wheels,** standing w/white mohair
coat w/grey stripes, glass eyes, worn
pink neck ribbon w/bell, pink felt ear lin-
ings, on small cast-iron wheels, original
ear button, 14" l. (wear).............................. **980**
**Cat on wheels,** very worn light mohair
w/bead eyes, worn pink neck ribbon

w/brass bell, standing w/front legs on
tiny cast-iron wheels, original button in
ear, 7 1/2" h. (repair, voice box silent).......... **413**
**Cow on wheels,** brown & white mohair
standing animal w/bead eyes, Steiff button in ear, on tiny cast-iron wheels,
10 1/4" l. (felt horns very worn &
wrapped w/string)........................................ **578**
**Dachshund on wheels,** standing dog
w/tan felt coat & glass eyes, leather collar, original button in ear, on tiny cast-
iron wheels, 16 1/2" l. (wear, moth holes,
damaged & repaired tail)............................. **385**
**Dog on wheels,** German Shepherd, cream
& ginger mohair w/glass eyes, embroidered nose, mouth & claws, steel frame,
wooden wheels, ca. 1920s, 20" l.,
16 3/8" h. (botton & left ear missing,
some fur & fiber loss, voice box not
working)....................................................... **288**

**Dog on wheels,** Spitz, standing position,
white mohair w/glass eyes, embroidered nose & mouth, excelsior stuffing,
steel frame, small spoked metal wheels,
1908, 22" l., 18 1/2" h. (button missing,
some fur & fiber loss, voice silent) .............. **690**
**Elephant,** "Jumbo," grey mohair, yes-no
type, standing on hind legs, jointed at
head & shoulders, jersey pads, glass
eyes, felt tusks, ear button & chest tag,
1970s, 10" h. ............................................... **201**
**Elephant on wheels,** grey mohair, white
felt tusks, red leather harness, red & yellow felt blanket, glass eyes, steel frame,
rubber-tired metal wheels, ear button &
tag, mid-20th c., 24 1/2" l. ........................... **431**
**Mallard drake,** "Stanic," airbrushed Dray-
lon fur, black plastic eyes, yellow felt bill,
button in wing, ca. 1973, 13 1/2" l.,
10 1/2" h. ..................................................... **230**
**Okapi,** velveteen, airbrushed coat, glass
eyes, mohair mane & accents on ears &
tail, ear button, 1960s, 11" h. ..................... **288**

*Giant Panda Steiff Toy*

**Panda,** standing upright, button in ear, ca. 1960s, 70" h. (ILLUS.) .............................. **1,870**

**Sheep on wheels,** standing animal w/wooly mohair coat, felt legs & face w/button eyes, worn neck ribbon w/bell, head turns, on small cast-iron wheels, 12 1/2" l. (one ear incomplete w/missing button) ....................................................... **935**

**Spider,** multicolored plush back, gold furry underbody, legs, antenna & mouth, black glass eyes, 1960s, 9" l. (button & tag missing) .................................................... **403**

**Stegosaurus,** "Dinos," yellow mohair belly, blue, emerald green, brown, magenta & yellow airbrushed body, green & black glass eyes, pink felt open mouth, green, blue & orchid felt back plates, yellow felt ears, 1960, 11" l. (one ear damaged, button missing) ........................................... **403**

*Two Large Steiff Teddy Bears*

**Teddy bear,** curly blonde mohair, black steel eyes, blank ear button, tan embroidered nose, mouth & claws, blonde felt pads, excelsior stuffing, w/original photo of bear & friends in a garden, some fur loss on muzzle, spotty moth damage on pad, ca. 1905, 20" h. (ILLUS. right) .......... **9,200**

**Teddy bear,** ginger mohair, fully jointed, black steel eyes, embroidered nose, mouth & claws, tan pads, excelsior stuffing, button missing, fur worn & fiber loss on muzzle, moth damage on pads, ca. 1905, 24" h. (ILLUS. left) ......................... **5,750**

**Teddy bear,** Polar bear, white mohair, 6' h. ... **4,370**

**Teddy bear,** miniature, beige mohair w/fully-jointed body, black bead eyes, embroidered nose & mouth, ear button, ca. 1905, 3 1/2" h. (some fur loss) ........................................................... **805**

**Teddy bear,** yellow mohair, glass eyes, embroidered nose, mouth & claws, ear button, fully jointed, no-pads-style, excelsior stuffing, ca. 1910, 7" h. (spotty fur loss) ....................................................... **748**

**Teddy bear,** golden mohair, shoe button eyes, black embroidered nose, mouth & claws, felt pads, fully jointed, excelsior stuffing, early, 10" h. (slight fur wear) ........ **1,035**

**Teddy bear,** "Teddy Baby," cream mohair, glass eyes, open mouth, embroidered nose & claws, synthetic suede pads, fully jointed, 11 1/4" h. (ear button missing) ........................................................ **1,150**

**Teddy bear,** gold mohair, black shoe button eyes, embroidered nose, mouth & claws, tan feet pads, fully jointed, ca. 1905, 12 1/2" h. (some spotty fur loss, body needs some stuffing) ....................... **1,725**

**Teddy bear,** light yellow mohair, black steel eyes, embroidered nose, mouth & claws, felt pads, fully jointed, excelsior stuffing, blank button, ca. 1905, 12 1/2" h. (extensive fur & pad loss, needs restuffing) ........ **1,265**

**Teddy bear,** beige mohair, glass eyes, embroidered nose, mouth & claws, felt pads, fully jointed, 13" h. (button missing some fur & fiber loss) ................................... **230**

**Teddy bear,** "Feed Me," rust mohair, glass eyes, unjointed, metal ring pulled on back of head opens mouth, metal box catches dry food, oil cloth bib, excelsior-stuffed head, ca. 1937, 15" h. ...................... **288**

**Teddy bear,** gold mohair, black steel eyes, embroidered nose, mouth & claws, beige felt pads, fully jointed, excelsior stuffing, ca. 1905, 16" h. (button missing, some fur & fiber loss, moth damage on pads) ...................................................... **2,415**

**Teddy bear,** ginger mohair, black steel eyes, embroidered nose, mouth & claws, fully jointed, excelsior stuffing, ca. 1905, 19" h. (fur & fiber loss on muzzle & ears, slight overall fur loss, replaced pads, button missing) ...................................................... **8,050**

**Teddy bear,** blond mohair, center-seam style, embroidered nose, mouth & claws, felt pads, fully jointed, excelsior stuffing, ca. 1905, 20" h. (spotty fur & fiber loss, fur soiled, button missing) ....... **11,500**

**Teddy bear,** blond mohair, jointed shoulders & hips, hump on back, black shoe button eyes, cloth pads on paws, black floss nose & mouth, excelsior-stuffed, unmarked, 20" h. (worn, especially on face, eye replaced, some mending, pads replaced) ..................................................... **575**

**Teddy bear,** blonde mohair, glass eyes, re-embroidered nose, mouth & claws, felt pads, excelsior stuffing, fully jointed, blank ear button, ca. 1910, 21" h. (button missing, extensive fur & fiber loss) .............. **805**

# STEINS

*Early Burl Walnut & Horn Stein*

**Burl walnut & horn-mounted,** cylindrical w/knobbed base ring below turned rings, the knobbed domed hinged cover set w/horn, heavy scroll handle w/thumb rest, Europe, late 17th c., 6 1/2" h. (ILLUS.) ................................................... **$2,185**

*Cut & Inscribed Glass Stein*

**Glass,** clear cut cylindrical form w/sawtooth bands & a large central cut round panel engraved w/the names of eight men, the hinged pewter cover w/eagle thumbrest & facet-cut glass insert w/engraved inscription, dated 1881, 1/2 L, 7 1/2" h. (ILLUS.) ....................................................... **235**

*Glass Dueling Society Stein*

**Glass,** clear panel-cut cylindrical sides w/heavy applied handle, the hinged pewter lid w/eagle thumbrest & porcelain insert coat of arms for a Dueling Society, ca. 1887, 1/2 L, 5 3/4" h. (ILLUS.) ....................................................... **595**

*Mold-blown Opaque Blue Glass Stein*

**Glass,** mold-blown blue opaque w/a bulbous ovoid form & overall diamond point pattern, hinged low-domed pewter lid & thumbrest, ca. 1875, 5 1/4" h. (ILLUS.) ........ **495**

*Tall Clear Mold-Blown Glass Stein*

**Glass,** mold-blown clear cylindrical body w/large oval punties & panels, applied clear glass handle, peaked domed hinged pewter lid & thumbrest, 1/2 L, 9" h. (ILLUS.) ............................................... **205**

*Small German Glass Stein*

**Glass,** student-type, clear panel-cut cylindrical sides w/hinged pewter-rimmed cover w/glass insert & applied strap handle, ca. 1889, .3 L, 5 1/4" h. (ILLUS.) ..... **145**

*No. 592 Mettlach Stein*

**Mettlach,** No. 592, pottery PUG, decorated w/a color tavern interior scene w/man & barmaid, early brown stamped mark, 1/2 L, 5" h. (ILLUS.)............................................ **225**

*Porcelain Stein with Landscape*

**Porcelain,** h.p. color panel w/a city & landscape titled "Scene of Gmunden v. Calvarrenberge," lithophane of a German maiden in the bottom, 1/2 L, 9" h. (ILLUS.)...................................................... **265**

*Porcelain Stein with Lithophane*

**Porcelain,** h.p. decoration of a letter from Bismarck below a classic urn, pointed dome hinged pewter cover w/cartouche thumbrest, band on the bottom w/a German inscription translating to "A Gift From Prince Bismarck," lithophane in the base, dated April 7, 1888, 1/2 L, 9 1/4" h (ILLUS.) .................................................. **1,200**

**Pottery,** remembrance-type, molded w/three panels of German military scenes in dark blue, brown & tan, hinged steeple-form pewter lid w/figural eagle thumbrest, bottom band reads "Mit Gott Fur Konig," ca. 1920s, 1/2 L, 9 3/4" h. (ILLUS. top next column) ............................ **310**

*German Military Remembrance Stein*

**Regimental,** high domed pewter lid w/soldiers loading cannon finial, figural eagle thumbrest, the sides h.p. w/inscriptions for the "6. Battallion Lebr. Rft. Der Feld Art (field artillary)," battle scenes on sides, dated 1904-06, 9 3/4" h. (ILLUS. right) ......................................................... **1,700**

*German Regimental Steins*

**Regimental,** porcelain w/a high domed pewter lid w/a seated soldier & grenade finial & figural eagle thumbrest, the sides h.p. w/inscriptions for the infantry Grenadiers Regiment #109, w/soldier's name, battle scenes & crest around sides, dated 1911-12, 9 3/4" h. (ILLUS. left) ......................................................... **1,070**

*German Reservists Stein*

**Reservist,** pottery w/large crowned "ER" within a green wreath on the front above an inscribed banner, tall steeple lid w/a figural locomotive finial indicating that was the reservist occupation, figural eagle thumbrest, lithophane in the bottom, 1/2 L (ILLUS.) .............................. **1,070**

*Dark Blue Stoneware Stein*

**Stoneware,** short bulbous form w/dark cobalt blue stripes alternating w/stripes of molded hops & wheat, loop handle, hinged low domed lid w/thumbrest, numbers on the base, .3 L (ILLUS.) ........ **75-150**

# TEDDY BEAR COLLECTIBLES

*Theodore (Teddy) Roosevelt had become a national hero during the Spanish-American War by leading his "Rough Riders" to victory at San Juan Hill in 1898. He became the 26th president of the United States in 1901 when President McKinley was assassinated. The gregarious Roosevelt was fond of the outdoors and hunting. Legend has it that while on a hunting trip, soon after becoming President, he refused to shoot a bear cub because it was so small and helpless. The story was picked up by a political cartoonist who depicted President Roosevelt, attired in hunting garb, turning away and refusing to shoot a small bear cub. Shortly thereafter, toy plush bears began appearing in department stores labeled "Teddy's Bear" and they became an immediate success. Books on the adventures of "The Roosevelt Bears" were written and illustrated by Paul Piper under the pseudonym of Seymour Eaton and this version of the Teddy Bear became a popular decoration on children's dishes.*

**Teddy bear,** miniature, ginger mohair, two-faced, black steel eyes, embroidered nose & mouth, comic face w/plastic tongue, metal nose, metal eyes, backed w/plastiform ringlets, fully jointed, Schuco, 1955, 3 1/2" h. .............................. **$518**

**Teddy bear,** brown wool, black shoe button eyes, embroidered nose & mouth, tan felt pads, jointed at shoulders & hips, excelsior stuffing, exterior metal joints, early, 9 1/2" h. (fiber damage on top of head & pads) .............................................. **115**

**Teddy bear,** light yellow mohair, blue shoe button eyes, embroidered nose, mouth & claws, beige felt pads, fully jointed, early, possibly Aetna, 12" h. (fiber & fur loss, repairs on muzzle & limbs) ........................... **345**

**Teddy bear,** blond mohair, glass eyes, embroidered nose, mouth & claws, velveteen pads, fully jointed, excelsior & kapok stuffing, possibly Joy Toy, Australia, 1920s, 14 1/2" h. (fur & fiber loss) .......... **115**

**Teddy bear,** light yellow mohair, black steel eyes, re-embroidered mouth, nose & claws, fully jointed, excelsior stuffing, probably Ideal, ca. 1919, 17" h. (spotty overall fur loss) ............................................. **374**

**Teddy bear,** beige mohair, glass eyes, embroidered nose, mouth & claws, shaved mohair pads, fully jointed, Schuco, mid-20th c., 18" h. (fur somewhat matted) ..................................... **288**

**Teddy bear,** gold mohair, glass eyes, applied twill nose, embroidered mouth & claws, beige felt pads, fully jointed, excelsior stuffing, Ideal, ca. 1919, 20" h. (minor fur loss) ............................................. **575**

**Teddy bear,** pink mohair, glass eyes, embroidered nose, mouth & claws, felt pads, fully jointed, excelsior stuffing, possibly Stevans Mfg. Co., ca. 1920s, 20" h. (two pads replaced, some fading, spotty fur loss) .......................................... **431**

**Teddy bear,** golden mohair, glass eyes, embroidered nose, mouth & claws, velveteen pads, fully jointed, excelsior & kapok stuffing, Chiltern, ca. 1958, 21" h. (some spotty fur loss) ................................... **173**

**Teddy bear,** yellow mohair, glass eyes, embroidered nose & mouth, football-shaped body, short arms & straight legs, Ideal, ca. 1920, 21 3/4" h. (spotty fur loss) ................................................................ **575**

**Teddy bear,** brown mohair, center seam sewn body, jointed limbs, stitched nose & mouth, large rounded ears, glass eyes, ivory felt paw pads, 23" h. (wear, ears loose) ..................................................... **358**

**Teddy bear,** worn gold mohair, jointed limbs, sewn mouth & nose w/glass eyes, felt paw pads, early 20th c., 23 1/2" h. (damage, repair) ............................................ **220**

**Teddy bear,** gold mohair, embroidered nose, mouth & claws, beige felt pads, fully jointed, excelsior stuffing, Ideal, ca. 1919, 25" h. (minor fur loss, ears need restitching) ................................................... **546**

**Teddy bear,** golden mohair, center-seam sewn body & jointed limbs, stitched nose & mouth on upturned snout, glass eyes, ivory felt paw pads, first half 20th c., 25" h. (worn, one paw pad worn & one replaced) ...................................................... **523**

**Teddy bear,** golden mohair, jointed limbs, glass eyes, stitched nose & mouth, pink felt paw pads, first half 20th c., 26 1/2" h. (some wear & repair) ................................. **550**

**Teddy bear,** light gold mohair, jointed limbs, stitched nose & mouth, glass eyes, ivory felt paw pads, squeak voice box, 27" h. (pads very worn) ...................... **358**

# TELEVISION SETS

*Admiral 10" Bakelite Console*

**Admiral,** 10" Bakelite console, 1948, no
cracks, 40" h. (ILLUS.) .............................. **$325**
**Admiral,** 10" Bakelite console, 40" high, no
cracks............................................................ **325**
**Admiral,** 10" Bakelite table top, no cracks ......... **65**

*Admiral 7" Bakelite*

**Admiral,** 7" Bakelite, 1948 w/"Chinese"
grille (ILLUS.) .............................................. **200**
**Admiral,** console w/radio, TV & phono-
graph, 1948, 11 x 20" ..................................... **75**
**Andrea 1-F-5,** 5" table tope, ca. 1937 ........... **3,500**
**Andrea VK-15,** 15" TV w/FM band, 1948.......... **100**
**Arvin 4080T,** metal, table top, 1948.................. **175**
**Automatic TV-16490,** large screen
wooden set, 1950s ......................................... **50**
**Automatic TV-710,** 7" console, 1947, rare ...... **650**
**CBS Columbia 12CC2,** color-drum set,
experimental, ca. 1951, very rare............. **3,000+**
**CBS Columbia 20C,** wooden B&W 20"
console ........................................................... **50**
**Crosley 307-TA,** 10" wooden table top,
1948 ............................................................... **175**
**Crosley 348-CP,** unusual 10" console
w/swivel tube, 1948....................................... **300**
**DuMont Model 80,** 1937 wooden table top,
two channel.............................................. **3,500+**
**DuMont RA-103 Chatham,** 1948 table top,
unusual shape............................................... **350**
**DuMont RA-103D,** square table top, 1949......... **75**

*DuMont RA-115*

**DuMont RA-115,** large wooden table top,
15" screen, 1951 (ILLUS.)............................... **75**
**DuMont RA-119 Royal Sovereign,** 10"
console, 1952, scarce .................................. **350**

*Emerson Wooden Table Top*

**Emerson,** 10" wooden table top, 1949
(ILLUS.).......................................................... **75**
**FADA 799,** 1948 heavy wooden table top........ **150**
**FADA 925,** 16" wooden table top, 1950 ............. **75**
**FADA TV-30,** 10" wooden table top, 1947 ....... **175**
**General Electric,** 10" Bakelite table top
from 1948, streamlined ................................ **350**
**General Electric,** 10" wooden table top,
1948 ............................................................... **75**
**General Electric,** 21" console, wide
wooden set, 1960s ......................................... **75**

*General Electric 812*

**General Electric 812,** 1950 square table
top, 12" screen (ILLUS.)................................. **50**

**General Electric HM-171,** table top w/5" screen, 3-channel (push buttons below the screen), from 1938 ............................ **3,500+**

**JVC 3240 Video Sphere,** spherical plastic TV w/chain on top & square plastic base, white .................................................................. **250**

*1960s Motorola*

**Motorola,** wide wooden console on spindle legs, 1960s (ILLUS.) ........................................ **75**

**Motorola 21-C2,** mid-1950s 21" wooden console on 4 legs ............................................ **50**

**Motorola 21T8,** large screen 1950s table top .......................................................................... **35**

**Motorola VK-101,** 1948 wooden console, AM/FM radio drops down ............................ **250**

**Motorola VT-73,** cloth covered portable 7" set ............................................................................ **135**

**National TV-10W,** wooden 10" table top, 1949 ...................................................................... **125**

**National TV-1625,** 16" console, 1950s .............. **75**

**National TV-7M,** metal 7" set, 1948, clean ...... **250**

**Panasonic TR-005,** flying saucer-shaped early 1970s, on pole, above small mini table top, unbroken ...................................... **550**

**Panasonic TR-535,** pop-up style small screen set......................................................... **50**

**Philco 48-1000,** 10" table top, w/off-set screen, from 1948 ........................................ **450**

**Philco 48-700,** 1948 heavy wooden table top with 7" screen, very clean ...................... **350**

*Philco Round-top*

**Philco 50T-1403,** round top wooden console, 1950 (ILLUS.) ...................................... **125**

**Philco Predicta console,** Barber-Pole, 1950s, wood, w/rounded back ...................... **550**

**Philco Predicta table top,** metal, ca. 1950s, clean & complete, working condition .................................................................. **350**

**Philco Predicta Tandem,** 2-pc. set, ca. 1960, 21" CRT tube on a long white cord, as found .............................................. **550**

**Pilot TV-37,** 3" fiber-board table top, 1947 cheaply made set, clean cabinet , complete ............................................................. **350**

**RCA 21S,** 1950s wooden console, large screen ................................................................ **75**

**RCA 621-TS,** deco styled 7" wooden table top, 1946 .............................................................. **500**

**RCA 630-TS,** RCA's first 10" post-war wooden table top, 1946 set, clean and complete...................................................... **250**

*RCA 721-TS*

**RCA 721-TS,** 10" round top set, 1947 (ILLUS.)........................................................ **175**

*RCA 8T244*

**RCA 8T244,** 1948 table top w/double doors (ILLUS.)........................................................ **150**

**RCA 9PC41,** buffet style 1949 projection set, pop-up screen ...................................... **125**

**RCA CT-100,** first mass-produced color TV, 15" console, complete ........................... **600**

**RCA TRK-12,** tall mirror-in-lid console, 1939 .................................................................. **4,000+**

**RCA TT5,** 5" table top, five channel TV, 1939 .................................................................. **4,000+**

**Scott 400A,** table top projection set, pop-up screen, 1948 ......................................... **350**

**Silvertone (Sears),** 21" large screen wooden console, 1950s ................................. **50**

**Silvertone (Sears) 125,** 10" table top, 1949....... **50**

**Silvertone (Sears) 9133,** wooden console, pull-out phonograph ...................................... **50**

*Sylvania Halolight*

**Sylvania Halolight,** 1959 console, white light surrounds screen (ILLUS.) .................. **225**

*Tele-Tone 7"*

**Tele-Tone 208,** cloth covered 7" portable, 1948 (ILLUS.) .............................................. **150**

**Zenith,** 16" rectangular screen concole TV, 1954 ................................................ **75**

**Zenith,** "porthole" table top, leatherette covered, round screen ................................. **250**

**Zenith,** "porthole" wooden combination w/phonograph, round screen, 1951 ............. **150**

# TEXTILES

## COVERLETS

**Jacquard,** double woven, one-piece, a central medallion & floral border, medallion spandrels w/label "P. Schum," royal blue, sage green, deep red & cream-colored natural white, 70 x 80" (some overall wear, light stains, puckering, fringe wear) .................................................... **$220**

**Jacquard,** single weave, two-piece, intricate floral medallions, floral & vintage borders w/"Made 1858," unusual colors of olive brown, navy blue, red & natural white, 66 x 80" (wear, fringe loss, minor stains) ...................................................... **220**

**Jacquard,** single weave, one-piece, large urns of flowers in the center, bird & Christian & Heathen borders, corners labeled "Daniel Bury, New Portage, Ohio 1845," navy blue, salmon pink & natural white, 70 x 80" (stains, very worn, small holes) ............................................... **358**

**Jacquard,** single weave, two-piece, rows of rounded floral medallions alternating w/starbursts in the center, eagle & tree borders w/"Union," corners signed "Elisa Thomas - Ashland. Wm. McClellan 1839," tomato red, navy blue & natural white, 70 x 80" (minor wear & stains) ........ **1,595**

**Jacquard,** single weave, two-piece, large leafy clusters w/peacocks feeding young, vintage & floral border band w/corners labeled "Made 1868," navy blue & natural white, 67 x 81" (stains, wear, some missing fringe) .......................... **330**

**Jacquard,** single weave, two-piece, floral medallions, vintage border & corners labeled "Jacob Carver, Ohio 1848," navy blue, teal blue, tomato red & natural white, 72 x 81" (minor stains) ...................... **880**

**Jacquard,** single weave, two-piece, tulip medallions in center, Christian & Heathen & bird borders, corners labeled "A. Hennings, Sugercreek, T. Stark County, Ohio 1845," navy blue, salmon pink, olive yellow & natural white, 72 x 81" (stains, wear, fading, fringe damage) .......... **385**

**Jacquard,** single weave, two-piece, floral medallions, vintage border & corners labeled "W. in Mt. Vernon, Knox County, Ohio by Jacob and Michael Ardner - 1855," navy blue, salmon red, pale gold & natural white, 74 x 82" (wear, some edge wear & fringe loss) .............................. **550**

**Jacquard,** single weave, two-piece, floral medallions & starflowers w/vintage & fruit borders, eagle corners labeled "Jacob Saylor, Salt Creek Township, Picaway, Co. Ohio 1859," navy blue & natural white, 74 x 84" (minor wear)............. **935**

**Jacquard,** single weave, two-piece, the center w/rows of large four-rose medallions, vintage & bird borders, corners labeled "Philip Bysel, Middletown, Holmes Co., Ohio 1842," rust red & natural white, 74 x 84" (stains, wear) ............... **715**

**Jacquard,** double woven, two-piece, floral medallions w/a double vintage border, navy blue & natural white, 76 x 84" (wear, stains, edge damage)........................ **193**

**Jacquard,** single weave, one-piece, flower-head medallions alternating w/smaller starbursts, double row floral borders & four star corners w/"J.B. 1857," magenta red, navy blue, olive tan & natural white, moth damage, stains, 78 x 85" (ILLUS. top next page) ............................................... **385**

**Jacquard,** rows of star medallions & four-leaf clusters alternating w/rows of four-rose clusters & spearpoint leaf clusters, vintage border w/trees & birds, corners labeled "Samuel Slaybaugh, Bucyrus, Crawford County, Ohio - 1849," red, green, blue & natural white, minor damage, 76 x 85" (ILLUS. bottom this column) ...................................................... **550**

*Flowerhead Medallions Coverlet*

*Star Medallions Jacquard Coverlet*

*Stars, Roses & Leaves Coverlet*

*Medallions & Blossomhead Coverlet*

**Jacquard,** double woven, two-piece, floral groups in center, vintage borders, corners labeled "Samuel Neily - Mansfield - Richland - Ohio 1846," salmon pink, navy blue & natural white, 72 x 86" (stains) ........................................................ **385**

**Jacquard,** double woven, two-piece, four-rose clusters within rings of small blossoms alternating w/geometric blossoms, delicate chain link & blossom border, navy blue & natural white, 74 x 86" (edge wear, stains, top edge frayed) ........... **275**

**Jacquard,** double woven, two-piece, large eight-point star medallions w/vine borders alternating w/oval medallions, double fruit basket & house borders, tomato red, natural white & navy blue, light stains, minor wear w/some fringe loss, top edge turned & sewn, 78 x 87" (ILLUS. top next column) ............................. **358**

**Jacquard,** double woven, two-piece, rows of large floral medallions in the center, seaweed & floral borders, corners dated "1848," dark navy blue & natural white, 71 x 88" (stains, wear, some fringe loss) ..... **385**

**Jacquard,** double woven, two-piece, four-rose medallions alternating w/large star-burst medallions & four-leaf blossom sprigs, blossomhead borders, signed in corners "Wove at Newark, Ohio by G. Stich 1846," bluish black & natural white, some wear, small holes, one more stained, 74 x 89 & 74 x 86", pr. (ILLUS. of one) ...................................................... **1,100**

**Jacquard,** single weave, one-piece, a central medallion w/four eagles, floral borders, border labeled "Henry Gabriel, Allentown, F.," navy blue, sage green, bright red & natural white, mid-19th c., 74 x 90" (wear, no fringe) ......... **358**

**Jacquard,** single weave, two-piece, floral, starflower & star medallions w/bird & tree borders w/houses & birds on bottom border, corners labeled "Somerset, Ohio 1846 - L. Hesse, Weaver," navy blue, tomato red, green & natural white, 74 x 90" (minor moth damage) ..................... **770**

**Jacquard,** double woven, one-piece, alternating rows of large vining leafy round & star-form blossoms alternating w/vining tulip-form blossoms, wide border band of large leafy blossoms, navy blue, deep red & natural white, attributed to Enon Valley, Pennsylvania, 19th c., 75 x 90" (minor stains, fringe wear)............................. **220**

**Jacquard,** one-piece, floral medallions & floral border, navy blue & rich red, 88 x 90" ............................................................ **440**

*Rose Clusters & Eagles Coverlet*

**Jacquard,** rows of four-rose medallions, swag border w/two-headed eagles, corners labeled "Peter Lorenz 1844," two shades of red, two shades of blue & natural white, wear, top edge rebound, 78 x 91" (ILLUS. of part) ............ **1,128**

**Jacquard,** double woven, one-piece, square center medallion w/four birds & floral & foliage borders w/lyres & buildings, tomato red & natural white, 19th c., 81 x 91" (minor wear, small holes, light stains)............................................................. **550**

**Overshot,** double woven, two-piece, summer-winter type, Snow Flake & Pine Tree patt., navy blue, deep red & natural white, old corner label "E.E.," 74 1/2 x 82 (overall & edge wear) .................................. **275**

**Overshot,** two-piece, plaid snowflake & pine tree patt., in red, teal blue & navy blue, 64 x 79" (wear, fringe damage) .......... **231**

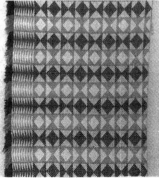

*Bow Tie & Diamond Optic Coverlet*

**Overshot,** two-piece, bow tie & diamond optic design in red, white & two shades of blue, 70 x 90" (ILLUS.) .............................. **413**

**Overshot,** double woven, two-piece, summer- winter type, a geometric design of rows of small crosses & plain blocks alternating w/rows of dotted blocks, navy blue, tomato red & natural white, found in Massachusetts, 19th c., 76 x 90" (wear, some small areas of damage, fringe worn in spots)..................................... **220**

**Overshot,** two-piece, plaid optical design in mauve, navy blue & cream, 66 x 92" (minor wear, age stains)................................. **165**

**Overshot,** Sunrise variant patt., red & white, 19th c., 69 x 93" (minor fiber wear) ............................................................. **173**

**Overshot,** two-piece, optical pattern in navy blue & natural white, 72 x 106" (minor stains) ............................................. **275**

# LINENS & NEEDLEWORK

*Battenberg is the common name for all types of laces formed by shaping a pre-made tape, usually machine made, to a design, and filling in spaces with needlework stitching. A wide variety of pre-made tapes can be used, ranging from plain cloth to elaborate segmented and scalloped tapes.Battenberg sold for a premium about five or more years ago, when it was one of the best known names. As more and more collectors discover tapes of lacework made with more sophisticated techniques, such as needle lace, bobbin lace, and fine quality drawnwork, prices for Battenberg and all tape laces have become much more realistic. Most forms of Battenberg still can be made today.Look at the quality of the tape, the connecting bars and filling stitches for clues that tell quality. Tapes made of poor quality cotton tend to shred along the edges. Look for bars covered with buttonhole stitches, or bars consisting of two or more twisted threads. Single threads looping between tapes tend to shift out of position, causing the lace to loose its shape.Appenzell is one of the names with the most cachet, especially since it was showcased in Scofield and Zalamea's book, 20th Century Linens and Lace (Schiffer, 1997). Because the name is so popular, many dealers apply it to anything remotely similar. Because prices tend to be high, make sure you are getting true quality. It is worth investing in a copy of the book, or at least checking it out at the library. Look for pieces with lots of exquisite embroidery, especially with figures, birds, and animals with lots of embroidery, especially with features worked in satin stitch. A very precisely stitched drawnwork mesh behind embroidered motifs is another characteristic. Swags of very tiny flowers worked in heavily padded satin stitch connect motifs and surround the drawn work areas.Crochet and Tatting are two of the most common types of craft laces of the last century. It is very important to note that crochet and tatting are distinctive types of thread manipulations. They should not be used as generic terms for lace.Take a good look in country craft shops, in gift shops, and in bed and table linen shops for the everyday handmade crochet doilies. Then, look in the antique and flea markets for something else. It doesn't take long to recognize the difference between handmade, which is still made by the boat-*

load, and the special vintage doilies with more difficult craftsmanship and more exotic designs.Quality
of the thread is another feature to look for. Most of
the cheap pieces that come from China, the Philip-
pines, and other foreign craft suppliers is made with
loosely spun, short-staple thread that has little resil-
ience, frays more readily, and is designed to be
used, enjoyed, and thrown away. European and
American pieces made from the last of the nineteenth into the twentieth century most often were
made of good quality cotton thread with high twist
and long staples, and stronger thread that produces
a crisp design.Damask is a technique where
threads carried across the surface of the woven
cloth create a silky, optical illusion of a design
against the plain background weave. The pattern is
reversible. The silk design appears against a matte
background on one side, on the other, the background is silky and the pattern matte. Because the
designs are so subtle, visible only in the shifting
candlelight, and because the linens require careful
washing and ironing, they often go for bargain
prices today.Fine linen or cotton fabric linens with
spectacular embroidery, lace insertions, cut work
patterns, and fine lace edgings are among the most
popular vintage linens. When choosing vintage table
linens with many different types of lace, embroidery,
drawnwork, and cutwork, make a point of looking
carefully at each element. Check to see if the connecting bars in the cutwork are breaking loose.
These are easy but tedious to repair. Look at the
stitching along the edge of cutwork. Fraying edges
on cutwork is difficult and expensive to repair, and
often means the tablecloth is nearing the end of its
useful days.Needle lace was made across Europe
for centuries and in China through the late nineteenth and into the early twentieth century. It travels
under many different names, especially Point de
Venice, or Venice lace. European needle lace with
gracefully shaped motifs, lots of beautifully worked
raised edges on the designs, lots of delicate shading or decorative accents in the dense clothlike
areas of motifs greatly add to the value. Chinese
needle lace, made for European trading companies
in the late nineteenth and early twentieth century,
usually does not sell for as much of a premium as
European work because the dense areas (flower
petals, leaves, etc.) rarely show any shading or
detailing and the complex background bars often
are twisting and curling. Needle lace with figures,
animals and birds worked into the background usually command a higher price.

**Bed sheets,** plain linen except for monogram "MH", very good condition,
66 x 80", pair .................................. **$61**
**Bedspread,** Normandy work, single bed
size, patchwork w/an area across the top
to serve as a sham, symmetrical design
of saucer-sized rounds of embroidered
white muslin, lace, & a wide mix of good
quality machine lace, entire bedspread
is piecework, edged w/machine lace in
unusual design, good condition,
78 x 110" (ILLUS. to next column) .............. **398**
**Bedspread,** Normandy work w/scattering
of embroidered & lace piecework across
one third of the net area in the center of
bedspread, deep ruffles of net down the
sides, 72 x 105" ........................................ **125**

*Normandy Work Bedspread*

**Bedspreads,** Normandy work, single bed
size, patchwork made of assorted hand
machine-made lace & embroidered fine
handkerchief-weight linen are all assembled by hand stitching, labeled "Made in
France", 16" drop ruffle edge on each
side, 71" sq., pair .................................. **765**
**Doily,** Battenberg w/floral design, 28" d. ........... **35**
**Doily,** crochet w/pineapple design, 35" d. ......... **25**
**Doily,** drawnwork of fine white cotton, good
design of tiny pinwheels closely worked
over the drawn threads, in 4" deep band
around edge, w/corner design in center
of cloth, 29" sq. ............................................ **30**
**Doily,** needle lace, ecru thread, Chinese
pinwheel design w/plain clothwork petals
alternating w/openwork stitching, 4" d. ............. **3**
**Doily,** needle lace, ecru thread, w/large
central rose design, 6" d. .............................. **10**

*Needle Lace Doily*

**Doily,** needle lace w/complex design of
scrollwork & flowers, some decorative
stitching in the clothwork, raised edges
add dimension, 6" d. (ILLUS.) .................. **25-30**
**Doily,** Princess tape lace, formed by hand
stitching loops & florets of scalloped &
segmented tapes to a machine-made
net, embellished w/embroidery,
4 1/2 x 12" ....................................................... **6**
**Doily,** tatted w/round motifs about 3" d.
assembled into a diamond shape .................. **14**
**Dresser scarf,** drawnwork edging, technique covers the exposed threads with a
dense pattern, making the drawnwork
both beautiful & reasonably durable,
good quality, small holes in the cloth
detract from the value, 24 x 38" .............. **25-45**
**Dresser scarf,** drawnwork w/an unusual
geometric design, 22 x 42" ..................... **75-85**
**Linen square,** w/deep swags of lace on
each corner, center embroidered w/Ital-
ian-style flowers & scrollwork, stitching
padded to add dimension, 30" sq. .................. **62**

*Needlework Napkins*

**Napkins,** embroidered, cutwork, drawnwork & lace embellished, set of 4
(ILLUS. of part)........................................ **15-25**
**Needlework family register,** chart of
names & dates above pious verses, a
willow tree & urn, hearts, flowers, trees,
geometric devices, surrounded by a
scalloped border containing flower buds
& leaves, a verse & dates added at a
later time, "Executed by Clarissa W.
Miller, aged 12 yrs," Ludlow, Massachusetts, early 19th c., 16 x 16 1/2" (minor
toning & staining) ..................................... **1,380**
**Piecework,** lace formed of cut cloth motifs
appliqued onto a net, some embroidery,
flower design w/scrollwork, 14 x 40" ............. **41**
**Pillow cover,** w/button back, trimmed w/1"
of drawnwork, good condition, 10" sq.
(minor foxing) ................................................ **10**
**Pillowcases,** cotton, w/3" edging in white
flowers w/blue accents, c. 1940s, good
condition, pr. (some minor staining) .............. **15**
**Placemats,** needle lace w/each showing a
different European castle scene worked
in decorative needle lace stitches, set of
12 .................................................................. **945**

*Normandy Work Placemats*

**Placemats,** Normandy work, consisting of
mostly handmade laces, good quality
piecework, 12 x 17", set of 6 (ILLUS. of
part).............................................................. **250**
**Runner,** Normandy work, patchwork of
handmade Vaienciennes bobbin lace &
other mostly handmade laces, central
motif is French embroidered whitework
w/birds & flowers, oval, 18 x 24" .................. **145**
**Show towel,** homespun linen w/cross-
stitch embroidery of stylized flowers &
inscribed "Marh B. Aby my name and
with my needle I sew the same - the
grass is green the flowers red, and this is
my name when I am dead 1839," in red,
blue, olive green & beige, lace trim at
bottom edge, 19 x 53" plus fringe (minor
wear) ........................................................... **330**
**Table runner,** machine imitation of filet
lace w/exceptional good design of roses
& irises worked into grid-like mesh, good
condition, 13 1/2 x 57"................................... **65**

**Table runner,** needle lace w/fanciful ladies
on swings in elaborate 18th c. dress,
several areas of elaborate decorative fill-
ing stitches, 26 1/2 x 58" ............................. **600**
**Tablecloth,** Appenzell w/design of cher-
ubs, 18th c. figures, swags of tiny flowers, designs highlighted w/lots of flat
satin stitch, padded satin stitch flower
swags add dimension, mint condition,
68 x 100" .................................................. **2,800**

*Battenberg Tablecloth*

**Tablecloth,** Battenberg w/bold design leaf
fronds w/grapelike clusters of buttonhole
stitch covered rings, central motif of tape
lace scrollwork scallops, 52" d., decent
condition, some careful mending
(ILLUS.)......................................................... **50**
**Tablecloth,** Battenberg w/embroidery &
cutwork center, edged w/plate-sized
round motifs of 12" of Battenberg tape
lace, 64" d. (needs mending) ......................... **45**
**Tablecloth,** crochet, many produced by
homemakers in the U.S. using patterns
typical of Eastern European designs,
early to mid-20th c. ................................. **50-150**
**Tablecloth,** crochet w/European-style
square tile-like motifs & scallop border,
creamy white, good condition, 88 x 96"........ **140**
**Tablecloth,** crochet w/traditional round
motifs, 58 x 78"......................................... **40-50**
**Tablecloth,** damask, banquet size, pure
Flemish linen w/Fleur-de-Lis pattern on
a spotted background, mid-19th c.,
includes 18 napkins, cloth 62 x 108",
napkins 33 x 40" (some repair & fraying) ..... **550**
**Tablecloth,** damask, cotton/rayon combination, pale yellow w/floral design, in box
labeled "Made in Japan", includes 12
napkins, ca. 1950s, cloth 64 x 104", nap-
kins 18" sq...................................................... **74**
**Tablecloth,** damask, pure Irish linen of
double damask w/floral design, includes
8 napkins, mid 20th c., cloth 62 x 78",
napkins 22" sq............................................. **195**

*Hardanger Tablecloth*

**Tablecloth,** Hardanger, Norwegian-style
embroidery w/square cutwork holes,

w/decorative filling stitches in some of the square-cut holes, good quality & condition, 48" sq., one well-mended area (ILLUS. of part)............................................ **235**

**Tablecloth,** homespun linen, overall small checkered plaid design in red, white & blue, hand-sewn center seam, hems w/one end pieced out, 44 x 80" .................... **275**

**Tablecloth,** mixed laces & embroidery, probably Chinese, little inserts of needle lace w/little flowers worked w/plain clothwork & openwork petals, relatively simple scrolling design of cutwork holes, minimal embroidery, 70 x 80"...................... **125**

*Needle Lace Tablecloth*

**Tablecloth,** needle lace, probably European, w/vague Oriental design of flower bowls, chrysanthemums, other large flowers, variety of decorative stitches, texture & quality of the stitching & thread suggest it was made in Zele, the Netherlands, deep beige colors, includes 12 matching napkins, mint condition, 68 x 108" (ILLUS. of part)............................ **950**

**Tablecloth,** Quaker Lace, machine lace, turn-of-the-century, w/floral center medallion, deep floral & swag border, 70 x 100" ........................................................ **96**

**Tablecloth or bedspread,** crochet w/traditional round motifs of flowers in the center & star like design surrounding, interesting floral scallop motifs filling the spaces between the rounds, 82 x 87" .......... **130**

**Tea towels,** Appenzell, w/18th c. dancing figures, pr. (few tiny holes in the linen)........... **85**

**Top sheet & pair of pillow cases,** cotton muslin w/machine embroidered flowers, ca. 1940s, 81 x 99" .......................... **35**

# NEEDLEWORK PICTURES

*Adam & Eve in Landscape Scene*

**Adam & Eve in landscape,** stitched overall w/a detailed landscape, in a central valley Adam & Eve stand flanking the apple tree, animals & two other fruiting trees two each side of them & a standing man on the left, two steep hills on each edge, each topped by trees & buildings, blue sky w/clouds, flowering sawtooth & diamond wide border band, inscrbied "Ann Maria Tius (?) her work age 1(?) January the 3, 1823," minor staining, losses, fading, framed, 15 x 20" (ILLUS.).................. **7,475**

*Emeline Orphon of the Castle Picture*

**Emeline Orphon of the Castle,** needlework & water-color, an oval landscape scene with two women & a gentleman near a large tree, a castle in the background, worked in shades of brown, tan, green & black, painted faces, hands & sky, black reverse-painted mat w/oval opening & gilt trim w/title across the bottom, early 19th c., framed, 25 x 32 1/2" (ILLUS.)..................................................... **4,070**

**Family register,** three alphabet panels above a family record flanked by flowering vines w/a meandering floral border, silk thread on linen, signed "wrought by Sarah Howe undere the care of L.B....aged 13 years Marlboro Aug 3, 1819," Massachusetts, 15 1/2 x 16" (fading, toning, silk thread loss in border) ....... **1,495**

**Flowers,** silk embroidery on linen, a bouquet of wild flowers below a verse framed by a meandering floral vine, the whole surrounded by a border of flowers & vines, inscribed "Mary Joy 1798 Eliza Jones," worked in gold, green, pink, white & brown thread, unframed, American, 18 1/2 x 23" (some staining & repairs) ......................................................... **632**

**Jesus & Mary Magdalene,** a scene of Jesus as a gardener meeting Mary Magdalene in the garden following the Resurrection, worked in a multi-layered format, solidly stitched in chenille & silk threads w/hand-painted silk features, cut & pasted to a painted silk sky, the entire oval picture pasted to a linen backing & mounted on a stretcher frame, in an eglomisé mat, framed, England, 19th c., 16 x 18 3/4" (toning, fading, repaint to the mat) ...................................................... **575**

**Landscape needlework on silk,** "Edgar & Matilda," a romantic couple in the foreground w/flowing banners & a flag on the left, a landscape w/trees on the right, water-color & sequin highlights, signed on the black églomisé mat "Sally Aldrich," America, early 19th c.,16" d. (minor fading & mat paint losses)................ **978**

*Fine Silk Memorial Picture*

**Memorial picture,** silk on silk, a scene w/ two large arched-over willow trees above leaf-trimmed urns w/lengthy sewn inscriptions on the right side, a young girl standing to their left & facing them, another taller tree above a third inscribed urn on the far left, New England, early 19th c., tacked down, foxing, minor fading, 17 5/8 x 21" (ILLUS.) .... **5,175**

**Needlework embroidery on silk,** depicting a mother & child seated in a tree-lined landscape, worked in silk, water-color on silk fabric in an oval format w/an églomisé mat, America, early 19th c., 9x10 1/2" including mat.............................. **920**

**Needlework embroidery on silk,** memorial to George Washington, depicted beneath a large willow tree, a young girl holding a wreath resting on a monument w/a plaque initialed "GW," silk & water-color on silk fabric, worked in an oval format, America, early 19th c., 16 1/4 x 18 1/4" (minor losses, staining) ... **1,955**

**Rebecca at the Well,** a landscape scene w/figures in Biblical dress, a man seated under a large leafy tree on the left of the well, a lady standing & holding a ewer of water to the right, buildings in the distance, solidly stitched crewel yarn & chenille threads & water-color on a silk ground, black eglomise framed at the center bottom in gold "Ann Bentley," probably England, early 19th c., framed, 14 x 14" (tear in the sky, minor needlework losses, paint loss to mat) ..................... **805**

**Silk memorial picture,** a large arching willow tree over a large classical monument w/a seated woman mourning beside it, landscape w/houses in the background, within a black églomisé mat w/gilt round opening & small gilt florets in each corner, signed across the bottom of the mat "By Elizabeth Shute 11 years old," ink highlights in scene, molded giltwood frame, early 19th c., 15 x 15 1/4" (minor scattered staining)..................................... **1,150**

# QUILTS

**Amish Basket patt.,** solid blues/black baskets, ca. 1935, 74 x 76"........................ **1,250**

**Amish Sunshine & Shadow patt.,** wide purple border, ca. 1940, 74 x 78".............. **1,250**

**Amish Turkey Tracks patt.,** solid colors, wide border, ca. 1930, full size ................... **850**

**Appliqued Album quilt,** composed of various printed & solid green, red, yellow, blue & orange fabrics in a pattern of sixteen squares depicting stars, baskets of flowers, floral sprays & pictorial scenes, the whole surrounded by a wide flower vine border, the white cotton field finely quilted in diamond, outline & starburst designs, several squares signed & dated, 1853, 76" sq. .................................. **5,462**

**Appliqued Album quilt,** composed of thirty medallions in rows, each a different design w/appliqued chintz & calico, solid colors & embroidery, well-quilted white fishscale background, old corner label reads "Made by Mrs. Betsey M. Moore, Presented to her daughter Varilla A. Bouldon - to her daughter Fanny G. Hurst to her daughter Kate Rankin Hurst (then in different hand) to Rankin Hurst," also a label from the "West Virginia Heritage Quilt Search Inc.," homespun backing, 74 x 87" (wear, stains, some faded fabrics, machine-sewn binding)................... **715**

*Appliqued Baltimore Album Quilt*

**Appliqued Baltimore Album patt.,** composed of various printed & solid green, red, blue, pink & orange fabrics in a design of sixteen squares each within a floral vine border, the squares containing a variety of wreath, urn & bouquet designs, the white cotton ground highlighted w/diamond & outline quilting, some staining & fabric loss, mid-19th c., 92" sq.(ILLUS.)........................................... **5,750**

**Appliqued Floral Medallion patt.,** four large pinwheel-style floral medallions w/leafy stems centered by a large four-petal blossom & surrounded by four-leaf crosses & a small pot of flowers at the center of each border, in teal blue, red & burnt orange on white, 19th c., minor stains, 86 x 90" (ILLUS. top next page)........ **688**

**Appliqued Nasturtium patt.,** composed of pieces in red & green on a white ground,

scalloped border, early 20th c., 76 x 90"
(staining) ....................................................... **173**

*Appliqued Floral Medallion Quilt*

*Fine Floral and Swag Quilt*

**Appliqued & pieced Floral and Swag patt.,** composed of printed & solid blue, maroon, beige, white & green fabrics arranged in a concentric design of zig-zags around stars & swags, vines & flowers centering a wreath, dated 1896, some discoloration, 70 x 78" (ILLUS.).......... **805**

**Appliqued Poinsettia & Christmas Cactus patt.,** repeating design of the floral motifs in red & green on a white quilted ground, dated "March 14, 1934," 62 x 68 1/2" (very minor fiber wear) ............. **230**

*Rose of Sharon Appliqued Quilt*

**Appliqued Rose of Sharon patt.,** four large stylized floral medallions in pink calico, solid red & teal green calico, meandering floral border, well-quilted w/trapunto wreaths in center, wear, edges frayed, some greens faded, small stains, 67 1/2 x 82 1/2" (ILLUS.) .................. **770**

**Basket patt.,** indigo, 1/4" stitching, ca. 1920s ...................................................... **1,200**

**Basket patt.,** multicolored baskets, ca. 1930, 74 x 76" ............................................ **350**

**Basket patt.,** composed of twelve blocks w/finely pieced footed bowl-form baskets overflowing w/a large bouquet of blossoms & leafy sprigs, spaced on a finely quilted white ground w/colored swag borders, several shades of pink & green w/maroon, grey & other colors, 78 x 94" (minor stains) ...................................... **825**

**Coxcomb patt.,** red & white, ca. 1920s ........... **650**

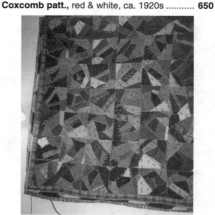

*Crazy Quilt*

**Crazy quilt,** lots of embroidery, ca. 1890 (ILLUS.)..................................................... **650**

**Crazy quilt,** velvets & silks, embroidered animals, ca. 1890, full size .......................... **850**

**Crib quilt,** Amish Stars & Snowballs patt., blues & blacks, ca. 1930, 34 x 58" .............. **450**

**Crib quilt,** embroidered animals, ca. 1940, 34 x 56" ..................................................... **125**

**Crib quilt,** Young Man's Fancy patt., indigo red, ca. 1910 ............................................... **450**

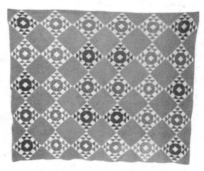

*Crown of Thorns Pattern Quilt*

**Crown of Thorns patt.,** composed of blocks of blue & black calico on white alternating w/blocks of olive green calico, overall wear, some repair & stains, 19th c., 74 x 88" (ILLUS.) ............................. **220**

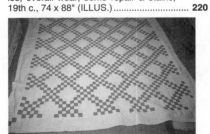

*Double Irish Chain Quilt*

**Double Irish Chain patt.,** turkey red, ca. 1930, full size (ILLUS.) ................................. **450**
**Double Wedding Ring patt.,** ca. 1930, full size ................................................................. **350**

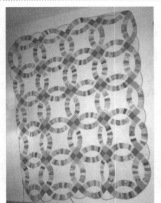

*Double Wedding Ring Quilt*

**Double Wedding Ring patt.,** ca. 1940, full size (ILLUS.) ............................................. **350**
**Dresden Plate patt.,** multicolored plates, ca. 1940, 74 x 76" ........................... **350**

*Drunkard's Path Quilt*

**Drunkard's Path patt.,** indigo, full size (ILLUS.) ...................................................... **700**

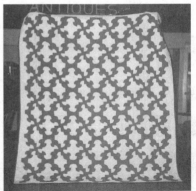

*Drunkard's Path Quilt*

**Drunkard's Path patt.,** red & white, ca. 1940s (ILLUS.) ............................................ **450**
**Early Folk Art patt.,** feed sack, appliqued flowers, full size ........................................... **375**

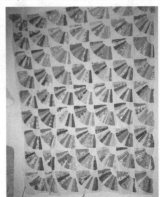

*Fan Quilt*

**Fan patt.,** ca. 1940, full size (ILLUS.)............... **350**
**Fan patt.,** feather stitching, ca. 1920s ............. **550**
**Fan patt.,** multicolored, ca. 1940, full size........ **375**

*Fence 'Round a Field Pattern Quilt*

**Fence 'Round a Field patt.,** brown center w/green & goldenrod criss-cross border, overall large diamond quilting, Holmes County, Ohio, minor stains, overall wear, 81 x 82" (ILLUS.).......................................... **303**

**Flower Basket patt.,** composed of red & green fabric baskets on a small figured ground, flowering vine border, patterned linen backing, mid-late 19th c., 81 1/2 x 83" (faded, staining) ....................... **403**

**Flower Garden patt.,** multicolored, chintz, 1890, rare.............................................. **750**

*Flower Garden Quilt*

**Flower Garden patt.,** multicolored gardens, ca. 1930s (ILLUS.) ........................ **375**

**Goose in the Pond patt.,** indigo blues, ca. 1920s, full size ............................................. **675**

**Harvest Sun patt.,** turkey red sun, ca. 1920s, full size ............................................. **450**

**House patt.,** composed of rows of stylized houses in several shades of blue print frabic on a white ground, 66 x 88" (overall wear & stains)......................................... **908**

**Irish Chain patt.,** composed of green calico & solid red patches w/white ground, some machine work, 63 x 79 1/2" (stains, minor overall wear) ......................... **440**

**Irish Chain patt.,** composed of red & green calico blocks on white, pink calico binding, 80" sq. (minor wear & stains).......... **468**

**Irish Chain patt.,** indigo blues, ca. 1920, full size ................................................. **650**

**Irish Chain patt.,** pastel pink, ca. 1940, full size............................................................. **350**

**Irish Chain patt.,** the design worked in red on white w/red, white, purple & green embroidery in each block, Stamford, New York, dated 1885, toning, very minor staining, 79 x 96" (ILLUS. top next column) .................................................... **1,610**

**LeMoyne Star patt.,** composed of various calico patches on a red & green ground, late 19th c., 66 1/2 x 80" (very minor staining)...................................................... **374**

*Unusual Irish Chain Pattern Quilt*

*Log Cabin Barn Raising Quilt*

**Log Cabin Barn Raising patt.,** wools, ca. 1890s (ILLUS.) ............................................. **750**

**Log Cabin Chevron patt.,** full size ................. **575**

*Log Cabin Pineapple Quilt*

**Log Cabin Pineapple patt.,** silks, ca.
1880s (ILLUS.) .............................................. **875**

**Log Cabin Straight Furrows patt.,** small
strips, ca. 1900s .......................................... **675**

**Log Cabin Sunshine & Shadow patt.,**
multicolored, ca. 1920s ................................ **550**

**Log Cabin ZigZag patt.,** 1/4" strips, ca.
1890s ........................................................... **575**

*Pieced Lone Star Quilt*

**Lone Star patt.,** composed of inner & outer
stars in red, medium blue & goldenrod
fabrics on white, finely quilted ground,
small black stains & age stains,
machine-sewn binding, 80 x 82"
(ILLUS.) ........................................................ **385**

**Mennonite Bars patt.,** wools, ca. 1880 ........ **1,200**

**Mennonite Basket patt.,** dark colors, ca.
1890 ............................................................. **750**

**Mennonite Crib quilt,** cotton, ca. 1900 .......... **550**

*Ornate Mosaic Diamond Quilt*

**Mosaic Diamond patt.,** composed of red,
blue, beige & pink chintz diamonds &
octagons arranged in a mosaic design,
the field highlighted w/octagonal, running diamond & chevron quilting, the
whole surrounded by a broad band of
floral chintz, some staining, 19th c.,
58 x 62" (ILLUS.) ........................................ **1,265**

**Nine Patch Checkerboard patt.,** composed of blocks in black, red, faded wine
red stripe & light blue alternating

w/khaki, Indiana Amish, 66 x 82" (worn,
fragile, some fabrics faded & frayed) .......... **385**

**Pine Tree patt.,** turkey reds, triple
border, ca. 1920 .......................................... **650**

*Pine Tree Pattern Quilt*

**Pine Tree patt.,** composed of blocks of tree
designs alternating w/solid blocks, in
shades of blue, green, black, brown, lavender, etc., machine-sewn binding,
made by Mrs. Mose Miller, Middlefield,
Ohio, very worn & faded, small tears 72"
sq. (ILLUS.) ................................................. **303**

**Pineapple patt.,** red & white, ca. 1920s .......... **650**

*Sailboats Quilt*

**Sailboats patt.,** ca. 1940, 74 x 76"
(ILLUS.) ....................................................... **575**

*Sampler Quilt*

Sampler quilt, red, blues & burgundies, ca.
1880s, 66 x 72" (ILLUS.) ........................... **1,750**

*Schoolhouse Quilt*

Schoolhouse patt., red & white, ca. 1900
(ILLUS.) .................................................... **1,500**
Star of Bethlehem patt., composed of var-
ious diamond-shaped patches w/large
potted flowering plants between each of
the eight star points, various plain &
printed cottons on a white ground, 19th
c., 85 x 88" (staining, fading, scattered
fiber wear) ................................................... **748**

*8-Pointed Star of Bethlehem Quilt*

Star patt., 8-pointed star of Bethlehem, ca.
1930 (ILLUS.) ............................................... **350**
Streak of Lightning patt., red & white, ca.
1930s .......................................................... **550**
Theme Quilt, butterflies, multicolored, ca.
1940s .......................................................... **575**
Theme Quilt, flags, ca. 1890s, full size ............ **650**
Theme Quilt, palm trees, ca. 1940s, full
size............................................................... **650**
Theme Quilt, patriotic, eagles & stars, ca.
1920s .......................................................... **650**
Theme Quilt, rodeo roundup, ca. 1940s,
full size ......................................................... **450**
Theme Quilt, schoolhouse, chintz, ca.
1880s, full size ......................................... **1,200**

Trip Around the World patt.,
multicolored, ca. 1940s, full size ................. **550**
Tulip patt., composed of red, green &
orange patches on a white cotton
ground, a LeMoyne Star border,
machine-pieced & hand-quilted, late
19th c., 80" sq. (minor staining)................... **489**
Yo Yo quilt, multicolored, ca. 1920s ............... **450**
Yo Yo quilt, multicolored, small pieces,
gated, full size ............................................. **650**
Young Man's Fancy patt., red & white, ca.
1920s .......................................................... **650**

# SAMPLERS

*Sampler with Alphabets & Houses*

Alphabets, family register & scene
w/house, on homespun linen, the top
third w/rows of alphabets & a small two-
story house on the right above several
rows of names & dates of family members above the inscription "Wrought by
Lucy Hildreth Bath Sept 4th AD 1810,"
the lower third w/a scene of a large
three-story Federal house on the left
next to a large flower shrub & a girl
w/flowers below a flock of flying birds
above on the right, surrounded by a
cross-stitch narrow border, framed, toning, fading, minor stains,
12 1/4 x 15 3/4" (ILLUS.)........................... **1,610**
Alphabets & family tree, silk on home-
spun linen, rows of alphabet on the
upper half, the lower half stitched in
large letters "Jane Dalloz. Francces Dalloz dide (died) on the 19 of November
aged 41, 1831 - John Strickling dide on
the 26 September, aageed 20, 1835,"
worked in shades of blue, brown, green,
tan & beige, framed, 8 3/4 x 11 3/4"
(stains) ........................................................ **440**
Alphabets, numerals & pious verses,
rows of letters & numbers above a
grouping of three pious verses above the
signature "Mary Stillman Sampler
Wrought In the year 1811 in her 14th

year," all within a vining floral border, on linsey woolsey, Massachusetts or New Hampshire, framed, 12 1/4 x 15 1/2" (fading, minor fiber wear) .......................... **2,185**

**Alphabets, numerals & scattered designs,** silk on a linen ground, various rows of large & small letters & numerals above a central inscription "Mary H Morrison, Nine Partners B. School, mo 1827," the lower half w/scattered designs of stylized blossoms, urns & baskets of flowers above a bottom wreath enclosing "MHM 1827," all within a meandering vine border, worked in shades of blue, green & black in a variety of stitches, inscribed on the back "A. Bulkley, Granville, NY, care of J. Moulton," unframed, 16 x 17" ........................... **3,162**

**Alphabets & pious verse,** an upper panel of alphabets & a pious verse above a lower panel of figural, foliate & animal designs, Greek key border, signed "Elizabeth Downess Work Aged 12 1824," on linen, framed, 12 3/4" sq. (minor repairs, toning, minor fiber wear) ............................ **690**

**Alphabets & pious verse,** rows of various styled alphabets below a top band w/two large tulip-like flowers flanking a dish of flowers, a lower wide band w/inscription "Mary Tufts her sampler made in the tenth year of her age 1794" followed by a pious verse, a bottom band w/large diamond devices flanking a central square w/a flowering tree & small birds, late 18th c., 15 3/4 x 22 1/4" (toning, fading, minor losses) ..................................... **1,380**

**Alphabets, pious verse & scenes,** wool on linen ground, rows of alphabets above a lengthy pious verse all across the center above vignettes including a young boy & girl flanked on one side by a floral sprig, a bird & a deer & on the other by a hunt scene, all within a wide zigzag, vining florals & Greek key borders, worked in shades of green, pink, blue & brown, signed "Sarah P. Crane in the 15th year of her age, at Morrisplain, Morris County, New Jersey, A.D. 1849. Novem.," unframed, 24 1/2 x 29" ............. **4,025**

**Alphabets, pious verse & varied designs,** the upper panel of alphabets & a pious verse above a lower panel of various architectural, bird, fruit & foliate designs, geometric floral border, signed "Juliaett Ballad Sampler Carmel Aged 11 years 1833," framed, 18" sq. (toning, scattered staining, minor fading) .............. **1,840**

**Alphabets & pious verse w/floral swags,** rows of letters above a short pious verse w/a large rose & ribbon swag above a pair of roses & the inscription "Paulina F. Freeman Aged 9 Years August 31, 1820," stylized vining floral border around top & sides, framed, 16 5/8 x 17 1/8" (toning, fading, minor scattered staining) .................................... **1,495**

**Alphabets & pious verses w/landscape,** the upper alphabet rows between undulating lines & floral blossoms over a pious verse above a band w/flower-filled

urns w/birds & small stags over a longer pious verse over a landscape band featuring a Garden of Eden scene w/Adam & Eve under the tree w/a snake, large birds perched on ground & other trees, small figures, birds & urns at the bottom flanked by inscription "Mary MacLeroy Her - Work aged 10 year 1741," probably Philadelphia, floral border, framed, 9 5/8 x 17 3/8" (toning, minor fading & staining).................................................. **8,050**

*Sampler with Alphabets & Scene*

**Alphabets, various objects & landscape,** the upper third in rows of alphabets above the inscription & bands of various objects including baskets of fruit, flowers, birds & trees, the lower band w/a detailed landscape including a two-story house beside a picket fence w/smaller buildings & urns of flowers on either side, a fruiting tree w/two birds in the center, zig-zag flowering vine border, inscribed "Elizabeth Saunders, Aged 10," toning, scattered staining, fading, framed, 15 1/4 x 17 1/2" (ILLUS.).............. **1,725**

*Roses & Arbor Family Tree Sampler*

**Florals, family register & monuments,** silk on homespun linen, a wide border across the top & upper sides of large rose blossoms & leaves w/blue bows above two leafy trees flanking a column-bordered arbor enclosing three wreaths w/genealogical information, willow trees, monuments & an empty reserve, signed & dated "Esther P. Payne 1828," Miss Cornwall's School, Glastonbury, Connecticut, framed, 18 x 24" (ILLUS.) ........ **19,550**

**Flowers, fruits & landscape w/pious verse,** a pair of potted flowers flanking rose clusters centered by the signature "Mary Jowett Work" above baskets of fruit flanking a central pious verse over a scene of Adam & Eve above a landscape centered by a large two-story brick house flanked by fir trees w/sheep & other animals across the front, all within a narrow vining border, probably Pennsylvania, ca. 1830s, beveled veneered frame, 24 x 25" (toning, minor losses, scattered staining)......................... **2,645**

**Inscription, pious verse & various designs,** silk on homespun linen, a central rectangular panel w/a long pious verse below various designs including a pair of birds flanking a vase of flowers & a pair of butterflies, a lower oblong reserve enclosing the inscription "Mary Ann Jones finished this Sampler in the ninth year of her age 1826," flanked by flowering sprigs & small stylized trees, all within a meandering floral border, worked in shades of green, brown, gold, yellow & white, framed, 15 x 18 3/8" (damage in lower left, small holes, minor stains)........................................................ **990**

**Inscription & various designs,** silk on homespun linen, a long narrow strip embroidered overall w/vertical bands of paired stylized designs of flowers, hearts, birds, crowns, butterflies, etc., inscribed across the top "Ann Wood's work 1840," in shades of yellow, blue, green, gold, white, brown & purple, old molded giltwood frame, 10 3/4 x 15" (minor stains) ........................................... **1,760**

*Sampler with Large Landscape Scene*

**Pious verse & large landscape w/house,** silk on homespun linen, a pious verse & inscription across the top above a large rectangular reserve showing a large two-story Georgian brick house flanked by willow trees & a Neoclassical maiden weeping over a monument, the whole bordered by a zig-zag floral vine, inscribed "Julian Wolff her work finished in the eleventh year of her age in the year of our Lord Eighteen hundred..15," probably Maryland, ca. 1814, framed, 17 x 17 1/2" (ILLUS.)............................... **5,750**

**Pious verse over landscape & inscription,** a long pious verse at the top flanked by tall flowering trees in urns over a vining floral band above a long landscape w/a willow tree & sheep to the left & a cottage & tree to the right above a delicate floral vine band above birds, crowns & branches over the inscription flanked by baskets of flowers, all within a thin floral border, inscribed "Elizabeth Holden, Aged 11 years 1824," worked in silk threads in shades of green, gold, brown, blue, yellow, white & black on a homespun linen ground, framed (stains)...... **880**

*Very Fine Silk on Linen Sampler*

**Pious verse w/wide floral border & house,** silk on homespun linen, the top & upper sides w/a wide flowering leafy vine border w/a central basket of flowers above a rectangular reserve enclosing a pious verse, at the bottom center a large scene of a yellow house w/green windows flanked by pine trees, inscribed across the bottom "Wrought by Diana Paine Stockbridge 1826 Age 9," worked in a variety of greens, blue, yellow, tan & brown silk stitches including cross, tent, satin, button hole, outline, couching & slanting Gobelin, Mary Cooper, instructress, framed, 16 1/4 x 17 1/4" (ILLUS.).. **25,300**

# TAPESTRIES

**Aubusson,** woven in muted tones of green & brown w/a multicolored flower-filled border, 19th c., 40 x 100" ........................ **3,335**

**Aubusson panel,** a long rectangular scene of 18th century maiden & youth in a landscape w/ruins, she wearing a pink dress crouched beside & tickling the sleeping youthful harvester, woven signature in the lower right "Croc Pere Fils & Jorrand, Aubusson," France, late 19th c., 53 x 91 1/4" ...................................... **4,025**

**Aubusson panel,** depicting a group of people in period costume fishing in the foreground w/ships in the distance, France, 18th c., 96 x 99" ...................................... **3,738**

**Brussels,** historical-type, depicting a story of Alexander the Great & showing a battle w/fallen soldiers & others on horseback, the general on his white rearing steed in the center, within a sumptuous fruiting & flowering border, after designs by Charles Le Brun, ca. 1660, 87 x 121"...................................... **28,750**

**Brussels Verdure,** large square landscape scene depicting a heavily wooded forest w/birds in the foreground trees & a village in the left distance, leafy scroll border, signed "E. Pannemaker," Flanders, late 17th c., 105 x 117".......................... **16,100**

**Continental,** mythological scene w/a lush landscape depicting Diana & her attendants after the hunt, possibly Brussels, late 17th - early 18th c., 74 x 88" (restorations) ..................................................... **7,475**

**Flemish Armorial,** incorporating in the center a large arms of Spain during their reign of Portugal, encircling the Order of the Garter, inscribed "Fortitudo" in top center & w/four armorial shields in the corners joined by trelliswork, first half 17th c., 87 x 89" ..................................... **37,375**

*Pair of Flemish Figural Tapestries*

**Flemish figural,** long narrow panels each woven w/standing female figures allegorical of Masuedeto & Zelotypa, putti below among leaves or scrolls, columnar borders, late 16th c., the two 113 x 151", pr. (ILLUS.)................................................. **8,625**

**Flemish Verdure,** a landscape w/a farmhouse in the middle distance, surrounded by lightly wooded landscape, within a flowering border centered above & below w/flower-filled baskets, late 17th c., 120 x 180" ......................................... **23,000**

**French Verdure,** a landscape scene w/a large leafy tree in the left foreground w/a bull & two goats nearby, a moted castle in the right distance, within a border of flowers & baskets, ca. 1680, 100 x 113" (ILLUS. top next column) ........................ **11,500**

*French Verdure Tapestry*

# THEOREMS

*During the 19th century, a popular pastime for some ladies was theorem painting, or stencil painting. Paint was allowed to penetrate through hollow-cut patterns placed on paper or cotton velvet. Still life compositions, such as bowls of fruit or vases of flowers were the favorite themes, but landscapes and religious scenes found favor among amateur artists who were limited in their ability and unable to do freehand painting. Today these colorful pictures, with their charming arrangements, are highly regarded by collectors.*

*Fine Early Watercolor Theorem*

**Basket of flowers,** water-color on paper, unsigned, American, 19th c., framed, 12 x 14 1/4" (toning, fading, minor staining) ............................................................. **$575**

**Basket of fruit,** free-hand water-color & stenciling on paper, a variety of fruits overflowing a basket, in shades of red, green, blue, yellow, brown, etc., on the back of marbleized paper, old frame, first half 19th c., 10 1/4 x 12 1/4" (minor damage) ......................................................... **1,650**

**Bouquet of flowers,** water-color on paper, a large varied & well executed group of flowers in varied colors against a brown ground w/uneven color, glued to under-

side of oval gold mat, beveled bird's-eye
maple veneer frame, first half 19th c.,
overall 22 x 26 1/4".................................... **660**

**Bowl of fruit,** water-color on paper, a large
wide shallow fluted bowl on a stepped
pedestal base filled w/large fruits &
leaves, a mat under the bowl, in a
molded painted yellow frame, toning,
minor staining, crease, first half 19th c.,
7 1/2 x 9 1/4" (ILLUS.)............................. **7,475**

**Bowl of fruit & compote of flowers,**
water-color on paper, a large varied
mound of stylized fruit in a low bowl
beside a footed compote overflowing
w/stylized flowers, faint signature, old
molded gilt frame, overall
25 1/4 x 31 1/4" (poor condition, tears,
old repairs) ..................................................... **385**

**Bowl of fruit w/birds & butterflies,** watercolor on velvet, a long gadrooned boat-
form bowl raised on bulbous short legs
w/bird feet, on a rectangular mat, the
bowl filled to overflowing w/various fruits
including large grape clusters, flying
birds & a butterfly above, another
perched butterfly, signed "Elizabeth
Robinson, painted in 1810," unframed,
20 x 21" (creases, tears at edge, toning,
staining & minor fading) ........................... **1,610**

**Cluster of fruits,** water-color on velvet, a
tall stack of mixed fruits including
grapes, cherries, peaches, pears &
strawberries in shades of green, yellow
& brown w/faded red & blue, old beveled
frame, 19th c., 14 1/8 x 16 1/2" .................... **660**

**Floral bouquet,** water-color on paper, cluster of flowers in shades of green, blue,
yellow & pink, signed on the back "Mary
Ann M.....Middlesbro. 1839. Miss Crosley's School," original beveled bird's-eye
maple frame w/gilded liner,
11 7/8 x 13 3/4" (stains, small hole,
minor damage to framd).............................. **523**

# TOBACCIANA

*Although the smoking of cigarettes, cigars &
pipes is controversial today, the artifacts of smoking
related items pipes, cigar & tobacco humidors,
cigar & cigarette lighters and, of course, the huge
range of advertising materials are much sought
after. Unusual examples, especially fine Victorian
pieces, can bring high prices. Below we list a cross
section of Tobacciana pieces.*

*The field of Tobacciana is a large one, consist-
ing of 90+ specialized hobbies from tobacco jars,
cigarette cards, cigar boxes, tobacco tins, pipes,
and much more. Like other collectibles, values are
highly dependent on where the item is sold, by
whom and to whom as well. A flea market booth in
a small town cannot expect to get the same prices
as a specialty dealer with a national clientele. Internet prices are likely to run the full gamut from high
to low.-Tony Hyman*

## ADVERTISING & STORE ITEMS

**Advertising figure,** Admiration cigars,
composition Indian vigorously striding

w/box of cigars under his arm, S.
Fernandez & Co., Tampa, ca. 1940s,
18" h. .................................................... **$150-250**

*Prince Albert Advertising Sign*

**Advertising sign,** tobacco, "'You'll Like it
Too!' Prince Albert," linen-backed, outdoor sign or indoor banner depicting
pipe smoker & Prince Albert can, 4 x 8',
excellent condition (ILLUS.) .................... **60-125**

*Robert Burns Advertising Sign*

**Advertising sign,** cigar, "Robert Burns 10¢
Cigar," lithographed on tin, 1901-1909,
24" d., very good condition (ILLUS.) ..... **450-800**

**Advertising sign,** snuff, paper, "Lorillard's
Snuff" above handsome red, white,
blue & black depiction of snuff-taking
seniors, reads "Won the Only Gold
Medal Awarded on Snuff at the Atlanta
Exposition" below, professionally
framed, intended for tobacconist's wall,
P. Lorillard, New York, ca. 1905-1910,
24 x 32".................................................. **300-450**

**Cigar box opener,** "El Verso Cigars" on
one side & "San Felice Cigars" on the
other, nickel plated, ca. 1950s, 3" l. .......... **15-30**

**Cigar store Indian,** full-size, wood, Indian
maiden holding bunch of cigars, fair
carving by unidentified workman, ca. late
19th century manufacture, repainted
before WWII, 5' h. including base.. **6,000-12,000**

*Bull Durham Tobacco Container*

**Tobacco container,** Bull Durham, card-board, designed to hold 64 cloth bags of smoking tobacco, intended as display pieces, various cowboy & racist Negro scenes, ca. 1910-1920s, excellent condition, widely reproduced (ILLUS.) .................................. **400-1,000 and up**

**Tobacco plug cutter,** counter-top, cast iron, figural of an imp, w/original paint, late 1800s, has been reproduced .......... **150-200**

# ASHTRAYS

*Ashtrays are just beginning to catch on with collectors, the result being a doubling in value in the last two years, and the end is not yet in sight. Prices here are aggressive, indicative of what these items are bringing in their best markets. Private parties and most dealers will buy and sell these at or below the low range given. To learn more about ashtrays, read Nancy Wanvig's Collector's Guide to Ashtrays, 2nd Edition.*

**Ashtray,** advertising, amethyst glass w/smooth bottom & white imprint "Hotel Fremont, Las Vegas, Nevada," ca. 1970s, 3 1/2" d. ............................ **5-10**

**Ashtray,** advertising, clear glass w/black imprint "Biloxi Belle Casino" (Biloxi, MS), after 1992, 3 1/4" ........................... **3-5**

**Ashtray,** advertising, clear glass, w/red on white imprint "The Fabulous Flamingo, The Showplace of the Nation, Las Vegas, Nevada" & artwork of flamingo w/head lowered, ca. 1947-1967, 4" d. ....... **15-25**

**Ashtray,** advertising, smoked glass, imprinted in red, "Flamingo Hilton, Las Vegas-Nevada" w/the three flamingos logo, after 1971, 4" d. ................................ **5-10**

*Bronze Dancer Ashtray*

**Ashtray,** bronze female dancer on shell or marble base, various shapes, sizes & poses, almost always women, generally nude, generally less than 6" h. (ILLUS.) ................................................ **100-250**

**Ashtray,** cast composition, ape in golfer's clothes, dismayed expression at missing short putt, painted, 8" h. ......................... **75-175**

**Ashtray,** ceramic, black panther on black ceramic base, gold colored trim, marked "Souvenir Boonville, New York," base 7" w. .......................................................... **8-20**

**Ashtray,** ceramic, black panther on black ceramic base, numerous variations trim,

pose & advertising (or lack of it), in various sizes from 3" to 10".............................. **5-40**

**Ashtray,** ceramic, in shape of the state of New York, w/decals picturing state capitol, state flower & state fish, ca. 1950s, approximately 5"......................................... **5-15**

**Ashtray,** ceramic, multicolored, shaped as a tobacco leaf w/three dimensional figures of Uncle Sam & Cuban man carrying a giant cigar, ca. 1920s, approximately 8" l., excellent condition..................................... **85-100**

*Poodle Head Ashtray*

**Ashtray,** ceramic, three-dimensional figure of poodle's head w/mouth open to receive cigarette, smoke comes out dog's eyes when cigarette left in ashtray, brown & white glaze (ILLUS.).................... **10-12**

**Ashtray,** ceramic, three-dimensional figure of Ubangi, smoke comes out his pursed lips when cigarette left in ashtray, brown glaze, approximately 7" h., unusual .......... **10-25**

**Ashtray,** chrome or Bakelite, pair of chrome birds, animals, or figures centered in an ashtray, pelicans & toucans being the most common of the dozen or so varieties found ...................................... **20-75**

**Ashtray,** glass, black bowl on pewter colored pedestal, unmarked, probably Art Metal Works/Ronson, base 6 1/2" d. bowl, 6 1/2" h. on pedestal .................... **400-500**

**Ashtray,** glass, clown laying on his back, multicolored, Italian, 7" long (repaired)...... **60-90**

**Ashtray,** glass, rubber dog lifting hind leg above cigarette in ashtray, on wooden base, transfer lettering reads "Do your cigarettes taste different lately?," base 7" l., perfect condition................................ **20-30**

*Leaping Swordfish Ashtray*

**Ashtray,** glass, swordfish leaping, light blue, Italian, 1950s, 5" tall (ILLUS.)......... **50-125**

**Ashtray,** seashell, oval shell w/nude woman sleeping inside, marked "Made in Guam," 6 x 5" ........................................ **40-75**

# CIGAR BOXES

*More than a million different cigar boxes exist. Included are about 200 very common brands. Among those that are the most common are Admiration, Alhambra, Antony & Cleopatra, Bayuk Ribbon, Bering, Brooks & Company, Chancellor, Chas Denby, Cinco, Corina, Cremo, Dutch Masters, El Producto, El Verson, Factory Seconds, Factory Smokers, Gold Label, Hav-A-Tampa, House of Windsor, Humo, King Edward, La Fendrich, Mark IV, Muriel, Phillies, Red Dot, Reynaldo, Robt Burns, Roi-Tan, Santa Fe, Thompson & Co., Van Dyke, (Old) Virginia Cheroots, Webster, White Owl, I & Wolf Bros. For more information about cigar boxes read Tony Hyman's Handbook of American Cigar Boxes.*

**Alcazar,** nailed wood/cardboard box of 50 cigars in four rows, label depicts famous race horse in full color, ca. 1950s, common, full, excellent condition (some minor external scuffing) ............................. **50-75**

**Black Hawk,** trimmed nailed wood box of 50, w/an attractive full color label depicting an Indian w/feathery headdress in a gold circle w/vignettes on both sides, Rocky Ford & Totem being the most common w/Indian themes, w/Black Hawk a distant third but regularly seen on the market ............................................. **35-60**

**Brooks & Co.,** Tebson/Coronas, standard boite nature box w/interlocked corners, hinges & clasp, collar & no paper label, popular national brand from 1920s through 1960s, near mint condition .............. **3-5**

**Cigar canister,** "Old Seneca Stogies," cov., tin by W.H. Kildow, Tiffin, Ohio, lithograph portrait of Native American w/full headdress by Continental Can Co., 4 1/4 x 5 1/2 (minor scrapes) ............... **385**

*Corina Larks Cigar Box*

**Corina Larks,** Western shape, sports or other size/shape boxes of 50 cigars, standard boite nature box w/hinges, clasp, collar & no or little inside label, Jose Escalante & Co., New Orleans, ca. 1940s & '50s, common, mint condition (ILLUS.) ......................................................... **3-5**

**Cyco Perfectos,** trimmed nailed wood box of 50 cigars, label depicts pretty girl &

oasis, made in South Dakota in late 1920s, very fine condition ......................... **20-40**

**Floradora,** nailed wood box of 100 cigars, label depicts bundle of three cigars held together w/pictorial band depicting woman's head, cigars priced at 3/10¢, P. Lorillard, factory 17, Virginia, ca. 1901-1909, excellent condition.......................... **50-60**

**Garcia y Vega,** wooden box in nearly 100 various sizes & shapes, label depicts woman carving initials in a tree, 1930s thru 1950s (with a blue tax stamp & white bonded warehouse stamp), prices vary depending on rarity............................. **5-30**

**Gay Boy,** nailed wood vertical box for 12 cigars, label depicts turn of the century dude, approx. 6" h. when opened, fine condition .................................................. **60-85**

*General U.S. Grant Cigar Box*

**General U.S. Grant,** nailed wood cigar box made to hold 100 cigars in six rows, overall lid & vertical end label, black & white outer label depicts General Ulysses Grant in Civil War uniform, plain white inner label, made by Wescott, Wise & Kent, Binghamton, NY, 1866, signature canceled 1866 revenue stamp in fine condition, handsome end label on an important box made between the war & his presidency (ILLUS.) .................... **175-300**

**Hermann Göring box with cigars made for Sonderanferligung Reichsmarschall Hermann Göring,** nailed wood box of 10 large cigars packed in glass tubes, inside label depicts Göring's crest in red & gold, German revenue stamp, Gildemann cigar factory, Berlin-Hamburg, ca. 1940s, excellent condition ................................................. **1,000-1,500**

**House of Windsor Palmas or Mark IV Magnates,** plastic box, either brown or black, designed to hold 50 cigars four rows deep, ca. 1970s & '80s, mint condition ......................................................... **3-5**

**King Edward Imperial,** wood or cardboard box of 50, w/label depicting the King, cigars priced from 2/5¢ to 8¢........................ **1-5**

**Merry Christmas,** book-shaped wooden box of 25 cigars packed two deep, F.M. Howell label depicts windblown pretty girl in Santa outfit carrying holly, unknown western New York cigarmaker, factory 973, 28th tax district ..................... **60-80**

**Metal box,** w/top picture frame inset w/various color pictures, hinges, clasp & inside mirror, known in green, red, other colors, w/a wide variety of subject matter on pictures from English cottages, French court scenes, sports, etc., held 100 cigars, box used by variety of Florida & Pennsylvania factories during 1930s, inside mirror had label glued on, but usually removed, excellent condition (cracked mirror) ........................................ **20-30**

*Miss Chicago Cigar Box*

**Miss Chicago,** box of 50, w/label depicting '40s style bathing beauty in wooden speedboat in Chicago River, skyline in background, mint condition (ILLUS.) ...... **80-125**

**Old Virginia Cheroots,** cardboard, w/predominantly blue label & small vignette of an elderly black man's face, this brand was one of the largest selling cheap cigars in America for almost 40 years, ....... **5-20**

**Old Virginia Cheroots,** wood, w/long 1883 tax stamp, w/predominantly blue label & small vignette of an elderly black man's face, this brand was one of the largest selling cheap cigars in America for almost 40 years, ...................................... **40-75**

**Phillies Perfecto,** tin box of 50 cigars packed four rows high, minor varieties; made by Bayuk Brothers, Philadelphia, ca. 1920s & 1930s, common, mint condition .................................. **5-10**

*The "Safety" Brand Cigar Box*

**"Safety" Brand (The),** standard trimmed nailed wood box of 50 cigars, w/inside label depicting red shirted man smoking a cigar while riding a balloon-tired bicycle, stock label used by many factories, fine condition (ILLUS.) ............................ **100-200**

**Sam'l Davis 1886,** wooden box, held 50 cigars packed in four rows, w/hinges, often w/a button clasp, no inside pictorial label, made by Sam'l Davis, Pennsylvania, ca. 1950s, mint condition ....... **3-5**

**Silver & mahogany w/jewels,** rectangular, the body raised on four berry feet w/foliage above, the hinged cover in repoussé & chased, the front w/a lock below a rose & ribbon thumbpiece mounted w/a sapphire, the top w/a wreath of roses enclosing a monogram "GL" set w/rubies & diamonds above the engraved dates "1814-1914" & "9/6," the interior lined w/mahogany, the key (broken) w/a rose, C.G. Hallberg, Stockholm, Sweden, 1914, 6 3/8 x 10", 4 1/8" h. ...................... **2,875**

**Uncle Sam's Delight,** trimmed, nailed wood box of 50, very large cigars for that period (1876-1886), 1883 tax stamp, full color inside label depicts Uncle Sam laying on ground, a bundle of cigars for a pillow, while smoking a three foot long cigar ...................................................... **400-750**

**Winsome Little Cigars,** flat tin of 10 cigars, depicts smiling woman on pillow, pre-WWI, approx. 3 1/2" wide ............... **125-200**

**Women's Rights Concha Regalia,** nailed wood box of 100 cigars, black & white label depicting street scene w/picketers from Democratic & Independent parties soliciting women's attention, John Rauch, factory 97 in the 6th tax district of Indiana, ca. 1880, excellent condition ... **400-600**

**Yellow Kid Reina Victoria,** nailed wood box of 100 cigars, colorful label depicts the Yellow Kid smoking a cigar, plus front page of New York Journal, signed by R.F. Outcault, ca. 1901-1909, unknown New York City cigarmaker, desirable box......................................... **600-800**

# CIGAR & CIGARETTE CASES & HOLDERS

*Cigar Cases*

Cigar case, aluminum, holds three cigars, decoration cut into the aluminum along w/inscription "Jamestown, 1907," apparently purchased or received as a prize at the Jamestown Exposition honoring the 300th anniversary of the first colony, 2 1/2 x 4 1/2" (ILLUS. bottom).................. **30-50**

Cigar case, nickel plated metal, w/space for name or inscription, ca. 1900-1930, 2 1/2 x 4 1/2" (ILLUS. top)........................ **15-30**

Cigar case, silver plated, gold wash inside, holds three cigars, minor decoration, ca. 1900-1930, 2 1/2 x 4 1/2" ........................ **25-50**

*Cigar Holder w/Battle Scene*

Cigar holder, leather & papier-maché, from 1820-1870, painting of battles, calamities, historic events; value dependent upon condition & the painting, most w/painted scenes, frequently marked "Segars" on the back, 5" long, more or less w/rounded ends (ILLUS.)............ **300-1,000**

Cigar holder, leather & papier-maché, from 1820-1870, painting of famous people, value dependent upon condition & the painting, most w/painted scenes, frequently marked "Segars" on the back, 5" long, more or less w/rounded ends .... **250-1,000**

Cigar holder, leather & papier-maché, from 1820-1870, painting of military scene, value dependent upon condition & the painting, most w/painted scenes, frequently marked "Segars" on the back, 5" long, more or less w/rounded ends... **150-300**

Cigar holder, leather & papier-maché, from 1820-1870, painting of nudes, value dependent upon condition & the painting, most w/painted scenes, frequently marked "Segars" on the back, 5" long, more or less w/rounded ends ....... **150-400**

Cigar holder, leather & papier-maché, from 1820-1870, painting of unknown men & women, value dependent upon condition & the painting, most w/painted scenes, frequently marked "Segars" on the back, 5" long, more or less w/rounded ends.................................... **100-200**

Cigar holder, leather & papier-maché, from 1820-1870, painting X-rated, value dependent upon condition & the painting, most w/painted scenes, frequently marked "Segars" on the back, 5" long, more or less w/rounded ends............ **400-1,000**

Cigarette case, sterling silver, rectangular w/rounded corners, gold-washed ovoid push button clasp, suspended on a silver link chain, gold-washed interior, engraved on front w/a name & date, Tiffany & Co., New York, New York, case 2 1/4 x 3 3/8" ................................................. **86**

*"Doublets Regal Size Cigarettes" Tin*

Cigarette tin, aluminum flat for 10 cigarettes, silver & blue, depicts 16th century soldier w/sword & shield, marked "Doublets Regal Size Cigarettes" (ILLUS.) ....... **30-60**

## LIGHTERS

*Evans Cigarette Lighter/Cigarette Case*

Evans cigarette lighter/cigarette case, mother-of-pearl squares, excellent condition, set of 2 (ILLUS.) .......................... **75-125**

Figural, Penguin, given by Patti Page, engraved w/her face & signed "Thanks, Patti Page," original box ........................... **40-60**

*Dachshund-shaped Figural Cigarette Lighter*

Figural, pot metal, shape of a dachshund, made to imitate its much more valuable Vienna bronze counterpart, tag w/1912 patent & marked "Austria," 4 1/4" l. (ILLUS.) ................................................. **50-100**

Ronson, pocket, Diana model, ca. 1950s ..... **10-20**

**Ronson,** table-type, Queen Anne model, ca. 1936-1959 ............................. **10-20**

# MATCHCOVERS

*Union Label Matchcover*

**Advertising,** "Union-Made Cigars," depicting the Cigar Maker's International Union of America & the 1940s Union Label; this union created more giveaways than any other, rare, Union matchcover only (ILLUS.) ........................... **5-12**

**Advertising,** "Union-Made Cigars," depicting the Cigar Maker's International Union of America & the 1940s Union Label; this union created more giveaways than any other, variety of celluloid items........................................................ **15-100+**

**Advertising,** Bell's Waterproof Wax Vestas, tin matchbox, w/slip-top & striker on bottom, litho in blue, white & tan w/three lines of lettering, English, ca. 1900-1910, approximately 2 3/4 x 1 1/2".......................... **5-20**

**Airline,** "Delta Air Lines" w/logo on front, blank saddle, small jets on back, dark blue, red & white, thirty-strike size ............. **5-10**

**Airline,** "Northwest Orient Airlines" w/tail of plane on front, "Northwest Orient Airlines" on saddle, "For Our Matchless Friends" w/logo & name on back, white, red & blue ...................................................... **5-8**

**Airline,** "Ozark Airlines" logo, on front, blank saddle, "We Make It Easy For You" & "Ozark Airlines" on back, "Stop Lite" inside, white, orange & black, back striker .......................................................... **3-5**

**Airline,** "TWA" w/airplane tail on front, blank saddle, "TWA" w/Texaco aircraft & star on back, gold, red & white...................... **4-7**

**Airline,** "United Airlines Coast to Coast" w/two-engine plane on front & back, "The Direct Midcontinent Route" on saddle, "Be Oil Wise Use Pennzoil" w/owls inside, red, white & blue, back striker.......... **6-11**

**Beer & Ale,** "Budweiser is for you (This)," on front & back, "Anheuser-Busch, Inc." on saddle, white, red & dark blue, back striker .......................................................... **4-8**

**Beer & Ale,** "Budweiser Light" on front, blank saddle, ad on back, silver, blue &

red, thirty-strike size, back striker, metallic...................................................................... **5-10**

**Beer & Ale,** "Coors, America's Fine Light Beer, Brewed With Pure Rocky Mountain Spring Water" on back, blank saddle, ad on front, stock design in red, white, blue & black ......................................... **5-8**

**Beer & Ale,** "Hamm's Beer" w/bear rolling log on front & back, "Theo. Hamm Brewing Co., St. Paul, Minn-San Francisco, Calif." on saddle, dark blue, light blue, white & red ................................................. **6-12**

**Beer & Ale,** "Hamm's Beer" w/buxom blonde holding tray on back, "Model Distributing Co., Denver Colo" on saddle, ad on front, stock design in yellow, black, red, white, blue & tan .............................. **12-19**

**Beer & Ale,** "Michelob, Weekends Were Made for" w/logo on front & back, blank saddle, black, red & gold, American Ace box ...................................................................... **5-8**

**Beer & Ale,** "Miller High Life Beer" & woman w/moon on back, ad on front, "The Best Milwaukee Beer" on saddle, stock design in red, blue, yellow white & black...................................................................... **8-14**

**Beer & Ale,** "Pabst On Tap" on saddle, Pabst Blue Ribbon logo & "What'll You Have?" on back, ad on front, stock design in green & black.............................. **5-10**

**Beer & Ale,** "Red Top Ale, Powerful Good" w/top & "Red Top Brewing Co., Cincinnati, Ohio" on back, "Red Top Ale" on saddle, ad on front, stock design in white, red, maroon & gold ............................ **5-8**

**Beer & Ale,** "Rheingold" w/short-neck bottle on front, "Rheingold Inn, Sun Valley, New York World's Fair" on back, locations on inside, ca. 1939 ......................... **7-11**

**Blacks,** "Black Cat, 557 West Broadway, New York" w/semi-clad black woman singer on front, "Dinner and Supper Continuous Entertainment" on back, Lion Match Corporation...................................... **8-15**

**Blacks,** "Kit Kat Club, 152 East 55th St, New York" w/black entertainers around name on front & back, "Telephone Eld. 5-0543" on saddle, light green, white & black, Lion Match Corporation ................. **15-20**

**Blacks,** "Lincoln Loan Service, Inc, Harrisburg, PA, Phone: 5219" w/two blacks throwing dice on back, red, black, green & yellow................................................................ **12-18**

**Blacks,** "Manuel's Taproom Lounge and Grill, 622-26 W. Ashley St., Jacksonville, Fla." w/black chef & black waiter carrying turkey, yellow & black, full length ............. **10-15**

**Blacks,** "Pick-A-Rib, Denver, Colo" on saddle, "Barbecue" w/black chef & "3100 E. Colfax at St. Paul, Phone: East 9925" on front, same w/"Speer and Broadway at 7th, Phone: Main 9562" on back, black & white.................................................................. **15-20**

**Blacks,** "Sherwood Rye" w/black waiter carrying tray w/bottle & two glasses, "De man who calls for Sherwood Rye Sure knows the bestest brand to buy!", dark blue, black & white, full length.................. **12-18**

*Baby Ruth Matchcover*

**Candy,** "Baby Ruth 5¢, Curtiss Candies," red, white & blue, full length (ILLUS.).......... **6-10**

**First Nite-Life match cover,** set of famous personalities on standard covers, colored in pastel, complete w/original strikers, Diamond Match Co., 1938, set of 24.. **20-40**

**Girlie,** Girlie Matchcover Catalog, No. 102, Mustang Ranch, drawing front & back, back striker.................................................. **5-10**

**Girlie,** Girlie Matchcover Catalog, No. 36, The Classic Cat, color photo of blonde nude, full-length, thirty-strike size.............. **15-18**

**Girlie matchbook cover,** w/original strikers, "It's great to be an American" on one side, pin-up girls by Merlin on the other, Maryland Match Company, ca. 1940, excellent condition ....................................... **3-8**

**Girlie set,** Arrow Match Company, Set No.1 of 5, "A Study of Photo Art" w/sitting or reclining photo nudes on each matchcover, ad on front, Girlie Matchcover Catalog p. 2, ca. 1950, the set ........ **18-23**

**Girlie set,** Diamond Match Co., Set No. 1 of 5, "I'm Ropin' You In," "Plenty on the Ball," "She'll Get Her Man," "The Right Bait Gets Results," "Well Equipped for Gold Digging," ad on front, Girlie Matchcover Catalog p. 11, ca. 1957, the set ...... **18-23**

**Girlie set,** Lion Match Co., Set No. 1 of 3, pen & ink drawings, ad on front, Girlie Matchcover Catalog p. 14, ca. 1951, the set .......................................................... **55-65**

**Girlie set,** Universal Match Corp., Set No. 1 of 5, "Inviting," "No Trespassing," "Sitting Pretty," "Slow Curves Ahead," "Temptation," ad on front, Girlie Matchcover Catalog p. 35, ca. 1954, the set ...... **11-17**

**NBC/CBS stars match cover,** famous radio personalities on standard match covers complete w/original strikers, Diamond Match Co., 1935, part of set................ **1-5**

**Political,** Dewey for President, cover w/photo of Dewey, ca. 1948...................... **10-15**

**Railroad,** "Burlington Northern" w/logo on front & back, blank saddle, green & white............................................................ **4-7**

**Railroad,** "New York Central System" on front, "New York Central" on saddle, "Travel & Ship by Dependable Rail" w/train on back, grey, red & white ................ **4-7**

**Railroad,** "Southern Pacific Streamlined Daylights" on front, blank saddle, colorful Deco-type train on back, yellow, red, green, white & black, front or back striker.... **9-15**

**Railroad,** "Virginia Railway" w/VGN logo on front, blank saddle, "A sure way to be sure, Route Virginian" on back, map inside, white, red & blue ........................... **10-12**

## PAPER GOODS

**Booklet,** George Washington, 6" x 9" published by Allen & Ginter, very colorful; there are more than 50 different similar albums produced in the 19th century by tobacco companies; topics include history, plants, animals, theater, sports, fish, etc. .................................................. **75-300**

**Cabinet photograph,** depicting front of Western cigar factory, large Punch store figure, five employees standing on wooden sidewalk, 1880s, approximately 4" x 6"............................................................. **150-250**

**Cigar bands,** mounted in album without glue, bands complete w/white tabs at end, more than half are pictorial bands of Presidents, animals, kings, famous persons, etc., approximately 1,000 in set ........................................................ **100-200**

**Postcard,** "A Modern Tobacco Factory, Tampa, Fla.," color ...................................... **3-5**

**Postcard,** picturing Julius Fecht Cigar Factory, Ottumwa, Iowa, unused, slight bruised, 1930s........................................ **15-30**

*Postcard Showing A Tobacco Buyer*

**Postcard,** real photo, black & white, shows tobacco buyer, reads "Our Mr. Levy Pres. Enterprise Cigar Co. Buying Havana in Cuba for the Celebrated Lord Stirling & Taking Cigars" (ILLUS.) ............. **10-20**

**Poster,** L & M cigarettes, featuring Matt Dillon & Miss Kitty from Gunsmoke, reads "They Said It Couldn't Be Done But L&M Did It!—Don't settle for one...without the other!," ca. 1960s, excellent condition....... **50-75**

## PERSONAL ITEMS

*Cigar Clipper Shaped Like A Man*

**Cigar clipper,** brass, shaped like scissors, made in U.S. & Europe, ca. 1890s-1920... **25-40**

**Cigar clipper,** shaped like man sitting on chamber pot, clip cigar by putting it in hole in his stomach, push down on his head & cigar trimming falls into chamber pot, European origin, turn-of-the-century, 6" h. (ILLUS.)................................ **150-400**

*Matchbox Grip & Matchsafe*

**Matchbox grip,** silver plated, three-sided, device for protecting matchboxes, w/embossed design of the United Brotherhood of Carpenters & Joiners of America, reads "See That This Label Appears On All Wood Work," 1 1/4 x 2 1/4", rare (ILLUS. bottom)........................................ **60-100**

**Matchsafe,** nickel plate & celluloid, tubular, advertises "Elect A. J. Cermak; Chicago needs a mayor," w/Cermak's picture, 2 1/4" l. x 3/4" d. ...................................... **75-125**

**Matchsafe,** nickel plated w/celluloid wraparound, depicts brewery worker's union label, reads "International Union of the United Brewery Workmen of America ask your Support against Prohibition As it is Detrimental to All," ca. 1920, 1 1/2 x2 1/2", excellent condition (ILLUS. top) **150-300**

## PIPES & CHEROOT HOLDERS

*To be considered in excellent condition, Meerschaum pipes should have no damage & should be smoothly colored, not mottled. The amber or plastic stem should be in place as, ideally, is the case in which it originally came. Briar pipes should show no evidence of reddish colored fill (it looks like clay) to correct blemishes. Pipes should not be dented around the bowl, the result of being banged to loosen tobacco.*

**Cheroot holder,** Meerschaum, straight stem, eagle w/banner in mouth, 5 1/3" long ...................................................... **125-175**

**Cheroot holder,** Meerschaum, w/carving of three nondescript dogs sitting sideways on straight stem, amber bit, approximately 3 1/2" l. (missing case)....... **35-50**

**Cheroot holder,** Meerschaum, w/amber stem, three deer w/large three-dimensional carving of antlers in crook of holder, exceptionally carved, ca. 1890-1910, 3 x 4 3/4" in original case, mint condition.................................................... **50-75**

**Cheroot holder,** Meerschaum, w/carving of two riders in hunting costume & seven dogs looking for a fox, seen peeking from around the bowl, bowl at 45 angle to stem, original fitted wooden case lined w/satin, covered w/split leather, inside marked "Paris," European origin, ca. 1890-1910, approximately 5" l............... **250-400**

**Pipe,** Meerschaum, w/slightly bent amber stem & bit, carved in the form of a hand holding a skull, good detail, stands upright when resting, without case, early 20th c. ..................................................... **100-175**

*Chinese Water Pipe w/Tools*

**Pipe,** water w/tools, made of paktong, Chinese origin, 20th c., approximately 10" h. (ILLUS.)..................................................... **50-125**

*Meerschaum Pipe w/Face of Napoleon*

**Pipe,** Meerschaum, carved w/face of Napoleon, excellent turn-of-the-century likeness, European origin, approximately 6" l. (ILLUS.) ....................................... **150-300**

*Meerschaum Pipe*

**Pipe,** Meerschaum, w/slightly bent plastic stem, w/two carved bare breasted ladies swooping about garlands of roses, European origin, ca. late 1800s, approximately 6 1/4 x4" (ILLUS.) ...................... **400-650**

**Pipe,** Meerschaum, carved in the form of an elephant w/bead eyes, approximately 14" l. w/plastic bit, no case, Turkish, ca. 1960-1990 ............................................. **60-150**

## SIGNS & SIGNBOARDS

**Sign,** embossed tin, advertising Trinidad y Hermano cigarettes, depicting Cuban plantation & pack of cigarettes, Cuban, 6 1/2 x 14 1/4" ..................................... **125-150**

**Sign,** paper, Red Man "First in America,"depicting Indian brave holding Bowie knife & package of Red Man, 12 x 18" ................................................ **125-150**

## SNUFF BOXES

**Boxwood,** carved in the form of a recumbent ram, Europe, 19th c., 3" l...................... **201**

**Burl wood,** round disk-form, the cover carved in low-relief w/a sea battle scene titled "Le Naufrage," machine-tooled back, early 19th c., 3 1/4" d.......................... **248**

**Burl wood,** round disk-form, the flat cover w/a gilded medallion under glass titled "Homage À Lafayette," tortoiseshell lining, early 19th c., 2 1/8" d. (minor edge damage & repair) ......................................... **413**

**Papier-maché,** round disk-form, the top w/a black lithographed & colored scene titled "The Reception of Genl. Lafayette at the City Hall New York," ca.1825, 3 1/2" d. (wear)............................................. **523**

**Silver,** modeled as a mouse, hinged cover on a base embossed w/scrolls & a country gentleman, gold-washed interior, 800 fine, 2 3/8" l., 1 3/4" h. .................................. **288**

## TOBACCIANA FOLK ARTS

*Glass Dish Covered w/Cigar Bands*

**Dish,** glass, covered w/cigar bands in carefully chosen geometric pattern. ca. 1910-1920, 6 1/2" d., excellent unfaded condition (ILLUS.).............................................. **25-50**

*Satin Cigar Ribbons Pillow*

**Pillow cover,** made from satin cigar ribbons. ca. 1900-1920, value depends on condition (no less than excellent is acceptable), the selection of ribbons & the artistry of presentation, 2' sq. (ILLUS.)..................................................... **75-250**

**Vase,** glass, covered w/cigar bands in random patterns, ca. 1910-1920, 6" h., excellent unfaded condition....................... **40-60**

## TOBACCO CARDS

*Tobacco cards became America's second collecting passion in the 1880s and continued to be popular for a quarter century in the U. S. and for 100 years in England. Numerous themes and brand names were involved, with the largest U. S. output coming from all the branches of American Tobacco Company. For more information about tobacco cards read Robert Forbes and Terence Mitchell's American Tobacco Cards Price Guide & Checklist.*

**Actors & Actresses,** cigarette cards, issued in various small sizes, black & white or sepia photographic images, more than 2,000 different, numbered & unnumbered, mostly Allen & Ginter, but other makers & brands as well, price per card ..................................................... **1-3**

**Actors, Actresses, Athletes,** cigarette cards, 500+ different, issued by Between the Acts Cigarettes, portraits inside an oval, advertising above, person identified below, price per card ............................ **3-8**

**Actors, Actresses, Athletes, Presidential Candidates,** cigarette cards, 500+ different, issued by Between the Acts Cigarettes, portraits inside an oval, advertising above, person identified below, Presidential Candidates, price per card ..................................................... **15-30**

**Animals,** cigarette cards, issued by Hassan Cork Tip Cigarettes, set of 80, price each ............................................................ **1-3**

**Bridge favors & place cards,** die cut, issued by Lucky Strike, clever portraits of actors & actresses as well as other subjects, easily recognizable by the holes for inserting Lucky Strike Cigarettes to stand them up, series of 80, price each................................................... **5-10**

**Coins of All Nations,** cigarette cards, set of 50 full color cards, depicting person in native dress & a full size coin, price each...... **3-5**

*Cowboy Tobacco Card*

**Cowboy Scenes,** cigarette cards, set of 25 full color cards issued by Duke for Honest Long Cut, price each (ILLUS.) ...... **12-20**

**Flags of All Nations,** cigarette cards, depicts flag & artifact from around the world, at least 10 different brands advertised on back, set of 100, price each............. **1-5**

**Gymnastic Exercises,** cigarette cards, set of 25 full color cards depicting women in revealing-for-the-day exercise suits, working out with dumbbells, etc., price each ........................................................ **7-15**

**Hard-A-Port brand,** cigarette cards, in the form of a deck of playing cards, each depicting a beautiful woman w/lots of leg & décolletté, full deck of 52 + Joker in original box...................................... **1,200-1,500**

**Hard-A-Port brand,** cigarette cards, in the form of a deck of playing cards, each depicting a beautiful woman w/lots of leg & décolletté, individual cards, price each .. **15-20**

**Kid's Brand pipe tobacco,** cigarette cards, in the form of a deck of playing cards, each depicting a beautiful woman in fancy attire, also seen under brand names Snipe & Red Boot, individual cards, price each...................................... **10-25**

**World's Champions,** Second Series, set of 50 cards issued by Allen & Ginter, full beautiful color, individual cards for baseball players & boxers can bring prices higher than the set's average price each ....... **30**

# TOBACCO PRODUCT TINS

*Smoking tobacco tins are among the more expensive tobacco collectibles. Plenty of tobacco tins are worth only a few dollars, but a surprising number are worth more than $100.00 and a significant handful worth $1,000.00 or more. Tobacco tins that are rusty, damaged, or badly scratched have no value. Condition is absolutely vital in the world of tin cans. A can worth $1,000.00 in mint condition may sit on your shelf unsold for years at $100.00 if it has condition problems.*

*To qualify as "excellent condition" the printed surface of the can should be unmarked or with slight soil and/or use wear outside the image area. The revenue stamp may be scratched or removed. A can is not "excellent" if the image is scratched or if "paint" (ink) is flaking off. Values given are for*
retail of cans in excellent condition. Cans in less than excellent condition retail for 25% to 50% of the prices shown.*

**Alumni Burley Cut,** vertical pocket tin in unusual concave configuration, predominantly silver tin with bust of man in cap & gown, United States Tobacco Co., Virginia, approximately 4 x 3 x 1", good condition............................................. **700-1,500**

*Bulwark Cut Plug Tin*

**Bulwark cut plug,** tin horizontal box, predominantly gold & blue, depicting a sailor looking through a spyglass, made in England by W.D. & H.O. Wills, approximately 6 x 4 x 1 1/2", excellent condition (ILLUS.) ..................................... **20-35**

**George Washington cut plug,** tin lunch box, w/wire & wood handle & metal clasp, R.J. Reynolds, Winston-Salem, NC, after 1910, common, approximately 7 1/2 x 4   1/2 x 4 1/2", excellent-mint condition.................................................... **30-40**

**Hi-Plane smooth cut tobacco,** vertical pocket tin, lithograph on tin in white on red background w/single engine, near mint condition ......................................... **25-45**

**Hi-Plane smooth cut tobacco,** vertical pocket tin, lithograph on tin in white on red background w/China Clipper, good condition............................... **200-1,000 and up**

**Just Suits cut plug,** tin lunch box, w/wire handle & metal clasp on end of box, Buchanon & Lyall, New York (div. of P. Lorillard, Virginia), after 1910, approximately 8 x 5 1/4 x 4", common, mint condition.................................................... **30-40**

**Lucky Strike cigarettes,** flat tin box called a "Flat Fifties," American Tobacco Company, regularly found in white, green, black, white & Christmas versions, approximately 6 x 4", full, near mint condition........................................................ **15-25**

*Lucky Strike Tin*

**Lucky Strike (smoking tobacco),** small green box w/red circle, some gold trim, "R.A. Patterson Tobacco Co. Rich'd, VA" (div. of American Tobacco Co.), ca. early 20th c., approximately 4 1/4" l., 3" w., excellent condition (ILLUS.) ............ **20-40**

*Niggerhair Tobacco Tin*

**Niggerhair Tobacco,** tin can w/bail handle & slip-top lid, black on brown, pictures South Sea Islander w/nose bone, earrings & predominant hair-do, American Tobacco Company, ca. 1920s -1946 when name changed to Biggerhair, approximately 6 3/4 x 5 1/2" d., common (ILLUS.) ......................................... **200-300**

**Prince Albert crimp cut (smoking tobacco),** vertical pocket tin & other configurations, in various sizes. R.J. Reynolds Tobacco Co., Winston-Salem, North Carolina, ca. 1910 to 1960s, full, near mint condition ...................................... **5-15**

**Prince Albert Now King (smoking tobacco),** "Now King" printed under portrait of Albert, most valuable as a vertical pocket tin (but known in other configurations), R.J. Reynolds Tobacco Co., Winston-Salem, North Carolina, ca. 1910s, good condition ....................................... **200-400**

**Rex pipe & cigarette tobacco,** vertical pocket tin, Spaulding & Merrick, Chicago (div. of Liggett & Myers), approximately 5 x 2" w., 5" h., excellent condition ........... **50-75**

*Stag Tobacco Tin*

**Stag tobacco,** small lightly oval upright pocket tin w/flip-top cover, predominantly red, depicting a large stag,

numerous other varieties of Stag are found (ILLUS.) ........................................... **50-75**

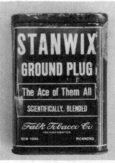

*Stanwix Ground Plug Tin*

**Stanwix ground plug,** vertical pocket tin w/flip-top lid, Falk Tobacco Co., Richmond, approximately 4 1/2 x 3 x 1", excellent condition (ILLUS.) .................. **150-250**

**White Ash cigar,** round wood grained tin can w/slip-top lid, newspaper-style black & white photo of Snyder in suit & tie is central oval image on can, originally held 50 5¢ cigars upright, made by Snyder in Pennsylvania, a large well-known company, ca. 1930s, approximately 5 1/2" h., common, excellent condition ...... **10-20**

# MISCELLANEOUS

*Many hundreds of items fall into the category of miscellaneous "Tobacciana." Prices are especially going up for ashtrays, cigarette cards, cigarette packs, cigarette dispensers, cigarette advertising, cigar boxes, & tobacco tags.*

**Box,** sterling silver, hinged, marked "Solace" in scroll on top, given as a prize in coupon contest held by Solace tobacco, 19th century, 3 1/2" x 2 1/4" x 1/2" ................................................... **200-300**

**Cigar,** in cellophane, w/band reading "Souvenir of National Convention, 1956 Chicago," 10 1/2" jumbo size ........................ **15-25**

**Cigar cutter,** sterling silver & 14k gold, small flattened rectangular form w/an overall basketweave design & an insert hole at one end, Tiffany & Co., New York..... **115**

**Cigar mold,** ten cigar size, hardwood, made by Miller, Dubrul & Peters, ca. 1880s through 1920s, common ................ **20-35**

*Elephant Cigarette Dispenser*

**Cigarette dispenser,** cast-iron, elephant dispenses cigarette under his belly when tail is cranked, holds approximately one pack in howdah on his back, known in red, black & green, ca. 1920s-1930s, 7" l. (ILLUS.)............................................. **50-75**

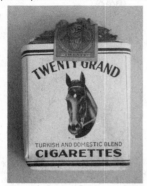

*Twenty Grand Cigarette Pack*

**Cigarette pack,** Twenty Grand, paper cup-type package, image on pack depicts race horse, printed brown on white (ILLUS.)...................................................... **5-10**

**Coin,** brass-like metal, picturing front of bull on one side, rear of bull on the other, marked "Heads you win, if you Smoke Bull Durham," 1 1/4" d. ................................. **2-5**

**Fan hanger,** round, cardboard, "Hambone," depicting cartoon black man flying plane in imitation of Charles Lindbergh, 7" d. ......................................... **35-50**

**Lux Super Fosforos match box,** cardboard box w/sliding drawer, label depicts baseball player, Cuban, ca. 1940s-1950s, good condition .............................. **10-20**

**Musical instrument,** made from cigar box & broom handle & other material, painted in Oriental motif, one metal string, 39" l. ............................................. **75-125**

**Package,** cardboard log cabin, for Sir Walter Raleigh smoking tobacco, complete w/fold down end, inside cardboard tray, lift up roof, 6 1/2 x 4.25" x 6" h. ........ **75-100**

**Package,** chewing tobacco, Plow Boy, unopened, 4 1/2" tall ................................. **20-40**

*Columbia Cigar Glass Paperweight*

**Paperweight,** glass, w/sepia ad for Columbia Cigar, eagle & flags, 4 x 2 3/4" (ILLUS.)................................................. **125-175**

**Pin,** enameled, shaped like tobacco leaf, celebrating 100th anniversary of Cuba's Partagas cigars, 1845-1945, 1 1/2" long ..... **8-15**

**Plate,** ceramic, "Hambone," depicting cartoon black man flying plane, marked Buffalo pottery (this is not advertising, not black memorabilia, & not Buffalo pottery; it is a contemporary fantasy piece being passed off as genuine, mostly at Southern & Midwestern auctions, now nationwide) 8" d. ................................................. **10-20**

**Tobacco box,** cov., brass & copper, oval, incised decoration w/figural scenes & verses, Holland, 18th c., 6 1/2" l.................. **173**

*Red Crest Tobacco Container*

**Tobacco container,** black pressboard, marked "Red Crest, Cut Plug," w/leather handle & buckle type latch, depicts a silver rooster, made by John J. Bagley & Company, 8 x 4 1/2", 4" h. (ILLUS.) ...... **250-400**

**Tobacco humidor,** cov., figural w/black man in shirt & neckerchief & top hat sitting on a cigar box, metal, ceramic, wood, the figure may be smoking a cigar or dipping snuff (about a dozen variants of this cigar box/figure type humidor are known, w/blacks more common than pixies & animals; widely reproduced: watch for sloppy painting, orange colored cigar box, or poor quality wood inside box), value for originals ................................... **200-400**

**Tobacconist's figure,** bust of Indian, beautifully cast hard rubber made to look like wood, late 1930s, 24" h. ................. **300-500**

**Tobacconist's figure,** bust of Uncle Sam, beautifully cast hard rubber made to look like wood, late 1930s, 24" h. ................. **500-600**

*Cigar Maker's Union Tray*

**Tray,** advertising Cigar Maker's Union & Union, tin 10 1/2 x 13 1/4", ca. 1902-1905 (ILLUS.) ........................................ **150-200**

# TOOLS

*Grandfather's old tool belt is no longer just a dust collector in the garage. From the wrenches, hammers and screwdrivers found inside to the catalog used to order them, tools and related items have become highly sought-after collectibles. Descriptions, pricing and photographs were supplied by Martin J. Donnelly Antique Tools.*

*Nickel Plated Anvil*

**Anvil,** Gem City Elevator Works, nickel plated w/raised cast letters, 3 1/2" l. (ILLUS.) .................................................... **$125**

**Axe,** Hibbard, Spencer & Bartlett Co., single bit, marked "Our Very Best," 36" l. .......... **175**

**Axe,** Kelly Axe & Tool Works, Charleston, No. 18722, dated "1912," 7" l. ...................... **125**

**Axe,** Kelly Axe & Tool Works, Charleston, No. 33628, single bit, individually registered, 30" l. .................................................. **115**

**Axe,** Lee, Colt & Anderson Hardware, Omaha, embossed double bit felling axe, ca. 1900, 9" l. ..................................... **365**

**Axe,** Plumb (Fayette R.), Philadelphia, belt style, marked "O.E.S. 1944," 18" l. ............... **395**

**Bevel,** Craftsman Wood Service Co., Chicago, "12 In 1" bevel w/original card, 6" l. ....... **45**

**Bevel,** Standard Tool Co., Athol, Mass, Stephen Bellows patent square, pat. March 11, 1884, 9" l. ..................................... **550**

**Brace,** Brown & Wells, plated beech w/improved button chuck, 13 1/2" l. ............ **425**

**Brace,** Flather (D.), Solly Works, Sheffield, anti-friction head, "John Bottom" pat., 13 1/2" l. ............................................... **235**

**Brace,** Morrison (J.H.), pat. Feb. 1, 1898, "The Challenge," intricate gearing, 19" l. (ILLUS. top next column) ...................... **745**

**Brace,** Stanley Tools, No. 2102-10, "Yankee" ratchet, 10" sweep, 10" l. ...................... **95**

**Caliper,** Athol Machine Co., Athol, Mass., hermaphrodite w/slide adjust leg, 4" l. ............ **45**

**Caliper,** Smith (E.G.), Columbia, Penna., No. 128, adjustable slide type, 6" l. ................ **85**

**Caliper,** Stevens & Co., Page & Hadley patent Feb. 8, 1870, 4" l. .............................. **135**

**Caliper,** Union Tool Co., Orange, Mass., quick-adjust, pat. June 13, 1914, 7" l. ............ **45**

**Caliper,** unmarked, "lady-leg" style w/circular joint, 6" l. ................................................ **1,050**

*The "Challenge" Brace*

**Carpenter's slick,** Buck Brothers, 3" w. blade, bulbous handle, 18" l. ........................ **145**

**Chisel,** Parr (Geo.), Buffalo, N.Y., heavy socket-framing type, 2" w., 12 1/4" l. .............. **55**

**Chisel,** Swan (James) Co. (The), heavy socket- framing, 2" w., 17" l. ........................... **95**

**Chisel,** Witherby (T.H.), heavy socket-framing type, 2" w., 12" l. ............................... **75**

**Drill,** push-type, nickeled lignum vitae knobs, A. H. Reid ........................................... **65**

**Gauge,** Peoria Corage Co., Peoria, Ill., rope & twine gauge w/full nickel plating, 5" l. ......................................................... **35**

**Gauge,** Starrett Co. (The L.S.S.), Athol, Mass., No. 45, adjustable depth, extra long body, 10" l. ...................................... **85**

**Hammer,** Atha Tool Co., No. 20, farrier's tool w/horseshoe logo, 13" l. ...................... **45**

**Hammer,** Belknap Hardware Co., Louisville, No. BG 47-7, claw style, 7 oz., 11" l. .................................................... **65**

**Hammer,** Cheney, Little Falls, N.Y., No. 885, nail-holding claw type w/original handle, 12 1/2" l. ...................................... **95**

**Hammer,** Heller Brothers Co., Newark, N.J., No. 523, claw type, adze eye, plain face, 16" l. .......................................... **155**

**Hammer,** Maydole (D.), Norwich, N.Y., ball peen style w/full nickel plating, 2 oz. size, 9" l. .......................................... **65**

**Hammer,** Maydole (D.), Norwich, N.Y., No. 120, ball peen style w/early imprint, 4 oz. size, original handle, 10 1/2" l. ...................... **35**

**Hammer,** Stanley Rule & Level, marked "Stanley's Standard," original decal, 16 oz. size, ca. 1920s-30s, 13 1/2" l. .................. **65**

**Hatchet,** American Ax & Tool Co., Glassport, marked "A.A. & T. Co." on head, pat. April 17, 1900, 15" l. .......................... **75**

**Hatchet,** Vaughn & Bushnell, Chicago, Ill., embossed lathing hatchet w/deeply etched logo, 13" l. ................................... **75**

**Level,** Davis Level & Tool Co., No. 2, cast iron w/filigree casting, 95% original black japanned finish, 12" l. .............................. **695**

**Level,** Goodell Pratt Company, No. 509, open-end style, 18" l. ................................... **65**

**Level,** Southington Hardware Co., torpedo-style, mahogany, ca. 1913, 9" l. ...................... **55**

**Level,** Stanley Rule & Level, No. 32, graduating w/green paper label on inside of
inclinometer dial, pat. April 21, 1863,
28" l. ............................................................ **895**

**Level,** Stanley Rule & Level, No. 41, ornate
brass top, pat. June 23, 1896, 3" l. ................ **65**

**Level,** Stanley Rule & Level, No. 93, brass
bound mahogany w/original decal,
"Sweetheart" trademark, 30" l. ..................... **195**

**Level,** Stanley Tools, No. 257, laminated
pine, non-adjustable, original box, 24" l. ........ **95**

**Level,** Starrett Co., (The L.S.S.), Athol,
Mass., No. 135, hexagon pocket-style,
full nickel plating, 3" l. ...................................... **25**

**Plane,** 26" jointer, "Stanley Rule & Level
Co., No. 132," ca. 1877 (old repair to
handle) .......................................................... **40**

**Plane,** 6 1/4" compass T-Rabbet, 1 1/2"
iron, ca. 1844, "W.H. Pond, New Haven"
(mark B-1) ...................................................... **35**

**Plane,** complex molder, Grecian Ovolo
w/filet, 1 1/2" iron, ca. 1827, "De Val-
court, 107 Elm, N. York," (mark B-1) .............. **75**

**Plane,** Fulton, New York, N.Y., No. 5320,
block style, metallic, pat. March 21,
1893, original box, 5 1/2" l. ......................... **115**

**Plane,** hollow No. 18, ca. 1832, "J.W. Farr
& Co. N. York" (mark D) ................................. **25**

**Plane,** hollow No. 8, ca. 1874, "D.R. Bar-
ton, Rochester, NY" (mark F) ......................... **20**

**Plane,** molding-type w/adjustable gate,
rosewood & boxwood w/ivory & brass
trim, stamped "Casey & Co. Auburn,
N.Y.," 19th c., 11" l. (wedge replaced) ......... **413**

**Plane,** panel plow, screw arm, ca. 1853,
"R.W. Booth, Cincinnati, OH" (mark A) .......... **75**

**Plane,** router-type, Stanley Model 71 1/2,
patent-dated "10/29/01" .................................. **95**

*Stanley Rule & Level Plane*

**Plane,** Stanley Rule & Level, No. 62, low
angle block style w/original box, 14" l.
(ILLUS.) .................................................... **2,745**

**Plumb bob,** Braunsdorf-Mueller Co., brass
w/B.M.C. logo, Newark, N.J., 4 oz., 4" l. ........ **75**

**Plumb bob,** Dietzgen Co., Eugene, Chi-
cago, No. 14, surveyor's, brass, 6" l. .............. **45**

**Plumb bob,** Leistner (P.), St. Charles, Missouri, millwright's w/reversible tip, 7" l.
(ILLUS. top next column) ............................. **545**

**Plumb bob,** Wells Screw Products Co.,
San Francisco, Calif., combination
Bakelite reel & plumb bob w/original box,
4" l. ............................................................. **125**

**Rule,** D. & S., Bangor, Maine, machinist's
bench, marked "O. Beers," 12" l. .................... **95**

*Early Midwest Plumb Bob*

**Rule,** Lufkin Rule Co. (The), No. 1206, aluminum zig-zag folding type, flat rolled
metal, 72" l. .................................................... **15**

**Rule,** Sawyer Tool Co., Ashburnham,
Mass., No. 4 bench rule w/multiple grad-
uations, 4" l. .................................................... **25**

**Rule,** Stanley Rule & Level, No. 36, two-
fold w/square joint, caliper, 6" l. ...................... **75**

**Rule,** Stanley Rule & Level, No. 64, four-
fold w/square joint, unbound, 12" l. .............. **185**

**Rule,** Stanley Rule & Level, No. 86, four-
fold, ivory & German silver, 24" l. ................. **395**

**Rule,** Stanley Tools, No. 36 1/2, two-fold
folding rule w/caliper, 12" l. ............................ **45**

**Rule & level,** Stanley Rule & Level, No. 96,
"Defiance" zig-zag folding type, 72" l. ............ **55**

**Saw,** Disston (H.) & Sons, Philadelphia,
Penn., No. 68, dovetail, 15 1/2" l. ................... **55**

**Saw,** Disston (Henry) & Sons, Philadelphia,
Penn., No. 9, double-swivel pruning
saw, 21" l. ....................................................... **55**

*"Young Rip" Hack Saw*

**Saw,** Edison Steel Works (The), Cleveland,
Ohio, hack saw, all-steel w/triangular
blade & original etching, "Young Rip,"
16 1/2" l. (ILLUS.) ........................................... **85**

**Saw blades,** Clemson Brothers Inc., Middletown, N.Y., No. 1218, blades
w/enameled box marked "The Star Hack
Saw, Clemson Bros. Inc.," 12 1/2" l. ............... **25**

**Screwdriver,** Millers Falls Company, No.
29 X, spiral ratchet type w/original box,
10 1/2" l. .......................................................... **45**

**Screwdriver,** Millers Falls Company, No.
852, permaloid handle, original box, 10"
blade, 16 1/2" l. ............................................... **35**

**Spoke shaves:** Herbert (A.E. ), Detroit, Mich., patternmaker's, solid bronze cast, original box, ca. 1920s, 3 1/2" l., the set ..... **195**

**Tape measure,** Stanley Rule & Level, No. 546, round casing, vertical reading, marked "patented," ca. 1947-57, 72" l. ........... **45**

**Trammels,** unmarked, cast brass in early-style knurling, marked w/owner's initials "JBO," 4 1/2" l., pr. ........................................ **115**

**Wrench,** Billings & Spencer Co. (The), nut wrench w/graduated center shaft, pat. Feb. 18, 1879, 6" l. ...................................... **55**

**Wrench,** Cellman Wrench Corporation, No. 91, quick-adjust style, "Polly, pat. April 17, 1923," 9" l. ............................................... **55**

**Wrench,** Elgin (The), pat. June 8, 1897, 7" l. ................................................................. **25**

*Nickel Plated Nut Wrench*

**Wrench,** Ellis, nickel plated nut wrench w/pivot head, pat. Nov. 3, 1903, 6" l. (ILLUS.) ........................................................ **365**

**Wrench,** La Gripper Wrench Co., Battle Creek, quick-adjust nut wrench, pat. June 28, 1898, 7" l. ..................................... **325**

**Wrench,** North Manufacturing Co., O.B., New Haven, Conn., cast iron, pat. Jan. 9, 1877, 6 1/2" l. ............................................ **95**

# TOOTHPICK HOLDERS
## CHINA, GLASS, METAL

*Personal hygiene was not a high priority with our Victorian ancestors. However, the more elite often carried a personal toothpick. This was typically a small slender case that held the "pick" which would be exposed for use by either sliding it out of the casing or twisting a portion of the case. Many of these were made of gold or silver and some were adorned with a gemstone. By the late Victorian years it had become fashionable to have a toothpick holder as part of the table setting. Wooden*

*toothpicks would be passed around the table following the meal and the guests would use them discretely hidden behind their linen napkin. These are the items that have become such a popular collectible. Toothpick holders were made from a wide variety of materials, but the most popular with collectors are of china, glass, or metal. Toothpick holder shapes are often confused with match holders, open sugars, and small vases. Match holders typically include a rough or ridged area for striking matches. Vases will typically be smaller around the neck to support the flowers with a larger area for the water reservoir. Toothpick holders have been widely reproduced and some have been "faked" by having the Heisey mark added to them or by having references to other glass manufacturers written on the ruby stained area.*

## CHINA

**Bisque,** boy standing by holder, good detail, decorated w/blue & gold ................... **$55**

**Bisque,** unpainted, rabbit by egg shell .............. **55**

**Delft,** Germany, blue church on white background ........................................................... **55**

**Germany,** handpainted floral, swirled mold ........ **30**

*Poppy Decorated Toothpick Holder*

**Germany,** two-handled, poppy decoration (ILLUS.) .......................................................... **160**

**Japan,** Geisha girl decoration ........................... **18**

**Nippon,** bulbous base w/two small handles near top rim, handpainted, lots of gold in decoration featuring people ........................... **60**

**Nippon,** large bulbous body w/three ball feet, sailboat decoration ................................. **85**

**Nippon,** short pedestal, handpainted floral decoration along top rim ............................... **24**

**Noritake,** Azalea patt. ...................................... **110**

**Old Ivory,** Selesia, white rose decoration ........ **235**

**R.S. Prussia,** pink & white roses, three handles ................................................................ **220**

*R.S. Prussia Toothpick Holder*

**R.S. Prussia,** Water Lily decor w/two handles (ILLUS.) ................................................ **190**

**Royal Bayreuth,** Rose Tapestry w/two handles & three feet ..................................... **375**

**Royal Bayreuth,** Sunbonnet Babies ironing..... **420**

*Royal Bayreuth Toothpick Holder*

**Royal Bayreuth,** Tapestry, portrait, w/two small handles & four small feet (ILLUS.)...... **395**

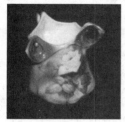

*Royal Bayreuth Toothpick Holder*

**Royal Bayreuth,** three small handles near top rim, floral decoration (ILLUS.) ................ **130**

## GLASS

**Alexis,** Fostoria, clear ........................................ 35
**Amberina,** Daisy Button, three feet................. 145
**Amberina,** Inverted Thumbprint, ring base shape ........................................................... 175
**Arched oval,** green w/gold.............................. 40
**Bellaire,** clear .................................................... 40
**Blazing cornucopia,** two handles, clear w/stained "eyes"................................................ 48
**Brazilian,** Fostoria, clear .................................... 45
**Bulging loops,** blue exterior, white interior...... 160
**Burmese,** art glass, figure mold w/crimped top, handpainted, rare .................................. 425
**Burmese,** art glass, square top, matte finish, handpainted ........................................ 425
**Burmese,** art glass, tri-corner, glossy finish, diamond quilted, very rare .................... 460
**Button Arches,** ruby stained ............................ 18

*Colorado Toothpick Holder*

**Colorado,** cobalt blue, no souvenir (ILLUS.)......................................................... 45
**Croesus,** Riverside, amethyst w/gold ............... 95
**Croesus,** Riverside, green w/gold...................... 95

**Elephant,** "Baby Mine", clear............................. 65
**Elephant head,** w/circus attire, clear................. 65
**Fancy loop,** Heisey, clear w/gold...................... 60
**Fancy loop,** Heisey, green w/gold .................. 190
**Florette,** glossy pink......................................... 130
**Flute,** clear ....................................................... 25
**Flute,** iridized amethyst ...................................... 95
**Flute,** iridized green........................................... 110
**Frog on lily pad,** clear ...................................... 55
**Gaelic,** clear ..................................................... 25

*Heart Toothpick Holder*

**Heart,** pink opaque, hard to find (ILLUS.)........... 90
**Heart band,** ruby stained ................................. 35
**Idyll,** blue opalescent ...................................... 300
**Iris w/meander,** green opalescent .................... 75
**Jefferson Optic,** amethyst w/enamel decoration ................................................................. 55
**Jefferson Optic,** custard.................................... 45
**Minnesota,** three handles, clear........................ 35
**Nearcut,** #2651, Cambridge, clear ................... 38
**Optic Thumbprint,** cranberry............................. 90
**Panelled Thistle,** Higbee, clear ........................ 40
**Pennsylvania,** clear........................................... 45
**Persian,** Fostoria, clear ..................................... 55
**Pleat & Bow,** milk glass w/enamel decoration .................................................................. 45
**Pomona,** fluted top w/filigree trim, first patent ............................................................ 290

*Preparedness Toothpick Holder*

**Preparedness,** clear, men in military uniforms on either side of the holder (ILLUS.)......................................................... 210
**Prince of Wales Plumes,** Heisey, clear........... 150
**Prince of Wales Plumes,** Heisey, ruby stained............................................................. 295
**Priscilla,** clear ................................................... 45
**Punty Band,** Heisey, ruby stained .................... 65
**Ring Band,** Heisey, Ivorina, custard ................. 65

**Royal Ivy,** Northwood, cranberry & vaseline spatter.......................................... 250
**Royal Oak,** Northwood, rubina, cranberry shading to clear, frosted............................. 180
**Saddle Over Barrel,** blue...................................... 65
**Scalloped Six-Point,** Duncan, clear w/gold....... 40
**Scalloped Skirt,** green w/enamel decoration ........................................................... 60
**Shoeshone,** clear.............................................. 35
**Sunbeam,** clear................................................. 40
**Sunbeam,** green ............................................... 65

*Tiffany Toothpick Holder*

**Tiffany,** Knotty Mold (ILLUS.)............................ 300
**Vermont w/Honeycomb,** aka Forget-Me-Not, green w/gold............................................. 65
**Waffle & Star Band,** clear................................... 45
**Waterford,** cut glass........................................... 50
**Windemere's Fan,** decorated black glass ......... 90
**Windemere's Fan,** decorated milk glass ........... 45

## METAL

**Bucket shaped,** open work at top, "Take your (pick axe)"............................................. 34
**Chick & Wishbone,** various versions by many different companies ......................... 25-45
**Silver plate,** bird sitting on rim, ........................ 45
**Silver plate,** dog w/red eyes sitting by holder, Tufts .................................................. 120
**Silver plate,** frog on one side, lizard on the other ...................................................... 65
**Silver plate,** square, two handles, very unusual, hard to find ..................................... 95
**Tacoma,** clear ..................................................... 45

## TOYS

**Airplane,** friction-type, lithographed tin, "Capital Airlines," four-motor, Viscount, Line Mar (Japan)...................................... **$182**
**Airplane,** friction-type, lithographed tin, sky cruiser-type, "Strato Airlines," plastic rudder, four-engine, elevator & motors, Louis Marx & Co., New York, New York (one engine loose) ........................................ 94
**Airplane,** lithographed tin, biplane, wooden cylinders & wheels, clicks & prop turns when pulled, stenciled designs on wings, attributed to Schieble, Z65 (repainted)......... 105
**Airplane,** pressed steel, single-engine monoplane, blue body, orange wings, Wyandotte Toys (Wyandotte, Michigan), 1930s, 18" wingspan, very good condition ................................................................ 197

**Airplane,** pressed steel, single-engine monoplane, Boycraft, all-original, near perfect decals, ca. 1930, 24" l. ..................... 743
**Airplane,** pressed steel, "Tri Motor Mail Plane," wheel-driven propellers, 18" wing span (repainted)................................... 176
**Airplane,** pressed steel, two-motor passenger plane, silver body, red wings, wooden wheels, Wyandotte Toys, 9 1/2" wing span ............................................................ 193
**Army airport tractor,** pressed steel, Tonka Mfg., ca. 1950s, 9" l. .................................... 105
**Army bulldozer,** pressed steel, Tonka Mfg., ca. 1950s, 13" l. ................................... 72
**Army jeep,** pressed steel, Tonka Mfg., ca. 1950s, 10" l. ............................................... 50
**Army troop carrier,** pressed steel, Marx & Co., ca. 1950, 19" l. (no canvas) .................. 33
**Auto race set,** "Mot-O-Run" magnetic highway, electric motor, oval track, toll booth & underpass to New York City, base lithographed w/scenes of a highway, farm, roads, gas station & railroad station, w/five tin vehicles, Louis Marx, copyright 1949, track 27" l., the set (scratches) ......................................................... 115
**Auto service station set,** "Uptown Service Center," lithographed metal w/plastic accessories, original box cover shows complete station w/young boy behind it all on an orange ground w/blue wording, notes in one corner "New 'Clip Lock' Easy Assembly," unused in box, No. 860, ca. 1970s, the set (some wear & damage to box) ............................................. 242
**Automobile,** boat-tailed Cabriolet, windup tin, "#8" on the side, ca. 1930s, 4 1/2" l........ 121

*Friction Action Lincoln Continental*

**Automobile,** Lincoln Continental, friction-type, lithographed tin, red w/silver trim, metal wheels, Japan, 1950s, very good condition, 11" l. (ILLUS.) ............................... 193
**Automobile,** Model A Ford, cast metal, made from hobby kit, Hubley Mfg. Co., 8" l. ....................................................................... 61
**Automobile,** sedan, pressed steel, "Toy Town Sedan," Wyandotte Toys, 21" l. (replacement doors) ...................................... 55

*Large Wyandotte Spring-Driven Auto*

**Automobile,** sedan, spring-driven, pressed steel, the long yellow sedan w/green roof & red-hubbed tires, pull-back spring motor, all original, very good condition, Wyandotte, 13 1/4" l. (ILLUS.)...................... **935**

*Bandai Battery-Operated Volkswagon*

**Automobile,** Volkswagon sedan, battery-operated, lithographed tin, grey w/silver metal trim & black & white tires w/metal hubcaps, Bandai (Japan), ca. 1960, very good condition, 10 1/2" l. (ILLUS.) .............. **110**

**Barn,** wooden, brick design on exterior, Morton E. Converse Co. (stalls gone) ............ **22**

**Battery-operated,** bunny reading while standings & turning pages in book, w/magnet in hand, Japan, 1950s, 8" h. .......... **61**

**Battery-operated,** flying saucer w/astronaut, Japan, 8" d. ........................................ **209**

**Battery-operated,** "Hy-Que the Amazing Monkey," tinplate, rubber & cloth, original box, T.N. (Japan), ca. 1960 (box damaged)...................................................... **219**

**Battery-operated,** "Magic Man," smoking clown in tinplate & cloth, w/controller & packing, w/original box, Marsuan (Japan), ca. 1960 ........................................ **316**

**Battery-operated,** "Professor Owl," tinplate, w/two disks & instructions, original box, Etco (Japan) ........................................ **431**

**Battery-operated,** "Rabbits Carriage (The)," plush grey mother rabbit in red checked skirt pushing a tin baby carriage w/little pink baby, w/original box, Japan, ca. 1950s, very good working order (slight fur discoloration)........................ **99**

**Battery-operated,** Santa Claus sitting on a roof next to a chimney, holds gifts & drums, mint in box...................................... **150**

*Shoe Shine Joe Battery-Operated Toy*

**Battery-operated,** "Shoe Shine Joe," hair-covered monkey-like figure seated polishing shoe & smoking a pipe, mint in original box, Japan, ca. 1950s (ILLUS.) ....... **220**

**Battery-operated,** "Snake Charmer," seated Indian man wearing turbin & playing pipe w/jar & snake in front of him

on the rectangular tin platform, cloth clothing, Line Mar, w/original box ................ **403**

**Battery-operated,** "Squawky the Parrot," tinplate & cloth parrot on a perch, w/tag, packing & original box, Louis Marx, ca. 1960 (wear to toy, box damaged) ................ **173**

**Battery-operated,** "Teddy the Artist," a plastic & cloth bear wearing a plaid jacket seated at a tin table & drawing, w/nine templates, two crayons, sketch book, packing & original box, Yonezawa (Japan), ca. 1960 ........................................ **403**

**Battery-operated,** "Tric-Cycling Clown," tinplate, rubber, plastic & cloth, w/packing & original box, Cragston (Japan), ca. 1960 ........................................................... **374**

**Battery-operated,** "Whistling Spooky Kooky Tree," lithographed tin, tree-trunk form w/plastic moving arms, leaves on top, moving eyes & mouth, Louis Marx, ca. 1960, 14 1/2" h. (some wear) ....... **690**

*Battery-operated Power Yacht*

**Battery-operated boat,** "Phillips 66" power yacht, hard plastic w/red upper decks & roof & white hull & trim, small Phillips sticker near the stern, w/original box w/lid forming marina dock, tear in box lid, takes 2 D-size batteries, ca. 1950s, 17 1/2" l., 5" h. (ILLUS.)................................. **209**

**Bell ringer toy,** cast wheels w/bell between them pulled by a tin horse, brown w/gold trim & red saddle, 5 1/2" l. ......................... **198**

**Bowling set:** 10 pins & 2 balls; wooden, turned design, the set..................................... **28**

**Bus,** friction-type, lithographed tin, sightseeing style, cream w/black striped sections along body, multiple open windows, bullet-form silver roof projections at front & rear, red headlights, rubber tires, lithographed interior, marked "I.Y. Metal Toys - Made in Japan," ca. 1950s, 16 1/2" l. (denting, spotting, scratches & soiling, non-working mechanism) ................ **149**

**Cap pistol,** cast iron, automatic-shape, patent-dated 6-29-09, Champion Hardware Co., 4" l................................................. **66**

**Cap pistol,** cast iron, single shot w/spur trigger cap well on top, 3 1/2" l. ..................... **44**

*Hubley Texan 38 Cap Pistol*

**Cap pistol,** cast metal & plastic, "Texan 38," silvered trigger & barrel, white plastic grips w/embossed black longhorn heads, Hubley, ca. 1950s, very good condition (ILLUS.) ........................................ **110**

**Circus cage wagon,** cast iron, painted in polychrome w/a red cage wagon holding a white polar bear, on yellow wheels, a driver on top & pulled by two white horses without riders, Kenton Hardware, early 20th c., unused in original box, 14" l. ..................................................... **550**

*German Clockwork Limousine*

**Clockwork mechanism,** limousine, lithographed tin, green & black chassis on green metal wheels, hood & doors open, forward, neutral & reverse action, real working pistons, complete, all-original, Moko (Germany), early 20th c., minimal fading, 9 1/2" l. (ILLUS.) ............................. **935**

**Clockwork mechanism,** motorcycle & rider, lithographed tin, driver in red, black motocycle, Germany, complete, works, early ........................................................ **1,100**

**Clockwork mechanism,** roadster, lithographed tin, "7" on side, Marklin (Germany), ca. 1930s, works, 15 1/2" l. (replaced fenders) ................................ **1,210**

**Coaster wagon,** "Peerless No. 400," painted & decorated wood, the pine body w/stenciled & painted decoration, long handle, red disk wheels w/solid rubber tires, Paris Mfg. Co. (South Paris, Maine), early 20th c., body 36" l ................. **173**

**Drum,** child's size, embossed tin w/eagle & banner in red, gold & blue japanning, wooden bands around sides, 10" d., 7 3/4" h. (heads damaged) ......................... **440**

**Drum,** child's size, tin, decorated w/flags in red, white, blue & gold-stenciled japanning, wooden bands, 6" d., 5 1/4" h. (heads worn) .............................................. **275**

**Earthmover,** pressed steel, Structo Mfg. Co., ca. 1590s, 17" l. (repainted) ................... **50**

**Erector set,** No. 8, w/locomotive parts, shovel, electric motor & instruction books, in wood case w/color lithographed label in lid, early 20th c., the set (rust, bending, other wear) ...................... **1,093**

**Farm set,** die-cast metal, African "Farm No. 1398," comprised of two mounted elephants, various European & native workers, horses, cattle, poultry, trees, fencing & hut, in original box w/cover, Heyde Miniatures (Dresden, Germany), 20th c., the set (incomplete, electrical tape on box) .................................................... **1,725**

**Farm yard set,** chromolithographed pressed cardboard, a house, family, animals & trees, No. 744/2, Herolin (Ger-

many), early 20th c., in maker's box w/label, box 12 3/4" w., the set (box bottom missing part of rim) ............................... **173**

**Fire ladder truck,** pressed steel, Smith-Miller Toy Co., ca. 1590s, 36" l. ................... **495**

**G.I. Joe doll,** "G.I. Joe Action Soldier," black hair, blue eyes, green fatigues w/button accents, green plastic cap, brown boots, metal dog tag, Army Manual, Boot Instructions, Gear & Equipment Manual, two sticker insignia sheets, G.I. Joe Club folder (snap on shirt loose, box & papers discolored) ........... **127**

**Kitchen stove,** electric, chrome & cream enamel, oven & two burners, Lionel, 11 1/2 x 25", 33" h. ................................... **1,093**

**Machinery hauler,** pressed steel, Structo Mfg. Co., ca. 1950, 13" l. .............................. **55**

**Marionette,** rabbit, rubber head, feet & hands, wearing skirt & long-sleeved blouse, ca. 1950 (skirt w/some holes) ........... **17**

**Military police outfit,** plastic, model of a Trooper, pistol, billy club, whistle, belt & holster & arm band, Carnell Mfg. Co., ca. 1950, near mint in original box ..................... **165**

*Old Cast Iron Motorcycle*

**Motorcycle,** cast iron w/rubber tires, driver in uniform, painted orange w/"Patrol" embossed on the side, worn paint, rust spotting, 6 1/2" l. (ILLUS.) ........................... **182**

*Tonka Allied Van Lines Truck*

**Moving van,** pressed steel, orange cab & trailer marked "Allied Van Lines" in black & white, ca. 1950s - 60s, Tonka (ILLUS.)..... **303**

*Pedal Fire Ladder Truck*

**Pedal vehicle,** pressed steel, hook & ladder fire truck, painted red & white, bell on hood & battery-operated headlight, AMF, 1950s, ladders missing, overall excellent (ILLUS.) ........................................................ **858**

**Penny toy,** lithographed tin, single yellow horse pulling a shell-form two-wheeled chariot, Germany, early 20th c., 5 1/4" l. (paint wear) .................................................. **242**

**Pile driver,** "Panama Pile Driver," pressed steel, gravity toy, w/falling ball-operated driver, patent-dated in December 1905, w/seven clay balls, Wolverine, 15 1/2" h. (paint flaking) ........................................... **230**

**Pop-up toy,** cowboy & horse, wooden jointed figures on wood block base, collapses when bottom is pressed ..................... **28**

**Pull toy,** horse & cart, painted wood, a silhouetted horse on small front wheel & w/hinged rear legs painted in original white & black w/red, black & green detail, pulling a cart w/canted sides nailed to the axle w/large spoked wheels, branded mark "Made by the S.A. Smith Mfg. Co. Battleboro, Vt. U.S.A.," first half 20th c., 20 1/2" l. (cart renailed to axle, corner of cart damaged) ................. **275**

**Pull toy,** horse on wheels, wood & composition, the standing animal w/a brown hair cloth covering, tack eyes & old colorful harness, on a narrow rectangular wood platform on tiny metal wheels, roach fur mane & bristle tail possibly old replacements, 19th c., 12 1/4" h.................. **220**

**Pull toy,** horse, papier-maché & wood, mounted on platform w/tiny tin wheels, late 19th - early 20th c., 8" l., 10" h. ............. **193**

**Pull toy,** lamb on platform, lambskin coat w/wool pile fabric face & glass eyes, loud "baa" when head is pressed down, on a narrow, thin green-painted rectangular wood platform w/tiny cast-iron wheels, 19th c., 16" l., 13 7/8" h. (felt damage on body, wool pile around left eye & upper fore legs).............................. **1,840**

**Pull toy,** lithographed tin, four men riding beams, up & down movement from cammed axle, Germany, early 20th c., 10" l. ...................................................... **193**

**Puzzle,** jigsaw-type, "A Chip of the Old Block," Johnward Dunsmore, 300 pcs., 1933 ......................................................... **20-30**

**Puzzle,** jigsaw-type, "A Council of War," Gordon Coutts, 280 pcs., 1940 ................. **20-40**

**Puzzle,** jigsaw-type, "A Matter of State," Clyde De Land, 300 pcs., 1933................. **20-30**

**Puzzle,** jigsaw-type, "A Ticklish Operation," R. James Stuart, 165 pcs., 1957...... **20-30**

**Puzzle,** jigsaw-type, "Advance Guard," Charles Russell, 252 pcs., 1936 .............. **35-40**

**Puzzle,** jigsaw-type, "An Interrupted Experiment," 320 pcs., 1955 ............................ **20-30**

**Puzzle,** jigsaw-type, "Artistic Bouquet," H. Dudley Murphy, 378 pcs., 1951 .................. **5-15**

**Puzzle,** jigsaw-type, "At Close of Day," G.B. Fox, 320 pcs., 1948.................................... **35-40**

**Puzzle,** jigsaw-type, "At Twilight," Frank Harper, 252 pcs., 1938.............................. **20-30**

**Puzzle,** jigsaw-type, "Bears," Joseph F. Kernan, 320 pcs., 1955 ............................. **35-40**

**Puzzle,** jigsaw-type, "Buffalo Hunt," Frederic Remington, 300 pcs., 1933 ............. **35-40**

**Puzzle,** jigsaw-type, "Canyon Sunrise," Stanley Walker, 378 pcs., 1937 ................. **5-15**

**Puzzle,** jigsaw-type, "Chums," Jane Freeman, 396 pcs., 1951.............................. **20-30**

**Puzzle,** jigsaw-type, "Collected From Rainbow's Rim," Hy Whitroy, 378 pcs., 1938 ..... **5-15**

**Puzzle,** jigsaw-type, "Colonial Days in Virginia," Charles M. Reylea, 357 pcs., 1933 ..................................................... **20-30**

**Puzzle,** jigsaw-type, "Come on Up," Leon Lippert, 192 pcs., 1933...................... **20-30**

**Puzzle,** jigsaw-type, "Cottage By the Bridge," Harry Hadland, 280 pcs., 1950...... **5-15**

**Puzzle,** jigsaw-type, "Country Vista," Walter M. Thompson, 252 pcs., 1939..................... **5-15**

**Puzzle,** jigsaw-type, "Dinner for Six," Mabel Rollins Harris, 378 pcs., 1934 ................... **20-30**

**Puzzle,** jigsaw-type, "Doctors of Science," Harold Mott-Smith, 300 pcs., 1933............ **20-30**

**Puzzle,** jigsaw-type, "Dreams Come True," Stanley Walker, 140 pcs., 1940 ................. **5-15**

*"Electric Ship" Puzzle*

**Puzzle,** jigsaw-type, "Electric Ship," Walter Greene, 300 pcs., 1933 (ILLUS.) ............... **5-15**

*"Fair Treasures" Puzzle*

**Puzzle,** jigsaw-type, "Fair Treasures," Charles M. Relyea, 120 pcs., 1933 (ILLUS). .................................................... **35-40**

**Puzzle,** jigsaw-type, "Farm Workers," Anthony Cucchi, 2562 pcs., 1943 ............. **20-30**

**Puzzle,** jigsaw-type, "Fire in the Barnyard," Thomas Hart Benton, 304 pcs., 1949 ....... **35-40**

*"Flushed" Puzzle*

**Puzzle,** jigsaw-type, "Flushed," Arthur Tait, 252 pcs., 1938 (ILLUS.) ........................... **20-30**

**Puzzle,** jigsaw-type, "Found," Edward Eggleston, 140 pcs., 1938 ............................... **20-30**

**Puzzle,** jigsaw-type, "Golden Galleon," Frederic Grant, 168 pcs., 1936 ........................ **5-15**

**Puzzle,** jigsaw-type, "Good Company," Donald Teague, 304 pcs., 1956 ............... **20-30**

*"Green River Buttes" Puzzle*

**Puzzle,** jigsaw-type, "Green River Buttes," Dey Deribcowsky, 400 pcs., 1937 (ILLUS.)...................................................... **5-15**

**Puzzle,** jigsaw-type, "Guardians All," H.H. Walters, 252 pcs., 1940 ........................... **35-40**

**Puzzle,** jigsaw-type, "Guardians of Freedom," Robert Skemp, 378 pcs., 1940 ....... **35-40**

**Puzzle,** jigsaw-type, "Hooking a Big One," Charles M. Reylea, 120 pcs., 1933 .......... **35-40**

**Puzzle,** jigsaw-type, "Hunter's Paradise," R. Atkinson Fox, 357 pcs., 1933 ............... **75-85**

**Puzzle,** "Hunting Pals," Anthony Cucci, 300 pcs., 1941 ................. **20-30**

**Puzzle,** jigsaw-type, "Hydro Project," Walter Greene, 300 pcs., 1933 .................. **5-15**

*"In Conference" Puzzle*

**Puzzle,** jigsaw-type, "In Conference," Ray Morgan, 216 pcs., 1933 (ILLUS.) .............. **35-40**

**Puzzle,** jigsaw-type, "Indian Summer," William Chandler, 168 pcs., 1936 ..................... **5-15**

**Puzzle,** jigsaw-type, "Jack Ashore," Henry Bacon, 300 pcs., 1933 ............................. **20-30**

**Puzzle,** jigsaw-type, "Keeping the Tryst," Frank Harper, 300 pcs., 1933 ................... **35-40**

**Puzzle,** jigsaw-type, "Lazy River," Federic Mizen, 252 pcs., 1950 ................................ **5-15**

**Puzzle,** jigsaw-type, "Let Me At 'Em," R. James Stuart, 378 pcs., 1942 .................. **35-40**

**Puzzle,** jigsaw-type, "Main Street," M. DeV. Lee, 252 pcs., 1949.................................. **35-40**

**Puzzle,** jigsaw-type, "Menace of the Air," Lynn Bogue Hunt, 165 pcs., 1933............. **20-30**

**Puzzle,** jigsaw-type, "Mother Love," Gene Pressler, 125 pcs., 1933 ......................... **50-60**

*"Mountain Chief" Puzzle*

**Puzzle,** jigsaw-type, "Mountain Chief," W. Langdon Kihn, 252 pcs., 1938 (ILLUS.) .... **20-30**

**Puzzle,** jigsaw-type, "Mountain Hues," Robert Wood, 378 pcs., 1937 ........................... **5-15**

**Puzzle,** jigsaw-type, "Mt. Moran," May Ferris Smith, 140 pcs., 1940.............................. **5-15**

**Puzzle,** jigsaw-type, "Nature's Power," Henry Lewis, 140 pcs., 1939................. **5-15**

**Puzzle,** jigsaw-type, "New England Winter Scene," George Durrie, 304 pcs., 1947 ...... **5-15**

**Puzzle,** jigsaw-type, "New World," John Newton Howitt, 280 pcs., 1948 ................ **20-30**

**Puzzle,** jigsaw-type, "No Time to Waste," Harold Anderson, 204 pcs., 1951............. **20-30**

**Puzzle,** jigsaw-type, "Off for the West," Wallace Robinson, 280 pcs., 1940.............. **5-15**

**Puzzle,** jigsaw-type, "Old Fashioned Garden," William M. Thompson, 252 pcs., 1939 ......................................................... **5-15**

**Puzzle,** jigsaw-type, "Part of Heart's Desire," R. Atkinson Fox, 209 pcs., 1933.. **75-85**

*"Radiant as a Rose" Puzzle*

Puzzle, jigsaw-type, "Radiant as a Rose," Arthur Frahm, 204 pcs., 1954 (ILLUS.) ..... **20-30**
Puzzle, jigsaw-type, "Red Demon of the Forest," Philip Goodwin, 465 pcs., 1933 .. **75-85**

*"Remembrance" Puzzle*

Puzzle, jigsaw-type, "Remembrance," Carle Blenner, 204 pcs., 1937 (ILLUS.) ...... **5-15**
Puzzle, jigsaw-type, "Seven New Playmates," Joseph F. Kernan, 280 pcs., 1948 ......................................................... **35-40**
Puzzle, jigsaw-type, "Slaking Their Thirst Together," Belmore Browne, 529 pcs., 1951 ......................................................... **20-30**
Puzzle, jigsaw-type, "Spanish Dancer," Edward Eggleston, 140 pcs., 1940 ........... **35-40**

*"Spirit of the U.S.A." Puzzle*

Puzzle, jigsaw-type, "Spirit of the U.S.A.," Harold Anderson, 376 pcs., 1941 (ILLUS.) ...................................................... **35-40**
Puzzle, jigsaw-type, "Springtime," George Ames Aldrich, 220 pcs., 1933 ..................... **5-15**
Puzzle, jigsaw-type, "Star Light-Star Bright," R. James Stuart, 378 pcs., 1943 .. **35-40**
Puzzle, jigsaw-type, "Starlight Trail," Walter Haskell Hinton, 252 pcs., 1941 ................. **20-30**
Puzzle, jigsaw-type, "Summer Pleasures," Annie Benson Muller, 252 pcs., 1937 ....... **20-30**
Puzzle, jigsaw-type, "Sunday Solo," Harold Anderson, 252 pcs., 1951 ......................... **20-30**
Puzzle, jigsaw-type, "Sunshine and Shadows," Rudolph Weber, 300 pcs., 1933 ........ **5-15**

Puzzle, jigsaw-type, "Surprise Attack," Anthony Cucchi, 280 pcs., 1951 ............... **20-30**
Puzzle, jigsaw-type, "Sweethearts," Mabel Rollins Harris, 262 pcs., 1937 ................... **20-30**
Puzzle, jigsaw-type, "Tender Care," Frank Van Vreeland, 308 pcs., 1933..................... **5-15**
Puzzle, jigsaw-type, "Thatch-Roofed Cottage," Aston Knight, 252 pcs., 1949 ............ **5-15**

*"The Bell's First Note" Puzzle*

Puzzle, jigsaw-type, "The Bell's First Note," J.L.G. Ferris, 465 pcs., 1936 (ILLUS.) ...... **20-30**
Puzzle, jigsaw-type, "The Critics," Charlie Dye, 437 pcs., 1952 ................................. **20-30**
Puzzle, jigsaw-type, "The Foundling," Hy Hintermeister, 378 pcs., 1939 ..................... **5-15**

*"The Little Rogue" Puzzle*

Puzzle, jigsaw-type, "The Little Rogue," Maud Tousey Fangel, 300 pcs., 1933 (ILLUS.)..................................................... **20-30**
Puzzle, jigsaw-type, "The Pack Train," Phillip Goodwin, 252 pcs., 1937 ...................... **75-85**
Puzzle, jigsaw-type, "The Part O' Heart's Desire," George McCord, 120 pcs., 1933.... **5-15**
Puzzle, jigsaw-type, "The Ship that Sank in Victory-1779," 465 pcs., 1936 .................. **20-30**
Puzzle, jigsaw-type, "The Touchdown," Hy Hintermeister, 252 pcs., 1937 ................... **20-30**
Puzzle, jigsaw-type, "Thoroughbreds," Gustave Muss-Arnolt, 378 pcs., 1937 ....... **35-40**
Puzzle, jigsaw-type, "Threesome," Frances Tipton Hunter, 378 pcs., 1950.................. **20-30**
Puzzle, jigsaw-type, "Time to Look," Emmett Watson, 378 pcs., 1954 ............... **20-30**
Puzzle, jigsaw-type, "To the Rescue," Walter Wilwerding, 378 pcs., 1940............ **20-30**
Puzzle, jigsaw-type, "Trophy of the Hunt," J.L.G. Ferris, 465 pcs., 1936..................... **20-30**
Puzzle, jigsaw-type, "Trouble on the Trail," Frank Hoffman, 378 pcs., 1938................. **20-30**

*"Twixt Love and Duty" Puzzle*

**Puzzle,** jigsaw-type, "Twixt Love and Duty," Jack Wittrup, 252 pcs., 1948 (ILLUS.) ...... **20-30**
**Puzzle,** jigsaw-type, "Two Friends," Adam Styka, 304 pcs., 1952............................... **20-30**
**Puzzle,** jigsaw-type, "Unfinished Painting," 378 pcs., 1942........................................... **5-15**

*"Well-Hooked" Puzzle*

**Puzzle,** jigsaw-type, "Well-Hooked," William Harnden Foster, 336 pcs., 1933 (ILLUS.).................................................. **20-30**
**Puzzle,** jigsaw-type, "Western Paradise," F. Grayson Sayre, 252 pcs., 1951.................. **5-15**
**Puzzle,** jigsaw-type, "Westward Ho," Arthur Frahm, 252 pcs., 1950 ............................ **20-30**
**Puzzle,** jigsaw-type, "Winning of the West," Frank Tenney Johnson, 375 pcs., 1939.... **20-30**
**Riding toy,** pony, brown & white plush, standing on four-wheel platform, steering handle, ca, 1950s, 18" l., 20" h.............. **121**

*Attacking Martian Robot*

**Robot,** battery-operated, "Attacking Martian," lithographed tin, black body & red feet w/printed controls on front, ca. 1950s, excellent condition, 11 3/4" h. (ILLUS.)....................................................... **148**

*Cragston's Mr. Robot Toy*

**Robot,** battery-operated, "Mr. Robot," lithographed tin w/clear plastic dome head w/red bubbles, red body w/black arms & controls on front, Cragston (Japan), near mint w/original cardboard headguard, original box w/minor damage, ca. 1950s (ILLUS.)...................................................... **1,155**
**Soldier,** painted wood, tin soldier-style standing on spindle, painted face & uniform w/tall black hat, William Doepke Mfg. Co........................................................ **22**
**Soldier set,** die-cast metal, including machine gunners, grenade thrower, pilot, doctor, nurse, stretcher bearers, casualty, soldiers in gas masks, two tents, Manoil, ca. 1930s, 22 pcs.................. **546**
**Soldiers,** cast lead, painted flat cast, some mounted, label on oval box says "No. 110 1/8, 10 stick pcs.," "Preussische Infanterie im Marsch" (Prussian Infantry Marching), made in Germany, the set............ **33**
**Soldiers,** die-cast metal, "American Infantry Marching 12th Regt. No. 169," comprising mounted officer, marching officer, standard bearer, drummer & eightteen infantrymen, Heyde Miniatures, in original box, 20th c., the set (box taped)............. **431**
**Tractor,** cast metal, "John Deere 4WD 8960 Limited Edition-Sept. '88, 1/2000," Ertl Toy Co., 16" l. ........................................ **138**
**Tractor,** cast metal, John Deere 8010 diesel 4wd custom, Ertl Toy Co., 15" l. ............. **215**

*Eska John Deere Tractor*

**Tractor,** pressed steel, John Deere model, green w/yellow trim & black rubber tires,

Eska, ca. 1950s, mint toy w/excellent original box (ILLUS.) .................... **787**

**Train accessory,** Lionel No. 124A railway station, tinplate w/two exterior & one interior light, grey base, two card arrivals signs (one sign replaced) ........................... **288**

*Train Street Light*

**Train accessory,** street light, Lionel Lines, double bulb, painted dark green, 1929, 9" (ILLUS.) ........................ **65**

**Train boxcar,** Lionel Lines, New York Central, No. 6464-125, 1954-56 ....................... **150**

**Train caboose,** Lionel Lines, No. 517, std. gauge, 1927-40 .......................................... **100**

*Lionel Double Roll Cable Car*

**Train car,** double roll cable car on flat bed, orange rolls tied down, grey body flat car, Lionel Lines #6561, 1950s (ILLUS.) ...... **100**

**Train cattle car,** Lionel No. 513, Standard gauge, 1927-38 .......................................... **175**

*Lionel Work Crane Car*

**Train crane car,** Lionel Lines, #6560, red w/smoke stack & control wheel on back, black crane arm w/large hook at end, 1950s-60s (ILLUS.) ..................................... **100**

**Train engine,** Lionel Lines 0-4-0 locomotive, No. 1061, 1963-64, 1969...................... **40**

**Train engine,** Lionel Lines 2-4-2 locomotive, No. 390/390E, Standard gauge, 1929-33....................................................... **800**

**Train engine,** Lionel Lines 2-6-4 locomotive, No. 2037, 1953-64............................... **125**

**Train engine,** Lionel Lines 4-6-4 locomotive, No. 2055, 1953-56............................... **225**

*Pennsylvania GG-1 Engine Car*

**Train engine,** Lionel Lines, Pennsylvania GG-1 locomotive, No. 18313, 1996 (ILLUS.) ....................................................... **375**

**Train engine,** Lionel Lines, Pennsylvania GG-1 locomotive, No. 2332, 1947-49 ......... **900**

*Lionel Locomotive & Coal Tender*

**Train engine & coal tender,** Lionel Lines, Locomotive No. 224E w/coal tender, 2-6-2 wheels, both black, 1940-1942 (ILLUS.)..... **400**

**Train engine & tender,** Lionel No. 384 (B) Standard guage 2-4-0 locomotive & No. 384-T tender, tinplate w/green lining (some retouching to tender top rail) ............ **633**

**Train engines,** Lionel Lines, Union Pacific GP-9 powered & dummy locomotives, No. 11956, 1997, the set ............................ **500**

*Lionel Lines Flatcar*

**Train flatcar,** w/pipes, Lionel Lines No. 6511, 1953-56 (ILLUS.)................................. **35**

**Train gondola car,** Lionel Lines, No. 212, Standard gauge, 1926-40 ........................... **175**

**Train handcar,** Lionel Lines, Mickey & Minnie Mouse, No. 1100, "O" gauge, 1935-37 ............................................................... **1,000**

**Train hopper,** Lionel Lines, No. 216, std. gauge, 1926-38 .......................................... **400**

*Republican Party Observation Car*

**Train observation car,** Lionel Lines, George Bush Whistle Stop, made for Republican Party campaign workers, uncatalogued 1992 (ILLUS.) ..................... **3,500**

**Train operating bascule bridge,** Lionel Lines, No. 313, 1946-49.............................. **550**

**Train operating crossing gate,** Lionel Lines, No. 77/077, "O" gauge, 1923-35.......... **50**

**Train operating gateman,** Lionel Lines, No. 145, 1950-66 ......................................... **550**

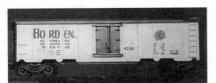

*Borden's Milk Car*

**Train operating milk car,** w/platform, Lionel Lines, Borden's, No. 9220, 1983-86 (ILLUS.)................................................ **125**

*Canada Confederation Train Engine*

**Train set,** Canada Confederation, Limited Edition HO set, engine white w/red stripes, marked "Canada—The Confederation Flyer" w/red Canadian maple leaf, 12 cars in set: engine, caboose & 10 cars representing each of the Canadian provinces, 1970s, rare (ILLUS. of engine only).............................................. **800**

**Train set,** Ives Standard gauge passenger set, includes motor No. 3236 locomotive in green, No. 184 Pullman club car & No. 186 observation cars in tan, the set (chips & scratches especially on cars)......... **575**

**Train set,** Ives Standard gauge passenger set, including No. 3241 NYC & HR electric locomotive, No. 184 buffet car & No. 186 observation car, finished in green, the set (roofs repainted, touch-ups on all pieces).......................................................... **288**

**Train set,** Lionel No. 294 outfit, electric, "O" gauge, all cars & transformer in original boxes, all very good condition, early 20th c., the set ...................................................... **935**

**Train set,** Lionel O-gauge Outfit No. 92, electric 152 New York Central 0-4-0 locomotive, 629 Pullman car, 630 observation carriages, No. 57 lamp post, No. 58 lamp post, No. 68 crossing sign, No. 89 flag pole, instructions & quantity of track, the set.............................................. **230**

**Train tank car,** Lionel Lines, No. 815, "O" gauge, 1926-42 ........................................... **100**

*Lionel Transformer Type ZW*

**Train transformer,** Lionel Lines, type ZW, 275 watts, handles four trains & whistles, 1948 (ILLUS.)............................................. **350**

**Truck,** cement mixer, pressed steel, Tonka Mfg., ca. 1950s, 15" l.................................... **127**

**Truck,** dump & plow, pressed steel, State Hi-Way Dept. truck, Tonka Mfg., ca. 1950s, 16" l. ...................................... **352**

**Truck,** dump, pressed steel, highway maintenance truck, Buddy L, 14" l. ................ **110**

**Truck,** dump, pressed steel, Mack, dark red paint, open cab w/lever action dump for back, metal tires w/hard rubber rims, worn Mack truck decal, Steelcraft, ca. 1930s, 25 1/2" l., 10 1/2" h. (paint loss, scratches)...................................................... **440**

*Smith Miller Dump Truck*

**Truck,** dump, pressed steel, reddish orange cab & dump box w/original decals, black rubber tires, Smith-Miller, ca. 1950s, all-original, very good condition (ILLUS.) ........................................ **330**

**Truck,** dump-type, cast iron, finished in greenish grey, Mack-style front, C-cab, driver, red spoked metal wheels, spring-operated bed w/swinging tailgate, possibly by Dent, ca. 1920s, 7" l. (paint loss) ....... **316**

**Truck,** dump-type, pressed steel, finished in black w/red chassis & wheels, open cab, front steering, decal on dashboard, hinged tailgate, Buddy L No. 201, ca. 1930s, 25" l. (lacks chain to winch, some scratches)................................................. **1,150**

*Cragston Gasoline Tanker Truck*

**Truck,** gasoline tanker, friction-type, pressed steel, yellow & red w/black rubber tires, "Shell" printed on the tanker, Cragston (Japan), ca. 1950s, w/original box, toy 6" l. (ILLUS.) ................................... **165**

*Walgreen's Ice Cream Truck by Marx*

**Truck,** ice cream delivery semi-truck & trailer, stamped steel, creamy white ground printed in blue on trailer "Walgreen's Ice Cream - Fresh Flavorful Delicious - It Tastes Better - Coast to Coast," the cab w/open windows & black grill printed w/"Walgreen Drug Co.," hard rubber wheels, rear door opens, Marx Toys, some rust spotting, scratches & soiling, 19 3/4" l. (ILLUS.)............................ 330

**Truck,** low-boy type, pressed steel, "Coast to Coast" on sides, Marx, ca. 1950, 25" l...... 110

**Truck,** machinery moving-type, pressed steel in black, red, yellow & silver, side labeled "Machinery Equipment Service" w/traversing crane, plastic motor & two wooden crates, w/original cardboard box marked "Machinery Moving Truck...," Marx, 1950s, 22" l. (truck w/rust & discoloration, box taped & water-stained)......... 173

**Truck,** oil tanker, tin friction-type, open cab, squatty oval tank marked "Dan-Dee Oil Truck," all-metal wheels, marked "J. Chein & Co. - Made in U.S.A.," 9" l. (paint chips, rust spotting, denting, scratches & soiling) ..................................... 413

**Wagon,** coaster-type, painted wood & steel, the low-sided rectangular bed w/old worn red & green paint w/"Pioneer" stenciled in small yellow letters, long hinged wooden handle w/steel grip & hinge, small wooden-spoked front wheels & larger rear wheels, late 19th - early 20th c., bed 34" l................................. 715

*Windup Celluloid Drummer Boy*

**Windup celluloid "Drummer Boy,"** boy wearing a pink hat & outfit, drum at front, w/original box, Japan, 10" h. (ILLUS.).......... 660

**Windup tin,** "Balky Mule," a cut-out colorful mule pulls a two-wheeled cart w/driver, Marx, w/original box, 8 3/8" l. (minor wear) ............................................................. 275

**Windup tin,** boy riding tricycle, Unique Art, runs, 9" h. (some paint missing across mouth & on stomach) ................................... 138

**Windup tin,** bus, "Inter-State Bus," double-decker, lithographed primarily in orange & yellow, right-hand driver, open top deck, rear staircase, metal wheels, model 109, Strauss, 10 1/2" l. (some scratches)................................................... 805

**Windup tin,** "Circus Monkey," tin monkey covered w/mohair & felt, Bestmaid,

Japan, w/original box, ca. 1950s, 4 5/8" h. ................................................................ 110

**Windup tin,** delivery wagon, "New Milk Wagon & Horse," lithographed tin w/closed wagon on metal wheels pulled by a brown horse, side of wagon reads "Toyland's Farm Products - Milk & Cream," original box, Louis Marx, toy 10 1/4" l. (slight wear to box & one flap detached) ............................................................ 489

**Windup tin,** "Sky Rangers," lithographed in color w/a monoplane & naval dirigible at opposite ends of a long bar atop a lighthouse & circling it when wound, dirigible & lighthouse decorated w/scenes of sailors, Unique, w/original box, 10" h. (scratches to toy, water stains on box)......... 345

**Windup tin,** "Zippo - The Climbing Monkey," colorful monkey figure climbs string, Louis Marx, original box, 9 1/4" h. (minor wear) ........................................................ 193

**Windup tin bus,** "Greyhound," dark blue horizontally ribbed body w/silver greyhound logo, movable front wheels, ca.1950s, Keystone Mfg. Co. (Boston, Massachusetts), 18" l. (some spotting, scratches & soiling) ...................... 358

**Windup tin "Kiddy Cyclist,"** boy on a tricycle, Unique Art Mfg. Co., ca. 1930s.......... 165

*Rodeo Joe Windup Toy*

**Windup tin "Rodeo Joe,"** color lithographed, cowboy driving a jalopy, Unique Art Mfg. Co. (New York, New York), complete, very good condition (ILLUS.)...................................................... 187

# WOODEN TOYS

*From the 1870s to the turn of the century, lithograph paper on wood blocks, pull toys & skill games were produced primarily by U.S. toy makers Rufus Bliss, Whitney S. Reed, Morton Converse, Milton Bradley & McLoughlin Brothers. For over 60 years, from the 1870s to 1935, Albert Schoenhut, a German emigrant from Philadelphia, produced toys for the American market, first specializing in toy pianos & later dolls, doll house furniture & dollhouses, wood-jointed circus, farm & comic figures, target games, advertising premiums & Rolly Dollies. From 1919-32, Schoenhut produced promotional replications of horse-drawn dairy wagons, including Sheffield, Hood & Alderney which were offered as premiums by those companies. In 1903 Albert*

Schoenhut purchased the invention of Fritz Mei-
necke, which included strung wood-jointed clowns,
animals & other circus figures including ringmaster,
animal tamer, circus strong man & acrobats. He
soon introduced tents, cages & wagons. By 1909
there were over 35 animals, 29 circus performers &
40 plus items of circus paraphernalia. Many posable figures had slotted hands & feet. Schoenhut's
trade name (Rolly Pollys) were for bottom weighted
painted composition figures that popped back up
when knocked down. Schoenhut also produced a
full line of these comic, clown & Santa Claus figurals from the 1890s to 1910. Schoenhut produced
Teddy Roosevelt "Adventures in Africa Series," a
lavish limited edition set, in 1910 to commemorate
the ex-26th president's triumphal return from an
African safari. Some of the wild animals from the
Humpty Dumpty circus were interchangeable,
although the scarce Gorilla & Zebu were introduced
in this series. Miscellaneous comic character doll
figures were made of wood & composition, wood or
ball-jointed posable figures. Skill games were
widely popular in the early 1900s & many were produced by German makers of papier-maché & wood.

# WOODEN TOYS

## ALBERT SCHOENHUT -TOY MAKER

### SCHOENHUT ADVERTISING TOYS
**Wagon,** advertisement type, Alderney
Dairy, painted wood, replication of actual
working dairy wagon, logos on side panels, pulled by dappled white horse on
small wheeled platform, 1929-32,
11 1/2" h. x 12" l. ...................................... 3,500
**Wagon,** advertisement type, Hood's Grade
"A" Milk, logos on side panels, white
horse on wheeled platform, 1929-31,
12" l. x 12 1/2" h. ...................................... 3,500
**Wagon,** advertisement type, Sheffield
Dairy, logos on sides, horse on wheeled
platform, 1929-32, 12" l x 12 1/2" h. .......... 3,500
**Wagon driver,** advertisement type, separate figures from wagon set, 7 1/2" h. .......... 750

### SCHOENHUT CIRCUS FIGURES

*Lion in Cage Wagon*

**Alligator,** glass eyes, Style I, 7" l. .................... 650
**Alligator,** hand-painted eyes, 12" l. .................. 400
**Arabian camel,** glass eyes, Style II w/open
mouth, ca. 1910-20 ...................................... 400

**Baby elephant,** wood w/cloth ears,
3" h. x 3 3/4" l. ............................................. 700
**Bactrian camel,** glass eyes, ca. 1910-20,
7" l. ............................................................. 850
**Buffalo,** painted eyes, Style IV w/molded
head, 8" l. .................................................... 800
**Cage wagon,** wooden cage on wheels
w/jointed wood lion (ILLUS.) ...................... 3,500

*"Humpty Dumpty Circus Bandwagon"*

**Circus bandwagon,** "Humpty Dumpty Circus Bandwagon," embossed wood, w/six
bandsmen, driver, pair of horses on
wheeled platform, donkey drawn clown
in chariot (ILLUS.) ....................................... 5,500
**Deer,** painted eyes, 6 1/2" l. ............................ 550
**Donkey w/blanket,** glass eyes, ca. 1910-
20, 9 1/2" l. .................................................. 250
**Elephant w/blanket,** glass eyes, ca. 1910-
20, 9" l. ....................................................... 250
**Gazelle,** (ILLUS. w/Lion, below) ................. 1,800
**Giraffe,** glass eyes, Style II w/closed
mouth, 1910, 11" h. ...................................... 450
**Hippopotamus,** glass eyes, one piece
head & neck, Style II, 9 1/2" l. ...................... 850
**Hippopotamus,** (ILLUS. w/Lion, below).......... 850
**Leopard,** glass eyes, Style I, ca. 1910, 7" l. ..... 650

*Circus Lion, Rhino, Gazelle & Hippo*

**Lion,** (ILLUS.) .................................................. 500
**Lion,** painted eyes, 1910, 8" w. ....................... 500
**Ostrich,** painted eyes, Style III w/flat-sided
head, 9 1/2" ................................................. 450
**Play set,** "Humpty Dumpty Circus," small
tent economy version which was offered
w/five or six basic figures ............................ 1,200
**Play set,** "Humpty Dumpty Circus," tent
w/cloth backdrops & grouping of circus
animals & performers ................................... 7,500
**Polar bear,** glass eyes, Style I, 8" l. .............. 1,700
**Reindeer,** wood w/leather antlers, glass
eyes, 7" sq..................................................... 600
**Rhino,** (ILLUS w/Lion, above) ......................... 550
**Tiger,** glass eyes, Style I, 1910, 7 1/2" l. .......... 550
**Wolf,** painted eyes, 7" l. .................................. 650
**Zebra,** glass eyes, 8" l. .................................... 750

## SCHOENHUT FARM & COMIC FIGURES & ANIMALS
**Barney Google & Spark Plug,** comic strip
characters, wood w/cloth outfit & blan-
ket, the pair (ILLUS.) .................................. 1,500

*Barney Google & Spark Plug*

**Bulldog,** leather tail, collar & ears, painted eyes, brindle color, 3 3/4" h. x 6 1/4" l. .......... **550**
**Bulldog,** leather tail & ears, painted eyes, white, 3 3/4" h. x 6 1/4" l. ............................. **475**
**Cat,** wood, painted eyes, ca. 1910-20, 5 1/2" l. .......................................... **950**
**Dutch couple Jolly Jiggers,** papier-maché & wood, w/cloth outfits, couple suspended on hooks dance on platform when board is compressed, 16" h. x 21" l. ........................................... **5,500**
**Farmer,** molded face w/wooden rake, 8" h. ....... **600**
**Goose,** painted eyes, Style I, 1910, 6 1/2" h. ...................................................... **450**
**Lamb (Mary's),** glass eyes, Style I, tiny bell on collar, 8" h. ............................................ **400**

*Maggie & Jiggs*

**Maggie & Jiggs,** comic strip figures, wood w/cloth outfits, Maggie has rolling pin, Jiggs has bucket of corned beef, the pair (ILLUS.) .................................................... **1,200**
**Mary,** Style I w/two-part head, original clothing, 8" h. .................................................. **650**

*Mary & Lamb*

**Mary & lamb,** w/wood feed crib (ILLUS.) ...... **1,400**
**Pig,** glass eyes, ball-jointed neck, Style I, 7" l. ............................................................. **700**
**Poodle,** glass eyes, cloth ruffle collar, Style II, 8" l. ...................................................... **450**

## SCHOENHUT ROLLY DOLLIES
**Bulldog,** hand-painted jointed wood on rounded base, 6 1/4" h. ............................ **2,500**
**Buster Brown,** 9 1/2" ...................................... **800**
**Chauffeur,** w/goggles & matching hat, 10 1/2" h. .................................................... **1,700**
**Clown,** painted papier-maché, black, Germany, 11 1/2" h. ........................................... **900**

*Clown on Horse*

**Clown on horse,** Germany, 6 1/8" (ILLUS.).. **1,200**

*Clown Rollies*

**Clowns,** five, painted composition, Germany, 6 1/4" to 15" h. (ILLUS.)................. **1,100**
**Keystone Cop,** 10 1/4" h. .............................. **750**
**Musical rabbit,** Germany, 8 1/4" .................... **350**

*Various Santa Claus Rollies*

**Santa Claus',** in various sizes (ILLUS.) ........ **7,700**

## SCHOENHUT TEDDY ROOSEVELT "ADVENTURE IN AFRICA SERIES"
**African native beater,** in cloth robe, carrying wooden spear, 1910 .......................... **1,500**
**Gorilla,** painted eyes, molded head, 9" h. ..... **3,000**
**Hyena,** painted eyes, 6" l. ............................... **350**
**Play set,** "African Safari" complete set, 25 wooden jungle denizens including Teddy Roosevelt, cameraman & native beaters w/colorful lithograph paper on wood jungle backdrop, 1910 (ILLUS.) .................. **15,000**

*"African Safari" complete set*

**Safari cameraman,** in cloth outfit w/small wooden camera around neck, 1910 .......... **1,500**

**Teddy Roosevelt,** individual figure in cloth outfit, kepi, rifle, 1910 ............................... **2,500**

**Zebu,** 1910, 7 1/2" ........................................ **1,650**

## LITHOGRAPHED PAPER ON WOOD TOYS

**Animals,** "Crandall's Menagerie," litho paper on wood, w/elephant, gorilla, toucan, camel, zebra, etc., in box w/paper label, patented 1867, 12 1/2" x 17 1/2" ..... **1,500**

**Boat,** "Monitor" Ironclad, litho paper on wood, R. Bliss, ca. 1870s .......................... **5,500**

**Boat,** "Noah's Ark," litho paper on wood, carved figurehead on prow, maker unknown, ca. 1910 ................................... **2,500**

**Bridge,** "(The) New York & Brooklyn Bridge," wood, w/operable bridge cars which move on pulley & string, ca. 1890, 49" overall, 1" x 4" w., 9 3/4" h. ................. **4,500**

**Circus cage wagon,** "Crandall's Happy Family," painted wood, w/15 wild animals, pull cord, ca. 1870s ........................ **3,000**

*"The Polar Bear"*

**Circus cage wagon,** "The Polar Bear," litho paper on wood, cage wagon w/trainer & polar bear figures, drawn by two dappled horses on wood wheels, R. Bliss, ca. 1880s (ILLUS.) .......................... **2,500**

**Coach,** "Pansy" Tally Ho Coach, litho paper on wood, R. Bliss, 1900, 31" w ................. **3,500**

**Construction toy,** "New Cathedral Construction Toy," wood, self-contained case for parts, books, blocks inscribed w/scriptural references, W.S. Reed, ca. 1870s ...................................................... **3,500**

**Figure,** "Quaker in Rocking Chair," litho paper on wood, attributed to R. Bliss, ca. 1890, 13" h. ...................................................... **650**

**Figure,** "Ye Hero of '76," wood, figure of Revolutionary patriot set in groove on wooden stand, Charles M. Crandall, ca. 1876 (U.S. Centennial related) ................. **3,500**

**Figures,** American Twin-Animal Ark, painted wood animals, R. Bliss, 1890, 17" l. (also came in 13" & 24" size) ........... **2,000**

**Figures,** Boy & Girl at School Desk, litho paper on wood, R. Bliss, ca. 1890s, figures 5 1/4" h, desk 5 1/4" w ...................... **2,500**

**Fire pumper,** litho paper on wood, horse drawn, detachable wood steam stacks & posts, W.S. Reed, ca. 1877, smaller than 15" l. ...................................................... **3,500**

**Fire pumper,** litho paper on wood, horse drawn, detachable wood steam stacks & posts, W.S. Reed, ca. 1877, 15" l. ............. **4,500**

**Historioscope,** "Panorama and History of America," litho paper & wood, w/hand crank to scroll pictures, views of Columbus landing through Civil War era, Milton Bradley, ca. 1870s ................................... **1,100**

**Historioscope,** "Panorama of Visit of Santa Claus to the Happy Children," litho paper & wood, w/hand crank to scroll pictures, Milton Bradley, ca. 1900 ............. **1,200**

**Hook & ladder,** litho paper on wood, double horses, two firemen, W.S. Reed, ca, 1890s ...................................................... **4,000**

**Horse-drawn carriage,** "Cinderella Coach," litho paper on wood, possibly Bliss, ca. 1890s, 10" l. ............................... **5,500**

**Sand toy,** "Black Musicians," pasteboard figures on wood, three black minstrels, activated by shifting sands, glass enclosed case, Henry Mencke patent, 1875 ...................................................... **2,500**

**Sand toy,** "General," litho paper, animated General swings saber when sand-activated, German, maker unknown, 1870s ...... **750**

**Ship,** "Terror" Coast Defense Monitor, litho paper on wood, R. Bliss, ca. 1910, 10" h. x 20" l. ...................................................... **1,200**

**Sleigh,** "Santa Claus Sleigh," litho paper on wood, pulled by reindeer, R. Bliss, ca. 1890, 12 3/4" l. ...................................... **2,500**

*"Santa Pulling Sleigh"*

**Sleigh,** "Santa Pulling Sleigh," sleigh is painted wood, Santa is composition w/cloth outfit, German, maker unknown, 8" l., 7" h. (ILLUS.) .................................... **1,200**

**Theater,** "Lime Kiln Club Theater," litho paper on wood, w/four minstrel players in box-like stage setting, R. Bliss, ca. 1870s ........ **8,500**

**Train,** "Central Park" trolley, litho paper on wood, W.S. Reed, 1878 ............ **6,500**

**Train,** "Empire Express," litho paper on wood, w/two engines, tender, two cars, alphabet blocks, R. Bliss, ca. 1890, 52" overall ........ **3,500**

**Train,** "Hercules Atlantic & Pacific," litho paper on wood, w/engine, tender, Milton Bradley, 1880 ............ **2,500**

**Train,** "Jackson Park Trolley," litho paper on wood, R. Bliss, ca. 1890s, 18" l. ........... **4,000**

**Train,** "(The) Reindeer Train," printed wooden engine, tender, four wooden cage cars, displays various wild animals, made to be assembled in puzzle fashion, Milton Bradley, 1800, 45" l. ........ **1,500**

*"U.S. Grant" Train*

**Train,** "U.S. Grant," litho paper on wood, engine & two parlor cars, attributed to R. Bliss, ca. 1880s (ILLUS.) ........... **2,500**

## MISCELLANEOUS COMIC CHARACTER DOLL FIGURES

**Betty Boop,** composition wood, jointed arms & legs, Cameo Doll Co., Fleischer Studios ........ **1,500**

**Fannie Brice,** molded swivel head, fabric clothes, Ideal Toy Co., ca. 1940s, 12 1/2" h. ........ **300**

**Howdy Doody,** composition, jointed arms & legs, copyright Bob Smith, ca. 1950s, 12 1/2" h. ........ **1,500**

**Jiminy Cricket,** wood flex doll w/umbrella, Ideal Toy Co., copyright Walt Disney, ca. 1950s, 6" h. ........ **500**

**King Little doll,** jointed wood, composition, Ideal Toy Co., ca. 1940s, 13" h. ........ **400**

**Pinocchio,** jointed wood, composition, copyright Walt Disney, ca. 1950s, 7 1/2" ........ **350**

**Superman,** jointed wood, composition, Ideal Toy Co., ca. 1950, 13 3/4" h. ........ **1,750**

## MISCELLANEOUS PUZZLES, SKILL GAMES

**Game,** "Brownies," nine pins, including Chinaman & policeman, Palmer Cox, pub. by McLoughlin Bros. ........ **850**

**Game,** "Golfers," including figural on long shafts, clubs, balls, boundary markers, bunkers, sand traps, felt putting greens, tee area, instruction manual, Schoenhut, 1910, clubs 36" l. ........ **3,500**

**Game,** Uncle Sam, litho paper on wood figures on bases, ca. 1890s, 11 3/4" h. ........ **850**

**Puzzle,** Uncle Sam, images on wood blocks in illustrated box, ca. 1890s, 10" w. x 11 1/2" l. ........ **950**

**Puzzle cubes,** "Yankee Doodle," six Thomas Nast cartoon images on all sides, forms six various images of Uncle Sam, in original wood box, ca. 1890s, McLoughlin Bros., 10 x 11 1/2" l. ........ **950**

**Skittles,** "Chief & Braves," nine papier-maché figures on wood bases, German, maker unknown, ca. 1890s, 9 to 9 1/2" h. ........ **8,500**

**Skittles,** "Hen & Chicks," painted wood & papier-maché, Germany, maker unknown ........ **1,500**

**Skittles,** "Sailors," hand-painted composition w/wood base, large wood ball, probably German, ca. 1890s, 10 1/2" h. ........ **2,600**

**Target,** litho paper on wood, pop gun & "harmless" ammunition, nine targets of people, animals, clay pipes, rubber ball, ca. 1910, 15" l. ........ **600**

**Target game,** "Trick Mule," W.S. Reed, 1880 ........ **850**

# TRAYS - SERVING & CHANGE

*Both serving and change trays once used in taverns, cafes and the like and usually bearing advertising for a beverage maker are now being widely collected. All trays listed are heavy tin serving trays, unless otherwise noted.*

*Americus Club Whiskey Tray*

**Americus Club Whiskey,** rectangular, metal, bottle in center, green background w/"Americus Club Whiskey - Henry Campe & Co., Inc." w/"San Francisco, Ca." at bottom, rim w/scroll & floral decoration on gold, lithograph by Chas. Shonk, Chicago, Illinois, minor crazing & surface rust on back only, 10 1/2 x 13 3/4" (ILLUS.) ........ **$231**

**Bartholomay Beer tip tray,** round metal, beautiful lady surrounded by clouds by Chas. Shonk Litho Co., Chicago, Illinois, border w/"Beers - Ales & Porter - In Kegs & Bottles," Bartholomay Brewery, Rochester, New York, 4 1/4" d. ........ **237**

**Clarke's Pure Rye tip tray,** tin, lithograph of bottle in center w/"Expressly for Family and Medicinal Use Only" on label & flanked by "Bottled - In Bond," red rim trimmed in gold w/gold lettering "Clarke's Pure Rye - The Largest Whiskey in the World," lithograph by Madein, Germany, unused condition, 4 1/4" d. ............................ **79**

**Dorne's Carnation Chewing Gum,** round tin lithograph showing package of gum & flowers in center w/"Taste the Smell," 4 1/4" d. (scuffs & dings) .............................. **105**

**Dr. Pepper,** rectangular, metal, pretty girl holding bottle in each hand w/"You'll like it too!" in upper corner, red border w/"Dr. Pepper" at top & bottom & "Drink a bite to eat" on each side, ca. 1940s (small shallow dents, light pitting & surface scratches) ..................................................... **605**

*E. Robinson's Sons Beer Tray*

**E. Robinson's Sons,** round, tin w/lithograph scene of factory w/train & wagons in foreground & "E. Robinson's Sons - Pilsner Bottled Beer" around border & "Haeserman M.M. Co. Litho, NY. Chic." at bottom, paint chips & crazing, 13 1/8" d. (ILLUS.) ....................................... **762**

**Golden Drops Lager Beer,** rectangular, tin, outdoor scene of men sitting at outdoor table drinking, marked "Decidedly Different" near top & "Two Rivers Beverage Co., Two Rivers, Wisconsin" at bottom, litho by American Can Co., 1 x 10 3/4 x 13 1/4" ........................................ **88**

**Hires,** round, metal w/lithograph depicting Josh Slinger, Hires soda jerk, in white suit, red tie, holding glass, "Hires 5¢" in red near center, Josh Slinger signature near bottom, red border w/"Things is getting higher but - Hires are still a nickel a trickle," 1915, 13" d. (heavy scratches, light chipping & wear) .................................. **138**

**Ideal Chocolate & Cocoa tip tray,** rectangular, tin, scalloped rim, box in center marked "Ideal Cocoa," w/"Once Tried" at top & "Always Used" below & "Ideal chocolates" on sides, brown & tan, minor scuffs & scratches,     2 1/4 x 3 1/4" (ILLUS. top next page) .................................. **100**

*Ideal Chocolate & Cocoa Tip Tray*

**Jno. T. Barbee Whiskey,** tin, oval, lithograph scene of people near log cabin taste testing some Old Barbee Whiskey w/"H. D. Beach Co. Coshocton, O." at bottom, Jno. T. Barbee & Co., Louisville, Ky., 13 1/2 x 16 1/2" ....................................... **110**

**John Hampden Havana Cigar tip tray,** metal, colorful figure of man in center, black rim w/gold lettering "John Hampden - Havana Cigar," Austria, 4 1/4" d. .......... **97**

**La Primadora Cigar,** glass, round w/bust portrait of beautiful lady in center w/scrollwork on both sides & bottom, 6" d. ............................................................. **165**

*McAvoys Malt Marrow Beer Tray*

**McAvoys Malt Marrow Beer,** round, tin w/lithograph showing small boy w/white shirt, blue knee pants, one brown shoe, the other foot bare, curly hair w/large cap, holding bottle & horn, brown & white dog behind him w/red script lettering "Malt-Marrow" in center, "McAvoy Beats 'Em All" around border, "Chas. W. Shonk Co. Litho Chicago" at bottom, razing, paint chips & soiling, 12" d. (ILLUS.) ..... **242**

**Red Raven tip tray,** rectangular metal, red bird, glass & product bottle shown w/"For Headache - For Indigestion" at top corners, "Red Raven" at borrom, Chas. Shonk Litho Co., Cicago, Illinois, 4 1/8 x 6 1/8" (minor crazing) ....................... **110**

*Ruhstaller Brewery Tray*

**Ruhstaller Brewery,** oval tin, lithograph showing man w/beard smoking pipe & sitting in arm chair near table, decorated border w/"Ruhstaller Brewery - Sacramento Cal." & "Ruhstaller Lager & Gilt Edge Steam Beer" upper center, minor scuff marks, surface rust on back, 13 1/2 x 16 1/2" (ILLUS.)............................. 330

**Slade's Products tip tray,** round, spin to win game type, white w/red trim, center marked "Don't Take chances - All Slade's Products are Sure Winners" w/four horse & rider figures around rim & marked "Mustard - Peanut Butter - Spices - Cream Tartar," unused condition, 4 1/4" d. ................................................. 55

**White Rock tip tray,** rectangular, tin, scene of pretty girl in white dress, kneeling on rock, lithograph by Chas. Shonk, Chicago, Illinois, marked "White Rock - The World's Best Table Water," 4 x 6" .......... 77

**Woodland Whiskey tip tray,** round metal w/lithograph of lady in blue dress & hat in waisted center scene flanked by bottles, by H.O. Beach Co., Coshocton, Ohio, 4 1/4" d. (edge scrapes & dings) ........ 358

**Wright & Taylor Old Charter Distillery,** round, tin lithographed w/scene of factory in background & girls wading in pond in foreground, circular insert w/bottle on right side, "Distillery, Louisville, Ky." at top center, border w/"Wright & Taylor - Old Charter Distillery," 12" d. (minor scratches, soiling & staining) ............ 363

# TRUMP INDICATORS

*A trump indicator is a device that was placed on the table during card games such as Whist and its successor, Bridge. They were to remind the players what the trump suit was. The earlier trump indicators from the 19th century, used in the game of Whist, had only the four suits of hearts, spades, diamonds and clubs. Later, in the game of Bridge, "No Trump" was added.*

*These gadgets are difficult to find and appear in many forms: people, animals, buildings, useful objects, etc. Some are made of beautiful porcelain while others are crudely made from metal and wood. The ones made from celluloid can be dated from the first half of the 20th century. One thing*

*trump indicators all have in common is their movable pointer or spinner displaying what card suit is trump.*

*As with so many items from the past, their usefulness has become outdated. In the modern game of Bridge, a player would probably be reminded "If you can't remember what the trump is, you shouldn't be playing Bridge." But, as gaming collectibles increase in popularity, the desirability of trump indicators will continue to score high.*

*Globe Trump Indicator*

**Brass,** model of a globe map, ring w/card suits around center (ILLUS.) ..................... $100

*Harp w/Celluloid Flip Cards*

**Brass,** ornate scrolling harp-form holder on domed base, celluloid flip cards w/suits (ILLUS.) .......................................................... 85

*Trump Indicator w/Enameled Base*

**Brass,** serpentine metal uprights suspending the suit flip cards, rectangular black enameled base (ILLUS.) ................................. 95

*Lady Bather Trump Indicator*

**Celluloid,** figural lady bather w/jointed arms pointing to suits in arch above (ILLUS.)...................................................... **250**

*Black Cat Trump Indicator*

**Celluloid,** model of a black cat, arched back & tail as pointer, green base (ILLUS.)...................................................... **250**

*Die Cube Trump Indicator*

**Celluloid,** model of a die cube, suit on each side, w/a built-in tape measure (ILLUS.) ...... **200**

*Celluloid Disk Trump Indicator*

**Celluloid,** model of a disk, turn ring to show suit, h.p. floral trim (ILLUS.) ........................... **35**

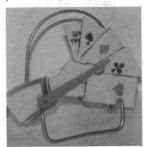

*Hand w/Cards Trump Indicator*

**Celluloid,** model of a hand holding cards, red pointer to suits (ILLUS.) ........................ **125**

*Playing Card Trump Indicator*

**Celluloid,** model of a playing card, disks indicate suits & numbers, h.p. floral trim (ILLUS.)...................................................... **95**

*Double Celluloid Wheels*

**Celluloid,** rounded & flattened frame w/scalloped top & rectangular foot, holds to small turn wheels (ILLUS.) ........................ **85**

*Clown On Ashtray*

**Ceramic,** ashtray, figural clown on back rim beside upright disk w/suits (ILLUS.)............. **125**

*Japanese Clown Ashtray*

**Ceramic,** ashtray, figural clown standing on back rim holding disk w/suits, iridized orange base, Japan (ILLUS.) ...................... **175**

*Wade Ashtray Trump Indicator*

**Ceramic,** ashtray, round w/upright metal frame w/flip suit cards, an enameled shield w/early ship at base of frame, blue glaze, Wade, England (ILLUS.).................... **135**

*Gnome Trump Indicator*

**Ceramic,** figural, gnome standing beside square block w/an opening to show suits, Germany (ILLUS.).............................. **250**

*Copper Souvenir Trump Indicator*

**Copper,** souvenir-type, low domed shape w/stamped souvenir scene at front & opening to show suit at rear (ILLUS.)........... **100**

*Seal Trump Indicator*

**Horn & wood,** rectangular wood base w/upright horn carved as a seal w/a projecting base holding flip suit cards (ILLUS.)...................................................... **125**
**Wooden,** barrel-shaped, pencil holders at top, w/ring of suits marked around the base ................................................................. **100**

*"Don't Forget The Kitty"*

**Wooden,** box-form, low rectangular form w/pull-out suit indicators, painted in inside "Don't forget the Kitty" w/black cat (ILLUS.)...................................................... **125**

*Inlaid Woods w/Flip Cards*

**Wooden,** finely inlaid domed base w/upright metal frame for suit flip cards (ILLUS.) .......................................................... **50**
**Wooden,** souvenir-type, twig base w/opening painted w/name, fence-form upright support for suit flip cards (ILLUS.).................. **95**

*Twig & Fence Trump Indicator*

# TRUNKS

*These box-like portable containers are used for transporting or storing personal possessions. There are many styles to choose from since they have been made from the 16th century onward. Thousands arrived in this country with the immigrants and more were turned out to accommodate the westward movement of the population. The popular dome-top trunk was designed to prevent water from accumulating on the top. Hinges, locks and construction, along with condition and age, greatly determine the values of older trunks.*

**Dome-top,** grain painted pine, shaded ochre color, iron lock America, 19th c., 24 x 9 3/4 x 11 3/4" (lid w/age cracks, minor paint loss)......................................... **$201**

*Early Grained & Painted Trunk*

**Dome-top,** painted & grained wood, the deep domed hinged top w/an iron hasp & lock, decorated overall w/various leafy vines & heart-shaped blossoms in sienna paint on an ochre ground, probably Vermont, early 19th c., cracks, minor paint wear & surface abrasions, 12 3/4 x 25 3/4", 13 1/4" h. (ILLUS.) ......... **2,990**

**Dome-top,** painted wood, the long rectangular hinged domed top opening to a well in the dovetailed base, the exterior covered w/yellow & burnt sienna fanciful grain painting in green & yellow bordered by simulated inlay banding, original surface, New England, early 19th c., 14 x 28", 12" h. (hardware partly missing) ..................................................... **259**

*Old Pine Dome-top Trunk*

**Dome-top,** pine, natural finish, wrought-iron latch & lock, tack trim, 19th c., 24" l., 9" h. (ILLUS.)................................................. **300**

**Dome-top,** rectangular, wood w/hide covering & leather trim w/brass studs, original brass bail handle & wrought-iron lock w/hasp, 9 x 18", 8 1/2" h. (hair mostly worn off top, some edge damage) ............... **110**

*Early Hide-covered Dome-top Trunk*

**Dome-top,** wood w/hide covering w/leather straps & decorative detail & brass stud bands, wrought-iron lock w/hasp & side handles, lined w/a two-tone blue wallpaper, some wear, 19th c., 10 x 18 1/4", 8 1/4" h. (ILLUS.)........................................ **330**

*Painted Poplar Tack-trimmed Trunk*

**Flat-top,** painted poplar, rectangular w/hinged lid, worn leather trim, tin corner braces & decorative brass tack trim w/initials "P.L.," worn printed cloth lining, old black paint, 19th c., 23 3/4" l. (ILLUS.)...................................................... **193**

**Flat-topped,** rectangular, wood w/hide covering & green leather trim w/brass tack borders, wrought-iron lock w/hasp & brass keyhole cover, interior lined w/wallpaper, 19th c., 9 1/4" l. (some wear) ..................................................... **193**

**Flat-topped,** rectangular, wood w/overall red & black leather covering decorated w/brass stud bands & original handle & lock w/hasp, lined w/marbleized paper, 19th c., 11 1/2" l. (leather hinges replaced) ..................................................... **385**

# WALL POCKETS

*Wall pockets became popular as early as the Victorian era. With their love of flowers, Victorians decorated whole walls with cascading vines from metal planters to hidden pockets behind tilted picture frames. Wooden, cardboard and ribboned paper pockets were put to practical use for such things as mail, notes and even as parlor slipper holders. However popular to the Victorians, the big "boom" came during the 1920s and 1930s introducing every and any imaginable type of wall pocket. While tapering off during the 1940s, they reemerged by the mid-50s and have been in production ever since.*

*All prices reflect wall pockets in top condition*

*Bird by Fulper Pottery*

**Apple on leaves,** ceramic, dark red apple, marked "McCoy" w/raised letters, ca. 1948, 7" h. ................................................. **$65**

**Arrowhead,** ceramic, dark green, mark incised "Creek" w/a stylized teepee, Creek Pottery of Checotah, OK, ca. 1970-76, 8" h. ...................................................... 45

**Bells,** ceramic, two attached red bells, marked w/Cleminsons seal in black ink, stamped "THE CALIFORNIA b CLEMINSONS HAND-PAINTED ©," 5" h. ................... 40

**Betty Boop on cone,** ceramic, white & gold luster w/Betty Boop walking w/her dog, white background w/gold flaring lip, marked "BETTY BOOP DES. L COPR BY FLEISCHER STUDIOS MADE IN JAPAN" w/red ink stamp, 5" h. .................... 125

**Bird,** ceramic, multicolored green w/long tail, marked "FULPER 375," made by Fulper Pottery, Trenton, NJ (ILLUS.) .......... 300

**Bucket w/roses,** ceramic, brown coloring, oak bucket-style w/top & bottom bands & two center roses, Woodrose patt., Weller Pottery, back incised "8" ............................. 100

**Bullet-shaped,** Tiffin satin glass, w/pointed base, U.S. Glass Co., Tiffin, Ohio, No. 16258, came in several colors including green, black, light blue, amethyst, amber & royal blue, 3 7/8" w., 9 1/4" h. ................... 100

**Butterfly,** ceramic, pale yellow, incised mark "NM" (Nelson McCoy), ca. early 1940s, 5 3/4" h. ........................................... 300

**Canoe,** vaseline glass, Daisy & Button patt., unmarked, 8" l. ................................ 80

**Car bud vase,** vaseline glass, made by McKee Glass Co., no markings, includes nickel-plated metal holder, 6" h. .................. 100

**Chef on stove,** ceramic, black chef sitting on side of old-style chartreuse cook stove, mark incised "Hollywood Ceramics ©," 6" h. .............................................. 75

**Cherub on cornucopia,** ceramic, cherub sitting on curved tail of white cornucopia w/pink roses & dark green leaves, marked "NR GERMANY" in blue ink stamp, 7 3/4" h. ........................................... 175

*Smiling Chinese Girl*

**Chinese girl,** ceramic, bust of smiling girl w/green clothing & chartreuse hat, marked "Royal Copley" in raised letters, 7 1/2" h. (ILLUS.)............................................. 45

**Cone,** ceramic, flaring lip in red luster, white luster body tapering to a point, w/long-tailed red, white & black bird perched on limb w/green white & red flower cluster off to side, marked "HAND-PAINTED JAPAN" w/red ink stamp, 7" h. ..................................................... 55

**Cone,** ceramic, tapering w/raised panels, pink & green, impressed "2008" & "Flame, Mark," Rookwood Pottery, ca. 1930 ...................................................... 250

**Cone,** glass, amber, sharply tapering paneled body coming to a point, trimmed w/silver inlay floral decoration, Fostoria, style No. 1881, 3" w., 8 1/4" h. .................... 125

**Cone,** glass, blue, sharply tapering paneled body coming to a point, Fostoria, style No. 1881, 3" w., 8 1/4" h. .............................. 75

**Cone,** glass, clear w/applied red coloring, tapering conical-style w/ribbing & pointed clear base, made by Jeannette Glass Co., No. 2930, ca. 1947-49, 3 1/2" w., 6 1/2 h. ....................................... 50

**Cone,** glass, green, sharply tapering paneled body coming to a point, Masonic emblem applied in gold leaf, Fostoria, style No. 1881, 3" w., 8 1/4" h. .................... 150

*Majolica Cone With Wicker Trim*

**Cone,** majolica, long slender tapering style, green w/wicker trimming, made by Joseph Holdcroft, Longton, England, ca. 1870-1920, 10 1/2" h. (ILLUS.) ................ **1,500**

**Cone,** vaseline glass w/scroll design tapering to point, made by U.S. Glass, 5" w. at top, 6 h. ......................................... **75**

**Cone w/handles,** ceramic, gold luster w/a large monarch butterfly above a small red butterfly, pointed lip flaring down to two side handles, marked "NORITAKE M HANDPAINTED MADE IN JAPAN" w/red ink stamp, 9 1/4" h. ............................. **225**

**Cornucopia,** ceramic, light pink, incised "RED WING 441," 7" h. .................................. **50**

*Elf on Bananas*

**Elf on bananas,** ceramic, bunch of yellow bananas w/red elf in center, mark incised "GILNER 19 © 50 CALF," made by Gilner Pottery, Culver City, CA, ca. 1950s, 7 1/2" h., 8" w. (ILLUS.) ...................... **45**

*California Pottery Fish*

**Fish,** ceramic, dark pink trimmed in black, w/large eyes & "swimming" to right, marked "Ceramicraft SAN CLEMENTE, CALIFORNIA" w/brown ink stamp w/marking in shape of artist's palette & three paint brushes, 8 1/2" h., 11" w. (ILLUS.).................................................. **30**

**Flour scoop,** ceramic, yellow w/embossed flowers, mark incised "USA CAMARK N-45," original price tag reads "$3.50," 10" l. ...................................................... **25**

**Flower,** ceramic, square, yellow w/green, mark incised "Walker - 958," California pottery, 5 x 5" ........................................... **20**

**Geese,** ceramic, two gold & two blue luster geese looking to side, marked "Made in Japan" w/black ink stamp, 6 1/2" h. ................. **75**

**Girl in tree,** ceramic, Hummel, No. 360/C, mark incised "M.I. Hummel" on front under girl & impressed "360/C" & "© Goebel 1958" on back ................................. **600**

**Grapes on leaf,** ceramic, purple grapes on chartreuse leaves, mark incised "Treasure Craft, Compton, California," 6" h., 6" w. ........................................................ **25**

**Grapes w/leaves,** ceramic, multicolored in soft pastel greens, browns & pinks, marked "Royal Bayreuth - T (in a shield) - 1794 BAVARIA" w/blue ink stamp & impressed "Deponiert," 9" h. ......................... **400**

*Harlequin Man*

**Harlequin man & woman,** ceramic, woman w/black mask, green bandana w/light pink flower & gold trimmed collar, man w/pink bandana, black mask & gold trimmed collar, marked "MADE IN JAPAN" w/red ink stamp, 6" h., the pr. (ILLUS. man only) .......................................... **85**

**Hat,** ceramic, yellow-weave w/brown rim & mauve flowers at bottom, marked "© Geo. Z. Lefton 4361" w/black ink stamp & "LEFTON TRADE MARK EXCLUSIVES JAPAN" w/red foil label, 6 3/4" h......... **50**

**Heart w/birds,** ceramic, heart-shaped w/two small yellow birds looking in opposite directions perched on leaves extending from red heart, three small yellow stars above, all on cream background w/brown shadowing, marked "Vv" w/blue ink stamp & incised "SU 23/0," Germany, 4" h. ..................................... **30**

**Hen,** ceramic, yellow w/red & green markings, made by Dan Davis, unmarked, California pottery, ca. 1950, 6" h. ................... **30**

**Horse collar,** ceramic, brown, mark incised "ROYAL DURAN - CALIF.," 10" h., 7" at widest point ..................................................... **50**

**Iron,** ceramic, glossy yellow w/pastel accents, Hull Pottery, Sun Glow patt., No. 83, ca. early 1950s ............................... **90**

**Iron on trivet,** ceramic, grey iron on black trivet, marked "McCoy U.S.A." in raised letters, ca. 1953, 8" h. ..................................... **75**

**Lily,** ceramic, double, turquoise, mark incised "AA VAN BRIGGLE Colo. Spgs," 5" h. ................................................................... **225**

**Lily w/handle,** ceramic, tapering curved trumpet shape w/leaves on base, powder blue, marked incised "NM," McCoy Pottery, ca. early 1940s, 6" h. ...................... **100**

**Limb w/blossoms,** ceramic, pink blossoms off top sides & one on bottom, Weller Pottery, Woodcraft patt., unmarked, ca. early 1920s, 8" h. ......................................... **135**

*Haeger Pottery Lavabo*

**Lion head lavabo,** ceramic, turquoise blue, Haeger Pottery, top piece marked "#R1504," top 9 1/2" w. x 14 1/2" h., bottom 16" w. x 6 1/4" h., 2 pcs. (ILLUS.) ......... **250**

**Love birds on trivet,** ceramic, white love birds on black trivet, marked "McCoy U.S.A." in raised letters, ca. 1953, 8" h. ......... **85**

**Mail box,** ceramic, green, embossed design w/"Letters" across top, marked "McCoy USA" w/raised letters, ca. 1951, 7" h. (ILLUS. top next page) ........................... **90**

**Mandolin,** ceramic, black, marked "RED WING U.S.A. M-1484" in raised letters & "ART POTTERY" on red & gold paper label, 15" h. ..................................................... **45**

*Mail Box by McCoy*

**Ming Tree patt.,** ceramic, blue base w/brown vining limbs, Roseville Pottery, marked in relief "Roseville U.S.A. 566-8," 8 1/2" h. ..................................................... **300**

*Morning Glory*

**Morning glory,** glass, medium blue, no markings, 7 3/4" h. (ILLUS.) ........................... **40**

*Oriental Girl*

**Oriental girl,** ceramic, wearing pink & black, sitting w/folded hands between two white pots decorated w/pink oriental lamp on each, marked "Weil Ware w/Burro - Made In California" w/black ink stamp & impressed "4045," made by California Figurine Co., founded by Max Weil, ca. 1940-55, 7 1/2" h., 6" w. (ILLUS.)...................................................... **40**

**Owl,** ceramic, brown, sitting on leaves w/wings extended back, mark impressed "GERMANY" & "1913," 7" h. .......................... **90**

**Owl in crescent,** ceramic, yellow, brown, green & red owl sitting in a red crescent, mark impressed "MADE IN JAPAN," 7" h.................................................................. **50**

**Owl in tree,** ceramic, brown, trumpet form w/owl on top & leaves on bottom, Wood-craft patt., Weller Pottery, impressed "Weller" & stamped "XX" w/brown ink, ca. 1920s-30s, 10" h.............................. **350**

**Parrot,** ceramic, mulberry, w/head to breast & single wing sweeping across front of body, mark incised "30 AA Van Briggle Colo Spgs," 7" h. ............................. **225**

**Parrot on basket,** ceramic, blue w/brown trim basket w/brightly colored parrot perched in center, marked "MADE IN JAPAN" w/black ink stamp, 6 3/4" h.............. **30**

*Baby Face Peace Lily*

**Peace lily w/baby face,** ceramic, baby face looking off to side w/green leaf behind peace lily, marked "PY-NC Japan" w/green ink stamp, 6" h. (ILLUS.)....... **25**

*Phoebe Head*

**Phoebe head,** ceramic, Prairie Green glaze, mark impressed "FRANKOMA" & incised "730 C P.M.," Ada clay, 7" h. (ILLUS.) ...................................................... **150**

**Pig bank,** ceramic, powder blue, No. 671, "Skedaddle," made by Morton Pottery Co., Morton, Ill., unmarked, 5" h. ................... **50**

**Pigtail girl,** ceramic, brown hair & closed eyes w/aqua bonnet & collar, marked "Royal Copley" in raised letters, 7" h.............. **45**

**Pine cones,** ceramic, double, green, Roseville Pottery, impressed "Roseville 1273-8," ca. 1931, 9" h................................ **300**

**Pirate,** ceramic, w/yellow & green shirt & grey headband, marked "Royal Copley" in raised letters, 8 1/2" h................................ **65**

**Pitcher,** ceramic, Bow-Knot patt., pink & blue, Hull Pottery, marked "U.S.A. Hull Art B-26-6" in raised lettering, includes round silver foil label marked "HULL POTTERY CROOKSVILLE, OHIO," ca. late 1940s, 6" h. .......................................... **250**

*Royal Copley Angel*

**Praying angel,** ceramic, blue w/grey wings, eyes closed w/head to left, Royal Copley, unmarked, 8" h. (ILLUS.) ................. **45**

**Rooster,** ceramic, yellow w/red & green markings, made by Dan Davis, unmarked, California Pottery, ca. 1950, 6 1/2" h. ................................................... **30**

**Scottie dog,** ceramic, white, blue bur-gundy, green or yellow, unmarked, Shawnee Pottery, ca. 1937-61, 9 1/2" h......... **60**

*Ceramic Shell*

**Shell,** ceramic, satin green, impressed "STANGLUSA3238,"6" h.(ILLUS.) ..... **125**

**Shell,** ceramic, Woodland patt., No. W13, dark pink, Hull Pottery, marked "W13-7 1/2 Hull U.S.A." in raised lettering, ca. late 1940s-early 1950s, 7 1/2" h. .................. **150**

**Teapot string holder,** ceramic, white decorated w/colorful yellow, black & red roosters, spout facing front for dispensing string, includes top wire handle & lid, marked "FREDROBERTS COMPANY. SAN FRANCISCO. MADE IN JAPAN" on blue paper label, approx. 5" h. .................. **70**

**Trumpet,** ceramic, matte green over red clay w/embossed top border in tapering trumpet-style, Peters & Reed Pottery, unmarked, 7" h. ............................................. **125**

**Trumpet,** ceramic, yellow, paneled tapering style, impressed "2957" & "Flame Mark," Rookwood Pottery, ca. 1926 ............ **275**

**Trumpet,** satin glass, narrow tapering trumpet-style w/pointed base, U.S. Glass Co., Tiffin, Ohio, No. 320, came in several colors including royal blue, black, canary yellow, green & light blue, 3 3/8" w., 9 1/8" h. ........................................... **80**

**Trumpet,** satin glass, pink w/h.p. flowers, narrow tapering trumpet-style w/pointed base, U.S. Glass Co., Tiffin, Ohio, No. 320, 3 3/8" w., 9 1/8" h. ................................ **100**

*Rose on Trumpet*

**Trumpet w/rose,** ceramic, brown tapering trumpet-style w/center yellow rose, scroll design on base, mark incised "Calif - USA," made by Marsh Industries of Glendale & Los Angeles, CA, ca. late 1950-80s, 9" h. (ILLUS.) ................................. **50**

**Tulip match holder,** ceramic, pink tulip w/green leaf hanger, marked "TULIP MATCH HOLDER ©Artist' Barn Fillmore, Calif" w/black ink stamp, "89¢" original price on back, approx. 3 1/2" h. ...................... **25**

**Vase,** ceramic, cylindrical shape w/multicolored flowers on white background w/blue ring at top, marked "CZECHO-SLOVAKIA" w/a dragon in black ink stamp, "$1.45" original price on back, 7 1/2" h. ........................................................ **75**

**Violin,** ceramic, white w/pink rose w/green leaves, trimmed in gold, marked "369" w/black ink stamp & "Lefton REG. U.S.

PAT. OFF. EXCLUSIVES JAPAN" on red foil label, 7 1/2" h. ...................................... **30**

**Wall phone,** ceramic, colors of yellow, red & green, impressed "U.S.A. 529," Shawnee Pottery, ca. 1937- 61, 6" h. ...................... **35**

**Water sprinkler,** ceramic, rooster design on white background w/brown spatter trim, marked "A Napco Ceramic JAPAN" on silver foil label & "S727R" on green ink stamp, 4 1/2" h. ......................................... **15**

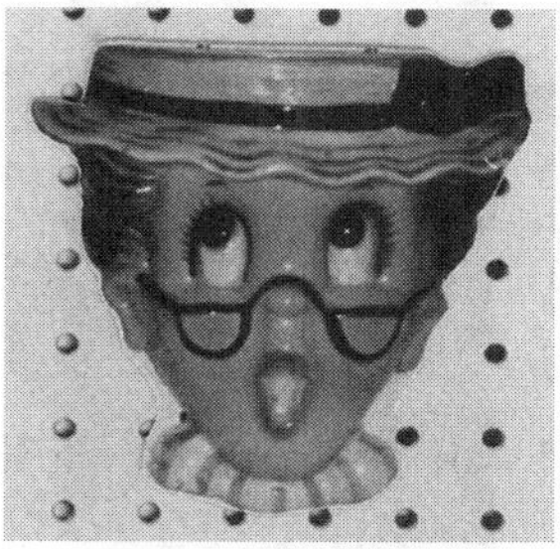

*Woman WIth Glasses*

**Woman w/glasses,** ceramic, woman w/reading glasses, yellow straw hat w/black ribbon & white & light blue striped collar, looking up w/mouth open, marked "Japan" w/paper label, 5" h. (ILLUS.) ........................................................... **30**

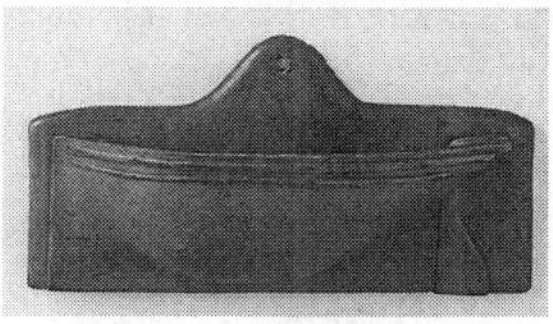

*Wooden Wall Pocket*

**Wooden,** red-painted carved pine & maple w/shaped backboard mounted w/pocket in form of half-hull, 19th c., losses to paint, 14" l., 7 1/4" h. (ILLUS.) .................. **1,725**

*Czechoslovakian Woodpecker*

**Woodpecker,** ceramic, woodpecker on limb, marked "Made in Czechoslovakia" w/red ink stamp, hand-drawn by Marvin Gibson, 7 1/2" h. (ILLUS.) .............................. **75**

**Woodpecker,** marigold carnival glass, tapering conical-form w/embossed woodpecker, made by Northwood Glass Co., unmarked, 8" h. ..................................... **125**

# WATCHES

## PENDANT WATCHES

*Smith Patterson Pendant Watch*

**Hunting case,** Art Noveau style, Smith Patterson Co., goldtone dial w/black Roman numerals, initialed case, chased & engraved griffin brooch, hallmarked for Bippart, Griscom & Osborn, 14k yellow gold (ILLUS.) ............................................. **$443**

## POCKET WATCHES

**Abbott Watch Co.,** 16 size, 17 jewels, gold jeweled settings, open face ................. **325-750**

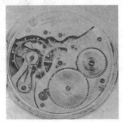

*Abbott Watch Co. Pocket Watch*

**Abbott Watch Co.,** No. 993932, 16 size, 17 jewels, gold jeweled settings, hunting case (ILLUS.) ....................................... **125-350**

*Adams & Perry Watch Co. Pocket Watch*

**Adams & Perry Watch Co.,** No. 1681, movement, 20 jewels, gold jeweled set-

tings, key wind & pendant set (ILLUS.)............................................ **2,000-4,000**
**Allison, J.H.,** No. 19, movement 16 jewels, gold train & escape wheel w/pivoted detent, key wind & key set ................ **600-1,500**

*American Watch Co. Pocket Watch*

**American Watch Co.,** Bridge Model, 16 size, 23 jewels, gold train, Adj.5P (ILLUS.)........................................ **1,100-2,500**
**American Watch Co.,** Model 1886, 16 size, 21 jewels, gold train, w/tadpole regulator ..................................................... **450-800**

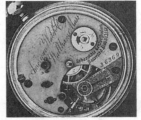

*American Watch Co. Pocket Watch*

**American Watch Co.,** No. 36369, Model 18KW, 18 size, 15 jewels, reversible center pinion, patented Nov. 30th, 1858 (ILLUS.)........................................ **2,400-5,000**
**American Watch Co.,** No. 5,000,297, Model 1888, 16 size, 19 jewels, gold jewel settings, gold train, high grade movement ............................................... **85-250**
**American Watch Co.,** No. 501,561, Model 16KW or Model 1868, 16 size, key wind & set from back, gold train ................ **400-1,000**
**American Watch Co.,** No. 80111, Model 1862, 20 size, 17-19 jewels, gold balance & escape wheel, gold jeweled settings, key wind, key set from back .. **2,000-4,000**

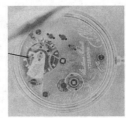

*Appleton, Tracy 20 Size Pocket Watch*

**Appleton, Tracy & Co.,** No. 125004, Model 20KW, 20 size, 15 jewels, w/vibrating hairspring stud (ILLUS.) .................. **1,400-2,800**

*Appleton, Tracy 18 Size Pocket Watch*

**Appleton, Tracy & Co.,** No. 1,389,078,
Model 1877, 18 size, 15 jewels, stem
wind, quick train, hunting case (ILLUS.).. **75-150**

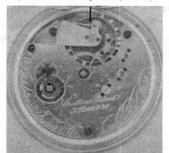

*Appleton, Tracy 16 Size Pocket Watch*

**Appleton, Tracy & Co.,** No. 140030, 15J,
16 size, w/vibrating hairspring stud, key
wind & set from back (ILLUS.) ........ **1,000-2,000**
**Appleton, Tracy & Co.,** No. 14,752, 1st
Serial No. 13,701, Model 1857, 18 size,
15-16 jewels, "Chronodrometer" on dial,
"Appleton Tracy & Co." or "P.S. Bartlett,"
key wind & set, 1/4 jump seconds... **2,000-4,000**

*Appleton, Tracy 20 Size Pocket Watch*

**Appleton, Tracy & Co.,** No. 250107, 20
size, 15-17 jewels, Fogg's safety pinion,
pat. Feb. 14, 1865, key wind & set from
back (ILLUS.) ........................................ **100-250**
**Bartlett, P.S.,** No. 13446, Model 1857, 18
size, 15 jewels, engraved on back "4 PR.
Jewels" ................................................. **150-300**
**Bartlett, P.S.,** No. 41597, Model 18KW or
1859, 11 jewels, key wind & set from
back................................................... **600-1,100**

*Canadian Railway Time Service Pocket
Watch*

**Canadian Railway Time Service,** No.
22,017,534, Model 1892, 18 size, 17
jewels, marked (ILLUS.)..................... **600-1,000**
**Crescent Street,** No. 552,526, Model
1870, 15J, 18 size, key wind & set from
back, this grade was the first American
watch to be advertised as a railroad
watch................................................: **150-400**
**Dennison, Howard, Davis,** No. 1205,
Model 1857, 18 size, 15 jewels, under
sprung, key wind ............................ **1,000-1,800**
**Grade 845,** No. 15,097,475, Model 1892,
18 size, 21 jewels, railroad grade, Adj.5P..... **300**

*Howard, Davis & Dennison Pocket Watch*

**Howard, Davis & Dennison,** 20 size, 15
jewels, 8 day, two mainsprings & gilt
movement, ca. 1852, the first 17 were
made for the officials of the company
(ILLUS.) ...................................... **30,000-80,000**
**Hunting case,** man's, Bautte (Jq. Fd.),
Geneve, white dial w/Roman numerals,
chased case w/bi-color floral bouquet on
one side & mixed metal & enamel decoration on reverse, scalloped edges, 18k
yellow gold (damaged enamel) .................. **260**

*Gruen Pocket Watch & Chain*

**Hunting case,** man's, Gruen, No. 96516, white dial w/black Arabic numerals, subsidiary seconds dial, chased & engraved case depicting a griffin, includes 48" l. trace link chain accented w/eight small cultured pearls & swivel hook, 14k yellow gold (ILLUS.).......................................... **575**

*Jurgensen Pocket Watch*

**Hunting case,** man's, Jurgensen (J. Alfred), No. 785, white procelain dial, subsidiary dial for seconds, fancy hands, highly jeweled movement, patent 1865, Copenhagen, 18k gold (ILLUS.)............... **3,000**

*J. Watson Pocket Watch*

**J. Watson,** No. 28,635, 18 size, 11 jewels, "Boston, Mass." engraved on movement, hunting case, key wind key set, ca. April 1863 (ILLUS.).................................. **1,000-2,500**
**Open-face,** man's, American Waltham, Riverside model, 16 size, double roller, gold-filled, pendant set, 15 jewel .......... **100-150**
**Open-face,** man's, Patek Phillippe & Co., No. 161442, Geneve, white dial, Roman numerals, 18k yellow gold, (missing bail) .............................................................. **575**
**Open-face,** man's, marked "H.H., Bevete S.G.D.G., Paris" on face, gold colored metal case w/white face in Roman numerals, lines indicate minutes between each numeral, one-piece thin gold hands, back depicts French cathedral, 1 5/8" d. ............................................... **210**

*Pennsylvania Special Pocket Watch*

**Pennsylvania Special,** No. 14,000,015, Model 1892, 18 size, 21 jewels (ILLUS.).......................................... **1,600-3,000**
**Sidereal,** Model 1892, 17J, 24 hour dial used by astronomers, marked "Sidereal" on dial ................................... **1,200-2,400**

*Vanguard Pocket Watch*

**Vanguard,** No. 10,533,465, Model 1892, 18S, 23J, diamond end stone, gold jewel settings, exposed winding gears (ILLUS.)................................................. **300-500**

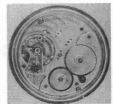

*Waltham Standard Pocket Watch*

**Waltham Standard,** No. 10,099,625, Grade 1892, 18 size, 19 jewels, Adj5P, open face, note engine & coal car (locomotive) engraved on movement (ILLUS.)......................................... **1,000-2,000**
**Waltham Watch Co.,** No. 778763, Model 1857, 18S, 15J, w/factory stem wind, Fogg's Patent ...................................... **200-325**

# WRISTWATCHES

**Abercrombie & Fitch,** 17 jewels, chronological., by Valj., 3 reg., 14K gold....... **900-1,200**
**Abercrombie & Fitch,** 17 jewels, chronological, by Valj., 3 reg., ca. 1950, stainless steel .............................................. **350-500**
**Abercrombie & Fitch,** 17 jewels, chronological, by Valj., 3 reg., stainless steel .. **350-500**

*Abercrombie & Fitch Seafarer Wristwatch*

**Abercrombie & Fitch,** Seafarer, chronological., waterproof, 18K gold (ILLUS.)......................................... **1,100-1,600**
**Abercrombie & Fitch,** Seafarer, chronological, waterproof, stainless steel ........ **350-500**

**Abra,** 15 jewels, curved case, c. 1930s, base metal................................................. **30-55**

**Abra,** 15 jewels, engraved case, c. 1930s, gold plate.................................................. **30-55**

**Abra,** 17 jewels, carved case, c. 1930s, base metal................................................. **30-55**

**Abra,** 17 jewels, engraved case, base metal ......................................................... **30-55**

**Abra,** 17 jewels, jump hour, stainless steel..................................................... **250-395**

**Abra,** 17 jewels, step case, c. 1930s, base metal ......................................................... **30-55**

**Baume & Mercier,** 17 jewels, curved, c. 1990s, 14K C&B.................................. **500 -800**

**Baume & Mercier,** 17 jewels, diam. mystery dial, c. 1950s, 14K white gold ........ **500-800**

*Baume & Mercier Wristwatch*

**Baume & Mercier,** 17 jewels, fancy lugs, auxillary second hand, c. 1955, 14k gold (ILLUS.)............................................... **250-400**

**Baume & Mercier,** 17 jewels, RF#49300, c. 1965, 14k gold................................. **150-225**

*Baume & Mercier Wristwatch*

**Baume & Mercier,** 17 jewels, seconds window, auto-wind, c. 1950s, base metal (ILLUS.)............................................... **100-175**

**Baume & Mercier,** 18 jewels, "Riviera", c. 1980s, 18k gold & stainless steel.......... **400-525**

**Baume & Mercier,** quartz, enamel dial, tank, c. 1990s, 14k gold ....................... **200-350**

*Baylor Wristwatch*

**Baylor,** 17 jewels, diamond on bezel & dial, c. 1948, 14k gold (ILLUS.) ................... **175-275**

**Baylor,** 17 jewels, hidden lugs, 14k gold... **125-195**

**Baylor,** 17 jewels, hidden lugs, gold filled ..... **40-75**

**Beltone,** 17 jewels, fancy hidden lugs, 14k gold ..................................................... **125-200**

**Boucheron,** man's, No. A250565, tankstyle w/reeded bezel & dial, invisible clasp, black leather Boucheron strap, French hallmarks, original leather pouch, 18k white gold .......................................... **2,128**

**Bueche Girod,** lady's, enlongated oval gold tone dial, rectangular bezel w/stylized hinge lugs, satin band, 18k yellow gold ................................................. **978**

*Man's Cartier Wristwatch*

**Cartier,** man's, rectangular convex white dial w/black Roman numerals, rounded gold bezel, black leather strap, 18k yellow gold (ILLUS.)...................................... **1,380**

**Doxa,** 17 jewels, cal. 1361, c. 1948, 14k gold ...................................................... **100-175**

**Doxa,** 17 jewels, center sec., c. 1949, gold filled.......................................................... **40-70**

*Doxa 17 Jewel Wristwatch*

**Doxa,** 17 jewels, center sec., stainless steel (ILLUS.) ............................................. **45-65**

**Doxa,** 17 jewels, chronog., 2 reg., c. 1942, gold filled ............................................... **250-400**

*Doxa 17 Jewel Wristwatch*

**Doxa,** 17 jewels, chronog., cal. 1220, c. 1940, gold filled (ILLUS.)........................ **175-275**

**Doxa,** 17 jewels, chronog., cal. 1220, c. 1940, stainless steel............................... **175-275**

*Doxa "Grafic" Date Wristwatch*

**Doxa,** 17 jewels, "Grafic" date, 14k gold
(ILLUS.) ................................................ **100-175**
**Driva,** 15 jewels, 5 min. repeater, 14k .. **3,000-4,000**
**Driva,** 15 jewels, repeater, repeats on
gong, repeater wound by bolt above
hand, c. 1930, stainless steel .......... **3,500-4,500**
**Driva,** 17 jewels, double teardrop lugs, c.
1945, 14k gold ..................................... **125-200**
**Gianmaria Buccellati,** man's, No. 46600J,
engraved dial w/black tracery enamel,
black leather strap, yellow gold clasp,
Italian hallmarks, 18k yellow gold .............. **6,900**
**Hamilton,** Foster model, leather band, gold
buckle, 14 k gold, 10 jewel .................... **300-550**
**Hilton W. Co.,** 17 jewels, chronological by
Venius W. Co., 18k gold ....................... **300-400**
**Hirco,** 17 jewels, center second-hand,
auto-wind, gold filled ............................... **30-70**
**Huguenin, E.,** 17 jewels, "Black Star,"
c. 1940, 14k gold .................................. **300-425**
**Hydepark,** 17 jewels, flip up top, 14k gold **400-550**
**Illinois,** 15 jewels, "Arlington also
Hawthorne," ca. 1929, gold filled .......... **175-250**
**Illinois,** 17 jewels, "Ardsley also
Hudson," ca. 1929, gold filled ............... **150-225**
**Illinois,** 17 jewels, direct read, ca. 1925,
aluminum, case ............................. **2,000-2,500**

*Illinois Direct Read Wristwatch*

**Illinois,** 17 jewels, direct read, ca. 1925,
chrome, case & band (ILLUS.) .............. **225-325**
**Illinois,** 17 jewels, Model 207 on Movement, model 250 on case, 14k gold ...... **300-425**
**Ingersoll,** Mickey Mouse, embossed
"Mickey's" on metal band, mint in box,
originally priced $2.95, ca. 1933 .......... **600-800**
**Lehman,** lady's, Uti movement, round goldtone dial w/ruby indicators, one-half
framed in graduating calibre-cut chan-
nel-set rubies, snake link bracelet,
French hallmarks, 18k yellow gold (dial
slightly discolored)..................................... **1,495**
**Omega,** Sea Master, embossed back, Man
on Moon, stainless steel band, manual
wind, ca. 1969 ........................................ **600-850**
**Rolex,** datejust, quick set, oyster stainless
steel band, 30 jewel, ca. 1970s .......... **900-1,100**
**Rolex,** lady's, Oyster Perpetual, date,
crenelated bezel, silvertone dial,
abstract indicators, sweep seconds
hand, magnifying glass on date aper-
ture, jubilee bracelet, stainless steel ......... **1,035**
**Rolex,** No. 16233, stainless steel, two-tone
18k gold, Jubilee bracelet, 31 jewel.. **2,100-2,500**
**Rolex,** No. 16610, stainless steel
w/subdate, flip lock, oyster band, 31
jewel ............................................... **1,850-2,350**
**Rolex,** No. 1675, GMT Master, stainless
steel, 30 jewel, ca. 1970s ............... **1,000-1,350**
**Rolex,** No. 2940, stainless steel, bubble-
back, original dial, ca. 1940s ........... **1,200-1,800**

**Rolex,** No. 2940, stainless steel, bubble-
back, re-done dial, ca. 1940s ............ **800-1,200**
**Rolex,** No. 5500, Air King, stainless steel,
heavy oyster bracelet, 26 jewel, ca.
1970s ................................................... **600-775**
**Tiffany & Co.,** lady's, "Atlas," Roman
numerals on bezel, original Tiffany & Co.
leather strap & blue felt pouch, 18k yel-
low gold (minor scratches to bezel).............. **978**
**U.S. Time,** Babe Ruth, Babe on dial,
leather strap, ca. 1948 (no box, fair con-
dition) .................................................... **225-300**
**Universal,** man's, Geneve, square black
abstract indicators, heavy mesh bracelet, 18k yellow gold (minor scratches to
crystal)......................................................... **460**

# WEATHERVANES & ROOF ORNAMENTS

*Roof glass was the creation of a gentleman from Crawfordville, Indiana in the late 19th century. Scores of pieces adorned the roof peak, front porch, front doors and windows of charming Victo-rian homes during the 1890s. All of these pieces carried the mark "Dec. 1, 91," the date of the origi-nal patent.*

*A range of colors was available including dark red, light and dark blue, green opaque glass, amber, white with a vaseline tint, and clear, which over the years has often turned a light purple due to exposure to sunlight.*

*Roof pieces slid into a bent metal (usually tin) track which was also stamped with the 1891 patent date. Large upside-down "J's" might be seen stand-ing, some 14" high, at the outer edges of the roof which was then lined with arrowhead-shaped pieces about 41/2" to 6" high. Where two peaks met, a double-wheel shape sometimes adorned the intersection. Also common were fan-shaped pieces that fit in the ninety degree angles of porch col-umns. These fans were sometimes used in groups of four to make a circular window for a door or hall-way.*

*Other unusual pieces included sections used above doorways and a glass ornament that was used in conjunction with a large 3' scrolled brace. This brace elevated itself above the roof crest arrowhead glass and held a ball in its center. The ball was designed in a Dot and Dash design that matched the pattern of the roof crest glass. This metal scrolling and the glass ball were not grounded like a lightning rod system and served a decorative purpose only.*

*Weathervanes were widely popular with Ameri-can farmers at a time when agriculture dominated the workforce of America in the 19th and early 20th centuries. This rooftop adjunct was not only decora-tive but provided a reliable guide to wind direction from afar. Today farming employs less than 5% of the American workforce but the old adage, "You can take the boy out of the farm, but not the farm out of the boy" still holds true as evidenced by the continued popularity of farm-related antiques. Today valuable old weathervanes adorn walls above fireplaces, in kitchens and family rooms and even, on a few rooftops.*

*As in the past, vanes in the forms of animals remain the most popular with collectors. Farmers sometimes used vanes which represented the stock they raised, so cows and horses were the most common forms, with chickens and pigs also widely seen. Eagles, of course, were popular with the patriotic-minded. Sheep, ears of corn and mules can also be found quite often but more rare are beavers, fish, and wolverines.*

*Today when you are looking at old weathervanes you are likely to find them with bullet holes since they were popular targets for little boys and hunters of the past. The rarest examples can be found in undamaged condition with an original finish and perhaps traces of original gilding.In addition to animal-form vanes, beautiful glass-tailed arrow vanes were popular. Found in basically two shapes, rectangular and kite-tail, the framed, colored glass was often etched. The six most common etched designs include:*

*1. -Company names such as Barnett, Electra, Kretzer, and Shinn*

*2.-Fleur-de-lis*

*3. d*

*5. Hearts and balls*

*6. Maltese cross*

*What better way to market your company name than perched high atop a few barns around the farming community? In fact, the design of the ball, the arrow and the system was a mark of the company that installed the system. Often reproduced, an original glass-tail vane should show the stains that result from the rusting of the frame around the glass, unless the arrow frame is of a later example made of aluminum*

*—Phil Steiner*

*Pricing:Current market prices for smaller vanes, dependent on the condition and rarity of form, may run as follows:*

**Arrow,** molded copper, on a mounting pole, America, late 19th c., overall 54" l., 12" h. (small crease & tear to feather ends) .......................................................... **$489**

*Arrow Weathervane*

**Arrow,** sheet metal, the silhouetted arrow cut w/circles, scrolls, fleur-de-lis & an arrowhead, mounted on a later metal rod

& base, some corrosion, late 19th c., 74 1/4" l., 18 1/2" h. (ILLUS.)..................... **1,725**
**Arrowheads,** 4 1/2" l. ......................................... **75**
**Arrowheads,** 6" l. ...................................... **100-175**
**Barnett Systems,** red script............................ **375**
**Bull,** sheet metal, silhouetted form w/head raised, worn old white & black repaint, 25" l. (battered, pipe rod holder reattached) ........................................................ **385**
**Bull,** molded & gilded copper, full-bodied animal covered in old weathered gilding, mounted on a repaired rod & a later black metal base, third quarter 19th c., 24 1/2" l., 17 1/4" h. ............................. **4,887**
**Chicken,** large, in perfect condition................. **500**
**Chicken,** small, in perfect condition ................ **350**

*Cod Fish Weathervane*

**Cod fish,** gilt copper, New England, late 19th century (a few minor dents), 30" l. (ILLUS.) .......................................... **1,500-2,500**
**Cow,** copper hollow body w/cast zinc head, standing on crossbar, 28" l. (old soldered repair, bullet hole repair, legs battered & wired to rod)................................. **2,750**
**Cow,** large, in perfect condition ....................... **375**

*Assorted Animal Weathervanes*

**Cow,** large, standing on end of arrow rod w/arrow point & pierced diamond "King" logo (ILLUS. center) .................................... **425**
**Cow,** molded & gilded zinc, standing full-bodied animal w/long pointed horns, on a shaped rectangular base tapering down to a short bar above the arrow directional, American, third quarter 19th c., 49 1/2" l., 50 1/2" h. .............................. **9,775**
**Cow,** small, in perfect condition........................ **225**
**Double-wheels** ............................................. **1,250**
**Ear of corn,** in perfect condition.................... **1,000**
**Electra** ............................................................ **350**
**Fan-shaped pieces** ....................................... **600**
**Fish,** wood w/lead & copper detail, a flat silhouetted board fish w/metal fins, plus iron hook, 31 1/2" l. ..................................... **523**
**Fleur-de-lis** ............................................. **175-225**
**Fruits, Autumn Varieties,** small folio, 1871, old frame, 2189 (stains, foxing).......... **165**

**Hearts & balls,** 18" - 24" .......................... **250-350**
**Horse,** circus, in perfect condition .................... **350**
**Horse,** circus-type, standing on end of arrow rod w/arrow point & pierced diamond "King" logo (ILLUS. bottom w/cow)..... **475**
**Horse,** common, in perfect condition............... **200**
**Horse,** copper (standing or running), in perfect condition .............................................. **500**
**Horse,** running, copper w/old greyish green patina, hollow body w/good detail, mounted on crossbar, 31" l. ...................... **3,080**
**Horse,** trotting, molded metal, mounted on a diagonally braced support w/a sheet metal broom-form terminal, old weathered painted surface, Maine, late 19th c., 22" h., 47" l. .............................................. **2,875**

*Horse Weathervane*

**Horse,** copper, Black Hawk, America, 19th c., verdigris surface, 26" l. (ILLUS.).... **800-1,200**
**Horse,** hackney-type, molded & gilded copper, the full-bodied figure of a running horse w/a zinc head & a cropped tail, w/old gilding, mounted on a later rod & a black metal base, third quarter 19th c., 30 1/2" l., 21" h. ........................................ **6,325**
**Horse,** prancing, molded & silvered zinc, the swell-bodied model of a horse w/sheet metal ears, ridged mane & stylized leaf fitted between its ears, mounted on a rod, third quarter 19th c., 40 1/2" l., 23" h. (minor repairs, tail loose) ....................................................... **9,200**
**Hunter,** sheet iron silhouetted figure of a hunter taking aim, painted black, late 19th - early 20th c., 25" l., 26 1/2" h. ......... **1,265**
**Krtezer** ........................................................... **300**
**Maltese Cross,** 18" - 24"........................... **250-350**
**Moon & comet** ....................................... **250-375**
**Pig,** large, in perfect condition, 14"................... **850**
**Pig,** medium, in perfect condition .................... **475**
**Pig,** small, in perfect condition.......................... **325**
**Plain,** kite-tail.................................................. **150**
**Plain,** rectangular ............................................ **165**

*Rooster Weathervane*

**Rooster,** copper, America, 19th c., 19 1/2" h. (ILLUS.).................................. **700-900**
**Rooster,** realistically molded silver-colored body standing on end of arrow rod w/arrow point & pierced diamond "King" logo (ILLUS. top w/cow) ............................... **500**
**Shinn** .............................................................. **300**
**Snowflake,** 18" - 24" .............................. **150-200**
**Star in diamond,** 18" ...................................... **275**

*Upside-down "J" Roof Glass*

**Upside-down "J,"** 14" h. (ILLUS.) ................ **1,000**

# WESTERN AMERICANA

**Advertisement,** "Cream of Wheat," original picture showing 1880s cowboy w/U.S. saddle bags riding up to mailbox marked "Cream of Wheat," by Wyeth, 32 x 42".... **$1,200**
**Autograph book,** red leather-bound w/gold edging & marked "Autographs," includes Buffalo Bill, "Arizona John" Burke & Kit Carson Jr., acquired at Manchester, N.H. performance, January 1875 .............................................................. **900**
**Bear trap,** Newhouse No. 5 ............................ **425**
**Bear trap,** Oneida, S. Newhouse, Kenwood N.Y., cast teeth w/drag ...................... **450**
**Belt,** thick leather w/heavy spotting design, marked "Made on 101 Ranch," size 48 ........ **425**
**Bit,** Crocket three-concho w/Oscar Crocket-style engraving .......................... **1,400**

*Inscribed "Pistol" Bit*

**Bit,** figural pistol, inscribed "W.F. Cody," Anchor (ILLUS.) ........................................ **3,000**

*G.S. Garcia Bit by Gutierrez*

**Bit,** full silver overlaid half breed w/large showy conchos, made by Gutierrez while working for G.S. Garcia, Elko, Nev., (ILLUS.) .......................................... **3,000**

**Bit,** silver & copper mounted gal-leg style, Buermann, all original ................................... **300**

**Bit,** silver & copper mounted w/inlaid mother-of-pearl, Kelly Brothers ................... **500**

**Bit,** silver heart, Oscar Crockett ....................... **550**

**Bit,** silver mounted w/copper Indian head concho, Kelly Brothers ................................ **600**

**Bit,** sterling inlaid kissing bird, G.S. Garcia (shows some wear) ..................................... **685**

**Book,** "Spur Marks" w/picture of spur illustrated by J.O. Bass on front cover, limited edition by N. Mitchell ............................ **450**

**Book,** "The James Brothers," illustrated first edition, copyright 1882 (wear) .............. **525**

**Book,** "The Story of the Wild West & Campfire Chats by Buffalo Bill," first edition w/250 original illustrations, copyright 1880 ............................................................ **275**

**Bosal,** signed Luis B. Ortega, braided by Ortega & Bob Mecate.................................... **550**

**Branding iron,** Teddy Roosevelt's hand-forged famous North Dakota Maltese Cross, includes "North Dakota Brand Record" book w/Maltese Cross on front cover ........................................................ **1,100**

*Braided Bridle*

**Bridle,** black & white top end, hitch braided in diamond pattern, horse hair, Deer Lodge Prison (ILLUS.)............................... **3,200**

**Calendar,** 1955, depicts cowgirl holding hat, marked "Newman's, Red Lodge, Montana" ...................................................... **105**

**Cartridge money belt,** rich, dark leather w/rectangular silver buckle, Charles E. Coggshall, Miles City, Mont., ca. 1895-1909 .......................................................... **1,300**

**Catalog,** marked "Al. Furstnow Saddlery Company" above bucking bronco & "Miles City, Montana USA" below, No. 36, ca. 1929 ............................................... **175**

**Catalog,** "The Lee-Saddles, Manufactured by F.C. Lee Saddlery" above bucking bronco w/"Pierre - So. Dakota" below, ca. 1934-35 ...................................... **225**

**Catalog,** "Visalia Stock Saddle Co., San Francisco. Cal.," No. 30, from Luis Ortega's personal collection, signed & stamped by Oretega, 1934.......................... **250**

*Batwing-style Chaps*

**Chaps,** batwing-style w/pinked edging, two-color leather, J.T. Irick, Casper, Wyo. (ILLUS.)............................................... **700**

**Chaps,** batwing-style w/tooled belt & 14 conchos, Otto Ernst, Sheridan, Wyo. ........... **550**

**Chaps,** fringed, shotgun-style in two-colored leather, S.C. Gallup Saddle Co., ca. 1889-1910.................................... **1,900**

**Chaps,** fringed, step-in style w/20 original conchos, R.T. Fraizer ............................... **4,740**

*Woolly Chaps*

**Chaps,** gold, woolly w/large carved belt, Visalia S.F. (ILLUS.)................................. **1,400**
**Chaps,** shiny black woolly w/diamond pattern belt, Bools & Butler, Reno, Nev., ca. 1920-30s ..................................................... **2,300**

*Cowboy Sprinkler*

**Cowboy sprinkler,** roping cowboy w/original paint, one of fifty made by Patch family, Virginia, ca. 1954 (ILLUS.) ..................... **900**
**Cowgirl outfit,** includes vest, fringed skirt, scarf, hat & boots, Pendleton Roundup souvenir....................................................... **135**

*Five-Star Cuffs*

**Cuffs,** heavy spotted five-Star Cuffs (ILLUS.) ..... **350**
**Cuffs,** "Lasso Em Bill," unused, in original box ............................................................. **125**
**Cuffs,** R.A. Bennett, Buffalo, N.Y., border stamped, ca. 1890-1925 ............................. **400**
**Cuffs,** stamped-basket style, marked "C.P. Shipley, Kansas City".................................. **300**
**Curry comb,** marked "Duplex Curry Comb, Anchor Brand, New Britain Conn., North & Judd Mfg. Co.," pat. 1909 ..................... **30**

**Gauntlets,** fringed w/beaded buffalo & diamond, pr. ...................................................... **600**

*Geometric Pattern Beaded Gauntlets*

**Gauntlets,** fringed w/embroidered star & fully beaded geometric pattern, pr. (ILLUS.)...................................................... **750**
**Hat,** black, circle-H w/Nutria fur, Hamley Saddle Company, Pendleton, Ore. ............. **625**
**Hat,** marked "Let er' Buck" & a cowboy riding a bronco on the crown, early Pendleton Roundup souvenir...................... **250**
**Hat,** Stetson, cowgirl marked w/Stetson stamp "Boss Raw Edge, Kettle Fresh, Made of Real Nutria Fur," Silverwoods Los Angeles store, 4 1/2" brim, 7 1/2 crown.......................................................... **850**
**Hat,** Stetson, cream w/white trim, bound rolled edge, 5" brim, 7" crown .................. **1,150**
**Hat,** Stetson, large, grey w/5" brim, 8" crown.......................................................... **850**
**Headstall,** silver mounted geometrical designs w/full sterling mounted California bit, extra quality braided reins & romel, ca. 1890-1910 .............................. **1,900**
**Headstall,** tooled w/Crockett heart bit & brass star conchos, C.P. Shipley, Kansas City ....................................................... **275**
**Holster,** hand-tooled double loop w/double cartouche, S.C. Gallup, Pueblo, Colo., ca. 1889-1910, rare .......................... **525**
**Holster,** tooled, J.W. Helder, Muskogee, Oka. & Cheyenne, Wyo., ca. 1931-32.......... **190**
**Holster w/belt,** basketweave stamping on both, Heiser holster w/Eubanks (Boise, Id.) belt ................................................... **100**
**Holster w/belt,** full stamped flap-style holster w/Heiser belt, Victor Ario, Great Falls, Mont., includes Colorado Dept. of Correction Badge ........................................ **150**
**Holster w/belt,** rawhide buck-stitching on Heiser holster w/George Lawrence belt ......... **70**
**Horn table,** stacked horns ornately decorated w/arrows, horse shoes, stars & geometric design all carved from horns (ILLUS. top next column) .......................... **2,200**
**Magazine,** "Buffalo Bill Bids You Good Bye, A Farewell Salute, Magazine And Official Review, Price 10¢ ," includes story about Cody's horse by Mark Twain & advertising for new automobiles, 1910........ **325**
**Movie poster,** early colorful lithograph of "Custer's Last Fight, The Greatest Wild West Feature," depicts Indians shooting rifles in front of fort w/Custer & Sitting

Bull in corners above, Quality Amusement Corp., ................................................. **425**

*Ornate Horn Table*

**Newspaper,** "The Cheyenne Daily Leader" Frontier Days Special Issue, Aug. 20-22, 1908, depicts roping cowboy on front w/"Wyoming - a State of Wonderful, Undeveloped Resources, Wyoming Development Number" ................................. **195**

*Buffalo Bill Photograph*

**Photograph,** Buffalo Bill Cody, by E.H. Rood, Denver, Colo., 7 x 9" (ILLUS.) ........... **700**
**Pipe,** ornate Meerschaum w/horse motif & case ......................................................... **210**
**Pomel bags w/inside holster,** tooled leaf design on rich medium brown leather, Main & Winchester, San Francisco, Calif., ca. 1849-1905 ................................. **4,500**
**Program,** "Buffalo Bill's Wild West," depicting Buffalo Bill in center oval w/a buffalo in lower right corner & Indian in lower left, 1888 (shows wear & fraying) ................. **220**
**Program,** "Stampede at Calgary Alberta 1912," personal rodeo program of champion bronco rider Eddie Watrin (shows wear & creasing) ........................................ **225**
**Ranger buckle set,** sterling silver w/14k gold bucking horse & rider, stars & longhorn, Comstock Colo., 1" w. ......................... **450**
**Reata,** braided, from Tom Mix Collection, 70' l. .................................................................. **550**
**Reata,** braided rawhide, 70' l. ........................... **270**
**Reata,** child's, fine quality braiding, 9' l. .............. **60**
**Reward poster,** "$50.00 REWARD - Wells Fargo & Company Express, will pay a reward of Fifty Dollars of the arrest and detention of JAMES E. BARRY," 1911 ........ **225**

**Rifle scabbard,** dark, smooth leather, P.A. Wilkerson, Buffalo, N.Y., ca. 1885-1930s ..... **400**
**Rifle scabbard,** stamped w/wide border, G.S. Garcia, Elko, Nev. ................................. **600**
**Saddle,** Cheyenne swell fork, stamped border, F.A. Meanea ......................................... **525**
**Saddle,** child's, Alfred Cornish, Omaha, Neb., 13" swells, 11 1/2" seat....................... **255**
**Saddle,** fully tooled w/eighteen large engraved heart conchos & silver-covered swells & cantle, Padgitt Brothers, Dallas, Texas ............................................. **1,200**
**Saddle,** R.T. Frazier, full stamped & tooled w/padded seat & nickel horn, rich light brown color ..................................................... **3,200**

*J.S. Collins Side Saddle*

**Saddle,** side-saddle style, original light brown coloring, slipper stirrup & original Collins-marked double cinches, J.S. Collins & Company, Cheyenne, Wyo., ca. 1876-1886 (ILLUS.).................................... **1,900**
**Saddle bags,** dark, smooth leather, J.G. Vandoren, Casper, Wyo., ca. 1900-1920s ....................................................... **400**
**Saddle bags,** fully tooled design, Connolly Bros., Billings, Mont. ................................ **1,400**

*Will Rogers Silk Scarf*

**Scarf,** silk, depicts Will Rogers in center oval, green background & cowboy motif border (ILLUS.) ........................................... **175**

**Spur straps,** bib-style w/early unique tooling, Victor L. Earmshield, Marysville, Calif., ca. 1875 ............................................. **500**

**Spur straps,** marked "Collins & Morrison, Omaha, Neb.," original conchos, ca. 1880s ........................................................ **150**

**Spurs,** bronze, Hercules buffalo head, 10-point rowels, Anchor, 1911 & 1912 pat. date, pr. ..................................................... **750**

**Spurs,** bronze, Hercules large double gal-leg style, 20-point rowels, Anchor, ca. 1880s, pr. ............................................... **1,100**

**Spurs,** bronze, Hercules star pattern, 10-point rowels, North & Judd, pr. ...................... **900**

**Spurs,** bronze, Hercules target pattern, 10-point rowels, Anchor, 1912 pat. date, pr. ..... **850**

**Spurs,** bronze, horse head, 10-point rowels, North & Judd, pr. .................................... **375**

**Spurs,** double mounted gal-leg style w/gold slippers & garters, silver-plated rowels & heart buttons, tooled straps w/sterling & gold buckle sets, McChesney, pr. ............ **3,300**

*Inlaid Sterling Silver Spurs*

**Spurs,** inlaid sterling silver, Visalia's version of G.S. Garcia's "Dandy Pattern," original tooled straps & marked conchos, 12-point rowels, pr. (ILLUS.) ..................... **5,400**

**Spurs,** silver, copper & brass mounted, gal-leg style, 6-point rowels, McChesney, pr. .............................................................. **1,050**

*Crockett Gal-Leg Style Spurs*

**Spurs,** silver diamond band pattern, gal-leg style, 8-point rowels, Crockett, pr. (ILLUS.) ...................................................... **3,000**

**Spurs,** silver inlaid crescent moon pattern w/star AB entwined mark, extra long chap guards, 10-point feathered rowels, August Buermann, pr. .............................. **3,800**

**Spurs,** silver mounted, entwined hearts & diamond pattern, 20-point rowels, Oscar Crockett, pr. ............................................. **2,000**

**Spurs,** silver mounted, large heart-shaped shank style, 6-point rowels, Kelly Brothers, pr. ...................................................... **6,750**

**Spurs,** silver mounted, shield pattern, 12-point rowels, McChesney, pr. ...................... **925**

**Stagecoach trunk,** dark brown leather w/padded top & clothing compartment in lid, includes Blackall's Somerville Express, Boston shipping tag, 1800s .......... **375**

**Stagecoach trunk,** salesman's sample size, leather-covered & tacked, soft lid w/inside top storage ................................... **450**

**Stagecoach trunk,** studded cowhide w/hinge lock, top marked "J. H." in oval w/studs, relined w/1830 dated newspaper .......................................................... **550**

**Tack bag,** large, canvas, front marked "Johnson Harness Shop of Dillon, Mont" above, "W. Christensen, Wisdom Mont" below .............................................................. **200**

**Tail holder,** Perfection Cow, pat. 1891 ............. **85**

*Tapaderos*

**Tapaderos,** fully tooled design, Al. Furstnow, Miles City, Mont., pr. (ILLUS.) ............. **500**

**Tether,** American Railway Express, "AMRYEX 30," rare 30 lb. style ................... **150**

**Trunk,** leather, studded w/forged latch, ca. 1750-1850s, 3' w., 17" h. ............................... **300**

**Vest,** four-button cowhide, marked "Made on 101 Ranch" w/101 ranch rivets, Indian camp scene w/big fire & marked "Marland Camp, Dec. 1-8, 1922" .................. **550**

**Watch,** American Waltham, gold hunting case w/longhorn on front, 17 jewel, Serial No.7823402, size 18, ca. 1892 ......... **600**

**Wolf trap,** Oneida, S. Newhouse, Lititz Pa., No. 114, exposed cast teeth ........................ **175**

# WESTERN CHARACTER COLLECTIBLES

*Since the closing of the Western frontier in the late 19th century the myth of the American cowboy has loomed large in popular fiction. With the growth of the motion picture industry early in this century, cowboy heroes became a mainstay of the entertainment industry. By the 1920s major Western heroes were a big draw at the box office and this popularity continued with the dawning of the TV age in the 1950s. We list here a variety of collectibles relating to all American Western personalities popular this century.*

*Buffalo Bill Poster*

**Buffalo Bill poster,** scene of cowboys & covered wagons, one marked "Pikes Peak or Bust" w/"Buffalo Bill Himself in Parade Every Morning 10:30 A.M." above scene & "Sells-Floto - Buffalo Bill - Santa Cruz - April 18" below, wood frame (ILLUS.) ..................................... **$2,200**

*Hopalong Cassidy Radio*

**Hopalong Cassidy radio,** Arvin, 1950, near mint (ILLUS.) ......................................... **458**
**Hopalong Cassidy wristwatch,** signed "Good Luck, Hoppy," U.S. Time, original display box .................................................. **330**
**Hopalong Cassidy alarm clock,** black w/red numerals & hands, picture of Happy & his horse on dial, U.S. Time .......... **193**

*Hopalong Cassidy & Topper Figures*

**Hopalong Cassidy & Topper figures,** plastic, Hopalong in black on white horse w/black trim w/original box, very good w/good box, Ideal (ILLUS.)............................. **90**

*Lone Ranger Boots*

**Lone Ranger boots,** child's, rubber, tan w/dark brown trim & spurs, Lone Ranger & Silver pictured on sides (ILLUS.) .............. **303**
**Lone Ranger first aid kit,** metal, by American Can Co., scene of Lone Ranger on Silver & holding lasso which frames "Official Lone Ranger First Aid Kit," 1938, 4" sq., 1 1/2" h. (minor scrapes) ........... **60**
**Lone Ranger ring,** "Rocket to the Moon" w/three rockets, premium offer, good .......... **300**
**Lone Ranger toy,** windup tin, Lone Ranger on rocker base, good, Marx ........................ **300**

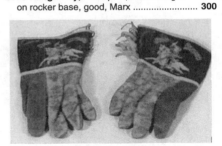

*Red Ryder Gloves*

**Red Ryder gloves,** red, blue & black cloth, design of Red Ryder on horseback at cuff, ca. 1950s, excellent condition, pr. (ILLUS.)........................................................ **55**

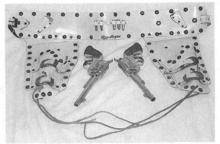

*Roy Rogers Double Gun & Holster Set*

**Roy Rogers cap guns with holsters,** ca. 1950s, Classy (ILLUS.) ................................ **798**
**Roy Rogers microscope ring,** good............... **110**

*Roy Rogers Paint Set*

**Roy Rogers paint set,** in original case, ca.
1950s, unused (ILLUS.) ............................... **121**
**Roy Rogers ring,** w/branding iron design,
good ............................................................ **95**
**Roy Rogers & Trigger flashlight,** metal &
plastic w/signal siren, good ........................... **50**

*Wild Bill Hickok Coloring Book*

**Wild Bill Hickok coloring book,** cover
w/scene of Wild Bill & his horse chased
by three Indians on horseback, ca. 1961,
Waldman Publishing Corp., published by
Playmore, Inc., unused (ILLUS.) ................... **20**

*Wild Bill Hickok Holster Set*

**Wild Bill Hickok guns & holsters set,**
double holsters w/cap guns in original
box, ca. 1950s, mint condition, Leslie
Henry (ILLUS.) ............................................. **935**

# WHISTLES
## STEAM WHISTLES

*The steam whistle was invented by Adrian
Stephens of Plymouth, England, in 1826. It was
designed only to "render clearly audible the escape
of steam from a safety valve." The steam whistle
was first used on a steamship in New England in
1837. The first whistles appeared on Mississippi
River paddlewheelers in 1844. They were simple
plain (single note) whistles. Two or more of these
plain whistles could be mounted together on a common manifold to create a pleasant sounding three-
bell chime. In 1877 the Crosby Steam Gage &
Valve Co. developed and patented the "Original
Single Bell Chime" whistle. As the name implies,
this is a cylindrical casting separated into three
chambers of different lengths, tuned to produce a
pleasant musical chord. In the early years, steam
locomotives were fitted with plain whistles, but by
the start of the 20th century, chime whistles were
routinely being installed.*

*American Chime Steam Whistle*

**American Shipbuilding,** ship, cylindrical
bell, separate valve design, plain single
note base tone whistle, long bell type
base, 10" x 36" (ILLUS.) .......................... **$3,000**

*Buckeye Chime Steam Whistle*

**Buckeye,** used inside factories or small outside applications, cylindrical chime bell, integral valve design, w/pull chord for whistle, 2" d. (ILLUS.) ............................ **150**

*"Mocking Bird" Variable Pitch Steam Whistle*

**Crane,** cylindrical "Mocking Bird" variable pitch bell, separate valve design, 5" d. (ILLUS.)...................................................... **500**

**Crosby,** cylindrical chime bell, integral valve design, plain single note whistle, note fancy acorn nut, 4" d. ........................... **200**

**Fitts,** United Water or Worcester, cylindrical chime bell, separate valve design, gong type whistle, vertical, 6" d. .................. **600**

*"Mocking Bird" Variable Pitch Steam Whistle*

**Lunkenheimer Co.,** cylindrical "Mocking Bird" variable pitch bell, integral valve design, w/spring loaded chain pull chord for whistle, works like a toy slide whistle, desirable, 2 1/2" d. (ILLUS.) .................. **300-600**

*Lunkenheimer Steam Whistle*

**Lunkenheimer Co.,** small boat or traction engine or steam roller, cylindrical chime bell, integral valve design, plain single note whistle, 3 1/2" d. (ILLUS.)..................... **250**

**Lunkenheimer Co.,** steamboat, cylindrical chime bells, separate valve design, w/pull chord for whistle, cast bronze manifold, very rare & desirable, 5", 6" & 8" d. ......................................................... **5,000**

*Powell Chime Steam Whistle*

**Powell,** ship or factory, cylindrical bell, separate valve design, plain single note whistle, 8" d. (ILLUS.).................................... **700**

*Schaeffer & Budenberg Whistle*

**Schaeffer & Budenberg,** locomotive or small ship, cylindrical chime bell, separate valve design, w/pull chord for whistle, 6" d. (ILLUS.) ........................................ **600**

*Horizontal Chime Steam Whistle*

**Sinker-Davis,** cast iron, cylindrical chime bell, separate valve design, gong type whistle, horizontal, 8" d. (ILLUS.) ............... **700**

*Star Brass Steam Whistle*

**Star Brass,** cylindrical chime bell, integral valve design, w/pull chord for whistle, rare & desirable 12" d. (ILLUS.) ...... **3,000-5,000**

*"Organ Pipe" Steam Whistle*

**Steven & Struthers,** cylindrical "organ pipe" bell, separate valve design, Glasgow, Scotland, popular in England, 6" d. (ILLUS.) ........................................................ **800**

**Unknown manufacturer,** steam locomotive, five-chime step-top bell, integral valve design, 6" d. .................................... **1,000**

# WINDMILL WEIGHTS

Windmill weights were manufactured primarily between about 1875 and 1925 for use as counterbalance or governor weights on windmills. Yet, until about 1985, few persons outside the Midwest had ever heard of them. Since that time, they have attracted interest from collectors of folk art and farm equipment as an art form and as a reminder of a way of life which has long since disappeared. This interest has resulted in a dramatic increase in their value and in a like decrease in availability.

Windmill weights, always cast in iron, with two exceptions, can be classified into two categories—counterbalance and governor or regulator weights. The counterbalance weights, which were utilized on vaneless mills as a method of counterbalancing the weight of the windmill's wheels, are primarily figural in form—horses, roosters, bulls, buffaloes, squirrels, spears, arrows, and stars, among others. The governor or regulator weights are primarily non-figural and attract interest primarily from windmill restorers and advanced collectors.

The windmill manufacturers, and farms using windmill weight-type windmills, were concentrated primarily in the Midwest. Hence, the vast majority of weights found today appear in farm sales or in local auctions in Nebraska, Kansas, Minnesota, and the Dakotas. As with most antiques and collectibles which attract and increase prices, reproductions and artfully repaired weights are now somewhat commonplace. Therefore, weight purchasers should be wary of getting "something for nothing" or of any weights which have new paint or new rust.

The following rules should be observed:

1. Don't purchase anything in new paint unless you can remove it to determine age and condition.

2. Avoid weights which have uniform grind marks on the edge.

3. Don't sandblast weights or remove old paint. Patina or surface is acquired through a long aging process by exposure to the elements and is highly regarded by collectors. Removing the paint or sandblasting destroys the character, personality, and historical significance.

4. Don't pass on items because they are not described in a book or because the actual weight or dimensions differ from that indicated in the book. New forms (or variations of known forms) are continually being discovered. Windmill weights were produced at foundries using unsophisticated production techniques (by today's standards).

5. Don't buy a weight because someone says it is rare—it frequently isn't rare or even a weight. I have seen "rare" short-tail horses (the most common forms) and have heard of camels, pigs, and rabbits (which to my knowledge do not exist).

6. Buy the very best you can afford. Don't sacrifice quality, rarity, and condition for price. The great pieces will almost always increase in value while the average or mediocre pieces almost always do not.

7. Lastly, talk to and deal with knowledgeable and reputable dealers. They are generally happy to share their knowledge and enthusiasm.

Values are estimated retail prices and are based upon form, condition and rarity. Prices tend to be higher in large metropolitan areas, such as the East Coast.

—Richard S. Tucker

*Battleship*

**Battleship,** Monitor, concrete & cast-iron frame & turret, 62 lbs., Baker Manufacturing Company, Evansville, Wisconsin, 12 1/2 (at bracket) x 28 3/4", 8" h., to top of turret (ILLUS.) ............................ **2,001-2,500**

*Bell*

**Bell,** rounded corners, 15 1/2 lbs., maker unknown, very rare, some rusting, 2 3/8 x 5 1/4", 5 1/2" h. (ILLUS.)...... **1,001-1,500**

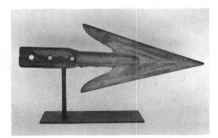

*Arrow*

**Arrow,** red paint, w/three small holes in the neck, 22 1/2 lbs. (including base), Leach Windmill Company, Joliet, Illinois, very rare, 1 3/8 x 25", 9 1/2" h. (ILLUS.)......................................... **$2,001-2,500**

*Bell, marked "6"*

**Bell,** marked "6," 43 lbs., Breyer Brothers, Whiting & Company, Waupun, Wisconsin, rare, 2 x 11 3/4", 14 1/2" h. (ILLUS.)........................................... **3,501-5,000**

*Buffalo with Molded 'Hair'*

**Buffalo,** w/molded 'hair,' 13 1/2 lbs. (without base), maker unknown, very rare, 1/2 x 16", 10 7/8" h. (ILLUS.) .. **3,501-5,000**

**Bull,** unmarked, 96 1/2 lbs., Fairbury Windmill Company, Fairbury, Nebraska, rare, original paint worn & rust, bull 1 1/2" x 24 1/4", 18" h., base 10 x 17 7/8", 3/4" h. ........................ **2,001-2,500**

*Fairbury Nebr. Bull*

**Bull,** marked "FAIRBURY NEBR.," 53 1/2 lbs. (including base), Fairbury Windmill Company, Fairbury, Nebraska, bull 5/8 x 24 1/2", 17 3/4" h., base 9 3/4 x 17 5/8", 3/8" h. (ILLUS.) .. **1,001-1,500**

*Bull*

**Bull,** thick w/separated tail, unmarked, 71 lbs. (including base), Fairbury Windmill

Company, Fairbury, Nebraska, rare, rusted, bull 1 1/4 x 24 1/2", 17 3/4" h., base 9 3/4 x 17 5/8", 3/8" h. (ILLUS.)........................................... **2,001-2,500**

*Canister*

**Canister,** marked "Fairbanks Morse," 17 1/2 lbs., Fairbanks, Morse & Company, Chicago, Illinois, rare, 11 3/4" d. (ILLUS.)........................................... **1,001-1,500**

*Cow*

**Cow,** white & black paint, w/embossed lettering "FAIRBURY" on side of cow, 54 lbs., Fairbury Windmill Company, Fairbury, Nebraska, very rare, cow 5/8 x 24 3/4", 17 5/8" h., base 9 3/4 x 17 5/8", 3/8" h. (ILLUS.)....... **2,001-2,500**

*Crescent Moon*

**Crescent moon,** points down, marked "AA13 - Standard," 14 1/2 lbs., F.W. Axtell Manufacturing Company, Fort Worth, Texas, rare, 2 1/8 x 10 1/2", 6 1/2" h. (ILLUS.) .................................. **251-500**

**Crescent moon,** points up, marked "A13 - SUCCESS," 24 lbs., Challenge Company, Batavia, Illinois, rare, 2 5/8 x 10 5/8", 6 1/2" h. .................................... **251-500**

**Disc,** 40 1/2 lbs., Baker Manufacturing Company, Evansville, Wisconsin, 3 x 10 1/4" ............................................ **Under 100**

*Eagle*

**Eagle,** 13 lbs., maker unknown, rare, 1/2 x 7 1/8", 15 3/4" h., 17" h. including lid (ILLUS.) ................... **5,000 and up**

**Governor weight,** marked "MFG BY BREYER BROS WHITING & CO WAUPUN WIS USA," 7 1/2 lbs., rare, 1 5/8 x 3 1/4", 5 5/8" h. .......................... **501-750**

**Governor weight,** model E S262, 17 1/2 lbs., U.S. Wind Engine & Pump Company, Batavia, Illinois, 7 7/8" d., 10 1/2" including bracket ................................... **100-250**

**Governor weight,** success, D17, 34 1/2 lbs., Hastings Foundry & Iron Works, Hastings, Nebraska, 8 1/2" d. ............... **100-250**

*Heart*

**Heart,** one of two sizes, marked "The Co. L. Houston Montgomery PA Patented June 1 1884 April 14 1885," maker unknown, 13 lbs., rare, 2 1/4 x 9 1/8", 10" h. (ILLUS.) ......................................... **3,501-5,000**

*Horse w/Long Tail*

**Horse,** long-tail w/large base, 57 1/2 lbs., Dempster Mill Manufacturing Company, Beatrice, Nebraska, rare, base 2 1/2 x 17 1/4", 21 1/2" h. (ILLUS.) ......................................... **2,501-3,500**

*Running Horse*

**Horse,** running, smaller version of two sizes, 33 lbs., attributed to Benjamin Danforth, Beatrice, Nebraska, rare, 1 1/2 x 19 1/2", 21 1/2" h. (ILLUS.) ........ **5,000 and up**

*Horseshoe*

**Horseshoe,** w/bar across middle, 17 1/2 lbs., maker unknown, 11/16 x 8 3/4" (including bracket), very rare, 10 3/4" h. (ILLUS.) ......................................... **3,501-5,000**

**Letter—B,** marked "Hildbreth Iron Works - Hildreth Neb," 54 lbs., Hildreth Iron Works, Hildreth, Nebraska, very rare,

2 5/8 x 12 3/4" (including bracket), 15 7/8" h. .................................... **5,000 and up**

*Ozark Letter "O"*

**Letter—Ozark "O,"** smallest of three sizes, 28 1/2 lbs., Breyer Brothers, Whiting & Company, Waupun, Wisconsin, rare, excluding base, 12" d. (ILLUS.) ........................................ **1,501-2,000**

*Letters—CWS*

**Letters—CWS,** 53 lbs. (including base), Cornell-Wigman-Searl Company, Lincoln, Nebraska, rare, weight 1 x 23", 10 7/8" h., base 12 x 18", 1/2" h. (ILLUS.)........................................... **3,501-5,000**
**Regulator weight,** Stover B13, 26 1/2 lbs., Stover Manufacturing Company, Freeport, Illinois, 2 3/4 x 7" ......................... **100-250**

*Rooster w/Long Stem*

**Rooster,** long-stem, marked "Hummer E 184" on tail, 9 1/2 lbs., Elgin Wind Power & Pump Company, Elgin, Illinois, 9 1/2 lbs., Elgin Wind Power & Pump Company, Elgin, Illinois (ILLUS.) .............. **751-1,000**
**Rooster,** yellow & red paint, marked "10 ft. No. 2" on tail, on red base, 34 lbs., Elgin Wind Power & Pump Company, Elgin, Illinois, 4 3/8 (at base) x 17", 15 3/4" h. ..................................................... **751-1,000**

*Rooster w/Barnacle-eye*

**Rooster,** barnacle-eye, white & red paint, 52 lbs., Elgin Wind Power & Pump Company, Elgin, Illinois, paint worn, 2 3/4 x 18", 18 1/2" h. (ILLUS.) ....... **3,501-5,000**

*Rooster w/Large Base*

**Rooster,** large base, red & white paint, marked "Hummer" on tail, 48 lbs., Elgin Wind Power & Pump Company, Elgin, Illinois, paint slightly worn, 4 3/8" (at base) x 17", 17 3/4" h. (ILLUS.)....... **1,501-2,000**

*Rooster*

**Rooster,** small mogul, one of three sizes, 60 lbs., 4 3/4 x 18 1/2", 18" h. (ILLUS.)............................................ **3,501-5,000**

*Rooster (A20)*

**Rooster,** duplex (A20), red & white paint, 64 lbs., Elgin Wind Power & Pump Company, Elgin, Illinois, paint worn, 2 1/2 x 19", 191/4" h. (ILLUS.) ....... **3,501-5,000**

*Woodmanse Rooster*

**Rooster,** Woodmanse, large, 63 lbs., Elgin Wind Power & Pump Company, Elgin, Illinois, some rust & paint worn, 3 3/4 x 18", 19 3/8" h. (ILLUS.)........ **1,001-1,500**

*Rooster*

**Rooster,** duplex, thick, red & white paint, 100 1/2 lbs., Elgin Wind Power & Pump Company, Elgin, Illinois, rare, paint worn, 4 3/8 x 19", 19 1/2" h. (ILLUS.) ....................................... **5,000 and up**

*Rooster w/Screw Leg*

**Rooster,** screw leg, 64 lbs., Elgin Wind Power & Pump Company, Elgin, Illinois, rare, 3 1/4 x 17 1/2", 20" h. (ILLUS.) ....................................... **5,000 and up**

*Shield*

**Shield,** decorated w/stars & stripes, 16 lbs. (including base), attributed to Challenge Wind Mill & Feed Mill Co., Batavia, Illinois, rare, excluding base, some rust & paint worn, 1 3/8 x 7 1/4", 8 3/8" h. (ILLUS.)........................................... **2,501-3,500**

*Spear*

**Spear,** embossed letters read "New Century Sauk Centre Minn," 34 1/2 lbs. (without base), maker unknown, rare, 2 x 15 1/4", 11" h. (ILLUS.) ............. **2,001-2,500**

*Spear Model 1912*

**Spear,** marked "MODEL - 1912," 39 lbs., Challenge Company, Batavia, Illinois, rare, 3 1/2 (at rear bracket) x 35 3/4", 14" h. (ILLUS.)................................. **3,501-5,000**
**Spear,** marked "Model 1913," 39 lbs., Challenge Company, Batavia, Illinois, 3 1/2 x 35 3/4", 14" h. ...................... **1,001-1,500**

*Squirrel*

**Squirrel,** 35 1/2 lbs., Elgin Wind & Pump Company, Elgin, Illinois, 3 (at base) x 13 3/4", 17" h. (ILLUS.)....... **3,501-5,000**

*Halladay Star*

**Star,** Halladay, five-pointed star, 38 1/2 lbs., U.S. Wind Engine & Pump Company, paint worn & some rusting, 2 3/4 x 14 3/4", 2 3/4" (ILLUS.).............. **501-750**
**Star,** (C24), five-pointed star w/remnants of white paint, 38 1/2 lbs., Flint & Walling Manufacturing Company, Kendellville, Indiana, rare, some rusting, 2 3/4 x 14 3/4", 14 3/4" h. (ILLUS. top next column) ............................................... **1,001-1,500**

*Star (C24)*

# WOOD SCULPTURES

*American folk sculpture is an important part of the American art scene today. Skilled wood carvers turned out ship's figureheads, cigar store figures, plaques and carousel animals of stylized beauty and great appeal. The wooden shipbuilding industry, which had originally nourished this folk art, declined after the Civil War and the talented carvers then turned to producing figures for tobacconist's shops, carousel animals and show figures for circuses. These figures and other early ornamental carvings that have survived the elements and years are eagerly sought.*

*"Rising Star" Cigar Store Figure*

**Boxer dancing figure,** pine, carved stylized figure of man w/articulated arms & legs, rotating head, painted brown, mounted on wood stand, late 19th c., 8 1/2" h. ................................................... **$1,495**

**Cigar store figure,** carved in the round & painted pine, small scale form of the performer "Rising Star," wearing a star diadem, fringed costume & high-button boots, holding a bunch of cigars in her left hand & standing on a crate marked "Cigars," America, third quarter 19th c., 57" h. (ILLUS.)......................................... **20,700**

**Cigar store figure of Indian Chief,** carved in the round & painted pine standing figure wearing a high colorful feathered headdress & a hide cloak over red & yellow costume, holding blocks of tobacco & bunches of cigars along w/a dagger, rectangular pedestal base, attributed to Samuel Robb, New York, ca. 1880, 66" h. ..................................................... **17,250**

*Carved Articulated Figure of Woman*

**Figure of woman,** carved pine, full-bodied female w/articulated joints & abstractly rendered facial features, mounted on white metal base, old natural color, probably Nebraska, ca. 1910, 37" h. (ILLUS.).. **1,955**

**Model of a foal,** carved & painted pine standing animal of slatted construction w/hollow head & body, solid carved legs, ears, mane & tail, Lexington, Kentucky, late 19th - early 20th c., 36" l., 35" h. ........ **9,200**

**Model of a rooster,** carved in the round & painted red pine stylized figure w/raised comb, mounted on black metal base,

America, late 19th - early 20th c., 18" l.,
18 1/2" h. ................................................ **9,200**

**Model of an American eagle,** carved
mahogany full-bodied, spread-winged
figure standing on cylindrical base, the
eyes fashioned of ebony & fruitwood,
signed on reverse "H. Winter," America,
20th c., by wing span 16 1/2" w.,
18 1/8" h. ................................................ **1,610**

**Ship figurehead,** carved in the round &
painted pine figure of Neptune, barechested, white-haired & grasping a blue
cloak, America, 19th c., 54" h. ................. **5,462**

*Ship Figurehead*

**Ship figurehead,** carved & painted pine
full-bodied figure of a dark-haired young
woman wearing a blue gown w/red &
white sashes tied around the waist &
holding a cluster of fruit & a rose in one
hand, America, 19th c., age cracks,
repainted, 56" h. (ILLUS.).......................... **9,775**

**Wall plaque,** carved in the half round &
painted pine, figure of an American
eagle w/talons grasping thirteen arrows
& an olive branch, a shield-shaped
breast plate & holding a banner in its
beak inscribed "E Pluribus Unum,"
America, third quarter 19th c.,
31 1/2 x 36 1/2" (ILLUS. top next
column) ................................................ **21,850**

**Whirligig,** carved & painted wood figure of
a man wearing a black jacket & blue
trousers, fitted w/rotating paddle arms,
America, early 20th c., 12" h. (some restoration to sheet metal paddles)................ **1,380**

*American Eagle Wall Plaque*

**Whirligig,** carved & painted figure of Native
American chief w/articulated eyes, nose
& mouth w/war paint & wearing a leather
headdress w/stylized feathers, a leather
skirt & boots w/black detailing, the
swinging arms terminating in green-
painted paddle baffles, swivelling on a
red-painted square base over a black-
painted compressed ball & stepped
plinth, America, 20th c., 17" h. ..................... **276**

*Whirligig Figure of Man*

**Whirligig,** carved & painted wood, stylized standing figure of man wearing a peaked cap, blue jacket, red vest & white trousers, the arms fitted as paddles that rotate, late 19th - early 20th c., 21" h. (ILLUS.) ...................................................... **6,325**

# WOODENWARES

*The patina and mellow coloring, along with the lightness and smoothness that come only with age and wear, attract collectors to old woodenwares. The earliest forms were the simplest and the shapes of items whittled out in the late 19th century varied little in form from those turned out in the American colonies two centuries earlier. A burl is a growth, or wart, on some trees in which the grain of the wood is twisted and turned in a manner which strengthens the fibers and causes a beautiful pattern to be formed. Treenware is simply a term for utilitarian items made from "treen," another word for wood. While maple was the primary wood used for these items, they are also abundant in pine, ash, oak, walnut, and other woods. "Lignum Vitae" is a species of wood from the West Indies that can always be identified by the contrasting colors of dark heartwood and light sapwood and by its heavy weight, which caused it to sink in water.*

*Also see KITCHENWARES.*

**Bowl,** burl, wide shallow round form w/flared sides, old soft finish, 6 3/4" d., 1 7/8" h. ...................................................... **$385**
**Bowl,** maple burl, deep rounded sides, deep honey-colored finish, 4" d., 2" h. ......... **138**
**Bowl,** turned & painted, flared sides, green w/later red trim, 19th c., 10 1/2" d., 3 1/4" h. (paint loss, dirt) ............................ **690**
**Bowl,** ash burl, deep curved sides on flat bottom, old soft finish, good color, 11" d., 4 3/8" h. (heavy interior wear) ..................... **880**
**Bowl,** birch, oblong w/deep sharply flaring sides, old worn patina, 10 1/2 x 18 1/4" l., 4 1/2" h. ......................................................... **116**

*Burl Bowl & Sugar Bucket*

**Bowl,** ash burl, deep rounded form w/protruding small rim handles, old worn patina, minor rim damage & small rim hole, 19th c., 13 1/2" d., 5" h. (ILLUS.) ......... **935**

**Bowl,** poplar, almond-shaped, old varnish finish, 12 x 19", 5" h. (wear & scratches from use, filled age crack in one end) ......... **182**
**Bowl,** ash burl, deep rounded turned sides w/a molded rim band, good old worn patina, 15" d., 5 1/4" h. ............................... **880**
**Bowl,** burl, primitive irregular rounded form w/widely flaring flattened sides, star-shaped patch in bottom, 19th c., 14 1/4 x 15 1/2", 5 1/2" h. ............................ **303**
**Bowl,** curly poplar, wide rounded form w/flat rim, refinished, 16" d., 5 1/2" h. ........... **248**
**Bowl,** ash burl, widely flaring rounded shape w/molded rim, good figure & good old patina,    19 3/4" d.,   5 3/4" h (age cracks, minor surface & edge damage) .... **1,540**
**Bowl,** turned, wide flat flaring sides tapering to a small round base, exterior w/old worn light blue paint, interior worn, 16 3/4 x 17 1/2", 5 3/4" h. ............................. **468**
**Bowl,** turned & painted wood, a wide shallow bowl w/slightly flared rim & turned band around the sides, raised on a wide turned pedestal foot, old red, black & yellow, 14 1/4 x 14 1/2", 6" h. ...................... **440**
**Bowl,** ash burl, deep rounded sides on a small flat base, wide flat rim w/incised rim band, good old finish, 15 1/2" d., 6 1/2" h. (minor age crack in rim) ............. **2,970**

*Large Hand-Tooled Burl Bowl*

**Bowl,** burl, hand-tooled, oval w/two open handles, known as an "Indians' Bowl," America,    18th    c.,    age    splits, 6 1/2 x 21 1/2 x 24 1/2" (ILLUS.) ............. **13,225**
**Bowl,** poplar, hand-turned, wide flaring rounded    sides,    old    brown    patina, 20 x 21 3/4", 6 1/2" h. ................................... **275**
**Bowl,** ash burl, deep rounded wide sides w/incised base band & grooved rim band, good figure, old scrubbed finish, 18 1/2" d., 7 3/4" h. (small natural crack in bottom) ................................................. **2,420**
**Bowl,** ash burl, deep oval boat-shaped form w/small flat bottom, old refinishing, 14 1/4 x 19", 8" h. (interior wear, glued V-shaped rim repair) ................................. **1,100**
**Bowl,** ash burl, deep rounded sides on a small flat base, good old finish, fissures are part of figure, 16" d., 16" h. ................. **1,210**
**Bucket,** painted, staved & hooped construction w/swing handle attached by wooden pegs, painted red, early 19th c., 9 1/4" d., 12" h. including handle (wear).... **2,185**
**Bucket,** cov., painted pine, stave construction w/two steel bands, tapering cylindrical form w/flat cover, old salmon red paint, 12 1/2" h. ............................................. **248**

**Butter churn,** painted, stave construction, tall gently tapering cylindrical form w/double wooden finger lappets at the bottom & one at the center & top edge, one stave forms upright rim handle, wooden lid & dasher, old worn red paint, 19th c., 24" h. (old repair in lid) ..................... **523**

**Candle box,** hanging-type, curly maple, rectangular open-topped form w/slightly pointed backboard w/hanging hole, cleaned down to traces of old brown, 19th c., 14 1/2" l. ......................................... **550**

*Pine Cookie Board*

**Cookie board,** pine, narrow rectangular board w/carved scene of Indian in circle w/long rifle & tomahawk, reverse w/pineapple in circle, old soft finish, 5 x 8" (ILLUS.)........................................................ **825**

**Cookie board,** beech, narrow rectangular board w/five carved scenes including a woman w/baby in crib, a woman at a well & a man w/knotted tree, old patina, some worm holes, 19th c., 3 1/2 x 28'.......... **220**

**Corset busk,** long flat hardwood slat w/rounded top end & notched bottom end, chip-carved w/designs including hearts, pinwheels, starflowers & the date "Octber 21, Day, Year 1768," light brown patina, 11 7/8" l. .......................................... **825**

**Cutlery tray,** painted & decorated, a molded rectangular bottom w/low canted sides w/a high central divider cut w/a high rounded central arch w/round cutout hand grip flanked by large upright scrolls, painted w/black scribed compass stars alternating w/circles against a ground of dots & wavy lines on mustard yellow, mid-19th c., 11 1/4 x 12 3/4" (minor paint wear, loss)............................. **8,625**

**Cutlery tray,** painted wood, rectangular w/canted sides, two compartments separated by a divider w/a shaped cutout & carved handle, molded rim & base, painted blue w/traces of red, America, mid-19th c., 9 1/2 x 13 1/2" (minor age splits)............................................................. **978**

**Cutting board,** pine, rectangular w/cut-out heart-shaped handle, old worn oiled finish, 6 3/4 x 13 1/2"........................................ **495**

**Dough box,** cov., painted poplar, rectangular top w/molded edges lifting above a deep box w/canted sides & base molding, worn old red paint, 19th c., 27" l. .......... **193**

**Dough box,** cov., poplar, splayed base w/square tapered legs, dovetailed case & one board top, old red repaint on base, 21 x 40", 28 1/2" h. ..................................... **468**

**Drying rack,** painted pine, two slender rectangular cross bars between slender straight uprights on shoe feet, old grey paint, mortised & pinned construction, 19th c., 19" w., 28" h. ................................... **413**

**Firkin,** stave construction w/tapering cylindrical sides, on stave extending above the rim & cut to form a flat handle, bentwood band around the rim & a bentwood lappet band around the bottom, old worn patina, 19th c., 5" d., 4 1/4" h. plus handle ....................................................................... **248**

**Jar,** cov., turned hardwood, footed squatty bulbous ring-turned base tapering gently to a wide mouth, fitted low domed cover w/turned button finial, wire bail handle w/wooden grip, brown varnish finish, attributed to Pease of Ohio, 19th c., 4 3/4" h. ...................................................... **578**

**Jar,** cov., turned slightly swelled cylindrical body w/low domed cover w/button finial, old yellow repaint, faded pencil inscription on bottom, 5" h. ..................................... **468**

**Jar,** cov., turned hardwood w/slightly tapering cylindrical body, ringed rim & ringed domed cover w/button finial, worn scrubbed finish varnished over, attributed to Pease of Ohio, 5 3/8" h. ................... **193**

*Turned Wood Jar*

**Jar,** cov., turned maple, footed bulbous base tapering gently to a wide mouth, fitted low domed cover w/turned button finial, fanciful feather design in reds & green on ochre ground, probably Ohio, first half 19th c., minor paint loss, old repaired crack, 6" d., 7" h. (ILLUS.)........... **2,645**

**Knife box,** mahogany, rectangular bottom w/deep gently canted sides w/scalloped rims, central divider w/arched center hand hole, dovetailed construction, old worn finish, 19th c., 10 x 14 1/4",

6 3/4" h. (minor age cracks, one corner chipped) ........................................................ **413**

**Kraut cutter,** walnut & hardwood, a long narrow rectangular board w/molded edges & oblong heart-shaped cut-out handle, angled metal blade, 22" l. ................ **440**

*Burl Mortar with Pestle*

**Mortar,** burl, bell-shaped tapering to pedestal base, together w/plain wood pestle, 7 1/4" h. 2 pcs. (ILLUS.) .............................. **440**

**Paddle,** burl maple, wide oblong & curved bowl w/a stem handle extending from back trim, old dark finish, 7 1/4" l. (wear in bowl) .......................................................... **193**

**Pitcher,** stave-constructed haystack-style, flat-bottomed w/tapering ovoid sides & rim spout, iron bands, handle & lip spout, old dark finish, 16" h. ................................... **495**

**Plate,** curly poplar, turned w/flanged rim & old natural patina, back inscription reads "This plate was made in 1880 by Wm. Ashton...," 8 3/8" d. ........................................ **110**

**Salt box,** cov., hanging-type, walnut, a rounded backboard tab w/large hole for hanging above the rectangular dovetailed box w/hinged cover, old worn finish, 17 x 17 1/2", 5 1/2" h. (bottom back corner damaged, hinges replaced) ............. **275**

**Salt dip,** painted & turned, footed, painted w/green, red & white stripes, 19th c., 3" d., 2 1/2" h. (some paint loss, dirt) .......... **316**

*Early Smoothing or Mangle Board*

**Smoothing or mangle board,** a long narrow rectangular board w/molded & chip-carved edges & a crude carved horse-form handle at one end, old dark green, black & red paint, initialed & dated "1787," insect & edge damage, probably Scandinavian (ILLUS.) ............................. **1,155**

**Sugar bucket,** cov., gently tapering cylindrical stave-constructed form w/two bands & flat fitted cover, swing bentwood bail handle, old salmon colored paint, 19th c., 10" h. plus handle ................. **413**

**Sugar bucket,** cov., stave construction w/double bentwood bands around the bottom & single band around the rim, flat fitted lid & bentwood swing handle, old red paint, copper tacks, minor edge damage, 11 3/4" d., 11 1/2" h. (ILLUS. bottom w/bowl) ............................................... **495**

**Sugar bucket,** cov., stave construction, tapering cylindrical form w/two single lappet bentwood bands around the body & a single lappet around the flat top, top branded "E.F. Lane & Co. Marlboro Depot, N.H.," old refinishing, 11 3/4" h. (some edge damage & age crack on cover) .......................................................... **165**

**Sugar bucket,** cov., painted, stave construction w/double wooden bands around the bottom & single band at the rim, flat fitted cover, bentwood swing handle, branded "Ephram Murdock," old blue repaint, 19th c., 12" d., 12" h. ............... **743**

**Sugar bucket,** cov., gently tapering cylindrical stave-constructed form w/two bands & flat fitted cover, swing bentwood bail handle, old cream-colored paint w/light blue beneath, 19th c., 14 1/4" h. plus handle .................................. **385**

**Tub,** turned & decorated poplar, deep thick cylindrical & slightly swelled sides, worn original red & yellow sponging, 10 3/4" d., 6" h. (wear, deep age cracks in bottom) ..................................................... **248**

# WORLD'S FAIR COLLECTIBLES

*There has been great interest in collecting items produced for the great fairs and expositions held through the years. During the 1970s, there was particular interest in items produced for the 1876 Centennial Exhibition and now interest is focusing on those items associated with the 1893 Columbian Exposition. Listed below is a random sampling of prices asked for items produced for the various fairs.*

## 1915 PANAMA-PACIFIC INTERNATIONAL EXPOSITION

*Ruhstaller's Lager Tray*

**Tray,** round, tin lithographed scene of lovely lady holding flower bouquet w/fair buildings & fountain in background, by Kaufman & Strauss, New York, Ruhstaller's Gilt Edge Lager, Sacramento, California, minor spots, 12" d. (ILLUS.)...... **$358**

## 1939-40 NEW YORK WORLD'S FAIR

**License plate,** self-framed tin, yellow w/black lettering, embossed "New York World's Fair 1939," 5 1/4 x 13 1/2" (soiling, scratches, staining & chips).................... **44**

## CENTURY OF PROGRESS 1933, CHICAGO

*The 1933-34 Chicago World's Fair (A Century of Progress) was conceived as a celebration of advances made in the century since the incorporation of the city of Chicago and drew over 40 million visitors. Situated on 427 acres on Northerly Island at the edge of Lake Michigan, the cite was known as "Rainbow City" for the colorful Esplanade of Flags and buildings in orange, red, yellow and pastels. The fair proved a testing ground for neon lighting with the focus on science undoubtedly accelerating improvements in transportation and communication. Key attractions were the Adler Planetarium (first of its kind in U.S.) and Ft. Dearborn historic site. Midway lures were the Skyway, Frank Buck's Jungle Camp, Thrill House of Crime and fan-dancer Sally Rand. Despite opening in the midst of the Depression and extending a second year to pay off debts, the CWF finished in the black, the first U.S. international exposition to make a profit.*

**Ashtray,** white metal, "1933 A Century of Progress" comet logo embossed in center, ornate scalloped border, 5" d. ................. **30**

**Cane,** metal cane head on wood, "Franklin D. Roosevelt" embossed along curve of handle, deep relief bust portrait in front of 8" attachment, 35" l. ................................ **110**

**Compact,** glitter covered white metal, "Hall of Science" embossed image on obverse ..................................................... **150**

*Embossed Crumbler Set*

**Crumbler Set,** embossed white metal, crumb pan & scraper w/scenes from fair (ILLUS.)......................................................... **20**

**Ephemera,** brochure, Arcturus Radio Tube Co., 16 pp. story of Arcturus lights which officially opened the fair, operating on energy from a ray that left star Arcturus during World's Colombian Expo in 1893 ........ **20**

**Ephemera,** brochure, Ford Pavilion handout, 24 pp., photos of Henry Ford's first shop, history of transportation from Chariot to '34 Ford, floor plan of pavilion ....... **20**

**Ephemera,** brochure, "Old Dutch Cleanser/Cleanliness Through the Ages", detailed history of cleansers .............. **15**

**Ephemera,** brochure, "Safety Glass" photographs of exhibit in Travel & Transportation building, cover shows Chicago White Sox pitching ace Lefty Grove attempting to break safety glass w/fast ball................................................................... **20**

**Ephemera,** brochure, "Sanifem/World's Fair Edition of Sex Relations," by D.S. Hubbard, maker of female hygiene capsule.................................................................. **25**

**Ephemera,** brochure, "United Air Lines at Century of Progress," photo of Boeing Mainliner at UAL pavilion & Transportation Building.................................................. **15**

**Ephemera,** flyer, "Happy Hours" handout w/velvet like cover promoting Ben Bernie Show ..................................................... **15**

**Ephemera,** foldout, "Stayform/A Century of Progress in Corsets," photographs of Stayform's exhibit................................... **15**

**Ephemera,** menu, "Black Forest Inn" large colorful menu w/fair views ............................... **20**

**Lamp,** Travel Building figural ceramic desk lamp w/silhouettes of trains, stagecoach, planes on shade, white building base, shade 3 1/2" ...................................................... **110**

**Mirror,** celluloid, oval, multicolor, "Bird's Eye View, Century of Progress, 1933," 3" w. ...................................................... **50**

**Mirror,** oval, celluloid, black & white, cartoon contrasting outhouse w/modern plumbing, "1833...1933", 3" w. ...................... **65**

**Napkin ring,** plated base metal, "Golden Pavilion of Jehol" black or dark blue image plus comet logo overprinted on white enamel, 3" d. ...................................... **25**

*Pin Tray*

**Pin tray,** white metal, "Century of Progress, 1933," white metal w/embossed images of buildings on Northerly Island, including Skyway ride (ILLUS.)................................. **15**

**Pinback,** black & orange, "Chicago's World's Restaurant Club/Member/World's Fair/Abie the Clown Cop" photo, 1 1/4" d. ...................................... **25**

**Pinback,** black & white, "Bring 'em Back Alive/Frank Buck's Jungle Camp," silhouette bust of Buck in helmet, 1 1/4" d......... **30**

**Pinback,** black & white, "Chicago's World's Fair/A Century of Progress," Mercury symbol with "I Will," "1933" on helmet, bird's eye view of Expo grounds, 3 1/2" d. ...... 30

**Pinback,** black & white, "I Have Seen the World Champion Log-Rollers" jugate photos of champions Pete Hooper & Sam Harris, 7/8" d. ...... 15

**Pinback,** blue on white, "Welcome Visitors," "1933 Century of Progress," comet logo, 2" d. ...... 20

**Pinback,** blue & white, "Boost Chicago's World's Fair," 3/4" d. ...... 15

**Pinback,** blue & white, "I Was There/1933 World's Fair," comet symbol, 7/8" d. ...... 15

**Pinback,** blue & white, "National Education Assoc./Chicago/1933," bust of Indian Chief & Mercury with "I Will" on Mercury's helmet, 1" ...... 25

**Pinback,** brown & white, "Polish Falcon Convention," illustration of flying falcon over waves, fair building in background, "July 9, 1933" at top, "World's Fair 1933," 1" d. ...... 15

**Pinback,** dark blue & white, New York Central Lines logo, "Century of Progress-- 1933," 1" d. ...... 20

**Pinback,** light green & black, "Arkansas Day/A Century of Progress," 1 1/4" d. ...... 20

**Pinback,** multicolored, "A Century of Progress/1934/Enchanted Island, Magic Mountain and Children's Theater", mountains in illustration, 1 1/4" d. ...... 20

**Pinback,** multicolored, "A Century of Progress/1934/See Midget City", illustration of village, 1 1/4" d. ...... 25

*"Indiana to Chicago/1933" Pinback*

**Pinback,** multicolored, "Indiana to Chicago/1933," American Legionnaire carrying map outline of Indiana, American Legion logo & cameo of man chopping tree, 3 1/2" l. (ILLUS.) ...... 35

**Pinback,** yellow & black, "Century of Progress Tours/Chicago,1933," stylized statue straddles Chicago skyline in silhouette, 7/8" d. ...... 20

**Pinback,** yellow & black, "Chicago's New Century Club/Mayor Edward J. Kelley, Chairman" stylized skyscrapers w/wings, large "C" insignia w/club inside bullseye, 1" d. ...... 25

**Pinball machine,** multicolored, "Jig Saw" pinball by Rock Ola, Chicago, fair logo, 1933, approx. 4' h. ...... 500

**Plaque,** multicolored in oval, Art Deco border in silver & black, "A Century of Progress" Northerly Island fair complex, 4 x 6" ...... 15

**Playing cards,** "A Century of Progress International Exposition/Chicago/1934," various CWF buildings pictured, Art Deco image, furled flags of many nations on box ...... 50

**Pocket knife,** "A Century of Progress, Chicago, 1933" embossed Chicago skyline on observe of handle, Ft. Dearborn on reverse, two blades, 3 1/4" l. ...... 55

**Pocket knife,** "A Mickey Mouse" pictured on white handle, "World's Fair Chicago/1933" printing, was never actually produced as a souvenir item for the fair, it is purely a fantasy item & has little value ...... 2

**Pocket knife,** blue plastic handle pocket knife, "Drink Coca-Cola in Bottles/World's Fair Chicago, 1933," Ideal, 3 1/2" l. ...... 50

**Pocket knife,** "Century of Progress 1933-34" official sterling silver pen knife, comet log on side, 2" l. ...... 45

**Pocket knife,** "Official Century of Progress" knife, Gits Bros., Chicago, retractable slot blade, 3 1/2" l. ...... 45

**Postcard,** "CBS Radio," black & white, illus. of inverted triangle-shaped microphone w/expo backdrop, "Covered by the Columbia Microphone for Millions of Radio Listeners" ...... 20

**Postcard,** "Dr. Ferguson's Toothland Puppet Show/Official Dentistry Exhibit," black & white ...... 15

**Postcard,** "Goodyear's Landing Field," Goodyear blimp landing at field w/Expo buildings, Lake Michigan shoreline; w/"Facts about Goodyear" ...... 20

**Postcard,** "Master Marble Shop on Enchanted Island/Millions of Marbles Used In Its Construction," black & white, illustration of building w/giant globe atop marquee, small lads in foreground are shooting marbles ...... 30

**Poster,** "Play...See...Hear...World's Fair Chicago, 1934," multicolored w/fuchsia, chartreuse hues, Sandor, surreal image of woman in hat amid montage of neon buildings, 25 x 38" ...... 650

**Poster,** "World's Fair Chicago/A Century of Progress," Scheffer, multicolor, Miss Columbia stands atop globe w/arms raised, Chicago skyscrapers, planes, blimps & spotlights crisscross beams over symbolic deities representing Science & Industry, reproduction, 24 x 36" ...... 300

**Puzzle,** "Century of Progress," wood, black & white, based on popular "Dad's Puzzler," sliding blocks have name designations including world wonders, airplanes, etc., lithographed box has fair scenes & "The Best Souvenir of Chicago/Take

One Home and Try to Solve It,"
5 x 5 1/2" ...................................................... **35**

*"Scrambled Eggs" Puzzle*

**Puzzle,** "Scrambled Eggs," wood, dark blue
w/gold & teal blue, Art Deco, gold,
orange & brown box, three-dimensional
painted puzzle, "Century of
Progress/1934" seal (ILLUS.)........................ **65**
**Puzzle,** "World's Fair Picture Puzzle," 300
cardboard pieces, multicolor, Rand
McNally, Chicago, 1932, H.J. Pettit - art-
ist, box 11 1/2 x 17 1/2".................................. **45**
**Refrigerator bottle,** "Hall of Science," pic-
ture embossed on pale green glass,
"Century of Progress, Chicago" in raised
letters, 8 1/2" h. ............................................. **25**
**Sewing kit,** "1934/A Century of Progress"
cylindrical white metal kit w/blue label
including thimble & needles, 3" h. .................. **20**
**Souvenir guidebook,** "A Century of
Progress Official Guide Book," 192 pp.,
Century of Progress Pub., Chicago,
1933 .............................................................. **15**
**Souvenir guidebook,** "Official Photo-
graphs of Century of Progress," Century
of Progress Pub., Chicago, 1933 .................. **20**
**Souvenir guidebook,** "Official Story and
Encyclopedia of A Century of Progress,"
compiled by Walter S. Franklin, Century
of Progress Pub., Administration Build-
ing, Chicago, 1933 ........................................ **25**
**Souvenir guidebook,** "Pictures of a Cen-
tury of Progress," R.H. Donnelly, Pub.,
Chicago, 1933 ............................................... **20**
**Teaspoon,** heavy silver plate, "Century of
Progress" comet logo, on narrow
tapered pointed handle .................................. **15**
**Teaspoon,** heavy silver plate, "Chicago
Tower/Hall of Science," narrow pointed
handle, approx. 6" .......................................... **20**
**Teaspoon,** silver plate, "Hall of Science"
embossed in bowl, winged Mercury
w/comet log, 6"............................................... **20**
**Teaspoon,** silver plate, "Travel & Transpor-
tation Building" image embossed in
bowl, "Science Court" along handle, 6" ......... **20**
**Textile,** handkerchief, blue & white, "1933"
comet symbol, "Japanese Silk" ................... **110**
**Textile,** handkerchief, red, white, blue &
black, "A Century of Progress," wide oval

bust of "President F.D. Roosevelt/June-
November, 1933" ............................................ **75**
**Textile,** handkerchief, red, white, blue &
black, "Chicago World's Fair" w/large
bust of F.D.R. figure ..................................... **110**

*Quilt w/Notable Figures of Past Century*

**Textile,** quilt, tan, brown & white,
"Progress/1888-1933," modern deity
atop building symbolizing "lighting the
way" various squares represent notable
figures including F.D.R., Thomas Edison, Charles Lindbergh, Abraham Lincoln & various inventions of past
century, 80 x 100" (ILLUS.) .......................... **700**
**Textile,** red, white, blue & black, "Souvenir
of World's Fair Chicago 1933," slanted
oval view superimposed over U.S. flag,
Northerly Island fair complex....................... **150**

*Textile w/Aerial View of Expo Grounds*

**Textile,** tapestry, blazing pink background
& fringe, "A Century of Progress" aerial
view of Expo grounds w/planes & dirigi-
bles aloft, 25 x 40" (ILLUS.) ........................ **125**
**Textile,** tapestry, dark brown & beige, "Chicago, 1833-1933" modern Chicago skyline w/Ft. Dearborn complex in
foreground (ILLUS. top next column) ............. **75**
**Timepiece,** "Chicago's World's Fair, 1833-
1933," Ingraham pocketwatch, etched

image of Chicago skyline & Ft. Dearborn on dial face, 2" d............................................. **85**

*Tapestry w/Chicago Skyline*

**Tin,** advertising-type, Art Deco design, dark blue & gold, De Met's Chocolates, Miss Liberty "I Will", scenes from the fair, 8 1/2" d.............................................................. **75**

**Tip tray,** advertising-type, lithographed tin plate, multicolor, Vapoo Shampoo, illustration of product, "Century of Progress" logo, 3" d.................................................... **65**

**Toy,** bank, "Administration Building," cast iron by Arcade, cream w/blue roof, "Century of Progress" in raised letters on obverse, "Chicago-1934" on rev., 4 1/2 x 7 1/2", 2" d....................................... **500**

*Ft. Dearborn Cast Iron Toy Bank*

**Toy,** bank, "Ft. Dearborn" maker unknown, cast iron, brown, 4 3/4 x 5 1/2", 4 1/2" d. (ILLUS.)......................................................... **300**

**Toy,** bank, "Ft. Dearborn" maker unknown, pot metal, brass finish (ILLUS top next page.)................................................................ **75**

**Toy,** bank, "Travel & Transportation Building" promotional premium for Preference Bank Service Co., NY, white metal w/bronze finish, base 3 1/2 x 5 1/4"............... **45**

**Toy,** camera, child's box camera w/leather-like paper cover on wood, original box w/"Century of Progress" comet sticker........... **45**

**Toy,** cap pistol, cast iron, orange & black, "Lone Star Ranger" lithographed, boxed set including pistol, leather holster & wooden bullets, box inscribed "Tower of Water-Chicago World's Fair," illustrated w/fair logo in background, 5 x 12".................. **50**

*Ft. Dearborn Pot Metal Toy Bank*

**Toy,** four-door Ford, Arcade, yellow cab, black trailer, 1933-34, special Chicago World's Fair edition, "Century of Progress" stenciled on roof, balloon tires, 6 7/8" l. ................................................. **250**

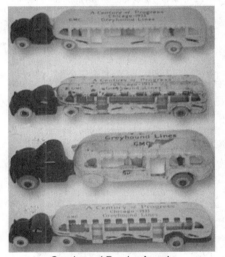

*Greyhound Bus by Arcade*

**Toy,** Greyhound Bus by Arcade, blue cab & white trailer, two-piece casting, "Century of Progress" logo on each side, GMC logo, 7 1/2" l. (ILLUS.) .................................. **200**

**Toy,** Greyhound Bus by Arcade, blue cab & white trailer, two-piece casting, "Century of Progress" logo on each side, GMC logo, 11" l. .................................................... **250**

**Toy,** Greyhound Bus by Arcade, blue cab & white trailer, two-piece casting, "Century of Progress" logo on each side, GMC logo, 12" l. .................................................... **300**

**Toy,** Greyhound Bus by Arcade, blue cab & white trailer, two-piece casting, "Century of Progress" logo on each side, GMC logo, 14" l. ...................................... **350**

**Toy,** Greyhound Bus by Arcade, white & blue painted cast iron, one-piece casting, "Century of Progress" logo on each side, GMC logo, 6" l. .................................... **150**

**Toy,** "Lincoln Logs," multicolored, J.L. Wright, Inc., wood construction logs w/illustration, Ft. Dearborn, official fair logo, original box 10 1/2 x 14". ...................... **110**

**Toy,** "Radio Flyer" wagon, pressed steel w/rubber rimmed wheels, orange "Century of Progress" w/black & gold sticker, advertising premium, 4 1/2" l. ....................... **110**

**Toy,** Studebaker Sedan by Matchbox, red, Century of Progress comet sticker, 2 1/2". ...................................................... **125**

**Toy,** "Tumble-Tumble," multicolored, seven-section lithographed cardboard fig. on wood ladder gravity toy, maker unknown, "Century of Progress" logo sticker, 6" h. ...................................... **45**

**Toy,** "World's Fair Bus," Kenton, blue w/white balloon tires, 1933, cast iron detachable, two-piece unit,10 7/8" l. ............ **300**

# WRITING ACCESSORIES

*Early writing accessories are popular collectibles and offer a wide variety to select from. A collection may be formed around any one segment pens, letter openers, lap desks or inkwells or the collection may revolve around choice specimens of all types. Material, design and age usually determine the value. Pen collectors like the large fountain pens developed in the 1920s but also look for pens and mechanical pencils that are solid gold or gold-plated. Also see: BOTTLES & FLASKS*

## INKWELLS & INKSTANDS

**Bronze well,** Renaissance style, cast as a satyr's head w/protruding chin & open mouth showing his tongue, wearing a leafy vine around his hair centered by a 'jewel' hinging to reveal the hollow interior, on an oval rope-twist base & three ball feet, medium brown patina, 19th c., 3 3/4" h. ...................................................... **$690**

*Viennese Bronze Figural Inkwell*

**Bronze well,** two kittens on a fringed rug, one recumbent w/front paws crossed, the other standing near & looking ahead w/startled expression, a cylindrical stool draped w/fabric w/hinged cover holding the ink pot, depatinated, impressed marks & "BERGM," by Bergman, late

19th c., Vienna, missing ink pot, 7 3/4" l. (ILLUS.) ................................................... **1,265**

**Cameo glass well,** square w/white floral decoration on citron ground, silver monogrammed lid, England, 4 3/4" h. ....... **1,925**

**Champlevé enamel well,** outlined w/enamel & enamel finial, onyx base, together w/pair of small etched crystal bud vases, probably Baccarat, fitted into champlevé enamel bases ........................... **275**

**China well,** w/attached undertray, ornate design w/floral decoration & gold scrolling, 6" w. .................................................. **110**

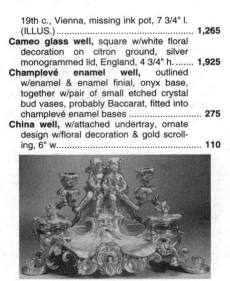

*Louis XV Style Inkstand*

**Gilt-bronze stand,** Louis XV Style w/two putti atop a mask mounted base w/scrolled candlebranches, covered inkwells, the shell-shaped base fitted w/drawer, late 19th c., 16" l., 9 1/2" h. (ILLUS.) ..................................................... **1,380**

*Gustave Michel Figural Inkwell*

**Gilt-bronze well,** modeled as two muscular nude men w/long shaggy hair, mustache & beard, engaged in physical struggle on edge of large oyster shell, inkwell w/hinged cover concealed in surrounding waters, signed "G. MICHEL" & impressed "SIOT-PARIS/Z108," by Gustave F. Michel (1851-1924), France, ca.1895, 6 1/2" h. (ILLUS.)........... **1,725**

**Jade & carnelian well,** green jade carved disk form base on small silver feet supporting cup-form green jade well bordered w/carnelian, inset flat green jade lid w/carved figural handle, probably Chinese, ca. 1900, 5 1/2" h. (ILLUS. top next column).............................................. **2,750**

**Loetz glass well,** Art Deco style w/hinged metal lid, circular cap evokes a winged insect, four organic shapes reach down to embrace slightly iridized green glass, 3 7/8" d., 3" h.............................................. **210**

*Oriental Jade & Carnelian Inkwell*

*Meissen Figural Inkstand*

**Porcelain stand,** figural sander & inkwell, the central chinoiserie figural group w/small well, scrolled footed base, late 19th c., Meissen, minor restorations, 9 1/2 x 14", 10" h. (ILLUS.) ...................... **4,025**

**Porcelain well,** cov., octagon-shaped, each panel w/stylized flowers, two openings for pens ..................................... **55**

**Porcelain well,** square base w/two open cylindrical wells, figural boy w/hands to face sitting on rolled-up carpet, German ...... **231**

**Sterling silver well,** traveling-type, square w/rounded corners, hinged cover engraved w/leafy scrolls & flowerheads, central monogram, cover opens w/front latch, interior w/further cover over fitted glass well, interior cover engraved w/presentation inscription, Gorham Mfg. Co., Providence, Rhode Island, retailed by Black, Starr & Frost, late 19th - early 20th c., 2 1/4" w., 1 1/2" h. ........................... **345**

## LAP DESKS & WRITING BOXES

**Writing box,** mahogany w/old finish, slant top w/one dovetailed drawer in end w/original brass bail handle, fitted inte-

rior w/two old inks & pen, writing surface recovered w/green felt, 9 1/2 x 15 3/4"......... **605**

**Writing box,** mahogany, rectangular w/hinged lid, fitted interior, old finish, Little Falls, New York, 16" l. ............................ **275**

**Writing box,** pine w/old mellow finish, cutout feet, slant top lift lid, one dovetailed drawer, 11 1/2 x 17", 16 1/4" h. .................... **440**

**Writing box,** walnut, rectangular dovetailed case, slant top lift lid w/low gallery & one interior dovetailed drawer, old refinishing, 19 1/2 x 19 3/4", 6 1/2" h. ...................... **413**

# LETTER OPENERS

*English Carved Ivory Letter Opener*

**Bronze,** Art Nouveau style, the handle molded in full-relief w/a maiden holding a bouquet of flowers, designed by V. Sabatier, signed "Fumiere et Cie - V. Sabatier," ca. 1900, 9 3/4" l. ......................... **690**

**Bronze & enamel,** Arts & Crafts style, tapering flattened rectangular handle w/graduating green enameled squares, impressed "Tiffany Studios - New York," 6 1/2" l. ......................................................... **575**

**Copper,** hand-hammered, Arts & Crafts style, elongated shield-form handle, marked by Dirk Van Erp, San Francisco, ca. 1920, 11 1/4" l. ...................... **230**

**Copper,** hand-hammered, Arts & Crafts style, the flat half-round top pierced w/an oak tree decoration, designed by Thomas McGlynn for Dirk Van Erp, San Francisco, ca. 1915, w/matching narrow rectangular tray w/pierced oak tree end handles, tray 3 5/8 x 10 12", 2 pcs. ........... **1,035**

**Copper, brass & silver,** Oriental motifs w/a long narrow rectangular handle cast & applied w/silver flying birds, the narrow oblong blade w/a diagonal band w/an applied silver fish, Kodzuka engraved decoration, Gorham Mfg. Co., Providence, Rhode Island, ca. 1885, 8 7/8" l. ...... **230**

**Copper & carnelian,** hand-hammered, Arts & Crafts style, top of handle composed of arched scrolls centering a teardrop-form carnelian stone, in the style of C.R. Ashbee, signed by H.E. Potter, ca. 1910, 7 1/2" l. .............................................. **172**

**Gilt- & patinated bronze,** Art Deco Egyptian-style, the handle in the form of a pharaoh's head, the blade w/hieroglyphics, designed & signed by A. Sadoux, France, ca. 1930, 9 1/4" l. ............................ **373**

**Gilt-bronze,** Art Nouveau-style, the handle carved & pierced w/a mistletoe design, designed & signed by Leroy, France, w/original fitted box, ca. 1900, 9 1/4" l. ......... **690**

**Ivory,** the handle boldly pierce-carved as a large entwined snake above an acanthus leaf & the flat long blade, England, ca. 1880, 12 1/2" l. (ILLUS.) .......... **431**

*Rare Russian Letter Opener*

**Silver & agate,** the handle cast in full-relief as a bear climbing a tree, palmette device at the base of the handle, flat tapering mottled brown agate blade, Russia, possibly by Fabergé impressed "FA - St. Petersburg," ca. 1908-17, 7 1/2" l. (ILLUS.) ........................................ **1,496**

**Silver & ivory,** Art Deco style, the flattened silver handle cast w/stylized drapery design at the top & scrolls & bands at the base, wide tapering ivory blade, marked by Georg Jensen Silversmithy, Copenhagen, Denmark, No. 125, ca. 1920, 10" l. ...................................................... **1,380**

**Sterling silver,** Arts & Crafts style, hand-hammered, curved & serpentine-edged sword-form pierced w/a row of small holes along the handle & top of the blade & pieced stylized leaves & buds at the base of the blade, marked by Dominick & Haff, ca. 1910, 8" l. .............................. **546**

**Sterling silver,** long gently curved & tapering form, the handle ornately cast w/pierced C-scrolls & the figure of a putto & dragon, marked by George Shiebler, ca. 1900, 14 1/4" l. .................... **1,495**

**Sterling silver & citrine,** the tip of the round handle set w/a large faceted tear-

drop-form citrine set into a cylindrical pierced & scroll-engraved mount above the flattened blade decorated w/scroll engraving around a long feather-like design, impressed mark of Mackay and Chisholm, Edinburgh, Scotland, ca. 1887-88, 10" l. .............................................. **431**

**Sterling silver & ebony,** the handle carved w/a stylized beaver, impressed mark of William Spratling, Taxco, Mexico, ca. 1950, 7 1/2" l. .......................................... **1,380**

*Art Deco Wrought-iron Opener*

**Wrought iron,** Arts & Crafts style, a long narrow rectangular form w/tapering blade, the handle pierced & carved w/a stylized branch design centered by a rectangular polished medallion inset w/a blue mottled stone, designed by Edgar Brandt, France, ca. 1900-10, 12 3/4" l. (ILLUS.) ...................................................... **2,830**

# MISCELLANEOUS

**Desk box,** pewter, hemispherical feet, two-part interior w/lift lids, one side w/ink & sander, lid scratch engraved "Boston Isaac Dupee, Aug. 31, 1833" (baffle on inkwell replaced, repairs) .......................... **193**

*Brass Desk Set*

**Desk set,** brass, oval base w/four feet, two candle sockets, sander & two compartments w/domed lids, late 18th - early 19th c., minor seam separation at gallery edge of base, 7 1/2" l. (ILLUS.) .................... **990**

**Pencil box,** pine, one piece w/worn old finish, sliding lid w/chip carving & "Betty x Lapham," 7 1/4" l. .......................... **303**

# INDEX